Educational Research

Educational Research

An Introduction
Fifth Edition

Walter R. Borg
Utah State University

Meredith Damien Gall
University of Oregon

Longman
New York & London

Educational Research: An Introduction, Fifth Edition

Longman, 10 Bank Street, White Plains, N.Y. 10606

Associated companies:
Longman Group Ltd., London
Longman Cheshire Pty., Melbourne
Longman Paul Pty., Auckland
Copp Clark Pitman, Toronto
Pitman Publishing Inc., New York

Executive editor: Raymond T. O'Connell
Development editor: Virginia L. Blanford
Production editor: Ann P. Kearns
Text design: Jill Francis Wood
Cover design: Paul Agule
Text art: Hal Keith
Production supervisor: Judi Millman

Library of Congress Cataloging-in-Publication Data

Borg, Walter R.
    Educational research.

    Includes bibliographies and index.
    1. Education--Research.   I. Gall, Meredith D.,
1942-   II. Title.
LB1028.B6   1989 370'.7'8   88-26594

ISBN 0-8013-0334-6

10-AL-959493

ACKNOWLEDGMENTS

We wish to express our appreciation to several colleagues for sharing their expertise as we prepared the fifth edition of *Educational Research*. Professor C. H. Edson advised us on the chapter on historical research; Professor David Flinders advised us on the sections of chapters 1 and 9 on postpositivistic philosophy of science and educational criticism; Professor Richard Rankin advised us on the section of chapter 14 on structural equation modeling; and Mr. Steven Stieber advised us on the chapter on data processing. We extend our appreciation to Ms. Joan Weston, who patiently taught Meredith Gall the CD-Rom version of the ERIC system.

CONTENTS

TO THE INSTRUCTOR

Educational research bears scant resemblance to the field of study that existed in 1963 when the first edition of this text was published. Since that time, the body of knowledge concerning educational research methods and the sophistication of the research process have increased greatly. One of our goals in the earlier editions was to provide the student with the essentials needed to carry through the entire research process, from identifying the problem to writing the thesis, and to introduce every research technique in common use so that the student could develop an understanding of educational research as a whole. A further goal was to present the essentials in clear, straightforward language that the average student could understand. These continue to be our goals, but we must confess that as educational research has become more complex and sophisticated, it has become much more difficult to achieve these ends. Our decision to add learning aids such as the Overview and Objectives sections to the third edition was influenced to a considerable extent by our feeling that as the field becomes more complex, the average student must be given more and more help in learning enough about educational research to plan and conduct research and to be an intelligent user of the research done by others.

Those of you who are familiar with the fourth edition will note that extensive revisions have been made to several chapters in this fifth edition. Chapter 1 has been completely rewritten. One of our goals for chapter 1 has been to give students an insight into the excitement and satisfaction that doing educational research can bring to the investigator. We have never been satisfied with our attempts to achieve this goal, but we keep trying.

We have retained our discussion of the contributions of educational research in this edition. The greatest change you will notice in chapter 1, however, is the introduction to the positivistic and postpositivistic philosophies of science and their application to education.

You will also notice that chapter 2 of the fourth edition, which discussed opportunities in educational research, has been omitted.

Part II, Planning Educational Research and Part III, Sampling and Measurement, have been updated in the fifth edition but have not undergone a major revision. In Part IV, chapter 9 has undergone a major revision, and chapter 10, designed to introduce students to the qualitative research model, is new. The qualitative and quantitative paradigms are compared and the methods of qualitative research are described.

Because the field of educational research has expanded to the point where it is no longer possible to cover all of the important aspects of research methodology in an introductory text, we have made a major effort to provide more annotated references that will help the student who needs additional information on some specific topic such as developing survey questionnaires, training interviewers, or conducting ethnographic research. We have tried to locate the most up-to-date sources for inclusion in the annotated reference sections, but have not hesitated to refer students to some of the older sources when we feel these provide valuable information. Similarly, we have retained some examples from the fourth edition when we have been unable to find a more recent example that we feel is as clear and to the point.

It has been a difficult problem to introduce students to the many new concepts that have become important in educational research without expanding the book into an encyclopedia. We are sure that you will find some topics in the fifth edition that you feel could have been omitted and others that you feel should have been given expanded treatment. Our past experience, however, indicates little consensus among persons who teach the research methods course concerning the amount of emphasis a given topic should receive. We note with regret that, despite our best efforts, the book has grown a bit larger. This seems an almost inevitable result of our attempt to give reasonable coverage to a rapidly expanding field of knowledge. Entire books are devoted to many of the topics that we deal with in a few pages, such as research ethics, qualitative research, meta-analysis, use of volunteer subjects, criterion-referenced measurement, and evaluation research—to mention but a few. We have not been satisfied merely to mention such topics in a few sentences because such cursory treatment fails to provide students with the knowledge base they need to understand the educational research process and apply it to their own research. Most students in education take only a single course in research methods, and if they do not get a good foundation in this course, it seems unlikely that they will ever become competent either in doing research or applying the research of others to their problems. Another reason we have tried to give a substantial introduction to all topics related to educational research is that many students keep this book for reference after completing the course. This is evident from the fact that few copies come onto the used book market.

The preparation of a text in educational research methods poses another problem because it is desirable to give the student a reasonable insight into statistical tools and measurement techniques as they apply to research, but to avoid covering the same ground typically dealt with in courses in statistics and educational evaluation. To deal with this problem we have followed essentially the same strategy used in previous editions. That is, we have emphasized the application of measurement and statistical techniques to problems of educational research. We have tried to give students enough information about these techniques so that they can recognize situations in which they should seek further information. Our treatment of statistical techniques continues to be as nontechnical as possible. We have tried to relate statistical techniques to the research designs with which they are commonly associated, but have avoided covering computation and formulas, which we regard as more appropriate for courses in statistics. It is our opinion that students should have at least one elementary course in statistics and one in educational measurement before taking the research methods course. However, we realize that prerequisites and degree requirements differ greatly from university to university. Therefore, we have tried to write this book so that students not having these prerequisites could still understand the book and gain a reasonable mastery of educational research methods.

As in the fourth edition, we have organized the chapters in the same sequence that the student follows in conducting a research project, starting with the selection of a research problem and ending with preparation of the research report. Nevertheless, we believe that students should read through the entire book before attempting to plan and carry out their own research projects. As each phase of a research project is tied very closely to every other phase, it is not possible to develop a text that permits the student to become fully competent in the initial steps of research before having gained some knowledge and insight into later steps. For example, a critical review of previous research is one of the early steps that the student must take in planning and carrying out a research project. However, the student is severely limited in the ability to evaluate previous research without some understanding of measurement, research design, and statistical analysis. In this edition we have again placed the chapter concerned with the critical review of research literature near the front of the book. We feel that it is desirable for the student to start this effort early in research training. We would suggest that the instructor assign several research articles for critical review during the course. The process of discussing articles in class and giving students feedback on their reviews will help a great deal in furthering their skills in this important area. As the student progresses through the course, the instructor's standards for the critical review assignments can be raised gradually so that a student who finishes the course will have developed sufficient skills in critical review to be prepared to review the literature for a thesis or dissertation. The authors have used this strategy in teaching their own research methods classes for several years and have found it to be effective.[1]

We have continued the pattern established in the third edition of starting each chapter with a brief overview of the chapter along with a list of specific learner objectives. A brief orientation is also provided at the beginning of each of the five parts. Because of the tremendous knowledge base that students must have before they can start functioning as educational researchers, you will find that the majority of the objectives relate to content mastery. You will also probably find that while some of these objectives are relevant to the needs and

---

1. An *Instructor's Manual* containing a test-item file, sample assignments, and suggestions for teaching the course is available free of charge from the publisher.

goals of your students, some are not. We would urge you to review the objectives carefully with your students, pointing out those that you regard as important and those that you feel are not important for your students. It may also be necessary for you to add objectives that we have not covered.

At the end of each chapter you will find a brief self-check test made up of 10 multiple-choice questions. These few items are designed to help students check whether they understand a sampling of the material covered in the chapter, and they are not intended to provide a coverage of all of the chapter objectives. You also will find a few application problems at the end of each chapter. These problems give students an opportunity to apply some of what they have learned in the chapter to problems frequently encountered by educational researchers. Again, the problems are meant to cover only a sampling of the chapter objectives. Our experience with these short tests, however, indicates that they are useful in helping students determine whether they understand and can apply the concepts that they have learned.

Note that we have included a Suggestion Sheet on the back end-paper of the book (after the index). The purpose of this sheet is to obtain feedback from students that we can use in subsequent revision of the book. Each student is asked to give feedback on one chapter, although he or she is free to comment on other chapters, too. The end of each chapter contains a brief statement indicating which students are to make comments on that chapter.

Please encourage students to complete the Suggestion Sheet. It is designed so that it can be torn out and mailed as a self-stamped envelope.

To an increasing degree educational researchers are utilizing the research methodologies that have been developed in the other behavioral sciences such as psychology, sociology, and anthropology. Therefore, although this book is aimed primarily at graduate students in the various areas of education, many of the research methods are equally relevant to students in other behavioral sciences. It is our belief that behavioral scientists are becoming more and more aware of the methodologies used by their peers in the other behavioral sciences. Although the main focus of each behavioral science will continue to be different, it seems likely that the same broad foundation of research methodology will undergird all these sciences.

We hope this new revision meets your students' needs. We have already started collecting material for our next revision and would appreciate any comments or suggestions you can give us to improve this book.

Walter R. Borg
Meredith D. Gall

TO THE STUDENT

The broad goal of this book is to help you, the graduate student in education, learn the essentials needed to carry out the entire research process from identifying your research problem to writing your thesis or dissertation. Because the research methods employed in the other behavioral sciences such as psychology and sociology are often similar to those used in education, students in these disciplines will also find this book helpful.

In educational research methods classes we have found two major groups of students. The larger group includes those who plan to carry out a research project and write a thesis or dissertation. There are, however, many students who use this book who are more interested in understanding and using the results of educational research than in conducting their own research. The knowledge base to be gained from this book is sufficient for students in both groups. The student who plans to be primarily a user of research information in the future needs this knowledge base in order to evaluate critically the research of others and translate available research evidence into plans of action that can be carried out in the schools. In order to evaluate research critically the student must know a great deal about the research process, must be able to identify strengths and weaknesses in the research, and must be capable of making judgments as to how these strengths and weaknesses might have affected the findings reported by the researcher.

In the past twenty-five years educational research has become much more complex and sophisticated. This has made it possible for researchers to make increasingly valuable contributions to educational practice, but it has also made the task of the graduate student in mastering this field more difficult. We have tried to make this task easier by writing this book in clear, straightforward language. For example, although we feel it necessary to tell you something about the more advanced statistical procedures that are now being used to analyze educational research data, we have attempted to do this without using technical language, mathematical jargon, or formulas. We have also tried to keep the book down to a manageable length by including only that information we feel is essential to the student. For example, entire textbooks, some larger than this book, have been written in areas such as survey research and evaluation research. In this book, these topics are each covered in one chapter. One result of our effort to weed out unimportant information has been that the amount of important information per page is often quite high, and you will find it difficult to assimilate the information in a single reading.

Because many research concepts and techniques are difficult for the beginning researcher to understand, we have included many examples to illustrate how these techniques have been applied in specific situations.

In order to help you organize the field of educational research in your own mind, we have included an introduction to each part of the book, an overview of each chapter, and a set of objectives for each chapter. The overview is designed to give you a quick picture of what you will learn in the chapter. This will help you learn and will also help you fit each chapter into the overall research picture. While the overview is aimed at providing a general orientation, the objectives tell you the specific information you should get from the chapter. All these objectives are not of equal importance. Which are most important to you depends on the goals you wish to achieve by taking the research methods course. If you are interested primarily in becoming a competent user of research to help solve day-to-day problems, your goals will differ somewhat from the goals needed to make research a major part of your educational career. You will find that most of the objectives are concerned with content mastery. This is because you need a large foundation of knowledge before you can move on to the application of this knowledge to carrying out research projects or using the research of others.

In order to help you get feedback on how well you have mastered the content of the chapter, you will also find a brief multiple-choice self-check test at the end of each chapter. These tests do not cover all important content in the chapter, but cover a sample of this content. If you do well on the self-check test, you probably know most other information covered in the chapter. The application problems at the end of each chapter help you determine whether you can apply the concepts you have learned to practical problems and questions frequently encountered by the beginning researcher. Again, the application problems provide only a small sample of possible applications that relate to what you have learned. However, the self-check test and application problems, although brief, should be sufficient to help you decide whether you have mastered the chapter or whether you should devote more study to it.

We would recommend that you use the following strategy for studying this book:

1. Read the overviews and part introductions.

2. Read the objectives for each chapter at least twice to fix them firmly in your mind. This will focus your attention on the most important content in the chapter.

3. Read a few pages of the text each day in order to keep abreast of the instructor's presentation. As you read the text, underline or in some other manner indicate the most important points and review these points frequently as your reading carries you further into the book. You should also make marginal notes as needed and should mark for future reference information that is especially pertinent to your own research plan. Watch for the terms in

boldface; these are important, and you should learn their meaning. As a rule, important terms are marked only the first time they are described or defined. Try to avoid falling behind in your reading of the text. Because the information level in this text is very high, you will find it difficult to master the important concepts if you try to read too large a segment of the text at a single sitting.

4. When you finish reading the chapter, read over the list of mistakes frequently made by beginning researchers. If you are planning your own research project, mark any of these that may be relevant.

5. Next, take the self-check test and check your answers. If you miss more than two of these items it may be wise to review again the main points that you have marked in the chapter.

6. Now, work through the application problems and again check your answers against the sample answer given in the back of the text.

7. Finally, turn back to the chapter objectives, read each one, and see if you have mastered the information related to that objective.

A good way to prepare for an examination is to read over the main points only (that is, the material you have underlined) for the chapters to be tested. This procedure will take much less time than you needed to read the chapters initially. After you have done this, work with another student who is taking the course. First, ask your fellow student questions based on the material you have underlined. Then, have your study mate ask you questions on the material he or she has underlined. Try to ask questions that require an understanding of the main ideas, not just a rote learning of important facts.

Finally, we have a request to make. We want very much to get your suggestions on how to improve this book in the future. The most useful suggestions are those that are specific. For example, it is difficult for us to use comments such as "this is a good book" or "this is a terrible book" in improving the next edition. On the other hand, specific comments such as "include more examples of null hypotheses" or "add a description of a study that used cluster sampling" can be very helpful.

We would like to get your specific suggestions on the entire book. However, this would take quite a bit of your time, so we are asking for your comments on only a single chapter. Which chapter you comment on will be determined by the first three letters of your last name. This will assure us of getting suggestions for improving all 21 chapters. Of course, if you want to comment on a different chapter or on more than one chapter, we will welcome all suggestions you can give us.

The Suggestion Sheet is printed on the back end-paper of the book (after the index) and can be cut out and made into a business reply mailer.

We hope you will find this book helpful not only in completing your graduate work but also in your later career. Good luck!

Walter R. Borg
Meredith D. Gall

REPRINT ACKNOWLEDGMENTS

The material cited below has been reprinted from other publications. We thank the authors and publishers for granting us permission to excerpt from their work.

Figure 1.1 is adapted from figure 1 of Walberg, Herbert, "Improving the Productivity of America's Schools," *Educational Leadership*, 1984, vol. 41, no. 8, p. 21.

Excerpts on pp. 84–85 are reprinted from Committee on Scientific and Professional Ethics and Conduct, "Ethical Principles of Psychologists," *American Psychologist* 36 (1981): 633-638. Copyright 1981 by the American Psychological Association. Reprinted by permission.

Figure 4.1 is reprinted from *Psychological Abstracts*, vol 74, no. 4 (April 1987), p. 1220. From American Psychological Association, publishers of *Psychological Abstracts* and the PsycINFO Database (Copyright © by the American Psychological Association).

Figure 4.2 is reprinted from *Resources in Education*, vol. 22, no. 4 (April 1987), p. viii. Washington, D. C.: Educational Resources Information Center.

Table 5.1 is reprinted from Cooper, Harris M., "Scientific Guidelines for Conducting Integrative Research Reviews." *Review of Educational Research*, Summer 1982, vol. 52, no. 2, pp. 291-302. Copyright 1982, American Educational Research Association, Washington, D. C. By permission of the publisher and author.

Excerpts on pp. 195–196 are reprinted from R. L. Rosnow and D. J. Davis, "Demand Characteristics and the Psychological Experiment," *Et Cetera* 34 (1977): 301-313. By permission of the author and publisher.

Excerpts on pp. 228–229 and 230–231 are reprinted from Robert Rosenthal and Ralph L. Rosnow, *The Volunteer Subject*, New York: John Wiley and Sons, Inc. 1975, pp. 195-196 and 198-199. By permission of the publisher and author.

Table 7.2 reprinted from G. C. Helmstadter, *Principles of Psychological Measurement*, © 1964, p. 85. By permission of Prentice-Hall Inc., Englewood Cliffs, NJ.

Tables 9.1 and 9.2 are adapted from table 1 and table 2 in Johnson, Dale M., and Smith, Blaine , "An Evaluation of Saxon's Algebra Text," *Journal of Educational*

Research, vol. 81, p. 100 and p. 101, 1987. Reprinted with permission of the Helen Dwight Reid Educational Foundation. Published by Heldref Publications, 4000 Albermarle St. NW, Washington, DC 20016. © 1987.

Figure 9.1 is adapted from figure 2 (p. 42) and figure 6 (p. 49) in Krathwohl, David R. *Social and Behavioral Science Research.* San Francisco: Jossey-Bass, 1985.

Table 9.6 and Figure 9.3 are reprinted from Leinhardt, Gaea, and Leinhardt, Samuel, "Exploratory Data Analysis: New Tools for the Analysis of Empirical Data." *Review of Research in Education,* vol. 8, 1980, pp. 89-92. Copyright 1980, American Educational Research Association, Washington, D. C. By permission of the publisher and author.

Table 13.2 is adapted from table 5 in Mitman, Alexis, et al., "Instruction Addressing the Components of Scientific Literacy and Its Relation to Student Outcomes," *American Educational Research Journal,* 1987, vol. 24, no. 4, p. 625.

Table 13.6 is adapted from table 2 in Basow, Susan A., and Silberg, Nancy T., "Student Evaluations of College Professors: Are Female and Male Professors Rated Differently?" *Journal of Educational Psychology,* 1987, vol. 79, p. 311.

Table 13.8 is adapted from table 3 of Shinn, Mark R.; Tindall, Gerald A.; and Spira, Deborah A., "Special Education Referrals as an Index of Teacher Tolerance: Are Teachers Imperfect Tests?" *Exceptional Children,* 1987, vol. 54, p. 37.

Excerpts on pp. 518–519 are reprinted from Sam Leles, "Using the Critical Incidents Technique to Develop a Theory of Educational Professionalism: An Exploratory Study," *Journal of Teacher Education* 19 (Spring 1968): 59-69. By permission of the publisher.

Table 14.5 is reprinted from table 3 in Krohn, Emily J.; Lamp, Robert E.; and Phelps, Cynthia G., "Validity of the K-ABC for a Black Preschool Population," *Psychology in the Schools,* 1988, vol. 25, p. 20.

Figure 14.4 is adapted from figure 1 in King, Suzanne, and Wolfle, Lee M., "A Latent-Variable Causal Model of Faculty Reputational Ratings," *Research in Higher Education,* 1987, vol. 27, p. 101.

Table 15.2 is adapted from tables 1 and 2 in Pratton, Jerry, and Hales, Loyde W., "The Effects of Active Participation on Student Learning," *Journal of Educational Research,* vol. 79, p. 213, 1986. Reprinted with permission of the Helen Dwight Reid Educational Foundation. Published by Heldref Publications, 4000 Albermarle St. NW, Washington, DC 20016. © 1986.

Table 15.3 is reprinted from table 1 in Castaneda, Sandra; Lopez, Miguel; and Romero, Martha, "The Role of Five Induced Learning Strategies in Scientific Text Comprehension," *Journal of Experimental Education,* 1987, vol. 55, p. 136.

Figure 16.3 is adapted from figure 1 in Edwards, Rosaland, "The Effects of Performance Standards on Behavior Patterns and Motor Skill Achievement in Children," *Journal of Teaching in Physical Education*, 1988, vol. 7, p. 96.

Figure 16.5 is adapted from figure 1 in Guza, D. S., and McLaughlin, T. F., "A Comparison of Daily and Weekly Testing on Student Spelling Performance," *Journal of Educational Research*, vol. 80, p. 375, 1987. Reprinted with permission of the Helen Dwight Reid Educational Foundation. Published by Heldref Publications, 4000 Albermarle St. NW, Washington, DC 20016. © 1987.

Figure 16.6 is adapted from figure 1 in Stern, George W., Fowler, Susan A., and Kohler, Frank W., "A Comparison of Two Intervention Roles: Peer Monitor and Point Earner," *Journal of Applied Behavior Analysis*, 1988, vol. 21, p. 107.

Figure 16.7 is adapted from figure 1 in Sharpley, Christopher F., "Some Arguments against Analyzing Client Change Graphically," *Journal of Counseling and Development*, 1986, vol. 65, p.157.

Table 16.9 is reprinted from "Pitfalls in the Measurement of Gains in Achievement," by Paul B. Diederich, by permission of the University of Chicago Press. Copyright © 1956 by the University of Chicago. Reprinted from *School Review* 64 (1956), table 1, p. 60.

Table 17.1 is adapted from table 1 in Lai, Morris K., et al., "A Nutrient Analysis of Students' Diets in the State of Hawaii," *Journal of Nutrition Education*, vol. 14, no. 2, 1982, p. 68. © Society for Nutrition Education.

Table 17.2 is reprinted from Egon G. Guba and Yvonne S. Lincoln, *Effective Evaluation* (San Francisco: Jossey-Bass, 1981), p. 28. By permission of the publisher.

Table 18.2 is adapted from the table in Cunningham, Lawrence J, "The Development and Validation of a High School Textbook on the Ancient Chamorros of Guam" (Ed. D. dissertation, University of Oregon, 1987). p. 95.

Table 21.1 is atapted from the table in Thorkildsen, Ron J, "An Experimental Test of a Microcomputer/Videodisc Program to Develop the Social Skills of Mildly Handicapped & Elementary Students" (Ph.D. dissertation, University of Oregon, 1984). p. 14.

Table 21.2 is reprinted from table 8 in Hall, Bruce W.; Ward, Annie W.; and Comer, Connie B., "Published Educational Research: An Empirical Study of Its Quality," *Journal of Educational Research*, vol. 81, p. 188, 1988. Reprinted with permission of the Helen Dwight Reid Educational Foundation. Published by Heldref Publications, 4000 Albermarle St. NW, Washington, DC 20016. © 1988.

Figure 21.2 is reprinted from figure 4 in Haensly, Patricia A.; Lupkowski, Ann E.; and McNamara, James F., "The Chart Essay: A Strategy for Communicating Research Findings to Policymakers and Practitioners," *Educational Evaluation and Policy Analysis*, 1987, vol. 9, p. 71.

Appendix A is reprinted from *CIJE* (regular monthly listing on p. vi), Phoenix, AZ: The Oryx Press. By permission of the publisher.

Appendix D is abridged from J. C. Flanagan's table of normalized biserial coefficients originally prepared for the Cooperative Test Service. Printed by permission of the author.

Appendix F is reprinted form *Test Collection*, Educational Testing Service, Princeton, NJ. By permission of the publisher.

Part I

EDUCATIONAL RESEARCH—THE FIELD

This part of the book consists of a single overview chapter. Its primary purpose is to help you understand why educational research is worth doing. We explain how educational research leads to new knowledge and how this knowledge contributes to policy-making and practice. Also, we review recent major changes in how educational research is done. You will find that important developments in the philosophy of science have led to expanded notions of what constitutes research knowledge and legitimate methods of inquiry.

In reading this chapter you will find that educational research is neither as useless nor as powerful as some people think. Rather, educational research is a very human and therefore fallible process, which nonetheless has some distinct advantages over personal knowledge.

AN OVERVIEW OF EDUCATIONAL RESEARCH

OVERVIEW

This chapter deals primarily with the question, Why do educational research? We address the question by considering how research contributes to knowledge about education and to the practice of education. Educational research is a form of scientific inquiry, and so the nature of science is discussed. This is followed by a description of the various types of research studies that are carried out by educational researchers and other social scientists. Finally, we present a case study of an educational research project to illustrate the personal satisfactions of doing research.

OBJECTIVES

After studying this chapter you should be able to:

1. State four types of research knowledge about education.
2. Give several examples of how research has contributed to knowledge about education.
3. Explain why it is difficult to apply educational research findings directly into practice.
4. Explain why basic research is worth supporting, even though it may not lead directly to improvement in educational practice.
5. Describe the basic tenets of positivistic scientific inquiry.
6. State four criticisms of positivistic scientific inquiry by postpositivistic philosophers.
7. Explain the problem of relativism in scientific inquiry, and how it can be avoided.
8. Describe three differences between positivistic and postpositivistic educational research.
9. Describe the purpose and characteristics of scientific theories.
10. Explain the three steps of the scientific method.
11. Identify several scientific disciplines and how they have contributed to knowledge about education.
12. Identify several bases for classifying educational research studies.
13. Describe several sources of personal satisfaction in doing educational research.

INTRODUCTION

A colleague suggested to us that if doctors were to lose their base of medical knowledge, most of them would have to stop working. They would have no idea how to treat anything other than common ailments. A surgeon, for example, could not perform open-heart surgery if he lacked research-based knowledge about heart functions, anesthesia, the meaning of symptoms, and the likely risks of particular courses of action. If educators were to suddenly lose the body of knowledge gained through educational research, however, their work would be virtually unaffected. Schools would continue to operate pretty much as they do now. It is hard to imagine a teacher who would refuse to teach students because he or she lacked research-based knowledge about the learning process and the effectiveness of instructional methods.

The point of our colleague's comparison of medicine and education is that research has relatively little influence on the day-to-day work of educators. Whether true or not, his assessment of educational practice raises an important question: Why do educational research? Like other researchers, we can state some of the taken-for-granted answers to this question. The major reason for educational research is to develop *new knowledge* about teaching and learning and administration. The new knowledge is valuable because it will lead eventually to the improvement of educational practice.

These are easy answers to the question, Why do educational research? But if you examine the question more closely, the answers do not seem satisfying. For example, what does "research" mean? A defense of educational research must depend on what is meant by this term. There are other issues, too. The matter of perspective seems important; individual researchers may be motivated to do research for one set of reasons, whereas society may support research for another set of reasons. Also, the relationship between research and improvement is much more complex than most people imagine. It seems unfair to dismiss research as irrelevant because some teachers do not see the application of a particular research finding to their classroom situation or because a particular research investigation results in negative conclusions.

The purpose of this chapter is to help you examine for yourself why educational research is worth supporting. The ideas presented in it will help you critically examine your preconceived notions about educational research. At the least, you will develop a better understanding of why thousands of educational researchers throughout the world believe in their work and continue to refine the methodologies presented in this book. Our own belief is that research is essential to the continued development and improvement of educational practice.

THE IMPROVEMENT OF EDUCATION THROUGH RESEARCH

Contributions of Research to Knowledge about Education

As we indicated above, the usual defense of educational research is that it develops new knowledge, which then is applied to the improvement of educational practice. In this section we consider whether research has contributed to *knowledge* about education. In the next section we consider whether this knowledge has had an impact on the *practice* of education.

To consider whether research has contributed to knowledge about education, we need to distinguish four types of research knowledge: (1) description, (2) prediction, (3) improvement, and (4) explanation.

Description

Many research studies involve the description of natural or man-made phenomena—their form, structure, activity, change over time, relation to other phenomena, and so on. Many important scientific discoveries have resulted from making such descriptions. For example, astronomers use their telescopes to develop descriptions of different parts of the universe. This process sometimes results in the discovery of stars and stellar events.

The descriptive function of research is heavily dependent upon instrumentation for measurement and observation. Researchers may work for many years to perfect such instruments—for example, the electron microscope, the galvanometer, and standardized tests of intelligence. Once the instruments are developed, they can be used to describe phenomena of interest to the researchers. For this reason, this book contains several chapters (7, 8, 11, and 12) concerned wholly or in part with instrumentation in educational research.

Descriptive studies have greatly increased our knowledge about what happens in schools. Some of the important books in education such as *Life in Classrooms* by Philip Jackson, *The Good High School* by Sara Lawrence Lightfoot, and *A Place Called School* by John Goodlad reported studies of this type.[1]

Some descriptive research is intended to produce statistical information about aspects of education that interest policymakers and educatiors. The National Center for Education Statistics specializes in this kind of research. Many of its findings are published in an annual volume called *Digest of Educational Statistics*. This center also administers the National Assessment of Educational Progress (NAEP), which collects descriptive information about how well the nation's youth is doing in various subject areas. A typical NAEP publication is *The Reading Report Card*,[2] which provides descriptive information about the reading achievement of 9- , 13- , and 17-year-old students in the 1970–71, 1974–75, 1979–80, and 1983–84 school year. On a larger scale, the International Association for the Evaluation of Educational Achievement (IEA) has done major descriptive studies comparing the academic achievement levels of students in many different nations, including the United States.[3]

1. Philip W. Jackson, *Life in Classrooms* (New York: Holt, Rinehart and Winston, 1968); Sara Lawrence Lightfoot, *The Good High School* (New York: Basic Books, 1983); John Goodlad, *A Place Called School* (New York: McGraw-Hill, 1983).
2. National Assessment of Educational Progress, *The Reading Report Card* (Princeton, NJ: Educational Testing Service, 1985).
3. For an overview of these studies, see T. Neville Postlethwaite, "International Association for the Evaluation of Educational Achievement," in *International Encyclopedia of Education*, eds. T. Husen and T. N. Postlethwaite (Oxford: Pergamon, 1985), pp. 2645–2646.

Prediction

Another type of research knowledge involves prediction, which is the ability to predict a phenomenon that will occur at time Y from information available at an earlier time X. For example, lunar eclipses can be predicted accurately from knowledge about the relative motion of the moon, earth, and sun. The next stage of an embryo's development can be predicted accurately from knowledge of the embryo's current stage. A student's achievement in school can be predicted fairly accurately by an aptitude test administered a year or two earlier.

Many prediction studies have been done by educational researchers to develop knowledge about factors that predict students' success in school and the world of work. One reason for doing this research is to *select* students who will be successful in a particular setting. For example, the Scholastic Aptitude Test (SAT) and similar measures are given to millions of high school students annually. Colleges use the test results, along with other data, to select students who have the best chance of success in their academic programs. Prediction research needs to be done to develop knowledge about how well these tests predict, whether they predict equally well for different groups of students (such as minority students), and whether new instruments can improve the predictability of success in particular settings.

Another purpose of prediction research is to *identify* students who are likely to be unsuccessful at a subsequent point so that prevention programs can be instituted. For example, there is much interest currently in high school dropouts, because only 75 percent of students nationally graduate from high school. By collecting different types of information about students at the sixth grade, for example, and following the students until they graduate from high school or drop out, researchers can determine which information provides the best predictions. This predictive knowledge can be used to identify sixth-graders who are at risk of becoming high school dropouts. These "at risk" students then can be put in special programs that are intended to eliminate the problems that result in nongraduation from high school.

Educational research has generated a large body of predictive knowledge about factors that predict student success or failure in various school and work settings. Procedures for doing predictive research are presented in chapter 14.

Improvement

The third type of research knowledge concerns interventions—programs, curriculum materials, and teaching methods—that improve student learning or some other valued outcome. Stated more generally, these studies are designed to develop knowledge about interventions that *control* a phenomenon of interest. For example, a physiologist might vary the placement of implanted electrodes in a rat's brain to determine whether this intervention affects a particular brain activity. If placement and activation of the electrode at a particular point in the brain (intervention X) leads reliably to a particular brain activity (phenomenon Y), we can say that electrode placement "controls" that brain activity. Because most interventions in educational research are intended to improve a valued outcome such as students' learning, we say that this research is oriented to improvement (rather than the more general, and neutral, goal of "control").

Many research studies are done to identify interventions, or factors that can be transformed into interventions, to improve students' academic achievement. Herbert Walberg and his colleagues synthesized nearly 3,000 such studies to identify interventions, or potential interventions, that improve students' performance on various measures of academic achievement.[4] The results of the synthesis are summarized in table 1.1.

The first column lists the interventions that were tested in the studies. Each intervention was the subject of many different studies. The second column is a statistic called *effect size*, which is discussed in chapters 4, 5, and 9. This statistic is a quantitative way of describing how well the *average* student who received the intervention performed relative to the *average* student who did not receive the intervention (or who received less of it). An effect size of 0 means that the average student receiving the intervention did no better or worse than the average student not receiving the intervention. Positive effect sizes mean that the average student receiving the intervention did better than the average student not receiving it. The larger the effect size, the more powerful is the intervention. Researchers consider effect sizes larger than .33 to have *practical significance*, that is, the effect is large enough to make a worthwhile difference in the outcome. Negative effect sizes mean that the average student receiving the intervention did less well than the average student not receiving it.

The third column in table 1.1 presents percentile equivalents to further help you interpret the meaning of the effect sizes. The percentile for reinforcement (88), for example, means that the average student receiving reinforcement, (i.e., the student scoring at the 50th percentile on an achievement measure following an intervention involving reinforcement) did as well on an achievement measure as a nonreinforced student who scored at the 88th percentile. In other words, reinforcing an average student typically moves the student from the 50th percentile to the 88th percentile. To illustrate further, if we look at table 1.1, we find that providing computer-assisted instruction typically moves an average student from the 50th percentile to the 59th percentile.

Walberg's synthesis of research shows that educational researchers have discovered many effective interventions for improving students' academic achievement. Further research is needed to refine these interventions to make them more effective across different educational settings and for different types

---

4. Herbert Walberg, "Improving the Productivity of America's Schools," *Educational Leadership* 41, no. 8 (1984): 19–27.

TABLE 1.1

Effects of Instructional Factors on Student Learning Outcomes

Method	Effect Size	Percentile
1. Reinforcement	1.17	88
2. Acceleration	1.00	84
3. Reading training	.97	83
4. Cues and feedback	.97	83
5. Science mastery learning	.81	79
6. Graded homework	.79	79
7. Cooperative learning	.76	78
8. Reading experiments	.60	73
9. Class morale	.60	73
10. Personalized instruction	.57	72
11. Home interventions	.50	69
12. Adaptive instruction	.45	67
13. Tutoring	.40	66
14. Instructional time	.38	65
15. Home environment	.37	64
16. Individualized science	.35	64
17. Higher-order questions	.34	63
18. Diagnostic prescriptive methods	.33	63
19. Individualized instruction	.32	63
20. Individualized mathematics	.32	63
21. New science curricula	.31	62
22. Teacher expectations	.28	61
23. Assigned homework	.28	61
24. Socioeconomic status	.25	60
25. Computer-assisted instruction	.24	59
26. Peer group	.24	59
27. Sequenced lessons	.24	59
28. Advance organizers	.23	59
29. New mathematics curricula	.18	57
30. Inquiry biology	.16	56
31. Homogeneous groups	.10	54
32. Class size	.09	54
33. Programmed instruction	−.03	49
34. Television	−.05	48
35. Mainstreaming	−.12	45

SOURCE: Data from Herbert Walberg, "Improving the Productivity of America's Schools," *Educational Leadership* 41, no. 8 (1984): 24.

of students. Also, research is needed to turn potential interventions into actual interventions. For example, classroom morale is not an intervention per se, but it is potentially manipulatable; that is, interventions probably can be developed to increase classroom morale, which in turn should improve student learning.

Improvement-oriented research knowledge is generated using causal-comparative, correlational, and experimental methods. In correlational research, natural variations in the intervention (for example, real-life situations where tutoring occurs or does not occur) are related to variations in student outcomes. In experimental research, the researcher deliberately manipulates the intervention (for example, creating a situation in which some students receive tutoring, and other students do not) to determine its effects on student outcomes. Procedures for conducting causal-comparative, correlational, and experimental research are described in chapters 13 through 16.

Explanation

The fourth type of research knowledge—explanation—is the most important of all in the long range. In a sense, this type of knowledge subsumes the other three. If researchers are able to explain a set of phenomena, it means that they can describe, predict, and control the phenomena with a high level of certainty and accuracy.

Research explanations take the form of *theories* about the phenomena being investigated. (The elements of theories, and procedures by which they are generated and tested, are discussed later in the chapter.) Several important theories have been developed by educational researchers. An example is the theory of educational productivity developed by Herbert Walberg on the basis of the research findings shown in table 1.1. His theory, which has some similarities to theories developed by Benjamin Bloom, John Carroll, Robert Glaser, and others, seeks to explain why some students learn more than others and how learning can be enhanced.

A graphic representation of the theory is shown in figure 1.1. We see that the theory explains how various factors are causally related to one another. Note that the factors do not refer to specific phenomena (for example, Johnny's score on the teacher's science test last Friday). The factors—called more precisely "theoretical constructs"—refer to elements common to many phenomena, such as "quality of instruction." In other words, they are mental representations of regularities in surface phenomena. Theoretical knowledge is important because it provides a succinct "formula" for predicting and controlling many different phenomena involving different persons and settings and occurring at different times.

In summary, educational research generates four important types of knowledge: descriptions of educational phenomena; predictions of educational phenomena; information about the effects of improvement-oriented interven-

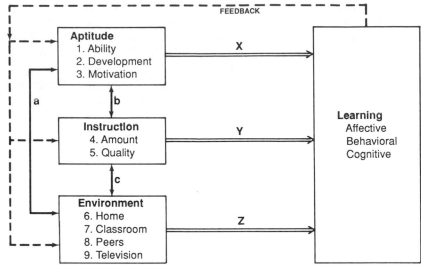

NOTE:
  Aptitude, instruction, and the psychological environment are major direct causes of
learning (shown as double arrows X, Y, and Z). They also influence one another
(shown as arrows a, b, and c), and are in turn influenced by feedback on the amount
of learning that takes place (shown as broken arrows).

Figure 1.1   Graphic Representation of a Theory of Educational Productivity
Source: Herbert Walberg, "Improving the Productivity of America's Schools," *Educational
Leadership* 41, no. 8 (1984): 21.

tions; and theories. One other type of knowledge, of a different order from
these, deserves mention. In reflecting on their work, educational researchers
keep developing new knowledge about how to design and conduct research.
Thus, research methodology keeps changing. For example, this edition of
Educational Research: An Introduction contains a greatly expanded coverage of
qualitative research methodology, reflecting important developments that have
occurred in this field over just the past five years. Many other advances in
research methodology are contained in this edition as well.

   A great increase in each type of research knowledge has occurred in the
modern era of educational research, dating back to around 1960. The increase
came about largely because the federal government began a serious effort to
fund educational research with the passage of the Cooperative Research Act of
1954. This act authorized the then U.S. Office of Education (USOE) to fund a
variety of research and development projects in universities and other educational agencies. From 1957 to 1963, USOE appropriations for educational
research and development averaged $20 million or less. In 1964, appropriations

increased to $37 million. In the following year they increased again, to over $100 million, where they stabilized for the remainder of the decade.[5]

Federal funding for educational research in the 1970s and 1980s varied depending upon the administration that was in power. Exact expenditures are difficult to determine because responsibility for educational research was dispersed across a variety of federal agencies, and the agencies involved kept changing in name and function. A conservative estimate of recent expenditures would be on the order of several hundred million dollars annually. As a percentage of total expenditures for education, this is a rather low amount; the percentage of expenditures for research on health and defense is much higher, for example. However, the availability of at least some federal funding for research through the 1970s and 1980s has led to a steady, if not dramatic, increase in research knowledge about education.

Contributions of Research Knowledge to the Practice of Education

The contributions of research to educational knowledge are easy to demonstrate through reviews of the research literature. The review summarized in table 1.1 is just one of many available reviews of accumulated research knowledge. (See chapter 4 for sources of published reviews.) It is much more difficult to determine whether the accumulation of research findings has made an impact on the practice of education. The reason is that many influences act on educational practice. Even when research knowledge attracts the attention of policymakers in education, they generally consider it as just one source of information to use in shaping a particular policy. Gene Glass makes this point well:

> Facts, even when accumulated into "research findings," seldom compel policies or political actions. Generally, findings are fragmentary or incomplete or, taken en masse, too incoherent to serve as justification for certain serious actions. Consider an example: When the judge in the Los Angeles desegregation case was confidently informed by sociologists that busing between the San Fernando Valley and downtown Los Angeles would result in the flight of 33% of the Anglo families from the public school system, he merely redrew the busing patterns so that the numbers of Anglos, Blacks, and Hispanics would balance after a third of the Anglos had fled the system. Policies grow out of "world views" and projections of possible futures, and these depend on many more things than research findings.[6]

5. For a discussion of the 20-year period of educational research following passage of the Cooperative Research Act, see David Krathwohl, "Improving Educational Research and Development," *Educational Researcher* 6, no. 4 (1977): 8–14.
6. Gene V Glass, "*What Works:* Politics and Research," *Educational Researcher* 16 (1987):9.

Glass's commentary raises the question whether the present situation should change so that research has a more direct impact on policy-making and practice. Our belief is that research should influence policy-making and practice, but only with the exercise of careful judgment. As you shall discover a bit later in the chapter, recent developments in the philosophy of science have sensitized researchers to the fact that most, if not all, research knowledge is value-laden. Therefore, putting a research finding into practice also means putting a particular set of values into practice.

For example, the interventions shown in table 1.1 are more or less effective in improving students' academic achievement, usually as measured by performance on standardized achievement tests. Using these research results as evidence for advocating one or more of the interventions, then, means also advocating high test performance as a valued outcome of schooling. There are other valued outcomes of schooling, however, such as curiosity, self-reliance, and humanitarian attitudes, that may not be promoted by these interventions. Thus, putting the research results into practice may implement, intentionally or inadvertently, one set of values rather than another.

D. C. Phillips, a philosopher of education, described this difficulty in putting research into practice as the "is/ought problem":

> Research findings take the form, roughly, of "X is Y" or "the probability of an X having the feature Y is p"; in other words, they are statements of the "is" form. On the other hand, implications for practice take the form such as, "person A ought to do Z to person B." In other words, they are statements involving an "ought" or "should" or some other locution involving the passing of a value judgment. But it is a point of logic that from statements only involving the use of "is," a conclusion involving "ought" or one of its locutions cannot validly be deduced. . . .[7]

To understand Phillips' point, we refer to a study on teacher enthusiasm discussed in more detail later in the chapter. One result of the study was that elementary students observed in the research were "on-task" approximately 75 percent of the time during instruction. This percentage is similar to results found in other research on student on-task behavior. This is a finding about what "is." However, the fact that students are not attentive some of the time does not necessarily mean they "ought" to be attentive more of the time. Perhaps it is natural and desirable for students to tune out instruction periodically. Even if more time on task is associated with higher achievement, perhaps students *ought* to be free to decide when and how they will attend to classroom instruction.

Questions involving "is" can be answered objectively by well-designed research. Questions involving "ought" are value-laden and can be resolved only

---

7. D. C. Phillips, "What Do the Researcher and the Practitioner Have to Offer Each Other?" *Educational Researcher* 9, no. 11 (1980): 19.

through dialogue and a decision-making process that includes interested constituencies. Researchers should not expect their findings about "is" to result in educational change immediately and without critical appraisal. Practitioners who look to research for prescriptive advice are similarly unjustified. It is much more sensible to use research knowledge about what "is" to inform dialogue about what "ought" to be—a dialogue that should be informed by other considerations as well.

Some educators believe that applied research should be given more funding support than basic research because it is more helpful to policymakers and practitioners. The reason that applied research is perceived to be more helpful is that it concerns improvement of actual practice; by contrast, basic research is more concerned with theory-building and the study of basic processes, such as the physiology and psychology of learning.

An important study done in the field of medicine should give pause to those who discount the value of basic research in education.[8] Julius Comroe and Robert Dripps started their study by identifying the 10 most important advances since the early 1940s in the treatment of cardiovascular and pulmonary diseases. (These diseases were selected because they account for more than half of all deaths in the United States each year.) The 10 advances are listed in the first column of table 1.2. With the assistance of 140 consultants, Comroe and Dripps identified the bodies of knowledge that needed to be developed through research before the 10 clinical advances could reach their present state of achievement. A total of 137 essential bodies of knowledge were identified, such as anatomy of cardiac defects, blood typing, monitoring of blood pressure, and management of postoperative infection.

The next step in Comroe and Dripps' investigation was to identify approximately 2,500 scientific reports that were important to the development of the 10 clinical advances. The list of reports was subsequently reduced to 529 essential reports, which were then subjected to detailed analysis. Each article was classified into one of six categories:

1. Basic research unrelated to the solution of a clinical problem
2. Basic research related to the solution of a clinical problem
3. Studies not concerned with basic biological, chemical, or physical mechanisms
4. Review and critical analysis of published work and synthesis of new concepts (without new experimental data)
5. Developmental work or engineering to create, improve, or perfect apparatus or a technique for research use
6. Developmental work or engineering to create, improve, or perfect apparatus or a technique for use in diagnosis or care of patients

8. Julius H. Comroe, Jr., and Robert D. Dripps, "Scientific Basis for the Support of Biomedical Science," *Science* 192 (1976): 105–111.

TABLE 1.2

Types of Research Reported in 529 Key Articles

Type	Basic: Not Clinically Oriented	Basic: Clinically Oriented	Not Basic	Review and Synthesis	Development: Research	Development: Clinical	Total
Cardiac surgery	34	23	19	0	3	11	90
Vascular surgery	9	7	14	3	0	21	54
Drug treatment of hypertension	42	16	21	2	0	0	81
Medical treatment of coronary insufficiency	21	20	22	1	1	3	68
Cardiac resuscitation	16	11	9	0	0	6	42
Oral diuretics	23	13	6	1	0	0	43
Intensive care[a]	—	—	—	—	—	—	—
Chemotherapy and antibiotics	12	18	21	1	0	2	54
Diagnostic methods	49	21	5	2	17	22	116
Prevention of poliomyelitis	3	12	3	0	1	0	19
Total	209	141	120	10	22	65	567[b]
Percentage of total	36.8	24.9	21.2	1.8	3.9	11.4	

SOURCE: Adapted from Julius H. Comroe, Jr., and Robert D. Dripps, "Scientific Basis for the Support of Biomedical Science," *Science* 192 (1976): table 6, p. 110.
[a] Because practically every key article in intensive care was also essential to other advances, these articles were assigned elsewhere.
[b] The total number of entries in the six categories (567) exceeds the total number of articles (529) because some key articles fit in more than one category.

Table 1.2 shows the number and percentage of key reports assigned to each of the categories.

The remarkable finding in this table is the high percentage of *basic* research studies (36.8 + 24.9 = 61.7%) that were essential to the development of current treatment of disease. Equally remarkable is the fact that more than a third (36.8%) of the essential studies were not even related to the practice of cardiovascular medicine. This result suggests that research can influence practice even when this is not its intent.

Our sense of the current situation is that an increasing number of educators are at least becoming aware of research knowledge concerning education. Popular education journals for practitioners such as *Educational Leadership* and *Phi Delta Kappan* regularly publish reports of important research studies. Moreover, teachers and administrators increasingly are required to take a master's level course in research methods that trains them how to read a research report and perhaps also to conduct a research study. Many of them go on to earn a doctorate, and in the course of doing so they get advanced research training and do a substantial research study for their doctoral dissertation.

Awareness of educational research is not sufficient to create positive attitudes toward research and the contribution it can make to the improvement of practice. There is still a long way to go before research has the respect and influence found in other professions such as medicine and engineering. Also, we have learned from research on educational change that the change process is very slow. Over the next twenty years or so, perhaps sooner, we expect to see increasing respect by practitioners for research knowledge, not as the sole guide to practice but as one basis, alongside personal judgment and experience, for making decisions.

THE NATURE OF SCIENTIFIC INQUIRY

The purpose of educational research is to discover new knowledge about teaching, learning, administration, and other educational phenomena. This statement appears straightforward, but a closer inspection raises questions. What do we mean by "knowledge"? What is the process by which knowledge is obtained? And what phenomena are worth acquiring knowledge about?

For much of this century, it would have been fairly easy to answer these questions. There were widely accepted techniques for formulating research problems, collecting data, and deciding whether the results constituted valid knowledge. These techniques collectively are called "the scientific method." In the past two decades, however, the waters have become muddied. Several developments have led educational researchers to call into question their methods and purposes.

One of these developments has been new ideas about the nature of scientific inquiry set forth by philosophers of science. Thomas Kuhn's book *The Structure of Scientific Revolutions*, published in 1962, stimulated many philosophers and researchers to rethink the assumptions underlying the traditional scientific method.[9]

Another development was the increasing interest of educational researchers in the methods of scientific inquiry used in disciplines other than psychology. Most of the original methods of educational research came from psychology. This is why many colleges of education have departments of educational psychology or are affiliated with departments of psychology. However, anthropology, sociology, history, economics, and other disciplines also have much to offer educational research. Some of their methods, such as ethnography (from the field of anthropology) and symbolic interactionism (from the field of sociology), are quite different from the methods of traditional educational research. The fact that these methods are so different, yet apparently legitimate, caused many educational researchers to consider their relevance to the study of problems relating to education.

Still another development was the increasing interest of educational researchers, with encouragement from practitioners, in phenomena not easily studied using traditional research methodology. As we shall see below, traditional research methodology is well suited to the study of overt behavior and forms of academic achievement measured by paper-and-pencil tests. It is less well suited to the study of nonobservables, such as teacher intentions, student cognitive processes, and school culture.

These three developments were instrumental in stimulating educational researchers to reexamine the nature of their scientific inquiry. The reexamination is by no means complete. Many issues remain unresolved, and researchers and philosophers continue to debate them in the professional literature. The purpose of the following discussion is to give you a sense of what the issues are and how they affect the content and organization of this book.

Positivism and the Scientific Method

The scientific method widely used in both the natural and social sciences is derived from a system of philosophy known as *positivism*. There are various schools of positivism,[10] but the one that has been most influential in this century is *logical positivism*.

9. Kuhn's book is described in the Annotated References at the end of this chapter.
10. For a brief description of different schools of positivism, see D. C. Phillips, "After the Wake: Postpositivistic Educational Thought," *Educational Researcher* 12, no. 5 (1983): 4–12.

Positivism is a system of philosophy that excludes everything from its consideration except natural phenomena and their interrelationships. One of the major principles of logical positivism is the *verifiability principle,* which states that something is meaningful if and only if it can be observed objectively by the human senses.[11] In other words, our knowledge claims about the world are not meaningful unless they can be verified through direct observation of the world. For example, if I make the knowledge claim that elementary school teachers ask mostly fact questions, that claim is meaningful and valid (if I am a logical positivist) only if I have made direct observations of teacher behavior. I must have defined the concept of "fact questions" in such a way that I, or anyone else, can identify instances of fact questions using only observable characteristics of teacher behavior.

Positivism, then, places a premium on observation of the world "out there." The researcher's values, interpretations, feelings, and musings have no place in the positivist's view of scientific inquiry. The researcher must be as objective as possible.

The scientific method that has dominated educational research right up to the present day is based on the principles of positivism. We shall explain the scientific method more fully in a later section of the chapter, but we introduce it here to show its basis in positivism.

The scientific method is commonly thought to include three major phases. The first phase is to formulate a hypothesis, which is a theoretically based knowledge claim about the relation between two or more constructs (which, in everyday terms, are called "concepts"). These constructs must be defined in such a way that they can be observed directly. For example, a construct such as "self-esteem" might be defined as a student's score on a paper-and-pencil instrument purporting to measure that construct. (Procedures for determining whether an instrument validly measures a construct are described in chapter 7.) In this case, the student's score on the instrument constitutes something that is directly observable.

The next phase of the scientific method is to deduce observable consequences of the hypothesis. For example, suppose our hypothesis is that teachers will be more likely to implement a new curriculum if it is consistent with their belief system than if it is not consistent. To test the hypothesis, we search for a new curriculum that is being introduced into a school district. Upon finding one, we analyze the curriculum and determine that it is based on a particular set of beliefs about student motivation for learning. We would deduce that, if the hypothesis is correct, teachers whose beliefs about student motivation are consistent with this curriculum will implement it to a greater degree than those teachers whose beliefs are inconsistent.

11. Something also can be meaningful to a logical positivist if it is a mathematical or logical tautology.

The third phase of the scientific method is to test the hypothesis by collecting data. We would administer measures of curriculum implementation and belief systems to all teachers who have been asked to use the new program. One way to analyze the resulting data would be to identify teachers who score very high (indicating belief consistency) or very low on the belief measure. Then the mean implementation scores of the high- and low-scoring teachers would be compared. If the hypothesis is valid, teachers scoring high on the belief measure should earn higher scores on the measure of implementation than the teachers scoring low on the belief measure.

As the above example illustrates, the scientific method is positivistic because its constructs and knowledge claims (hypotheses) are grounded in presumably objective observations of the world.

Positivistic and Postpositivistic Philosophies of Science

The positivistic approach to scientific inquiry has served educational research well. Much of the knowledge that we have acquired about education has resulted from its application. Nonetheless, some philosophers have found flaws in the assumptions underlying positivistic science. Their analysis of these flaws has led to revised views of what constitutes legitimate scientific inquiry. These revised views form what can be called a postpositivistic philosophy of science.

Criticism of positivistic science generally focuses on four of its assumptions. First, positivism assumes that hypotheses derived from theories can be confirmed or disconfirmed through objective, neutral observations. In other words, these observations (called "observation statements" or "O-reports" by positivists) must be independent of the theory they are designed to test. Otherwise the observations will be biased in favor of the theory.

Critics of this assumption point out that there is no such thing as a theory-free observation. For example, suppose we wish to test the hypothesis that gifted children whose academic achievement is below their potential are more likely to have emotional disorders than are gifted children achieving at their potential. What objective, neutral observations allow us to test this hypothesis? A moment's reflection will demonstrate that our theories, whether explicit or implicit, will influence how we define and measure the constructs of giftedness, achievement, and emotional disorder. One group of researchers might make observations based on a particular theory involving these constructs and find support for the hypothesis. Another group of researchers might make observations based on a different theory and reject the hypothesis.

Apparently, then, observations are always "theory-laden," a term coined by critics of positivism. Thus, there is no absolute, independent test that can be made of a hypothesis derived from a theory.

The second assumption of positivism is that the observations used to test the validity of knowledge claims are value-free. If the observations are not value-free, the findings of a "scientific" study may reflect the values of the researcher rather than something that is true about the world. For example, Nazi "researchers" were able to demonstrate that Germans were the master race. However, their research data (i.e., their "observations") were anything but value-free.

Critics of positivism argue persuasively that there is no such thing as a value-free observation, especially in the social sciences. Kenneth Howe states the case this way:

> Value judgments may not be excluded from the arena of rational criticism in general or from the conduct of research in particular. No researcher, whatever the field, can avoid value commitments (whether or not such commitments are acknowledged). It is absurd, for example, to suggest that the physicists participating in the Manhattan Project to develop nuclear weapons were engaged in a value-free enterprise. It is even more absurd to suggest that social research can be value-free because social research is *doubly value-laden*. Not only is social research circumscribed by values that determine things such as funding and how research results should be used . . . the very concepts social researchers employ are evaluative of human behavior.[12]

Howe's point about the evaluative nature of concepts (what we refer to above as "constructs") undermines the positivistic assumption that constructs can be defined so as to allow for neutral, objective observation. Consider concepts commonly used by educators and educational researchers: academic achievement, self-esteem, intelligence, ability, talent, learning style, study skills, achievement motivation, internal locus of control. Each of these concepts is the subject of research because there is a constituency that values it, and they value it in a way that influences how the concept is defined and measured.

In fact, there are those who accuse mainstream educational research of working against needed social changes because it focuses on helping students achieve taken-for-granted academic goals.[13] These goals represent the values of the dominant class in society. By helping teachers and students achieve these goals better, educational research is helping to perpetuate these values, which are not in the best interests of the underclass.

This criticism has strongly influenced the work of educational historians. In the chapter on historical research (chapter 19), you will find that some

12. Kenneth R. Howe, "Two Dogmas of Educational Research," *Educational Researcher* 14, no. 8 (1985): 10–18.
13. For a discussion of this criticism, see Jonas F. Soltis, "On the Nature of Educational Research," *Educational Researcher* 13, no. 10 (1984): 5–10.

historical researchers (called "revisionist historians") have rewritten the history of some periods of American education based on a values framework different from previous "mainstream" historians.

Criticism of the value-laden nature of positivistic science does not seem applicable to present-day educational research. Most educational researchers, whether they have a positivistic or postpositivistic orientation, are sensitive to the value-laden and ethical character of their investigations. In fact, an entire chapter of this book (chapter 3) is concerned with ethical and human relations factors involved in educational research.

The third assumption of positivistic science that has been criticized is its requirement that tests of knowledge claims are restricted to observable phenomena. In educational and social science research, this usually means the observable behavior of the persons being studied, their performance on tests, or their responses to paper-and-pencil measures of such constructs as attitudes, interests, and classroom climate. (Note that test performance and responses to paper-and-pencil measures can be "observed" and scored objectively.) Research done by behaviorists such as B. F. Skinner is strongly positivistic because it focuses exclusively on behavior and excludes all internal phenomena as outside the province of scientific inquiry.

Many of the phenomena of interest to educational researchers, however, are not directly observable. These phenomena include intentions, feelings, and cognitions of individual persons. Group phenomena such as shared norms and values, school climate, and school culture are also of interest to researchers. No convincing reason exists to believe that observable behavior is any more "real" than these internal phenomena.

The final assumption of positivism is that "the world out there" is generally consistent across settings and time periods.[14] Thus, if researchers test a knowledge claim in one setting and find support for it, they are likely to feel confident that the knowledge claim will be true in other places and at other time periods.

This asssumption is probably reasonable for knowledge claims about the natural world, but critics of positivistic science argue that it is unlikely to apply to the kinds of social behavior that educational researchers study. In fact, we doubt that any educational researcher, whether operating in the positivistic or postpositivistic tradition, accepts this assumption. Rather, most researchers acknowledge the extreme variability that exists across individuals, social groups, and cultures. For example, it is common for researchers to include in their research reports a statement about the need for their findings to be replicated

14. Phillips, "After the Wake," claims that this is not an assumption of positivism, but other researchers claim that it is; for example: Frederick Erickson, "Qualitative Methods in Research on Teaching," in *Handbook of Research on Teaching*, 3rd ed., ed. Merlin C. Wittrock (New York: Macmillan, 1986), pp. 119–161.

using different populations and situations. Also, most researchers realize that because observations are inherently value-laden, particular knowledge claims may lose their validity as the values of a society change over time.

Despite these criticisms of the asssumptions underlying positivism, positivistic science lives on. In fact, most of the research concepts and procedures described in this book are positivistic in nature. But alongside positivism has emerged a **postpositivistic philosophy of science.** Philosophers of this persuasion accept as givens that science is theory-laden and value-laden and that it is possible to acquire knowledge about phenomena not directly observable by the senses.

Research methodologies rooted in postpositivistic philosophy of science are being used increasingly in educational research. (Chapter 10 discusses them in some depth.) They show promise of yielding important new knowledge about education. Yet there is a major problem with postpositivistic philosophy that raises questions about the validity of the theories and knowledge claims that it legitimates.

The problem is this: If all observation is theory-laden, as postpositivistic philosophers argue, how can we hope to find a common ground of neutral observational data by which to judge the validity of competing knowledge claims derived from different theories? For example, how can we judge whether the theory of evolution is more valid than the theory of creationism? Researchers from each theoretical camp can define constructs and select observational data that support their theory and refute the other.

Postpositivistic philosophy seems to give credibility and status to all sorts of theories and methods of inquiry, for example, astrology and research based on theories of a master race. All are on an equal footing with theories associated with traditional scientific methods, because there is no way to test which theory is more valid. Thus, we are left with a *relativistic* view of the world, meaning that what we take to be true is a function of the particular theoretical framework we have chosen to adopt.

Relativism is not very appealing, so there has been some effort by postpositivistic philosophers and researchers to avoid it. Thus, D. C. Phillips pointed to "historical evidence that the settling of a theoretical dispute *can* take place; usually, however, it is a long drawn-out business, a battle of attrition. Nevertheless, the dispute eventually is settled. Gradually a case is built up that favors one position rather than another."[15] As an example, Phillips notes that very few people nowadays accept the theory that the earth is flat. The round-earth theory is widely accepted as true based on the weight of accumulated evidence in its favor.

Indeed, the weight of accumulated evidence is very important in building the case for particular knowledge claims and theories. Educational researchers,

15. Phillips, "After the Wake," p.11.

whether operating in the positivistic or postpositivistic traditions, spend a lot of time reviewing the research literature relating to the knowledge claims that interest them. Techniques for reviewing the literature on education, especially the research literature, are described in chapter 4.

James Garrison proposed another way besides the weight of accumulated evidence to avoid the dangers of relativism. He appealed to the use of "practical deliberation" to judge the claims of competing theories.[16] In Garrison's view, those competent to deliberate include educational theorists, researchers, and educational *practitioners*. We can raise the question, however, about who is to make the judgment as to which members of these groups are competent to engage in "practical deliberation."

So far as we know, no absolute standard exists for judging which of several competing theories is correct. Some individuals seem willing to live with the problem. For example, there are those who accept both creationism and evolutionism, or who feel that both should be taught in the schools on an equal footing. Our own view is more aligned to that of Phillips. Over a long period of time, theoretical disputes do seem to get resolved, usually by resort to the weight of empirical evidence. Even research methods grounded in postpositivistic philosophy probably will live or die, over the long haul, by this standard. If these methods do not yield evidence that holds up under continued scrutiny and empirical testing by scientists and the larger community, they are not likely to survive.

Positivistic and Postpositivistic Research in Practice

The effects of postpositivistic philosophy of science are being felt increasingly in the world of educational research. A new generation of educational researchers influenced by this philosophy is refining their methods and publishing their research results. The previous edition of this book (1983) contained only brief descriptions of these methods. This edition has a chapter exclusively on this type of research (chapter 10), and other chapters have new or expanded sections on particular methods. For example, chapter 17 was substantially rewritten to include developments in qualitative evaluation.

Many labels have been used to distinguish between traditional research methods and these new methods (or old methods newly embraced because of their consistency with postpositivistic thinking): positivistic versus postpositivistic research;[17] scientific versus artistic research;[18] confirmatory versus dis-

16. James W. Garrison, "Some Principles of Postpositivistic Philosophy of Science," *Educational Researcher* 15, no. 9 (1986): 12–18.
17. Phillips, "After the Wake."
18. Elliot Eisner, "On the Differences Between Scientific and Artistic Approaches to Qualitative Research," *Educational Researcher* 10, no. 4 (1981): 5–9.

covery-oriented research;[19] quantitative versus interpretive research;[20] and quantitative versus qualitative research. The quantitative-qualitative distinction seems most widely used, and therefore we use it in this and subsequent chapters.

Both quantitative researchers and qualitative researchers go about scientific inquiry in different ways. How different is difficult to determine. Abraham Kaplan observed that the way in which researchers actually go about their work (what he calls "logic-in-use") is not the process implied in the reporting of their studies (what he calls "reconstructed logic").[21] The way in which typical researchers do their work is flexible, open, and sometimes intuitive. Published reports of their work are formal, linear, and leave out much of the process and anomalies encountered.

Thus, the following characterization of quantitative and qualitative research is general. In practice, the differences between the two approaches may not be as extreme as those presented here.

Relation to Self

Quantitative researchers attempt to keep themselves from influencing the collection of data. Instruments with established psychometic properties, such as achievement tests (see chapter 8) and standardized observation schedules (see chapter 12), are used to collect data. Statistical methods (see chapter 9) are used to analyze the data and draw conclusions. In other words, quantitative researchers attempt to be objective, meaning that they wish to develop an understanding of the world as it is "out there," independent of their personal biases, values, and idiosyncratic notions.

In contrast, qualitative researchers view themselves as a primary instrument for collecting data. They rely partly or entirely on their feelings, impressions, and judgments in collecting data. They also rely heavily on their own interpretations in understanding the meaning of their data. Their findings often are reported in the form of verbal descriptions (from whence probably came the label "qualitative research") rather than in the form of quantitative summaries of the type yielded by statistical analysis.

Relation to Research Participants

Quantitative researchers try to maintain positive interpersonal relations with the administrators, teachers, students, and others whom they study. (Chapter 3 includes a section on human relations factors in educational research.) At the

19. Bruce J. Biddle and Donald S. Anderson, "Theory, Methods, Knowledge, and Research on Teaching," in *Handbook of Research on Teaching*, 3rd ed., ed. Merlin C. Wittrock (New York: Macmillan, 1986), pp. 230–252.
20. Erickson, "Qualitative Methods."
21. Abraham Kaplan, *The Conduct of Inquiry* (San Francisco: Chandler, 1964).

same time, they strive to be personally detached so that their observations are as objective as possible. Detachment is achieved by using objective instruments (for example, achievement tests, rating scales, observation schedules, and interview guides) for collecting data from the people they are studying.

Qualitative researchers, however, often interact closely with those involved in their study. The research data arise out of these interactions in the form of what people reveal to the researcher and the researcher's impressions. In fact, those being studied may be included as participants in the design of the study and interpretation of the results. W. R. Torbert labeled this process "collaborative inquiry" and argued that it improves the validity and usefulness of a study's findings.[22] The reason is that many of the phenomena of interest to researchers are internal events such as perceptions and feelings rather than overt behavior. The only way to get an accurate understanding of these internal states, according to qualitative researchers, is to form a personal relationship with those being studied.

Concern for Generalizability

Quantitative researchers acknowledge the presence of individual fluctuations in human behavior, but they also believe that there are general laws that hold across individuals. For example, quantitative researchers assume that there are principles of learning that hold across large classes of people, if not entire cultures, and that can be discovered through research. Thus, quantitative researchers are likely to study a population or sample of people, rather than a few individuals. Procedures for forming samples are an important part of quantitative research methodology (see chapter 6).

Qualitative researchers, however, are more likely to study the individual case. Each individual, each school, each culture is likely to have an idiosyncratic set of values, feelings, and beliefs that can only be discovered through intensive, interactive study of that individual, school, and culture. The way in which these internal states affect behavior may vary from one case to the next, and from one historical period to the next. Therefore, although qualitative researchers sometimes generalize across cases, they do so with much caution. Some qualitative researchers take the extreme position that all generalization is impossible. If this position is taken, it is difficult to justify doing research at all.

Other differences between quantitative and qualitative research are explained in chapter 10. Our purpose here is primarily to illustrate how positivistic and postpositivistic philosophies support quite different types of research.

What does all this mean for you as a student of educational research? For

22. W. R. Torbert, "Why Educational Research Has Been So Uneducational: The Case for a New Model of Social Science Based on Collaborative Inquiry," in *Human Inquiry: A Sourcebook of New Paradigm Research*, eds. P. Reason and J. Rowan (New York: Wiley, 1981), pp. 141–151.

one thing, it means that you will need to become conversant with both types of research in order to read the research literature. Although most articles in research journals reflect the quantitative tradition, some articles report qualitative research, and their number is likely to increase substantially over the coming years.

In becoming aware of the philosophical basis underlying research, you should also be sensitive to the fact that research is very much "a personal and social process," as Jerome Allender described it.[23] Like other forms of human endeavor, then, research is uncertain and prone to error. Therefore, you need to learn how to read reports of research—whether quantitative or qualitative—critically. Chapter 5 presents guidelines for doing so.

You will also need to decide what kind of research to do for your thesis or dissertation. Will you do qualitative or quantitative research? Even within qualitative and quantitative research, there are distinct methodologies, some of which may appeal to you more than others. Ideally, you would select a research problem amenable to investigation by a methodology that suits your interests and philosophy. As you will find in the next chapter, however, additional factors need to be considered in selecting a research problem to investigate for a thesis or dissertation.

SCIENTIFIC THEORIES AND METHODS

Scientific Theories

As we discussed above, theory-building is the most important purpose of research. That is because theories encompass the other purposes of research: description, prediction, and control/improvement. Therefore, some researchers devote a great deal of effort to building and testing theories that explain educational phenomena.

Many definitions of the term *theory* are available. For our purposes we will define **theory** as a system for explaining a set of phenomena by specifying constructs and the laws that relate these constructs to each other. To explain this definition, let's consider Jean Piaget's theory of intellectual development. Piaget's theory is familiar to most educators and has had a substantial influence on American curriculum and instruction.

First, note that Piaget's theory is a *system* in that it consists of a set of constructs. The system is loose in that the constructs were developed and changed in the many treatises that Piaget and his colleagues wrote over a period

---

23. Jerome S. Allender, "Educational Research: A Personal and Social Process," *Review of Educational Research* 56 (1986): 173–193.

of many years. Other researchers have attempted to pull the theory together by writing concise descriptions of it. These concise descriptions are representations of the system.

The theoretical system is designed to explain a set of phenomena: the behavior of infants and children with respect to their environment. For example, Piaget would observe how children of different ages responded to a particular task. The children's responses constituted phenomena to be explained by the theory.

The theory provides an explanation of phenomena by first specifying a set of theoretical constructs. A **theoretical construct** is a concept that is inferred from observed phenomena. It can be defined constitutively or operationally. A **constitutively defined construct** is one that is defined by referring to other constructs. For example, the Piagetian construct of conservation can be defined as the ability to recognize that certain properties of an object remain unchanged when other properties of the object (e.g., substance, length, or volume) undergo a transformation. Note that in this definition "conservation" is defined by referring to other constructs (e.g., "property," "transformation," or "length").

An **operationally defined construct** is one that is defined by specifying the activities used to measure or manipulate it. For example, the construct "conservation" (defined constitutively above) could be defined operationally by referring to a particular task, for example, pouring a constant amount of liquid into different-sized containers and asking a child whether the amount of liquid remains the same.

In conducting investigations, researchers are more likely to use the term *variable* than the term *construct*. A **variable** can be thought of as a quantitative expression of a construct. Variables usually take the form of scores on a measuring instrument. Researchers need to be careful to use instruments that yield reliable and valid scores on *variables* that relate to *constructs under investigation*.

The final part of our definition of *theory* states that it specifies laws relating constructs to each other. For example, Piaget theorized that there are four major stages of intellectual development: sensorimotor, preoperational, concrete operations, and formal operations. These stages are constructs defined constitutively and operationally by Piaget. Piaget proposed the law that these constructs are related to each other as an invariant sequence: The sensorimotor state is always followed by the preoperational stage; the preoperational stage is always followed by the concrete operations stage; and the concrete operations stage is always followed by the formal operations stage. Two examples of laws from other theories are: (1) A behavior (construct) will be more likely to recur if followed by a reinforcer (construct) than if not followed by a reinforcer; (2) achievement (construct) will increase as a function of the amount of instructional time (construct) on content relevant to the test (construct). Each of the constructs in a well-developed theory will be connected to the other constructs by laws.

Theories serve several useful purposes. First, theoretical constructs identify commonalities in otherwise isolated phenomena. Piaget's theory, for example, pulls together many isolated infant behaviors as instances of sensori-motor intelligence. In other words, theoretical constructs identify the universals of experience so that we can make sense of experience. Second, the laws of a theory enable us to make predictions and to control phenomena. Because astronomers have a well-developed theory, they can make very accurate predictions about the occurrence of eclipses and other phenomena in the universe. Because special educators work from a well-developed theory of learning (sometimes called a "behavioral theory of learning"), they can make instructional interventions that dependably lead to positive changes in student behavior.

The constructs and laws of a theory have important heuristic functions. One heuristic function is to organize the isolated findings of research into a powerful explanatory network. Consider, for example, the theory graphically displayed in figure 1.1. It organizes into a coherent whole the findings of nearly three thousand studies that explored many isolated variables. The theory is elegant in its simplicity (a property of good theories), yet it explains a highly diverse set of phenomena.

The other important heuristic function of theory is to identify areas for further research. Research results that do not fit the theory will force the researcher to revise the theory and then to collect new data to test the revised theory. For example, Walberg's theory of educational productivity proposes that:

> The first five essential factors [shown in figure 1.1] appear to substitute, compensate, or trade-off for one another at diminishing rates of return. Immense quantities of time, for example, may be required for a moderate amount of learning if motivation, ability, or instructional quality is minimal. Thus, no single essential factor overwhelms the others; all appear important.[24]

Suppose further research discovered that one of these five factors, if present only to a moderate degree, produced a high amount of learning, even though the other factors were minimal. This finding would force a reexamination and revision of the theory. Another possibility is that further research would continue to validate the theory for certain educational contexts, but not others. In this scenario, the theory would need to be revised to account for these discrepant findings. In this way, theories change over time and gradually may be replaced by other theories that have greater explanatory power. Freudian theory at one time was used to explain children's behavior, but it gradually became displaced by Piagetian theory, which provided better explanations of a more diverse array of children's behavior. More recently, behavioral theories of

24. Walberg, "Improving the Productivity," p. 22.

learning have been giving way to cognitive or cognitive-behavioral theories of learning.

Theory might make a particularly important contribution to education because it emphasizes the micro-processes underlying surface phenomena. For example, we find in table 1.1 that reduction in class size generally has a positive effect on student academic achievement. But why? *Class size* is a macro-construct; it has relatively little explanatory power. Small classes probably are good because they bring into play instructional processes that are not present in large classes. Researchers could build and test theories to identify these underlying instructional processes. Knowledge about such processes might enable educators to design interventions that are more reliable and more powerful, but less expensive, than reduction in class size.

Scientists sometimes speak of "small" and "large" theories. A small theory might be developed to account for a limited set of phenomena (e.g., antecedents and consequences of teacher morale). A large theory might account for many phenomena (e.g., behavioral theory and Freud's theory). Also, a theory might "grow" as it incorporates more constructs to explain more phenomena. A researcher might start with a small theory of academic achievement. As more determinants of achievement are discovered, the researcher can enlarge the theory to accommodate them.

The Scientific Method

In traditional positivistic research, theories can be developed and tested in two different ways. One way is to conduct research atheoretically, meaning that the researcher collects data with no particular theory in mind. The researcher simply poses a set of research questions and seeks to answer them by collecting relevant data. Eventually, this or some other researcher might take the accumulation of these atheoretical findings and generate a theory that explains them. Walberg's theory, which is shown in figure 1.1, is of this type. It seeks to explain the findings of literally thousands of studies, many of which were atheoretical.

The other way to proceed is to start by formulating a theory and then test it by collecting relevant data. As we stated above, this process has three steps: (1) formulation of a hypothesis, (2) deduction of observable consequences of the hypothesis, and (3) testing the hypothesis by making observations (that is to say, by collecting research data).

These three steps are illustrated in a study conducted by Brian Mullen.[25] The study involved a theory developed by social psychologists called *self-attention theory*. This theory concerns self-regulation processes that occur when a

---

25. Brian Mullen, "A Self-Attention Perspective on Discussion," in *Questioning and Discussion: A Multidisciplinary Study*, ed. J. T. Dillon (London: Ablex, 1988), pp. 74–89.

person becomes the object of his or her attention. Self-consciousness and embarrassment are manifestations of self-attention processes at work; however, other manifestions do not have this affectively negative state associated with them.

One purpose of self-attention theory is to explain the effect of groups on the individual. The theory states in part that when individuals are in groups of people like themselves, they become more self-attentive as the size of the group decreases. This is because the smaller group becomes more of a focal point for the individual's attention, and as a result, the individual is led to compare himself or herself with the standards represented by the group.

How can we test whether this theory is correct? Researchers do so by formulating a **hypothesis,** which is a tentative proposition about the relation between two or more theoretical constructs. In Mullen's study, the hypothesis was that individuals would be more self-attentive in smaller groups than in larger groups. The two theoretical constructs in this hypothesis are "group size" and "self-attention." They were hypothesized to be in inverse relation to each other, meaning that as group size decreases, self-attention increases.

The next phase in the scientific method is to deduce observable consequences of the hypothesis. To engage in deduction, the researcher needs to find a real-life or simulated simulation. In Mullen's case, he had available a set of transcripts of 27 high school discussions varying in size of discussion group. He operationally defined self-attention in this context as the use of first-person-singular pronouns ("I," "me") by students whenever they spoke in the discussion groups. Group size was measured by counting the number of students in each discussion group.[26] Thus, Mullen had a situation in which he could determine observable consequences of the hypothesis. Each construct specified in the hypothesis was operationally defined and measurable using the data available to him.

The third step of the scientific method is to test the hypothesis by collecting data. Using the transcripts and other data available to him, Mullen counted the number of students and number of first-person-singular pronouns in each discussion. Mullen then related the two sets of numerical data (group size and pronouns) to each other by using the statistical method called *correlation*, which you will read about in chapter 14. The statistical analysis yielded the hypothesized result: A higher frequency of first-person-singular pronouns existed in the smaller discussion groups than in the larger discussion groups.

Mullen's study illustrates how the scientific method can be used to test a theory. Because the hypothesis was supported, that part of the theory to which it relates is strengthened, meaning that we can be a bit more confident that the theory provides a good explanation of how individuals act in social situations.

---

26. Actually, a more complex measure of group size, called the Other–Total Ratio, was computed, but in this study it corresponded closely to the count of the number of students in each group.

Despite the power of the scientific method to test the validity of knowledge claims (i.e., hypotheses), it has several weaknesses. One of them is that the researcher may deduce inappropriate observable consequences from the hypothesis, and thus make an inappropriate test of the hypothesis. For example, Mullen assumed that first-person-singular pronouns were an operational measure of self-attention. Such may not be the case. Other theorists and researchers, therefore, need to check each study carefully to determine whether appropriate measures and situations were used. It is especially important to make these checks when the empirical results do not support the hypothesis. One would not want to reject a hypothesis, and with it a basically sound theory, simply because it was put to an inappropriate test. Procedures for making these checks of published studies are described in chapter 5.

The other weakness of the scientific method is more difficult to overcome. The weakness is that any observable result potentially can support multiple, sometimes conflicting, theories. That is why a researcher can never "prove" a theory, only "support" it. In the case of Mullen's study, he acknowledged several alternative theoretical explanations of his observed results, and he noted that the results of his study did not conclusively eliminate any of them as untenable.

As we discussed above in the section on scientific inquiry, alternative theories of certain events tend to get resolved by the weight of evidence accumulated over time supporting one or the other. Thus, Mullen noted in his report that other researchers have used self-attention theory successfully to predict conformity, prosocial behavior, loafing behavior, antisocial behavior, participation in religious organizations, stuttering in front of audiences of varying sizes, lynch mob behavior, and discussion behavior of the President of the United States and his aides. Self-attention theory, then, does not stand or fall by Mullen's results alone. The soundness of the theory must be judged by the total weight of the evidence.

In summary, theories can be developed by posing and testing atheoretical research questions or by posing and testing theory-based hypotheses. Specific procedures for posing research questions and hypotheses are described in chapter 2.

Scientific Disciplines

A **scientific discipline** is an organized field of inquiry that seeks to explain a distinctive domain of phenomena using its own theories, constructs, and methods of investigation. Anthropology, psychology, economics, and chemistry are examples of what we mean by the term *scientific discipline*.

Is educational research a scientific discipline according to this definition? The answer is no. The field of educational research has largely developed by borrowing from other scientific disciplines. In fact, many of the most important contributions to educational research have come from individuals trained in a scientific discipline. Prominent examples come to mind: Jerome Bruner (psychology), Margaret Mead (anthropology), Lawrence Cremin (history), Michael Scriven (philosophy), and William Labov (linguistics).

The following is a list of scientific disciplines and a representative contribution that each has made either to knowledge about education or to a method of inquiry that can be used in educational research:

1. Anthropology: the ethnographic method
2. Biology: the genetic basis for individual differences in intelligence
3. Computer science: the study of artificial intelligence
4. Economics: cost-benefit analysis of educational policies
5. History: the study of school reform movements
6. Linguistics: social-class differences in language patterns of children
7. Mathematics: statistical analysis of data from samples
8. Physiology: brain structures that support intellectual functions
9. Political science: political influences on school boards

TYPES OF EDUCATIONAL RESEARCH

Just as there is not a single scientific method, so too there is not just one type of educational research. In fact, educational research includes many kinds of investigation. We present here several typologies for classifying educational research. The typologies are useful for analyzing published research and for thinking about the research you might undertake for your thesis or dissertation.

Topic

Educational research can be classified by the phenomena investigated. Some of the major topics investigated by educational researchers are: learning processes, cognitive abilities, classroom teaching methods, student personality and motivation, school climate, administrative leadership, school finance, programs for special groups of learners (e.g., learning disabled, gifted), teacher education, curriculum development, subject matter instruction (e.g., reading, mathematics, writing). Many education journals specialize in practice and research relating to one of these topics.

Purpose

As we discussed above, educational research has four primary purposes: description, prediction, control/improvement, and explanation. Because explanation subsumes the other three purposes, we set it aside and discuss it in the next section on exploration and confirmation. This leaves us with three primary purposes of research.

Some educational research studies have more than one purpose, but usually one is dominant. For example, most educational experiments have the purpose of improving student learning or other valued outcome, but some of them also include careful descriptions of the situation being studied.

Exploration versus Confirmation

Some research studies are exploratory in nature. These studies tend not to be guided by hypotheses, because the researcher does not have sufficient understanding of the phenomena to form conjectures about relationships between constructs. For example, you may be curious about the current status of educators' attitudes toward the use of microcomputers in instruction. In this case you would state the purpose as a question or objective rather than as a hypothesis. (The distinction among research questions, objectives, and hypotheses is described in chapter 2.)

Other research studies are more *confirmatory* in nature. The researcher already has a hunch based on theory, prior research, or personal observation. For example, you may have reason to believe that educators' attitudes toward microcomputer education are related to their prior training in microcomputers and to their self-concept about mathematics ability. Your conjectures can be stated as hypotheses and tested. The research results will support or fail to support the hypotheses.

Exploratory research tends to study many variables and their relationships in order to further understanding of the phenomena. Confirmatory research tends to be theoretically based and focused on a limited set of well-measured variables.

Basic versus Applied Research

Basic research focuses on fundamental structures and processes with the goal of understanding them. For example, a basic research project might concern the identification of different learning styles that students use to process difficult textbook material. Applied research focuses on structures and processes as they appear in educational practice, with the goal of developing knowledge that is directly useful to practitioners. An example of an applied research project would be a study to test the effectiveness of a published software program for teaching typing skills.

Both basic and applied research can make use of the range of research designs presented in this book. Exceptions are evaluation research methodology (chapter 17) and educational R & D (see chapter 18), which are used exclusively, or almost exclusively, to answer applied research questions.

PERSONAL MOTIVATION FOR DOING EDUCATIONAL RESEARCH

Thus far we have dealt with the public, institutional basis for supporting educational research. Our discussion involved such matters as the nature of scientific inquiry and the relationship between research knowledge and educational practice. Now we consider the personal reasons why researchers choose to investigate education. What satisfactions are to be derived from undertaking a research project and seeing it through to completion?

We use as an example three doctoral dissertations that were completed under our direction over the past decade.[27] Each of them was an experiment in which teachers were trained to make more enthusiastic presentations in class. The three doctoral students were Edward Bettencourt, Max Gillett, and James Denight.

The first dissertation project began when Edward Bettencourt initiated discussions with us about possible research ideas. His attention soon turned to teacher enthusiasm. During the time that he was a school principal, he observed that the teachers whom he considered effective were very enthusiastic about their work. Bettencourt believed strongly that enthusiasm was important in elementary school teaching. Together we recalled instances of principals who said that they hired teachers based on their level of enthusiasm in the interview situation.

The next step was for Bettencourt to start thinking about whether there was research evidence to support his beliefs. He decided to initiate a review of the literature to answer the question, Are enthusiastic teachers really more effective than nonenthusiastic teachers? He was helped in his search by a published review, which surveyed empirical research on teacher enthusiasm up to about 1970.[28] His post-1970 search uncovered an important dissertation study by Mary Collins. A report of this study was published in the *Journal of Teacher Education*.[29]

Collins had identified observable indicators of teacher enthusiasm and had demonstrated that her training procedure reliably increased preservice teachers' enthusiasm level. Her measure of teacher enthusiasm consisted of a five-point rating scale for each of eight enthusiasm indicators: (1) rapid uplifting, varied

27. The "we" in this example refers to Meredith Gall and his three dissertation advisees. The three dissertations are: Edward M. Bettencourt, "Effects of Training Teachers in Enthusiasm on Student Achievement and Attitudes" (Ed.D. dissertation, University of Oregon, 1979); Maxwell H. Gillett, "Effects of Teacher Enthusiasm on At-Task Behavior of Students in Elementary Classes" (Ph.D. dissertation, University of Oregon, 1980); James A. Denight, "Effects of Teacher Enthusiasm Training on On-Task Behavior and Attitudes of Students in High School" (Ed.D. dissertation, University of Oregon, 1987).
28. Barak Rosenshine, "Enthusiastic Teaching: A Research Review," *School Review* 78 (1970): 499–514.
29. Mary L. Collins, "Effects of Enthusiasm Training on Preservice Elementary Teachers," *Journal of Teacher Education* 29 (1978): 53–57.

vocal delivery; (2) dancing, wide open eyes; (3) frequent, demonstrative questions; (4) varied, dramatic body movements; (5) varied, emotive facial expressions; (6) selection of varied words, especially adjectives; (7) ready, animated acceptance of ideas and feelings; and (8) exuberant overall energy level. Ratings were made by trained observers, who studied videotapes of the teachers' classroom performance. The observers did not know whether a particular videotape was made before or after training, or whether a teacher was in the trained or untrained group. Collins' study was important because it provided a good operational definition of teacher enthusiasm and an empirically validated training program.

At this point Bettencourt was entertaining several research ideas. It happened that the author of the pre-1970 review, Barak Rosenshine, was visiting our university, and so we discussed with him the relative merits of the various research ideas. He argued that the most important problem in this area was whether teacher enthusiasm was sufficiently potent to cause students to improve their academic achievement. Previous research on this problem generally produced positive results, but most of the studies were methodologically weak. Collins' definition of teacher enthusiasm and training procedures overcame the most serious weaknesses of these studies.

As a result of this discussion, Bettencourt decided to test two hypotheses relating to teacher enthusiasm. The first hypothesis was that teachers trained in Collins' procedures would become more observably enthusiastic than teachers not so trained. The test of this hypothesis provided a replication of Collins' original findings. The second hypothesis was that students of enthusiasm-trained teachers would achieve at a higher level than students of untrained teachers.

Bettencourt planned to have the trained and untrained groups teach the same curriculum unit in order to control for academic content. The unit was to be a few weeks long so as not to disrupt the teachers' regular curriculum. Bettencourt's dissertation advisers were familiar with a suitable unit that had been developed for another research project. He contacted the director of that project and obtained his permission to use the unit's materials and achievement tests. Meanwhile Bettencourt phoned Collins and obtained her assistance in setting up the training program and the procedures for making objective ratings of teacher enthusiasm. He also obtained an agreement with the directors of the university's Resident Teacher Program (a special internship program for newly certified teachers) to incorporate the experimental training conditions as part of the internship coursework.

Before discussing Bettencourt's results, we need to introduce the two other dissertations that grew out of this study. In reviewing videotapes of Bettencourt's teachers after training, we observed that students of the trained teachers appeared more attentive and on-task during instruction. Max Gillett, another doctoral student interested in teacher enthusiasm, became intrigued by the possibility that teacher enthusiasm training might have a positive effect on student on-task behavior. He decided to conduct an experiment to test the hypothesis that students of enthusiasm-trained teachers would exhibit a higher level of on-task behavior than students of untrained teachers. He also tested Bettencourt's first hypothesis, thus providing a second replication of Collins' findings. His operational definition of on-task behavior was based on previous studies of other investigators. Gillett used another sample of teachers from the same internship program from which Bettencourt drew his sample.

James Denight, a more recent doctoral student, reviewed the two studies, both of which involved elementary teachers and their classes. Denight, who has a background as a secondary school principal and teacher, wondered whether the enthusiasm training procedures would be effective with secondary teachers. Therefore, he designed an experiment very similar to Gillett's, except that the trained and untrained groups were experienced secondary teachers. Thus, his study constitutes a third replication of Collins' findings about teacher's enthusiasm level before and after training, and a replication of Gillett's findings regarding student on-task behavior (which are presented below).

In addition, Denight tested two other hypotheses: that students taught by enthusiasm-trained teachers will have a more positive attitude toward their teacher; and that these students will have a more positive attitude toward the teacher's lessons.

The results of the test of the first hypothesis are presented in table 1.3. The means (M) shown in this table are the mean scores of each group on five-point scales that observers used to rate the teachers' use of the eight enthusiasm indicators. Higher scores on the scales mean a higher level of enthusiasm. The results shown in the table indicate that, although the trained teachers in each study started at different overall levels of enthusiasm, they all ended at approximately the same level. None of the untrained groups of teachers changed in their enthusiasm level over the course of the experiment. Thus, the four studies replicate each other nicely and provide considerable empirical support for the effectiveness of Mary Collins' training procedure.

TABLE 1.3

Enthusiasm Level of Teachers before and after Training

Teacher Sample	Pretraining M	Posttraining M
Collins	1.24	2.98
Bettencourt	1.89	2.65
Gillett	2.43	2.84
Denight	2.59	2.96

Bettencourt's hypothesis about the effect of teacher enthusiasm training on student achievement was not supported by the results. The classes of trained and untrained teachers made very similar gains on the achievement test: For trained teachers, the class mean pretest and posttest scores were 22.88 and 28.83 (gain of 5.95 points); and for untrained teachers, the corresponding scores were 23.73 and 29.59 (gain of 5.86 points).

Gillett and Denight, however, obtained positive results for their hypothesis concerning the effect of teacher enthusiasm training on student on task behavior. In fact, the results shown in table 1.4 indicate that students of trained teachers were more on-task during both teacher-led instruction and seatwork. The on-task measure shown in this table is the percentage of students rated to be on-task by trained observers. The percentage is the average of ratings made every few minutes for an entire class period.

Denight's two hypotheses concerning the attitudes of students of trained and untrained teachers were unsupported by the results. Both groups of

TABLE 1.4

Percentage of On-Task Students in Classes of
Enthusiasm-Trained and Untrained Teachers

	Percentage of On-Task Students during Teacher-Led Instruction	
	Trained Teachers	Untrained Teachers
Gilett's study		
Pretraining M	76.62	75.41
Posttraining M	87.17	76.98
Denight's study		
Pretraining M	77.69	74.65
Posttraining M	83.61	77.04
	Percentage of On-Task Students during Seatwork	
	Trained Teachers	Untrained Teachers
Gillett's study		
Pretraining M	71.56	81.51
Posttraining M	85.88	69.71
Denight's study		
Pretraining M	69.27	83.30
Posttraining M	84.86	76.46

students had virtually identical mean scores on each administration of the attitude scales, and there was no change in attitude from the pretraining administration to the posttraining administration.

We found, then, that the results supported several of the hypotheses, and disconfirmed others. The disconfirmed hypotheses can be just as exciting and informative as the supported hypotheses because they lead researchers to reexamine their theories and speculations. Consider Bettencourt's failure to find an effect of teacher enthusiasm on student achievement. This result puzzled us because other researchers had obtained positive results concerning the enthusiasm-achievement relationship.

When Gillett's results came in, we were even more puzzled. His results concerning the enthusiasm–on-task relationship suggested that we should have found the effect we were looking for. The reason is that other research investigations have found that student on-task behavior has a positive effect on student achievement. Therefore, in Bettencourt's study, teacher enthusiasm training should have increased student on-task behavior, and in turn, student academic achievement.

We continued to puzzle about the negative finding in Bettencourt's study as we started writing a report of both studies for publication. Barak Rosenshine and other colleagues suggested that we might obtain useful clues by reanalyzing the curriculum unit and reports of previous studies. Our reanalysis led us to make two discoveries. First, the curriculum unit in Bettencourt's study relied heavily on supplementary curriculum objectives and inquiry-oriented activities. By contrast, regular mathematics instruction in elementary school emphasizes basic skills and drill-and-practice.[30] We came to the realization that the atypicality of the curriculum unit could have masked the effects of teacher enthusiasm training.

The second discovery came in rereading previous experiments involving manipulation of teacher enthusiasm level. Four of the previous experiments had demonstrated a positive effect of teacher enthusiasm on student achievement. Only one previous experiment and Bettencourt's experiment had found an absence of effect. We discovered that the few experiments with positive results have one feature in common. The comparison treatment (the no-training condition) in each study required the teacher to purposefully act in a nonenthusiastic manner. For example, in one of the comparison treatments the teacher "read an entire speech from a manuscript" and "made no gestures or direct eye contact and held vocal inflection to a minimum."[31] In the two experiments reporting no effect, however, the comparison groups of teachers were given no special instructions. They were allowed to use their natural teaching style.

30. This point was documented in J. T. Fey, "Mathematics Teaching Today: Perspectives from Three National Surveys," *Mathematics Teacher* 72 (1979): 490–504.
31. W. Coats and V. Smidchens, "Audience Recall as a Function of Speaker Dynamism," *Journal of Educational Psychology* 57 (1966): 189-191.

This analysis suggests that the four experiments obtained positive results because an elevated level of teacher enthusiasm was compared with a depressed level of enthusiasm. Bettencourt may not have obtained positive effects because an elevated level of teacher enthusiasm was compared with a natural, nondepressed level. In other words, the difference between treatments was not sufficiently large to produce an effect on student achievement.

Our reflections on the studies by Bettencourt, Gillett, and Denight have led us to pose new hypotheses and questions for further research. One hypothesis is that teacher enthusiasm training would show an effect on student achievement if used with teachers with depressed affect about their work (e.g., stressed or burned-out teachers). The teachers selected for training from this group should develop elevated levels of enthusiasm relative to their nontrained, low-affect colleagues.

On another issue, we were surprised to find that the effect of enthusiasm training on students' on-task behavior was just as strong during seatwork, when teachers presumably have less opportunity to exhibit enthusiastic behavior. We would like to do further research to learn why this might be so. One line of speculation is that the nonverbal aspects of teachers' instruction convey important messages to students. If this is true, we would like to learn what messages are conveyed by teacher enthusiasm and whether the messages have the capacity to motivate student work even when the teacher is not directly communicating to all students (e.g., during seatwork). Still other issues for further research concern the duration of enthusiasm training effects, the reasons why Denight did not find an effect of teacher enthusiasm training on student attitudes, and how our operational definition of enthusiasm relates to other possible definitions.

The experiments by Bettencourt and Gillett have been presented at national conventions of the American Educational Research Association, published in a professional journal,[32] and included in a major review of research on teacher enthusiasm.[33] As a result, we have become acquainted with other researchers interested in investigating teacher-enthusiasm phenomena. Denight's study, which was just completed as a dissertation, will be prepared for presentation to the broad community of researchers and practitioners.

These examples of research illustrate the factors that motivate certain individuals to pursue scientific inquiry. First, researchers value the power of scientific inquiry to provide a check on personal belief, common sense, and ordinary observation. In our case we believed that enthusiasm is a desirable

32. Edward M. Bettencourt, Maxwell H. Gillett, Meredith D. Gall, and Ray E. Hull, "Effects of Teacher Enthusiasm Training on Student On-task Behavior and Achievement," *American Educational Research Journal* 20 (1983): 435–450.
33. A. Guy Larkins, C. Warren McKinney, Sally Oldham-Buss, and Allison C. Gilmore, *Teacher Enthusiasm: A Critical Review* (Hattiesburg: The University of Southern Mississippi, 1985).

teacher trait, but we also wanted to subject this belief to a research test. Second, the researcher is motivated by curiosity. Collins demonstrated that level of teacher enthusiasm can be elevated, but we were curious about whether we could obtain the same effect. Our curiosity was also aroused by anomalies in our data: Why wasn't there an effect on student achievement? Why did students' on-task behavior during seatwork improve?

The joy of discovery is another source of motivation for doing research. We were pleased to discover that Collins' training procedure held up under three replications. We were excited, too, to discover plausible reasons why an effect on academic achievement did not occur.

The profession of educational research also has its sources of satisfaction for the individual. First, there is the satisfaction of knowing that we have contributed to knowledge about education. The Bettencourt, Gillett, and Denight experiments are now part of the literature on teacher enthusiasm.

Second, there is the satisfaction of thinking that our work may one day influence the practice of teacher education. Perhaps teacher educators will incorporate our work, along with the contributions of other researchers, in designing training in affective skills for prospective teachers.

Third, there is the satisfaction of being members of the educational research community. We have been in communication with other interested researchers through their writings, personal conversations, phone calls, and professional associations. Educational researchers seldom work in isolation. If the problem is of sufficient importance, you will find other researchers working on it. There are many "invisible colleges" of researchers around the world working right now on important problems in education. Finally, professional researchers receive professional recognition for their contributions. Educators who do research are generally respected by their colleagues and by the community. If you are working in a college or university setting, research contributions are generally a major basis for awarding promotion and tenure.

THE STUDY OF EDUCATIONAL RESEARCH

The purpose of this chapter was to help you understand *why* educational research is worth doing. Most of the following chapters describe *how* to do educational research. However, "book knowledge" of these tools and concepts will not turn you into a competent researcher. It is essential that you acquire experience in doing research. The usual way to accomplish this goal is to apprentice yourself to an experienced researcher. We highly recommend that you seek out such opportunities. We also recommend that you read research reports in education journals as you study this book. We provide many examples of published research, but you are advised to supplement them by looking for additional examples.

As you read this text, we recommend that you think about research projects you might want to undertake. A replication-and-extension project is quite feasible for the beginning researcher. Replication allows research to be self-correcting, as we saw in the case of the four experiments on teacher enthusiasm. If replication studies produce consistent results, confidence in the hypothesis and in the theory from which the hypothesis was derived is strengthened. If inconsistent results are obtained, the researchers will need to determine whether there was a problem in research methodology or in their theorizing.

Replication studies need not literally repeat the conditions of a previous study. The replication can duplicate critical elements and also extend the inquiry into new domains. That is why we advocate replication-*and-extension*. Replication is discussed further in chapter 9.

In reading this text, you should reflect on your personal orientation to the various research methods presented in it. You may find that you are more inclined to experimentation, or that you prefer descriptive research. You may find that you are more sympathetic to the perspectives and methods of quantitative research, or that your bent is toward qualitative research. You need to find a niche in it that is compatible with your interests, values, and strengths.

ANNOTATED REFERENCES

Biddle, Bruce J., and Anderson, Donald S. "Theory, Methods, Knowledge, and Research on Teaching." In *Third Handbook of Research on Teaching*, ed. Merlin C. Wittrock. New York: Macmillan, 1986.

A well-documented perspective on the nature of scientific inquiry, theory-generating, types of research knowledge, and the relationship between research and practice. Recommended highly for the student who seeks a deeper understanding of the topics introduced in this chapter.

Gage, N. L. *Hard Gains in the Soft Sciences: The Case of Pedagogy*. Bloomington, IN: Phi Delta Kappa Center on Evaluation, Development, and Research, 1985.

Reflects Gage's accumulated wisdom about how research has contributed to knowledge about teaching and teacher education. Gage helped initiate the modern era of educational research by editing the first *Handbook of Research on Teaching* in 1963. The last chapter contains an insightful discussion of how different research strategies and perspectives produce different kinds of knowledge about teaching.

Kuhn, Thomas S. *The Structure of Scientific Revolutions*. Chicago: University of Chicago Press, 1962.

A classic essay that changed the way people think about the nature of science and scientific progress. Kuhn argued that a scientific discipline progresses cumulatively within an agreed-upon paradigm until anomalies unexplained by the paradigm provoke a scientific revolution and the creation of a new paradigm. The notion of paradigm paved the way for and legitimized postpositivistic research approaches in the social sciences.

Phillips, D. C. *Philosophy, Science, and Social Inquiry.* Oxford: Pergamon, 1987.

A highly readable, book-length discussion of philosophical controversies that were presented in this chapter. The author considers the various criticisms that postpositivists direct at positivistic science, and attempts to refute them. He presents a compelling view of how researchers follow a "tentative and meandering course" toward scientific knowledge.

Richardson-Koehler, Virginia. "What Happens to Research on the Way to Practice?" *Theory into Practice* 26, no. 1 (1987): 38–43.

Provides an insightful analysis of problems that have occurred in using research findings to make policies about schooling and teaching. The author observes that research findings by themselves are not a sufficient basis for change. She describes elements of an effective change process that have been identified in recent research.

Travers, Robert M. W. *How Research Has Changed American Schools: A History from 1840 to the Present.* Kalamazoo, MI: Mythos Press, 1983.

Offers a fascinating account of the history of educational research, concluding that it has had an "immense impact" on education. The historical account supports the view of postpositivistic researchers and revisionist historians that educational research is value-laden and has been used to support prevailing social values and beliefs.

U.S. Department of Education. *What Works: Research about Teaching and Learning.* Washington, DC: U.S. Department of Education, 1986. (To order, write to: What Works, Pueblo, Colorado, 81009.)

Glass, Gene, V. "*What Works.* Politics and Research." *Educational Researcher* 16, no. 3 (1987): 5–10.

Useful to students who wish to get a broad overview of what research has discovered about improving school management, classroom instruction, and parental involvement in education. Each of the 41 research generalizations is followed by comments on how it can be applied in practice and by a list of relevant research reports.

Glass states in his review of this publication that it is "the most widely read document in the history of educational research" (p. 5). He skillfully analyzes the value-laden character of the research findings selected for the pamphlet, and he concludes that they represent a historical-conservative political philosophy.

SELF-CHECK TEST

Circle the correct answer to each of the following questions. An answer key is provided on page 883.

1. Research knowledge about how educational videodiscs affect students' attitude toward the course in which they are used is an example of
   a. description.
   b. prediction.
   c. improvement/control.
   d. explanation.
2. Educational research findings tend not to affect practice directly because
   a. research findings tend to be value-free.
   b. research findings derive almost entirely from basic research.
   c. policymakers tend to see no value in research findings.
   d. policymakers tend to view research findings as just one source of information for making decisions.
3. Comroe and Dripps' study of medical advances demonstrated the importance of
   a. political influences on what gets researched.
   b. applied research in generating hypotheses for theory-testing.
   c. basic research in bringing about improvements in medical practice.
   d. the interaction between researchers and practitioners in bringing about medical advances.
4. The verifiability principle emphasizes the value of
   a. objective observation.
   b. personal introspection.
   c. group consensus.
   d. group interpretation.
5. A postpositivistic researcher would view the concept of learning disorder as
   a. generalizable across cultures.
   b. theory-free.
   c. value-laden.
   d. value-free.
6. The use of standardized tests, detachment from the persons being studied, and interest in finding general laws are characteristics of
   a. postpositivism.
   b. positivism.
   c. relativism.
   d. qualitative research.
7. The statement, "Aptitude will be measured by the quantitative scale of the Scholastic Aptitude Test (SAT)," is an example of a(n)
   a. theoretical law.
   b. operationally defined construct.
   c. constitutively defined construct.
   d. hypothesis.
8. In the scientific method, hypotheses are tested
   a. before theoretical constructs have been defined.
   b. before a theory has been specified.
   c. before observable consequences of the hypothesis have been specified.
   d. after observable consequences of the hypothesis have been specified.

9. Up to the present time, educational research has been influenced
   a. only by psychology.
   b. only by mathematical statistics.
   c. only by scientific disciplines that involve the study of learning processes.
   d. by a wide variety of scientific disciplines.
10. A study that tested a hypothesis derived from a theory about how brain chemistry affects short-term memory would be an example of
   a. basic research.
   b. applied research.
   c. exploratory research.
   d. descriptive research.
11. The experiments on teacher enthusiasm presented in this chapter illustrate
   a. the study of a previously unexplored phenomenon in education.
   b. literal replication of previous research.
   c. replication-and-extension of previous research.
   d. the use of theory to guide research.

APPLICATION PROBLEMS

The following problems are designed to give you practice in applying significant concepts and research procedures explained in chapter 1. They do not have a single correct answer. For feedback, you can compare your answers with the sample answers on pages 885–886.

1. Suppose the federal government decides to fund a new program for training high school students in study skills. Some educators argue that all of the appropriated funds should be used to develop model programs and materials, to train teachers in summer institutes, and to hire additional school staff. Other educators argue that at least 15 percent of the appropriations should be allocated for research on study skills. What defense could you offer for this "15 percent for research" proposal?
2. Quantitative and qualitative researchers have different perspectives on their relation to self, on their relation to research participants, and on generalizability of research findings. Briefly review these two perspectives, and provide a defense for the value of each perspective.

SUGGESTION SHEET

If your last name starts with letters from Aa to Bal, please complete the Suggestion Sheet at the end of the book while this chapter is still fresh in your mind.

Part II

PLANNING EDUCATIONAL RESEARCH

Planning is the most important step in any research project. The most polished procedures and sophisticated statistical analyses cannot salvage a study that is poorly planned. The first step in planning is to identify a significant problem to attack. In this section you learn how to locate a research problem and how to develop a research plan that will permit you to collect rigorous evidence related to your problem.

In planning your study you must pay careful attention to the ethics and legal rules of research. Most educational research involves the use of human subjects. Failure to follow ethical guidelines not only can cause the researcher legal problems but may do serious harm to the subjects who participate in educational research.

Research evidence is cumulative. Many researchers contribute small pieces to a puzzle until, finally, a comprehensible "picture" emerges. In order for you to plan a research project that will contribute a new piece to the "picture," you must carefully study and interpret the pieces other researchers have contributed. This process is called "reviewing the literature" and is an essential part of planning your research. Researchers who attempt to sidestep a thorough review of previous research often end up following a path that others have found to be a dead end or repeating a study that someone else has done better.

Perhaps your most difficult task in reviewing the research of others is evaluating their work and deciding, in view of its limitations, how the findings fit into the overall picture of research related to the problem you are trying to investigate. How well you can carry out this critical review is determined to a large extent by how much you know about educational research methods. Thus, although you will be able to identify a research problem, start your literature search, and develop a tentative research plan after you have read the four chapters in this part, your critical evaluation of the key studies related to your problem and your final research plan should be delayed until you have finished studying this book.

<table>
<tr><td>

2

</td><td>

DEVELOPING
THE RESEARCH PROPOSAL

</td></tr>
</table>

OVERVIEW

Chapter 2 introduces you to several important skills that are needed to write an educational research plan and to conduct the project itself. First, we suggest several approaches to help you identify possible research problems and select an appropriate problem for your own research project. Next, you are given an outline to use in developing your research proposal systematically. This section deals briefly with each major part of the research plan: the problem, hypotheses, measures, subjects, research design, and data analysis.

The advantages of developing a chronological list of procedures for your research project are also discussed. Many students prepare their research plan section by section and do not give enough attention to the problem of fitting the sections together. We discuss this problem and illustrate a method for developing a related plan. If your research plan is fairly complex, the use of a procedure such as PERT (Program Evaluation and Review Technique) helps you better understand your research and avoid many of the errors and miscalculations often made by inexperienced researchers. We introduce you to the PERT technique and ask you to consider the advantages of conducting a pilot study prior to the main investigation in order to test and revise the research plan.

OBJECTIVES

After studying this chapter you should be able to:

1. Describe your areas of interest in education and current research problems that are under investigation in these areas.
2. Explain the advantages and disadvantages of working on a team project.
3. Discuss the reasons for replicating significant studies.
4. Use a variety of procedures to locate unsolved research problems in a given area of education.
5. List and describe the topics that need to be included in a sound research plan.
6. Describe the advantages of a research plan.
7. Write directional hypotheses, null hypotheses, and questions that relate to a given research problem.
8. Apply four criteria to the development and evaluation of hypotheses.
9. Demonstrate the relationship among the hypotheses, measures, and analysis procedures in a research plan.
10. Describe PERT and how it can be used in research planning.
11. State at least three reasons for including a pilot study in a research project.

INTRODUCTION

In this chapter we will give you an overall introduction to the task of locating a suitable research problem and building a proposal designed to address your problem. Although you are not yet ready to prepare a proposal, we believe that this overview will help you see how each step in the research process is related, thus helping you learn and understand the process.

The list below provides a very brief outline of the steps you will follow in developing a research proposal. The remainder of this chapter helps you carry out the initial step, and the remainder of the text takes you through the entire research process.

Selecting and Defining the Research Problem

1. *Identify problem area.* What area relates best to your current interests and future professional goals? (chapter 2)
2. *Build preliminary knowledge base.* Read secondary sources to get an overview of what is known and what questions in your problem area need further exploration. (chapter 4)
3. *Identify specific problem and write your problem statement.* What question will you address? What variables will you measure? Why is this problem important? (chapter 2)
4. *Review previous research.* Locate, evaluate, and synthesize previous research and theory and relate your findings to your problem. (chapters 4,5)

Outlining the Research Plan

5. *Formulate hypotheses or objectives.* What specific questions will you address in order to shed light on your problem? (chapter 2)
6. *Select possible measures.* Locate and evaluate measures of the variables to be studied and select the most appropriate. (chapters 8,9)
7. *Select research subjects.* Identify the population to which your research will apply; decide on the size of your sample and how subjects will be selected. (chapter 6)
8. *Specify the research design.* Study the types of research and decide which is most appropriate for your problem. (chapters 11–19)
9. *Select analysis procedures.* Review statistical tools and decide which will best test your hypotheses, given your subjects, measures, and research design. (chapters 10, 13, 14, 15, or 16 depending on research design)
10. *Specify research activities.* Describe in chronological order and in as much detail as you can the specific steps you must take to carry out the proposed research. Check the entire proposal for ethical and legal compliance. (chapter 3)

As you progress through this text you will master the concepts and skills needed to develop the research proposal that you will submit to your thesis or dissertation committee and that will subsequently guide your research.

The text is organized in about the same order that one follows in developing a research plan and subsequently conducting your study. Thus, many students develop each section of their proposal as they complete the relevant section of the text, ending the course with a well-thought-out plan.

SELECTING AND DEFINING A RESEARCH PROBLEM

The graduate students' research problem for their thesis or dissertation usually focuses on an educational phenomenon that they wish to describe, an event that they have observed and will attempt to explain, or a problem for which they will try to develop a solution. The research problem often is phrased as a question such as:

1. What changes can I make in reading instruction to increase the interest of Chicano children in my class?
2. What mistakes do students make most often in solving long-division problems?
3. Some children never volunteer answers during recitation even when I am sure they know the correct answer. Why is this?

The ultimate value of your research project is probably determined more by the imagination and insight that goes into the research problem than by any other factor. Therefore, the selection of a research problem for the master's thesis or doctoral dissertation is a very important step. Often, eager to get started on research work, the student seizes upon the first research idea that comes along. A student who begins a research problem before giving the choice much careful study and thought is likely to lose many important advantages.

The very process of seeking a research problem is an important step in your professional maturation. At the outset, you may see no problems, or from first explorations into the research literature conclude that research has already solved all the problems in education. Your first ideas for research may be naive; a closer check will reveal that they have already been thoroughly explored. As you continue to search, however, insight into the literature becomes sufficiently broad so that you can see research problems in everything you read. This point is not reached without a considerable amount of scholarly work in the research literature, but once achieved, you have taken a significant step.

One reason that students seize upon the first idea they encounter is that very often they go too far in their graduate program before starting to search for a suitable research problem. You have had years of experience in taking courses and thus the classwork involved in your graduate program is a familiar experience and one that you are reasonably confident you can complete successfully. In contrast, the research aspect of the graduate program is new and different and something that you may be strongly tempted to put off. Every university has a lengthy list of "allbuts" among its graduate students—those who have completed *all* work for an advanced degree *but* the thesis or dissertation. A great many such students never obtain their advanced degrees. It is usually desirable for graduate students to gain some insight into research and to commence the search for a suitable problem as soon as possible after entering graduate work, even if they do not plan to carry out a project until they near the end of their work.

In looking for a research problem, bear in mind some of the possible outcomes of your research effort in preparing you for your profession. The review of the literature provides you with an understanding of the work that has already taken place relating to your problem area and prepares you to carry out a project that will add to the facts and information that have been accumulated by previous research workers. Because of the extensive reading you must do in your problem area, you will usually build up a sizable fund of knowledge. Thus, in order that this knowledge may be of significant future value, you should attempt to develop a research problem in an area that is closely related to your professional goals. For example, a student who plans to teach elementary school will profit much more from a research project in some area such as child development or the learning of elementary school subjects than in an area involving secondary education, adolescent development, or school administration.

Another reason for the selection of a topic closely allied to your interest is that the research project provides an opportunity to do significant independent work in a problem area that will better prepare you for professional work and will incidentally make you a more desirable prospect for employment. Although most of them do not produce research findings of major significance, many master's theses do produce worthwhile information that makes a small but definite contribution to the field of knowledge. Because there are many significant problems in education for which we require further knowledge, you should resist the temptation to do research that is essentially trivial or that can contribute nothing to educational knowledge. Students often rationalize carrying out a trivial study by saying that the real purpose of the master's thesis is to provide practice in independent work, and the results cannot be expected to be of any scientific value. Generally, once a significant project has been identified, it requires no more time and effort to carry out than a trivial project or one that repeats work that has already been adequately done. The difference between the trivial project and the significant project is not the amount of work required to carry it out, but the amount of thought that the student applies in selection and definition of the problem.

Another factor that you should consider in selecting a problem is that you will not only gain valuable knowledge and experience in the problem area you select, but if you carry out a worthwhile piece of research, it may be possible to publish the results in a professional journal. Publishing an article based on your thesis adds significantly to your professional status.

In defining a research problem, do not hesitate to entertain ideas and approaches that represent a departure from conventional educational practice. Researchers often overlook or reject promising ideas because they are strange or conflict with some of the individual's biases. B. F. Skinner provides us with an excellent example of the degree to which narrow thinking can stifle unusual ideas. During World War II, Skinner worked with a group of psychologists on a project aimed at conditioning pigeons to operate a guidance system for missiles.[1] The pigeons were conditioned to peck at a particular type of target that they viewed on a screen, such as a ship or length of coastline. If the target was not at the center of the screen, the pigeons' pecking provided a guiding signal to change the course of the missile. The device was developed to a high level of efficiency and became nearly foolproof even under unfavorable conditions. It required no materials in short supply, and once the pigeons had been conditioned the behavior persisted for long periods without reinforcement. In several demonstrations before scientific committees the conditioned pigeons performed perfectly, yet the project was abandoned because it was impossible to convince the dozen or so distinguished physical scientists on the evaluation committee that the behavior of a pigeon could be adequately controlled. To these men, who were accustomed to thinking in terms of servomotors, rheostats, and electrical circuits, the idea of using a live organism to carry out the task of missile guidance was too fantastic to be taken seriously, even when they were confronted with evidence that the pigeons could do the assigned task. Although none of us can be completely freed from the shackles of our environment, preconceptions, and prejudices, the researcher seeking a research problem should remain aware of the existence of these impediments and should make a conscious effort to avoid their influence. As Skinner points out, "One virtue in crackpot ideas is that they breed rapidly and their progeny show extraordinary mutations." Thus, even the wildest idea may, if pursued, lead eventually to a unique and often practical approach to a scientific problem.

The First Step

The first step in locating a specific problem for the dissertation or thesis is to identify the broad problem areas that are most closely related to your interests and professional goals. You will find it a profitable experience to write down in as much detail as possible the type of work you wish to do upon completion of

1. B. F. Skinner, "Pigeons in a Pelican," *American Psychologist* 15 (1960): 28–37.

graduate training and the specific aspects of this work that most interest you. The process of writing down this information will help you clarify your goals and interests. Very often you will find that these goals are somewhat less clear in your mind than you may have supposed. Typical broad areas of interest that might be listed are high school counseling, teaching art to children in the primary grades, social problems of adolescents, remedial reading in the elementary school, relationships between teachers and principals, and intramural programs in physical education.

After one or more such areas of professional interest have been identified, you are ready to seek out specific problems in these areas that could form the basis for your thesis.

Working on a Team Project

Thirty years ago almost no money was available for the support of educational research. Most research projects were small-scale studies carried out by university faculty members, and in many instances the faculty member did all the research including such tasks as administering and scoring tests used in the project. Since that time, however, money available for educational research has increased tremendously. Now most universities are receiving financial support for educational research in the form of contracts and grants from federal agencies and private foundations, and the projects being carried out are much wider in scope and often involve a team of research workers rather than a single scientist. The graduate student often has an opportunity to participate in one of these extensive research projects as a member of a team. As a rule, such projects are developed by faculty members, and portions of the project are given to graduate students to complete. Completion of the allotted portion of the project then constitutes the research for the master's thesis or doctoral dissertation.

Working on team projects has both advantages and disadvantages. Perhaps the most important advantage is that financial support is usually available for working on such a project. This support may cover as little as paying for test administration or providing needed materials or clerical assistance, but in many cases it also involves a scholarship or research assistantship that is sufficient to meet expenses while you are completing your graduate work. The team project also offers you an opportunity to participate in a bigger and more sophisticated study than would be the case if you were working independently. These studies usually involve more complex research designs and more advanced statistical procedures, and thus you learn more about these than you would otherwise. You also have a chance to learn something about the workings of team research, and because most major projects are now carried out by teams, this insight may prove valuable in future work. You can also learn much from other members of the research team. Each team member brings a different background of training and experience to the project, and therefore the team can often produce a more polished research effort than is the case with a single investigator.

Participation in a team research project also has disadvantages, however. Perhaps the most important of these is the loss of the opportunity to find and develop an individual problem. In team research, the project is usually created and designed by the faculty member who is directing it. At worst, graduate students involved in team projects are little more than clerks who carry out various tasks without fully understanding what they are doing or why it is being done. Even in team projects where you are asked to do significant independent work—and this is usually the case—you may not get firsthand experience in all aspects of developing and carrying out a research plan. Second, the problem being studied by a research team may not be closely allied with your interests, nor may it contribute directly to your future professional work, as would be the case if you designed and carried out an independent project.

Whether you carry out a small independent project or participate in a larger team project, the experience you gain through independent scholarship and research is perhaps the most important aspect of your graduate program. A significant piece of work done at this level can add materially to your professional maturity, may improve your employment opportunities, and start you on the path to recognition and high professional status in your chosen field.

A Reading Program

Perhaps the most satisfactory method of locating specific problems within the scope of your broad interests is through a systematic program of reading. Let us say, for example, that you plan to teach in the elementary schools and are particularly interested in problems related to working with bright children at that level. First, you would check the library card catalogue to locate current textbooks in this field. If you have selected a field in which no complete textbooks have been written, you will usually find chapters dealing with your interest area in some of the introductory texts used in general education and psychology courses. Select two or three textbooks and review pertinent chapters in each. This will give you some background information about your area of interest and also some insight into various subtopics in the field, a knowledge of current practices, and a brief summary of recent research. This preliminary reading will help you narrow your focus to one or more specific subtopics. If your broad interest is in working with bright, elementary-level children, you may decide to develop a research problem dealing with the creative abilities of bright children, or you may decide to study the development of bright children in the primary grades. These topics are of course still much too broad for a specific research problem, but this initial narrowing permits you to explore the areas you have selected in somewhat greater depth by reading additional materials that deal specifically with the narrower subject. You may also obtain valuable information by checking these topics in such sources as the *Review of Research in Education*, the *Review of Educational Research*, and the *Handbook of Research on Teaching*.[2]

This additional reading will usually result in the identification of a number of tentative research problems that are sufficiently limited and specific to form a possible basis for your work. In the example used here, you might develop specific research topics in the area of social development of bright students in the elementary schools such as the following: (1) relationships between intelligence and sociometric choice among sixth-grade children, (2) development of interest in the opposite sex in elementary children between grades four and six, (3) social activities of bright children as compared with those of average children in 10 fifth-grade classrooms, and (4) social adjustment problems in extremely bright children in the intermediate grades.

Research Based on Theory

Perhaps the approach most likely to produce an outstanding thesis or dissertation is to formulate a research problem that will test a theory related to your area of interest.

In simple terms a **theory** is an explanation of behavioral or physical events. The more "powerful" a theory is, the more events can be explained by it. Psychoanalytic theory is considered by some researchers to be powerful because it provides an explanation for a vast range of behavior from infancy to old age, from the behavior of normal persons through the continuum of mental illnesses. Theories consist of generalizations (in the physical sciences, usually called laws) and constructs. A **law** or **generalization** is a statement of a relationship between two or more events; generalizations can be used to predict events. For example, the statement that individual tutoring results in increased school achievement is a generalization. Assuming it is true, we can predict that a particular student, given tutoring, will show a gain in achievement. A **construct** is a type of concept used in scientific research to describe events that share similar elements. Motivation, achievement, learning ability, intelligence, and value are all examples of constructs. Constructs are usually defined in operational terms, that is, in terms of the "operations" needed to measure them. For example, the construct "intelligence" is usually defined in terms of scores derived from administration of an intelligence test. Motivation may be defined in terms of changes in subjects' performance after they receive "motivating" instructions. These operational measures of constructs are usually called *variables* because the level or

2. Bibliographic information for these references can be found in the Annotated References at the end of chapter 4.

degree to which different subjects display the construct varies and because values or numerals can be assigned to different levels. Theoretical research usually consists of testing a hypothesis (a speculation about the relationship between two or more variables) that is derived from a theory.

Many areas of education have virtually no theoretical foundation. In areas, however, where the problems of education cut across other behavioral sciences, such as psychology or sociology, an increasing amount of pertinent theoretical work can be found. Some of these areas of overlapping concern are learning, motivation, language development, behavioral management, attitude development, and social class. A good example of an educational research problem derived from theory in another behavioral science, psychology, is provided by a recent study of changes in school-related attitudes.[3] In this study, Robert Steiner tested a hypothesis related to attitude change derived from the theory of cognitive dissonance developed by Leon Festinger.[4] Simply stated, cognitive dissonance is a state of tension that occurs when an individual simultaneously holds two cognitions (i.e., attitudes, ideas, or beliefs) that are logically inconsistent or in conflict. According to Festinger's theory, this dissonance is unpleasant, and the individual experiencing it is motivated to reduce it. With regard to attitude change, Festinger's theory would indicate that if an individual has an attitude we want to change, such as racial prejudice, we can create cognitive dissonance by exposing the person to ideas that are incompatible with his or her attitude or inducing the person to behave in a manner contrary to his or her original attitude. This in turn will create dissonance, and in order to reduce this dissonance, the individual will shift his or her original attitude so that it will be more consistent with the behavior we have induced. The theory also suggests that the level of cognitive dissonance experienced by the individual is related to the degree of attitude change that is likely to occur. That is, a greater degree of dissonance will lead to greater attitude change in order to reduce the dissonance.

In Steiner's study, a measure of attitude toward science was administered to a sample of ninth-grade science students. Steiner then divided his group into students having high (HS) versus low (LS) attitudes toward science. Students in these groups in turn were randomly assigned to experimental and control treatments. Each student in the experimental treatment prepared a short videotape extolling science and advocating that students enroll in science. According to Festinger's theory, this behavior would cause substantial cognitive dissonance for the LS students, whose initial attitude toward science was low. The behavior could also cause some dissonance (presumably less) among

---

3. Robert L. Steiner, "Induced Cognitive Dissonance as a Means of Effecting Changes in School-Related Attitudes," *Journal of Research in Science Teaching* 17, no. 1 (1980): 39–45.
4. Leon Festinger, *A Theory of Cognitive Dissonance* (Stanford, CA.: Stanford University Press, 1957).

students in the HS group if their videotape behavior was more favorable to science than their initial attitude was. The control group was not exposed to any treatment, and so it would be expected that their attitudes would not change. After the treatment phase, an attitude scale was again administered to all subjects, and changes in attitudes between the pre- and post-measures were analyzed. It was found that the attitudes of the control group remained virtually the same on the two measures, as expected. The attitudes toward science of subjects in the experimental groups improved significantly between the pre- and post-measures. Contrary to expectation, however, gains made by the LS and HS groups were not significantly different. Therefore, the theory of cognitive dissonance was partially supported in that the cognitive dissonance generated by the treatment did result in higher scores. The theory was not fully supported because the LS group did not change their attitudes more than the HS group did.

This study is typical of research designed to test behavioral science theory in that it produced some relevant evidence but did not provide a definitive test of the theory. As research of this kind slowly accumulates, the scientist gains an increasingly better understanding of the theory, which in turn leads to changes in the theory and eventually to its general acceptance or rejection.

However, we should note that even though a number of studies might produce evidence confirming a theory while no disconfirming evidence is found, the theory is never fully accepted because the possibility of disconfirming evidence in the future always exists. On the other hand, one study that produces disconfirming evidence calls for revision or rejection of the theory.[5]

Several advantages accrue to conducting theory-based research in education. First, the theory tends to focus the direction of the research. Without some viable theory to serve as a guide, many studies address trivial questions or contribute nothing to the slow accumulation of knowledge needed for advancement of a science of education. Second, a theory can provide a rational basis for explaining or interpreting the results of research. Studies without a theoretical foundation often produce results that the investigator is at a loss to explain. Eventually such studies can help in the development of a theory, but their impact on our understanding of the phenomena being studied is much less clear and immediate than for theory-based research. Still another advantage of good theories is that they enable the researcher to make predictions about a wide range of situations. For example, cognitive dissonance could be employed to attempt to change a wide range of attitudes.

In summary, a valuable technique for defining a research problem is to derive a hypothesis from a theory in one of the behavioral sciences and then to test the hypothesis in a relevant educational context.

---

5. See David R. Krathwohl, *Social and Behavioral Science Research* (San Francisco: Jossey-Bass, 1985), for a discussion of how scientific theory is developed and confirmed.

Replication

Another strategy that can be used to locate a research problem is to select a previous study for replication. In the behavioral sciences, where we are usually unable to maintain the level of experimental control that is possible in the physical sciences, important studies should always be replicated before their findings are accepted by the scientific community. Therefore, you can often make a valuable contribution by repeating an important research project that someone else has carried out. In order to make a significant contribution, however, you must carefully search the literature to find a study that is appropriate for replication. There is no point in replicating a trivial study or one that is so poorly designed that the results cannot be accepted with any confidence. There are, however, several valid reasons for carrying out replications, and you should locate a study for which one of these reasons is relevant. Among the reasons for carrying out a replication are the following:

1. *To check the findings of a major or milestone study.* Occasionally a study is reported that either produces new and surprising evidence, reports findings that conflict strongly with previous research, or challenges a generally accepted theory. The replication of studies of this kind is very useful because these studies help confirm or disconfirm the validity of the new evidence. If supported by replication, such studies often open up a new area of investigation or have a major impact upon educational practice. Studies of this sort are often discussed in graduate seminars, as well as in literature reviews such as those that appear in editions of the *Handbook of Research on Teaching* or in issues of the *Review of Educational Research.* An example of a study that has had a major impact in the educational community is the work of David Wiley and Annegret Harnischfeger.[6] Based on their reanalysis of data obtained from Coleman's sixth-grade sample in Detroit, these researchers concluded that lengthening the school year by 10 days, increasing the school day to six hours, and raising the average daily attendance to 95 percent would bring about major achievement gains, including a 65 percent gain in reading comprehension and a 34 percent gain in mathematics achievement. This study dramatically illustrated the importance of time as a factor in school learning and stimulated many studies that further explored the influence of time in the schools. Considerable controversy also developed over the validity of Wiley and Harnischfeger's findings. This creates an ideal situation for replication, since their findings were both important and controversial.[7]

2. *To check the validity of research findings across different populations.* The typical research study in education is carried out with a small sample of

---

6. David E. Wiley and Annegret Harnischfeger, "Explosion of a Myth: Quantity of Schooling and Exposure to Instruction, Major Educational Vehicles," *Educational Researcher* 3, no. 4 (1974): 7–12.

7. For a recent replication of this research, see Abraham H. Daniels and Emil J. Haller, "Exposure to Instruction, Surplus Time, and Student Achievement: A Local Replication of the Harnischfeger and Wiley Research," *Educational Administration Quarterly* 17, no. 1 (1981): 48–68.

individuals representing a single population. Without replication we are unable to determine the degree to which findings that emerge from such research apply to other populations. For example, Charles Fisher and his colleagues studied the relationship between specific teacher behaviors and the achievement of second- and fifth-grade pupils in mathematics and reading. The researchers found that teachers' use of academic monitoring was negatively related to reading achievement but positively related to mathematics achievement. They also found several teaching behaviors that were positively related to the achievement of fifth-grade students but negatively related to second-grade achievement.[8] Clearly, it is unsafe to generalize research findings on effective teaching techniques across grade levels or subject areas without first doing replication studies. Similarly, findings for male populations may or may not apply to females, and findings valid for one racial or ethnic group may or may not be valid for other groups.[9] Thus, replications provide us with a very valuable tool for determining the degree to which research findings can be generalized across populations.

3. *To check trends or change over time.* Many research results in the behavioral sciences depend in part on the environment in which the individual functions. Thus, research findings on racial attitudes that were valid 20 years ago may be invalid today. Replication is a useful tool for checking earlier findings and identifying trends. For example, a study of curricular trends in high schools surveyed 234 principals in 1979, replicating a 1974 survey.[10] Comparisons of the 1974 and 1979 data revealed trends in 20 areas such as departmentalization, use of independent study, and moral education. These trend data give us interesting insights into where the secondary curriculum appears to be going.

If you can locate a survey conducted several years ago that covers topics of current interest, it is fairly easy to conduct a replication that will reveal interesting trends and that will increase our understanding of the questions addressed.

4. *To check important findings using different methodology.* In any research project there is a possibility that the observed relationships are an artifact of the methodology used by the researcher and are not due to a true relationship between the phenomena being studied. A true relationship should emerge regardless of the measures and methods used as long as they are reasonably

8. C. W. Fisher, N. N. Filby, R. Marleave, L. S. Cahen, M. M. Dishaw, J. E. Moore, and D. C. Berliner, *Teaching Behaviors, Academic Learning Time and Student Achievement: Final Report of Phase III-B, Beginning Teacher Evaluation Study* (San Francisco: Far West Laboratory for Educational Research and Development, 1978).

9. For an example of a cross-cultural replication, see A. C. Ramirez, R. T. Garza, and J. P. Lipton, "The Fear-Affiliation Relationship," *Journal of Cross-Cultural Psychology* 11 (1980): 173–188.

10. Mary P. Tubbs and James A. Beane, "Curricular Trends and Practices in the High School: A Second Look," *High School Journal* 64, no. 5 (1981): 203–208.

valid and appropriate. Thus, a very useful form of replication is to repeat important studies using different methodology. For example, a study by Wayne Piersel, Gene Brody, and Thomas Kratochwill found that disadvantaged minority-group children shown a videotape designed to give them a favorable experience with the test situation before being given an intelligence test earned significantly better scores than did similar children not shown the videotape.[11] This is an important finding because its application would reduce the likelihood of disadvantaged minority children being given spuriously low test scores, which psychologists suspect often happens. Leslie Raskind and Richard Nagel replicated this study but improved the research methodology by using examiners who did not know which children were in the experimental and control groups and by showing an unrelated videotape to the control group.[12] These features of experimental design, which were not present in the earlier study, reduced the likelihood of obtaining spurious results. Using the same intelligence measure (WISC-R), Raskind and Nagel found no significant IQ differences between the experimental and control groups. This suggests the results of the earlier study could have been due to deficiencies in research methodology. Because the children in the two studies were drawn from different populations, however, additional replications would be desirable before drawing any firm conclusions.

In conclusion, we have seen that replication gives us a much sounder basis for judging the validity of a research finding than is possible when only a single study is available. Moreover, replications that study individuals drawn from different populations, during different times, and using different methods contribute greatly to the confidence we may have in generalizing the research findings. Clearly, the more broadly we can apply a research finding to educational practice, the more valuable that finding will be.[13]

There has been a trend in recent years to conduct more replications of educational research. You should give this option careful thought because it offers significant advantages for thesis and dissertation studies.

Other Methods of Identifying Research Problems

If you still have not located a problem after using the approaches just presented, a number of other approaches may be tried. One of these is to observe carefully the existing practices in your area of interest. For example, a student interested

11. Wayne C. Piersel, Gene H. Brody, and Thomas R. Kratochwill, "A Further Examination of Motivational Influences on Disadvantaged Minority Group Children's Intelligence Test Performance," *Child Development* 48 (1977): 1142–1145.
12. Leslie T. Raskind and Richard J. Nagel, "Modeling Effects on the Intelligence Test Performance of Test-Anxious Children," *Psychology in the Schools* 17 (1980): 351–355.
13. The degree to which research findings can be generalized across people, settings, and times is called *external validity*. This construct will be discussed at length in later chapters.

in human relations problems in the public schools may observe faculty meetings, committee activities, and other situations where such problems may arise. These observations will often provide ideas and insights that can lead to a worthwhile research project. The student may observe that in faculty meetings some principals are much more effective than others in enlisting cooperation and developing enthusiasm among teachers. This observation might lead to a comparison of the methods of principals who are successful with those who are unsuccessful in obtaining teacher cooperation.

Another valuable source of research ideas is found in the advanced courses that you take in your graduate program. In graduate seminars, important research articles are often critically reviewed in class and important research questions are raised. In many textbooks, questions are also brought up for which we have no answers. Some textbooks even go so far as to list problems that require additional research. The brief reviews of research published in the *Review of Educational Research* almost always list specific areas in which further study is needed.

When searching for a problem, keep a notebook of research ideas. Whenever an interesting idea comes up in reading or class discussions, make a brief note of the idea and its source. The source will be useful if you decide to probe more deeply into the idea. This approach not only produces many potential thesis and dissertation problems but also makes you increasingly perceptive to possible problems, so that you see many you would previously have overlooked.

Do not hesitate to consult with professors at your college or researchers at other institutions who are working in areas related to your interests. Because they may have carried out research on a particular problem over a period of years, these people are likely to have developed a sensitivity to important unsolved problems in their field. For example, the authors have worked over the last several years on the development of training programs to improve the classroom skills of inservice teachers. As a result of this experience, we have identified a number of research problems concerning the teacher's role in the classroom. Little is known, for example, about the effect of many teacher behaviors on student performance. Does the teacher's use of higher cognitive questions in classroom discussions relate to student behavior and achievement? What is the effect of individual or small-group tutoring on student achievement? Also, little is known concerning the frequency with which certain teacher behaviors occur in the classroom, for example, how frequently teachers use tutoring, role-playing, or discussion of controversial issues, and at what grade levels these techniques are most used. Another type of research problem concerns identification of variables affecting development of teaching skills. We know, for example, that the use of models facilitates skill development. However, certain variables, such as sex and status of the model, may enhance or lessen the effectiveness of modeling. By consulting with researchers in your own area of interest, you may be able to identify problems of similar importance to the advancement of a particular field of study.

Graduate students in education have the advantage of working in an area where they have gained much experience during their years as students. Very often graduate students can recall problems encountered in their own educational experiences and from one of these problems develop a worthwhile research plan. Newspapers and popular magazines are sometimes valuable sources of research ideas. These periodicals often report at length on educational problems that are currently considered of major importance and usually report the opinions of educators and others in public life concerning these problems. These reports usually contain assertions, suggestions, and criticisms, the merits of which can be checked by research. For example, public debate in recent years concerning the need for changes in the methods of teaching reading has stimulated many research projects aimed at trying and evaluating some of the ideas and proposals that have been put forth.

OUTLINING A RESEARCH PROPOSAL

Purpose of the Research Plan

After having identified a specific research problem that appears to be satisfactory, you should outline a research plan in as much detail as possible. The project is still tentative at this point because your review of the literature has yet to be completed, and this review almost always leads to some changes in the research plan. The tentative outline, however, can do much to clarify your thinking and will also give direction to your review of the literature and your study of educational research. In order to plan a research project, you must have tentatively identified a problem, read a substantial amount of the research and theoretical literature relevant to your problem, and have a good basic knowledge of the educational research process. As this is only the second chapter of this text, you may wonder how you can be expected to be ready to prepare a research plan at this point. The fact is that you are probably not ready to develop a finished plan, but you should still start a preliminary plan, following the outline presented earlier in this chapter and based on the information described in the next few pages. Your preliminary plan will surely contain many blank spaces and many ideas that you will later change. The deficiencies of your plan will become apparent to you as you progress through this book. As you learn more about such topics as reviewing the literature, sampling, educational measurement and research design you can immediately apply this knowledge to the gradual refinement of your preliminary plan.

Most graduate students have two major goals in their study of the process of educational research. First, they want to develop the skills and knowledge they will need to plan and carry out their own research. Second, they must be able to apply their knowledge of the research process to the critical evaluation and interpretation of the research of others. Only by understanding the work of previous researchers can you build upon this work and move ahead, if only by a small amount, the frontiers of educational knowledge. If you keep these two broad goals in mind as you progress through this book, ideas and information presented will have much more meaning.

The tentative research plan should contain the following sections: introduction and problem description, statement of the objectives or hypotheses, listing of possible tests or measures to be used in the study, description of the proposed sample, research design, a chronological description of the procedures to be used in carrying out the project, and plans for carrying out analysis of data to be collected.

An important advantage of a research plan is that it compels students to state all their ideas in written form so that they can be evaluated and improved upon by the researcher and others. Even a simple research project contains many elements, and it is easy to overlook some of them unless they are all written down in a systematic manner. The authors recall an instance in which a written plan helped to stop a student from making a serious error in his research project. In discussing the proposed project with the student, we found the research design satisfactory. When the research plan was read later, however, we discovered that the student planned to have teachers try a new teaching technique with unfamiliar pupils rather than with pupils from their own classes. This procedure would confound the effect of the new teaching technique with the effect of working with unfamiliar pupils. Subsequently the student was advised to change the research design to avoid this error.

Another advantage of a detailed research proposal in written form is that it can easily be submitted to several professors and consultants for their comments and suggestions. Furthermore, the final plan can be used as a guide for conducting the research project. Otherwise you will need to rely on memory and may forget important details of the project when carrying it out.

Introduction and Problem Statement

Research proposals usually start with an introductory section that states the research problem, briefly reviews the most relevant research and theoretical literature, and states why you believe the problem to be important and what contribution you expect to make to educational knowledge and practice. This section typically covers the first four activities listed in the outline in the Introduction of this chapter.

By the time you start writing your research plan, you should be well along in your efforts to convert your initial research idea into a clear, specific, and manageable research problem. You will recall that the development and clarification of the research problem usually progresses as you build a stronger foundation of knowledge through a reading program. This program should start with books that pull together much information in a few pages, but by the time you have selected a specific problem, it should also include a review of the most relevant research articles that have appeared in recent journal issues.

Knowledge and understanding should be demonstrated through a brief review of the most important research and theoretical work relating to your problem. Usually a discussion of 10 to 20 key references is sufficient to help the members of the thesis committee fit your problem into the context of other work in this area. These few references, however, should be selected carefully from an extensive review of previous research and the findings fitted together to provide an integrated picture of the field of knowledge. If this brief review appears to be a disjointed recitation of the studies cited, as is often the case, the reader may well question your understanding of the problem you propose to study.

You are also expected to describe how your proposed study will contribute to educational knowledge. You should try in this section of your introduction to build a bridge between your expected outcomes and major educational problems and needs. If you have found any survey data that establish or document the importance of your problem, it should be presented.

For example, if your problem is concerned with remedial reading, surveys that report a large number of poor readers could be cited to demonstrate the need for additional research. Quotations from experts in the field that emphasize the importance of your problem area or the need for further research can also be used to help build a justification for your proposed research topic.

Briefly, the introduction and problem statement should have the following characteristics:

1. It should be written in clear, nontechnical language, avoiding jargon. Try to stimulate the reader's interest.
2. The problem should be sufficiently limited in scope to be a manageable thesis or dissertation problem.
3. The problem should be carefully fitted into the broader context of current theory and relevant research. Avoid making assumptions or unsupported claims or statements.
4. The significance of the problem should be addressed; that is, does it explore an important question, meet a recognized need, or make a useful contribution to knowledge?
5. The problem should be clearly and logically related to the hypotheses that follow.

In preparing the introductory section of the research proposal, you should bear in mind that the impression this section makes upon the members of the thesis committee will do much toward shaping their attitudes about you and the remainder of your plan.

Formulating Hypotheses or Objectives

In our day-to-day activities we are often faced with problems for which we must gather information and seek answers. In order to focus our information gathering we try to identify possible solutions or explanations to our problem and then gather the information needed to see if a given explanation is correct. These "educated guesses" about possible differences, relationships, or causes are called *hypotheses*.

For example, suppose that your car will not start. You know that there is a cause-and-effect relationship between availability of gasoline and running of the engine. Therefore, your first hypothesis may be that you are out of gas. When you note that the gauge indicates half full, you tentatively reject this hypothesis. Next, you hypothesize that you have gasoline but it is not reaching the carburetor. To test this hypothesis, you disconnect the gasoline line from the carburetor and operate the starter to see if gasoline is pumped out of the line. If so, you reject this hypothesis. Your next hypothesis may be that no electricity is reaching the spark plugs. This can be tested by removing a spark plug wire, operating the starter, and checking to see if a spark jumps from the wire to the engine. You can continue to formulate and test new hypotheses until the problem is solved.

This simple process that we use to attack our day-to-day problems is similar to the approach an investigator may use to attack a problem in educational research. First, the investigator hypothesizes a relationship between two or more variables, or a difference between two or more treatments. The investigator then collects evidence related to the hypothesis and examines the evidence to decide whether or not to reject the hypothesis. For example, a first-grade teacher may have noted that one of the pupils in class appears to be making no progress in reading. Careful observation of this child plus a review of previous research in this area may suggest several possible causes for this problem. These possible causes may be stated as hypotheses. The teacher may then design and carry out a program aimed at testing each hypothesis by manipulating the possible cause and then checking the child's progress in reading.

Educational research problems tend to be more complex than "troubleshooting" your car. The first-grade pupil is infinitely more complex than an automobile engine, and consequently most educational problems are likely to have multiple causes that may interact in unexpected ways and are likely to differ from child to child. Nevertheless, formulation of an hypothesis, and gathering of relevant evidence to test the hypothesis, is usually the most productive approach to throwing light on educational problems.

Before we leave our car and take the bus, let us look a bit more closely at the process we went through in attacking the "won't start" problem. First, it is important to state our problem as precisely as possible. For example, "the car won't go" is not as good a problem statement as "the starter will turn over the engine but the engine will not start." Once we have stated our problem clearly we can formulate hypotheses, that is, possible explanations or solutions to the problem. Note, however, that you must know something about the process you are studying in order to formulate good hypotheses. For example, if you did not know that gasoline must reach the carburetor in order for the engine to run, you would not be likely to formulate the hypothesis that gasoline is not reaching the carburetor. Similarly, in educational research you will be unable to formulate good hypotheses unless you know something about the phenomenon you propose to study. Furthermore, the more you know about your topic before you conduct your research, the better will be your hypotheses and the greater will be your chances of producing useful new knowledge related to your problem. This is one reason why a careful review of relevant literature is essential to the development of a sound research plan.

Although knowledge is a crucial ingredient to the formulation of good hypotheses, imagination is equally important. Investigators who make a real effort to look at their problem in new ways or organize relevant previous knowledge into new configurations are likely to gain perspectives and insights that other investigators have missed. When generating hypotheses, researchers must allow time to think through all the alternatives they can identify. Graduate students, who are typically in a great hurry to finish their research, often settle for the first promising approach or hypothesis they think of. It is always a serious mistake to hurry the planning phase of research. This is a time for careful thought, reading, and discussions with professors and fellow students. Research planning, even when done with care, requires only a small percentage of the total effort required to carry out a research project. In many cases a hastily planned project that produces nothing of value takes longer to carry out than a carefully planned project because of the mistakes, false starts, and need to repeat or replan that are an inevitable consequence of poor planning.

Because our society is highly evaluative, students often reject unique ideas that with further development would form the basis for promising hypotheses. In the initial stages of generating hypotheses, you should be noncritical. That is, you should first generate as many ideas as possible and only then should you start examining the ideas critically.

Educational researchers can often generate more imaginative hypotheses and procedures if they look at the knowledge, ways of attacking problems and methods for gathering data that have been developed in other disciplines such as sociology, psychology, economics, history, and anthropology. For example, a number of recent studies of classrooms and school systems have generated interesting new knowledge by using procedures borrowed from anthropology.[14]

The graduate student who has formulated a well-thought-out set of hypotheses has taken a major step on the road to an effective study. Such hypotheses place clear and specific goals before the researcher and provide a basis for selecting relevant samples, dependent variables, and research procedures to meet these goals. Many studies in education fail to produce useful knowledge because the researcher plunges ahead before developing a clear and specific set of hypotheses.

Directional and Null Hypotheses

Hypotheses may be stated in two forms, directional and null. The **directional hypothesis** states a relationship between the variables being studied or a difference between experimental treatments that the researcher expects to emerge. For example, the following are directional hypotheses:

1. Pupils of low ability in ability-grouped classrooms will receive significantly higher scores on a measure of inferiority feelings than pupils of low ability in random-grouped classrooms.
2. There is a positive relationship between the number of older siblings and the social maturity scores of six-year-old children.
3. Children who attend preschool will make greater gains in first-grade reading achievement than comparable children who do not attend preschool.

In contrast to the directional hypothesis, the **null hypothesis** states that no relationship exists between the variables studied or no difference will be found between the experimental treatments. For example, in null form, the aforementioned hypothesis could be stated thus: "There will be no significant difference between the scores on a measure of inferiority feelings of low ability pupils in ability-grouped classrooms and low-ability pupils in random-grouped classrooms." The null hypothesis does not necessarily reflect the scientist's expectations, but is used principally because it is better fitted to our statistical techniques, many of which are aimed at measuring the likelihood that a difference found is truly greater than zero.

Note that regardless of whether directional or null hypotheses are stated, the differences or relationships hypothesized refer to *population* differences, not

---

14. See Leona M. Foerster and Dale Little Soldier, "Applying Anthropology to Educational Problems," *Journal of American Indian Education* 20, no. 3 (1981): 1–6; and John U. Ogbu, "School Ethnography: A Multilevel Approach, *Anthropology and Education Quarterly* 12, no. 1 (1981): 3–29. This topic is also discussed in chapter 10.

sample differences. Stated another way, the null hypothesis, in the form usually used in education, states that no difference exists, and the statistical tools test this hypothesis by determining the probability that whatever difference is found in the research subjects is a true difference that also is present in the population from which the research samples have been drawn. You may be confused by the null hypothesis because it appears senseless to hypothesize the exact opposite of one's expectations. This is a disadvantage of the null form, because the researcher's expectations, based as they are upon considerable insight into other research and theory, often make the study clearer to the person reading the research report. Some researchers overcome this problem by using both a **working hypothesis** that reflects their expectations based on theory or previous research and a **statistical hypothesis** that is usually in the null form and is set up to make testing of the working hypothesis statistically more precise.

Directional hypotheses can also be tested as statistical hypotheses. However, your statistical hypothesis should be stated in the directional form only when there is little or no possibility that the findings will yield a difference or relationship in the opposite direction. This is because the null hypothesis and the directional hypothesis call for different statistical treatment, the first requiring what is called the two-tailed test of significance and the second requiring a one-tailed test. The two-tailed test assumes that the difference could occur in either direction—that is, either the ability-grouped or random-grouped children could have significantly greater inferiority feelings. The one-tailed test on the other hand assumes that, if a difference occurs, it can occur in only one direction. See chapter 13 for a discussion of one-tailed and two-tailed tests.

Some investigators state their problem in the form of a question instead of stating a working hypothesis. The aforementioned hypothesis stated as a question might read: "Is there a significant difference between the scores on a measure of inferiority feelings of a group of low-ability pupils in ability-grouped classrooms as compared with low-ability pupils in random-group classrooms?" The question form is often the easiest for the inexperienced research worker to use because it states specifically the question that the research will attempt to answer. In writing the research results, you may organize your report so as to answer the questions that you have posed.

In some research carried out in education, especially descriptive studies, it is appropriate to list objectives rather than hypotheses. A survey, for example, aimed at determining the extent of differences in the salaries of university professors in different fields of learning could test a hypothesis such as "There will be no significant differences between the mean salaries of faculty members of comparable ranks in different areas of learning." In a study of this sort, however, it is probably more desirable merely to state the objectives of the study as follows: "The objectives of this research are (1) to study the salaries paid professors of comparable academic ranks in different fields of learning and (2) if differences are found to exist, to attempt to identify the factors that appear to contribute to the observed differences."

Criteria for Good Hypotheses

If hypotheses are to be of maximum value to the researcher, they should satisfy the following four critera:

1. *The hypothesis should state an expected relationship between two or more variables.* In correlational studies, that is, those in which data on two or more variables are collected on the same individuals and correlations are computed, a direct relationship is usually stated in the hypothesis. For example, a directional hypothesis for a correlational study might state: "There is a significant positive relationship between peer-group acceptance and attitude toward school of sixth-grade boys."

In experimental studies, where an experimental treatment such as a new reading program is administered to one group of subjects but not to another group, differences between the treatments are usually hypothesized. For example, a null hypothesis for an experimental study might state: "There will be no significant difference in the reading achievement of first-grade pupils trained with Experimental Program A and comparable pupils trained with Conventional Program B." Although this hypothesis deals with an expected difference, it also indirectly suggests a relationship. Namely, it implies a relationship between characteristics of the two reading programs and reading achievement. Thus, either directly or indirectly, a good hypothesis is concerned with an expected relationship between two or more variables.

In addition to stating a relationship, the hypothesis may also briefly identify the variables and the population from which the researcher plans to select his sample. Some researchers provide a good deal of specific information about subjects and variables in their hypotheses as in this example: "Success in engineering as measured by a composite score based on income, patents held, and scholarly publications is positively related to freshmen scores on the Garnett College Test in Engineering Science for a random sample of 100 engineers who graduated from the University of Minnesota during 1976." As a rule, however, do not include such information because it lengthens the hypothesis statement and tends to make it less clear.

2. *The researcher should have definite reasons based on either theory or evidence for considering the hypothesis worthy of testing.* After completing the review of the literature, you will have detailed knowledge of previous work relating to your research project. In many cases you will find conflicting research results so that your hypothesis cannot agree with all available information. In general, however, your hypothesis should not conflict with the preponderance of previously reported information.

In addition to being in agreement with knowledge already established within the field, hypotheses should be formulated in accordance with theories in education or psychology. When this is possible, the results of the research will contribute to the testing of the theory in question. In many areas of education so little research has been done that reasonably conclusive information is not available. In this case educational theory may form the only basis for developing the hypothesis. You must always have some basis in theory or fact for your hypotheses. Occasionally, we find a study in education that has used the "shotgun approach." In this approach the research worker tries all the measures one can in the hope that something will yield useful results. This approach should be avoided because it uses measures for which no hypotheses have been developed. Many dangers are involved in applying such research results to educational practice. When we do not have some understanding of why a particular relationship exists, there is always a danger that factors are operating that may be detrimental to the educational program.[15]

3. *A hypothesis should be testable.* Hypotheses are generally stated so as to indicate an expected difference or an expected relationship between the variables studied in the research. The relationship or differences that are stated in the hypotheses should be such that measurement of the variables involved can be made and necessary statistical comparisons carried out in order to determine whether the hypothesis as stated is or is not supported by the research. Do not state any hypothesis that you do not have reason to believe can be tested or evaluated by some objective means. For example, the authors recall a "hypothesis" prepared by a teacher who wished to evaluate a high school course in civics. It was "to determine whether this course will make the student a better adult citizen." Such an objective would be very difficult to test because it would require (1) waiting until pupils taking the course had become adult citizens, (2) setting up criteria to determine how good a citizen each pupil had become, (3) evaluating each adult in terms of the criteria established, and then, perhaps most difficult of all, (4) determining what aspects of the adult citizenship of the former pupils could be directly attributed to the civics course. We can see from this example that such hypotheses are much easier to state than they are to evaluate by objective means. The hypotheses of inexperienced research workers in education often fail to meet the criterion of testability because relationships are stated that cannot be measured using today's tests. A similar mistake made frequently by graduate students is to state hypotheses in terms that would require many years to test.

4. *The hypothesis should be as brief as possible consistent with clarity.* In stating hypotheses the simplest and most concise statement of the relationship expected is generally the best. Brief, clear hypotheses are easier for the reader to understand and also easier to test. The question "Is a student counseling program desirable and economically feasible at the elementary school level?" reflects the sort of fuzzy thinking that handicaps many studies in education. A program can be "desirable" or "undesirable" from a very large number of different viewpoints. No specific guides are given about what aspect of the guidance program is to be studied. The second part of the question dealing with

---

15. A discussion of the "shotgun approach" can be found in chapter 14.

the economic feasibility is determined largely by the individual school district's financial resources. In order to develop a meaningful hypothesis from this question we would need to determine first the specific aspects of the elementary school counseling program that the research worker plans to study. Let us say he wished to provide counseling for three classes of sixth-grade pupils and not provide counseling for three other classes in a large elementary school and then compare his two groups on such variables as the number of behavior problems reported by the classroom teachers, the incidence of truancy, and the pupils' stated attitudes toward school. In this case perhaps three specific hypotheses would be the best approach. Stated in the null form these might be:

1. Sixth-grade pupils receiving counseling will not be signficantly different in the number of behavior problems reported by the teacher from sixth-grade pupils not receiving counseling.
2. Sixth-grade pupils receiving counseling will not be significantly different in incidence of truancy from sixth-grade pupils not receiving counseling.
3. Sixth-grade pupils receiving counseling will not be significantly different in their stated attitudes toward school from sixth-grade pupils not receiving counseling.

In the aforementioned example the broad general question has been changed to three specific null hypotheses, each stating a specific relationship between two variables. It is usually desirable to state your hypotheses in this more precise form. The advantage of stating a hypothesis for each relationship to be studied is that this procedure is simple and clear. The testing of multiple hypotheses involving several relationships leads to some confusion because portions of the hypothesis may be supported by the research evidence and other portions may not be supported. In writing the results of the experiment, you will find it possible to present a more easily understood picture of your findings if each hypothesis has stated only a single relationship.

Considering Alternate Hypotheses

Once you have formulated your hypotheses, carefully consider the following question: "If my research results support the relationship that I have stated in my working hypothesis, what factors, other than the variables manipulated in my research, could have brought about this result?" For example, suppose you plan a study designed to compare the effectiveness of two reading programs in improving the reading comprehension of first-graders. Your working hypothesis is that children who study Program A will obtain higher reading comprehension test scores at the end of first grade than will children who study Program B. You select 10 first-grade teachers in School 1 to teach Program A, a new program. Program B, which is already in use in your district, will be used by 10 teachers in School 2. What are some of the reasons, other than the superiority of Program A, that could result in children in Program A classrooms obtaining higher scores on the reading comprehension test? Let us consider a few possibilities:

1. School 1 has a more extensive prereading program in kindergarten than does School 2. Thus, the children in School 1 are better prepared for first-grade reading and do better for that reason.
2. Teachers who try Program A in School 1 are more enthusiastic and highly motivated than those who continue to use Program B in School 2. Often a new program tends to generate teacher enthusiasm.
3. School 1 serves a neighborhood of higher socioeconomic status than that served by School 2.
4. The items on the Reading Comprehension Test fit the content of Program A better than the content of Program B and therefore are biased in favor of Program A.

We could list many more alernate hypotheses, but these few should be enough to illustrate that many factors other than the effectiveness of Program A could account for the research results. In effect, each alternate hypothesis constitutes a flaw in your research design that will cast doubt on your research findings.

The reason for stating alternate hypotheses when planning your research is that once you have identified these alternatives, the research design can often be changed in ways that eliminate each alternate hypothesis. For example, consider alternate hypothesis 4 as stated above. The Reading Comprehension Test bias could be eliminated by selecting another test that fit the content of Programs A and B equally well, or by analyzing the content of the two programs and omitting test items that were covered in one program but not the other.

As you learn more about research design you will become increasingly capable of identifying alternate hypotheses and adjusting your research proposal to eliminate them.

Selecting Possible Measures

The next step in preparing the tentative research plan is to make a listing of possible measures. You probably have had courses in educational measurement that have provided some background in the types of measures available and sources of information about educational measures. This topic is covered briefly in chapters 8 and 9. Very often the process of identifying possible measures will require you to clarify your objectives and eliminate hypotheses for which no measures are available or can be developed. After measures have been identified, evaluate them and select the most appropriate.

Selecting Research Subjects

You should then describe the subjects you will require for your study. At this point, consider carefully the chance of obtaining the type and number of subjects you need. If your study is concerned with individuals who occur only rarely in the general population, be particularly careful to determine whether or not subjects are actually available to do the work you have planned. For example, studies of highly gifted children, say those with IQs above 160, are extremely difficult to carry out unless you have a very large population to draw from because children at this IQ level occur very rarely in the general population. Your method of selecting your sample should also be considered and tentatively decided upon. Careless selection of subjects is an error often found in educational studies. Considerations involved in selecting a sample of subjects are discussed in chapter 6.

Specifying the Research Design

Next, describe your tentative research design. Become familiar with the various types of research designs in chapters 10 to 19, and be sure that the design you plan to use will permit testing the hypotheses. Students often give little thought to the design of their projects until too late.

Selecting Analysis Procedures

A tentative plan for analysis of the research results is very important because this plan may have a considerable bearing upon the number of subjects needed, the measures and scoring procedures used, and the methods of recording the data. Yet many students give no thought to analysis until the data are collected. Then they find that no analysis procedures fit their data very well, and often they discover that the only procedures that can be used to salvage the study are complex ones that they must then learn to use.

In no area is lack of foresight so costly and disastrous as in doing research. Careful planning saves time in the long run and results in much better research. Students should complete their course in research methods prior to starting the work on their research problem, because much of the knowledge needed to carry out even the first steps in a research problem requires an understanding of the overall field of educational research.

Specifying Research Activities

After you have spelled out your measures, subjects, design, and analysis, add to your research plan a chronological list of procedures that you will follow in carrying out your study. This list should be as detailed as possible. In addition to describing each activity, give the approximate date when the activity will be completed, and also estimate how many working hours will be required to carry out the activity. Compiling this chronological list forces you to think through the entire research process and may alert you to problems that you might otherwise overlook. The following types of problems are often identified as a result of compiling a chronological list of procedures:

1. In order to start the research in October, school officials must be contacted during the summer.
2. The collection of pretest data must be speeded up or the experimental treatments will extend into the Christmas holiday.
3. Standardized tests to be administered must be ordered as soon as possible to assure their arrival by the time needed.
4. The posttests cannot be given by one person in the number of days available.
5. The research cannot be completed during the time remaining in the current school year.
6. At least three observers will be needed to collect the classroom observation data in the time allotted.
7. Some of the activities to be done by the researcher during the first month of the project must be rescheduled because they will require 200 hours and only 80 hours are available.

Fitting the Proposal Together

In their initial attempts to develop a research plan, students often focus on each section of the plan in turn, and give too little attention to relationships among the various sections. As a result, it is not uncommon to find research plans in which errors such as the following occur:

1. An hypothesis is listed that cannot be tested by the measures described later in the plan.
2. The "Measures" section of the plan includes measures that are not related to any of the hypotheses or objectives. This happens frequently in correlational studies in which the careless researcher adds a few extra measures in the hopes that something interesting will emerge, or because the schools from which he has sampled already use the measures, or for some other reason.
3. Inappropriate analysis procedures are stated. Students who do not think through their analysis often list several analysis techniques and hope that one or the other will be accepted by the thesis committee.

One way to avoid errors such as those mentioned above is to construct a table in which the hypotheses are listed in the left-hand column, the measures to be used to test each given hypothesis are described in the center column, and

TABLE 2.1

Procedure for Checking Relationships among Hypotheses, Measures, and Analysis

Hypothesis	Measures	Analysis
1. There is no relationship between overall achievement and popularity for sixth-grade boys.	1a. Achievement: total battery score on the California Achievement Tests. 1b. Popularity: a sociometric choice instrument in which each student lists names of his or her five best friends.	1. Product moment correlation between 1a and 1b.
2. When the effects of achievement differences are controlled, there is no relationship between popularity and self-concept of sixth-grade boys.	2a. Achievement: as in 1a. 2b. Popularity: as in 1b. 2c. Self-concept: Tennessee Self-Concept Scale.	2. Partial correlation between 2b and 2c, partialing out 2a.

NOTE: The problem of this study is to determine relationships between peer-group popularity and characteristics of sixth-grade boys.

the method of analysis is given in the right-hand column. An example of such a table for a correlational study is given in table 2.1. This procedure is especially useful in helping the student think through studies that have a large number of objectives or hypotheses. For example, in descriptive questionnaire surveys, items are often included in the questionnaire that do not relate to any research objective and are often stated in a form that makes analysis difficult. By matching test items with hypotheses in a table, you are assured that all objectives are covered in your questionnaire and that no items are included that do not relate to an objective.

Using PERT in Research Planning

In the planning of research several procedures have been developed over the past 20 years. Many of these techniques were developed to improve planning for the development of complex weapons systems. They can be employed in any research or development activity, however, and are especially useful in planning large-scale projects. In educational research, **PERT (Program Evaluation and Review Technique)** is the most widely used of these planning systems. In effect, PERT is an extension of the chronological list of procedures typically included in an educational research plan.[16] By using PERT, the researcher can (1) clearly see the relationships among the various activities making up the research, (2) check one's progress and identify activities that must be changed or speeded up in order to keep the project on schedule, and (3) focus on potential or actual problems involved in carrying out the project.

The first step involved in using PERT is to identify all goals that must be reached in the process of carrying out the project. Broad goals are first identified, and these are subsequently broken down into as many specific activities and subgoals as possible. For example, one broad goal in a study of the relationship between student attitudes and achievement could be to develop a scale to measure student attitudes toward school. This could be broken down into the activities and subgoals as shown in figure 2.1.

Having made a breakdown such as this for the entire project, you can now draw a network in which the various events or subgoals are arranged in order, beginning with the first day of the project and ending with the last day. Figure 2.1 shows a PERT network for the development of the attitude scale mentioned earlier. Each circle represents one subgoal or event. The initial event, *a* in figure 2.1, is to "start scale development." The circles are connected by lines, which represent the activities that must be carried out to achieve the following subgoals. Activities that can be carried out simultaneously are drawn parallel to each other, while those that must be done in sequence are drawn end-to-end. A dashed line is called a "dummy activity" and is used mainly to connect the completion of one broad goal or event and the start of the next. In drawing the PERT network, make decisions about the sequence of events and how you will allocate time to accomplish them. Note that each of these activities is highly specific and deals with only one small aspect of the process of developing the needed attitude scale. It is much easier to estimate accurately how much time will be involved in achieving each specific subgoal than to estimate the work involved in achieving the broad goal without making this detailed breakdown of activities.

The next step in PERT is to make time estimates. For each subgoal make three time estimates: optimistic (*a*), the time that will be needed to achieve the subgoal if everything goes well; most likely (*m*), best estimate of time needed; and pessimistic (*b*), the time needed if everything goes wrong that can go wrong. These estimates are usually expressed in weeks and made to the nearest tenth of a week. Figuring a five-day week, each half day equals one-tenth of a week (.1).

16. Flowcharts can also be used in research planning. See K. M. Evans, *Planning Small-Scale Research,* 3rd ed. (Windsor, Berkshire, England: NFER-Nelson, 1984) for a research planning flowchart.

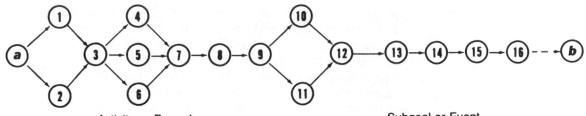

Activity or Procedure	Subgoal or Event
	a. Start scale development
1. Search literature for attitude scales	1. Complete search
2. Review attitude scaling procedures	2. Complete review
3. Select procedure to be used	3. Complete selection
4. Construct scale items	4. Complete item construction
5. Assemble prototype scale	5. Complete scale assembly
6. Arrange field test of prototype scale	6. Complete arrangements
7. Field-test prototype scale	7. Complete field test
8. Score scale	8. Complete scoring
9. Item-analyze scale	9. Complete item analysis
10. Revise prototype scale	10. Complete revision
11. Arrange field test of revised scale	11. Complete arrangements
12. Field-test revised scale	12. Complete field test
13. Score revised scale	13. Complete scoring
14. Item-analyze revised scale	14. Complete item analysis
15. Make final revision of scale	15. Complete final revision
16. Duplicate final scale for use	16. Finish duplication
	b. Start next major activity

Figure 2.1   PERT Network Showing Development of an Attitude Scale

Researchers who have made the three estimates for a given subgoal use the following formula to compute the expected elapsed time (t_e) to be spent in work planning:

$$t_e = \frac{a + 4m + b}{6}$$

For example, for activity 6, "arrange field test of prototype scale," the researcher may estimate that if all goes well (*a*) one can make the arrangements in one-half day. However, it will probably (*m*) take a full day by the time telephone contacts are made, appointments are set up, and necessary meetings are held. If the necessary persons are difficult to contact, if appointments cannot be made on the same day, and if meetings take longer than anticipated, the researcher estimates that four and one-half days (*b*) will be needed to complete this task. Using the formula

$$t_e = \frac{.1 + (4 \times .2) + .9}{6} = \frac{1.8}{6} = .3$$

the researcher arrives at .3 weeks or 1.5 days as the time estimate.[17]

Figure 2.1 represents the PERT network for only one major step in a research project. In developing a network for the entire project, each major goal would be broken down; the resulting network would combine many networks such as figure 2.1 in chronological order to produce the network for the entire project. Since this final network will be quite complex even for a typical thesis or dissertation plan, you may want to begin by constructing a PERT network that shows only the major goals or events. Then this network can be expanded by breaking down each broad goal, as was done in figure 2.1.

THE PILOT STUDY

A preliminary trial of research measures and techniques is essential to the development of a sound research plan. Whenever possible this preliminary trial should be enlarged into a **pilot study.** In a pilot study the entire research procedure is carried out, including analysis of the data collected, following closely the procedures planned for the main study. Pilot studies are carried out with fewer subjects than will be employed in the main study. For some pilot studies two or three subjects are sufficient, and you rarely need to include more than 20 subjects.

In addition to serving all the purposes of the usual tryout, such as improving data-collecting routines, trying scoring techniques, revising locally developed measures, and checking the appropriateness of standard measures, the pilot study provides additional knowledge that leads to improved research:

1. It permits a preliminary testing of the hypotheses that leads to testing more precise hypotheses in the main study. It may lead to changing some hypotheses, dropping some, and developing new hypotheses when called for.
2. It often provides ideas, approaches, and clues not foreseen prior to the pilot study. Such ideas and clues greatly increase the chances of obtaining clear-cut findings in the main study.
3. It permits a thorough check of the planned statistical and analytical procedures, thus allowing an appraisal of their adequacy in treating the data.

---

17. Note that the formula arbitrarily gives the greatest weight to the researcher's best estimate.

Needed alterations also may be made in the data-collecting methods, so that data in the main study may be analyzed more efficiently.

4. It greatly reduces the number of treatment errors because unforeseen problems revealed in the pilot study may be overcome in redesigning the main study.

5. It may save a major expenditure of time and money on a research project that will yield nothing. Unfortunately, many research ideas that seem to show great promise are unproductive when carried out in the field or laboratory. The pilot study almost always provides enough data for the research worker to make a sound decision on the advisability of going ahead with the main study.

6. In many pilot studies it is possible to get feedback from research subjects and other persons involved that leads to important improvements in the main study. Although the pilot study should follow the main study procedures for the most part, variations such as trying alternate instruments and procedures and seeking feedback from subjects on the treatment, measures, and other aspects of the research are usually desirable. In deciding what variations are appropriate, you should remember that the pilot study is not an end in itself but is only a means by which the main study can be improved.

7. In the pilot study, the research worker may try out a number of alternative measures, and then select those that produce the best results for the main study with some tentative evidence that they would be productive. If you plan to continue beyond the master's degree, the master's research may sometimes serve as a pilot study for later research to be carried out as part of a doctoral program. The less research experience you have, the more likely you are to profit from the pilot study. Because of this, you should attempt a pilot study whenever possible.

MISTAKES SOMETIMES MADE IN PLANNING RESEARCH

1. The researcher puts off selection of a problem until completing all or most of the courses.

2. Uncritically accepts the first research idea thought of or that is suggested.

3. Prepares fuzzy or untestable hypotheses.

4. Hurries the planning of the research and, as a result, ends up with a poorly designed study that contributes nothing to educational knowledge.

5. Fails to carry out a preliminary trial of the measures and, as a result, makes serious mistakes when collecting data for the study.

6. Fails to conduct a pilot study and, as a result, encounters many unforeseen problems that weaken the research.

7. Overlooks important steps in preparing a chronological list of procedures.

ANNOTATED REFERENCES

Behling, John H. *Guidelines for Preparing the Research Proposal*, rev. ed. Lanham, MD: University Press of America, 1984.

Aimed both at the graduate student who wants to develop a thesis proposal and the professional educator who wants to prepare a grant proposal. The Research Proposal Outline and the Guidelines for the Research Proposal provide a detailed, step-by-step description of the process. The section on methodology is much too brief to be of any value to those who are not already familiar with this topic. It can, however, help remind the writer of the bases that must be covered in a proposal.

Carlow, C. D. "The Application of Psychological Theories to a Curriculum Development Project: An Example." *Educational Psychologist* 12 (1976): 36–48.

Describes how the learning theories of Ausubel and the motivation theories of White and Berlyne were used as guides in the development of an elementary school mathematics curriculum. The author demonstrates how the theoretical constructs were directly applied, modified, and combined in developing the curriculum. This paper provides a good example of how theory can be applied to the development of curriculum materials, which in turn could be used in research to test the theories involved.

Cook, Desmond L. *Program Evaluation and Review Technique—Applications in Education*. Lanham, MD: University Press of America, 1979.

Provides a description of PERT and gives examples of PERT charts for all of the major kinds of educational research. Much useful information is also provided on implementation of PERT on educational research and development projects. Students who intend to use PERT in planning their thesis or dissertation studies should read this book.

Davitz, Joel R., and Davitz, Lois L. *Evaluating Research Proposals in the Behavioral Sciences*, 2nd ed. New York: Teachers College Press, 1977.

Contains clear and simple guidelines that a student can use to evaluate a research plan. The authors pose questions that focus the student's attention on important aspects of the research plan, discuss each question briefly, and provide a reference to which the student may go for further information. There is also a chapter on the language of research that contains definitions of many terms the student will encounter in reviewing research literature.

Foster, Carol, and Lent, James R. "Application of Program Evaluation and Review Technique (PERT) Within a Curriculum Development Project." *Journal of Special Education Technology* 8(1) (1986): 47–58.

Provides a useful model for those who want to use PERT on the planning of their research. A 34-event PERT chart was developed for a three-year curriculum development project. When the PERT projections were compared with actual progress it was found that the mean actual time required was within one month of the original estimate.

Lester, James D. *Writing Research Papers: A Complete Guide,* 4th ed. Glenview, IL: Scott, Foresman, 1984.

Presents the current guidelines of the Modern Language Association on style and format for writing research papers. Major sections deal with finding a topic, using the library, taking notes, writing the paper, and format. Much practical information is provided. Most students will find the sections dealing with writing and format especially useful.

Madsen, David. *Successful Dissertations and Theses.* San Francisco: Jossey-Bass, 1983.

Takes the student through many of the steps involved in completing a thesis or dissertation. In addition to providing help in areas such as selecting a research topic and preparing the research proposal, the author also addresses aspects of the process not typically covered, such as working with the advisory committee, defending the thesis, and adapting it for publication. Two sample proposals are included: one for an historical study and one for an experimental study. This book is not designed to teach students how to carry out research; rather, it focuses on steps preceding and following the research activity such as preparing a proposal and writing the thesis.

PERT. The following references give additional examples of educational applications of the Program Evaluation and Review Technique:

Colvin, George M., and Fielding, Anthony F. "A PERT Application to Curriculum Planning." *Educational Technology* 15, no. 10 (1975): 9–20.

The authors describe a modified PERT technique that can help school administrators in curriculum planning, evaluation, and decision making.

Gallagher, Stephan M. "A New Systems Tool: PER-flo." *Educational Technology* 19, no. 7 (1979): 38–40.

In the proposed system, flowcharting is combined with PERT to develop PER-flo. An example of the method is given.

Hai, D. M. "PERT in Higher Education: An Application for Doctoral Students." *Educational Technology* 17, no. 8 (1977): 33–36.

The author used the PERT procedure to plan her Ed.D. dissertation and other activities necessary for the completion of her degree program. This article provides a useful model for graduate students.

SELF-CHECK TEST

Circle the correct answer to each of the following questions. An answer key is provided on page 883.

1. For the researcher, a negative aspect of working on a team project is
   a. lack of financial support for team projects.
   b. lack of opportunity to find and develop one's own project.
   c. the complexity of a team project compared to an individual project.
   d. the interaction required with the other team members.
2. Borg and Gall state that perhaps the most satisfactory method that a graduate student can use to locate specific research problems is to
   a. work in conjunction with state departments of education.
   b. initiate many action research projects.
   c. conduct a systematic reading program.
   d. maintain contacts in professional educational organizations.
3. A theory is said to be "powerful" if it
   a. is extremely accurate.
   b. provides an explanation for a large number of events.
   c. has a high degree of reliability.
   d. is valid.
4. A concept used in scientific research to describe events with similar elements is
   a. theory.
   b. generalization.
   c. construct.
   d. principle.
5. A statement of a relationship between two or more events that can be used in prediction is called a
   a. principle.
   b. developmental theory.
   c. concept.
   d. generalization.
6. Speculations about the relationship between two or more variables are called
   a. theories.
   b. hypotheses.
   c. principles.
   d. constructs.
7. When the experimenter has a reasonably high expectation concerning the relationship that exists between the variables, it is most appropriate to state the hypothesis in the _____ form.
   a. directional
   b. interrogative
   c. null
   d. objective
8. "There will be no significant difference between the scores on a measure of achievement of high- and low-anxious students" is a hypothesis written in the _____ form.
   a. directional
   b. interrogative
   c. null
   d. objective
9. Borg and Gall list several criteria of good hypotheses. Which of the criteria does the following hypothesis most violate?
   Hypothesis: The upper-division courses in civics will produce better adult citizens than the lower-division courses in civics.
   a. Hypotheses should be worthy of testing.
   b. Hypotheses should be testable within a reasonable period.

c. Hypotheses should be brief.
d. All of the above are correct.
10. A pilot study is often helpful because it
   a. permits a preliminary testing of the hypotheses.
   b. provides the researcher with ideas, approaches, and clues.
   c. permits a check of procedures with the possibility of revision where needed.
   d. All of the above are correct.

APPLICATION PROBLEMS

The following problems are designed to give you practice in applying significant concepts and research procedures explained in the chapter. Most do not have a single correct answer. For feedback, compare your answers with the sample answers on pages 886–887.

1. State three of your areas of interest in education. For each area of interest, state two problems currently being investigated by researchers. Select one of the problems and write a null hypothesis, a directional hypothesis, and an objective that fit the problem.
2. Without referring to the textbook, if possible, make a sequential list of the topics usually covered in a research plan.
3. A graduate student claims that it is not necessary to make up a research plan for a study the student intends to do. The student prefers to take each phase of the project as it comes; a plan would only inhibit him and keep him from improving the study as it progressed. What two advantages of a detailed written research plan could you point out to this student?
4. Consider the following statement and hypothesis:
   Several questionnaire studies of ability grouping have indicated that teachers believe such grouping to be harmful to the self-concept of students who are placed in low-ability groups. Eminent clinical psychologists have also questioned the value of ability grouping on the same grounds. However, no experimental studies have ever been done to test this view. It is the goal of our study to measure the self-concept of a group of low-ability children and then place them in ability-grouped classes and see whether their self-concepts change. *It is our hypothesis that no significant changes will take place, since we believe that any loss of self-concept occurring because of ability grouping will be offset by a gain because the students will be better able to compete in the ability-grouped class.*
   What criteria, if any, does the hypothesis fail to meet? Which, if any, does it satisfy?
5. A graduate student claims that it is not necessary for her to do a pilot study prior to conducting an experiment for her doctoral dissertation. Her experiment is primarily a replication of a previously published study, with a few modifications. What are at least three arguments in favor of doing a pilot study, even under these conditions?

SUGGESTION SHEET

If your last name starts with letters from Bam to Bor, please complete the Suggestion Sheet at the end of the book while this chapter is still fresh in your mind.

| **3** | # ETHICS, LEGAL CONSTRAINTS, AND HUMAN RELATIONS |

OVERVIEW

In conducting an educational research project, one must never lose sight of the special requirements and problems involved in working with people. The human relations aspect of educational research is particularly important when the project is carried out in the public schools. If schoolchildren are the subjects, it is necessary to obtain the understanding and cooperation of school administrators, teachers, parents, interested community groups, and the subjects themselves. Thus, the procedures section of the research plan should describe how you intend to gain school cooperation, how you will deal with potential human relations problems that may arise, and what precautions you will take to ensure that the plan meets the ethical standards and legal requirements established for behavioral science research. These topics are discussed in this chapter.

OBJECTIVES

After studying this chapter you should be able to:

1. Identify aspects of a research situation that involve ethical questions or principles.
2. State and discuss five ethical principles of research that have been developed by the American Psychological Association.
3. Describe five strategies that can be used to assure the confidentiality of research data.
4. Discuss the pros and cons of using deception in behavioral science research, and explain factors the researcher should consider before using deception.
5. Describe the legal constraints to educational research imposed by federal law.
6. Describe categories of research that are exempt from review by the Institutional Review Board.
7. State the conditions under which the Institutional Review Board can waive the requirement for informed consent.
8. Discuss the kinds of questions the researcher must answer when presenting a research plan to school officials.
9. State steps that can be taken to protect the rights of individuals who are to serve as subjects in a research project.
10. Define dehoaxing and desensitizing, identify research situations where these are required, and describe what steps should be taken to dehoax or desensitize research subjects.

ETHICAL PRINCIPLES

In recent years the ethical aspects of behavioral research have been of increasing concern to the Congress, scientists, private citizens, and institutions that support this research. In part, this concern reflects the great growth of behavioral research and its impact on people's lives. Although most researchers have acted in an ethical manner, there have been occasional abuses of individuals' rights.[1]

The American Psychological Association recently published 10 ethical principles for the conduct of research activities with human participants. In planning a research project, you should study these principles carefully:

The decision to undertake research rests upon a considered judgement by the individual psychologist about how best to contribute to psychological science and human welfare. Having made the decision to conduct research, the psychologist considers alternative directions in which research energies and resources might be invested. On the basis of this consideration, the psychologist carries out the investigation with respect and concern for the dignity and welfare of the people who participate and with cognizance of federal and state regulations and professional standards governing the conduct of research with human participants.

a. In planning a study, the investigator has the responsibility to make a careful evaluation of its ethical acceptability. To the extent that the weighing of scientific and human values suggests a compromise of any principle, the investigator incurs a correspondingly serious obligation to seek ethical advice and to observe stringent safeguards to protect the rights of human participants.

b. Considering whether a participant in a planned study will be a "subject at risk" or a "subject at minimal risk," according to recognized standards, is of primary ethical concern to the investigator.

c. The investigator always retains the responsibility for ensuring ethical practice in research. The investigator is also responsible for the ethical treatment of research participants by collaborators, assistants, students, and employees, all of whom, however, incur similar obligations.

d. Except in minimal-risk research, the investigator establishes a clear and fair agreement with research participants, prior to their participation, that clarifies the obligations and responsibilities of each. The investigator has the obligation to honor all promises and commitments included in that agreement. The investigator informs the participants of all aspects of the research that might reasonably be expected to influence willingness to participate and explains all other aspects of the research about which the participants inquire. Failure to make full disclosure prior to obtaining informed consent requires additional safeguards to protect the welfare and dignity of the research participants. Research with children or with participants

1. John G. Adair, R. CL. Lindsay, and James Carlopio, "Social Artifact Research and Ethical Regulations: Their Impact on the Teaching of Experimental Methods," *Teaching of Psychology* 10(3)(1983): 159–162. These researchers found greatly increased coverage of research ethics in recent research methods textbooks, which reflects an increasing concern with this topic.

who have impairments that would limit understanding and/or communication requires special safeguarding procedures.

e. Methodological requirements of a study may make the use of concealment or deception necessary. Before conducting such a study, the investigator has a special responsibility to (i) determine whether the use of such techniques is justified by the study's prospective scientific, educational, or applied value; (ii) determine whether alternative procedures are available that do not use concealment or deception; and (iii) ensure that the participants are provided with sufficient explanation as soon as possible.

f. The investigator respects the individual's freedom to decline to participate in or to withdraw from the research at any time. The obligation to protect this freedom requires careful thought and consideration when the investigator is in a position of authority or influence over the participant. Such positions of authority include, but are not limited to, situations in which research participation is required as part of employment or in which the participant is a student, client, or employee of the investigator.

g. The investigator protects the participant from physical and mental discomfort, harm, and danger that may arise from research procedures. If risks of such consequences exist, the investigator informs the participant of that fact. Research procedures likely to cause serious or lasting harm to a participant are not used unless the failure to use these procedures might expose the participant to risk of greater harm, or unless the research has great potential benefit and fully informed and voluntary consent is obtained from each participant. The participant should be informed of procedures for contacting the investigator within a reasonable time period following participation should stress, potential harm, or related questions or concerns arise.

h. After the data are collected, the investigator provides the participant with information about the nature of the study and attempts to remove any misconceptions that may have arisen. Where scientific or human values justify delaying or withholding this information, the investigator incurs a special responsibility to monitor the research and to ensure that there are no damaging consequences for the participant.

i. Where research procedures result in undesirable consequences for the individual participant, the investigator has the responsibility to detect and remove or correct these consequences, including long-term effects.

j. Information obtained about a research participant during the course of an investigation is confidential unless otherwise agreed upon in advance. When the possibility exists that others may obtain access to such information, this possibility, together with the plans for protecting confidentiality, is explained to the participant as part of the procedure for obtaining informed consent.[2]

In educational research carried out by graduate students, the principles relating to informed consent (*d*), deception (*e*), debriefing subjects at the end of the study

2. Committee on Scientific and Professional Ethics and Conduct, "Ethical Principles of Psychologists," *American Psychologist* 36 (1981): 633–638. Copyright 1981 by the American Psychological Association. Reprinted by permission of the publisher and author.

(*h* and *i*), and protecting confidentiality of research data (*j*) are the ones most likely to be violated.[3,4]

Informed Consent

The protection of individual privacy in educational research involves two factors: the consent of the individual as to what will be disclosed to the researcher, and the confidential use of research data collected on individuals. The researcher should obtain the individual's consent before gathering data on the person. In the case of schoolchildren, the consent of parents and appropriate school personnel should be obtained. Ideally the subject should receive some explanation of the tests and experimental procedures to be used. This explanation must satisfy the subject that participation is important and desirable and that it is to the subject's advantage to cooperate.

There are occasions, however, when it would invalidate research findings to tell individuals beforehand the purpose of the study and the type of information they will be expected to provide during the course of the research project. For example, in some experiments it may be necessary to give individuals false information in order to experimentally arouse or decrease their motivation. Nevertheless, even in this situation the researcher should obtain the individual's consent to be in the experiment and should tell the subjects that they will be informed of the experiment's purpose *after* the study is completed.

Another way of resolving this dilemma is proposed by J. E. Atwell. He suggests that when the validity of research results would be jeopardized by informing subjects about the research, the investigator may obtain "implied consent." To do this, a sample drawn from the population to be studied is fully informed on every aspect of the proposed research. If the individuals in the sample agree by a large majority to be subjects in the study, the researcher can assume that other persons from the same population would also agree. The researcher then selects subjects from this population, but does not seek informed consent from the actual subjects.[5]

There is clear evidence that the results of some studies can be drastically altered if research subjects are informed of all details about the research. For example, in a study by J. H. Resnick and T. Schwartz, volunteer subjects were

3. It is interesting that codes of ethics adopted by European psychologists are generally similar to the APA principles. See H. Schuler, "Ethics in Europe," in *Ethics of Human Subject Research,* ed. A. J. Kimmel (San Francisco: Jossey-Bass, 1981), pp. 41–48.
4. Students who plan to conduct qualitative research should consult: American Anthropological Association, "Proposed Code of Ethics Would Supersede Principles of Professional Responsibility," *Anthropology Newsletter* 25 (1984): 2. Also see the Annotated References in this text for other sources dealing with ethics in qualitative research.
5. J. E. Atwell, "Human Rights in Human Subjects Research," in A. J. Kimmel, ed., *Ethics of Human Subject Research* (San Francisco: Jossey-Bass, 1981).

placed in two groups. They were given cards containing a verb and the six pronouns *I, we, you, they, she, he,* and were asked to construct sentences using the verb and one pronoun.[6] During the last 80 of 100 trials, the investigator reinforced the subjects with verbal approval each time the subject constructed a sentence that began with *I* or *we,* to determine the effects of the reinforcement. The results showed that the use of "I-we" sentences increased for uninformed subjects and decreased for informed subjects. In this study, fully informing the subjects led to serious distortion of the results. But should the need to learn more about human behavior take precedence over the need to inform subjects, even in studies like this, where no conceivable harm or danger to the subjects is possible? The pros and cons raised when such studies are considered in relation to ethical standards certainly merit careful consideration.[7]

Federal regulations related to informed consent are discussed later in this chapter.

Confidentiality

Once research data have been collected, the researcher should make certain that no one has access to the data except the researcher and possibly a few co-investigators. Research subjects, of course, should be told at the outset who will have access to the data. Whenever possible, names of subjects should be removed from data-collection instruments and replaced by a code. This procedure is particularly important to follow when the data are to be stored for a relatively long time. Take particular care with data that conceivably could be subpoenaed. Unfortunately, in most states educational research data do not have privileged status (as does communication between husband and wife, lawyer and client, etc.). Confidentiality must be further protected by not using names of individuals in any publications that result from the research project.

You can avoid problems relating to invasion of privacy by including procedures in your research design for individual consent and preservation of confidentiality, and if you carry out your project in an ethically responsible manner. Carefully guard confidentiality of research data by either (1) collecting research data so that no one, including the researcher, can link the data to specific subjects; or (2) using some sort of linkage system, such as substituting numbers for names, so that only a person who has access to a closely guarded key can identify data for a specific subject. The first approach is regarded as

---

6. J. H. Resnick and T. Schwartz, "Ethical Standards as an Independent Variable in Psychological Research," *American Psychologist* 28 (1973): 134–139.
7. For another study that clearly shows a distortion of results caused by informed consent, see Gerald T. Gardner, "Effects of Federal Human Subjects Regulations on Data Obtained in Environmental Stressor Research," *Journal of Personality and Social Psychology* 36 (1978): 628–634.

ethically preferable, but if often reduces the effectiveness of the research. In many projects, the researcher must retain some means of identifying subjects. For example, in longitudinal studies where data are gathered on the same subjects over a long period of time, much valuable information is lost if the responses of specific subjects cannot be identified. Similarly, many cross-sectional studies gather data from a variety of sources. These data often need to be linked in order to have a clear picture of the phenomena being studied. Such linkage is difficult unless some means of identifying subjects is retained for at least a short time.

For studies dealing with nonsensitive issues, careful linkage procedures should be set up and closely guarded. The scientific benefits usually outweigh the slight risk of a breach in confidentiality. When research deals with controversial or sensitive topics, however, confidentiality is much more important, and very sophisticated procedures may be needed to minimize the danger of a breach.[8]

Behavioral scientists generally agree that subjects should be given assurances of confidentiality by the researcher, and that these assurances should be rigidly adhered to. Evidence shows that an absolute assurance of confidentiality increases the number of subjects willing to cooperate in research.[9] This is especially true when sensitive topics, such as sexual intercourse or marijuana use, are involved.[10]

In recent years many strategies have been developed to assure confidentiality. Because these strategies often go beyond the needs of most graduate students, we here summarize only a few of the most widely used ones:

1. *Ask subjects to furnish information anonymously.* This strategy virtually eliminates the possibility that individuals can be linked to their responses. If it is necessary to determine who has responded (an important consideration in questionnaire surveys), include a separate postcard with the questionnaire and request the respondent to return the card after returning the questionnaire. This provides a check of who has responded, thus permitting follow-ups of nonrespondents; but because the postcard and questionnaire are mailed separately, it is not possible to link the two and identify a given respondent's questionnaire.

2. *Use an identifier that can be destroyed as soon as the individual's response is received.* This approach is often used in surveys where it is necessary to follow up on nonrespondents. In questionnaire studies, the questionnaire may be designed so that the respondent's name or code number can be torn off as soon as the questionnaire is received and before responses are tabulated.

8. For a detailed discussion of confidentiality, see Robert F. Boruch and Joe S. Cecil, *Assuring the Confidentiality of Social Research Data* (Philadelphia: University of Pennsylvania Press, 1979).
9. National Academy of Sciences, Committee on Federal Statistics, *Report of the Panel on Privacy and Confidentiality as Factors in Survey Responses* (Washington, DC: NAS, 1979).
10. Eleanor Singer, "Informed Consent: Consequences for Response Rate and Response Quality in Social Surveys," *American Sociological Review* 43 (1978): 144–162.

3. *Use a third party to select the sample and collect data.* In some sensitive areas, knowledge that the individual belongs to a target population can be a breach of confidentiality regardless of the individual's responses. For example, suppose you want to study a sample of child abusers. It may be necessary to ask clinicians working with child abusers to randomly select cases from their active files, administer your measure to the selected cases, and, without identifying subjects, turn over these measures to you. This way, you do not know who is in your sample and of course cannot link names to responses.

4. *Have subjects make up their own code numbers or aliases.* When data must be collected over a period of time or when several measures must be administered to each subject, the data can be linked by having each subject make up an alias based on information not available to the researcher. The subject then puts the alias (rather than his own name) on all measures related to the research. For example, Robert Boruch and Joe Cecil recommend a number code based on the birth dates of respondents' parents.[11] Another possibility is to have the subject arrive at a four-digit "secret number," such as the odd digits in the subject's Social Security Number, the month and day of a friend's birth, the last four digits on the subject's auto license, house number from a previous residence, and so on. Since no one but the subject knows how this number was arrived at, it would be nearly impossible to identify the subject from this number.

The alias need only be a word or number the subject can reconstruct if he or she forgets it and be based on information that is almost certain to be different for all respondents.

5. *Data contamination or randomized response.* This approach involves introducing a random error into subject responses so that a certain number of subjects give untrue responses. For example, suppose the investigator wants to estimate how many girls in a target population have had sexual intercourse before age 12. Each subject is asked the question but is told to cast a die before answering. If the number 1 comes up, the subject is to give a false response, that is, indicate that she has had intercourse when in fact she has not, or vice versa. The respondent is protected because the researcher has no way of knowing whether the respondent has given a true or false response. However, the researcher does know that for a large sample, one-sixth of the responses will be false; knowing this, the researcher can estimate closely the number who have had intercourse before the age of 12. This approach can be used in direct interviews and in telephone and mail surveys.

Various combinations of approaches that employ anonymity, a third party, aliases, and randomized responses have been proposed. If the few strategies described in this chapter do not meet the confidentiality needs of your research, Boruch and Cecil should be consulted.[12]

---

11. See the Annotated References at the end of this chapter.
12. See the Annotated References at the end of this chapter.

Deception

Many studies in the behavioral sciences could not be carried out unless the investigator withheld information or deceived the subjects. Robert Menges reviewed published reports of about 1,000 psychological research studies and found that about 19 percent of them provided inaccurate information to subjects.[13] Only 3 percent gave subjects complete information. The percentage of studies giving inaccurate information varied greatly for different psychological journals. For example, 47 percent of articles in the *Journal of Personality and Social Psychology* used deception compared with only 3 percent in the *Journal of Experimental Psychology*. Clearly, different research areas require different amounts of deception. The ethical problems of using deception depend largely on the risk to subjects.

There are a number of reasons why deception is used. Edward Diener and Rick Crandall classify these reasons as methodological or practical considerations, ecological validity, ethical considerations, and lack of negative effects.[14] In some studies it would be very difficult to find naturalistic situations in which the behavior being studied will occur. For example, a study of student responses to another student's cheating is much easier to observe and control if the "cheater" is a confederate.

In many studies, even though the needed data could be collected in naturalistic situations without deception, practical considerations such as limited time and money lead the researcher to use deception. Suppose, for example, you were studying teacher reactions to serious student misbehavior, such as open defiance of the teacher. Such behavior occurs rarely in most classrooms, and the cost of having observers stay in the classroom long enough to see a reasonable number of cases where student defiance occurred would be very high.[15] If student confederates are employed without the teacher's knowledge, however, open defiance can occur whenever desired by the researcher. Of course, unless the teacher is deceived, the teacher's reactions will not be natural, and the results will be of little value.

Ecological validity, which is discussed at length in chapter 15, is the degree to which the results of an experiment can be generalized from the set of environmental conditions created by the researcher to other environmental conditions. If a subject is aware that he or she is participating in an experiment, or if the environment of the experiment is markedly different from the natural environment to which we would like to apply our results, then the subject's responses may differ from the subject's natural responses, and this will produce

---

13. Robert J. Menges, "Openness and Honesty Versus Coercion and Deception in Psychological Research," *American Psychologist* 28 (1973): 1030–1034.
14. See the Annotated References at the end of this chapter.
15. Walter R. Borg and Frank R. Ascione, "Classroom Management in Elementary Mainstreaming Classrooms," *Journal of Educational Psychology*, 74 (1982): 85–95.

spurious results. Deception often must be practiced in order to elicit spontaneous and natural behavior so that findings may be more safely generalized to natural situations.

In some experiments it is more ethical to deceive subjects than to subject them to pain or other adverse experiences that would result if deception were not used. The classic study of obedience by Stanley Milgram provides a good example.[16] In this study subjects were ordered to administer increasingly severe electric shocks to another individual in the context of a learning experiment. The dependent variable was the level of shock the subject was willing to administer before refusing to continue further. Actually, the person supposedly being shocked was a confederate, and no shocks were administered. It was clearly more ethical to deceive the subjects than to allow the victim to be shocked. In Milgram's initial experiment, 26 of the 40 subjects followed orders and administered what they thought was the maximum shock of 450 volts.

Most deceptions employed in behavioral research pose little or no risk to the subject. Many researchers consider such deceptions justified if the investigation promises to add to scientific knowledge. Some research indicates that most adults do not object to deception per se,[17] although a small percentage of adults surveyed found certain forms of deception objectionable.[18]

One way to estimate the effects of deception prior to starting your research is to select a group similar to your research subjects, give them a description of the experimental conditions, and ask them to imagine how they would react to the planned deceptions. A study comparing the reactions of passive role-players (PRPs) to subjects who actually took part in the research has demonstrated that PRPs were quite accurate in predicting how actual participants would feel about the deception employed.[19]

Some researchers are opposed to deception on the grounds that it is unethical and morally wrong to deceive anyone as part of a research project. Others oppose deception for more practical reasons. Probably the strongest argument against deception is that its use is widely known among such groups of potential subjects as college students. This awareness tends to make subjects suspicious and distrustful of researchers. If researchers are perceived as liars or deceivers, it seems inevitable that the long-term effects on science will be negative, and can lead to overt subject resistance and covert efforts to sabotage a study by giving spurious or unnatural responses.

16. Stanley Milgram, "Behavioral Study of Obedience," *Journal of Abnormal and Social Psychology* 67 (1963): 371–378.
17. Edwin A. Rugg, "Ethical Judgements of Social Research Involving Experimental Deception," *Dissertation Abstracts International* 36 (1975): 1976.
18. D. W. Wilson and E. Donnerstein, "Legal and Ethical Aspects of Non-Reactive Social Psychological Research: An Excursion into the Public Mind," *American Psychologist* 31 (1976): 765–773.
19. Marilyn Aitkenhead and Jackie Dordoy, "What the Subjects Have to Say," *British Journal of Social Psychology* 24 (1985): 293–305.

Other arguments against deception are that it often creates as many methodological problems as it solves and that it deprives the subject of the information needed to give informed consent to participate in the research.

Still another problem arises because there is a strong probability that some of the subjects will see through the deception and will respond differently from naive subjects.[20]

After a thorough review of the arguments regarding deception, Diener and Crandall recommended that researchers consider the following factors before undertaking investigations in which deception is used:

1. Researchers should decide whether research deception is ever ethically defensible and whether a particular deception could have detrimental effects on themselves or on subjects. The potential results of the study must seem important enough to justify the ethical cost of lying.
2. The research should not create negative effects in subjects outside the realm of the study itself, such as cynicism or resentment or lessened altruism in real-life situations.
3. Deceptions should not be practiced when they are not necessary for effective completion of the research.
4. When subjects are exposed to potential harm or surrender substantive rights, informed consent is a necessity. Deception should not undercut subjects' rights to be informed beforehand about risks.
5. Safeguards such as debriefing should be used to minimize potential negative outcomes.[21]

Dehoaxing and Desensitization

An ethical question that is receiving increased attention in the behavioral sciences concerns the responsibilities of the researcher to debrief subjects who have participated in an experiment. Douglas Holmes points out that debriefing is of two types, *dehoaxing* and *desensitizing*.[22]

In **dehoaxing,** the researcher must convince subjects who have been deceived as part of an experiment that they have, in fact, been deceived so that the deception can do no future harm to the subject. For example, in a study in which students were given fraudulent test scores in order to measure the effect of these scores on their aspiration level, it would be the responsibility of the researcher to convince the subjects that they had been deceived. If subjects

20. For an interesting study related to this problem, see Joseph Horvat, "Detection of Suspiciousness as a Function of Pleas for Honesty," *Journal of Personality and Social Psychology* 50 (1986): 921–924.
21. Diener and Crandall (1978), p 96. See Annotated References at the end of this chapter.
22. See the Annotated References at the end of this chapter.

believe that the false scores are correct, this belief could permanently damage their self-esteem and academic aspirations. Simply telling subjects that they have been deceived is often not sufficient. In this case, some form of demonstration might be needed to *convince* subjects and thus remove the undesirable effects of the experiment.

Desensitization is defined by Holmes as "the process of helping subjects deal with new information about themselves acquired as a consequence of the behaviors they exhibited during the experiment" (p. 868). For example, in a study of obedience, if subjects exhibit some behavior, such as administering electrical shocks to another person because the experimenter told them to do so, the knowledge that they did this might cause subjects grave concerns and doubts about themselves. Holmes discusses two approaches that have been used to deal with this problem. One approach is to suggest that the subjects' behavior resulted from the circumstances of the experiment and was not due to defects in the character or personality of the subjects. A second approach is to point out that the subjects' behavior is not abnormal or unusual. In effect, these approaches provide the subjects with rationalizations that make it possible for them to accept a behavior that is in conflict with their own self-perceptions or ideas of right and wrong. In studies of this sort, experimenters may be tampering with the lives of subjects in ways that they might be unable to control and may cause damage they will be unable to correct. Before research that will require desensitization is initiated, look very carefully into the ethical issues involved, proceed slowly and deliberately, and stop work if any serious risk to the subjects appears to be developing.

LEGAL CONSTRAINTS

In recent years, laws have been enacted to place certain legal constraints on the educational researcher. For the most part these laws require the researcher to follow procedures designed to protect the research subject. Generally the procedures are in harmony with the ethical standards that behavioral scientists have developed for themselves and have observed for a number of years. Such laws have the advantage of providing a lever that can be used against the few researchers who do not follow ethical research practice. Perhaps the greatest danger of such laws is that rigid and bureaucratic interpretation can stifle many valuable research activities.

Because laws in this domain are quite recent, the process of clarification and interpretation is still under way. Also, additional legislation will almost surely be enacted within the near future. Therefore, although the following pages accurately report the status of legal constraints as they exist in 1989, the researcher should check on the most recent changes to assure that a law is not unwittingly violated or a new interpretation of one of the laws has not been made.[23]

The Family Educational Rights and Privacy Act of 1974

The Family Educational Rights and Privacy Act of 1974, commonly known as the **Buckley Amendment,** is designed to protect the privacy of students' educational records. One of its major provisions, which is important to educational researchers, is that in most cases data may not be made available in a personally identifiable manner from school records unless there is written consent by the parents or by the student in the case of postsecondary students or persons at least 18 years of age. The written consent must be signed and dated by either a parent or eligible student and must include a specification of the records to be disclosed, the purpose for the disclosure, and the persons to whom the disclosure is to be made.[24]

There are several exceptions to the written consent requirement. One of these is that school personnel with "legitimate educational interest" are exempted. Thus, graduate students carrying out research in their own school or district on a topic that is of interest to the district would probably be exempted from the written consent requirement. Also exempted are organizations conducting studies for local and state educational agencies for the purpose of developing, validating, or administering predictive tests, administering student-aid programs, and improving instruction. Because much educational research is concerned either directly or indirectly with improving instruction, students doing such research may be exempted from the written consent requirement. This exemption would be at the discretion of the local institution, and therefore it would be necessary for the researcher to convince local authorities that the proposed project qualifies.

If researchers are given access to school records, they must conduct their research in such a manner that the personal identification of students and their parents by unauthorized persons would not be possible. The purposes of the research must be made known and information that identifies individuals must be destroyed when no longer needed for the purpose for which the study is conducted.

For many research projects in education the researcher does not need information that personally identifies the subject. For example, if a study were

---

23. A recent study of published research suggests that legally mandated constraints such as informed consent and freedom to withdraw are still not observed by many researchers. See John G. Adair, Terrance W. Dushenko, and R. C. L. Lindsay, "Ethical Regulations and Their Impact on Research Practice," *American Psychologist* 40, no. 1 (1985): 59–72.
24. See Weinberger and Michael (1977) in the Annotated References at the end of this chapter.

concerned with comparing the reading comprehension of pupils in 15 first-grade classrooms who were trained with Reading Program A and pupils in 15 other first-grade classrooms who were trained with Reading Program B, the school district could legally supply the researcher with lists of pupil scores in reading comprehension, identifying only the classrooms. Under these conditions parental consent to furnish these scores would not be required. In designing studies in which school records will be used, the researcher should try to plan the research in such a way that personally identifiable data are not needed.

Although final rules were published in June 1976 (see Annotated References), the Department of Education may publish additional regulations concerned with the Buckley Amendment as it refers explicitly to educational research.

The National Research Act of 1974

The National Research Act of 1974 provides for the review by an Institutional Review Board of behavioral research (including educational research) that involves human subjects. At present the main function of this act is to provide a mechanism for reviewing research proposals from the standpoint of protection of human participants. The concern for protecting research participants originally focused on biomedical research where risks are generally more clear-cut than in educational research.[25] In fact, very few studies in education expose subjects to any risk whatsoever. For example, a recent study of 23 evaluation research projects in several behavioral science areas failed to find any studies in which subjects were exposed to physical or mental risks.[26] **Risk** is broadly defined as exposure to the possibility of physical, psychological, or social injury as a consequence of participating as a subject in research, development, or related activity.

Most universities have established their own Institutional Review Board to conduct reviews in compliance with this act. The main function of these boards is to determine whether human participants will be placed at risk and, if so, whether the risk to the participant outweighs the importance of the information to be collected. The Institutional Review Board must also obtain assurances that the rights and welfare of participants will be adequately protected, that informed consent will be secured, and that the conduct of the research will be reviewed at

25. Even in biomedical research, injury to research subjects is a very rare occurrence. For a thorough discussion of this topic, see President's Commission for the Study of Ethical Problems in Medicine and Biomedical and Behavioral Research, *Compensating for Research Injuries*, 1, *Report* (Washington DC: Government Printing Office, 1982).
26. Evelyn Perloff and Judith K. Perloff, "Ethics in Practice," *New Directions for Program Evaluation* 7 (1980): 77–83.

timely intervals. The current definition of informed consent emphasizes the need for voluntary, uncoerced consent and for the freedom of research participants to withdraw from the research project without prejudice.

The regulations related to the National Research Act that are of most interest to educational researchers were published in the *Federal Register* on January 26, 1981, by the Department of Health and Human Services. A minor revision of these regulations was published in 1983,[27] and work is now underway to make further revisions and develop a model federal policy that would be followed with some variations by all federal agencies.[28] A survey of virtually all federal agencies that conduct or fund research that involves human subjects was carried out in 1981.[29] With a few minor exceptions, the survey found that all agencies substantially conform to the Health and Human Services regulations. Therefore, if you are doing research involving human subjects for any federal agency, you can safely use the HHS regulations as a guide.[30]

These regulations limit the requirement that research proposals be approved by an Institutional Review Board to proposals that receive funds from the Department of Health and Human Services. The regulations also name several types of research that are exempt from review because they involve "minimal risk" to human subjects. It should be noted that the Department of Health and Human Services takes the position that, although they are not legally required to, institutions should afford review and other human-subject protections regardless of source of funding. Among the categories of research that are exempt from the regulations are:

1. Research conducted in established or commonly accepted educational settings, involving normal educational practices, such as (*a*) research on regular and special education instructional strategies, or (*b*) research on the effectiveness of or the comparison among instruction techniques, curricula, or classroom management methods.
2. Research involving the use of educational tests (cognitive, diagnostic, aptitude, achievement) if information taken from these sources is recorded in such a manner that subjects cannot be identified directly or through identifiers linked to the subjects.
3. Research involving survey or interview procedures, except where all of the following conditions exist: (*a*) Responses are recorded in such a manner that

27. Office for Protection from Research Risks *Protection of Human Subjects* Code of Federal Regulations 45 CFR 46, Washington, DC: U.S. Government Printing Office, March 8, 1983.
28. Office of Science and Technology Policy, "Proposed Model Federal Policy for Protection of Human Subject." Washington, DC: *Federal Register* 51, no. 106, June 3, 1986, 20204–20217.
29. President's Commission for the Study of Ethical Problems in Medicine and Biomedical and Behavioral Research, *Protecting Human Subjects, Partial Preliminary Draft*, 9 October 1981.
30. See C. R. McCarthy, "The Development of Federal Regulations for Social Science Research" in Kimmel, ed., *Ethics of Human Subject Research*.

the human subjects can be identified directly or through identifiers linked to the subjects; (*b*) the subject's responses, if they became known outside the research, could reasonably place the subject at risk of criminal or civil liability or be damaging to the subject's financial standing or employability; and (*c*) the research deals with sensitive aspects of the subject's own behavior, such as illegal conduct, drug use, sexual behavior, or use of alcohol. All research involving survey or interview procedures is exempt, without exception, when the respondents are elected or appointed public officials or candidates for public office.

4. Research involving the observation (including observation by participants) of public behavior, except where all of the following conditions exist: (*a*) Observations are recorded in such a manner that the human subjects can be identified directly or through identifiers linked to the subject; (*b*) the observations recorded about the individual, if they became known outside the research, could reasonably place the subject at risk of criminal or civil liability or be damaging to the subject's financial standing or employability; and (*c*) the research deals with sensitive aspects of the subject's own behavior such as illegal conduct, drug use, sexual behavior, or use of alcohol.

5. Research involving the collection or study of existing data, documents, records, pathological specimens, or diagnostic specimens if these sources are publicly available or if the information is recorded by the investigator in such a manner that subjects cannot be identified directly or through identifiers linked to the subjects.[31]

As is the case with most federal regulations, these exempt categories are difficult to interpret.[32] For example, nearly all educational research could be exempt from review under the first category because it is logical to assume that (*a*) and (*b*) are merely examples of many similar activities. Because many kinds of tests including attitude scales, personality measures, and adjustment measures are used in "normal educational practice," one can conclude that studies using these measures in school settings are exempt from review. However, the second category appears to limit exemption to "cognitive, diagnostic, aptitude, achievement" tests and then only if subjects cannot be identified.

Such inconsistencies are eventually ironed out by the bureaucracy. In the absence of clear explanations, many researchers interpret such regulations in whatever way best suits their purposes. Nevertheless, if you have questions about whether your research is exempt from review, you should check with a

---

31. Office for Protection from Research Risks, *Protection of Human Subjects,* Code of Federal Regulations 45CFR46, Washington, DC: U.S. Government Printing Office, March 8, 1983, p. 4, section 46.101.

32. For an interesting discussion of these regulations, see J. J. Thomson et al., "Regulations Governing Research on Human Subjects—Academic Freedom and the Institutional Review Board," *Academe* 67 (1981): 358–370.

member of the Institutional Review Board (IRB) at your university for the latest interpretation of the regulations.

The regulations also identify several kinds of research that can be reviewed through an "expedited review procedure" in which only one IRB member reviews the proposal. The one member may approve the proposal, but only a vote of the entire board may disapprove. Most of the provisions for expedited review refer to biomedical research. The following categories, however, are relevant to behavioral science areas such as experimental psychology and physical education:

1. Recording of data from subjects 18 years of age or older using noninvasive procedures routinely employed in clinical practice. This includes the use of physical sensors applied either to the surface of the body or at a distance that do not involve input of matter (e.g., injections) or significant amounts of energy (e.g., electric shock) into the subject or an invasion of the subject's privacy. It also includes such procedures as weighing, testing sensory acuity, electrocardiography, electroencephalography, thermography, detection of naturally occurring radioactivity, diagnostic echography, and electroretinography. It does not include exposure to electromagnetic radiation outside the visible range (for example, X rays, microwaves).
2. Voice recordings made for research purposes, such as investigations of speech defects.
3. Moderate exercise by healthy volunteers.
4. The study of existing data, documents, records, pathological specimens, or diagnostic specimens.
5. Research on individual or group behavior or characteristics of individuals, such as studies of perception, cognition game theory, or test development, where the investigator does not manipulate subjects' behavior and the research will not involve stress to subjects.
6. Research on drugs or devices for which an investigational new drug exemption or an investigational device exemption is not required.

Informed Consent

Another requirement of the National Research Act is that investigators obtain the "informed consent" of subjects to participate in the research to be conducted. Current regulations state that the requirement for informed consent can be waived if the IRB finds either:

(a) that the only record linking the subject and the research would be the consent document and the principal risk would be potential harm resulting from a breach of confidentiality. Each subject will be asked whether the subject wants documentation linking the subject with the research, and the subject's wishes will govern; or (b) that the research presents no more than minimal risk of harm to subjects and involves no procedures for which written consent is normally required outside the research context.

If your research involves minimum risk and uses procedures for which written consent is not normally required, you may justifiably ask the IRB at your university to waive the informed consent requirement.

If your study is such that you must obtain informed consent, you should prepare a letter that contains the following basic elements:

1. A statement that the study involves research, an explanation of the purposes of the research and the expected duration of the subject's participation, a description of the procedures to be followed, and identification of any procedures which are experimental;
2. A description of any reasonably foreseeable risks or discomforts to the subject;
3. A description of any benefits to the subject or to others which may reasonably be expected from the research;
4. A disclosure of appropriate alternative procedures or courses of treatment, if any, that might be advantageous to the subject;
5. A statement describing the extent, if any, to which confidentiality of records identifying the subject will be maintained;
6. For research involving more than minimal risk, an explanation as to whether any compensation and an explanation as to whether any medical treatments are available if injury occurs and, if so, what they consist of, or whether further information may be obtained;
7. An explanation of whom to contact for answers to pertinent questions about the research and research subjects' rights, and whom to contact in the event of a research-related injury to the subject;
8. A statement that participation is voluntary, refusal to participate will involve no penalty or loss of benefits to which the subject is otherwise entitled, and the subject may discontinue participation at any time without penalty or loss of benefits to which the subject is otherwise entitled.[33]

A copy of the letter should be given to each subject for his or her signature and then returned to you. These signed copies should be kept on file in case you must later prove that consent was obtained.

---

33. Office for Protection from Research Risks, *Protection of Human Subjects*, Code of Federal Regulations 45 CFR 46, Washington, DC: U.S. Government Printing Office, March 8, 1983, p. 9, section 46.116.

For some subjects, it is preferable to give an oral presentation covering the aforementioned points and then have subjects sign a short form. If this approach is more appropriate for your research, check the regulations for detailed instructions.

Other informed consent provisions may be required for some studies. If your study involves more than minimum risk to the subjects, you should study the most recent regulations carefully and follow them in order to protect yourself from legal action.

The National Commission for the Protection of Human Subjects was created by the National Research Act and is responsible for developing guidelines, criteria, definitions, and mechanisms required to implement the act.[34]

The Privacy Act of 1974

At present, this act is not relevant to the work of most graduate students because its provisions are aimed primarily at protecting individuals from threats to individual privacy coming from the federal government. Nevertheless, there is considerable sentiment for extending the act's provisions, in modified form, to private and public institutions.

Some contractors who carry out research for the federal government are liable under the provisions of this act. However, persons who have received federal research grants do not currently come under the Privacy Act. Probably the safest approach for the educational researcher is to maintain very careful control of any research evidence, such as test scores, that can be linked to individuals, following the procedures described earlier in this chapter.

HUMAN RELATIONS

Questions about Your Research

There are several rules that you should observe if you plan to select subjects from the public schools. First, have a thorough and detailed research design that you can explain in terms that administrators, teachers, and parents can understand. Many school administrators are doubtful of the value of educational research and are likely to be critical in their appraisal of the research design. If you have failed to think through your design carefully, you may find yourself

---

34. Students seeking the most recent information on guidelines and regulations related to the National Research Act and the Protection of Human Subjects, should write to the Office for Protection from Research Risks, Building 31, Room 4B09, National Institutes of Health, 9000 Rockville Pike, Bethesda, MD 20892.

unable to answer questions put to you by educators, and this failure will almost certainly lead to a decision by school administrators not to participate in the study.

Before approaching parents or school administrators, have thorough and convincing answers prepared to questions that are likely to arise. Questions you should expect to answer include, What is the purpose of this study? What do we hope to learn from it? Are the findings likely to be worthwhile? Is the study important to education? If you cannot convince school personnel that your work is worthwhile and likely to produce useful results, you may well be unable to obtain cooperation. Schools generally cooperate in research projects because educators feel a professional responsibility. Research projects almost always cause school personnel a certain amount of inconvenience and extra work, and unless you can convince these individuals that your research is worth the extra effort and inconvenience, cooperation will probably not be obtained.

Another question that school personnel usually bring up in evaluating research projects is, Will the results of this research apply directly to our school? In other words, school administrators are interested in the direct returns that they may obtain from the research project. One direct return, of course, is that any research data obtained will have greater application to the schools in which the research has been done than it will to other schools. To be of significant value, however, the research must be designed to obtain findings that can be applied beyond the situation in which the work was carried out. If results can be applied only to the isolated situation and the specific subjects upon whom the experiment was conducted, then there is little value in doing such work. The fact remains, however, that a research project will be *more* applicable to the specific situation in which the experiment is carried out than to similar situations in other schools.

Very often school personnel are interested in other possible advantages that they may obtain from the research. These differ depending on the project, but they can include such things as test scores that can be used by the school in guidance and other regular activities, new curricular material, visual aids, and improved administrative procedures. Some studies also involve the use of special measures that the school cannot afford to administer but that can be useful if administered by a research worker. These include such things as intelligence tests, individually administered projective measures, and depth interviews. For example, one of the authors of this text recently carried out a research project that included administering the TAT[35] to a sample of low-achieving children. Because this measure was given on an individual basis and required a clinical psychologist for administration and scoring, the cost would have been too great for most school districts. This test identified a number of

35. Thematic Apperception Test: a projective personality measure in which the subject is shown pictures and makes up a story around each picture.

children who appeared to have serious emotional disturbances. The school district was then able to arrange for help for these children. Point out any such possibilities of direct advantage to the schools, as this is often a major consideration of school administrators in deciding whether to cooperate with the research.

Administrators will wish to know in considerable detail just what the school's role and responsibility will be in the research project. How much time will be required of the subjects? At what part of the school year must this time be scheduled? Will adjustments to the testing schedule be possible if other school activities interfere? Can subjects be tested in their classroom or will it be necessary to take subjects from their classes to another room? Will teachers be required to administer any of the tests or measures? Will it be necessary for the schools to provide pencils, answer sheets, lap boards, or other materials? Think through such questions carefully before approaching the school administrator. The price that the school generally must pay to participate in educational research is measured in the aforementioned terms, and the administrator must weigh the possible advantages to the school and to the profession against the losses in time, extra adjustments that must be made, and possible expenses to the school district.

At this point we caution you against making compromises with the administrator that weaken the research design. For example, if a random sample of subjects within the school is required for a research project and the school administrator suggests that volunteers be taken instead, explain in detail the disadvantages of using volunteers and attempt to win the administrator over to paying the additional price in inconvenience that is required to obtain the random sample. If the administrator insists upon changes that seriously weaken the research design, it is wiser to attempt to carry out the study elsewhere than to carry it out with disabling restrictions. In general, follow the rule that *all* concessions should be made that do not seriously weaken the scientific value of the study and *no* concessions should be made that do so compromise the research.

One question that administrators may not mention but that may concern them greatly is: "Will the results of this research reflect unfavorably upon my school?" You should bring this question up and discuss it objectively. As most educational research is aimed at discovering general principles and insights rather than the yielding of specific information about the participating schools and subjects, results can usually be prepared in such a way that they will not reflect unfavorably upon the schools used in the study. These results are generally reported in professional research journals, and the study is customarily described without identifying the specific schools involved. School administrators especially need reassurance when your study is such that school personnel may be anxious about their pupils' potential performance. Even if research results reflect unfavorably on participating schools, you should emphasize in all public statements that by cooperating in the research project, school personnel have shown themselves interested in improving their service. In fact, educators who admit that their schools are not perfect and who are seeking ways to improve them are more to be commended than those who are blind to shortcomings or who seek to hide deficiencies rather than correct them.

School administrators will also be concerned with the specific measuring instruments that will be used in the research. Show samples of these measures to teachers and administrators in order that they may examine them carefully, and be prepared to answer any questions concerning the measures and to explain the specific purpose of each measure in the research. The only case where you should not make such explanations is a study where administrator or teacher knowledge of the measures might result in bias or contamination of the research results. For example, you probably should not provide teachers with more than a brief examination of an achievement test to be used, because some teachers, usually those who are insecure or who feel that poor performance by their pupils will reflect unfavorably upon themselves, will coach pupils on correct answers if they have the actual test in hand.

Many psychological measures used in educational research projects are difficult for school administrators to understand. If you use such measures, be prepared to explain very thoroughly the purpose of these measures and to provide evidence that the measure is valid and useful. In examining these measures, administrators often have in mind the possible responses that parents may make to them. If the measure contains items that may cause unfavorable reactions from parents or community groups, you need to have very strong justification for its use. You should also carry out public relations work with the groups concerned prior to the use of such measures. You should avoid using measures that cannot be defended on the basis of appropriateness to the study and psychological significance, and before research is begun you should obtain approval from school authorities for all measures to be used.

In discussing a proposed research project with school personnel, you need to ensure that all parties understand specifically what their responsibilities are. Try to bring up any questions that may lead to future misunderstandings. Keep careful notes during planning meetings. Once you feel that all parties understand their roles in the project, compose a letter that spells out the agreement in specific terms and send this letter to the superintendent or principal involved for confirmation.

On major studies a more formal process to maintain good site relations is called for. Susan Paddock and John Packard describe four phases of a site relations program they employed in a large-scale education project.[36] If, like many students, you plan to carry out part of a large-scale research project for

---

36. Susan C. Paddock and John S. Packard, "On the Conduct of Site Relations in Educational Research," *Educational Researcher* 10, no. 3 (1981): 14–17.

your thesis or dissertation study, you shoud carefully review the Paddock and Packard article.

Following Channels

When working with any administrative hierarchy, such as a school district, it is very important to follow appropriate channels of authority. If you plan to use subjects from more than one school, you generally need first to obtain approval from the district superintendent or from the assistant superintendent in charge of research. After obtaining such approval, visit each school concerned and present your ideas to the principal. If the principal objects strongly to testing pupils in the school, the superintendent will usually support the principal, even though the superintendent has given tentative approval for the project. Even if the superintendent were inclined to force the principal to cooperate, such an arrangement would create a situation in which it would be very difficult to carry out effective research. The interest and cooperation of all persons concerned with the research is necessary if it is to be carried through to a successful conclusion.

After the principal and superintendent have been briefed concerning the purposes of the research and the procedures to be followed, you usually will need to meet with teachers in the schools and to obtain their interest and cooperation. Often a faculty meeting can be devoted to the research topic, and you can present your plans and get the responses of the teachers at this time. Teachers and school administrators frequently will see problems or difficulties in the research plans that you have not recognized. Solicit and follow the suggestions of school personnel whenever this may be done without compromising some scientific aspect of the research.

In most studies parents should also be informed concerning the nature of the study and given an opportunity to express their opinions. This may often be done by presenting your plans at PTA meetings in the schools involved. The purposes of the study and the procedures should be discussed as frankly as possible, omitting only information that could lead to compromising the study in some way. In addition to such a presentation, you will usually need to prepare a letter explaining the study. This letter is sent home to parents of all children who will participate as subjects and should provide a place where the parent may sign to signify approval of the child's participation in the research. In preparing your letter, check on the legal requirements to obtain "informed consent," given earlier in this chapter, and be sure your letter meets these requirements.

The degree of rapport that you must build up with other community groups is dependent to a great extent upon the nature of the study. Studies dealing with areas such as achievement, which are generally regarded as a major aspect of the school's business, need a less extensive public relations program than studies involving such areas as personality and social adjustment, where the role of the school is less clear and where some of the measures to be employed might be resented or misunderstood by the parent.

Not only should you establish good working relationships before starting your research, but you should also maintain these relationships during the time the research is carried on. If they have problems or questions that go unanswered, teachers may refuse to cooperate or may even sabotage your work by doing such things as complaining to parents that your research is interfering with class work, or taking children on field trips on days when you have scheduled testing. Keep teachers and others who are involved in your project informed of your progress and alerted to coming events in the research plan. In small-scale projects, you should personally keep in contact with participating teachers and administrators. In large-scale projects, periodic reports and newsletters should be sent to teachers, parents, and other interested persons. A sample letter, similar to one sent to teachers participating in a project conducted by the senior author, has been reproduced in figure 3.1.

Much research is possible only because of warm personal relationships between the educational researcher and school personnel. If you develop a sincere interest in the problems of practitioners and a respect for their ideas and points of view, you will gain insights that will improve your research plans and you will also receive a level of cooperation that makes it possible to complete your project when the going gets rough. Often you can provide help for school administrators and teachers such as helping them locate new curriculum materials, conducting a brief literature search related to a current school problem, helping prepare a research proposal for state or federal funding, or helping to analyze a test that is being considered for the district's evaluation program. Researchers who freely give help when they can build up a credit balance that greatly simplifies many of the problems associated with doing research in the public schools. The researcher who is regarded in the schools as a friend and colleague has a much easier time than one who is regarded as an outsider with unknown motives.

Dealing with Public Relations Problems

In spite of your best efforts to establish good rapport with concerned groups, public relations problems arise occasionally in educational field studies. A frequent problem involves protests over measures used in the research. Such protests are usually made by small but vocal groups of citizens who are primarily interested in obtaining publicity. Often local newspapers, in the quest for more sensational news stories, will encourage such groups by giving their protests wide and sometimes biased coverage. Most of these protests can be traced back

UTAH STATE UNIVERSITY · LOGAN, UTAH 84322-2810

DEPARTMENT OF PSYCHOLOGY
(801) 750-1460

May 20, 1988

Dear Mrs. Oliver:

With your valued assistance we have just finished collecting data for the second year of the Utah ability-grouping study. I realize that this research has caused you inconvenience and has taken time from your classes. I assure you that we are aware of the problems that such a study causes in the cooperating schools and shall continue to try to reduce these problems during the remaining two years of the study. I'm afraid that it is inevitable that progressive school districts, such as your own, that choose to support research and strive to find better ways of educating our youth must always pay for their leadership by accepting the problems that major research projects always bring.

I am pleased to tell you that we already have enough important results to indicate that this research is well worth the effort, the problems, and the inconveniences. Our work to date has yielded important new knowledge about ability grouping. The remaining two years of the study will certainly teach us more and will also give us a chance to check the results we have already obtained.

The work under way in the Utah study is one of the first extensive long-term evaluations of ability grouping, and I assure you that through your cooperation you are making a real and important contribution to the teaching profession.

Although I know you have been working closely with Mrs. Johnson from our staff, my deepest regret is that I have had little opportunity to meet personally with the teachers cooperating in this research. I know that many of you have questions about the study that I could answer. I am also sure that you have suggestions and ideas that would help us make this research better. I plan to visit each cooperating school before we start collecting data next year and hope that you will jot down ideas and suggestions so that we may discuss them at that time.

In closing, permit me to thank you again for your patience and cooperation. I am looking forward to meeting with you and exchanging ideas during the coming year.

Sincerely,

Walter Borg

Walter R. Borg

Figure 3.1   Sample of a Letter Sent to a Participant in a Field Research Project

to the fact that items occur in many psychological tests, the purpose of which cannot be easily explained to the lay person. Many psychological tests in such areas as personality, mental health, social adjustment, attitudes, and interests are still in the early stages of development, and not even their strongest advocates would claim them to be highly valid measures. In many cases, however, such measures are the best available and must be used if research in a particular area is to be carried forward.

If your project is given biased coverage in news stories, make an attempt to provide reporters with your side of the story. Point out the procedures that are being used to protect individual privacy. These procedures should include obtaining prior consent and assuring confidentiality of data.

ETHICAL AND HUMAN RELATIONS MISTAKES SOMETIMES MADE BY EDUCATIONAL RESEARCHERS

1. The researcher fails to follow proper channels in setting up a study in the public schools.
2. Has not prepared answers for questions likely to be asked by school administrators about the research project.
3. Weakens the research design by making changes for the administrative convenience of the schools from which subjects are to be drawn.
4. Establishes good rapport and then loses it by failing to maintain communication.
5. Uses measures that cannot be defended to critics of the research.
6. Does not follow correct procedures for obtaining informed consent from parents or subjects.
7. Fails to set up adequate safeguards to ensure the confidentiality of research data.
8. Does not carry out effective debriefing of research subjects.

ANNOTATED REFERENCES

American Anthropological Association. "Proposed Code of Ethics Would Supersede Principles of Professional Responsibility." *Anthropology Newsletter* 25, no. 7 (1984): 1–2. See also: American Anthropological Association, *Professional Ethics*, Washington, DC: American Anthropological Association, 1983.

These two sources describe the current and proposed ethical standards of the American Anthropological Association. The student who plans to conduct qualitative research should review these statements of ethics.

Beauchamp, Tom L.; Faden, Ruth R.; Wallace, R. Jay, Jr.; and Walters,

LeRoy, eds. *Ethical Issues in Social Science Research*. Baltimore: Johns Hopkins University Press, 1982.

An excellent source for students who want to explore ethical issues in depth. The 19 chapters are divided into five parts: Foundations, Harm and Benefit, Informed Consent and Deception, Privacy and Confidentiality, and Government Regulation. Because different authors have contributed different chapters, the reader is exposed to differing points of view.

Boruch, Robert F., and Cecil, Joe S. *Assuring the Confidentiality of Social Research Data*. Philadelphia: University of Pennsylvania Press, 1979.

By far the most comprehensive and informative reference on confidentiality we have located. The brief section on confidentiality in this chapter is based primarily on this source. Many interesting and ingenious methods of maintaining confidentiality while gathering needed research data are discussed, and examples are given. Although focusing primarily upon the mailed questionnaire and interview, many of the strategies suggested are equally appropriate for other kinds of research.

Committee on Ethical Standards in Psychological Research. *Ethical Principles in the Conduct of Research with Human Participants*. Washington, DC: American Psychological Association, 1973.

Lists principles that are nearly identical to those from the more recent source quoted in the text. Each principle is described in detail, incidents related to the principle are presented, and a discussion of each principle is provided. An excellent source for the student who needs help in weighing the pros and cons of a course of action related to any of these principles.

Department of Health, Education, and Welfare. "Privacy Rights of Parents and Students—Final Rule on Education Records." *Federal Register* 41 (1976): 24662–24675.

Indispensable for students who plan to use school records in their research and school administrators responsible for school records. The sections on formulation of institutional policies and disclosure of personally identifiable information are of special interest to the researcher.

Diener, Edward, and Crandall, Rick. *Ethics in Social and Behavioral Research*. Chicago: University of Chicago Press, 1978.

Clearly and systematically deals with the ethical issues that concern behavioral scientists. For each issue, the authors explore the main ideas, arguments, and relevant research evidence and come to a conclusion. They also provide very useful guidelines for the researcher faced with an ethical problem or question.

Holmes, Douglas S. "Debriefing after Psychological Experiments: I. Effectiveness of Postdeception Dehoaxing." *American Psychologist* 31 (1976): 858–867.

Holmes, Douglas S. "Debriefing after Psychological Experiments: II. Effectiveness of Postexperimental Desensitizing." *American Psychologist* 31 (1976): 868–875.

These two articles discuss the debriefing of research subjects and review research on the effectiveness of efforts to dehoax and desensitize subjects at the end of experiments. The articles will be useful to researchers planning studies that involve deception or that cause subjects to engage in behavior that may result in psychological discomfort.

Kimmel, A. J., ed. *Ethics of Human Subject Research.* San Francisco: Jossey-Bass, 1981.

Presents information on codes of ethics and federal regulations related to human subject research. The last five chapters, which deal with ethical problems and place ethical issues in a theoretical and philosophical context, are especially recommended.

President's Commission for the Study of Ethical Problems in Medicine and Biomedical and Behavioral Research. *Protecting Human Subjects.* Washington DC: Government Printing Office, 1981.

Biennial report summarizing the results of a 1980 survey of 83 federal agencies regarding their rules governing research on human subjects. The commission found a considerable lack of uniformity and recommended that all agencies adopt the current Health and Human Services regulations. The report summarizes the current rules of all federal agencies supporting research with human subjects. The responses of federal agencies to violations of the regulations were also studied, and five case studies involving violations are discussed in some detail. Nine recommendations were made by the commission as a result of the study, and these are likely to lead to future changes in regulations related to human-subject research. This is a useful report for researchers interested in the current human-subject regulations and the operation of the commission.

May, Wanda T. *On the Potential to Be an Unethical Researcher of Children.* Paper presented at the annual meeting of the American Educational Research Association, Washington, DC, 1987.

Discusses children's rights and researcher responsibilities in qualitative studies. The author explores consent, researcher's role and confidentiality, methodology and data collection, and reciprocity within the context of a two-year case study of third- and fourth-graders in art classes. Several ethical dilemmas that frequently arise in classroom research are reviewed. Although the author is concerned with qualitative research, most of the ethical problems discussed can arise in any study involving classroom observation or interviewing. The paper's reference list includes several recent sources for the student who wants to learn more about this topic.

Reynolds, Paul D. *Ethical Dilemmas and Social Science Research.* San Francisco: Jossey-Bass, 1979.

Deals with three major topics: investigators' responsibilities and participants' rights, restrictions on investigators' autonomy, and social scientists' relations with society. The ethical problems of most interest to graduate students, such as informed consent, deception, and participants' rights, are analyzed. The book attempts to help the social scientist analyze moral dilemmas by emphasizing the major relevant issues. In other words, scientists are encouraged to think through the arguments for themselves rather than rely on prescriptions, which this book does not provide.

Reynolds, Paul D. *Ethics and Social Research.* Englewood Cliffs, NJ: Prentice-Hall, 1982.

Deals with ethical issues that arise in the conduct of social science research. Each chapter starts with an example of research and gives an example of how to analyze the research for important ethical issues. Both overt research and covert research are discussed. Codes of ethics for several social science professional organizations, such as the American Psychological Association and American Sociological Association, are given along with federal guidelines and legal constraints.

Seiber, Joan E., ed. *The Ethics of Social Research,*Vols. 1 and 2. New York: Springer-Verlag, 1982.

Designed to provide researchers with a greater awareness of research problems requiring ethical decisions, decision criteria and choice alternatives, evidence that sound ethical solutions can be achieved, and effective role models. Volume 1 is concerned with ethical problems encountered in surveys and experiments, whereas Volume 2 focuses on ethnographic field research. Volume 2 also discusses the regulation of research and the role of the Institutional Review Board. These texts are excellent sources of information for both quantitative and qualitative researchers.

Stoltz, Stephanie B. *Ethical Issues in Behavior Modification.* San Francisco: Jossey-Bass, 1978.

In 1974 the American Psychological Association set up a commission to study ethical issues in behavioral modification and to make recommendations. The commission completed its work in 1976, and this book is the result. It deals in depth with major ethical questions in a variety of settings including the schools. Students planning research that involves behavior modification should read this book carefully.

Weinberger, J. A., and Michael J. A. "Federal Restrictions on Educational Research: A Status Report on the Privacy Act." *Educational Researcher* 6, no. 2 (1977): 5–8.

This series of articles provides a brief but excellent coverage of current federal legislation and its apparent effects upon educational research. Students interested in this topic should start with these articles, but since the situation in this field is changing rapidly, should also seek out the most recent developments.

SELF-CHECK TEST

Circle the correct answer to each of the following questions. An answer key is provided on page 883.

1. If explaining the reason for the research to subjects before data collection will invalidate the research, the experimenter should
   a. not disclose any information about the object of the research.
   b. inform them anyway, since their cooperation is vital.
   c. tell the subjects they will be informed at the completion of the research.
   d. give reasons other than the true reasons for the research.

2. Because in the school setting the researcher must have the cooperation of parents, teachers, students, and administrators, it is important that the researcher
   a. conduct as much research as possible in the laboratory setting.
   b. ask the superintendent to explain the research to all involved.
   c. devise a plan to gain and maintain school cooperation.
   d. work only in settings where immediate cooperation is available.

3. Concerning confidentiality of research data, the researcher should
   a. make certain no unauthorized individuals have access to the data.
   b. inform the subjects about the persons who will have access to the data.
   c. remove names from data-collection instruments and replace with a code.
   d. All of the above are correct.

4. If a college student agrees to participate in a research project and then, after completing part of the work, drops out,
   a. the student should be penalized in some way, such as lowering his or her grade in a college class.
   b. the student should be required to provide another person as a substitute.
   c. nothing should be done since the student has the right to withdraw.
   d. the student is legally committed to complete the project and should be informed of this fact.

5. The protection of individual privacy in educational research involves two factors: consent of the individual as to what shall be disclosed to the researcher, and
   a. the length of time during which data collected are to remain confidential.
   b. confidential use of research data collected on individuals.
   c. the need for all data to be collected anonymously.
   d. disclosure based only upon significance of findings of study.

6. A graduate student is employed as a research assistant in a psychological experiment involving deception. In studying the research plan she notices that no debriefing is planned. What should she do?
   a. Since she is not in charge of the project, she has no ethical responsibility and therefore should do nothing.
   b. If professional ethics are violated, she has a responsibility and therefore should bring up the ethical question and see that it is resolved.
   c. Although she has no ethical responsibility, she should suggest that the investigator look into the ethical question but should not pursue the matter any further.
   d. She should resign her assistantship in order to protect her ethical position.

7. Under current federal regulations, which of the following types of research is *not* exempt from review by the Institutional Review Board (IRB)?
   a. Research conducted in established or commonly accepted educational settings that involves normal educational practices.
   b. Research involving the use of educational tests if subjects cannot be identified.
   c. Research collecting voice recordings for research purposes, such as investigations of speech defects.
   d. Research involving surveys or interviews of public officials.

8. The main purpose of the Privacy Act of 1974 is
   a. to protect subjects from questions asked in research projects that might invade their privacy.
   b. to give individuals the right to refuse to participate in research projects.

      c. to protect individuals from invasion of privacy by the federal government.

      d. to require educational researchers to remove names from test answer sheets and similar materials.

9. In experiments in which subjects have been deceived, what is the ethical responsibility of the investigator?

      a. Inform subjects before the study that the experiment involves deception but do not identify what the deception is.

      b. Give subjects a written sheet at the end of the study that states that the study involved deception. The specific deception should not be described since this may damage future research.

      c. The investigator must inform the subjects in writing at the end of the study of the specific nature of the deception.

      d. The investigator must inform subjects of the deception at the end of the study and also carry out other activities such as demonstrations in order to convince subjects that they have been deceived.

10. A major provision of the "Buckley Amendment" is that

      a. in most cases data from school records cannot be released without consent of the parent (or subject if over 18).

      b. public schools cannot use data in their records for educational research.

      c. schools may not release educational records to state education agencies.

      d. all student records must be reviewed each year by the schools, and data not essential to the school operation must be destroyed.

APPLICATION PROBLEMS

The following problems are designed to give you practice in applying significant concepts and research procedures explained in chapter 3. Most of them do not have a single correct answer. For feedback, you can compare your answers with the sample answers on pages 887–888.

1. You plan to conduct a research project in which you will give tests to high school students and teachers in a particular school district. You are now meeting with the district superintendent to explain the purpose of the project. The superintendent asks you, "You plan to use students and teachers as subjects in an experiment. What steps are you taking to protect their rights as individuals?" What are two desirable steps that you could mention?

2. School people usually do not understand the nature of educational research. Therefore, the researcher only needs to inform superintendents, principals, and teachers about the general purpose of his research project. They need not be informed of specifics, such as tests to be administered, number of students to be involved, how the results will be reported, etc. Is this a sound position to take? Support your answer.

3. In a study of truthfulness, you set up research conditions that make it possible to detect certain lies that could not be detected under normal conditions. At the end of the study, several subjects appear to be very upset when they discover that they have been caught in lies. As the investigator, what responsibility do you have to the subjects? Suggest steps you could take to meet this responsibility.

4. Suppose you have carried out a study in which you have given students incorrect scores on a test of algebra aptitude that they have taken (some higher and some lower than the correct scores) to see if this information would affect their responses on a vocational interest test to vocations such as engineering, which require mathematics. Describe the procedure you would use to debrief the students at the completion of the study.

5. Suppose that you plan a research project designed to determine whether the use of fairly large rewards (values above $50, such as a bicycle, portable radio, record player) administered during Grade 7 can bring about significant longterm improvement in the school attitudes, attendance, and achievement of junior high school students who have a history of truancy and underachievement dating back at least three years. The school has gathered attendance and achievement data yearly for several years. You will administer an attitude measure at the end of the sixth grade to obtain a pretreatment measure of this variable. Your reward program will be carried out in Grade 7. Data on attitude, attendance, and achievement will be routinely collected each year and will be compared at the end of grades 7, 8, 9, and 10 with data collected for grades 4, 5, and 6. A comparable control group will be employed that will receive small rewards (values up to $5) such as free time for preferred activities, tickets to athletic events, magazines, and phonograph records. Students who meet the research criteria will be assigned randomly to the two treatments. List ethical and legal steps you should include in your research plan.

SUGGESTION SHEET

If your last name starts with letters from Bos to Cam, please complete the Suggestion Sheet at the end of the book while this chapter is still fresh in your mind.

4 REVIEWING THE LITERATURE

OVERVIEW

An educational researcher who would advance scientific knowledge must first identify and understand the research that has already been done in the field of interest. This chapter is designed to help you acquire the skills needed to conduct a thorough and systematic review of the research literature in your area of interest. Several reasons for conducting a review of literature are given, such as seeking to delimit the research problem and to identify new approaches. A systematic method of reviewing the educational research literature is described. Also discussed are the most important reference books and services that provide reviews, indexes, and abstracts of completed research studies.

OBJECTIVES

After studying this chapter you should be able to:

1. Describe the difference between primary and secondary sources and locate examples of each. How is each typically used in the educational research process?
2. State and explain briefly six reasons for conducting a review of literature before starting a research project.
3. Conduct a review of the research literaure on a given topic, following the three steps presented in this text.
4. Locate relevant articles in *Education Index, Psychological Abstracts, Current Index to Journals in Education,* and *Resources in Education* on a given research topic.
5. Describe at least four major preliminary sources specifically intended for use in educational research.
6. Plan a computer search of *Resources in Education, Current Index to Journals in Education,* or *Psychological Abstracts* on a given topic in educational research.
7. Read a research article and prepare a bibliographic citation and a note card that follows the models given.
8. Develop a system for coding research literature on a given topic.
9. Describe ways to obtain references not available in your university library.

INTRODUCTION

The review of the literature involves locating, reading, and evaluating reports of research as well as reports of casual observation and opinion that are related to the individual's planned research project. This review differs in a number of ways from the reading program often used to locate a tentative research project. First, such a review is much more extensive and thorough because it is aimed at obtaining a detailed knowledge of the topic being studied, while the reading program is aimed at obtaining enough general knowledge and insight to recognize problems in the selected area.

Secondary Sources

The reading program generally uses textbooks, encyclopedias, and other secondary source materials. **Secondary source** materials in education include any publications written by an author who was not a direct observer or participant in the events described. For example, most of the material found in textbooks of Roman history are secondary source materials because the author has merely compiled the reports of others and rearranged these reports into a textbook. Most of the content of textbooks in education and psychology is also secondary source material.

Let us suppose that an individual wishes to write a textbook on methods of teaching remedial reading. The prospective author does an exhaustive review of the literature in this field, noting the results of all experiments and weighing and evaluating these results in terms of various approaches to remedial reading instruction. Then, on the basis of the interpretation of the various research reports and articles one has read, the author prepares the textbook. If, in the textbook, the author also reports the results of experiments that the author has carried out, then this portion of the textbook would be considered a primary source. That portion, however, that is based on interpretations of the work of others would be classified as a secondary source. Secondary sources are useful because they combine knowledge from many primary sources into a single publication. A good textbook, for example, combines the work of many other persons and simplifies or eliminates much of the technical material that is not of interest to the general reader, thus providing a quick and relatively easy method of obtaining a good overall understanding of the field.

Primary Sources

The **primary source** differs from the secondary source in that it is a direct description of an occurrence by an individual who actually observed or witnessed the occurrence. In educational research this generally means the description of the study by the individual who carried it out.

The principal disadvantage to the research scholar of using secondary sources is that it is never possible to be sure what changes have been made by the secondary source author. In the process of simplifying and combining the results of many studies, the author of a textbook or other secondary source report may slant his or her interpretation of the primary source to agree with his or her own views and will omit material that the person reviewing the literature needs to know. Thus, a review of the literature should be based, whenever possible, upon primary sources. Most secondary sources, such as textbooks, contain a bibliography listing the sources from which the material was obtained so that the student can usually locate the primary source.

Importance of the Review

The review of the literature is an important part of the scientific approach and is carried out in all areas of scientific research, whether in the the physical, natural, or social sciences. Such reviews are also the basis of most research in the humanities. In fields such as history, the review of literature not only gives the scholar an understanding of previous work that has been done, but the results of the review actually provide the data used in the research. Historical studies in education, which we will discuss in a later chapter, are based almost entirely upon a careful study of existing printed knowledge in the field.

The review of the literature in educational research provides you with the means of getting to the frontier in your particular field of knowledge. Until you have learned what others have done and what remains still to be done in your area, you cannot develop a research project that will contribute to furthering knowledge in your field. Thus the literature in any field forms the foundation upon which all future work must be built. If you fail to build this foundation of knowledge provided by the review of the literature, your work is likely to be shallow and naïve, and will often duplicate work that has already been done better by someone else. Although the importance of a thorough review of the literature is obvious to everyone, this task is more frequently slighted than any other phase of research. Research workers are always tempted to let a sketchy review of the literature suffice so that they can get started sooner on their own research project. However, you should make every effort to complete a thorough review before starting your research because the insights and knowledge gained by the review almost inevitably lead to a better-designed project and greatly improve the chances of obtaining important and significant results. Often the insights gained through the review will save as much time in conducting the project as the review itself required.

PURPOSES OF THE REVIEW

Although the general purpose of the review is to help you develop a thorough understanding and insight into previous work and the trends that have emerged, the review can also help you in reaching a number of important specific goals.

Delimiting the Research Problem

The review of literature can help in both limiting and more clearly defining your research problem. Many studies attempted by graduate students are doomed to failure because the researcher has not limited the problem to an area small enough and sufficiently specific to work with satisfactorily. Selecting a limited problem and treating it well is far better than attempting the study of a broad general problem and doing it poorly. Many graduate students also commit themselves to research problems before they have adequately thought them out. A fuzzy or poorly defined problem can sometimes result in the student collecting data and then learning that the data cannot be applied to the problem one wishes to attack. Before starting your review of the literature, do sufficient background reading from secondary sources to permit a tentative outline of your research problem. The review of the literature will then provide you with the knowledge you need to convert your tentative problem into a detailed and concise plan of action.

Seeking New Approaches

In the process of reviewing the literature, you not only should learn what work has been done but should also be alert to research possibilities that have been overlooked. The unique experience and background of a given individual may make it possible for that person to see a facet of the problem that other research workers have not seen. Such new viewpoints are likely to occur most frequently in areas where little research has been done, but even in well-researched areas someone occasionally thinks of an approach that is unique and creative. A good example is C. E. Thompson's classic study of administration of the Thematic Apperception Test (TAT) to black subjects.[1] Prior to this study, many clinicians were administering the standard TAT cards to clients regardless of racial background. Persons pictured on the standard TAT cards are white, and Thompson saw that the use of these cards with black subjects might well lead to different responses because of perceptual differences. In his research he developed a comparable set of cards in which blacks were substituted for whites in the TAT pictures and found that his hypothesis was correct. Although hundreds of research projects had been carried out using the TAT prior to Thompson's work, his special insight led to a unique and valuable contribution to our knowledge of this important instrument.

1. C. E. Thompson, "The Thompson Modification of the Thematic Apperception Test," *Rorschach Research Exchange and Journal of Projective Techniques* 13 (1949): 469–478.

Avoiding Sterile Approaches

In reviewing the literature, be on the lookout for research approaches in your area that have proved to be sterile. Not uncommonly, literature reviews will produce several very similar studies done over a period of years, all of which employ approximately the same approach and all of which failed to produce significant results. One or two repetitions of an unproductive approach can be justified on the grounds that these confirm the previous finding that the area is unproductive. Repetitions beyond that, however, serve no useful purpose and generally suggest only that the persons repeating the study have not done an adequate review of the literature.

Insight into Methods

The review of the literature can also provide insight into the methods, measures, subjects, and approaches used by other research workers and can thus lead to significant improvement of your design. A mistake many graduate students make when reading research reports is to give scant attention to anything but the results reported. Very often a study that has little to contribute in the way of results can help a great deal by suggesting methods and useful approaches. For example, discussions of the various measures used can help you decide which of these measures would be best suited for your own research. A sampling pattern discussed by one research worker can help other research workers in the field avoid the same difficulties, and insights into research methods gained in one study can help subsequent investigators design studies leading to more significant research findings.

For example, a study concerned with training in-service teachers to use specific classroom management skills found that although the teachers could be taught to use a set of three specific skills in one week of instruction and practice, their use of the skills was awkward and unnatural.[2] The training program was revised and four weeks were added during which teachers did nothing but practice the skills they had learned earlier. This change resulted in much more effective teacher performance.[3] The methodological insights gained in these studies would be useful to any researchers concerned with training teachers in classroom skills.

---

2. Walter R. Borg, "Changing Teacher and Pupil Performance with Protocols," *The Journal of Experimental Education* 45, no. 3 (1977): 9–18.
3. Walter R. Borg and Frank R. Ascione, "Classroom Management in Elementary Mainstreaming Classrooms," *Journal of Educational Psychology* 74, no. 1 (1982): 85–95.

Recommendations for Further Research

The authors of research articles often include specific suggestions and recommendations for persons planning further research in the field. These suggestions should be considered very carefully because they represent the insights gained by the research worker after experience in the problem area. Specific research topics are often suggested that are particularly useful in helping you delimit the research problem.

Sampling Current Opinions

Although research reports make up the most important source of information that you should cover, you need also study newspaper accounts, nontechnical articles, and opinion articles related to your topic. Such articles occasionally contain unique ideas that can be tested through research and also help the research worker gain insight into those aspects of the problem area that are considered critical or controversial by educators. For example, a study of opinion articles in the field of ability grouping shows that most of the disputes among educators regard the possible effects of ability grouping on the child's *personality* and *social development*. Yet nearly all the research reported in the field of ability grouping is concerned with the *achievement* of children in ability-grouped situations. These studies contribute valuable knowledge, but they have had little effect on the judgments of most educators. Only research that presents objective data concerning the variables that educators consider critical is likely to have any effect on their decisions to establish or support an ability-grouping program.

SCOPE OF THE REVIEW

Perhaps the greatest frustration encountered by graduate students carrying out their first review of literature is generated by their attempt to determine what they should and should not read. Unfortunately, no pat formulas exist that we can give to help you make this decision. Obviously you should read all those studies that are closely related to your research problem. The decisions that will cause you difficulty involve those studies that are only partially related to your problem, or that are related only to one phase of the problem.

Relatively new research areas usually lack an organized body of secondary-source information to provide general background and thus require a more stringent and broader review, in which even those studies that are only peripheral to the main area of your own problem should be read, to provide you with the foundation of knowledge you will require.

For example, suppose you are interested in the causes of "teacher burnout." Because widespread interest in this phenomenon is fairly new in education, you should probably read most of the studies in the broad area of "burnout" and occupational stress even if they are not closely related to your topic. An article that discusses ways to train teachers to cope with stress, for instance, although only peripheral to the causes of teacher burnout, should probably be checked. Studies that deal with the causes of burnout in other professional groups, such as nurses and social workers, should also be reviewed. In new research areas like this one, you may find no more than two or three studies that are very close to your topic. Your search must therefore be broader, to provide you with sufficient insight into your problem.

In more thoroughly explored areas, where research activity has extended over a longer period of time and where much of the early work is covered in secondary sources, you can usually develop adequate insight into your chosen field by reading only those studies that are closely related to your research topic. In such areas, much more information is available, and you can cover a narrower topic range in greater depth. A study in a more thoroughly explored area might, for instance, be concerned with the effectiveness of high school counseling in bringing about certain personality changes as measured by the Thematic Apperception Test (TAT). In this area, you would find studies that relate personality changes to counseling and involve the use of various personality instruments, and you should cover all of these. In addition, some studies using the TAT in other related research areas should be read; for example, studies involving changes in personality during psychotherapy. As the TAT is a well-established instrument that has been used in a great many research projects, you should not try to read *all* research involving its use, however. In fact, over 2,000 references dealing with the TAT have been listed in the *Mental Measurement Yearbooks*. Most of these would be of little value in carrying out the research described previously. Considerable background reading on the TAT in secondary sources, however, would be desirable.

CONDUCTING A REVIEW OF THE LITERATURE

Although a review of the literature is a preliminary step in all scientific research, the methods of conducting a review differ from field to field to some extent. The method that is described in detail in this section is one that works well in the field of education. This method has been developed over a number of years, and we advise you to follow it closely until you have built up sufficient experience to make intelligent adaptations.

Step One—Listing Key Words

In most sciences, abstracts or indexes are available that cover most material published in the science in question. In education, the most useful sources are *Resources in Education, Current Index to Journals in Education, Psychological Abstracts,* and *Education Index.* These sources are organized by subject. Therefore, you need to identify *key words* related to your topic, in order to look up these key words in the index to locate sources of information related to your topic. For example, let us say that you wish to search *Education Index* for studies related to the following question: What are student and teacher attitudes toward handicapped children in elementary mainstream classrooms?[4] Your first step in reviewing the literature would be to make a list of key words that relate to this question. Your first list might include the following: Attitudes, Mainstream Classrooms, Mentally Handicapped Children, Emotionally Disturbed Children, and Learning-Disabled Children. This preliminary list of key words will almost certainly be incomplete and will be changed when the actual search of *Education Index* begins. It does, however, provide a starting point, and as many possible key words as you can think of should be listed in order to reduce the likelihood of important studies being overlooked. Key words for *Resources in Education* and *Current Index to Journals in Education* are contained in the *Thesaurus of ERIC Descriptors,* which is described later in this chapter. Key words for searching *Psychological Abstracts* are listed in the *Thesaurus of Psychological Index Terms.*

Step Two—Checking Preliminary Sources

References, such as indexes and abstracts, that are intended to help one identify and locate research articles and other primary sources of information are called *preliminary sources.* (See Annotated References for complete bibliographic data on preliminary sources described in this section.) Many of the preliminary sources that are likely to be of help to you in reviewing the literature in education and related fields are discussed in this section. We first discuss manual search procedures. However, some of these preliminary sources can be searched by computer. The procedure for conducting a computer search is described later in this chapter.

Education Index

Education Index provides an up-to-date listing of articles published in hundreds of education journals, books about education, and publications in related fields. Both an author and subject index are included, that is, each article is listed once

---

4. Mainstream classrooms are those in which mildly handicapped children are placed in regular classrooms with nonhandicapped children for all or part of the school day.

under its subject and again under the name of the author. *Education Index* is published monthly, except for July and August. It lists only the bibliographical data concerning each article or book reference. The year for *Education Index* runs from September to the following June. For the current quarter each of the monthly issues must be searched, but these monthly issues are combined quarterly, and the quarterly issues in turn are combined in a yearly volume for the immediate past year. Most reviews of the literature in education cover a minimum of 10 years, but for some studies you may need to search a longer period. In this case, *Education Index*, which has been published since 1929, is especially valuable.

You should develop and follow a systematic method of searching *Education Index* for the period of the review. We have found that preparing a checklist of key words, such as that shown in table 4.1, is an effective method for ensuring a systematic search. After preparing this checklist, start with the most recent issue of *Education Index* and look up each key word. In this process, be alert for other possible key words that you might want to add to your list to provide more complete coverage.

To check each key word in the *Index*, look up the word and read the titles of articles listed under it. If you find titles that indicate articles that deal with some phase of your topic, copy the bibliographical data (author, title, and source of publication) on a 3×5 index card. Use a separate card for each article or other reference. You may find it difficult to judge the contents of an article from its

TABLE 4.1

Sample of Checklist Used in Searching *Education Index*

Key Words	Volume			
	12/86*	9/86	Volume 36	Volume 35
Attitudes, elementary school students'	√[a]	√	√	√
Attitudes, teachers'	√	√	√	√
Attitudes toward the handicapped	√	√	√	√
Mainstreaming	√	√	√	√
Mentally handicapped children	N[b]	N	√	√
Emotionally disturbed children	N	√	N	N
Learning-disabled children	N	N	√	√
Student opinion	N	N	N	Drop.

[a] Indicates volume checked and bibliography cards made.
[b] Indicates volume contained no usable references under key word.
* This is a quarterly compilation covering October, November, December, 1986.

title, and many articles for which you prepare bibliography cards will later prove to contain nothing pertinent to your topic. In deciding whether or not to prepare a card and check a particular article, you should generally assume that it is better to check an article that proves useless than to overlook an article that may be important. Thus, when in doubt, prepare a card and check the article.

After checking titles under key words and making up bibliography cards, place a check on your checklist. If you have found nothing under a given key word after checking several volumes of *Education Index*, drop the word from your checklist.

In the above example, a review of several volumes of *Education Index* would suggest that some of the original key words are appropriate, some are unproductive and can be eliminated, some do not fit the subject and must be changed, and some new ones must be added. *Attitudes* would be replaced by three more specific phrases: Attitudes, Elementary School Students; Attitudes, Teacher; and Attitudes Toward the Handicapped. *Mainstream Classrooms* would be changed to mainstreaming, and *Mentally Handicapped* to Mentally Handicapped Children. *Student Opinion* would be added, as opinions are closely related to attitudes, and studies of student opinion may therefore prove relevant.

The revised list of key words is given in table 4.1.

Psychological Abstracts

Another valuable preliminary source in education is *Psychological Abstracts*. This reference, published monthly by the American Psychological Association, contains abstracts of articles appearing in over 1,000 journals and other sources in psychology and related areas. Every issue has 16 sections, each covering a different area of the field. The monthly issues also include brief subject and author indexes.

Sections that are most pertinent to research in education are Developmental Psychology, Psychometrics, and Experimental Psychology (Human). Coverage in these areas is very thorough, and many journals that are predominately educational, such as *Elementary School Journal, Harvard Educational Review,* and *Journal of Reading Behavior,* are covered. You should select key words for your *Psychological Abstracts* search from the *Thesaurus of Psychological Index Terms,* which you can find in the reference section of your library. Although this Thesaurus was not developed until 1973, the terms you select will, for the most part, be satisfactory for searching earlier volumes, for the *Thesaurus* includes most of the 800 index terms used before 1973. Always look up the index term *bibliography* in *Psychological Abstracts;* under this heading, you will find a listing of bibliographies on a wide variety of subjects. If you can locate a recent bibliography in your area of interest, it will be of great help to you in carrying out your review of the literature. We will discuss other sources for bibliographies later in this chapter.

11926. Pliner, Susan & Hannah, Mary E. (U Detroit) **The role of achievement in teachers' attitudes toward handicapped children.** *Academic Psychology Bulletin,* 1985(Win), Vol 7(3), 327–335. —Examined 83 elementary education teachers' attitudes toward 4 types of handicapped children (orthopedically impaired, visually handicapped, hard of hearing, and emotionally disturbed) as a function of the child's level of achievement. Ss were given descriptions of 2 children in each category, one achieving at grade level and one 2 yrs below grade level. Ss were asked to make placement decisions from a list of options. Unlike previous research that has reported negative attitudes on the part of teachers toward handicapped children, results indicate that teachers hold negative attitudes (as indicated by placements in more restrictive environments) toward this group only when the child's level of achievement is low. When achievement was at an acceptable level, teachers were positive (as indicated by placements in regular classroom with resource/consultant services) toward the handicapped. (19 ref) —*Journal abstract.*

Figure 4.1   Sample Entry
Source: Reprinted from *Psychological Abstracts* 74, 4 (April 1987): 1220.

Two volumes of *Psychological Abstracts* are currently published each year, one covering the January to June issues and one covering the July to December issues. Separate volumes of subject and author indexes are published for each volume of abstracts. In using *Psychological Abstracts,* turn first to the subject index to check key words. The subject index volumes do not contain complete bibliographical data such as are found in *Education Index* but do provide 10 to 15 word descriptions of the subject. You will find a number after each of these brief descriptions. This number refers to the number assigned to the abstract. Write down the abstract numbers for all articles that appear to relate to your topic and then look these up in the abstract volume.

For example, in the April 1987 monthly issue (Vol. 74, No. 4) under "handicapped (attitudes toward)" we find six abstract numbers.[5] A check of these abstracts produces the reference shown in figure 4.1.

Note that, in addition to the bibliographical data needed to locate the original article, the entry shown in figure 4.1 provides a brief but informative abstract. These abstracts are very helpful because they assist you in making a decision about whether or not a given article actually pertains to your research. This decision is much easier to make on the basis of an abstract than solely on the basis of the bibliographical data supplied in *Education Index.* After reading the abstract, decide whether the article is pertinent and, if it is, record the bibliographical data on your 3 × 5 card.

When the research topic is exclusively education, such as school lunch programs, little is gained from checking *Psychological Abstracts.* In areas relating to educational psychology, on the other hand, you may decide to check both

5. Note that the monthly issues for the current year are always searched first.

Psychological Abstracts and *Education Index* to be assured of getting full coverage in your field. When you use both these sources, check *Psychological Abstracts* first because of the advantage of an abstract over a bibliographical entry only. You may want to use a checklist like the one in table 4.1 in searching *Psychological Abstracts* as well.

The *Cumulated Subject Index to Psychological Abstracts* is also a helpful reference for the student who wishes to conduct an exhaustive long-term search. The initial volumes cover the years 1927 through 1960, which makes it possible for you to find all references on a given subject in one place, without searching 34 separate volumes. Two supplements cover the period from 1961 to 1969, and subsequent volumes cover three-year periods to the present. If you wish to search all references by a given author, a companion set of volumes, titled the *Author Index to Psychological Index, 1894–1935* and *Psychological Abstracts, 1927–1958*, is also available. Supplements to the *Cumulative Author Index* are being published periodically to bring this reference up to date.

Educational Resources Information Center (ERIC)

ERIC, an acronym for the Educational Resources Information Center, was initiated in 1965 by the U.S. Office of Education to transmit the findings of current educational research to teachers, administrators, researchers, and the public. Two very useful preliminary sources are published by ERIC. These are **Resources in Education (RIE)** and **Current Index to Journals in Education (CIJE).** Although ERIC abstracts some of the same documents as *Education Index* and *Psychological Abstracts*, it includes many documents not abstracted by these services. For example, *RIE* provides abstracts of papers presented at education conferences, progress reports of ongoing research studies, studies sponsored by federal research programs, and final reports of projects conducted by local agencies such as school districts and Title III centers, which are not likely to appear in education journals. Thus, *RIE* will be valuable to the student in providing an overview of the most current research being done in education. In contrast, many of the studies currently referenced in *Education Index* and *Psychological Abstracts* were completed several years previously because of the time lag between completion of the study, publication in a journal, and abstracting by the service.

ERIC provides a variety of services to the researcher through its central office and 16 clearinghouses. Each clearinghouse is responsible for cataloguing, abstracting, and indexing relevant documents in its subject area. In addition, each clearinghouse publishes its own newsletters, bulletins, and bibliographies. We suggest that you write to the clearinghouse in your area of interest to obtain information that may help you in locating pertinent research literature and in planning your study. The addresses of the 16 clearinghouses can be found in Appendix A.

The abstracts prepared by each clearinghouse appear in the monthly ERIC publications *RIE* and *CIJE*. *RIE* includes approximately 1,000 document abstracts in each issue, classified by subject area, institution, and accession number. To use *Resources in Education*, first select key search terms in your area of interest. To assist the user in identifying search terms, ERIC has published a *Thesaurus of ERIC Descriptors*, which lists all terms used to classify ERIC documents by subject; for a given subject area, it provides synonyms, narrower terms, broader terms, and related terms. For example, the general search term "dropouts" is further analyzed into such terms as "high school dropouts," "potential dropouts," "dropout identification," and "dropping teaching."

After selecting the appropriate descriptors, search the subject index in the monthly issues of *Resources in Education* for the current year and in the semiannual index volumes for previous years. When you locate a reference in the subject index that relates to your topic, copy the ED number given at the end of the bibliographical data. Then look up each ED number in the Document Résumés section, where you will find a description of the reference such as the sample entry shown in figure 4.2. Notice in this figure that the Document Résumé contains a great deal of useful information in addition to the usual brief abstract.

If you wish to obtain the full document that is abstracted in the entry, you can order it through the ERIC Document Reproduction Service. A Reproduction Service price is listed in the Document Résumé for each entry. If you need an *RIE* document quickly, you can order it by computer using the ORBIT or DIALOG systems, which are available through most university libraries. See a current issue of *RIE* for detailed instructions. Whether you order by mail or by computer, the document can be ordered on microfiches, which are small sheets of microfilm, each containing up to 60 pages of text, or in hard copy form at about 70 percent of the document's original size. The advantages of microfiches are their low cost and small size; however, they require a special microfiche reader, which enlarges the image to normal page size. Most libraries now have these special readers. Most university libraries also maintain a collection of ERIC microfiches, so you needn't order them through the Reproduction Service unless you want a personal copy.

Since 1969 ERIC has also published *CIJE*, which indexes nearly 800 education journals and journals in related fields and includes more than 1,000 articles each month. Like *RIE*, *CIJE* is published monthly and cumulated semiannually. The monthly numbers contain a subject index, an author index, and a main entry section. First, select descriptors related to your topic from the *Thesaurus of ERIC Descriptors* and, then, search the subject index and note the relevant EJ reference numbers. Then look up these numbers in the main entry section, which provides the same information as is given in the Document Résumés in *RIE*. Compared with *Education Index*, *CIJE* has the advantages of a more comprehensive index (based on the *Thesaurus of ERIC Descriptors*), multi-

SAMPLE RESUME

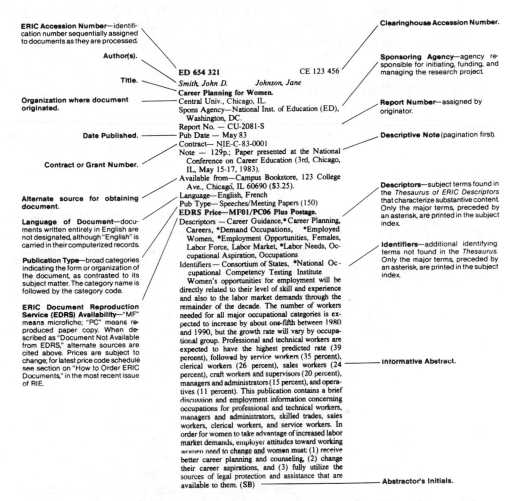

ERIC Accession Number—identification number sequentially assigned to documents as they are processed.

Author(s).

Title.

Organization where document originated.

Date Published.

Contract or Grant Number.

Alternate source for obtaining document.

Language of Document—documents written entirely in English are not designated, although "English" is carried in their computerized records.

Publication Type—broad categories indicating the form or organization of the document, as contrasted to its subject matter. The category name is followed by the category code.

ERIC Document Reproduction Service (EDRS) Availability—"MF" means microfiche; "PC" means reproduced paper copy. When described as "Document Not Available from EDRS," alternate sources are cited above. Prices are subject to change; for latest price code schedule see section on "How to Order ERIC Documents," in the most recent issue of RIE.

Clearinghouse Accession Number.

Sponsoring Agency—agency responsible for initiating, funding, and managing the research project.

Report Number—assigned by originator.

Descriptive Note (pagination first).

Descriptors—subject terms found in the *Thesaurus of ERIC Descriptors* that characterize substantive content. Only the major terms, preceded by an asterisk, are printed in the subject index.

Identifiers—additional identifying terms not found in the *Thesaurus*. Only the major terms, preceded by an asterisk, are printed in the subject index.

Informative Abstract.

Abstractor's Initials.

ED 654 321   CE 123 456
Smith, John D.   Johnson, Jane
Career Planning for Women.
Central Univ., Chicago, IL.
Spons Agency—National Inst. of Education (ED),
    Washington, DC.
Report No. — CU-2081-S
Pub Date — May 83
Contract— NIE-C-83-0001
Note — 129p.; Paper presented at the National
    Conference on Career Education (3rd, Chicago,
    IL, May 15-17, 1983).
Available from—Campus Bookstore, 123 College
    Ave., Chicago, IL 60690 ($3.25).
Language—English, French
Pub Type— Speeches/Meeting Papers (150)
EDRS Price—MF01/PC06 Plus Postage.
Descriptors — Career Guidance,* Career Planning,
    Careers, *Demand Occupations, *Employed
    Women, *Employment Opportunities, Females,
    Labor Force, Labor Market, *Labor Needs, Oc-
    cupational Aspiration, Occupations
Identifiers — Consortium of States, *National Oc-
    cupational Competency Testing Institute
    Women's opportunities for employment will be
directly related to their level of skill and experience
and also to the labor market demands through the
remainder of the decade. The number of workers
needed for all major occupational categories is expected to increase by about one-fifth between 1980
and 1990, but the growth rate will vary by occupational group. Professional and technical workers are
expected to have the highest predicted rate (39
percent), followed by service workers (35 percent),
clerical workers (26 percent), sales workers (24
percent), craft workers and supervisors (20 percent),
managers and administrators (15 percent), and opera-
tives (11 percent). This publication contains a brief
discussion and employment information concerning
occupations for professional and technical workers,
managers and administrators, skilled trades, sales
workers, clerical workers, and service workers. In
order for women to take advantage of increased labor
market demands, employer attitudes toward working
women need to change and women must: (1) receive
better career planning and counseling, (2) change
their career aspirations, and (3) fully utilize the
sources of legal protection and assistance that are
available to them. (SB)

Figure 4.2   Sample Entry from *Resources in Education* and Identifying Characteristics
SOURCE: Reprinted from *Resources in Education*, all numbers.

disciplinary journal coverage, and abstracts of the articles indexed. *Education Index* covers a much longer time span of journal publication (1929 to date) than does *CIJE* (1969 to date).

For most educational topics, the most productive strategy for conducting exhaustive review would probably be to search *RIE* and *CIJE* for the years 1969 to date, search *RIE* and *Education Index* for the years 1966 to 1968, and then search *Education Index* from 1965 back as far as you plan to extend your review. The typical literature review for a thesis or dissertation, however, focuses primarily on the most recent 10 years.

Other Useful Preliminary Sources

Several preliminary sources are useful for locating certain kinds of information needed in some literature reviews or for searching specific subject areas. Those that are often useful to the researcher in education are described below.

The Citation Indexes

Let us suppose that in the course of your review of literature you have located two or three key references that were published several years ago. It is often very useful if you can trace the effects of these earlier works on subsequent research. Also, if your review has uncovered a controversial article, you can gain valuable insights by reading what later authors say in support or opposition. An easy way to locate later works that have cited such an article is to look up each key author in **Science Citation Index (SCI)** or **Social Science Citation Index (SSCI),** depending on the field of study. *SCI* covers the literature of Science, Medicine, Agriculture, Technology, and the Behavioral Sciences; *SSCI* covers literature of the Social, Behavioral, and Related Sciences. Articles in psychology are cited in both indexes, but work in education is most likely to be cited in *SSCI*.

You would start your search of *SCI* or *SSCI* with the year the key reference was published and check all volumes up to the current one. Under the name of the author of the key reference with which you are concerned you will find bibliographical data for all sources that have cited the key reference. For example, Arther R. Jensen's famous article from the 1969 *Harvard Educational Review* entitled "How Much Can We Boost I.Q. and Scholastic Achievement?" was cited in two articles in the 1986 volume of *SCI*. In checking *SSCI* for 1986 we find 20 articles listed that have cited the Jensen article, reflecting the heavier behavioral science coverage. A review of these articles would give you a clear picture about current thinking regarding this controversial topic.

In using these indexes you should check each author's name with both given initials, only the first initial, and no initials; for example, Jensen, A. Jensen, as well as A. R. Jensen. If an author cites the article as by A. Jensen, that is the way it will be listed in the *Index*. In compiling the Indexes, the A. Jensen citations are not combined with the A. R. Jensen citations, even though, since the same article is cited, they are obviously the same man. In *SSCI* for 1986, the *Harvard Educational Review* article is cited once under "A. Jensen," once under

"Jensen," and 18 times under "A. R. Jensen." If we wanted to check all articles that had cited Jensen's 1969 article, we would, of course, have to check *SCI* back to 1969, and *SSCI* back to its beginning in 1973.

National Technical Information Service (NTIS)

There is a considerable lag between the time a research project is completed and the time it is indexed in the preliminary sources, such as *Psychological Abstracts*. If a researcher wants information on recently completed and ongoing research projects in an area of interest, *NTIS* is the best preliminary source available. To use *NTIS*, see the section of this chapter dealing with computer searches.

Literature Related to Measures

Because all research involves measurement, you often need to obtain information on educational measures that are relevant to your own research, or are reported in the research of other investigators. Two widely used sources are described below:

Mental Measurements Yearbooks

The *Mental Measurements Yearbooks* are very valuable if you wish to locate articles related to published tests that you are considering for use in your own research. In addition to providing bibliographies, the yearbooks also print critical reviews of many of the measures listed.[6]

Test Critiques

Test Critiques, in seven volumes, have attempted to provide information on the most widely used psychological, educational, and business tests. Over 700 tests are reviewed in these volumes and additional volumes are expected. Each test has been reviewed by a specialist knowledgeable about tests in the area. The reviews are quite detailed, averaging about six pages in length. A typical review starts with an Introduction, which contains a detailed description of the measure; a Practical Applications section, which includes information on appropriate subjects, administration, scoring and interpretation; Technical Aspects such as validity and reliability are then covered and finally an overall critique is provided. There are four indexes: Test Titles, Test Publishers,

---

6. The most recent, *The Ninth Mental Measurements Yearbook* (1985), is published by the Buros Institute of Mental Measurements at the University of Nebraska. Many published measures have been in use for several years and are reviewed in earlier editions of the *Mental Measurements Yearbook*.

Authors-Reviewers, and Subject. The indexes in Volume 7 cover the tests reviewed in all seven volumes.[7]

These two sources as well as other references to educational and psychological measures will be discussed in greater detail in a later chapter.

Abstracts and Indexes in Content Areas Related to Education

Child Development Abstracts and Bibliography covers articles in this area that are drawn from over 170 publications in medicine, psychology, biology, sociology, and education. Each issue includes abstracts under six major subject headings, as well as an author index and subject index. These are combined into annual volumes.

Sociological Abstracts is published five times each year. Journals dealing mainly with sociology are fully abstracted, whereas those concerned with related areas such as anthropology, education, and political science are abstracted selectively. Each issue contains subject, author, and source indexes in addition to abstracts that are similar in format to *Psychological Abstracts*. The subject index is also similar to *Psychological Abstracts*, listing the abstract numbers for each citation after a brief description of about 10 to 15 words.

Exceptional Child Education Resources (ECER) have been published quarterly since 1969 by the Council for Exceptional Children. More than 200 journals are regularly searched for material concerning exceptional children. The format is similar to that used in *Current Index to Journals in Education* since the Council operates the ERIC Clearinghouse on Handicapped and Gifted Children. However, many journals searched for *ECER* are not covered by *CIJE*. Each issue contains subject, author, and title indexes, and the final issue each year contains indexes for the entire volume.

State Education Journal Index has been published twice a year since 1963. This is a subject index that provides bibliographical data on articles published in over 100 state education journals, such as *Alabama School Journal, California School Boards*, and *Oregon Education*. This index focuses on periodicals not covered in other indexes such as *Education Index*. Very brief annotations are provided for articles with misleading titles. The journals indexed cover a wide range of educational subjects but are probably most useful for topics of state concern such as federal aid, collective bargaining, state education agencies, and teacher certification.

Business Education Index is a combined author-subject index of articles in the field of business education published annually since 1940. Articles from about 60 periodicals are indexed along with the books and some theses relevant to business education.

7. Daniel J. Keyser and Richard C. Sweetland, eds., *Test Critiques*, Vols. 1 (1984), 2–4 (1985), 5 (1986), 6–7 (1988) (Kansas City, MO: Test Corporation of America, 1984–1988).

Educational Administration Abstracts have been published since 1966. There are four issues a year. Approximately 140 journals containing articles related to educational administration are reviewed and abstracted. Abstracts are classified into 42 content areas. An author index and journal index are included in each issue, but no subject index is provided. A listing of recently completed dissertations in educational administration is generally included in each issue.

Physical Education Index has been published quarterly since 1978. It is a subject index covering about 170 periodicals, both domestic and foreign, that deal with physical education and related topics.

Bibliographies and Reviews of Research Literature

Recently, the improved procedures developed by Gene Glass and others to pull together research evidence have stimulated interest in literature reviews.[8] If you can locate a recent review of literature related to your research topic, you can get a useful overview with little effort. The quality of such reviews varies, however, and you should look at reviews critically before accepting the conclusions of the reviewer. J. T. Guthrie provides some useful guidelines for evaluating review articles.[9] Gregg Jackson's analysis of 36 randomly selected review articles can also be a help to students who want to know more about this topic.[10]

Bibliographic Index

An early step in searching preliminary sources is to consult *Bibliographic Index*, a subject list of bibliographies that have been published separately or as parts of books or journals. About 2,600 periodicals are regularly searched for bibliographic materials. The format is similar to the *Education Index* except that only references which contain a bibliography of 50 or more citations are listed. If the bibliography is annotated, the abbreviation "annot" is given. If you can locate a recent annotated bibliography on your topic, you will save much of the labor of searching the preliminary sources.

Review of Educational Research

Review of Educational Research is published quarterly by the American Educational Research Association. A typical issue contains five to seven critical, integrative reviews of research literature bearing on important topics and issues. Recent issues have reviewed research on such topics as educational objectives, teacher

---

8. See chapter 5 for a discussion of techniques for integrating research findings.
9. John T. Guthrie, "Reviews of Research," *Reading Teacher* 34 (1981): 748–751.
10. Gregg B. Jackson, "Methods for Integrative Reviews," *Review of Educational Research* 50 (1980): 438–460.

decisions, college teaching, and student ratings of instruction. Each article includes an extensive bibliography. Graduate students should check the most recent five years of this journal to see if a review has been published in their area of interest. If so, the relevant review and bibliography will give you an excellent start on your own search of the literature.

Review of Research in Education

The purpose of the *Review of Research in Education* is to present critical essays that survey and synthesize research in important problem areas. The first volume in this annual series was published in 1973 and contains nine essays in the areas of Learning and Instruction, School Organization, History of Education and Research Methodology. Subsequent volumes have covered such topics as Child Development and Educational Intervention, Economics of Education, Comparative Education, Teacher Effectiveness, and Application of Cognitive Psychology to Education. Essays are written by leading educational researchers and provide thorough and perceptive overviews of the areas covered.

Encyclopedia of Educational Research

The fifth edition of the *Encyclopedia of Educational Research*, a monumental work, became available late in 1982. This is perhaps the best single source of information on educational research currently available. The four volumes are organized into 19 major topics ranging from Agencies and Institutions Related to Education to Teachers and Teaching. The 317 contributors are among the nation's leading educational researchers. The student planning a review of the literature should start by reading relevant entries in this encyclopedia.

The International Encyclopedia of Education: Research and Studies

The International Encyclopedia of Education: Research and Studies consists of nine volumes containing 1,448 articles in over 5,600 pages, plus a volume of indexes. In the first nine volumes entries are listed alphabetically by subject. A typical entry will contain about four pages including a brief bibliography. Students interested in a given topic should first consult the subject index. A check of the Classified List of Entries is also recommended. The index volume also contains a List of Contributors, that is, persons writing the entries, and an author index, that is, all authors cited in the articles.

This important work is truly international, with contributors from virtually every country in the world, and coverage of most of the world's major educational journals. There is also an article for virtually every country, which describes its educational system. For example—a three-page article on Vanuatu and a four-page article on Trinidad and Tobago are included.

Educators' Handbook—A Research Perspective

Educators' Handbook—A Research Perspective is designed to provide teachers and administrators with a practical review of educational research in which the technical aspects of research methodology are deemphasized. Each of the 25 chapters is written by educational researchers with research experience in the chapter topic. An extensive bibliography is included in each chapter. The book is divided into five sections: What Should I Teach?, How Should I Teach It?, What Should I Know About My Students?, The School, and Professional Issues.

NSSE Yearbooks

The yearbooks of the National Society for the Study of Education (NSSE) contain major overviews of important educational topics. Recent yearbooks have been concerned with such topics as classroom management, adolescence, microcomputers in education, and social studies. Each yearly volume consists of two books dealing with different major areas of education. The typical book contains 10 to 12 chapters concerned with different aspects of the topic. Chapter authors, who are recognized authorities, attempt to give a clear picture of the state of knowledge in the field by focusing on a few major research and theoretical articles. Exhaustive bibliographies, such as are found in the *Review of Educational Research*, are usually not included in the yearbooks. However, if your area of interest has been the focus of a recent yearbook, you may find an excellent overview of important research findings, current approaches to studying the topic, and the thinking of leaders in the field.

Handbook of Research on Teaching, Third Edition

The Handbook of Research on Teaching, Third Edition, contains excellent reviews of virtually every aspect of research on teaching. The 35 chapters are organized under five major areas that deal with Theory and Method of Research on Teaching, Research on Teaching and Teachers, The Social and Institutional Context of Teaching, Adapting Teaching to Differences Among Learners, and Research on the Teaching of Subjects and Grade Levels. The chapters are written by recognized authorities, and each includes a very comprehensive bibliography. Reading the chapters related to one's topic provides an excellent introduction to the literature for any student who plans to do research on teaching.

Annual Reviews of Psychology

The *Annual Reviews* typically contain several chapters that deal with areas of psychology such as counseling psychology, attitudes, and human learning that are pertinent to many educational research topics. An annual volume usually consists of approximately 20 chapters. Each chapter deals with recent research in one topic of psychology and includes an extensive bibliography covering important work in that area. An author index, subject index, and cumulative indexes are included in each volume. Students interested in problems related to some aspect of psychology should check the most recent five volumes for reviews pertinent to their work.

Preliminary Sources Covering Theses and Dissertations

Because many theses and dissertations are never published, a check of the following is necessary for a thorough coverage of the research literature.

Dissertation Abstracts International

Dissertation Abstracts International (DAI) is a monthly compilation of abstracts of doctoral dissertations submitted by nearly 400 cooperating institutions, mostly in the United States and Canada but also including a few institutions from other countries. It has been published in various forms since 1938 when it first appeared as *Microfilm Abstracts*. At present there are three sections: Section A contains dissertations in the humanities and social sciences including education; Section B covers the sciences (including psychology) and engineering, and Section C publishes abstracts of doctoral and postdoctoral dissertations accepted at European institutions. The abstracts within each issue of Section A are organized into 32 major content areas, one of which is Education. There are 35 subtopics under the Education content area such as "adult," "art," "higher," and "teacher training." Students interested in checking dissertations in one of these subtopics of education should check the table of contents to locate pages containing relevant abstracts.

Each monthly issue also contains a keyword title index in which the bibliographic entries are classified and arranged alphabetically by important key words contained in the title. To search a specific topic check the key word title index to locate relevant abstracts. For example, a student who is interested in the social development of preschool children could check "social," "development," and "preschool" in the key word title index; read the titles listed under each key word; and copy the page numbers for abstracts related to her topic. The student would then read each of the selected abstracts. Abstracts in education vary in length up to a full page and usually give a good coverage of the essentials of the dissertation. Any dissertation covered in **Dissertation Abstracts International** may be purchased from University Microfilms International on either microfilm or Xerox, the order number being given at the end of the abstract.

Comprehensive Dissertation Index

Comprehensive Dissertation Index provides a subject and author index covering virtually every doctoral dissertation accepted in U.S. and Canadian universities from 1861 through 1972, a total of nearly a half-million entries. More than 86,000 of the entries are in the area of education. Since 1972, yearly supplements have been published to keep the *Index* up to date. A 10-year cumulation for the years 1973–1982 has also been published, which is somewhat easier to use than the annual supplements. This reference source would normally be used in conjunction with *Dissertation Abstracts International*. First check the subject index and note the bibliographical data on any dissertations that appear related to your topic, as well as the volume and page of *DAI* on which the abstract of a given dissertation can be found. Once you have recorded this information on all relevant dissertations, read the abstracts. The final step is to obtain microfilm copies of any dissertations that are sufficiently important so that they can be studied in detail.

Master's Theses in Education

Master's Theses in Education has been published annually since 1951. Master's theses are listed under about 40 major educational topics covered in the table of contents, such as Achievement and Progress, Adult Education, Delinquency, and Higher Education. Only the author, title, and institution are given. The coverage is quite complete, however, listing nearly all institutions in the United States and Canada that offer master's degrees in education. Earlier volumes contain an Author Index, a Subject Index, and an Institutional Index in which theses written at a given institution may be located. However, since 1980, only the Institutional Index is included. Any theses that appear to be very closely related to your proposed topic may be obtained through interlibrary loan.

Masters Abstracts International

Master's theses available from University Microfilms International, about 1,500 per year, starting in 1962, are summarized by their authors in *Master's Abstracts*. Entries are grouped by field of study and indexed by key words and author names. There are subtopics under Education that cover most major educational areas. Scan the table of contents to locate areas related to your interests.

Preliminary Sources Covering Periodicals and Newspapers

Education is a topic of wide general interest, and as a result much is written about it in popular magazines and newspapers. If your research topic is in an area that has received public attention, the following sources should be checked.

Reader's Guide to Periodical Literature

The *Reader's Guide,* published in New York by H. W. Wilson Co., 1900 to date, is an author and subject index similar in format to *Education Index* but covering general and nontechnical periodicals published in the United States. The magazines that are indexed change from time to time because the aim is to maintain a good subject balance and to overlook no major field rather than provide exhaustive coverage. At present about 200 magazines are being indexed. *Reader's Guide* is an excellent source for studying the layperson's views on education. Because many of the magazines covered have wide circulation, their influence upon public opinion can be significant.

Social Sciences Index

Published in New York by H. W. Wilson Co., 1974 to date, the *Social Sciences Index* is an author and subject index that covers approximately 350 English-language periodicals in the social sciences, including many foreign publications. It is a good source of references concerning how education is viewed by social scientists in fields such as anthropology, economics, environmental science, law, medical science, and sociology.

The New York Times Index

Published from 1851 to date, the *New York Times Index* provides an index of news printed in the *New York Times.* It is primarily a subject index but is extensively cross-referenced; it is also referenced by the names of persons covered in news stories. Brief summaries of most articles are given, along with date, page, and column of the issue in which the story may be found. This index is an excellent source of current information about education and permits studying the development of educational issues and events that could not be traced as accurately through any other source. We recommend you look up some current topic that interests you, such as federal aid to education, school building programs, or racial integration, in order to get some insight into the value of this index as a source of educational information. Most university libraries have the *New York Times* on microfilm, so searching this source is fairly easy once relevant articles are located in the *Index.*

Facts on File

Facts on File, Inc., published in New York from 1941 to date, summarizes news reported in more than 50 foreign and U.S. newspapers and magazines. This is a weekly digest of world news that is indexed twice monthly. Indexes are cumulative through the year. The weekly digests are combined into a yearbook along with an annual index. Material from newspapers, magazines, broadcasts, government reports, and so forth are processed daily to produce the weekly digest. Material is indexed by subject and names of persons appearing in the news. Date of the event, page, and location on page in the digest section of the yearbook are given. Because the yearly index and weekly digests are bound together in one volume, *Facts on File* permits the student to locate and read summaries of important educational news stories without going to another source. It is much easier to use than *The New York Times Index*, but coverage is less thorough.

Sources of Information on Educational Materials

In planning a research project researchers are often interested in locating curriculum materials or educational products that will be useful in their research. Many graduate students carry out studies in which two groups of pupils are trained using different instructional programs and materials in order to determine which results in greater gains in pupil achievement. For example, comparisons between different first-grade reading programs or conventional versus "new" mathematics programs are often conducted and can make a useful contribution since they provide evidence that can be used by educators to help make curriculum decisions.

Because the review of literature must often be concerned with locating educational materials that can be employed in research, this section briefly describes several major sources of information that index such materials. If you fail to locate needed materials in these sources, you will find other catalogues and indexes of educational materials in the reference section of your college library.

NICEM Indexes

Published in Albuquerque, New Mexico, by Access Innovations, Inc., with current volumes dated from 1980 to 1985, *NICEM Indexes* (The National Information Center for Educational Media) contains a set of indexes that lists audiovisual educational materials in eight nonbook formats such as educational films, film strips, audiotapes, videotapes, slides, and overhead transparencies. Each index includes a subject guide, an alphabetical guide by title, and a producer-distributor code so that the reader can determine what items are available in his area of interest and where they may be obtained. A very brief description of each entry is included in the alphabetical guide.

Audio Video Market Place

Published annually in New York by R. R. Bowker, *Audio Video Market Place* covers about 4,500 producers of audio visual learning materials. Entries include name of organization, address, phone number, name of one or more executives, and list of products, services, or interests. There is an alphabetical index.

Educators' Guide to Free Films (and others as listed below)

From Educators Progress Service in Randolph, Wisconsin, *Educators' Guide to Free Films* is published annually. This series of guides covers free films, filmstrips, guidance materials, science materials, social studies materials, teaching aids, audio and video materials, and health, physical education, and recreation materials. They are revised annually, and because a large percentage of the items listed change from year to year, you need to refer to the latest edition. The guides usually include brief descriptions and are indexed by title, subject, and source.

Many indexes and guides to educational materials are listed in *The Directory of Directories.*[11] The latest edition to this guide should be checked for new sources of educational materials and for specialized sources not described in this chapter.

Educational Film Locator

Educational Film Locator, published in New York by R. R. Bowker in 1980, contains annotations and complete bibliographic data on over 40,000 films available from the Consortium of University Film Centers.

The Educators' Handbook of Interactive Videodiscs

Educators' Handbook of Interactive Videodiscs is a comprehensive list of videodiscs for educators.

The Elementary School Library Collection, 15th edition

Edited by Lois Windel of Brodart Co., Greensboro, North Carolina, 1986, *The Elementary School Library Collection* is a classified catalogue of books, filmstrips, recordings, videocassettes, and microcomputer software for preschool to sixth-grade children.

---

11. See the Annotated References at the end of this chapter.

Conducting a Computer Search

In a comprehensive review of the literature, a computer search can be used to accomplish step 2 of the manual search process; that is, checking preliminary sources. You must still read the references that you select from the computer search, and you should make notes following essentially the same procedures described in this chapter. This work, however, is made easier because computer searches often provide printouts of abstracts; these belong to you and can be used to reject references that are not close enough to your topic to be read. If you receive a computer printout of your serarch, the bibliographical data and abstracts of the articles you plan to read can be cut out and pasted onto note cards, and you are thereby saved the effort of copying this information from a preliminary source. In many cases you will have to make additional notes when you read the reference to supplement the abstract obtained in the computer search, but the savings in time will still be significant.

A manual search of preliminary sources is a dull, time-consuming activity that the computer can carry out in a matter of minutes at low cost. Most of the computer search services described in this chapter mail the computer printouts shortly after the on-line search is completed so you usually receive them within ten days or less. For searches that involve only a few references, a printout may be obtained immediately from the terminal at which you are conducting the search. This procedure, however, becomes expensive for long searches since it greatly increases the time that the terminal is connected to the computer, that is, on-line time.

Manual searches are difficult to conduct for problems that involve several concepts that must all be present in a reference in order to fit the researcher's needs. For example, a problem such as "the effects of television violence on the aggressive behavior of preschool children" involves four major concepts: *television, violence, aggression,* and *preschool children.* In a manual search, you would have to search at least one of these concepts (e.g., television) very thoroughly and then read the abstracts or the articles themselves to find references in which the other three concepts are also present. The computer can search designated preliminary sources in a matter of seconds to locate references in which all four concept terms are present.

Where Can You Have a Computer Search Conducted?

Many universities have terminals that link them to one of the information retrieval systems such as **DIALOG Information Services,** or the SDC/ORBIT system. You should visit the reference section of your library and see if a terminal is available. If not, many organizations provide computer searches of ERIC, which includes *RIE* and *CIJE* and is probably the most useful single data base for researchers in education. Having an on-line terminal available speeds up the computer search process, permits you to check the number of relevant references and to get other information that will usually result in a better search. If an on-line terminal is not available, commercial information retrieval services provide order forms on which you can list your problem, descriptors, and other information. These forms are then mailed to the service center where the information is fed into the computer and the search is carried out.

The cost of a computer search varies with the service used, the data base searched, and the length of the search. On-line computer time ranges from about $30 to $120 per hour, while the cost of printouts of the selected citations ranges from 10 cents to 35 cents for each citation. Careful planning of the search is essential in order to keep on-line computer time to a minimum. It is usually advisable to go over your search strategy with the person who operates the terminal before going on-line. A typical ERIC search on the Lockheed DIALOG system including a printout of 200 abstracts that is mailed to you will cost about $35.

The ERIC data base is also available on compact disc. We anticipate that many university libraries will purchase these discs, which should further reduce the cost of conducting searches.

In addition to ERIC, many other data bases can be very useful for reviewing literature on research problems. For example, there are currently more than 140 data bases available in the DIALOG system. A few of those most relevant to behavioral science research are listed below.[12]

Exceptional Child Education Resources (*ECER*) (1966 to present) focuses on the education of handicapped and gifted children. References are indexed using ERIC descriptors. This data base covers published and unpublished literature and is a valuable supplement to ERIC since only about one-fourth of the *ECER* citations are duplicated in ERIC. Information can be obtained from the Council for Exceptional Children, 1920 Association Drive, Reston, VA 22091.

PsycINFO (1967 to present) is essentially the computer form of *Psychological Abstracts*. The data base covers the world literature in psychology and related behavioral sciences. References are indexed using the *Thesaurus of Psychological Index Terms*. Many of the descriptors in this thesaurus differ from the ERIC descriptors. Check to see which descriptors best fit your problem. You may want to search both data bases. For further information contact the American Psychological Association, 1200 Seventeenth Street NW, Washington, DC 20036.

PsycALERT is a companion file to *PsycINFO*. It provides full bibliographic data for all material subsequently included in *PsycINFO*. Items are entered in

---

12. For a complete list of data bases available in DIALOG, check the most recent *Database Catalog* published by DIALOG Information Services.

PsycALERT very promptly and thus this file is useful for searching the most recent sources. Once complete data have been prepared, an item is transferred to *PsycINFO* and dropped from *PsycALERT*.

Dissertation Abstracts On-Line (1861 to present) is based on material from *Dissertation Abstracts International* and *American Doctoral Dissertations*. It is a definitive subject, title, and author guide to virtually every American dissertation, thousands of Canadian dissertations, and many from institutions abroad. Abstracts are included for most dissertations completed after January 1980. You may search this source using DIALOG or use the DATRIX system by obtaining an order form from University Microfilms, 300 North Zeeb Road, Ann Arbor, MI 48106. List key words and other information about your topic, mail your order form, and you will receive a printout giving the title, author, degree date, and university for each reference. The issue and page reference in *Dissertation Abstracts International* (*DAI*) is also given if the dissertation has been abstracted. For dissertations completed before 1980, you must locate the abstracts you need to read in *DAI*.

Federal Research in Progress data base provides access to information on ongoing and recently completed federally funded research projects in all fields, including the behavioral sciences. Data for each project typically include project title, funding organization, performing organization, principal investigator, period covered, funding level, and a brief summary of the work to be performed. This information can be useful in avoiding duplication of research effort, learning about current work, and locating possible funding sources for similar work. For further information contact the National Technical Information Service, 5285 Port Royal, Springfield, VA 22161.

In addition to the aforementioned, there are many data bases in the DIALOG system that are occasionally useful to researchers in the behavioral sciences. Among these are:

A-V ONLINE gives a comprehensive coverage of nonprint educational material such as films, filmstrips, audio tapes, and phonograph records. File currently contains nearly 400,000 items.

Child Abuse and Neglect (1965 to present) contains more than 15,000 records related to this topic.

Magazine Index (1973 to present) privides a very broad coverage of general magazines. Over 435 popular magazines are covered.

Medline (1966 to present) is produced by the U.S. National Library of Medicine. It currently contains over 5.2 million records and is a major source of biomedical literature. This data base is often useful to students doing research in physical education.

Mental Health Abstracts (1969 to present) covers worldwide information related to mental health. Sources include over 460,000 records from 1,200 journals published in 41 countries.

National Newspaper Index (1979 to present) indexes virtually everything printed in the *Christian Science Monitor,* the *New York Times,* and the *Wall Street Journal.*

NEWSEARCH (current month only) is a daily index of more than 2,000 news items from over 1,700 newspapers and other news sources. It is an excellent source for current news.

SOCIAL SCISEARCH (1972 to present) indexes every significant item from the 1,500 most important social science journals throughout the world plus selected items from 3,000 additional journals. Based on *Social Science Citation Index.*

Sociological Abstracts (1963 to present) covers the world's literature in sociology and related disciplines. Covers more than 1,200 journals and other sources.

Steps in Conducting an On-Line Computer Search

The following steps have been carried out using the DIALOG system as an example. This system contains the data bases that are usually the most important for educational research problems. The same procedure can be used, with some adaptation, for conducting on-line searches with other systems.

1. *Define research problem.* To conduct a successful search you must write a short but precise statement of your research problem or topic. If your description is too general your search will probably produce a great many items that are not closely related to your problem and that will increase the cost. A statement such as "the academic self-concept of handicapped children in the elementary school" describes the researcher's interest in a few words and is written in terms that will help focus the search, such as *handicapped, self-concept, elementary.* In contrast a topic such as "the self-concept of schoolchildren" is not precise enough to describe a viable research problem.

2. *State specific purpose of search.* Literature searches are conducted for several reasons. You should think through the precise purpose of your search since you will use different approaches for different kinds of searches.

Most searches are conducted as part of an exhaustive review of literature to be included as part of your thesis or dissertation. This kind of review must be very sharply focused but usually should include all relevant references for the past 10 years. All relevant narrow descriptors are chosen when possible, and the computer is instructed to locate references that contain combinations of descriptors, which further narrows the search. How narrow your search should be is determined partially by your topic, as discussed earlier in this chapter.

The computer can also be useful in assisting in a preliminary review of literature conducted to locate possible research problems. A computer search can locate recent references in your area of interest; these in turn can assist in limiting and better defining the problem. Usually such searches use broader descriptors and fewer combinations of descriptors since you have not yet settled on a narrow problem. To avoid getting very large numbers of references, it is advisable to instruct the computer to select only the 10 to 30 most recent references for each descriptor or descriptor combination.

Computer searches can also be helpful in updating a review of literature. It is not uncommon for graduate students to take two or three years after completing the review of literature to complete a research project and write their thesis or dissertation. By this time the review will be somewhat out of date. Using the same descriptors employed in the initial search, you can update your review by instructing the computer to select only those references published since your initial computer search was conducted.

3. *Select data base.* The next step is to select one or more data bases that are most relevant to the research problem. For most educational studies a search of the ERIC data base will produce most of the relevant literature. For the self-concept problem given as an example above, a search of *Exceptional Child Education Resources* and *Psychological Abstracts,* both of which are also available in the DIALOG system, could be added to ERIC to give a more complete coverage or could be used instead of ERIC.

4. *Select descriptors.* Using the procedures prescribed for your data bank, select the descriptors, index terms, or key words (all synonymous terms) that best describe your problem in terms the computer will accept. Remember that the *exact* terms used in indexing the materials into the system must be used. If you spell a descriptor incorrectly or make some similar error such as adding an *s,* the computer will not recognize the descriptor and will report no references.

Using the *Thesaurus of ERIC Descriptors 11th Edition* we would locate the descriptors that would fit our study of "the academic self-concept of handicapped children in the elementary school." First we would find that there is no descriptor for academic self-concept. Instead, we find *self-concept* and *self-esteem,* both of which seem to fit our topic. Since there is no source available that gives precise definitions of the ERIC descriptors, we have no way of knowing how a reviewer decides to use one of these descriptors or the other. In this case it is best to include both in our search and to instruct the computer to select articles that use either. We also find two broad descriptors that could be used for handicapped schoolchildren. These are *handicapped children* and *handicapped students.* However, we find that both of these broad descriptors are listed as "invalid" descriptors, which means they are no longer used to described current sources. We are advised to use the broad descriptor "disabilities," or preferably select more narrow descriptors that identify the specific disabilities we are most interested in. When we check the list of more narrow terms (NT) under "disabilities" we find *learning disabilities* and *mild mental retardation.* We decide that these are the two groups we are most interested in. Our final descriptors are *elementary school students,* and *elementary education.*[13]

13. In the ERIC system the reviewer must include an "educational level" descriptor. The appropriate mandatory descriptor for our example would be *elementary education.* Although *elementary school students* better fits our problem it is advisable to use both since some reviewers will use the mandatory descriptor in place of *elementary school students.*

If we decided to use the *Psychological Abstracts* data base instead of ERIC, we would find the following in the *Thesaurus of Psychological Index Terms, Fifth Edition: self-concept, self-perception, self-esteem, educable mentally retarded, learning disabilities,* and *elementary school students.* Note that, although similar, these index terms are not identical to our ERIC descriptors.

5. *Plan the computer search.* In planning your search it is usually best to start with combinations of descriptors that produce references that precisely fit your needs. Descriptors may be combined using *and* and *or.* For example, using the six ERIC descriptors: (1) *self-concept,* (2) *self-esteem,* (3) *learning disabilities,* (4) *mild mental retardation,* (5) *elementary school students,* and (6) *elementary education* we can instruct the computer to select references having the following combination of descriptors:

(1) Self-Concept   (3) Learning Disabilities   (5) Elementary School Students

or   *and*   *or*   *and*   *or*

(2) Self-Esteem   (4) Mild Mental Retardation   (6) Elementary Education

For the computer, we would print this combination as (1 or 2) and (3 or 4) and (5 or 6). This asks the computer for any reference that includes a combination of either *self-concept* or *self-esteem* and either *learning disabilities* or *mild mental retardation* and *elementary school students* or *elementary education.* Notice that *or* connections tend to increase the number of references selected since there are more references that have one descriptor *or the other* than have either by itself. But *and* connections tend to reduce the number of selections since only references that have *all the descriptors* connected by *and* would be selected. We have limited the three sample searches described below to a few descriptors. A far more complete search may be achieved if more descriptors are selected and sets of related descriptors are connected with *or.* This procedure is illustrated in figure 4.3.

Our search of the above combination produced 74 references, which indicates that our search was satisfactory for a typical thesis review. Often, when three or more descriptors are connected with *and,* the search will produce very few references, although the few produced will be on target.

You will recall that for research topics on which much work has been done, a narrow search is called for, whereas for topics on which little has been done the search must cover a broader area. In our example, if our initial search had been too narrow, we could have broadened it by removing the grade-level descriptors, that is, *elementary school students* and *elementary education.* When we ask the computer for references having (1 or 2) and (3 or 4), we find that there are 342 references. This search would produce many references that would not be relevant, but would also produce some that could provide valuable background information. In most cases a search that produces 342 references is too broad.

In order to provide more insight on how the various data bases are related, we then repeated our initial search using the *Exceptional Child Education Resources (ECER)* data base. This search located 103 references, of which 46 duplicated those found in the ERIC search.

We then carried out a third search using the *PsycINFO* data base. The index terms selected were (1) *self-concept,* (2) *self-perception,* (3) *self-esteem,* (4) *educable mentally retarded,* (5) *learning disabilities,* and (6) *elementary school students.* The search we conducted may be written (1 or 2 or 3) and (4 or 5) and (6). Note that this is essentially similar to the ERIC and *ECER* searches. We located 82 references, only 17 of which were duplicated in either the ERIC or *Exceptional Child Education Resources* searches. Forty of the references located by *PsycINFO* were dissertations, which are not adequately covered in the ERIC data base. These results suggest that in order to obtain a complete search it is advisable to check all relevant data bases.

The importance of using combinations of descriptors is illustrated by the fact that the ERIC search produced 7,054 references with the *learning disabilities* descriptor and 9,973 references with the *self-concept* descriptor. Obviously, using a single descriptor will usually result in a very broad search and will produce many references that are of no importance to the researcher.

Broad versus Narrow Descriptors

One of the rules for assigning ERIC descriptors requires that a document be indexed to the specific level of subject matter covered. In other words, the reviewer should select the most specific descriptor that fits the subject matter of the article or document. This means that an article dealing with *speech handicaps* would not be given the additional descriptor *disabilities,* unless it deals with *both* disabilities in general and also with *speech handicaps.* This often confuses the researcher, who is likely to assume that a general term such as *teaching* would also be assigned to all the narrow terms under teaching such as *diagnostic teaching, creative teaching,* and *peer teaching.* In terms of planning a search, this rule means that in order to get the most complete coverage of your topic, you may choose to include both the broad descriptors and the narrow descriptors that are directly related to your research problem. Using broad descriptors, however, may result in your locating some references that are not closely related to your problem. Such references may provide useful background data or may help place your problem in a broader context, but they will usually be less important than those you locate using more specific descriptors. For example, in our ERIC search related to *self-concept,* if we used the broad descriptor *disabilities* instead of the two narrow descriptors *learning disabilities* and *mild mental retardation,* we would locate more references (82 versus 74) but many of these would deal with children having disabilities in which we are not interested.

In addition to descriptors, ERIC reports are also classified by *author,* by

File   1:ERIC—66087/JULY

SET	ITEMS	DESCRIPTION
?S SELF-CONCEPT		[Each descriptor is entered; the computer (C) assigns a set number (S_1, etc.) and reports how many references in the system have this descriptor.]
S1	9973	SELF-CONCEPT (INDIVIDUALS' PERCEPTIONS OF THEMSELVES)
?S SELF-ESTEME		
S2	0	SELF-ESTEME Misspelled descriptor, C reports 0 items]
?S SELF-ESTEEM		
S3	3084	SELF-ESTEEM (INDIVIDUALS' VALUE JUDGMENTS OF THEMSELVES)
?S LEARNING DISABILITIES		
S4	7054	LEARNING DISABILITIES (CATEGORY IN FEDERAL LEGISLATION REFERRING TO . . .)
?S MILD MENTAL RETARDATION		
S5	2746	MILD MENTAL RETARDATION (INTELLECTUAL FUNCTIONING THAT RANGES TWO TO . . .)
?S ELEMENTARY SCHOOL STUDENTS		
S6	9485	ELEMENTARY SCHOOL STUDENTS (NOTE: COORDINATE WITH THE APPROPRIATE MANDA . . .)
?S ELEMENTARY EDUCATION		
S7	35384	ELEMENTARY EDUCATION (EDUCATION PROVIDED IN KINDERGARTEN OR GRADE . . .)
?C (1 OR 3) AND (4 OR 5) AND (6 OR 7)		[C is asked how many items are in this set, i.e., have this combination of descriptors.]
S8	74	(1 OR 3) AND (4 OR 5) AND (6 OR 7) [There are 74 items in this set.]
?C (1 OR 3) AND (4 OR 5)		
S9	342	(1 OR 3) AND (4 OR 5) [When we omit the two grade level descriptors, the number of items increases to 342.]
?C 9/MAJ		
S10	66	8/MAJ [We ask C how many of the items in Set 8 have descriptors 1, 3, 4, 5, 6, 7 as major descriptors. There are 66.]
?LIMIT8/1977	1987	[We ask C how many of the 74 items in Set 8 were published from 1977 to 1987]
	74	8
	325637	PY = 1977 : PY = 1987
S11	62	8/1977–1987 [62 of the 74 items were published from 1977 to 1987.]

Figure 4.3   Sample Computer Search, Illustrating Various Search Techniques

?LIMIT11/MAJ [We ask C how many of the 62 items in Set 11 have descriptors 1, 3, 4, 5, 6, 7 as major descriptors.]

    S12   55   11/MAJ [There are 55 that have major descriptors.]

?LIMIT12/EJ [We ask C how many items in Set 12 come from CIJE (EJ).]

    S13   39   12/EJ [39 of the 55 items come from CIJE. The remaining 16 items therefore come from RIE.]

?S SLOW LEARNERS [We enter a new descriptor that we believe may help locate additional relevant references.]

    S14   594   14 [There are 594 items with "slow learners" as a descriptor.]

            2746   5 [There are 2746 items with "mild mental retardation," Set 5 as a descriptor.]

    S15   556   14-5 [We believe that the descriptors "slow learners" (Set 14) and "mild mental retardation" (Set 5) might be applied to the same references. We ask C how many references have "slow learners" as a descriptor but NOT (shown by minus sign) "mild mental retardation." There are 556, indicating that the two descriptors are usually not applied to the same references.]

?C (1 OR 3) AND 15

    S16   20   (1 OR 3) and 15 [We ask C how many references have Set 1 (self-concept) or Set 3 (self-esteem) and Set 15 (slow learners minus mild mental retardation). There are 20 which we may want to check.]

?S ACADEMIC(W)SELF(W)CONCEPT [We ask C how many items in ERIC have the term "academic self-concept" some place in the entry (i.e., title, abstract, etc.). This is a proximity search.]

    S17   105   ACADEMIC(W)SELF(W)CONCEPT [There are 105; we may want to check those that also include Sets (4 or 5) and (6 or 7). This is done later in our search; see Sets 23 and 24.]

?S PIERS(W)HARRIS(W)SELF(W)CONCEPT(W)SCALE/ID [We ask C how many items in ERIC have the name of this test as an identifier (ID).]

    S18   0   PIERS(W)HARRIS(W)SELF(W)CONCEPT(W)SCALE/ID [No items have this identifier.]

?S SELF(W)ESTEEM(W)INVENTORIES/ID [We ask C how many items have the name of this test as an identifier (ID).]

    S19   0   SELF(W)ESTEEM(W)INVENTORIES/ID [No items have this identifier. Searching identifiers is often nonproductive; Proximity searches are recommended instead.]

?S SEI [Proximity search—How many items have SEI some place in the ERIC entry? SEI is the name commonly used for the Self-Esteem Inventories.]

    S20   14   SEI [There are 14 references that contain this term.]

Figure 4.3   (continued)

?S PIERS(W)HARRIS
      S21   157   PIERS(W)HARRIS [Proximity search: How many items in ERIC
                             have this term in the entry? This term is
                             commonly used in the literature to refer to the
                             Piers Harris Self-Concept Scale.]
?S PIERS(W)HARRIS/ID [How many ERIC items have this term as an identifier (ID)?]
      S22   74   PIERS(W)HARRIS/ID [74 items have this term as an identifier.
                             Note that the proximity search (Set 21)
                             produced many more references than the
                             identifier search (Set 22).]

?
?C (4 OR 5) AND 17 [This search aims at locating references that are closely "on target,"
                i.e., directly concerned with academic self-concept.]
      S23   8   (4 OR 5) AND 17 [There are 8 references in this set.]
?C (6 OR 7) AND 23 [How many of Set 23 are relevant to the elementary level?]
      S24   5   (6 OR 7) AND 23 [There are 5 items in this set.]
?S DISABILITIES [This is a broad descriptor, entered to show effect of using broad
                descriptors.]
      S25   21106   DISABILITIES (PHYSICAL, MENTAL, OR SENSORY IMPAIRMENTS
                          THAT . . .) [Note the very large number of items having this
                          broad descriptor.]
?C (1 OR 3) AND 25
      S26   479   (1 OR 3) AND 25 [This search combines the two self-concept
                          descriptors with the broad "disabilities"
                          descriptor.]
?C (6 OR 7) AND 26 [This search incorporates the two elementary descriptors with the
                previous search.]
      S27   82   (6 OR 7) AND 26 [There are 82 references; many will be off
                          target because of using the broad descriptor.]
?S DT = 040 [How many dissertations, i.e., document type 040, are in ERIC data base?]
      S28   2586   DT = 040 [There are 2586 dissertations in the ERIC file. This is
                          only a small fraction of dissertations in Education and related
                          fields that have been completed since ERIC was started and shows
                          that ERIC is a poor source for dissertations.]
?C8 AND 28 [How many dissertations in the ERIC data base are related to our problem as
           described by Set 8?]
      S29   0   8 AND 28 [There are no dissertations in ERIC data base in
                          problem area described by Set 8.]
?C9 AND 28   [How many dissertations in the ERIC data base are related to the
                          broader problem as described by Set 9?]
      S30   0   9 AND 28 [No dissertations in file on topic of Set 9.]
?C (1 OR 3) AND 28 [How many dissertations on self-concept or self-esteem?]
      S31   92   (1 OR 3) AND 28 [There are 92.]

Figure 4.3   *(continued)*

institution, and by *identifier*. For most computer searches these classifications are of little value. However, if you know that much important work in your area of interest has been conducted by a specific author or at a specific institution, you may want to search these classifications. Identifiers include terms such as *geographical locations, trade names, equipment names, specific theories, tests*, and *testing programs*. These may be useful in some searches, but we have found them of little value in the kinds of computer searches usually conducted by graduate students.

6. *Conduct the search.* Once you are on-line, the first step is to enter your descriptors and determine how many references are available under each descriptor. For example, in the ERIC search on self-concept, we found the following frequencies: self-concept, 9,973; self-esteem, 3,084; learning disabilities, 7,054; mild mental retardation, 2,746; elementary school students, 9,485; and elementary education, 35,384. (See figure 4.3.)

The next step is to enter each of your planned combinations of descriptors and ask the computer how many references are available for each combination. Next, you may decide to have the computer print out the bibliographical data on 5 to 10 of the references in a given combination to see what sort of references have been selected.

You would then select a combination of descriptors that will produce between 50 and 200 items and instruct the computer to send you a printout. Before proceeding, study figure 4.3 carefully. It shows how our sample search was entered into the computer and illustrates many of the techniques that you can employ in conducting a computer search. The information in brackets has been added to help you understand the process. For some data bases such as ERIC, you can request titles with ED or EJ numbers, complete bibliographical data, or complete bibliographical data plus an abstract. When available, the abstracts are usually worth the additional cost; for a DIALOG search of ERIC, the cost is 10 cents per citation for bibliographical data only and 14 cents for bibliographic data plus abstract. If you need only the ED and EJ numbers and the title, you can have these printed out on-line at no extra cost except contact time.

7. *Review the printout.* Once you have received the printout of references located in your computer search, study the abstracts and proceed with the rest of your literature review, using the procedures described in this chapter. If, in checking the bibliographies of articles you read, you locate important references that were not found in your computer search, study these carefully and try to determine why they were missed.

Researchers are often suspicious of computer searches because of having carried out a search in which references that they knew were relevant to their topic did not appear. The usual reasons for this are (1) the researcher's failure to use a sufficient number of related terms with "or" connectors, and (2) the reviewer's failure to select the correct descriptors. Keep in mind the process that is employed in preparing abstracts and selecting descriptors for a given article.

The article is assigned to one of the ERIC clearinghouses and someone who is presumably knowledgeable on the subject reads the article, prepares the abstract, and selects the descriptors. Unfortunately, both the preparation of the abstract and decision as to which descriptors are relevant are quite subjective. Therefore, if the same article were assigned for review to a half dozen different persons, it is unlikely that any two of these persons would include the same material in their abstract or would list exactly the same descriptors. This subjectivity is clearly illustrated by the two *CIJE* printouts from the ERIC system shown in figure 4.4.

A close look at these references confirms that they are two different reviews of the same article. However, if you read the two abstracts, you will see that they have very little in common. A look at the descriptors is even more surprising. The first review lists nine descriptors, whereas the second review lists only six descriptors. Note furthermore that only four of the descriptors, "autism," "middle schools," "peer teaching" and "program descriptions" are common to the two reviews. This clearly illustrates the fallibility of this system.

EJ282648   EC152054
Peer Tutors Help Autistic Students Enter the Mainstream.
Campbell, Ann; And Others
Teaching Exceptional Children, v15 n2 p64–69 Win   1983
Available from: Reprint: UMI
Language: English
Document Type: JOURNAL ARTICLE (080); PROJECT DESCRIPTION (141)
A peer-tutoring program in which tutors were taught behavioral techniques as well as background information through a board game format was successful in promoting school. Peer tutors helped to promote positive attitudes among students and teachers. (CL)
Descriptors: * Attitude Change; * Autism; Behavior Modification; Middle Schools; * Peer Influence; * Peer Teaching; Program Descriptions; Student Attitudes; Teacher Attitudes

EJ274446   EC151160
Peer Tutors Help Autistic Students Enter the Mainstream.
Campbell, Ann; And Others
Teaching Exceptional Chidren, v15 n2 p64–69 Win   1983
Available from: Reprint: UMI
Language: English
Document Type: JOURNAL ARTICLE (080); PROJECT DESCRIPTION (141)
The peer-tutoring program was initiated at the Belle Vue (Florida) Middle School as an effective way of bringing autistic students into contact with the mainstream. (SW)
Descriptors: * Autism; Mainstreaming; Middle Schools; * Peer Relationship, * Peer Teaching; Program Descriptions

Figure 4.4   Two CIJE Entries on the Same Article

Unless you are very thorough in planning the computer search, you may miss a great many important references. Therefore you may well want to conduct a second search after becoming more familiar with the field of study.

Proximity Searching

Proximity searching, also called *full text searching*, is a procedure for searching the citations entered in the data base for specific words or phrases. This technique is very useful (1) when you want to search a very narrow and sharply defined topic or (2) when there are no descriptor terms that really fit your topic.

Proximity searching may be carried out with any of the DIALOG data bases, although the coverage may differ from one data base to another. The search may be carried out for single words, phrases, or for two or more words that appear in close proximity in the material searched. These words do not have to be descriptor terms; any combination of words can be used.

You may also conduct a full text search using terms that have been truncated so that only the root term remains. For example, a search of the root term *librar* would locate references containing any variation of that root term, such as *library, libraries, librarians,* thus providing a broader coverage of relevant citations.

For ERIC, the material searched for each reference includes the title, descriptions, identifiers, and abstract. For example, suppose we are interested in studies concerned with homeless people. Because no descriptor for homeless people is included in the ERIC *Thesaurus,* we select the descriptors *economically disadvantaged* and *housing needs.* We find that there are 2,483 items with the first as a descriptor, 354 with the second, but only 11 items when *economically disadvantaged* is joined with *housing needs* using an "and" connector. This combination seems to be about as close to our topic as we can get, using regular descriptors. A search of these 11 items would probably produce some references related to homeless people, but some of the 11 would also be "off target."

You will obtain much more sharply focused citations if you carry out a full text or proximity search using the words "homeless people." In conducting a proximity search, different instructions can be given to the computer so that different criteria will be met before a citation is selected. For example, if the "W-limiter" is used, one of the selected words (*people*) must directly follow the other (*homeless*) in order for the reference to be selected. If the "F-limiter" is used, both words must appear in the same field (for example, both words must be somewhere in the title). If the "C-limiter" is used, the selected words must only appear someplace in the citation. Thus, the limiters can be used to broaden or narrow the search as desired.

When we searched *homeless* (W) *people,* we located 41 references. These citations were virtually all "on target," thus providing much better coverage of available literature than was obtained from combining the descriptors *economically disadvantaged* and *housing needs*.[14]

For most educational topics closely relevant descriptors or combinations of descriptors will be found in the ERIC *Thesaurus*, and in this case a search of these descriptors is the best choice. Proximity search, however, is a very useful tool when descriptors that are closely related to your topic are not available or when you need a few references that are sharply focused on a very specific topic.[15]

Proximity searching is also an excellent way to locate references that provide information on measures you plan to use in your research. For example when we conducted a proximity search of *Piers (W) Harris* (the name usually used for the Piers Harris Self-Concept Scale) we located 157 references (see Set 21 in figure 4.3).

Step Three—Reading and Noting Selected References

Bibliography Card

During your search of the preliminary sources, prepare a bibliography card for each book or article that you believe might contain material pertinent to the review. Although information included in the bibliographical data for a given citation is always about the same, these data can be recorded in many different formats. Before starting your review of the literature, check the rules in effect at your college concerning acceptable format for the bibliography section of the thesis or dissertation. Some schools permit you to use any format that is generally acceptable in your field of study. Other schools have a specific format that must be followed by all graduate students. If your school permits the use of any form that is acceptable in your field, the easiest approach will be for you to use the format of the preliminary source from which you expect to obtain most of your references. *Current Index to Journals in Education* is the most productive source for most students working in education, and therefore its format is advantageous to use when permitted. Most of the references will come from the subject index of *CIJE*, and articles listed by subject give the title of the book or article before the author's name. For your bibliography card, the author's name (last name first) should be listed before the title. This change is necessary because it is much more convenient for you to maintain your note-card file in

14. As of January 1986, "Homeless People" was added to the ERIC system as a descriptor. New descriptors are regularly added to the system. To find out what descriptors have been added since the current edition of the *Thesaurus*, check the most recent issue of *RIE* or *CIJE*.
15. For another example of a proximity search see Set 17 in figure 4.3. In this case, even though the descriptors "Self-Concept" and "Self-Esteem" are fairly close to our topic, a proximity search of *Academic (W) Self (W) Concept* is more sharply focused and produced a few very relevant references when combined with descriptors (4 or 5) and (6 or 7).

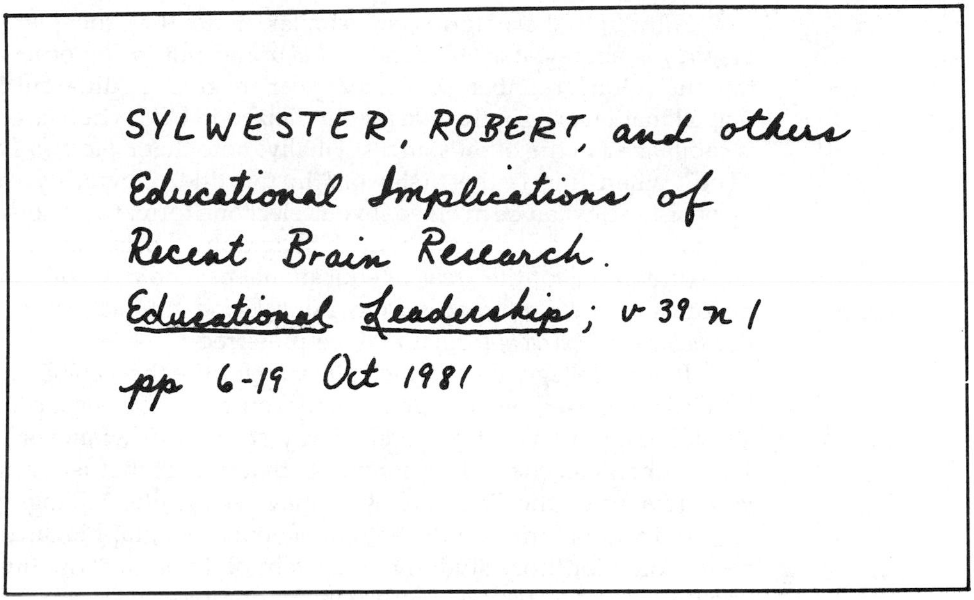
SYLWESTER, ROBERT, and others
Educational Implications of
Recent Brain Research.
Educational Leadership; v 39 n 1
pp 6-19 Oct 1981

Figure 4.5 Sample Bibliography Card in *CIJE* Format

alphabetical order by author, and the bibliography as prepared for your thesis normally will be listed in this order. It is advisable to print the author's name; misspelled names are a common source of errors and are difficult to detect when proofreading.

Figure 4.5 shows a bibliography card in the *CIJE* format. If this format is chosen, the bibliographic data from articles found in other sources, such as *Education Index* and *Psychological Abstracts*, should be converted to the *CIJE* format. Let us compare bibliographical data for an article as it appears in *CIJE*, *Education Index*, and *Psychological Abstracts:*

Current Index to Journals in Education:
Battista, Michael The Interaction between Two Instructional Treatments of Algebraic Structures and Spatial-Visualization Ability. *Journal of Educational Research;* v74 n5 p337–41 May-Jun 1981 (Reprint: UMI)
Education Index:
BATTISTA, Michael Interaction between two instructional treatments of algebraic structures and spatial-visualization ability. J Educ Res 74:337–41 My/Je'81
Psychological Abstracts:
Battista, Michael. (Purdue U) The interaction between two instructional treatments of algebraic structures and spatial-visualization ability. *Journal of Educational Research,* 1981 (May-Jun), Vol 74 (5), 337–341.

Although these forms are similar, note that the *Journal of Educational Research* is abbreviated in *Education Index* and not in the other two sources and that the volume number, pages, and year are given in different format. Note also that all main words in the title are capitalized in *CIJE* whereas only the first word is capitalized in the other sources. Finally, note that *Education Index* format omits "The" when this is the first word in the title. Obviously, many errors and inconsistencies can be avoided if you select one format and convert all references to that format when making up bibliography cards. Students reviewing the literature in one of the areas of educational psychology will normally obtain the majority of their references from *Psychological Abstracts,* and in this case, the *Psychological Abstracts* format may be preferred.

If your college has specified a format for the thesis bibliography that differs from the one used by your preliminary sources, the easiest procedure is to copy all bibliographic data from preliminary sources in whatever form it is found. Then, when you check the reference to determine whether or not it is relevant to your review of the literature, you may recopy the bibliographic data in the required school format at the bottom of your bibliographic card. You will need to do this only for those studies that contain pertinent information; usually, that is one out of every three or four preliminary references.

Accuracy is extremely important in preparing bibliography cards. A mistake in copying the data can often cause a great deal of extra work. For example, if you incorrectly copy the name of a journal, the date, volume or page numbers, you will fail to find the article when checking the source. Then you will be faced with the problem of trying to determine which part of your bibliographic citation is incorrect. These mistakes are easy to make unless you take special care. As you may well have covered a large number of preliminary sources, a mistake in the early stages may mean a lengthy second search. Even if you make an error in some portion of the bibliographic data that does not interfere with your locating the actual material, such as misspelling the author's name, the error is still serious, for you will probably repeat it in your thesis. Nothing reflects more unfavorably on the scholarship of a research worker than frequent errors in bibliographic data.

Using the Library

Now that you have completed your search of preliminary sources and have assembled a set of bibliography cards, the time has come to start checking these references in the library. The majority of your references will probably be in professional journals, because these are the principal outlets for primary source research articles.

If you visit several academic libraries, you will find two common arrangements for shelving and handling professional journals. Newer and smaller libraries often have these journals on open shelves in the reference area along with desks or tables that students can use when reading the journals. This system is simplest for you, for you can locate the journals you need, read them, and usually make copies, all in the same area.

Older and larger university libraries, on the other hand, usually have their professional journals shelved in closed stacks. Ordering these materials through basic library procedures can waste a great deal of your time. If you are using a closed-stack library, we advise you to obtain a stack permit and examine the layout of the library, to determine what method of obtaining materials will require the least amount of time. In a library where periodicals in a given field are all shelved in a central location and where study space is available in the stacks, you will probably want to work in the stacks. Some libraries, however, do not permit students to enter the stacks, and some, because of space limitations, shelve journals in such a way that they are difficult to find and cannot be used in the immediate area in which they are shelved. In this case, you can usually save time by making out a call slip for about 10 periodicals and then, while waiting for the library clerk to return with your requests, making out another call slip for a second group of 10. While the clerk hunts down your second group, you can scan and make notes on the first group, and so on. Because a certain percentage of references that you ask for will prove to have nothing relevant, or will be lost, checked out, or in the bindery, you should always submit call slips for 10 or more references at a time.

Many professional journals are now available on microfilm. Libraries are making increasing use of this format because it is less expensive and requires less space than storing printed journals. Check the room in your library where microfilms and microfiches are stored. Most university libraries have equipment available for copying microfilm onto regular-sized sheets of paper; this is useful if you need a copy of an article or report for later reference.

Few of us except the most experienced reference librarians have a complete grasp of the many resources available in the typical university library. Most university libraries conduct tours for students at the beginning of each year or semester, and you will almost surely learn something new if you take such a tour. Also, don't hesitate to ask questions; librarians as a group tend to want to help whenever possible.

Obtaining Materials Not Available Locally

You will almost certainly find that some of the materials you wish to examine are not available in your college library. There are several ways to obtain these materials, and you shouldn't give up merely because a source is not immediately available. The quickest way to obtain copies of articles published in professional journals is to write directly to the author and ask for a reprint of the article. Authors usually have such reprints and are willing to send a reprint to anyone requesting it. *Do* send a stamped, self-addressed envelope with your request.

Reprints thus received are your personal property and should be kept in your file so that you may recheck them if necessary. The main problem in writing for reprints is obtaining the author's address. *Psychological Abstracts* usually provides such addresses. This information is not given in *Eudcation Index*, however. A great many authors may be located by checking the various professional directories that are available, such as *Who's Who in American Education, Biographical Directory of the American Psychological Association*, and *American Educational Research Association Directory of Members*. Your reference librarian can usually suggest other directories if an individual is not listed in any of the above sources.

If you are unable to obtain a reprint of an article from its author, the next step is to see if the needed journal is available in another library in the vicinity. In large population centers where several colleges or universities are located within a small geographical area, you can usually find the materials you need at another local library. In areas where other libraries are few and far between, you may obtain needed materials through interlibrary loan. Check your library's policies on interlibrary loan; many libraries place restrictions on this service because it is rather expensive.

Often you may wish to examine a thesis or dissertation that is available only through the school library where the work was actually done. Such studies may be obtained through interlibrary loan, or microfilm copies of most dissertations may be obtained from University Microfilms, Inc. (Ann Arbor, Michigan). Microfilm copies of a dissertation can often be obtained at less expense than borrowing the dissertation itself through interlibrary loan. Even when it proves more expensive, microfilm is often preferable, since the copy need not be returned and is available for future reference.

You can usually obtain either microfilm or photostatic copies of any reference not available at your own library. The librarian at your library will locate the needed materials and arrange for their reproduction, but the cost of reproduction and shipping is usually yours. This varies considerably, usually from 15 cents to 35 cents per page, so having material photocopied is generally more practical for short articles than for books or lengthy documents. If, however, the reference appears to be of major importance, you should obtain it by some means. The satisfaction of knowing that you have done a thorough and scholarly review of the literature will more than compensate for the expense.

Taking Notes on Research Articles

Check through your bibliography cards and identify those covering studies that appear most important to your review of the literature. Then begin your review by checking the most recent of these important studies. The reason for starting with the most recent is that these, having earlier research as a foundation, are likely to be more valuable. By reading the most important articles first, you quickly build up a reasonably deep understanding of your problem, and this makes it possible for you to profit more from the subsequent study of articles that are only peripherally related to your topic. This insight makes it much easier for you to fit these less important studies into the overall picture you are building of your field through the literature review.

When you finally open the journal to an article you wish to check, first read the abstract. Most research articles begin with a brief abstract or end with a summary. By reading these, you can usually determine whether or not the article contains any information that would justify reading the entire article. If, after reading the abstract or summary, you decide that the article is pertinent, first check the accuracy of your bibliographical data, because the source where you obtained these data might have been in error. Then record the same bibliographic data on the top of a 5×8 note card and take notes on the article as you read it. In order to save time, you may abbreviate the bibliographical data on this second card.

In a research article, the writer attempts to present the essential materials in as brief a form as possible. You will find that the average research article is only five or six pages long and thus takes little time to read, and that the majority of research articles follow a standard pattern that further reduces the time needed to review them. This format usually includes (1) a brief introduction, (2) the hypotheses to be tested, (3) a statement of the procedure including a description of the subjects, measures used, and research design, (4) a section giving the findings, and (5) a summary and conclusions. In taking notes, be as brief as possible without omitting anything that you feel you may want to use in the design of your study or the preparation of your research report. A brief outline of the reference using short sentences or phrases with headings for the problem or hypothesis, procedure, findings, and conclusions will usually be sufficient.

The procedures and findings usually require the most detailed notetaking. In order to make comparisons among related studies later on, record the number of subjects, sampling methods, treatments (independent variable), measures employed (dependent variable), research design, and any other procedure worthy of attention.

Findings should also be reported in some detail, especially for studies that are very relevant to your problem. Both significant and nonsignificant findings should be recorded, along with levels of significance for the former. In order to combine studies and draw an overall picture of the findings, it is useful to categorize studies as significant ($+$), nonsignificant ($+$), nonsignificant ($-$), and significant ($-$). The meta-analysis technique developed by Gene Glass and his associates provides a more sophisticated method of combining the results of related studies. If you plan to use this method, record the means and standard deviations of the experimental and control groups in experimental and quasi-

OLEJNIK, S. F. and DOEYAN, J. D. Soliciting teacher participants for classroom research. _Journal of Educational Research_, 1982, 75(3), 165-168.

Problem. Effects on teacher interest to participate in a res. proj. of the following 3 variables: (1) nature of the res., i.e., exp. vs. non-exp. (in exp., teachers randomly assigned to treatment; in non-exp. could choose treatment); (2) monetary reward vs. no reward; (3) time required to participate, i.e., ~4 hours vs. 4-12 hours over 2-week period.

Procedure. Subj. were 58 teachers, gr. 2-8. 15 teachers gr. k, 1, & special subject dropped after data collected. Randomly assigned to 8 treatments, N per cell 5-11. Each tr. contained desc. of 5 proposed studies. Desc. identical except that the 3 ind. variables were manipulated.

Findings. ANOVA gave sig. higher interest for groups getting honorarium (10% level); NSD exp vs non-exp, NSD time, no interactions were sig.

Conclusions. Financial incentive sig. increased teacher interest in participating.

Comments. Request for teacher commitment instead of interest would be more realistic. Cell sizes small. Dropping k, 1, & spec. teachers indicates poor planning.

Figure 4.6 Sample Note Card

experimental studies and the product-moment correlations in correlational studies.[16]

It is also desirable for you to record your own evaluation of the study and to note how it may relate to your research while the article is still fresh in your mind. In addition to your outline of the study, it is often profitable to record promising or unusual techniques employed in the study, new measures that may be of use, interesting theoretical points, and a critical evaluation including apparent weaknesses that make the results questionable. This critical evaluation of the research is important because you will often find several research reports that test similar hypotheses but yield different results. Unless you can make a critical evaluation of the research, it is difficult to determine which of the conflicting results is more likely to be correct. Chapter 5 presents a detailed discussion of methods for critically evaluating research articles (see figure 4.6 for a sample note card).

Taking Notes on Opinion Articles

In education many of the articles that you encounter will not be reports of research projects, but will describe the experiences or opinions of the author concerning some educational topic. Opinion articles do not follow the research article format and usually do not contain a summary. When checking the opinion article, first scan the article to get some idea of its content. One method of scanning is to read only the first sentence in each paragraph. After scanning, decide whether the article contains material of importance. If so, read the entire article. An abstract of the opinion article can usually be prepared most quickly using a sentence outline approach.

Quotations

When reading articles be alert for quotations that might be useful in preparing the review of the literature for your thesis or dissertation. If you find material you may wish to quote, the material to be quoted should be copied very carefully on the note card, enclosed in quotation marks, and the page from which the quote was taken noted. Most systems of referencing require that the page be given for direct quotations, and this also facilitates checking the quotation if necessary.

Students often use far too many quotations in their reviews. A good rule to follow is to copy for possible quotations only materials that are stated very skillfully, or in very concise terms, or are typical and clear reflections of a particular point of view you wish to illustrate in your thesis. After copying a

---

16. See chapter 5 for a discussion of meta-analysis.

quotation, recheck to be sure that you have copied it exactly. Inaccurate quotations are a serious reflection on the scholarship of the writer, and it is almost certain that some of the quotations will be checked for accuracy by the faculty members who read the thesis.

Classifying Articles You Read

In reading articles for your review of the literature, you should keep constantly in mind the objective of your research and should attempt to relate the material you read to your research plan. Do not restrict yourself to the narrow study of only that research that is closely related to the work you are planing. Very often studies that are only partially related to your work will give you new theoretical viewpoints and acquaint you with new tools and methods that can be profitably applied to your research plan.

In reviewing the literature, you will usually find that the articles you read can be classified into several categories. For example, in doing a review of literature in the field of ability grouping, one of the authors found some articles that compared the achievement of students in ability-grouping and random-grouping systems, some articles that made comparisons of sociometric scores and social status measures between the two systems, some that discussed methods of grouping, and so on. In carrying out your review, be alert for such natural subdivisions because they form a basis for classifying note cards.

A Coding System

As some such pattern for your review emerges, develop a system of coding that will permit you to indicate what type of material is contained on a given note card. The coding system adopted by the research worker will be different for each review of the literature. An example of a coding system used by one of the authors in a review of the literature in ability grouping may be helpful in developing your own coding. These codes are generally placed in the upper-right-hand corner of the note card.

+   An important study
S   Studies dealing with social interaction
A   Studies dealing with achievement of pupils in different grouping systems
G   Studies describing grouping systems and studies discussing problems involved in grouping, such as individual variability, and so forth
B   Studies relating grouping to behavior problems
P   Studies relating grouping to personality adjustment, personality variables, and self-concept

Using such a code is helpful in several ways. It makes you actively aware of the major areas of concentration in your topic. It makes it possible for you to check quickly your notes on a specific portion of the literature, and it makes the job of writing up your review of the literature much easier. The more extensive studies, of course, may contain material relating to two or three subtopics. These are recorded by indicating all the codes for subtopics.

MISTAKES SOMETIMES MADE IN REVIEWING RESEARCH LITERATURE

1. The researcher carries out a hurried review of the literature to get started on the research project. This usually results in overlooking previous studies containing ideas that would have improved the student's project.
2. Relies too heavily upon secondary sources.
3. Concentrates on findings when reading research articles, thus overlooking valuable information on methods, measures, and so forth.
4. Overlooks sources other than education journals, such as newspapers and popular magazines, which often contain articles on educational topics.
5. Fails to define satisfactorily the topic limits of the review of the literature. Searching too broad an area often leads to the student becoming discouraged or doing a slipshod job. Searching too narrow an area causes students to overlook many articles that are peripheral to their research topic but contain information that would help them design a better study.
6. Copies bibliographic data incorrectly and is then unable to locate the reference needed.
7. Copies far too much material onto note cards. This often indicates that the student does not have a clear understanding of the project and thus cannot separate important from unimportant information.
8. Fails to use all relevant narrow descriptors when conducting a computer search.

ANNOTATED REFERENCES

Jackson, Gregg B. "Methods for Integrative Reviews." *Review of Educational Research 50* (1980): 438–460.

Critically analyzes procedures used by reviewers of the educational research literature. Because your thesis or dissertation will include a literature review, you can learn much from studying this article. The study analyzes 36 randomly sampled review articles and relates the findings to 6 basic tasks involved in conducting an integrative review: (1) selecting questions or hypotheses for the review, (2) sampling research articles to be reviewed, (3) describing the characteristics of the studies, (4) analyzing the findings, (5) interpreting the results, and (6) reporting the review. Jackson's work identifies many deficiencies frequently found in literature reviews and suggests effective ways to overcome these deficiencies. A brief but informative discussion of meta-analysis is also included.

Brandhorst, Ted, and Eustace, Joanna, eds. *Directory of ERIC Information Providers*. Washington, DC: Educational Resources Information Center, May 1986 (ED 275 329).

Lists organizations that provide their users with access to the ERIC data base and its related resources. This includes organizations that provide computer searches of ERIC, hold collections of ERIC microfiche, and collect various ERIC publications. Entries include name and address of organizations, population served, data bases available, cost, and other information. Available free of charge from ERIC Processing and Reference Facility, 4350 East-West Highway, Suite 1100, Bethesda, MD 20814.

Woodbury, Marda L. *A Guide to Sources of Educational Information*, 2nd ed. Washington, DC: Information Resources Press, 1982.

Comprehensive guide to virtually every type of information related to education. It contains detailed descriptions of more than 700 sources, plus backup chapters on how to locate them and how to use them. Among the kinds of sources included are dictionaries, encyclopedias, bibliographies, abstracting and indexing services, instructional materials, tests and assessment instruments, and many more.

Abstracting and Indexing Sources

The following sources are useful in locating research articles that have been published in psychology, education, and related fields.

Author Index to Psychological Index, 1894–1935 and Psychological Abstracts, 1927–1958. Boston: Hall, 1960.

Bibliographic Index. New York: H. W. Wilson, 1938 to date.

Mitchell, James V. Jr., ed. *The Ninth Mental Measurements Yearbook*. Lincoln, NE: The Buros Institute of Mental Measurements, 1985.

Business Education Index. New York: Delta Pi Epsilon Fraternity through Gregg Division, McGraw-Hill, 1940 to date.

Child Development Abstracts and Bibliography. Washington, DC: Society for Research in Child Development, 1927 to date.

Comprehensive Dissertation Index. Ann Arbor, MI: University Microfilms International. Covers dissertations 1861 to date.

Cumulated Subject Index to the Psychological Abstracts, 1927–1960. Boston: Hall, 1966. Several supplements have been published.

Cumulative Author Index to Psychological Abstracts First Supplement 1959–1963. 2 vols. Boston: Hall, 1965. Several additional supplements have been published.

Current Index to Journals in Education. Phoenix, AZ: Oryx Press, 1969 to date.

Dissertation Abstracts International. Ann Arbor, MI: University Microfilms International, 1938 to date.

Education Index. New York: H. W. Wilson, 1929 to date.

Educational Administration Abstracts. Columbus, OH: University Council for Educational Administration, 1966 to date.

Exceptional Child Education Resources. Reston, VA: Council for Exceptional Children, 1969 to date.

Psychological Abstracts. Washington, DC: American Psychological Association, 1927 to date.

Resources in Education. Washington, DC: Educational Resources Information Center, 1966 to date.

Science Citation Index. Philadelphia: Institute for Scientific Information, 1961 to date.

Social Science Citation Index. Philadelphia: Institute for Scientific Information, 1973 to date.

Sociological Abstracts. New York: Sociological Abstracts Inc., 1954 to date.

State Education Journal Index. Westminster, CO: L. S. Ratliff, 1963 to date.

Reviews of Research Literature

The following sources are helpful to the student in gaining a quick overview of research in education or psychology.

Annual Review of Psychology. Palo Alto, CA: Annual Reviews, 1950 to date.

McMillan, James H., ed. *Annual Editions: Educational Psychology 87/88,* 3rd ed. Guilford, CT: Dushkin, 1986. Fourth edition scheduled for late 1988; subsequent editions at 18–24-month intervals.

Review of Educational Research. Washington, DC: American Educational Research Association, 1931 to date. Published five times a year.

Review of Research in Education. Itasca, IL: F. E. Peacock (a publication of the American Educational Research Association), 1973 to date. Annual volumes.

Husen, Torsten, and Postlethwaite, T. Neville. *The International Encyclopedia of Education: Research and Studies.* New York: Pergamon, 1985.

Richardson-Koehler, Virginia. *Educators' Handbook—A Research Perspective.* New York: Longman, 1987.

Wittrock, Merlin C., ed. *Handbook of Research on Teaching,* 3rd ed. New York: Macmillan, 1986.

Yearbook of the National Society for the Study of Education. Chicago: University of Chicago Press, 1902 to date. Published annually.

Directories

The following directories will help you locate the addresses of professional workers in education and psychology. This information is needed in order to obtain reprints of articles not available in the local library. If the following directories do not produce the needed information, check under "Directories" in recent issues of *Education Index, Guide to American Educational Directories,* or *Guide to American Directories* for additional sources. If your library does not have a directory you need, check with faculty members or local educators who may be members of the association publishing the directory.

American Educational Research Association: Directory of Members. Washington, DC: American Educational Research Association. Published biannually.

This is a complete roster of over 10,000 members with titles and addresses.

1986 APA Membership Register. Washington, DC: American Psychological Association. Published at irregular intervals.

The 1985 edition of this directory provides a biographical listing. The *1986 Register* contains only names, addresses, phone numbers, and membership status for over 63,000 members.

Ethridge, James M., ed. *The Directory of Directories,* 5th ed. Detroit: Information Enterprises, 1987.

Organizes directories into 15 subject areas, one of which is education. A revised edition will be published every two years with supplementary issues between editions. A subject index and title index are provided. Students will find it well worth their while to scan the 27 pages in the education section. The information provided for each directory includes address and phone number of publisher, persons or institutions covered, information included in entry, how directory is arranged (e.g., alphabetical), and what indexes are provided.

The National Faculty Directory 1989. Detroit: Gale Research Co. Published annually since 1970.

An alphabetical list, with departments and full institutional addresses, of about 650,000 members of teaching faculties at junior colleges, colleges, and universities in the U.S. and some Canadian institutions. Since much educational research is conducted by faculty members, this source is very useful in locating current addresses of researchers.

SELF-CHECK TEST

Circle the correct answer to each of the following questions. An answer key is provided on page 883.

1. The general term applied to publications that contain descriptions of educational research by an author who was not a direct observer or participant is " _____ source."
   a. secondary
   b. primary

    c. preliminary

    d. review

2. If an author of a textbook reports results of his own experiments, that portion of the text would be considered a _____ source.

    a. review

    b. primary

    c. secondary

    d. preliminary

3. A good rule to follow is to develop a reading program based on _____ sources to locate a tentative research problem followed by a review of the literature based on _____ sources.

    a. primary/secondary

    b. secondary/primary

    c. secondary/preliminary

    d. preliminary/secondary

4. The initial step in reviewing the literature is to

    a. make a list of key words related to the study.

    b. take notes on research articles.

    c. check the preliminary sources.

    d. study opinion articles to gain insight into the problems related to the study.

5. *Education Index, Psychological Abstracts,* and *Resources in Education* are all examples of _____ sources.

    a. preliminary

    b. primary

    c. reference

    d. secondary

6. Unlike *Education Index* and *Psychological Abstracts,* the ERIC system includes abstracts of

    a. conference papers.

    b. final reports of school district studies.

    c. progress reports of educational research studies.

    d. All of the above are correct.

7. The purpose of the *Review of Educational Research* is to

    a. provide bibliographies of research completed in each calendar year.

    b. summarize the research literature on a variety of educational topics.

    c. produce a current index to the major preliminary sources in education.

    d. all of the above are correct.

8. The best source of bibliographies of research on published tests is

    a. *Mental Measurements Yearbooks.*

    b. *Review of Educational Research.*

    c. *Bibliographic Index.*

    d. *Dissertation Abstracts.*

9. The purpose of DATRIX is to help the researcher by

    a. preparing article abstracts that contain sample size, research design, and statistical techniques used.

    b. selecting ERIC documents on a given topic.

    c. selecting doctoral dissertations on a given topic.

    d. providing names of other researchers doing current studies on a given topic.

10. Probably the most often used preliminary source covering popular periodicals and newspapers is

    a. *The New York Times Index.*

    b. *Sociological Abstracts.*

    c. *Reader's Guide to Periodical Literature.*

    d. *Facts on File.*

APPLICATION PROBLEMS

The following problems are designed to give you practice in applying significant concepts and research procedures explained in the chapter. Most of them do not have a single correct answer. For feedback, you can compare your answers with the sample answers on pages 888–890.

1. Select a research topic in which you are interested and locate a primary and secondary source related to it. Enter the bibliographic data on the two sources and explain why each is a primary or secondary source.
2. Suppose you wanted to conduct a manual search of research literature related to the effect of praise on the sharing behavior of young children.
   a. Check the *Thesaurus of Psychological Index Terms* and list key index terms related to praise and sharing that you could check in *Psychological Abstracts*.
   b. Check the *Thesaurus of ERIC Descriptors* and list key descriptors you could use in checking *RIE* and *CIJE*.
   c. Check *Psychological Abstracts* and locate one article that appears relevant to this topic. Make up a bibliography card.
3. Graduate students often find it helpful to learn something about the research work of faculty members with whom they are working. Select one member of your graduate committee or a faculty member in your major department and collect the following information:
   a. List articles published by the faculty member over the past five years and make up bibliography cards.
   b. Check how many times each article has been cited by other authors over the past two years.
   c. Read the article cited most frequently and prepare a note card.
4. Locate an article on experimental procedures published in 1976 by Harold W. Richey.
   a. Prepare a bibliography card.
   b. Prepare a note card on this article.
5. Suppose that a researcher wanted to carry out a computer search of the ERIC data base in order to locate references related to the question "What teaching techniques make a difference in learner achievement?" Following the procedures in this chapter, make up a search plan using all relevant descriptors in *and/or* relationships such as the example given on pages 142–149.

SUGGESTION SHEET

If your last name starts with letters from Can to Cop, please complete the Suggestion Sheet at the end of the book while this chapter is still fresh in your mind.

5 CRITICAL EVALUATION OF RESEARCH

OVERVIEW

This chapter introduces you to techniques for critically evaluating research reports and combining your findings into an integrated picture of knowledge related to your topic. Because your own research must build upon the previous work in your field, it is essential that you be able to interpret this work. Often you will find two studies in the literature that report conflicting results. When this occurs, you must be able to analyze the articles and interpret the findings in light of the strengths and weaknesses of the two studies. Particularly, you should estimate how design flaws and research biases could have affected the results of each study. This chapter provides techniques to analyze research reports for evidence of (1) deliberate bias or distortion, (2) nondeliberate bias, (3) sampling bias, (4) failure to consider important variables, (5) use of weak or inappropriate measurement procedures, (6) observer bias, (7) the Hawthorne and John Henry effects, (8) contamination, and (9) demand characteristics that could distort the research results.

OBJECTIVES

After studying this chapter you should be able to:

1. Identify sections of research reports and aspects of research design that indicate possible bias or contamination.
2. Describe three procedures for combining and interpreting research evidence related to your topic.
3. Describe aspects of a research report that may indicate deliberate bias.
4. Describe ways in which a researcher can unintentionally bias his or her results.
5. Describe four types of situations that indicate sampling bias.
6. State the four questions that one should ask when evaluating measurement tools used in research projects.
7. Explain the Hawthorne Effect, the John Henry Effect, and demand characteristics, and identify research situations in which these effects may occur.
8. Explain the function of placebos in research.
9. Explain the concepts of statistical and practical significance, and use them to evaluate the significance of findings reported in research.
10. Describe sources of bias that can influence the results of interview and observational data.

INTRODUCTION

The research worker must build the research upon the knowledge accumulated by previous researchers, and a major goal of the review of the literature is to establish this foundation. Nevertheless, soon after starting a first review of the literature, you will discover that instead of a solid foundation, the previous research appears to provide a foundation of shifting sands. The findings of similar studies will often be contradictory, leaving you at a loss to decide which, if any, to accept. This problem must usually be resolved through a critical evaluation of the previous research in which the strengths and weaknesses of each study are carefully weighed, and the results are combined to produce an overall picture.

Research Quality

Although the quality of educational research is improving, evidence still indicates that much of the research published has important weaknesses that should be considered by the reviewer in weighing research results. Perhaps the most extensive study on the quality of educational research is the work of Caroline Persell.[1] Her study included all articles published in a single year in American behavioral science and education journals plus all papers presented at an annual meeting of the American Educational Research Association. This provided a total of 1,100 papers from which a sample of 390 papers was selected. A national panel of 39 outstanding researchers each evaluated 11 papers, the eleventh paper for each researcher being one that was evaluated by several other researchers in order to obtain estimates of the reliability of the ratings. Each paper was rated on a 5-point scale on a number of variables. A total of 43 percent of the papers were rated below average or incompetent in terms of their contribution to theory; 35 percent were rated at this level on their contribution to practice; and 39 percent on their use of research methods. These results are generally in agreement with an earlier study by E. Wandt[2] of 125 articles; and a study by N. E. W. Ward, B. W. Hall, and C. F. Schramm that evaluated a sample of 121 articles published in 44 journals.[3] Even if we discount some of these findings on the grounds that experienced researchers have high standards and tend to be critical, the conclusion remains that a substantial percentage of studies published in education have serious deficiencies.

In Persell's study the judges indicated reasons for their ratings of below

1. Caroline H. Persell, *Quality, Careers and Training in Educational and Social Research* (Bayside, NY: General Hall, 1976).
2. Edwin Wandt, ed., *A Cross-section of Educational Research* (New York: David McKay, 1965).
3. N. E. W. Ward, B. W. Hall, and C. F. Schramm, "Evaluation of Published Educational Research: A National Survey," *American Educational Research Journal* 12 (1975): 109–128.

average or incompetent. Of the 178 papers that received poor ratings on theory or practice, the judges thought that 59 percent dealt with an important problem but contributed little to its understanding, while 25 percent dealt with unimportant problems. For papers that received low ratings on methodology, the most frequently cited reasons were poor data analysis (25 percent), poor research design (24 percent), and poor data collection (15 percent). Other reasons for low ratings included poor reporting, poor interpretation, and inadequate analysis. Correlations between ratings in the three rating areas were high, ranging from .68 to .91. This suggests that papers that are weak in one area tend to be weak in the others. Or, put another way, a substantial number of papers were generally weak across the rating areas.

A more recent study compared the quality of research articles published in the *Journal of Educational Research*, (*JER*) in 1970 with those published in 1980.[4] The following quality criteria were applied: statistics used, source of funding, experimental versus nonexperimental, focus of research topic, number of subjects, affiliations of researchers, track record of researchers, number and recency of references and number of citations of *JER* articles in other journals. Of the 13 quality indicators used, eight showed marked improvement. Especially noteworthy was an increase in the use of more sophisticated statistics, number of references cited, and use of experimental research design.

Analyses of educational research tend to be directed primarily to weaknesses rather than strengths and therefore obscure the fact that many good studies are being conducted. This emphasis on the weaknesses of educational research is continued in many research methods courses in which the student is often asked to evaluate poor articles critically. One reason that instructors select weak articles for students to evaluate is probably to emphasize the danger of accepting research findings uncritically, which can, of course, lead to misinterpretations and unsound decisions. Also, during the time graduate students are learning about research methods, they can more easily detect the obvious weaknesses found in poor articles than the more subtle weaknesses found in better articles. Since both good and poor research is reported in the educational literature, your real task is to evaluate the articles that are relevant to your problem, give more weight to the better research, and estimate how the results of a given study might have been altered due to weaknesses in the research process. You can then combine the results into an accurate composite picture of the state of knowledge in your area of interest.

Mistakes, oversights, and biases may occur at any stage of the research process, from the initial steps taken in problem definition to the final phases of statistical analysis. The research worker's effectiveness in detecting these errors

4. Charles K. West, Colleen Carmody, and William M. Stallings, "The Quality of Research Articles in the *Journal of Education Research,* 1970 and 1980," *Journal of Educational Research* 77, no. 2 (1983): 70–76.

is dependent for the most part upon two factors: knowledge and understanding of the total research process in education, and knowledge in the specific field of his review. Thus, this chapter should properly be studied after one has mastered the next thirteen chapters, which cover the entire research process. Because the chapters are arranged sequentially in terms of the skills required at each step of the research process, however, it is placed here. Skill in critical evaluation of research is needed early in the research process so that you can determine the strengths and weaknesses of previous research in your area of interest. Students who cannot properly evaluate the weaknesses of previous research may well repeat them in their own research project. In contrast, students who can avoid these weaknesses stand a good chance of making a substantial contribution to their area of interest.

Each topic discussed here is covered more fully in a later chapter. Therefore, if you cannot understand a particular topic, you are advised to look it up in the index and read ahead in the appropriate chapter. Also, you may profit by supplementing your reading of this chapter with study of the research evaluation checklist presented in Appendix B.

Systematic Literature Analysis

One of the most important and difficult tasks that you must complete before starting your research is to pull together the research findings that are relevant to your topic, extract useful knowledge, and draw some general conclusions. Many procedures can be used to combine research findings of related studies and estimate the overall significance of the combined results.[5] We will discuss three quantitative procedures that differ in difficulty and information required, and compare them with the traditional narrative review method. We should emphasize that all these methods assume either an exhaustive review of literature or the selection of a representative sample of studies related to a given topic or hypothesis. If a biased sample of studies is selected, then the combined results of the studies will also be biased.

The Traditional Review

Prior to the landmark article by Gene Glass on meta-analysis in 1976, (see Annotated References) virtually all reviews followed the traditional pattern. Such reviews usually involve locating relevant studies that have reported statistically significant results and reviewing these studies using a narrative

5. See R. Rosenthal in the Annotated References at the end of this chapter.

style. More emphasis is given to the better studies, and the better narrative reviews also attempt to pull together the significant results into a composite picture of the state of knowledge in the area reviewed, often using a table to summarize findings or a simple quantitative procedure such as counting the number of significant versus nonsignificant studies (i.e., vote counting). Such reviews have been criticized by many researchers as being subjective, not using specific criteria for inclusion of studies in the review, and placing too much emphasis on statistical significance as the sole criterion of evaluating results. The most serious weakness, however, is that most traditional reviews have not employed a statistical procedure for combining the results of all relevant research into a single quantitative estimate of treatment effect. Light and Pillemer (see Annotated References) clearly illustrate the deficiencies of narrative reviews by describing two reviews of studies related to the effect of environment on the IQs of adopted children. Although the two authors reviewed the *same* group of studies, they reached *opposite* conclusions.

Vote Counting

The first approach and by far the easiest to use was recommended by Gregg Jackson.[6] One version of this method involves classifying all studies into four categories: (1) significant positive results; that is, in the direction hypothesized (+), (2) nonsignificant (+), (3) nonsignificant (−), and (4) significant negative results (−). Even when there are no individual studies reporting significant results, if the nonsignificant results are nearly all in the same direction this trend may be significant. For example, suppose you locate 30 studies that relate to a specific hypothesis. If 25 studies report findings in the hypothesized direction but nonsignificant, and 5 report nonsignificant findings in the opposite direction, the trend for the 30 studies is significant at the .001 level in the hypothesized direction. In addition to being easy to use, this method permits the classification of virtually all studies. More precise methods of combining research findings require additional information, and studies not reporting this information cannot be classified. Either the sign test or chi-square can be used to determine the statistical significance of the combined data.[7] Its greatest weakness is that it considers only the direction of the effect for each study and includes no estimate of its *magnitude*. A serious limitation of vote counting is that a large number of studies are needed to obtain an accurate composite picture.

6. See the Annotated References at the end of chapter 4.
7. Although simple to use, the vote-counting procedure can produce misleading results, failing to detect an effect even when a fairly large effect size is present. See Larry V. Hedges and Ingram Olkin, in the Annotated References at the end of this chapter.

The Chi-Square Method

An approach advocated by N. L. Gage takes into account the size of the sample and the magnitude of the relationship or difference reported in each study.[8] The model is based on the fact that any p value can be transformed into a chi-square with two degrees of freedom. This method involves first converting whatever inferential statistics are reported in each study (e.g., t, F, r) into exact probability (p) values by checking the appropriate statistical tables.[9] The probability values are next converted to chi-square values.[10] Because chi-square values and degrees of freedom (df) are additive, the chi-squares and dfs for all studies are then summed. To determine the overall level of significance of the studies being combined, it is only necessary to check in a regular chi-square probability table for the summed values of chi-square and degrees of freedom.

The main limitation of the chi-square method is that it is based on the assumption that the studies being combined are independent of one another. In many studies, several significance tests are carried out on the same subjects. These tests are not independent, so the investigator must include only one probability value for each study. Gage suggests that the least significant result from each study be used, since this will lead to the most conservative conclusion. Another option would be to compute the probability value for the finding in each study that is most relevant to your problem.

Meta-Analysis

In recent years, the meta-analysis approach developed by Gene Glass and his colleagues (see Annotated References) has been widely adopted by researchers. This method involves converting the findings of each study to an *effect size* (Δ). For studies that compare an experimental and control group, the effect size is computed by subtracting the mean score of the control group on the dependent variable from the experimental group mean and dividing by the control group standard deviation.[11] Similar formulas have been developed to convert most inferential statistics, such as t-ratios, F-ratios, percentages, and correlation coefficients to an effect size. The mean of the effect sizes for all studies included

---

8. See N. L. Gage, *The Scientific Basis of the Art of Teaching* (New York: Teachers College Press, 1978), chap. 1.
9. There are also computer programs available that convert a given statistical finding into an exact probability value.
10. The formulas for converting p to chi-square are given in Lyle V. Jones and Donald W. Fiske, "Models for Testing the Significance of Combined Results," *Psychological Bulletin* 50, no. 5 (1953): 375–382. A table for converting p to chi-square may be found in Mordecai H. Gordon, Edward H. Loveland, and Edward E. Cureton, "An Extended Table of Chi-Square for Two Degrees of Freedom for Use in Combining Probabilities From Independent Samples," *Psychometrika* 17, (1952): 311–316.
11. $\Delta = \dfrac{\overline{X}_{Exp} - \overline{X}_{Con}}{SD_{Con}}$

in the research review is then calculated to estimate the typical effect of the phenomenon under study. For example, a meta-analysis of the effects of psychotherapy on alcoholism combined the results of twenty experiments in which control groups were employed.[12] The dependent variable in this analysis was "success rate," which was usually defined as abstinence or near abstinence. Success rates for experimental and control groups in each study were compared to estimate the effect of treatment. The average success rate for experimental groups was 51 percent versus 33 percent for control groups. This represents a difference of .96 standard deviation. These results suggest that the overall effect of psychotherapy is positive. A correlation of .49 was found between the hours of therapy provided in each experiment and the success rate. The reviewers also examined kinds of therapy and duration of the effect. Certainly the methods of quantification used in this meta-analysis give the reviewer a better understanding of the effects of psychotherapy than would emerge from less sophisticated methods of data integration, such as vote counting.

Compared with other methods of integrating research data, the meta-analysis technique has advantages and disadvantages. Several authors, including Gregg Jackson, Robert Rosenthal, Robert Slavin and Frederic Wolf have discussed advantages and limitations of this procedure that should be considered by anyone who plans to conduct a meta-analysis.[13] Glass and his associates devoted a chapter in their book to the most common criticisms of their procedure and give well-thought-out arguments to counter them. Despite the limitations of meta-analysis, it is currently the best available method for cumulating and integrating the results of research.

Perhaps the most persistent criticism of meta-analysis is the inclusion of data from poor studies.[14] In meta-analysis all studies that provide evidence related to the question under investigation are included, regardless of quality. Glass justifies this approach by pointing out that methodologically weak studies often report results similar to those found in stronger studies; by combining the results of all studies, these results can be accepted with more confidence. Even when the results of strong and weak studies do not agree, Glass argues that including all results will give the reviewer a better understanding of the phenomenon under investigation than if weaker studies are eliminated at the outset.

This argument is valid under the condition that the investigator looks at the results of his meta-analysis in depth. If a mean effect size is computed

12. H. J. Schlesinger, E. Mumford, and G. V Glass," A Critical Review and Indexed Bibliography of the Literature to 1978 on the Effects of Psychotherapy on Medical Utilization" (Department of Psychiatry, University of Colorado Medical Center, Denver, 1978).
13. See the Annotated References at end of chapters 4 and 5.
14. See Robert E. Slavin, "Best-Evidence Synthesis: An Alternative to Meta-Analysis and Traditional Reviews," *Educational Researcher* 15, no. 9 (1986): 5–11. This article discusses the problem of research quality and suggests an alternative to meta-analysis.

without giving close attention to the findings of specific studies, serious misinterpretations of the data could result. For example, one of the authors once did an exhaustive review of research literature related to ability grouping. Most of the studies located were one-year studies in which ability grouping was the "new innovation," while conventional grouping was the control condition. These one-year studies generally found that ability grouping resulted in higher student achievement. However, these studies were probably biased by the Hawthorne Effect. A few methodologically superior studies extended over several years and were, therefore, less subject to the Hawthorne Effect. These studies generally found no significant differences in achievement between the two grouping systems. If a meta-analysis of all studies had been done, the large number of weak studies would have produced a spurious effect favoring ability grouping.

When weak studies have larger *random errors* than strong studies, their inclusion in the meta-analysis would probably not affect the overall picture. But, when a large number of weak studies have the same *systematic bias*, their inclusion can substantially distort the average effect size obtained.

Literature Analysis as Research

In recent years an increasing number of students have reported a literature analysis (mostly meta-analyses) for their thesis or dissertation, instead of conducting primary research. The conduct of a rigorous literature analysis makes a significant contribution to our understanding of research on a particular problem. Also, because of the huge number of research reports now available, integrative research reviews such as meta-analyses are very useful in helping researchers keep up with the current state of knowledge in their interest areas.

For the student who is considering doing an extensive analysis of research literature, Harris Cooper[15] provides a very useful set of guidelines. He conceptualizes the research review as a scientific inquiry involving five stages that parallel those in primary research: problem formulation, data collection, data evaluation, analysis and interpretation, and public presentation. He then describes threats to validity that can occur at each stage. For example, in discussing data collection he identifies two potential sources of invalidity, both dealing with sampling. First, the reviewer may select a sample of research studies that is not representative of the total set of studies conducted on his research problem. Second, the individuals used in the selected studies may not be representative of the population to which results are to be generalized. Some characteristics of the population may be missing, while others may be overrepresented. Cooper also suggests ways of protecting the validity of the literature analysis at each stage.

15. See H. Cooper (1984) in the Annotated References at the end of this chapter.

TABLE 5.1

The Integrative Review Conceptualized as a Research Project

Stage Characteristics	Stage of Research				
	Problem Formulation	Data Collection	Data Evaluation	Analysis and Interpretation	Public Presentation
Research question asked	What evidence should be included in the review?	What procedure should be used to find relevant evidence?	What retrieved evidence should be included in the review?	What procedures should be used to make inferences about the literature as a whole?	What information should be included in the review report?
Primary function in review	Constructing definitions that distinguish relevant from irrelevant studies.	Determining which potentially relevant studies to examine.	Applying criteria to separate "valid" from "invalid" studies.	Synthesizing valid retrieved studies	Applying editorial criteria to separate important from unimportant information.
Procedural differences that create variation in review conclusions	1. Differences in abstractness of definition. 2. Differences in operational detail.	Differences in the research contained in sources of information.	1. Differences in quality criteria. 2. Differences in the influence of non-quality criteria.	Differences in rules of inference.	Differences in guidelines for editorial judgment.
Sources of potential invalidity in review conclusions	1. Narrow concepts may make review conclusions less general. 2. Superficial operational detail may obscure interacting variables.	1. Accessed studies may be qualitatively different from the target population of studies. 2. People sampled in accessible studies may be different from the target population.	1. Nonquality factors may cause improper weighting of study information. 2. Omissions in study reports may make conclusions unreliable.	1. Rules for distinguishing patterns from noise may be inappropriate. 2. Review-based evidence may be used to infer causality.	1. Omission of review procedures may make conclusions irreproducible. 2. Omission of review findings and study procedures may make conclusions obsolete.

SOURCE: Reprinted from Cooper, Harris M., "Scientific Guidelines for Conducting Integrative Research Reviews." *Review of Educational Research*, Summer 1982, vol. 52, no. 2, pp. 291–302. Copyright 1982, American Educational Research Association, Washington D.C. By permission of the publisher and author.

Cooper's guidelines for conducting an integrative review are summarized in table 5.1. In planning a review, you should read Cooper's article and refer to this table. For example, suppose you have developed a tentative literature review plan and want to evaluate its soundness. Using Cooper's procedure, you would analyze four main aspects of the plan (the four Stage Characteristics of the first column of table 5.1). Consider one such aspect, "Research question asked." You would check the soundness of your research question formulation by answering the five questions across the top row of the table. If your plan deals adequately with all the questions and procedures listed in table 5.1, you may feel confident that you will produce a thorough and valid integrative review of the findings related to your research question.

FACTORS TO CONSIDER IN EVALUATING RESEARCH

Formulation of the Research Hypothesis or Objective

In critically evaluating a research project, you should determine whether the research hypothesis or objective is specific and clearly stated. An ambiguous, broadly stated hypothesis is a sign that the researcher has not analyzed the problem in sufficient detail. Suppose the only statement of the researcher's hypothesis is that use of audiovisual materials in lectures will result in gains in student achievement. This hypothesis leaves many important questions unanswered. What types of lectures? What types of student achievement? What is the rationale or theoretical basis for the hypothesis? The unfortunate consequence of ambiguous, broadly stated hypotheses is that they yield only ambiguous, broadly stated conclusions when the study is completed. Suppose the hypothesis were not confirmed. What can one conclude about the value of audiovisual materials in lectures? Very little, since the hypothesis as stated provided little basis for expecting either positive or negative results. Therefore, as a first step in evaluating a research project, we advise you to examine critically whether the researcher's hypothesis or objective was developed specifically from theory and previous research findings, and whether it meets the criteria presented in chapter 2.

Deliberate Bias or Distortion

The goal of research must be the discovery of scientific truth. Unfortunately, a few persons who carry out educational research are more interested in obtaining evidence to support a particular viewpoint than in discovering truth. Whenever you have reasons for wanting your research to support a particular viewpoint, the likelihood of bias is greatly increased. Occasionally a researcher will be so emotionally involved with a topic that the researcher deliberately slants findings or even structures a design to produce a predetermined result.[16] Such cases of deliberate bias are usually easy to detect because the same emotional involvement that motivates the individual to bias the work is usually reflected in the individual's research report. Studies that are introduced with "this study was conducted to prove" must be considered suspect. Scientists do not carry out their work to prove a point, but to get an answer.

The use of emotionally charged words or slanted or intemperate language is the most obvious indicator of a biased viewpoint. For example, in reviewing the literature on aptitude testing, the authors found an article entitled "The Reign of ETS" (Educational Testing Service).[17] Since the word "reign" in this context appeared slanted, we were not surprised to find that article was highly critical of ETS and aptitude testing. Only quotations and studies illustrating the weaknesses of testing were cited. An unbiased article would have reviewed research on both sides of the issue in order that readers could weigh the pros and cons and come to their own conclusions.

Occasionally, one encounters an article in which the investigator appears to be deliberately trying to mislead the reader. For example, misleading statistics are sometimes found in reports of survey research in which results are reported in percentages. In reviewing survey studies, pay close attention to the number of cases upon which the percentages are based. If the number of cases is not reported, you should view the results with suspicion because they may be based on very few cases. To illustrate, David Martin discussed some misleading statistics published by the Children's Defense Fund in a report entitled *Children Out of School in America*.[18] The report stated that of all the secondary students who had been suspended more than once in census tract 22 in Columbia, South Carolina, 33 percent had been suspended two times and 67 percent had been suspended three or more times. Actually, the survey had found only three children in the entire census tract who had been suspended more than once. One of these children had been suspended twice and the other two children three or more times. Another part of the report stated that 25 percent of the 16- and 17-year-olds in a housing project in Portland, Maine, were out of school. The fact is that only eight children were surveyed, and two of them were found to be out of school. This example demonstrates that very impressive percentages reported in survey research may be virtually meaningless if they are based on only a few cases. Such percentage data are especially suspect if published by an organization that is attempting to prove a point or build a case supporting a particular point of view.

16. P. Evans, "The Burt Affair—Sleuthing in Science," *APA Monitor*, no. 12 (1976): 1, 4.
17. Allan Naire et al., "The Reign of ETS," *Today's Education* 69 (1980): 58–64.
18. David L. Martin, "Firsthand Report: How Flawed Statistics Can Make an Ugly Picture Look Even Worse," *American School Board Journal* 162, no. 3 (1975): 57–59.

The reader may also be misled by studies that report research results to several decimal places, thus creating the illusion that these results are highly accurate. W. P. Dickson attributes this tendency to the fact that many computer programs print the results of statistical analyses to several decimals.[19] Few, if any, measures employed in education are sufficiently accurate to justify reporting results to more than two decimal places.

Another form of deliberate bias occurs when researchers focus on surprising or newsworthy findings, while minimizing weaknesses in the research that reduce the validity or generalizability of the findings. Often the complete research report clearly states the limitations of the research, but these are omitted in speeches, shorter articles for "popular consumption," or news interviews. As a result, the researcher gets a good deal of publicity and the public is misled. Other researchers invariably challenge such biased reporting, but these challenges, however valid, are rarely reported in mass media.[20]

Even when a scientist attempts to report his findings objectively, they will usually be distorted by mass media in order to make them brief, interesting, and "more newsworthy." Thus, you are well advised to believe nothing about scientific research that you read in the newspapers until you have checked the facts in the original research report.

Nondeliberate Bias

Remember that we are all products of an environment that subtly shapes and distorts our perceptions in innumerable ways. As a result, biases can influence the work of even the most competent scientists without their awareness of what is happening. Sir Francis Galton, for example, argued in his treatise *Hereditary Genius* that the English were superior intellectually to Africans because in almost every instance of conflict between the two, the English won. He overlooked the fact that the English had guns and the Africans had spears. To a less biased observer, differences in weaponry rather than differences in intelligence would be a more tenable explanation of the English victories.[21]

The researcher who has an emotional stake in the outcome of the research is especially susceptible to bias. Many persons who are emotionally involved with the topic of their research will not deliberately bias this research. Nevertheless, a strong likelihood of bias exists because individuals may unconsciously slant their work in a hundred different ways. They may make certain systematic

19. W. P. Dickson, "Insignificant Figures, Statistical Insignificance, and Misconclusions," *Journal of Research in Science Teaching* 10, no. 2 (1973): 183–185.
20. See Russell H. Weigal and Jeffrey J. Pappas, "Social Science and the Press, A Case Study and Its Implications," *American Psychologist* 36 (1981): 480–487, for an interesting report of this form of bias and the contribution to it by the news media.
21. See Frank P. Besag, "Social Darwinism, Race, and Research," *Educational Evaluation and Policy Analysis* 3 (1981): 55–69, for a discussion of racism as an influence in educational research.

"errors" in sampling, in selecting measures, in scoring the responses of subjects, in the way they treat subjects, in observations of performance, in recording of research data, and in analyzing and interpreting results, all of which tend to favor the outcome they want.

Objectivity is always difficult to attain in the behavioral sciences and is probably impossible when you are emotionally involved with your topic. You should try to avoid working in such areas whenever possible. If your position is such that you must do research in an area where you are involved emotionally, have your design checked by several other researchers for omissions or unconscious biases. One of the authors was once directed to conduct a study comparing the effectiveness of second lieutenants who had received commissions through the Officer Candidate School (OCS) of the U.S. Air Force with those who had received commissions through the ROTC. Realizing some bias in favor of the OCS graduates, he had the design carefully checked by other psychologists. One phase of the experiment called for a comparative rating of the effectiveness of officers from the two groups in drilling a company of basic trainees. Officers to be evaluated were to be instructed to report to the drill field in khaki uniform. Raters were not to be told the source of the commission of the officers being rated. One psychologist, upon reviewing these plans, pointed out that the officers who had graduated from OCS would be immediately recognized, as they were required to have their khaki shirts tailored to a close fit, whereas the ROTC officers wore loose-fitting shirts, which they purchased from the post exchange. Although trying, at least on the conscious level, to avoid bias in this research, the author had "forgotten" this difference in uniforms when designing the research. This clue to the source of commission would have permitted the raters to have reflected their biases in their ratings. In summary, look for the following clues when attempting to locate possible biases in a research report:

1. Does the phraseology used suggest that the research worker is inclined to favor one side of the question?
2. Is emotional or intemperate language of either a favorable or an unfavorable nature employed?
3. Does the person hold a theoretical position or have a stake in a particular point of view, or does the researcher belong to a group (racial, vocational, religious, political, ethnic, etc.) that would predispose the person in a given direction about the subject of the research?

Sampling Bias

All the points that must be remembered in setting up the procedures for selecting a sample for your own research should be applied to evaluating the sampling techniques used by other researchers. Sampling bias in one form or another probably weakens more educational studies than any other factor. (Sampling techniques are discussed in chapter 6.) Let us review some forms of sampling bias that should be looked for in evaluating the research of others.

1. *Did the study use volunteers?* Volunteer groups are rarely representative, differing at least in motivation level from nonvolunteers. Motivation is, of course, an extremely important variable in most educational research. A basic weakness of most questionnaire studies is that the persons responding are essentially "volunteers," who may differ greatly from the nonresponding subjects. The results of studies using volunteer groups can probably be safely applied to other volunteer groups, but not to the population from which the volunteers were drawn. In many field studies, however, such as research on teaching effectiveness, the results will probably be applied to volunteers in other teaching situations, so the use of volunteers is appropriate.

Because of the legal and ethical constraints discussed in chapter 3, many studies cannot be carried out with human subjects unless the informed consent of the subjects (or their parents in the case of minors) has been obtained. It is therefore pointless to reject all research that employs volunteers, since in most instances the choice is either to use volunteers or not do the research. Instead, review the characteristics of the volunteer sample reported by the researcher.

Consider these characteristics along with the information given in chapter 6 on frequently found characteristics of volunteer samples. This will permit you to draw tentative conclusions about the population from which the volunteers were obtained. In effect you can ask: "In what ways have the results of this study probably been altered because of the use of volunteers?" You can then reassess the results so as to determine their probable relevance to the population. Such adjustments, of course, will be crude approximations, but they still give you useful insights about the population. For example, in a study of the vocational aspirations of young adults, a volunteer sample might be expected to have higher aspirations than the population because volunteers are likely to be better educated, of higher social-class status, more intelligent, and higher in need for achievement.[22] Of course, these would not be characteristics of all volunteer samples, and your interpretation of the results should also reflect information provided by the researcher about the specific volunteer sample.

2. *Have subjects been lost?* Studies reporting losses of subjects in one or more of the groups involved can usually be expected to have sampling bias. The reason for this bias is that subjects are not lost on a random basis. The subjects lost will generally be different from the ones who remain with the study until its completion. The nature and magnitude of these differences, and therefore their effect upon the research results, are difficult to estimate. Another source of bias when subjects are lost in experimental studies is that different levels of attrition occur in experimental and control groups. For example, subjects in the experi-

22. See R. Rosenthal and R. L. Rosnow (1975) in the Annotated References at the end of this chapter.

mental group are often required to complete a time-consuming treatment such as participating in a remedial writing program, while no special demands are made on the control group. Under these conditions the rate of attrition often will be much higher for the experimental group. Thus, even if the two groups were closely comparable at the outset, they may differ considerably at the end of the study because of this difference in attrition.

3. *In an effort to get subjects who differ in the variable being studied, have groups been selected that also differ in other important respects?* Causal-comparative studies often suffer from this form of sampling bias. Some of the early studies of relationships between cigarette smoking and lung cancer illustrate such bias. The "heavy smoker" samples were obtained in large cities, the "nonsmoker" samples came from rural areas. These two groups were vastly different in many factors other than smoking, such as living habits, amounts of impurities in the air breathed, and pressures of daily life. With sampling biases of this magnitude, it would be difficult for such studies to link lung cancer to smoking with any degree of confidence.

4. *Are subjects extremely nonrepresentative of the population?* Few educational studies are able to employ truly random or representative samples of national populations. Yet, unless samples are extremely biased, the results often have important implications for the population. For example, although no one would assert that a sample of poor readers taken from the different school districts in Los Angeles County is representative of the nation as a whole, a study involving this sample may well have national implications. This is because most American public schools have much in common, and pupils in a large heterogeneous area such as Los Angeles County who are having reading problems are probably quite similar to pupils in other areas of the country. As the sample becomes less heterogeneous and less representative, however, the general significance of the findings diminishes. Subjects from a single district may lead to a less useful study because of unique district policies concerning reading instruction. On the other hand, a study using subjects from an obviously nontypical school district, such as one in which 80 percent of the students are Hispanic, may have no general implications because of the nonrepresentative nature of the group and the relationship between bilingualism and reading difficulties. Similarly, a study of attitudes toward blacks using a sample from New Orleans, or a study of attitudes toward smoking using a sample from Salt Lake City, would produce little information of general significance, although such studies might throw much light on the situation in the area sampled. Since most studies are unable to employ broad representative samples, the investigator can help the reader interpret the findings by describing the sample in detail with emphasis upon the characteristics of the sample that are probably different from the broad population.

In some studies much more care is devoted to obtaining a representative experimental group than a representative control group. This difference probably stems from the erroneous notion of inexperienced researchers that the experimental group is far more important and that any subjects will serve for the control group. This form of bias often occurs in experimental studies of some types of exceptional children, such as the severely retarded, who occur rarely in the general population. In this case the investigator uses all the available exceptional children in the experimental group and then draws the control group from the normal population. All subjects in an experimental study should be drawn from the same population. Because the performance of the experimental group must be weighed against the control group, a biased control group can obviously lead to erroneous results. Thus, careless selection of the control group should be watched for. In reviewing the research of others, remember that nonrepresentative samples do not produce data of general significance; rather, they often yield results that are misleading and can lead to serious blunders if applied to the general population. When such a study is read, the findings must be interpreted with the sampling bias in mind.

Have Important Variables Been Overlooked?

The environments in which most educational studies are carried out are extremely complex, and as a result investigators cannot control, and for that matter are usually not aware of, all the variables in the situation that might affect their results. Nevertheless, researchers should be able to identify and should attempt to control the most important variables that relate to their research. Many studies are found in education that have overlooked or failed to control important variables. Such studies usually produce misleading results because the influence of the uncontrolled variable upon the dependent variable cannot be assessed. For example, many early studies comparing the effectiveness of televised instruction with conventional classroom instruction failed to control preparation time and teaching ability. The usual procedure was to select the best teacher available and give this person the full day to prepare a TV lesson. Progress of TV pupils was then compared with progress of pupils in conventional classrooms having average teachers who taught the usual four to six classes daily. The results, which were loudly hailed as proof that television had some intrinsic merit that greatly increased learning, were in fact nothing more than a demonstration that better teachers who have more preparation time do a better job. Better-controlled studies concerned with TV instruction showed little or no difference compared with conventional classroom instruction.

A study by C. R. Atherton attempted to compare the achievement of three groups of college students who had been exposed to the same content with lecture, discussion, and independent study methods.[23] Students in the lecture

---

23. C. R. Atherton, "Lecture, Discussion, and Independent Study Instructional Methods Revisited," *Journal of Experimental Education* 40 (1972): 24–28.

and discussion treatments were exposed to the material for three 50-minute periods. But students in the independent study treatment were given the material and *told* to study it for three hours during the week. There was no real control on how much time they devoted to study or when they studied. Therefore, students in this group could have studied more than three hours or not at all and could have studied immediately before their achievement was measured or immediately after they received the materials. This failure to control study times makes any comparison of the effectiveness of the three treatments meaningless.

David Warden describes several cases in which studies of children's language have provided conflicting results.[24] For example, a study by E. Clark found that two- to five-year-old children were deficient in their comprehension of the prepositions *in, on,* and *under* when they were required to place objects at locations specified by the prepositions (e.g., *on* the table or *under* the cot).[25] Clark had overlooked the fact that his procedure not only required comprehension of the prepositions but also involved the additional task of manipulating the objects. When R. Grieve and his associates separated comprehension from manipulation of the objects, they were able to demonstrate that two- and three-year-olds did comprehend these prepositions.[26]
Inasmuch as each of us brings a different background of perception and experience to focus upon a given problem, it is not surprising that one person may overlook the importance of a variable that is immediately apparent to another. The best way to avoid overlooking important variables in your own research is to have your design studied and criticized by several other researchers before starting to collect data. The previous research that you review also exposes you to a number of different viewpoints about your research area and reduces your chances of overlooking or failing to control an important variable. Many such oversights can be traced to a careless and inadequate review of the literature.

Critical Evaluation of Measurement Techniques

Many of the weaknesses and limitations of educational research can be attributed to the inadequacies of our measures. The tools and techniques of educational measurement available to us are often crude and of doubtful validity. A thorough check of all tests and measurement techniques reported in

24. David A. Warden, "Experimenting With Children's Language," *British Journal of Psychology* 72 (1981): 217–222.
25. E. Clark, "Non-linguistic Strategies and the Acquisition of Word Meaning," *Cognition* 2 (1973): 161–182.
26. R. Grieve, R. Hoogenraad, and D. Murray, "On the Young Child's Use of Lexis and Syntax in Understanding Locative Instructions," *Cognition* 5 (1977): 235–250.

all the studies you review would be a very time-consuming task, and we do not recommend it for students doing their first review of the literature. You should make a check, however, of the measures used in any studies that are of major importance in your review. Check thoroughly any study that has yielded findings that make an important contribution to your area of review or have an important bearing on your own research design. This review not only helps you interpret relevant research but also helps you select measures for your own research. If standard measures are cited with which you are not familiar, you should study a specimen set, consult the *Mental Measurements Yearbooks,* and check other sources of information (to be discussed in chapter 7). If the measure used is new or has been developed for the research being evaluated, obtain a copy and weight the measure carefully against your own knowledge of test development techniques and the theoretical constructs upon which the measure is based. You can only evaluate the findings of the research you read after you have carefully appraised the measurement tools that produced these findings and considered the probable effects of flaws in these instruments.

Let us briefly summarize some of the questions that you should ask when evaluating the measurement tools in research closely pertinent to your own topic.[27]

1. *What reliability data are available?* Reliability studies give us information on the degree to which a measure will yield similar results for the same subjects at different times or under different conditions. In other words, they provide us with an estimate of consistency. Several procedures can be used to estimate reliability, and the type of reliability calculated and the reliability coefficient should both be checked. Because tests of very low reliability have large errors of measurement, they often obscure differences or relationships that would be revealed by the use of more reliable instruments. Thus, you should carefully consider the possible effects of low reliability on reported results of studies you evaluate and should not reject a promising hypothesis for your own study because of negative findings based on unreliable measures.

2. *What validity evidence is available?* As we shall show in chapter 7, there are four major types of validity. Study the validity evidence carefully because interpretation of the research results hinges on the validity of the measures upon which these results are based. The absence of extensive validity data in a new measure does not mean the measure lacks validity, but it definitely limits the interpretations that can be made. Many inexperienced research workers accept standardized educational measures at face value and assume that these measures are valid, although little evidence is put forth by the test publisher to support this assumption. In the case of measures of dubious validity it is generally safer to consider the results reported to be tentative at best.

---

27. The procedures for evaluating tests are discussed in chapter 7.

3. *Is the measure appropriate for the sample?* In evaluating the research of others, you should remember that even a well-standardized and generally accepted measure will have little value if applied to an inappropriate sample. A typical mistake made by inexperienced researchers is to use a measure that is more appropriate for some subsamples of the research group than others, therefore biasing results in favor of the subsamples whose background gives them an advantage on the measure. Occasionally tests are employed that are either too easy or too difficult for the majority of the sample measured. For example, a study of achievement of children at different ability levels will have little meaning if the test used has too low a ceiling, thus limiting the level of achievement that a superior student can display.

4. *Are test norms appropriate?* Many educational research projects compare the performance of the research sample with normative data that have been provided with the measure. If normative data are to be used, the comparability between the research group and the test norm group should be checked. Some tests, although generally applicable to the sample tested, have single items that are invalid. Some of the older intelligence tests, for example, have drawings of such objects as automobiles, airplanes, and telephones that are so different in appearance from the form familiar to today's children that the test item so illustrated may have lost much of its validity. Such errors, although not immediately apparent to most adults, have a significant influence on test scores.

Subtle forms of measurement bias may also make significant differences in research findings. For example, the authors recently encountered a questionnaire being used in an educational follow-up study in which the respondent was to rate various aspects of a school attended using five quality levels. The quality levels provided were "excellent," "superior," "very good," "average," and "below average." You will note that, on this scale, average is not located in the middle of the alternate choices. When asked why the choices were arranged in this way, the research worker stated that he had observed in previous questionnaires that more responses occur above the average line of the scale, and he had, therefore, provided an extra classification on the above-average side. He was surprised to find that the ratings he had obtained in this follow-up study were somewhat higher than those obtained in previous studies of the same school. When using the quality levels just mentioned, the mean response fell between the "superior" and "very good" categories as compared with a mean response between "average" and "good" in previous studies. This suggested a higher evaluation of the course of study being followed up. Actually, however, the errors of leniency and central tendency (see chapter 12) would lead most respondents to rate a course of study average or slightly above average if they had no strong feelings about it one way or the other. Because most people consider the average rating to be the one that falls in the middle, when the research worker changed the names of the categories, the respondents continued to check the middle category or the one adjacent to and higher than the middle. Thus, in terms of the mean position of the responses on a 5-point scale, no change occurred, but in terms of the adjectives employed, there was an apparent improvement in the respondents' evaluation of the school. Use of unbalanced response choices in which more opportunities are available for a favorable response than for an unfavorable response will tend to yield responses with a favorable bias. The danger of such biases is well known to experienced measurement specialists, and errors of the sort just described are more likely to be found in measures developed specifically for the research project by an inexperienced researcher. If the use of such measures is reported in research projects pertinent to your field of interest, request copies in order that you may study them for biases of the sort previously described.

Observer Bias

Human beings have a disturbing tendency to see what they want to see, hear what they want to hear, and remember what they want to remember. **Observer bias** has been recognized as a problem by workers in the physical sciences for centuries, and techniques to control such bias are routinely included in physical science experiments. Workers in the behavioral sciences not only have attempted to control observer errors, but also have studied these biases and found them to be much more subtle and complex than physical scientists had imagined.

J. Rostand tells a remarkable but true story that illustrates the dangers of observer bias, even in scientific areas such as physics that deal with phenomena that are much simpler, more concrete, and more adaptable to measurement than are the elusive substances of the behavioral sciences.[28] This example deals with the N ray, which was discovered by a distinguished French physicist, René Blondlot, while investigating X rays, which had been discovered a short time earlier by Röntgen. After discovering the N ray, Blondlot went on to study its characteristics. He found the ray increased the brightness of any luminous object. A Nernst filament was found to be a rich source of N rays and produced a radiation so intense that Blondlot doubted that anyone with eyes could fail to see it. In fact, of the many persons who were permitted to observe these rays, Blondlot reports only three or four who failed to see them. As his experiments continued, Blondlot discovered that the sun was a source of N rays. He learned that N rays could be stored in certain substances such as quartz and later reemitted. Further experiments revealed that external stresses caused certain substances to emit N rays. Finally, Blondlot set up a series of careful experiments using three independent measures that resulted in measuring the wavelength of the N ray. The results of measurements using the three different approaches

28. Jean Rostand, *Error and Deception in Science* (New York: Basic Books, 1960).

were highly consistent. By February 1904, photographs had been taken that showed the effect of N rays on an electric spark. Upon this discovery Bordier, lecturer at Lyons Medical School, rebuked the few doubters who had not been able to see the N ray by pointing out:

> Such observers have only themselves to blame; no doubt they used faulty techniques or else the source of radiation was impaired; in any case, the existence of N rays will never again be put in doubt, particularly now that their action has been recorded *photographically*, i.e., by a purely objective method. (Rostand, 1960, p. 18)

Other researchers now began to report extensive findings from their experiments on the N ray. The experiments of one scientist revealed that sound vibrations gave rise to N rays; another found N rays emitted from a magnetic field, another from liquefied gases, and so on.

Charpentier, professor of biophysics at Nancy, discovered that N rays were liberated from the muscles and nerves of living animals and concluded that these rays might play a fundamental role in biology. Because N rays were emitted from nerves, studies of the anatomy of the nervous system became possible and were started. This technique, of course, had very important implications for medical science. For example, research workers soon discovered that changes in N radiation occurred as a consequence of certain diseases of the nervous system.

In 1904, less than two years after Blondlot had reported his original work, an imposing body of knowledge had been amassed concerning the N ray. Yet we hear nothing about N rays today. The fact is that *the N ray does not and never did exist*, and within a few short months after these later discoveries, the entire edifice erected by Blondlot and his colleagues had tumbled down.

> Doubting voices had been raised from the very beginning of Blondlot's discovery and some specialist objections had never been silenced effectively. Still, no amount of doubting or criticism had been able to halt the triumphant progress of the new science. All the world had clearly observed a phenomenon that had never existed. Then, almost overnight, the hypnotic spell was broken.
>
> The Nancy group and some of its faithful managed to put up some slight resistance, but the whole business was dropped and buried once for all. N-rays, N_1-rays, and physiological radiations would never again grace the pages of scientific journals, in which they had cut so marvelous a figure. . . .
>
> The most astonishing facet of the episode is the extraordinarily great number of people who were taken in. These people were not pseudo-scientists, charlatans, dreamers, or mystifiers; far from it, they were true men of science, disinterested, honourable, used to laboratory procedure, people with level heads and sound common sense. This is borne out by their subsequent achievements as Professors, Consultants and Lecturers. Jean Becquerel, Gilbert Ballet, Andre Broca, Zimmern, Bordier—all of them have made their contribution to science.

No less extraordinary is the *degree of consistency, and of apparent logic that pervaded the whole of this collective delusion;* all the results were consistent, and agreed within fairly narrow limits. . . .

While we have no evidence that flattery or deception was at the roots of the discovery of N-rays, we may take it that the urge to make new discoveries, so powerful in all men of science, played a considerable role from the very start. Coupled with this urge were *preconceived ideas, and autosuggestion* together with the desire to break new ground.

The remarkable history of N-rays is full of morals both for the individual, and also for the social psychologist.[29]

Although observations are sometimes deliberately biased by the researcher with an ax to grind, the more serious danger is from biases of which the researcher is unaware, such as those that occurred in research on the N ray. These undeliberate and unconscious observer biases are often not detectable from the usual research report that appears in the professional journal. For example, an interviewer may unconsciously give the subject subtle signs of approval and disapproval of different responses that will tend to encourage the subject to give the approved answer whether it is true or not. Although the information available is too limited for you to expect to detect many such biases, you should, nonetheless, search carefully for evidence of their existence, and weigh their possible effects when they are discovered.

The methods of descriptive research, especially interview and observation studies, are perhaps most susceptible to observer bias. Let us review some of the main sources of such bias that the student should watch for in critically evaluating descriptive research:

1. Does the interview guide contain leading questions? Is it structured in such a way to give the subject clues as to the preferred answer?
2. Does the observer's or interviewer's method of recording behavior or responses permit undue emphasis upon behavior that is in accordance with observer biases or expectations? The use of tape recordings greatly reduces danger of this bias.
3. Do methods of recording behavior require that the observer or interviewer draw inferences about the meaning of the behavior being observed? In general, the more inferences the observer must draw, the more the likelihood of bias. For example, an observer can usually record low-inference data such as the number of questions a teacher asks more accurately than high-inference data such as a rating of the cognitive level of each teacher question or a rating of the teacher's voice modulation used in asking each question.

29. Ibid., pp. 27–29.

4. Are questions asked that might threaten, embarrass, or annoy some respondents, thus leading them to give false or unsatisfactory replies?

5. Does the observer know the expected outcomes of the research? If the observer knows that the group being observed has been exposed to treatment that is expected to bring about certain changes in behavior, one is more likely to see these changes than when observing a group that has not been exposed to the treatment. In a review of four studies of observer errors, Rosenthal reported that over 70 percent of the recording errors found in these studies were biased in the direction of the observers' hypotheses.[30] Recent experiments that deliberately manipulate observers' expectations further confirmed this kind of bias.[31]

EFFECTS RELATED TO THE RESEARCH SITUATION

The Hawthorne Effect

In experiments involving human subjects, a great many subtle influences can distort research results. If individuals are aware that they are participating in an experiment, for example, this knowledge may alter their performance and therefore invalidate the experiment. Studies carried out at the Hawthorne Plant of the Western Electric Company first called attention to some of these factors.[32] In one of these studies the illumination of three departments in which employees inspected small parts, assembled electrical relays, and wound coils was gradually increased. The production efficiency in all departments generally went up as the light intensity increased. Experimenters found, however, that, upon decreasing the light intensity in a later experiment, the efficiency of the group continued to increase slowly but steadily. Further experiments, with rest periods and varying the length of working days and weeks, were also accompanied by gradual increases in efficiency whether the change in working conditions was for the better or for the worse. Apparently the attention given the employees during the experiment was the major factor leading to the production gains. This phenomenon is referred to by psychologists as the **Hawthorne Effect.** The factory workers who carried out the same dull, repetitive task month after month were stimulated and motivated by the attention and concern for their well-being displayed by the research workers. A new element

30. See R. Rosenthal and R. Rosnow in Annotated References at the end of this chapter.
31. See Ennio Cipani and Vicki A. Waite, "Experimenter Bias Effects: A Direct Replication," *Perceptual and Motor Skills* 51 (1980): 129–130.
32. Fritz J. Roethlisberger and William J. Dickson, *Management and the Worker* (Cambridge, MA: Harvard University press, 1939).

had been added to their dull existence—not illumination or the other variables that the researchers were studying, but the researchers themselves.

The term Hawthorne Effect has come to refer to any situation in which the experimental conditions are such that the mere fact that the subject is aware of participating in an experiment, is aware of the hypothesis, or is receiving special attention tends to improve performance. Certainly many educational experiments report changes and improvements that are due primarily to the Hawthorne Effect. For example, research in which one group of teachers continues with the same teaching methods it has previously employed while another group is trained in a new method and receives considerable help and attention in implementing this method will usually result in changes in teacher performance or pupil achievement favorable to the new methods. Many school districts, in the process of trying out new methods, frequently set up a one-year experiment in which the new method is introduced to a limited number of pupils. The results of such experiments are almost certainly influenced by the Hawthorne Effect because teachers usually approach a new method with some enthusiasm; and the students, aware that they are being taught by a new and different method, are also likely to display more interest and motivation than usual. The influence of the Hawthorne Effect can be expected to decrease as the novelty of the new method wears off, and, therefore, studies extending over a period of two or three years can be relied upon somewhat more in evaluating the effectiveness of a new technique.

The most common research strategies employed to assess the magnitude of the Hawthorne Effect (and thus remove the effect from the experimental effect) employ various kinds of control groups. For example, suppose that a control group (H) is added for whom such variables as time, effort, interest, attention, novelty, and awareness of participation are essentially equal to the experimental group (X). Then the difference in outcomes on the dependent variable between control group H and a notreatment control group (C) would represent Hawthorne Effect; and the difference between control group H and experimental group X would represent treatment effect with Hawthorne Effect removed.[33]

It is interesting that attempts to manipulate the Hawthorne Effect experimentally often have failed to produce evidence of the effect.[34] However, there is much indirect evidence that the effect operates in some studies. The prudent

33. See John G. Adair, Donald Sharp, and Cam-Loi Huynh, "Hawthorne Control Procedures in Educational Experiments: A Reconsideration of Their Use and Effectiveness" (Paper presented at the Annual Meeting of the American Educational Research Association, Washington, DC, April 1987), for an analyses of procedures used to control Hawthorne Effect.
34. See John G. Adair (1984) in the Annotated References at the end of this chapter. Also see Desmond L. Cook, *The Impact of the Hawthorne Effect in Experimental Designs in Educational Research* (Washington, DC: U.S. Office of Education, 1967). Also see Robert H. Bauernfeind and Carl J. Olson, "Is the Hawthorn Effect in Educational Experiments a Chimera?" *Phi Delta Kappan* 53 (1973): 271–273; and Patricia A. Rubeck, "Hawthorne Concept—Does It Affect Reading Progress?" *Reading Teacher* 28 (1975): 375–379.

researcher should take steps to reduce the special attention given the subjects, the novelty of experimental treatments, and the awareness of participation in a research project that may contribute to this effect. Such precautions will improve the research design whether or not the Hawthorne Effect occurs.

The John Henry Effect

The legend of John Henry tells of a black railroad worker who pitted his strength and skill at driving steel railroad spikes against a steam driver that was being tested experimentally as a possible replacement for the human steel drivers. The **John Henry Effect** refers to a situation often found in educational research in which a control group performs above its usual average when placed in competition with an experimental group that is using a new method or procedure that threatens to replace the control procedure. This phenomenon is probably quite common in educational studies in which a conventional teaching methodology is being compared with a new methodology. Teachers in the control group feel threatened by the new methodology and make a strong effort to prove that their way of teaching is as good as the new method.

This effect was named and described by Robert Heinich in 1970 while reviewing studies that compared television instruction with regular classroom teaching. He found that the classroom teachers in the control group often made a "maximum" effort, and thus their students' performance matched the performance of students who viewed televised instruction.[35] Since Heinich's work, several studies have been conducted in which the John Henry Effect appears to have operated because unusual effort in the control group has been observed, and control subjects matched or exceeded the performance of experimental subjects. Gary Saretsky, who conducted much of the study of this phenomenon, concluded that the John Henry Effect is likely to occur when an innovation is introduced in such a manner as to be perceived as threatening to jobs, status, salary, or traditional work patterns.[36]

One of the authors of this text encountered this phenomenon in a study in which teachers who had been trained in verbal skills designed to improve pupil achievement were compared with teachers who had not received the training. In order to provide comparable pupil achievement data, a one-week curriculum unit was developed, and teachers in both experimental and control groups were asked to teach this unit. Observation indicated that not only were the control-group teachers devoting a great deal of time to their preparation to teach the unit, but they were also observed to be using many of the skills that had been

35. Robert Heinich, *Technology and the Management of Instruction* (Washington, D.C.: Department of Audiovisual Instruction, 1970).
36. See Gary Saretsky (1975) in the Annotated References at the end of this chapter.

taught to the experimental-group teachers. A questionnaire sent to both groups of teachers revealed that over half of the control-group teachers had obtained some of the training materials from the experimental group. At the outset of the study, the experimental-group teachers had been asked not to share any training materials with the control teachers. However, it is obviously difficult for teachers to refuse requests of their colleagues, since many of the experimental-group teachers did make the training materials available. The result, of course, was to reduce the apparent effects of the training, since the control-group teachers were obviously making a major effort to prove that they were as good as the experimental-group teachers and had learned many of the same skills that had been taught to the experimental group.

The John Henry Effect in educational studies probably reflects in part the competitive desire to prove that "I can do just as well as those people who are being trained." It is also probable that persons who know that they are members of a control group feel psychologically threatened by a situation in which they feel they are likely to come out second best.

Saretsky provides convincing evidence that the John Henry Effect resulted in a marked increase in the achievement in control-group classrooms when these classrooms were compared with classrooms in which performance contracting was employed.[37] He obtained data on performance of the control subjects for the two years prior to the experimental year. These data showed that during the experimental year control-group gains in mathematics as measured by standardized tests were much higher than in the two preceding years. Because performance contracting is very threatening to teachers, it seems obvious that the control teachers made a very strong effort during the year of the experiment.

It is fairly easy to confuse the John Henry Effect with the Hawthorne Effect. The two have somewhat opposite effects on an experiment, however, because the Hawthorne Effect reflects the impact of being part of an experiment upon the experimental group's performance, whereas the John Henry Effect reflects the impact upon the control group in experiments where the experimental group is perceived as competing with or threatening to surpass the control group.

The Pygmalion Effect

This effect takes its name from a controversial study by Robert Rosenthal and Lenore Jacobson, reported in *Pygmalion in the Classroom*.[38] These researchers demonstrated that teachers' expectations about their students' intelligence in

37. Gary Saretsky, "The OEO P.C. Experiment and the John Henry Effect," *Phi Delta Kappan* 53 (1972): 579–581.
38. Robert Rosenthal and Lenore Jacobson, *Pygmalion in the Classroom* (New York: Holt, Rinehart and Winston, 1968).

some cases appeared to bring about changes in the students' intelligence test scores. Thus, the term **Pygmalion Effect** has come to refer to changes in the subject's behavior that are brought about by the experimenter's expectations. The effect has been replicated in some studies, but not in others. In any case, the possibility that this effect can occur should alert researchers to the importance of *not* conveying *their expectations* to the subject.

Demand Characteristics

An important characteristic of human subjects when they are participants in an experiment is that they do not perceive their participation as an isolated event but instead try to relate it to past experience and the total context of the experimental situation. In other words, they are likely to be sensitive to all aspects of the research environment and to use cues present in that environment to come to conclusions as to what the experiment is attempting to achieve, what is expected of them as subjects in the experiment, and what the researcher hopes to find. M. T. Orne has used the term **demand characteristics** to describe all the cues available to the subject regarding the nature of the research.[39] These can include rumors about the research, the setting, instructions given to the research subject, the status and personality of the experimenter, subtle clues provided by the experimenter, and the experimental procedure itself.

Orne and his associates have carried out a number of studies designed to explore the effects of demand characteristics on the performance of subjects. In one of these studies, the demand characteristics were deliberately manipulated in order to measure their effects on the outcome of an experiment.[40] Both groups of subjects were told that the study was designed to determine the effectiveness of the lie detector. However, one group was told that it was not possible to detect lying in the case of psychopathic personalities or habitual liars. The investigators hypothesized that this group would want to be detected in order to demonstrate that they were not psychopaths or habitual liars. Instructions for the other group stipulated that while it is extremely difficult to deceive the lie detector, this can be done by highly intelligent, emotionally stable, very mature persons. These instructions would create a desire on the part of the subjects to deceive the lie detector in order to appear highly intelligent, emotionally stable, and mature. The results show very large differences in the hypothesized direction between the number of persons whose lies were detected and not detected in the two groups. Since all other conditions of the experiment were identical for the two groups, this would clearly illustrate the tremendous power

39. Martin T. Orne, "Demand Characteristics and the Concept of Quasi-Controls" in *Artifact in Behavioral Research,* eds. R. Rosenthal and R. L. Rosnow (New York: Academic Press, 1969).
40. Lawrence A. Gustafson and Martin T. Orne, "Effects of Perceived Role and Role Success on the Detection of Deception," *Journal of Applied Psychology* 49 (1965): 412–417.

of demand characteristics to lead to markedly different behavior on the part of subjects.

Orne suggests three ways that the researcher can gain insight into the demand characteristics of an experiment. This information is necessary to estimate the possible effects of these cues on the performance of subjects or to determine how to restructure the research to eliminate research conditions that can distort results. The first of these is to interview subjects after the experiment in order to learn their perceptions of the experimental situation. A second procedure is to conduct preinquiry interviews with a group of subjects from the same population that will be employed in the experiment. In this case, the experimental procedures are explained to the preinquiry group in such a way as to provide them with the same information that would be available to the experimental subject. The preinquiry group, however, does not go through the experimental procedure. Participants are then asked to produce data of a type similar to what they would have produced if they had actually been subjected to the experimental treatment. If the data produced under these conditions are similar to the data obtained in the experiment, it shows that subjects in the actual experiment could have guessed what was expected of them. In a third procedure, subjects are asked to behave as if exposed to the experimental treatment, which they did not actually receive. In this case, a naive experimenter observes these "simulators," but is unaware of the fact that they are simulating the experimental effects. Since the simulators are given no information about the experiment other than that which would be available to the actual research subjects, they must guess what the subjects might do in the experimental conditions. If their behavior is similar to that of the real subjects, it would indicate that the regular subjects could be responding to the demand characteristics rather than to the experimental treatment in the same manner as the simulators.

A number of behavioral scientists have recently studied demand characteristics, their theoretical foundation, and procedures that can be used to minimize their effect. Much of this work has been reviewed by Ralph Rosnow and D. J. Davis.[41] They concluded that in order for demand characteristics to affect research findings, two requirements must be met. First, the demand characteristics must be "received" by the subject, that is, the subject must be sensitive to or aware of the experimental conditions. Second, the subject must be motivated to respond to the demand characteristics. The most common response is probably to acquiesce, that is, to play the role of a "good subject." Some subjects may be counter-acquiescent, however, and may perform in a manner opposite to the way they perceive the investigator's expectations or desires. Of course, both types of response tend to distort the results of the research.

---

41. See the Annotated References at the end of this chapter.

To reduce the subject's response to demand characteristics, Rosnow and Davis recommend that the researcher use procedures (1) to reduce the clarity of the demand characteristics, (2) to generate alternative demand characteristics that will not influence the research findings, and (3) to reduce the subject's motivation to respond to the demand characteristics. Specific procedures that can help achieve these three goals are summarized below.

Procedures for Reducing Artifact Influences in Laboratory Settings.[42]

I. Receptivity Manipulations
   A. Minimize demand clarity
      1. Measure the dependent variable in a remote setting not obviously connected to the treatment setting.
      2. Measure the dependent variable removed in time from the treatment.
      3. Avoid pretesting by using posttest only or interchangeable group designs.
      4. Use unobtrusive measures.
      5. Use "blind" procedures; that is, keep the experimenter's knowledge of the research to a minimum.
      6. Standardize and restrict the experimenter's communication with the subjects. (Since the experimenter is the main channel for communicating demand characteristics, minimize the experimenter's capacity to transmit such information.)
   B. Generate alternative demands
      1. Elicit false hypotheses about the purpose of the experiment. The false demand characteristics should be selected so that they will not interfere with possible research outcomes.
      2. Have the subjects play the role of experimenter's aide. This increases the probability that the subject will focus on the false demand characteristics as he or she plays the role of "experimenter."
II. Motivational Manipulations
   A. Give feedback of compliant behavior in a set of preexperimental trials.
   B. Maintain subject anonymity.
   C. Make the experimental setting and procedures low-keyed.
   D. Disclose the use of deception and enlist the subject's support.
   E. Use "bogus pipeline" to get subjects to monitor their behavior and reject demand-compliant responses. In the "bogus pipeline" subjects are told that a physiological monitoring device used in the experiment can detect

---

42. Adapted from Ralph L. Rosnow and D. J. Davis, "Demand Characteristics and the Psychological Experiment," *Et Cetera* 34 (1977): 301–313.

when they are lying, thus motivating them to give honest responses rather than responses that acquiesce to demand characteristics.

F. Use measures that require behavioral commitment as opposed to verbal report of commitment. For example, asking for a commitment to donate blood is more likely to elicit an honest response than merely asking for a verbal response indicating willingness to do so.

The effect of the cues available in the experimental situation upon the performance of subjects is probably a more important factor in psychological laboratory studies, such as Orne carried out, than in naturalistic field studies of the type frequently carried out in education. Furthermore, the college students who were the subjects in Orne's studies are probably much more perceptive of the demand characteristics of the experiment and more likely to respond to these cues than a child in an educational research project would. Nevertheless, in all likelihood changes in a subject's behavior related to the research situation occur to a degree in most studies in which the subject is aware of the fact that he or she has participated in an experiment. For example, Orne points out that in studies in which subjects see themselves as being evaluated, they will usually behave in such a way as to make themselves look good. This attempt to look good under research conditions is common in educational studies and is an important factor in both the Hawthorne Effect and the John Henry Effect.

PLACEBOS

A **placebo** is a chemically inert substance administered in the same manner as the drug or active substance under investigation. Placebos are employed in medical research and in educational and psychological studies in which the effects of various substances on human behavior are being tested. The purpose of the placebo is to make it impossible for subjects to determine whether or not they are receiving the active substance under study as this knowledge may have an effect upon their behavior. Many studies have demonstrated that if one group of subjects receives some sort of attention, such as the administration of a drug, while the control group receives no comparable attention, some of those receiving the drug will react in ways that cannot be explained by the chemical or medical effects of the drug. Although relatively little is known about the psychological factors causing such reactions, it seems likely that the human contact with the researcher and the subject's expectation that something will occur as a result of the substance received contribute significantly.

The results of drug studies that do not use placebos are always subject to doubt because the proportion of the effect that is attributable to psychological factors and the proportion that is caused by the drug cannot be determined. The placebo, in effect, acts as a control, permitting the psychological factors to operate. The physical or behavioral changes brought about by the active substance cannot operate in control-group subjects because the active substance is not present in the placebo. Therefore, in effect, changes caused by the active substance equal the experimental group changes minus the control group changes.[43]

In recent years the term *placebo* has been used in a broader sense to describe a control treatment that gives subjects the same amount and kind of attention as the experimental treatment but is unrelated to the dependent variable. For example, in a recent study aimed at reducing depression in children, the placebo treatment was of the same duration and in a similar format as the experimental treatments, but dealt with problems unrelated to depression.[44]

Even when placebos are used, researchers have found that if the experimenter knows which subjects received the active substance and which subjects received the placebo, this knowledge can lead to observer bias. For example, the researcher unconsciously may give the subject subtle cues, such as watching for reactions more attentively in cases where subjects have received the active substance. Therefore, most studies aimed at evaluating the effects of drugs or other substances now employ what is called the "doubleblind" technique, in which neither the experimenter nor the subject knows when the active substance or when the placebo is being taken. Obviously, in order to achieve this degree of control, the placebo must be identical to the active drug in those characteristics that may be compared by the subject, such as appearance and taste.

Although placebos play a useful role in helping to control psychological variables, many researchers fail to recognize that the control is still subject to error. If subjects know the active drug being used and its probable effect, those subjects who receive the placebo may react in the manner expected. For example, if subjects know that the active drug is a sleeping pill, they may exhibit a drowsy reaction to the placebo. The fact that these control subjects react like the subjects who received the drug would not negate the possibility of real drug effects. This error, of course, cannot occur if subjects do not know the expected effect of the drug being used.

Medical studies have demonstrated that there is considerable individual difference in reaction to placebos. Some individuals tend to react to placebos, while others do not. For example, some hospital patients will consistently report a reduction in pain following the administration of an inert substance, whereas others will not. Persons may show either a positive or negative reaction to the

43. Note that this is essentially the same strategy often used to control Hawthorne Effect. Relationships among Hawthorne Effect, John Henry Effect, and Demand Characteristics are discussed by John G. Adair (1984); see Annotated References.
44. L. Butler, S. Miezitis, R. Friedman, and E. Cole, "The Effect of Two School-Based Intervention Programs on Depressive Symptoms in Preadolescents," *American Educational Research Journal* 17 (1980): 111–119.

placebo. H. K. Beecher found that the incidence of relief reported in fifteen studies involving medical placebos ranged from 15 to 58 percent. However, he also found 35 different toxic effects that occurred after the administration of placebos.[45]

Persons who respond to placebos are referred to as "placebo reactors." There is some question as to whether this is an enduring trait or whether it varies with the situation; that is, a person may be a placebo reactor in one situation but not in another.[46] In small sampling studies, there is always a possibility that the control group will contain a larger number of placebo reactors than the experimental group. If this is the case, the results of the experiment may be negative, even though the active substance being tested has a definite effect upon the experimental subjects. Some studies have shown that if placebo reactors are screened out, significant differences sometimes emerge that would not show up otherwise.[47] As yet we know very little about the degree to which some persons are consistently placebo reactors, or whether such persons differ in personality or other respects from individuals who do not react to placebos. Some evidence suggests that these differences do exist, and until we know more about placebo reaction, differences in consistency can considerably distort research findings involving small samples.[48]

Placebos in Educational Research

Few studies in educational research employ placebos to control psychological factors.[49] In educational research, however, psychological factors can differentially affect experimental and control groups in situations where no treatment is given the control group. Therefore, it is advisable to use a "placebo treatment" for control groups so that the experimental and control conditions are psychologically similar for all subjects. For example, if a new remedial mathematics program is being administered in experimental classrooms, the researcher could introduce a new music appreciation program of similar duration into control classrooms. The music program would have no effect on mathematics achieve-

45. H. K. Beecher, "The Powerful Placebo," *American Medical Association Journal* 159 (1955): 1602–1605.

46. Patricia J. Aletky and Albert S. Carlin, "Sex Differences and Placebo Effects: Motivation as an Intervening Variable," *Journal of Consulting and Clinical Psychology* 43, no. 2 (1975): 278.

47. H. K. Beecher, A. S. Keats, F. Mosteller, and L. Lasagna, "The Effectiveness of Oral Analgesics (Morphine, Codeine, Acetylsalicylic Acid) and the Problem of Placebo 'Reactors' and 'Nonreactors,'" *Journal of Pharmacology and Experimental Therapeutics* 109 (1953): 393–400.

48. L. Lasagna, J. Mosteller, J. M. von Felsinger, and H. K. Beecher, "A Study of the Placebo Response," *American Journal of Medicine* 16 (1954): 770–779.

49. For a recent study that used placebos in educational research, see Carol K. Whalen et al., "A Social Ecology of Hyperactive Boys: Medication Effects in Structured Classroom Environments," *Journal of Applied Behavior Analysis* 12 (1979): 65–81.

ment, but would make the two treatments more similar because all classrooms are trying out a new program.

In evaluating educational research, you should be alert to studies that employ control groups that do not receive the treatment or recognition given to the experimental group. These studies are much more susceptible to the Hawthorne Effect and the John Henry Effect than those in which some sort of control treatment is employed.

EXPERIMENTER AND STATISTICAL CONTAMINATION

Contamination refers to any situation in which data that should be kept independent to satisfy the requirements for sound research have in some way become interrelated. Faulty research design often permits contamination to occur in educational studies. Contamination, in turn, tends to bias the results of the study. We discuss various ways in which contamination can weaken research design in later chapters. The major sources of contamination, as they affect interpretation of published research, are described below.

Experimenter Contamination

Experimenter contamination usually arises when the research worker has knowledge of the subject's performance on the independent variable, and this knowledge influences the observation of the behavior of the subject on the dependent variable. Let us suppose, for example, that we are doing a study of the relationship between the amount of conflict present in the home environment of the child (independent variable) and behavior in the classroom involving direct and indirect aggression (dependent variable). If the observer collected data on conflicts in the home prior to carrying out the classroom observations, there would be a strong possibility that knowledge of the child's home environment would influence the researcher's interpretation of the child's aggressive behavior in the classroom. In other words, if the researcher had hypothesized that children coming from home environments involving conflicts would display more direct aggression in the classroom, he or she would tend to look for signs of direct aggression in these children and would be likely to see more direct aggression and interpret questionable behavior as direct aggression.

Experimenter contamination is not limited to studies in which the researcher uses observational techniques. Any situation that requires the research worker to obtain data (interviews, individual testing, etc.) on one variable that could influence his perception of another variable is subject to this form of contamination.

Statistical Contamination

Statistical contamination occurs when data that have in some way become related are treated as being independent in the statistical analysis. An example of statistical contamination was encountered by one of the authors in the work of one of his doctoral candidates. The student was carrying out a study of characteristics related to success of elementary school principals. The design called for the participation of each person to be evaluated in six role-playing situations. In each situation the subject was evaluated independently by two raters on a number of pertinent behaviors. These specific evaluations were combined in order to provide an overall evaluation of the individual as a principal. In carrying out the analysis, the student found a high correlation between observer ratings in the specific area of "human relations skills" and the overall evaluations of the individual's effectiveness. From this correlation he concluded that "human relations skills' constituted by far the most important factor in the effective performance of elementary school principals. He had failed to realize, however, that because the overall rating also included the rating of human relations skills, which was the most heavily weighted of the specific rating areas, he was in effect correlating human relations skills with itself to the extent that it was part of the overall rating. Such correlations are, of course, spurious and indicate statistical contamination.

CRITICAL EVALUATION OF STATISTICAL ANALYSES

As part of Wandt's study of the quality of educational research articles, which we referred to previously, a panel of experts was asked to identify shortcomings of articles that were rated "revise" or "reject." The two most frequently cited shortcomings were that the results of statistical analyses were not clearly presented and that incorrect statistical methods were used to analyze data. Gallagher's review of research in science education also cited inappropriate statistical treatment of data as a frequent error.[50] Therefore, we advise you to check carefully the appropriateness of statistical analyses presented in journal articles.

The first step in evaluating the statistical analyses used in a study is to see what information is reported. Many studies fail to report the minimum statistical information needed to evaluate the findings that have been reported. To illustrate, a survey of 33 randomly selected research articles by Alan Michalczyk and Lloyd Lewis found that 14 failed to report the standard deviation.[51] The

50. James J. Gallagher, "A Summary of Research in Science Education for the Years 1968–1969: Elementary School Level," *Journal of Research in Science Teaching* 9, no. 1 (1972): 19–46.
51. Alan E. Michalczyk and Lloyd A. Lewis, "Significance Alone Is Not Enough," *Journal of Medical Education* 55 (1980): 834–838.

mean and standard deviation scores on each variable for each group of subjects involved in a study are essential to estimating the magnitude of treatment effects.

Other information that should be given in a research report includes the alpha level selected to reject the null hypothesis, the significance level of the obtained results, the sample size, and the specific statistical procedures employed.

If the researchers have reported this information, the next step is to check the results for possible errors. Many types of errors may be present in the statistical analysis of research data. As you acquire more training and experience with statistical tools, you will become increasingly able to detect such mistakes. Often statistical errors occur simply because the researcher does not know how to use a particular statistical technique. For example, researchers may use a t-test to determine the statistical significance of a difference between mean scores, and in the process of doing the computations, they will compute the wrong degrees of freedom. Also, the wrong statistical technique may be selected. The researcher may select a parametric statistical technique even though the distribution of scores is badly skewed; when this situation occurs, a nonparametric technique should be used. Another weakness of some statistical analyses is that they are carried out only for the total sample and not for subgroups as well. For example, the researcher may find a significant correlation between two variables in a sample of students. Assuming adequate sample size, the researcher should then determine whether the correlation also exists for selected subgroups, such as boys versus girls and students at different grade levels.

Errors frequently occur in the interpretation of statistical findings. Researchers often have a tendency to confuse the statistical significance of research results with their practical significance. An illustration of this point can be found in a study of readability of science materials.[52] In this generally well-designed study, the investigator determined the effect on student comprehension of rewriting a sixth-grade science textbook to a third-grade level of readability. The experimental group received the rewritten reading material, while the control group received the original text. On a test of comprehension of the reading passages, it was found that the experimental group scored significantly higher ($p<.05$) than the control group. There is no problem with the statistical analysis so far. However, on the basis of this finding, the investigator recommends that sixth-grade science textbooks be rewritten by publishers and by teachers during summer writing conferences. Is this recommendation, which entails a good deal of work for educators, warranted by the statistical findings? When we look at the data more closely, we find that the comprehension test administered to all students contained 129 items. The mean scores of the experimental and control groups on this test were 75.97 and 73.48, respectively. Thus, there is a difference

52. D. L. Williams, "Rewritten Science Materials and Reading Comprehension," *Journal of Educational Research* 61 (1968): 204–206.

of only 2.5 items between the two groups on a test containing 129 items. The difference is statistically significant, but this can be attributed to the fact that a very large sample (417 students) was used. Even a very small difference between mean scores is likely to be statistically significant with this large a sample. In short, the research results achieve statistical significance, but they can hardly be said to have significance for educational practice. In critically evaluating research, make a point of checking that the investigator has not "overinterpreted" the results of the statistical analyses.

MISTAKES SOMETIMES MADE IN CRITICALLY EVALUATING RESEARCH

1. The researcher gives equal weight to good and weak studies.
2. Fails to pull together evidence from all related studies in order to get an overall understanding of the state of knowledge.
3. Does not use a quantitative procedure such as meta-analysis to determine overall effect size.
4. Fails to weigh the possible effects of sampling bias in appraisal of the reported research results.
5. Overestimates the importance of research findings that are statistically significant but have no practical significance.
6. Does not detect important errors and then repeats these errors in his or her own research.
7. Conducts critical evaluation too late to apply what has been learned to one's own research.
8. Overlooks situations that permit observer bias to occur.

ANNOTATED REFERENCES

Adair, J. G., and Spinner, B. "Subjects' Access to Cognitive Processes: Demand Characteristics and Verbal Report." *Journal for the Theory of Social Behaviour* 11 (1981): 31–52.

Analyzes the demand characteristics that seem to have operated in several studies. The behavior and verbal reports of research subjects are discussed in the context of demand characteristics theory. Perhaps more useful to the researcher is the authors' discussion of ways to improve the verity of self-report information gathered from research subjects. Among the strategies discussed are (1) the "funnel questionnaire," which begins with very general questions and gradually becomes more specific; (2) concurrent probing, in which subjects report on the strategy used; (3) "think aloud," in which each subject describes his or her thought processes as the subject goes through the problem at hand; and (4) videotape reconstruction, in which subjects are shown a replay of the experiment to help them recall their cognitions.

Adair, John G. "The Hawthorne Effect: A Reconsideration of the Methodological Artifact." *Journal of Applied Psychology 69,* no. 2 (1984): 334–345.

An interesting narrative in which the author reviews the original Hawthorne studies, discusses differences in definitions of the Hawthorne Effect, describes controls for this effect reported in current field studies, and raises questions about the adequacy of these controls. The article is based for the most part on analyses of 40 studies that employed controls for Hawthorne Effect, and 13 studies that were designed to produce Hawthorne Effect so it could be studied.

Chang, Lin, and Becker, Betsy J. "A Comparison of Three Integrative Review Methods: Different Methods, Different Findings?" Paper presented at the Annual Meeting of the American Educational Research Association, Washington, DC, April 1987.

Compares three different methods for integrating research: vote counting, tests of combined significance, and analysis of effect size. Literature dealing with the statistical properties of the three methods is discussed. An example is used to illustrate differences in results emerging from these methods. Effect size analyses are found to be more informative than the other two approaches.

Cooper, Harris M. *The Integrative Research Review: A Systematic Approach.* Beverly Hills, CA: Sage, 1984.

Conceptualizes the integrative research review as a form of scientific inquiry similar in many ways to the primary research process. Five stages in conducting an integrative research review are discussed: problem formulation, data collection, data evaluation, analysis and interpretation, and reporting. The functions, sources of variance, and potential threats to validity are described for each stage. The author has provided an excellent model for the scholar who wants to conduct an integrative review. This book is strongly recommended to students who want to develop a better understanding of the integrative review process.

Glass, Gene V. "Primary, Secondary, and Meta-Analysis of Research." *Educational Researcher 5,* no. 10 (1976): 3–8.

A classic article in which Glass first builds a case for a quantitative procedure for combining research results. He then illustrates his meta-analysis procedure by describing two analyses that have been carried out. In one of these concerned with the effect of four kinds of psychotherapy, 800 effect sizes were computed from 375 studies comparing subjects who received therapy with control group subjects. An average effect size of .68 was obtained, which clearly demonstrates that psychotherapy does "work." This analysis provided an answer to a question that had been hotly debated by psychologists for many years. Glass points out that without some quantitative method such as meta-analysis it would be virtually impossible for a reviewer to grasp the overall effect as found in these 375 studies.

Glass, Gene V; McGaw, Barry; and Smith, Mary L. *Meta-Analysis in Social Research,* Beverly Hills, CA: Sage, 1981.

The authors describe the problems involved in reviewing and integrating research and explain in some detail how to use meta-analysis. Frequent examples, drawn from meta-analysis studies by the authors and others, are provided. In the final chapter, the four most frequent criticisms of meta-analysis are discussed.

Hedges, Larry V., and Olkin, Ingram. *Statistical Methods for Meta-Analysis.* New York: Academic Press, 1985.

A technical treatment of the statistical issues concerned with integrating independent studies. The introductory chapter provides a good review of the problems of using statistical procedures in meta-analysis. Vote-counting methods—their use and limitations—are discussed in chapter 4. Much of the remainder of the book is concerned with a sophisticated discussion of effect sizes in meta-analysis. Recommended for the advanced student.

Hunter, John E.; Schmidt, Frank L.; and Jackson, Gregg B. *Meta-Analysis: Cumulating Research Findings Across Studies.* Beverly Hills, CA: Sage, 1982.

Defines meta-analysis as any method of averaging results across studies, and therefore covers a variety of methods in addition to the Glass procedure. The authors emphasize procedures for distinguishing between true variance across studies and variance due to sampling error, measurement error, and restriction in range. They point out that in many cases, once adjustments are made for errors and limitations, they have found no variance in results across studies. When this occurs, a very clear overall picture emerges. This book is very useful to the student who wants to develop an in-depth understanding of meta-analysis procedures.

Katzer, J.; Cook, K. H.; and Crouch, W. W. *Evaluating Information–A Guide for Users of Social Science Research,* 2nd ed. Reading, MA: Addison-Wesley, 1982.

The purpose of this book is to teach students in the social sciences how to read and evaluate research information. The text avoids technical and procedural details and attempts to explain principles in nontechnical language. The evaluation process proposed by the authors is based on the "error model," which focuses on sources of errors, kinds of errors, and ways that researchers can control errors. A step-by-step evaluation guide is provided along with a list of questions the student should ask in evaluating a research article.

L'Hommedieu, Randi; Menges, Robert J.; and Brinko, Kathleen T. *Putting the "But" Back in Meta-Analysis: Issues Affecting the Validity of Quantitative Reviews.* Paper read at the Annual Meeting of the American Educational Research Association, Washington, DC, April 1987.

Describes some of the problems encountered in conducting a meta-analysis and makes some useful recommendations.

Light, Richard J., and Pillemer, David B. *Summing Up, the Science of Reviewing Research*. Cambridge, MA: Harvard University Press, 1984.

Discusses the weaknesses of narrative reviews and then moves on to provide guidelines for conducting quantitative reviews. First the authors address issues related to organizing the review, next specific review procedures are presented and evaluated, then the inclusion of qualitative data in the review is discussed, and finally several examples are described to illustrate the procedures. The authors also propose a 10-item checklist for evaluating reviews. This book is very readable, making frequent use of examples to illustrate and clarify.

Millman, Jason, and Gowin, D. B. *Appraising Educational Research: A Case Study Approach*. Englewood Cliffs, NJ: Prentice-Hall, 1974.

Contains nine educational research articles covering a variety of educational topics and research procedures. Special notes and a detailed critique are provided for each article. The critiques were developed and modified on the basis of comments supplied by over 800 students and provide an excellent model for students who are studying the critical review process.

Persell, Caroline. *Quality, Careers and Training in Educational and Social Research*. Bayside, NY: General Hall, 1976.

Explores the dimensions of quality in educational research, reports on the evaluation of nearly 400 recent studies, and deals with specific flaws. Seven articles are included that give the reader insights into the range and nature of recent research in education. Information is also given on the amount of research being carried out in each of the broad areas of education.

Rosenthal, Robert. "Combining Results of Independent Studies." *Psychological Bulletin* 85, no. 1 (1978): 185–193.

Describes nine procedures that can be used to combine the probabilities obtained from two or more independent studies to determine the overall significance of the combined results. Each method is described, and its use is illustrated. The advantages and limitations of each method are given, as are suggestions as to when each method is applicable.

Rosenthal, Robert. *Meta-Analytic Procedures for Social Research*. Beverly Hills, CA: Sage, 1984.

A very readable book that clearly describes the process of meta-analysis in enough detail so that the reader can conduct a meta-analysis or evaluate meta-analyses conducted by others. The final chapter, which discusses the major criticisms of meta-analysis, will be especially useful to the student who wants to evaluate this procedure. Special attention should be given the Binomial Effect Size Display as a method of estimating the practical importance of a given effect size.

Rosenthal, Robert, and Rosnow, Ralph L., eds. *Artifact in Behavioral Research*. New York: Academic Press, 1969.

All research is subject to error. Nevertheless, the complexity of human subjects and their interaction with human experimenters leads to an array of subtle and complex errors in the behavioral sciences. This book provides the best single source available on these errors. Included are chapters on topics such as suspiciousness of the experimenter's intent, pretest sensitization, demand characteristics, interpersonal expectations, and evaluation apprehension.

Rosenthal, R., and Rosnow, R. L. *The Volunteer Subject.* New York: Wiley, 1975.

Because it is very difficult to obtain nonvolunteers for most research, it is important for behavioral scientists to understand volunteer subjects and use them effectively. This book builds upon the extensive research of the authors but also pulls together other important research on the volunteer subject. Topics covered include characteristics of the volunteer, suggestions for reducing volunteer bias, and implications for interpreting research findings. This is an essential source for the researcher who works with human subjects.

Rosnow, Ralph L., and Davis, D. J. "Demand Characteristics and the Psychological Experiment." *Et Cetera* 34 (1977): 301–313.

An excellent discussion of demand characteristics, factors that mediate these phenomena, procedures for reducing their influence on research results, and ways to detect their occurrence. Many useful references are provided.

Saretsky, Gary. "The John Henry Effect: Potential Confounder of Experimental vs. Control Group Approaches to the Evaluation of Educational Innovations." Paper presented at the annual meeting of the American Educational Research Association, Washington, DC, 2 April 1975 (ED 106 309).

Starts with a brief historical review of resistance to innovation. The author then reviews a number of factors that bias research, such as the halo effect, the placebo effect, and the Hawthorne Effect. He then discusses the John Henry Effect and describes several studies in which this effect seems to have occurred. Available on *RIE* microfiche.

Wolf, Fredric M. *Meta-Analysis: Quantitative Methods for Research Synthesis.* Beverly Hills, CA: Sage, 1986.

Written in clear nontechnical language, this work provides an excellent introduction for the beginning student. It discusses the advantages and criticisms of meta-analysis, introduces the reader to effect size, and describes ways of reducing bias. The 13 Guidelines for Practice given in the last chapter should be carefully studied by anyone planning to conduct a quantitative review of research literature.

SELF-CHECK TEST

Circle the correct answer to each of the following questions. An answer key is provided on page 883.

1. Of the following, the factor that most often weakens educational research studies is
   a. deliberate distortion.
   b. sampling bias.

    c. inaccurate statistical analysis

    d. inaccurate computer programming.

2. Loss of subjects during the course of a research project usually introduces bias because

    a. the resulting sample is too small.

    b. they are not lost on a random bias.

    c. descriptive statistics cannot be used on the resulting data.

    d. All of the above are correct.

3. If a research study cites standard measures concerning which the reader is unfamiliar, one should

    a. consult the *Mental Measurements Yearbooks*.

    b. disregard the study.

    c. try to interpret the study as carefully as possible.

    d. disregard the portion of the study related to the unknown standard measure.

4. Measurement tools are likely to invalidate the research findings if they are

    a. too easy or difficult for the majority of the research sample.

    b. administered only to a volunteer group of subjects.

    c. developed by the researcher.

    d. known to have high reliability.

5. Observer bias may be reduced by

    a. carefully structuring an interview guide.

    b. use of audiotape recordings.

    c. reducing the amount of inference required by the observer.

    d. All of the above are correct.

6. Technically, the chemically inert substance administered in the same manner as a drug under investigation is called a

    a. reactor.

    b. contaminator.

    c. placebo.

    d. catalyst.

7. Observer contamination arises when the research worker is

    a. influenced in the observation of an independent variable by knowledge of subjects' performance on a dependent variable.

    b. poorly instructed concerning the task.

    c. not thoroughly knowledgeable concerning the experiment.

    d. All of the above are correct.

8. Screening "placebo reactors" out of research studies has served to

    a. decrease observer bias.

    b. reveal significant differences not otherwise shown.

    c. eliminate deliberate bias.

    d. reduce statistical contamination.

9. A common error in statistical analysis is to select a parametric technique even though

    a. the sample size was very large.

    b. the sample included only volunteers.

    c. the distribution of scores was badly skewed.

    d. test scores were derived from observational data.

10. If a researcher finds a small difference in test scores between a large sample of experimental subjects and a large sample of control subjects, it is likely that the difference will be

    a. statistically significant and have practical significance.

    b. not statistically significant, but have practical significance.

    c. statistically significant, but not have practical significance.

    d. of no consequence for determining the statistical or practical significance of the research findings.

APPLICATION PROBLEMS

The following problems are designed to give you practice in applying significant concepts and research procedures explained in the chapter. Most of them do not have a single correct answer. For feedback, you can compare your answers with the sample answers on pages 891–892.

1. What sampling biases appear to be present in the following description of procedures used to select subjects? In order to determine the effects of a new discussion method on the achievement of college students, 156 psychology majors enrolled in an undergraduate course in educational psychology were selected to participate in the study. Each subject was assigned to one of four sections, each taught by a different instructor. Two sections were randomly designated as experimental and two as control. Because the course is required for graduation, the population consisted of sophomores, juniors, and seniors. Most of the subjects were commuters from the local community. Of the 75 students initially enrolled in the experimental course, 58 completed all course requirements. Totals for the control group were 81 and 78, respectively. Nine of the students in the treatment group who failed to complete did enough coursework to earn a passing grade, and the other eight dropped the course shortly after hearing the requirements. In the control group, three students dropped the course for administrative reasons.

2. Identify possible bias or contamination in the following hypothetical studies.
   a. In recent years a number of investigators have suggested that heredity plays an important role in determining individual differences in intelligence. The purpose of the research reported herein is to prove the invalidity of this racist belief once and for all. Underline indicators of bias, and state what type(s) of bias appear(s).
   b. An investigator hypothesizes that primary-grade female teachers who have young children of their own (ages 3–9) will display more warmth and understanding in the classroom than those who have no children. He selects 30 teachers who have young children and 30 who have no children. All are female and teach primary grades (i.e., K–3). He then observes each teacher for two hours and rates the teacher on "warmth" and "understanding" using a 5-point scale for each trait. He then compares the mean scores of the two groups of teachers on "warmth" and "understanding" to test his hypothesis. What type(s) or bias or contamination appear(s) to be present?

3. Prior to the start of the school year, students who have preregistered will be randomly assigned to the four first-grade classrooms. Two of these classrooms will then be randomly assigned to treatment and two to control conditions. In the treatment classrooms each child will be given a multivitamin supplement in the 4-oz. serving of orange juice normally given to all children at 10:00 A.M. daily.
   a. Is this study subject to the Hawthorne Effect? If so, why?
   b. Is a placebo needed? If so, why?

4. An investigator carries out a correlational study designed to identify variables that relate to success in solving word problems in mathematics. He administers a word-problem test to 1,000 high school seniors, all of whom have completed second-year algebra with passing grades. He obtains a correlation of .17 between word-problem test scores and a test in which the subjects are shown pictures of common objects (such as book, pencil, bell, knife, etc.) and their speed in naming the objects is measured. This correlation is statistically significant at the .01 level. Is the relationship of practical significance for predicting success in solving word problems? Explain your answer.

5. A professor of elementary education develops a special 10-week program of role playing and simulated teaching problems to train teachers to improve their explaining skills. She wants to evaluate the effectiveness of this program by determining whether teachers who

are trained in these skills obtain better pupil achievement than teachers who are not. She explains the study at a district teachers' meeting and locates 40 teachers who are willing to participate. These teachers are randomly divided into two groups. Group A is given the training and group B is not. Six teachers drop out of group A at the end of the second week. At the end of the program, pupil achievement tests would be given in the classrooms of all 34 teachers who remain.

a. Is sampling bias present in this study? Discuss.
b. Could the Hawthorne Effect occur? Why?
c. Could the John Henry Effect occur? Why?
d. How could the study be changed to reduce these effects?

SUGGESTION SHEET

If your last name starts with letters from Cor to Doc, please complete the Suggestion Sheet at the end of this book while this chapter is still fresh in your mind.

Part III

SAMPLING AND MEASUREMENT

One of our main goals in educational research is to obtain valid knowledge about some aspect of education and to apply that knowledge to a defined population. We almost never collect data from all individuals who make up our population, however. Instead, we select a sample of subjects from that population for study. The procedures we use in selecting our sample are very important because they determine the extent to which we can apply our findings to the population from which our sample was drawn.

Our measurement procedures in research are no less important than sampling procedures. All science uses measurement, and the progress of a given science is determined to a large extent by the accuracy of the instruments developed to measure variables in its domain. Because educational research is concerned with the human subject, by far the most complex organism on our planet, the problems of educational measurement are much more difficult that those of other sciences. Many of the measures currently available to the educational researcher are of questionable validity. The findings reached through use of such measures are therefore also of questionable validity. To improve this situation, researchers need to develop a thorough understanding of educational measurement principles and a knowledge of how to locate, evaluate, and interpret educational measures.

6 POPULATIONS AND SAMPLES

OVERVIEW

Usually researchers cannot investigate the entire population of students or educators in whom they are interested. They must limit their investigation to a small sample. Among the most crucial decisions that confront researchers, then, is the selection of a sample of subjects who are representative of the population to which they wish to generalize research findings. Researchers often make errors in selecting their samples. Three major errors are discussed. You are then given procedures for using a variety of sampling techniques and their rationale. Because most educational research must be conducted with volunteer samples, the characteristics of volunteers are discussed along with suggestions for interpreting research data collected on such samples. Next you are presented with a number of factors to be considered in determining how many subjects you should include in your research design. Since the educational researcher desires that the findings have as great an impact as possible on the field of education, it is imperative that serious consideration be given to the sampling procedure. Once a decision is made with respect to sampling, the degree of generalizability of the findings to students and educators other than those included in the actual project is likewise fixed.

OBJECTIVES

After studying this chapter you should be able to:

1. Discuss three common errors in selecting samples.
2. Describe the procedure for generalizing from the sample to the accessible population and from the accessible population to the target population.
3. Define *sample attrition* and explain how it can be reduced.
4. Describe the procedure for selecting a simple random sample from a defined population.
5. Describe the procedure for selecting a stratified sample from a defined population.
6. Describe the procedure for selecting a cluster sample from a defined population.
7. Describe seven types of situations in educational research that require a fairly large sample.
8. Estimate the sample size needed for a particular research problem.
9. Give two reasons why volunteers are likely to constitute biased samples in research projects.
10. Distinguish between known characteristics of volunteer and nonvolunteer samples.

The usual purpose of educational research is to learn something about a large group of people by studying a much smaller group of people. The larger group we wish to learn about is called a **population,** whereas the smaller group we actually study is called a **sample.** In this chapter we will discuss how populations are defined and how samples are selected.

COMMON MISTAKES IN SAMPLING

A common mistake in educational research is to investigate persons from the appropriate population simply because they are available. For example, a researcher might select all subjects from one school because one happens to know the school principal and is sure that the principal will grant permission to do the study in that school. The problem with this strategy is that the research results cannot be applied with much confidence to other subjects who are members of the same population. Suppose that you have selected all subjects from one school, and subsequently find that subjects exposed to teaching method A learn significantly better than subjects exposed to teaching method B. A principal in another school can legitimately raise the question: "How do I know that teaching method A will be superior in my school?" Generalization from one school to another or from one sample of students to another is risky, unless you have selected subjects by means of appropriate sampling techniques.

A worse error is to select subjects who are not even in an appropriate population for the contemplated research, merely because they are easily available. For example, many studies on the effects of different types of psychological counseling or therapy are conducted using normal college students who have no need for counseling but who are drafted as subjects merely because they are students in a class of psychology. It is doubtful whether the responses of such students to counseling bear any relationship to responses of persons in the real target population, that is, persons who seek counseling because of series emotional problems.

College sophomores, who are available but often inappropriate, have been the subjects for so much research in education and psychology that the use of sophomores in research projects finds its way into many of the jokes about research workers in these fields. Some studies suffer relatively little from using available subjects. For example, exploratory studies on the effects of drugs upon behavior may not be seriously weakened by the use of available subjects. Whenever the research worker wishes to generalize the results to specifically defined populations, however, the use of subjects merely because they are available is inappropriate.

Many educational field studies are biased because the research worker chooses experimental and control groups from different populations. For example, some early studies on the effectiveness of TV instruction used high school students receiving conventional instruction as a control group, but used adults who wanted to complete their high school education in home study as an experimental or TV-instruction group. The age, interests, motivation, and dropout rates for the two groups are very different, thus making the results of such studies meaningless.

Occasionally identification of a suitable sample is sufficiently time-consuming and expensive to warrant the use of shortcuts. Nevertheless, the possible effects of shortcuts should be carefully studied before they are used. Terman's famous study of "gifted children" provides an example of a sampling shortcut that seriously affected the research results.[1] In this study Terman wished to locate 1,000 children with IQs over 140 on the Stanford-Binet Intelligence Scale. The Stanford-Binet test is expensive and time-consuming to administer. Therefore, rather than test many pupils who had little chance of obtaining a score of 140, Terman decided to ask teachers to suggest the names of students whom they considered superior. Only those students nominated by a teacher were tested. The difficulty with this procedure is that teachers tend to underestimate the intelligence of pupils who create disturbances and are not cooperative in the classroom. Thus, Terman's sample does not include this type of individual, and as a result of this shortcut in selecting the original sample, all the findings of his important study must be qualified. Terman's results, instead of being applicable to gifted children in general, refer primarily to a particular type of gifted child.

The method of selecting a sample is critical to the whole research process. If research findings are not generalizable to some degree beyond the sample used in the study, then the research cannot provide us with new knowledge, cannot advance education as a science, and is largely a waste of time.

The sample should be selected by some process that permits us to assume that the sample is *representative* of the population from which it has been drawn on those variables that are relevant to the research we are planning to conduct. By "representative" we do not mean identical. The only way we could be certain that the sample was identical to the population would be to take the entire population for our "sample." Instead, we define a sample as representative if we have drawn the sample in a manner that makes it probable that the sample is approximately the same as the population on the variables to be studied. The word "approximately" implies some degree of difference between the sample and the population. We can never be sure of the magnitude of this difference unless we have measured the entire population and compared the population and the sample. We do know, however, that the probable size of this difference is closely related to the size of the sample. The sample ideally should be large enough that the investigator can be confident, within a reasonable limit, that if he should draw a different sample of the same size and using the same procedures he would obtain approximately the same result in his research.

This difference between the characteristics of a sample and the characteristics of the population from which the sample was drawn is called *sampling error* and can be estimated for random samples. As indicated above, sampling error is a function of the size of the sample, with the error being largest when the sample

1. Lewis, M. Terman, ed., *Genetic Studies of Genius*, vol. 1, *Mental and Physical Traits of a Thousand Gifted Children* (Stanford, CA: Stanford University Press, 1926), p. 21.

is small. Research findings based on a sample of two or three subjects are apt to be highly unreliable.[2] If we were to study another sample of this size, it is quite likely that different findings would be obtained. It is important to select a sample of adequate size in order to produce research data that reliably approximate the data that would be obtained if the entire population were studied.

This chapter discusses sampling techniques that enable you to select a sample that is representative of a larger population. We also discuss procedures that you can use to determine the sample size needed for a given study. Although our discussion is concerned primarily with the selection of subjects for a research project, you should note that the sampling techniques discussed here also pertain to the selection of events or objects for research. For example, sampling techniques would be used if you wished to select a sample of class periods for systematic observation, or a sample of textbooks in order to do a content analysis.

DEFINING THE POPULATION

Sampling means selecting a given number of subjects from a defined population as representative of that population. One type of population distinguished by educational researchers is called the **target population.** By target population, also called **universe,** we mean all the members of a real or hypothetical set of people, events, or objects to which we wish to generalize the results of our research. The advantage of drawing a small sample from a large target population is that it saves the time and expense of studying the entire population. If the sampling is done properly, you can reach conclusions about an entire target population that are likely to be correct within a small margin of error by studying a relatively small sample.

The first step in sampling is to define the target population. Typical populations from which educational research samples might be drawn include school superintendents in Utah; practice-teaching supervisors in state-supported teachers' colleges; bilingual children in the primary grades of the San Antonio city school district; pupils failing algebra in New York City schools; and seniors graduating from American public high schools in June 1989. These examples illustrate that the target population may represent a large group scattered over a wide geographical area or a small group concentrated in a single area.

The researcher can seldom draw a representative sample from a target population such as all first-grade pupils in public schools in the United States. In

2. Certain kinds of research can be conducted with very few cases or even a single case. This topic is discussed in chapter 16.

order to obtain a representative sample of this broadly defined population, you would need to develop a complex method of selecting cases from different areas, different-sized communities, and different types of schools.

Obviously the selection of such a sample and collection of data from it would involve a tremendous amount of work and expense. Instead, you must usually draw your sample from an **experimentally accessible population** such as all first-grade pupils in the San Francisco school district.[3] Even though the sample is selected from the accessible population, you may want to know the degree to which the results can be generalized to the target population. This type of generalization requires two inferential leaps. First, you must generalize the results from the sample you actually studied to the accessible population from which you selected the sample. Second, you must generalize from the accessible population to the target population. The leap from sample to accessible population presents no problem if a **random sample** of the accessible population was obtained, that is, a sample in which all members of the population had an equal chance of being selected. If the sample was not formed randomly, you must gather data about the sample and the population on characteristics critical to the study. Often such data are available in school records, but some testing may also be necessary. You will rarely be able to obtain all data that would be useful, but you should obtain comparative information on as many critical variables as possible with the resources you have at your disposal. These data will demonstrate that the sample is either biased or unbiased. If the sample is unbiased, you can safely generalize the results to the accessible population. If, however, the sample is biased, you must report the nature of the bias and discuss how this bias is likely to affect the results.

In order to make the second leap from the accessible population to the target population, you must gather data to determine the degree of similarity between the two populations. It is possible to gather comparative data on a very large number of variables. However, if you are able to demonstrate that the accessible population is closely comparable to the **target** population on a few variables that appear most relevant to the study, you have done much to establish **population validity.** That is, you have established that the accessible population is reasonably representative of the target population. For example, suppose you want to compare the achievement of first-grade pupils who are taught with two different reading programs. If you select a random sample from the accessible population of first-graders in the San Francisco schools but can demonstrate by comparing local test data with national test norms that San Francisco first-graders are not significantly different from first-graders nation-wide on such important variables as reading readiness, verbal IQ, chronological age, and socioeconomic status, then you have established a degree of population

3. See Glenn H. Bracht and Gene V Glass, "The External Validity of Experiments," *American Educational Research Journal* 5, no. 4 (November 1968): 437–474, for a more detailed discussion.

validity. This means that you can generalize your results from the accessible to the target population with reasonable confidence. Often financial limitations or the nature of the research problem limit us to sampling the student population of a single school district. Studies based on this narrow accessible population are, of course, less generalizable than those based on broader populations, but may still have implications for other educators if it can be demonstrated that this population is reasonably similar to the target population on a few critical variables.

To identify all the members of a defined population is beyond the scope of most research projects. For example, identifying by name all fifth-grade teachers even in a single state would be a major undertaking. Thus, researchers usually rely on published lists, called *sampling frames*, of various populations that are of interest to educators. Most researchers will be able to draw samples from accessible populations only at the state or district level. Contact the state or district education office to find out if the office has a list of persons in the population that interests you. For administrative purposes, state and district education departments usually maintain lists of information about schools, such as school addresses, grades, enrollment, and names of principals and teachers. In certain instances, you may wish to consult a national association or national directory, even though the defined population is at the state or district level. For example, suppose you wished to survey a sample of educational researchers in a given state. You might obtain a current membership directory from the American Educational Research Association and mark all the members residing in that state. From this defined population, you might then select a sample of educational researchers. The *Guide to American Educational Directories* is a helpful source for locating directory lists that can be used to define populations.[4]

In using any published list to define a population, check to determine whether the list is complete and up to date. School enrollment and memberships of organizations are constantly changing, so frequent updating of population lists is necessary. Also, keep in mind that membership in most organizations is voluntary. Thus, the researcher who uses an organization directory to define a population faces the risk of selecting a biased sample, since joiners of organizations may differ in important respects from nonjoiners. Should this be the case, you should probably define the accessible populations as all members of a given organization rather than as all members of the profession or group which the organization serves.

Two studies have been done to evaluate the degree to which research articles meet criteria of population validity. J. E. Permut and co-workers used four criteria to evaluate a sample of 460 articles on marketing research.[5]

4. B. T. Klein, *Guide to American Educational Directories*, 5th ed.(Rye, NY:Todd Publications,1980).
5. J. E. Permut, A. J. Michel, and M. Joseph, "The Researcher's Sample: A Review of the Choice of Respondents in Marketing Research," *Journal of Marketing Research* 13 (1976): 278–283.

1. A clear description of the *population* to which the results are to be generalized should be given.
2. The *sampling procedure* should be specified in enough detail so that another investigator would be able to replicate the procedure. This should include at a minimum *(a)* the type of sample (simple random, stratified, convenience, etc.), *(b)* sample size, and *(c)* geographical area. In most educational studies, other descriptive data, such as sex, age, grade level, and socioeconomic status, should also be included.
3. The *sampling frame,* that is, the lists, indexes, or other population records from which the sample was selected, should be identified.
4. The *completion rate,* which is the proportion of the sample that participated as intended in all of the research procedures, should be given.

Only 10 percent of the studies reviewed by the researchers met all four criteria. In a similar analysis of 297 studies in communication research, Dennis Lowry also found that only 10 percent met these criteria.[6] Although other data may be needed to establish the population validity of a given study, you should try, as a minimum, to include data that satisfy the four criteria that we have seen above.

SAMPLING TECHNIQUES

As we have already mentioned, sampling involves the selection of a portion of a population as representative of the population. To help ensure that the sample is representative, the ideal solution, which we know to be seldom achieved, is to select a random sample from the target population. A random sample is one in which each individual in the defined population has an *equal* chance of being included.

We should note that the use of sampling techniques can be quite complicated. This is particularly true when these techniques are used to draw a random sample from a national population. However, sampling from a national population usually occurs only in survey research, such as public opinion polls. Samples used in experimental, causal-comparative, or correlational research are generally drawn from a much more limited accessible population, such as all the elementary school teachers in a particular school district.

6. Dennis T. Lowry, "Population Validity of Communication Research: Sampling the Samples," *Journalism Quarterly* 56, no. 1 (1979): 62–68, 76.

Simple Random Sampling

The usual definition of a *simple random sample* is that it is a procedure in which all the individuals in the defined population have an *equal* and *independent* chance of being selected as a member of the sample. By "independent" is meant that the selection of one individual does not affect in any way the selection of any other individual. A more precise definition of a simple random sample is that it is a process of selection from a population that provides *every sample of a given size* an equal probability of being selected. This is technically correct, since in the process of selecting cases, the selection of each individual changes slightly the probability for the next case being selected. For example, suppose there are 1,000 sixth-grade pupils in our accessible population, and we want to select a simple random sample of 100. When we select our first case, each pupil has one chance in 1,000 of being selected. Once this pupil is selected, however, there are only 999 cases remaining so that each pupil has one chance in 999 of being selected as our second case. Thus, as each case is selected, the probability for being selected next changes slightly because the population from which we are selecting has become one case smaller. For all samples of any given size selected from this population, however, the overall probability (i.e., the sum of individual probabilities) would be the same.

The main purpose for using random sampling techniques is that random samples yield research data that can be generalized to a larger population within margins of error that can be determined statistically. Random sampling is also preferred because it permits the researcher to apply inferential statistics to the data. Inferential statistics enable the researcher to make certain inferences about population values (e.g., mean, standard deviation, correlation coefficient) on the basis of obtained sample values. If a random sample has not been drawn from a defined population, however, the logic of inferential statistics is violated and the results of inferential statistics must be interpreted with much more caution. We discuss the relationship between sampling and inferential statistics later in this chapter and again in chapter 9.

Various techniques can be used to derive a simple random sample. Suppose the research director of a large city school system wishes to obtain a random sample of 100 pupils currently enrolled in the ninth grade from a population of 972 cases. First, he would obtain a copy of the district census for ninth-grade pupils and assign a number to each pupil. Then he might use a **table of random numbers** to draw a sample from the census list. (A table of random numbers can be found in Appendix C.) Generally these tables consist of long series of five-digit numbers generated randomly by a computer. Table 6.1 is a small portion of a typical table.

To use the random numbers table, randomly select a row or column as a starting point, then select all the numbers that follow in that row or column. If more numbers are needed, proceed to the next row or column until enough

TABLE 6.1

A Typical Table of Random Numbers

Row	1	2	3	4	5	6	7	8	9	10
1	32388	52390	16815	69298	82732	38480	73817	32523	41961	44437
2	05300	22164	24369	54224	35983	19687	11052	91491	60383	19746
3	66523	44133	00697	35552	35970	19124	63318	29686	03387	59846
4	44167	64486	64758	75366	76554	31601	12614	33072	60332	92325
5	47914	02584	37680	20801	72152	39339	34806	08930	85001	87820
6	63445	17361	62825	39908	05607	91284	68833	25570	38818	46920
7	89917	15665	52872	73823	73144	88662	88970	74492	51805	99378
8	92648	45454	09552	88815	16553	51125	79375	97596	16296	66092
9	20979	04508	64535	31355	86064	29472	47689	05974	52468	16834
10	81959	65642	74240	56302	00033	67107	77510	70625	28725	34191

Column

numbers have been selected to make up the desired sample size. In effect, you may start at any random point in the table and select numbers from a column or row or diagonally if you wish.

Suppose, in our example, the researcher selects row 1 column 5 as his starting point in the above table and selects numbers vertically. Since there are 972 cases in our illustrative city school system, he needs only to use the last three digits of each five-digit number. If the table of random numbers reprinted here were used, the researcher would select the 732nd pupil on the census list, the 970th pupil, the 554th pupil, and so on. He would skip the number 983 since there are only 972 cases in his population. This procedure would be followed (with a much larger table of random numbers, of course) until a sample of 100 pupils had been selected.

If a small population is used, another method of selecting a simple random sample is sometimes followed. This method involves placing a slip of paper with the name or identification number of each individual in the population in a container, mixing the slips thoroughly, and then drawing the required number of names or numbers.

Simple random sampling is well illustrated by a study involving the collection of a national random sample of secondary physics teachers.[7] The researchers responsible for this curriculum evaluation study wished to avoid using a nonrandom sample consisting largely of "volunteer" teachers. This procedure, typical of many curriculum evaluation studies, makes it difficult to generalize the findings of the curriculum evaluation to other groups of teachers, especially nonvolunteers, who might be required to teach the new curriculum. The researchers first purchased a list of the names and addresses of 16,911 physics teachers compiled by the National Science Teachers Association. They point out in their report that this is the most comprehensive population list of high school physics teachers available, although it is not complete; it was based on responses received from 81 percent of all secondary schools in the United States. Thus, their population was not "all high school physics teachers" but rather "all high school physics teachers on the 1966 NSTA list." Each teacher on the population list was assigned a number according to his or her ordinal position on the list. Then a table of random numbers was used to select a total of 136 teachers. These 136 teachers were sent letters inviting them to participate in the study, but it was only possible to contact 124 of them.

Eventually 72 of the original 136 teachers agreed to participate in the study according to the conditions specified. Another 46 teachers were unable to participate for various reasons. In order to determine whether their final sample was biased, the researchers decided to compare several characteristics of the 72 accepting teachers against those of the 46 nonacceptors. When this comparison

7. W. W. Welch, J. J. Walberg, and A. Ahlgren, "The Selection of a National Random Sample of Teachers for Experimental Curriculum Evaluation," *School Science and Mathematics* 69 (1969): 210–216.

was made, the researchers found that significantly more acceptors than nonacceptors worked in larger schools and taught the Physical Science Study Committee (PSSC) physics course. The researchers interpreted these differences as indicating that the accepting teachers were more likely to be those who taught in large schools where previous innovations had been accepted. Thus, although they attempted to obtain a truly "random" sample, their actual sample was somewhat biased in favor of teachers working in innovative schools, and consisted of volunteers since only half the teachers contacted chose to participate. Nevertheless, the researchers' final sample was probably more representative than the samples used in most curriculum studies, and it was possible to generalize the study's findings to a national population of physics teachers, with certain qualifications.

Incidentally, the study just described illustrates another problem that sometimes occurs with research samples. Of the 72 accepting teachers, 46 were assigned to the experimental group teaching the new physics curriculum, and the remaining 26 were assigned to the control group. During the course of the year-long evaluation study, 10 teachers were lost from the experimental group and 5 were lost from the control group for various reasons—death, quitting one's job, transfer to a new position, and so forth. Whenever a research project extends over a considerable period of time, there is likely to be attrition of subjects. Not only can attrition lead to bias in the research sample (since those who leave the study may differ in important ways from those who persist), but also the reduced sample size can make it more difficult to find statistically significant differences. Thus, if the research study makes considerable demands on subjects or lasts over a long period of time, it is advisable to include more subjects in the random sample than are needed in order to provide for possible attrition. It is also important to take any steps possible to keep attrition to a minimum.

The human relations procedures described in chapter 3 can do much to reduce attrition, as can the 10 steps for increasing the rate of volunteering given later in this chapter. Some attrition may reflect careless or poorly planned techniques for gathering, processing, and analyzing research data. Loss of data often occurs because the subject is not contacted by the data gatherer or the subject does not provide all the information needed for analysis. Much attrition in school research is the result of student absences on testing days or incorrectly completed measures. Prompt checking of data, careful recordkeeping, and a systematic follow-up procedure can greatly reduce this problem.[8] Great care is required at all stages of data collection, processing, and analysis if attrition is to be reduced and valid data obtained.

In summary, simple random sampling is a powerful technique for selecting

8. See Gloria Marshall, "Methods for Minimizing Attrition in Field Studies" (Paper presented at the annual meeting of the American Educational Research Association, San Francisco, 22 April 1976), for a discussion of attrition in longitudinal studies.

a sample that is representative of a larger population. Nevertheless, it is rarely possible to study a simple random sample that is perfect. Even if a simple random sample is initially selected, some subjects will probably refuse to cooperate and others will be lost through attrition, leaving you with a sample that is not truly random.

Systematic Sampling

As with simple random sampling, the technique of *linear systematic sampling* is used to obtain a sample from the defined population.[9] This technique can be used if all members in the defined population have already been placed on a list. Suppose you want to select a sample of 100 pupils from a census list of 1,000 pupils. To use systematic sampling, first divide the population by the number needed for the sample (1,000 ÷ 100 = 10). Then select at random a number smaller than the number arrived at by the division (in this example, a number smaller than 10). Then, starting with that number (e.g., 8), select every tenth name from a list of the population.

Systematic sampling is a slightly easier procedure to use than is simple random sampling. It differs from simple random sampling in that each member of the population is not chosen independently. Once the first member has been selected, all the other members of the sample are automatically determined.

Systematic sampling can be used instead of simple random sampling if you are certain that the population list is not in some periodic order. If there is any possibility of periodicity in the list (that is, if every *n*th person on the list shares a characteristic that is not shared by the entire population), then simple random sampling should be used instead.

Stratified Sampling

In many educational studies, the sample should be selected in such a way that you are assured that certain subgroups in the population will be represented in the sample in proportion to their numbers in the population itself. Such samples are usually referred to as *stratified samples*. Let us say, for example, that we wish to conduct a study to see if there are significant differences on Thematic Apperception Test aggression scores of pupils at different ability levels from ability-grouped sixth-grade classrooms. Under this grouping system, pupils are classified into three levels on the basis of general intelligence and placed in classrooms accordingly. In this case, if we were to define the population as all

9. This is the most widely used form of systematic sampling. For a description of other forms, see Richard M. Jaeger (1984) in the Annotated References at the end of this chapter.

sixth-grade pupils in the district being studied and select a random sample, our random sample may not include a sufficient number of cases from one of the three ability levels. In this research we must also consider the possibility that girls will react differently in terms of aggression scores than will boys. In order to avoid a sample that does not include a sufficient number of pupils of each sex at each ability level, a stratified sample can be selected. All sixth-grade pupils in the district would be divided into one of the following six groups: superior boys, superior girls, average boys, average girls, slow boys, and slow girls. Sub-samples would then be selected at random from each of the six groups, or strata.

Proportional stratified sampling is usually used, that is, the proportion of subjects randomly selected from each group is the same as the proportion of that group in the target population. Therefore, if slow girls made up 8 percent of the sixth-grade population, they should also make up 8 percent of the sample. If this procedure is not followed, any analysis based on the total sample (i.e., all six groups combined) will produce inaccurate information. Suppose, for example, that we randomly selected 100 pupils from each of our six groups. Any statistics, such as the mean, that we computed on these 600 pupils would not accurately reflect the population since the proportion of average pupils in the population is higher than the proportion of superior or slow pupils, and even within ability levels, the proportion of boys and girls is different. However, when we are concerned primarily with the strata, and we do not plan to compute means or other statistics for the entire sample, we can select an equal number of cases from each of the strata.

In proportional stratified sampling, the size of the sample is usually determined by the minimum number of cases we decide is acceptable in the smallest subgroup. If we decide that the smallest must contain 30 cases, then we select a total sample large enough so that the correct proportion of our smallest subgroup will equal 30. For example, if 8 percent of our sample must be slow girls and this subsample must be 30 cases, then our total sample would be 375 (i.e., $30 \div .08$).

Stratified samples are particularly appropriate in studies where the research problem requires comparisons between various subgroups. In summary, stratified sampling procedure assures the research worker that the sample will be representative of the population in terms of certain critical factors that have been used as a basis for stratification, and also assures the researcher of adequate cases for subgroup analysis.

Cluster Sampling

In **cluster sampling** the unit of sampling is not the individual but rather a naturally occurring group of individuals. Cluster sampling is used when it is more feasible or convenient to select groups of individuals than it is to select individuals from a defined population. This situation occurs when it is either impractical or impossible to obtain a list of all members of the accessible population. Suppose, for example, that one's defined population consists of all residents over the age of 18 in a particular city. Simple random sampling or systematic sampling could be used if an up-to-date, complete census of all the city's individuals and their ages were available. If not, then cluster sampling is advisable.

The city might be divided into areas containing 16 square blocks. Each area would be listed and numbered, and the areas to be sampled would be drawn at random. All individuals who meet the age requirement in each sample area would be studied, excepting those who cannot be reached or who are un-cooperative. Thus, the unit of sampling is a 16-square-block area rather than the individual citizen.

Multistage cluster sampling is a variant of cluster sampling. Once the square block areas have been randomly selected, the researcher can further reduce the sample size by only studying a random sample in each square-block area. For example, the researcher might list the addresses of all houses in the area and then study the residents of ten randomly selected houses in each 16-block area included in the sample. In essence, multistage cluster sampling consists of two or more cycles of listing and sampling. Several sampling stages or cycles may be carried out in order to arrive at the subjects to be ultimately included in the sample.

Cluster sampling is sometimes used in educational research with the classroom as the unit of sampling. Suppose that you wish to administer a questionnaire to a random sample of 300 pupils in a population defined as all sixth-graders in four school districts. Let us say that there are a total of 1,250 sixth-graders in 50 classrooms, with an average of 25 pupils in each classroom. One approach is to draw a simple random sample using a census list of all 1,250 pupils. In cluster sampling, though, you would draw a random sample of 12 classrooms from a census list of all 50 classrooms.[10] Then you would administer the questionnaire to every pupil in each of the 12 classrooms.

The main advantage of cluster sampling is that it saves time and money. The use of this technique enables you to confine questionnaire administration to 12 of the 50 classrooms. If simple random sampling were used, you might have to arrange for access to all 50 classrooms, even though in some of these classrooms you might have selected only one student for the sample. Disadvantages of cluster sampling are (1) that it is less accurate than simple random sampling because in a simple random sample there is only one *sampling error*, whereas in multistage sampling there is a sampling error at each stage, and (2) that the conventional formulas for computing statistics on research data

---

10. Twelve classrooms would be selected because there are an average of 25 pupils in each classroom, and the desired sample is 300 pupils.

cannot be used.[11] Also, the statistics are less sensitive to population differences. Nevertheless, these disadvantages must be weighed against the considerable savings in time and money that can result from using cluster sampling.

Besides the sampling techniques described above, which are sufficient for most educational research, a variety of more sophisticated techniques are intended primarily for use in large-scale survey research. See the Annotated References section of this chapter for sources that deal with these procedures.

VOLUNTEER SAMPLES

Random sampling of broad populations is possible for survey research in which slight demands are made on the subjects. For example, most public opinion polls are able to obtain random samples since they typically ask only a few questions and take only a few minutes of the respondent's time. Demands on the subject are much greater in most educational research; consequently, even if the researcher selects a random sample, he can rarely get cooperation from all the subjects selected. (You will recall that when some subjects refuse to participate in a study, the remaining subjects no longer constitute a random sample because persons who agree to participate are likely to be different from those who do not.) For educational studies that employ other methods than survey, such as correlational or experimental research, the demands on the subject are usually much greater, and consequently it is virtually impossible to obtain the cooperation of all subjects selected by random sampling.

Furthermore, as you learned in chapter 3, legal and ethical constraints require you to obtain informed consent from human subjects (or their parents in the case of minors) before involving them in a research project.

As a result of the aforementioned conditions, nearly all educational research must be conducted with volunteer subjects. We know that volunteer subjects are likely to be a biased sample of the target population since volunteers have been found in many studies to differ from nonvolunteers.[12]

There is a considerable body of research on the characteristics of volunteers. Robert Rosenthal and Ralph Rosnow have conducted an excellent review of research in this area and have identified a number of characteristics that have been found to occur in studies of volunteer subjects.[13] Conclusions about

11. For statistical formulas to be used with data obtained from a cluster sample, we advise you to consult Leslie Kish (1965). See Annotated References at the end of this chapter for complete bibliographic information.
12. Some studies comparing nonvolunteers or random samples with volunteer samples have found little difference. See, for example, C. M. Achilles and M. N. Lintz, "Random Notes on Randomness: A Survey Concern." (Paper presented at the Annual Meeting of the Mid-South Educational Research Association, Memphis, TN, November 1986, ED 279715.)
13. See Rosenthal and Rosnow (1975) in the Annotated References at the end of this chapter.

distinguishing characteristics are listed at four levels of confidence depending on the accumulation of research evidence that supports each conclusion. Within each category the conclusions are listed in order starting with those having the strongest evidence supporting them.

CONCLUSIONS WARRANTING MAXIMUM CONFIDENCE

1. Volunteers tend to be better educated than nonvolunteers, especially when personal contact between investigator and respondent is not required.
2. Volunteers tend to have higher social-class status than nonvolunteers, especially when social class is defined by respondents' own status rather than by parental status.
3. Volunteers tend to be more intelligent than nonvolunteers when volunteering is for research in general but not when volunteering is for somewhat less typical types of research such as hypnosis, sensory isolation, sex research, small group and personality research.
4. Volunteers tend to be higher in need for social approval than nonvolunteers.
5. Volunteers tend to be more sociable than nonvolunteers.

CONCLUSIONS WARRANTING CONSIDERABLE CONFIDENCE

6. Volunteers tend to be more arousal-seeking than nonvolunteers, especially when volunteering is for studies of stress, sensory isolation, and hypnosis.
7. Volunteers tend to be more unconventional than nonvolunteers, especially when volunteering is for studies of sex behavior.
8. Females are more likely than males to volunteer for research in general, but less likely than males to volunteer for physically and emotionally stressful research (e.g., electric shock, high temperature, sensory deprivation, interviews about sex behavior).
9. Volunteers tend to be less authoritarian than nonvolunteers.
10. Jews are more likely to volunteer than Protestants, and Protestants are more likely to volunteer than Roman Catholics.
11. Volunteers tend to be less conforming than nonvolunteers when volunteering is for research in general but not when subjects are female and the task is relatively "clinical" (e.g., hypnosis, sleep, or counseling research).

CONCLUSIONS WARRANTING SOME CONFIDENCE

12. Volunteers tend to be from smaller towns than nonvolunteers, especially when volunteering is for questionnaire studies.
13. Volunteers tend to be more interested in religion than nonvolunteers, especially when volunteering is for questionnaire studies.
14. Volunteers tend to be more altruistic than nonvolunteers.
15. Volunteers tend to be more self-disclosing than nonvolunteers.
16. Volunteers tend to be more maladjusted than nonvolunteers, especially when volunteering is for potentially unusual situations (e.g., drugs, hypnosis, high temperature, or vaguely described experiments) or for medical research employing clinical rather than psychometric definitions of psychopathology.

17. Volunteers tend to be younger than nonvolunteers, especially when volunteering is for laboratory research and especially if they are female.

CONCLUSIONS WARRANTING MINIMUM CONFIDENCE

18. Volunteers tend to be higher in need for achievement than nonvolunteers, especially among American samples.
19. Volunteers are more likely to be married than nonvolunteers, especially when volunteering is for studies requiring no personal contact between investigator and respondent.
20. Firstborns are more likely than laterborns to volunteer, especially when recruitment is personal and when the research requires group interaction and a low level of stress.
21. Volunteers tend to be more anxious than nonvolunteers, especially when volunteering is for standard, nonstressful tasks and especially if they are college students.
22. Volunteers tend to be more extraverted than nonvolunteers when interaction with others is required by the nature of the research.[14]

The degree to which these characteristics of volunteer samples affect research results depends on the specific nature of the investigation. For example, a study of the level of intelligence of successful workers in different occupations would probably yield spuriously high results if volunteer subjects were studied, since volunteers tend to be more intelligent than nonvolunteers. On the other hand, in a study concerned with the cooperative behavior of adults in work-group situations, the tendency for volunteers to be more intelligent may have no effect on the results, but the tendency for volunteers to be more sociable could have a significant effect. It is apparent that the use of volunteers in research greatly complicates the interpretation of research results and their generalizability to the target population, which includes many individuals who would not volunteer.

The work of Rosenthal and Rosnow provides us with valuable information that should be considered carefully when planning a study in which volunteer subjects are to be used. Review the characteristics listed above and for each ask such questions as: How relevant is this characteristic to the dependent and independent variables to be employed in my study? If relevant, how would the difference between volunteers and nonvolunteers on this characteristic be likely to influence the research results? Are any data available on my target population for checking whether these characteristics are present among the volunteers I will employ as subjects? The first two questions often can be answered on the basis of knowledge about the variables in your study that you gain during a review of previous research. You can also get help on these questions by

14. Ibid., pp. 195–196.

discussing them with members of your research committee or other faculty members who have worked in your area of interest.

With regard to the third question, Rosenthal and Rosnow suggest two methods, which they refer to as *exhaustive* and *nonexhaustive*. In the exhaustive approach, all potential subjects are compared on as many relevant variables as possible in which volunteers and nonvolunteers may differ. For example, suppose you plan to ask for volunteers from a sophomore general psychology class to participate in a study of client responses to different interview techniques used in counseling, such as directive versus nondirective. Among the characteristics identified by Rosenthal and Rosnow, differences in such variables as need for social approval, conformity, and authoritarianism may lead to differences in volunteer and nonvolunteer responses in the planned research. You could first measure all students on these variables by administering appropriate tests to the class, then call for volunteers, and then compare the scores of volunteers and nonvolunteers to determine how the groups differ on these variables. When working with student samples, you may not need to administer measures on all relevant variables, since most schools and colleges routinely administer batteries of tests to all students, and these data can be drawn on for comparisons between volunteers and nonvolunteers.[15]

In the nonexhaustive method, data on nonvolunteers are not available, but data are available on subjects who differ in their willingness to volunteer. For example, you can compare the scores of easy-to-recruit volunteers and hard-to-recruit volunteers on some critical variable such as intelligence and then extrapolate to obtain an estimate of the intelligence of nonvolunteers in the target population. Easy-to-recruit volunteers may be those who volunteer repeatedly over a period of time, those who will volunteer without being offered an incentive such as money, or those who respond more promptly to requests for volunteers (such as newspaper advertisements or letters).

These procedures for obtaining information about characteristics of a specific volunteer sample, when combined with the general characteristics of volunteers described by Rosenthal and Rosnow, are of great assistance to the researcher in interpreting findings and generalizing to nonvolunteer populations. In reviewing research on the volunteer subject, Rosenthal and Rosnow also identified 10 situational variables that tend to increase or decrease the rates of volunteering. These findings form the basis for the following suggestions for increasing the rate of volunteering and thus reducing the volunteer bias:

SUGGESTIONS FOR IMPROVING RATE OF VOLUNTEERING

1. Make the appeal for volunteers as interesting as possible, keeping in mind the nature of the target population.

---

15. The researcher may need to obtain the student's permission, however, to obtain data from these records. See chapter 3.

2. Make the appeal for volunteers as nonthreatening as possible so that potential volunteers will not be "put off" by unwarranted fears of unfavorable evaluation.

3. Explicitly state the theoretical and practical importance of the research for which volunteering is requested.

4. Explicitly state in what way the target population is particularly relevant to the research being conducted and the responsibility of potential volunteers to participate in research that has potential for benefiting others.

5. When possible, potential volunteers should be offered not only pay for participation but small courtesy gifts simply for taking time to consider whether they will want to participate.

6. Have the request for volunteering made by a person of status as high as possible, and preferably by a woman.

7. When possible, avoid research tasks that may be psychologically or biologically stressful.

8. When possible, communicate the normative nature of the volunteering response (i.e., volunteering is the normal thing to do).

9. After a target population has been defined, an effort should be made to have someone known to that population make the appeal for volunteers. The request for volunteers itself may be more successful if a personalized appeal is made.

10. In situations where *volunteering* is regarded by the target population as normative, conditions of public commitment to volunteer may be more successful; where *nonvolunteering* is regarded as normative, conditions of private commitment may be more successful.[16]

Most of these suggestions will not only increase the rate of volunteering but will also reduce attrition in both volunteer and nonvolunteer samples. You should consider these suggestions very carefully, for following them will reduce volunteer bias and also result in better research planning.

RANDOM ASSIGNMENT

In experimental studies obtaining a random sample is usually impossible because the typical treatment makes considerable demands upon the subject's time. You usually must work with volunteers unless you can incorporate your treatments into the regular school program and thus avoid the requirement of obtaining "informed consent" (see chapter 3). However, even in situations where random sampling is impossible, you may often use random assignment. In **random assignment,** the subjects who will participate in the experiment are assigned randomly to the different experimental treatments.

16. Rosenthal and Rosnow (1975), p. 198. See the Annotated References at the end of this chapter.

Let us suppose that you want to compare the effectiveness of two second-grade reading programs in a large city school system. You locate five schools that are willing to participate and obtain permission from 90 percent of the parents of first-grade pupils for their children to participate during Grade 2. You then randomly assign 48 pupils in each school to two classrooms, one to use each reading program. This provides a total sample of 240 children, with 120 for each of the two treatments. This approach is far superior to identifying two intact classes in each school and randomly assigning *classes* rather than *individuals* to the two treatments. Random assignment does not assure that the sample is representative of the accessible population, but it does ensure that children who receive the different experimental treatments are reasonably comparable.

To use random assignment in experimental studies in the public schools you must usually make arrangements sufficiently in advance so that students can be randomly assigned to classes at the start of the school year. Once classes are established it is virtually impossible to move pupils from one class to another in order to satisfy the needs of your research.

Even when random assignment is employed, some degree of difference may be expected to occur between groups. For example, one group may contain subjects who are more intelligent, more highly motivated, or in other ways different from the subjects in other groups in the experiment. Such errors may be large in groups made up of few cases, but may be expected to decrease as the number of subjects increases. Let us say that we wish to compare the achievement of a group of ninth-grade pupils taught algebra using an inductive method with the achievement of another group taught algebra using a deductive method. We could randomly assign 50 pupils who wish to take algebra to two classes at the start of the term and assign algebra teachers of comparable experience to teach the classes. In this experiment chance differences between groups may be expected to be large because only one class of 25 pupils is involved in each group. If, among the 50 subjects, there were two very brilliant students, and if these two students were both assigned to the same group (as could easily occur in the random assignment process), the achievement of these students could be high enough to raise the mean achievement of their entire group by several points.

Two approaches can be utilized to reduce the likelihood of this kind of error. One is to employ larger groups. For example, if 10 classes of 25 subjects were to be included in each group, instead of one class, the chances of the 20 brightest students all being assigned to groups being taught by the same method would be remote. The other approach is to check your groups for "outliers," that is, subjects who do not appear to fit into the groups, and eliminate these cases from your sample. The use of random assignment in experimental studies is discussed further in chapter 15.

SAMPLE SIZE

Important Considerations

A problem that must be faced in planning every research project is to determine the size of the sample necessary to attain the objectives of the planned research. The general rule is to use the largest sample possible. The rule is a good one because, although we generally study only samples, we are really interested in learning about the population from which they are drawn. The larger the sample, the more likely is its mean and standard deviation to be representative of the population mean and standard deviation. Sample size is also closely connected with statistical hypothesis testing. The larger the sample, the less likely we are to obtain negative results or fail to reject the null hypothesis when it is actually false. (We discuss this relationship between sample size and hypothesis testing in more depth in chapter 9, when we consider the theory underlying statistical hypothesis testing.)

In most research projects, financial and time restrictions limit the number of subjects that can be studied. In correlational research it is generally desirable to have a minimum of 30 cases. In causal-comparative and experimental research, it is desirable to have a minimum of 15 cases in each group to be compared. For survey research Seymour Sudman (see Annotated References) suggests that there be at least 100 subjects in each major subgroup and 20 to 50 in each minor subgroup whose responses are to be analyzed. In deciding on sample size, several factors should be considered. As a rule, larger samples are necessary under the following conditions:

1. *When many uncontrolled variables are present.* In many research studies, it is impossible for the investigator to control some of the important variables that could have an effect upon the research findings. Under these conditions research workers can have more confidence in the findings if they employ large samples. The large random sample, if attainable, is the best solution since it ensures to some extent that the uncontrolled variables will themselves be operating randomly for the different groups being studied and therefore will not have a systematic effect upon the results. Teaching ability, for example, is a difficult variable to control but is important in many educational studies. If a study of teaching methods involves only two teachers, one using method A and one method B, teaching-ability differences may cause more change in achievement than method differences. On the other hand, if 15 or more teachers are randomly assigned to each method, teaching-ability differences are more likely to "randomize out," thus permitting us to appraise method differences.

2. *When small effect sizes are anticipated.* In research projects in which only small differences on the dependent variable are expected among the various groups being studied, or in correlational studies where small relationships are

expected, it is desirable to use large samples. For example, a teacher may have developed a set of visual aids to help in teaching certain mathematical concepts. Such aids usually cannot be expected to make a large difference in student achievement. In order to evaluate these aids, large samples of pupils using and not using the aids would have to be compared. If small samples were used, the larger standard errors of the sample statistics could obscure small but important differences.

3. *When groups must be broken into subgroups.* Many educational research projects not only involve general comparisons of the different treatment groups but also can contribute additional worthwhile knowledge if these major groups are divided into subgroups and further comparisons are made. Let us suppose that we are carrying out a study of the possible effects of an extracurricular program upon the attitudes of high school students toward school. Ten schools having no organized extracurricular programs could be selected, and in five of these schools such a program could be developed. We might administer a pretest of student attitudes before the extracurricular program was introduced, and after a period of one or two years, administer final measures to determine what changes had taken place in student attitudes toward school. We might then compare attitude changes occurring in the schools that had adopted an organized program with the changes that occurred in the schools in which no extracurricular program had been present. After an overall analysis of these comparisons had been made, however, we might wish to compare the effects of the extracurricular program upon different groups in order to develop further understanding of the data. For example, we may hypothesize that girls' attitudes would be changed more markedly than boys' attitudes by the introduction of such a program because girls value social activities more highly at the high school level. This would require dividing the groups by sex and making further comparisons. We might then wonder if students at different socioeconomic levels might respond differently to the extracurricular program. Perhaps such a program would lead to favorable attitude changes on the part of middle-class students and unfavorable changes on the part of lower-class students. Again we would need to subdivide the original sample on the basis of social class in order to conduct this further analysis.

Such analyses often provide worthwhile knowledge and interesting theoretical insights, but they can be carried out only if the original groups are large enough so that, after such divisions are made, the subgroups still have sufficient numbers of cases to permit a statistical analysis. In the preceding example, a group of 100 students might be adequate to make the overall comparisons of the effects of the extracurricular program. However, in dividing the 100 cases into groups on the basis of sex and socioeconomic status, we may find that only 7 of the subjects can be classified as lower-class girls. This would indicate that 100 cases are not sufficient for subgroup analysis.

A mistake commonly made by inexperienced research workers is to select a sample that would be large enough for division into the anticipated subgroups only if the subgroups are equally represented in the sample. If there is an unequal representation, such as in the above example, we may have an insufficient number of cases in some groups to carry out the statistical analysis planned. This problem usually can be avoided by stratified sampling. But even with stratified sampling, because you cannot always predict all subgroups you may want to study, a large number of cases is also desirable.

4. *When high attrition is expected.* Perhaps the best basis for estimating attrition is to check the losses experienced in similar previous research. The duration of a study is a major factor in the amount of attrition to be expected. Robert Goodrich and Robert St. Pierre estimated that 20 percent attrition per year is a realistic level for planning.[17] Thus, attrition in longitudinal studies often exceeds 50 percent.[18] Attrition can be reduced by the following strategies:

a. Keep demands made upon the subject to the minimum necessary.
b. Fully inform subjects about your study, emphasizing its importance.
c. Before subjects start participating, obtain a strong commitment from them to complete their part in the research.
d. Make frequent contacts with subjects in order to maintain interest and rapport.

5. *When a high level of statistical significance, statistical power, or both are required.* The level of significance of a statistical test is closely related to sample size. Therefore, fewer subjects are needed to reject the null hypothesis at the .05 level than at the .01 level. In exploratory studies, many researchers employ an alpha (significance level) of .10 because such studies are often carried out with small samples.

Statistical power is the probability that a given statistical test will result in rejection of a false null hypothesis. Statistical power is enhanced by a large sample size.[19]

6. *When the population is highly heterogeneous on the variables being studied.* If every person in the population were exactly alike on the variable studied, a sample of one would be sufficient. As the population becomes more variable, however, larger samples must be used in order that persons having different amounts of the characteristic in question will be satisfactorily represented.

17. Robert L. Goodrich and Robert G. St. Pierre, *Opportunities for Studying Later Effects of Follow Through* (Cambridge, MA: ABT Associates, 1979)
18. For a discussion of factors affecting sample size, see Robert G. St. Pierre, "Planning Longitudinal Field Studies: Considerations in Determining Sample Size," *Evaluation Review* 4, no. 3 (June 1980); 405–415.
19. For a discussion of statistical power, see Jacob Cohen, *Statistical Power Analysis for the Behavioral Sciences* (New York: Academic Press, 1977).

7. *When reliable measures of the dependent variable are not available.* The reliability of a measure refers to its capacity to yield similar scores on the same individual when tested under different conditions or at different times.[20] The reliability of measures used in educational research differs greatly. Measures of variables such as academic achievement, reading comprehension, typing speed, and visual acuity are usually much more reliable than measures of variables such as personality, honesty, or self-concept. Nevertheless, research in many important areas of education must be done with measures of low reliability or not done at all, simply because the science has not yet advanced to the point where more reliable measures have been developed.

Measures that are less reliable have a larger error of measurement. This topic is discussed further in a later chapter; here it is sufficient to know that for an achievement test with a reliability of .95 and a standard deviation of 10, there is about once chance in three that an individual's true score will differ by more than 2.2 points from the score he obtains when he takes the test. In contrast, if the reliability had only been .50, there is the same probability that his obtained score will differ from his true score by more than 7.1 points. You can see that a test with a reliability of .50 is a rather crude measure and, because of its large error of measurement, may not be sufficiently sensitive to detect small differences. In studies that must employ measures of low reliability, you have little chance of detecting small differences if you use a small sample. As sample size increases, your chance of detecting small differences or slight relationships improves.

Suppose we wanted to study the difference between the adult height of males born in Germany in 1944–1946 and the heights of their brothers born in 1954–1956 to determine possible effects of diet on growth. If we use a highly accurate measure of height we can detect a much smaller difference than if we use a crude measure, such as a yardstick. Also, if a difference exists, it would be more likely to show up if we measure a sample of 1,000 pairs of brothers than if we measure only 50 pairs.

Small Sample Studies

In many educational research projects, small samples are more appropriate than large samples. This is often true of studies in which role-playing, depth interviews, projective measures, and other such time-consuming measurement techniques are employed. Such techniques cannot be used in large sample studies unless considerable financial support is available. However, a study that probes deeply into the characteristics of a small sample often provides more

20. Reliability is discussed further in chapter 7.

knowledge than a study that attacks the same problem by collecting only shallow information on a large sample. For example, a number of studies have attempted to discover the reasons why many superior college students drop out of college. Most of these studies have consisted of little more than classifying the one-sentence responses made by students on the dropout cards they complete for the registrar. Our knowledge of related studies in sociology and social psychology would lead us to doubt whether students give their true reasons for dropping out of college on such a card. Many students write down a convenient or socially acceptable reason regardless of their true reason for withdrawal. Other students are not fully aware of the true reasons why they are dropping out. One of the authors once participated in a research project in which superior students dropping out of Utah State University were given a carefully planned in-depth interview. These interviews, carried out by a trained psychologist, revealed that the student's true reasons for dropping out of college were almost always different from the reasons stated on the registrar's dropout card. Although it involved fewer than 50 superior dropouts, this study produced insights into the reasons for withdrawal from college that probably could never be obtained by the shallower approach employed by many studies.[21]

In other studies very close matching of subjects on the critical variables concerned in the study is possible, and under these conditions, small sampling studies often yield the information sought more efficiently than large sampling studies. The classic study by H. H. Newman, F. N. Freeman, and K. J. Holzinger on the intelligence of identical twins is a good example of such a study:[22] Because identical twins have the same genes, they are ideal for studying the relative influence of heredity and environment upon various human characteristics. One phase of this study, although concerned with only 19 pairs of separated identical twins, provided information on the relative influences of heredity and environment upon intelligence that would have been difficult to obtain with large samples of less closely matched subjects.

Estimating Needed Sample Size

Many graduate students carry out studies in which they employ small samples to study variables that are related to each other to a low degree. Their research is doomed to producing negative results because the small differences they are likely to obtain will not be statistically significant with a small sample.[23] In such

21. This study was conducted by Luna R. Brite.
22. H. H. Newman, F. N. Freeman, and K. J. Holzinger, *Twins: A Study of Heredity and Environment* (Chicago: University of Chicago Press, 1937).
23. See chapter 11 for a further discussion of sample size.

cases, if the student had carefully thought through the chances of success before starting, the student could have revised the plan so as to increase either the power of the treatment or the sample size and thus improve his or her chances of obtaining significant results.

A procedure such as described in the next few pages, although providing only a rough estimate of minimum sample size, should be followed when designing your research.

First, we will consider the procedure for estimating sample size when two groups are to be compared on the dependent variable in order to determine if they are significantly different. Experimental and causal-comparative studies are usually carried out to explore problems of this kind.

The first step is to study carefully related research that has used the same or a closely related dependent variable in order to determine the approximate amount of difference in this variable one might expect to find in one's own study.[24] For example, suppose you are planning a study designed to measure the effect of a new classroom management program on the attitudes toward school of sixth-grade pupils in inner-city schools. You locate three similar studies, each of which used different classroom management programs. However, these programs are all fairly similar to the program you plan to use. Since each study used a different measure of attitude toward school (the dependent variable), you must first review the studies and determine the standard deviation reported for each measure. If different standard deviations are reported for the experimental and control groups, the average will be sufficiently accurate for the estimation to be made. Next you should record the difference between the mean scores of the experimental and control groups for each study. Then, for each study, divide this difference by the standard deviation to determine the difference in standard deviation units. Finally, estimate the power of the treatments used in the three studies. Length of treatment is usually a good estimate of power, but there are many other factors you might consider, such as (1) Did all subjects regularly participate, or was participation irregular? (2) How well were treatments controlled; that is, did the investigator have methods of ensuring that the subjects actually did what they were intended to do? (3) Did the treatment employ procedures that appear effective? For example, in most cases a treatment in which the subjects perform a task is more effective than a treatment where the subjects read about the task. There are of course many other factors that would give clues to the effectiveness of a specific treatment, and you should try to make the best estimate you can. This estimate is then used to estimate how effective your treatment is likely to be compared with those used in previous research. The data on standard deviation, difference, and treatment for our three hypothetical studies is given below:

24. This is usually called *Effect Size* and abbreviated ES.

	A	B	C	D
	Standard Deviation of Dependent Variable	*Difference between Means on Dependent Variable*	*Difference in SD (B/A)*	*Length of Treatment*
Study 1	16	6	.38	40 hrs. over 8 wks.
Study 2	12	5	.42	32 hrs. over 4 wks.
Study 3	19	5	.26	16 hrs. over 2 wks.

You might reason that in your study the experimental groups of teachers will be trained 48 hours over 12 weeks and tested on the Jones School Inventory, which according to the test manual has a standard deviation of 14. Since your treatment appears to be more powerful than those used in studies 1, 2, or 3, you would estimate that the difference between your experimental and control groups in mean scores on the Jones School Inventory will be about half of a standard deviation, or 7 points (i.e., .50 × 14). Thus, the following values should be substituted into the formula for estimating the number of cases (N) you will need for each group in the research.[25]

N = number of cases needed in each group to achieve a difference significant at the .01 level. (This is want you want to estimate.)
s = 14 (standard deviation)
t = 2.7 (*t*-test value needed for significance at .01 level with about 45 cases)
D = 7 (estimated difference between mean scores of experimental and control groups)

$$N = \frac{2s^2 \times t^2}{D^2}$$
$$N = \frac{(2 \times 14^2) \times 2.7^2}{7^2} = \frac{392 \times 7.29}{49} = 58.32$$

The formula indicates that you will need 58 cases in each of the two groups.

25. This formula assumes that the standard deviation for both groups will be the same and that the experimental and control groups will be of the same size. Since the formula only provides a rough estimate, these assumptions would usually be acceptable.

A critical point in this estimate, of course, is estimating the size of D, the difference between the means. We advise you to be conservative in this estimate. If you have no previous research upon which to base this estimate, carry out a small-scale pilot study and use your results to estimate D. A pilot study is almost always a desirable step, for reasons explained in chapter 2.

If you are planning a study involving more than two treatments, select the two treatments for which you expect the largest mean difference and carry out the above procedure for each pair of groups separately. Then decide on your group size by considering all of the N values that you obtain.

Correlational Studies

If you are planning a correlational study, the process of estimating the number of cases needed is much easier. You would again estimate the probable size of the correlation you are likely to obtain based on previous research plus (if possible) the results of a pilot study. Then using table 6.2, you can go down the r

TABLE 6.2

**Approximate Number of Cases Needed for a
Correlation of a Given Level to Be Statistically
Significant at the .01 Level**

r	N
.80	9
.75	11
.70	13
.65	15
.60	18
.55	21
.50	26
.45	32
.40	42
.35	52
.30	70
.25	100
.20	150
.15	300

Source: Adapted from Henry E. Garrett, *Statistics in Psychology and Education*, 6th ed. (New York: David McKay, 1966), table 25, p. 201.

column until you come to the estimated correlation and then read the number of cases you will require in the *N* column to be statistically significant.

Since both the described procedures provide only estimates, the .01 level of significance is used. Thus, even if you are a bit optimistic in your expectations, you still have a good chance to obtain a difference that is significant at the .05 level, which is the alpha level selected by most graduate students.[26]

MISTAKES SOMETIMES MADE IN SAMPLING

1. The researcher fails to define the accessible and target populations and to provide evidence of their similarity.
2. Uses a sample too small to permit statistical analysis of interesting subgroups.
3. Fails to use the stratified sampling technique when needed to obtain adequate samples of subgroups.
4. When using volunteer subjects, fails to determine how they differ from nonvolunteers and fails to consider these differences in interpreting the findings.
5. Changes the sampling procedure in order to make data collection more convenient for the schools involved.
6. Does not allow for attrition in selecting the sample size.
7. Selects a sample that is not appropriate for the research project.
8. Selects the experimental and control groups from different populations.

ANNOTATED REFERENCES

Babbie, Earl R. *The Practice of Social Research*, 4th ed. Belmont, CA: Wadsworth, 1985.

A good source for students who plan to conduct survey research. Contains a chapter on survey sampling procedures and a chapter that gives examples of four sample designs.

Jaeger, Richard, M. *Sampling in Education and the Social Sciences*. New York: Longman, 1984.

Discusses the basic concepts underlying sampling theory and describes various forms of random, stratified, systematic, and cluster sampling in considerable detail.

Kalton, Graham. *Introduction to Survey Sampling*. Beverly Hills, CA: Sage, 1983.

---

26. For other methods of estimating sample size, see the Annotated References at the end of this chapter.

Describes the various sampling procedures and also addresses topics such as sampling frames, sample size, and nonprobability sampling. Although written primarily for the survey researcher, much of the information is relevant to other methodologies.

Kish, Leslie. *Survey Sampling*. New York: Wiley, 1965.

In spite of its age, still a basic reference on the use of sampling techniques in the social sciences. The discussion is fairly technical, but it is well worth consulting before the student attempts to use one of the sampling techniques presented in this chapter.

Olejnick, Stephen F. "Planning Educational Research: Determining the Necessary Sample Size." *Journal of Experimental Research* 53, no. 1, 40–48 (1984).

Discusses the problem of estimating needed sample size. Four factors affect this estimate: significance level selected for alpha, statistical power, the analysis procedure, and the estimated effect size. Two tables are provided that the student can use to estimate minimal sample size, given desired level of significance, statistical power, statistical tool to be used, and estimated effect size. Several references relevant to the sample size problem are cited.

Rosenthal, Robert, and Rosnow, Ralph L. *The Volunteer Subject*. New York: Wiley, 1975.

Should be required reading for serious students, since virtually all educational research must be conducted with volunteer subjects. It pulls together available research evidence on the characteristics of volunteer subjects and discusses the implications of this research for interpreting research findings in studies in which volunteers are used. The situational determinants of volunteering are also reviewed and suggestions are made for reducing volunteer bias.

Sudman, Seymour. *Applied Sampling*. New York: Academic Press, 1976.

An excellent source for the educational researcher who plans to carry out survey research. The chapters on small-scale sampling and sample size are especially valuable for the graduate student. The latter chapter explores the question of information versus cost and provides useful formulas for estimating optimum sample size.

SELF-CHECK TEST

Circle the correct answer to each of the following questions. An answer key is provided on page 883.

1. A common error in selecting a sample of research subjects is to
   a. select whatever persons are readily available.
   b. select a sample that is too large for the scope of the research problem.
   c. rely only on stratified sampling.
   d. use tables of random numbers which are not truly random.

2. All the members of a real of hypothetical set of persons, objects, or events are called the
   a. population.
   b. random sample.
   c. stratified sample.
   d. collection.
3. The first step in sampling is to
   a. define the population from which the sample is to be drawn.
   b. determine whether the sample is to be stratified.
   c. determine sample size.
   d. identify desired characteristics of the sample.
4. If the researcher defines his population in a narrow fashion, the research results will be
   a. useless.
   b. generalizable to a limited population.
   c. generalizable to a broad population.
   d. of no theoretical value.
5. A random sample
   a. is one in which each member of a population has an equal chance of being chosen.
   b. must be large in number.
   c. can be selected only by using a specially designed computer program.
   d. All of the above are correct.
6. The main reason for using random sampling techniques is to select a sample that will
   a. include the correct number of subjects.
   b. be stratified.
   c. yield generalizable research data.
   d. yield research findings that are statistically significant.
7. Systematic sampling may be used instead of simple random sampling if the
   a. population list is in nonperiodic order.
   b. sample size is small.
   c. population is heterogeneous.
   d. expected differences are small.
8. In cluster sampling the unit of sampling is the
   a. individual.
   b. population.
   c. naturally occurring group of individuals.
   d. population after having been subgrouped on characteristics not related to the research.
9. Compared to simple random sampling, the main advantage of cluster sampling is the
   a. degree of randomness it achieves.
   b. accuracy of sampling it achieves.
   c. reliability of research findings to which it leads.
   d. saving in time and money.
10. Large samples must be used when
    a. few uncontrolled variables are present.
    b. small differences are anticipated.
    c. subgroup analysis is not going to be conducted.
    d. the population is highly homogeneous.

APPLICATION PROBLEMS

The following problems are designed to give you practice in applying significant concepts and research procedures explained in the chapter. Most of them do not have a single correct answer. For feedback, you can compare your answers with the sample answers on pages 892–893.

1. An investigator plans to select a simple random sample of 100 subjects from the population of all fifth-grade pupils attending public schools in Utah. List the steps that she might take to obtain this sample.
2. An investigator wishes to analyze the verbal praise used by primary-grade teachers in a large-city school district. Since he wants an adequate sample of teachers of both sexes and at three different levels of experience, he decides to collect a stratified sample by selecting 20 teachers from each stratum. List the steps he would take in selecting this sample. He does not plan to combine his subgroups for analysis so proportional numbers are not necessary.
3. An investigator wishes to study oral reading performance of second-grade children in a large school district. A total of 3,172 second-grade children are enrolled in 104 classrooms in the district. The investigator wishes to obtain a total group of 100 subjects using a two-stage cluster sampling technique. Describe the steps she would take in selecting her sample.
4. An investigator plans to study the effects of learning a problem-solving strategy upon the mathematics achievement of sixth-grade students. He will select a sample of students and randomly assign half of them to the experimental group and half to the control group. All subjects will be given a pretest of mathematics achievement. The experimental group will receive a one-hour lesson which teaches a problem-solving strategy that students can follow when trying to solve word problems in mathematics. The control group receives no special training. Since he expects the problem-solving training to work best with the brighter students, the investigator will divide both his groups in terms of IQ using the following categories: (1) below 90, (b) 90–110, (c) 111–130, (d) above 130. He administers a mathematics achievement posttest two months after treatment to all subjects. What are two reasons why a fairly large sample size is required for this project?

5. What are four procedures in the following research description that are likely to cause sampling bias?

    An investigator teaches three sections of Remedial English for freshman in a large state university. A colleague teaches three sections of regular Freshman English. The investigator has developed a 20-hour program to teach rules of spelling. She gives a spelling test in her sections and in her colleague's sections. Next she selects 63 students from her sections and 36 from her colleague's sections who score below 50 percent on the test. She describes her program to her sections and asks the 63 low scorers to take the program by attending special sessions one hour per day for four weeks. Fifty-one agree to do so. The 36 students in her colleague's sections are used as a control group and receive no special treatment. At the end of four weeks, 26 of her students have completed the spelling program while the remainder have missed from 1 to 18 of the special sessions. She administers a spelling posttest to the 26 treatment subjects and the 36 control subjects and compares their gains since the pretest.

SUGGESTION SHEET

If your last name starts with letters from Dod to Fis, please complete the Suggestion Sheet at the end of the book while this chapter is still fresh in your mind.

7 SELECTION AND ADMINISTRATION OF TESTS

OVERVIEW

Standardized tests are often used in educational research projects to measure factors such as school achievement, aptitude, self-concept, and attitudes. Most tests used in educational research are norm-referenced. In recent years, however, domain-referenced tests of achievement have gained much attention. Among the important characteristics of tests discussed in this chapter are validity, reliability, conditions of administration, normative data, and alternate forms. Four kinds of test validity are discussed: content validity, predictive validity, concurrent validity, and construct validity. Also, we present three methods for determining test reliability and discuss their relationship to standard error of measurement. A discussion of factors to consider in selecting a test for a research project follows, such as the amount of testing time available, whether to use individual or group measures, and how to select between available measures. The chapter concludes with a presentation of guidelines on how to use tests in the context of an educational research project.

OBJECTIVES

After studying this chapter you should be able to:

1. Describe the four distinguishing characteristics of a standardized test.
2. Describe four types of test validity and identify the type of test validity that should be determined for different research problems.
3. Describe three types of test reliability and identify the type of test reliability that should be determined for different research problems.
4. Interpret the standard error of measurement and describe how it relates to reliability.
5. Describe three problems that arise when the researcher shortens a standardized test.
6. Describe the main steps the researcher must take to develop a measure.
7. Describe item-analysis procedures related to difficulty index, item validity, and item reliability.
8. List five major criticisms that have been made of educational tests.
9. Describe three procedures for ensuring that standard conditions for test administration are met.
10. State at least one procedure for handling each of these testing problems: gaining subjects' cooperation; eliciting maximal performance; obtaining honest answers on personality inventories; and giving test results to those who ask for them.
11. Give three reasons why generally it is not advisable to use school-collected test data in a research project.

TESTS IN EDUCATIONAL RESEARCH

In educational research we are usually concerned with one of three major goals. Descriptive research, which includes most surveys, is aimed at describing the characteristics of a population or an educational phenomenon. Correlational and causal-comparative research explore relationships between two or more variables. Experimental research is concerned with the effects of manipulating variables.

Measurement plays an important role in each of these types of educational research. Any procedure that produces objective and quantifiable information is a form of measurement. In education such procedures include interviewing, observation, and the administration of questionnaires and tests. In this chapter we focus on tests, since they are by far the most widely used procedure for collecting information in educational research. Tests come in a variety of types, such as written and oral, norm-referenced and domain-referenced, individual and group. A test can be broadly defined as any instrument for assessing individual differences along one or more given dimensions of behavior.

Most tests used in the behavioral sciences are **norm-referenced.** Briefly, this means that the test produces a score that tells us how the individual's performance compares with other individuals. The manuals for these tests provide the user with tables of norms based on the scores obtained by relevant groups of subjects who have been tested by the test developer. Interpretations based on relative performance are very useful for most of the characteristics we study in the behavioral sciences, such as anxiety, creativity, dogmatism, or racial attitudes.

For some kinds of performance, such as achievement, a measure that tells what the subject knows in absolute terms is often more useful than one that describes his or her performance in relative terms. For example, it is sometimes more useful to know that a student can read sample articles from a typical newspaper and be able to explain 90 percent of what has been read than to know that the student reads better than 62 percent of a sample of other fifth-grade pupils.

In recent years, **domain-referenced tests,** which measure the learner's absolute level of performance in a precisely defined content area or "domain," have been used to an increasing degree to measure achievement-related performance. This chapter emphasizes standardized norm-referenced measures because these are used in the vast majority of educational research. But it also introduces you to domain-referenced tests because these are more useful for many studies involving achievement or mastery of special skills.

Educational researchers also may develop tests to meet the special needs of a research project. Test development is a difficult process that often requires more training than the typical graduate student in education has acquired. In many cases, however, graduate students can use measures developed by other researchers, which, although not published, may be carefully developed.

To a degree all the aforementioned measures are "standardized." A **standardized test** is one (1) that produces very similar results when different persons administer and score the measure following the instructions given and (2) for which normative data are present to describe how subjects from specified populations perform. Not only have standardized tests become a basic part of methodology in educational research, but also their practical applications have become increasingly important in society. Think, for example, of the many tests you have taken as you progressed through the American school system— intelligence tests, teacher-made and published measures of school achievement, the Scholastic Aptitude Test, and the Graduate Record Examination. If you sought guidance in deciding upon an academic major and career, you probably completed tests pertaining to vocational interests and personality.

CHARACTERISTICS OF STANDARDIZED TESTS

As mentioned above, standardized tests have a number of important social applications for the classification, selection, evaluation, and diagnosis of persons. Our discussion focuses only on their uses in educational research, however. We begin by considering some of the defining characteristics of a standardized test.

1. *Objectivity*. The **objectivity** of a standardized test depends on the degree to which it is uninfluenced or undistorted by the beliefs or biases of the individuals who administer and score it. Prescientific measures and the measures used in the less mature sciences tend to have relatively little objectivity. Two individuals may use the same measure and arrive at two different observations or scores. In fact, the development of a science may be traced in terms of the progress it has made in recognizing the possibility of personal errors in measurement and in ruling them out to a greater and greater degree.[1]

The degree of objectivity of standardized tests in education can usually be determined by analyzing whether the administration and scoring procedures permit bias to occur. In our later discussion of individually administered tests (particularly projective techniques such as the Rorschach Inkblot Technique and the Thematic Apperception Test), we show how the conditions of administration and scoring provide a number of opportunities for bias to occur. Not surprisingly, then, these techniques usually do not yield high estimates of interobserver reliability. In contrast, multiple-choice tests are generally con-

1. For further review of experimenter errors and their effects on behavioral sciences, see chapter 15.

sidered much more objective since they are self-administered in large part, and all scorers can apply a scoring key and agree perfectly. In fact, these types of standardized tests are often called "objective tests."

2. *Conditions of administration.* It should be apparent that a test is of limited value if its developers do not specify all the directions to be given in administering the test. For example, a standardized test typically includes such information as how much time is allowed for the test, whether guessing is penalized, whether instructions can be repeated, and how student questions are to be answered. The directions may also include specification of how much personal interaction (e.g., establishing rapport) is allowed between the tester and the subjects. An important advantage of using standardized tests in your research project is that if you produce significant research findings, other researchers will be able to replicate and expand on your work because they can create the same conditions of administration by consulting the test manual.

3. *Normative data.* The process of collecting normative data on a test is an important part of the process of standardization. Generally a test developer will administer his test to a carefully defined sample (or several samples, usually varying in sex and age) and collect a set of raw scores. Individual scores are then related to the performance of the group as a whole by compiling a table of **test norms.** Often the raw scores are converted to **percentile ranks.** Given a particular raw score, the table of norms based on percentile ranks enables one to determine the percentage of individuals in the standardization group who received the same or a lower raw score. Table 7.1 is a typical table for converting raw scores to percentile ranks.

The table of norms is very helpful because, usually, you are interested in a subject's performance relative to the group rather than the subject's absolute performance. However, you should observe several precautions in using tables of norms prepared by developers of standardized tests. First, check to determine whether your sample is comparable to the standardization group on which the table of norms is based. Suppose that you are testing a sample of 12-year-olds with an aptitude test standardized on a group of high school seniors. If you use the table of norms for that group, you will seriously underestimate the average level of your group. Moreover, the test may be inappropriate for your sample and consequently will yield spurious scores.

Although percentile scores are useful because they are easily understood by the layperson, they cannot be used for the computation of statistics. This is because percentile ranks are not linear transformations of raw scores.[2] Therefore, you should convert percentile scores to standard scores for the purpose of statistical analysis. Many standardized tests in use today are provided with a table of norms based on standard scores. Essentially, **standard scores** are a set of

2. This problem is discussed in most textbooks on statistics.

TABLE 7.1

Norms Based on Percentile Ranks

Raw Score	Percentile Rank	Raw Score	Percentile Rank
48		34	44
47		33	40
46		32	36
45	99+	31	30
44	96	30	22
43	93	29	18
42	90	28	15
41	87	27	11
40	81	26	7
39	76	25	4
38	71	24	3
37	65	23	1
36	56		
35	49		

transformed scores derived from the mean and standard deviation of the raw scores. The topic of standard scores is developed further in our discussion on analysis of research data in chapter 20.

You have probably noted that the degree of confidence that can be placed in a table of norms depends on the care with which standard conditions of administration and scoring have been specified by the test developer. For example, if the tests on which normative data are based are scored by two individuals, one of whom is biased to assign lower scores, the resulting table of norms will reflect this bias and therefore will present an inaccurate picture of the distribution of test scores with a given population.

4. *Reliability and validity.* In addition to the characteristics of objectivity, standard conditions of administration, and normative data, standardized tests can also be described in terms of their reliability and validity. These important test characteristics are discussed next.

WHEN IS A TEST VALID?

In selecting a standardized test for use in a research project, you will want to make a thorough review of the evidence regarding the test's validity. A commonly used definition of validity is that it is the degree to which a test measures what it purports to measure. However, this general definition does not take into account the fact that there is more than one kind of test validity. The prospective test user should ask not "Is this test valid?" but "Is this test valid for the purposes to which I wish to put it?"

Without standards for validity, tests can be misused and may actually have deleterious effects on the person being tested. For example, an unscrupulous test developer might claim, without benefit of supporting evidence, that a particular test predicts vocational success. If the scores from this invalid test are taken at face value by high school counselors, the result could be that many students will be erroneously advised to avoid vocations for which they had aptitude or pursue vocations for which they were unsuited. In general, the dangers arising from the use of invalid tests in research are less serious than those that can occur by using such measures to make educational decisions in the schools.

Researchers sometimes use measures of low or unknown validity because no better measures are available. Most researchers are careful to point out such weaknesses and tend to be cautious in interpreting their results and drawing conclusions. Invalid tests can lead to erroneous research conclusions, which in turn can influence educational decisions. For this reason the American Psychological Association has published guidelines for determining test validity.[3] In this set of guidelines and in the field of educational measurement generally, four types of test validity are recognized—content, concurrent, predictive, and construct. Concurrent and predictive validity are sometimes grouped together and called *criterion-related validity* because they relate to the ability of a test to measure an individual's behavior on some other variable, called a *criterion*. We will also briefly discuss face validity. Because the typical graduate student is probably familiar with these terms, our discussion will emphasize their relevance to the design of a research project.

Content Validity

Content validity is the degree to which the sample of test items represents the content that the test is designed to measure. Content validity should not be confused with *face validity*, which refers to the evaluator's appraisal of what the content of the test measures. For example, if a test purports to measure reading achievement and if the items appear to deal with relevant content in this area, the test can be said to have face validity. In contrast to face validity, which is a subjective judgment that the test *appears* to cover relevant content, content validity is determined by systematically conducting a set of operations such as

3. See *Standards for Educational and Psychological Testing* in the Annotated References at the end of this chapter.

defining in precise terms the specific content universe to be sampled, specifying objectives, and describing how the content universe will be sampled to develop test items. Note that a test need not cover *all content* in a given course of study to be content valid, but must cover a *representative sample* of this content.

Content validity is important primarily in achievement testing and various tests of skills and proficiency, such as occupational skills tests. For example, a test of achievement in ninth-grade mathematics will have high content validity if the items covered on the test are representative, in type and proportion, of the content presented in the course. If test items cover topics not taught in the course, ignore certain important concepts, and unduly emphasize others as compared with their treatment in the course, the content validity will be lower. Unlike some types of validity, the degree of content validity is not expressed in numerical terms as a correlation coefficient (sometimes called a *validity coefficient*). Instead, content validity is appraised usually by an objective comparison of the test items with curriculum content.

Because content validity is concerned with the match between the content of *your course* and the test you are using, you will usually need to carry out your own content-validity analysis. A recent study comparing the content of the four most popular mathematics textbooks with the four most commonly used standardized achievement tests showed that the match between textbook and test content ranged from 21 percent to 50 percent. This means that in the worse case the student only had an opportunity to study 21 percent of what was tested. Clearly with content validity this low the achievement test provides a very inaccurate picture of what students have learned.[4]

Often the test manual will describe the techniques used to arrive at the test content. Thus, researchers interested in selecting a measure of ninth-grade mathematics achievement that is appropriate for their particular sample should determine whether the test developer derived test items from the same textbook or one similar to that studied by their sample.

Content validity is particularly important in selecting tests to use in experiments involving the effect of teaching methods on achievement. Suppose, for example, you are interested in doing a research project to determine whether an inquiry method of teaching social studies concepts is superior to a noninquiry method. The research project may involve training two groups of sixth-grade teachers to use one or the other method for one school term. At the end of the semester, a test of social studies achievement would be administered to determine whether the two teaching methods lead to different amounts of learning. To make a proper comparison, you would need to administer an achievement test that is representative of the content covered during the term; in other words, the test should have a high content validity, otherwise you cannot

---

4. See Andrew Porter, "Do Tests and Textbooks Match?" *IRT Communication Quarterly* 7, no. 3 (1985): 1, 4.

confidently draw conclusions from the study. If the hypothesis states that an inquiry approach leads to superior learning, but the specific content that was learned is not measured by the achievement test, the hypothesis has not been given a fair test.

In many studies, the objectives of the different methods or experimental treatments are not identical. In such cases, you should check the content validity very carefully to be sure that the measure selected is equally valid for all treatments. Obviously, a measure that is more valid for treatment A than for treatment B will produce results that spuriously favor the former. This problem occurred in some of the first research projects comparing the "new" mathematics program with the traditional curriculum. These studies yielded misleading findings because the content validity of the achievement tests used to assess outcomes was not carefully considered. The usual finding was no difference between the two curricula. However, the content of most mathematics achievement tests about a decade ago emphasized computational skills. With the development of new achievement tests with more emphasis on test items sampling basic concepts, research studies began to show that both curricula led to similar achievement in computational skills but that students in the "new" math curriculum showed superior achievement in their understanding of mathematical concepts. If you are planning a project involving comparison of the effects of several treatments (e.g., different teaching methods) on achievement, then you should select a test whose content is similar to that used in the treatments.

Predictive Validity

Predictive validity is the degree to which the predictions made by a test are confirmed by the later behavior of the subjects. Much educational research is concerned with the prediction of success in various activities. The usual method of determining predictive validity is to administer the test, wait until the behavior that the test attempts to predict has occurred, and then correlate the occurrence of the behavior with the scores of the subjects on the test. Let us take an algebra aptitude test as an example. Suppose that such a test were designed to be administered near the end of the eighth grade to predict success in ninth-grade algebra. At the end of the ninth grade, the test scores would be correlated with a measure of algebra achievement, such as grades in the algebra class or an algebra achievement test. In this case the algebra grades or the achievement test scores would be called **criterion measures.** The correlation between the algebra aptitude test and the algebra achievement test provides us a measure of the predictive validity of the aptitude test, that is, the degree to which its prediction of students' success in algebra was borne out by their later performance. In estimating criterion-related validity, the choice of a criterion and the measurement procedures used to obtain criterion scores are important and should always be checked when selecting measures for research. For example, the use of principal ratings as a criterion for a test of teacher competence would be a poor choice as such ratings have generally been found to be unreliable and invalid. In other words, studies of criterion-related validity are no better than the criterion measure that has been used.

It is important to assess the predictive validity of a standardized test before deciding whether to use it in making practical decisions requiring forecasts, such as selecting students for college. Predictive validity is also important in many research projects. As an illustration, suppose that you are interested in planning a research project to identify variables that predict success among high school students in doing remedial tutoring with younger students. In deciding which tests to include in your test battery, you might well look for measures that have been shown to have predictive validity in similar situations. For example, you might find that the Strong-Campbell Interest Inventory is a good predictor of which high school students will chose to major in education at college. On the basis of this evidence, you might include this vocational interest inventory in your test battery in expectation that it would predict this new criterion, that is, success in remedial tutoring.

The student who plans to assess the validity of a test in predicting a particular criterion should be familiar with the concepts of base rate and cross-validation. Base rate is the proportion of persons who meet the criterion out of the total number of persons in the population. To illustrate, suppose that your project involves the use of personality tests to predict students who will be arrested for delinquency during a particular school year. Suppose further that the incidence of delinquency is 5 percent of the particular student population in which you are interested. Thus, in a sample of 100 students it is likely that 5 will become delinquent, and 95 will remain nondelinquent. You can see that with this base rate, you can predict delinquency correctly 95 percent of the time simply by predicting that everyone in the sample will be nondelinquent. Although a valid personality test might further increase the predictability of delinquency under these conditions, the practical value of the test will be slight. The implication of this example is that you should only attempt to predict a criterion whose base rate of incidence is not exceptionally high or low.

In many prediction studies, a number of tests are used to predict a specific criterion. The researcher can then develop a prediction equation (see chapter 14) based on some or all of these tests that will yield a higher validity coefficient than the correlation between any one test and the criterion. This prediction equation may be spuriously high, however, because it capitalizes on chance fluctuations in the data. Therefore, to determine the value of the prediction equation it is necessary to cross-validate by administering the same tests to a new sample drawn from the same population. Generally, the validity coefficient obtained in the initial study will shrink somewhat for the new sample.[5]

Concurrent Validity

A second type of criterion-related validity is called concurrent validity. The **concurrent validity** of a test is determined by relating the test scores of a group of subjects to a criterion measure administered at the same time or within a short interval of time. The distinction between concurrent and predictive validity depends on whether the criterion measure is administered at the same time as the standardized test (concurrent) or later, usually after a period of several months or more (predictive.).

In designing a research project, you may well be interested in locating a short, easily administered objective test that has high concurrent validity with a criterion which, although important, is more difficult to measure. For example, if you are interested in measuring intelligence, it might be quite impractical to use the Wechsler Intelligence Scale for Children or the Stanford-Binet Intelligence Scale, each of which must be individually administered and requires one or more hours of testing time. Even though these tests have considerable standardization data and much evidence of predictive and construct validity, it is much more economical to administer one of several brief, objective, group tests of intelligence that have high concurrent validity when compared with the Stanford-Binet or the Wechsler scales.

Tests with high concurrent validity can often be used as a substitute for ratings of a particular personality characteristic. One of the authors planned a research project to determine whether anxious college students showed more preference for female role behaviors than less anxious students.[6] To identify contrasting groups of anxious and nonanxious students, it might have been necessary to have a large sample of students evaluated for clinical signs of anxiety by experienced clinical psychologists. However, the author was able to locate a quick, objective test, the Taylor Manifest Anxiety Scale, which has been demonstrated to have high concurrent validity with clinical ratings of anxiety in a college population. The author saved considerable time conducting the research project by substituting this quick, objective measure for a procedure that is time-consuming and subject to personal error. Nevertheless, if the test's concurrent validity had been established with groups other than students, such

5. For an example of a predictive validity study, see Gregory P. Darakjian and William B. Michael, "The Long-term Comparative Predictive Validities of Standardized Measures of Achievement and Academic Self-Concept for a Sample of Secondary School Students," *Educational and Psychological Measurement* 43 (1983): 251–260.
6. Meredith D. Gall, "The Relationship Between Masculinity-Femininity and Manifest Anxiety," *Journal of Clinical Psychology* 25 (1969): 294–295.

as military personnel or psychiatric inpatients, then the author would have had no justification for substituting this test for clinical ratings or other measures of anxiety. When you are deciding which measures to use in a research project, you should seriously consider using a brief standardized test before resorting to measures that require complicated administration and scoring procedures.

In evaluation of a test's concurrent validity, you need to assess the adequacy of the criterion (as is true in evaluation of a test's predictive validity). Occasionally a test will be validated against another test rather than against a meaningful real-life criterion. There is little value in knowing that one test of anxiety, for example, correlates highly with a criterion test of anxiety, unless the criterion test itself has been demonstrated to have significant construct or predictive validity. If the criterion is valid, so presumably is the other test that correlates highly with it.[7]

Construct Validity

Construct validity is the extent to which a particular test can be shown to measure a hypothetical construct, that is, "a theoretical construction about the nature of human behavior."[8] Psychological concepts—such as intelligence, anxiety, creativity—are considered hypothetical constructs because they are not directly observable but rather are inferred on the basis of their observable effects on behavior. In order to gather evidence on construct validity, the test developer often starts by setting up hypotheses about the characteristics of persons who obtain high scores on the measure as opposed to those who obtain low scores. Suppose, for example, that a test developer publishes a test that claims to be a measure of anxiety. How can one determine whether the test does in fact measure the construct of anxiety? One approach might be to determine whether the test differentiates between psychiatric and normal groups, since theorists have hypothesized that anxiety plays a substantial role in psychopathology. If the test does in fact differentiate the two groups, then we have some evidence that it measures the construct of anxiety.

A variety of procedures may be used to establish the construct validity of a test, yet many published tests have only a limited amount of evidence to indicate that they are indeed measuring the constructs that they purport to measure. Construct validity is a particularly important factor to consider in planning a research study that proposes to test a hypothesis. For example, suppose that you plan to test the hypothesis that creative children will be able to state more

---

7. For an example of a concurrent validity study, see Lawrence J. Dolan, "Validity Analyses for the School Attitude Measures at Three Grade Levels," *Educational and Psychological Measurement* 43 (1983): 295–303.
8. *Standards for Educational and Psychological Testing* (1985), p. 9. See the Annotated References at the end of this chapter.

meanings of a word than will noncreative children. To test this hypothesis, you will need to ask yourself whether your hypothesis presupposes a particular concept of creativity, for example, potential or actualized creativity, artistic or scientific creativity, creativity as process or creativity as product.

On occasion you may plan a research project in which it is not important to consider construct validity. This is the case when the primary purpose of the research is to find predictors of a criterion on an empirical basis without resort to theory. Here the concern is to identify tests that have predictive validity for a particular purpose. The construct validity of the tests is not necessarily relevant. In fact, researchers not uncommonly determine a test's predictive validity in one study and then investigate the test's construct validity in later studies.[9]

Face Validity

Face validity is concerned with the degree to which a test *appears* to measure what it purports to measure, whereas the other forms of test validity we have described *provide evidence* that the test measures what it purports to measure. Thus, although face validity can never take the place of the other forms of test validity, it is still important because most people react more favorably to tests having high face validity. Nevo suggests that tests having face validity are more likely to:

Bring about higher levels of cooperation and motivation while subjects are taking the test.

Reduce feelings of dissatisfaction or injustice among low scorers.

Help convince potential users (e.g., teachers and school administrators) to implement the test.

Improve public relations, as laypeople can more easily see the relationship between the test and the performance or characteristic it purportedly measures.[10]

For example, face validity is low for many personality measures. Such measures often contain items that validly differentiate between normal and maladjusted groups but do not *appear* to be related in any way to the maladjustment in question. Persons tested with such measures often reject the results or refuse to cooperate because they cannot perceive any relationship

9. For an example of a construct validity study, see Kenneth C. Caillet and William B. Michael, "The Construct Validity of Three Self-Report Instruments Hypothesized to Measure the Degree of Resolution for Each of the Six Stage Crises in Erickson's Developmental Theory of Personality," *Educational and Psychological Measurement* 43, no. 1 (1983): 197–209.
10. See Baruch Nevo, "Face Validity Revisited," *Journal of Educational Measurement* 22, no. 4 (1985): 287–293.

between the test and the maladjustment. Thus, face validity can be an important consideration in selecting tests for use in situations where subject acceptance is essential. However, a test can *appear* to be valid when evidence for the other kinds of test validity indicates it is not. Therefore, let us emphasize again that face validity can only supplement information about predictive, concurrent, construct, or content validity of a test and can *never take the place of such information.*

DETERMINING TEST RELIABILITY

Reliability, as applied to educational measurements, may be defined as the level of internal consistency or stability of the measuring device over time. When two forms of a test are administered to the same sample of individuals, or when the same test is administered on two occasions, the same individuals will usually obtain different scores. These differences are in part attributable to *errors in measurement.* As such errors become larger, the reliability of the test becomes lower.

There are several methods of estimating reliability, most of which call for computing a correlation coefficient between two sets of similar measurements. Suppose we wished to measure students' knowledge of physics. A physics achievement test consisting of one multiple-choice item would be highly unreliable. Some students may know quite a bit about physics, yet may not happen to know the answer to this particular test item; in contrast, some students whose achievement level in physics is low may happen to know or guess the correct answer. Also, if we had selected a different item, the results would probably have been much different. Thus, the one-item test is susceptible to many chance factors and therefore is not a "reliable" estimate of the students' level of achievement in physics.

Reliability is an extremely important characteristic of tests, and it must be carefully considered in selecting measures for research purposes. The level of reliability you should require from the tests you select is determined largely by the nature of the research in which you plan to use these measures. If the research project is such that you can expect only small differences between your experimental and control groups on a variable measured by the test, then you need to use a test of high reliability. Conversely, if large samples are to be used and if the mean test scores are expected to differ materially for the experimental and control groups, then you may select a measure of relatively low reliability and still be reasonably sure that the test will discriminate adequately. The reason a test of high reliability is required in the first situation and not the second is that when only small differences are likely to be found, a test of low reliability may be too crude to reveal these differences. For example, let us say we wished to measure the height of two samples of adult men, but had only a crude

TABLE 7.2

Range and Median Values of Reliabilities Reported for Various Types of Measures

Type of Test	Number of Reliabilities	Value of Reported Reliabilities		
		Low	Median	High
Achievement batteries	32	.66	.92	.98
Scholastic ability	63	.56	.90	.97
Aptitude batteries	22	.26	.88	.96
Objective personality	35	.46	.85	.97
Interest inventories	13	.42	.84	.93
Attitude scales	18	.47	.79	.98

SOURCE: Reprinted from G. C. Helmstadter, *Principles of Psychological Measurement,* © 1964, p. 85. Reprinted by permission of Prentice-Hall, Inc., Englewood Cliffs, NJ.

measuring device, such as the span.[11] Let us further suppose that the true mean difference in height between the groups is one-half inch. One is unlikely to detect this small a difference because the span is a fairly unreliable measure; a person may not extend his hand to the same length each time, and if more than one person does the same measuring, their hands probably will not be of the same size. However, if the true mean difference in heights between the two groups of men is four inches, the taller group is more likely to be accurately distinguished from the shorter group despite the unreliability of the span as a measuring device.

The reliability of a test is much easier to establish than its validity. Therefore, if no specific information on reliability is provided in the test manual, you may safely assume that the reliability of the test is low. A helpful list of representative reliabilities of standardized tests has been prepared by G. C. Helmstadter[12] and is reproduced in table 7.2. It should be noted that the values of the reliabilities vary with the type of characteristic being measured. A check by the author of a sample of tests that are reviewed in the *Ninth Mental Measurements Yearbook* and *Test Critiques* indicates that reliabilities have not changed significantly from the averages reported in table 7.2

A point that must be watched for in evaluating test reliability is that many tests yield a number of subscores in addition to a total score. This is the case for some intelligence and achievement tests that provide subscores in order to give a

11. The distance from the tip of the thumb to the tip of the little finger when extended.
12. G. C. Helmstadter, *Principles of Psychological Measurement* (Englewood Cliffs, NJ: Prentice-Hall, 1964), table 8, p. 85.

profile of the student's performance in the various areas making up the test. However, reliability is often reported only for the total score. Therefore, the subscores must be used cautiously unless reliability data are available for them. When such data are not available, you will have difficulty making an intelligent appraisal of the worth of the subscores. You may be sure that all or most of these subscores will have lower reliabilities than the total test reliability. The reliability coefficients of the subscores, however, may differ considerably, with some being as reliable as the total test and others being of such low reliability that they should not be used in the planned research.

The reliability of a standardized test is usually expressed as a coefficient. Reliability coefficients vary between values of .00 and 1.00, with 1.00 indicating perfect reliability, which is never attained in practice, and .00 indicating no reliability. The reliability coefficient reflects the extent to which a test is free of error variance. Error variance may be defined as the summed effect of the chance differences between persons that arise from factors associated with a particular measurement. These factors might include wording of the test, the person's mood on the day the test is administered, the ordering of the test items, or the content that is used. The closer a reliability coefficient is to the value of 1.00, the more the test is free of error variance and is a measure of the true differences among persons in the dimension assessed by the test.

Reliability coefficients can be obtained by several different approaches, and each type has a somewhat different meaning. A description of the types in common use follows.

Coefficient of Equivalence

This method of calculating reliability may be used whenever two or more parallel forms of a test are available. This method is often called *alternate form reliability* and is computed by administering two parallel forms of the test to the same group of individuals and then correlating the scores obtained on the two forms in order to yield a reliability coefficient. The two forms of the test may be administered at a single sitting, or an interval may be scheduled between the two administrations. Some interval between the administration of the forms is usually desirable, especially if the alternate forms are nearly identical, as is the case with some achievement measures. This interval tends to reduce practice effects that may be an important factor if the two forms of the test are administered at the same sitting. Administering the two forms at different times also results in some differences in both the setting and in the state of mind of the individuals who are tested. Therefore, the reliability obtained is usually lower, but reflects better the testing situation that exists in most research projects. At the present time, the **coefficient of equivalence** is the most commonly used estimate of reliability for standardized tests. It is very widely used with standardized achievement and intelligence tests.

Coefficient of Stability

This form of reliability is useful when alternate forms of the test are not available or not possible to construct. To calculate the **coefficient of stability,** sometimes called *test-retest reliability*, the measure is administered to a sample of individuals, and then after a delay the same measure is again administered to the same sample. Scores obtained from the two administrations are then correlated in order to determine the coefficient of stability. The most critical problem in calculating this form of reliability is to determine the correct delay between the two administrations of the measure. If the retest is administered too quickly after the initial test, students will recall their responses to many of the items, which will tend to produce a spuriously high reliability coefficient. On the other hand, if the retesting is delayed for too long a period, there is a good possibility that the student's ability to answer some items will change. For example, the student may pass through a period of development or learning and thus be better prepared to answer questions on the retest.

Coefficient of Internal Consistency

Several methods can be used to estimate the internal consistency of a test. Unlike other procedures for computing test reliability, internal consistency can be determined from a single administration of a single form of the test. The commonly used methods of computing internal consistency are the *split-half* or *subdivided test*, the Kuder-Richardson *method of rational equivalence*, and Cronbach's *Coefficient Alpha. Hoyt's Analysis of Variance Procedure* is less often used.

The most widely used method of estimating internal consistency is through the split-half correlation. To determine the **coefficient of internal consistency,** the test whose reliability is under investigation is administered to an appropriate sample. It is then split into two subtests, usually by placing all odd-numbered items in one subtest and all even-numbered items in another subtest.[13] The scores of the two subtests are then computed for each individual, and these two sets of scores are correlated. The correlation obtained, however, represents the reliability coefficient of only half the test, and since reliability is related to the length of the test, a correction must be applied in order to obtain the reliability of the entire test. The Spearman-Brown prophecy formula is used to make this correction.[14]

The **method of rational equivalence,** which also provides an estimate of internal consistency, is the only widely used technique for calculating reliability

13. Other methods of splitting the test are sometimes used, such as a logical division of the test into two sets of comparable items.
14. See William A. Mehrens and Irving J. Lehmann (1987) in the Annotated References at the end of this chapter for a discussion of this formula.

that does not require the calculation of a correlation coefficient. This method gets at the internal consistency of the test through an analysis of the individual test items. It requires only a single administration of the test. A number of formulas have been developed to calculate reliability using this method. These are generally referred to as the Kuder-Richardson formulas, after the authors of an article in which these formulas were first discussed.[15] The formulas in this article are numbered, and the two most widely used are usually referred to as K-R 20 and K-R 21. Items must be scored dichotomously (that is, right or wrong) in order to use these formulas.

Formula 20 is considered by many specialists in educational and psychological measurement to be the most satisfactory method of determining reliability. This formula is being used to an increasing degree to determine the reliability of standardized tests.

Formula 21, a simplified approximation of formula 20, is of value primarily because it provides a very easy method of determining a reliability coefficient. The use of formula 21 requires so much less time than other methods for estimating test reliability that it is highly appropriate for use in teacher-made tests and short experimental tests being developed by a research worker. One desirable aspect of the Kuder-Richardson formulas is that they generally yield a lower reliability coefficient than would be obtained by using the other methods described. Thus they can be thought of as providing a minimum estimate of reliability of a test.

Cronbach's **Coefficient Alpha** (α) is a general form of the K-R 20 formula that can be used when items are not scored dichotomously. For example, some multiple-choice tests and essay tests include items that have several possible answers, each of which is given a different weight. In this case, Alpha is the appropriate method for computing reliability.[16]

Hoyt's Analysis of Variance Procedure is occasionally mentioned in the research literature. It is rarely used, however, because it produces exactly the same results as K-R 20 and is more difficult to compute.

A Comparison of the Methods of Estimating Reliability

Although the different methods of estimating reliability usually produce similar results, there are usually some differences because different methods take into account different sources of error. Reliability coefficients based on one administration of the test, or of different forms of the test at a single sitting, exclude two sources of error that are present in many research situations where single

15. M. W. Richardson and G. F. Kuder, "The Calculation of Test Reliability Coefficients Based upon the Method of Rational Equivalence," *Journal of Educational Psychology* 30 (1939): 681–687.
16. See Lee J. Cronbach, "Coefficient Alpha and the Internal Structure of Tests," *Psychometrika* 16 (1951): 297–334.

administration is not possible. First, individuals differ from day to day on many subtle variables such as mood, level of fatigue, and attitude toward the test. Second, in spite of your best efforts to maintain standard conditions, when tests are given on different occasions many small variations are likely to occur in the testing situation. For example, the administrator may read the instructions more rapidly, a light may burn out in the test room, or the school band may march past the classroom window.

The coefficient of stability, in which subjects are administered the same test on two different occasions, fails to reflect a different source of error because of the fact that the subjects are exposed to the same items on both occasions. The items on a particular test constitute only a small sample of all items that could be written in the area the test covers. The specific items on a single test are likely to discriminate in favor of some students and against others. This error will show up if the split-half or parallel-form reliability is computed since the two sets of scores that are correlated are based on different samples of items. However when the test-retest method is used, this source of error is not taken into account.

Only when a combination of equivalence and stability is employed, that is, when different forms of the test are administered with a time interval between, are all three of these sources of error taken into account. Thus, this method provides a more conservative estimate of reliability and one that reflects the conditions that maintain in most educational research projects. Because reliability data are fairly easy to collect, many standardized tests report reliability coefficients obtained from several different methods. In this case, you should consider which of the aforementioned sources of error will be present in your research and should use, if available, the reported estimates of reliability that take these sources into account.

Standard Error of Measurement

The various forms of reliability give an overall estimate of test consistency that is very useful in comparing different tests that you may want to consider for use in a research project. However, for interpreting test scores, the standard error of measurement is a more useful tool.[17] An individual's test score is likely to contain a certain amount of measurement error. The **standard error of measurement** allows you to estimate the range within which the individual's true score probably falls. For example, suppose the test manual for an algebra aptitude test reports that the alternate form reliability coefficient (r_{11}) is .85, for a norm group of 300 eighth-grade students, and the standard deviation of the test scores

---

17. Also called the *standard error of the obtained score.*

(s) is 14. To compute the standard error of measurement (s_m) we use the following formula:

$$s_m = s\sqrt{1 - r_{11}}$$

Substituting the given values into this equation we have

$$s_m = 14\sqrt{1 - .85}$$
$$= 14\sqrt{.15}$$
$$= 14 \times .387 = 5.42$$

Since s_m is normally distributed, we can estimate the probability that an error of a given size will occur. The relationship between errors and the normal probability curve is covered in elementary statistics textbooks and is discussed briefly in a later chapter. At this point it is sufficient for you to know that about two-thirds of all test scores will be within plus or minus one standard error of measurement of their true score and about 95 percent will be within ± two s_m. In the above example, if a student obtained a score of 86 on the algebra aptitude test, there would be 2 chances in 3 that the true score would be between 80.58 and 91.42 (i.e., 86 ± 5.42); and 95 chances in 100 that the student's true score would lie between 86 ± 2 × 5.42 (86 ± 10.84 or 75.16 and 96.84).

It is clear from the formula that the size of s_m is inversely related to the reliability coefficient; that is, as the reliability becomes higher, the error becomes smaller. If the algebra aptitude test had had a reliability of .96, the s_m would have been 2.8; while if the reliability had been .57, the s_m would have been 9.18. Thus, you can see that tests of low reliability are subject to large errors. Under these conditions an individual's true score on the test may vary by a large number of score points from the score obtained.

Standard error of measurement helps us to understand that the scores we obtain on educational tests are only estimates and can be considerably different from the individual's "true score." With this in mind we can avoid the blind faith in test scores that many educators seem to have. We can see, for example, that there may be no real intelligence difference between two pupils who receive IQ scores of 97 and 102. Standard error of measurement can also be regarded as an index of a test's reliability. In fact, as we have seen, the standard error of measurement can be determined directly from the reliability coefficient and the standard deviation of the test scores. The standard error of measurement cannot be used to compare the reliability of different tests, however, although the reliability coefficient can be used for this purpose.[18]

18. For a more detailed discussion of the standard error of measurement, see Richard H. Williams and Donald W. Zimmerman, "On the Virtues and Vices of the Standard Error of Measurement," *Journal of Experimental Education* 52, no. 4 (1984): 231–233.

DOMAIN-REFERENCED TESTS

Most achievement tests used in the public schools evaluate the performance of the individual relative to the performance of a well-defined group that was tested in order to develop the test norms, that is, the norm group. Such tests are called **norm-referenced tests.** Their main goal is to differentiate clearly among students at different levels of achievement. For example, a norm-referenced test in arithmetic achievement will typically contain items on addition, subtraction, multiplication, and division, ranging from easy to very difficult problems involving each operation. Note that arithmetic is broadly defined and that the student's score on the test, although telling how well the student compares with other students in overall arithmetic achievement, often tells little about the student's specific strengths and weaknesses. For example, consider the test performance of three students: Student A does very well on addition and subtraction, average on multiplication, and zero on division; student B answers about one-third of the items correctly in all four operations; student C gets all subtraction and division problems correct, except those that require regrouping (i.e., borrowing), and misses all addition and multiplication problems that require adding 9 plus 7. These students differ greatly on their specific strengths and weaknesses, yet all could obtain exactly the same score on a norm-referenced test of arithmetic achievement.

A **domain-referenced test** is one that draws a random or stratified sample of items from a very precisely defined content area or domain for which the content limits are clearly specified, such as "all arithmetic problems involving the addition of three two-digit whole numbers." Note that this domain is much more narrow and precisely defined than is "arithmetic achievement" on a norm-referenced test. To obtain a broader estimate of the learner's arithmetic achievement, we would have to define several domains and develop a test to measure the learner's mastery of each. Broadly defined domains lead to heterogeneous content and should be avoided since the resulting test is likely to show that the learner has mastered some aspects of the domain but not others. Such results are less clear and less appropriate for criterion-referenced interpretation than are results based on precise definition of narrow domains.

One major function of domain-referenced tests is to estimate the learner's "domain status," that is, precisely what is the learner's level of performance and specific deficiencies in the domain covered by the test? Another function of such tests is to make criterion-referenced decisions. Once a domain has been defined and items developed, a performance criterion can be established, such as, "Given a sample of problems requiring the addition of three two-digit whole numbers, all students will reach or exceed the 90 percent accuracy level." Scores are then interpreted in reference to this criterion. Domain-referenced tests that are interpreted in terms of students reaching or not reaching an established criterion are called **criterion-referenced tests.**

Norm-Referenced versus Domain-Referenced Achievement Measures

Whether you decide to use norm-referenced or domain-referenced achievement measures depends on the specific questions you want to explore. Norm-referenced achievement tests can be used to answer questions such as the following:

1. Where does John stand in reading achievement compared to other children in his first-grade class and compared to the national norm group of first-grade children reported in the test manual?
2. How does the overall arithmetic achievement in Ms. Smith's class compare with that in Ms. Jones's class?
3. How does the science achievement of fifth-grade pupils in Salt Lake City school district compare with the national norms, or with pupils in the Ogden city school district?

Domain-referenced tests can provide answers to some of the aforementioned questions, but are not as useful for comparing relative achievement in a broadly defined content area as are norm-referenced measures. Domain-referenced measures, however, since they deal with a much more specific content domain, are more useful in answering such questions as:

1. What is John's level of knowledge in the domain; that is, what percentage of addition problems of a given type can we expect him to solve correctly?
2. What are his specific deficiencies in the domain? Domain-referenced tests are much more useful for diagnosis of specific learning difficulties than are the typical norm-referenced achievement tests.
3. How is Cheryl progressing relative to her past performance? This question is usually important in self-pacing or individualized instructional programs.
4. What are the specific strengths and weaknesses of a given school program or curriculum; for example, what specific objectives are we achieving with our new first-grade reading program and what objectives are not being attained? Needs assessments, which examine differences between desired and actual learning status of students in a given school or district, often ask questions of this sort.
5. What specific changes in pupil performance have occurred as a result of changing the curriculum?

In summary, when we want information about student achievement *relative to other students,* we should select norm-referenced measures. When we want to diagnose difficulties or find out what students have achieved *in absolute terms,* we should select domain-referenced measures.

Reliability

Reliability of a domain-referenced test is defined as the consistency of the test in making estimates of the examinee's levels of mastery of the test's domain. The correlational methods most often used to determine the reliability of norm-referenced tests are not suitable for domain-referenced tests because the correlation coefficient is not appropriate for comparing sets of scores having little variability, as is the case in domain-referenced tests. Norm-referenced test items are selected to produce maximum variability since the purpose of such tests is to discriminate clearly among students at different achievement levels. In fact, items that nearly all students answer correctly are eliminated from norm-referenced tests. On the other hand, the selection of items for a domain-referenced test is concerned only with selecting items that fit into the domain as defined. Items that everyone answers correctly are not eliminated if they fit into the domain. Therefore, if the training program has been successful, students will vary little on a domain-referenced test because most students answer most items correctly. In the addition example given earlier, the goal was to bring all students up to the 90 percent mastery criterion. You can see that if this goal is achieved, there will be relatively little variability in the total test scores. In contrast, norm-referenced test items generally are selected at or near the 50 percent difficulty level, which produces maximum variability in the total test scores.

There are procedures for determining reliability of criterion-referenced measures that roughly parallel the split-half, test-retest, and alternate form methods used with norm-referenced tests.

You will recall that the user's main concern in criterion-referenced measures is whether or not students have achieved the criterion established. Reliability estimates compare different forms of the measure on their agreement in placing students into two groups: those who reached the criterion, and those who did not. Reliability is usually reported in terms of percentage of agreement rather than as a correlation coefficient, as is the case with norm-referenced measures.[19]

Validity

Because domain-referenced measures are generally aimed at measuring achievement, evidence of content validity is important. Several procedures have been developed that are generally similar to methods used to establish content

19. For specific procedures for computing the reliability of domain-referenced tests, see Victor R. Martuza, *Applying Norm-Referenced and Criterion-Referenced Measurement in Education* (Boston: Allyn & Bacon, 1977), chap. 17. Another useful source on this topic is Jason Millman, "Reliability and Validity of Criterion-Referenced Test Scores," in *New Directions for Testing and Measurement; Methodological Developments*, ed. R. Traub (San Francisco: Jossey-Bass, 1979). See also Ronald A. Berk, "A Consumer's Guide to Criterion-Referenced Test Reliability," *Journal of Educational Measurement* 17, no. 4 (1980): 323–349.

validity of norm-referenced achievement tests. For example, R. Hambleton and his associates have developed the following procedure:

1. Select two content specialists.
2. Give each specialist the domain definition (which is a very specific description of the content domain to be tested) and the test items.
3. Have each expert independently rate the relevance of each item to the domain definition using a 4-point scale ranging from "not relevant" to "very relevant."
4. These data are then entered into a table and used to compute a measure of interrater agreement and an index of content validity.[20]

FACTORS TO BE CONSIDERED IN TEST SELECTION

Adjusting to Available Testing Time

A dilemma faced by many graduate students in planning their research is administering satisfactory measures of the variables that are important to their problem within the testing time they can obtain from their subjects. It is desirable to use the most valid and reliable measures available, but when the testing time for these measures is added up, the total often exceeds the time available.

The amount of time available to test research subjects is almost always limited. Suppose you are working with a public school sample, and a total of one hour is available for testing. You may want to administer several measures; however, one of these measures requires an hour to complete. You may find in reading the test manual or reviewing the literature that a short form of the test, requiring perhaps half the time of the long form, is available. Or you may discover another test that is somewhat less reliable but requires only half the administration time. This savings in time permits you to administer one or more additional measures, which may make an important contribution to your research.

The reliability of a test is related to its length. The more items in a test, the better estimate we can make of the person's true score, which would be his or her score on a test of infinite length. Because the reliability coefficient indicates the extent to which a test reflects the true score variance, it follows that a shorter test will usually be less reliable. However, since the test developer usually retains the best items in the short form, the loss in reliability is in fact often slight. For example, a recent study of the Beck Depression Inventory found that

20. A description of this procedure and others for determining content validity of domain-referenced measures may be found in Martuza, *Applying Norm-Referenced Criterion—Referenced Measurement in Education*, 1977.

the standard form (21 items) had a reliability of .85, whereas the short form (13 items) had a reliability of .83.[21]

Many standardized tests in areas such as achievement and intelligence have very high reliability coefficients, typically above .90, and some loss in reliability can be accepted when the measures are to be used for research purposes. When measures such as achievement tests are administered as part of the regular school testing program, the results are usually used for diagnosis or counseling of *individual* students. In contrast, most educational research projects are concerned with comparing the performance of *groups* of students. Because group performance is more stable than individual performance, lower test reliabilities are acceptable for group research.

If there is no short form available for a test you wish to use and if an acceptable shorter test cannot be located, you have one final option. You may be able to shorten the measure yourself. You can estimate the reliability of a shortened version of the test using the general form of the Spearman-Brown Prophecy Formula.[22]

For example, suppose you located an achievement measure with a reliability of .90 that required approximately three times as much administration time as you have available. Using the Spearman-Brown formula, you would find that if you reduce the length of the test to one-third its original length, the estimated reliability would drop to .75. This level of reliability is still acceptable for many research projects.[23]

Reducing the length of a standardized test, however, should be considered only after other alternatives have been exhausted, for you must deal with three important problems if you decide to shorten a standardized test.

First, you must be sure that in the process of shortening the test, you do not bias its content and therefore seriously lower its validity. If the test is in an area such as mathematics achievement, where each concept is covered by several test items, you can usually reduce the length without making significant changes in the range of content covered. For tests of this kind, if you wish to reduce the length by half, you may often simply select every second item; or by two-thirds, every third item; and so on.[24]

For many tests, however, this simple approach is not sufficient. If you feel

21. William M. Reynolds and Jonathan W. Gould, "A Psychometric Investigation of the Standard and Short Form Beck Depression Inventory," *Journal of Consulting and Clinical Psychology* 49 (1981): 306–307.
22. This formula can be used to estimate reliability of either a longer or a shorter form of the same test. See William A. Mehrens and Irving J. Lehmann (1987), p. 65, in the Annotated References at the end of this chapter.
23. As the expected differences between the groups studied and the size of the groups increases, you can afford to accept some reduction in test reliability.
24. For a simple procedure for developing a short form, see L. Biggers, "An A Priori Approach for Developing Short Forms of Tests and Inventories," *Journal of Experimental Education* 44 (1976): 8–10.

this is the case, then you should select at least three judges who are experts in the test area and have them analyze the items and identify pairs or groups of similar items. You can then draw the desired number of items from these groups. This process will permit you to shorten the test without making significant changes in its character and coverage. You may, however, have some difficulty obtaining the cooperation of qualified judges and establishing an objective procedure they can follow in identifying comparable items.

The second problem you must deal with if you choose to shorten a standardized test is that of obtaining permission from the publisher. As most such tests are copyrighted, you cannot ethically or legally copy parts of the test without permission. Some publishers are sufficiently supportive of research to give their permission if they believe the research evidence will contribute to a better understanding of the test in question. Others will charge for permission to copy or will require that you purchase copies of the test in question. In some cases, if the author or the publisher believes that shortening the test will seriously reduce validity, permission will be denied. In any event, you can see that obtaining permission can be a slow and frustrating process.

A third problem is that data on norms, validity and reliability that have been gathered on the original test can be applied to the shortened version only with great caution, if at all. Thus, you must collect new normative data if needed in your study, you must recompute reliability, and you should collect data from a sample of subjects who are administered in both the original test and your revision, with a time interval, in order to have some basis for establishing the degree of comparability of the two measures.

You can see that shortening a standardized test for use in a research project adds up to a considerable amount of extra work, which can be avoided if a satisfactory existing measure can be found.

Individually Administered versus Group Tests

Both group tests and individually administered tests are available for measuring many intellectual and personality characteristics. A group test is one that has been constructed so that a sample of subjects can take the test all at one time; the test giver distributes the tests, reads direction, and may time it if it is a speed test. Such tests usually yield objective scores and consist of items of the yes-no, multiple-choice, or true-false type. By definition the individual test is one in which the tester measures one subject at a time. Most projective tests, such as the Rorschach Inkblot Technique, and some measures of intelligence, are of this type.

Individually administered measures should be selected only when they make an essential contribution to the research project. This is usually the case when you are interested in studying *process* rather than *product*, that is, *how* children respond to certain test items rather than what their total score is. Most standardized tests represent a product approach to measurement. An achievement test in mathematics, for example, usually yields a single score or set of scores that sums up an individual's performance on the test. Of course, it is important to have a measure of the product of performance, but there are also situations in which it is important to know the process by which an individual earned a particular score on the test. Why did the individual miss particular items on an arithmetic test? Did he or she guess, or was the person careless in doing computations, or did the person lack understanding of basic mathematical concepts, such as regrouping as used in subtraction problems (e.g., $38 - 19 = \square$)? The test would need to be individually administered in order to assess these aspects of a subject's performance. Tests developed in a clinical setting, such as the Rorschach Inkblot Technique and the Thematic Apperception Test, often are individually administered so that the clinician can measure not only a subject's responses but can also learn why the subject gave a particular response. Thus, if you are interested in such topics as the problem-solving techniques of fifth-graders and eighth-graders, or identification of reading disorders in low-achieving students, you probably will need to use individually administered measures in your research.

The nature of the sample will also determine whether individually administered tests are necessary. Very young children, for example, usually cannot be tested as a group because their attention span is limited and they do not have the reading skills required by group tests. Other groups, such as the retarded or physically handicapped, may also need to be tested individually. Delinquents and potentially recalcitrant groups may require individual testing if there is reason to believe that their performance on a group test will be unreliable.

Individually administered tests generally have a number of disadvantages for the beginning researcher. First, specialized training is often required to administer such tests. If you are unable to administer the test yourself, you probably will have to incur the expense of hiring experienced testers. This in itself presents a problem, for research has established that, for most projective measures, the tester affects the results. As we shall find later in this chapter, more than one tester must usually be employed to control for a possible tester effect. Second, these tests generally cannot be scored with the objectivity of group tests. Hence, you may need more than one scorer in order to increase reliability. Third, scores yielded by many individually administered tests are not immediately interpretable, but require interpretation by a trained educational or clinical psychologist.

The fact that individually administered tests have a number of disadvantages compared to group tests does not mean that you should rule out using them in your research project. Because they are difficult to use, however, you should select them only when they make an essential contribution to your research.

Selecting between Measures of the Same Variable

Much of what we have presented in this chapter is designed to help you make decisions about what measures you will use in your research project. Not uncommonly, students search for a measure of a particular variable, only to find that several such measures are available. Which measure should you select? The answer to this question is complex. Some alternative measures can be ruled out because they are unsuitable for your sample of subjects. Others may be found deficient in test reliability and validity or will require too much time. Yet occasionally situations arise when you have a number of seemingly appropriate measures from which to select.

To consider an example of such a situation, suppose that you wish to investigate the hypothesis that creative college students will do better than noncreative students in courses in which grades are based primarily on essay tests, but no difference in grades is expected between the two groups in college courses that rely primarily on multiple-choice exams for grading purposes. To test this hypothesis, you will need to measure individual differences in creativity among college students. A review of the literature would indicate that creativity in college students has been measured by a number of tests, including the Remote Associates Test, the Barron-Welsh Figure Preference Test, and the Myers-Briggs Type Indicator. These tests all have favorable evidence regarding reliability and validity. Which of these tests should you select for your research project? If you have not already done so, you should examine the rationale of your hypothesis at this point very closely. Perhaps your rationale is that grades on essay tests reflect in part the ability to generate novel ideas about a given topic, whereas grades on multiple-choice tests emphasize the ability to assimilate facts. In this case the Remote Associates Test may be the best test to use because it measures the ability to generate remote associations to words. (Of course, if another test could be located that had been demonstrated to predict creativity in essay writing, this would be the test to use.) If, on the other hand, you cannot arrive at an exact definition of creativity, then perhaps you should consider doing an empirical study rather than a hypothesis-testing study. In this case you might want to select several measures, including those mentioned here, to correlate with grades in the two types of courses.

To summarize, selecting between alternate measures of the same or ostensibly the same variable involves several considerations: suitability for one's sample of subjects, appropriateness in terms of testing conditions such as administration time, evidence regarding the tests' reliability and validity, and the way in which each test measures the variable with which one is concerned.

Is the Test Appropriate for Your Research?

Evaluate a test carefully before deciding on its appropriateness for your research sample. Some of the considerations involved in this evaluation have been discussed already under other headings.

Check the reading level of the test, particularly if it will be used by elementary school children. Occasionally one finds a test that the manual describes as usable at a particular grade level but that includes many words not generally known by students at that level. Such a test would be invalid since the score would depend to some degree on vocabulary and reading ability rather than on ability in the characteristic the test purports to measure.

In selecting an aptitude or achievement test, judge its appropriateness in terms of the general aptitude or achievement level of your research sample. Each test is designed to work most efficiently at a particular level. Some tests claim to be usable over a fairly wide age or grade range, but such measures are generally more accurate at the center of their range than at the extremes. If it is not appropriate for the level of subjects to be tested, a test will not discriminate; that is, it will fail to reflect differences that exist among the subjects. A test that is too easy discriminates poorly because most subjects will receive perfect or near-perfect scores. For example, if we administer a third-grade arithmetic test to ninth-grade pupils, all but the poorest ninth-grade pupils will obtain nearly perfect scores. We cannot determine from this test how much arithmetic a ninth-grade pupil knows. Average students, above-average students, and highly superior students will all receive about the same score on the test. The same, of course, is true of a test that is much too difficult or advanced for the subjects. In this case, all but a few superior students will receive very low scores.[25]

In many research projects, the test norms provided by the publisher are used in some phase of the research. If they are to be used, these norms must be based on subjects who are reasonably comparable to the research subjects. Also, the test's reliability and validity data should have been collected on samples comparable to the one that will be used in the research. The importance of this point is illustrated by a study using the California F-Scale, a measure of authoritarianism, to predict plant workers' performance.[26] The researchers noted that most of the construct-validity studies on the F-Scale were based on urban middle-class Americans. They predicted that this measure would not be valid for subjects born and reared in rural environments. To test this prediction, the researchers measured plant workers' productivity before and after an experimental treatment in which the workers were extensively interviewed and observed by so-called researchers. The hypothesis was that increases in produc-

25. To get a sense of how tests are designed to be appropriate for particular populations varying in ability, read Lee J. Cronbach, *Essentials of Psychological Testing*, 4th ed. (New York: Harper & Row, 1984).
26. Stephen M. Sales and Ned A. Rosen, "Subcultural Variations in the Validity of the California F-Scale," *Educational and Psychological Measurement* 27 (1967): 1107–1114.

tivity would be positively correlated with presence of authoritarian trends, as measured by the F-Scale, in urban but not in rural workers, since the so-called researchers would be perceived as authority figures toward whom authoritarian personalities would be likely to respond positively. As hypothesized, a statistically significant correlation of +.39 was found between the F-Scale and productivity increases for the workers born and reared in an urban environment. For the subsample *born and reared in a rural environment*, however, a nonsignificant correlation of +.04 was found.

This study makes the point that a test may be valid for one population but not for another. Therefore, you should make certain that a particular test's validity data are appropriate for your sample of subjects before deciding to use it in your research project.[27]

DEVELOPING MEASURES

The development of new measures in the behavioral sciences is a complex and difficult process that you should not attempt until you have had training in educational and psychological measurement. The development process, although generally similar for all measures, differs in many specifics depending upon the kind of measure to be developed. For example, the process of developing a multiple-choice achievement test in American history is much different than that involved in developing an attitude scale designed to measure teacher attitudes toward handicapped children.

Steps in the Process

It is beyond the scope of this book to provide detailed information on the test development process. The following brief outline is designed to give you some insight into the general process of test development. Additional steps are necessary for some types of measures. The Annotated Reference section lists sources that provide more detailed coverage on test construction.

1. *Define objectives.* Any test development effort should start with careful thought about the specific outcomes that the measure is to achieve. Construction of achievement tests requires careful description of the knowledge or skills that the test should measure. In attitude scale construction, a clear definition of the attitude to be measured and a statement on how the results of the measure will be used are needed.

2. *Define the target population.* The target population should be defined in detail since characteristics of the target population must be considered in many

---

27. For more information on differential validity, see Cameron Fincher, "Differential Validity and Test Bias," *Personnel Psychology* 28, no. 4 (1975): 481–500.

of the decisions that must be made on such questions as item type, reading level, test length, and type of directions.

3. *Review related measures.* Much can be learned by a careful study of tests that measure similar characteristics. An in-depth review of a few relevant measures will provide many ideas on methods for establishing validity, how different types of items can be applied, what levels of validity and reliability can be expected, and possible formats.

4. *Develop an item pool.* Before starting to write test items, the developer should make a number of decisions, such as: What types of items should be used? How long should the test be? How much emphasis should be given to each aspect of the characteristic or content area to be measured?

A great deal of information is available in the measurement literature on procedures for writing test items. The process of writing items is much more complex than generally thought, with many pitfalls. Thus, the next step in developing an item pool is to develop some skill in writing items. Several of the references given at the end of this chapter give information on item writing. Since many of the prototype items will be found unsatisfactory when the test is tried out, it is usually necessary to write at least twice as many items as will be needed on the final form of the test.

Many strategies are used by professional test developers to obtain items. For example, achievement tests for the public schools are sometimes developed by bringing a group of outstanding teachers to a central location and paying them to define the content area and to develop prototype items.

5. *Prepare a prototype.* The first form of the test puts into effect the earlier decisions on format, item type, etc. The test is usually somewhat longer than the final product since one can expect that many items will be discarded after tryout. The prototype test represents the developer's best judgment about what form the test should take.

6. *Evaluate the prototype.* Often the first step in evaluating the prototype is to obtain a critical review by three or more experts in test construction. This review usually identifies needed changes and raises many questions that can be answered only by a tryout of the test. The prototype is then field-tested with a sample from the target population. It is usually desirable to have a sample of 100 or more subjects in order to obtain good enough data for item analysis, and whenever possible larger samples should be used. However, when small or difficult-to-reach populations are involved, the researcher must often settle for smaller samples.

Item Analysis

After the data are collected, an item analysis is conducted. The general purpose of the item analysis is to identify good and bad items. The specific analysis and interpretation depends upon the nature of the test. For example, in developing norm-referenced achievement tests the item analysis is usually concerned with the difficulty level of each item and its ability to discriminate between good and poor students.

The **difficulty index** is usually computed for cognitive measures such as aptitude and achievement tests. It is simply a tally for each item of the number of subjects who answered the item correctly, divided by the total number of subjects taking the test. For most norm-referenced achievement measures the ideal item difficulty level is.50, that is, half the subjects respond correctly. An exception is when the test has been designed to discriminate among subjects at a given cutoff point. Suppose, for example, that a vocational school wanted to develop a driving aptitude test to select students to be trained in truck driving. If they wanted to select the top 25 percent of the applicants, this could be done more accurately using items with a difficulty index of .25. For measures in which the subject can obtain a certain number of correct answers by guessing, a correction may be made to the difficulty index.

Item validity is the correlation between subjects' responses to a particular item and their scores on the criterion measure. The validity coefficient therefore tells the degree to which correct responses on the given item relate to the subjects' performance on the criterion measure. The usual procedure for determining item validity is:

1. Compute the score of each subject on the criterion measure.
2. Select the 27 percent of the subjects who obtain the highest criterion score and the 27 percent who obtain the lowest criterion score.
3. For each of these two groups, tally the proportion who answer the first item correctly.
4. Using the proportions, consult the table in Appendix D to determine the item-validity coefficient.[28]
5. Repeat steps 3 and 4 for each item on the test.

Item reliability is the correlation between subjects' responses to a particular item and their total test score. To determine item reliability the same steps are followed as for item validity except that total score on the test being developed is used instead of the score on the criterion measure. For example, suppose you have carried out steps 1–3, using total test score, and have determined that .86 of the upper 27 percent group answered item 1 correctly as opposed to .50 of the lower group. We read along the top of the table in Appendix D until we come to 86.[29] We then read down the left hand column until we come to 50. At the intersection of the 86 column and the 50 row we find .42. This is the item-reliability coefficient.

28. The coefficients in the table are normalized biserial correlations. Other types of correlation are more appropriate under some conditions.
29. Decimals have been omitted from this table.

Study the references given at the end of this chapter before attempting to interpret these coefficients. The main purposes of the item analysis are to select valid and reliable items of appropriate difficulty level and to identify items that need revision.

7. *Revise measure.* On the basis of the experience gained in the field test and the results of the item analysis, the prototype test is revised and preparations are made for a field test of the revised measure. This cycle of field test and revision may have to be repeated several times in order to develop an effective instrument.

8. *Collect data on test validity and reliability.* Some data on the validity and reliability of the test will be obtained during development. The main effort is usually delayed until the instrument is in final form, however, since data on earlier forms cannot be applied to the final form because of the revisions that have taken place. The *Standards for Educational and Psychological Testing* published by the American Psychological Association (see Annotated References) can provide useful guidelines on the kinds of data that should be collected. Tests developed for use in a single research project rarely meet all these standards, but a review of the standards can still provide many helpful ideas—especially with regard to reliability and validity.

You can see from this brief outline that developing a new measure is difficult and time-consuming. It is a task that graduate students should not undertake until they have had adequate training in educational measurement. The progress of any science is closely linked to the development of new and better measures of the phenomena that are its concern. The rigorous development and validation of a new measure, therefore, can be a significant contribution to knowledge. Such an effort is, in itself, often an acceptable problem for the thesis or dissertation.

USING TESTS IN RESEARCH

Establishing Standard Conditions

Part of the meaning of the term *standardized test,* as we noted earlier, is that the test developer has specified the same conditions (directions, materials, timing, etc.) for every person who will take the test. Without standard conditions of administration, tables of norms and studies reporting validity and reliability would be worthless to the user. Similarly, your research findings can make no scientific contribution if you do not ensure standard conditions of administration for the tests used in your project.

The importance of this aspect of research procedure can be illustrated by a study investigating tester effects on the Stanford-Binet Intelligence Scale.[30] Six female and seven male testers administered the Stanford-Binet to a sample of four-year-old minority-group children. It was found that the children tested by females earned a significantly higher mean IQ (89.61) than those tested by males (83.19). Thus, it appears that some of the variance in these children's IQ scores is attributable to the testers rather than to "true" individual differences in intelligence. In this sense, the IQ scores are unreliable. The purpose of establishing standard conditions of administration is to reduce error variance (such as that attributable to tester characteristics) and at the same time increase true score variance.

The problem of tester effect is of particular concern with individually administered tests because the tester has ample opportunity to bring his or her personality into the testing relationship.[31] To control for tester effect, employ experienced testers and employ more than one of them. The data collected by each tester can then be compared to determine whether the findings have been influenced by tester effect. For example, suppose you are interested in comparing the intelligence of 30 sixth-grade students nominated as showing signs of creativity with 30 students nominated as noncreative. Further, suppose that four experienced examiners are employed to test the subjects. Each examiner will then test 15 randomly assigned students, half (7 or 8) in each group. Using analysis of variance (see chapters 15 and 16) you can then determine whether the testers affected the results. You may find that some testers obtained higher IQ scores than did others, or that there is an interaction; that is, for some testers creative children score higher on the Stanford-Binet. In summary, when a tester is a potential source of variance, employ more than one tester.

Standard conditions of administration are also extremely important for group tests. The test manual will usually provide specific directions for the tester to read to the group being tested. Read these directions carefully before entering the test session. Otherwise you may find yourself in the unhappy situation of being unable to answer subjects' questions, even though answers are contained in the test manual; or you may employ a test procedure that you find afterward is nonpermissible.

Although tests vary widely in conditions of administration (e.g., whether speed is emphasized, whether students are encouraged or discouraged to guess, and so on), two sets of conditions should remain constant across tests. First, subjects should be tested in a comfortable physical environment. An overcrowded classroom, poor lighting, and excessive outside noise may all increase the

30. Victor J. Cieutat, "Examiner Difference with the Stanford-Binet I.Q.," *Perceptual and Motor Skills* 20 (1965): 317–318.
31. For a review of studies on experimenter effects, of which tester effect is one aspect, see Robert Rosenthal and Ralph S. Rosnow, *Artifact in Behavioral Research* (New York: Academic Press, 1969).

size of errors in subjects' scores. Second, the physical and mental state of the person or persons being tested should be a paramount concern. Someone who is overly anxious or fatigued is not likely to turn in a representative performance on a standardized test. To minimize such effects on subjects' performances, take care not to test subjects at unusual times (e.g., orientation week, examination week, end of the school year), and, as a general rule, do not administer more than one or two tests in a single session.

Motivating and Gaining Subjects' Cooperation

The subjects' cooperation is important if test results are to be meaningful. Before administering a test, ask yourself: How can I enhance the amount of cooperation I will receive from my subjects? What might motivate students to turn in a maximal or typical performance on the measures I will administer?

Some answers to these questions have been given in the previous section. A comfortable physical environment and the consideration for subjects' mental and physical state are likely to increase the cooperation they will give. Another important consideration is that the tester be very familiar with the test directions. It can be very annoying for a subject to be tested by someone who fumbles with materials, who appears uncertain, or who makes obvious errors. Subjects are likely to feel that if the research were of any importance, the tester would be more conversant with test materials and directions. Feeling that the research lacks significance, subjects may take a haphazard approach to the testing; as a consequence their test scores will be unreliable.

An obvious way to gain familiarity with a particular test outside of a formal research testing session is to "pretest" the measure. Enlist the cooperation of a few friends or subjects and practice the testing procedures on them. One of the authors had to train eight testers to administer a test individually as part of a research project. As none of the testers were familiar with the test, they were asked to study the directions first and then asked to practice administering it to the author until their proficiency reached an acceptable level.

To increase the likelihood that you are sampling subjects' maximal performance (as on tests of aptitude or achievement), attempt to make the testing a reinforcing event for the subject. In the case of elementary and high school students, you can often do this by gaining the cooperation of the students' teacher beforehand.[32] Students often have a strong need to please their teacher; thus, you might request the teacher to tell her students that the test is important and that they should try to do their best on it. College and graduate students are usually intrinsically motivated to do well on tests. To increase the cooperation of these groups, the authors have found that a good technique is to tell them that

32. Procedures for gaining the cooperation of school and other officials are discussed in chapter 3.

you will reveal the purpose of the research and discuss the results after the testing is finished. This appeals to subjects' sense of curiosity and serves as a reinforcer for them to cooperate in taking the tests. Another good technique is to make the testing appear important; using a stopwatch and reading directions from a manual are likely to make subjects feel that their performance is of significance to the tester.

In administering tests of personality, questionnaires, and attitude scales, the tester is often faced with the problem of persuading subjects to depict themselves in a typical, honest manner. Some items in these tests may ask subjects to give personal information that they feel uncomfortable about revealing. Make it clear to subjects before the testing session begins that under no circumstances will data collected on any individual be revealed to anyone. You may also want to remind subjects that test scores will be reported in group form only. To protect subjects' sense of privacy and anonymity further, we recommend that you assign code numbers to all subjects. If you plan well beforehand, you should be able to arrange the test session so that subjects can write a code number on their tests instead of their names.

The testing of preschool and primary-grade students presents special problems. Trained testers should be employed to administer the research measures to these groups; otherwise the resulting test scores are likely to be quite unreliable. Test manuals often contain special directions to be used when testing these age groups.

Older students will often ask whether it is appropriate to guess on a test of aptitude or achievement. Usually the test manual contains directions to be given to subjects on this matter. If a subject persists in asking questions about guessing after the directions have been read, however, or if the manual contains no directions, do not attempt to influence the subject. When this situation arises, your response should be something like, "Do what you think is best" or "Use your judgment."

Occasionally after a testing session is ended, one or two subjects will ask if they can have access to their test results. As a rule, you should not provide subjects with this information. Most subjects will be satisfied if they are told that the tests were administered for a research project and therefore can be used only for that purpose. If some subjects persist, you can recommend that they go to the school counselor or campus counseling center where they will be able to receive professional assistance.

Scheduling and Administering Tests in the Schools

If you plan to administer tests in the schools as part of your research project, your success will depend on how carefully the scheduling of tests meets the conditions that prevail in most schools. First, do not schedule excessively long testing sessions. Consider the nature of the test and motivation of the students in setting up a testing session. Research suggests that children in the upper elementary grades should be tested no more than 90 minutes in a single session, and that single sessions should not extend beyond three hours for students at the secondary level. The ideal testing times for most students are probably about one-half of these time limits. If testing is to be scheduled for more than one school period, it is usually necessary and desirable to schedule breaks. These breaks may be scheduled between tests or even during a nontimed test. Two or three minutes is usually sufficient to permit the students to stand at their chairs, stretch, and talk.

In setting up the schedule, attempt to complete all testing within a reasonably short period. If the testing program is stretched out over a period of several weeks, as is sometimes the case when large samples must be tested, there is some danger that the testing situation will be somewhat different for those persons tested last as compared to those persons tested first. In the case of achievement measures, for example, students tested last will have had additional time in which to achieve, and may therefore earn higher scores than pupils tested early in the program. Avoid testing near holidays or too close to the end of the school year. The excitement attending the holiday can make a significant difference in the attitude of students concerning the testing. Testing during the last month of the school year often causes problems because students are less likely to be attentive to the test, and it may be difficult to arrange makeup tests prior to the end of the term. Also, because numerous special programs and extracurricular activities are scheduled at this time, many students will be absent from the testing.

Whenever possible, students should be tested in small groups. The regular classroom unit is probably the most desirable group to test because the students are in a familiar environment and the group is small enough so that the test administrator can maintain good control over the situation. Testing in large groups, on the other hand, makes it difficult for the administrator to answer questions or to collect materials, and a single giggle can result in the test situation degenerating into chaos and confusion.

Although you will often be unable to achieve an ideal testing situation, attempt to set up the most favorable situation possible. If experimental and control groups are to be tested separately, as if often the case, you should also attempt to equalize as much as possible the situation faced by the two groups. For example, to test all experimental subjects in the morning and all control subjects in the afternoon would be undesirable because students are often less alert and less highly motivated during the afternoon session. It would be similarly undesirable to test all experimental subjects during the first week of the testing program and all control groups during the second week. To whatever extent such scheduling variables can be equalized between the experimental and control groups, this should be done.

During the scheduling session, you should also come to an agreement with the school principal involving such questions as: What help will the school provide for the testing program? How will makeup tests be scheduled and who will administer them? What role will the classroom teacher play in the testing program? How will disciplinary problems that occur during the testing period be handled? This last question is especially important because a prompt and efficient means of handling disciplinary problems often makes the difference between maintaining and losing control of the testing situation. If testing is to be carried out in the classroom, you should also visit each teacher who will be involved and discuss the teacher's role in the testing. Under certain conditions, you might feel it would be more desirable for the teacher to be absent during the testing session; in other situations, the teacher might assist as a proctor and be responsible for disciplinary problems. The teacher's role should be decided on the basis of the needs of the specific study, but it should always be fully understood by both teacher and researcher before the session begins.

If you have done a thorough job of pretesting and preparing for the testing program in which you will collect your data, you will have little to do during the actual testing session except to follow closely the procedure you have developed and tried. In the event that some unusual or unforeseen situation arises during the testing period, make careful notes of what occurs in order to determine later whether the occurrence has introduced factors or biases that will reduce the value of the data.

Using Test Data Collected by Schools

You may find yourself under pressure in carrying out research for the master's thesis to use test data already collected by the schools. This is generally not advisable for several reasons. First, the measures available are often not those that are most appropriate for the research project. Second, you may wish to include some subjects in your sample who have not taken the test. Third, you do not know the conditions under which the test was administered and, of course, you had no control over these conditions. We urge you therefore to select and administer the measures that seem most appropriate for your research whenever this is possible and to avoid using data not collected under your control.

The Social Significance of Testing

In the last 50 years the testing movement has had a major impact on American society. Each year literally millions of tests are administered for the purpose of making important decisions about individuals—Who shall be admitted to college and to what college? Who shall be selected to fill a particular job opening? Who needs to be hospitalized for mental illness? Therefore, the researcher planning to use standardized tests needs to realize some of the ethical issues that have arisen in connection with the testing movement.

The early 1960s witnessed a rash of books attacking tests.[33] Chief among their criticisms of testing were these:

1. *Invasion of privacy.* Some tests, particularly those dealing with personality, ask individuals to reveal information usually considered personal. The individual's right to privacy is generally considered to be a basic American value.

2. *Accessibility of test data.* Test scores are not usually made available to the individual tested, yet important decisions about the person are often made on the basis of these scores. This situation gives testers a potentially large degree of power over an individual's destiny and may make the individual feel helpless and under the control of testers.

3. *Rigid use of test scores.* Critics complain that testers make no allowance for change in the individual or in the environment. Although an individual may earn low achievement scores during a particular school year, this does not mean necessarily that this person will continue to be a low achiever. Also, the individual's environment is often a changing one, and therefore test predictors may only be valid for a short period of time and within a limited environmental setting.

4. *Types of talent selected by tests.* Tests generally sample only a few of the aptitudes and personality traits important for success in a given area. Thus, if aptitude tests alone are used to select individuals for college, this practice may discriminate against individuals who do not have high scores on the aptitudes measured by these tests but who do have a high level of creativity or artistic aptitude. A related criticism is that tests can perpetuate the status quo rather than encourage change. For example, if college admission is determined only by scholastic aptitude tests, only persons of high scholastic aptitude will complete college. These graduates, now in a position of power, may continue the use of the same tests to select students who are similar to themselves. This approach to test use may keep individuals out of college who might bring about productive changes in the college system.

5. *Unfairness to minority groups.* Some aptitude and intelligence tests are criticized as unfair to minority groups because they contain test items pertaining to experiences that these groups may not have enjoyed. Therefore, minority groups will earn undeservedly low scores on these tests and not be selected for schools and jobs that would help them improve their social and financial status.

---

33. Among those authors who criticized the testing movement most severely were Hillel Black, *They Shall Not Pass* (New York: Morrow, 1963); Martin L. Gross, *The Brain Watchers* (New York: Random House, 1962); and Banesh Hoffman, *The Tyranny of Testing* (New York: Crowell-Collier, 1962). These books appear to reflect deliberate bias as discussed in chapter 5.

The degree to which widely used intelligence measures such as the Wechsler Intelligence Scale for Children (WISC) and the Stanford-Binet discriminate against minority-group children is not clear at this time. Two major court cases (*Larry P.* v. *Riles* and *P.A.S.E* v. *Hannon*) have examined this issue. In the former case the court ruled in 1979 that these measures were culturally biased, whereas in the latter case the court ruled in 1980 that the same measures did not discriminate against black children.

Recent federal legislation has required that tests used to identify handicapped children be selected and administered so as not to discriminate racially or culturally. In response to this requirement, Mercer and Lewis devised a set of tests and procedures, the System of Multicultural Pluralistic Assessment (SOMPA), which is designed to provide a fairer way of assessing children from different ethnic and cultural backgrounds.[34] Although professionals are not fully in agreement on the effectiveness of SOMPA, it appears to be a significant step toward achieving a comprehensive nondiscriminatory assessment.[35]

In summary, the claim that many tests are unfair to minority groups is probably valid. However, work is progressing to eliminate or greatly reduce this discrimination.[36]

6. *Low predictive validity.* A criticism often heard in recent years is that many tests simply do not do the job they were designed for. Aptitude tests such as the Scholastic Aptitude Test and the Graduate Record Examination are often criticized because of their low validity for predicting both educational and vocational success. It is true that many such measures, when used alone, do a poor job of prediction. Nevertheless, critics often overlook the fact that most prediction studies, such as prediction of success in college, are based upon several variables of which the aptitude test is only one. The validity of the entire battery of measures is often high enough to make reasonably accurate predictions of the future success of the applicant.[37]

Although they are primarily addressed to situations in which tests are used to make practical decisions affecting individuals' lives, these criticisms are sometimes applied to research projects involving testing. This is particularly true when tests are administered in the public schools. In one unfortunate episode in Houston, Texas, the answer sheets to six sociometric and psychological measures that had been administered to some 5,000 ninth-grade students were

34. Jane Mercer, *"SOMPA": Technical Manual* (New York: Psychological Corporation, 1979).
35. For an extensive discussion of SOMPA, see *School Psychology Digest* 8 (1979). The entire issue is devoted to this topic.
36. See Laura Hines, "Nondiscriminatory Testing: The State of the Art," *Peabody Journal of Education* 58, no. 2 (1981): 119–124.
37. See Allan Naire et al., "The Reign of ETS," *Today's Education* 69 (1980): 58–64, for a discussion of most of the arguments against aptitude testing. Note, however, that this article presents only one side of the issue. Two pamphlets published by ETS that refute many of Naire's claims are: *Test Use and Validity* (Princeton, NJ: Educational Testing Service, 1980) and *Test Scores and Family Income* (Princeton, NJ: Educational Testing Service, 1980).

ordered burned by the school board. In this instance, accounts indicated that parents objected to having their children respond to such items as: "I enjoy soaking in the bathtub." "Sometimes I tell dirty jokes when I would rather not." "Dad always seems too busy to pal around with me."[38]

In another episode, in spite of a thorough and well-planned public relations program, a similar problem arose. In this case the research program dealt with mental health and was being carried out by a foundation that was well established and had good rapport in the community. An extensive public relations program was carried out, including meetings and discussions with school boards, superintendents, administrative personnel, school nurses and teachers, religious leaders, PTA groups, the Lions Club, and other civic groups. The research worker's difficulty started because a local right-wing group was currently involved in a campaign opposing the "mental health movement."

> The man who spearheaded this opposition was also a member of the American Legion and later read a statement along the same lines at a P.T.A. panel on which members of the research team appeared. He accused us of implanting "Red" ideas in children's minds and said our "Guess-Who" technique was a way of "fingering" certain children (designating them at an early age so they would be marked for life for our own ulterior motives).[39]

The authors have had some experience with a similar protest movement, and when this experience is compared with the previously described situations, it appears that all three have a number of things in common. First, individual test items are generally attacked without reference to their context or psychological foundations. Second, such attacks are usually led by small extreme groups of one sort or another. In the authors' experience, the protest group was made up almost entirely of a close-knit group of health-food faddists. Another characteristic of all three of these situations is that although it was vigorous and noisy, the protesting group did not represent any significant parent group. In the Houston episode, tests were returned to a number of small school districts—the Spring Branch Board of Education decided to destroy the answer sheets only of pupils whose parents objected to the testing. Six weeks after that decision, only 11 parents out of the possible 750 requested that the answer sheets be destroyed. In the second episode discussed, a similar offer was made and only three parents, those who started the original protest, requested that their children's records be destroyed. In the authors' experience, approximately 5,000 children were tested, and in spite of the considerable bedlam raised by the

---

38. Gwynn Nettler, "Test Burning in Texas," *American Psychologist* 14 (1959): 682–683.
39. Leonard D. Eron and Leopold O. Walder, "Test Burning II," *American Psychologist* 16 (May 1961): 239.

small protesting group, only one parent came forward to request that her child's test papers be destroyed.

In dealing with such problems, a number of points might be worth mentioning. First, remember that in many instances these protests are led by people who are not truly concerned about the testing but wish to use it merely as a vehicle to gain publicity or gratify some personal need. Second, it is impossible to explain adequately to a lay group the function of many items used on psychological tests. It is doubtful whether you should ever attempt to debate the merits of specific test items. Instead, explain how the test was developed and attempt to demonstrate that the test as a whole is valid and useful. Third, it is important to take all action that seem appropriate at the very outset of any such protest. If the research is well designed and the measures are justified, those parents who are truly concerned can generally be convinced of the value of the study, thus depriving the extreme group of their support. Work closely with the newspapers and do everything possible to acquaint them with your side of the question. Finally, it is wise to offer to withdraw children from the study if the parents examine the tests and make a written request that their children be withdrawn, even though they had earlier given permission to test their children.

It should be clear by this point that the use of tests in a research project is not a matter to be taken lightly. You should be aware of the main criticisms of testing and realize that tests can be used to advance scientific knowledge, or can be abused by those who are unethical or who are poorly trained.

MISTAKES SOMETIMES MADE IN SELECTING AND ADMINISTERING TESTS

1. The researcher fails to evaluate measures thoroughly before selecting those to be used in his research.
2. Uses a table of norms that is inappropriate for the research sample.
3. Does not evaluate carefully the criteria that have been used to determine the validity of a particular test.
4. Does not consider the problem of base rate in determining a test's predictive validity.
5. In attempting to measure a particular construct, selects a test on the basis of its name rather than its demonstrated construct validity.
6. Uses a norm-referenced achievement test in a study where a domain-referenced test would be more appropriate.
7. Selects measures of such low reliability that true differences between research groups are hidden by the errors of measurement.
8. Fails to consider the human relations aspect of testing.

9. Attempts to develop his or her own measure without first gaining skills in test construction.
10. Does not attempt to control for possible tester effects, particularly when a test is administered individually.
11. Does not study the test manual carefully before administering a test.
12. Attempts to administer too many tests in a single testing session.

ANNOTATED REFERENCES

Test Development Standards and Item Writing

Brown, Frederick G. *Measuring Classroom Achievement.* New York: Holt, Rinehart and Winston, 1981.

Especially useful for the teacher or researcher who finds it necessary to develop an achievement test. Guidelines for writing different kinds of test items are brief and clear. Also included are chapters on planning a test and analyzing test scores and items. The book takes a practical, how-to-do-it approach and provides many examples.

Committee to Develop Standards for Educational and Psychological Testing, *Standards for Educational and Psychological Testing,* Washington, DC: American Psychological Association, 1985.

A very valuable source for both test developers and students who want to evaluate tests for use in research or in the field.

Gronlund, Norman E. *Constructing Achievement Tests,* 3rd ed. Englewood Cliffs, NJ: Prentice-Hall, 1982.

A good basic text on achievement test construction. It is written in simple, easy-to-understand language and contains clear step-by-step guidelines on item development.

Hopkins, Kenneth D., and Stanley, Julian C. *Educational and Psychological Measurement and Evaluation,* 6th ed. Englewood Cliffs, NJ: Prentice-Hall, 1981.

Mehrens, William A., and Lehmann, Irving J. *Using Standardized Tests in Education,* 4th ed. New York: Longman, 1987.

Good introductory texts on educational measurement. Both provide brief but useful guidelines on test development and item analysis and will be useful to the student who needs to develop a basic understanding of this field.

Roid, Gale H., and Haladyna, Tom M. *A Technology for Test-Item Writing.* New York: Academic Press, 1982.

Deals with test-item writing for criterion-referenced tests. The initial section introduces the student to criterion-referenced testing and its relationship to instruction. The main body of the book provides practical guidance on item writing, which is supported by numerous examples, and describes the rationale and procedures for six prominent item-writing methods. The final section is concerned with methods for the review and analysis of test items. In addition to being an extremely practical guide to item writing, the book pulls together virtually all the recent research on this topic. This is probably the best source currently available in this area.

Test Statistics

Guilford, Joy P., and Fruchter, Benjamin. *Fundamental Statistics in Psychology and Education*, 6th ed. New York: McGraw-Hill, 1977.

Provides an excellent coverage of the statistical aspects of validity, reliability, item analysis, and test norms. Chapters 17, 18, and 19 should be studied by students who plan to develop a measure.

Domain-Referenced Tests

The field of domain-referenced testing is expanding and changing rapidly. Thus, the student who wants the most recent information in this field should carry out a computer search of the ERIC data base. The ERIC Clearinghouse on Tests, Measurement, and Evaluation at Princeton, NJ 08540, and the Instructional Objectives Exchange, Box 24095, Los Angeles, CA 90024, are excellent sources of up-to-date information in this field. Since many measurement texts do not cover this topic, several references are given here.

Berk, Donald A. "A Consumer's Guide to Setting Performance Standards in Criterion-Referenced Tests." *Review of Educational Research* 56, no. 1 (1986): 137–172.

A difficult problem in developing criterion-referenced tests is establishing the criterion or standard that learners should meet. This review identifies and briefly describes 38 methods for setting or adjusting standards. Two types of criteria are discussed: technical adequacy and practicability. Each method is compared on six technical adequacy criteria and four practicability criteria and given an overall rating. Strengths and weaknesses of each method are also presented. This is an excellent source for the student who is faced with the problem of setting standards.

Berk, Ronald A., ed. *A Guide to Criterion-Referenced Test Construction*. Baltimore: Johns Hopkins University Press, 1984.

Each chapter is written by a recognized authority. Most of the information needed to construct a criterion-referenced test is given, including specifying the domain, generating test items, item analysis, validity, and reliability.

Educational Testing Service. *Criterion-Referenced Measures, Grade 7 and Above*. Princeton, NJ: Educational Testing Service, various years.

One of a large series of *Test Collection Bibliographies* published by the Test Collection Division of ETS. This bibliography lists and provides brief annotations on more than 160 criterion-referenced measures. These bibliographies are regularly updated.

Haertel, Edward. "Construct Validity and Criterion-Referenced Testing." *Review of Educational Research* 55, no. 1 (1985): 23–46.

Starts with a comparison of norm-referenced and criterion-referenced achievement tests. The author then compares psychological with achievement constructs and discusses the steps necessary to carry out construct validation of a criterion-referenced achievement test. An example of the process is then provided. A good source for the student who wants to develop expertise in the development of criterion-referenced measures.

Klein, S. P., and Kosecoff, J. *Issues and Procedures in the Development of Criterion-Referenced Tests.* Princeton, NJ: ERIC Clearinghouse on Tests, Measurement and Evaluation, September 1973 (ED 083 284).

Describes the basic procedures for development of criterion-referenced tests including item construction and selection, improving item quality, and content validity. Also reports the results of a survey of current efforts in criterion-referenced testing by test publishers. This section contains descriptions of some of the criterion-referenced tests available such as the Prescriptive Mathematics Inventory developed by the California Test Bureau.

Popham, W. James. *Criterion-Referenced Measurement.* Englewood Cliffs, NJ: Prentice-Hall, 1978.

A highly readable introduction to criterion-referenced test development and use by one of the leaders in the field. An excellent discussion of the deficiencies of norm-referenced tests is provided. The chapters related to the development of criterion-referenced measures, preparing specifications for criterion-referenced tests, and practical application of these measures in instruction and evaluation are especially useful.

Validity, Reliability, and Test Criticism

Benson, Jeri. "A Redefinition of Content Validity." *Educational and Psychological Measurement* 41, no. 4 (1981): 793–802.

Suggests that the way items are written, item format, test instructions, and item readability all have an impact on content validity, and briefly reviews the research literature on these topics.

Cronbach, Lee J., and Meehl, Paul C. "Construct Validity in Psychological Tests." *Psychological Bulletin* 52, no. 4 (1955): 281–302.

A classic article, still one of the best discussions of construct validity.

Green, Bert F., ed. *Issues in Testing: Coaching, Disclosure, and Ethnic Bias.* San Francisco: Jossey-Bass, 1981.

Deals in considerable depth with three important issues. The effects of coaching and the effectiveness of different forms of coaching are explored. Test bias and the detection of biased test items are discussed. The problem of equating alternate forms of a test brought about by test disclosure requirements is considered and alternatives are probed.

 Haney, Walt. "Validity, Vaudeville, and Value—A Short History of Social Concerns Over Standardized Testing." *American Psychologist* 36, no. 10 (1981): 1021–1034.

Traces publications related to educational testing that appeared in the popular book and periodical literature over a 70-year period. It places many of the current criticisms of testing into historical perspective. Each of the major debates that have concerned educational testing is discussed. Any student interested in testing will find this article interesting and informative.

Yalow, Elanna S., and Popham, W. James. "Content Validity at the Crossroads." *Educational Researcher* 12, no. 8 (1983): 10–14, 21.

Explores several current questions related to content validity. The importance of content validity in court cases concerned with job certification, and the legality of high school graduation tests is reviewed. Curriculum validity and instruction validity and their relationship to content validity are also examined. The need to develop common metrics for content validity is further discussed.

SELF-CHECK TEST

Circle the correct answer to each of the following questions. An answer key is provided on page 883.

1. The degree to which a measure is undistorted by the beliefs or prejudices of the individual using it reflects the _____ of the measure.
   a. validity
   b. objectivity
   c. consistency
   d. reliability
2. A table of norms enables the researcher to
   a. determine the construct validity of a test at a glance.
   b. compare the relative reliabilities of two or more tests.
   c. determine whether a subject's score was drawn from a defined population.
   d. compare a subject's score with the scores of a defined sample.
3. The degree to which a test measures what it purports to measure reflects its
   a. objectivity.
   b. validity.
   c. stability.
   d. reliability

4. If a sample of test items adequately represents the subject matter of a given curriculum, the test is said to have _____ validity.
   a. construct
   b. predictive
   c. content
   d. concurrent

5. A test which yields scores that are found to be highly correlated with subjects' later behavior is said to have high _____ validity.
   a. concurrent
   b. rational
   c. predictive
   d. content

6. The type of test validity that is assessed by comparing subjects' scores on a test with their scores on some other measure within a short time interval is called _____ validity.
   a. correlational
   b. rational
   c. concurrent
   d. predictive

7. The degree to which a test measures a given hypothetical construct reflects its _____ validity.
   a. content
   b. rational
   c. internal
   d. construct

8. If the researcher is most concerned with the content validity of a test, the best source of information would be
   a. *Psychological Abstracts.*
   b. the test itself.
   c. *Mental Measurements Yearbooks.*
   d. *Review of Educational Research.*

9. Which of the following was a criticism of testing often heard in the early 1960s?
   a. invasion of privacy
   b. low reliability of the test data
   c. inflexible use of test scores
   d. too broad sampling of talents

10. It is not advisable to use test data collected by the schools for research purposes because
    a. the measures are often inappropriate.
    b. it is too expensive.
    c. test conditions are too rigidly controlled.
    d. students have knowledge of the test prior to its administration.

APPLICATION PROBLEMS

The following problems are designed to give you practice in applying significant concepts and research procedures explained in the chapter. Most of them do not have a single correct answer. For feedback, you can compare your answers with the sample answers on pages 893–894.

1. An investigator has developed a new technique to teach eighth-grade students the characteristics of positive and negative numbers. She wishes to evaluate her technique by

using it to teach group A while using group B, which receives conventional instruction on positive and negative numbers, as a control. She needs a mathematics achievement test to measure the posttraining performance of the two groups. She considers the XYZ Test of Mathematics Achievement. In checking the test manual, she finds that when this test was administered to a sample of eighth-grade students at the end of the academic year, the test scores correlated .72 with their end-of-year grades in mathematics. No other validity evidence was given in the test manual.

   a. What type of validity evidence was given in the test manual?
   b. What type of validity is most relevant to the proposed study? Why?

2. An investigator has developed an algebra aptitude test to be given to eighth-grade students to determine which ones are likely to succeed in ninth-grade algebra. To validate his test, he administers it to 100 randomly selected eighth-grade students, all of whom are then placed in ninth-grade algebra the following term. At the end of the term he computes a correlation coefficient between aptitude scores and the achievement scores, the latter taken from an algebra achievement test given at the completion of the course.

   a. What type of validity did the investigator study?
   b. What type of validity is most relevant for this test? Why?

3. To determine the reliability of a new high school science achievement test, the developer selects a random sample of 1,000 high school students, administers both form A and form B of the test to all subjects, and computes a correlation coefficient of .92. What type of reliability did she obtain?

4. For each of the following situations indicate whether an individual measure or a group measure would be more appropriate and why.

   a. An investigator wishes to study the reading speed and reading comprehension of a random sample of 100 freshmen entering a large state university for the fall semester.
   b. An investigator wishes to study the ability of retarded children (ages 6 to 9) to describe the content of pictures shown to them.

5. State at least one procedure for handling each of these testing problems.

   a. A researcher is planning to administer several aptitude tests to groups of college students as part of a research project. What can he do to increase the likelihood that students will give their maximum performance?
   b. A researcher wants to administer a measure of sex attitudes to high school and college students. What can she do to increase the likelihood that students will give frank, honest responses?

SUGGESTION SHEET

If your name starts with letters from Fit to Gor, please complete the Suggestion Sheet at the end of the book while this chapter is still fresh in your mind.

8 TYPES OF STANDARDIZED TESTS

OVERVIEW

You need to become familiar with the great variety of tests that have been developed. With this familiarity, you will be much more likely to select the measures that are most appropriate for your research project. This chapter tells you how to locate information about tests and dicusses ten important types of standardized tests. Since it would be a vast undertaking for you to review all available measures, this chapter contains information about using the *Mental Measurements Yearbooks* as well as major sources of information on unpublished measures. The *Yearbooks* contain descriptions and reviews of nearly all published tests in psychology and education and greatly simplify the task of test selection.

OBJECTIVES

After studying this chapter you should be able to:

1. If given a research problem, locate an appropriate measure in the *Ninth Mental Measurements Yearbook* and state at least three reasons for selecting the measure.
2. Evaluate a standardized test on the combined basis of date supplied by the test publisher and information given in the *Mental Measurements Yearbooks* and *Test Critiques*.
3. List six sources of information on standardized tests and describe the kind of information that may be obtained from each source.
4. Describe at least one advantage and one disadvantage of self-report personality measures.
5. List at least one widely used test of each of the following types: intelligence, aptitude, achievement, diagnostic, creativity, personality, projective, self-concept, attitude, and vocational interest.

HOW TO LOCATE INFORMATION ABOUT TESTS

Before selecting a particular test, accumulate as much information as possible about it. Students often hastily decide upon a test in planning research and then find themselves plagued with difficulties in using the test and interpreting the findings. Suppose, for example, that you wish to test the hypothesis that empathy is an important trait for success in school counseling. You form two groups of counselors rated as successful and unsuccessful and administer a test of empathy. Since an accurate measure of empathy is crucial to testing your hypothesis, if the measure you select is found to be invalid by those who might evaluate the research—editors of educational journals or professional counselors—then the findings that result from such a study are cast into immediate doubt.

You will want to know how to obtain information about tests for another reason. In reviewing the research done by others in your field of interest, you cannot make sound judgments concerning the findings without having access to information about tests used to measure the research variables. The following are widely used, accessible sources of information about tests.

The Test Manual

The *test manual* provides you with much of the information that you need to evaluate the standardized test. Among the questions that the manual helps to answer are the following:

What is the theoretical construct or rationale upon which the test is based?
What are the recommended uses of the test?
What validity data are available? What types of validity have been studied? Is the evidence of validity sufficient for use in the planned research?
What reliability data are available? Is the measure sufficiently reliable to meet the needs of the planned research?
For what types of subjects is the test appropriate?
What conditions of administration are necessary to use the test?
Does the test require special training for interpretation?
Is a shorter form of the test available that will yield substantially the same results?

Although test manuals can provide much useful information to the student interested in evaluating a particular standardized test, the student must be able to evaluate the test manual itself. For example, test manuals will occasionally omit evidence regarding validity or reliability that is unfavorable to the test and that might dissuade potential purchasers.[1]

Some standardized tests, particularly those that have been extensively researched, are likely to pass through several revisions. You should be certain, therefore, that your test manual is appropriate for the test version that you are evaluating.

1. *Standards for Educational and Psychological Testing* (Washington, DC: American Psychological Association, 1985) gives a good summary of information that should be included in test manuals.

Reference Sources of Information about Tests

The Mental Measurements Yearbooks

A very important source of information on standardized tests, the *Mental Measurements Yearbooks* are published periodically; the most recent of the series is the *Ninth Mental Measurements Yearbook,* published in 1985.[2] This is a completely new work that supplements the earlier editions. The current edition lists 1,409 tests and contains 1,266 critical test reviews and over 20,000 references on the construction, use, and limitations of the specific tests included in this edition.

The *Mental Measurements Yearbooks* can be used to obtain information on specific tests that you have located elsewhere, or they can help you locate tests that are available in a particular field. The *Yearbooks* are also very valuable tools for checking on tests that others have used in their research. The *Yearbooks* have three indexes: to get information on a specific test, look up the test in the Index of Titles; to locate available tests in a particular subject area, consult the Classified Subject index; to identify a test that measures a specific variable, the Score Index is the best place to begin.

When you find tests in any of the indexes that interest you, note the number of the test and check each number in the Tests and Reviews section of the book. Under the test number, you will find a brief listing of practical information, such as the types of subjects who may be administered the test, the scores yielded by the test, administration time, cost, and publisher. Following these data you will usually find a number of references containing information about the test. Several hundred such references may be available for the more widely used tests. A quick examination of these references will often reveal several that are of particular relevance to your research project. Reviews are available for many of the tests listed. These reviews are perhaps the most valuable feature of the *Mental Measurements Yearbooks* because they provide you with an evaluation of the test by one or more authorities in the field. They are usually written by persons who have worked extensively in the field with which the test is concerned and are designed specifically to provide test users with appraisals that can help them in evaluating the test. The reviews are generally critical and address most of the essential elements important in test evaluation, thus providing you with a sounder evaluation than you could make for yourself.

ETS Test Collection

If you fail to locate the measures you need in the *Mental Measurements Yearbooks,* your next step should be to search the relevant parts of the Educational Testing Service (ETS) collection. This is the most extensive collection of tests and other

---

2. See the Annotated References at the end of this chapter.

measurement devices available, consisting of more than 14,000 instruments, both published and unpublished. ETS established this collection to assist researchers and others who need test information.[3] You may obtain specific information by writing or phoning ETS. In most cases, however, the best way to use this collection is to purchase the *Test Collection Bibliography* that relates to your interests and then order microfiche copies of the most promising measures described in the *Bibliography*.[4] Bibliographies are constantly being updated and so are more likely to contain the latest information than the *Mental Measurements Yearbooks*.

At present, annotated ETS bibliographies are available in more than 200 areas. The description of each measure in the bibliographies includes title, author, publication date, target population, and publisher or source. Because many tests cited in educational research literature are not available commercially, ETS makes them available on microfiche. The microfiche may be purchased for individual measures or for sets of 50 to 100 measures. Many university libraries have purchased these sets, so check with your reference librarian before purchasing microfiches.

Test Critiques

Test Critiques, a seven-volume work by Keyser and Sweetland dating from 1984 to 1988, contains critiques of tests selected by specialists in the given areas, and therefore the more widely used measures are usually reviewed. Each review includes five sections: An Introduction, which describes the test in detail with relevant developmental background; a Practical Application/Uses section, which provides information on administration, scoring, and interpretation; a section on Technical Aspects, which is concerned primarily with reliability and validity; an overall Critique, which is very useful in helping you evaluate the test; and a brief list of References dealing with the measure and related topics. On average, seven to eight pages are devoted to each measure, and a great deal of information is provided. The seven volumes currently available cover over 700 measures, and subsequent volumes are planned at six- to nine-month intervals. In using these volumes, the best approach is to check the most recent volume, since it contains cumulative indexes that cover all volumes. If you are looking for evaluation data on a test located elsewhere, use the test titles index. If you are trying to locate tests in a particular subject area, use the subject index.

These volumes, along with the *Ninth Mental Measurements Yearbook*, are the best sources of evaluation information on available tests. The main advantage of *Test Critiques* is the thoroughness of the information provided for each measure.

---

3. See the Annotated References at the end of this chapter.
4. See Appendix F for a listing of available *Test Collection Bibliographies*.

Its main limitation is the small number of measures covered thus far. As new volumes become available, this limitation will be largely overcome.

Tests—A Comprehensive Reference for Assessments in Psychology, Education, and Business, 2nd Edition

Tests—A Comprehensive Reference (edited by Sweetland and Keyser, 1986) provides information on more than 3,000 tests. The information on each test includes a statement of the purpose of the test, a description of the test, administration time, grade range, scoring information, cost, and publisher. Tests are listed under three major headings: Psychology, Education, and Business and Industry. Each of the sections is in turn divided into several specific subsections. For example, subsections under Education include such areas as Academic Subjects, Achievement and Aptitude, Intelligence, Reading, and Special Education.

To use this reference to locate tests in a given area, check the table of contents and locate the relevant subsection. Then turn to this subsection and scan the information given. For example, if you were looking for measures designed to identify first-grade children with learning disabilities you would check "Learning disabilities" in the table of contents. Tests in this area are described on pages 576 to 589 in the references. You could then identify specific measures that would meet your needs by scanning the information provided on these pages. The book also contains several indexes, including a test title index, an author index, and a listing of out-of-print tests. Unfortunately, there is no subject index or score index.

This volume is an excellent source for *locating* tests relevant to your needs. However, it is not useful in *evaluating* tests, as no information on reliability, validity, or norms is included.

The Test Developer

The best source of recent information on a test is often the test developer. Because there is a considerable lag between the completion of research and its publication, the developer will often have information on the test that has not been printed and is also likely to know of other researchers who have recently used the measure. Contacting the developer is especially useful in getting the latest data on recently developed tests, for which there may be very little published data on validity and other important characteristics but much unpublished data. Thus, we advise you to write to the test developer and request any information that has not yet appeared in print. If your letter explains the purposes for which you wish to use the test, the test developer will in all probability be cooperative. One reason for this cooperation is that the developer may be able to add the findings from your research project to those he or she has already collected.

The Test Itself

One of the most important sources of information about standardized tests is the test itself, particularly if you are concerned about questions of face validity, content validity, or the appropriateness of the test for your sample. The test manual may claim, for example, that a particular test is appropriate for fifth-grade students. Your examination of a copy of the test may reveal, however, that the reading level is beyond that of the fifth-graders whom you are planning to test. Or suppose that your research entails the evaluation of two methods for teaching reading. In selecting a test of reading achievement to evaluate the effectiveness of the two methods, you may find that the test manual and the *Mental Measurements Yearbooks* do not provide enough information about the reading content covered by the test. The best source of information to determine whether the reading content covered by the test is representative of that included in your training materials is a copy of the test itself.

Other Sources

In addition to the sources of test information listed above, other compilations are included in the Annotated References at the end of this chapter. Refer to these if your search of the sources mentioned above does not locate a suitable measure for your study.

If these additional sources also fail to turn up a suitable measure, you can design and carry out a computer search of the most relevant data bases, using the procedures described in chapter 4. An ERIC clearinghouse for tests and measurements at the Educational Testing Service in Princeton, New Jersey, feeds much information into the ERIC system. If the computer search fails, your final alternatives are to change your research topic or to develop your own measure.

How to Obtain Copies of Tests

Once you have decided on the standardized test (or tests) you wish to use, you will need to obtain a number of copies of each test. If the test is distributed through a publisher such as Science Research Associates or the Psychological Corporation, you should purchase copies from them. The publisher and purchase price of particular tests can be found in the most recent edition of *Mental Measurements Yearbooks*. College counseling and testing centers often have catalogues issued by test publishers that provide such information as well. Under no circumstances should you obtain a single copy of a test and then duplicate or mimeograph copies; this constitutes a violation of copyright and is illegal. Occasionally a test with all its items will appear initially in a professional publication; if there is no copyright reference, you may duplicate such a test with the author's permission for use in a research project. In any case, we advise you to write the test's developer to provide information about your project and to request any information not in the published article pertaining to the test's validity, reliability, administration, and scoring.

The qualifications needed to administer, score, and interpret tests vary greatly from test to test. Some require little more than the ability to read and understand the manual; others require a substantial amount of special training and supervised practice. *Standards for Educational and Psychological Testing* specify that the test manual should state any special qualifications required to administer and interpret a test. In order to ensure that tests are used by qualified personnel, test publishers have the ethical responsibility to check a prospective purchaser's qualifications. The test publisher may require sponsorship by a psychologist or educator holding the doctorate if a graduate student plans to purchase certain tests. Your thesis chairman or committee members are likely candidates to serve as sponsors.

TYPES OF STANDARDIZED TESTS

In planning a research project, you need to be familiar with the wide variety of standardized tests that have been published. In this chapter, standardized tests are classified into 10 main types. Because the number of tests is so many, we shall describe only a few examples of each type. We selected these examples because they are used frequently in educational research.

Intelligence Tests

Intelligence tests provide an estimate of general intellectual level by sampling a person's performance on a variety of tasks. These tasks may include word definition, mathematical problem solving, general knowledge, and short-term memory of digits. Most intelligence tests yield a single global score of performance on these tasks. This score is called the IQ (intelligence quotient). Some intelligence tests also yield subscores such as verbal IQ and nonverbal IQ; subscores may also be provided for specific intellectual functions, such as spatial relationships, verbal ability, numerical reasoning, and logical reasoning. However, students who plan to use subscores in their research analysis should carefully check to determine whether they are supported by sufficient evidence of construct validity and reliability.

Intelligence tests are held in high regard by educational researchers and school personnel because of their success in predicting school achievement. In fact, they are often called scholastic aptitude tests because the majority of them measure those aspects of intelligence that appear to be required for success in school learning.

Measures of intelligence may take the form of group or individually administered tests. The group intelligence tests have the advantage of low cost, and these tests provide a measure of scholastic aptitude that is satisfactory for most research purposes. Perhaps the most serious weakness of the group intelligence test is its inability to identify pupils in the group who are ill, negative toward the test, or suffer from some handicap that will cause them to make spuriously low scores. The individual tests overcome this difficulty because the examiner can usually determine by the student's answers and general behavior whether extraneous factors that would tend to lower the student's score are entering the testing situation. Another disadvantage of group testing that can seriously distort research results in studies involving young children or children of below-average achievement is that most of these tests depend to a considerable degree on the student's ability to read and students whose reading ability is low will generally receive a spuriously low test score.

The disadvantage of the individual test, of course, is expense. A trained examiner requires about an hour to administer the usual individual intelligence test to a single pupil. Individual tests also require considerable training to score and take much longer to score than do group tests, most of which are machine-scorable. In spite of these disadvantages, you should use individual intelligence tests whenever your subjects are such that you have reason to doubt the accuracy of results obtained from group tests. You should reduce the size of your sample to permit individual testing rather than test a large sample with a group measure of questionable validity.

Of the individually administered measures of intelligence, the Stanford-Binet Intelligence Scale is perhaps the best known. It is more suitable for the testing of children than of late adolescents and adults. A primary reason for the usefulness of the Stanford-Binet in educational research and practice is the considerable amount of evidence that has been collected regarding its validity and reliability. In recent years, though, the Wechsler Scales have achieved increasing prominence in the field of testing. This is perhaps due to the fact that these scales yield a number of useful subscores in addition to an overall IQ score. The Wechsler Adult Intelligence Scale (WAIS) is suitable for the testing of late adolescents and adults. The Wechsler Intelligence Scale for Children (WISC) is a downward extension of the WAIS and is suitable for the testing of children between the ages of 5 and 15. The most recent test in this series is the Wechsler

Preschool and Primary Scale of Intelligence (WPPSI), which was published in 1967. It was designed for the testing of children between the ages of four and six and a half.

A number of group tests of intelligence are available. Some of these are actually a series of tests. The reason for developing series of tests is that a single group test can usually sample only a restricted range of difficulty in content. For example, a group test to assess the intellectual performance of fifth-graders would be totally inadequate to assess high school seniors: The items would be so easy that the test would not discriminate differences in intellectual level for the latter group. Therefore, a series of tests of comparable content are developed for various grade levels. As an illustration, the School and College Ability Tests (SCAT) have forms available for grade 3.5–6.5, 6.5–9.5, and 9.5–12.9. Because they are comparable in content and in unit of measure, these forms make possible the study of intellectual development over many years in school and the comparing of intellectual performance of children at different grade levels. Other widely used group intelligence tests are the Kuhlmann-Anderson Tests, the Lorge-Thorndike Intelligence Tests, and the Otis-Lennon School Ability Test.

Culture-Fair Tests of Intelligence

As we pointed out previously, tests have been criticized because they may discriminate unfairly against minority groups within a culture.[5] Test developers have responded to this criticism by constructing tests that purport to be "culture-fair," which means that words and facts that are culturally linked have been eliminated. Consequently, most of these tests do not require the subject to use language. Among the intelligence measures developed to eliminate or reduce cultural bias are the Goodenough-Harris Drawing Test and the Culture Fair Intelligence Test.

Although the culture-fair testing movement has been gaining increasing favor by educators, there is reason for some caution in accepting the concept of a culture-fair test. For example, a growing body of evidence suggests that verbal tests may actually be more culture-fair than nonverbal tests. Also, some psychologists and educators have argued that it is meaningless to construct tests that eliminate differences between groups, if these are true differences. Instead, training such as that provided by Project Head Start should be used to eliminate these differences.

---

5. Examples of books critical of intelligence testing are Alan Gartner, Colin Greer, and Frank Riessman, eds., *The New Assault on Equality, I.Q., and Social Stratification* (New York: Harper and Row, 1974); and Benjamin Fine, *The Stranglehold of the I.Q.* (New York: Doubleday, 1975).

Aptitude Tests

Aptitude tests are aimed at predicting the student's later performance in a specific type of behavior. Tests are available to measure aptitudes for many specific school subjects such as foreign language, art, music, and mathematics. Examples of such tests are the Orleans-Hanna Algebra Prognosis Test, and the Metropolitan Readiness Tests. Aptitude tests to measure skills needed in various occupations are also available. These include tests of sensory capacities, mechanical aptitude, and aptitude for selling.

A major trend in educational testing has been the development of test batteries that measure a wide range of aptitudes that are related to vocational and scholastic success. For example, the General Aptitude Test Battery (GATB) developed by the U.S. Employment Service measures these aptitudes: intelligence; verbal, numerical, spatial, form perception; clerical perception; motor coordination; finger dexterity; and manual dexterity. The student's scores on these aptitudes yield a profile that can be compared with profiles of successful persons in various occupations in order to locate types of work for which the student has the aptitude required for success. The Differential Aptitude Tests (DAT) are another frequently used test battery for counseling and research with high school students and adults. Eight aptitudes are measured by the DAT: verbal reasoning, numerical ability, abstract reasoning, clerical speed and accuracy, mechanical reasoning, space relations, spelling, and language use. Validity studies have demonstrated the value of the DAT in predicting students' scholastic success and vocational choice.

You should follow the usual evaluation procedures in the selection of aptitude tests for research purposes. Predictive validity is especially important in aptitude tests because they are primarily concerned with prediction of future behavior. Aptitude tests are often used in educational research initially to equate groups that are to receive two different experimental treatments. For example, let us say we wish to compare the effectiveness of two methods of teaching ninth-grade algebra. If the students to be used in the experiment are initially different in terms of algebraic aptitude, the group with the higher aptitude might learn more regardless of the method. Therefore, in order to evaluate the effectiveness of the two methods, we would want either to equate the two groups being studied by matching students on algebraic aptitude or to make statistical adjustments for initial differences found by the aptitude test. By using one of these methods, you can be more confident that achievement differences measured at the end of the study are due to differences in method than if you had no knowledge of the initial aptitude of the two groups.

Aptitude tests also are used in research to identify students of a particular aptitude level for special study. For example, you may wish to identify students who have very low aptitude for learning a foreign language in order to determine whether a method could be developed to teach foreign language effectively to students at this level.

Achievement Tests

Because learning is one of the major goals of education, measures of amount learned (i.e., achievement) are often used in educational research. Many standardized achievement tests are available. Some are intended to measure the student's knowledge of specific facts, whereas others, especially the more recent tests, attempt also to measure the student's understanding and mastery of basic principles. Although achievement tests have been criticized on social grounds, they are probably the most valid, reliable, and useful measures available to the educational researcher.

Administration time for different achievement tests varies greatly; some test batteries take as little as 30 minutes, whereas others require two days of testing to administer the entire battery. Achievement test batteries also differ in subject-matter coverage. The Wide Range Achievement Test, for example, contains tests in the areas of reading, spelling, and arithmetic, and requires less than 30 minutes to administer. In contrast, the intermediate level of the Metropolitan Achievement Test provides 7 scores related to reading, 6 scores related to language, and 8 scores related to mathematics and may require as long as 10 hours to complete.

In selecting an achievement test or battery for your research project, you first should decide what areas of achievement to measure and then evaluate the tests that purport to measure achievement in these areas. You should also consider carefully the research questions you want to answer and decide whether norm-referenced or domain-referenced achievement tests are more appropriate. These two types of tests were discussed in chapter 7. Because there is usually limited time available for testing in the public schools, it is often necessary to administer single achievement tests rather than an entire test battery. As a rule you will administer only tests measuring achievement in the content areas specified in the research problem.

In addition to studying the evaluations available in source books such as the *Mental Measurements Yearbooks* and evaluating the test manual, you should administer the test to yourself (even if it is at the elementary school level) in order to check the instructions and gain an insight into the specific content covered. A major problem in developing achievement tests is to select content sufficiently common to the curriculums of most school systems so that the test will have a satisfactory level of content validity. It is much more difficult to achieve content validity in areas such as social studies than in areas such as arithmetic where the sequence and content is reasonably standard. A test may be very well constructed and receive good reviews in the *Mental Measurements*

Yearbooks and still be inappropriate if it does not fit the content covered in the schools to be used in the research.

In selecting an achievement test or battery to be used in more than one school district, the problem of content validity is increasingly acute because tests may fit the curriculum of one district better than the other. In this case obtained differences in achievement may be due to differences in content validity rather than actual differences brought about by the research conditions. Very often, some of the newer achievement batteries, which place more emphasis upon principles and less upon specific facts, are more appropriate for use in studies involving more than one district. Another aspect of content validity that you should check when examining the test is the degree to which the test is up-to-date. Some achievement tests that were excellent several years ago are considerably less valid today. A common weakness found in the older tests is that illustrations of devices that have changed in physical appearance, such as the airplane, the automobile, and the telephone, may be so outdated that many students in today's schools would not even recognize them.

Another factor you should consider in selecting achievement measures for research is the test battery already being used by the schools from which the research sample will be drawn. Almost all school districts now administer achievement tests on a regular basis as part of their program of self-evaluation and improvement. Generally, using the same battery for research that is being used for other purposes in a particular school or district is undesirable, unless a very close control of the testing situation is possible. Achievement testing is psychologically threatening to many teachers, who fear that a poor performance by their students on the test reflects on their own abilities as teachers. Thus, if teachers have copies of the test at their disposal, they will not infrequently provide their pupils special preparation in areas and sometimes even on specific items covered by the test. Selecting your own measure reduces the likelihood of the teacher's giving this sort of special assistance to pupils.

Finally, consider the *test ceiling* when selecting an achievement measure. If the test is too easy for some pupils, they will score close to the test ceiling or maximum score. As a result, the test cannot reflect gains made by such pupils and does not provide an accurate indication of their achievement level. This problem often occurs in studies that extend over several years, where the measure chosen is appropriate at the start but the ceiling is too low to provide an accurate measure at the end of the study.

When research conditions call for a measure of very specific knowledge, you may need to develop an achievement test for use in the research project. In this case a domain-referenced test is often more appropriate than a norm-referenced test, because domain-referenced tests typically provide a more complete coverage of the content domain. The principal advantage of the locally developed achievement test is that it can be tailored to the precise content area with which you are concerned. The disadvantages are the additional time required to construct such a test and the fact that most research workers cannot bring a locally developed test to the high technical level attained by standardized tests.[6]

Diagnostic Tests

Occasionally the aim of a research project will be to evaluate the effectiveness of a remedial program. In this situation the researcher may find it helpful to use one of the variety of diagnostic tests that are available to identify students in need of remediation.

Diagnostic tests are a form of achievement test. However, an achievement test typically yields a single score indicating the student's general level of achievement in a given subject. Some diagnostic tests in common use are the Stanford Diagnostic Reading test, the Stanford Diagnostic Mathematics Test, and the Diagnostic Screening Test: Spelling. There are several advantages to administering diagnostic tests in research or remedial programs. First, students who share a specific deficiency in a subject can be identified; otherwise, students might be selected whose deficiencies vary widely, even though they earn the same score on a general achievement test. Second, the use of diagnostic tests is helpful in planning individualized remedial instruction, an approach advocated by many educators. A disadvantage of some diagnostic tests, however, is that the subscores have low reliabilities and are highly intercorrelated with one another. A researcher who can locate a suitable domain-referenced test should consider it since such measures are usually very useful for diagnosis.

Measures of Creativity

The identification and nurture of creative talent has become a major concern of educational researchers in the last two decades. Note surprisingly, many new measures of creativity have been developed during the same period of time. A primary reason for this upsurge of research in creativity is that educators have become increasingly interested in the role of nonintellectual factors, such as creativity and personality characteristics, in school achievement.[7]

Most measures of creativity are intended to assess the aptitudes and personality traits that contribute to creative achievement. They are not direct

6. Many interesting developments have occurred in achievement measurement in recent years, such as the emergence of mastery testing and criterion-referenced testing, the renewed emphasis on basic skills, and the increase of public involvement in testing. The student who wants to learn more about such developments is referred to W. B. Schrader, ed., *Measuring Achievement: Progress over a Decade* (San Francisco: Jossey-Bass, 1982), and Isaach I. Bejar, *Achievement Testing, Recent Advances* (Beverly Hills, CA: Sage, 1983).
7. It should be noted, however, that some measures of creative aptitude have been found to be highly correlated with traditional measures of scholastic aptitude.

measures of creative achievement itself. One of the major contributors in this area is J. P. Guilford, who has constructed a number of tests measuring divergent thinking processes. Some of these tests are Word Fluency (the person writes words each containing a specified letter); Brick Uses (the person lists uses for a common brick); Expressional Fluency (the person composes 4-word sentences, given only the initial letters, for example, H____ r____ t____ s____); Plot Titles (the person composes plot titles, which are rated for their cleverness). Another major research effort was directed by E. P. Torrance; one outcome of this work was the development of the Torrance Tests of Creative Thinking. Because they were developed within a school context, these tests are frequently used by educational researchers in projects involving students at all grade levels. There are also a great many experimental tests of creativity. Perhaps the best source of information about available creativity measures is the ETS test collection bibliography entitled "Creativity and Divergent Thinking."

Self-Report Measures of Personality

Many measures of personality rely on self-report to assess individual differences in traits, needs, adjustment difficulties, and values. These measures are used frequently in educational research to describe the personality characteristics of different groups of concern to educators, such as underachievers, minority groups, exceptional children, and members of a particular profession. They are also used to identify certain personality types for use in studies concerned with interrelationships between personality characteristics and other variables, such as intelligence, school achievement, or popularity.

Some of these measures are referred to as "general inventories" because a single instrument is used to measure a variety of personality traits. The inventory seeks information about the individual's personality by asking questions or requiring the subject to respond to statements. Because a number of variables are assessed at the same time, there are usually several hundred of these statements. Consequently, most subjects will require an hour or more to complete a general inventory. One of the principal advantages of the personality inventory is its low cost and ease of administration and scoring. The questions or statements are almost always in objective form, such as yes-no or multiple choice, a format that permits them to be scored by computer or with a template.[8] However, a few of these measures require training in order to interpret particular variables. For example, you would have no difficulty administering the Minnesota Multiphasic Personality Inventory (the MMPI), since it is virtually

8. A template or window key is placed over the test paper. Holes in the key focus the test scorer's attention on the correct answers. This speeds up the scoring process and reduces errors.

self-administering and can be objectively scored. But suppose you found that one of your research groups scored significantly higher on the Pt scale (psychasthenia) than a comparison group. Unless you have had training in the MMPI or can consult with someone who has had this training, you probably will be unable to interpret the significance of this findings.

One of the potentially serious disadvantages of personality inventories stems from the fact that they are based on self-report. Like most self-reporting devices, they are only accurate to the degree that the self-perceptions are accurate and to the degree that the person is willing to express them honestly. This problem has been, and continues to be, a matter of concern to many educational and psychological researchers.

Unless you establish rapport with the subjects, some may respond in a random fashion or deliberately lie or distort their answers. If such spurious answer sheets are not detected and omitted from the data analysis, they can lead the researcher to invalid conclusions. Many inventories contain a "lie scale" or "carelessness" index that helps identify spurious answer sheets. These vary in effectiveness, but some detect over 80 percent of randomly answered response sheets. For example, O'Dell developed a "carelessness" index for the Sixteen Personality Factor Questionnaire that correctly selected 88 percent of randomly completed answer sheets.[9]

There is ample evidence that self-report measures are subject to faking. This is not surprising because the link between the item and the construct it attempts to measure is rather obvious for most self-report personality tests. Some test developers have tried to reduce faking by using more subtle items. However, there is research evidence that casts doubt on the degree to which faking is reduced by this method.[10]

Another variable that leads to spurious responses is called *response set*. If self-report inventories are to be used effectively in practical applications and in research settings, it is important to investigate the extent to which subjects are responding to the content of each item and the extent to which their responses are determined by a general "set." Three types of "response sets" have been extensively researched: social desirability, or the set to present oneself in a favorable light; acquiescence, or the set to respond "true," no matter what the content of the inventory item may be; and the set to respond deviantly. If you have good reason to believe that your sample may be motivated to fake or give atypical answers, then you should not use a self-report inventory.

We pointed out in the previous chapter the increasing frequency of attacks on tests as an invasion of privacy. This is particularly true of personality

9. J. W. O'Dell, "Method for Detecting Random Answers on Personality Questionnaires," *Journal of Applied Psychology* 55 (1971):380–383.
10. Ronald R. Holden and Douglas N. Jackson, "Subtlety, Information, and Faking Effects in Personality Assessment," *Journal of Clinical Psychology* 37 (1981):379–386.

measures. You should therefore carefully review the personality inventory you are considering to see if it contains items that might cause public relations difficulties with parents or community groups. For example, administering an inventory to junior high school students that contained questions dealing with sexual conduct might cause serious repercussions in the community and make it impossible for you to complete the research. If such items are essential to the research objectives, you should be prepared to carry out extensive public relations work before and during the study.

The following self-report measures of personality are used frequently in educational research.

General Inventories

Minnesota Multiphasic Personality Inventory (MMPI). This inventory was developed by determining which items out of a 550-item pool differentiated empirically between particular psychiatric groups and normal groups. In addition to the original scales (e.g., hypochondriasis, depression, schizophrenia), many other variables can be assessed, including response sets and scales of ego strength, anxiety, and repression-sensitization. The *Mental Measurements Yearbooks* list over 5,000 references on the MMPI, many of them relevant to educational research. The MMPI may be an appropriate instrument to use when you are interested in measuring various aspects of personality adjustment in late adolescents and adults.

The California Psychological Inventory (CPI). Although the CPI draws heavily on the MMPI item pool, its aim is to measure traits thought to be relevant to interpersonal behavior and intellectual functioning. Whereas the MMPI was developed for use in psychiatric settings, the CPI is oriented primarily to the assessment of normal persons. Some of its 18 scales are dominance, sociability, responsibility, good impression, flexibility, intellectual efficiency, and achievement via independence. The CPI can be used with high school and adult populations. Approximately 1,400 references related to this measure are listed in the *Mental Measurements Yearbooks.*

The Edwards Personal Preference Schedule (EPPS). This inventory measures 15 needs based on Murray's need system. One of the merits of the EPPS is that an attempt has been made to control for the response set of social desirability by having subjects decide between pairs of statements of equivalent social desirability. Some of the 15 scales are autonomy, dominance, intraception, and abasement. Norms on the EPPS are available for college students and adults.

The Sixteen Personality Factor Questionnaire (16 P.F.). This inventory is different from those already described in that its scales were developed by the method of factor analysis. Some of the personality dimensions measured by the scales are reserved versus outgoing, affected by feelings versus emotionally stable, practical versus imaginative, relaxed versus tense. Primarily used for research purposes, the 16 P.F. can be administered to subjects who are age 16 or older.

Specific Personality Variables

In addition to the general personality inventories just described, a group of measures are available which focus on a single personality variable or small set of related variables. Sample measures in a few areas of interest to educational researchers are described below.

Rokeach Dogmatism Scale. Although designed to measure the variable of closed-mindedness, this scale is often used in educational and psychological research as a measure of general authoritarianism. A sample item is: "When it comes to differences of opinion in religion we must be careful not to compromise with those who believe differently from the way we do." (Agreement with this item is scored in the direction of closed-mindedness.)[11]

Fundamental Interpersonal Relations Orientation-Behavior (FIRO-B). This brief inventory is based on William Schutz's theory of small-group behavior.[12] It measures the strength of one's expressed inclusion, control, and affection, and the extent to which one wants these behaviors from others. FIRO-B can be administered to persons of high school age and older. There is also a form of this scale (FIRO-BC) that can be administered to children in grades 4 to 8.

Study of Values. This inventory attempts to determine the predominant value system of the person tested. The Study of Values yields six scores indicating the relative strengths of the dominant values that shape the individual's personality: theoretical, economic, aesthetic, social, political, and religious.

Locus of control. This variable is concerned with the degree to which individuals believe they are in control of the events of their lives (internal locus of control) or that external forces largely determine these events (external locus of control). The child's locus of control influences the youngster's behavior in school and therefore is of interest to researchers. A number of experimental measures have been designed to explore this concept (see the ETS "Locus of Control Bibliography"). The *Academic Achievement Accountability Scale*, developed by Margaret Clifford, is useful because it is designed to measure locus of control as it relates to academic outcomes. It may be administered to grades 3 through 8 and requires only about 20 mintues.

If you are interested in a measure of only one personality characteristic, first check the *Ninth Mental Measurements Yearbook* to see if a published measure is available. The score index of the *Yearbook* is useful in locating measures that yield a score on a specific variable. If you cannot find a measure of the variable of

---

11. This scale may be found in Milton Rokeach, *The Open and Closed Mind* (New York: Basic Books, 1960).
12. William C. Schulz, *FIRO: A Three-Dimensional Theory of Interpersonal Behavior* (New York: Holt, Rinehart & Winston, 1958).

interest, check the general inventories to see if any of these measure the variable in which you are interested. If so, you can either administer the entire inventory or, using the scoring key, extract the items that measure the variable and administer only those items. You should obtain the publisher's permission before using the latter approach, for these inventories are usually copyrighted. Use the test norms for the variable with caution if you administer only part of the inventory, for there is likely to be some difference in response when items measuring a single variable are taken out of the context of the entire inventory.

If you cannot find a suitable measure of the variable in a general inventory, check the list of ETS bibliographies and the other source books described earlier in this chapter, as well as those listed in the Annotated References.

If all these strategies fail to produce a satisfactory measure, carry out a computer search of the specific personality construct, using the ERIC or *Psychological Abstracts* data base.

Checklists

Some self-report measures of personality take the form of checklists. A collection of items is presented to the individual, who is asked to check those items that are applicable to herself. A great many checklists have been used in educational research.

The Adjective Checklist (ACL). This measures consists of 300 adjectives. The person checks as many of these adjectives as are self-descriptive. The ACL data can be used to compare groups on the frequencies with which they endorse particular adjectives. The ACL can also be scored on 37 scales that assess such personality variables as aggression, self-confidence, dominance, and personal adjustment. The ACL is a useful research instrument, as it yields a considerable amount of information in a relatively short period of time (it can be completed in 15 or 20 minutes). Also, the ACL can be used by subjects to describe themselves or to describe another person or group.

Mooney Problem Checklist. This measure contains a list of problems that a student may have. The student simply checks off those problems applicable to himself. This checklist may be administered to students in grades 7 and up.

Projective Techniques

The term *projective technique* was popularized by L. K. Frank.[13] It was his contention that the use of instruments such as the Rorschach Inkblot Technique, with its amorphous stimuli and freedom of response, would reveal the individual's inner thoughts, fantasies, and idiosyncratic structuring of reality. One of the

---

13. L. K. Frank, "Projective Methods for the Study of Personality," *Journal of Psychology* 8 (1939):349–413.

purported advantages of projective techniques over self-report inventories is that they are less subject to faking.

The most widely used projective techniques are the *Rorschach Test* and the *Thematic Apperception Test* (TAT). In the Rorschach, the subject responds to a set of inkblots, whereas in the TAT the subject responds to a set of pictures. These measures have been widely used in psychological research. The *Mental Measurements Yearbooks* list over 5,000 studies that have employed the Rorschach Test.

In spite of the popularity of projective tests we would recommend that they be used with caution in a research project because, as a rule, these measures require extensive training and experience to administer, score, and interpret. Should you decide to employ the Rorschach or similar projective techniques in your project, you should employ fully qualified persons to administer, score, and interpret the results.

A recent development in the field of projective techniques is the construction of group-administered instruments to measure classic Rorschach variables. The most widely used of these instruments is the Holtzman Inkblot Technique (HIT), which, from a psychometric point of view, is far superior to the Rorschach. Unlike the Rorschach, where subjects may give as many or as few responses to each stimulus as they choose, the number of responses that the subject can give to each Holtzman card is controlled. Most of the Holtzman scoring variables have satisfactory reliability. The disadvantages of the HIT are that training is needed to interpret the scoring variables and that some of these variables seem to reflect verbal productivity rather than basic personality characteristics.

Measures of Self-Concept

The *self* or *self-concept* may be defined as the set of cognitions and feelings that each of us has about ourself. Researchers may want to measure self-concept for various reasons. You may want to investigate, for example, the effect of various educational practices on students' self-concept, or whether students' self-concept is a determinant of school performance.

Interest in self-concept has increased markedly in recent years, and many measures are available for research in this area. A few measures that provide information on self-concept are listed in the Personality section of *The Ninth Mental Measurements Yearbook*. Because most self-concept measures are not available from regular test publishers, however, the sources for unpublished tests are more useful for locating them. For example, *Tests and Measurements in Child Development: Handbook II* lists 45 self-concept measures, and *Measures for Psychological Assessment* lists 113 measures in this area. (See the Annotated References at the end of this chapter.)

The two ETS Bibliographies on Self-Concept (grades 4 through 6 and grades 7 through adult) list approximately 200 measures.

Attitude Scales

Scales are frequently developed to measure the individual's attitude toward a particular group, institution, or institutional practice. An attitude is usually thought of as having three components: an affective component, which consists of the individual's feelings about the attitude object; a cognitive component, which is the individual's beliefs or knowledge about the attitude object; and a behavioral component, which is the individual's predisposition to act toward the attitude object in a particular way.

A review of research on the effectiveness of attitude measures as predictors of behavior indicated that general attitude measures are not very accurate predictors of specific behavior.[14] However, recent work suggests that specific behavior can be predicted from measures of attitude toward the specific behavior.[15]

Several different procedures have been used to develop measures of attitude. On a Thurstone-type scale, the individual expresses *agreement* or *disagreement* with a series of statements about the attitude object. On a Likert-type scale, the individual checks one of five possible responses to each statement: strongly agree, agree, undecided, disagree, strongly disagree. Sometimes the Semantic Differential is used to assess attitudes. The individual gives a quantitative rating of an attitude object on a variety of bipolar adjectives, such as fair-unfair, valuable-worthless, and good-bad. Guttman scaling, interviews, and open-ended questionnaires are examples of other methods used to measure attitudes.

Attitudes are often measured in educational research because of their possible predictive value. For example, you may be interested in measuring students' attitude toward high school, since this variable might predict which students will be high school dropouts. An important study concerned with this use of attitude scales was done by Tittle and Hill.[16] They compared the effectiveness of various types of attitude scales (Likert, Guttman, Semantic

---

14. For more information on this topic, the student should refer to M. Fishbein and I. Ajzen, *Belief, Attitude, Intention, and Behavior: An Introduction to Theory and Research* (Reading, MA: Addison-Wesley, 1975); and I. Ajzen and Martin Fishbein, "Attitude-Behavior Relations: A Theoretical Analysis and Review of Empirical Research," *Psychological Bulletin* 84 (1977): 888–918. These authors suggest an alternative to the three-component model.

15. For a recent review of research on the relationship between attitudes and behavior, see Daniel J. Canary and David R. Seibold in the Annotated References at the end of this chapter, under Attitudes section.

16. Charles R. Tittle and Richard J. Hill, "Attitude Measurement and Prediction of Behavior: An Evaluation of Conditions and Measurement Techniques," *Sociometry* 30 (1967): 199–213.

Differential, Thurstone, Self-Rating) in predicting objective indices of voting behavior. The Likert scale was superior to all the other scale types; it yielded a mean correlation coefficient of .54 with the objective indices of voting behavior.

In reviewing the research literature related to your topic, you may come across an attitude scale that you can use in your project, for researchers often develop their own attitude scales. A number of attitude scales are listed in *Measures for Psychological Assessment* (see the Annotated References at the end of this chapter), which purport to measure attitudes toward such things as authority, change, death, health, job, mental illness, and school. However, the ETS bibliographies are the best source for locating attitude scales. There are 15 of these bibliographies listing attitude measures in areas such as Attitudes Toward Curriculum, Racial Attitudes, Children's Attitude Toward Parents, and Attitude Toward School.

Sometimes you may wish to measure an attitude for which no scale is available. For example, one of the authors found it necessary to develop a scale to measure teachers' attitudes toward ability grouping. You can develop satisfactory attitude scales if you follow closely the procedures outlined in textbooks on this subject (see Annotated References). The Likert technique is usually the easiest method of developing scales needed in research projects.

Attitude scales are direct self-report measures and so have the usual disadvantages of this type of instrument. The primary disadvantage is that we can never be sure of the degree to which the subject's responses reflect his or her true attitudes. Under certain conditions, for example, when the individual's attitude is in conflict with the social norm, that person may go to considerable lengths to hide his or her true attitude. Less direct attitude measures are needed to overcome this difficulty, but to date few such measures have been developed.

Measures of Vocational Interest

Vocational interest inventories have proved to be of considerable value to educational researchers. They are used to investigate how students come to develop specific vocational interests, and they also provide an indirect assessment of personality characteristics (e.g., an individual interested in banking is likely to have a different personality structure from an individual interested in art as a career).

Vocational interest inventories typically require the individual to express an interest in various types of people, sports, hobbies, books, and other aspects of daily life. One of the first of these measures to achieve wide use and acceptance was the Strong Vocational Interest Blank (SVIB). Strong conducted a long-range research program demonstrating that occupational groups could be reliably differentiated on the basis of measured interests, that the same characteristic patterns of interest are found in different samples of the same occupational groups, that interest patterns are very stable over time, and that individuals who entered occupations for which they had obtained high SVIB scores were more likely to remain in the occupation than were individuals who entered occupations for which they had scored low. The current version of the SVIB is known as the Strong-Campbell Interest Inventory (SCII). To date this measure can be scored on a total of 264 scales, including 23 basic interest and 207 specific occupational scales.

Since the SCII primarily measures interest in professional and business occupations, this instrument is probably not appropriate for the researcher investigating the interests of students who are not college-bound. Measures such as the Minnesota Vocational Interest Inventory, the Career Assessment Inventory, and the Career Guidance Inventory are more likely to be useful in such cases because for the most part they cover occupations such as building trades, baker, and truck driver, which do not require a college education.

The Kuder General Interest Survey was developed to measure the individual's interest in 10 broad vocational areas rather than specific occupations. These areas are outdoor, mechanical, computational, scientific, persuasive, artistic, literary, musical, social service, and clerical. It can be administered to students in grades 6 through 12.

The Kuder Occupational Interest Survey is also widely used in counseling and research. This measure can be administered to students in grades 10 to 16 and to adults.

There are 126 scales for specific occupational groups, and 48 scales for college major groups.

Although the Strong and Kuder inventories are the most widely used measures of vocational interest, several others have been developed and are more appropriate for some research projects. Consult the *Mental Measurements Yearbooks* and other sources of test information before selecting a vocational interest measure for your research project.

MISTAKES SOMETIMES MADE IN USING STANDARDIZED TESTS

1. Researcher selects the first test that is found rather than systematically selecting the test most appropriate for the research problem.
2. Uses subscores from a test without checking their validity and reliability.
3. Does not check the content of an achievement test to determine whether it corresponds to the content covered in the schools that will be used in the research.
4. Selects a test instrument, such as the Minnesota Multiphasic Personality Inventory, that the researcher is not qualified to administer and interpret.
5. Fails to check the content of a personality test to determine whether it is likely to cause public relations difficulties.

ANNOTATED REFERENCES

The following references contain test compilations, descriptions, reviews, or other data that can be useful to the researcher. The most important references are described in the chapter. Others are described below, while only bibliographical data are given for the rest. Students should also consult the list of *Test Collection Bibliographies*, published by Educational Testing Service, given in Appendix F.

General (includes tests in most of the major areas of measurement)

Chun, K.T.; Cobb, S.; and French, J.R.P., Jr. *Measures for Psychological Assessment: A Guide to 3,000 Original Sources and Their Application*. Ann Arbor: Institute for Social Research, University of Michigan, 1974.

Contains experimental measures for the most part. Although no measures developed since 1970 are included, many of those included are still currently in use.

Comrey, A.L.; Backer, T.E.; and Glaser, E.M. *A Sourcebook for Mental Health Measures*. Los Angeles: Human Interaction Research Institute, 1973.

Contains descriptions of about 1,100 measures related to mental health drawn from sources dating from 1968 to 1972.

ETS Test Collection Catalog. Princeton, NJ: Educational Testing Service, 1986.

Lists 200 Test Collection Bibliographies and more than 800 unpublished tests that are available on microfiche.

Goldman, B.A., and Busch, J.C. *Directory of Unpublished Experimental Mental Measures*, Vol. 2. New York: Human Sciences Press, 1978. See also Vol. 1, published in 1974.

Contains information on 1,034 tests that were located by the authors in 42 professional journals dating between 1970 and 1972.

Johnson, Orval G. *Tests and Measurements in Child Development: Handbook II*. San Franscisco: Jossey-Bass, 1976.

The earlier volume by O.G. Johnson and J.W. Bommarito entitled *Tests and Measurements in Child Development: Handbook I*, published in 1971, is also useful.

These handbooks cover over 1,200 unpublished measures, this is, measures not published by regular test publishers or included in *The Mental Measurements Yearbooks*. The authors searched 148 journals for the period 1956 through 1965 for *Handbook I* and 1966 through 1974 for *Handbook II* to locate measures that can be administered to subjects from birth to age 18.

Keyser, Daniel J., and Sweetland, Richard C., eds. *Test Critiques*, Vols. 1–7. Kansas City, MO: Test Corporation of America, 1984–1988.

Mitchell, James V. Jr. *The Ninth Mental Measurements Yearbook.* Lincoln: University of Nebraska Press, 1985.

The earlier *Yearbooks* are also useful.

Straus, Murray A., and Brown, Bruce W. *Family Measurement Techniques: Abstracts of Published Instruments, 1935–1974.* Minneapolis: University of Minnesota Press, 1978.

Contains information on 813 instruments concerned with measuring characteristics of the family. An abstract is provided for each test.

Sweetland, Richard C., and Keyser, Daniel J., eds. *Test—A Comprehensive Reference for Assessments in Psychology, Education, and Business,* 2nd ed. Kansas City, MO: Test Corporation of America, 1986.

Attitudes

Aiken, Lewis R. "Attitude Measurements and Research." *New Directions for Testing and Measurement 7* (1980):1–24.

Provides a brief but informative review of the current status of attitude measurement. The major approaches as well as several less well known techniques for measuring attitudes are described. Reliability and validity of attitude measures are discussed. Several theories of attitude development and change are briefly reviewed, and an extensive list of references is provided.

Canary, Daniel, J., and Siebold, David R. *Attitudes and Behavior.* New York: Praeger, 1984.

First section describes the procedures used by the authors in carrying out their literature review and provides an overview of research and theory on the nature of attitudes and their relation to behavior. Remainder is an annotated bibliography that provides an excellent coverage of the research and theoretical literature in this area. A subject index relates the references reviewed to 13 content categories.

Henerson, Marlene E.: Morris, Lynn L.; and Fitz-Gibbon, Carol T. *How to Measure Attitudes.* Beverly Hills, CA: Sage, 1978.

Gives considerable attention to methods of attitude measurement other than the usual self-report scales, such as interviews, surveys, using written accounts such as journals and diaries, observations and sociometric techniques. Major attention is also given to developing your own attitude measures. This is a short, practical, and readable "how to do it" book with many examples and illustrations.

Mueller, Daniel J. *Measuring Social Attitudes.* New York: Teachers College Press, 1986.

Discusses each of the major methods of attitude scale construction. Steps are clearly described and examples are given. Procedures for determining reliability and validity are described. Methods of attitude measurement, other than the five major procedures, are briefly described. This is a very useful handbook that covers the essentials in a book of just over 100 pages.

Rajecki, D.W. *Attitudes, Themes and Advances.* Sunderland, MA: Sinauer, 1982.

Presents an overview of attitude research, discusses the structure and function of attitudes, and reviews methods of attitude measurement. Also reviews research on several major topics such as attitudes and prosocial behavior, and attitude-behavior consistencies. A good source for the student who seeks a foundation in attitude theory and research.

The Classroom Situation

Borich, Gary D., and Madden, Susan K. *Evaluating Classroom Instruction—A Sourcebook of Instruments.* Reading MA: Addison-Wesley, 1977.

Gives a comprehensive coverage of instruments used in teacher behavior research from 1954 through 1975.

Although this book is now over 10 years old, most of the measures described are still in use. Measures are classified into nine categories according to who supplies information about whom. Categories include, for example, measures "about the teacher from the pupil" and measures "about the pupil from an observer." This classification system is very helpful to the researcher who is looking for a particular type of measure.

Projective Techniques

Semeomoff, Boris. *Projective Techniques.* New York: Wiley, 1976.

Provides a very thorough coverage of the Rorschach Test and the Thematic Apperception Test as well as derivatives of these two measures. Projective techniques such as the Family Relations Indicator, the Structured Doll Play Test, and Lowenfeld Mosaic Test, and many others are covered in sufficient detail so that researchers can make a preliminary decision on whether a given measure meets their needs.

Self-Concept Measures

Beane, James A., and Lipka, Richard P. *Self-Concept, Self-Esteem, and the Curriculum.* Boston: Allyn & Bacon, 1984.

Provides a good introduction to self-concept with special emphasis on enhancing student self-perceptions in the schools. A brief section on measuring devices focuses on observation of school behavior and unobtrusive self-concept indicators.

Wylie, R.C. *The Self-Concept: A Review of Methodological Considerations and Measuring Instruments,* Vol. 1. Lincoln: University of Nebraska Perss, 1974; Vol. 2, *The Self-Concept, Theory and Research on Selected Topics.* Lincoln: University of Nebraska Press, 1979.

Among the most scholarly works concerned with self-concept. In volume 1 the author discusses self-concept theories, explores methodological problems that commonly occur in self-concept research, analyses problems in self-concept measurement, and reviews many of the self-concept measures that are in general use. In volume 2 the author reviews much of the substantive research related to various aspects of self-concept and its correlates. Among the topics discussed as they relate to self-concept are socioeconomic class; sex, racial and ethnic variables; family variables; and achievement. Very extensive bibliographies are included in both volumes. Although no longer current, these volumes are an excellent source for any serious student of self-concept.

SELF-CHECK TEST

Circle the correct answer to each of the following questions. An answer key is provided in page 883.

1. Sampling performance on a variety of tasks that include word definition, mathematical problem solving, general knowledge, and short-term memory of digits is typical of _____ tests.
   a. achievement
   b. special aptitude
   c. intelligence
   d. creativity
2. Intelligence tests are held in high regard by educational researchers and school personnel because of their
   a. standardized formats.
   b. success in predicting school achievement.
   c. generalized format.
   d. instructional efficiency.
3. The most serious weakness of group intelligence tests is
   a. their inability to identify students who are performing at lower than capacity.
   b. the difficulty of creating a table of norms for test scores.
   c. the administration of the tests in a confidential manner.
   d. the interpretation of test results.
4. Tests aimed at predicting the student's later performance on a specific type of skill are termed _____ tests.
   a. projective
   b. achievement
   c. aptitude
   d. self-concept

5. In selecting an achievement test for a research project, the first step is to
   a. refer to the *Mental Measurement Yearbooks*.
   b. decide what it is that is to be measured.
   c. evalaute tests that are available.
   d. pretest the instruments with individuals like your sample but not part of the sample.
6. Tests which are similar to achievement tests but which yield more data concerning the individual are labeled _____ tests.
   a. diagnostic
   b. personality
   c. inventory
   d. projective
7. A potentially serious disadvantage of personality inventories is that they are
   a. expensive.
   b. difficult to score.
   c. difficult to administer.
   d. based on self-report.
8. Social desirability and acquiescence are examples of
   a. self-concepts.
   b. projective techniques.
   c. response sets.
   d. Likert-type scales.
9. One purported advantage of projective techniques over self-report inventories is they are
   a. less subject to faking.
   b. easier to score.
   c. less difficult to administer.
   d. cheaper.
10. One disadvantage of attitude scales is that
   a. they usually have low test-retest reliability.
   b. they usually have low construct validity.
   c. subjects' responses may not reflect their true attitudes.
   d. they require highly trained raters to ensure accurate scoring.

APPLICATION PROBLEMS

The following problems are designed to give you practice in applying significant concepts and research procedures explained in the chapter. Most of them do not have a single correct answer. For feedback, you can compare your answers with the sample answers on pages 894–895.

1. Locate tests in the *Ninth Mental Measurements Yearbook* that measure study skills. You are planning a study of the relation of study skills to achievement. You plan to test a random sample of students at grades 4 through 12.
   a. Which Index(es) in the *Yearbook* would you check to locate measures of study skills?
   b. List the tests and test numbers you locate that measure study skills. Place an asterisk in front of those that provide a study skills score for the entire grade range of your study (i.e., 4–12).
   c. Why would the Bristol Achievement Tests: Study Skills (171) probably not be appropriate for your research project?
2. A researcher wishes to make a general personality assessment of the 100 high school seniors who will participate in his research project. Both the California Psychological

Inventory (CPI) and the Holtzman Inkblot Technique (HIT) measure the type of variables in which he is interested.

    a. What is one advantage that the CPI, a self-report measure, probably has compared to the HIT?

    b. What is one probable disadvantage of the CPI compared to the HIT?

3. List at least one standardized test that it would be appropriate to administer in each of the following situations (select tests described in this chapter):

    a. A researcher has only about 30 minutes of group testing time, and she wants to determine possible differences between a sample of high test-anxious students and a sample of low text-anxious students on a variety of personality dimensions. What would be an appropriate test to administer to the students?

    b. A researcher wants to determine the effectiveness of providing diagnostic information about students' arithmetic skills to teachers at the beginning of the school term. What would be an appropriate test to administer to the students?

    c. A researcher needs to obtain a measure of intelligence or scholastic aptitude for his project. The test will be administered to a group of ethnic-minority children, and he knows the community is suspicious about testing. What would be an appropriate test to administer to the students in this situation?

    d. A researcher wants to test the hypothesis that graduating college seniors who have had joint majors (e.g., English and history) have a wider range of vocational interests than students who have majored in a single subject. What would be an appropriate test to administer to this group?

4. A researcher is asked by school district personnel to collect data for a period of three years to determine whether its plans to improve third-grade reading skills are successful. The researcher decides to administer the same reading achievement test at the end of the school year for the following three years. As she examines various achievement tests for possible use in the study, what are three aspects of their content that she should judge carefully?

5. Suppose you plan to conduct a study in which 30 mentally handicapped 4-year-old children would be given a special program designed to improve their self-help skills. You decide to use a rating scale or checklist that has a test-retest reliability of at least .80. Using *Tests and Measurements in Child Development: Handbook II*, locate two measures that might be appropriate for this study.

SUGGESTION SHEET

If your last name starts with letters from Gos to Hav please complete the Suggestion Sheet at the end of the book while this chapter is still fresh in your mind.

Part IV

RESEARCH DESIGN
AND METHODOLOGY

Researchers are constantly developing new procedures for investigating questions and hypotheses about education. If enough researchers use the procedures for a long enough period of time, these procedures tend to become formalized and legitimated by the research community.

Many of these formalized, legitimated procedures have become associated with one or the other of two major traditions in educational research methodology. One tradition emphasizes *quantitative* measurement and analysis. The other emphasizes *qualitative* measurement and analysis. The next two chapters introduce you to the major concepts and procedures of each tradition. Parts V and VI of the book provide a more specific description of the methods used by researchers working within each tradition.

The term "research design" is central to the following chapters. In its broad sense, research design refers to all the procedures selected by a researcher for studying a particular set of questions or hypotheses. The term is generally used, however, to refer specifically to the researcher's choice of quantitative or qualitative methodology, and how, if at all, causal relationships between variables or phenomena are to be explored.

QUANTITATIVE RESEARCH DESIGN AND STATISTICAL ANALYSIS

OVERVIEW

The chapter begins by describing the characteristics of quantitative research, which is research that is rooted in the positivistic approach to scientific inquiry. We emphasize the point that each part of a quantitative research design is important; if any part is deficient, the entire design is weakened. The notion of causality is examined, because one of the main purposes of quantitative research is to detect causal relationships between variables. The remainder of the chapter concerns statistical techniques for analyzing quantitative data. These statistical techniques are used to (1) describe educational phenomena, (2) make inferences from samples to populations, and (3) identify psychometric properties of tests. Furthermore, we discuss techniques for exploring data, handling missing data, and deciding whether to analyze data at the individual or group level.

OBJECTIVES

After studying this chapter you should be able to:

1. Explain why each link in Krathwohl's chain of reasoning model is important in testing hypotheses or answering research questions.
2. Distinguish between different patterns of causation commonly explored in educational research.
3. Explain the different levels of analysis involved in the study of causal relationships.
4. Describe how descriptive, causal-comparative, correlational, and experimental designs differ in their power to reveal causal relationships.
5. Distinguish between the various types of scores used in research.
6. Compare the relative advantages and disadvantages of the mean and the median.
7. Interpret the meaning of the standard deviation in relation to the normal curve.
8. Distinguish between the various types of bivariate and multivariate correlational statistics.
9. Describe the statistical tools that can be used to analyze test validity, test reliability, and item characteristics.
10. Describe how a test of statistical significance is used to decide whether to reject or accept the null hypothesis.
11. Interpret the meaning of a given level of statistical significance (p).
12. Describe the factors involved in doing a statistical power analysis.
13. Interpret the meaning of confidence limits.

14. Distinguish among literal, operational, and constructive forms of research replication.
15. Interpret the meaning of effect size as a measure of the practical significance of research results.
16. Interpret stem-and-leaf displays in exploratory data analysis.
17. Explain the problems in data analysis caused by missing data.
18. Distinguish between situations in which the individual score or the group mean is the preferred unit of statistical analysis.
19. Explain why multilevel analysis of educational research data is sometimes desirable.

The term *quantitative research* refers to investigations that are rooted in a positivistic approach to scientific inquiry. (Positivism is discussed in chapter 1). Most educational research is of this type. In this chapter we discuss the fundamentals of quantitative research design. We also discuss the major statistical procedures used to analyze the various types of data that are yielded by quantitative research. The next two parts of the book (chapters 11 through 19) present specific quantitative research designs. Also, the preceding chapters of this text present in-depth discussions of specific elements of quantitative research design; for example, sampling and testing.

THE NATURE OF QUANTITATIVE RESEARCH DESIGN

The fundamental purpose of educational research is to develop new knowledge about educational phenomena. More precisely, the purpose of educational research is to develop our confidence that particular knowledge claims about educational phenomena are true or false.

How do researchers go about building the confidence of the general community that a knowledge claim is true or false? From the perspective of quantitative research, the answer to this question is to collect evidence that supports or refutes the knowledge claim. This evidence is in the form of objective observations of relevant phenomena. (You will recall from chapter 1 that the essential feature of positivistic research is its reliance on observations of the world "out there" to test knowledge claims.) These observations constitute the research data—the "evidence"—for testing a knowledge claim. The stronger the research evidence, the more certain we can be that the knowledge claim is true or false. At some critical point of certainty, the knowledge claim is no longer considered a claim, but rather is accepted as "knowledge."

Researchers attempt to design a study so that it will yield the strongest possible evidence to support or refute a knowledge claim. **Research design,** then, can be defined as a process of creating an empirical test to support or refute a knowledge claim. Some research designs are stronger than others. The purpose of this chapter and much of the book is to help you design the strongest possible research design so that you and others can be confident that the knowledge claim you have tested is true or false.

The above discussion provides a simple description of research design. The actual process of designing a research study is more complex. David Krathwohl developed a model of research design that reflects this complexity.[1] His model specifies a sequence of steps, or "links," that form a "chain of reasoning."

Figure 9.1 illustrates the chain of reasoning model. It is depicted as a series of links to convey the notion that each step in the process of testing a knowledge claim is dependent on the soundess of the preceding step. Also, each step in the chain must follow rationally from that which precedes it, or the total research design is weakened.

Any test of a knowledge claim has two parts to it. The first part is to test whether the knowledge claim is true of the particular situation that the researcher has chosen to observe. The second part is to test whether the knowledge claim is likely to hold true in other situations. This is a test of the knowledge claim's *generalizability*. A research study needs to be designed so that both parts of a knowledge claim are given the strongest test possible within the resources available to the researcher.

The 9 steps of the chain of reasoning model shown in figure 9.1 can be illustrated using a research study that evaluated an innovative, but controversial algebra textbook.[2] John Saxon, a former Air Force Academy engineering instructor, criticized existing algebra textbooks as being ineffective and developed his own. Unable to find a commercial publisher for it, he published it himself. The text is currently widely used, and many claims for its effectiveness have been made. Two researchers, Dale Johnson and Blaine Smith, set out to test the merit of these claims.

1. *Conclusions from previous studies.* The first step in designing a research study is to review previous research findings. Perhaps evidence already exists that would support the knowledge claim being tested. If so, the previous evidence, combined with new evidence, would increase our confidence that the knowledge claim is true.

In the case of the algebra text study, Johnson and Smith searched for existing evidence on the effectiveness of Saxon's text. They concluded that the "studies showed mixed results"[3] with respect to the text's effectiveness in promoting students' cognitive achievement. But they also noted that many of these studies employed weak research designs, and so the knowledge claim that Saxon's text is superior to other algebra texts had not been given a fair test. Furthermore, Johnson and Smith found no existing evidence concerning the effects of Saxon's test on students' attitude toward mathematics, even though

1. David R. Krathwohl, *Social and Behavioral Science Research* (San Francisco: Jossey-Bass, 1985).
2. Dale M. Johnson and Blaine Smith, "An Evaluation of Saxon's Algebra Text," *Journal of Educational Research* 81 (1987): 97–102.
3. Ibid., p. 97.

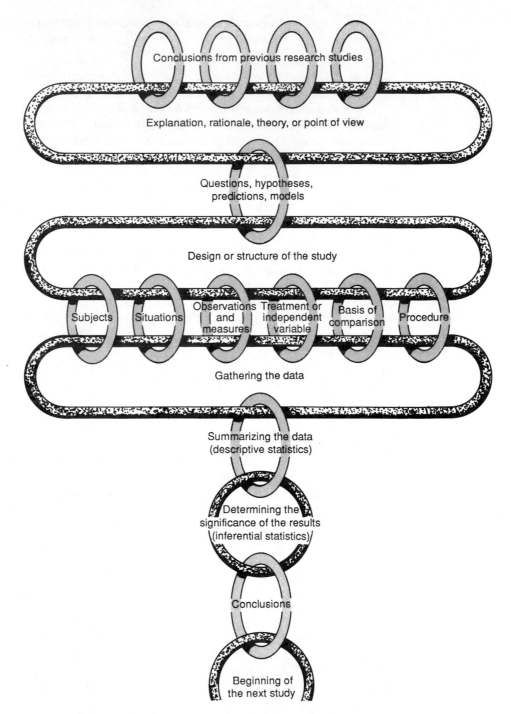

Figure 9.1   Krathwohl's Model of the Chain of Reasoning in Quantitative Studies

Source: Adapted from figures 2 and 6 in David R. Krathwohl, *Social and Behavioral Science Research,* San Francisco: Jossey-Bass, 1985, pp. 42 and 49, respectively.

the development of a positive attitude toward mathematics is an important goal of mathematics instruction.

2. *Explanation, rationale, theory, or point of view.* A knowledge claim gains in credibility if it is grounded in a plausible rationale rather than coming out of "the clear blue." Acknowledging this point, Johnson and Smith reviewed the rationale for Saxon's approach to writing his textbook. They found that Saxon sought to correct three deficiencies of existing algebra texts: poor organization, confusing writing style, and lack of distributed practice. Saxon's text remedied each of these deficiencies. Also, Johnson and Smith found existing research evidence to support Saxon's remedies. Thus, there are reasonable grounds to think that his textbook would be more effective than competing textbooks.

3. *Questions, hypotheses, predictions, models.* The next step in testing a knowledge claim is to state it in a form that it can be tested in and that is related to the previous steps in the "chain of reasoning." This point may seem obvious, but occasionally a researcher will formulate research hypotheses or questions that are totally unrelated to the research literature that was reviewed.

In the Johnson and Smith study, two hypotheses were formulated and expressed in null form:

H_0^1:   There will be no differences between experimental and control groups on mathematics attitude measures.

H_0^2:   There will be no difference between experimental and control groups on mathematics achievement when prior achievement is statistically controlled.[4]

Note that the hypotheses were stated in a form that allowed for an empirical test of their validity. The experimental group is the group that is to use the Saxon text, and the control group is the group that is to use a conventional algebra text.

4. *Design of the study.* This step in the "chain of reasoning" involves the design of the empirical test of the knowledge claims. The research design needs to be sound; otherwise, the results of the test will be rejected as unsound. In fact, as we noted above, Johnson and Smith rejected the results of some previous studies of Saxon's text because the research designs were faulty.

The design of Johnson and Smith's study is described in the published report, including details about sampling, experimental procedures, and measurement. Readers can study this information and decide for themselves whether the research design would be likely to lead to sound conclusions about the knowledge claims that were tested.

5. *Gathering the data.* Once the empirical test has been designed (step 4 above), it must be executed. Various problems that might compromise the integrity of the empirical test can occur at this step. The teachers might not use

4. Ibid., p. 99.

the textbooks in the way intended, data might get lost, some students might fail to complete all of the measures, and so on. In the Johnson and Smith study, the experimental classes were found to have higher initial achievement than did the control classes, even though classes were assigned randomly to the experimental and control conditions. This unforeseen problem was corrected in the data analysis and thus did not pose a serious threat to the test of the knowledge claims.

6, 7. *Summarizing the data,* and *Determining the statistical significance of the results.* In quantitative research, as the term implies, the gathered data are in numerical form. These numbers have little meaning in themselves; they must be analyzed using statistical techniques to determine whether they support the knowledge claims.

The statistical analysis usually involves two tests. First, the data are analyzed to provide a summary description of the situation that was studied. Second, the data are analyzed using inferential statistics to determine whether the observed results generalize to other situations (specifically, to the population represented by the sample). Tables 9.1 and 9.2 present the results of the statistical analyses for the Johnson and Smith study. We explain the meaning of the information in these tables in later sections of the chapter that deal with specific statistical techniques.

You will find that much of this chapter and the chapters in Part V concern statistical analysis. In addition, you will probably take several courses on statistics as part of your graduate program. This is because the selection and

TABLE 9.1

Differences between the Experimental and Control Groups on Measures of Attitudes toward Mathematics

Attitude	Experimental M	Control M	t-Value
1. Self-confidence in mathematics	17.3	19.2	2.86*
2. Pleasure of mathematics	19.3	20.9	2.89*
3. Motivation	19.7	21.5	2.71*
4. Study habits and attitudes	18.4	18.9	1.14
5. Attitude toward textbook	9.1	11.9	3.00*
6. Overall attitude (combined 1–5)	234.4	252.5	3.38*

SOURCE: Adapted from table 1 in Dale M. Johnson and Blaine Smith, "An Evaluation of Saxon's Algebra Text," *Journal of Educational Research* 81 (1987):100.
NOTE: A lower score indicates a more positive attitude.
*$p < .05$

TABLE 9.2

Differences between the Experimental and Control Groups on Subscales of the Comprehensive Assessment Program High School Algebra I Test

Subscale	M		Adj. M		SD		F
	Experimental	Control	Experimental	Control	Experimental	Control	
Polynomials	5.29	5.09	5.21	5.16	1.87	2.04	0.04
Exponents and radicals	4.76	4.43	4.68	4.50	2.10	2.19	0.49
Definitions and theory	1.75	2.07	1.78	2.03	1.16	1.35	4.59*
Linear equations and inequalities	3.42	3.28	3.36	3.33	1.68	1.80	0.02
Systems and coordinates	2.42	2.49	2.39	2.51	1.51	1.72	0.36
Radicals and quadratics	2.64	2.56	2.60	2.60	1.51	1.61	0.00
Word problems	2.15	2.12	2.11	2.15	1.17	1.19	0.12

SOURCE: Adapted from table 2 in Dale M. Johnson and Blaine Smith, "An Evaluation of Saxon's Algebra Text," *Journal of Educational Research* 81(1987):101.
* $p < .05$.

application of appropriate statistical analyses involve many complicated considerations. Yet, by referring to figure 9.1, you can see that statistical analysis constitutes just a few links—albeit important links—in the total chain of reasoning in a research study.

8. *Conclusions.* The researcher must examine the results of the data analysis and decide whether the knowledge claim is supported or not. Johnson and Smith concluded from the statistical results shown in tables 9.1 and 9.2 that Saxon's algebra textbook was no more effective than a conventional algebra textbook in improving students' algebra achievement, but that it did develop more positive student attitudes toward mathematics.

In deciding whether a knowledge claim is supported by the results, the researcher also needs to consider and eliminate alternative explanations of the results. For example, Johnson and Smith found that students using Saxon's textbook had more positive attitudes toward mathematics at the end of the school year than did students using a conventional text. This finding supports the knowledge claim that Saxon's text is effective in developing positive student attitudes toward mathematics. Johnson and Smith, however, suggest another explanation of the observed result, namely, that students using the Saxon text had more positive attitudes toward mathematics at the end of the year because they had more positive attitudes than did the other students at the beginning of the school year. Because data on student attitudes at the beginning of the school year were unavailable, the researchers cannot reject this alternative explanation.

Therefore, the knowledge claim that the Saxon text promotes positive attitudes is cast in doubt and must be put to further experimental testing if someone feels that the claim is sufficiently important to support or refute it.

Another task at this step in the chain of reasoning is to draw conclusions about the generalizability of the knowledge claim to situations other than the one observed. Unfortunately, Johnson and Smith provide little information about the sample other than to note that it was a "rather select sample of students from an academic perspective,"[5] because they scored on average at the 73rd percentile on a measure of mathematics achievement administered at the start of the school year. Also, the Saxon text was compared with just one other algebra textbook. Therefore, the knowledge claim supported by the study (that the Saxon text was not more effective in promoting algebra achievement) is rather restricted in generalizability.

9. *Beginning of next study.* Once a study is completed, it is reported in some form and thereby becomes part of the research literature. The report itself can affect the credibility of the knowledge claims that were tested. The omission of critical details of the research design, use of biased language, flaws in reasoning, and other problems can make it difficult for the reader to accept the researcher's knowledge claims.

Weaknesses in a study's research design, or questions raised by the findings, often provoke the need for new studies. The researchers who did the study themselves may note this need. For example, Johnson and Smith stated:

> . . . the data of this study do not provide an indication about long-term effects (if any) of the use of the Saxon text. If one assumes that cognitive achievement *follows* any change in attitude, it could be conjectured that the experimental group students might show differential improvement in subsequent years. This cannot be answered by the present data.[6]

An observation such as this often provides the impetus for another study, either by the original researchers or by other researchers. Thus, there is a chain of reasoning not only within a study but also across studies as researchers pursue a line of research in which each study builds logically on studies that preceded it.

Krathwohl's chain of reasoning model demonstrates the critical importance of each step in creating and executing a quantitative research study and interpreting the data it generates.[7] If any step is faulty, the entire study is compromised. Also, the model demonstrates that the process of formulating and testing knowledge claims involves personal judgment, interpretation, creativity, and rational persuasion at each step. Quantitative research is not, as

5. Ibid., p. 101.
6. Ibid., pp. 100–101.
7. Although Krathwohl's model primarily refers to quantitative research design, he demonstrates in his book that it also can be applied, with modifications, to qualitative research design.

some people think, a mechanical process in which impersonal data-collection instruments are used to collect numerical data that are then churned through a computer, which spews forth a precise, unequivocal finding.

In describing the nature of quantitative research design, we have used as an example the case where the researchers started with a knowledge claim and then designed a study to test it. Another possibility is to generate data first and then have a knowledge claim arise from the results. Krathwohl's chain of reasoning applies to this situation as well. The difference is that the knowledge claim arises near the end of the chain, and so the researcher (and reader) must reason back through the earlier steps, or links, in the chain to determine whether there was any flaw that might weaken the credibility of the resulting knowledge claim.

Types of Research Design

Most quantitative research in education can be classified as one of two types—descriptive studies and studies aimed at discovering causal relationships. **Descriptive studies** are primarily concerned with finding out "what is." Examples of questions that might be studied by means of a descriptive approach are: Do teachers hold favorable attitudes toward the "new" mathematics? What kinds of activities occur in sixth-grade art classes and how frequently do they occur? What have been the reactions of school administrators to innovations in teaching the social sciences? Have first-grade textbooks changed in readability over the last 50 years? Observational and survey methods are frequently used to collect descriptive data.

Although description is an important goal of educational research, most of the studies involve discovering causal relationships. Typical causal problems investigated by educational researchers are: What factors *determine* choice of college major? What *causes* underachievement? Does this new instructional strategy *lead to* increased learning when compared with conventional instructional strategies?

We may distinguish between research designs in terms of their effectiveness in establishing causal links between two or more variables. The **causal-comparative method** is aimed at the discovery of possible causes for the phenomenon being studied by comparing subjects in whom a characteristic is present with similar subjects in whom it is absent or present to a lesser degree. However, this research design can only be used to explore causal relationships, not confirm them.

Suppose that you are interested in testing the hypothesis that anxiety impairs performance on timed aptitude tests. If a causal-comparative design were used, you might select contrasting groups of high- and low-anxious students, and then compare their performance on a timed aptitude test. Suppose we found that the high-anxious group indeed did have lower test scores on the average than did the low-anxious group. Although this finding is consistent with the research hypothesis, an alternative causal hypothesis is possible, namely, that poor performance on timed aptitude tests (and perhaps other academic tests) is likely to cause anxiety. Thus, the research results do not tell us whether anxiety causes impaired performance or whether impaired performance causes anxiety.

A similar problem occurs in correlational designs. **Correlational studies** include all research projects in which an attempt is made to discover or clarify relationships through the use of correlation coefficients. Like the causal-comparative method, correlational studies tell the researcher the magnitude of the relationship between two variables A and B, but they cannot be used to determine whether A causes B, B causes A, or whether a third variable, X, causes both A and B.

The **experimental research** design is ideally suited to establish causal relationships if proper controls are used. The key feature of experimental research is that a treatment variable is manipulated. For example, the study of algebra textbooks described above employed an experimental design. The treatment variable was type of textbook. Some students were assigned to read Saxon's textbook, whereas other students were assigned to read a conventional algebra textbook.

The experiment is the most powerful research design for identifying causal relationships. If administration of one treatment (A) results in a different outcome than the other treatment (B), we can conclude that treatment A caused the observed effect. Experiments are not always conclusive, however. For example, in the algebra textbook study, Saxon's textbook caused more positive student attitudes toward mathematics to occur at the end of the school year than did the other textbook. Possibly, however, students using Saxon's textbook had more positive attitudes at the beginning of the school year, and this is what caused them to appear more positive at the end of the school year. The research design was not sufficiently strong to rule out this alternative causal explanation.

If you are doing a research study for the master's or doctoral degree, you will probably use one of these three research designs—causal-comparison, correlation, or experiment. Therefore, in this and chapters 13 through 16 we will discuss at length how to use each design properly. Analysis of the data is also part of your research design; therefore we will discuss the statistical techniques most commonly used with each research design.

THE NATURE OF CAUSAL RELATIONSHIPS

One of the primary purposes of research, as we stated above, is to discover causal relationships between variables. But what does it mean to say that one thing *causes* another? Philosophers through the centuries have struggled with this question. For example, philosophers known as logical positivists[8] rejected the very notion of causality on the grounds that it is nonobservable. They argued that it is sufficient to speak of *functional relationships* between variables. This view also has been espoused by some educational researchers.[9]

Several issues and assumptions concerning causality affect the design of quantitative research studies. One of them involves the way in which variables influence each other. (The terms "influence" and "affect" are used here as synonyms for "cause.") Researchers assume that variables can form a variety of causal patterns, as illustrated below:

1. A → B
2. A → B → A → B
3. C → A → B
4. A → B
   C ↗
5. A → B
   ↑ ↗
   C
6. ┌─────────┐
   │ A → B │
   └─────────┘
      ↑
      C

To understand these patterns, let us hypothesize that teacher praise positively affects student learning. The first causal pattern shown above applies to this hypothesis: praise (A) positively affects (→) student learning (B).

An alternative hypothesis is that teacher praise and student achievement have a reciprocal influence, such that teacher praise causes students to learn more (A → B); students' learning gains cause teachers to praise more (B → A); and so on. This is the second causal pattern shown in the illustration above.

Suppose we hypothesize that teacher training (C) causes teachers to praise students more often (A), which in turn increases student learning (B). Our hypothesis is that teacher training does not affect student learning directly, but rather *indirectly* through increased frequency of teacher praise. This is the third causal pattern shown above.

The fourth causal pattern involves situations where two or more variables independently affect B. For example, we can hypothesize that teacher praise (A) and student ability (C) each affect student learning (B). The fifth causal pattern shown above is a slightly more complex pattern. An example of it would be the hypothesis that student ability (C) affects the amount of praise that

8. The positivistic philosophy of science is discussed in chapter 1.
9. Robert M.W. Travers, "Letter to the Editor," *Educational Reseacher* 10, no. 6 (1981):32. For a rebuttal to Travers, see Robert H. Ennis, "Abandon Causality?," *Educational Researcher* 11, no. 7 (1982):25–27.

teachers give students (A) *and* student learning; and that teacher praise (A) also affects student learning (B) independently of student ability (C).

The final causal pattern shown above is commonly found in educational research. It applies to cases in which A is hypothesized to affect B differently under various conditions of C. For example, we can hypothesize that teacher praise affects student learning (A → B), but only for students of average or low ability (one condition of C); for students of high ability (another condition of C), teacher praise has no effect (i.e., A does not affect B).

The following chapters explain how to select an appropriate research design and statistical procedure for testing each type of causal hypothesis described above. If an appropriate design and statistical procedure are not chosen, it may not be possible to make the desired causal inferences from the research data that were collected.

Causation is inferred when changes or variations in B (effect) are preceded by changes or variations in A (cause). It often happens, however, that several other phenomena occur at the same time as A, as illustrated below:

$$
\begin{array}{l}
A \\
C \\
D \\
E
\end{array} \!\!\!\!\longrightarrow B
$$

We may infer incorrectly that C, D, and E influence B because they precede B closely in time and space. Superstitions occur in this fashion. For example, a person with a winning lottery ticket realizes that it was purchased late at night. Thereafter, this person only purchases lottery tickets late at night, superstitiously thinking that time of day has something to do with sales of winning lottery tickets.

In the case of educational research studies, several possible preceding events (A, C, D, E) may be plausible causes of B. For example, in the algebra textbook study, the experimental group students were observed to have more positive attitudes toward mathematics than control group students at the end of the school year. This effect (B) plausibly could be attributed to teachers' use of Saxon's algebra text (A), teacher enthusiasm about the opportunity to try something new and be part of an experiment (C), subtle cues from the experimenter that Saxon's text is superior to conventional texts (D), more positive attitudes toward mathematics among experimental group students even before using Saxon's text (E), or some other cause. Suppose that all of these phenomena occurred prior to B. The researchers would need to decide whether it was necessary to design studies to determine whether each factor is an actual or spurious cause of the observed effect B.

Another issue in determining causal relationships among variables concerns the *level* at which causal phenomena are to be investigated in educational research. If the level is too *micro* or too *macro*, the resulting causal inferences may be of little use to educators. For example, researchers have found that students from families having high socioeconomic status (SES) tend to have better academic achievement than students from low SES families.[10] SES is a macro variable because it subsumes a lot of information about family structure and functions. Even if researchers determine that the relationship between SES and student achievement is causal, it is of little practical use to educators. It simply is not within their power to raise the SES level of their students' families.

Researchers therefore need to conduct studies at the level of *manipulable* causes. For example, in studying students' familities, researchers can observe how parents of different SES levels interact with their children. Suppose evidence accumulates that parental interaction patterns are causally related to students' school performance. This knowledge would be useful to educators and policymakers, because parental interaction patterns are potentially manipulable. For example, the interaction patterns identified as effective through research can be taught in parent education programs.

Consider also the case of the algebra textbook study. The researchers studied causal relationships at a manipulable level, because if Saxon's textbook was found to be effective, it would be fairly easy for educators to adopt it as a course text. Furthermore, much useful knowledge would be gained by conducting follow-up investigations to determine which feature, or features, of the text caused it to be effective. Was it the spaced reviews, the writing style, or the text organization? Suppose the spaced reviews were found to account for most of the observed effect. This is not only a manipulable causal factor but also one that is highly generalizable. Curriculum developers in any subject area can incorporate this feature in their instructional materials.

Studies of manipulable causal factors are not necessarily more valuable than studies of micro or macro causal factors. Basic research, which usually focuses on micro-processes, can be just as valuable as applied research, which focuses on manipulable factors.[11] The important point to keep in mind is to be aware that different causal levels can be investigated, and therefore you should select a level that is appropriate to the research problem that interests you.

WHAT YOU SHOULD KNOW ABOUT STATISTICS

To analyze research results effectively, researchers need to have four kinds of information about statistical tools. They need to know: (1) what statistical tools are available; (2) under what conditions each tool is used; (3) what the statistical results mean; and (4) how the statistical calculations are made. Let us take a brief

10. Research evidence on the relationship between SES and student academic achievement is summarized in the form of an effect size statistic in table 1.1 (variable 24) in chapter 1.
11. The study of basic and applied research in medicine by Comroe and Dripps, reviewed in chapter 1, illustrates this point well.

look at these types of information and see how they will be discussed in this and the next chapters.

What Statistical Tools Are Available?

One of the most serious weaknesses of research studies is to fail to make maximum use of the data collected. Obviously, the more statistical techniques with which you are familiar, the more varied are the analyses that you can apply to your research data. This capability is important, since most research data can be subjected to more than one type of statistical analysis. Each analysis sheds a different light on the research data.

As an example of this principle, researchers usually will calculate and analyze the mean of the posttraining achievement scores of students who have received different instructional methods. This analysis will reveal whether a group of students exposed to one instructional method learned more, on the average, than a group of students exposed to a different method. But the analysis should not stop there. The standard deviations of the groups' scores should be calculated to determine whether the instructional methods caused the students to become more similar to each other (i.e., more homogeneous) or more different from each other (i.e., more heterogeneous) in their performance. Other types of statistical analysis, to be discussed elsewhere, also can be applied to these data.

There are three main types of statistical techniques. As the name implies, **descriptive statistics** (also called *summary statistics*) are used to "describe" the data we have collected on a research sample. The mean, median, and standard deviation are the main descriptive statistics; they are used to indicate the average score and the variability of scores for the sample. The advantage of descriptive statistics is that they enable the researcher to use one or two numbers (e.g., the mean and standard deviation) to represent all of the individual scores of subjects in the sample. Columns 2 and 3 in table 9.1 present the mean scores of the experimental and control groups in the algebra textbook study.

Inferential statistics, the second type of statistical technique, are used to make inferences from sample statistics to the population parameters.[12] Inferential statistics are important in educational research because we typically study a sample or samples, yet we wish to reach conclusions about the larger populations from which they were drawn. In other words, inferential statistics allow us to *generalize* from the situation that was studied to the situations not studied. The *t* values shown in table 9.1 and the *F* values shown in table 9.2 are inferential statistics.

---

12. Descriptive information, such as the mean, median, and standard deviation, is referred to as *statistics* if computed from the scores of a sample of subjects. The same information is referred to as *parameters* if computed from the scores of the entire population.

The third type of statistical technique is called **test statistics.** As the name implies, test statistics are mathematical methods for describing and analyzing the psychometric properties of tests and other instruments. In the algebra textbook study, the researchers reported that the internal reliability of the total instrument used to measure students' attitudes toward mathematics was .96. This is a test statistic.

This chapter presents the range of descriptive, inferential, and test statistics commonly used in educational research. Many of them are discussed in greater depth in other chapters.

Under What Conditions Are Statistical Tools Appropriate?

One characteristic of a sound research plan is that it specifies the statistical tools to be used in the data analysis. Statistical tools should be decided upon *before* data have been collected, because different tools may require that the data be collected in different forms. For example, analysis of variance or analysis of covariance may become annoyingly complicated and difficult to interpret if the various cells (i.e., the various comparison groups to which subjects are assigned) have markedly different numbers of subjects.

Researchers sometimes use a statistical technique that is inappropriate for their data. A researcher might try to determine whether the mean scores of three or more groups are significantly different from each other by performing *t*-tests on all possible pairs of means. For example, if there are four groups (A, B, C, D), the researcher would perform six *t*-tests (A vs. B, A vs. C, A vs. D, B vs. C, B vs. D, C vs. D). This procedure is incorrect. The proper statistical tool is analysis of variance, which compares all groups to one another simultaneously. If the analysis of variance is statistically significant, special post hoc *t*-tests may be used to detect significant differences between pairs of means. This procedure is described more fully in chapter 13.

Occasionally a statistical tool is used when the data to be analyzed do not meet the conditions required for the tool in question. For example, most tests of statistical significance are based on the assumption that the measured characteristics are normally distributed in the population. The assumption of normality is justified for most variables studied in educational research, but when not justified, nonparametric or "distribution-free" methods should be used. These methods make no assumptions about the shape of the distribution. We discuss these topics further in later chapters.

What Do the Statistical Results Mean?

After appropriate statistical tools have been selected and applied to the research data, the next step is to interpret the results. Interpretation must be done with care. The results of statistical analyses are sometimes misinterpreted even when the researcher has selected an appropriate statistical tool and made the necessary calculations without error.

The most common problems occur in interpreting the meaning of the p value associated with an inferential statistic. The proper interpretation of p values is discussed later in the chapter.

How Are Calculations Made?

This question is concerned with the mathematical procedures involved in the use of statistical formulas. The mathematical procedures demand the majority of time in most statistics courses and are not within the scope of this book. Most statistical calculations are laborious but not difficult.[13] Therefore, in this book you should direct your attention to learning what statistical tools are available, when they are used, and what the results mean after they are used. With this knowledge you can make most of the statistical decisions that are necessary at the time that you develop your plan for a research study.

TYPES OF SCORES

Measurements in educational research are usually expressed in one of five forms: the continuous score, the rank, the artificial dichotomy, the true dichotomy, and the category. We need to recognize the differences between these scores, since the form in which the data are expressed usually determines our choice of a statistical tool. For example, if you had collected continuous scores on two groups, you would probably analyze group differences by calculating mean scores and by computing a z or Student's t. However, if the measurements were in the form of categories, you would analyze group differences by a chi-square (χ^2) test in which relative frequencies of category occurrence are compared.

Before deciding on a method of statistical analysis, you should determine the form of your research data. The five types of scores cited above are discussed in the next sections.

Continuous Scores

Continuous scores are values of a variable that has an indefinite number of points along its continuum. Intelligence tests, personality inventories, and most other standardized measures employed in educational research yield continuous

___

13. See the Annotated References at the end of this chapter for textbooks that present statistical computations and theory.

scores. In the algebra textbook study described at the beginning of the chapter, the attitude and achievement measures that were used yielded continuous scores.

In practice, continuous scores are usually limited to whole numbers, but in theory, fractional scores must be possible for the variable to be considered continuous. For example, in the measurement of IQ, a person may theoretically obtain a score at any IQ point within the broad range of IQs possessed by human beings. This not only means it is possible for a person to obtain a score of 101 while another person obtains a score of 102, but it also means that theoretically it would be possible to find a person who would perform slightly better than a person at 101 IQ and slightly lower than a person at 102 IQ.

A student's performance on each item of a test is usually summed to yield a total **raw score,** which is a form of continuous score. Raw scores, in the absence of other information, are difficult to interpret. For example, what does it mean that a student achieved a raw score of 30 items correct on a 50-item test? This raw score can represent good, poor, or average performance depending upon how other students scored or upon our expectations of how a particular student should have scored.

Because raw scores are difficult to interpret, they often are converted to "derived" scores, also a form of continuous score. **Derived scores** aid interpretation by providing a quantitative measure of each student's performance relative to a comparison group. Age equivalents, grade equivalents, percentiles, and standard scores are examples of derived scores.

Age equivalents and **grade equivalents** are average scores on a particular test for people who are at the same age or grade level. In constructing a new test, the test developers may administer it to a large group of people (sometimes called the standardization sample), and then determine the average score obtained by persons at each age or grade level. These average scores are organized into tables of age and grade norms. Suppose a researcher administers the test to a sample of beginning fifth-graders (mean age of 11.3 years) and determines that they have a mean score of 56.7 on the test. Referring to the table of norms in the test manual, the researcher may find that in the standardization sample a score of 57 (56.7 would be rounded off to this number) was the average score earned by sixth-graders and by students who were 12.7 years of age. The researcher could conclude, on the basis of these norms, that the students in his sample were of above-average ability.[14]

Another form of derived score is the **percentile.** Percentiles are obtained by computing the percentage of persons whose score falls below a given raw score. For example, if 50 percent of the sample obtain a raw score of 16 or below, then anyone obtaining a raw score of 16 would be at the 50th percentile. Manuals for

14. The conclusion assumes that the research sample was drawn from the same population as the standardization sample.

published tests sometimes contain percentile equivalents for raw scores based on the standardization sample.

A **standard score** is a form of derived score that uses standard deviation units (described later in this chapter) to express an individual's performance relative to the group's performance. The Z score is a type of standard score frequently used in educational research. The first step in calculating a Z score is to subtract the mean score of the total group from a person's raw score $(\chi - M)$. The next step is to divide the result by the standard deviation of the group. For any distribution of raw scores, Z scores have a mean of zero and a standard deviation of 1.00. Also, Z scores are continuous and have equality of units. Thus, a person's relative standing on two or more tests can be compared by converting the raw scores to Z scores.

Because Z scores can yield negative numbers (e.g., a person who is one standard deviation below the group mean would earn a Z score of -1.00), researchers sometimes convert raw scores to standard scores yielding only positive numbers. For example, T scores have a mean of 50 and a standard deviation of 10. The Stanine scale, developed by the U.S. Air Force, has a mean of 5 and standard deviation of 2. The 1960 version of the Stanford-Binet scales yields standard scores having a mean of 100 and a standard deviation of 16.

If you have administered a test for which age, grade, or percentile equivalents are available, it is advisable to report both the raw scores obtained by your research sample *and* the equivalents. Age, grade, and percentile equivalents provide useful information about your research sample by showing how their performance compares to the standardization sample. Equivalents should not be used in data analyses involving descriptive or inferential statistics, however. The reason for not using equivalents in these analyses is that they have unequal units. For example, if you refer to the normal curve in figure 9.2 (shown later in the chapter), you will find that there is the same range of scores from the 15th percentile (actually the 15.87th percentile) to the 50th percentile as there is from the 2nd percentile to the 15th percentile.[15] Thus, if the mean of a test is 50 and its standard deviation is 10, a person with a score of 50 and a person with a score of 40 would be about 35 percentiles different from each other. However, two other persons with the same raw score difference of 10, but having raw scores of 40 and 30, would only be about 13 percentiles different from each other.

Because of the inequality of age, grade, and percentile units when applied to most variables in educational research, either raw scores or standard scores should be used in data analyses involving descriptive or inferential statistics.

---

15. This analysis of the inequality of percentile units assumes that the raw scores are normally distributed.

Rank Scores

Some types of educational data are available only as ranks, for example, a student's high school graduation rank. A **rank score** expresses the position of a person or object on a variable, relative to the positions held by other persons or objects. In some educational research it is easier to rank individuals than to assign quantitative scores to them. For example, ranking procedures are used very commonly in the evaluation of teachers. A researcher may ask principals or teacher supervisors to rank a given group of teachers in terms of their effectiveness. The **rank scores** may then be used to form subgroups of effective and ineffective teachers, or the scores may be correlated with another variable thought to be related to teacher effectiveness.

Dichotomies

The term **dichotomy** refers to a variable that has only two values. For example, pass-fail grades are a dichotomous variable because the students can earn only one of two scores: pass or fail. An **artificial dichotomy** results when individuals are placed into two categories on the basis of performance on a continuous variable. We can see that the dichotomy of pass-fail grades is artificial because if we carefully tested the individuals who complete a given course of study, we would find that their test scores would make a continuous distribution ranging from those persons who learned a great deal to those persons who learned little or nothing. The point at which we divide this continuous variable into pass-fail groups is based upon an arbitrary cutting point or criterion. If we compare the person who barely passes and the person who barely fails, we find that these individuals are very similar and yet are viewed as very diferent because their scores happen to lie near the cutoff point.

When individuals are divided into two groups on the basis of a true difference on the variable, the dichotomy is referred to as a **true dichotomy.** The true dichotomy differs from the artificial dichotomy in that it is not necessary to establish any arbitrary cutting point for dividing the cases into two groups.

Gender is probably the true dichotomy must frequently used in educational research. Many studies are concerned with differences between males and females in learning patterns, verbal fluency, personality, and other measurable characteristics. In these studies one of the variables is usually of a continuous nature, such as scores on a verbal fluency test. The other variable is gender, which is a true dichotomy.

Categories

The term **category** is used to refer to values of a variable that can yield more than two discrete, noncontinuous scores. (If there were only two categories, the variable would be an artifical or true dichotomy.) For example, student participation in high school athletics could be recorded in such categories as: (1) earned letter in varsity sports, (2) participated but did not earn letter, (3) participated in intramural sports, (4) participated in physical education classes, or (5) did not participate in any athletics.

Some of the variables that we wish to measure in educational research can be expressed only in the form of categories. For example, in studies of eye-hand dominance individuals are usually classified into one of these categories: left-left, left-right, right-left, and right-right. These characteristics cannot be measured meaningfully in any of the other score forms without changing the nature of the variable being studied.

DESCRIPTIVE STATISTICS

Measures of Central Tendency

A **measure of central tendency** is a single numerical value that is used to describe the average of an entire set of scores. For example, 136 experimental group students and 140 control group students participated in the algebra textbook study described in the first section of the chapter. We would have difficulty getting even a crude picture of each group's performance on the attitude and achievement measures by examining the scores of each of these students. However, by calculating a central tendency statistic (the mean score of each group), the researchers obtained an easily interpreted description of the "typical" or "average" performance of each group.

The mean, median, and mode are measures of central tendency. The **mean** is calculated by dividing the sum of the scores by the number of scores. The **median** is the middle score in the distribution of scores. The **mode** is the most frequently occurring score in the distribution. The scores reported in columns 2 and 3 of table 9.1, and in columns 2 and 3 of table 9.2, are mean scores. The M in the top row of each table is an abbreviation for "mean."

The mean is generally considered the best measure of central tendency. One of its advantages over the median and mode is that it is more stable. Thus, if we study several samples drawn from the same population, the means are likely to be in closer agreement than the medians.

When a distribution of scores is symmetrical, the mean and the median are located at the same point on the distribution. When the distribution has more extreme scores at one end than at the other—that is, when it is skewed—the mean will always be in the direction of the greater number of extreme scores. In this situation, the median will reflect more accurately the average performance of the sample, as can be seen in the following example:

Distribution A	*Distribution B*
8	27
6	6
5	5
5	5
4	4
3	3
3	3
3	3
1	1
Mean = 4.2	Mean = 6.3
Median = 4.0	Median = 4.0

The two distributions differ by a single score. In the first distribution, both the mean and the median accurately represent average performance. In the second distribution, however, only the median provides an accurate representation of average performance. Just one person earned a score as high as or higher than the mean (6.3), even though the mean, as a measure of central tendency, is intended to represent "average" performance. As we shall discuss later in the chapter, this person (the one whose score was 27) is called an "outlier."

When a distribution is highly skewed, as in distribution B, both the mean and the median should be reported. Special statistics (presented in most textbooks of statistical methods) can also be used to describe quantitatively the skewness and shape of the distribution of scores. Generally, though, a visual presentation of the distribution of scores, as in the example in the preceding paragraph, is sufficient.

Measures of central tendency are calculated for continuous scores and ranks. Categorical data, including dichotomies, are summarized by creating frequency distributions, as in the following example:

Category	*Frequency*	*(%)*
Students earning letter in varsity sports	21	(11)
Students participating, but not earning letter	37	(19)
Students participating in intramural sports	115	(61)
Students not participating in athletics	16	(8)
	189	

The most frequently occurring category is easily determined by inspecting the frequency distribution. Also, the frequency of individuals or events in each category as a percentage of the total is readily determined.

Measures of Variability

Variability is the amount of dispersion of scores about a central value, such as the mean. If all persons had the same or similar scores on a test, this variability would hold little interest for educational researchers. However, the fact that there usually is variability about a mean score leads them to ask, "Why do some subjects earn low intelligence scores, while others earn high scores? What accounts for this variability?" or "This educational program leads to increased achievement for some students but not others; what factors might account for this variability in achievement outcomes?" It is this concern to understand variability, or individual differences, that forms the basis of much educational research. Thus, the measurement of variability plays a central role in research design and statistical analysis.

The **standard deviation** (usually abbreviated SD) is the measure of variability most often reported in research studies. Basically, the standard deviation is a measure of the extent to which scores in a distribution, on the average, deviate from their mean. Thus, one step in the calculation of the standard deviation is to subtract each score from the mean. The resulting deviation scores are then squared and entered into a formula to yield the standard deviation. Columns 6 and 7 in table 9.2 report the standard deviations of the experimental and control groups' scores on the achievement subtests in the algebra textbook study.

The standard deviation is popular as a measure of variability because it is stable, that is, repeated samples drawn from the same population are likely to have similar standard deviations. Also, in the analysis of research data, the standard deviation is needed in order to compute other statistics. The standard error of measurement, product-moment correlation, and many other statistical tools are based partially on the standard deviation. The standard deviation also forms the basis for various types of standard scores, such as Z scores, T scores, and Stanine scores, described earlier in this chapter.

The mean and standard deviation, taken together, usually provide a good description of how members of a group scored on a particular measure. For example, if we know that a group of subjects has a mean score of 10 on a test, and a standard deviation of 2, we can infer that approximately 68 percent of the subjects earned scores between 8 and 12, and that approximately 95 percent of the subjects earned scores between 6 and 14.

We can use the standard deviation to make the inference described above because of the relationship between the standard deviation and the normal curve. The **normal curve** (also known as the normal probability curve) is a frequency polygon—that is, the height of the curve at a given point indicates the proportion of cases at that point. An example of a normal curve is shown in figure 9.2. This curve shows that the majority of individuals measured are clustered close to the mean. As we move farther and farther from the mean,

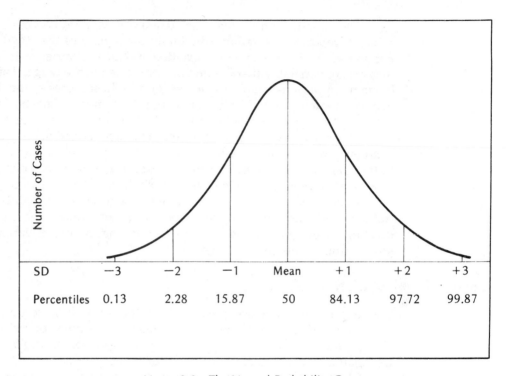

SD	−3	−2	−1	Mean	+1	+2	+3
Percentiles	0.13	2.28	15.87	50	84.13	97.72	99.87

Figure 9.2   The Normal Probability Curve

fewer cases occur. The curve for most measures of complex human characteristics and behavior has a shape similar to that shown in figure 9.2.

The baseline shown in figure 9.2 has been divided into a number of equal units. Each unit is one standard deviation in length. We can show mathematically that, if a distribution of scores forms a normal curve, each standard deviation above or below the mean will include a fixed percentage of the scores. (These percentages are shown as percentiles in figure 9.2.)

Suppose that in one set of normally distributed scores, the mean is 3.0 and the standard deviation is 1.5. In another set of normally distributed scores the mean is 25.0 and the standard deviation is 5.0. Even though the values of the mean and standard deviation of the two sets of scores vary, the properties of the normal curve can be used to infer the dispersion of scores. For example, figure 9.2 indicates that approximately 16 percent of the scores will be one standard deviation or more above the mean (i.e., at the 84th percentile or higher). In the first set of scores, approximately 16 percent of the scores will be 4.5 (3.0 + 1.5) or larger. In the second set of scores approximately 16 percent of the scores will be 30 (25.0 + 5.0) or larger.

The variance, rather than the standard deviation, is occasionally given in research reports. The **variance** is simply the square of the standard deviation. For example, if the standard deviation is 4.0, the variance is 16.0. Another measure of variability that is sometimes reported is the **range.** This measure, as its name implies, is simply the lowest and highest scores in the distribution. It may be of interest to report the range, but the standard deviation also should be reported, since it provides important additional information about variability.

Occasionally continuous data are presented as a frequency distribution. A **frequency distribution** is a list of each score on a measure and the number of individuals who earned each score. For example, a frequency distribution would report the number of students who scored 30 on a test, the number of students who scored 31, the number of students who scored 32, and so forth. The frequency distribution can be inspected to determine the most frequently occurring score (i.e., the **mode**) and also the dispersion, or variability, of other scores around this central value.

Correlational Statistics

The descriptive statistics presented in the preceding sections involve the description of scores on a single variable. In some types of research, however, we are interested in describing the relationship between *two or more* variables. Correlational statistics are often used for this purpose.

The **bivariate correlation coefficient** is a statistic that enables us to describe in mathematical terms the strength of relationship between two variables (e.g., student attentiveness in class and school achievement). There are many types of correlation coefficients. Selection of the appropriate coefficient depends upon the form of the scores (continuous, ranked, dichotomous, or categorical) that are to be related to each other.

Researchers are increasingly turning their attention to the use of **multivariate correlational methods.** These methods allow us to describe and explore the relationship between three or more variables. This capability is important, because the variables in which educational researchers are most interested (e.g., school achievement) usually are not affected by a single factor. Rather, they are affected by a complex of factors (e.g., home environment, personal characteristics, prior school experience), which themselves may influence each other in complex ways.

There are several multivariate correlational methods. **Multiple linear regression** is a statistical technique for exploring the strength of relationship between several independent variables (singly or in combination) and one dependent variable. **Canonical correlation** is similar to multiple linear regression, except that more than one dependent variable is included in the analysis. A **discriminant function** also is similar to multiple linear regression; it is used when the dependent variable is a dichotomous variable expressing group membership (e.g., college graduate vs. high school graduate). **Partial correlation** and **part correlation** are techniques used to describe the strength of relationship between two variables after the influence of one or more other variables on one (part) or both (partial) of the variables has been removed statistically. Finally, **factor analysis** is a statistical method for determining whether a set of variables can be reduced to a smaller number of factors. For example, if a researcher has administered achievement tests measuring 30 different variables to a group of subjects, factor analysis can be used to determine whether each variable measures a different type of achievement or whether two or more variables contribute to the measurement of the same type of achievement.

Correlational statistics and their use in correlational research are discussed more fully in chapter 14. A list of correlational statistics and their respective uses is presented in table 9.3.

TABLE 9.3

Table of Correlational Statistics

Bivariate Statistics	Purpose
Product-moment correlation	Used to describe the strength of relationship between two variables
Rank-difference correlation	
Kendall's *tau*	
Biserial correlation	
Widespread biserial correlation	
Point-biserial correlation	
Tetrachoric correlation	
Phi coefficient	
Contingency coefficient	
Correlation ratio	
Multvariate Statistics	**Purpose**
Multiple linear regression	Used to describe the strength of relationship between several independent variables and one dependent variable
Discriminant function	
Canonical correlation	Used to describe the strength of relationship between several independent variables and several dependent variables
Partial correlation	Used to describe the strength of relationship between two variables after the influence of a third variable has been controlled
Part correlation	
Factor analysis	Used to determine whether a set of variables can be reduced to a smaller number of factors

Test Statistics

Statistics of various types can be used to describe and explore the psychometric properties of tests and other educational measures. Selection of the appropriate statistic depends upon the type of psychometric property being investigated. As indicated in chapter 7, psychometric properties of tests can be classified into three types: test validity, test reliability, and item characteristics.

Test validity is often investigated by calculating the correlation between subjects' test scores and their scores on a criterion measure. The resulting correlation coefficient (sometimes called a **validity coefficient**) indicates the magnitude of relationship between the two sets of scores. Any of the two-variable correlational statistics listed in table 9.3 can be used to calculate a validity coefficient; selection of the appropriate coefficient depends upon the form of the scores in the variables to be correlated. In the case of predictive validity, a special statistic, called the **standard error of estimate,** can be calculated to determine the margin of error to be expected in an individual's predicted score based on his or her score on the predictor measure.

The reliability of a test can be estimated by several methods, as discussed in chapter 7. Each method requires the calculation of a correlation coefficient. Different sources of error variance are controlled by each of the methods of reliability: split-half, test-retest, Kuder-Richardson, alpha. The selection of the appropriate reliability method also depends upon the form of the test scores (e.g., continuous, dichotomous).

Several types of statistics can be used to analyze characteristics of items in a test. The same statistics are also helpful in constructing and selecting items to be incorporated into a new test. These statistics are applied to each test item, one at a time. **Item validity** is determined by correlating subjects' scores on an individual item with their scores on a criterion measure. Because item scores are usually dichotomous (e.g., right-wrong, agree-disagree), biserial correlational statistics are often used to determine item validity. Another approach to determining item validity is to calculate the **index of discrimination,** which is based on an analysis of the proportion of persons in contrasting criterion groups who pass each item.

Item reliability is determined by correlating subjects' scores on an individual item with their total test score. Correlational statistics, especially biserial coefficients, are used to determine item reliability. (Item validity statistics use total test score on a *different* measure rather than total score on the test of which the item is a part.)

Finally, in test construction, it is important to calculate the **index of item difficulty,** which simply is the percentage of persons passing the particular test item.

A summary list of the test statistics presented above is included in table 9.4. Each of them is discussed in more detail in chapter 7.

TABLE 9.4

Table of Test Statistics

Statistic	Purpose
Validity coefficient	Used to describe the strength of relationship between test scores and scores on a criterion measure
Standard error of estimate	Used to describe the margin of error to be expected in an individual's predicted score on a criterion measure based on his test score
Reliability coefficient	Used to describe the item consistency or stability of a test
Item-validity coefficient	Used to describe the strength of relationship between item scores and scores on a criterion measure
Index of discrimination	Used to describe the validity of a test in terms of the persons in contrasting groups who pass each item
Item-reliability coefficient	Used to describe the strength of relationship between an item score and total test score
Index of item difficulty	Used to describe the percentage of persons who correctly answer a particular test item

STATISTICAL INFERENCE

The Null Hypothesis

Rarely in educational research can we study every member of a specified population, for example, all sixth-grade students in the United States. Generally, measurements are made on a sample of subjects randomly drawn from a defined population. However, the research findings based on a random sample are of little value unless they can be used to make *inferences* about the defined population.

Consider the example of the researchers who did the algebra textbook study. They found that the students in their sample who used Saxon's algebra textbook had more positive attitudes toward mathematics than did students who used a conventional algebra textbook. But the researchers were not just interested in this sample of students. They wanted to know whether their finding would hold true of the *population* of students with characteristics similar to their sample.

The researchers' concern can be stated in the form of the following questions: "Is this a chance finding? Is it possible that if we studied new samples of high school students using Saxon's textbook or a conventional algebra textbook that we would find similar differences in attitudes? If we inferred that this is a 'true' difference between the entire population of students using one or the other textbook, how likely is it that our inference is false?"

Statisticians have developed a mathematical procedure, called statistical inference, that enables researchers to answer these questions. The initial step in statistical inference is to establish a null hypothesis. The **null hypothesis** states that *no* difference will be found between the descriptive statistics compared in one's research study.[16] For example, one of the null hypotheses in the algebra textbook study was:

H_0^1:   There is no difference between the population of students using Saxon's text and the population of students using a conventional algebra text in their mean scores on mathematics attitude measures.[17]

After formulating a null hypothesis, the researcher carries out a test of statistical significance to determine whether the null hypothesis can be rejected (i.e., to determine whether there actually is a difference between the groups). As we shall find in the next section, this test enables us to make statements of the type: "If the null hypothesis is correct, we would find this large a difference between sample means only once in a hundred experiments. Since we have found this large a difference, then quite probably the null hypothesis is false. Therefore, we will reject the null hypothesis and conclude that the difference between sample means reflects a *true* difference between population means."

The Test of Statistical Significance

A **test of statistical significance** is done to determine whether the null hypothesis can be rejected. Suppose that the null hypothesis stated above is correct, meaning that the mean attitude scores of the population of students using Saxon's textbook and the population of students using a conventional algebra textbook are the same. Even so, we would probably find a difference if we measured a random sample from each population. If fact, if we selected many random samples of a given size, the differences between mean scores would form a **standard error curve,** which has the same characteristics as a normal curve.

The difference scores in a standard error curve have a mean of zero and a standard deviation whose value depends on the population standard deviation. Assume that the standard deviation of population difference scores on the overall attitude measure (item 6 in table 9.1) is 10. Thus, if we studied many samples of students using Saxon's textbook and many samples of students using

16. Null hypotheses are also discussed in chapter 2.
17. This is a slight rephrasing of the researcher's statement in order to highlight the purpose of a null hypothesis.

a conventional algebra textbook, and each time subtracted the mean attitude score of one group from the other, about 68 percent of the time these difference scores would have a value between +10 and −10 (one SD above and below the mean). About 95 percent of the time the difference scores would have a value between +20 and −20.

In the algebra textbook study, the researchers selected just one sample of students using Saxon's text and students using a conventional algebra text. They observed a mean difference of 18.1 points between the groups on the overall attitude measure. To test the null hypothesis, we need to pose and answer the question: How often would a difference score of this magnitude or larger be found between samples drawn from two populations whose means are the same?

Because we do not know the population means and standard deviations that are necessary to answer this question, we must estimate them using the sample means and standard deviations. These sample statistics are combined in such a way as to yield a critical ratio, also called a *t* value (or *z* value if the samples are large). The *t* value indicates how often a difference score of a given magnitude between samples of a given size would occur when there is no true population difference.

In the algebra textbook study, the *t* value for the overall attitude measure was 3.38 (see column 4 of table 9.1). This large a *t* value indicates that if there was no difference in attitude between the population of students using Saxon's text and the population of students using a conventional algebra text, we would obtain this large or a larger difference less than once in every thousand samples studied. As this is an extremely unlikely event, the researchers rejected the null hypothesis in favor of an alternative hypothesis, namely that there is a true difference in attitude between the population of students using Saxon's text and the population of students using a conventional algebra text.

The ***t* distribution** (or the *z* **distribution** if the sample is large) is used to determine the level of statistical significance of an observed difference between sample means. Generally, educational researchers will reject the null hypothesis if the *t* value reaches a significance level of .05.[18] Occasionally, the more stringent .01 level is chosen for rejecting the null hypothesis, and in exploratory studies the .10 level may be used.

You should note that when the .10 level is chosen, there is one chance in 10 that the researcher will reject the null hypothesis when, in fact, it is correct. If the significance level of .01 is chosen, however, there is only one chance in 100 that this would occur. The rejection of the null hypothesis when it is correct is called a **Type I error.** Obviously, if we lower the significance level required to

18. For an explanation of why the .05 level is commonly chosen, see Michael Clowles and Caroline Davis, "On the Origins of the .05 Level of Statistical Significance," *American Psychologist* 37 (1982):553–558.

reject the null hypothesis, we reduce the likelihood of a Type I error. At the same time, we increase the likelihood of a **Type II error,** that is, the failure to reject the null hypothesis ("no difference") when there is, in fact, a difference.

Interpretation of Significance Tests

Tests of statistical significance are frequently misinterpreted, and because these tests play such a large role in research design, we will consider their proper interpretation and common misinterpretations.

Researchers commonly establish the level of significance (usually .10, .05, or .01) after the statistical analyses have been completed. A z or t value will be computed, and the researcher will refer to a significance table to determine how "significant" it is. However, the logic of statistical inference dictates that the significance level be established *before* a z or t value is computed. You should make a decision at the outset of your study that if you find a difference between samples that exceeds a given significance level (for example, .05), the null hypothesis will be rejected. You cannot properly wait until after the statistical analysis to reject the null hypothesis at whatever significance level the t or z happens to reach.

The level of significance used to decide whether to accept or reject a null hypothesis is called **alpha.** The level of significance actually obtained in the study is called the **probability value** and is indicated by the symbol p. (The p values are given at the bottom of tables 9.1 and 9.2.)

The p value has been subject to a number of misinterpretations. Some researchers believe that the p value indicates the probability that the differences found between groups can be attributed to chance. For example, if you found that a mean difference of five IQ points between groups of subjects was significant at the .01 level, you might erroneously conclude that there is one chance in 100 that this is a chance difference. The proper interpretation of such a finding is that the null hypothesis can be rejected (assuming that the .01 level of significance had been established beforehand), since the mean difference of five points exceeds the mean difference that we would find once in a hundred samples if the population mean difference was zero.

Another misinterpretation is that the level of significance indicates how likely it is that your research hypothesis is correct.[19] For example, suppose that you had hypothesized that inquiry teaching will result in greater student achievement than expository teaching. If the difference between the mean achievement scores is found to be significant at the .01 level, you might conclude that the probability is 99 percent ($1.00 - .99 = .01$) that your hypothesis is correct. However, the level of significance only helps to make a decision about

19. The research hypothesis states that a difference between groups will be found, whereas the null hypothesis states that no difference will be found.

rejecting the null hypothesis; it has only an indirect bearing on the confirmation of your research hypothesis. For example, you may find a significant difference between two groups but not for the reason suggested by your hypothesis. Similarly, you may find too small a difference between groups to reject the null hypothesis, but your research hypothesis may still be correct. A Type II error may have occurred, or the measures used to test the hypothesis may have been inadequate.

Still another misinterpretation of p values is to think that they indicate the probability of finding the same research results if the study were repeated. You might think, for example, that if a difference between the means of two groups is significant at the .05 level, a comparable difference will be found 95 times in every 100 repetitions of the study. However, even if the difference between means that we obtained in our study is a true population difference and is highly significant, we might still find considerable variations in the amount of difference from repetition to repetition of the study. In short, the level of significance cannot be used to predict the results of future studies in which the conditions of the original study are replicated; it can only be used to make a decision about rejecting the null hypothesis.

Perhaps the most common and most serious misinterpretation of the test of significance is to confuse the level of signficance (i.e., the p value) of the research results with the practical and theoretical significance of the research results. The level of significance is influenced to a considerable degree by the number of individuals tested in the research project. Thus, the larger the sample size, the smaller the difference needed to reach a given level of significance. For example, with a sample of 1,000 subjects, a correlation coefficient of .08 is significant at the .01 level. In contrast, a correlation coefficient of .42 with a sample of 22 subjects is only significant at the .05 level. However, the latter coefficient has more practical significance because its magnitude is larger.

As we have already observed, the test of significance is concerned with the inferences that we wish to make from sample statistics to population parameters. Thus, a test of significance is made when we wish to determine how probable it is that the differences we have found between our samples will also be found in the populations from which they were drawn. Therefore, to use the test of significance properly, we should use it only with samples randomly drawn from a specified population. However, researchers sometimes do not specify the population or do not use random sampling techniques, and thus the sample may not be representative.

On occasion a test of statistical significance is used when the entire population has been studied. For example suppose that a researcher defined all males and all females at a particular college as two populations. Then suppose the reseacher finds, as hypothesized, that the females have higher gradepoint averages than the males. In this situation it is meaningless to use a test of statistical significance. The difference between gradepoint averages is a *true* difference because the entire populations have been studied rather than samples drawn from their respective populations.

The use of statistical significance in educational research is sometimes criticized.[20] One criticism is that educational researchers seldom work with samples randomly drawn from defined populations, even though random sampling is a requirement for using statistical significance tests. Another criticism is that the tests are often misinterpreted, as we indicated above. The p value is taken as a measure of the worth of a study rather than for what it really is: a basis for rejecting the null hypothesis. The third criticism is that the "power" of statistical significance tests in educational research tends to be low. (The concept of statistical power is discussed a bit later in the chapter.)

We believe that each of these criticisms is legitimate, yet they do not justify complete discontinuation of statistical significance testing. The tests are quite helpful under conditions of random sampling and high statistical power. Conversely, the tests should be used with caution or not at all under conditions of nonrandom sampling or low statistical power. Our recommendation is that researchers should be wary of accepting a difference or relationship as real on the basis of one study, no matter how statistically significant the results are. A significant p in a study is cause for optimism, but replications of the study should be done to get additional assurance that the observed result is real. Also, other indices should be calculated in each study to set p values in proper perspective. We discuss these indices—effect size, measures of correlation, and confidence intervals—later in the chapter.

Types of Significance Tests

Thus far in our discussion of inferential statistics we have been concerned with how to determine whether the difference between two sample means reflects population differences. A significance test based on the calculation of a t or z value is appropriate for this purpose. Other significance tests are available for answering other questions involving inference from sample statistics to population values (also called *population parameters*).

Occasionally a researcher is interested in determining whether a *single* statistic, such as a sample mean or correlation coefficient, is significantly different from a specified population value. A z or t value is calculated to determine whether this kind of inference is justified. Also, a z or t value can be calculated to determine whether the proportions (e.g., the percentage of "yes"

20. S. Alan Cohen and Joan S. Hyman, "How Come So Many Hypotheses in Educational Research Are Supported? (A Modest Proposal)," *Educational Researcher* 8, no. 11 (1979):12–16; R.P. Carver, "The Case Against Statistical Significance Testing," *Harvard Educational Review* 48 (1978):378–399; see also Michael Oakes, in the Annotated References.

answers to a questionnaire item) in two samples differ significantly from each other, whether two correlation coefficients differ significantly from each other, and whether two change scores differ significantly from each other.

Analysis of variance is an inferential technique with many applications. For example, it can be used to determine whether three or more sample means are significantly different from one another.[21] Analysis of variance results in an *F* value, which if statistically significant, tells us that the means are likely to have been drawn from different populations. However, analysis of variance does not specify which of the three or more sample means differ significantly from one another. Special post hoc *t*-tests are used for this purpose. Duncan's multiple-range test is an example of a post hoc *t*-test.

Analysis of variance is used frequently in experimental research involving complex factorial designs. Depending upon the complexity of the factorial design, two or more *F* values can be generated from a single analysis of variance. The *F* values indicate whether sample means of the various factors represented in the experiment (e.g., treatments, sex of subjects, ability levels) differ significantly from one another, and whether the various factors interact significantly with one another.

The analysis of variance technique also can be used to test the statistical significance of an hypothesized trend. This application is called **trend analysis.** For example, you may form five groups varying in perceptual ability (very low, low, average, high, very high), and hypothesize that students at each level will do better on a reading comprehension task than will students in the ability level just below it. Trend analysis can be used to test this hypothesis.

Still another application of analysis of variance is in the determination of whether two or more sample variances differ significantly from each other. In certain situations, you may wish to do an analysis of variance that controls for other differences that may exist in the samples being compared. **Analysis of covariance** can be used for this purpose if certain statistical assumptions are satisfied. The last column of table 9.2 shows the *F* values for a series of analyses of covariance, one for each of the achievement subtests. Only one of the *F* values is statistically significant (the Definitions and Theory subtest).

The analysis of covariance in table 9.2 controlled for students' achievement scores at the beginning of the school year. Columns 2 and 3 in table 9.2 show the experimental and control groups' actual mean scores at the end of the school year. Columns 4 and 5 show their mean scores at the *end* of the school year, adjusted for their mean scores at the *beginning* of the school year. The two groups in fact had different mean scores at the beginning of the school year. The

---

21. Analysis of variance also can be used to determine whether two means differ significantly from each other. In this situation, analysis of variance will yield the same result as the calculation of a *t* or *z* value.

TABLE 9.5

Table of Inferential Statistics

Tests of Statistical Significance (Parametric)	Purpose
t-test Critical ratio (z)	Used to determine whether two means, proportions, or correlation coefficients differ significantly from each other; also used to determine whether a single mean, proportion, or correlation coefficient differs significantly from a specified population value
Analysis of variance	Used to determine whether mean scores on one or more factors differ significantly from each other, and whether the various factors interact significantly with each other; also used to determine whether sample variances differ significantly from each other
Analysis of covariance	Similar in use to analysis of variance, except that the influence of one or more independent variables on the dependent variable is controlled
Trend analysis	Used to test the statistical significance of an hypothesized trend
Duncan's multiple-range test Scheffé's test	Used, following a significant F ratio in analysis of variance, to test the statistical significance of differences between particular group means or combinations of group means
Confidence limits	Used to estimate a population value, based on what is known about a sample value
Nonparametric Tests	**Purpose**
Mann-Whitney U-test	Used to determine whether two uncorrelated means differ significantly from each other
Wilcoxon signed-rank test	Used to determine whether two correlated means differ significantly from each other
Kruskal-Wallis test	Used to determine whether three or more mean scores on a single factor differ significantly from each other
Chi-square test	Used to determine whether two frequency distributions differ significantly from each other

adjusted mean scores in columns 4 and 5 are approximations of the mean scores that the two groups would have earned had they started with equal achievement at the beginning of the school year.

The tests of statistical significance presented above make certain assumptions about the form of the research data. If these assumptions are not satisfied, it may be more appropriate to use one of the **nonparametric tests of statistical significance.** The chi-square test is commonly used when the research data are in the form of categories or dichotomies rather than continuous scores or ranks. The Mann-Whitney U-test, the Wilcoxon signed-rank test, and the Kruskal-Wallis test are nonparametric substitutes for the t-test for uncorrelated means, the t-test for correlated means, and one-way analysis of variance, respectively.

A summary list of tests of statistical significance is presented in table 9.5. These tests are discussed in more detail in chapters 13 through 16.

Statistical Power Analysis

Researchers rarely desire to prove the null hypothesis. They do not wish to demonstrate that there is no difference between groups, or no correlation between variables, or no difference between treatments. Instead, researchers usually conduct studies because they want to find differences and relationships. For example, researchers are more likely to become interested in investigating a method of instruction because they believe it may be superior to conventional practice than because they believe it is no different from conventional practice.

Given researchers' interest in discovering differences and relationships, they will want to maximize the likelihood of rejecting the null hypothesis (which posits *no* difference or relationship) when the null hypothesis in fact is false. Fortunately, options are available to researchers for accomplishing this goal. **Statistical power analysis** is a procedure for studying the likelihood that a particular test of statistical significance will be sufficient to reject a false null hypothesis. **Statistical power** is the probability that a particular test of statistical significance will lead to the rejection of a false null hypothesis.

Statistical power analysis requires access to mathematical tables, but we can provide an overview of how the procedure works.[22] First, it is a fact that statistical power increases automatically with sample size. In other words, the larger sample, the smaller the difference or relationship needed to reject the null hypothesis. For example, if you obtain a correlation coefficient of .25 between two variables in a sample of 47 students, you cannot reject the null hypothesis at the .05 level of significance. If you obtained the same coefficient (.25) but with a larger sample ($N = 62$), you would be able to reject the null hypothesis at the .05 level of significance.

The second determinant of statistical power is the level of significance (p) at which the null hypothesis is to be rejected. Statistical power can be increased by raising the level of significance. Thus, a test of statistical significance with p set at .10 is more powerful than the same test with p set at .05. ("More powerful"

22. Tables for statistical power analysis are in Jacob Cohen, *Statistical Power Analysis for the Behavioral Sciences*, rev. ed. (New York: Academic Press, 1977).

means that it is easier to reject the null hypothesis at the .10 level than at the .05 level.) In practice, p is usually set at .05. However, some researchers feel that it is permissible to set p at .10 in exploratory studies to increase statistical power. A p of .10 increases the risk of Type 1 error, but it also might spotlight a potentially important difference or relationship that would have been overlooked had a lower p value been set.

The third determinant of statistical power is whether directionality is specified in the research hypothesis.[23] Directionality refers to the fact that observed differences and relationships can go in two directions. For example, in an experiment, treatment A can be better than treatment B (one direction), or treatment B can be better than treatment A (the other direction). However, we might be able to argue, on the basis of theory or previous research findings, that treatment B cannot possibly be better than treatment A. If we can reject this "direction" in advance of doing the experiment, we can increase statistical power by doing a one-tailed test of statistical significance.

The fourth determinant of statistical power is **effect size,** which is the magnitude of a difference or relationship in a sample or population.[24] To understand how effect size influences statistical power, you need to keep two facts in mind. First, it is a fact that the greater an observed difference or relationship, the lower is the level of significance (p) associated with it. For example, an r of .38 in a sample of 20 students is significant at the .10 level. In contrast, an r of .44 in the same size sample is significant at the .05 level. Thus, the null hypothesis can be rejected at the conventional significance level (.05) with an r of .44, but not with an r of .38.

Because the magnitude of r affects significance level, we need to ask what determines the magnitude of r. This leads us to the second fact: A researcher is more likely to obtain a large effect size in a sample when there is a larger effect size in the population. Returning to our example, suppose the value of r is .65 in the population from which the sample of 20 students was drawn. It is likely, then, that samples drawn from this population will tend to yield similarly large values of r. Conversely, if the population value of r is small (for example, $r = .30$), samples drawn from this population will tend to yield similarly small values of r. In brief, if the population value of r is large, it will be easier to reject the null hypothesis than if the population value is small.

The effect size in a population is beyond the researcher's control. One researcher may decide to study an instructional method (A_1), which in the population is much more effective than another instructional method (B_1). Another researcher may decide to study method A_1 supplemented by a technique (A_2), which in reality is just slightly better than method A_1 without

23. Research hypotheses are described in chapter 2. Directionality (one-tailed versus two-tailed) of statistical significance tests is described in chapters 13 and 14.

24. The concept of effect size is also discussed in chapter 4 (see section on meta-analysis). Later in the chapter, effect size is discussed as an index of practical significance.

the technique. Both studies may be worth doing for different reasons. Yet, assuming that both researchers use the same sample size and significance level, the first researcher is more likely to reject his null hypothesis ($A_1 = B_1$) than the second researcher, even though her null hypothesis ($A_2 = A_1$) is also false.

What can the second researcher do to increase the power of her statistical significance test? She can establish a higher probability level for rejecting the null hypothesis, or can increase sample size. Exercising both options will increase statistical power even more.

Researchers use statistical power analysis to understand how the four factors described above—sample size, significance level, directionality, and effect size—influence the ability of a statistical significance test to reject the null hypothesis.[25] By manipulating one or more of these factors, we can increase the power of our statistical significance test. As we stated above, mathematical tables are available to show how changes in each factor increase or decrease statistical power.

SUPPLEMENTS TO SIGNIFICANCE TESTS

Tests of statistical significance should be supplemented by other procedures to explore further the statistical and practical significance of research data. Two of the procedures discussed here—calculation of confidence limits and replication studies—are concerned primarily with clarifying the statistical significance of research results. The other procedure—calculation of effect size—is intended to clarify the practical significance of research results.

Confidence Limits

Researchers sometimes calculate **confidence limits** (also called *confidence intervals*) in addition to testing for statistical significance. Confidence limits provide a method for estimating population values, based on what is known about sample values. For example, suppose that we know that the mean test score for a sample of subjects is 75. The sample mean and standard deviation can be used to estimate a range of values (the confidence limits) that are likely to include the true population mean. If our calculations reveal that the 95 percent confidence limits for the sample mean are 68 and 83, we can infer that there is a high likelihood that the true population mean lies between 68 and 83. Stated more precisely, we can infer that if we collected data on 100 research samples similar to the one we actually studied, only 5 of them would contain confidence limits

25. There are additional determinants of statistical power analysis, but we have described the main ones here.

that did not include the true population mean. In practice, we usually study a single research sample, but by calculating 95 percent confidence limits, we can be reasonably certain that ours is not in the 5 percent of sample means whose confidence limits do not contain the true population mean.[26]

A typical experiment will yield two posttreatment means—one for the experimental group and one for the control group. If we calculate confidence limits for each mean, we will have an easily interpreted measure of whether the observed difference between two means indicates a true difference between the populations represented by the samples. Suppose the experimental group mean is 24 with 95 percent confidence limits of 20 and 28. The control group mean is 15 with 95 percent confidence limits of 12 and 18. Given these limits, we can conclude that the true mean of the experimental population is quite unlikely to be lower than 20, and the true mean of the control population is quite unlikely to be higher than 18. Thus, it appears that the experimental group "truly" outperformed the control group in this hypothetical study.

Now consider what happens under a different set of conditions. Suppose the experimental group mean remains the same (24), but the 95 percent confidence limits are 17 and 31. The control group mean also remains the same (15), but the 95 percent confidence limits are 7 and 23. Thus, the true mean for the experimental population is likely to be as low as 17, and the true mean for the control population is likely to be as high as 23. Thus, we cannot disregard the possibility that the two population means are the same, with a likely value between 17 and 23.

Confidence limits are a branch of inferential statistics in that they enable the researcher to make an inference from a sample statistic to a population value. Hence, they are included in the summary list of inferential statistics in table 9.5. Tests of statistical significance also involve inference from sample statistics to a population value, but their purpose is to provide a basis for deciding to accept or reject a null hypothesis. In published research, tests of statistical significance are almost always reported. In addition, a few researchers will report the confidence limits for key statistics.

Replication of Research Results

Tests of statistical significance are used to help researchers to draw conclusions about the validity of a knowledge claim on the basis of a single study. In other words, if the null hypothesis is rejected, we conclude that the knowledge claim (i.e., the research hypothesis) is true. If the null hypothesis is accepted, we conclude that the knowledge claim is false.

26. Sometimes the 99 percent confidence limits are calculated.

In reality, researchers generally do not draw such extreme conclusions. This is the case even if the obtained level of statistical significance is extremely low (e.g., $p = .001$). One reason is that it is difficult to rule out all possible alternative explanations of the result. Another reason is that flaws in research design and execution creep into most studies. Thus, many researchers do not reach final conclusions about the validity of a knowledge claim on the basis of a single study and a single test of statistical significance. The significance test only serves to increase or decrease their confidence in their knowledge claims. They, or other reseachers, repeat the study in order to test further the validity of the knowledge claim.

Replication is the process of repeating a research study with a different group of subjects using the same or similar methods. Results of a study are more "significant"—in the sense of inspiring confidence that they represent differences or relationships in the population—if a new study yields similar results, or if the present study repeats the findings of past research. Consider the case of mastery learning, the effectiveness of which has been demonstrated in many experiments.[27] Suppose you decide to conduct a new experiment to determine whether mastery learning is superior to conventional instruction in a situation not previously investigated. As predicted, the experimental group that received instruction based on mastery learning principles earned a higher mean score on the posttest than the comparison group, but the difference was not statistically significant. You are safe in concluding that this is most likely a true difference because it replicates a consistent set of previous findings.

In fact, we can demonstrate that statistical significance is multiplicative across studies. Two or more studies using the same methodology can each yield nonsignificant results, but if the results of each study are in the same direction, the p values from the statistical significance tests can be multiplied. For example, if the p value in each of two studies is .20, their combined probability is .04 (.20 × .20). Thus, the null hypothesis (which would be the same in both studies) can be rejected at the .04 level of sigificance.

If possible, you should attempt to replicate your research project, particularly if your findings show promise of making a substantial contribution to knowledge about education. If you are able to replicate your findings, they are of much more "significance" to other educational researchers than a statistically significant but weak finding (e.g., a correlation of .20 significant at the .01 level) obtained in the original study. A replicated finding is strong evidence against the possibility that a Type I error (rejection of the null hypothesis when it is true) occurred in the original study.

Replication also provides other kinds of evidence, depending upon the

27. James H. Block, Helen Efthim, and Robert Burns, *Creating Effective Mastery Learning Schools* (New York: Longman, 1988).

type of replication study that is carried out. David Lykken distinguished three types of replication:

> *Literal replication* . . . would involve exact duplication of the first investigator's sampling procedure, experimental conditions, measuring techniques, and methods of analysis; asking the original investigator to simply run more subjects would perhaps be about as close as we could come to attaining literal replication and even this, in psychological research, might often not be close enough.
>
> In the case of *operational replication*, on the other hand, one strives to duplicate exactly just the sampling and experimental procedures given in the first author's report of his research. The purpose of operational replication is to test whether the investigator's "experimental recipe"—the conditions and procedures he considered salient enough to be listed in the "Methods" section of his report—will in other hands produce the results that he obtained.
>
> In the quite different process of *constructive replication*, one deliberately avoids imitation of the first author's methods. To obtain an ideal constructive replication, one would provide a competent investigator with *nothing more than* a clear statement of the empirical "fact" which the first author would claim to have established, and then let the replicator formulate his own methods of sampling, measurement, and data analysis.[28]

Literal replication, which you can carry out yourself, can be used to evaluate whether a Type I error might have occurred in the original study. Operational replication is particularly important for experiments in which the researcher must determine the effectiveness of a procedure to improve learning. For example, suppose you trained teachers in the use of the inquiry method and found that this method led to greater student achievement than conventional teaching methods. If other researchers can then use your training procedures and materials and find similar achievement gains, we may conclude that the inquiry method is a superior instructional strategy. If operational replicaton does not support the original findings, then we would probably conclude that the effectiveness of the training procedure and materials is limited to the original researcher. Obviously, an educational procedure or product that holds up after an operational replication has more practical significance for the improvement of education than one that works only in the hands of the original researcher.

The third type of replication, constructive replication, increases the validity of theoretical studies in education. Suppose you hypothesize that the presence of anxiety leads to a decrement in academic performance. To test this hypothesis, you need to select or construct measures of anxiety and of academic performance. The hypothesis becomes increasingly credible when it is demon-

28. David T. Lykken, "Statistical Significance of Psychological Research," *Psychological Bulletin* 70 (1968):155–159.

strated that the relationship between the two variables holds up after several constructive replications in which different operational measures of one or both of two variables are used each time. For example, if a particular measure of anxiety predicts decrements in gradepoint average for each year of college, decrement in performance on a particular examination, and decrement in scores on an aptitude test, the hypothesis is more credible and powerful.

Replication studies unfortunately are seldom done by educational researchers.[29] Yet it is an important strategy for determining the significance of results obtained in a particular study. As we indicated in chapter 2, as a beginning researcher, you should seriously consider replicating and extending previous studies rather than trying to investigate a previously unresearched problem.

Effect Size

If tests of statistical significance are inappropriate for making inferences about the practical significance of research results, what can be used in their place? The approach currently favored is to calculate an effect size (ES). We discussed effect size earlier in the chapter with respect to its use in statistical power analysis. Also, the calculation and interpretation of ES were discussed in chapter 4 as part of a method called *meta-analysis* for reviewing a set of research studies on a particular problem. An example of effect sizes derived from a meta-analysis is presented in chapter 1 (see table 1.1).

Still another use of ES statistics is as an aid to interpreting the results of a single study. For example, suppose an experiment has been done comparing two methods of instruction. The mean score of the experimental group students on a posttest measure of academic achievement is 56, and the corresponding mean score of the control group is 47. The mean difference between the groups is 9 points. Is this difference large enough to have significance for the practice of education? Perhaps. Using the ES approach, you would divide the mean difference (9 points) by the standard deviation of the control group on the posttest. If the standard deviation happens to be 9, the ES will be 1.00 (9-point mean score difference divided by the standard deviation of 9).

An ES of 1.00 means that the average student in the experimental group scored at the 84th percentile of the control group distribution. This appears to be an impressive result. We must check, though, that the posttest measured an important outcome of learning. Also, the impressiveness of the result is dependent on the absolute difference in points between the 84th percentile and

29. James P. Shaver and Richard S. Norton, "Randomness and Replication in Ten Years of the *American Educational Research Journal*," *Educational Researcher* 9, no. 1 (1980):9–15.

50th percentile of the control group distribution. In this case there is a 9-point difference between the two percentiles, which may have modest significance in a 70-item test.

The concept of ES is not new, but only recently has its use in educational research become popular. It is a helpful method for assessing the practical significance of relationships and group differences, as long as it is not applied unthinkingly. The meaning of ES is dependent on the measures used, the absolute difference between group means, the shape of the score distribution, the subjects in the sample, and possibly other factors. In sum, there is no simple answer to the problem of determining practical significance of research results. The ES is just an aid to interpretation, albeit an important aid.

PROBLEMS IN STATISTICAL ANALYSIS

The Need for Exploratory Data Analysis

A common problem in data analysis is to calculate the usual descriptive statistics (mean and standard deviation) before carefully examining the individual scores collected in the study. The data in some research studies are "untouched by human hands" in the sense that they are entered onto computer cards by keypunchers; the cards then are entered into the computer, and a computer program generates the descriptive and inferential statistics specified by the researcher. Thus, the researcher is denied the opportunity to examine the "raw" data. As a result, the researcher may overlook important patterns and phenomena revealed by the individual scores.

Statistical techniques for examining patterns and phenomena in individual scores have been developed in recent years, most notably by the statistician John Tukey.[30] These techniques are not widely used, but they are worth studying because they have revealed new insights about the nature of data often collected in educational research. The techniques are known collectively as **exploratory data analysis,** which is a method for "discovering unforeseen or unexpected patterns in the data and consequently [for] gaining new insights and understanding of natural phenomena."[31]

Once the research data have been collected and quantitifed, exploratory data analysis can begin. An essential tool of exploratory data analysis is the **stem-and-leaf display,** which is a convenient method for displaying all of the individual scores on a particular measure. Table 9.6 presents a conventional

---

30. See the Annotated References at the end of this chapter.
31. Gaea Leinhardt and Samuel Leinhardt, "Exploratory Data Analysis: New Tools for the Analysis of Empirical Data," in *Review of Research in Education*, Vol. 8, ed. David C. Berliner (Washington, DC: American Educational Research Association, 1980), p. 86.

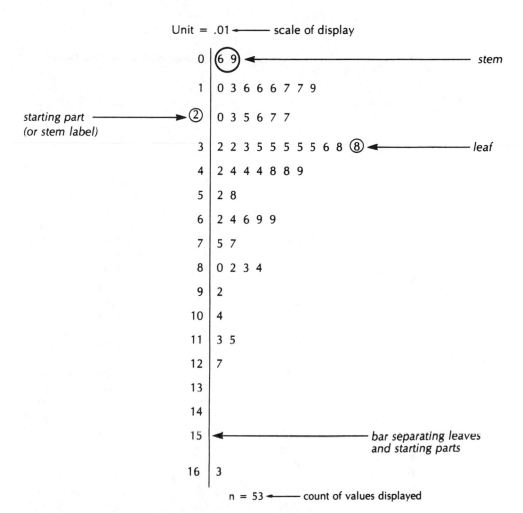

Figure 9.3 Example of a Stem-and-Leaf Display. Note that the display is of the data in column 5 of table 9.6. For example, the first score of column 5 (0.33) is represented in the fourth line of the stem-and-leaf display. Each leaf in the display can be converted to a regular score by placing the stem label to the left of it and then by multiplying by .01. For example, the bottom-most leaf is 3. Placing the stem label to the left of it yields the number 163. Multiplying this number by .01 results in a score of 1.63, which is the score of the eighth student in column 5.

Source: Gaea Leinhardt and Samuel Leinhardt, "Exploratory Data Analysis: New Tools for the Analysis of Empirical Data," in *Review of Research in Education*, Vol. 8, ed. David C. Berliner (Washington, DC: American Educational Research Association, 1980), p. 92. Copyright 1980, American Educational Research Association, Washington, DC. Reprinted by permission of the publisher and authors.

TABLE 9.6

Example of Computer Printout of Raw Data

Sequential Location	CUR	School	Words	Silent	Overlap
1	0.00	1.00	2489.00	0.33	48.65
2	0.00	1.00	3755.00	0.80	94.59
3	0.00	1.00	3346.00	0.58	95.95
4	0.00	1.00	3057.00	1.27	44.59
5	0.00	1.00	7002.00	0.84	93.24
6	0.00	1.00	748.00	1.04	97.30
7	0.00	1.00	1462.00	0.36	54.05
8	0.00	1.00	9562.00	1.63	90.54
9	0.00	1.00	4434.00	0.44	91.89
10	0.00	1.00	4295.00	1.15	94.59
11	0.00	2.00	4426.00	0.82	86.49
12	0.00	2.00	1632.00	0.02	6.76
13	0.00	2.00	1626.00	0.92	54.05
14	0.00	2.00	2886.00	0.83	44.59
15	0.00	2.00	484.00	0.35	52.38
16	0.00	2.00	483.00	0.35	53.57
17	0.00	2.00	1867.00	0.25	83.43
18	0.00	2.00	1437.00	0.10	4.05
19	0.00	2.00	1162.00	0.35	6.76
20	0.00	2.00	1676.00	0.38	2.70
21	0.00	2.00	1218.00	0.44	6.76
22	0.00	3.00	0.00	0.52	87.84
23	0.00	3.00	0.00	0.32	81.08
24	0.00	3.00	4713.00	0.27	94.59
25	0.00	3.00	2823.00	0.23	89.19
26	0.00	3.00	1093.00	0.16	25.68
27	0.00	3.00	2560.00	0.17	22.97
28	0.00	3.00	3036.00	0.38	94.59
29	0.00	3.00	4423.00	0.75	98.65
30	0.00	3.00	5811.00	1.13	94.59
31	0.00	3.00	2948.00	0.19	71.62
32	1.00	4.00	198.00	0.48	100.00
33	1.00	4.00	198.00	0.66	97.30
34	1.00	4.00	293.00	0.42	82.43
35	1.00	4.00	293.00	0.25	87.84
36	1.00	4.00	198.00	0.77	85.14
37	1.00	4.00	253.00	0.69	100.00
38	1.00	4.00	253.00	0.64	100.00
39	1.00	4.00	32.00	0.13	64.86
40	1.00	5.00	20.00	0.35	39.19

TABLE 9.6 (*continued*)

Sequential Location	CUR	School	Words	Silent	Overlap
41	1.00	5.00	999.00	0.62	58.11
42	1.00	5.00	20.00	0.11	52.38
43	1.00	5.00	67.00	0.16	18.92
44	1.00	5.00	20.00	0.35	5.41
45	1.00	5.00	0.00	0.06	39.29
46	1.00	5.00	0.00	0.09	42.86
47	1.00	5.00	67.00	0.48	32.43
48	1.00	5.00	419.00	0.17	24.32
49	1.00	6.00	88.00	0.27	20.27
50	1.00	6.00	212.00	0.44	52.70
51	1.00	6.00	88.00	0.32	10.81
52	1.00	6.00	212.00	0.69	44.59
53	1.00	6.00	212.00	0.49	39.19

Source: Gaea Leinhardt and Samuel Leinhardt, "Exploratory Data Analysis: New Tools for the Analysis of Empirical Data," in *Review of Research in Education*, Vol. 8, ed. David C. Berliner (Washington, DC: American Educational Research Association, 1980), p. 89. Copyright 1980, American Educational Research Association, Washington, DC. Reprinted by permission of the publisher and authors.
Note: The first column is the student's identification (ID) code. The second column is the ID code for the curricular approach that each student received. The third column is the student's school ID code. The fourth column is number of words read by the students in a three-day period. The fifth column is a measure of silent reading time. The sixth column is a teacher prediction measure.

display of individual scores provided by a computer program. The scores are from a group of learning disabled students who participated in an experimental reading curriculum. The problem with such a display is that it is difficult to "see" the data. Patterns and departures from the patterns are not easily detectable.

Now examine the same set of 53 scores summarized in a stem-and-leaf display in figure 9.3. Each digit to the right of the vertical line represents a student's score. If you wish, you can transform each digit (technically a "leaf") by a few simple calculations into the individual's actual score.

One advantage of a stem-and-leaf display is that you can easily see the shape of the distribution of scores. It is apparent in figure 9.3 that the scores do not form a normal distribution. Most of the scores are at the lower range of values, clustering around a value of approximately .30. Because the score distribution is skewed in this direction, you should be alert to the possible need to use statistics that do not assume a normal curve distribution: for example, the median and range, and the various nonparametric statistics.

Another advantage of a stem-and-leaf display is that it provokes questions about the data. For example, looking at figure 9.3, you might speculate about the factors that caused most students to be at the lower end of the scale, while a minority of students scored at the upper end of the scale. You might be able to formulate a hypothesis about these factors and test it using available data. Otherwise, the hypothesis might provide the basis for designing a new study.

The third advantage of exploratory data analysis is that it facilitates the detection of outliers. An **outlier** is a research subject whose scores differ remarkably from the general pattern established by other subjects in the sample. The student with a score of 1.63 in figure 9.3 is clearly an outlier. If you identify an outlier, you should check whether an error occurred in calculating the outlier's score. Some subjects show up as outliers simply because the researcher misplaced a decimal point or transposed the subject's score on another variable while preparing the data for computer analysis.

If the outlier's score is not attributable to a calculating error, you need to search elsewhere for an explanation. Perhaps the outlier was not exposed to the same conditions as the other subjects in the sample, as was the case in figure 9.3:

> In the actual research project from which these data were drawn; it was independently determined that the child on whom this outlier value was measured was, for administrative reasons, not under the control of the classroom teacher and was not, therefore, exposed to the same treatment as the other members of the class. He was ultimately removed from the study.[32]

The decision to eliminate one or more outliers from a research study is problematic. Even one or two outliers can distort the results yielded by conventional statistics, unless the sample is large. You should not eliminate outliers just for this reason, though. Outliers should only be eliminated for good cause, as in the case of the student described above. If outliers are left in the sample, consider analyzing the data using both parametric and nonparametric statistics. Comparison of the results yielded by these statistical tools will yield information about how much an outlier, or outliers, are distorting the data.

In the example above, there would be little argument about the decision to call the student with a score of 1.63 an outlier. But how about the student with a score of 1.27 in figure 9.3? Or the students with scores of 1.13 and 1.15? It is not clear that they should be considered outliers. Statistical techniques that yield quantitative decision rules for identifying outliers are available.[33] In reporting a study's findings, note the occurrence of outliers and how they were handled in the data analysis.

32. Ibid., pp. 153–154.
33. Ibid.

Missing Data

Missing data are items of information that the researcher intended to collect as part of the research design but that, for one reason or another, are not available for the data analysis. Missing data may occur simply because the researcher lost the data through his or someone else's carelessness. In large-scale research, tests may be administered to hundreds of students. Even though a particular student was present for testing, his or her test can become lost in the process of handing it to the test administrator, in the process of returning it to the central data collection center, in the process of keypunching an ID code, or in the process of the computer analysis. Because the loss of data complicates and may weaken the statistical analysis, caution should be exercised to ensure that the data are not lost through avoidable human error.

Missing data also can occur if a subject selected for the research sample refuses to participate in all or part of the study. Even if a subject agrees to participate, the subject may be unavailable at the time(s) that data are collected. The likelihood of missing data becomes more probable as the number of data collection sessions increases, simply because there are more opportunities for subjects to become ill or be called away by other commitments. Students tend to come down with the flu or other illness at the same time. If a substantial number of students are absent from school or are unavailable for a scheduled data-collection session, it probably is better to reschedule the session than to have incomplete data for the statistical analysis. This is not a rigid rule, however; in certain studies, the data may be uninterpretable unless they are collected at a specific time. In this situation, the better compromise may be to collect data from a partial sample, if the resulting data can be analyzed to yield interpretable findings.

Missing data are particularly challenging when several different tests have been administered on several occasions to the same groups of subjects. Consider the group of scores for two different tests administered at two intervals to an experimental and control group depicted in table 9.7. Missing data are indicated by the symbol —.

The researcher had planned to perform a separate analysis of covariance for each test. Time 1 scores are the covariate, and the difference between experimental and control mean scores at time 2 is to be analyzed for statistical significance.

How should the missing data be handled? One solution is to eliminate incomplete cases, so that only subjects with time 1 and time 2 data are included in the statistical analysis. This solution would entail the loss of four experimental subjects and four control subjects in analyzing test A data, and the loss of three experimental subjects and two control subjects in analyzing test B data. However, note that different subjects would be eliminated across the two tests, such that the experimental and control groups would not have quite the same

TABLE 9.7

Missing Data in Two Tests Administered to Experimental and Control Groups

	Test A				Test B			
	Experimental Group		Control Group		Experimental Group		Control Group	
Subject I.D.	Time 1	Time 2	Time 1	Time 2	Time 1	Time 2	Time 1	Time 2
001	5	7	4	5	—	37	38	40
002	4	—	4	4	42	63	—	51
003	8	12	—	7	53	71	45	43
004	—	17	15	—	36	63	55	55
005	6	—	4	3	15	17	38	50
006	10	13	8	10	52	—	63	64
007	3	5	5	7	49	45	—	36
008	7	5	5	5	38	—	50	48
009	—	10	10	—	47	65	36	40
010	12	17	9	—	50	54	47	51

composition across the two samples. If you wish to include only those subjects who have complete data for both tests and both test sessions, even more data are lost. For example, the experimental group would include only three complete cases (003, 007, 010)! Another solution is to estimate the missing data by plugging the group mean into each cell or by using a regression analysis to estimate more precisely the missing values. The decision to use one solution or another involves complex considerations. In this type of situation, we recommend that you call upon the services of an expert statistician.

The best solution obviously is to avoid missing data. Extra effort to ensure that all data required by the research design are collected will save effort later in the statistical analysis phase of the study. Note, too, that beyond a certain point, missing data may hopelessly compromise the research design. In this situation, the only alternatives are to abandon or to repeat the study.

The Unit of Statistical Analysis

Educational researchers may study individuals as they learn in isolation, as they learn independently but within a group setting, or as they learn in a group. These distinctions are important to consider in deciding whether to use the individual learner or a group of learners as the unit of statistical analysis. The **unit of statistical analysis** is the sampling unit replicated within a research study. If the student is the sampling unit, then each student added to the sample can be considered a replication of the phenomena to be described, correlated, or experimentally manipulated.

The effect of the statistical unit on research results is illustrated by the following example. Suppose the relative effectiveness of two teaching methods, A and B, is to be compared by having them used in different classrooms. Ten sixth-grade classrooms, two from each of five schools, are selected for the experiment; one class in each school is randomly assigned to teaching method A and the other to teaching method B for a period of two months. Hypothetical posttest scores of individual students following the experimental period are shown in table 9.8. Elementary classrooms typially have 20 or 30 (or more) students, but to simplify the data presentation, the table shows classes containing between 5 and 8 students.

TABLE 9.8

Posttest Scores of Students under Two Teaching Methods

Method A (N = 32)				
School 1 Class 1	School 2 Class 2	School 3 Class 3	School 4 Class 4	School 5 Class 5
18	25	28	17	22
22	18	27	19	24
27	29	29	23	30
15	30	30	18	15
9	19	24	24	27
24	M = 24.2	26	M = 20.2	21
M = 19.2		31		29
		27		28
		M = 27.8		M = 24.5
Method B (N = 34)				
School 1 Class 6	School 2 Class 7	School 3 Class 8	School 4 Class 9	School 5 Class 10
25	16	19	22	21
22	25	21	20	29
18	18	28	24	18
18	23	16	19	14
20	15	15	18	22
22	9	21	21	M = 20.8
M = 20.8	22	14	15	
	M = 18.3	12	17	
		M=18.3	M = 19.5	

In this experiment the purpose of the statistical analysis is to determine whether the posttest scores of students who received teaching method A are significantly different from the posttest scores of students who received teaching method B. A critical ratio or t value can be calculated to test for statistical significance. The issue is, What is the unit of statistical analysis—the individual student or the classroom group? If the unit is the individual student, there are 32 students in teaching method A who can be compared with 34 students in teaching method B. If the class is used as the unit, there are only five class means for teaching method A to be compared with five class means for teaching method B.

Note, too, that the descriptive statistics vary as a function of the unit of analysis. The mean and standard deviation of scores in teaching method A are 23.6 and 5.42, respectively, when the student is the unit of analysis. In contrast, the mean and standard deviation of the group means (19.2, 24.2, 27.8, 20.2, 24.5) are 23.2 and 3.49, respectively, when the group is the unit of analysis.

Some researchers have recommended that the class mean should be used as the unit of analysis in the kind of experiment illustrated in table 9.8. Kenneth Hopkins demonstrated, however, that the individual student should be used as the unit of analysis in conducting tests of statistical significance.[34] He recommended doing a certain type of analysis of variance in which the classroom and experimental treatment are considered "factors" (the concept of factor is explained in chapter 16). In the experiment illustrated in table 9.8, the 10 classes constitute one factor and the teaching methods A and B constitute another factor. Hopkins demonstrated the appropriate form of analysis of variance to be used for experimental designs of different levels of complexity.

This discussion of the unit of statistical analysis highlights the fact that education occurs at many levels: individual students (e.g., tutorial instruction), small groups within classrooms (e.g., reading groups), classrooms, schools, school districts, regions, states, and even nations. You need to decide which of these levels include the phenomena of interest to you. Leigh Burstein argued that educational researchers should consider several levels at once in designing a study:

> Schooling activities occur within hierarchical organizations in which the sources of educational influence on students occur in the groups to which an individual belongs. These groups (learning group within classrooms, classrooms within schools, schools with districts, families within communities, schools within communities) influence the thoughts, behavior, and feelings of their members. This hierarchical stucture gives rise to multilevel data.[35]

34. Kenneth D. Hopkins, "The Unit of Analysis: Group Means Versus Individual Observations," *American Educational Research Journal* 19 (1982):5–18.
35. Leigh Burstein, "Issues in the Aggregation of Data," in Berliner, ed., *Review of Research in Education*, p. 158.

By "multilevel data" Burstein means data that can be analyzed at more than one level of schooling. For example, if a researcher collects data on three classrooms within a school, the data can be analyzed at two levels: classroom (each classroom has a score, or set of scores, associated with it) and school (the mean score of the three classrooms on a variable yields some data about the school as a whole).

There is no correct level(s) of schooling on which research should be focused. Instead, each of you will need to develop a theory or explanation for the particular phenomena that interest you. The theory or explanation will serve as a guide for deciding the level or levels to be included in the data collection and analysis. For example, suppose you are interested in the effects of teacher praise on students. You might focus on the incidence of praise statements delivered to the class as a whole. In this case, you would need to study a sample of classes and would use the class as the unit of analysis. Another possibility is for you to focus on teacher praise given to individual students. In this case, you might measure the number of praise statements directed by the teacher to each student in the classroom. The student then would be the unit of analysis, and the sample size would be the number of students in the classroom. If you studied more than one classroom, each classroom could be considered an independent replication of the study.

Another example is provided by the case of eductaional researchers who are interested in studying the effects of school principals. Suppose you hypothesize that the principals' emphasis on teacher supervision influences the morale of teachers in the school. This hypothesis should be tested by using the school as the unit of analysis. You would need to form a sample of school principals, one per school, and measure the principals' emphasis on teacher supervision and the overall morale of the teaching staff. Suppose, instead, you are interested in whether principals vary in their supervision of individual teachers, and whether these variations are related to individual differences in teacher morale. The individual teacher is the unit of analysis in this situation.

It is important to note that both units of analysis (principal and teacher) can be studied if the data are collected appropriately. Suppose you measure emphasis on teacher supervision in terms of number of supervisory visits with teachers during a school year. If the data are collected for each teacher, you would know the number of supervisory visits per teacher and each teacher's morale. You can also aggregate the data to obtain a measure of the principal's general emphasis on teacher supervision and an overall measure of teacher morale in this school. (Aggregation in this case is the process of obtaining the mean score of teachers on each variable—supervisory visits and morale.)

If the data are collected in this way, they can be subjected to multilevel analysis. For example, you can determine the relationship between supervisory visitation and teacher morale within schools and across schools. Also, you can determine whether there is more variability in principal supervision or teacher morale within schools or across schools.

Policy studies in education are concerned with even larger units of analysis than the ones described in the preceding examples. Researchers working on the National Assessment of Educational Progress aggregate student data to the state level so that they can study differences between states in the educational attainments of their students. Researchers involved in the International Association for the Evaluation of Educational Achievement aggregate student data to the national level so that they can compare differences in education between nations of the world.[36]

The problem of selecting an appropriate unit or units of analysis is indeed complex. The most critical step is to think through the phenomena that you wish to study. Consider especially whether the subjects in the sample are acting alone or whether their actions are affected by some larger group of which they are a member. Once you have developed a working theory of the phenomena, you are advised to consult an experienced statistician to help you select appropriate procedures for data collection and analysis. Multilevel analysis should be considered as an option.

MISTAKES SOMETIMES MADE BY RESEARCHERS

1. The researcher does not make sure that each step in a research design is logically related to the others.
2. Does not consider the different ways in which the variables to be studied might be causally related to each other.
3. Selects a statistical tool that is not appropriate for the proposed analysis.
4. Collects research data before deciding on a statistical tool for analyzing the data.
5. Uses only one statistical tool when several can be applied to illuminate different aspects of the data.
6. Uses parametric statistics when the data grossly fail to meet the necessary assumptions.
7. Misinterprets the meaning of an obtained p value.
8. Overstates the importance of small differences that are statistically significant.
9. Initiates statistical analyses before carefully examining the individual scores collected in the study.
10. Does not adjust statistical analyses to account for missing data.
11. Uses the individual as the unit of analysis when it is more appropriate to use the group mean as the unit.

36. These research programs are briefly described in chapter 1.

ANNOTATED REFERENCES

Bruning, James L., and Kintz, B.L. *Computational Handbook of Statistics*, 3rd ed. Glenview, IL: Scott, Foresman, 1987.

Provides easy-to-follow computational procedures for most of the statistical techniques presented in this chapter. An excellent resource for the practicing researcher.

Cook, Thomas D., and Campbell, Donald T. *Quasi-Experimentation: Design & Analysis Issues for Field Settings*. Chicago: Rand McNally, 1979.

Chapter 1 provides a brief review of the major philosophical positions on the nature of causation. The authors show how these positions have affected the way in which educational researchers typically conduct experiments to demonstrate causal relationships. The second author, Campbell, co-wrote with Julian Stanley one of the definitive works on educational experimentation (see chapter 15 of this text).

Hays, William L. *Statistics for the Social Sciences*, 3rd ed. New York: Holt, Rinehart and Winston, 1981.

For the student who wishes a deeper understanding of the theoretical and mathematical bases of educational research statistics, a well-organized reference book with comprehensive coverage of the major topics in statistics: sets, probability theory, descriptive statistics, hypothesis testing, chi-square, analysis of variance, correlation, and nonparametric statistics.

Linn, Robert L. "Quantitative Methods in Research on Teaching." In *Handbook of Research on Teaching*, 3rd ed., ed. Merlin C. Wittrock. New York: Macmillan, 1986, pp. 92–118.

Provides an expanded, mathematically oriented treatment of topics covered in chapter 9: research design, notions of causality, statistical techniques, and units of statistical analysis. The student who can follow the author's mathematical reasoning will profit from his discussion of the strengths and weaknesses of different research designs and statistical tools.

Oakes, Michael. *Statistical Inference: A Commentary for the Social and Behavioral Sciences*. New York: Wiley, 1986.

Creates an argument for the abandoment of inferential statistics in favor of calculating confidence limits. In the process of doing so, the author provides an insightful explanation of the nature of inferential statistics, their role in testing knowledge claims, and how they have been misused by researchers.

Tukey, John W. *Exploratory Data Analysis*. Reading, MA: Addison-Wesley, 1977.

This landmark book presents an alternative view of how educational research data should be analyzed. Conventional data analysis emphasizes summarizing the data in a few descriptive statistics and testing the null hypothesis. Tukey's procedures emphasize exploring the shape of score distributions and unusual phenomena within data.

SELF-CHECK TEST

Circle the correct answer to each of the following questions. An answer key is provided on page 883.

1. According to Krathwohl, the first step in designing a research study is to:
    a. formulate the precise knowledge claim to be tested.
    b. design an empirical test of the knowledge claim.
    c. review evidence from previous studies relating to the knowledge claim.
    d. develop a rationale for the knowledge claim to be tested.
2. The division of individuals into two categories on the basis of performance on a continuous variable is called a(n)
    a. artificial dichotomy.
    b. ranking.
    c. true dichotomy.
    d. artificial ranking.
3. The amount of dispersion of scores about a central value can be measured by the
    a. mean.
    b. standard deviation.
    c. median.
    d. p value.
4. If a group of students has a mean score of 20 on a test and a standard deviation of 4, approximately two-thirds of the scores lie between _____ and _____ .
    a. 16, 28
    b. 18, 22
    c. 16, 24
    d. 12, 28
5. The rejection of the null hypothesis when it is correct is called a Type _____ error.
    a. Alpha
    b. Beta
    c. I
    d. II
6. The p value indicates
    a. whether the null hypothesis can be accepted or rejected.
    b. how likely it is that one's research hypothesis is correct.
    c. the probability that the results would be the same if the study were repeated.
    d. All of the above are correct.
7. Confidence limits are useful because they
    a. yield the probability of making a Type I error.
    b. provide a more stable test of statistical significance than the F ratio.
    c. determine the presence of outliers in research data.
    d. enable inferences from sample statistics to population values.
8. In operational replication the researcher
    a. deliberately avoids imitation of the original researcher's procedures.
    b. attempts to duplicate exactly all of the original researcher's procedures.
    c. only attempts to duplicate the original researcher's sampling and experimental procedures.
    d. deliberately avoids the Type I errors made by the original researcher.
9. For any distribution of raw scores the mean and standard deviation of z scores are _____ and _____ , respectively.
    a. 1, 0
    b. 0, 1

    c. 0, 0

    d. 1, 1

10. The use of the student as the unit of statistical analysis is most justified when
    a. the sample size is small enough to warrant the *t*-test.
    b. the variation between group means is statistically significant.
    c. intact classrooms have been assigned to the experimental treatments.
    d. each student has received the treatment independently of every other student in the sample.

11. The experimental group has a mean and standard deviation of 10.8 and 2.6, respectively. The control group has a mean and standard deviation of 8.0 and 1.4, respectively. Effect size is
    a. 2.0.
    b. 2.6.
    c. 1.4.
    d. 1.2.

12. The power of a statistical significance test is affected by
    a. sample size.
    b. the *p* value used to reject the null hypothesis.
    c. estimated effect size.
    d. All of the above are correct.

13. Stem-and-leaf displays are useful for
    a. estimating missing data.
    b. detecting outliers.
    c. estimating effect size.
    d. computing Type I error.

APPLICATION PROBLEMS

The following problems are designed to give you practice in applying significant concepts and research procedures in the chapter. For feedback, you can compare your answers with the sample answers on page 895.

1. A researcher is interested in studying the relationship between a principal's instructional leadership (A), teacher morale (B), school climate (C), and (D) student achievement. Suggest two ways in which these variables might be causally related to each other.

2. Indicate whether the mean or the median would be a more accurate measure of central tendency in the following situation, and state why.

    You are interested in the average gain that can be made by students taking a speed-reading course. A reading test was given to 250 students before and after taking the course. In looking over the scores, you notice that most students have gained 100 to 300 words per minute. However, there are about 40 students who have really made outstanding gains ranging from 600 to 1,000 words per minute. Mean or median? Why?

3. What type of score is each of the following?
    a. Students are divided into two groups: those who have blue eyes and those who have brown eyes.
    b. These two groups of students are then measured on the time required for their eyes to adjust to different amounts of light.
    c. Each subject is also classified as a heavy smoker (31+ cigarettes per day), moderate smoker (20 to 30 cpd), light smoker (1 to 19 cpd), or nonsmoker.
    d. Each subject is classified as either having normal vision (20/30 or better) or below-normal vision (poorer than 20/30).

4. A study is carried out to test the relative effectiveness of two sixth-grade mathematics programs. A group of 120 sixth-grade pupils is randomly assigned to 4 classrooms. Two classrooms use program A and two use program B. At the end of training all subjects are given a 200-item mathematics test (reliability .97) that closely follows the content covered in the two programs. The mean achievement score for students in program A is 108.7 items correct, as compared with 106.2 for program B. This difference is statistically significant at the .05 level. Is the difference of practical significance?

5. A researcher has completed a study in which an experimental group of 60 college students was formed into pairs and then required to ask each other questions in preparation for an examination. A control group of 60 students was requested to quiz themselves in preparation for the same examination. Students' scores on the examination formed the dependent variable. What is the appropriate unit of statistical analysis for determining whether the examination performance of the experimental group differed from that of the control group?

SUGGESTION SHEET

If your last name starts with letters from Haw to Jaa, please complete the Suggestion Sheet at the end of the book while this chapter is still fresh in your mind.

OVERVIEW

The qualitative research model was developed primarily in the social sciences and has been applied to educational problems only in recent years. In this chapter we will describe the main characteristics of qualitative research and the qualitative and quantitative research models. We will also introduce you to participant observation and ethnographic interview, the main methods used by qualitative researchers. Qualitative research methods are largely subjective in that they rely heavily upon the investigator's skills of observation and interpretation to provide valid information. Therefore, much training and experience is needed to carry out this kind of research.

OBJECTIVES

After studying this chapter, you should be able to:

1. Explain the different assumptions that underlie the naturalistic and positivistic research models.
2. Describe the main characteristics of qualitative research.
3. Describe the main elements of the value system of ethnographic researchers.
4. Explain the advantages and disadvantages of ethnographic research.
5. Describe the criteria that can be used to evaluate studies using participant observation.
6. State the main steps taken to carry out a participant observation study.
7. Describe nonparticipant observation and some of its characteristics.
8. Describe three kinds of interviews used by qualitative researchers.
9. State rules that qualitative researchers should consider in conducting interviews.
10. Describe the process of analytic induction.
11. Define external validity and internal validity and describe threats to each that are often present in qualitative studies.
12. Describe types of case studies used in qualitative research.
13. Describe errors that can occur in subject responses when reactive measures are used.
14. Describe the kinds of research for which qualitative methods are most appropriate.

THE QUALITATIVE RESEARCH MODEL

Educational research has been built largely on the research traditions and methods that were initially developed in the physical and biological sciences. This model is variously called "quantitative," "conventional," "traditional," or "positivistic" research. In the behavioral sciences this model is best exemplified by the research of experimental psychologists. Most of the research methods discussed in this text are based upon this model and reflect some of the assumptions upon which the positivistic paradigm has been built.

In the past 20 years, however, another paradigm for conducting educational research has slowly gained acceptance. This model was developed by anthropologists and sociologists and is usually called "qualitative," "naturalistic," "ethnographic," "subjective," or "postpositivistic" inquiry. In this text, we will generally use the terms "quantitative" and "qualitative" to distinguish these two paradigms, except when referring to the work of an author who uses different terms. Although descriptions of qualitative research methods given by different authors vary considerably, Burgess points out that most writings devoted to this style of inquiry emphasize participant observation and in-depth interviews that allow the researchers to learn first-hand about the social world.[1]

The purpose of this chapter is to introduce you to the qualitative research model and tell you a little about the methods usually used in qualitative research. Qualitative research is much more difficult to do well than quantitative research because the data collected are usually subjective and the main measurement tool for collecting data is the investigator himself. Therefore, before you can conduct qualitative research effectively you will need extensive training and practice in the methods you plan to use. This chapter *will not* be sufficient to prepare you to conduct qualitative research.

The Two Paradigms

Both qualitative and quantitative research have philosophical foundations, characteristics, and techniques that make them ideally suited for the exploration of some questions and inadequate for the investigation of others. Marion Dobbert points out in her book *Ethnographic Research* that

> All scientific procedures have their weaknesses because they are designed to do one thing and not others. Anthropological procedures are designed to study cultures, societies, or institutions as wholes. Consequently, they cannot be used to study certain kinds of detailed matters of intracultural significance. A person using strictly the field-based methodology to be described in this book cannot predict presidential-election outcomes, will never discover the relation between income and gross national product, and will be unable to measure reading abilities of school children or to find out whether the whole word or phonics method adds more to such ability.[2]

1. See R. G. Burgess, 1985, in the Annotated References at the end of this chapter.
2. M. L. Dobbert, *Ethnographic Research: Theory and Application for Modern Schools and Societies* (New York: Praeger, 1982), p. 7.

Thus, in reading this chapter, you should try to gain an understanding of the kinds of questions that qualitative research is best able to address. Keep in mind as you read that both qualitative and quantitative paradigms are legitimate forms of scientific inquiry.

Perceptions of the qualitative versus the quantitative research paradigms range all the way from assertions that the two approaches are incompatible and in direct conflict (e.g., Lincoln and Guba)[3] to the more moderate position that each model is best suited to certain research questions and in many cases a combination of the two approaches is superior to either (e.g., Reichardt and Cook).[4] In fact, two large-scale research projects, the Beginning Teacher Evaluation Study[5] and the ORACLE Project,[6] have successfully used a combination of quantitative and qualitative methodology. It is interesting to note that in both of these studies the quantitative data provided the basic research evidence while the qualitative data were used to round out the picture and provide examples. However, studies also have been conducted in which the main focus was on qualitative inquiry and quantitative research was given the supporting role. In comparing the highly structured observational data with the ethnographic observational data collected in the ORACLE Project, the authors reported that the two observational methods generally produced very similar findings.[7]

Reichardt and Cook have discussed the qualitative versus quantitative question at some depth and have rejected the argument that the two paradigms are incompatible.[8] In fact, they describe several benefits that can be gained by using the two methodologies in combination. Although they look at the two paradigms from the standpoint of evaluation research, virtually everything they say can be applied to all aspects of educational research. They conclude about the qualitative-quantitative debate:

> But while the debate has served a very useful purpose, it has also been partly dysfunctional. In large part, the way the debate is currently being argued serves to polarize the qualitative and quantitative positions and to foster the belief that the *only* available option is a choice *between* these two extremes. It is as if the pendulum must swing to either one side or the other. The currently perceived overemphasis on quantitative methods can then only be corrected by an equal but opposite emphasis on qualitative methods. Of course, once qualitative methods have been

3. Y. S. Lincoln and E. G. Guba, *Naturalistic Inquiry* (Beverly Hills, CA: Sage, 1985).
4. C. S. Reichardt and T. D. Cook, "Beyond Qualitative Versus Quantitative Methods," in *Qualitative and Quantitative Methods in Evaluation Research*, eds. T. D. Cook and C. S. Reichardt (Beverly Hills, CA: Sage, 1979).
5. See C. Denham and A. Lieberman, eds., *Time to Learn* (Washington, DC: National Institute of Education, 1980).
6. See M. Galton and J. Willcocks, *Moving From the Primary Classroom* (London: Routledge & Kegan Paul, 1983).
7. See Galton and Delamont, 1984, in the Annotated References in this chapter.
8. Reichardt and Cook, "Beyond Qualitative Versus Quantitative Methods."

put to the test as thoroughly as quantitative procedures have been in the past, the qualitative methods will be found to be just as fallible and feeble. If the dichotomization between the methods is maintained, the pendulum will swing back toward quantitative procedures in an inevitable backlash. Undoubtedly this too would be found unsatisfactory, so the pendulum would swing back again, and so on. Thus the current debate keeps the pendulum swinging between extremes of methods and extremes of dissatisfaction.

The solution, of course, is to realize that the debate is inappropriately stated. There is no need to choose a research method on the basis of a traditional pardigmatic stance. Nor is there any reason to pick between two polar-opposite paradigms. Thus, there is no need for a dichotomy between the method-types and there is every reason (at least in logic) to use them together to satisfy the demands of evaluation research in the most efficacious manner possible.[9]

Students who want to learn more about these two models of inquiry should examine critically the claims of extremists on both sides who attempt to label one model as "old research" and the other as "new research," who maintain that the two paradigms are diametrically opposite and incomparable, or who suggest that there is only one "right way" to do research in the social and behavioral sciences.

In their definitions of naturalistic research, social scientists often discuss two dimensions. First is the degree to which the investigator influences or manipulates the conditions under which the behavior is studied. Second is the degree to which units are imposed upon the behavior being studied by the investigator. At one end of the continuum on these two dimensions is rigorous experimental research such as is carried out in the psychological laboratory. In this type of research the behavior being studied is controlled and manipulated as completely as possible and precise objective units of measurement are imposed by the investigator upon the behavior being studied. At the other end of this continuum is qualitative or naturalistic research in which the investigator exerts no influence and conducts no manipulation of the behavior being studied and imposes no *a priori* measurement units on the outcome.

Let us now take a closer look at these two different models of inquiry and compare the assumptions upon which they are based. To review, the quantitative research model forms the basis of the scientific method and was developed initially from research in the physical and biological sciences. The qualitative model has emerged primarily from the social sciences. It is based upon assumptions that are in most cases nearly opposite to the assumptions underlying positivism. These assumptions seem to better fit the realities of behavioral science inquiry than do the positivistic assumptions *as they emerged from the*

9. Ibid., pp. 26–27.

physical sciences. However, we must recognize that researchers in the behavioral sciences have identified many of the problems of using the quantitative research model and have adjusted their methods of inquiry so that many of the criticisms of this model simply do not apply to well-designed quantitative research.

Comparison of the Assumptions Underlying Qualitative and Quantitative Research Models

Qualitative and quantitative research models are based on very different sets of assumptions. Lincoln and Guba have identified five salient areas related to research in which the naturalistic and positivistic models differ. A brief discussion of some of their ideas may help the reader to understand how the two models differ.[10] Readers familiar with the educational research literature may notice that the research designs used by many investigators do not fit either model to the exclusion of the other but instead use some combination of these paradigms.

1. The nature of reality:
   a. *Positivistic model*. There are human characteristics and processes that constitute a form of reality in that they occur under a wide variety of conditions and thus can be generalized to some degree. Different variables related to a complex process may be studied independently. For example, the effects of teacher behavior on pupil learning can be studied without studying all of the other variables that influence pupil learning. Such inquiry can gradually merge into a composite picture of the phenomenon being studied. Finally, when sufficient inquiry has been carried out, the phenomenon can be predicted and controlled at levels that substantially exceed chance.
   b. *Naturalistic model*. There are no human characteristics or processes from which generalizations can emerge. Instead, each subject or phenomenon is different and can only be studied holistically. Since the total setting in which the phenomenon occurs is never the same, it is unlikely that prediction or control will ever be achieved although some level of understanding may be reached. Attempts to break a complex phenomenon into parts and to study these parts separately cannot succeed.

10. The authors have attempted to interpret the work of Lincoln and Guba with emphasis on its significance to the educational researcher. An attempt has been made to present a balanced look at the two paradigms. Because Lincoln and Guba are advocates of the naturalistic model, our brief introduction, which strives for balance, may not accurately reflect their views. Interested students should read sources listed in the Annotated References at the end of this chapter to get a balanced picture of the relative merits of the two models.

2. Relationship of the researcher to the research subject:
   a. *Positivistic model.* The researcher can function independently of the subject to a major degree, although some interaction is probably inevitable. Various research strategies are employed to minimize the effects of this interaction upon the research findings.
   b. *Naturalistic model.* The researcher and the research subject interact to influence one another and are inseparably interconnected.
3. The possibility of generalization:
   a. *Positivistic model.* The ultimate goal of research is to develop a body of knowledge in the form of generalizations that will hold at least to some degree over time and in contexts similar to those in which the generalizations were developed.
   b. *Naturalistic model.* The aim of inquiry is to develop a body of knowledge that is unique to the individual being studied, and that can be used to develop working hypotheses about the individual.[11]

It should be noted that many sociologists and anthropologists do not agree with Lincoln and Guba's position on generalization. For example, in discussing the natural-history foundations of ethnographic research, Dobbert states:

> The origins of this approach are found in the work of Darwin (considered the father of the modern natural history method), who learned its elements through studies of the geology and biology of his day. The essence of the natural history approach is careful and painstaking observation, guided by informed questions *and followed by generalization based upon the grouping of observed facts and then by a testing of the derived generalization through further observation.* [Italics added.]
>
> In anthropology, the facts observed are the interactions, actions, and statements of individuals, which are then grouped according to similarities.[12]

4. The possibility of causal linkages:
   a. *Positivistic model.* Given sufficient research with valid measures (which is rarely the case), every action or effect can be explained by a cause or combination of causes that precede the effect in time.
   b. *Naturalistic model.* All elements in the situation are in a state of mutual simultaneous interaction so it is impossible to distinguish causes from effects.
5. The role of values in inquiry:
   a. *Positivistic model.* Values can impact upon research procedures in many ways. Inquiry should be made as value-free as possible through the use of sound research design and objective data-collection procedures.

---

11. Lincoln and Guba, *Naturalistic Inquiry.*
12. Dobbert, *Ethnographic Research,* pp. 8, 9.

b. *Naturalistic model.* Research is value-bound because inquiries are inevitably influenced by the values of the researcher, the choice of theory, the methodology employed, and the values inherent in the context of the inquiry.

CHARACTERISTICS OF QUALITATIVE RESEARCH

The Naturalistic Inquiry Perspective

Lincoln and Guba,[13] Burgess,[14] Reichardt and Cook,[15] and others have described the characteristics of qualitative research. These descriptions give the reader a good overall picture of this methodology. The following 10 characteristics of qualitative research are generally accepted by workers in the various disciplines who employ this methodology.

1. *Research involves holistic inquiry carried out in a natural setting.* Thus, qualitative research is virtually always field research in which the investigator tries to study all elements present in the setting in which the inquiry takes place. This emphasis on studying the whole setting in order to understand reality is perhaps the most important characteristic of the qualitative research paradigm and results in much investigation being aimed at an understanding of the social, cultural, and historical setting in which the investigation occurs.

2. *Humans are the primary data-gathering instrument.* The qualitative researcher prefers to rely on human powers of observation rather than on measurement instruments such as paper-and-pencil tests. The main rationale for using the human observer is that no nonhuman instrument is sufficiently flexible to adapt to the complex situation as it evolves and to identify and take into account biases that result from the interactions and value differences between the "instrument" and the subject. Although the human observer is the primary data gatherer in qualitative research, many researchers collect supplemental data with more objective instruments such as questionnaires and paper-and-pencil tests.

3. *Emphasis on qualitative methods.* You will learn in chapter 12 that human observers and interviewers can employ highly quantitative procedures. However, in the various methodologies that fit the qualitative research paradigm, qualitative data-gathering procedures are obviously preferred because they are considered more amenable to the diversity of "multiple realities" one finds in a complex field situation.

---

13. Lincoln and Guba, *Naturalistic Inquiry.*
14. See the Annotated References at the end of this chapter.
15. Reichardt and Cook, "Beyond Qualitative Versus Quantitative Methods."

4. *Purposive rather than random sampling.* By purposely selecting a wide range of subjects to observe, including deviant cases who are often missed by random sampling or rejected as "outliers" in quantitative research, the qualitative researcher will be more likely to uncover the full array of "multiple realities" relevant to an inquiry. Many quantitative researchers overlook the fact that a great deal can often be learned by a careful study of the nontypical subject. Questions such as Why does this subject respond differently? and What implications do these differences have in developing theory? can be very productive in advancing research knowledge.

5. *Inductive data analysis.* Instead of deductive analysis, which focuses on testing preconceived hypotheses, the qualitative researcher studies the data inductively in order to reveal unanticipated outcomes. In other words, the qualitative researcher first gathers the data and then tries to develop understanding and draw generalizations.

6. *Development of grounded theory.* A major characteristic of qualitative research is its emphasis on "grounded theory." Theory that is "grounded in the data," that is, developed from the data, is viewed as superior to *a priori* theory because it will more accurately reflect the data.[16] Also, *a priori* theory may well limit and bias the perceptions of the observer. It should be noted, however, that many quantitative researchers recognize the value of grounded theory and carry out pilot studies in order to develop theoretical constructs that are subsequently tested using quantitative methods.

7. *Design emerges as the research progresses.* In qualitative inquiry, the investigator starts with a very tentative design (or in some cases none at all) and develops the design as the inquiry progresses. This permits adapting the design to include variables that were not anticipated prior to the start of observation. The rationale for emergent design is that it is impossible for enough to be known ahead of time to develop an adequate research design.

8. *Subject plays a role in interpreting outcomes.* Because the qualitative researcher usually attempts to reconstruct reality from the frame of reference of the subjects, it follows logically that the respondents may in some cases be better able than the investigator to understand the complex interactions that have been observed and account for the influence of local values on these interactions. Quantitative researchers with behavioristic orientations often overlook the fact that much can be learned from human subjects simply by asking for their perceptions.

9. *Utilization of intuitive insights.* Although most researchers develop hunches and intuitive insights from their interactions in the research situation, qualitative researchers place more emphasis on tacit or intuitive knowledge. They believe that such knowledge must be given legitimacy because of the

---

16. See Peter Woods, "Ethnography and Theory Construction in Educational Research," in *Field Methods in the Study of Education*, ed. R. G. Burgess (Philadelphia: Falmer, 1985) for a discussion of this topic.

complexity of the situation and the fact that much of the interaction with the subject occurs at the subjective or intuitive level. Whereas qualitative researchers consider such feelings as legitimate knowledge, the quantitative researchers use such insights and feelings as the basis for framing hypotheses that can then be explored objectively. They do not consider the hunches themselves as a form of knowledge.

10. *Emphasis on Social Processes.* Qualitative studies focus upon social processes and the meanings that participants attribute to social situations.

The Ethnographic Research Perspective

Many of the concepts, values, and methods that undergird the qualitative research paradigm can be traced to ethnographic research. This method was designed by anthropologists and is sometimes called the *anthropological field-study approach.* A look at the ethnographic method will give you a better undestanding of the origins and meaning of the characteristics of qualitative research listed above.

An *ethnography* can be defined as an in-depth analytical description of an *intact* cultural scene. Anthropologists have usually used the participant observation method in their ethnographics in order to obtain the insider's viewpoint. The main characteristic of ethnographic research is that the observer uses continuous observation, trying to record virtually everything that occurs in the setting being studied. The participant observer sometimes makes an audio or video recording and analyzes it after the observation. Or the researcher may make brief notes during the observation and enlarge on these immediately after the observation.

For most educational studies, such as those concerned with classroom interactions, educational researchers generally have used nonparticipant observation because a more complete and accurate record is obtained. The specific procedure usually followed by the nonparticipant observer is to make lengthy handwritten notes that give a continuous account of the classroom activities and interactions (see figure 10.1).

Some qualitative researchers in education collect data over a much shorter period of time than is customary in anthropological field studies. Such deviations from the procedures developed by anthropologists have resulted in rather severe criticisms of educational researchers using ethnographic techniques. Educational researchers also have been accused of using ethnographic techniques without accepting or understanding the values that the ethnographers consider an essential part of this methodology.[17]

Anthropologists employ ethnographic techniques within the context of a

17. See D. M. Fetterman, "Ethnography in Educational Research: The Dynamics of Diffusion," *Educational Researcher* 11, no. 3 (1982): 17–22.

Protocol Number: 06
Name of Researcher: Gail
Date of Observation:
Subject of Observation:

	2nd Grade Class, Open Class-
	1. room, with two team teacher and two other adults, this
	2. is a joint observation with Elizabeth. I will be
	3. observing two reading groups today, simultaneously,
	4. including 9 children. Out of the 9 children, 2 are
	5. girls, 7 are boys.
	6.
8:30 Noise level 2	7. At 8:30 the noise level is 2. The children have just been
	8. let into the classroom, taking their coats off and
	9. wandering around the room. Several boys are in the corner
	10. fighting, and some girls are sitting on the floor
	11. doing a puzzle. The teacher is walking back and forth
	12. in the back of the classroom not attending the children.
	13. The noise continues and the children are running
	14. around. There is much confusion in the room. The teachers
8:35	15. stand at the desk talking to one another. At 8:35,
	16. Mrs. Tyler leaves the room. The team teacher
	17. stays seated behind the classroom at her desk. At 8:40
	18. Mrs. Tyler comes back into the room. She walks to the
	19. desk at the far-left-hand side of the classroom,
	20. which is a round table, and sits on the edge. She says,
	21. "Blue Group, get your folders and go up in the front.
	22. Green Group, come here." Noise level drops to 1, and
	23. the children begin to follow her orders. She says,
	24. "Anybody lose a quarter." No one responds, and she
	25. repeats the question again with irritation in her voice.
	26. She says, "I know someone lost a quarter
	27. because it was found in the coat room. Look in your
	28. pockets and see." No one says anything. She now
	29. stands up and pulls a pile of workbooks from across the
	30. table over to her. They are the _____ reading work-
	31. books. She opens one of them on the top and says,
	32. "Ah Daniel!" She says this with a loud sharp voice.
	33. She continues, "Your work yesterday was not too bad
	34. but you need some work. Evidently there are still some
	35. words you don't understand." She thumbs through the rest
	36. of his lesson. Danny is standing at the outside of
	37. the circle around her, not listening to what she is saying.
	38. Mrs. Tyler now stands and gives instructions to the Green
	39. Group. She tells them to go through 8 through 13, reading
	40. the two stories between those pages and to go over the
	41. work in the workbooks that she is about to give back.

Figure 10.1   Sample of a Continuous Observation Protocol

Source: From William J. Tikunoff, David C. Berliner, and Ray C. Rist, *Special Study A: An Ethnographic Study of the Forty Classrooms of the Beginning Teacher Evaluation Study Known Sample.* Technical Report #75-10-5(A) (San Francisco: Far West Laboratory for Educational Research and Development, 1975).

value system that is quite different from the values of most other behavioral scientists. The main elements of this value system are:

Phenomenology: The researcher must develop the perspectives of the group being studied, that is, the researcher must adopt the "insider's" viewpoint.

Holism: The researcher must attempt to perceive the big picture or the total situation rather than focusing upon a few elements within a complex situation as is usually done in quantitative educational research.

Nonjudgmental orientation: Judgments, hypotheses, or preconceptions may distort what the researcher sees; hence, the emphasis is on recording the total situation in qualitative terms without superimposing one's own value system.

Contextualization: All data must be considered only in the context of the environment in which it was gathered.

Ethnographers do not start with specific hypotheses. In fact, they try to put aside specific expectations or preconceptions in order to avoid the risk that these will bias what they see in the observational situation. They are likely to start with a broad theoretical framework or with tentative working hypotheses that may provide some general guidelines to the observer about what behavior may be important. Only after insights and theoretical constructs emerge from the field notes will the qualitative researcher begin to focus his or her observations. For example, an ethnographic study of elementary classrooms used the categories that emerged from the protocols of an earlier study to focus the perceptions of the observers (see table 10.1). Note that these questions focus the observer but contain no preconceived hypotheses.

Detailed notes are needed because the ethnographer believes that only through the study of a complete sociocultural system such as a school, a classroom, a PTA chapter, or a teachers' union can the system and the behavior of individuals in the system be understood. In other words, the ethnographer rejects the study of the individual outside of the context in which the individual functions. As the observational data accumulate, the researcher tries to develop hypotheses that help to explain or understand the phenomena observed.

Such hypotheses, therefore, are much more thoroughly *grounded* in the real world than are many of the hypotheses that emerge from armchair speculation in the behavioral sciences. As we indicated earlier in the chapter, these hypotheses are often referred to as *grounded theory* or *grounded hypotheses*. Thus, the ethnographic method tends to generate hypotheses that can then be tested using further observation or other methods such as correlational or experimental research.[18]

18. See G. E. Overholt and W. M. Stallings, "Ethnographic and Experimental Hypotheses in Educational Research," *Educational Researcher* 5, no. 8 (1976): 12–14.

TABLE 10.1

Major Categories in Henry's Cross-Cultural Outline of Education

I. On what does the educational process focus?

II. How is the information communicated (teaching methods)?

III. Who educates?

IV. How does the person being educated participate?

V. How does the educator participate? (What is his attitude?)

VI. Are some things taught to some and not to others?

VII. Discontinuities in the educational process.

VIII. What limits the quantity of information a child receives from a teacher?

IX. What forms of conduct control (discipline) are used?

X. What is the relation between the intent and the results of education?

XI. How long does the process of formal education last?

SOURCE: From W. J. Tikunoff, D. C. Berliner, and R. C. Rist, *Special Study A: An Ethnographic Study of the 40 Classrooms at the Beginning Teacher Evaluation Study Known Sample* (San Francisco: Far West Laboratory for Educational Research and Development, 1975). The table is based on Jules Henry, "The Cross Cultural Outline of Education," *Current Anthropology* 4 (1960): 269–305.

To summarize, the ethnographic method has a number of advantages and disadvantages.[19] Among the advantages:

1. It provides a very complete picture of the environment being studied, and because these studies usually extend over many months, they give a longitudinal perspective not present in most educational research.
2. It is more likely than other research methods to lead to new insights and hypotheses.
3. The hypotheses or theories that are developed are grounded solidly in observational data gathered in a naturalistic setting.
4. Because the observer does not start with specific hypotheses, the observer is less likely than the conventional observer to overlook phenomena that do not fit one's expectations.

Some of the disadvantages of the ethnographic method are:

1. A very alert and sophisticated observer who can write clearly and rapidly is needed. Even if persons with considerable training in sociology or anthropol-

19. See J. P. Goetz and M. D. LeCompte, *Ethnography and Qualitative Design in Educational Research* (New York: Academic Press, 1984).

ogy are employed, it is still necessary to train them further in observational techniques.

2. A great many hours of observation are needed to understand the environment being studied. Most ethnographic studies extend over several months and some more than two or three years. This necessity makes the original research very costly and also makes it very difficult for other scientists to replicate the research.

3. The observational records ("field notes") tend to be very long and therefore difficult to quantify and interpret.

4. Because the observations are subjective and because checks of interrater reliability usually cannot be made, the observer's biases may seriously distort the findings.

5. It is virtually impossible to observe and write down all behavior as it occurs in a natural setting such as the classroom. Thus, the observer is constantly called upon to make instant decisions on what to write down and what to omit.

6. The observer often becomes an active participant in the environment being studied. This can lead to role conflicts and emotional involvement, which can reduce the validity of the data being collected.

METHODS IN QUALITATIVE RESEARCH

Participant Observation

The *participant observer*, by virtue of being actively involved in the situation being observed, often gains insights and develops interpersonal relationships that are virtually impossible to achieve through any other method. The level of this participation may be varied. In *complete participation* the individual becomes a full member of the group and the role of observer is concealed. Or the observer's role may be somewhat open but the observer may *function primarily as a participant*, keeping one's observational activities as unobtrusive as possible. This level is commonly used in studies of organizational behavior such as those often carried out by industrial psychologists. Or the researcher may *function primarily as an observer* but may participate enough to gain rapport with the group and develop a better understanding of the group's functions and relationships. This level is typical of such anthropological studies as the work of Margaret Mead.

Complete participation, although sometimes the best way to collect accurate information, involves many problems. Perhaps the most serious of these is the ethical problem of deception and the reaction that will occur if the deception is discovered. Another problem that must be considered when observing small groups is that the observer's participation may significantly modify the phenomenon one is studying. Also, the participant observer may become emotionally involved and lose objectivity, in which case the data collected will be of dubious value. The observer will also have difficulty recording observations and must rely on memory or use hidden recording equipment. Finally, the complete participant cannot take advantage of many special situations that arise without risking detection. For example, contacts with persons who are rejected by the group may provide valuable information but must be limited in order to preserve the observer's own group status. Thus, complete participation is less often used than the more moderate levels described above.

Although participant observation is not widely used in educational research, the method is well suited for the investigation of many educational problems. For example, studies of the organizational structure of school districts, teachers' unions, and other educational organizations, and studies of effective group interaction such as in team-teaching situations or parent-teacher activities seem appropriate for this method.

Criteria for Evaluating Participant Observer Studies

To realize the advantages of this method, studies using participant observation must reach certain standards. Louis Smith developed the following criteria to judge the validity of studies in which participant observation is used:[20]

1. *Quality of direct on-site observation.* Smith noted that individuals, organizations, and groups often "mask" what is really going on from the researcher. Masking is much more difficult to do with participant observers than with other kinds of data collection, such as questionnaires.

2. *Freedom of access.* In doing participant observations in the school setting the researcher must have broad access. For example, if a school administrator succeeds in steering the observer to particular schools, teachers, or events, then biased data will probably be gathered. Similarly, free access to attend classes, meetings, and so forth unannounced and without prior arrangements is necessary to obtain a normal, unbiased picture of phenomena in a natural setting.

3. *Intensity of observation.* A great many hours of participant observation are needed when this method is used. As the amount of direct observation increases, the chances improve of obtaining a valid and credible picture of the phenomena being studied. As intensity increases, the data are likely to improve for a number of reasons. First, the likelihood of "faking" or "putting on an act" is decreased. Second, as schools operate over long, established cycles—the semester or year—it is necessary to observe the entire cycle in order to gain a complete picture.

20. L. M. Smith, "An Evolving Logic of Participant Observations, Educational Ethnography, and Other Case Studies," in *Review of Research in Education*, Vol. 6, ed. L. S. Shulman (Itasca, IL: F. E. Peacock, 1978).

4. *Qualitative and quantitative data.* Although in the past ethnographic data have been almost entirely qualitative, there is a trend in educational ethnography today to collect both qualitative and quantitative data. The use of recordings, such as videotape, permits both qualitative and quantitative analysis. Smith considers arguments about which of these two forms of data should be used to be "pseudo-issues" and sees a gradual merging of the two views.

5. *Triangulation and multimethods.* These procedures refer to the strategy of using several different kinds of data-collection instruments, such as tests, direct observation, interview, and content analysis, to explore a single problem or issue. Although educational ethnography is built primarily upon participant observation, this method should be supplemented by other data-collection procedures if possible.

Shipman[21] has pointed out that each social researcher is likely to concentrate on different aspects of a "confused reality," which is too complex to study in its entirety. A partial solution to understanding this complex reality is *triangulation of methodology,* that is, using several methods to study the same object. Shipman maintains that when the investigator uses only one method, the result is "a one-dimensional snapshot of a very wide and deep social scene" (Shipman, 1981, p. 147). Triangulation can also be achieved by collecting essentially the same data from different samples, at different times, and in different places. In this sense, triangulation is simply a form of replication that contributes greatly to our confidence in the research findings regardless of whether qualitative or quantitative methodology has been employed.

6. *Sampling of data.* Because the participant observer cannot see everything that is relevant in the situation being studied, some procedure for getting a representative sample of the total data universe is necessary. The first step is to get an overview of the total territory that is relevant to the observer's goals. In a school this could include the principal, parents, teachers, students, and non-teaching staff in a variety of settings such as the classroom, faculty lounge, cafeterias, and playground. Then, with the total amount of observation time in mind, the observer can develop a sampling plan that covers the entire territory to some degree.

Margaret LeCompte and Judith Goetz point out that in most social situations, such as a classroom, the stream of interaction is too complex and too subtle for the participant observer or even a team of observers to record everything that happens.[22] Thus, the participant observer realistically is limited to recording only those phenomena that are most relevant to the topic being studied. However, participant observers must be sensitive not only to what they are *including* in their protocols, but also what they are *excluding*. These inclusion-exclusion criteria may change as both the research topic and concep-

21. M. Shipman, *The Limitations of Social Research,* 2nd ed. (New York: Longman, 1981), p. 147.
22. M. D. LeCompte and J. P. Goetz, "Problems of Reliability and Validity in Ethnographic Research," *Review of Educational Research* 52, no. 1 (1982): 31–60.

tual framework evolve, as the data begin to emerge as a daily flow of events and activities, as the participant observer develops intuitive reactions and hunches, and as the overall picture comes together.

7. *Unobtrusive measures.*[23] The participant observer should be alert to unobtrusive cues that provide insights into the behavior being observed. Such cues can do much to provide the observer with a clearer picture of what is going on. For example, a teacher who is always late for appointments with the observer may be giving an important cue about his or her attitude, and this could be probed.

Questions Explored in Participant Observation

Researchers engage in a variety of activities when acting as participant observers. They watch what the subjects do, listen to what they say, and interact with subjects in order to be socialized into the group under investigation. Specifically, participant observers focus their watching and listening to answer questions such as the following:

1. *Who* is in the group or scene? How many people are there, and what are their identities and relevant characteristics? How is membership in the group or scene acquired?
2. *What* is happening here? What are the people in the group or scene doing and saying to one another?
   a. What behaviors are repetitive and which are irregular? In what events, activities, or routines are people engaged? What resources are used in these activities, and how are they allocated? How are activities organized, labeled, explained, and justified? What differing social contexts can be identified?
   b. How do the people in the group behave toward one another? What is the nature of this participation and interaction? How are the people connected or related to one another? What statuses and roles are evident in this interaction? Who makes what decisions for whom? How do the people organize themselves for interactions?
   c. What is the content of their conversations? What subjects are common and which are rare? What stories, anecdotes, and homilies do they exchange? What language do they use for communication, both verbal and nonverbal? What beliefs do the content of their conversations demonstrate? What formats do the conversations follow? What processes do they reflect? Who talks and who listens?
3. *Where* is the group or scene located? What physical settings and environments form their contexts? What natural resources are evident and what technologies are created or used? How does the group allocate and use space and physical

---

23. Unobtrusive measures are measures that can be taken without alerting the subjects that they are being measured. Many behaviors that occur in the field situation, such as facial expressions, tone of voice, and so on, can give the observer insights about the phenomena being observed.

objects? What is consumed and what is produced? What sights, sounds, smells, tastes, and feeling sensations are found in the contexts that the group uses?

4. *When* does the group meet and interact? How often are these meetings and how lengthy are they? How does the group conceptualize, use, and distribute time? How do participants view their past and future?

5. *How* are the identified elements connected or interrelated—either from the participants' point of view or from the researcher's perspective? How is stability maintained? How does change originate and how is it managed? How are the identified elements organized? What rules, norms, or mores govern this social organization? How is this group related to other groups, organizations, or institutions?

6. *Why* does the group operate as it does? What meanings do participants attribute to what they do? What is the group's history? What symbols, traditions, values, and world views can be found in the group?[24]

Steps in Participant Observation

Norman Denzin lists the following steps in carrying out a participant observation study:[25]

Step 1: Before actual field contacts and observations begin, formulate a general definition of the problem. Adopt a theoretical perspective, review the relevant research literature, and write an initial statement of research and theoretical objectives.

Step 2: Next, select a field setting, largely determined by the formulation of the problem as stated in step 1. The design should be flexible, so that multiple settings can be considered for later observations.

Step 3: Upon selection of the research setting, make initial field contacts. Establish entree, make public the purpose of the study to certain persons, and start initial observations.

Step 4: In this phase the initial implementation of step 1 occurs. Working definitions of key concepts are developed, and multiple research methods are employed. Statistical data on the setting and participants are gathered, documents are analyzed, and the historical context of the setting is documented.

Step 5: By this phase, field research is progressing. Informants will have been selected, approached, and instructed, and interviews will be solicited. Early theoretical formulations will now be tested, reformulated, and tested again. Negative cases will be sought as the general method of analytic induction is followed.

Step 6: General categories for data analysis are developed as hypotheses are formulated and tested. Indicators of key concepts are now being developed and refined as a scheme for coding and analysis takes shape.

24. Goetz and LeCompte, *Ethnography and Qualitative Design,* pp. 112–113.
25. See N. K. Denzin, in the Annotated References at the end of this chapter.

Step 7:   Complex sets of propositions are developed and validated with multiple methods and varieties of data. Comparison groups are selected to further specify the causal propositions as a sequential, explanatory network is developed.

Step 8:   This is the conclusion of the study, although additional observations may be made as necessary. Role disengagement occurs as the field workers begin to withdraw from continuous day-to-day observations. The actual writing of the research report now begins, and all earlier notes and observations are incorporated into a final picture of the events and processes studied. This phase is kept deliberately open-ended, since the observers may be drawn back for supplemental data. (Denzin, 1978, p. 202)

Nonparticipant Observation

The nonparticipant observer minimizes interactions with the subjects being observed and attempts to obtain as complete a record as possible of behavior relevant to the observer's interests. The main advantages of nonparticipant observation are that it is less obtrusive than participant observation and less likely to be distorted by the emotional involvement of the observer. On the other hand, certain kinds of information, such as the subject's attitudes and perceptions, are much more difficult to obtain by the nonparticipant observer. In qualitative research, nonparticipant observation typically involves accurate minute-by-minute accounts of what the subjects do and say. These are usually called "protocols" or "steam-of-behavior chronicles." An example of a protocol made in a second-grade classroom is given in figure 10.1. Because of the limitations of this method, Pelto and Pelto recommend that protocols or stream-of-behavior chronicles obtained by the nonparticipant observer should be validated using interactive methods such as participant observation or key-informant interviewing.[26] Also, in most field situations some participation in the observed situation is virtually inevitable. Thus, it is important for the observer to keep a record of any interactions that occur and estimate their possible consequences.

Occasionally the nonparticipant observer uses more structured procedures such as the interaction analysis procedures developed by Ned Flanders.[27] When structured observation forms are used the quantitative observation methods described in chapter 12 are appropriate. However, most qualitative researchers reject these procedures because they are too narrow.

26. P. J. Pelto and G. H. Pelto, *Anthropological Research: The Structures of Inquiry,* 2nd ed. (New York: Cambridge University Press, 1978).
27. N. Flanders, *Analyzing Teaching Behavior* (Reading, MA: Addison-Wesley, 1970).

Characteristics of Nonparticipant Observation

1. Procedures must keep observer involvement to a minimum. Strive for a detached, neutral approach.
2. The location and behavior of both the observer and the observer's equipment should be as unobtrusive as the field situation permits.
3. This method is usually used after interactive methods, such as participant observation, have indicated what specifics should be observed.
4. This method is much more sharply focused than are the interactive methods used in qualitative research.

The Informant Interview

Participant observation is usually considered the basic method of qualitative research. However, most researchers advocate data collection by more than one method, which as we said earlier is called method triangulation. The use of triangulation helps to demonstrate validity and open up new perspectives about the topic under investigation.

As you will learn in chapter 11, interviews can be classified in terms of the amount of structure imposed. Most interviews conducted by quantitative researchers are classified as structured, in which the interviewer closely follows an interview guide, or semistructured, in which some deviation from the interview guide is permitted. In contrast, in the unstructured interview, an interview guide is not used and the interviewer has almost complete latitude in deciding what questions to ask. The unstructured interview best fits the qualitative paradigm. However, researchers who have developed insights about a given social group, such as participants in a university seminar, primarily through participant observation, may check these insights by use of structured or semistructured interviews.

Elements in the Ethnographic Interview

James Spradley defines ethnographic interviews as a series of friendly conversations in which the investigator gradually introduces new ethnographic elements in order to gain the information sought.[28] In order to maintain rapport and avoid the atmosphere of an interrogation, these elements must not be introduced too quickly. If rapport begins to deteriorate the researcher should shift back to the

28. J. P. Spradley, *The Ethnographic Interview* (New York: Holt, Rinehart, and Winston, 1979).

friendly conversation mode. Spradley describes the three most important ethnographic elements in the interview as follows:

1. *Explicit purpose.* The researcher should have a specific purpose for the interview and should make this clear to the informant so the person knows where the interview is going. While avoiding an authoritarian stance, the researcher should gradually take control and direct the talk into those channels that will discover the relevant knowledge of the informant.

2. *Ethnographic explanations.* During the entire series of interviews the researcher must provide ethnographic explanations to the informant. These are concerned with explanations of what the project is all about, statements about why the researcher is writing things down or making a tape recording, encouragement to the informant to describe the informant's culture in his or her own terms, and explanations of the interview process and the reasons for asking various kinds of questions.

3. *Ethnographic questions.* The questions asked are, of course, the reason for the interview. What is asked, how it is asked, and how topics are followed up determines the quality of the field notes and the ethnographic record that is subsequently written. Spradley describes over 30 kinds of ethnographic questions, which he organizes into three main categories: *descriptive questions*, which are aimed at eliciting respondents' perceptions of some aspect of their culture; *structural questions*, which help the interviewer discover how respondents organize or structure their knowledge or perceptions; and *contrast questions*, which enable the researcher to discover the dimensions of meaning that respondents employ to distinguish the objects and events in their world.

Kinds of Ethnographic Interviews

Judith Goetz and Margaret LeCompte identify three forms of interviewing used by qualitative researchers: key-informant interviews, career histories, and surveys.[29]

Key-Informant Interviews

Key informants are members of the group under study who have special knowledge or perceptions that are not otherwise available to the researcher. In some cases they are chosen because they are able to observe in situations not available to the ethnographer. They are often nontypical in that they have more knowledge, better communication skills, or perspectives different from other group members. For example, in studying the social structure of a fifth-grade classroom, the role of an adult as a participant observer is likely to be severely

29. See Goetz and LeCompte, *Ethnography and Qualitative Design.*

limited. Even as a nonparticipant observer, the adult might miss much information that is known intuitively by the participants. In this case, the researcher may interview a few students who are in leadership roles, are more intelligent and mature than their peers, and are willing and able to communicate their perceptions. These key informants may provide insights that no amount of observation would reveal. Goetz and LeCompte point out that, because key informants tend to be reflective individuals, they may provide insights into processes, sensitize the researcher to value dilemmas, and help the researcher see the implications of specific findings.[30]

However, problems arise in using key informants. The very qualities that make these persons key informants also make them nontypical, so care must be taken to select a representative group of informants and to check findings by other methods. Because the key informant has the power to define to some degree the topics to which the investigator will have access, there is always a danger that the researcher will be manipulated by the informant. For example, Burgess describes a teacher informant who attempted to use him to get information about her promotion and to convey her views to the principal.

Another problem that Burgess discusses is the need to protect the informant who gives the investigator confidential information that could harm the informant if the informant were identified as the source. This problem becomes even more difficult if an informant gives the investigator information about unethical or illegal activities. For example, let us suppose a teacher tells the researcher that other teachers on the faculty are using cocaine during school hours. Should the researcher protect the informant or pass on the information to the principal (who may also be a key informant)? Burgess maintains that the researcher's obligation to the teacher outweighs any obligation to the administration and thus the researcher should not pass on this information.[31]

These two brief examples illustrate the fact that the use of key informants can pose many difficult human relations problems and ethical issues. The student who is interested in qualitative research is again cautioned that these methods require extensive training and experience.

Career History Interviews

This type of interview aims at eliciting a narrative from the subject that provides a broad account of the subject's professional life. In education, for instance, career histories of successful teachers may provide in-depth information about aspects of the teaching profession that could not be obtained by other data-

30. Ibid.
31. R. G. Burgess, "In the Company of Teachers: Key Informants and the Study of a Comprehensive School," in *Strategies of Educational Research: Qualitative Methods,* ed. R. G. Burgess (Philadelphia: Falmer, 1985).

collection procedures. For example, Katherine Newman carried out interviews of 10 experienced public school teachers to determine their perceptions of their career development.[32] Two in-depth interviews were conducted for each teacher. The first part of each interview was unstructured; the second part was semistructured. Two types of data analyses were conducted. To get a holistic picture, a biography was written for each teacher. The data from the interviews were then analyzed to get answers related to specific aspects of the teachers' career such as decision to become a teacher, job satisfaction, and inservice education. Several interesting stages of career development emerged. Note that in this study, both quantitative and qualitative data were collected and were subjected to both quantitative and qualitative analysis.

Survey Interviews

In qualitative studies, surveys are usually based upon data obtained from previous unstructured procedures such as participant observation. An interview guide is then developed from these data. Goetz and LeCompte[33] describe three kinds of survey interviews. The first is the *confirmation survey*, which is a structured interview (or questionnaire) that produces evidence to confirm earlier findings. This is, of course, a form of triangulation and helps establish the concurrent validity of the observational data previously collected. Such surveys are especially useful in large-scale studies where in-depth interviewing cannot be carried out for all subjects. Like all self-report data, however, confirmation survey data are sometimes inaccurate indicators of actual behavior. Therefore, findings should be corroborated by observational data.

Another form of survey interviewing used by ethnographers is the *participant construct* interview that is used to learn how informants structure their physical and social world. The result is a set of category systems used by the participant. For example, LeCompte asked kindergarten children to tell her all of the things they thought they and their teachers could do in kindergarten.[34] From their responses she developed a typology of the children's perceptions of student and teacher roles.

In some cases, *projective techniques* may be used in survey interviews.[35] This is appropriate where it is impossible to observe the participants reacting to the actual situation under study. A variety of stimuli such as photographs, drawings, or games can be used to elicit reactions or determine patterns of social

32. K. K. Newman, "Middle-aged Experienced Teachers' Perceptions of Their Career Development," *Dissertation Abstracts International* 39 (1978): 4885A–4886A.
33. See Goetz and LeCompte, *Ethnography and Qualitative Design.*
34. M. D. LeCompte, "The Civilizing of Children: How Young Children Learn to Become Students," *The Journal of Thought* 15, no. 3 (1980): 105–126.
35. Pelto and Pelto, *Anthropological Research.*

interaction that cannot be observed in the natural setting. For example, social interactions between children and abusive parents could be studied in this way.

Interviewing Rules for Qualitative Researchers

Most authors who discuss the use of interviews in qualitative research provide a list of suggestions or rules for conducting such interviews. The following list has been compiled from several sources.[36] Note that most of these rules also apply to interviews carried out in quantitative studies.

1. Frame the same question in different time dimensions. For example, in interviewing teachers about classroom management you could ask: How did you respond to open student defiance when you first started teaching? How do you now respond? How do you believe you will respond after you have gained another five years' experience?
2. Pose questions in language that is clear and meaningful to the subject.
3. During the exploratory phase of a study, qualitative researchers may use deliberately ambiguous questions to increase response variability and determine respondent meanings and interpretations without cueing the subject.
4. Avoid leading questions. However, in some cases a leading question may be asked that contains a deliberate assumption designed to provoke a subject reaction.
5. Ask questions that contain only a single idea.
6. Use open-ended questions as these elicit richer qualitative responses.
7. Effective probing is necessary to produce more complete information. Probes can be used for getting further elaboration, explanation, clarification, and completion of detail.
8. The interviewer should talk less than the respondent. As a rule, the less the interviewer talks, the more information is produced.
9. Save complex or controversial questions for the latter part of the interview after rapport has been established.
10. Pilot-test the interview in order to improve questions, identify kinds of probes needed, and develop a sequence that makes sense and maintains interest.
11. Use a conversational mode in the interview, that is, a mode similar to everyday conversation. This mode communicates empathy, encouragement, and understanding and elicits trust and a relaxed atmosphere.

36. See Goetz and LeCompte, *Ethnography and Qualitative Design*; M. Q. Patton, *Qualitative Evaluation Methods* (Beverly Hills, CA: Sage, 1980); and L. Measor, "Interviewing: A Strategy in Qualitative Research," in *Strategies of Educational Research: Qualitative Methods*, ed. R. G. Burgess (Philadelphia: Falmer, 1985).

Case Study

The case study, in its simplest form, involves an investigator who makes a detailed examination of a single subject or group or phenomenon. Until recently, this approach was rejected by many educational researchers as unscientific, mainly because of its lack of research controls. However, the increased acceptance of qualitative research methods such as educational ethnography and the use of participant observers has revived the case-study approach. In fact, some researchers consider case study, participant observation, and ethnography as essentially synonymous.[37] In any event, case studies often incorporate a variety of qualitative data-collection methods.

The case-study approach has had a long history in educational research and has also been used extensively in other areas of research such as clinical psychology and the study of individual differences. For example, much of the work of Sigmund Freud and Jean Piaget employed case studies.

Most case studies are based on the premise that a case can be located that is typical of many other cases, that is, the case is viewed as an example of a class of events or a group of individuals. Once such a case has been located, it follows that in-depth observations and collection of other data about the single case can provide insights into the class of events from which the case has been drawn. Of course, there is no way of knowing how typical the selected case really is, and it is therefore rather hazardous to draw any general conclusions from a single case study. However, this problem can be greatly reduced by multiple-case studies involving several replications of the single case study, as recommended by Robert Yin.[38] The main justification for case studies in quantitative research has been that they have the potential to generate rich subjective data that can aid in the development of theory and empirically testable hypotheses.[39] However, qualitative researchers regard the case study as an important research method in its own right, and believe that it need not be limited to generating hypotheses.

A case study requires the collection of very extensive data in order to produce an in-depth understanding of the entity being studied. Shallow case studies, some of which are still being done in education, have little chance of making any useful contribution to educational thinking. For example, a case study recently reported in the literature involved interviewing one teacher for less than 10 hours and observing in the teacher's classroom for two class periods. Information sources for an intensive case study include *public archival records* such as actuarial records, political and judicial reports, government documents, and media accounts; *private archival records* such as autobiographies,

37. L. M. Smith, "An Evolving Logic."
38. See R. K. Yin in the Annotated References at the end of this chapter.
39. See R. E. Stake, "The Case Study Method in Social Inquiry," *Educational Researcher* 7 (1978): 5–8, for an interesting philosophical article supporting the case-study method.

diaries, and letters; and *direct response data* such as questionnaires, and interviews that are usually administered by the researcher in order to obtain specific information, perceptions, and opinions that are relevant to the study.

Several kinds of case studies can be found in the social science literature. These include:

1. *Historical case studies of organizations.* These studies trace the development of an organization over time. Studies of experimental schools such as *Summerhill* are often of this kind.[40] This type of case study usually relies heavily upon interviews and documents.

2. *Observational case studies.* These studies usually focus on an organization, such as a school, or on some part of an organization, such as a classroom. A group of individuals who interact over a period of time is usually the focus of the study. Such studies are concerned with ongoing groups and generally use participant observation as the major data-collecting tool. A recent case study of a newly desegregated junior high school is an example of this method.[41] The authors were interested in determining the impact of the school on students' thinking about human differences related to race, social class, and gender. The study extended over three years and included observations in classrooms and other school settings, and interviews with students, teachers, and administrators. Because of the complexity of the school, case studies of this kind usually employ a variety of qualitative and quantitative methods over a long period of time.

3. *Oral histories.* These are first-person narratives that the researcher collects by extensive interviewing of a single individual. For example, a case study could be used to help understand an educational phenomenon like the one-room school or to trace the development of a program for handicapped children as seen by a teacher closely involved in this area over a period of 20 to 30 years.

4. *Situational analysis.* In this form of case study a particular event is studied from the viewpoint of all the major participants. For example, an act of student vandalism could be studied by interviewing the student involved, the student's parents, teachers, peers, the school principal, and the juvenile court judge. When all of these views are pulled together, they provide a depth of perception that can contribute significantly to understanding the event being studied.

5. *Clinical case study.* This approach is aimed at understanding a particular type of individual, such as a child with a specific learning disability. Such case studies usually employ clinical interviews and observations but may also involve testing and other forms of data collection. The usual goals are to better

40. A. S. Neill, *Summerhill* (New York: Hart, 1960).
41. See C. E. Sleeter and C. A. Grant, "Race, Class, and Gender in an Urban School: A Case Study," *Urban Education* 10, no. 1 (1985): 31–60.

understand the individual and the disability and identify possible treatments. Teachers also conduct clinical case studies. For example, a case study might be conducted by a teacher to determine why a given child is having difficulty with reading.[42]

VALIDITY OF QUALITATIVE METHODS

External Validity

The *external validity* of participant observation and other qualitative research methods, that is, the degree to which the findings can be generalized to the population from which the participants were drawn, has been frequently criticized.[43] Critics have pointed out that analysis of a few cases that are not randomly chosen from the target population leads to bias because of the unique characteristics of the cases chosen. The degree to which the sample is representative of the population from which the sample was drawn is called *population validity*, which is one aspect of external validity. If population validity cannot be established, as is often the case in qualitative research, then the investigator must be very cautious in generalizing his results. LeCompte and Goetz point out that information on the typicality of the phenomena being observed helps provide evidence of external validity in qualitative studies.[44] Designs that involve collecting data at several sites also provide such evidence.

Another threat to external validity found in many qualitative studies is called *experimenter effect*. This is the degree to which the biases or the expectations of the observer have led to distortions of the data. Because qualitative methods such as participant observation and interview are highly subjective, they are more subject to such biases than are most of the methods used by quantitative researchers. Denzin and other sociologists have recommended the use of "analytic induction" to deal with the problem of generalizability.[45] Analytic induction is the process of searching for propositions that apply to all cases of the problem under analysis. The steps in this process are:

1. A preliminary description or definition of the phenomenon to be explained is formulated.
2. A hypothetical explanation of that phenomenon is formulated.

42. For a recent example of a case study in education, see J. Raim and R. Adams, "The Case Study Approach to Understanding Learning Disabilities," *Journal of Learning Disabilities* 15 (1982): 116–118.
43. See chapter 15 for a discussion of external and internal validity.
44. LeCompte and Goetz, "Principles of Reliability and Validity."
45. See N. K. Denzin in the Annotated References at the end of this chapter.

3. One case is studied in light of the hypothesis, in order to determine whether or not the hypothesis fits the facts in that case.
4. If the hypothesis does not fit the facts, either the hypothesis is reformulated to fit the facts, or the phenomenon to be explained is redefined so that the negative case is excluded.
5. If the hypothesis does fit the facts, it is tested against additional cases. Practical certainty may be attained after a small number of confirming cases has been examined, but the discovery of one negative case disproves the explanation and requires a reformulation.
6. This procedure of examining cases, redefining the phenomenon, and reformulating the hypotheses is continued until a universal relationship is established, that is, one that fits all cases not excluded. During this process, each negative case calls for a redefinition to exclude the case or a reformulation of the hypothesis to fit the case.[46]

This is a very rigorous process that leads to strong evidence that the hypothesis, as finally reformulated, is generalizable. Its most serious limitation is that, while it can be used to study phenomena that either occur or do not occur, it is difficult to use in the study of continuous variables. In the social and behavioral sciences, most of the variables we study are continuous, that is, they are found in different degrees along a continuum.

Internal Validity

Qualitative research methods have also been criticized for weak internal validity, that is, the degree to which the research findings can be distorted by extraneous variables. *Internal validity* is an important consideration in all research. A number of threats to internal validity have been identified by researchers and are discussed in some detail in chapter 15. When a study is subject to internal validity threats it is difficult for the researcher to discriminate between results that indicate a true relationship and results that are artifacts of the research process. These threats apply both to quantitative and qualitative research.

Perhaps the most serious extraneous variables or biases, that is, internal validity threats, in qualitative research are *history, maturation, experimental mortality,* and *instrumentation.* History refers to extraneous variables external to the subjects that are present during the course of the study and distort the results. Maturation refers to changes in the subject that occur during the study. Experimental mortality refers to loss of subjects during the course of the study. All three of these threats become more serious as the length of the study

---

46. Adapted from W. S. Robinson, "The Logical Structure of Analytic Induction," *American Sociological Review* 16 (1951): 812–818.

increases. Because most qualitative studies extend over a long time period they are especially susceptible to these problems.

Instrumentation refers to errors or biases that are introduced when the instruments used to collect research data are thought to remain constant, but in fact change. As the researcher is the main instrument for collecting data in most qualitative studies, biases, changes in perception and subjectivity can all bring about changes in the "instrument," that is, the observer or interviewer. Changes in what is observed, and how it is interpreted, can be very serious threats to validity. Unless such changes are carefully recorded, which requires a great deal of insight on the part of the observer, data collected early in a study will not be comparable to data collected later.

Both Denzin and LeCompte and Goetz discuss the problems of external and internal validity in qualitative research at some length and should be referred to by the interested student.[47] They point out that many of the internal and external validity threats have a different meaning in the qualitative and quantitative paradigms. For example, experimental researchers try to control history (i.e., changes in the social group that occur during the course of the study) whereas qualitative researchers often study history as a focus of their research. Qualitative researchers often use somewhat different strategies to deal with internal and external validity threats than do quantitative researchers, and it is not entirely fair to measure the validity of qualitative research using the quantitative research yardstick.

WHEN IS QUALITATIVE RESEARCH MOST APPROPRIATE?

Many scientists who have studied qualitative and quantitative research methodologies have concluded that each paradigm is well suited for the study of certain kinds of problems. We will now consider some of the types of research questions in education that are appropriate for study with qualitative methods.

Qualitative Research Questions

In terms of broad research questions, Erickson, Florio, and Buschman suggest that qualitative methods are best at seeking answers to the following five questions:

1. What's happening in this field setting?
2. What do the happenings mean to the people involved in them?

47. See Denzin in the Annotated References at the end of this chapter, and LeCompte and Goetz, "Principles of Reliability and Validity."

3. What do people have to know in order to be able to do what they do in the setting?
4. How does what is happening here relate to what is happening in the wider social context of this setting?
5. How does the organization of what is happening here differ from that found in other places and times?[48]

The authors give several reasons why educational researchers need to address these questions. They point out that the most obvious aspects of everyday life in educational settings tend to become invisible because they are so habitual. These need to be rediscovered in order to understand the educational setting. Qualitative methods such as participant observation can provide the concrete detail needed for understanding. In much educational research we overlook the fact that events that appear the same may have distinctly different local meanings. Qualitative methods are probably the best means we have for discovering these local meanings.

These methods are also well suited to discover the relationship between a given educational setting and its immediate social context. For example, teacher behavior in the classroom is affected by what happens in the broader social systems such as the school, the district, and the community, and these systems must be taken into account when studying the local scene.

In looking beyond the local setting, the investigator can compare the way different activities and problems are handled in other places and other times. The perspective developed by such comparisons can help the researcher identify the genuine possibilities for change as well as the genuine constraints.

Qualitative Research Applications

Let us now look at some aspects of educational research for which qualitative methods seem especially appropriate:

1. *Theory development.* A major criticism of education is the dearth of educational theory. Even when we consider that much educational practice is supported by theory from other behavioral sciences such as psychology and sociology, much of what we do in education still has no theoretical basis whatsoever. Qualitative research methods such as long-term observation (both participant and nonparticipant) are especially effective in the development of grounded theory and could make major contributions to many areas of educational theory.

48. F. Erickson, S. Florio, and J. Buschman, *Field Work in Educational Research* (East Lansing: Michigan State University, Institute for Research on Teaching, 1980): ED 196 882.

2. *Defining important variables.* In many areas of education we have only a very sketchy understanding of the variables that relate to important educational outcomes. For example, we still know very little about the impact of different teacher behavior patterns and strategies upon student outcomes such as achievement even though quantitative researchers have given this area a great deal of attention over the past 20 years. Because of their emphasis upon holistic longitudinal approaches and efforts to maintain a nonjudgmental orientation, qualitative researchers have the potential for discovering new variables that have been overlooked by quantitative researchers.

3. *Hypothesis generation.* Qualitative methods such as nonparticipant observation, key-informant interviews, and case studies can be extremely valuable in helping researchers develop new ideas and hypotheses about their areas of interest. These methods can open up many new areas of investigation if researchers can rid themselves of preconceived notions.

4. *Organizational structures and problems.* Educational researchers have generally neglected the many social and organizational structures that are an important part of the educational scene. Qualitative methods have long been used by sociologists and anthropologists to study such phenomena. Until we better understand the total environment in which education takes place, our psychological studies are likely in many instances to produce puzzling and contradictory results.

5. *Studying new phenomena.* When new ideas, theoretical constructs, or behavioral syndromes emerge they are often poorly defined and not well understood. For example, suppose a new classification of handicapped children is tentatively identified. Qualitative research methods such as case study are probably the best means available to describe the new phenomenon and help develop an understanding of it. Often an in-depth study of one individual using observation and interview will give a far better understanding than will a shallow survey of 100 subjects.

These are but a few of the areas in education where qualitative studies can make an important contribution. For additional ideas and viewpoints see the Annotated References.

MISTAKES SOMETIMES MADE BY QUALITATIVE RESEARCHERS

1. Researchers attempt to use qualitative methods for which they are not adequately trained.
2. Depend entirely on participant observation rather than using methods triangulation.
3. Allow preconceived ideas and expectations to influence their observations.
4. Observe for much too short a time.

ANNOTATED REFERENCES

Bromley, D. B. *The Case-Study Method in Psychology and Related Disciplines.* New York: Wiley, 1986.

Focuses on concepts and procedures appropriate to case studies in psychology. The "quasi-judicial," nonexperimental method and its use in investigating individual cases is discussed. After giving an interview and a brief historical orientation to the case-study method, the main case study procedures and problems are discussed. Most chapters include cases selected to illustrate the various aspects of case-study methodology.

Burgess, R. G., ed. *Strategies of Educational Research: Qualitative Methods.* Philadelphia: Falmer, 1985.

Focuses specifically on the application of qualitative research methods to educational problems. Several chapters are especially useful, dealing with such topics as participant observation with pupils, key-informant interviewing with the teachers, and use of archives and other qualitative methods in the study of curriculum and educational policy.

Denzin, N. K. *The Research Act: A Theoretical Introduction to Sociological Methods,* 2nd ed. New York: McGraw-Hill, 1978.

Provides considerable insight into qualitative research methodology, much of which has roots in sociology. The chapters on naturalistic inquiry, participant observation, and nonreactive methods are especially useful.

Galton, M., and Delamont, S. "Speaking with Forked Tongue? Two Styles of Observation in the ORACLE Project." In *Field Methods in the Study of Education,* ed. R. G. Burgess. New York: Falmer, 1984, pp. 163–189.

Describes the use of highly structured observation and an ethnographic observation in a single large-scale study. The results from the two observational methods generally agreed. However, some problems were encountered in between-method triangulation, training the ethnographic observers, and in deciding how to merge the findings from the two paradigms.

Goetz, J. P., and LeCompte, M. D. *Ethnography and Qualitative Design in Educational Research.* Orlando, FL: Academic Press, 1984.

An excellent source for the graduate student who wants to learn more about qualitative research or is preparing to do a qualitative study. The characteristics of ethnographic research and its relationship to theory are discussed. Then the qualitative research process is described in order, starting with conceptualization and ending with analyses and interpretation of data.

Kirk, J., and Miller, M. L. *Reliability and Validity in Qualitative Research.* Beverly Hills, CA: Sage, 1986.

Concerned primarily with issues related to the scientific status of field data. The major focus is upon applying the psychometric concepts of reliability and validity to qualitative research. The authors provide a balanced discussion of qualitative and quantitative methods and make the case that the social sciences are fully as "scientific" as the physical sciences.

Lincoln, Y. S., and Guba, E. G. *Naturalistic Inquiry*. Beverly Hills, CA: Sage, 1985.

Concerned mainly with a theoretical and philosophical comparison of the positivistic and naturalistic research paradigms. The authors advocate the naturalistic model, disparaging quantitative research methodology. A good source for the student who is interested in exploring the merits of naturalistic inquiry.

Pollard, Andrew. "Opportunities and Difficulties of a Teacher-Ethnographer: A Personal Account." In *Field Methods in the Study of Education*, ed. R. G. Burgess. Philadelphia: Falmer Press, 1984, pp. 217–223.

Experiences of a participant observer in collecting qualitative research data while employed as a full-time teacher. The author discusses problems encountered and does so in an interesting narrative style. A useful chapter for teachers who contemplate using this method in their classrooms.

Spindler, G., ed. *Doing the Ethnography of Schooling*. New York: Holt, Rinehart and Winston, 1982.

Looks at the school from the viewpoint of the anthropologist. A variety of interesting qualitative studies are reported along with some theoretical and methodological chapters.

Van Maanen, J., ed. *Qualitative Methodology*. Beverly Hills, CA: Sage, 1983.

Focuses upon the use of qualitative methods in organizational research. The chapters on the ethnographic paradigm, triangulation, and studying organizational cultures will be of special interest to the student who wants to develop a better understanding of qualitative research.

Yin, R. K. *Case Study Research, Design and Methods*. Beverly Hills, CA: Sage, 1984.

An excellent source for the student who wants to conduct a case-study research project. The author's orientation, however, is quantitative, not qualitative. It is designed to serve as a guide to the investigator who is trying to use the case-study approach as a rigorous research method.

SELF-CHECK TEST

Supply the correct answer to each of the following questions. An answer key is provided on page 883.

1. Which of the following assumptions is usually considered basic to the qualitative research model?
   a. Variables related to a complex process may be studied independently.
   b. The researcher can function independently to a major degree.
   c. It is not possible to distinguish causes from effects.

    d. The impact of the researcher's values can be minimized through the use of sound research design.

2. For each of the following statements, indicate whether it is characteristic of the positivistic (P) or naturalistic (N) model:

    _____ a. After sufficient research has been conducted, the phenomena studied can be predicted at levels that exceed chance.

    _____ b. The researcher must try to study all elements present in the research setting.

    _____ c. Given sufficient research, every effect can be explained by a cause or causes that precede it in time.

    _____ d. The human observer is the primary data-gathering instrument.

3. Purposive sampling is a characteristic of qualitative research. This means that qualitative researchers

    a. establish the purpose of the study and omit subjects who don't fit.

    b. eliminate "outliers" from the sample.

    c. sample so as to obtain a wide range of subjects.

    d. select only nontypical subjects.

4. Qualitative researchers emphasize the development of "grounded" theory. This means

    a. the theory must be developed from the data.

    b. a firm groundwork of theory must be established before research can start.

    c. only subjects who are on the turf can develop theory.

    d. the theory must build upon the research design that has been selected.

5. The primary data-collection method in ethnographic research is

    a. content analyses of case histories.

    b. participant observation.

    c. objective tests (either written or oral).

    d. semistructured interview.

6. An important element in the value system that anthropologists consider essential to ethnographic research methodology is

    a. researchers must strive to separate themselves from the viewpoint of the group being studied.

    b. researchers must not be submerged in the big picture.

    c. researchers must focus on the few key elements related to their hypothesis.

    d. researchers must maintain a nonjudgmental orientation.

7. An important advantage of the ethnographic method is that

    a. it is highly efficient because only one observer is needed over a brief time span.

    b. it is more likely than other methods to lead to new insights and hypotheses.

    c. field notes are much easier to interpret than are quantitative research data.

    d. participant observation data collection used in this method are more objective and free of bias than are other forms of measurement.

8. In qualitative research, triangulation may be defined as

    a. the technique of using several kinds of data-collection instruments to study a single problem.

    b. the method of collecting different data from three samples of subjects.

    c. the method of focusing all investigation on a single dimension of the social scene.

    d. the method of classifying key informants on three critical dimensions.

9. An important difference between participant observation and nonparticipant observation is

    a. the participant observer is less obtrusive because he or she is part of the group.

    b. the nonparticipant observer is less likely to become emotionally involved in the research situation.

    c. the nonparticipant observer can usually get data more easily in sensitive areas such as the subjects' attitudes.

    d. the observations of the participant observer are much more sharply focused.

10. An important rule to follow in conducting key-informant interviews is
    a. key informants must be kept completely separate from the group being studied.
    b. key informants should be chosen who are as typical of the group as possible.
    c. persons who are more intelligent or mature than other group members lack insight and are poor key informants.
    d. choose key informants who are able to observe in situations not available to the researcher.

APPLICATION PROBLEMS

The following problems are designed to give you practice in applying significant concepts and procedures in the chapter. For feedback, you can compare your answers with the sample answers on pages 894–895.

1. The following is a brief narrative describing the methods used in a qualitative research project. What criticisms would a qualitative researcher probably make of these procedures?
   This study is concerned with the social structure of a fifth-grade class made up of the following racial and ethnic groups: 12 white, 8 black, 4 Hispanic, 2 oriental, and one Native American (Ute Indian). The researcher's first step was to state the following hypothesis: "There is no relationship between race and leadership status in the classroom." He then selected a random sample of 10 students to observe over a one-week period and designed an observation form in which he checked each selected student for the number of leadership remarks made by that student.
2. Evaluate the following participant observer study using the criteria given in this chapter:
   This study is to be carried out in an inner-city high school. It is aimed at studying teacher interactions with each other and with students in as many school-related situations as possible including faculty meetings, class meetings, and informal interaction in the cafeteria, teachers' lounge, on the playground, and in the halls. Two participant observers have been employed half-time as teachers in the school and will observe for one school year. No one in the school has been informed of the study. The two participant observers will be involved in complete participation as faculty members.
   Concurrent with the participant observations, two investigators would conduct survey interviews of all teachers and with a sample of students. Key-informant interviews would also be conducted at regular intervals with a group of key informants that includes teachers, students, and other school personnel.

SUGGESTION SHEET

If your last name starts with letters from Jab to Kee, please complete the Suggestion Sheet at the end of the book while the chapter is still fresh in your mind.

Part V

BASIC TYPES OF EDUCATIONAL RESEARCH

The following chapters present the major research designs used in quantitative research. Some of the topics are also relevant to qualitative research, notably the measurement tools used in survey and observational research and the issues involved in establishing causality when studying relationships between variables.

Some of the research designs allow for more rigorous investigation of causal relationships than do others. Rigor is not the only consideration, however, because the more rigorous designs call for a level of control of the research situation that is often impossible to achieve in educational research. Also, as control of the research situation increases in rigor, it usually becomes more difficult to generalize the findings to real-life situations. Thus, the selection of a research design typically involves a compromise among what is most rigorous, what is most natural, and what is most feasible.

11 THE METHODS AND TOOLS OF SURVEY RESEARCH

OVERVIEW

This introduction to survey research is the first of several chapters concerned with different types of quantitative educational research. In subsequent chapters you will be considering observational, historical, causal-comparative, correlational, and experimental research. You begin your study of survey research by considering the various types of knowledge that can be generated by analysis of survey data. Often surveys are used simply to collect information, such as the percentage of respondents who hold or do not hold a certain opinion; however, surveys can also be used to explore relationships between different variables. The main focus of the chapter is on the questionnaire and the interview as specific tools of survey research. You will be presented with specific techniques for preparing questionnaires and interview guides. Also, you will learn techniques for using them effectively in your research projects. Finally, because questionnaires and interviews are both aimed at gathering similar kinds of data, their relative advantages and disadvantages are compared so that you will be able to select the technique that is most appropriate for your project.

OBJECTIVES

After studying this chapter you should be able to:

1. If given survey data measuring different variables, determine whether the variables are related to each other in terms of time-bound or time-ordered association.
2. Compare cross-sectional and longitudinal surveys.
3. Define trend studies, cohort studies, and panel studies.
4. If given the objectives of a survey, write both closed-form and open-ended questionnaire items to measure them.
5. State the rules for constructing questionnaire items.
6. State the rules related to questionnaire format.
7. Write a letter of transmittal for a questionnaire survey using the guidelines recommended.
8. Describe procedures for dealing with nonrespondents after the initial letter of transmittal and after follow-up techniques have been tried.
9. Decide when it is appropriate to use the interview technique rather than a questionnaire.
10. Describe specific sources of error in interview studies that can be traced to predispositions of the respondent, the interviewer, and the interview procedures.
11. Give the rules for conducting interviews.
12. State the advantages and disadvantages of telephone interviewing.
13. Discuss the advantages of computer-assisted telephone interviewing (CATI).

14. If given the objectives of an interview study, develop an interview guide to gather data on these objectives.
15. State at least one advantage and one disadvantage of note taking and tape recording as data-collection methods in interviews.
16. State several procedures for facilitating effective communication between the interviewer and respondent.

INTRODUCTION

The Survey as a Form of Educational Research

Survey research is a distinctive research methodology that owes much of its recent development to the field of sociology. Considered as a method of systematic data collection, though, the survey has a long historical tradition. As far back as the time of the ancient Egyptians, population counts and surveys of crop production were conducted for various purposes, including taxation. The contribution of twentieth-century sociologists such as Lazarsfeld, Hyman, and Stouffer was to link instruments of data collection (e.g., questionnaires and interviews) to a logic and to statistical procedures for analyzing these kinds of data.

The information collected by surveys can be of various types. The Gallup poll is probably the best-known survey used to sample public opinion. Market researchers employ surveys to evaluate product acceptance and use. Among the scientific disciplines, researchers in economics, anthropology, psychology, and public health make frequent use of surveys to collect information relevant to interests and problems in their fields.

Studies involving surveys account for a substantial proportion of the research done in the field of education. For example, Lazarsfeld and Sieber did a content analysis of educational research appearing in 40 journals in 1964 and found that about a third of them involved use of the survey method.[1] A wide range of educational problems can be investigated in survey research, as illustrated by this list of recent studies:

Laminack, Lester L., and Long, Betty M. "What Makes a Teacher Effective—Insight from Preservice Teachers." *Clearing House* 58, no. 6 (1985): 268–269.

Turner, Lynn. "The Impact of Educational Reform Legislation on the Instructional Role of ETSSC Principals." *Catalyst for Change* 15, no. 2 (1986): 25–30.

1. Paul F. Lazarsfeld and Sam D. Sieber, *Organizing Educational Research* (Englewood Cliffs, NJ: Prentice-Hall, 1964).

Gorton, Richard A., and Burns, James. "Faculty Meetings: What Do Teachers Really Think of Them?" *Clearing House* 59, no. 1 (1985): 30–32.

El Tom, M. E. A. "Aspects of Mathematics Education in Some Third World Universities." *Educational Studies in Mathematics* 17, no. 2 (1986): 165–191.

Shadden, Barbara B., and Raiford, Carolyn A. "Communication Education and the Elderly: Perceptions of Knowledge and Interest in Further Learning." *Communication Education* 35, no. 1 (1986): 23–31.

Local school districts sometimes need to do surveys. The comprehensive **school survey** explores and evaluates many aspects of the school system, such as buildings, maintenance, administrative procedures, financial support and procedures, teaching staff, learning objectives, curriculum, and teaching methods. Such surveys are usually carried out by a team of visiting specialists from universities and other school systems. Another type of survey, the school census, is conducted so that administrators can predict the educational needs their schools will be called upon to meet in future years. Local surveys are also used for the purposes of internal evaluation and improvement.

In performing a research project for completion of an advanced degree, you might well consider employing the survey approach to investigate a particular educational problem. However, you should be aware that surveys involve considerably more than administering a questionnaire to describe "what is." It is unfortunate but true that many research workers in education hold surveys in low esteem because they believe that surveys are limited to description.[2] In fact, though, survey research utilizes a variety of instruments and methods to study relationships, effects of treatments, longitudinal changes, and comparisons between groups. In this chapter we discuss the basic design in survey research, the cross-sectional survey, as well as the principal survey tools: the mailed questionnaire, face-to-face interview, and telephone interview. Although this chapter will introduce you to survey research, it will not provide all of the information needed to plan and conduct an effective survey. However, the Annotated References include many excellent sources for the student who wants to conduct a survey study.

Data-Collection Tools in Surveys

Data-collection tools are used in survey research to obtain *standardized* information from all subjects in the sample. If you wish to determine your subjects' socioeconomic status, for example, you must administer the same instrument to all subjects. You cannot determine the socioeconomic status of half the sample

---

2. Surveys have also been criticized on philosophical and technical grounds. See D. A. deVaus in the Annotated References at the end of this chapter for a brief review of these criticisms.

using one set of questions and then change questions to collect the same information for the remaining sample. Also, the conditions of administration must be as similar as possible for each subject in the sample.

The information collected by survey instruments is assumed to be quantifiable. In the case of multiple-choice questionnaire items, the information is quantified at the time it is collected. If open-ended questions are used, the "open-ended" information that is obtained must be codified so that it can be analyzed and reported quantitatively.

The questionnaire and individual interview are the most common instruments for data collection in survey research. Accordingly, detailed steps in constructing and administering questionnaires and interview schedules are presented in this chapter. However, you should be aware of the other methods that can be used to collect survey information. The telephone interview is one such method, and it has important advantages that we will discuss later in this chapter.

Another technique for collecting survey information is to examine records. For example, students' files often contain much information of interest to the researcher: parents' ages, income, occupations, marital status, the student's school attendance, course grades, extracurricular activities. Examination of records has the advantage of being relatively complete and quick, since all the relevant information is usually stored in one location. Of course, you should be sensitive to the issue of invasion of privacy if this technique is used. Clearance from all involved groups should be obtained before proceeding to examine records. Depending on the situation, these groups may include the research subjects, the subjects' parents, and the administrators who have compiled the records.

The Cross-Sectional Survey

In the **cross-sectional survey,** standardized information is collected from a sample drawn from a predetermined population. (If information is collected from the entire population, the survey is called a **census.**) As we discussed in chapter 6, the sampling techniques most commonly used in educational surveys are simple random, stratified, or cluster sampling. Another basic feature of the cross-sectional survey is that the information is collected at one point in time (although the actual time required to complete the survey may be one day to a month or more).

Survey data from a cross-sectional survey can be analyzed by a variety of methods. The particular method or methods that you select will depend on the types of inferences you wish to make from your data.

Descriptions of Single Variables

The simplest use to which survey data can be put is a description of how the total sample has distributed itself on the response alternatives for a single questionnaire item. These are sometimes called the "marginal tabulations." For example, newspapers often report the result of public-opinion polls in terms of marginal tabulations; 50 percent of the sample were in favor of a particular governmental policy, 30 percent disagreed with it, and 20 percent were unsure or had no opinion.

Survey research in education often yields this type of normative description. As an illustration, we may consider a study by W. G. Trenfield that was designed to investigate the degree of interest of high school students in participating in adult civic activities.[3] A Likert-type scale of 30 items, each describing a different civic activity, was administered to a sample of 300 students randomly drawn from a population of approximately 4,000 high school students in a Texas school district. Students were asked to describe their degree of interest in participating in each activity on a 5-point scale. In the data analysis, the mean score of the entire sample on each attitude item was determined. This form of data analysis provides an interesting description of students' civic interests. We find, for instance, that these students are most likely to express their civic interest by voting in national elections and by signing a petition to be presented to a public official. They are least likely to express interest in running for public office and in attending night classes to improve their ability as a citizen.

Descriptions of this type may provide important leads in identifying needed emphases and changes in school curricula. Also, we should note that since proper sampling procedures were employed, Trenfield was able to generalize his descriptive findings from the sample to the population from which they were drawn.

Exploring Relationships

In addition to their value for determining the distribution of a sample on a single variable, surveys can be used to explore relationships between two or more variables. Students who are aware of the possibilities for investigating relationships in their survey data will make a more substantial research contribution than students who limit their data analysis to single variable descriptions.

Questionnaire items may refer to past, present, or future phenomena. If

3. W. G. Trenfield, "An Analysis of the Relationships Between Selected Factors and the Civic Interests of High-School Students," *Journal of Educational Research* 58 (1965): 460–462.

you study relationships between questionnaire items that refer to the same point in time, you are engaging in what is known as **"time-bound association."** If the items can be temporally ordered relative to each other, then the data analysis is referred to as **"time-ordered association."**

For example, suppose we wanted to study the relationship between the school-related interests and vocational interests of high school seniors. A questionnaire dealing with these two areas of interest could be administered to a sample of high school seniors and the relationships could be determined by computing correlation coefficients. Since the interest scores in both areas would be measures of the student's interests at a single point in time, namely the time when the questionnaire was administered, the results would be a time-bound association. However, suppose a similar survey were carried out with a sample of high school graduates who were asked to report their current vocational interests and recall what their school-related interests *had been* during their senior year. This questionnaire would provide time-ordered data since the person's school-related interests were reported for a different time than were the vocational interests even though all data were collected at a single point in time.

If survey data are time orderable, then hypotheses with cause-and-effect *implications* can be tested. For example, A. Huettig and J. M. Newell used the survey method to study whether amount of training in modern mathematics would result in more positive attitudes toward this subject. A sample of 115 elementary school teachers were administered a questionnaire designed to collect information about their teaching experience and attitudes about modern mathematics. They responded to 31 Likert-type attitude statements, and the data were analyzed in terms of whether 60 percent or more of each subgroup had a positive or negative attitude on each item. The hypothesis was considered confirmed because it was found that teachers with more training in modern mathematics were likely to respond favorably to more attitude items than teachers with little or no training.[4]

Although surveys of this type can identify *possible* cause-and-effect relationships, it would be erroneous to conclude from these data alone that training in modern mathematics *results in, leads to,* and *causes* these more favorable attitudes. Only an experiment with appropriate controls can determine with a high degree of certainty that the relationship between these two variables is causal. In survey research, though, there is a strategy that can be used to strengthen our confidence that two variables that are correlated with each other (such as amount of training and positiveness of attitudes toward modern mathematics) are also causally related. This strategy consists of attempting to

4. See A. Huettig and J. M. Newell, "Attitudes Toward Introduction of Modern Mathematics Program by Teachers with Large and Small Number of Years' Experience," *Arithmetic Teacher* 13 (February 1966): 125–130.

find another variable that could explain the relationship between the two original variables. If we cannot find a variable that explains away the relationship, then we can be more confident, though not certain, that the relationship is causal-temporal.

Another way to increase our confidence in time-ordered survey data is to replicate the survey with another sample drawn from the same population. If the findings of the second survey are about the same as the first, we can be much more confident that they represent a true relationship rather than one that occurred because of sampling and/or measurement errors.

We should note, however, that replication has no bearing on the problem of *direction* of causality; that is, we still have no way of knowing whether training in modern mathematics leads teachers to form more positive attitudes toward this subject (irrespective of their original attitudes) or whether teachers with positive attitudes toward modern mathematics seek out training in the subject. To answer these questions an experimental approach is necessary. The experimental design would involve measurement of attitudes before and after training of an experimental and control group.[5]

An investigator who uses cross-sectional survey data to explore time-ordered relationships must be aware of a serious source of error: Respondents may not remember accurately information related to a previous time. Such errors are likely to become larger as you delve farther into the past. Also, although factual information may be recalled accurately, the respondent's recollection of past attitudes or opinions may be distorted by present attitudes. For example, a teacher may be able to remember the number of black children she had in her class three years ago, but if her attitude toward black children has changed, she may not recall accurately her attitude of three years ago.

In summary, the value of survey research of the type carried out by Huettig and Newell is that while it cannot establish causal relationships with any degree of certainty, it can be used to explore a variety of relationships (e.g., between training and attitudes) in a relatively economical way. If important relationships are found, then questions about causality can be resolved by means of an experiment.

The Longitudinal Survey

In **longitudinal surveys,** data are collected at different points in time in order to study changes or explore time-ordered associations. This design is, of course, superior to the collection of time-ordered data in a cross-sectional survey because the data are not distorted by the faulty recollection of the respondents.

5. This type of research design is discussed in chapters 15 and 16.

Three longitudinal designs are commonly employed in survey research: trend studies, cohort studies, and panel studies. These differ mainly in terms of the respondents who are studied at different points in time.

In **trend studies** a given *general* population is sampled at each data-collection point. The same individuals are not surveyed, but each sample represents the same population. For example, if you wanted to study trends in the use of pocket calculators in the teaching of high school mathematics, you would select a sample each year from the current membership directory of a national mathematics teachers association. Each year you would send questionnaires to the sample selected and would compare responses from year to year. Although the population of mathematics teachers would change from year to year, and different mathematics teachers would be surveyed each year, if appropriate sampling procedures such as random sampling were used, the responses could be regarded as representative of the population of mathematics teachers from which the samples were drawn. You would then compare responses from year to year to determine what trends were present.[6]

In **cohort studies** a *specific* population is followed over a period of time. Trend studies sample general populations such as high school students or voters in school bond elections, which are constantly changing in terms of the specific individuals who are members of the population. In cohort studies, however, a specific population such as members of the 1985 graduating class at Stanford University is sampled throughout the course of the survey. Suppose, for example, we wanted to study the yearly vocational progress of all elementary school teachers who were granted California teaching certificates in 1987. We would list the names of all members of this population and at each data collection point would randomly select a sample from this list. Thus, although the population would remain the same, different individuals would be sampled each year to determine vocational progress.

In **panel studies** the investigator selects a sample at the outset of the study and then at each subsequent data-collection point the same individuals are surveyed. Because panel studies follow the same individuals over time, you can note changes in specific individuals and can therefore explore possible reasons why these individuals have changed. Such individual changes cannot be explored in trend or cohort studies since different individuals make up the sample at each data-collection point.

Loss of subjects is a serious problem in panel studies, especially if the study extends over a long period of time. For example, in one large-scale panel study that followed a national sample of twelfth-grade students into adulthood, a response rate of 61.9 percent was obtained for the one-year follow-up, 37.9

6. The National Assessment of Educational Progress is an example of a major trend study. For a description of this study, see Frank B. Womer and Wayne H. Martin, "The National Assessment of Educational Progress," *Studies in Educational Evaluation* 5 (1979): 27–37.

percent after 5 years and 27.9 percent after 11 years. This study used a variety of procedures, including an annual newsletter to keep track of subjects, and sent four mailings at each follow-up period.[7]

Not only does the number of subjects become smaller, but the remaining subjects may be a biased sample because those who drop out are likely to be different from those who continue to cooperate in the study. In the aforementioned example, respondents to the 11-year follow-up were as much as one-half of a standard deviation higher in general academic aptitude than nonrespondents, reflecting a very serious bias.

Many trend and cohort studies are carried out using earlier data collected by other researchers. For example, if a survey of the vocational interests of seniors in Chicago high schools had been carried out in 1978, another researcher could collect comparable data in 1988 and compare the two sets of data in a trend study. In some areas of education such as vocabulary, mastery of number facts, or attendance, you may be able to locate several studies that have collected comparable data at different points in time. Such data, when combined with current data, can provide insights into an important educational trend. Recent investigations have used this approach to study the downward trend in achievement in the public schools.

In conducting replications of this type, try to use the same questions and format as in the earlier surveys. There is some evidence and much practical experience to indicate that small changes in question wording can produce large effects on answers.[8]

STEPS IN CONDUCTING A QUESTIONNAIRE SURVEY

With careful planning and sound methodology, the mailed questionnaire can be a very valuable research tool in education. The next few pages will introduce you to the major steps that must be taken to carry out a successful questionnaire survey. These include: (1) **defining objectives,** (2) **selecting a sample,** (3) **writing items,** (4) **constructing the questionnaire,** (5) **pretesting,** (6) **preparing a letter of transmittal,** and (7) **sending out your questionnaire and follow-ups.** Analysis of the results and preparing the research report are covered in later chapters.

Although this section can give you a basic grasp of the survey research process, it cannot give you the in-depth knowledge necessary to conduct high-quality surveys. The Annotated References at the end of this chapter

7. Lauress L. Wise, "The Fight Against Attrition in Longitudinal Research" (paper presented at the annual meeting of the American Educational Research Association, New York, 4–8, April 1977).
8. For more information on this topic, see Robin M. Hogarth, ed., *Question Framing and Response Consistency* (San Francisco: Jossey-Bass, 1982).

include several excellent sources for the student who wants to develop a better understanding of survey research.

Defining the Questionnaire Objectives

The first step in carrying out a satisfactory questionnaire study is to define your problem and list specific objectives to be achieved or hypotheses to be tested, by the questionnaire.[9] It is not uncommon for graduate students to develop a questionnaire before they have a clear understanding of what they hope to obtain from the results. Unless you are able to state specifically and in detail what information you need, what you will do with this information after you get it, and how each item on the questionnaire contributes to meeting your specific objectives, you have not thought through your problem sufficiently.

Students often start with a broad topic such as "education of handicapped children," which must be focused much more sharply before it can form the basis for a satisfactory survey. DeVaus (see the Annotated References) has suggested five questions that can help focus your survey topic:

1. What is the time frame of your interest? Are you interested in current practices, or do you want to study trends in handicapped education over a period of years?
2. What is the geographical location of your interest? Do you want to study handicapped education in a given state or region, in the United States as a whole, or do you want to compare the status of handicapped education in different countries?
3. Are you interested in a broad descriptive study or do you want to specify or compare different subgroups? For example, will you focus on specific subgroups of handicapped children?
4. What *aspect* of your topic do you want to study? Are you interested in effective teaching strategies, legal constraints, cost, training of teachers, class size or some other variable as it relates to handicapped education?
5. How *abstract* is your interest? For example, are you interested in reporting facts or do you want to interpret the facts, relate the facts to a broad social context, or develop theory from the facts?

In preparing your objectives or hypotheses you should keep in mind the methods of data analysis that you will apply to the returned questionnaires. Suppose that you are interested in surveying the extent of usage of ability grouping in the schools of your state. The first objective of your study might be to determine the percentage of schools in the state that are using some form of

---

9. See Patricia Labaw in the "Questionnaires" section in the Annotated References for a discussion of the importance of hypotheses in survey research.

ability grouping. Therefore, you should include items in the questionnaire that will elicit reliable information from each school regarding its use of ability-grouping systems. Of course, the objectives of your study need not be limited to describing the current situation in the schools. You might consider surveying your sample on such questions as: how administrators of schools with ability grouping think their grouping practices can be improved, whether administrators of schools without ability grouping have previously tried to institute an ability-grouping system, and how the community has reacted to the idea of ability grouping in its schools.

In our discussion of the cross-sectional survey, we pointed out that survey data can be used to achieve objectives other than description of how the responses of the total sample are distributed on each questionnaire item. In a survey of ability-grouping practices, one objective may be to investigate differences between types of schools. For example, the survey data could be analyzed to determine whether urban schools are more or less likely than suburban or rural schools to have an ability-grouping system. The study of relationships between variables may also be an objective. As an illustration, one could investigate the relationship between the schools' achievement test scores and the presence or absence of an ability-grouping system. As we discussed earlier in this chapter, it is possible to describe such relationships as instances of time-bound association, that is, no inference is made about a causal relationship between the two variables. However, the exploration of *possible* causal relationships can be an objective of your study if the data are time-orderable. For example, you may hypothesize that schools which send a large proportion of their students to college will be more likely to institute an ability-grouping system than schools in which the percentage of college-bound students is low. To test this hypothesis, data should be collected about presence or absence of an ability-grouping system in each school and the percentage of college-bound students in each school.[10]

To summarize, surveys can have a variety of objectives. These objectives need to be identified at the outset of the study, otherwise you will find it very difficult to make sound decisions regarding selection of a sample, construction of the questionnaire, and methods for analyzing the data.

Selecting a Sample

Once your objectives or hypotheses are clearly stated, you should identify the target population from which your sample will be selected. The most obvious consideration involved in selection of subjects of a questionnaire study is to get people who will be able to supply the information you want. Very often the

10. If such a study were to be done, the percentage of college-bound students should be based on data collected by the schools *prior* to the institution of an ability-grouping system.

group that will have the data you want is immediately apparent. But in some cases, if you do not have a thorough knowledge of the situation involved, you may send your questionnaire to a group of persons who do not have the desired information. For example, a graduate student seeking data on school financial policies sent questionnaires to principals of a large number of elementary schools. Many of the questionnaires returned were incomplete, and few specific facts of the sort wanted were obtained. This study failed because the trend in recent years has been for the superintendent and staff to handle most matters concerning school finance. Inasmuch as the principals who received the questionnaire had little specific knowledge concerning this topic, they were unable to supply the information requested on the questionnaire.

Salience of the questionnaire content to the respondents is not only necessary to obtain accurate information but also has a significant influence on the rate of response. A review of 181 surveys using questionnaires judged to be "salient," "possibly salient," or "nonsalient" to the respondents revealed that for the salient studies the return averaged 77 percent, as compared with 66 percent for those judged possibly salient and 42 percent for those judged nonsalient.[11]

Most questionnaire studies conducted in education are aimed at specific professional groups. Once you have established that the professional group selected actually has access to the information you wish to obtain, you can survey the entire group or you can select a sample from the population.[12] Many professional groups in education have special organizations or societies, and in some cases a random selection of names from the directory of organization members gives a satisfactory group. A list of the members of the population you want to sample is called a *sampling frame*. However, most available sampling frames do not contain *all* members of the population. There may be a tendency for the more competent members of the professional group to belong to the organization, thus leading you to select a biased sample, so use such sampling cautiously.

State public school directories are more satisfactory for selection of subjects because they list all persons involved in public education in the state and are usually up to date. When the population is very large, such as all elementary school teachers in the United States, and no complete name list is available, it is usually necessary to use a multistage procedure to obtain a random sample. The first stage in obtaining a nationwide sample could be to select randomly a specified number of school districts. Since most districts print rosters of their teachers, the next step would be to request a copy of the rosters from districts

---

11. See Heberlein and Baumgartner in the Annotated References at the end of this chapter.
12. A variety of sampling procedures is employed in survey research. These are briefly described in chapter 6. For more detailed information on sampling for survey research, see Annotated References at the end of this chapter.

selected in the first stage. A specified number of teachers could then be randomly selected by name from each roster.

As we have discussed previously, it is often desirable to obtain responses from several specific categories of persons within the professional group being sampled. For example, you may wish to compare responses dealing with use of pupil-centered instruction gathered from teachers with different amounts of professional experience. If this is your objective, then it is desirable to use stratified sampling in order to select subsamples of sufficient size from different levels of population.

If the data from different subsamples are to be combined at some stage of the analysis, the number of subjects selected from each subsample should be proportionate to the number of subjects from each subsample in the population. For example, suppose the population of elementary school teachers includes 78 percent women and 22 percent men; then, if we stratify by sex, the proportion of women and men in our sample should be 78 percent and 22 percent, respectively. We could also maintain the correct proportions in combining our data by selecting the same number of men and women in our sample by weighting the women's responses .78 and the men's responses .22. Finally, if the men's and women's responses were to be *compared* but *not combined*, it would not be necessary for the two subsamples to be proportionate.

Constructing Questionnaire Items

Many of the questionnaires that are received in the mail by principals, superintendents, and other educators appear to have been thrown together by the graduate student during the short break between lunch and a two o'clock class. This haphazard type of questionnaire has led many school administrators to develop negative attitudes about the questionnaire as a research approach. Some of the more harassed administrators deposit the questionnaires they receive in the wastebasket with little more than a quick glance. This attitude, of course, presents an obstacle that you must and can overcome by the careful construction and administration of your questionnaire. Each item on your questionnaire must be developed to measure a specific aspect of one of your objectives or hypotheses. You should be able to explain in detail *why* you are asking the question and *how* you will analyze the responses. Also, you should make an effort to frame your questions in language that respondents will understand. This is why we recommend identifying your target population *before* you start writing questions.

It is a good idea to make up dummy tables that show how the item-by-item results of your questionnaire will be reported. These tables can contain information such as planned data breakdowns, response categories, and titles. In fact, the dummy tables can be complete except for the results that you can quickly add after your analysis has been completed.

Questions may be of either the **closed form** in which the question permits only certain responses (such as a multiple-choice question), or the **open form** in which subjects make any response they wish in their own words (such as an essay question). Which form will be used is determined by the objective of the particular question. Little research on the relative merits of closed and open questions has been reported. What evidence is available suggests that the two formats produce very similar information.[13]

In some studies, the qualitative nature of the information sought makes it necessary to use open-form questions. Most researchers employ interviews rather than questionnaires to gather qualitative data. However, when you must use a mailed questionnaire with open-form questions, the response rate would probably be improved by using a variation in questionnaire methodology that was employed in a study by Yahya and Moore.[14] They developed a questionnaire that was aimed at collecting qualitative data using open-form questions requiring lengthy replies. Respondents were sent a blank audio cassette along with the questionnaire, and asked to record their responses on the tape. Using four follow-ups, a 97 percent response rate was achieved. Reactions to taping their answers were solicited from the respondents. Respondents indicated that: (1) taping saved time, (2) it was useful for gathering large amounts of data, (3) they were more at ease in disclosing information, and (4) they felt the method was efficient and encouraged response. It appears that this method has some of the advantages of the interview for collecting qualitative data with open-form questions and yet would be less costly, especially if respondents were sampled over a wide geographical area. Obviously, respondents must have a cassette recorder available to them. However, recorders are used so widely in education that this would not be a problem for most surveys.

Generally, though, you should design the questions in closed form so that quantification and analysis of the results may be carried out efficiently. Let us suppose you wish to know the size of the teacher's home town so that you can compare teachers from different-sized towns in terms of interests and vocational goals. There are several ways that this question could be asked. Perhaps the poorest technique would be to ask, "What is your home town?" This question requires that you be able to read the person's reply and look it up in an atlas to determine the population. A technique that would be somewhat better would be to ask, "What is the population of your home town?" In this case you could classify the responses into population categories such as those used by the U.S. Census Bureau. A still better means of obtaining this information would be to ask, "What is the population of your home town? (Check one.)"

13. See Norman M. Bradburn, "Question-Wording Effects in Surveys," in *Question Framing and Response Consistency*, ed. Robin M. Hogarth (San Francisco: Jossey-Bass, 1982).

14. Ismail B. Yahya and Gary E. Moore, *On Research Methodology: The Cassette Tape as a Data Collection Medium* (paper presented at the Southern Research Conference in Agricultural Education, Mobile, AL, March 1985). ED 262 098.

_____ rural, unincorporated
_____ incorporated, under 1000
_____ 1,000 to 2,500
_____ 2,500 to 5,000
_____ 5,000 to 10,000
_____ 10,000 to 50,000
_____ 50,000 to 250,000
_____ over 250,000

This latter technique would provide you with the information you want in immediately usable form, thus requiring less effort on your part, while requiring no more effort by your subjects.

Perhaps the best method of determining the multiple-choice categories to use in closed questions is to ask the question in essay form of a small number of respondents, and then use their answers to develop the categories for the multiple-choice item that will be included in the final form of the questionnaire. In multiple-choice areas where a certain number of unexpected responses might occur, an "other" choice can be used along with a space for explanation. For example, suppose that you are interested in provisions made for gifted pupils in elementary schools. First, you could ask a small number of respondents the question "How are gifted pupils in your school identified and what provisions are made for them? Please be specific and indicate the extent to which each technique was employed during the past school year." Examination of the respondents' answers will probably suggest a limited number of categories which can be incorporated into multiple-choice items, for example:

1. Do you have a systematic program for identifying gifted children in your school?_____ _____If yes, what means of identification do you use?   yes   no
   _____ a. Group intelligence test
   _____ b. Individual intelligence test
   _____ c. Achievement battery
   _____ d. Aptitude battery
   _____ e. Teacher ratings
   _____ f. Other (specify)_____
   _____

2. What provisions were made for gifted pupils in your school during the past school year? (Check appropriate answers.)
   _____ a. Acceleration (grade skipping)
   _____ b. Ungraded program
   _____ c. Ability grouping
   _____ d. Enrichment
   _____ e. Special classes
   _____ f. Other (specify)_____
   _____

Depending on the specific objectives of the questionnaire, other questions could be added concerned with such matters as the number of pupils at each grade level who skipped a grade, the number of pupils in special classes, the criteria for establishing ability-grouped sections, and others.

In constructing questionnaire items, avoid, whenever possible, questions that may in some way be psychologically threatening to the person answering. For example, a questionnaire sent to school principals concerning the morale of teachers at their schools would be threatening to some principals because low morale suggests that the principal is failing in part of his or her job. When receiving a questionnaire containing threatening items, a person usually does not return it. If one does return it, little confidence can be placed in the accuracy of the reply because of the person's ego involvement in the situation.

Many of the rules for constructing questionnaire items are similar to rules for constructing items for objective tests that are found in most textbooks in educational measurement. Among these are the following:

1. Clarity is essential; ambiguity must be avoided. If your results are to be valid an item must mean the same thing to all respondents. For example, terms like "several," "most," and "usually" have no precise meaning and should be avoided. In his study of respondents' interpretation of questionnaire items, William Belson obtained 28 different interpretations of the word "usually." Only 60 percent of the interpretations reflected the approximate intent of the investigator.[15]

2. Short items are preferable to long items because short items are easier to understand. Avoid questions that are unnecessarily detailed.

3. Negative items should be avoided as they are misread by many respondents; that is, the negative word is overlooked, resulting in the respondent giving an answer that is opposite to the person's real opinion.

4. Avoid "double-barreled" items, which require the subject to respond to two separate ideas with a single answer. An item such as "Although labor unions are desirable in most fields, they have no place in the teaching profession" cannot be answered with the usual closed-question format (such as strongly agree, agree, no opinion, disagree, strongly disagree) by a person who disagrees with one part of the item and agrees with the other part.

5. Do not use technical terms, jargon, or "big words" that some respondents may not understand. Remember, clarity is especially important in questionnaires since the respondent is usually reached by mail and has no one available to explain unclear items.

6. When a general and a related specific question are to be asked together, it is preferable to ask the general question first. If the specific question is asked

15. See Belson in the Annotated References at the end of this chapter.

first, it tends to narrow the focus of the following general question and to change responses to the general question.[16]

7. Finally, it is very important that an effort be made to avoid biased or leading questions. If the subject is given hints as to the type of answer you would most prefer, there is some tendency to give you what you want. This tendency is especially strong when the letter of transmittal that accompanies the questionnaire has been signed by someone that the subject is eager to please.

Questionnaire Format

The questionnaire and cover letter are the main sources of information that the subject will refer to in deciding whether or not to complete your questionnaire. The following rules of questionnaire format have been developed from experience and research in this field and should be considered carefully.[17]

1. Make the questionnaire attractive. This can often be achieved by using colored ink or colored paper, by laying out the front page in an artistic manner, by careful composition and use of white space, and by using a high-quality reproduction method such as laser printing.
2. Organize and lay out questions so the questionnaire is as easy to complete as possible.
3. Number the questionnaire items and pages.
4. Put name and address of person to whom form should be returned at beginning and end of questionnaire even if a self-addressed envelope is included.
5. Include brief, clear instructions, printed in bold type.
6. Use examples before any items that might be confusing or difficult to understand.
7. Organize the questionnaire in some logical sequence. For example, you may decide to group together related items or those that use the same response options. If you ask time-ordered questions, such as respondents' employment history, follow chronological order.
8. When moving to a new topic, include a transitional sentence to help respondents switch their trains of thought.
9. Begin with a few interesting and nonthreatening items. *Do not* start the questionnaire with an open-form item that requires considerable writing.
10. Do not put important items at the end of a long questionnaire.
11. Put threatening or difficult questions near the end of the questionnaire.

---

16. See Howard Schuman and S. Presser, *Questions and Answers in Attitude Surveys: Experiments on Question Form, Wording, and Context* (New York: Academic Press, 1981).
17. See Berdie and Anderson in the Annotated References at the end of this chapter.

12. Avoid using the words "questionnaire" or "checklist" on your form. Many persons are prejudiced against these words.

13. Include enough information in the questionnaire so that items are meaningful to the respondent. Items that are interesting and clearly relevant to the study will increase response rate. Length also has a small effect on response rate, so the questionnaire should be as short as possible consistent with the objectives of the study. A regression analysis of response rates obtained in 98 questionnaire studies showed that, on average, each page added to a questionnaire reduced the number of responses by about 0.5 percent.[18]

Attitude Measurement in Questionnaires

Most questionnaires deal with factual material, and in many cases each item is analyzed separately to provide a specific bit of information that contributes to the overall picture that you are attempting to obtain. Thus, it is possible to look upon the questionnaire as a collection of one-item tests. The use of a one-item test is quite satisfactory when you are seeking out a specific fact, such as teacher salary, number of baseball bats owned by the physical education department, or number of students failing algebra. When questions get into the area of attitude and opinion, however, the one-item test approach is extremely unreliable. A questionnaire dealing with attitudes must generally be constructed as an attitude scale and must use a number of items (usually at least 10) in order to obtain a reasonable picture of the attitude concerned.[19]

If you are planning to collect information about attitudes, first search the literature to determine whether a scale suitable for your purposes has already been constructed.[20] If a suitable scale is not available, you will need to develop one. Likert scales are probably the most common types of attitude scales constructed. If you develop an attitude scale for your survey project, it should be pretested in order to collect reliability and validity evidence. Also, you should investigate in your pretest whether the sample of subjects has sufficient knowledge and understanding to express a meaningful opinion about a particular topic. For example, you might want to learn the attitudes of a sample of teachers or administrators toward some of the newer developments in education, such as criterion-referenced evaluation, performance-based teacher education, and mainstreaming. If a sizable proportion of the sample is not adequately familiar with these developments, the attitude responses will be of questionable value.

One method of dealing with subjects who are not familiar with a particular topic is to include a "no opinion" category as one of the response alternatives for

---

18. See Heberlein and Baumgartner in Annotated References at the end of this chapter.
19. A discussion of the attitude scale as a type of standardized test can be found in chapter 8.
20. See the Annotated References for chapter 8.

each attitude item. The disadvantage of this method is that subjects with little or no information about a particular topic will often still express an opinion in order to conceal their ignorance or because they feel social or professional pressure to express an opinion. This point is illustrated by an interesting study dealing with interview surveys.[21] A total of 625 respondents in three Iowa urban communities were interviewed about their attitudes regarding nine persons (e.g., Barry Goldwater, John F. Kennedy) and seven organizations (e.g., CORE, John Birch Society). The respondents could express a favorable or unfavorable attitude on six Likert-type categories, or they could use a seventh category to express no knowledge of a particular person or organization. To determine whether respondents would express an attitude toward an organization about which they were uninformed, the interviewers asked for their opinion of a nonexistent organization called the League for Linear Programs. To their surprise the interviewers found that 10 percent of the sample expressed a favorable or unfavorable attitude toward this organization about which it was impossible for them to have any knowledge! It was further found that this same 10 percent of the sample were also more likely to express attitudes toward the other organizations and persons rather than check the "don't know" category. They also were more likely to express favorable attitudes and to have less formal education than the rest of the sample.

The implication of these findings is that the respondents' knowledge and expertise is an important factor in interpreting attitude data. Therefore, when planning a questionnaire survey involving attitude measurement you should investigate respondents' familiarity with each attitude object covered in the survey. One technique for doing this is to administer an information test to a small sample of respondents similar to those to be queried in the main survey, to determine whether they are capable of expressing an informed opinion about the persons, organizations, or educational practices mentioned in the attitude or opinion items. Another strategy often used is to include several information questions at the beginning of an attitude questionnaire to screen out respondents who display little or no knowledge of the attitude object.

Effect of Anonymity on Questionnaire Response

In most educational studies, respondents are asked to identify themselves. Anonymity is sometimes called for if data of a personal nature or data that may be threatening to the individual are requested. A questionnaire dealing with sexual behavior, for example, may receive more honest responses if the subject remains anonymous.

The anonymous questionnaire poses many research problems. Follow-ups

21. Irving L. Allen, "Detecting Respondents Who Fake and Confuse Information About Question Areas on Surveys," *Journal of Applied Psychology* 50, no. 6 (1966): 523–528.

are difficult and inefficient because nonresponding individuals cannot be identified. Furthermore, you may not be able to make some of the statistical breakdowns of the group that may be desirable. For example, in a study of teacher-principal relationships, you may want to divide the respondents into men and women teachers, married and unmarried teachers, and teachers with different amounts of experience, and then compare the responses of these different groups. In the anonymous questionnaire, breakdowns of this sort that were not anticipated and provided for in the questionnaire cannot be made. Often the desirability of analyzing certain subgroups separately is not apparent until the data are collected.

The essential question that must be answered, however, is whether anonymity is necessary to get accurate replies. The research on this problem suggests that the need for assuring anonymity varies from one research situation to another and that it is influenced by such variables as respondent's age and sex and the content of the questionnaire. In a study of attitudes toward religion, Francis randomly assigned 300 ten- and eleven-year-old children to three groups.[22] All subjects were administered an attitude scale that included a lie detection scale. One group was instructed to write their names on the front page, another group was told to write their initials in the top right corner of the first page and then fold over the corner, while a third group was instructed specifically not to write their names. All subjects were told that their replies would be confidential and that no one at either school would read them. Differences between the groups on both the attitude scale and the lie scale were very small, none approaching significance.

Because attitude toward religion is a sensitive topic, this study suggests that anonymity is not as important as some researchers have suggested. Anonymity has been found to affect responses in other studies, however. Therefore the safest approach is to conduct a small-scale pilot study that closely duplicates the procedures to be used in the main study and to compare subject responses under anonymous versus identified conditions. The results can then be used to decide whether anonymity is necessary for the specific study to be conducted.

If a pilot study cannot be conducted, the factors to be considered in deciding whether identification is to be asked for are the importance of identification in the analysis of results, the level of maturity of the respondents, the degree to which questions involve answers that the respondent might be reluctant to give if he or she is identified, the probable effect of anonymity on the number of returns, and the procedures that can be used in the analysis of results.

22. Leslie Francis, "Anonymity and Attitude Scores Among Ten- and Eleven-Year-Old Children," *Journal of Experimental Education* 49 (1981): 44–76.

Pretesting the Questionnaire

In addition to the preliminary check that you make of your questions in order to locate ambiguities, you should carry out a thorough pretest of your questionnaire before using it in your study. For the pretest you should select a sample of individuals from a population similar to that from which you plan to draw your research subjects. For example, if you were concerned with mechanical aids used for teaching foreign languages in California high schools, you could pretest your questionnaire using a sample of foreign-language teachers employed in another state. The pretest form of the questionnaire should provide space for the respondents to make comments about the questionnaire itself so they may indicate whether some questions seem ambiguous to them, whether provisions should be made for certain responses that are not included in the questionnaire, and other points that can lead to improving the instrument.

A useful pretesting strategy was proposed by William Belson. Respondents are asked to repeat their understanding of the meaning of the question in their own words. Questions can then be revised and retested until they are understood by all or most members of the pretest sample.[23] Except for changes required to collect pretest feedback, the techniques for administering the questionnaire during the pretest should be essentially the same as planned for the main study. When there is some doubt as to which of two questions or two approaches might be most useful, try both on portions of the pretest sample. The number of cases in the pretest sample need not be large. If the subjects are taken from a well-defined professional group, such as school superintendents, as few as 20 cases will often be sufficient. For more heterogeneous groups, such as persons paying property taxes or parents with one or more children in elementary school, a larger pretest group is advisable.

When the pretest results are in, first check the percentage of replies obtained. Educational studies generally can be expected to yield a higher percentage of replies than questionnaires sent to random samples of the general population because the educational questionnaire usually aims at a reasonably homogeneous group, and this makes it possible to prepare an appeal to the group for cooperation, which is more likely to be successful. If, in checking the percentage of replies, you have received less than 75 percent of the pretest sample, you will probably need to make major changes in the questionnaire or in the procedures for administering it. The next step is to read the subjects' comments concerning the questionnaire. These comments often give specific information on how the questionnaire can be improved. Then, check the responses item by item. If you find items that are often left blank or answered in

---

23. William A. Belson, "Respondent Understanding of Survey Questions," *Polls* 3 (1968): 1–13.

ways that you did not predict, the item was probably misinterpreted by some of the subjects.

You are now able to do a brief analysis of the pretest results. This will give you a chance to determine whether the methods you have planned to use for summarizing and quantifying the data will work satisfactorily. Also, the pretest results may suggest additional questions to you. For example, if sharp disagreement is found in the responses to a particular item of the questionnaire, you may want to construct additional items that will help you understand the reasons for this disagreement.

After the preceding procedure has been completed and all improvements made in the pretest questionnaire, you are ready to administer your revised questionnaire to the sample you have selected.

Precontacting Your Sample

Contacting respondents before sending a questionnaire has been found in several studies to increase the response rate. The precontact can take the form of a letter, postcard, or telephone call. Evidence to date suggests that telephone contacts are the most effective.[24] Such contacts usually identify the investigators, discuss the purpose of the study, and request cooperation. Respondents return a self-addressed postcard indicating their willingness to cooperate. Such precontacts are effective probably because they alert the respondents to the imminent arrival of the questionnaire, thus reducing the chance that it will be thrown out as "junk mail." Precontacts may also put a more personal or human face on the research. Finally, having once agreed to cooperate, the respondent is under some psychological pressure to do so when the questionnaire arrives.

The Letter of Transmittal

Your major problem in doing a questionnaire survey is to get a sufficient percentage of responses to use as a basis for drawing general conclusions. Perhaps the most important single factor in determining the percentge of responses you will obtain is the letter of transmittal used with your questionnaire. This letter must be brief but yet must convey certain information and impressions to the subjects if you are to obtain a satisfactory percentage of responses. First, it is essential that you give the subjects good reasons for completing your questionnaire and sending it back to you. A brief assurance of confidentiality should be included; it is especially important if any sensitive questions are to be asked. When highly sensitive or potentially threatening

---

24. See Arnold S. Linsky in the Annotated References at the end of this chapter for a review of 12 studies on this topic.

questions are included in your questionnaire, a specific description of how confidentiality will be maintained should be added.

Whenever possible, the purposes of the study should be explained briefly and in such a way as to make the subject feel that the study is significant and important. If your questionnaire is aimed at a group with specific professional ties, such as mathematics teachers, you should probably make some reference to the person's professional status and his or her feelings of affiliation with this group. In some cases a certain amount of subtle flattery is also useful in preparing the letter of transmittal. This is usually accomplished by stressing the importance of the subjects' professional group and the value of the information the group can supply. Research has shown that both altruistic and egoistic appeals are effective in increasing response rate.[25] An offer to send the respondent a copy of the results is often effective. If made, however, such a promise should be honored; neglect of such matters is not ethical and will weaken future studies involving persons in your sample.

If possible, it is also desirable to associate your study with some professional institution or organization with which individuals in your sample might be expected to identify. For example, superintendents within a particular state might be expected to respond favorably to a letter signed by the state superintendent, the state or national president of a superintendents' association, or the dean of education at the state university. If your study is well designed and deals with a significant problem, it is usually possible to have someone sign your letter of transmittal who will represent a favorable authority symbol to the persons responding.

If your questionnaire is not aimed at a specific professional group, responses are more difficult to obtain because specific appeals cannot be made. Under these conditions you might slant your appeal along the lines that you might expect even the members of a widely diversified group to have common views, such as patriotism and a desire to improve the community. If your study is one where these general appeals are obviously inappropriate, the best approach is probably an appeal to the individual's sense of humor. For example, several years ago a national magazine wished to obtain information from its readers on the extent to which they used commercial flying in pursuing their sports activities. As the subscribers were a highly heterogeneous group having very little in common except subscription to this periodical and as the topic was not one where a general appeal could be expected to work, the magazine sent their very brief questionnaire along with a letter of transmittal on which was glued a dime. The letter of transmittal started out by asking the person to take a

25. For a brief review of literature on letters of transmittal and questionnaire design, see J. G. Odom, "Validation of Techniques Utilized to Maximize Survey Response Rates" (Paper presented at the annual meeting of the American Educational Research Association, San Francisco, 8–12 April 1979). ED 169 966.

coffee break at the expense of the magazine and while drinking the coffee to check off answers on the attached postcard.[26] This sort of approach is likely to get a good response because it amuses the subject while making very modest demands upon the subject's time.

Another alternative that has proven effective is to include a small cash reward or a premium such as a ballpoint pen with your letter of transmittal. Several studies have explored the effect of enclosing a small cash reward with the questionnaire. Such rewards, usually ranging from a quarter to a dollar, have consistently increased the response rate, as have small gifts or premiums. Usually the reward should be given as a token of appreciation rather than as payment for the respondent's time. Since most studies dealing with cash rewards are over 20 years old, it may be that inflation has weakened the effect of small rewards.[27] A recent study that offered a reward of $2 to complete a 25-page questionnaire got a quicker reply from persons offered the reward, but the eventual response rate was about the same.[28]

One of the items contained in the letter of transmittal is a request that the questionnaire be returned by a particular date. Set this date so that the subject will have sufficient time to fill out and return the questionnaire without rushing or inconvenience, but on the other hand, will not be likely to put it aside to do later as is the tendency if too generous a time allowance is given. A satisfactory rule of thumb would be to calculate the probable mailing time and allow the individual an additional week or less to complete the questionnaire and return it. Included with the questionnaire and the letter of transmittal should be a stamped, self-addressed envelope so that the individual can respond with a minimum of inconvenience.

There is some evidence to indicate that the type of mailing also has an effect on the response rate. Special-delivery mailing has been found more effective than first-class mail, which in turn is more effective than third-class mail. The use of hand-stamped envelopes also has been found in several studies to produce more returns than postal-permit envelopes.

The neatness and composition of your questionnaire and accompanying material is an important factor in determining the number of replies. The more expensive methods of duplication are usually worth the extra cost. A letter of transmittal reproduced by the offset process on letterhead paper and signed with a different color ink will command more attention than one poorly dittoed on cheap paper. If a word processor is available, individually typed letters, differing only in the names and addresses of the recipients, can be produced at a

26. Yes, there was a time when you could buy a cup of coffee for 10 cents!
27. See Linsky, and Heberlein and Baumgartner in the Annotated References at the end of this chapter for reviews of studies offering cash rewards and premiums.
28. V. J. Shackelton and J. . Wild, "Effects of Incentives and Personal Contact on Response Rate to a Mailed Questionnaire," *Psychological Reports* 50 (1982): 365–366.

Letterhead paper ——▶ OKLABAMA STATE UNIVERSITY
Collegetown, Oklahoma
M. A. Brown, President

College of Education
February 1, 1983   I. B. Smith, Dean

Typed with same
machine used in ——▶ Mr. A. B. Jones
cutting offset stencil   Superintendent of Schools
                             Mediumtown, Oklahoma

Duplicated using word   Dear Sir:
processor or offset
process to look like ——▶   The attached survey instrument concerned with proce-
individually typed letter   dures used in selecting elementary school principals is part of a
                              statewide study being carried on cooperatively by the State De-
Purpose of study   partment of Public Instruction and Oklahoma State University.
                              This project is concerned specifically with determining the
                              present status of principal selection in our state. The results of
Importance of ——▶   this study will help to provide preliminary criteria to be used
study   for developing better selection procedures and for improving
                              the administrator training program at Oklabama University.

Importance of   We are particularly desirous of obtaining your responses
respondent ——▶   because your experience in principal selection will contribute
                              significantly toward solving some of the problems we face in
                              this important area of education. The enclosed instrument has
                              been tested with a sampling of school administrators, and we
                              have revised it in order to make it possible for us to obtain all
                              necessary data while requiring a minimum of your time. The
Reasonable but   average time required for administrators trying out the survey
specific time limit   instrument was 9.5 minutes.
                                 It will be appreciated if you will complete the enclosed
Special delivery   form prior to February 10th and return it in the stamped, spe-
further stresses   cial delivery envelope enclosed. Other phases of this research
importance ——   cannot be carried out until we complete analysis of the survey
                              data. We would welcome any comments that you may have
Assurance of   concerning any aspect of principal selection not covered in the
confidentiality ——▶   instrument. Your responses will be held in strictest confidence.

Offer results ——▶   We will be pleased to send you a summary of the survey
Thank ——▶   results if you desire. Thank you for your cooperation.
respondent
                                                                    Sincerely yours,

Print in different color to
appear personally signed   ————————————————————▶

Signed by important educator ——————————————————————▶
rather than graduate student   I. B. Smith, Dean

Enc.
sjc
                    Figure 11.1   Sample Letter of Transmittal

low cost. These letters are superior to the best offset copies and have the added advantage that small changes can be made at a reasonable cost in each letter to make it more individualized. A sample letter is shown in figure 11.1.

Follow-Up Techniques

A few days after the time limit that you have set in your letter of transmittal, it is usually desirable to send a follow-up letter along with another copy of the questionnaire and another self-addressed envelope to individuals who have not responded.[29] Since your original letter of transmittal failed with the nonrespondent group there is no point in sending the same letter again. Instead, try to change your approach and use a different basis for making your appeal for cooperation. For example, if you used a personal appeal in your initial letter, you may want to try a professional appeal in your first follow-up letter.

The follow-up letter should generally assume the tone that you are sure the individual wished to fill out the questionnaire, but perhaps because of an error on your part or some oversight, it was overlooked. The follow-up letter should then go on to point out again the importance of the study and value of the individual's contribution to this important project, using different language and emphasis from your original letter. Postcard reminders have also been used, and in some cases they have been found as effective as letters. However, in one carefully conducted experimental study the investigators found that a form letter with another copy of the questionnaire obtained up to 7 percent more responses than a postcard with the same message.[30]

As a rule, if careful attention is given to the design of the questionnaire, the letter of transmittal, and follow-up letter, a sufficient percentage of subjects will respond. In cases where a very high percentage of response is required, you may need to conduct further follow-ups using different approaches. A second follow-up letter will generally bring in a few percent of the sample but if a new approach is used, it might bring in the additional cases needed. On some occasions as many as four follow-up letters are used. Figure 11.2 shows the pattern of responses reported in a review of 98 experimental studies in this area. Although the reviewers point out that results varied considerably from study to study, these average percentages give a reasonable indication of what can be expected from different numbers of follow-ups. A few of the studies reviewed

29. Research suggests that if funds permit, a questionnaire should be included in the second mailing. See Thomas A. Heberlein and Robert Baumgartner, "Is a Questionnaire Necessary in a Second Mailing?," *Public Opinion Quarterly* 45 (1981): 102–108.
30. Blaine R. Worthen and E. J. Brezezinski, "An Experimental Study of Techniques for Increasing Return Rate in Mail Surveys" (Paper presented at the annual meeting of the American Educational Research Association, New Orleans, February 1973).

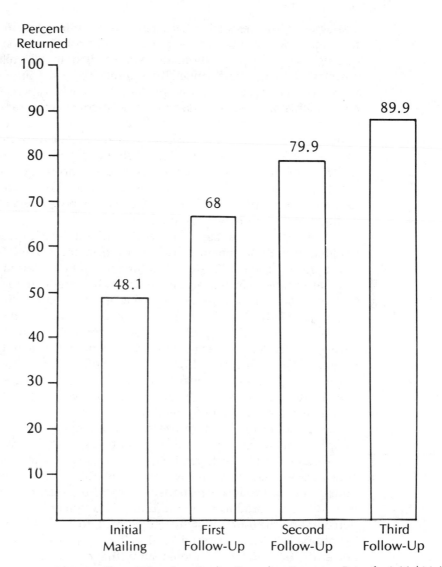

Figure 11.2   Response Rates Taken from Studies Recording Response Rates for Initial Mailing and Different Numbers of Follow-ups.

used four or more follow-ups, but this did not lead to a significant increase in returns over three follow-ups.[31]

Let us now examine a study that illustrates a variety of follow-up

31. See Heberlein and Baumgartner and the Annotated References at the end of this chapter.

strategies.[32] The researcher was particularly interested in whether follow-up techniques would increase the percentage of college dropouts responding to a questionnaire. This questionnaire was mailed to all college men who had enrolled at a large state university a number of years prior to the study. Three waves of mail resulted in a 67 percent mail-back response. In the first wave, respondents were sent a questionnaire, a cover letter, and a stamped return envelope. The second wave of mail came 20 days later, when the nonrespondents were sent the same enclosures again except for a new cover letter. The third wave of mail resulted when a reminder card was sent out. At this point different follow-up techniques were used to encourage mail-backs by the 383 resistant nonrespondents. All nonrespondents whose phone number could be located were telephoned. Those who could not be reached by phone were sent a certified letter and new questionnaire.

The use of the telephone and certified mail as follow-up techniques resulted in an 82 percent mail-back return from the 383 resistant nonrespondents in this study. The total mail-back return was thereby raised to 94 percent of the original sample, which is an unusually high percentage for this type of survey. One further point is worth noting regarding respondents who had been college dropouts. Had follow-up techniques been discontinued after the first three waves of mail-back response, college dropouts would have comprised 23 percent of the respondents. After the telephone calls and certified mailings, college dropouts accounted for 31 percent of the total number of respondents. Since college dropouts possessed special characteristics of interest to the investigator, it was worth the additional follow-up time in order to get a more adequate representation of them.

In a more recent study, researchers sought to contact the parents of a sample of about 5,000 male adults who had graduated from high school seven years earlier. The questionnaire, which was concerned with post-high-school education and employment, was very brief, fitting on a regular postal card. The initial mailing produced responses from 56.6 percent of those contacted. The first follow-up produced an additional 22.5 percent, the second follow-up 7.4 percent, and the third follow-up 5.5 percent, for a total response of 92 percent. A telephone interview after the third follow-up provided data on an additional 4 percent.[33] In contrast, a national study that employed a much longer questionnaire obtained a total response of only about 25 percent, even though a very extensive effort was made to reach the subjects.[34]

It is clear from the research we have discussed that although the number of

32. Bruce K. Eckland, "Effects of Prodding to Increase Mail-Back Returns," *Journal of Applied Psychology* 49 (1965): 165–169.
33. See Sewell and Hauser in the Annotated References at the end of this chapter.
34. Wise, "The Fight Against Attrition in Longitudinal Research."

follow-ups is a major factor in response rate, many other factors also influence it.[35]

What to Do about Nonrespondents

After the responses have been obtained, you face the problem of analyzing your results. The question that usually arises at this point is "How would the results have been changed if all subjects had returned the questionnaire?" If only a small percentage of your subjects failed to respond, this question is not critical. If more than 20 percent are missing, however, it is very likely that most of the findings of the study could have been altered considerably if the nonresponding group had returned the questionnaire and had answered in a markedly different manner from the responding group. This could be the case if the nonresponding group represents a biased sampling; that is, if those people who did not respond to the questionnaire are in some measurable way different from those who did respond. A common sampling bias of this type is that persons having a good program are more likely to respond than those having a poor program. For example, a questionnaire dealing with the physical education program at the elementary school level will get a higher percentage of responses from those schools having programs that the respondents believe to be above par. School administrators are often reluctant to admit the deficiencies of their schools and therefore fail to return questionnaires in which these deficiencies would be revealed.

Several studies have investigated whether personality and intellectual differences exist between respondents and nonrespondents.[36] The general finding of these studies is that respondents and nonrespondents do not differ on any significant personality dimensions. However, nonrespondents tend to have achieved less academic success than respondents.

If more than 20 percent of the questionnaires are not returned, it is desirable to check a portion of the nonresponding group even though this checking usually involves considerable effort. The ideal method of checking is to select a small number of cases randomly from the nonresponding group and then interview these subjects in order to obtain the necessary information. If the questionnaire has been sent over a wide geographical area, face-to-face interviewing of a random selection of nonresponding cases is usually not possible. Under these circumstances you can get some insight into the nature of the

---

35. Students who plan to conduct a questionnaire survey should read the relevant Annotated References at the end of this chapter before developing their research plans.
36. See Robert Rosenthal and Ralph L. Rosnow, *The Volunteer Subject* (New York: Wiley, 1975), for a review of these studies.

nonresponding group by checking those persons who are within a reasonable distance. However, telephone interviewing is usually a good alternative to personal interviews, is less costly, and is not subject to geographical limitations. If the questionnaire is too long to cover in an interview, a random sample of questionnaire items (10 or 20) can be asked.

In most educational surveys of the sort conducted by graduate students, 20 cases are adequate to check the nonresponding group. After data have been obtained from these cases, compare the responses of this group to each item with the responses of those who replied initially to determine whether the nonresponding sample is biased. If this sample of nonresponding subjects answers the questions in about the same manner as the responding group, you may probably safely assume that the responding group is an unbiased sample of those to whom you mailed the questionnaire. If this sample, however, is considerably different in their responses, note these differences and discuss their significance in reporting the results of the responding sample.

THE INTERVIEW AS A RESEARCH TOOL

You will see from the following that many of the steps in conducting an interview study are essentially the same as those for conducting a study that uses the mailed questionnaire as the primary data-collection tool. Stewart and Cash have described 10 steps that should be taken in planning and conducting a survey interview. We will summarize these briefly and then discuss some of them in greater detail.

Step 1: *State the Purpose*

The first step is to write a statement describing the general purpose of the research. In writing this statement, be aware of the various research designs that can be used in the cross-sectional survey to gather different kinds of information. The purpose determines the nature of the interview because different purposes require different levels of structure, different kinds of questions, and different interviewer qualifications.

Step 2: *Review Relevant Literature*

As is true of all research, interview studies must be built upon the findings of previous studies. Earlier surveys are especially useful as they will often permit the investigator to explore changes over time.

Step 3: *Select a Sample*

A sample of respondents should be selected using appropriate survey sampling techniques. A serious weakness of interview studies done by graduate students is the usual necessity of using small samples. Remember that the dangers of a biased sample are particularly serious when only a small number of individuals can be included in the research. After a sample has been selected, try to obtain some commitment of cooperation from these individuals before the interviewing starts.

Step 4: *Structure the Interview*

In order to expose all respondents to a "nearly indentical" experience, the opening statement, interview questions, and closing remarks should be structured. This helps to ensure that you will get reasonably comparable data from all respondents. You should also develop a preliminary system for coding responses and tabulating results at this time.

Step 5: *Develop Questions*

Because *unplanned* explanations by the interviewer change the interview situation, each question must be carefully phrased so that all respondents will understand what is wanted, and so the responses will lend themselves to tabulation and analysis. Once questions have been written, an interview guide can be developed.

Step 6: *Select and Train Interviewers*

Decide how many interviewers are needed, what special qualifications are required, what personal characteristics are important, and what training is needed to conduct effective interviews with the respondents who will be surveyed. Carry out selection and training.

Step 7: *Conduct Pretesting*

No amount of careful planning will ensure a successful interview study. Pretesting will nearly always reveal flaws in your questions, inadequacies in your coding system, gaps in interviewer training, and other problems that must be solved before research data can be collected.

Step 8: *Conduct the Interviews*

If pretesting and interviewer training have been adequate, few problems should emerge. Observe a sample of interviews either directly or with videotape to ensure that the planned procedures are being followed and to deal with any unanticipated problems that might arise.

Step 9: *Code and Tabulate*

Develop a system for coding responses during steps 4 and 5, and check it during steps 6 and 7. For open-form questions you may get some responses that did not occur during pretesting. This requires further study and revision of your coding system.

Step 10: *Analyze and Interpret Results*

Your preliminary plans for analysis should be developed during step 5. However, once the data have been tabulated you will probably need to do additional analysis to explore questions that have emerged. Once analysis is completed you must decide what conclusions may be supported, what limitations must be imposed, and what generalizations to the population are justified. The possible meaning of unanticipated results must also be considered.

Now that we have an overview of the interview study, let us look at some specific aspects of this kind of research in more detail.[37]

Advantages and Disadvantages of the Interview

The interview as a research method in survey research is unique in that it involves the collection of data through direct verbal interaction between individuals. This direct interaction is the source of both the main advantages and disadvantages of the interview as a research technique. Perhaps its principal advantage is its adaptability. The well-trained interviewer can make full use of the responses of the subject to alter the interview situation. As contrasted with the questionnaire, which provides no immediate feedback, the interview permits you to follow-up leads and thus obtain more data and greater clarity. The interview situation usually permits much greater depth than the other methods of collecting research data. A serious criticism of questionnaire studies is that they are often shallow, that is, they fail to probe deeply enough to provide a true picture of opinions and feelings. In contrast, the skilled interviewer,

---

37. See Charles J. Stewart and William B. Asch, Jr. in the Annotated References at the end of this chapter.

through the careful motivation of the subject and maintenance of rapport, can obtain information that the subject would probably not reveal under any other circumstances. Such information may be difficult to obtain because it usually concerns negative aspects of the self or negative feelings toward others. Respondents are not likely to reveal this type of information about themselves on a questionnaire and will only reveal it in an interview situation if they have been made to feel comfortable by a skillful interviewer.

The advantages of the interview over the mailed questionnaire in certain situations were shown in a study by Robert Jackson and J. W. M. Rothney.[38] These investigators conducted a follow-up study of 890 high school students, some of whom had received intensive counseling. The entire sample was sent a four-page mailed questionnaire five years after its high school graduation. A subsample of 50 cases was then drawn for a personal interview in which the same items that appeared on the questionnaire were asked. The information collected by means of the two techniques was then compared. It was found that a higher proportion of the sample completed each interview item than the corresponding questionnaire item. Also, 98 percent of the planned interviews were completed, compared with 83 percent of the mailed questionnaires. Two experienced counselors read and evaluated the questionnaire and interview data for evidence of personal problems. The mean number of problems yielded by the interview data was 8.82, whereas the corresponding figure for the questionnaire data was only 2.82. Thus it appears that under favorable conditions the interview tends to yield more complete data and also more data regarding negative aspects of the self.[39]

Another finding of this study was that respondents were fairly consistent when their interview and questionnaire responses to fact or yes-no items were compared. A study by W. Bruce Walsh[40] yielded a similar finding. This investigator compared the relative accuracy of the interview and questionnaire in collecting factual data from a college sample (e.g., gradepoint average, number of failed courses, quarter hours completed). The interview and questionnaire proved to be of comparable accuracy when the data collected by each method were compared with the records on file at the unviersity. As it is considerably less expensive than interviewing, the mailed questionnaire is usually used when factual, unambiguous information is to be collected. However, as the study by Jackson and Rothney indicates, the interview is likely

---

38. Robert M. Jackson and J. W. M. Rothney, "A Comparative Study of the Mailed Questionnaire and the Interview in Follow-Up Studies," *Personnel and Guidance Journal* 39 (1961): 569–571.
39. These findings are generally supported by a more recent study; see J. Legacy and F. Bennett, "A Comparison of the Mailed Questionnaire and Personal Interview Methods of Data Collection for Curriculum Development in Vocational Education," *Journal of Vocational Education Research* 4, no 3 (1979): 27–39.
40. W. Bruce Walsh, "Validity of Self-Report: Another Look," *Journal of Counseling Psychology* 15 (1968): 180–186.

to yield more complete information when open-ended questions pertaining to negative aspects of the self need to be asked.

Although it has a number of important advantages over other data-collection tools in certain situations, the interview does have definite limitations as a research tool. Because it is easier to ask questions than to administer tests or conduct observations, the interview is often misused to collect quantitative data that can be measured more accurately by other methods.[41] For example, college gradepoint averages obtained from the registrar are much more accurate than those obtained by asking students. Another important limitation of the interview stems from the nature of the process. The flexibility, adaptability, and human interaction that are unique strengths of the interview also allow subjectivity and possible bias that in some research situations are its greatest weakness. The interactions between the respondent and the interviewer are subject to bias from many sources. Eagerness of the respondent to please the interviewer, a vague antagonism that sometimes arises between interviewer and respondent, or the tendency of interviewers to seek out answers that support their preconcieved notions are but a few of the factors that may contribute to biasing of data obtained from the interview. These factors are called *response effects* by survey researchers.

Response Effect

Response effect is the tendency of the respondent to give inaccurate or incorrect responses, or more precisely is the difference between the answer given by the respondent and the true answer. For example, respondents asked their annual income may give an incorrect reply for any of a great many reasons. They may forget some sources of income such as stock dividends, they may be ashamed of or wish to hide some income such as money won gambling, they may want to impress the interviewer and therefore exaggerate their income, and so on.

C. H. Weiss discussed several potential sources of error present in the interview situation.[42] Three of these are basic and should be carefully considered in planning your study, designing your interview guide, and selecting and training your interviewers. The first can be traced to *predispositions of the respondent*. A few examples of respondent predispositions that can lead to errors include:

1. The respondent is suspicious of or hostile to the research.
2. Is indifferent or not motivated to cooperate.

---

41. See Robert M. Guion and Andrew S. Imada, "Eyeball Measurement of Dexterity: Tests as Alternatives to Interviews," *Personnel Psychology* 34 (1981): 31–36, for an example of a misuse of the interview.
42. For more detailed treatment of this topic, see C. H. Weiss, "Interviewing in Evaluation Research," in *Handbook of Evaluation Research*, vol. 1, eds. Elmer L. Struening and Marcia Guttentag (Beverly Hills, CA: Sage, 1975).

3. Lacks the information the interviewer is seeking
4. Wants to please the interviewer or be accepted by the interviewer.
5. Wants to present him or herself in favorable terms.

To reduce these sources of error, carefully study your target population, try to identify predispositions that are likely to be present, and then design your study so as to eliminate or minimize their effect. For example, if you suspect your respondents are likely to be hostile (e.g., a juvenile delinquent sample), try to develop procedures to reduce this hostility and build satisfactory rapport.

The second source of error relates to *predispositions of the interviewer* and includes:

1. Being uncomfortable with the people one is interviewing.
2. Being ill at ease in the environment in which one is working.
3. Allowing one's own opinions to influence what one hears and/or records.
4. Being unable to establish rapport with the respondents.
5. Having stereotyped expectations of what people are like and what they will say.

Obviously, you must select interviewers very carefully and train them thoroughly in order to avoid or eliminate such predispositions. Perhaps most important is the need to select interviewers who can relate to the respondents in a positive fashion. An interviewer who might do a fine job of interviewing successful teachers may be totally unsuited to interview unmarried pregnant teenagers.

There is, in fact, some evidence to indicate that matching interviewers and respondents on variables such as social class, race, age, and sex is likely to produce more valid responses.[43] Some researchers have also recommended selecting interviewers from the respondent target population, and there is some evidence to support this strategy.[44]

The third source of error relates to the *procedures used in conducting the study*. Examples of a few procedures that can lead to errors include:

1. The way the study is explained to the respondent.
2. The methods used for gaining the respondent's cooperation.
3. The length of the interview.
4. The place where the interview is held.
5. The presence of other people during the interveiw.

43. For examples of the kind of research that has explored these variables, see Anton J. Nederhof, "Impact of Interviewer's Sex on Volunteering by Females," *Perceptual and Motor Skills* 52 (1981): 25–26; and Herschel Shosteck, "Respondent Militancy as a Control Variable for Interviewer Effect," *Journal of Social Issues* 33, no 4 (1977): 36–45.
44. See Carol H. Weiss, "Research Organizations Interview the Poor," *Social Problems* 22, no. 2 (1974): 246–258.

Careful planning and small scale tryouts are essential in developing procedures that will produce good cooperation and accurate responses. A good way to start is for you to place yourself in the role of the respondent and try to identify elements in the research situation that could be disturbing. Discussing the research procedures with a few subjects from the respondent population, who will not be included in the sample, is also very useful in helping you see your research from the respondent's point of view. Finally, a pretest of the interview with a few respondents with frequent probes of their perceptions and feelings is recommended.

Survey researchers have conducted considerable research to determine the conditions under which response effects are most likely to occur. Many variables related to the nature and structure of the interview situation, the characteristics of the interviewer, and the characteristics of the respondent have been explored. The most comprehensive review of research in this field is that of Seymour Sudman and Norman Bradburn.[45] They analyzed evidence of response effects for threatening and nonthreatening questions about respondent behavior and for attitudinal questions. Response effects were generally largest for threatening questions (i.e., questions about which many respondents are reluctant to talk). For example, in face-to-face interviews, 47 percent of persons identified as drunk drivers gave distorted responses to questions on this topic. Sudman and Bradburn identified three sources of response effects: characteristics of the interview format, characteristics of the interviewers, and characteristics of the respondents. Characteristics of the interview format were most important in influencing response to the three kinds of questions (threatening, nonthreatening, and attitudinal).

Threatening Questions

Norman Bradburn, Seymour Sudman, and their associates carried out an extensive series of experimental studies on response effects, built on the conceptual framework of their earlier research review.[46] This work focused on threatening questions, since it is with this type of question that response effects are most serious.

The design of the interview format or structure was again found to be the most important factor in generating response effects. The following findings emerged from this research and should be carefully considered when planning an interview in which sensitive or threatening topics are to be covered:

1. There was no consistent advantage to using a particular method of data collecting. Results obtained from face-to-face interviews, telephone inter-

45. See the Annotated References at the end of this chapter.
46. See the Annotated References at the end of this chapter.

views, and self-administered questionnaires were generally similar, although each method was superior under certain specific conditions.

2. Open-ended questions using a long introduction to the topic and wording familiar to the respondent obtained much higher levels of reporting and smaller response effects than short, closed-form, standard questions.

3. Asking questions about the behavior of friends in conjunction with questions about the respondents' own behavior increased responses.

4. The presence of third parties during an interview generally made little difference in responses obtained.

5. Assuring respondents of absolute confidentiality increased their willingness to answer threatening questions.

6. More detailed information and truthful introduction to questionnaires had no effect on overall response rates or responses to individual questions.

7. If a signed consent form is needed, it is preferable to ask for a signature *after* the interview is completed.

8. If an interviewer *expects* to have difficulties with the questions to be asked, he should not be employed in the study. Such interviewers in fact have more difficulties and obtain less accurate and complete responses.

This series of studies produced additional findings, which you are advised to examine if you plan to use interviews in your research project.

The Interview Guide

You must develop a guide to be used during the interview. This guide makes it possible to obtain the data required to meet the specific objectives of the study and to standardize the situation to some degree. The **interview guide** lists, in the desired sequence, the questions that are to be asked during the interview, and it provides guidelines to the interviewer on what to say at the opening and closing of the interviews. The questions are usually asked exactly as they appear on the guide.

Whenever possible, the guide should be structured to require a minimum of writing by the interviewer. In trying out the preliminary form of the interview guide, you will usually find that most answers to a given question can be placed in a few categories. Even though the actual responses in a given category differ in detail, they are all essentially the same answer and can therefore be classified together. If these typical response categories are listed under the item, the interviewer simply checks the category a respondent's answer fits into and writes down only the unusual answer that does not fit into a category.

If probes are likely to be needed, it is desirable to list acceptable probing questions so that all respondents will be exposed to the same interview situation. Interviewers must be given some latitude in dealing with unusual problems or responses. However, more comparable data will be obtained if you anticipate such situations and provide the interviewers with standard ways of dealing with them. The form that the interview questions will take depends upon the level of structure of the interview, that is, the amount of direction and restriction imposed by the interview situation. An interview can be thought of as being highly structured, semistructured, or unstructured. Of course, within a single interview, the questions asked by the interviewer may vary along this entire continuum. Certain types of information, such as the limited specific facts or opinions collected in public-opinion polls, call for a highly **structured interview** situation. In these studies the interviewer usually asks each respondent a brief series of questions that can be answered either yes or no, or by selecting one of a set of alternate choices. The respondent's answers are not followed up to obtain greater depth, and the level of structure in this case is such that the data could be collected quite satisfactorily with a mailed questionnaire. The main advantage of the interview over the mailed questionnaire for this type of data collection is that the interviewer is likely to get responses from more of the persons in the sample selected and will get fewer "don't know" and unusable responses than would occur on a questionnaire. The disadvantage, of course, is the greater expense of collecting data.

Researchers in education generally include some highly structured questions in their interview guide, but they will aim primarily toward a semistructured level. At this level the interviewer first asks a series of structured questions and then probes more deeply, using open-ended questions in order to obtain more complete data. Suppose you are trying to understand the relationship between the student's high school experiences and the student's college achievement. First you may ask a sample of college students structured questions having to do with the size and location of their high schools, their grades, extracurricular activities, courses taken, and so forth. Then you may probe by asking open-ended questions, such as "How well do you think your high school experience prepared you for college?" and "If you could repeat your high school experience, would you want to do anything different on the basis of what you have learned in college so far?" After the respondent gives his or her initial reaction to these questions, you can use the resulting information to probe deeper for additional insight into your central concern, namely, the relationship between high school experiences and college achievement. The **semistructured interview,** therefore, has the advantage of being reasonably objective while still permitting a more thorough understanding of the respondent's opinions and the reasons behind them than would be possible using the mailed questionnaire. The semistructured interview is generally most appropriate for interview studies in education. It provides a desirable combination of objectivity and depth and often permits gathering valuable data that could not be successfully obtained by any other approach.

The **unstructured interview** is best illustrated by the client-centered approaches used in clinical psychology and psychiatry. In this type of interview, the interviewer does not employ a detailed interview guide but has a general plan and usually asks questions or makes comments intended to lead the respondent toward giving data to meet the interviewer's objectives. Unstructured interviews are generally called for in situations where the type of information sought is difficult for the subject to express or is psychologically distressing to the individual. Because of the threatening nature of topics usually covered by unstructured interviews, this procedure must constantly adapt to the respondent and is highly subjective and time-consuming. Graduate students can very seldom employ the unstructured interview in their research because skillful use of this technique requires a great deal of training and experience.

In developing the interview guide and conducting interviews, you should carefully observe a few common-sense rules:

1. Try out the guide in a few interviews in order to check vocabulary, language level, respondents' understanding of questions, and respondents' reactions to the interview. A pedantic or poorly phrased question can antagonize respondents and greatly reduce the validity of the data obtained. These first tryouts should be done by the researcher as he or she will gain a feel for the interview procedure that cannot be gained if someone else does this work.

    During the tryout, do some in-depth questioning to determine the respondent's understanding of questions that seek anything more than simple and obvious responses. In a recent study of subjects' understanding of survey questions, William Belson found that for the 29 questions he evaluated, on average only 29 percent of the respondents in his study interpreted the questions within permissible limits of the intended interpretation. These questions were designed to incorporate difficulties frequently found in survey questionnaires. The very high level of misinterpretation found by Belson illustrates the need to check respondents' interpretations *very* carefully during the tryout of your instrument.[47]

2. Interact with the respondent as an equal. Don't talk down to respondents, and don't try to court their favor.

3. If sensitive questions are to be asked, remind the respondent that answers will be held in strict confidence. If the respondent seems to hesitate, explain specifically the procedures that will be used to assure confidentiality.

4. Never hint, either by specific comment, tone of voice, or nonverbal cues such as shaking the head, to suggest a particular response. The interviewer must maintain a neutral stance on all questions to avoid biasing the responses.

47. See Belson in the Annotated References at the end of this chapter.

Interviewer Training

Even for highly structured interviews, the interviewers must be trained if reliable and objective information is to be obtained. The amount of training needed increases as the depth of the interview increases and structure decreases.

The training usually is carried out in two phases. In the first phase the trainees study the interview guide and learn about the interview conditions, logistics, necessary controls and safeguards, variables being studied, and similar information. Before conducting any interviews, interviewers should become so familiar with the interview guide (wording, format, recording procedures, and allowable probes) that they can conduct the interview in a conversational manner without hesitating, backtracking, or needing to reread or study the guide.[48] The researcher's expectations should not be discussed with the interviewers for this can bias the interviewers' perceptions.

In the second phase, research on interviewer training suggests that the trainees should conduct practice interviews and receive corrective feedback until their performance becomes standardized and reaches the desired level of objectivity and reliability.[49] Videotape recordings of practice interviews are very effective in providing models of the correct interview procedures and in giving corrective feedback. The tape can be replayed several times and trainees can improve the coding system, locate procedural errors, suggest better procedures, and discuss alternative ways of dealing with problems that arise.

Recording the Interview

Note taking or tape recording are the usual methods for preserving the information collected in the interview. Before choosing one of these methods, the interviewer will need to consider carefully the advantages and disadvantages of each.

If note taking is employed, duplicate a supply of interview guides containing the questions to be asked during the interview and typical responses derived during the tryout of the guide listed under each question. Provide space for the interviewer to add any necessary information or to write down answers that do not fit one of the usual response categories. As each question is answered by the respondent, the interviewer simply checks the appropriate response category and jots down any additional information as necessary. The

---

48. See Henry S. Dwyer, *The Interview as a Measuring Device in Education*, TM Report 56 (Princeton, NJ: Educational Testing Service, 1976), for a discussion of interviewing and a list of common-sense rules.
49. For a review of research related to interviewer training, see Mark D. Spool, "Training Programs for Observers of Behavior: A Review," *Personnel Psychology* 31 (1978): 853–888.

interview guide should of course allow more space after open-ended questions than after closed-form questions, which can be answered in a few words. The chief advantage of the note-taking method is that it facilitates data analysis, since the information is readily accessible and much of it has already been classified into the appropriate response categories by the interviewer. Because the respondent's answers are recorded beside the appropriate questions on the interview guide, it is easy for you to go through the guides, processing all the data for each question separately in a relatively short period of time.

One disadvantage of the note-taking method is that it may disrupt the effectiveness of the communication between interviewer and respondent. Whether this happens is to some extent dependent on the type of question being asked. When interviews include a large number of unstructured questions, involve extensive probing to get more depth, or produce answers that do not fit into a set of predeveloped categories, the note taking can require so much time that it is impossible to maintain rapport with the resondent.

When questions deal with simple factual information, respondents expect their answers to be written down and may become annoyed or offended if they are not. On the other hand, if respondents are asked to reveal sensitive or confidential information, taking notes may distract or upset them and prevent them from giving information they otherwise might have given. If confidential information is desired, the interviewer should carefully prepare the respondent. It is particularly important to stress the fact, before the formal interview begins, that the information provided by the respondent will be anonymous and reported only in group form (that is, combined with the data of other respondents). Another way to avoid the possibly disruptive effect of note taking is for the interviewer to consider delaying this procedure until after the interview is completed and the respondent has left the setting. However, the delay may lead the interviewer to forget important details; for instance, details that disagree with the interviewer's expectations. Of course, even if the note taking is done during the interview, the interviewer may unconsciously emphasize responses that agree with the interviewer's expectations and fail to record responses that do not.

The use of tape recorders has several advantages in recording interview data for research. Most important perhaps is that it reduces the tendency of interviewers to make an unconscious selection of data favoring their biases. The tape-recorded data can be played back more than once and can be studied much more thoroughly than would be the case if data were limited to notes taken during the interview. It is also possible to reanalyze the taped interview data to test hypotheses not set up in the original study. For example, interview data originally taped to study the interests of college freshmen could be reanalyzed to study their grammatical errors. Finally, it is possible with tape-recorded data for a person other than the interviewer to evaluate and classify the responses. This permits calculation of a reliability coefficient for the interview data. Reliability estimates can be made by comparing interviewer evaluations with evaluations of another research worker using the tape only, or by comparing initial interviewer evaluations with evaluations made by the same interviewer at a later date based on playback of the taped interview. In well-designed interview studies, these reliability coefficients may be as high as .90. The tape recorder also speeds up the interview process because there is no necessity for extensive note taking, although some minimal notes may be desirable. For example, some record of gestures might be appropriate in certain interview situations.

The principal disadvantage of using a tape recorder with the interview is that the presence of the tape recorder changes the interview situation to some degree. In interviews involving information of a highly personal nature, respondents may be reluctant to express their feelings freely if they know that their responses are being recorded. The interviewer should carefully explain the purpose of the recording and gain the confidence of the respondent, so as to minimize any undesirable effects of having the interview recorded. In interviews not aiming primarily at the collection of research data, it is seldom necessary to record the results. The opportunity to calculate reliability coefficients and the gain in objectivity provided by the taped record are very important factors, however, in research, and therefore using a tape recorder should be seriously considered for research interviews.

Telephone Interviewing

The use of the telephone in interview studies has greatly increased in recent years. As interviewers' salaries increase, the cost of long-distance telephone calls becomes competitive, and we can expect more interview studies to use this medium. Many universities now have WATS lines, which further reduce long-distance charges.

One major study used identical questionnaires to gather data from face-to-face interviews and telephone interviews and found that the latter cost about half as much.[50] In many educational surveys where members of the target population are spread over a large geographic area, such as all superintendents in the Rocky Mountain states, the cost advantage of telephone interviewing would be much greater. Although reduced cost is probably the greatest advantage of the telephone method, there are some other significant advantages.

1. You can select subjects from a much broader accessible population than would be the case if interviewers traveled to the location of each respondent.

50. See Graves and Kahn in the Annotated References at the end of this chapter.

2. Since all interviewers can work from a central location, monitoring of interviews and quality control is much easier. Automatic data entry and computer-assisted interviewing are also possible when all interviewers telephone from a central location.

3. Occasionally in regular interview studies interviewers do not actually carry out assigned interviews but instead fake the data. This is much less likely under the controlled conditions possible in telephone interviewing.

4. In telephone interviewing, when no one answers little cost is incurred, making frequent callbacks feasible.

5. Many groups, such as business people, school superintendents, and teachers, are easier to reach by telephone than by personal visits.

6. Telephone interviewing provides access to dangerous neighborhoods and to security buildings where interviewers are not admitted.

The relative advantages of telephone and face-to-face interviews have been studied by researchers. There is some evidence that telephone interviews can be used to collect sensitive data. One major study found that for nonthreatening questions, respondents' distortions were slightly higher for telephone interviews than for face-to-face interviews. For threatening questions, the reverse was true.[51] Although it would seem easier to establish rapport in a face-to-face interview, the physical presence of the interviewer may stimulate response distortion.

Obviously hanging up a phone is easier than ejecting an interviewer from one's home or office. However, some investigators have been successful in completing a very high percentage of telephone interviews, even when dealing with sensitive topics. In one carefully controlled study by Graves and Kahn completed interviews were obtained from 74 percent of the sample in personal interviews and 70 percent in telephone interviews.[52] Because this study used the same questionnaire for the personal and telephone interviews it was possible to compare the distribution of responses for the two methods. The results were generally very similar over a wide range of topics and item formats.

The most serious problem with telephone interviewing is that some households (about 2 to 4%) do not have telephones, thus eliminating them from the accessible population, while other households (about 5%) have two or more phone lines, thus increasing their probability of being sampled.

For certain populations like the working poor, eliminating persons without phones could bias the sample. For most adult populations such as school teachers, however, the number of persons not having a telephone would be very small, and their omission from the accessible population would probably not

51. See Bradburn, Sudman, and associates in the Annotated References at the end of this chapter.
52. See Graves and Kahn in the Annotated References at the end of this chapter.

introduce a significant bias. States also differ in telephone saturation from 82 percent to 100 percent, so regional bias could occur in national surveys.[53]

Another consideration in planning your sample for a telephone survey is that many persons have unlisted numbers. If the study involves random samples of persons within a given geographical area, this problem can be overcome. Select four-digit numbers from a table of random numbers and add these to the exchange (i.e., the first three numbers); dial the numbers, and you will reach both listed and unlisted numbers.[54] Graves and Kahn report that random digit dialing reaches approximately 90 percent of all American households, while an area probability sample, such as is used for personal interviews, provides access to about 95 percent of all dwellings.[55]

Another problem that could make telephone interviewing more difficult is that many companies now use the telephone to sell their products but cloak their sales pitch in the guise of a telephone survey. This practice will surely make many persons more resistant to legitimate surveys.

In summary, research has shown that telephone interviewing reaches nearly the same proportion of the target population, obtains nearly as high a percentage of returns, and produces comparable information at about one-half the cost of personal interviews.[56]

Computer-Assisted Telephone Interviewing[57]

Only a few years ago microcomputers cost tens of thousands of dollars, and so the use of these machines was relegated to special purposes. Recently the price of microcomputers has dropped drastically. At present, several excellent machines are available for below $500, and the lower limit is not yet in sight!

Microcomputers are increasingly accepted as part of our everyday life. Small as the machines are, they can be a powerful tool in educational research. Microcomputers can be used to gather, analyze, and display research data.

The microcomputer can be used to gather data in several ways. Three examples are: automated data gathering, where the subject sits at the computer solving a problem, carrying out a learning task, or playing a game; computer-

---

53. See Paul J. Lavrakas in the Annotated References at the end of this chapter for more detailed information on telephone saturation.
54. See M. Hauck and M. Cox, "Locating a Sample by Random Digit Dialing," *Public Opinion Quarterly* 38 (1974): 253–256.
55. See Graves and Kahn in the Annotated References at the end of this chapter. For a discussion of the pros and cons of random digit dealing versus directory sampling, see Jennifer D. Franz, *Sampling for Telephone Surveys: Do the Results Depend on Technique?* (paper presented at the Annual Meeting of the American Educational Research Association, Washington, DC, April 1987).
56. For a more thorough discussion of telephone interviewing, see Paul J. Lavrakas, and James H. Frey in the Annotated References at the end of this chapter.
57. This section was prepared by Carl F. Berger, Mark Shermis, and Paul Stemmer, School of Education, University of Michigan. Dr. Berger and his associates have done a great deal of research and development on the use of microcomputers in educational research.

assisted data gathering, where the microcomputer is used by the researcher to gather data; and computer-assisted interviewing.

One of the most effective uses of the microcomputer is to assist in gathering information in telephone interviews. While computer-assisted telephone interviewing (CATI) may seem a trivial use of the computer, its use virtually eliminates two major sources of errors in interviews, namely, recording data in the wrong place on the form and asking the wrong questions. Most telephone interviews require the interviewer to jump to a different part of the form depending on the response of the person interviewed. For example, if the question is "Are you employed?" a response of yes might indicate that this response be recorded and that the interviewer turn three pages to a set of questions on mode of employment. If the interviewer fails to turn three pages, inappropriate or embarrassing questions may follow with the possible result of a badly shortened interview! Using a microcomputer, a program can be developed that not only records the subject's responses but also branches to the next question the interviewer should ask. Thus, as the interviewer types *yes* into the microcomputer, the response *yes* is recorded, and the computer is programmed to jump three pages in the computer program and display the first question on modes of employment. Not only does the researcher not have to worry about turning the pages but the interviewer does not even see the questions that are inappropriate. To the interviewer the next question that appears is the one needed. Response accuracy generally climbs with such computer-assisted interview techniques because the interviewer can concentrate on responses rather than worry about a wrong decision on what question to ask next.

Because of these and other advantages, an increasing number of researchers are turning to computer-assisted telephone interviewing. In using CATI, the interview guide or survey instrument is stored on a magnetic disk and questions are displayed individually for the interviewer in program-controlled sequences on a terminal. Responses to individual items are entered on the terminal keyboard. Specific applications of CATI vary, but precoded answers are generally recorded by alpha-numeric codes, while answers to open-ended questions, respondent qualifications, and interviewer notes are typed out in full. Also, respondent answers can be stored in data files, which are continuously updated as interviewing and coding proceed.

Nicholls,[58] Groves, Berry, and Mathiowetz[59] and Frey[60] highlight several advantages of CATI over standard telephone interviewing techniques.

58. See W. Nicolls, "Computer Assisted Telephone Interviewing," *Computer Center Newsletter* 3, no. 1 (1980) (University of California at Berkeley).
59. See R. M. Groves, M. Berry, and N. Mathiowetz, "Some Impacts of Computer Assisted Telephone Interviewing on Survey Methods," in American Statistical Association, *Proceedings of the Section on Survey Research Methods, Houston, Texas, 11-14 August 1980* (Washington, DC: American Statistical Association, 1980), pp. 519–524.
60. See James H. Frey in the Annotated References at the end of this chapter.

1. Question branching is controlled by the system. This permits using more complex survey instruments and eliminates an important form of interviewer error.
2. The computer can be programmed to produce an earlier answer or stored information needed for response to a subsequent item, thus aiding interviewer and respondent recall.
3. CATI systems require the investigator to spell out clear and explicit procedures that were formerly unspecified.
4. "Wild codes" (codes that do not have any meaning) can be detected while the interview is in progress and resolved by questions directed by the computer to either the interviewer or the respondent.
5. Close supervision is possible by monitoring both the interview conversation and interview entries. There is also an opportunity to have an additional interviewer simultaneously code the interview. Comparison of the codes given by each interviewer for the same interview can then be made to look for inconsistencies and to estimate interrater reliability.
6. Call-backs, retries, and appointment call-backs automatically come up at designated times.
7. Checks on the consistency of respondent replies to reveal response sets or discrepancies can be easily applied.
8. Since data entry and error checking are concurrent, the system can produce a fully cleaned (error-free) data file ready for analysis shortly after the completion of field work.

In order to have a fully functioning CATI system, the computer needs to perform some or all of the following functions:

1. Random digit dialing (RDD)
2. Storage and retrieval of telephone lists
3. Automatic dialing
4. Presentation of questions
5. Code checking and storage of responses
6. Input and merging to a dataset
7. Interviewing management

Because of the complexities of tasks required by CATI, such systems were initially developed for use with large computers. With the advent of more sophisticated microcomputers with 16-bit memory, CATI systems are beginning to be developed for them, too. For example, Berger, Shermis, and Stemmer have demonstrated a microcomputer application to a statewide vocational education follow-up survey.[61]

61. See Carl F. Berger, Mark L. Shermis, and Paul Stemmer, "Data Gathering Using Microcomputers" (American Educational Research Association Training Session, New York, April 1982). Also see James H. Frey in the Annotated References for a discussion of CATI.

Effective Communication in Interviews

Interview questions must be framed in language that ensures effective communication between the interviewer and the respondent. The respondent must fully undestand the language in which the question is framed. In those educational research studies where respondents are professional educators, the problem of phrasing questions in language common to both interviewer and respondent is not usually serious, but for studies involving interviews with lay people, the educational jargon we in the profession know and use can seriously block effective communication. For example, if a question such as "What is your opinion of homogeneous grouping in the public schools?" were asked, many of the persons answering would not have a clear undertanding of the term "homogeneous grouping." Often respondents are reluctant to admit that they don't understand the meaning of the question. The fact that they have been asked the question implies that they should understand it, and rather than admit their ignorance, they may give an evasive or noncommital answer.[62] To avoid this difficulty, the interviewer should explain technical terms in plain language before asking for the respondent's opinion. Also, it is advisable to ask a few information questions about the topic first. If the respondent cannot answer the information questions, then the opinion item can be skipped since the respondent's answer will have little value or meaning.

Occasionally graduate students are carried away by their enthusiasm for a research idea and ask for information that no one could reasonable be expected to have. An example of this was an interview study proposed recently by a graduate student that would ask college students to recall conversations the students had during their childhood with teachers or other adults that exerted a major influence on the moral values and educational and vocational goals of the students. The graduate student believed that there are certain critical moments in everyone's childhood when the words of a parent or teacher become a major factor in determining the future goals and behavior of the child. Such a theory may be valid, but the line of questioning planned by the graduate student called for a level of recall as well as a level of insight that few persons could be expected to possess. Another error frequently made in educational studies is to ask parents to comment on technical aspects of education about which they have little or no knowledge. For example, an interview study carried out to learn the parents' opinions of different methods of teaching reading could produce very little useful information. Many of the parents would probably have opinions concerning the teaching of reading, but for the most part these opinions would have little foundation except their limited personal experiences.

Effective communication between interviewer and respondent is facilitated

62. You may recall our discussion earlier in the chapter of the study by Allen (see note 21), who found that 10 percent of a sample expressed an opinion about a bogus organization, the League for Linear Programs, rather than check the "don't know" category.

if the respondent appreciates the purpose of each question that is asked. With the help of the interviewer, respondents develop an idea of the purpose of the interview, and if they can see no connection between their perception of the purpose and a question that is asked, they are likely to react negatively. They may become suspicious of the interviewer and wonder whether the interview actually has some purpose other than the one they have been told. Inasmuch as respondents cannot be sure of what this hidden purpose is, suspicions are aroused, and one is immediately placed on guard. Under these circumstances answers will be evasive and respondents' attitude guarded or hostile. On the other hand, respondents may consider such questions as indicative of a lack of ability or of poor planning on the part of the interviewer. In this case respondents are likely to feel that their participation is a waste of time. This loss of confidence in the interviewer is serious in that it is often followed by a refusal to cooperate. If the status of the respondent is higher than that of the interviewer, a special effort must be made to avoid questions that respondents can interpret as wasting their time. The problem of questions that appear irrelevant arises often in studies involving psychological data, such as personality. Indirect questioning is often necessary in this area, and unless considerable groundwork is laid by the interviewer, resistance by the respondents will be encountered.

There are a number of other techniques that the skillful interviewer can use to promote effective communication with the respondent. Before the formal interview begins, engage the respondent in a few minutes of small talk to help the person relax and to establish rapport. Assure the respondent that all statements will be held in strictest confidence and be used for research purposes only. In some instances it may be desirable to use subtle social pressure to impress on the respondent the importance of the interview. For example, the interviewer might make a statement such as "I am doing this study in collaboration with Dr. _____ at the state university in order to learn how men in your position feel about these issues." Once the interview has been initiated, other techniques may be helpful in maintaining respondent cooperation and participation. After the respondent has completed an answer, the interviewer can sometimes elicit additional information by pausing before asking the next question or by saying, "Tell me more about that." Of course, it is undesirable to contradict or appear to cross-examine the respondent, for the person may become threatened and deceptive in answering further questions. If the respondent does appear to be threatened by a particular question, change the subject; at a later point in the interview, it may be possible to raise the subject again in such a way that the respondent is not threatened. Finally, it is inadvisable to ask too many closed-form questions in succession or to change the subject of the interview too frequently. Otherwise a respondent may feel that the interview is not necessary and that the interviewer is not interested in obtaining the respondent's own views in depth.

Leading Questions

A factor that often biases the results of interview studies is the use of leading questions. A leading question is any question that, because of its phrasing, leads the respondent to consider one reply more desirable than another. Let us say, for example, that we were interviewing a random sampling of voters concerning their attitudes toward federal aid to education. After establishing whether the respondent was familiar with the issue of federal aid to education, a reasonable question might be, "What is your opinion of federal aid to education?" A question that might be classified as moderately leading would state, "Do you favor federal aid to education?" This question is a little easier for the respondent to answer in the affirmative than the negative. A more serious attempt to lead the respondent would result in a question such as "In view of the dangers of federal control, do you feel that federal aid to education is advisable?" Here the resondent is strongly motivated to give an unfavorable response to federal aid. Questions can be slanted even further by the use of emotionally toned words to which the individual is inclined to react for or against with little thought for the basic issue involved. Such a question might be, "Do you favor federal aid to education as a means of providing each child with an equal educational opportunity?" In this case the concept of "an equal opportunity for all" is likely to elicit favorable replies.

The Respondent's Frame of Reference

Each person is the product of an environment that is unique. Words recall different experiences and have different shades of meaning for each of us. Unless the interviewer establishes a common ground for communication—a common frame of reference—these differences can seriously interfere with the communication process. If the respondent's frame of reference is different from that of the interviewer, replies are likely to be misinterpreted. For example, if a group of mothers was asked, "What do you think of the teacher your child has this year?" one might answer in terms of the teacher's personal appearance, another may think of the teacher's willingness to help on a PTA committee, another may have never seen the teacher but may feel that her child is not getting proper reading instruction, while another may have had a conference with the teacher the day before about her child's misbehavior and think of nothing but this meeting in making an evaluation. Thus, we can see that unless the interviewer and respondent are using the same frame of reference, many difficulties can arise when obtaining interview data. In research perhaps the most desirable solution to this problem is to specify the frame of reference wanted by the interviewer. The preceding question could be placed in a specific frame of reference by asking, "What do you think of the way your child's teacher handles parent-teacher conferences?"

Pretest of the Interview Procedures

Although the interview can provide us with valuable data, we need to remember that it is a highly subjective technique. When this technique is used in research, all possible controls and safeguards must be employed if we expect to obtain reasonably objective and unbiased data. A careful pilot study is the best insurance you have against bias and flaws in design. After the interview guide has been developed, a pilot study should be conducted to evaluate and improve the guide and the interview procedure and help the interviewer develop experience in using the procedure before any research data for the main study are collected. The number of subjects interviewed in the pilot study need not be large—10 to 20 are sufficient for most educational studies. The interviewer can usually determine from the progress of the last few pilot interviews whether more are needed to improve the procedures further. The subjects interviewed in the pilot study should be taken from the same population as the main study sample whenever possible and from a very similar population when research design does not permit drawing from the main study population.

The pilot study should be carried out with specific objectives in mind. The interviewer should determine from the pilot study whether the planned procedures actually produce the data desired. The interviewer should be alert to communication problems, evidence of inadequate motivation, and other clues that suggest a rephrasing of questions or revision of procedure.

The pretest can also be used to identify threatening questions. Bradburn and Sudman define a question as threatening when 20 percent of respondents feel that most people would be very uneasy talking about the topic. This criterion can be employed by investigators in the pretest to identify such questions. Such items should then be omitted or revised if possible. However, if these items are essential to the research, which is often the case, then the techniques recommended by these authors can be employed to reduce response effects.[63]

Several methods of opening the interview should also be tried and perfected. Unwillingness of the respondent to cooperate generally indicates that the techniques that have been established are not sufficient for motivation and maintenance of rapport. The pilot study also gives the interviewer an opportunity to evaluate his or her methods of recording the interview data and to determine whether adequate information is being recorded, whether the recording method causes excessive breaks in the interview situation, and whether the mechanics of reporting can be improved.

During the pilot study, you also should assess carefully the methods you have planned to use for quantifying and analyzing your interview data. If the pilot study results indicate that data obtained cannot be quantified or are not

---

63. See Bradburn, Sudman, and associates in the Annotated References at the end of this chapter.

falling into the areas anticipated, the interview procedures must be revised until satisfactory quantification and analysis are possible.

Tape recording of pilot study interviews is especially important even if the tape recorder is not to be used during the regular interview procedure. By playing back the interview, the interviewer can gain many insights into his or her handling of the questions and will be made aware of problems that may have escaped the interviewer during the interview situation.

MISTAKES SOMETIMES MADE IN SURVEY RESEARCH

Survey Research in General:

1. Researcher does not formulate clear, specific objectives for the research.
2. Relates data-gathering procedure to objectives in only a general way and thereby fails to get quantitative data specific to the problem.
3. Selects sample on the basis of convenience instead of attempting to obtain a random sample.
4. Analyzes survey data one variable at a time instead of analyzing relationships, longitudinal changes, and comparisons between groups.

Questionnaire Studies:

5. Researcher uses a questionnaire to investigate problems that could be better studied with other research techniques.
6. Gives insufficient attention to the development of the questionnaire and fails to pretest it.
7. Asks too many questions, thus making unreasonable demands on the respondent's time.
8. Overlooks details of format, grammar, printing, and so on that give the respondent an unfavorable first impression.
9. Fails to check a sample of nonresponding subjects for possible bias.

Interview Studies:

10. Researcher does not adequately plan the interview or develop a detailed interview guide.
11. Does not conduct sufficient practice interviews to acquire needed skills.
12. Fails to establish safeguards against interviewer bias.
13. Does not make provisions for calculating the reliability of interview data.
14. Uses language in the interview that is not understood by the respondents.
15. Asks for information that the respondent cannot be expected to have.

ANNOTATED REFERENCES

Survey Research

deVaus, D. A. *Surveys in Social Research.* Boston: George Allen & Unwin, 1986.

Covers all the major steps in survey research from formulating a research question to conducting the data analysis. The chapters on analysis are recommended since they deal with analysis procedures in clear, nontechnical language and provide frequent examples.

Fowler, Floyd J., Jr. *Survey Research Methods.* Beverly Hills, CA: Sage, 1985.

Provides a great deal of practical information on survey research. All major aspects of questionnaire surveys and survey interviewing are briefly discussed. The chapter on ethical issues in survey research is recommended since this topic is overlooked by most authors in this area.

Jolliffe, F. R. *Survey Design and Analysis.* New York: Wiley, 1986.

Provides a good description of survey sampling procedures, and a discussion of methods of processing and surveying the results. Chapter 3 also gives a useful review of nonsampling errors, including methods of dealing with nonresponse, and item nonresponse.

Kalton, Graham. *Introduction to Survey Sampling.* Beverly Hills, CA: Sage, 1983.

Contains information a student will need in selecting and applying a sampling procedure to a survey. Different kinds of sampling procedures are described. Nonresponse, analysis, and sample size are briefly addressed. Two examples of survey research are discussed.

Orlich, Donald C. *Designing Sensible Surveys.* Pleasantville, NY: Redgrave, 1978.

Deals briefly with most aspects of survey research including interviews, questionnaires, construction of survey items, sampling, research designs, data processing, and writing the research report. A very practical guide, containing many examples. Highly recommended for students who plan to conduct a survey.

Sudman, Seymour, and Bradburn, Norman M. *Response Effects in Surveys.* Chicago: Aldine, 1974.

Pulls together virtually all the research on response effects. Many variables related to the interview process such as degree of structure, question length, and topic of the study are discussed. The effects of memory and the effects of interviewer and respondent characteristics on response to different kinds of questions are also reviewed. Comparisons are also made of the relative effectiveness of the questionnaire and the interview for gathering various kinds of survey data. A very thorough bibliography is included.

Questionnaires

Belson, William A. *The Design and Understanding of Survey Questions,* Aldershot, England: Gower, 1981.

In this study 29 experimental questions designed to study respondent interpretations were imbedded in 4 questionnaires. The questions were administered to a total of 265 subjects in an initial interview. A second in-depth interview was then conducted with each respondent to determine how the experimental questions asked during the first interview had been understood. The researcher then very carefully analyzed the interpretations of each item. This study gives the reader many useful insights into the questioning process and is a valuable guide to the design of better questions.

Berdie, D. R., and Anderson, J. F. *Questionnaires: Design and Use.* Metuchen, NJ: Scarecrow Press, 1974.

Filled with useful information on designing and carrying out a questionnaire study. The sections on item construction and procedures to stimulate responses are especially valuable. The appendices contain four sample questionnaires, follow-up letters, and a case history of a questionnaire study. Finally, an extensive annotated bibliography is provided that includes most important references on questionnaires published over the past 30 years.

Heberlein, Thomas A., and Baumgartner, Robert. "Factors Affecting Response Rates to Mailed Questionnaires: A Quantitative Analysis of the Published Literature." *American Sociological Review* 43 (1978): 447–462.

Linsky, Arnold S. "Stimulating Responses to Mailed Questionnaires: A Review." *Public Opinion Quarterly* 39 (1975): 82–101.

These two reviews summarize a large amount of research information that can help a researcher maximize response rate on a questionnaire survey. Linsky has written a conventional review of research literature from 1935 to the time of his article. For most of the major areas he presents data related to response rates in tabular form, which helps the reader see the overall patterns of research evidence. In contrast, Heberlein and Baumgartner used a procedure similar to Glass's meta-analysis to combine the results of 98 experiments concerned with response rates. Their multiple regression analysis is especially useful in revealing the effects of combining various strategies for increasing response rates. They have also developed an interesting model that can be used to predict the final response rate an investigator can expect to obtain, based on such variables as saliency, use of cash incentive, and number of follow-ups to be used. The student planning a questionnaire survey should give both articles careful attention.

Labaw, Patricia. *Advanced Questionnaire Design.* Cambridge, MA: Abt Books, 1980.

Presents a great deal of practical information that emerges from the considerable experience of the author; written in conversational style and illustrated with clear and relevant examples. The chapters on hypotheses are especially recommended.

Schuman, Howard, and Presser, S. *Questions and Answers in Attitude Surveys: Experiments on Question Form, Wording, and Context*. New York: Academic Press, 1981.

Describes a series of experiments that manipulated a number of question-form variations to learn their effect on results obtained on survey questionnaires. Among the variations studied were: open vs. closed questions, encouragement vs. discouragement of "don't know" responses, variations in question order, and changes in the tone of wording. Their results indicate that even minor differences in wording can bring about major differences in responses. The context in which the question is asked also was found to have a substantial effect on answers received. These findings are especially important for researchers doing longitudinal surveys or replicating earlier studies, but should be studied by anyone doing survey research.

Sewell, W. H., and Hauser, R. M. *Education, Occupation, and Earnings*. New York: Academic Press, 1975.

A large-scale follow-up survey of about 5,000 male high school seniors several years after graduation. The sections describing the research procedures provide a good model for this type of research.

Sudman, Seymour, and Bradburn, Norman M. *Asking Questions: A Practical Guide to Questionnaire Design*. San Francisco: Jossey-Bass, 1982.

An extremely practical guide to writing questions for use in structured questionnaires and interview guides by authors with very strong backgrounds in survey research. Chapters focus on framing both threatening and non-threatening questions, knowledge questions, and attitude questions. Most chapters start with a checklist of main points, followed by many examples. Should be required reading for anyone planning to conduct either a questionnaire or an interview study.

Interviews

Bradburn, Norman M.; Sudman, Seymour; and Associates. *Improving Interview Method and Questionnaire Design*. San Francisco: Jossey-Bass, 1981.

Reports the results of a series of large-scale experimental studies carried out over a seven-year period by the National Opinion Research Center at the University of Chicago and the Survey Research Laboratory of the University of Illinois. These studies investgated the response effects related to threatening questions in survey research. Anyone planning to conduct survey research on sensitive topics will profit greatly from a careful study of this important work.

Graves, R. M., and Kahn R. L. *Surveys by Telephone: A National Comparison with Personal Interviews*. New York: Academic Press, 1979.

Describes an excellent experimental study designed to compare the results of a personal interview survey ($N = 1{,}548$) with two telephone surveys (Ns of 865 and 869), all conducted simultaneously. The questionnaires employed in the two modes were essentially identical. The researchers explored most of the important questions related to these two interview modes. This is the best research we have located on this topic, and the book is strongly recommended to anyone planning an interview study.

Gorden, Raymond L. *Interviewing Strategy, Techniques and Factors*, rev. ed. Homewood, IL: Dorsey Press, 1975.

Presents a detailed treatment of interviewing, including such topics as locating and contacting respondents, selecting interviewers, taking notes, planning the interview, arranging topics, and dealing with resistance. The interview is also compared with other data-gathering procedures such as observation and use of questionnaires.

Stewart, Charles J., and Cash, William, B., Jr. *Interviewing: Principles and Practices*, 3rd ed. Dubuque, IA: William C. Brown, 1982.

First four chapters introduce the reader to the interview process and structure, and the phrasing of questions. The remaining chapters deal with various kinds of interviews. Most relevant for educational researchers is the discussion of the survey interview.

Survey Research Center. *Interviewer's Manual*, rev. ed. Ann Arbor: Institute for Social Research, University of Michigan, 1976.

Provides much useful information on the use of interviews in survey research. Specific instructions are given on such topics as making initial contact with the subject, asking questions, probing, and recording responses. Many examples are given.

Tolar, Alexander, ed. *Effective Interviewing*. Springfield, IL: Thomas, 1985.

Each chapter discusses a different type of interview. Most of the types described can be employed in educational research such as the behavioral interview, the oral history interview, and the research interview. Should be checked by students planning an interview study.

Weiss, Carol H., "Interviewing in Evaluation Research." In *Handbook of Evaluation Research*, ed. Elmer L. Struening and Marcia Guttentag. Beverly Hills, CA: Sage, 1975.

Although focused on evaluation research, the information on interviewing given in this chapter would be very useful in planning any type of interview study. The author's presentation is readable, well-organized, and complete.

Telephone Interviews

Frey, James H. *Survey Research by Telephone*. Beverly Hills, CA: Sage, 1983.

Provides an excellent comparison of the advantages and disadvantages of mailed questionnaires, face-to-face interviews, and telephone interviews. Discusses sampling procedures including several methods of random-digit dialing. Design of the interview guide and administration of a telephone survey are also discussed. The section on computer-assisted telephone interviewing (CATI) will be especially useful to students who are planning this type of survey.

Lavrakas, Paul J. *Telephone Survey Methods, Sampling, Selection, and Supervision*. Beverly Hills, CA: Sage, 1987.

Focuses mainly on sampling procedures and the supervision of telephone interviewing. It does not deal with other aspects of survey research such as framing questions, estimating errors, and data analysis. Recommended for any student who wants to conduct a telephone survey.

SELF-CHECK TEST

Circle the correct answer to each of the following questions. An answer key is provided on page 884.

1. The goal of the data-collection tools used in survey research is to
   a. obtain standardized information from all subjects in the sample.
   b. gather as much data as possible in the shortest period of time.
   c. collect only information that will prove to be significant.
   d. collect nonquantified data.
2. The most commonly used instruments for data collection in survey research are the
   a. questionnaire and standardized test.
   b. questionnaire and individual interview.
   c. individual interview and situational testing.
   d. standardized test and critical-incident technique.
3. The term "time-bound association" indicates that the variables being studied
   a. refer to future events.
   b. refer to psychological processes that will hold constant over time.
   c. are measured at the same point in time.
   d. correlate highly with each other.
4. The first step in conducting a questionnaire survey is to
   a. select the sample.
   b. define the population from which the sample is to be taken.
   c. list specific objectives to be achieved by questionnaire.
   d. construct questionnaire items.
5. The most basic consideration involved in selecting subjects for a questionnaire study is the
   a. size of sample.
   b. identification of a group that has the desired information.
   c. definition of method used for data collection.
   d. identification of data analysis techniques.
6. In writing a letter of transmittal to accompany a mailed questionnaire, the researcher is advised to
   a. avoid associating the research project with a professional institution.
   b. request that the questionnaire be returned by a certain date.
   c. avoid setting a time limit for return of the questionnaire.
   d. state that follow-up techniques will be used if the questionnaire is not returned by a certain date.

7. Compared with the mailed questionnaire, the principal advantages of the interview are
   a. low cost and high adaptability.
   b. adaptability and depth of information collected.
   c. objectivity and ease of administration.
   d. ease of administration and high reliability of information collected.
8. The research interview has the following disadvantage(s):
   a. Considerable training is required to administer the interview.
   b. It is a time-consuming and expensive technique.
   c. It is subject to interviewer bias.
   d. All of the above are correct.
9. The principal disadvantage of tape recording a research interview is
   a. its relatively high cost.
   b. the complexity of its operation.
   c. the change that it produces in the interview situation.
   d. the low validity of tape-recorded data compared to the validity of the note-taking technique.
10. It is good interview technique to
    a. ask leading questions.
    b. avoid engaging in small talk before starting the formal interview.
    c. cross-examine respondents if they seem deceptive.
    d. make sure that respondents understand the purpose of each question asked.

APPLICATION PROBLEMS

The following problems are designed to give you practice in applying significant concepts and research procedures explained in the chapter. Most of them do not have a single correct answer. For feedback, you can compare your answers with the sample answers on pages 896–897.

1. Suppose that you are doing a survey to determine college seniors' plans for the year immediately following June commencement. Your first step is to write sample closed-form and open-ended items for pilot testing.
   a. Write a closed-form questionnaire item in multiple-choice format that you think will elicit the desired information. Include at least five choices in the item statement.
   b. Write an open-ended questionnaire item that you believe will also elicit the desired information.
2. The open classroom is a relatively new development in American education. A researcher decides to survey the attitudes of elementary school teachers toward this new approach to instruction. She develops an attitude scale for this purpose. A colleague advises that she should also give the teachers a short test to determine what they know about the open classroom. Why might the colleague have made this recommendation?
3. A graduate student has designed a survey questionnaire that will serve as the main data-collection instrument of his dissertation. He plans to send the questionnaire to a random sample of textbook publishers throughout the United States. He prepares the following letter, which is to be sent to each publisher along with a copy of the questionnaire:

Dear Sir:
   The enclosed questionnaire will take only a few minutes of your time to complete. The purpose of the questionnaire is to collect data for my doctoral dissertation in the

Department of Education at the University of Ingleside. My field of specialization is curriculum development.

A prepaid addressed envelope is enclosed for return of the questionnaire. If you have any questions about the study, I will be happy to answer them. Thank you for your cooperation.

Sincerely,
ARTHUR JONES

What are three ways in which the content of this letter can be improved?

4. A researcher has received back 72 percent of the questionnaires that she sent to a sample of high school counselors. What are three methods the researcher can use to contact nonrespondents to request that they return their questionnaire?

5. A researcher wishes to survey a sample of parents in a school district to determine their satisfaction or dissatisfaction with particular schools. He has included the following questions in his interview guide:

   1. How many children do you have?
   2. What are their ages?
   3. What school(s) do they attend?
   4. How long have they attended the school(s):
   5. What do you like best about the school(s) your children attend?
   6. What do you like least?
   7. What kinds of contact have you had with your children's teachers and other school staff?

   a. Do these questions constitute a structured interview, semistructured interview, or an unstructured interview?
   b. Why do you think the researcher organized the questions into the above sequence?
   c. Which questions will most likely require probing by means of open-ended questions?

SUGGESTION SHEET

If your last name starts with letters from Kef to Lev, please complete the Suggestion Sheet at the end of the book while this chapter is still fresh in your mind.

12 THE METHODS AND TOOLS OF OBSERVATIONAL RESEARCH

OVERVIEW

Many methods can be used to collect research data relating to human behavior. In chapter 10 we introduced you to a variety of qualitative research methods including participant observation. Although productive for some kinds of research, these methods involve a level of subjectivity that provides few safeguards against bias by the investigator or observer. In the previous chapter you considered the methods and tools of survey research, principally the questionnaire and the interview. It was shown that one of the principal disadvantages of these techniques is that individuals tend to bias the information they offer about themselves. The problems of observer bias and self-report bias can be overcome to a considerable degree by using a set of techniques that can be grouped under the general heading of *systematic observational research methods*. The purpose of chapter 12 is to give you information concerning the collection of systematic observational data. It covers topics such as use of standard observational forms, use of audiotape and videotape recorders to collect data, training of observers, and procedures for reducing observer bias. Also discussed are the use of situational testing, observations by untrained groups, computer-assisted observation, and the technique of content analysis.

OBJECTIVES

After studying this chapter you should be able to:

1. If given a broad characteristic such as "friendliness," identify specific behaviors that might be indicative of this characteristic and prepare low-inference items for use in an observation schedule.
2. State at least one advantage and one disadvantage of using a standard observational schedule in a research project.
3. Describe some of the factors to be considered in selecting observers.
4. If given a particular observation schedule, establish a procedure for training observers in its use.
5. Describe the types of factors that reduce the reliability and validity of observational data.
6. Describe precautions that the researcher should take to reduce observer bias, rating errors, and contamination.
7. Define "nonreactive measure" and describe the errors that can occur when reactive measures are used in educational research.
8. If given a research variable, identify at least one nonreactive measure that could be used to assess it.

9. Define situational tests and identify appropriate situational tests for use in particular research projects.
10. Describe how anecdotal records, sociometry, supervisory ratings, and critical-incident technique can be used in educational research.
11. Describe the steps a researcher takes in planning a content analysis.
12. If given a particular construct and a body of written material, develop appropriate content-analysis procedures for measuring this construct.

STEPS IN COLLECTING OBSERVATIONAL DATA

In preceding chapters we discussed standardized tests, survey questionnaires, and interviews as methods for collecting research data. These methods are similar in their reliance on self-report as the basic source of data. Although as a rule self-reports can be obtained easily and economically, people often bias the information they offer about themselves, and sometimes they cannot accurately recall events and aspects of their behavior in which the researcher is interested.[1]

In this chapter we are concerned primarily with *systematic observation*. In systematic observation a trained observer employs a predefined observation form. Concern for reliability and the use of methods that permit replication by other investigators are the essential elements of this type of research.

The observational method, if used properly, overcomes the limitations of the self-report method. Sechrest, for example, has argued that social attitudes, such as prejudice, should be studied by means of naturalistic observations, since self-reports of these attitudes are often biased by the set to give a socially desirable response.[2] Prejudice has been studied naturalistically by observing the seating patterns of black and white students in college classes.[3] Even when bias is not present in self-report data, the observational method usually yields more accurate quantitative data than could be obtained by self-report. For example, many educators have noted that in class discussions teachers dominate the talk at the expense of student participation. But what are the actual percentages of teacher and student talk in these discussions? It is unlikely that teachers or students could provide accurate self-report information on this question. However, an observational study in which an audiotape recorder or videotape recorder was used could yield precise quantitative data.

1. In a review of six studies in which both observational and self-report data were collected on the same specific behaviors, none reported a clear relationship between the two types of data. See Colin M. Hook and Barok V. Rosenshine, "Accuracy of Teacher Reports of Their Classroom Behavior," *Review of Educational Research* 49, no. 1 (1974), 1–12.
2. Lee Sechrest, "Naturalistic Methods in the Study of Social Attitudes" (Paper presented at APA Annual Convention, 1966).
3. Donald T. Campbell, William H. Kruskal, and William P. Wallace, "Seating Aggregation as an Index of Attitude," *Sociometry* 29 (1966): 1–15.

Although they overcome some limitations of self-report instruments, observational techniques have potential limitations of their own. In observational studies the experimenter attempting to study complex behavior patterns often finds that the more straightforward behaviors, which can be objectively observed and recorded, are only slightly related to the complex behaviors one wishes to study. Thus, one is faced with the choice of getting objective data that is of little value because of its limited relationship to a complex behavior or getting data more closely related to the complex behavior one is studying but finding it of limited value because of its subjectivity. Obtaining data related to complex behavior that is objectively observable and yet pertinent to the problem requires careful planning.

Another problem that must be faced in conducting the observational study is the degree to which the presence of the observer changes the situation being observed. In observations of classroom behavior, for example, a change in the behavior of both the teacher and class members usually occurs when an observer enters the room. Classrooms in laboratory schools are often provided with adjacent rooms fitted with one-way screens so that observations can be carried on without disturbing the situation. Occasionally studies are conducted in which the observer visits the classroom a number of times before recording any observational data so that the class will become accustomed to being observed and will react normally when the research data are actually collected.

In some cases the observer's role can be disguised so as to direct less attention to the presence of an experimenter. In fact, any changes in the observational situation that will make the observation less obtrusive and appear more a part of the regular classroom situation will reduce reactivity. Very often graduate students with limited control over the situations that they wish to observe find it difficult to solve this problem satisfactorily.

The time factor often makes observational research difficult for the graduate student. This method of gathering data is time-consuming, and the student usually finds it difficult to make enough observations of a sufficiently large sampling of individuals to provide reliable data. To provide reasonably sound data and to permit reliability estimates, observational studies usually require that at least two independent observers record data on the situation being observed. This again poses a problem for graduate students who must often rely entirely on their own resources for obtaining research data.

In addition to the aforementioned practical limitations, systematic classroom observation has been criticized on the grounds that only qualitative methods such as we discussed in chapter 10 can provide a meaningful picture of the classroom. A more basic criticism is that most educational questions simply cannot be explored by using empirical research procedures. Such criticisms ignore the fact that much useful knowledge about educational questions has already been produced by systematic observation and other forms of quantitative research, and generally reflect a lack of understanding of what quantitative research can and cannot do.[4]

Defining Observational Variables

Developing systematic observational measures for your research project is difficult. This section presents some techniques for developing and simplifying observational measures. To illustrate these techniques, we will use as an example a research problem that requires observation of behavior. Suppose our research problem is to determine whether a particular type of workshop in modern mathematics affects what teachers do in their classrooms.

This broad statement of the problem suggests some type of classroom observations, but these cannot be specified until several decisions are made.

First, we need to limit the number of observations that will be made. Because of the problem, observations will be limited to teachers' daily mathematics class, probably an hour or less. This still includes too broad a range of behavior. It would be quite unrealistic to expect an observer to record everything that transpires in a classroom for an hour. Even in a minute's time many different kinds of activities may occur. In order to determine what the observer should look for, we need to develop hypotheses or expectations about the effect of the workshop in classroom teaching. At this point we should be able to limit the focus of the observations considerably. Suppose that our main hypothesis is that teachers who have had workshop training in modern mathematics will spend more time explaining new mathematical concepts than teachers without this training. If this is the case, the observation process is simplified considerably, since the observer need only focus on the teacher rather than on students and teacher simultaneously. However, the total length of observation may need to be increased beyond a single class period. Teachers with workshop training may spend as much time as teachers without training in explaining a new concept on the first day, but they may spend more days developing a complete explanation. To detect this difference, observations over a period of several days, perhaps a week, may be necessary.

The first step then is to narrow or focus your observation by referring to your hypotheses or expectations for the pertinent variables to be observed and recorded. The next step is to define a behavior unit and a time unit. This process may in turn result in a still more focused range of observation. For the present example, it would be necessary to decide what behavior or behaviors constitute an ''explanation of a new mathematical concept.'' We may decide to define

4. See Paul Croll in the Annotated References at the end of this chapter for a discussion of these criticisms. For an extreme statement of the anti-research position, see Kieran Egan, *Education and Psychology* (New York: Teachers College Press, 1983).

explanation as "all teacher statements that define some aspect of the new concept, that present examples of the concept, or that direct students to perform tasks pertaining to the concept." In this case we might decide to make the individual sentence the basic unit of observation, which would enable us to express research findings in the following form: "Teachers with workshop training uttered _____ sentences to explain the new mathematical concept compared with _____ sentences for teachers without this training."[5] Next, it is necessary to define a precise time unit based on the total length of the observation. In our example the time unit might reflect a week's period of instruction in mathematics class, or about four hours. Thus, research findings would now be stated in this form: "In four hours of observed mathematics instruction, teachers with workshop training uttered _____ sentences compared with _____ sentences for teachers without this training." Now, ratios can also be expressed thus: "Ten explanatory sentences were uttered per hour of class time."

Three types of observational variables may be distinguished: descriptive, inferential, and evaluative. Descriptive variables have the advantage that they require little inference on the part of the observer. Consequently, they generally yield reliable data. Researchers often refer to such variables as "low inference" variables. For the present research example, we might want to have observers record all utterances of certain key phrases as each teacher explains a mathematical concept, such as regrouping. (These phrases include "place value," "base ten," "expanded notation," "renaming.") This is a purely descriptive task, and thus there would be high agreement between observers recording the behavior of a given teacher. Other observational variables require the observer to make an inference before a variable can be scored. For example, observers may be asked to record the self-confidence with which a teacher explains a mathematical concept. Some teachers may speak with a good deal of confidence, whereas others may appear uncertain, confused, or anxious because their understanding of the topic is weak. Confidence, uncertainty, confusion, and anxiety are not behaviors but rather are inferences made from behavior. These are often referred to as "high inference variables." It is much harder to collect reliable data when observers are asked to make inferences from behavior.

Related to inferential variables are evaluative variables. These also require an inference from behavior on the part of the observer, but in addition, the observer must make an evaluative judgment. For example, we may be interested in obtaining ratings of the quality of the teacher's explanation of a mathematical concept. Quality ratings are not behavior but rather are inferences made from behavior. Because it is difficult to make reliable observations of evaluative variables, we need to collect examples of behavior that define points along the

---

5. To simplify the process of recording, it might be desirable to just observe the time spent uttering such sentences. Thus, minutes and seconds become the basic unit of observation.

continuum of excellent-to-poor explanations and use these in training the observers.

You will note that as we progress from low inference, to high inference, to evaluative variables, the observers' task becomes more complex. Reid has pointed out that any changes in the observational task that make it more complex tends to lower observer reliability or agreement. He has devised several methods of estimating the complexity of the variables to be observed.[6]

To ensure accurate recording, observers should be required to score only one behavior at a given point in time. For example, most observers would find it quite difficult to record certain aspects of the teacher's talk and at the same time record the percentage of children who appear to be paying attention to the teacher. Consequently, the reliability of both sets of observations would probably be low.

Recording Observational Information

New formats for recording observational data are continually being developed. Most recording procedures, however, can be classified into four major categories: (1) duration recording, (2) frequency-count recording, (3) interval recording, and (4) continuous recording.

Duration Recording

In **duration recording** the observer simply uses some timing device, such as a stop watch, to measure the elapsed time during which the target behaviors occur. In many studies, the observer records time for a single behavior, such as the length of time a given student is out of his seat. However, if you are interested in duration of time during which several behaviors are emitted by a single subject, these can be recorded by a single observer if they generally do not occur at the same time. For example, the observer could record the length of time a given pupil was on-task, off-task but not disruptive, mildly disruptive, or seriously disruptive. Duration recording can be used to observe the amount of time several pupils emit a single behavior if it is a behavior that not more than one pupil will emit at the same time. For example, the duration of pupil verbal responses to teacher questions can be recorded for several pupils if, as a rule, only one pupil responds at a time. Reliability of duration recordings can be estimated by computing a correlation coefficient for the sets of duration scores that two observers recorded for a group of subjects. For example, each of the two

6. See J. B. Reid, ed, *A Social Learning Approach to Family Intervention: Vol. II, Observation in Home Settings* (Eugene, OR: Castalia Press, 1978) for a discussion of the research evidence supporting this position.

independent observers might record each pupil's seconds of verbal input during a one-hour classroom discussion; you would enter the two sets of scores into the raw score formula for the Product-Moment correlation. The resulting correlation coefficient is the inter-observer reliability of the duration data. Either the time of the two observers for each specific incident or cumulative time can be compared. In the latter case, the shorter time is usually divided by the longer time in comparing the two observers. For example, if observer A reported 82 minutes of out-of-seat behavior while observer B reported 96 minutes, the estimate of *interobserver agreement* would be 82/96 or .85. Interobserver reliability and interobserver agreement are not the same; and there are several ways that each may be computed. Therefore, you need to specify which you have computed and what method was used in the computation.[7]

Frequency-Count Recording

In **frequency-count recording** the observer records each time the target behavior or behaviors occur. Usually, a tally sheet or a counting device such as a wrist counter is used. If the target behavior occurs at very high frequency, an observer may be able to record only one behavior. However, observers can be trained to tally several moderate to low-frequency behaviors. Frequency counts are most useful in recording behaviors of short duration and those where duration is not important. For example, one of the authors conducted a study in which observers were trained to tally 13 teacher behaviors related to classroom management, such as goal-directed prompts, concurrent praise, and alerting cues. As the behaviors were of short duration and were such that more than one could not occur at the same time, interobserver reliabilities were satisfactory, ranging from .71 to .96 for the 13 behaviors.[8]

Interval Recording

Interval recording involves observing the behavior of the **target subject** (i.e., the subject being observed) at a given interval. For example, in the Flanders Interaction Analysis System the observer checks the behavior of the target subject each three seconds and records which of 10 specific behaviors the subject is emitting at each interval. All classroom behavior can be classified into one of the 10 Flanders categories.[9] Length of interval varies with nature of the behaviors being observed but usually ranges between 10 seconds and one

7. For more information, see Ted Frick and Melvyn I. Semmel, "Observer Agreement and Reliabilities of Classroom Observational Measures," *Review of Educational Research* 48 (1978): 157–184.
8. Walter R. Borg, "Changing Teacher and Pupil Performance with Protocols," *Journal of Experimental Education* 45, no. 3 (1977): 9–18.
9. Ned A. Flanders, *Analyzing Teaching Behavior* (Reading, MA: Addison-Wesley, 1970).

minute. In the simplest systems, the observer tallies whether the subject is or is not emitting a single target behavior at each interval; for example, a pupil is either on-task or not on-task. In more complex systems, such as Flanders's, all behavior is classified into a set of categories and the appropriate behavior is tallied at each interval. Such systems usually permit you to study the sequence of behavior. Also, multiplying the frequency of a given behavior by the time interval gives an estimate of duration.

But although interval recordings reflect both the frequency and the duration of the observed behavior, they do neither with the same level of accuracy as procedures that focus on one or the other. For this reason this method has been criticized by some researchers.[10]

Continuous Recording

In **continuous recording** the observer records all the behavior of the target subject (or subjects) during each observation session. This method does not usually focus on a specific set of behaviors. Typically, the observer writes a **protocol,** which is a brief narrative in chronological order of everything that the subject does or everything that occurs in a given setting such as a classroom, a faculty meeting, a reading group, or an arithmetic lesson. This approach is often used in exploratory studies to help the researcher identify important behavior patterns that can subsequently be studied using one of the other methods of recording. As it is virtually impossible to record everything, the observer must be very perceptive and must have a clear understanding of the kinds of behavior that are likely to be important when the protocols are analyzed. To analyze the protocols, the researcher reads them, sets up a content analysis system that fits the data, and then rereads and classifies the observed behavior into the system the researcher has developed. Continuous observation is also used in ethnographic research, which we discussed in chapter 10.

Time Sampling

Time sampling involves selecting intervals out of the total time available for observation and then observing only during the selected periods. This procedure can be used in conjunction with any of the four recording techniques we have just described. The intervals may be selected either at random or on a systematic basis. Random selection provides representative data for behaviors that can occur at any point in the total observational period. For example, an investigator could randomly select a one-hour period each day in which the

---

10. See D. P. Hartmann and D. D. Wood, "Observational Methods," in A. S. Bellack, M. Hersten, and A. E. Kazdin, eds., *International Handbook of Behavior Modification and Therapy* (New York: Plenum, 1982).

teacher's use of questions would be observed, since questioning behavior occurs throughout most of the school day. On the other hand, if you were interested in the ways teachers greet their pupils, a fixed period, perhaps the first 15 minutes of the school day, would be selected for observation.

The Observation Form

Once the observational variables to be used in the research study are identified, you need to develop a form on which they can be recorded. A paper-and-pencil observational form can accommodate a variety of scoring procedures. Perhaps the most common scoring procedure is to use a form that describes the behaviors to be observed in considerable detail so that the observer can check each behavior whenever it occurs. This form of scoring requires a minimum of effort on the part of the observer and can usually be developed so as to require the observer to make few inferences. The first item of the observation form presented in figure 12.1 is of this type. This scoring procedure is fairly easy for the observer to use, particularly if the categories are well defined and do not require a high level of inference.

Some studies require that the observer not only record the behavior as it occurs, but also evaluate it on a rating scale. Item 2 of the sample observation form is of this type. It is obvious that this scoring procedure requires a higher level of inference on the part of the observer. The observer must not only record the behavior but must also evaluate it, and this is much more difficult to do objectively. If you use a rating scale as part of your scoring procedure, you should avoid the common mistake of attempting to obtain excessively precise discrimination from the observer. Most human behavior studied in educational research cannot be reliably rated on more than five levels. The 3-point rating scale, breaking the behavior observed into such categories as "above-average," "average," and "below average," is often as fine a discrimination as can be made with satisfactory reliability. Five-point rating scales, however, are often used in educational research and can be employed effectively in observing well-defined behavior. It is almost never advisable to attempt to obtain ratings for finer than a 5-point scale. Furthermore, the more inference the observer must use in making the rating, the fewer rating levels should be employed. An "Officer Effectiveness Report" that was employed by the U.S. Air Force provides the ultimate example of attempting fine discriminations in the evaluation of characteristics that, at best, can only be differentiated roughly. This instrument, for example, required the senior officer to make an evaluation on the individual's cooperativeness. Fifteen levels of cooperativeness were provided by the scale. It is doubtful whether a complex behavior requiring as high a level of inference as "cooperativeness" can be accurately discriminated at more than three levels by most observers.

1. Check each question asked by the teacher into one of the following categories (observe for the first fifteen minutes of the class hour):

	Frequency	Total
a. Asks student to solve a problem at blackboard.	xxxx	4
b. Asks student to solve a problem at his seat.	xxxxxxx	7
c. Asks students if they have any questions or if they understand.	xx	2
d. Other.	xxxxx	5
	Grand Total	18

2. Each time the teacher asks a student to solve a problem, rate its level of difficulty on a 5-point scale.

	Frequency	Total
1. Difficult	xxx	3
2.	x	1
3. Average	xxxxx	5
4.	x	1
5. Easy	x	1
	Grand Total	11[a]

[a] The sum here should equal the sum of categories *a* and *b* in item 1.

Figure 12.1   Sample Observation Form

Figure 12.1 illustrates the way the observers' recording task can be made more simple and accurate by providing a checklist. The first item of the sample observation form in figure 12.1 could have required the observer to write down each question that is asked by the teacher. As teachers ask questions fairly frequently, the observer would need to do much writing; if the writing demand is excessive, the accuracy of the observer's report is likely to be affected adversely. The use of the four categories that appear in the sample observation form is preferable since the observer's task is simplified and the resulting data are in quantitative form.

Pilot Testing

After a prototype of the observation form has been developed, try it out in a number of situations similar to those to be observed in the research and correct any weaknesses you discover. A common weakness in prototype forms is that they require the observer to record more kinds of behavior or watch more subjects than can be done reliably. Although observers can be trained to record 20 or more different behaviors, a great deal of training is needed when the number of behaviors exceeds 10.

Similarly, the more subjects the observer must watch, the more difficult the task becomes and as a result the data obtained will be less accurate. In many studies better data will be obtained if the observer watches a random sample of subjects rather than all subjects in the observed situation. For example, in classroom observation the observer can obtain more reliable data on a random sample of six pupils than if called upon to observe every pupil in the class.

Another weakness found in prototype observation forms is that the behaviors to be observed are not defined in sufficient detail. These definitions are used by the observer to determine whether or not a given behavior occurred. They should be detailed and specific and give examples of the behavior taken from observations made by the researcher. They should also give examples of behaviors that are similar but should *not* be recorded so that the observer can compare these with situations that occur during observations. Usually an instruction sheet is attached to the observation form so that these detailed definitions and guidelines are always available to the observers. During observer training these instructions are refined further, as we will discuss later in this chapter.

Standard and Experimental Observational Schedules

Instead of developing your own observational schedule for a research project, you may prefer to use one of the many **standard observational schedules** that have been developed by educational researchers. In planning an observational study, you should consider the various advantages of using one of these schedules. First, as is true of standardized personality and aptitude tests, standard observational schedules have usually reached a stage of development where they are valid and reliable measuring instruments. Second, use of a standard schedule saves you the considerable amount of time that it takes to develop your own schedule. Third, because most of these standard schedules have been used in a number of research studies, you can compare your findings with those obtained by other researchers using the same instrument. The obvious disadvantage of standard schedules is that they sometimes do not include all the variables that you are interested in measuring. However, in this case you can use just the part of the schedule that you need, keeping in mind that previously reported reliabilty and validity data will not apply if only part of the instrument is used.

The standard observational schedules that have been developed vary in complexity, the type of behavior they record, and the settings in which they can be used. An exhaustive coverage of classroom forms is provided in *Mirrors for*

Behavior and *Evaluating Classroom Instruction* (see Annotated References). These references are both over 10 years old, but many of the instruments described are still in use.

A good way to locate more recent observation instruments that you can use in your research is to conduct a brief computer search of the ERIC and PsycINFO data bases. You should link the observation descriptor (ERIC: "Classroom Observation Techniques"; PsycINFO: "Observation Methods") with descriptors for the specific behavior you want to observe, using "and" connectors.

The ETS Test Collection Bibliography entitled "Systematic Observation Techniques" is also an excellent source for locating observation schedules. You will recall that these bibliographies are frequently updated. The current bibliography describes over 100 observation forms aimed at measuring a wide range of variables. While most are focused on various aspects of teacher and/or student behavior in the classroom, others deal with such diverse areas as personality characteristics, marital interactions, counselor-client verbal behaviors, and ward adjustment of neuropsychiatric patients.

We should note that many of the observation forms you will find through computer searching or the ETS Bibliography are experimental forms developed for use in a research project. Many of these, however, are carefully developed and comparable to standard observational schedules.

A good illustration of the research contribution that standard observational schedules can make is provided by Wayne Herman's study of how a six-week social studies unit was taught in classrooms of above-average, average, and below-average ability students.[11] Flanders's system of interaction analysis and Medley and Mitzel's OScAR (Observation Schedule and Record) were used to observe classroom interaction. Several interesting differences in teachers' instructional style were found between the three types of classrooms. Analysis of the observational data collected using the Flanders system (which classifies all classroom verbal behavior) showed that teachers of above-average students tend to use more indirect techniques[12] than do teachers of average and below-average students. Also, teachers very infrequently criticize above-average and average students, but criticize below-average students to a moderate extent. Another finding was that above-average students tend to talk more than average and below-average students, who, in turn, do not differ from each other in talkativeness. The OScAR data provided somewhat different insights into classroom interaction. The reason is that this observational schedule classifies different behaviors (primarily classroom activities) from the Flanders system. Analysis of the OScAR data indicated that teachers of above-average students

11. Wayne L. Herman, Jr., "An Analysis of the Activities and Verbal Behavior in Selected Fifth-Grade Social Studies Classes," *Journal of Educational Research* 60 (1967): 339–345.
12. Indirect techniques include accepting feelings, praising students, accepting student ideas, and asking questions.

spend only half as much class time (7.7 percent) using illustrations[13] as teachers of average students (20.8 percent). Teachers of below-average students rely on illustrations most of all (41.5 percent of class time). Herman's interpretation of this finding is that "this progression should appear because as the intelligence level of the groups decreases there is more need for concrete instructional materials of a visual nature, such as maps, pictures, blackboard, and three-dimensional activities" (pp. 342–343). Further analysis of the OScAR data indicated that students of above-average ability spend more total class time (30.8 percent) in independent seatwork than do students of average (10.6 percent) or below-average (12.6 percent) ability. This finding suggests that above-average students are more independent and less in need of teacher direction.

It should be apparent from this summary of Herman's research project that use of standard observational schedules, such as the Flanders system and OScAR, can yield important insights into the nature of classroom interaction.

Use of Audiotape and Videotape Records

In some situations it is impractical to collect observational data at the same time the critical behavior is occurring. If several of the behaviors to be rated occur at the same time or closely together, the observer's task can be complicated to the point that her observations lose validity. For example, the observer may be required to rate each teacher and student response on one or more dimensions. If teacher-student interaction occurs with high frequency, the observer is likely to be frustrated in her attempts to record all the necessary observational data. Also, we have already noted that observational ratings differ in the level of inference required of the observer. When ratings require a high level of inference, an observer will probably want an opportunity to study the behavior carefully before making a rating. However, in a live observational setting, there is no chance to have several "instant replays" of a critical event. Another situation in which it may be impractical to collect observational data at the time the behavior occurs is when you want to check on the reliability of observers' ratings. We have discussed elsewhere the desirability of reporting the interrater reliability of observational data; otherwise you have no way of knowing the extent to which observations reflect the biases and idiosyncrasies of a single observer. However, it is not always possible to have two or more observers present at the same time to observe the events on which ratings are to be made. A similar situation occurs when you wish to have specially qualified observers rate samples of behavior. As an illustration, suppose that you wish to describe and rate the techniques that children use in the process of drawing pictures. Art teachers are probably the best qualified to make observations, but they may not be free to observe at the time the children are working on their pictures.

Obviously all the situations just described present obstacles to your using

13. Illustrations include maps, pictures, and blackboard activities.

the observational method. Audiotape and videotape recorders may help to overcome these obstacles. When recorders are used, observers no longer need to make ratings at the time particular events are occurring. These events may be recorded on audiotape or videotape so that they can be replayed several times for careful study or for several observers to rate at their convenience. Another advantage of recording observations is that the recordings permit you to obtain data on behavior that you did not anticipate you would need at the outset of your study. For example, in a study of teacher praise, you may notice midway through your observations that teachers are using kinds of praise remarks that you did not anticipate in planning your observation form. If you have recorded the observations, you can replay them and reclassify the praise statements so as to include the types of praise not listed on your original observation form.

Consider carefully the advantages of these recording techniques if you are planning to do an observational study. At the same time you should note certain disadvantages. Videotape recorders provide a fairly complete record of behavior, but they are not easy to obtain, and videotape is fairly expensive.[14] Audiotape recorders are much more accessible, but they are limited to recording verbal behavior; also, it is often hard to identify and differentiate among speakers when listening to audiotape. In certain situations technical competence is required in order to obtain satisfactory video/audio recording. For example, you may need to have more than one microphone and to adjust the camera frequently so that a reasonably complete record of classroom behavior can be obtained.

If these disadvantages are overcome, recording behavior so that it can be observed and rated at a later time is highly desirable. Sometimes it is not possible to obtain enough videotape or audiotape recorders to use in the main data-collection phase of your study. However, if they are available, one or two recorders can be used to collect samples of behavior to facilitate the development of an observation form and the training of observers. The recordings can be replayed as often as necessary, thus making it easier to develop observational categories and to test the reliability with which observers can use these categories in rating behavior.

Another possibility when a limited amount of videotape is available is to make typed transcripts of the videotaped records. Once the transcript has been made, the videotape can be erased and reused. This approach is especially useful when sophisticated analysis of language is required or when the observer is working with a complex category system or one requiring a high level of inference. Typed transcripts of videotape have been used in many of the

---

14. Many universities have audiovisual centers from which videotape recording equipment may be borrowed. Also, if your research is being carried out in the public schools, needed equipment may sometimes be borrowed from the schools involved.

Stanford University studies on microteaching and have yielded highly reliable data.[15]

Selecting and Training Observers

Select persons to work as observers with care, for careless or unmotivated observers can destroy the most carefully planned study.

Some research evidence shows that observers who produce the most reliable data tend to be persons of above-average intelligence and verbal fluency who are highly motivated to do a good job.[16] Our experience indicates that women in the 30 to 45 age range who have some college education, whose children are all of school age, and who are seeking temporary part-time employment tend to make good observers. They typically know something about the local schools and relate well to teachers and other school personnel. They are easily motivated and fit well into a schedule that only demands two or three hours a day and can be adjusted to fit with their other responsibilities. College students are also used as observers in many studies. This work provides valuable experience for students who are majoring in education or psychology. The biggest problem in using college students is scheduling the observations around their class schedules. Because of the scheduling problem and the tendency for students not to show when they have a test or assignment due in one of their classes, you should train enough students to have adequate backup. Structured observations often become boring if more than two hours a day is scheduled, and boredom, fatigue or loss of motivation usually lead to less reliable observational data.

After the observation form has been developed and tried out on a small scale to correct its more serious deficiencies, it should be employed to train the individuals who will conduct the observations required by the research. The first step in the training is to discuss the observation form with the observers, describing each item sufficiently to develop a thorough understanding of what is to be observed and how it is to be recorded. Usually brief and precise definitions of each behavior to be observed should be included on the form or on a separate instruction sheet. The trainee should become very familiar with the form and behavioral definitions before moving to the next level of training. It is usually desirable to test the trainee on this basic information to ensure his or her mastery. This test also provides a good device for eliminating persons who lack motivation, as they will do poorly on the test and, if they are employed, are

15. These studies are described in Walter Borg, Marjorie Kelley, Philip Langer, and Meredith Gall, *The Minicourse: A Microteaching Approach to Teacher Education* (Beverly Hills, CA: Macmillan Educational Services, 1970).
16. See Donald P. Hartmann in the Annotated References at the end of this chapter.

likely to do poorly on the observational task as well. Then make videotape recordings of situations similar to those to be observed in the study and replay these *before* the training sessions to fill out the observation form and to be sure that examples of the behaviors to be observed are present. Next, start the training session by showing 10 to 15 minutes of the videotape. Stop the recorder each time one of the behaviors to be scored occurs, call the trainees' attention to the behavior, and discuss specifically *why* this event fits the definition of the behavior in question. This process of relating actual examples of each behavior to the behavioral definitions helps give each trainee a clear understanding of what is to be observed.

The next step is to set up practice observations in which all observer trainees participate. The videotapes made earlier can be used in the practice observations. Show a brief segment of the videotape, instructing the trainees to record each behavior on the observation form as it occurs. Be sure that trainees are seated so that they cannot see each other's forms, since you wish to determine how accurately each trainee can *independently* record what he or she has seen. After the videotape has been played, you should individually check each trainee to determine if he or she has correctly tallied the behaviors observed using the observation form you completed earlier as a criterion. If the observers disagree with each other or with the criterion, as is usually the case, replay the videotape, stopping at each behavior to explain how it should have been recorded, and why. During these discussions the observers' instruction sheet should be revised to include any clarifications that come about as a result of using the observation form. Usually, a few special rules will also be developed during this time to help the observers make decisions about how to record unusual behavior that was not foreseen when the observation form was developed.

During the practice sessions, watch for other deficiencies in the observation form or instructions. Common problems include (1) requiring the observer to record too many behaviors, (2) including behaviors on the form that cannot be reliably identified by the observers, even after extensive training, and (3) poor format that slows down recording or causes observer errors or omissions. Sometimes your observation form will include two behaviors that are quite similar. Thus, when borderline cases occur, the observers have difficulty deciding which behavior to record. This problem can be resolved in several ways. The two behaviors can be combined into one redefined behavior, or, if it is essential to get data separately on the two behaviors, a rule can be established to resolve borderline cases. Such cases can be placed in a "can't decide" category, or can be assigned to the two categories alternately, or can be assigned to the two categories randomly by flipping a coin.

The process of practice and feedback should be repeated with different videotape segments until you reach the desired level of agreement among the observer trainees. For tallying highly specific descriptive behavior, such as counting the number of times the teacher smiles, the percentage of agreement between observers should be above 90 percent. When the observer must make inferences or evaluations about the behavior being observed, however, 70 to 80 percent agreement is usually considered satisfactory. To determine the level of agreement, check whether observers agreed or disagreed on each behavior that should have been recorded during the observation and divide the number of agreements by the total of agreements and disagreements.[17] Start the training with short segments, but as the observers gain expertise use longer segments until the later phases of training are being conducted for periods that are the same length as the observations that will be conducted in the study.

After the observers have been trained by observing videotape recordings, it is desirable for them to practice further in the setting where they will actually carry out their observations, for example, regular classrooms. They should not, of course, practice in classrooms that will be used in the research, but in similar classrooms. If possible, videotape recordings of these practice sessions should be made so that after the observation the recording can be replayed and discussed. Research on observer training has demonstrated that programs such as those we have recommended result in accurate and reliable oservational data.[18]

Once the observers have been trained to the desired level of agreement and accuracy, start the observations promptly since a delay will result in some loss in observer skills. If the observations are to extend for more than one week, you should hold a weekly refresher training session for the observers. If this is not done the observational data will become less reliable since the observers will gradually lose the common frame of reference they developed during training. This "observer drift" can be a major source of error in observational studies. If each observer interprets and records the same behavior differently, it is obvious that no objective information will be produced.

Research evidence also suggests that observers should be checked frequently during the course of the study to keep them performing at a satisfactory level. Taplin and Reid compared "decay" in reliability for three groups of observers: (1) those who were told they would not be checked, (2) those told they would be spot-checked at regular intervals, and (3) those told they would be checked on a random basis. The random-checked group maintained the highest level of reliability followed by the spot-checked group and the not-checked group.[19] Since the spot-checked group performed very well in the

17. A weakness of "percentage of agreement" is that some of the agreement is due to chance. An agreement statistic that corrects for chance (Cohen's kappa) is described in Roger Bakeman and John M. Gottman in the Annotated References at the end of this chapter.
18. See Mark D. Spool, "Training Programs for Observers of Behavior: A Review," *Personnel Psyhology* 31 (1978): 853–888, for a review of research on this topic.
19. P. S. Taplin and J. B. Reid, "Effects of Instructional Set and Experimenter Influence on Observer Reliability," *Child Development* 44 (1973): 547–554.

sessions where they knew they *would* be checked, and very poorly in the sessions where they thought they *would not* be checked, the problem seems to be one of motivation. Therefore you should do what is possible to maintain high levels of motivation. For example, you should try to convince the observers of the importance of their task, schedule sessions so as to avoid observer fatigue, inform them that you will check their performance on a random basis, carry out frequent random checks, and give them frequent feedback on their reliability.

During the training period, in addition to computing percent of agreement for each session, interrater reliability coefficients may be calculated after every ten practice sessions in order to estimate the degree to which observers are developing a common frame of reference. These correlations are usually computed separately for each behavior across the 10 sessions. All observers are compared, pair by pair, to determine if certain observers consistently disagree with their colleagues or if certain behaviors cannot be reliably observed. Interrater reliabilities should reach at least .70, and much higher reliabilities can be obtained if training is adequate, motivation is maintained, and observations are of specific behavior.

As the training progresses, some observers will probably be found who cannot develop a reliable frame of reference. Some persons seem to be unable to interpret consistently the behavior they observe or in the same way that it is interpreted by the rest of the group. After a reasonable training period, it is usually advisable to replace these persons with other observers.

Reducing Observer Effect

Research suggests that observers are sometimes not very objective in their use of observational schedules. When this situation occurs, the research data will reflect the biases and characteristics of the observer rather than the observational variables that you seek to measure. It is also well documented that the presence of the observer can affect the behavior of those being observed. As a consequence, the research data may reflect atypical rather than naturally occurring behavior. The student planning an observational study should be aware of these unwanted observer effects and take steps to remove or reduce them. They include:

1. *The effect of the observer on the observed.* Unless concealed, the observer is likely to have an impact on the observed. For example, an observer entering a classroom for the first time probably will arouse the curiosity of the students and possibly the teacher. The resulting inattentiveness of the students to the teacher may not reflect their usual behavior and thus may provide nonrepresentative observational data. To reduce this effect the observer should not record any observations for at least the first five or ten minutes that he or she is in the classroom. In some cases the experimenter may need to make several visits to the classroom before students take the intrusion for granted and behave as if the

observer were not present. It is also advisable for the teacher to prepare students beforehand for the observer's visit and to introduce the visitor when she or he enters the classroom. This procedure is usually sufficient to satisfy student curiosity and to restore the normal classroom situation within a few minutes.

A more serious problem caused by the presence of the observer occurs when the person or persons being observed are influenced in their behavior by the observer's intentions. Suppose the purpose of an observational study is to record the number and length of dyadic interactions between teacher and student in art classes. If they learn that this is the purpose of the study, teachers will probably increase the frequency of their dyadic interactions, particularly if they are led to believe that this is desirable behavior. As a result, the research data based on recorded observations will be nonrepresentative of the teachers' actual classroom behavior and thus possess little or no validity. Therefore we advise you to meet with the teachers before observations are made. At this meeting inform the teachers candidly that they cannot be told the nature of the research project because this might affect their behavior. Also reassure them that the data will be kept confidential and will not reflect unfavorably on the individuals who participate.

It is also good procedure to tell the teachers that after the observational data have been collected, they will be informed of the study's purpose. Occasionally while the study is in progress a teacher will attempt to learn the purpose of the research from the observer or to secure a copy of the observation form. The training of observers should include directions not to give this information to teachers while the study is in progress and to report such attempts to you.[20]

2. *Observer bias.* This type of bias refers to systematic errors that are traceable to characteristics of the observer or of the observational situation. In contrast to random errors, which are distributed around "true" scores or values, bias usually produces errors in a single direction, yielding scores that are consistently too high or too low. We doubt whether any observations we conduct are completely free from bias, and there is evidence to suggest that in many studies that have a high potential for bias, the investigators do not take sufficient precautions to avoid it.[21]

In the observation process, observers bring to bear all their past experience, and as these past experiences will differ for each observer, it will lead to different perceptions of the situation, different emphases, and different interpretations. Biases, of course, have a much greater chance of operating when the

---

20. For a more complete discussion of observer presence effects, see Gerald R. Patterson, *A Social Learning Approach: Vol. 3, Coercive Family Process* (Eugene, OR: Castalia Publishing Co., 1982), pp. 53–58.
21. J. A. Salvia and C. J. Mersel, "Observer Bias: A Methodological Consideration in Special Education Research," *Journal of Special Education* 14 (1980): 261–270, reviewed 153 studies having a high potential for bias and found that only 22 percent reported adequate safeguards.

observer is called upon to draw conclusions or make involved inferences from the behavior observed. Possible sources of bias should be looked for and eliminated if they are found. For example, to use an observer who was prejudiced against blacks in a study observing the creative ability of black children and white children in a nursery school would clearly be unwise. The person's bias would almost certainly lead to seeing more creative behavior among white children and either ignoring, misinterpreting, or minimizing the creative efforts of black children in this group. In addition to racial and ethnic biases, many other subject characteristics have been shown to bias the ratings of some observers. These include social class, physical attractiveness, and labels such as "emotionally disturbed" or "mentally retarded."[22]

The best method to control for the possible presence of observer bias is to check carefully for bias during training when comparative data are available on all observers, and to eliminate any observers whose data appear to be biased. A further safeguard is to assign two observers to each situation to be observed. Generally the combined records of two or more observers provide more reliable data than the record of a single observer. The extent of interobserver agreement can be determined by computing the appropriate statistic. Usually a measure of correlation or a percentage of agreement is obtained. (Correlational statistics are discussed in chapter 9.) When more than one observer is used, each should work independently. If observers work together, one usually influences the other, and the judgments of this observer are therefore given more weight because they are reflected in the other's ratings. Also, when observers work together, each observer's ratings are contaminated by the judgments of the other observer, thus making reliability coefficients spuriously high. In many studies it is not possible to employ two observers for every observation. In this case enough observations are carried out with two observers to check interrater reliability and the rest are conducted with one observer.

3. *Rating errors.* In our discussion of standardized measures of personality, we noted that the validity of these measures is sometimes weakened by the presence of response sets. Some persons will give a socially desirable response to a personality item irrespective of the item's content. Thus, the person's score on the test is more a reflection of a response set than whether that person possesses the personality trait measured by the test. A similar situation is found sometimes with observational rating scales. As a result, several kinds of systematic errors are often found in observational data. Three common errors of this sort are called *error of leniency, error of central tendency*, and *halo effect*.

Some observers assign the same rating to the majority of research subjects even when there are obvious individual differences among them. For example, some observers have a tendency to rate most individuals at the high end of the

---

22. See Salvia and Mersel, "Observer Bias," for a brief review of research on this topic.

scale. This tendency is called the **error of leniency**. In studies where the research worker has an opportunity to train observers thoroughly and has complete control over the situation, the error of leniency is rarely a problem. In many observational studies, however, research workers have relied upon observers over whom they have little control. As an illustration, studies of teacher effectiveness often use the school principal as an observer. It is rarely possible in studies of this sort to train the observers sufficiently to rule out errors of leniency and other rating errors. Therefore, if at all possible the research worker should attempt to train impartial observers.

Another error common in observational ratings is the **error of central tendency**. This error is caused by the inclination of the individual to rate the persons observed at the middle of the scale. Sometimes observers will rate everyone near the average to avoid making difficult decisions. This tendency should be watched for during training. This error is also made in cases where some of the behaviors to be rated have not occurred during the observation. The observer, feeling the need to register some sort of information on the form, rates the individual at the average, or center, of the rating scale.

Still another error frequently encountered is the so-called **halo effect**. This is the tendency for the observer to form an early impression of the person being observed and to permit this impression to influence his or her ratings on all behaviors involving the given individual. For example, if the observer forms an initially favorable impression of the person being observed, the observer will tend to rate the individual favorably in subsequent performance areas. An initially unfavorable impression can lead to the opposite effect. All three errors—leniency, central tendency, and halo effect—are most likely to occur when the observer must draw inferences or evaluate abstract qualities rather than record specific behaviors. Thus, these errors occur more easily when the observer rates such characteristics as "cooperativeness," "integrity," and "interest in the job" than when she or he rates specific behavior such as "shakes hands with the visitor," "rises from the chair when the visitor enters the room," and "offers the visitor a chair."

The magnitude of these errors can be so large when subjective high-inference variables are observed that the resulting ratings are virtually meaningless. For example, a recent study of the ratings of student-teachers by cooperating teachers showed such high levels of halo effect and error of leniency that the validity of the entire rating system was called into question. The student-teachers were rated on 5-point scales in such subjective areas as "attitude" and "personality." The *mean* "attitude" rating of the 161 student-teachers who participated in this study was 4.85 out of a possible 5.[23]

23. See LeAdelle Phelps, Charles D. Schmitz, and Blaine Boatright, "The Effects of Halo and Leniency on Cooperating Teacher Reports Using Likert-Type Rating Scales," *Journal of Educational Research* 79, no. 3 (1986): 151–154.

4. *Contamination.* A frequent flaw in observational studies is contamination. While bias is usually the result of predispositions of the observer, **contamination** occurs when the observer's knowledge of one aspect of a study tends to corrupt by contact the observer's perception of data recorded in another aspect of the study. The most common source of contamination is the influence of the observer's knowlege concerning the performance of the subjects on one of the variables being studied on his or her observation of another variable. Let us say, for example, that we are doing a study of the human relations skills of successful elementary school principals. Unsuccessful and successful principals could be identified by a composite evaluation made by teachers, parents, and school superintendents. It may then be possible to observe the performance of the successful and unsuccessful principals in faculty meetings and evaluate them on certain human relations skills. If, however, the persons observing the faculty meetings are aware of which principals have been classified as successful and which as unsuccessful, this knowledge will almost certainly influence their perceptions of the principal's behavior.

Contamination is an especially serious problem in master's degree studies because one graduate student often collects all data involved in the study. If the student is aware of the dangers of contamination, however, ways can usually be found to avoid it. For example, if we are studying relationships between academic achievement and leadership in the classroom, observations of leadership behavior could be carried out before achievement data are gathered; or the achievement test could be administered, if necessary, but not scored until leadership ratings are completed.

But suppose the achievement data were needed to identify students to be observed, for example, high and low achievers. In this case the achievement test could be scored, and another person, not connected with the study, could write down the names of the high and low achievers in random order and give this list to the observer. Any of these approaches would make it impossible for the observer's perceptions of leadership behavior to be influenced by knowledge of the subject's achievement level.

Observer expectations are also a powerful source of contamination. Research has demonstrated that an observer's expectations can have a significant effect on how one interprets and records what one sees. For example, in a study by Anita Kolman, different observer groups were shown identical videotapes of nursery children at play and were asked to record instances of aggression.[24] One group of observers was told it was viewing middle-class children and to expect a large amount of aggression (MC); another group was told it was viewing lower-class children and to expect a high level of aggression (LC). The third group was told nothing about the children or what level of aggression to expect

24. Anita Sue Kolman, "Definition of the Situation and Observer Bias" (paper presented at the annual meeting on the Midwest Sociological Society, April 1975). ED 118600.

(CON). Significant differences were found among the three observer groups. The MC observers did see more aggression than the CON observers, which supports the researchers' hypothesis. However, the LC observers saw *less* aggression than the CON observers, a result that was counter to the hypothesis. Remember, all observers were looking at the same videotapes. One of the videotapes showed clear examples of aggression, while the other showed more ambiguous situations that required more observer judgment. More bias occurred when observers viewed the ambiguous situations as the researchers had hypothesized. Thus, both observer expectations and the ambiguity of the observed situation led to increased bias, but in the case of the LC group, the bias was not in the expected direction.

In an earlier study by Karlton Skindrud, although observers remembered the expectations conveyed by the researchers, these expectations had no effect upon their observations of a videotape of deviant child behavior in a family situation.[25] The author believed no observer contamination occurred because mature, well-trained observers were used. Observer bias or contamination are most likely to occur when observers are not adequately trained, when the observational task is difficult, when behavior to be observed is defined in global or ambiguous terms, and when observer drift from standard code definitions is not controlled.

Observer expectations can also distort results when some form of pre- and post-observations are to be made. If one knows the expected outcomes of the experimental treatment, the observer may watch more closely for these outcomes on the post-treatment observations. This effect can be avoided by having the observer score tape recordings or typed transcripts of the classroom situation. Under these conditions you should wait until both pre- and post-treatment recordings have been made and then assign tapes or transcripts to observers in random order so that they do not know whether they are observing a pre-treatment or post-treatment recording. An even better method is the "doubleblind" technique in which all tapes or transcripts are number coded and neither the observers nor the person distributing them to the observers knows which tapes or transcripts were made at the beginning and which at the end of the study.

Table 12.1 summarizes the major observer effects and errors that must be controlled or avoided in planning and carrying out observational research. Review these and consider the following precautions that should be taken to minimize these observer effects and errors.

1. Structure the observational situation so that the observer is as unobtrusive as possible.

25. Karlton D. Skindrud, *An Evaluation of Observer Bias in Experimental-Field Studies of Social Interaction* (Eugene: Oregon Research Institute, 31 July 1972). ED 072105.

TABLE 12.1

Ten Important Observer Effects and Errors

Type	Description	Example
1. Effect of observer on the observed	Person(s) observed change their behavior because they are aware of the observation	A teacher uses more praise and less sarcasm in order to create a better impression.
2. Effect of observer on the setting	Presence of the observer may lead to anxieties or expectations that change the climate of the observed situation	Spontaneity may be suppressed and the classroom atmosphere may become more formal.
3. Observer personal bias	Systematic errors traceable to characteristics of the observer or the observational situation.	An observer who believes welfare recipients are lazy underreports their work activities.
4. Error of leniency	When using a rating scale, observer tends to make most ratings at the favorable end of the scale.	A principal rates all of teachers in the school as "outstanding" on a 5-point scale.
5. Error of central tendency	When using a rating scale, observer tends to make most ratings around the midpoint.	Observer is asked to make high-inference judgments on variables such as "dedication," and avoids the task by rating everyone "average."
6. Halo effect	Observer's initial impression distorts later evaluations or judgments of the subject.	Observer is impressed by teacher's warm interactions with children and subsequently rates the teacher high on teaching skills.

7. Observer omissions	Because the observation system includes variables that occur very rapidly or simultaneously, the observer overlooks some behavior that should be recorded.	Observer is required to classify all teacher and student remarks into 15 categories. During a heated class discussion several students talk at once and observer is overwhelmed.
8. Observer drift	The tendency for observers to gradually redefine the observational variables, so that the data collected do not reflect the original categories.	Observers are asked to rate teacher enthusiasm, but as each observes different teachers their definitions of enthusiasm gradually drift apart.
9. Reliability decay	Toward end of training, observer reliability is high, but in the field, as monitoring and motivation decrease, observers become less reliable.	Observer Jones is assigned to record teacher reinforcement in Ms. Smith's classroom, 4 hours a day for a week. As fatigue and boredom increase, Jones' reliability drops.
10. Contamination	The observer's knowledge of one aspect of a study influences his or her perception of events observed in another part of the study. Observer expectations are a common form of contamination.	The experimental group of kindergarten children is given special training in social skills that is withheld from the control group. The observer knows which group has received training and is more alert to social skills displayed by children in the experimental group.

SOURCE: Adapted from Carolyn M. Everton and Judith L. Green, "Observation as Inquiry and Method," in Merlin C. Wittrock, ed., *Handbook of Research on Teaching*, Third ed. (New York: Macmillan, 1986).

2. Explain the common rating errors to the observers and structure the observation schedule to minimize these errors.

3. Be sure the observation schedule does not require the observer to record more data or record at a higher rate than can be done accurately.

4. Make the observational task as objective as possible. Avoid requiring the observer to make evaluations, interpretations, or high-level inferences.

5. Give the observer as little information as possible about your hypotheses, research design, and expectations.

6. Do not reveal to the observer information about the characteristics of your subjects, such as social class, IQ, or composition of experimental and control groups, that the observer does not need to know.

7. Train observers to a high level of reliability and objectivity, and retrain as necessary to avoid observer drift.

8. Monitor observers on a random basis to minimize reliability decay.

9. Construct your observation form to minimize recording errors.[26]

10. Check for bias when training observers, and eliminate those who submit biased observations.[27]

Computer-Assisted Observation[28]

The observation of behavior in educational and psychological research yields a wealth of valuable information. However, it is a complicated and labor-intensive process. The complexity of behavior and of observation methods leads to technical errors, such as miscoding, as well as problems in achieving and maintaining satisfactory interrater agreement.

Tools have been devised to alleviate some of the technical problems of research observation. For many years, computers and event-recording devices have been used in controlled laboratory studies of animals and in the study of human behavior.[29] More recently, microcomputers[30] handheld recording devices, and even hand-held calculators have been used as tools in observational

26. A review of recording errors in 21 studies by Robert Rosenthal, "How Often Are Our Numbers Wrong?" *American Psychologist* (1978) 1005–1008, found an error rate of about 1 percent. Two-thirds of the errors found were in a direction favoring the researcher's hypothesis.

27. An informative review of observer bias is provided by A. E. Kazdin, "Artifact, Bias, and Complexity of Assessment: The ABC's of Reliability," *Journal of Applied Behavioral Analysis* 10 (1977): 141–150.

28. This section was written by Carl Berger, Mark Shermis, and Paul Stemmer, University of Michigan.

29. See J. G. Baker and G. Whitehead, "Technical Note: A Portable Recording Apparatus for Rating Behavior in Free-Operant Situations," *Journal of Applied Behavior Analysis*, no. 5 (1972): 191–192.

30. See R. A. Owings and C. H. Fiedler, "Measuring Reaction Time with Millisecond Accuracy Using the TRS-80 Microcomputer," *Behavior Research Methods and Instrumentation* 11 (1979): 589–591.

data collection.[31] This section describes the use of a microcomputer in combination with the Behavioral Event Recording Package (BERP) as a data-collection and storage encoder for observational studies. BERP features a multichannel event-recording and data-storage device. Ten user-defined keys act as 10 independent timing devices (stopwatches) while also recording event sequences.

Our experience indicates that this package can be extremely helpful and cost-effective when used with videotape observation. To bring a microcomputer into a classroom might be too obtrusive in some instances. Under these conditions, a keyboard number pad adaptation (with a long ribbon cable) or a handheld calculator would seem to be a less obtrusive means of event recording. However, handheld calculators lack a clock for timed study, and the information must be later transferred to computer storage media.

The BERP package features real-time error prevention. Wild codes are simply not permitted. The direct storage of the data reduces the number of steps required, thereby decreasing the likelihood of error in the transfer process. The ease of use of this system appears to show great promise in increasing interrater agreement. Previous research has shown that event-recording devices generally improve rater accuracy.

The number of keys allows for ten simultaneous behavior codings. This number was chosen so that the observer need only be trained so that each finger represents an event. An experienced user need not look away from the event being recorded.

The package can provide evidence of systematic errors, thus providing a means of observation training.[32] The program could be modified to make a total training package, or without modifications, the data may be used in training to provide the observer-trainees with feedback on Interval-by-Interval and Occurrence Agreement.

In the typical observational study the microcomputer can help with several of the necessary steps. During the observation itself, recording is much easier using the computer than entering data into a manual observation form. When one of the selected behaviors occurs, the observer presses the key that represents the behavior being observed. Pressing the key a second time records the cessation of that behavior. The microcomputer stores the sequence of behaviors as they occur and records the duration of each event. If a second behavior starts before the first is finished, the observer presses the key for the second behavior, and the microcomputer keeps track of both. The BERP permits

31. See Jeffrey L. Edleson, "An Inexpensive Instrument for Rapid Recording of In Vivo Observations," *Journal of Applied Behavior Analysis* 11, no. 4 (1978): 502.
32. See George C. Thornton and S. Zorich, "Training to Improve Observer Accuracy," *Journal of Applied Psychology* 65 (1980): 351–354.

recording data on 10 different behavioral categories simultaneously and timing and recording the duration of each. Without the computer, it would be virtually impossible for the observer to record this amount of information. Because the observer's task is greatly simplified when aided by the microcomputer, there is much less chance of the observer missing events or making coding errors. As the observational task becomes more demanding, the microcomputer's contribution becomes increasingly important since observer errors made during manual recording increase greatly as the demands of the situation approach the observer's capacity to respond.

Several of the steps usually required when conducting an observational study in which data are collected manually and analyzed by a large computer can be done in part or in total by the microcomputer. Steps that can be handled by the microcomputer include:

1. *Recording and timing* the events being observed and transcribing the data onto coding sheets.
2. *Transferring the data* from the coding sheets into computer storage, ready for data analysis.
3. *Cleaning up the data* by locating coding errors and detecting "wild codes," which are codes that have no meaning in the coding system being used.
4. *Aggregating and analyzing the data*.
5. *Interpreting the results of data analysis*. Microcomputers have the capacity to produce a variety of graphic data representations, which can greatly help the researcher in understanding his results. Often the cost of doing this activity on a large computer is prohibitive.

Microcomputers offer the promise of an efficient and cost-effective tool. We have found that the micro is most cost-effective when it is used to perform several types of information processing, such as word processing, telecommunication, networking to larger computers, data analysis, graphic representation, and data gathering and storage.

Nonreactive Measures

All research requires some measurement. In educational research, paper-and-pencil tests are the dominant form of measurement, but methods such as interviews and questionnaires are also widely used. A major problem encountered in using such measures with human subjects is that the subjects are aware that they are being measured and often react in ways that tend to produce inaccurate or distorted information. In our discussion of demand characteristics (see chapter 5), we mentioned that the typical research subject uses cues from the research environment to come to conclusions about the purposes of the research and the expectations of the researcher. Because different subjects perceive and react to the research situation in different ways, a variety of errors may be introduced.

A main source of cues available to the subject are the measures employed in the research. Measures vary greatly in their degree of reactivity, that is, the degree to which the subject is aware of being measured and of the information the measure is attempting to obtain. The more reactive a measure is, the greater is the potential for distortion by the subject. For example, a self-esteem scale currently in use includes these items: "All in all, I am inclined to feel that I am a failure" and "I wish I could have more respect for myself."[33] Although many subjects will respond honestly, the purpose of the items is not difficult to discern; the *potential* for distortion is therefore large.

Potential Errors

E. J. Webb and his associates identified several errors in subject responses that can occur as a result of using reactive measures.[34] Briefly these errors include:

1. *The guinea pig effect.* This effect occurs because of the subject's awareness of being tested. Although it does not necessarily follow that awareness leads to measurement errors or distortion, the probability of such errors increases as the subject's awareness of being measured increases.

2. *Role selection.* When subjects are selected for participation in research, they are forced into a role-defining decision, that is, "What kind of person should I be as I respond to these questions?" If the role selected by the person as research subject differs from his or her role in similar natural situations, then the person's responses will be invalid, even though the subject is not giving dishonest answers. For example, in a study of air force officers, one of the authors found considerable differences between their responses to situational test questions related to on-the-job activities and their actual behavior in similar real situations. Interviews revealed that in framing their situational test answers, most adopted the role of officers "who always follow air force regulations to the letter." In real situations most adopted the role of officers who ignored or "bent" the regulations when common sense so dictated.

In situations where the test results are to be used to make some decision that affects the individual (such as admission to college, selection for a new job, or parole from prison) people will probably play the role they consider most likely to show them in a favorable light. In such situations, reactive measures are likely to produce very inaccurate results.

3. *Change due to reactive measurement.* Another problem that occurs when

33. John P. Robinson and Phillip R. Shaver, *Measures of Social Psychological Atitudes* (Ann Arbor: University of Michigan, Institute for Social Research, 1973), p. 83.
34. See Webb and co-workers in the Annotated References at the end of this chapter.

using reactive measures is that the initial measure may bring about real changes in what is being measured. For example, a scale designed to measure racial attitudes may, by the use of direct statements, make the subject more sensitive to some of the illogical aspects of racial prejudice and consequently change that person's attitudes. Such change obviously introduces an error into the research procedures that can lead to invalid conclusions about the effect of the experimental treatment.

4. *Response sets.* Finally, subjects often develop response sets when answering questions on reactive measures. For example, a response set frequently adopted by subjects is the *acquiescence set*—the tendency to agree rather than disagree. Any such response pattern clearly introduces an error into the subject's responses.

These errors do not occur when nonreactive (or "unobtrusive") measures are used. *Nonreactive measures* are characterized by the fact that the data are collected in a natural setting, and the subjects are unaware that they are being measured. For example, suppose you are interested in studying how teachers individualize instruction. To measure this variable you might give the teacher a questionnaire, interview the teacher, or observe the teacher and record behavior that relates to individualization. Because individualization of instruction is generally regarded as desirable, the teacher may exaggerate the use of individualization in responding to a questionnaire or interview. When an observer is present, the teacher may "put on an act" and display behavior that is far from typical.[35]

Although you can take some steps to reduce the teacher's reaction, such as establishing rapport and giving the teacher assurances of confidentiality, the potential for reaction would remain. Another approach to this measurement problem would be to look for nonreactive measures of individualized instruction. One possibility would be simply to record the variety of textbooks and workbooks in use in each classroom. If the teacher is individualizing instruction, he or she should be using a wider variety of curriculum materials than a teacher who instructs a class as an undifferentiated group. Another unobtrusive measure would be the written work that students complete during a class period. In a classroom that has individualized instruction, students will be working on different assignments, whereas in a conventional classroom all students will be working on the same assignment. Therefore, you can measure the extent of individualization in the classroom by counting the number of different assignments being worked on by students during a particular period of time.

35. This tendency for individuals to act differently when they are aware of being evaluated is clearly shown in a study by Terry L. Weech and Herbert Goldhor, "Obstrusive Versus Unobtrusive Evaluation of Reference Service in Five Illinois Public Libraries: A Pilot Study," *Library Quarterly* 52, no. 4 (1982): 305–324.

Educational researchers have not exploited the uses of nonreactive measures to a significant degree, yet the classroom and other educational settings contain many artifacts that can be used to measure research variables.

One of the authors has worked with a number of nonreactive measures in school settings. In one project where the objective was to estimate student attitude toward school authority, the principal mentioned over the school public address system that there was a great deal of littering in the school halls and urged students to use wastebaskets. The weight of litter collected from halls the day before the announcement was compared with that collected the day after the announcement. A reduction was considered indicative of a favorable attitude toward the principal, while an increase suggested a negative attitude. Samples of such measures may be found in Appendix E.

Webb and his co-workers have collected many examples of unobtrusive measures used in research studies. Some of them are listed here to suggest their usefulness as a substitute for behavioral observations, interviews, or questionnaires:

The floor tiles around the hatching-chick exhibit at Chicago's Museum of Science and Industry must be replaced every six weeks. Tiles in other parts of the museum need not be replaced for years. The selective erosion of tiles, indexed by the replacement rate, is a measure of relative popularity of exhibits.

The accretion rate is another measure. One investigator wanted to learn the level of whiskey consumption in a town which was officially "dry." He did so by counting empty bottles in ash cans.

The degree of fear induced by a ghost-story-telling session can be measured by noting the shrinking diameter of a circle of seated children.

Chinese jade dealers have used the pupil dilation of their customers as a measure of the client's interest in particular stones, and Darwin in 1872 noted this same variable as an index of fear.

Library withdrawals were used to demonstrate the effect of the introduction of television into a community. Fiction titles dropped, nonfiction titles were unaffected.

The role of rate of interaction in managerial recruitment is shown by the overrepresentation of baseball managers who were infielders or catchers (high-interaction positions) during their playing days.

Sir Francis Galton employed surveying hardware to estimate the bodily dimensions of African women whose language he did not speak.

The child's interest in Christmas was demonstrated by distortions in the size of Santa Claus drawings.

Racial attitudes in two colleges were compared by noting the degree of clustering of Negroes and whites in lecture halls.[36]

36. See Webb and co-workers in the Annotated References at the end of this chapter.

In addition to being effective substitutes for conventional educational measures, nonreactive measures are very useful as supplements to such measures. A serious threat to our ability to generalize research findings is the possibility that these findings are due, at least in part, to the unique characteristics of the instrument we used to measure the variables being studied.[37] If we use several different kinds of instruments to measure the same variables, and if similar results are obtained from these different instruments, then we can be much more confident that our results are valid. Nonreactive measures are especially useful when used in conjunction with conventional reactive measures because they usually employ much different measurement approaches.

Limitations

Although nonreactive measures seem to have some important advantages as tools in educational research, they also have some limitations that must be considered.

Validity

Validity can be a problem for many nonreactive measures. As Webb and his colleagues point out, it is often difficult to determine just what is being measured. For example, the lost-letter technique (a nonreactive measure) has been used frequently to estimate attitudes related to sensitive topics such as political elections because a direct approach probably would not produce valid responses. In the lost-letter technique, large numbers of letters are addressed to organizations that reflect different attitudes on an issue. These letters are then "lost," that is, dropped in various locations designed to sample the geographical area (such as a city) being studied.

The technique is based on the assumption that a person who finds a letter is more likely to mail it if the address represents a candidate or attitude that he or she supports. Thus, the rate of returns for letters representing different attitudes should reflect the percentage of persons holding each attitude in the community under investigation. In several election studies, however, the proportion of letters returned failed to predict the election results, thus raising doubts about the validity of the technique.

It has been hypothesized that some addresses arouse more curiosity in the finder than others and that letters with these addresses are more likely to be opened and read than mailed. This hypothesis was supported in a recent study. Letters were addressed to Education Research Project, Marijuana Research

---

37. The degree to which the results of an experiment can be generalized (that is, applied to other situations and samples) is called external validity. This concept is discussed in chapter 15.

Project, and Sex Research Project. Letters addressed to Education Research Project were most often returned. Letters addressed to Sex Research Project were least often returned, and of those that were returned, more had been opened.[38] Because curiosity and other variables may affect the return rate, the lost-letter technique cannot safely be assumed to provide a valid measure of attitudes.

Reliability

Reliability can sometimes be a problem with many nonreactive measures; many of these measures are essentially similar to a one-item test or to one question from a questionnaire. Even for nonreactive measures for which reliability can be computed, the data are of limited use to other researchers because most such measures are designed to study a very specific attitude or question and are rarely used more than once. In contrast, conventional measures, such as achievement tests, personality inventories, and attitude scales, are used in many studies. Over a period of time a useful body of knowledge about the measure is developed.

Sensitivity

Sensitivity of measurement is a further problem with nonreactive measures. Many nonreactive measures deal with dichotomies such as mail versus don't mail, support versus oppose, or volunteer versus nonvolunteer. Such data are much less sensitive than a Likert-type attitude scale that measures the individual's level of agreement along a continuum that typically includes 5 or 7 points.

The lack of sensitivity in nonreactive measures can be overcome somewhat by developing *sets* of nonreactive measures that attempt to measure different facets of the same question or attitude. This is not as easy as it may seem, however, and brings us to some of the practical limitations of nonreactive measures. First, a great deal of creativity is required to think of ways to measure phenomena nonreactively. Second, if a set of nonreactive measures is used, much more time and effort are required than if a direct measure of the same variable was administered. Third, because nonreactive measures are generally unique to a single research project, no compilations (such as the *Mental Measurements Yearbooks*) are available to the researcher who wants to use them.

38. Lee Sechrest and J. B. Grove, "The Lost-Letter Technique: The Role of Curiosity" (unpublished manuscript, Florida State University, 1980). For another interesting application of this technique, see David P. Farrington and Barry J. Knight, "Stealing from a Lost Letter: Effects of Victim Characteristics," *Criminal Justice and Behavior* 7, no. 4 (1980): 423–435.

Ethical Considerations

Because the subjects are usually not aware that they are being measured, two ethical questions are particularly relevant to the use of nonreactive measures. These are *informed consent* and *invasion of privacy*. In most educational studies, data are gathered in public places such as classrooms. Observations or collections of nonreactive data in public settings are usually not regarded as an invasion of privacy. Data collection in public areas where individuals would expect their behavior to be private, such as public toilets, however, has been challenged as an invasion of privacy. At the extreme is "spying" on an individual's private behavior, such as placing listening devices in the subject's home, which is clearly an invasion of privacy.

Informed consent poses a difficult problem, for the main purpose of nonreactive measurement is to gather data without the awareness of the subjects. In many studies using nonreactive measures, such as the lost-letter technique, it would be impossible to identify beforehand persons who would pick up the lost letters and obtain their consent. If the nonreactive measure is such that it poses a physical or psychological risk to the subjects—such as a study of the behavior of high school students when they see a research confederate who appears to be drowning in the swimming pool—then conducting the study without informed consent would be considered unethical. However, consider studies where no risk to the subjects is present, where the anonymity of the subjects is maintained, where it is impossible to conduct the study under informed consent conditions, and where the study promises to produce significant benefits or especially valuable knowledge. Under these conditions, the investigator would probably be justified in proceeding without informed consent.

One way to meet the informed consent requirement is to inform the subjects that data about them will be collected unobtrusively but not tell them what data will be collected or how it will be collected. Researchers usually suggest that the data can best be collected if they "fade into the woodwork" and do not interfere with the activities of the subjects. Formal consent is then sought largely on the basis of the subjects' trusting the researcher. The researcher agrees to share the data with the subjects after the study is completed—usually in the form a report that protects the individual's right to confidentiality and privacy.[39]

In summary, if the requirements of privacy and informed consent are absolute or inviolate then nonreactive measures could never be used. However, a more reasonable position is that ethical principles place limits on what can be

---

39. See Webb and co-workers in the Annotated References at the end of this chapter for a discussion of the ethical questions related to use of nonreactive measures. Also see Flora I. Ortiz, *Is Unobtrusive Ethical?* (paper presented at the Annual Meeting of the American Educational Research Association, Montreal, Quebec, April 11–15, 1983).

done, and the investigator and others must look closely at the specifics of the planned research to decide whether a significant violation of these principles will occur.

CONTRIVED OBSERVATIONS

Naturalistic Contrived Situations

Two kinds of contrived observations[40] are used in behavioral science research. In the first, which employs **naturalistic contrived situations,** the researcher intervenes in a natural situation in a manner that cannot be detected by the subject; thus, the naturalness of the situation is preserved. In the second, *situational testing,* the situation is totally artificial, and the subject is aware of this fact. The main reason for manipulating the situation is to assure that the events of interest to the researcher will occur. In simple naturalistic observations many hours of observation might be required to record one two-minute event. For example, suppose you want to observe the responses of teachers to such behavior as cheating, fighting, or open defiance by pupils. Since these behaviors occur at a very low frequency in most classrooms, a great deal of observer time would be needed to gather data on a reasonable sample of such behavior. By using pupil confederates, contrived situations can be set up to collect the necessary data in a reasonably short time.

Another advantage of establishing contrived situations to be observed is that the level of intensity of the situation can be manipulated. For example, in a study of pupil cheating, opportunities to cheat involving several levels of risk can be set up. In fact, the classic studies of Hartshorne and May on pupil cheating employed just such situations.[41] Observing behavior at several specific and clearly defined levels of intensity, while fairly easy in contrived situations, is in many cases virtually impossible in natural situations.[42]

There are two serious limitations to observing in contrived situations. First, in many cases believable situations cannot be contrived without arousing the suspicion of the subjects. Second, difficult ethical problems may arise because of the deception involved. When one or both of these problems rule out the use of naturalistic contrived observation, a similar technique, situational testing, can be employed.

40. See Webb and co-workers in the Annotated References at the end of this chapter for a discussion of contrived observation.
41. H. Hartshorne and M. A. May, *Studies in the Nature of Character:* Vol. 1, *Studies in Deceit* (New York: Macmillan, 1928). These classic studies and others by the same authors made extensive use of contrived observation. The ingenuity of their work still sets a standard for this field.
42. For a recent example of a study using contrived observation, see Robert D. Foss and Carolyn B. Dempsey, "Blood Donation and the Foot-in-the-Door Technique: A Limiting Case," *Journal of Personality and Social Psychology* 37 (1979): 580–590.

Situational Testing

Situational testing is another form of contrived observation in which the subjects are aware of the fact that they are playing a role. The research worker devises a situation and assigns appropriate roles to the subjects, who are asked to play these roles to the best of their ability. Typically, all participants except the person being tested have been trained to play their roles. These roles create a situation to which the person being tested must respond in some way such as making a decision or trying to resolve a conflict. The situations are aimed at bringing out the specific types of behavior that the researcher is interested in observing. Originally developed by social psychologists to study leadership behavior and small-group interaction, situational testing has many applications for the educational researcher. For example, many studies have attempted to identify the factors related to successful teaching or successful administrative behavior through the use of personality inventories and other paper-and-pencil measures. The results of these studies have been disappointing, probably because it is difficult to break down the complex behavior patterns that teachers or principals display in their work, and study them piece by piece. Situational testing permits a study of the total behavior pattern and thus seems more likely to provide insight into the characteristics required for success in complex activities.

Like other forms of contrived observation, situational testing has advantages over the observation of behavior in natural settings. By setting up the situation, you can control, to a greater degree than is usually possible in the naturalistic contrived situation, the behavior that is likely to occur. This permits you to focus the observation on behavior that appears to be critical in the area being studied. In order to observe such critical behavior in a natural situation, the observer may need to be present for weeks or even months.

The artificial situation also permits much more careful training of the observers. Inasmuch as you have a good idea of the types of behavior that will occur, you can develop observational rating forms that fit the situation specifically and can train your observers in the specific situations that they will later observe in the collection of research data. Because a number of subjects can be exposed to essentially the same situation (although each, of course, will respond differently), it is much easier to obtain comparable data on the behavior through this technique than through observation of behavior in natural situations or naturalistic contrived situations.

In situational tests the subjects are usually aware of the observer's presence, although in some cases the observer watches through a one-way mirror. In naturalistic contrived situations, the observations in many cases are covert, and hidden recording devices are used to collect the data. Both approaches can produce satisfactory data, but generally it is easier to develop an effective observational procedure in situational testing because of the higher degree of control by the researcher.

The principal criticism of situational testing is that the situation itself is artificial and therefore may not give an accurate indication of how the individual would behave in a natural situation. In other words, can data obtained in artificial situations be generalized to natural or in vivo situations?[43] In using role-playing situations in research the authors have been impressed by the degree to which subjects appear to forget that they are involved in an artificial situation. Particularly in situations that lead to emotional interaction between the subject and actors, it appears that most subjects become deeply involved in the situation, and many seem to forget, at least for the moment, that the situation is an artificial one.

Perhaps the principal disadvantage of situational testing for the graduate student is the time required to develop and carry out a project using this technique. Small-scale situational studies, however, can be carried out by the graduate student. For example, parent-teacher conference situations could be developed and used in a study of teacher behavior. In research problems concerned with human relations, situational testing offers perhaps the best chance of producing meaningful data.

One variation of situational testing that is somewhat easier to carry out is to use written situations. Describe the situations you want to study in some detail and ask subjects to tell how they would react if faced with the described situation. This method is much less costly than using situations that involve role-playing and also makes it possible to expose the subjects to a much wider range of situations in the time available.[44] The obvious limitation of written situations is that subjects *tell* how they would react instead of actually reacting. Our experience with written situations indicates that at least for some kinds of situations, the responses are not very highly correlated with what the subjects would actually do. Subjects can often describe a response that they cannot carry out. For example, our research on military leadership showed that when faced with a situation requiring the subjects to plan and carry out an escape from a prisoner-of-war compound, many subjects who could describe how they would conduct an escape on a written situational test could not actually get their

43. Generalizability, also called external validity, is a problem in virtually all research. For a discussion of this problem as related to role-playing, see C. D. Spencer, "Two Types of Role Playing—Threats to Internal and External Validity," *American Psychologist* 33, no. 3 (1958): 265–268.

44. See Kenneth A. Dodge, Cynthia L. McClaskey, and Esther Feldman, "Situational Approaches to the Assessment of Social Competence in Children," *Journal of Consulting and Clinical Psychology* 53, no. 3 (1985): 344–353. The authors have developed a measure that includes 44 written social situations that discriminate between rejected aggressive children and adaptive children. Considerable data on validation are reported.

plans accepted by other "prisoners" and carry out the escape in a role-playing situation.

Several types of situational tests might be adapted to educational research. We will briefly discuss three of these: the leaderless-group discussion, team problem-solving activities, and individual role-playing situations.

Leaderless-Group Discussion

In a **leaderless-group discussion**, a group of subjects (usually six or eight) is given a problem and asked to discuss this problem and arrive at possible solutions. Observers record the behavior of the different group members. The technique of the leaderless-group discussion is said to have been developed originally around 1925 to study leadership behavior in the German army.[45] More recently, this technique has been used to study decision making and interaction in various military groups, student groups, and executive groups in business. Its value is that it provides a good simulation of important situations that occur in real life. For example, the behavior of school board members in a leaderless-group discussion working on a problem presented them by the researcher is probably quite similar to the behavior of these same individuals as they tackle the problems they confront in real-life school board meetings. Consequently, ratings of leadership, cooperation, and teamwork made on the basis of observations of leaderless-group discussions have been found to have high predictive validity.

There is, however, evidence that coaching can significantly improve performance in leaderless-group discussions and therefore research using this technique should eliminate opportunities for coaching to occur, or manipulate coaching as an independent variable.[46] In education this technique could be used to study such problems as decision making by school boards, leadership behavior among schoolchildren at different levels, and teacher interaction in faculty meetings.

Team Problem Solving

In team problem solving a team is usually presented with a problem that it is called upon to solve. This method differs from the leaderless-group discussion in that in addition to discussing solutions, the team arrives at a solution and attempts to carry it out. Problems involving the escape of the team from a prison compound or getting the team across a difficult physical barrier have been used

45. H. L. Ausbacher, "History of the Leaderless Group Discussion," *Psychological Bulletin* 48 (1951): 383–391.
46. See Paul M. Kurecka et al., "Full and Errant Coaching Effects on Assigned Role Leaderless-Group Discussion Performance," *Personnel Psychology* 35 no. 4 (1982): 805–812.

in research by military psychologists. Observers may be assigned to evaluate total team activities or to evaluate the behavior of individual members of the team. This technique has been used for the most part in the study of military leadership.[47] However, it could be applied to research in a number of educational areas, such as studies of player interaction in team sports, studies of group behavior in high school clubs, and studies of work groups in parent-teacher projects.

Individual Role-Playing

The individual role-playing situation is a form of situational testing that is generally aimed at collecting research data in a situation where only one research subject is involved, usually in a key role. The situation may also involve actors who are trained to play other roles necessary to bring out the subject's behavior that is to be evaluated. Subjects are usually given material that describes the situation in which they are to work and sometimes discusses the nature of the problem they will attempt to solve and the identity of other persons who will participate. Subjects study this material prior to the start of the situation, arrive at a solution or method of handling the problem, and then attempt to carry out this solution in the role-playing situation. In observing subjects' behavior in the situation, it is possible to evaluate subjects' decisions, but more important, it is also possible to evaluate their skill in carrying them out. For example, one of the authors participated in a study aimed at developing criteria for measuring the effectiveness of elementary school principals.[48] In this study each subject played the role of a principal in several different situations aimed at revealing different aspects of the behavior important in the elementary principal's position. Six situations were developed. In each of these the person being tested took the part of the principal. Actors were trained to take other roles called for. In one of these situations, the person tested was given the following instructions:

Instructions to Principal

You are the principal of a large elementary school of about 1,000 pupils, from kindergarten to sixth grade, in a city of about 30,000 population. The schools in the city are up-to-date, progressive, and have a high rating. The people in the community are proud of their schools and support them enthusiastically.

47. Ernest Tupes, Walter R. Borg, and A. Carp, "Performance in Role-Playing Situations as Related to Leadership and Performance Measures," *Sociometry* 21 (1958): 165–179.
48. Walter R. Borg and J. A. Silvester, "Playing the Principal's Role," *Elementary School Journal* 64 (1964): 324–331.

There is a Mr. Jones waiting to see you about getting his son registered in school. Mr. Jones is a successful businessman who is active in civic affairs, is well liked, and has a lot of influence in the community. He is proud of his children (two of them are already in school), and he is interested in giving them every opportunity to grow and develop.

It seems that, when he attempted to enroll his son in kindergarten, the son was turned down because he was five hours too young. Ms. Roberts was so busy enrolling new pupils that she did not have time to discuss the matter with Mr. Jones and just told him that his son did not come up to the age requirement. Mr. Jones was a little disturbed and has asked you for an appointment to discuss the matter. He will probably try to get you to make an exception for his child.

You have had problems before on the age requirements for enrollment, so take a few minutes to think it through. The superintendent is out of town for 10 days, and a decision has to be made before he returns.

Main Points:
1. Mr. Jones is an important man in the community.
2. Entrance age requirements or some other entrance requirements are necessary.
3. You are proud of your school and its high rating.
4. You cannot afford to have the public unhappy about the school.
5. You have 15 minutes to spend with Mr. Jones, and you should make a decision within the time limit.

The actor trained to play the role of Mr. Jones had the following instructions:

Instructions to Actor

You are a successful businessman in a community of about 30,000 population. You are active in civic affairs and interested in the progress of the community. You are generally well liked and have considerable influence.

You are the father of three children and are very proud of your family and interested in their welfare. Two of your children are already in school and are well adjusted and doing very good work. You have your own set of cumulative records on each child that you keep up-to-date. These records are complete and show that your children are superior.

Your youngest boy, Edward, was just turned down when you tried to get him enrolled in the kindergarten because he was five hours too young. This disturbed you because the records you received from the private nursery school Edward has been attending show that his IQ is 136; he is well above the average in physical size and development; he is socially well adjusted; he is in excellent health; and is an active, alert, and happy boy.

You know he is ready for school and that he will make a good adjustment. You feel that it is in the child's best interest to start now, and if they will not take him into the public schools you will have to enroll him in a private school. You do not want this extra expense, and besides you are a taxpayer and have donated a lot of time and money for public welfare and feel that your children have a right to public education.

You think that the chronological age rules used to determine who is ready for school is old-fashioned and silly, and you know that your boy is more ready to enter kindergarten than 90 percent of the children being enrolled.

You did not like the way Ms. Roberts turned you down when you tried to get Edward enrolled because she did not take time to listen to the reason why you thought Edward was ready for school. So you decided to go to the principal about it. This bothers you because you are a busy man, and you do not like to waste time over something that seems so unreasonable and wrong.

You are not acquainted with the principal, Mr. Smith, but you are well acquainted with the superintendent of schools. You know the superintendent is a reasonable man and you tried to see him, but he is out of town for a few days, and this enrollment has to be taken care of now or it will be too late.

When you go the principal's office, you present your problem and wait for his reaction.

There are several possible approaches the principal might follow:

1. He might dogmatically say no. If he does, threaten to make a public issue of it. You have rights as a taxpayer; your boy is superior, and so forth. Just do not take no for an answer. Do not hesitate to show your anger under those circumstances.
2. He may try to win you over without yielding—here again you should point out that your boy is better prepared for kindergarten than most of the children who were accepted because he has been in private nursery school and the test results show him to be superior.
3. He may refuse to yield but agree to study the policy and see how exceptions could be made. But your boy is ready now and the policy could be studied and rules made for exceptions later.
4. He may accept Edward if it is kept quiet, as a special favor, and so on. You do not want any underhanded admission because the boy is qualified to go in the "front door," on his own merits, and so on.
5. He may accept Edward without qualifications. If he does, tell him that your neighbor has a boy who has been in the same nursery school that Edward attended. There is a complete set of records showing that this boy is superior also. He is only 15 days younger than Edward, and his parents would like to get him enrolled also.

Keep in mind that you are an important man, that the records show that Edward is superior, that his experience in the private nursery school gives him an added advantage, that you think the chronological age rule is no good, and that other superior children should also be allowed in.

Situations such as these seem to provide a better basis for evaluating some of the complex human-relations skills needed by a principal than any number of trait-oriented personality, aptitude, or interest measures.

A highly significant study using role-playing situations to study school administrator behavior was carried out at Columbia Unviersity.[49] In this study the subjects were introduced to a mythical school district through the study of handbooks, motion pictures, and participation in meetings, and then each played the role of a principal attempting to solve administrative problems related to the school and district.

In a more recent study, students at different grade levels ranging from first grade through college played the role of teachers in evaluating student achievement. Important insights into the way that students perceive teachers emerged.[50]

Observations Made by Untrained Groups

Most of our discussion of observational studies to this point has been concerned with closely controlled scientific observation. In many educational studies, however, it is not possible to maintain this control over the observational situation. We now discuss techniques that provide less precise scientific data and are to some extent less direct, as they are based on the observations and recollections of special groups whom we cannot train thoroughly or control closely. This type of observation is much more likely to be subjective and biased. Nevertheless, in many instances the very subjectivity of the observations may be of value to the resarcher. For example, the leadership ability of students could be determined by trained adult observers. However, nominations of leadership ability by a student's peers may be of more value in predicting a student's later standing in the student's pccr group, even though these nominations are not based on objective observations.

49. John K. Hemphill, Daniel E. Griffiths, and Norman Fredericksen, *Administrative Performance and Personality: A Study of the Principal in a Simulated Elementary School* (New York: Teachers College Press, 1962).
50. See Oren Harari and Martin V. Covington, "Reactions to Achievement Behavior from a Teacher and Student Perspective: A Developmental Analysis," *American Educational Research Journal* 18 (1981): 15–28.

The Anecdotal Record

One technique used quite commonly in education is the **anecdotal record**. Anecdotal records are generally based on teacher observations and involve descriptions of behavior that the teacher considers typical of the individual described. With some training teachers can provide anecdotal records of considerable value to the scientist. The anecdotal record should be an objective description of the child's behavior without interpretations by the observer. In preparing the instructions and forms of anecdotal records, the research worker should strive toward as great objectivity as possible. Unless teachers are trained they often produce records that are general appraisals of their students rather than anecdotes that describe the way a child behaved in a specific situation. The most serious danger in anecdotal records is that the teacher will write these records while emotionally upset about the incident being described. For example, in compiling anecdotal records dealing with disciplinary problems and misbehavior, the teacher is much less likely to be objective than an observer who is not directly involved in the disciplinary situation.[51]

Sociometric Techniques

Sociometric techniques are designed to measure the social structure of a group and to appraise the social status of each individual with respect to other members of his group. A number of different techniques can be used to collect these data. In the usual approach, each group member is asked to select persons in the group most preferred on the basis of a specific criterion. For example, members may be asked to indicate the three persons with whom they would most like to work on a committee assignment. In studies involving classroom groups, pupils are often asked to indicate persons with whom they would most like to do an assignment, near whom they would prefer to have their desks, and so on.[52] J. L. Moreno, in the earliest development of sociometric measurement, used such methods as a means of rearranging groups of schoolchildren so that they could study together more harmoniously.[53] Occasionally selections of least preferred individuals are also made. This has generally been considered necessary to identify rejected children—the group usually regarded as most in need of help.

51. For an example of how anecdotal records can be used to collect objective classroom data, see James Levin, James Nolan, and Nancy Hoffman, "A Strategy for Classroom Resolution of Chronic Discipline Problems," *NASSP Bulletin* 69 (1985): 11–18.
52. For a recent example of a study using sociometric techniques to measure pupil peer relationships, see Thomas F. Tyne and William Geary, "Patterns of Acceptance-Rejection Among Male-Female Elementary School Students," *Child Study Journal* 10 (1980: 179–190.
53. J. L. Moreno, *Who Shall Survive?* (New York: Beacon, 1953).

Although the use of negative selection criteria has been questioned on ethical grounds, there is research evidence that such choices have no effect on children's peer interactions.[54] However, a recent study has developed a method of identifying rejected children without using negative nominations, which accurately identifies over 90 percent of rejected children. This method involves joint use of positive nomination and rating scale measures.[55]

In another version of the sociometric technique, individuals are asked to identify persons whom they believe have chosen them. The choices that they believe were made can then be compared with actual choices in order to obtain an indication of a person's insight into his or her social position. Still another type of sociometric measure is the "guess who test." These measures contain descriptions of various social roles, and subjects are asked to indicate the group member who best fits each role. For example, the researcher might present a group of students with these descriptions:

"This student would make a good class president."
"This student would be the most fun at a party."
"This student is the smartest in my class."
"If I had difficulty with arithmetic, I would ask this student for help."

The instructions would direct each student to write down the names of one or two students who fit each description.

Sociometric techniques are often used to measure popularity among students in a classroom. Because popularity among one's peers is an important personal attribute, many researchers have investigated factors that might be related to popularity as measured by sociometric techniques. An interesting study of this type was carried out by J. W. McDavid and H. Harari.[56] They investigated whether people, like objects, tend to be judged favorably or unfavorably by their labels, that is, by their first name. Their sample consisted of 59 fourth- and fifth-graders who belonged to one of four youth groups at a community center. These students were asked to indicate on a 3-point scale how much they liked or disliked each of 49 different names (being all the first names of those children in the sample). Two social desirability ratings were completed for each name. One rating (SDI) was the mean of the ratings made by the members of the youth group to which a particular student belonged. The other rating (SDO) was the mean of the ratings made by nonmembers of the youth

54. See Maureen Hayvren and Shelley Hymel, "Ethical Issues in Sociometric Testing: Impact of Sociometric Measures on Interaction Behavior," *Developmental Psychology* 20, no. 5 (1984): 844–849.
55. See Steven R. Asher and Kenneth A. Dodge, "Identifying Children Who Are Rejected by Their Peers," *Developmental Psychology* 22, no. 4 (1986): 444–449.
56. John W. McDavid and Herbert Harari, "Stereotyping of Names and Popularity in Grade-School Children," *Child Development* 37 (1966): 453–459.

group; the purpose of this rating was to minimize the possibility that students would rate a name in terms of an actual person whom they knew rather than as a label. Once these social desirability ratings of names had been obtained, the popularity status of each student was established by the sociometric technique of having students nominate others with whom they would like to play together, and so on. The correlation between a student's popularity and the social desirability of his or her name was high (r for SDI was .63, and r for SDO was .49), leading McDavid and Harari to conclude that "the child who bears a generally unpopular or unattractive name may be handicapped in his social interactions with his peers" (p. 458).

Supervisory Ratings

Ratings, such as those made of teachers by their principals or of principals by their superintendents, provide a commonly used method of gaining data concerning the behavior of subjects in educational research. Supervisory ratings, of course, are difficult to conduct on a scientific and tightly controlled basis. In some studies the supervisor makes special observations as part of the research plan, but as the supervisor has already formed an opinion of his or her subordinates prior to the time these observations are made, this opinion will inevitably have an effect upon the observational ratings even if she or he tries to be objective. Under these conditions we may be sure that observed behavior that agrees with the observer's bias is most likely to be noted and recorded. "Halo effect" also operates strongly in this type of evaluation. In many cases, however, the behavior of the individual as seen through the eyes of the supervisor, although different perhaps from the objective behavior of the individual, still has an important meaning in educational research. For example, you may be interested in studying factors related to promotion or nonpromotion of teachers. Principals' ratings of the teacher's competence may be an important factor in predicting promotion and therefore should be obtained, even though in some instances these ratings may not be objective.

The Critical-Incident Technique

One form of observational rating that has been employed to a considerable degree in recent years is the **critical-incident technique** developed by John Flanagan.[57] This technique, as usually applied, involves studying the performance of one group of individuals (such as teachers) by asking another group of individuals (such as principals) to describe "critical incidents" that relate to the performance of the first group. In vocational studies, the informants are usually

---

57. John C. Flanagan, "The Critical-Incident Technique," *Psychological Bulletin* 51 (1954): 327–358.

supervisors, but the method can be used whenever a group can be identified that has information about the performance of another group.

The researcher usually uses interviews to obtain from the supervisor descriptions of the subject's specific behavior patterns that are considered to be critical to the skills being studied. Some studies of military leadership ability, for example, have used the critical-incident technique. One of the authors once had the opportunity to read hundreds of the critical incidents collected by Flanagan in his research on military leadership. In reading these incidents, it was apparent that many of the incidents recorded would not be considered "critical" by a psychologist, because they were global evaluations and general comments about the subject's performance rather than specific incidents involving the subject. Perhaps the most serious problem encountered in using the critical-incident technique is to obtain incidents from the individuals interviewed that seem to be truly critical to the behavior or skills being studied. If incidents can be collected that are truly critical, that truly differentiate between successful and unsuccessful behavior, then this method can be a very useful research approach.

The critical-incident technique seems to be well suited to many educational problems, particularly those involving the qualifications of school administrators and teachers. In one such study, the researcher was interested in how educators viewed professionalism in the field of education.[58] Specifically, Leles was concerned with whether educators have the same notion of professional and nonprofessional behaviors as do other occupational groups. The critical-incident technique permitted collection of a large amount of data on this subject. Leles asked teachers, administrators, counselors, and others to recall an incident that involved nonprofessional conduct on the part of an educator. The use of the critical-incident technique was a simple yet effective alternative to training observers and having them carry out lengthy observations of professional and nonprofessional conduct in a variety of educational settings. To give an idea of the data that can be collected by this technique, some of Leles's reported incidents are presented in the following paragraphs:

> In coaching, we are often asked to do things for administrators. Once last year, a friend of mine who was a coach had to chauffeur women around to various schools. These women were very influential, and the administrators were afraid of them, so the coaches more or less became ambassadors of goodwill to them. We hated every minute of it.

> My principal took a master copy from my files (book report form), had copies made, and then presented them to our faculty meeting as his own idea. This was done without my knowledge or permission, although the form was original with me. Other teachers reported similar incidents with the same principal.

58. Sam Leles, "Using the Critical Incidents Technique to Develop a Theory of Educational Professionalism: An Exploratory Study," *Journal of Teacher Education* 19 (Spring 1968): 59–69.

A teacher who, while chairman of the Salary Committee, used classroom time to carry on duties related to that position. This was an elementary situation, and the children were put to work at busy work. This same teacher, who exercises a good deal of control over many of the personnel, voices long and loud protests over teachers associating with custodial help, etc. This, she says, is unprofessional.

Many teachers in my building have children standing in the halls because they are unable to cope with their behavior in the classroom. I believe that much of this stems from failure to provide for individual differences and the discipline in the classroom.

Several instrumental music teachers in the area are receiving 10 percent kickbacks from the musical instrument dealers who sell instruments to their students. Such awards (in confidence of course) are made in a direct cash handout or accumulated into something like a grand piano.

What seems to me to be unprofessional behavior is the discussion by teachers in the teachers' lounge. By this I mean discussing students in a derogatory manner.

Arriving late and leaving early. There have been examples of teachers who do not show up at the school at an appropriate time—time enough to enable students to talk with the teacher if necessary before classes—and they leave immediately after the last bell—again not permitting the students an opportunity to talk with the teacher.

English teacher approaches superintendent and board of education with regard to large classes and the lack of time to work with children on their writing of themes. She wanted more help or fewer students. Superintendent answered by accusing her in presence of board of education of not being able to handle classes. Some superintendents do not want problems to exist and will deny their existence. (Leles, 1968, pp. 67–68)

CONTENT ANALYSIS

Types of Studies Employing Content Analysis

"**Content analysis** is a research technique for the objective, systematic, and quantitative description of the manifest content of communication."[59] The raw material for the research worker using the content-analysis technique may be any form of communication, usually written materials, but other forms of

59. Bernard Berelson, *Content Analysis in Communication Research* (Glencoe, IL: Free Press, 1952), p. 18.

communication such as music, pictures, or gestures should not be excluded. Textbooks, high school compositions, novels, newspapers, magazine advertisements, and political speeches are but a few of the sources available. Content analysis is often used in conjunction with observational studies. The researcher tape records classroom verbal behavior, for example, makes a typed transcript from the audiotape, and then analyzes the content of the transcript in order to measure variables that have been formulated by the researcher.

Most content analyses in education have been aimed at answering questions directly relating to the material analyzed. These analyses have generally been concerned with fairly simple classifications or tabulations of specific information. Content analyses of pupil compositions, for example, can give us a classification of grammatical and spelling errors as well as information on the frequency of different types of errors. This information can be directly applied to the revision of English courses or the development of remedial programs. A content analysis of current textbooks in first-year algebra can tell us such things as What topics are covered by all books? What emphasis is placed on each topic? In what sequence are topics usually presented? What mathematical terms are introduced? What system of symbols is most frequently used? Such textbook analyses are often carried out by test publishing companies that produce standardized achievement tests in order that their tests can be constructed to have high content validity. Among the important early content analyses carried out in education were simple frequency counts of words in order to identify those words most commonly used in the English language.[60] Such word lists then formed the basis for determining the readability of textbooks and for the development of elementary reading textbooks and spelling lists. However, readability is a function of other factors besides frequency of word occurrence. Therefore, later researchers attempted a more complex content analysis of textbook materials in developing readability formulas.[61] Other areas of education that have been studied using content analysis include the analysis of propaganda; the sociological effects of reading; the treatment of blacks in history textbooks, the Soviet Union in American textbooks and nationalism in children's literature; television programs; the readability of books and newspapers; and the social ideas in McGuffey readers.[62] We can see from these examples that content analysis can be a valuable tool for obtaining certain types of information useful in identifying or solving educational problems.

60. Edward L. Thorndike, *A Teacher's Word Book of the Twenty Thousand Words Found Most Frequently and Widely in General Reading for Children and Young People,* rev. ed. (New York: Teachers College Press, 1932).

61. Irving Lorge, "Predicting Readability," *Teachers College Record* 45 (1944): 404–419; and Rudolf Flesch, *How to Test Readability* (New York: Harper & Row, 1951).

62. See Berelson, *Content Analysis,* pp. 199–200, for an extensive listing of research using content analysis prior to 1950.

Whereas most early studies employing content analysis relied on simple frequency counts of objective variables (e.g., spelling errors), recent studies more often aim at using content analysis to gain insights into complex social and psychological variables. Such studies are much more difficult to carry out than the simple frequency studies and often depend on a researcher's high level of sophistication in psychology, sociology, or other behavioral sciences.

For example, a study compared the kinds of words used by black children aged three, four, and five.[63] Such research can give us valuable insights into theoretical issues related to the development of affective and cognitive processes in young children. This study also employed a computer to conduct the content analysis and tried out wireless microphone-transmitters to gather samples of the children's language. The use of modern technology can remove most of the tedious and time-consuming operations that have been required by earlier content analyses and should permit researchers to work with larger samples and explore more complex relationships.

Recent content-analysis studies consider not only content frequencies but also the interrelationships among several content variables, or the relationship between content variables and other research variables. An early illustration of this trend in content analysis is provided by Zahorik's study of the types of feedback statements that teachers use to inform students about the adequacy or correctness of their responses.[64] Teacher feedback includes statements such as "All right," "Fine," "Why did you say that?" and "Could anyone give us another point?" To study teacher feedback behavior, Zahorik tape recorded and transcribed discussion lessons of third-grade and sixth-grade teachers. The content of these discussions was then analyzed by means of an instrument developed for the study, which contained 25 categories for classifying teacher feedback. In the first part of the data analysis, Zahorik simply computed the frequencies with which different types of teacher feedback were given. Then, more sophisticated analyses of the content data were made. Teachers' use of different types of feedback was related to grade level of the classroom, purpose of the lesson (introduction-readiness discussions versus development discussion), teachers' use of questions, and quality of student answers. Such analyses can yield valuable insights into the nature of classroom interaction. One of the main findings of Zahorik's study, for example, was that teacher's verbal feedback tends to be rather limited in variety and depth: "Only a few types of feedback are used with regularity and these types may be less informational than others which are used infrequently" (p. 149). Such a finding might serve as

63. James C. Montague, Jr., "A Preliminary Methodological Verbal Computer Content Analysis Study of Preschool Black Children," *Journal of Educational Research* 69 (1976): 236–240.
64. John A. Zahorik, "Classroom Feedback Behavior of Teachers," *Journal of Educational Research* 62, no. 4 (1968): 147–150.

the basis for improving teachers' instructional practices. Zahorik raises the possibility that a wider variety of types of feedback, including types that seem to carry more information, would benefit learners. He suggests that teachers develop wide feedback repertoires, including more emphasis on elaborate types of praise, direct negatives such as simple reproof-denial, reasons or explanations as to why a comment had or lacked value, and clues or prompts regarding what to do next to improve a response. These types of feedback should improve the learning process, since they give learners a clearer idea of the worth of their responses.

Planning a Content-Analysis Study

Specifying Objectives

The first step in planning a content-analysis study is to establish specific objectives to be achieved or hypotheses to be tested. Content analyses usually aim at achieving one of the following kinds of objectives:

1. *Produce descriptive information.* For example, a content analysis of themes found in history textbooks used in Soviet schools provided descriptive information that gave us a better understanding of what the average Soviet citizen knows about history and how he or she might interpret current international situations.[65] Most content analysis in education is aimed at producing descriptive information.

2. *Cross-validate research findings.* Content analysis is a useful tool to check research findings obtained from studies using other methods, such as the interview. For example, the findings of a study of the written communication deficiencies of college freshmen based on interviews with professors of English could be checked by conducting a content analysis of a sample of freshman compositions. We can place much more confidence in research evidence that holds up when the research is replicated using a different methodology. Because content analysis is nonreactive and often less costly than other methodologies, this approach is well suited for replication.[66]

3. *Test hypotheses.* Content analysis can be used to explore relationships and to test theories. For example, a recent study by Richard Brown used content analysis of newsmagazine coverage of the family-planning issue to test Lewin's theory of gatekeeping.[67]

---

65. Charles D. Cary, "Natural Themes in Soviet School History Textbooks," *Computers and the Humanities* 10 (1976): 313–323.

66. For an article that discusses the use of content analysis in conjunction with other research methodologies, see Joan E. Broderick, "A Method for Derivation of Areas for Assessment in Marital Relationships," *American Journal of Family Therapy* 9 (1981): 25–34.

67. See Richard M. Brown, "The Gatekeeper Reassessed: Return to Lewin," *Journalism Quarterly* 56 (1979): 595–601.

Locating Relevant Data

Once objectives have been spelled out, the next step in the content analysis is to locate data that are relevant to these objectives. Klaus Krippendorff observed that anything connected with the phenomenon that interests the researcher qualifies as data for content analysis.[68] In most content analysis studies in education, the relationship between the content to be studied and the research objective is clear and direct. However, you should be alert to subtle and indirect relationships that can provide information relevant to your hypotheses.

A recent study of changes in black identity and self-image provides an excellent example of the content analysis of indirect evidence.[69] The researchers hypothesized that the black power movement that started in the mid-1960s led to a positive change in black identity and self-perception. They reasoned that if such a change had taken place, a search of black publications would reveal a decrease in advertisements for hair straighteners and skin-bleaching cremes and an increase in advertisements offering Afro wigs or using models with Afro hairstyles. They then conducted a content analysis of 272 issues of *Ebony* magazine to determine the number and proportion of such advertisements for each year from 1949 to 1972. The results in fact demonstrated major changes, starting around 1966, in the numbers of advertisements of the selected types. For example, the annual mean number of ads for hair straighteners was 9.69 from 1961 to 1966 and 6.51 from 1967 to 1972. Similarly, a very sharp increase in ads featuring Afro hairstyles or wigs started in 1967. This study shows that content analysis can employ unobtrusive and indirect measures to draw inferences about attitudes and behavior. In many cases this indirect approach to sensitive issues probably produces more valid information than direct methods such as interview or questionnaire.

Most content-analysis studies are based on data that are already available. However, you can also generate data relevant to your objectives by administering questionnaires, having your subjects write essays, or making interview transcripts and then analyzing the context of these data. For example, in one study 1,000 students were asked to respond in writing to the question "What does cigarette smoking mean to you?" The content of the responses was then analyzed and compared for students at different grade levels and for smokers and nonsmokers.[70] A study of this kind could provide valuable insights of how students perceive cigarette smoking, which in turn could suggest strategies for reducing this behavior.

---

68. See Krippendorff in the Annotated References at the end of this chapter.
69. See J. Spencer Condie and James W. Christiansen, "An Indirect Technique for the Measurement of Changes in Black Identity," *Phylon* 38 (1977): 46–54.
70. See Ian M. Newman and Vincent S. DiSalvo, "Use of a Computer-Based Content Analysis Technique," *Journal of School Health*, 50, no. 4 (1980): 214–217.

Gathering Contextual Evidence

Having selected the data you intend to analyze, you must next establish an empirical link between the data selected and the inferences you plan to make from these data. In other words, create a rationale that the content-analysis data are really related to your objective or hypothesis. The usual ways of providing this contextual evidence include presenting a theory or model, reviewing previous research, or citing expert opinion that supports the relationship between the data and the objectives upon which the study is based.

For example, in the study of black identity just discussed, the authors cite expert opinion and previous research to support their contention that the "natural look" is related to the quest for black identity. However, the investigators have still taken a rather large inferential leap in equating a change in advertising in *Ebony* magazine to a change in black identity. Alternate hypotheses might also explain the changes in the number of ads related to Afro hairstyles, hair straighteners, and skin-bleaching cremes. For example, (1) some of these products may have contained substances that led the Food and Drug Administration to ban their use; (2) the Afro style may be a fashion fad that has nothing to do with black identity, although it does result in more Afro ads and fewer hair-straightener ads; (3) *Ebony* may be read primarily by a certain group of blacks (e.g., middle class), and the results of the study may not reflect a general change in black identity.

We are not suggesting that any of these alternative hypotheses are correct. The point is that as the content-analysis data become less directly linked to the research objectives, demonstrating that these data really measure what the researcher thinks they measure becomes more difficult. Thus, there are both advantages and disadvantages to the use of indirect data in content-analysis studies.

Developing a Data Sampling Plan

The next step in planning a content-analysis study is to develop a plan to obtain a representative sample of the universe of possible data that has been identified. Content analyses can be misleading or biased if the research worker does not use satisfactory methods for selecting the sample of content to be studied. In many content analyses, all content specifically pertinent to the research problem is studied. For example, an analysis concerned with the educational theories of a single author would usually be conducted by analyzing all the writing of the author in question. Content analyses dealing with topics that draw from a very large body of documentary materials, however, usually select material to be analyzed by some sampling technique. A study of trends in educational philosophy as reflected in newspaper editorials over the past 50 years would involve a very large volume of "raw material." In this case a sampling technique would be used to reduce the content to be analyzed to manageable size. One might, for example, limit one's selection to newspapers published every fifth year; thus, only 10 years of newspaper publishing need be considered rather than all 50 years. Next, one might use a table of random numbers. If the numbers 125, 5, 300 appeared, one would examine newspapers published on the 125th, 5th, and 300th day of the year. One could go through the table of random numbers until a specified number of editorials on educational philosophy had been selected for each year.

A problem faced in many content-analysis studies is that all the data in the universe are not available. Of course, some data are unavailable for accidental or random reasons. These do not usually pose a problem because in most cases another unit can be randomly selected to replace the missing one without incurring any serious danger of bias. For example, a librarian may have misfiled an occasional issue of a daily newspaper.

In some cases, however, there are nonrandom reasons for the survival of certain kinds of data and the loss of other kinds. For example, in cleaning out his files, a psychiatrist may retain files of patients with whom he was successful and destroy files for those with whom he has failed because he hopes someday to incorporate his successful cases in a book. On the other hand, his colleague in the next office may do just the opposite because she has no plans to write a book and believes that her failures may eventually return for additional treatment. In either case, the data that remain are a biased sample of the universe. Such bias is referred to by Krippendorff as "self-sampling bias."[71] If you suspect that self-sampling bias has occurred, make a special effort to obtain the missing data; if this fails, try to determine why the data are missing and how their absence may affect the representativeness of the sample.

Sampling data for a content-analysis study may employ any of the sampling procedures discussed in chapter 6. However, random sampling is generally the best procedure and is much easier to achieve in content analysis than in most other kinds of research.

Developing Coding Procedures

Once the content has been selected using appropriate sampling techniques, a coding or classification system needs to be developed for analyzing the content. When possible, use a coding system that has already been developed in previous research. First, this option saves the time needed to develop your own system, which for most content-analysis studies is a difficult and time-consuming task. Also, the use of available content-analysis dictionaries or standard coding categories permits comparisons with other studies that have

---

71. See Krippendorff in the Annotated References at the end of this chapter.

used the same system. Consequently, the research project is more likely to make a contribution to theory and knowledge in the field under investigation. A number of content-analysis dictionaries have been developed; check these carefully to see if one of them meets your needs. For example, the *Harvard III Psychosociological Dictionary* is frequently used in conjunction with content analysis in both psychology and sociology. This dictionary includes content categories in such areas as persons, roles, cultural objects, cultural processes, psychological processes, and social-emotional actions.[72]

If you cannot locate a content-analysis dictionary or classification system that fits your research, you will have to develop your own because it is necessary to define content categories that measure the variables indicated by the research objectives or hypotheses. For example, if you were interested in the frequency of positive and negative self-references in first and last counseling interviews, you would need to develop a set of categories and rules for deciding what types of statements are to be scored. Objective categories such as specific words (e.g., all occurrences of the word "I") are relatively easy to develop and score. Content categories involving inference or evaluation on the part of the rater are more difficult to develop. As content analysis usually depends on frequency counts, it is very important to control for the length of the communication. For example, you may find that clients of student counseling services make more negative self-references in the first interview than in the last interview. Before interpreting this finding, you must examine the length of interviews to make sure they are comparable. Clients may talk more in the first interview than in the last interview. Thus, the apparent change in frequency of negative self-references can be attributed to the change in clients' talkativeness.

After initial development of the content classification system, determine whether several raters can use it with a high degree of interrater reliability. If interrater reliability is low, you will need to identify points of ambiguity in the content classifications system and clarify them. Sometimes it is helpful to develop a set of scoring rules in order to increase the reliability with which the classification system can be used. This was the case in a study carried out by one of the authors.[73] The hypothesis was that creative persons would be more sensitive to aesthetic, dynamic, and affective properties of objects than noncreative persons. To test the hypothesis, he compared the frequency with which creative persons used certain kinds of noun modifiers (adjectives, participles, predicate adjectives) in describing Rorschach inkblots with the frequency of

---

72. For an example of a study that used this content analysis dictionary, see J. C. Montague, Jr., E. C. Hutchinson, and E. Matson, *Computerized Verbal Content Analysis of Institutionalized Versus Community Retarded Children* (Little Rock: University of Arkansas, 1973), ED 085949.
73. Meredith D. Gall, "An Investigation of Verbal Style in Creative and Noncreative Groups" (Ph.D. dissertation, University of California, Berkeley, 1968).

noun modifier use by noncreative persons.[74] In order to ensure that raters would reliably tally appropriate noun modifiers, he made up a set of rules for scoring noun modifiers to resolve the ambiguities that had become apparent in initial development of the classification system. The following lists the rules for scoring noun modifiers:

Rule 1: Noun modifiers usually immediately precede or follow a noun, or they immediately follow: is, are, looks, appears, seems.

Rule 2: Words immediately preceding or following nouns are almost always scored as a noun modifier if they end in -ed, -ing, -en, -y, -some, -like, -ful.

Rule 3: Do not score these adjectives or adjectives of the type: a, an, the, this, that, these, those, his, her, our, your, my, its, their, some, any, no, other.

Rule 4: Do not score adjectives having to do with number, such as first, second, one, two, few, many, each, both, every.

Rule 5: Do not score adjectives referring to location on the blot (e.g., "the *top* part of the blot looks like. . .") or on an object percept (e.g., "looks like the *top* part of a beetle") such as top, bottom, upper, lower, side, back, entire, whole.

Rule 6: Score such adjectives as "huge," "tremendous," "tiny," but do not score these specific words: big, large, small, little.

Rule 7: Do not score color words, such as white or black. The exceptions are combination colors, such as "blue-gray" (which is scored as one word) and words like "reddish."

Rule 8: Do not score adjectives that are an integral part of a noun phrase, such as praying mantis, United States. However, the adjective "high" in the phrase "high heels" is scored, since it refers to a particular style of shoes.

Rule 9: Only those noun modifiers that reflect one or more of the seven qualities previously stated are to be scored. This means that several types of adjectives are not scored, such as location (e.g., "marine life"), general class of human, animal, or inanimate (e.g., "human figures," "bearskin rug," "cloud formation," "anatomical shape"), critical-evaluative words (e.g., "obvious," "strange," "appropriate," "fantastic").

Rule 10: The noun modifiers that are not usually scored because of rule 9 are scored if they modify a quality noun (e.g., "a sense of *anatomical* form," "an *underwater* quality").

---

74. For example, in describing one of the Rorschach inkblots, a creative architect said, "It's *live* and *growing, soft* and *fragile* . . . could move in the wind." By contrast, a noncreative person might say, "Just looks like an inkblot . . . side things look like two animals."

By the use of such rules, the investigator was able to achieve near-perfect agreement between raters in scoring Rorschach protocols for appropriate noun modifiers. Interrater reliability is very important in content analyses in which human coders are employed and should always be computed and reported.

Planning Analysis Procedures

The final step in planning a content analysis is to decide upon the specific analytical procedures to be used. As in most other research, statistical procedures are needed to summarize the data and aid in its interpretation.

By far the most common method of summarizing content-analysis data is through the use of absolute frequencies, such as the numbers of specific incidents found in the data, and relative frequencies, such as the proportion of particular events to total events. Descriptive statistics such as the mean, median, and standard deviation are also used to compare the occurrences of different events. In content analyses that explore relationships, simple cross tabulations or chi-square analysis are often used because these techniques are suited to the analysis of categorical data.[75]

The Computer in Content Analysis

In the past 20 years the computer has revolutionized content analysis. Many common operations, such as tallying word frequencies, are extremely dull and time-consuming when done by hand and can be carried out with great speed and accuracy and at small cost by computers. This permits the analysis of large sets of data that would be practically impossible using manual procedures. The technology is approaching the point where, using optical readers, it will soon be possible to transfer the entire works of an author from the printed page directly into the computer with virtually no human interface.

Perhaps the most serious problem the content analyst must overcome in using computers is the need to develop highly detailed computer programs to take the place of the coding instructions that would be used by human coders. While the human coder can interpret, draw inferences, and apply common sense to the making of coding decisions, the computer cannot do anything it is not programmed to do. Thus, developing a computer program to code content-analysis data requires us to think through the process much more carefully than would be required if human coders were to be employed.

Fortunately, a number of computer programs have already been developed for use in content analysis. Perhaps the most widely used of these is the General

---

75. A variety of multivariate techniques, such as discriminant analysis and cluster analysis, are also used. See Peter R. Monge and Joseph N. Capella, eds., *Multivariate Techniques in Communication Research* (New York: Academic Press, 1980).

Inquirer.[76] These programs (1) identify systematically instances of words and phrases specified by the researcher, (2) count occurrences, (3) print and graph tabulations, (4) perform statistical analyses, and (5) sort and regroup sentences according to whether they fit a particular category system.[77] For example, you can store spelling lists from different textbooks in the computer, then have the computer print out a variety of research data such as a set of words common to every spelling list, a set of words unique to each spelling list, a readability index computed for each spelling list, and even a classification of the words in each list by themes and types (e.g., sports, science, adjectives, number of syllables).

We should like to note, finally, that the content-analysis technique is very well suited for small-scale educational research projects, and we are surprised that more students do not carry out content-analysis studies. Obtaining communications such as textbooks and newspapers is usually easier than obtaining research subjects. There is less opportunity to bias the data-collection process, since communications are usually "nonreactive." Also, communications can be analyzed directly, wheras one generally needs to collect data first from subjects by means of interview, standardized test, or observation before proceeding to the data-analysis phase of the research project. In short, the content-analysis technique can provide a basis for research projects that are significant yet economical in terms of time and money. Although we have learned much about word frequency, spelling and grammatical errors, and textbook content, we know almost nothing about the more subtle effects of the different forms of educational communication upon the personality, goals, and values of our youth.

MISTAKES SOMETIMES MADE IN OBSERVATIONAL RESEARCH

1. The researcher does not sufficiently train observers and thus obtains unreliable data.
2. Uses an observation form that requires too much from the observer.
3. Fails to take adequate precautions to avoid having observers disturb or change the situation they are to observe.
4. Asks observers to make excessively precise discriminations among behaviors.

76. See P. J. Stone et al., *The General Inquirer: A Computer Approach to Content Analysis* (Cambridge, MA: M.I.T. Press, 1966). For a study using the General Inquirer, see E. Aries, "Sex Differences in Small Group Behavior" (Paper presented at the conference on Sex Roles in American Society, Troy, New York, 1 May 1976), ED 136089.
77. Stone et al., *The General Inquirer.* Also see Newman and DiSalvo, "Use of a Computer-Based Content Analysis Technique," for a brief description of other computer programs used in content analysis.

5. Does not use at least two observers in order to determine interrater reliability.
6. Does not ensure that observers work independently of each other.
7. Allows contamination of data collection to occur.
8. Does not use random sampling techniques when appropriate.
9. Allows observer drift and reliability decay to occur.

ANNOTATED REFERENCES

Observation

Bakeman, Roger, and Gottman, John M. "Observing Interaction." In *An Introduction to Sequential Analysis*. New York: Cambridge University Press, 1986.

The authors' main theme is that the collection of sequential data in observational studies permits the researcher to test many hypotheses that cannot be tested with the typical nonsequential methods of observation. However, most of the topics in the book, such as developing a coding scheme, recording behavioral sequences, and assessing observer agreement, are relevant to any study that employs systematic observation. A good source for students who plan to conduct an observational study.

Boehm, A. E., and Weinberg, R. A. *The Classroom Observer—A Guide for Developing Observation Skills*. New York: Teachers College Press, 1977.

Provides a brief and practical introduction to classroom observation. Most of the major parts of an observational study are discussed including problem definition, behavioral categories, sampling behavior, and recording behavior.

Croll, Paul. *Systematic Classroom Observation*. Philadelphia: Falmer Press, 1986.

A good source for the student who wants to learn more about observational research. Discusses the design and conduct of observational research and the analysis of observational data. Provides useful examples.

Evertson, Carolyn M., and Green, Judith L. "Observation as Inquiry and Method." In Merlin C. Wittrock, ed., *Handbook of Research on Teaching*, 3rd ed. New York: Macmillan, 1986.

Recommended to any student who is considering an observational study for a thesis or dissertation. After a brief historical orientation, the authors explore the observation process. Four broad systems of recording observational data are then discussed in detail. The authors are especially skillful in using tables to summarize, and figures to illustrate, important processes. An extensive reference list is included.

Hartmann, Donald P., ed. *Using Observers to Study Behavior*. San Francisco: Jossey-Bass, 1982.

Focuses on a few major topics, including a discussion of the reactive factor that can distort observational data and ways to control it, steps to be considered in designing an observational study, the process of training observers, and the analysis of observational data.

Schatzman, Leonard, and Strauss, Anselm L. *Field Research.* Englewood Cliffs, NJ: Prentice-Hall, 1973.

Discusses field research from the viewpoint of the sociologist. A practical guide, dealing with such topics as entering the environment to be observed, getting organized, watching, listening, recording, and analyzing data. A useful source for the student who plans to use interviews or observations in research.

Observational Instruments

Borich, G. D., and Madden, S. K. *Evaluating Classroom Instruction: A Sourcebook of Instruments.* Reading, MA: Addison-Wesley, 1977.

Reviews a large number of instruments that can be used to evaluate teacher and pupil behavior. Many are observation forms. Most of the information that a researcher needs to select an instrument is provided.

Herbert, J., and Altridge, C. "A Guide for Developers and Users of Observation Systems and Manuals." *American Educational Research Journal* 12 (1975): 1–20.

Proposes 33 criteria that can be used to evaluate observation instruments. These criteria are useful to the researcher who wishes to select an instrument from those available as well as providing guidelines for the researcher who plans to develop his or her own instrument. Each criterion is discussed, and many examples are given.

Simon, Anita, and Boyer, E. Gil. *Mirrors for Behavior III: An Anthology of Observation Instruments.* Wyncote, PA: Communications Materials Center, 1974.

Originally published in 1967 in 6 volumes and covers 26 observation instruments. Volumes 7 through 14, published in 1970, cover 53 additional instruments. Two supplemental volumes to the 1970 edition covered an additional 12 observation systems. This 1974 anthology covers observation instruments selected from fields such as group dynamics, psychotherapy, medicine, industry, and anthropology, as well as providing an extensive examination of instruments related to education. A total of 99 observation systems are examined, which deal with a wide range of phenomena including cognitive and affective processes, nonverbal behaviors, and interactions with materials. Brief abstracts are provided on the 99 systems that help the reader locate instruments that may meet particular needs. These are followed by a more detailed treatment of each system, which briefly describes the system on eight dimensions and also defines the categories of behavior that are observed. Most of the systems are described in more detail in the earlier volumes. For example, the Flanders System of Interaction Analysis, perhaps the most widely used system, is given 3 pages in the 1974 edition whereas the entire observer's manual (51 pages) is included in the 1967 edition.

Nonnreactive Measures

Sechrest, Lee, ed. *Unobtrusive Measurement Today.* San Francisco: Jossey-Bass, 1979.

Contains several interesting chapters concerned primarily with the use of unobtrusive (nonreactive) measures in a variety of research situations. The chapters on designing unobtrusive field experiments and on using nonverbal behaviors as unobtrusive measures are especially recommended.

Webb, E. J.; Campbell, D. T.; Schwartz, R. D.; Sechrest, L.; and Grove, J. B. *Nonreactive Measures in the Social Sciences.* Boston: Houghton Mifflin, 1981.

Second edition of the classic reference in this area. A variety of nonreactive measures including physical traces, archives, and observation are discussed. The chapters on the ethical problems and limitations of such measures, which were not included in the first edition, are especially useful to the investigator who is considering the use of nonreactive measures in a research project.

Content Analysis

Krippendorff, Klaus. *Content Analysis: An Introduction to Its Methodology.* Beverly Hills, CA: Sage, 1980.

Systematically covers the major steps in planning and conducting a content analysis. Students planning a content-analysis study should first read the final chapter, "A Practical Guide," and then read other chapters as needed. The author's style is difficult and requires careful study and rereading.

SELF-CHECK TEST

Circle the correct answer to each of the following questions. An answer key is provided on page 884.

1. Observational methods of data collection are often useful when
   a. the researcher needs a data-collection system that is more economical than self-reports.
   b. subjects are apt to bias self-reports.
   c. subjects can accurately recall events.
   d. the Hawthorne Effect is likely to occur.

2. A major disadvantage of observational research is that
   a. it is easily biased by the subject.
   b. no standardized observational instruments are available.
   c. the presence of the observer changes the situation.
   d. only the most simple behaviors can be observed.
3. The "halo effect" is most apt to occur when the observer is required to
   a. evaluate abstract qualities.
   b. record specific behaviors.
   c. record descriptive variables.
   d. operate from a concealed position.
4. Observer contamination means that a person observes the occurrence of a variable
   a. without prior training in observing that variable.
   b. without realizing the need to control for the error of central tendency.
   c. with prior knowledge of the statistical techniques to be used in analyzing the data.
   d. with knowledge of subjects' performance on other variables.
5. Asking individuals to assume certain roles in a setting devised by the researcher and then observing the individuals in these roles describes one kind of
   a. peer evaluation.
   b. critical-incident testing.
   c. situational testing.
   d. supervisory rating.
6. Collecting data on a group by asking each member to select persons in the group most preferred by that person on the basis of a specific criterion describes the _____ technique.
   a. sociometric
   b. anecdotal
   c. critical-incident
   d. supervisory rating
7. The error most often noted in supervisory ratings is the
   a. error of central tendency.
   b. halo effect.
   c. conscious observer bias.
   d. placebo effect.
8. Research analysis of transcripts from audiotapes of classroom verbal behavior is called _____ analysis.
   a. content
   b. critical-incident
   c. sociometric
   d. anecdotal
9. A recent trend in content analysis research is to
   a. compare content frequencies.
   b. study the relationship between content variables and other research variables.
   c. compare the types of words most frequently used in the English language with those used in other languages.
   d. compute readability indices for school textbooks.
10. Selection of a sample of material for content analysis
   a. cannot be done, since the entire population of material must be studied in order to draw valid inferences.
   b. will determine the objectives of the research project.
   c. cannot be done by using a random sampling technique.
   d. should be done by using a random sampling technique.

APPLICATION PROBLEMS

The following problems are designed to give you practice in applying significant concepts and research procedures explained in the chapter. Most of them do not have a single correct answer. For feedback, you can compare your answers with the sample answers on pages 897–898.

1. a. Some educators believe that enthusiasm is an important characteristic of the good teacher. Nevertheless, enthusiasm is a "high-inference" variable. Name three observable teacher behaviors that you think are indicative of enthusiasm in classroom teaching.

   b. Suppose that one behavioral indication of teacher enthusiasm is use of facial expressions such as smiles, laughter, or raised eyebrows. Write an observation-schedule item that could be used for observing this behavior during a 20-minute class discussion.

2. A researcher plans to train five observers to use the Flanders Interaction Analysis system, which is a standard observational schedule. Her schedule of training includes the following steps to be carried out at a series of meetings with the observers.

   a. Explain the 10 categories of the observation form.

   b. Explain how teacher or student behavior is coded on the observation form every three seconds.

   c. Have the observers score three videotapes of classroom interaction and compare their scoring of each tape with the researcher's criterion scoring.

   d. Provide the observers with their classroom observation assignments.

   What important step has been omitted from the researcher's training plan?

3. A researcher is interested in testing the theory that children learn by imitating the behavior of others. To test the theory, he asks one group of teachers to act exceptionally neat in their class for a period of weeks, for example, conspicuously taking time to arrange their desks neatly. He asks another group of teachers to act sloppy for a similar period of time. The researcher's prediction is that children who have "neat" teachers will be acting more neatly at the end of the experiment than will children exposed to "sloppy" teachers. What is one unobtrusive measure of children's degree of neatness that could be used in this experiment?

4. Suppose that you wish to test the hypothesis that high school students' popularity with their peers is related to indices of mental health, such as freedom from anxiety and positive self-image. What are two methods involving untrained observers that could be used to measure peer popularity?

5. A researcher wants to determine whether the thought level of students' essays improves from the first to fourth year of college. She has available a collection of essays written by the same students over a four-year period of college attendance. What are three aspects of essay writing style that could be analyzed to yield a measure of thought level? Why these particular aspects?

SUGGESTION SHEET

If your last name starts with letters from Lew to May, please complete the Suggestion Sheet at the end of the book while this chapter is still fresh in your mind.

13 EXPLORING RELATIONSHIPS BETWEEN VARIABLES: THE CAUSAL-COMPARATIVE METHOD

OVERVIEW

The causal-comparative method is used to explore causal relationships between variables prior to, or as a substitute for, doing an experiment. It involves comparing samples that are different on a critical variable but otherwise comparable. For example, juvenile delinquents have been compared with nondelinquents who are drawn from the same population in order to identify possible causes of delinquent behavior. In the first part of the chapter we discuss advantages and disadvantages of using this type of research design. Next, we provide detailed techniques for conducting a causal-comparative study, particularly in the critical area of selecting appropriate comparison groups. The second half of the chapter deals with statistical techniques for analyzing the research data yielded by this method.

OBJECTIVES

After studying this chapter you should be able to:

1. Explain the relationship between causal-comparative, correlational, and experimental research.
2. Describe three interpretations that can be made if a relationship between two variables, A and B, is discovered through causal-comparative research.
3. State plausible alternative hypotheses to challenge a research hypothesis in a causal-comparative design.
4. Form meaningful subgroups, given an initially defined sample of subjects to be used in causal-comparative research.
5. Explain the use of the extreme groups method in causal-comparative research.
6. Define suitable comparison groups, given an initially defined group in which a particular characteristic is present.
7. Interpret the t value resulting from a t-test for the difference between means, and describe how this test would be used in causal-comparative research.
8. Describe situations in causal-comparative research in which it is necessary to use the t-test for correlated means rather than the t-test for independent means.
9. Compare the meaning of t values resulting from a one-tailed and two-tailed t-test, and describe situations in which each test would be used.

10. Interpret the *t* value resulting from a *t*-test for a single mean, and describe how this test would be used in causal-comparative research.
11. Interpret the *F* values resulting from an analysis of variance, analysis of covariance, and multivariate analysis of covariance; describe how these tests of statistical significance would be used in causal-comparative research.
12. Interpret the *F* value resulting from a test for differences between variances; describe how this test would be used in causal-comparative research.
13. Describe situations in causal-comparative research in which it is necessary to use nonparametric tests of significance rather than parametric tests.
14. Interpret the results of a chi-square test, and describe how this test would be used in causal-comparative research.
15. Interpret the results of the Mann-Whitney *U* test, the Wilcoxon signed-rank test, and the Kruskal-Wallis test; describe how these tests would be used in causal-comparative research.

INTRODUCTION

The Study of Relationships between Variables

As we stated in chapter 9, educational research is done either to describe educational phenomena or to discover relationships between variables. The relationships between variables of greatest interest to educators are those involving cause and effect. The discovery of cause-and-effect relationships between variables is very useful in theory building and educational improvement. For example, if we find that a particular type of instruction improves student problem solving, that knowledge can be used to develop a theory of problem-solving instruction or to develop an effective curriculum that incorporates this type of instruction.

The causal-comparative method is one approach to exploring cause-and-effect relationships between variables. In a sense, it is not a method at all, but rather a particular way of analyzing relational data. The correlational method, discussed in chapter 14, provides another approach to exploring cause-and-effect relationships. Like causal-comparative research, the distinguishing characteristic of correlational studies is the way in which the data are analyzed. We will discuss the similarities between causal-comparative and correlational research again at the end of the chapter. Also, we advise you to read this chapter and chapter 14 together so that you can see the connections between the two methods.

The causal-comparative method was more widely used years ago than it is now, because the statistical techniques associated with this method—primarily the *t*-test and analysis of variance—were well known to researchers then. In recent years, however, researchers have discovered that correlational statistics, especially multiple regression, can do everything that the *t*-test and analysis of variance can do and more. Correlational statistics are particularly useful for studying relationships between three or more variables. Because educational processes typically reflect complex interactions between numerous variables, it is no wonder that researchers now rely on correlational statistics.

Even though correlational research is increasingly popular, we recommend that you learn the causal-comparative method in depth. The statistics associated with the causal-comparative method (especially the *t*-test and analysis of variance) are still widely used in experimental research. Therefore, we will make repeated reference to these statistical techniques in our subsequent discussion of experimental designs (chapters 15 and 16). Also, some relational data are better understood by the *t*-test, analysis of variance, or similar technique than by correlational statistics. For example, relationships involving dichotomous groups (e.g., boys versus girls) or categorical groups (e.g., elementary school administrators versus junior high school administrators versus middle school administrators) are more easily interpreted using the statistical tools presented in this chapter. Finally, you may find it easier to understand the logic of discovering cause-and-effect relationships between variables if you study the causal-comparative method first. The correlational method is ultimately a more powerful approach, but for many beginning researchers it is not as easily understood as the causal-comparative method.

Advantages and Disadvantages of Causal-Comparative Studies

The **causal-comparative method** is aimed at the discovery of possible causes and effects of a behavior pattern or personal characteristic by comparing subjects in whom this pattern or characteristic is present with similar subjects in which it is absent or present to a lesser degree. For example, the causal-comparative method can be used to study the causes of high academic achievement (a behavior pattern) or the effects of ethnic background (a personal characteristic). This method is sometimes called **ex post facto research,** because causes are studied after they presumably have exerted their effect on another variable.

The causal-comparative method is used instead of the experimental method because many of the cause-and-effect relationships in education that researchers wish to study do not easily permit experimental manipulation. A causal-comparative study by Gary Green and Sue Jaquess illustrates this point.[1] These researchers were interested in the effect of part-time employment by high

1. Gary Green and Sue Norvill Jaquess, "The Effect of Part-Time Employment on Academic Achievement," *Journal of Educational Research* 80 (1987): 325–329.

school students on their academic achievement. Their sample included 477 high school juniors who either were unemployed or employed at least 10 or more hours per week at the time of the study.

Note that the researchers did not experimentally manipulate employment. It would be virtually impossible for them to ask some students to work part-time and to ask other students not to work, so that they could observe the effects of employment. Their only recourse was to observe the effects of *natural* variations in employment. By *natural*, we mean that variations in employment were observed under conditions that did not involve any artificial arrangement, including experimentation by the researchers. An advantage of the causal-comparative method, then, is that it allows researchers to study cause-and-effect relationships in situations where experimental manipulation is not possible.

A disadvantage of the causal-comparative method is that it is difficult to establish causality on the basis of the collected data. Consider, for example, the results of the employment study, which are shown in table 13.1. Employed and nonemployed students earned similar grade-point averages (GPAs), but nonemployed students earned significantly higher ACT scores. (The ACT—from the American College Testing Program— is similar to the Scholastic Aptitude Test, which many high school students take when applying for college admission.)

Do these results show there is no cause-and-effect relationship between high school employment (cause) and student academic achievement (effect)? The results shown in table 13.1 support that conclusion because the difference in

TABLE 13.1

Academic Achievement and Extracurricular Participation of Employed and Nonemployed Students

Variable	Employed Students M	Nonemployed Students M	t	p
1. GPA	2.66	2.78	.81	.42
2. ACT score	17.13	18.93	2.22	.02
3. Extracurricular participation (hours per week)	6.21	8.30		.05[a]

SOURCE: Adapted from Gary Green and Sue Norvill Jaquess, "The Effect of Part-Time Employment on Academic Achievement," *Journal of Educational Research* 80 (1987): 327–328.
[a] The researchers did not report the *t* value for this variable—only that the difference was statistically significant. Significance is conventionally established at the .05 level.

GPA between the employed and nonemployed groups is slight and statistically nonsignificant. It is possible, however, that employed students took easier courses than nonemployed students. Had they taken courses as difficult as those taken by the nonemployed students, their GPA might have been significantly lower. Because the researchers did not examine the variable of course difficulty,[2] we cannot conclude for certain from the observed results that employment has no effect on GPA.

The significant result for the ACT variable suggests that high school employment *causes* poor performance on the ACT. Several other causal interpretations are possible, however. For example, it may be that students who find that they have low aptitude for college study are likely to become interested in the world of work instead, and so they seek part-time employement while still in high school. In this interpretation, a third variable (aptitude for college study) is seen as the cause of both high school employment and ACT performance. Still another interpretation is that parent behavior is the primary causative factor. Some parents may encourage their children not to seek part-time employment and to prepare for college instead; other parents may discourage their children from planning for college (perhaps because of the expense involved) and instead encourage them to earn money through part-time employment.

Given the plausibility of these alternative interpretations, we would be going out on a limb to recommend that working students should stop employment if they want their ACT scores to improve. Further research is needed to test the merits of the alternative interpretations. If they are refuted, we would have a more secure basis for claiming that employment causes a decrement in ACT performance.

Alternative interpretations must be considered as well in explaining the significant relationship between employment and extracurricular participation shown in table 13.1. It seems likely that employment causes students to devote less time to extracurricular activities. Yet it is also plausible that students who are less interested in extracurricular activities (as indicated by a low amount of time spent on them) are likely to turn their energies elsewhere, including part-time employment. In this interpretation, extracurricular participation causes employment, not the other way around.

In summary, the major advantage of causal-comparative research designs is that they allow us to study cause-and-effect relationships under conditions where experimental manipulation is difficult or impossible. Another advantage is that many such relationships can be studied in a single research project; for example, table 13.1 shows relationships involving four different variables. The

2. The researchers compared the grades of employed and nonemployed students in one required class, thereby presumably controlling for differential course difficulty. This, however, is a weak test of the differential course difficulty hypothesis.

major disadvantage of causal-comparative research designs is that determining causal patterns with any degree of certainty is difficult.[3] An observed relationship between variables *A* and *B* can mean that *A* causes *B*, *B* causes *A*, or a third variable *C* causes both *A* and *B*.

PLANNING A CAUSAL-COMPARATIVE STUDY

Statement of the Research Problem

The steps in a causal-comparative research project are illustrated in a recent study of scientific literacy at the junior high school level.[4] Alexis Mitman, John Mergendoller, Virginia Marchman, and Martin Packer investigated the relationship between variables involving teacher instruction (cause) and variables involving students' scientific literacy (effect). The concept of scientific literacy, as used in this study, includes five components: (1) mastery of science content, (2) positive attitudes toward science, (3) understanding of the societal impact of science, (4) the process of science reasoning, and (5) the sociohistorical development of science.

The initial step in a causal-comparative study is to speculate about the causes of the phenomena that interest you. Your speculations can be based on previous research findings and theory, and on your own observations of the phenomena. In the study mentioned above, Mitman and her colleagues speculated that the development of students' scientific literacy might be influenced by teachers' verbal and written instruction. They speculated that

> instruction in typical classes would emphasize the transmission of science content during recitation and seatwork activities. It was thought that, if this were the case, teachers' main opportunity to facilitate the scientific literacy of their students would be to suggest meaningful contexts for science content during verbal presentations, reinforced by attention to the same contexts on written assignments. Teacher provision of meaningful contexts for lesson concepts during instructional explanation has been shown to enhance student acquisition of appropriate schemas in other subject areas (Duffy, Roehler, Meloth, and Vavrus, 1986).[5]

After possible causes of the phenomena have been identified, they should be incorporated into the statement of the research problem. As you will recall,

---

3. Causation and variations in causal patterns are discussed in chapter 9.
4. Alexis L. Mitman, John R. Mergendoller, Virginia A. Marchman, and Martin J. Packer, "Instruction Addressing the Components of Scientific Literacy and Its Relation to Student Outcomes," *American Educational Research Journal* 24 (1987): 611–633.
5. Ibid., p. 613.

the research problem is usually stated in the form of research objectives or hypotheses. In the study we have been considering, the researchers formulated and tested the following hypothesis: ". . . it was hypothesized that the extent and consistency with which teachers contextualized science content should have a direct and measurable influence on students' acquisition of the five components of scientific literacy . . ."[6] The term "contextualized" in this hypothesis means teacher presentation of scientific content in a context that is meaningful to students. (For example, a teacher might put into context the scientific concept of ecosystem by showing students that the relationship between local industries and local resources reflects an ecosystem in action.) In the researchers' hypothesis, teacher presentation of science content in context is the cause, and acquisition of scientific literacy is the effect. We discuss the researchers' empirical test of this hypothesis a bit later in the chapter.

You should attempt to state and test alternative hypotheses about other factors that might explain observed differences between two groups. For example, in the study by Mitman and colleagues, students' level of scientific literacy at the end of the school year might plausibly be influenced not only by the quality of the teacher's instruction, but also by their level of scientific literacy at the start of the school year. In other words, students who knew more about science at the outset might learn new content more easily than students starting with a weak knowledge base. Thus, students' level of scientific literacy in September (cause) might influence the level of scientific literacy that they achieve by the following June (effect).

The research results can confirm more than one alternative hypothesis. This is a common occurrence because complex behaviors such as student learning are often determined by a variety of factors. The magnitude of difference between the two groups on each measure can be examined to determine which factor, or set of factors, appears most likely to cause the phenomenon being studied.

The testing of plausible alternative hypotheses is called **strong inference.**[7] Whenever possible, it should be used in causal-comparative research to formulate the variables on which the comparison groups are to be contrasted. You can then select measures of these variables on a rational basis, instead of relying on the "shotgun approach" in which a large number of measures are administered because they appear interesting or are available. Also, the use of alternative hypotheses provides you with a helpful reminder that the findings of a causal-comparative study, no matter how well done, are subject to various causal interpretations.

6. Ibid., p. 614.
7. J. Platt, "Strong Inference," *Science* 146 (1964): 347–353.

Selecting a Defined Group

After the research problem has been stated, the next step in the causal-comparative method is to define the group that possesses the characteristic one wishes to study. Procedures used to define this group will determine the meaning and applicability of the results. Underachievers, for example, might be defined conceptually as pupils whose achievement is less than would be expected from their measured aptitude. An operational definition, however, must be much more precise. It must specify the measure of achievement to be used, the measure of aptitude to be used, and the degree of difference between them that is to be considered indicative of underachievement. Studies that appear at first glance to be similar may really be different because of differences in procedures for defining the samples.

Another problem is whether the underachievers obtained by applying the operational definition are likely to be reasonably homogeneous in terms of factors causing underachievement. Can we identify types of underachievers who are underachieving for different reasons, or are the same causes likely to be operating for all underachievers? This is an important question for you to ask. Suppose your hypothesis is that a basic cause of high school underachievement is poor personal adjustment. Further suppose that, in actuality, underachievement in English is due to difficulties in personal adjustment, but that underachievement in mathematics is totally unrelated to this factor. If you fail to discriminate between English and mathematics underachievers in selecting your sample, you will seriously weaken your chances of finding any support for your hypothesis. Having treated all underachievers as a homogeneous group, you will probably find no difference between them and a comparison group (e.g., a normally achieving or overachieving group) on a measure of personal adjustment. Had you tested the hypothesis using only underachievers in English, however, you would probably have found significant differences between English underachievers and an appropriate comparison group on a measure of personal adjustment.

Even in this instance, you may need to define your group further. For example, there may be sex differences in the factors leading to underachievement in English. We might find that problems in personal adjustment are a factor in underachievement for females but not for males. If this were the case, further data analysis would reveal differences between female underachievers in English and an appropriate comparison group of females, whereas no differences would be found for male underachievers in English.

The preceding discussion suggests that the success of a causal-comparative study depends on the investigator's skill in selecting groups that are homogeneous with respect to certain critical variables. Therefore, you should ask yourself this question: Is this a homogeneous group or can further subgroups be defined? A few examples of subgrouping follow:

1. first-grade teachers	1. male vs. female teachers
2. juvenile delinquents	2. delinquents who commit crimes against property vs. delinquents who commit crimes against persons
3. computer educators	3. computer educators who have received inservice training in this field vs. those who are self-taught
4. school administrators	4. school superintendents vs. assistant school superintendents

Often the review of the literature will provide ideas about the types of subgroups that need to be formed if significant differences are to be found. If you plan to study a characteristic not researched previously, common sense and reasoning based on psychological or educational theory can be used to form homogeneous subgroups.

In the study of scientific literacy described above, Mitman and her colleagues identified two groups of teachers who varied in the extent to which they taught science content in a meaningful context. Their procedure for identifying the two groups started with the selection of a total sample of 11 teachers and the students in one of their seventh-grade life science classes. Each teacher was observed teaching two different life science topics. Trained observers coded the amount of time that each teacher spent making explicit statements refering to a science context in teaching each topic. An example of a "context-enriched" statement is as follows:

> "All right. We now know about the four different blood types. Being able to identify each person's blood type is an important part of today's medicine our medical technology. This is because when people are ill and need blood transfusions, it is critical that they receive compatible blood. To see how blood typing works, we're going to test ourselves—just as they would in a hospital."[8]

The researchers recorded the percentage of total instructional time that each teacher made such context-enriched statements. The five teachers with the highest percentages were identified as high-context-use teachers, and the six teachers with the lowest percentages were identified as low-context-use teachers, as shown in table 13.2.

Because their sample was small, they did not define subgroups from these initially defined groups. Had a larger sample been available, they might have

8. Mitman et al., "Instruction Addressing the Components of Scientific Literacy," p. 617.

TABLE 13.2

Teachers' Total Percentage of Presentation Time Devoted to Science Context

Group	Teacher ID	Percentage of Presentation Time Addressing Contextual Components
Low-context-use teachers	2	0
	3	0.2
	6	0.7
	7	0.5
	8	0.5
	10	1.2
High-context-use teachers	1	11.0
	4	3.8
	5	4.0
	9	4.0
	11	3.5

SOURCE: Adapted from table 5 in Alexis L. Mitman, John R. Mergendoller, Virginia A. Marchman, and Martin J. Packer, "Instruction Addressing the Components of Scientific Literacy and Its Relation to Student Outcomes" *American Educational Research Journal* 24 (1987): p. 625.

considered forming subgroups based on the teacher's gender or understanding of science. Another possibility would be to break the high-context-use group into two subgroups: teachers who generally make good context-enriched statements, and teachers who generally make weak context-enriched statements. (The importance of studying the quality of teachers' references to context is highlighted later in the chapter.)

Inspection of table 13.2 indicates that the sample only included one teacher (ID 1) who placed much emphasis on science context (11% of presentation time). The number of such teachers in the sample could have been increased if the researchers had selected a much larger sample, for example, 100 teachers. It would be prohibitively expensive in most research projects, however, to collect observational and study test data on this large a sample.

The **extreme groups method** can be used to solve this problem in some situations.[9] In the study we have been considering, the researchers found that students' reports of their teachers' references to scientific context were moderately correlated ($r = .34$) with teachers' observed references. The students were

9. For a technical discussion of the extreme groups approach and its relationship to the correlational method, see Edward F. Alf, Jr., and Norman M. Abrahams, "The Use of Extreme Groups in Assessing Relationships," *Psychometrika* 40 (1975): 563–572.

particularly accurate in identifying the teachers who made the most and least references to scientific context. Now, it is much less expensive to have students fill out a questionnaire on their teachers' context use than to observe teachers directly. Researchers could select a sample inexpensively by first administering the questionnaire to the classes of, let's say, 100 different teachers. Then they could select the 10 teachers who were reported by students to have the highest context use and the 10 teachers who were reported by students to have the lowest context use. The other 80 teachers would be eliminated from further investigation. The resulting sample of 20 teachers most likely would include a greater number of teachers with very high and very low context use than would a sample of 20 teachers drawn at random from the population.

Selecting Comparison Groups

Once you have selected a homogeneous group having the characteristic you wish to study, the next step is to select a group not having this characteristic in order to permit comparisons. The population from which the comparison sample is to be selected is usually defined to be similar to the characteristic-present group except for the variable being studied. In the study of scientific literacy described above, the comparison group of low-context-use teachers was drawn from the same pool of teachers as the high-context-use teachers. Presumably the two groups were similar in all respects except for their use of context-enriched statements while teaching science.

Suppose one finds that the two groups differ significantly on an extraneous variable. For example, suppose the high-context-use teachers generally had more years of teaching experience than did the low-context-use teachers. In this case, if students of the high-context-use teachers were found to develop greater scientific literacy than students of low-context-use teachers, we could not be certain whether this effect was due to the teachers' use of context-enriched statements or to their teaching experience.

One way to solve this problem would be to use a **matching procedure.** The researcher would take each high-context-use teacher and *match* this teacher with a low-context-use teacher having the same amount of teaching experience. This procedure, however, might require a time-consuming search for a sample of low-context-use teachers that could be matched with the high-context-use teachers on this variable.

Matching procedures usually create more problems than they solve. You cannot be certain that you have selected the most important variable or variables on which to match subjects. Also, you may not be able to find suitable matches for some members of the characteristic-present sample. Therefore, the preferred procedure is to try to select the characteristic-present and comparison samples randomly from the same population, and then to control for other variables through the use of analysis of covariance, which is described later in the chapter.

Data Collection

No limitations exist on the types of measuring instruments that can be used in causal-comparative studies. Standardized tests, questionnaires, interviews, and naturalistic observations are all useful for collecting data about cause-and-effect factors. In the study we have been describing, the researchers used an observational procedure to determine the percentage of time that each teacher used to provide a context for science content:

> Observers kept a continuous written record of major class events and activities during every observed class period. Observers noted the clock time on these records at the beginning and end of each activity segment. . . . Observers also audiotaped each class period . . . observers used the above written records and narrative descriptions to [calculate] the amount of time teachers devoted to different kinds of [presentation] activities. . . . Following this initial calculation of total presentation time, observers calculated the percentage of this time devoted to content-only versus context-enriched instruction.[10]

Researchers also administered several measures to assess learning outcomes relating to scientific literacy:

> Students completed three science measures both at pretest (beginning of the school year) and posttest (end of the school year). . . . The Life Science Questionnaire tapped students' knowledge of science content—i.e., life science achievement. The Science Process Survey tapped students' understanding of the reasoning process of science and, to a lesser extent, the social-historical development of science. Finally, the Feelings toward Science Survey assessed . . . students' feelings toward science classes, vocational and educational intentions in science, feelings toward science in general, and interest in science activities outside of class.[11]

Data Analysis

The first step in an analysis of causal-comparative data is to compute descriptive statistics for each comparison group in the study. These generally will include the group mean and standard deviation. In the study of scientific literacy, each teachers' use of context-enriched statements was reported as a percentage (see table 13.2). Students' scores on the scientific literacy measures were reported as mean gains from beginning of the school year to end of the school year, as shown in table 13.3.

The next step usually is to do a test of statistical significance. The choice of a significance test depends on whether the researcher is interested in comparing

10. Mitman et al., "Instruction Addressing the Components of Scientific Literacy," p. 617.
11. Ibid., pp. 618–619.

TABLE 13.3

Performance on Scientific Literacy Measures of Students Taught by Teachers High or Low in Context Use

Scientific Literacy Measure	Mean Gain Score		t Value	p Value[a]
	High-Context Use	Low-Context Use		
Feelings toward science classes	−.194[b]	−.080	−1.40	0.82
Vocational and educational intentions in science	−.174	−.216	.48	.316
Feelings toward science in general	−.132	−.118	− .18	.431
Interest in science activities outside of class	−.045	−.072	.44	.329
Knowledge of life science	2.148	2.102	.10	.460
Understanding of scientific process	1.191	.582	1.69	.046

[a] One-tailed probabilities are reported.
[b] Negative mean gains indicate lower posttest than pretest score.
SOURCE: Adapted from Alexis L. Mitman, John R. Mergendoller, Virginia A. Marchman, and Martin J. Packer, "Instruction Addressing the Components of Scientific Literacy and Its Relation to Student Outcomes," *American Educational Research Journal* 24 (1987): 626.

groups with respect to mean score, variance, median, rank scores, or category frequencies. You should be familiar with the various significance tests, which were introduced in chapter 9 and are presented more fully here. Also, note that many of the same significance tests can be used in analyzing data from experimental designs, which are presented in chapter 15.

STATISTICAL ANALYSIS: THE *t*-TEST

The *t*-Test for Differences between Means

The basic rationale for testing the significance of the differences between two sample means was explained in chapter 9. You may find it helpful to reread the sections that describe the standard error of the mean, the null hypothesis, and the test of statistical significance. We showed that the *z* distribution, which follows the normal curve distribution of differences between sample means, can be used to test the null hypothesis that there is no difference between population means. It is appropriate to use the z distribution when large samples are studied ($N = 30$ or larger). When small samples are studied ($N = 29$ or smaller), it is advisable to use the **t-test** instead. Most statistics textbooks provide separate tables listing significance levels for the z and the t distributions.

The t-test is probably the most commonly used statistical tool in causal-comparative studies. Many research problems require a great deal of time and money, and so including many subjects in the sample is not possible. In the study of scientific literacy that we have been considering, a large amount of data was collected on each teacher and his or her life science class. The researchers' resources only allowed them to collect such data on 11 teachers, 5 of whom were classified as making more use of context-enriched statements and 6 of whom were classified as making less use of context-enriched statements.

The t-test makes three assumptions about the scores obtained in causal-comparative research. The first assumption is that scores form an interval or ratio scale of measurement. The second is that scores in the populations under study are normally distributed. The third is that score variances for the populations under study are equal.

Statisticians have conducted research to determine what happens when the assumptions underlying the t-test and other parametric statistics are violated. They have found that these tests provide accurate estimates of statistical significance even under conditions of substantial violation of the assumptions.[12] If you are concerned about score distributions in your data, you should consider doing both a t-test and its nonparametric counterpart—either the Mann-Whitney U test or the Wilcoxon signed-rank test. If the two tests yield different results because the data depart substantially from t-test assumptions, you can just report the results of the nonparametric test.

The t-tests for the scientific literacy measures in the study by Mitman and her colleagues are shown in table 13.3. One statistically significant difference was observed, although surprisingly it was in the direction opposite to that which was predicted. Students of low-context-use teachers were found to make a greater gain in understanding of science process than did students of high-context-use teachers. In attempting to explain this unanticipated result, researchers found that teachers' context-embedded statements were often incomplete or confusing. Therefore, they surmised that

> because teachers' references to these components often were deficient and unsystematic, it is possible that teachers who made more references to the contextual components actually detracted from students' learning. This, in turn, might lead to lower student performance on measures designed to test their scientific literacy directly.[13]

---

12. For an extended discussion of this problem, see C. A. Boneau, "The Effects of Violations of Assumptions Underlying the t-Test," *Psychological Bulletin* 57 (1960): 49–64.
13. Ibid., p. 628.

A researcher may wish to compare groups on many variables. Each comparison requires a separate *t*-test. As shown in table 13.3, the classes of the high- and low-context-use teachers were compared on six scientific literacy measures, requiring a total of six *t*-tests. As the number of *t*-tests increases, however, so does the risk of a Type I error. For example, suppose two groups are compared on 20 variables, resulting in 20 different *t*-tests. Almost certainly one of the comparisons will yield a significant *p* (assuming *p* is set at .05) even if there is no difference between the populations represented by the samples on any of the variables. To understand how this happens, think about coin-tossing. On any given toss of a coin, your probability of the coin turning up heads is .50. But the probability is much higher (.9) that you will turn up a head at least once if you toss the coin 10 times.

To summarize, you can increase your chances of finding a significant difference between groups on some variable by comparing the groups on many variables. Unfortunately, you also increase the risk of committing a Type I error. To avoid this problem, you can set the significance level low (e.g., *p* = .01). The preferred option, though, is to use a statistical technique called *multivariate analysis of variance*, which is described later in the chapter.

The problem of multiple *t*-tests is more serious when you are doing an exploratory study in which variables are included because they are interesting or because measures of them are easily available. Some of the group differences on these variables are likely to reflect chance effects. The more such variables, the more likely is one to be statistically significant. Multiple *t*-tests are much less a problem if the direction of the group difference on each variable has been predicted prior to data collection based on theory or previous research findings. Such research is less likely to include variables that do not reflect real differences between the populations represented by the sample groups.

Correlated and Uncorrelated Means

There are two kinds of *t*-tests for determining the significance of differences between sample means. Your choice of one of these *t*-tests depends on whether the scores of the two groups are correlated or dependent. In the study of scientific literacy, the two groups of teachers (high and low context use) were selected from the same population of teachers. The two groups are independent of each other, however. In other words, there is no reason to expect that the scientific literacy scores of classes taught by the two groups of teachers are related to each other. Therefore, the mean scores of the two groups can be tested by the **t-test for independent means.**

If the two groups of teachers had been matched on a variable, a different type of *t*-test would be used. For example, in discussing matching procedures earlier in the chapter, we suggested the possibility that years of teaching experience might influence teachers' ability to help students achieve scientific literacy. This variable (teaching experience) can be controlled by matching each teacher in the characteristic-present group with a teacher in the comparison group having the same amount of teaching experience. In this case, the scientific literacy scores of students taught by the two groups would be related to each other. Therefore, the difference between the mean scores of the two groups should be tested by the **t-test for correlated means.** The advantage of this *t*-test is that it results in a smaller standard error than the *t*-test for independent means. Consequently, one's chances of detecting a significant difference between mean scores for samples of a given size are increased. To think of it another way, the *t*-test for correlated means has more statistical power than the *t*-test for uncorrelated means.

One-Tailed versus Two-Tailed Tests of Significance

The ends of a normal curve (i.e., where it approaches the baseline) are called the *tails of the distribution.* When we compare two means to determine whether they are significantly different, we are checking the degree of overlap between the tails of the standard error curves of these two means (see chapter 9 for a discussion of standard error curves). Notice that in figure 13.1(a) mean A is significantly higher than mean B because almost no overlap exists between the two error curves, whereas in figure 13.1(b) some overlap exists. There is a good chance that mean C would be higher than mean D in some repetitions of the research. For example, in some repetitions of the study, mean C may move to C-1 and mean D to D-1, reversing the relationship between C and D.

In research comparing two groups, group B may prove to be superior to group A, but we must not ignore the possibility that the reverse will be true. In figure 13.1(a) we are comparing the overlap between tail B-2 of error curve B and tail A-1 of error curve A to determine whether the means are significantly different. If mean B had been higher, however, we would compare the overlap between tail B-1 and tail A-2. A **two-tailed test of significance,** in which both tails of the error curve are considered, allows the researcher to determine the significance level of differences between two means in either direction, that is, A greater than B, or B greater than A.

In some studies, we can be almost positive that if a difference is observed, it will be in the hypothesized direction. In the study of scientific literacy, the researchers hypothesized that if differences between classes of high- and low-context-use teachers were found, they would favor the high-context-use group. Therefore, one-tailed *t*-tests were used, as shown in table 13.3.

The main advantage of the **one-tailed test of significance** is that a smaller critical ratio (*t* or *z* value) is needed to be statistically significant. Inexperienced researchers often use the one-tailed test where it is not justified in order to make their results appear more significant. You should avoid the one-tailed test unless quite certain that its use is justified.

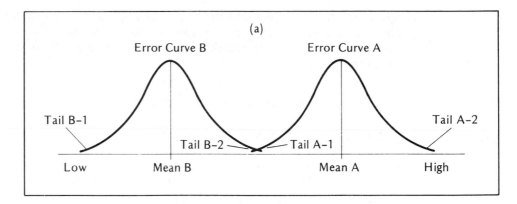

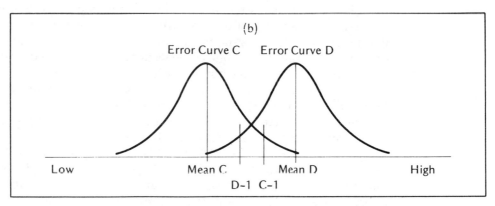

Figure 13.1   Error Curves and Statistical Significance

The *t*-Test for a Single Mean

In most causal-comparative research, we are interested in comparing the mean scores of two samples to determine whether they are significantly different from each other. The *t*-tests for independent means or for correlated means is used for this purpose. Occasionally, however, we are interested in whether a sample mean differs significantly from a specified population mean. For example, suppose you investigate a sample of twelfth-grade students who share a particular characteristic (such as being college-bound). You administer the Wechsler Adult Intelligence Scale to each student, and find that the mean IQ score is 109. As part of the data analysis, you may wish to determine whether this sample mean deviates significantly from the population mean. Assuming a population mean of 100, we may use the **t-test for a single mean** to determine whether this difference (109 − 100) is statistically significant.

Generally, population means are not known in educational research. Some standardized tests provide norms based on very large samples, however. The means of these samples are usually close approximations of their respective population means. Also, population norms are available for some physical measures (e.g., height, weight, strength) that may be of interest to the educational researcher.

STATISTICAL ANALYSIS: ANALYSIS OF VARIANCE

Comparison of More than Two Means

As we have already indicated, causal-comparative research may involve the study of more than two groups. In a study by Sidney Strauss and Efraim Bichler, four groups of children varying in age were compared to determine whether there is a natural development in understanding the properties of the arithmetic mean (M).[14] The four groups took various tests measuring different properties of the mean such as: The sum of the deviations from the mean is zero; the mean does not necessarily equal one of the values that was summed; and the mean can be a fraction that has no counterpart in physical reality.

Descriptive statistics for each age group's performance on the combined tests is shown in table 13.4. The difference between the mean scores of the four groups could be tested for statistical significance by performing six t-tests, which would compare: (1) 8-year-olds with 10-year-olds; (2) 8-year-olds with 12-year-olds; (3) 8-year-olds with 14-year-olds; (4) 10-year-olds with 12-year-olds; (5) 10-year-olds with 14-year-olds; and (6) 12-year-olds with 14-year-olds. The total number of t-tests increases dramatically with each additional comparison group. For example, if the number of groups is five, a total of 10 comparisons can be made.

Instead of doing many t-tests, researchers usually start by doing a simple analysis of variance. The purpose of **analysis of variance** in this situation is to determine whether the groups differ significantly among themselves on the variables being studied.[15] If the analysis of variance yields a nonsignificant F ratio (the ratio of between-groups variance to within-groups variance), the computation of t-tests to compare pairs of means is not appropriate. An exception to this rule occurs when the researcher, before data collection, hypothesizes that a specific pair of means differs significantly from each other.

In the study by Strauss and Bichler, the analysis of variance did indicate that the four groups differed significantly from each other. The F value was 10.31, which is statistically significant ($p < .00001$).[16]

14. Sidney Strauss and Efraim Bichler, "The Development of Children's Concepts of the Arithmetic Average," *Journal for Research in Mathematics Education* 19 (1988): 64–80.
15. In more technical terms, analysis of variance is used to determine whether between-groups variance is significantly greater than within-groups variance.
16. The analysis of variance in Strauss and Bichler's study included several other variables (also known as *main effects*). They are not described here in order to simplify our explanation of this statistical technique.

TABLE 13.4

Descriptive Statistics for Children's Total Scores on Tests of Arithmetic Mean Properties

Age Group	M	SD
8-year-olds	1.41	.21
10-year-olds	1.57	.14
12-year-olds	1.67	.18
14-year-olds	1.75	.17

SOURCE: Adapted from Sidney Strauss and Efraim Bichler, "The Development of Children's Concepts of the Arithmetic Average," *Journal for Research in Mathematics Education* 19 (1988): 71.
NOTE: Scores in this table are the average of students' scores across seven tests of understanding of arithmetic mean properties.

If the *F* ratio is statistically significant, the researcher can do *t*-tests to determine which group means differ significantly from one another. However, you should note that a special type of *t*-test is used following analysis of variance. The standard error of this *t*-test is derived from the variances of all the groups rather than from the variances of the two specific groups being compared. Also, if you have not planned to make specific comparisons *before* undertaking the research, then a **t-test for multiple comparisons** should be used. There are several *t*-tests for multiple comparisons, including Duncan's multiple-range test and the techniques developed by Newman-Keuls, Tukey, and Scheffé. These special *t*-tests take into account the probability that the researcher will find a significant difference between mean scores simply because many comparisons are made on the same data.

In the study by Strauss and Bichler, the Scheffé method for making post hoc comparisons was used. The researchers found that "a Scheffé test with an alpha level of .01 indicated significant differences between each of the age groups."[17] In other words, all possible comparisons of mean scores were statistically significant.

Analysis of variance also allows us to compare subgroups that vary on more than one variable (also called **factors** or **main effects**). To illustrate this point, let us consider a study of student evaluations of college professors by Susan Basow and Nancy Silberg.[18] The main purpose of the study was to determine whether there is a bias in the evaluation of professors such that female professors are given lower ratings than male professors. Each of 16 female professors at a private college in the northeastern United States was

17. Strauss and Bichler, "The Development of Children's Concepts," p. 71.
18. Susan A. Basow and Nancy T. Silberg, "Student Evaluations of College Professors: Are Female and Male Professors Rated Differently?" *Journal of Educational Psychology* 79 (1987): 308–314.

TABLE 13.5

Ratings of Male and Female Professors on Scholarship by Male and Female Students

Sex of Student	Sex of Professor				All Professors
	Male		Female		
	M	SD	M	SD	M
Male	11.7	3.1	12.9	3.1	12.3
Female	12.0	3.1	11.9	3.2	11.0
Male and female combined	11.9		12.4		

SOURCE: Adapted from Susan A. Basow and Nancy T. Silberg, "Student Evaluations of College Professors: Are Male and Female Professors Rated Differently?", *Journal of Educational Psychology* 79 (1987): 311. NOTE: Lower scores indicate more positive evaluations. Score range = 5–25, except for overall teaching ability, for which the range = 1–5.

matched with a male professor of similar rank, teaching field, and years of experience at the college.[19] Each of the professors was evaluated by his or her students on six rating scales during the fifth or sixth week of the semester. The researchers recorded the sex of each student who completed the rating scales.

Some of the descriptive statistics reported by the researchers are shown in table 13.5. Each rating of the professors' quality of scholarship is classified in two ways: (1) the rating is of a male or female professor; (2) the rating was made by a male or female student. A single analysis of variance enabled the researchers to determine whether each of these variables (sex of professor; sex of student) affected the ratings. First, the mean rating of all male professors (11.85) was compared with the mean rating of all female professors (12.43). The F value for this analysis was 7.71, which is statistically significant ($p < .01$).[20] It appears that male professors receive higher ratings for scholarship than do female professors. (Keep in mind that in this study lower ratings indicate more positive evaluations.)

The same analysis of variance yielded a test of the statistical significance of the difference between the mean ratings of male students (12.30) and female students (10.97), irrespective of the sex of the professor being rated. The

19. The purpose of matching procedures was described earlier in the chapter in the section, "Selecting Comparison Groups."

20. You should note that the comparison of male and female professors involves two groups. Therefore, the difference between the mean scores of the two groups can be tested for statistical significance by a *t*-test. Indeed, analysis of variance for two groups is identical to a *t*-test. The equivalence is represented mathematically by the equation $F = t^2$.

obtained F value of 3.92 is statistically significant ($p < .05$). It appears that female students give their professors higher ratings for scholarship than do male students.

The same analysis of variance yields still further information. This information concerns whether the interaction between the two variables of sex of professor and sex of students is statistically significant.[21] A significant **interaction** means that the effect of one variable is dependent on the effect of the other variable. This is the case for the statistical results shown in table 13.5. The F ratio of 9.67 for the teacher-sex by student-sex interaction was statistically significant ($p < .01$).

Inspection of table 13.5 reveals the nature of the interaction. Male students overall rated professors lower (12.3) on scholarship than did female students (11.0). However, this statement is misleading. In fact, male students only rated female professors lower than did female students (12.9 versus 11.9). In other words, ratings of professors by male and female students are affected by (that is, "interact with") the sex of the professor whom they are rating.

The analysis of variance used to compare the mean test scores of children shown in table 13.4 is sometimes called a **one-way analysis of variance** because the subgroups differ on one factor, namely, age. The analysis of variance used to compare the mean scores shown in table 13.5 is sometimes called a **two-way analysis of variance** because the subgroups differ on two factors, namely, sex of student and sex of professor. Three-way and even four-way analyses of variance can be done, depending upon the complexity of the data. For example, if each student in the study of professor ratings had been classified further as high achieving or low achieving, a three-way analysis of variance might be done. Each rating would be classified on three factors: sex of professor being rated; sex of student making the rating; and achievement level of student making the rating.

The number of levels represented by each factor is sometimes used to describe a particular analysis of variance design. One can say that a "2 × 2 factorial analysis of variance design" was used to compare the various mean scores shown in table 13.5, because there are two levels of one factor (male and female professors) and two levels of another factor (male and female students).

Further variations in analysis of variance designs are not described here because they involve complex statistical considerations. You should consult an expert statistician to ensure that the correct analysis of variance design is selected if you plan to use this statistical procedure in your study. We also suggest that you read the sections pertaining to analysis of variance in chapter 15. If employed properly, analysis of variance is a powerful technique. A single set of calculations allows you to test the statistical significance of several

---

21. The concept of interaction is discussed further in chapter 16 in the section on aptitude-treatment interaction.

comparisons and interactions among groups of subjects who vary on one or more factors.

Analysis of Covariance

In doing causal-comparative studies, researchers sometimes need to determine whether a difference between two groups on a particular variable can be explained by another difference that exists between the two groups. Suppose your hypothesis is that seventh-grade boys make more grammatical errors in writing class papers than seventh-grade girls. A sample of papers written by the two groups is scored for grammatical errors, and a *t*-test shows that the mean number of errors is significantly greater for the boys than for the girls.

At this point you need to ask the question, "Can this obtained difference be explained in terms of some other variable on which the groups might differ?" In other words, alternative hypotheses need to be tested. You might consider the length of the students' papers as a possible explanatory variable. Suppose the sample of boys is found to write significantly longer papers than the sample of girls, thus increasing their opportunity to make grammatical errors. You now need to determine whether controlling for initial differences in writing productivity eliminates the obtained difference in mean number of grammatical errors.

The statistical technique of **analysis of covariance** is used to control for initial differences between groups.[22] The effect of analysis of covariance is to make the two groups equal with respect to one or more control variables. If a difference is still found between the two groups, we cannot use the control variable to explain the effect. In our example, suppose you found that boys still made significantly more grammatical errors than girls after using analysis of covariance to control for initial differences in writing productivity. You would be able to conclude that the sex difference in grammatical errors was not due to the fact that boys write longer papers.

Analysis of covariance is useful in causal-comparative studies because the researcher cannot always select comparison groups that are matched with respect to all relevant variables except the one that is the main concern of the investigation. Analysis of covariance provides a post hoc method of matching groups on such variables as age, aptitude, prior education, and socioeconomic class.

Research data need to satisfy certain statistical assumptions before analysis of covariance can be applied.[23] These assumptions, such as homogeneity of

---

22. Correlational techniques similar to analysis of covariance (partial and part correlation) are described in the next chapter.
23. The assumptions are discussed in an article by Janet Elashoff (see the Annotated References at the end of this chapter).

regression, can be checked empirically, but the computations are complex. Inexperienced researchers are advised to consult an expert statistician if they plan to use analysis of covariance.

Multivariate Analysis of Variance

Multivariate analysis of variance (usually abbreviated MANOVA) is a statistical technique for determining whether several groups differ on *more than one* dependent variable. MANOVA is quite similar to the *t*-test and to analysis of variance. The only noteworthy difference between the techniques is that the *t*-test and analysis of variance can only determine whether several groups differ on one dependent variable.

Each subject included in a MANOVA will have a score on two or more dependent variables. These scores are represented by a mathematical expression called a **vector.** Each subject in the study has a vector score. Also, a mean vector score can be calculated for a group of subjects. This mean vector score is called a **centroid.** The purpose of MANOVA is to determine whether there are statistically significant differences between the centroids of different groups.

The concept of representing several dependent variables by a single vector can be understood in a nontechnical way. Consider the case of two groups—high- and low-achieving students—who have been measured on two dependent variables: attitude toward their present school and attitude toward being engaged in further schooling. Each student's scores can be expressed in the form (6, 8), indicating that a student has a score of 6 on the first variable and a score of 8 on the second variable. The scores can also be represented on a graph. Each single point on the graph represents a student's scores on two variables. Suppose the graph points (comparable to "vector" scores) for high-achieving students tend to occupy a different space on the graph than the points for the low-achieving students. The purpose of MANOVA, in a sense, is to determine whether these two "spaces" differ significantly from each other.

Our example has been of two dependent variables represented on a two-dimensional graph. You might try imagining the case of three dependent variables and how each subject's vector of scores on them can be represented by a single point on a three-dimensional graph.

The first step in doing a MANOVA should be to test the assumption of the equality of group dispersions. If a nonsignificant F is obtained, we can conclude that the assumption is satisfied. (Researchers sometimes skip this step because MANOVA is robust, meaning that the assumption can be violated to an extent without violating the validity of the test.) The next step is to do a test of the statistical significance of the difference between group centroids. The most commonly used test for this purpose is **Wilks lambda** (λ). This test yields an F value, which can be looked up in an F ratio table to determine its level of statistical significance. If a significant MANOVA *F* is obtained, we can then do an analysis of variance on each dependent variable to determine which of these variables are statistically significant and contributing to the overall MANOVA *F*. Although unlikely, it is possible to obtain a significant MANOVA *F* without finding a significant *F* in any of the analyses of variance.

A typical causal-comparative study will include a substantial number of dependent variables. Our preceding discussion should not be construed to mean that all of the variables must be tested for statistical significance by a single MANOVA. You should group the variables into clusters (that is, vectors) that include educationally or psychologically related variables. Each cluster of variables can be analyzed by a separate MANOVA.

The use of MANOVA in causal-comparative research is illustrated by the study of college professor ratings that we described a bit earlier in the chapter. You will recall that table 13.5 presents the mean ratings of the professors on the factor of scholarship. In fact, the students rated the professors on six factors: scholarship, organization/clarity, instructor-group interaction, instructor-individual student interaction, dynamism/enthusiasm, and overall teaching ability. The mean ratings of male and female professors on all six factors is shown in table 13.6.

TABLE 13.6

Descriptive Statistics for Ratings of Male and Female Professors by Male and Female Students

	Male student				Female student			
	Male professor (n = 275)		Female professor (n = 278)		Male professor (n = 284)		Female professor (n = 243)	
Variable	M	SD	M	SD	M	SD	M	SD
Scholarship	11.7	3.1	12.9	3.1	12.0	3.1	11.9	3.2
Organization/clarity	10.7	3.3	12.1	3.9	11.1	3.4	11.2	4.2
Instructor-group interaction	11.8	3.2	12.5	3.5	12.1	3.2	11.9	3.6
Instructor-individual student interaction	10.7	3.3	11.6	3.5	10.7	3.6	11.1	3.7
Dynamism/enthusiasm	9.6	3.6	11.6	4.0	10.0	3.8	10.7	4.1
Overall teaching ability	2.2	0.8	2.6	1.0	2.2	0.8	2.4	1.0

SOURCE: Adapted from table 2 in Susan A. Basow and Nancy T. Silberg, "Student Evaluations of College Professors: Are Female and Male Professors Rated Differently?" *Journal of Educational Psychology* 79 (1987): 311.
NOTE: Lower scores indicate more positive evaluations. Score range = 5–25, except for overall teaching ability, for which the range = 1–5.

Basow and Silberg, the researchers who did the study, analyzed the group mean differences shown in table 13.6 for statistical significance by the use of MANOVA. The six rating scales were considered to be a cluster of related variables. The F ratios for the MANOVA are shown in the second column of table 13.7. The significant F for teacher sex (10.40) means that male and female professors had significantly different mean scores on the vector representing the six rating scales. The F ratios for the ANOVAs (analysis of variance) shown in columns 4–9 of table 13.7 indicate which of the six rating scales yielded significantly different mean scores for male and female professors.

The MANOVA yielded a nonsignificant F for student sex (1.29), meaning that male and female students did not differ significantly in their mean score on the vector representing the six rating scales. Despite the nonsignificant MANOVA F, the researchers reported the F ratios for the ANOVAs performed on the individual rating scales. One of them—the F for Scholarship—is significant. Because the MANOVA F was nonsignificant, however, one should be cautious about interpreting this sex difference in student ratings. It may well be a chance finding. As the number of F ratios that are calculated increases, so does the likelihood of obtaining a significant F by chance.

Finally, we see that the MANOVA F for the teacher-sex by student-sex interaction (2.54) in table 13.7 is statistically significant. This result means that the sex difference in the students' scores on the vector representing the six rating scales is dependent on the sex of the professor being rated.

TABLE 13.7

Multivariate Analysis of Variance Summary for Ratings of Male and Female Professors by Male and Female Students

Multivariate ANOVA[a]			Univariate ANOVA[b]					
Source	F		1	2	3	4	5	Overall
Teacher sex	10.40***	F	7.71**	10.63**	1.44	9.11**	34.64***	39.71***
Student sex	1.29	F	3.92*	1.15	0.45	1.85	1.12	3.72
Teacher sex × Student sex	2.54*	F	9.67**	9.33**	4.62*	1.79	8.62**	7.10**

Source: Adapted from Susan A. Basow and Nancy T. Silberg, "Student Evaluations of College Professors: Are Female and Male Professors Rated Differently?," *Journal of Educational Psychology* 79 (1987): 310.
Note: Univariate analyses are on Scholarship, Organization/Clarity, Instructor-Group Interaction, Instructor-Individual Student Interaction, Dynamism/Enthusiasm, and overall teaching ability.
[a] $dfs = 6, 1071$.
[b] $dfs = 1, 1076$.
* $p < .05$. ** $p < .01$. *** $p < .001$.

MANOVA is a useful statistical technique because it helps the researcher see the data in a multivariate perspective. Well-defined groups, such as those studied in causal-comparative research, are unlikely to differ from each other because of a single, superficial trait or ability. Rather, groups are likely to differ in some respect because of many interrelated differences in their personal background. MANOVA helps the researcher conceptualize and analyze the nature of these multiple influences.

The correlational counterpart of MANOVA is canonical analysis, which is described in the next chapter. Either technique can be used to analyze data that consist of one or more independent variables and two or more dependent variables. Although one does find instances of MANOVA in the literature, canonical analysis appears to be becoming the method of choice among educational researchers.

Tests for the Difference between Variances

The standard deviation and its square, the variance, are two statistics for describing the variability of scores obtained from a sample of subjects. You might want to do a statistical test to determine whether the variances in scores for two samples differ significantly from each other, just as you might want to determine whether the mean scores differ significantly. There are two main reasons for doing this test. The first reason is that most of the commonly used statistical tests—including the *t*-test for differences between means—assume that the variances of the two samples are approximately equal. If the score variances of two samples differ markedly, then one of the nonparametric tests discussed later in this chapter should be used.

The second reason for testing variance homogeneity between two samples is that your hypothesis may concern the variability of sample scores. For example, you might hypothesize that college graduates are more like one another in scholastic aptitude than college dropouts. The rationale might be that all college graduates are apt to be fairly intelligent but that, for various reasons, both students of high and low aptitude may leave college before graduation. To test this hypothesis in a causal-comparative study, you would administer a measure of scholastic aptitude to a sample of college graduates and a sample of college dropouts. Next you would do a statistical test to determine whether college graduates have less variable scores on the aptitude measure than do the college dropouts.

The statistical tool used to test for significance of differences between variances is analysis of variance, which is the same tool used to test for differences between several means. The larger the *F* ratio, the less likely it is that the variances of the populations from which the samples were drawn are equal. If the F ratio exceeds the significance level you have set, you would reject the null hypothesis (stating equality of variances) and conclude that the obtained difference between the sample variances is a true one.

You should be aware that several statistical tests are available for comparing differences between variances. If the two sets of scores are obtained from independent samples, the **test for homogeneity of independent variances** is used. If the two sets of scores are obtained from repeated measures on a single sample or from two matched samples, then the **test for homogeneity of related variances** is used. Should you wish to determine whether the variances of more than two sets of scores differ significantly from one another, the **F maximum test for homogeneity of variance** can be used.

STATISTICAL ANALYSIS: NONPARAMETRIC TESTS

Advantages and Disadvantages of Nonparametric Tests

The tests of statistical significance discussed in the two previous sections are known as **parametric statistics.** A parameter, you will recall, is a population score, whereas a statistic is a score for a sample randomly drawn from the population. Parametric statistics make certain assumptions about population parameters. One assumption is that the scores in the population are normally distributed about the mean; another assumption is that the population variances of the comparison groups in one's study are approximately equal. When large deviations from these assumptions are present in the research data, parametric statistics should not be used. Instead, one of the **nonparametric statistics** should be selected since, as their name implies, they do not make any assumptions about the shape or variance of population scores.

Parametric statistics assume that the scores being analyzed are derived from a measure that has equal intervals. As we explained in chapter 9, most continuous measures meet this criterion. Measures that yield categorical or rank scores, however, do not have equal intervals, and so one of the nonparametric statistics should be used for data analysis. We discuss the common types of nonparametric statistics in the following sections.

When research data meet the assumption of being interval scores but do not meet the assumptions of normal distribution and variance homogeneity, we still advise you to use one of the parametric statistics presented earlier in the chapter. The main reasons for recommending the use of parametric statistics in these situations are that: (1) studies have shown that moderate departure from the theoretical assumptions has very little effect upon the value of the parametric technique,[24] (2) nonparametric statistics are generally less powerful, that is, they require larger samples in order to yield the same level of significance; and (3) for many of the problems encountered in educational research, suitable nonparametric tests arc not available.

The Chi-Square Test

Chi-square (χ^2) is a nonparametric statistical test that is used when the research data are in the form of frequency counts. These frequency counts can be placed into two or more categories. The chi-square test was used to analyze data resulting from a study of special education referrals by Mark Shinn, Gerald Tindal, and Deborah Spira.[25] These researchers were interested in determining whether teachers are biased in their referrals of students for special education services because of reading difficulties. Their sample included all students in a large midwestern city referred for such services over approximately one school year. The number of referred students, grouped by grade level, ethnicity, and sex, is shown in the second column of table 13.8. For example, the table shows that 79 white students and 65 black students in grade 2 were referred for special education services because of reading difficulties during the school year.

The next step in the study was to determine the number of students who should have been referred if there was no bias in the referral process. Shinn and his colleagues examined normative data on a reading test administered to a large random sample of regular education students in the district. Specifically, they examined students who scored at the 16th percentile or below on the test. Test scores this low indicate severe reading difficulties. Now, the researchers reasoned that if there was no sex bias in the teacher referral process, the proportion of boys to girls referred for special education services for reading remediation should not differ from the proportion of boys to girls scoring at or below the 16th percentile on an objective reading test. Similarly, they reasoned that if there was no ethnic bias in the teacher referral process, the proportion of white to black students who were referred should not differ from the proportion of white to black students scoring at or below the 16th percentile on the test.

As shown in table 13.8, the researchers used the chi-square test to determine the statistical significance of the difference between the observed frequencies of referrals (column 2) with the frequencies that would be expected

24. Refer to the discussion earlier in the chapter on the effects of violating assumptions underlying the t-test.
25. Mark R. Shinn, Gerald A. Tindal, and Deborah A. Spira, "Special Education Referrals as an Index of Teacher Tolerance: Are Teachers Imperfect Tests?" *Exceptional Children* 54 (1987): 32–40.

TABLE 13.8

Chi-Square Test of Observed and Expected Referral Rates by Ethnic Background and Sex of Student

Group	Observed	Expected	X^2
Ethnic status			
Grade 2 White	79	78.3	
Grade 2 Black	65	53.9	2.36
Grade 3 White	48	52.4	
Grade 3 Black	45	39.5	1.14
Grade 4 White	63	68.3	
Grade 4 Black	52	34.5	*9.27
Grade 5 White	46	55.1	
Grade 5 Black	44	33.7	*4.64
Grade 6 White	24	36.6	
Grade 6 Black	31	20.1	*10.30
Sex			
Grade 2 Male	106	76.1	
Grade 2 Female	45	74.9	*22.4
Grade 3 Male	78	66.3	
Grade 3 Female	45	56.7	*4.5
Grade 4 Male	79	60.1	
Grade 4 Female	47	65.9	*12.6
Grade 5 Male	64	58.8	
Grade 5 Female	41	46.2	1.0
Grade 6 Male	40	37.1	
Grade 6 Female	25	27.9	.53

SOURCE: Adapted from table 3 in Mark R. Shinn, Gerald A. Tindal, and Deborah A. Spira, "Special Education Referrals as an Index of Teacher Tolerance: Are Teachers Imperfect Tests?" *Exceptional Children* 54 (1987): 37.
* Indicates results significant beyond the .05 level

from the normative data for students scoring at or below the 16th percentile on the objective reading test (column 3). Six of the 10 chi-square coefficients are statistically significant. For example, more than twice as many boys as girls (106:45) in the second grade were referred for special education services.

However, the proportion of boys to girls who scored low on the objective reading test (76.1 : 74.9) was virtually the same. These results suggest a sex bias in teachers' referral of students for special education services.

When the frequency data are grouped into more than four cells, a more complex chi-square test is done. You also should be aware that when the expected frequency in any cell is less than five, a correction needs to be applied to the regular chi-square test. (Apply Yates' correction, or do a Fisher exact test.) In the process of doing a chi-square test, you might also compute a **phi coefficient** (for a fourfold table) or a **contingency coefficient** (for more than four cells). These correlation coefficients provide an estimate of the magnitude of the relationship between the variables in a chi-square table.[26]

The chi-square test is most often used when the categories into which frequencies fall are discrete rather than continuous. Let us suppose we want to determine whether large families contribute more or fewer than the expected number of students dropping out of school before graduation. The number of children is a discrete variable because, for example, a family can have 3 or 4 children but not 3-1/2. Dropping out of school is also a discrete variable because it either occurs or does not occur. Under these conditions, chi-square is the appropriate test of statistical significance.

Chi-square is equally useful when the traits or characteristics being considered are actually continuous variables that have been categorized. For example, GPA is a continuous variable because it can take on any value within a given range (usually between 0.00 and 4.00). It is also possible to convert GPA into meaningful categories such as high GPA (3.50–4.00), average GPA (2.50–3.49), and low GPA (0.00–2.49). The difference between the frequency of different groups of students in each of these GPA categories can be tested for statistical significance using the chi-square test.

Other Nonparametric Tests

Of the nonparametric tests of significance, chi-square is probably the most frequently used by educational researchers in causal-comparative studies. Other nonparametric tests are sometimes used, particularly when the research data are in the form of rank-order scores or interval scores that grossly violate the parametric test assumptions of normality and homogeneity of variance.

The **Mann-Whitney U test** can be used to determine whether the distributions of scores of two independent samples differ significantly from each other. If U is statistically significant, it means that the "bulk" of scores in one population is higher than the bulk of scores in the other population. The two populations are represented by the two independent samples on which the U

26. The phi coefficient and contingency coefficient are discussed also in the next chapter.

test is made. This test is generally used when the assumption of homogeneity of sample variances underlying the *t*-test is violated. A recent study, however, found that even when the assumption is violated, the *t*-test provides a better test of the null hypothesis when the sizes of the two sample groups are unequal and the smaller sample has the larger variance.[27]

The **Wilcoxon signed-rank test** is used to determine whether the distributions of scores in two samples differ significantly from each other when the scores of the samples are correlated (either through matching or because repeated measures are taken on the same sample). The Wilcoxon test is analogous to the *t*-test for correlated means except that it makes no assumptions regarding the shape of the score distribution or homogeneity of variance between the two sets of scores. If more than two groups of subjects are to be compared, a nonparametric one-way analysis of variance (the **Kruskal-Wallis test**) can be used.

INTERPRETATION OF CAUSAL-COMPARATIVE FINDINGS

The process of interpreting causal-comparative findings can be illustrated using the study of scientific literacy discussed earlier in the chapter. You will recall from table 13.3 that classes taught by the high-context-use teachers made significantly less gain in their understanding of the scientific process than did classes taught by low-context-use teachers. We can conclude from these results that there is a reliable negative relationship between teachers' use of context-enhanced statements and students' development of scientific literacy.

Can we reach beyond this conclusion and infer that context-enhanced statements cause a decrement in students' development of scientific literacy? The results are consistent with this interpretation, but because this was a causal-comparative study, other interpretations must be considered as well. For example, as we stated above, the researchers found that most of the teachers' context-enhanced statements were confusing or incomplete. Perhaps confusing, incomplete statements *of any type* cause decrements in students' development of scientific literacy. In this case, teacher references to context appear to have an effect on scientific literacy only because they are confusing, incomplete statements, which is the real cause of the effect.

Another interpretation of the results is that students who have difficulty in developing scientific literacy cause teachers to help them by making more context-enhanced statements. In other words, student performance affects teacher behavior, rather than the reverse. The researchers did not present the

27. Donald W. Zimmerman, "Comparative Power of Student *t* Test and Mann-Whitney *U* Test for Unequal Sample Sizes and Variances," *The Journal of Experimental Education* 55 (1987): 171–174.

pretest scores of the two groups of students, so we do not know whether one group was more science-illiterate than the other and therefore possibly more difficult to teach. Thus, the interpretation is neither supported nor refuted by the reported results. This is the basic problem of causal-comparative studies. They are good for revealing possible causal relationships between variables, but they do not provide strong evidence about the nature of the causal pattern.

Two procedures can be used to improve the interpretability of causal-comparative studies. First, as we discussed earlier in the chapter, alternative hypotheses should be formulated and tested whenever possible. Second, the relationships between all of the variables in the study can be examined using the technique of path analysis, which is discussed in the next chapter.

The most powerful method for demonstrating the causal properties of causal-comparative findings is to do experiments. The presumed cause, or causes, of the outcomes being studied would be manipulated. For example, in the study of scientific literacy, teachers' use of the technique of providing a meaningful context for the scientific content being taught was hypothesized to have an effect on students' development of scientific literacy. An experiment could be designed in which a group of teachers is trained to use this technique with attention to both quantity and quality of use. (Training in quality of use is especially important, because the present study found that teachers rarely use the technique appropriately.) Another group of teachers would not receive the training. If the hypothesis is valid, we would expect to see the students of trained teachers make greater gains in scientific literacy than students of untrained teachers.

We wish to emphasize once again that both causal-comparative research and experiments have advantages. A single causal-comparative study can reveal the relationships among a substantial number of variables. Experiments then can verify the causal properties of the most promising relationships discovered.

THE CAUSAL-COMPARATIVE
METHOD AND CORRELATION

We noted at the outset of the chapter that the causal-comparative method and the correlational method are similar in certain respects. Both methods are nonexperimental in that they do not involve manipulation of a treatment variable. Also, in both methods the researcher studies the relationship between variable X and variable Y. The major differences between the two methods are in the measurement of variable X and in the analysis of the resulting data.

These differences can be illustrated by considering the study of part-time employment among high school students, which was discussed at the start of the chapter. In that study, employment was a dichotomous variable having two values—present (employed) and absent (nonemployed). If the researchers had wished, they could have conceptualized employment as a continuous variable. To measure the variable, they could have requested students to list the average number of hours and minutes that they were employed each week during the school year. In this case, both variable X (employment) and variable Y (e.g., GPA) would be continuous variables. The resulting data are best analyzed using correlational statistics, which are described in the next chapter. In the actual study by Green and Jaquess, the data were analyzed by t-tests because variable X was a dichotomous variable used to form groups of employed and nonemployed students.

The t-test and other tests of statistical significance described in this chapter do not tell the researcher the magnitude of the relationship between variable X and variable Y. Therefore, researchers sometimes first analyze causal-comparative data to determine whether observed differences are statistically significant. If a statistically significant difference is found, the researcher will compute one of the correlational statistics presented in the next chapter to determine the magnitude of the relationship between the two variables. A bivariate statistic such as the product-moment correlation coefficient is usually computed following a t-test. The correlation ratio (eta) is computed following analysis of variance. The phi coefficient or contingency coefficient can be computed as part of the process of doing a chi-square test.

MISTAKES SOMETIMES MADE IN DOING CAUSAL-COMPARATIVE RESEARCH

1. The researcher assumes the results of causal-comparative research are proof of a cause-and-effect relationship.
2. Does not form homogeneous groups to be compared. After the initial groups have been defined, does not form subgroups on the basis of age, gender, socioeconomic status, or similar variables.
3. Uses the wrong sampling distributions when testing the statistical significance of data obtained from small samples.
4. Does not use the correct t-test when comparing independent means or correlated means.
5. Does a one-tailed test of statistical significance when a two-tailed test should be done.
6. When comparing several means, does not do an analysis of variance prior to determining which group means differ significantly from each other.
7. Does not control for initial differences between groups that might explain the differences that are found.
8. Neglects to use a nonparametric test of significance when the data grossly violate the assumptions of parametric statistical tests.

ANNOTATED REFERENCES

Amick, Daniel J., and Crittenden, Kathleen S. "Analysis of Variance and Multivariate Analysis of Variance." In *Introductory Multivariate Analysis,* eds. Daniel J. Amick and Herbert J. Walberg. Berkeley, CA: McCutchan, 1975.

Describes the uses and mathematical bases for the following statistical techniques: one-way analysis of variance, tests for homogeneity of variance, factorial analysis of variance, and multivariate analysis of variance. Also, the authors show how these techniques relate to each other.

Bruning, James L., and Kintz, B. L. *Computational Handbook of Statistics,* 3rd ed. Glenview, IL.: Scott, Foresman, 1987.

Provides a step-by-step computational guide for these statistical tests frequently used in causal-comparative studies: *t*-test for a difference between a sample mean and a population mean; *t*-test for a difference between two independent means; *t*-test for a difference between two correlated means; one-way analysis of variance; test for difference between variances of two independent samples; test for difference between variances of two related samples; test for differences among several independent variances; Duncan's multiple-range test; test for significance of difference between two proportions; Mann-Whitney *U* Test for independent samples; Wilcoxon signed-rank test for related samples; simple and complex chi-square tests; phi coefficient and contingency coefficient.

Campbell, Donald T., and Stanley, Julian C. "Experimental and Quasi-Experimental Designs for Research," In *Handbook of Research on Teaching,* ed. N. L. Gage. Chicago: Rand McNally, 1963.

Available as a separate reprint from the *Handbook.* Primarily about experimental design, although the concluding section discusses ex post facto research, including causal-comparative designs. The authors stress the problems involved in drawing causal inferences from ex post facto data.

Elashoff, Janet D. "Analysis of Covariance: A Delicate Instrument." *American Educational Research Journal* 6 (1969): 383–399.

Discusses the purpose of analysis of covariance and its advantages and limitations; also describes the assumptions about the data which must be satisfied if analysis of covariance is to be used correctly. Procedures for checking these assumptions in a set of data are given.

Siegel, Sidney. *Nonparametric Statistics for the Behavioral Sciences.* New York: McGraw-Hill, 1956.

Nonparametric techniques have a number of advantages that make them particularly well suited for certain data of the behavioral sciences. These techniques make no assumptions concerning the population distribution, are easy to compute, and are particularly useful with small samples such as are often used by the graduate student. This text presents nonparametric techniques in a form that can be understood by the average behavioral scientist who lacks advanced mathematical training. Siegel's emphasis is upon research application of these techniques, and he strengthens his presentation with many interesting examples taken from the behavioral sciences. Although some of the techniques presented such as chi-square and Spearman's *rho* are treated in most textbooks on educational and psychological statistics, many of the techniques covered in this text are not generally found in these sources.

SELF-CHECK TEST

Circle the correct answer to each of the following questions. An answer key is provided on page 884.

1. The main situation in which a researcher would use a causal-comparative design rather than an experimental design is when
   a. random sampling is not possible.
   b. experimental manipulation is not possible.
   c. use of standardized tests is not possible.
   d. young children are the subjects of the research.
2. One of the main limitations of causal-comparative research is that
   a. it is more expensive than other types of research.
   b. control groups cannot be studied.
   c. cause-and-effect generalizations are difficult to draw from the research data.
   d. null hypotheses cannot be tested.
3. In most statistical analyses of causal-comparative data, the first step is to compute
   a. correlations.
   b. means and standard deviations.
   c. ranges.
   d. variances.
4. If sample size is greater than appropriate for the *t* test, the appropriate statistical tool is the
   a. *F* test.
   b. analysis of covariance.
   c. correlation coefficient.
   d. *z* distribution.
5. One of the assumptions that the *t*-test makes about scores obtained in causal-comparative research is that
   a. score variances for the populations under study are equal.
   b. means of the scores are equal.
   c. population means do not differ.
   d. score variances for the populations under study are not equal.
6. If a researcher matches subjects between groups, the appropriate *t*-test is the *t*-test for
   a. independent means.
   b. equal variances.
   c. correlated means.
   d. unequal means.
7. If a researcher conducting causal-comparative research is almost certain that any detected change will be in a hypothesized direction, it is appropriate to use the
   a. two-tailed *t*-test.
   b. analysis of covariance.
   c. one-tailed *t*-test.
   d. correlation coefficient.

8. A post hoc method for matching groups on certain variables is the
   a. analysis of covariance.
   b. multiple regression equation.
   c. *t*-test for correlated means.
   d. *t*-test for independent means.
9. Multivariate analysis of variance is used to detect statistically significant group differences in
   a. vectors of independent variables.
   b. vectors of dependent variables.
   c. correlations between dependent variables.
   d. correlations between independent and dependent variables.
10. The most important characteristic of nonparametric statistics is that they
    a. make no assumption about the variance of the population scores.
    b. demand that scores in the population be normally distributed about the mean.
    c. require equal population variances.
    d. can be used only with interval scales of measurement.
11. The purpose of computing a correlational statistic following a *t*-test or analysis of variance is
    a. to determine whether the sample variances are equal.
    b. to determine the magnitude of the relationship between the variables.
    c. to determine the directionality of the observed differences.
    d. All of the above are correct.

APPLICATION PROBLEMS

The following problems are designed to give you practice in applying significant concepts and research procedures explained in the chapter. Most of them do not have a single correct answer. For feedback, you can compare your answers with the sample answers on pages 898–899.

1. Define a suitable comparison group for each of the following defined groups.
   a. High school mathematics teachers with high scores on authoritarianism.
   b. Bilingual first-grade children of Mexican ancestry.
   c. Fourth-grade Pueblo Indian boys who have attended school only on the reservation.
2. An investigator studies the difference in achievement of third-grade children who learned to read using the "phonetic" method and those who learned to read using the "look-say" method. Children in the two groups were matched on scholastic aptitude. What type of *t*-test should the investigator use to analyze the results? Why?
3. You hypothesize that low-achieving children who receive special tutoring will make significantly greater achievement gains than those who spend an equal amount of time in the regular classroom. Would this hypothesis be tested with a one-tailed or a two-tailed test of significance? Why?
4. An investigator is interested in learning whether attendance at an authoritarian high school tends to produce authoritarian students. He locates two high schools that are located in very similar neighborhoods serving similar racial and socioeconomic groups. School A employs a rigid authoritarian structure, and both teachers and administrators have higher than average scores on a measure of authoritarianism. School B employs a democratic administrative structure with major student involvement in running the school. Both teachers and administrators in School B have lower than average scores on a test of authoritarianism.

a. In a pilot study the investigator randomly selects 25 students from each school and administers a 40-item scale of authoritarianism to them. What statistical technique should be used to analyze these data?

b. Each high school has 12 extracurricular activities that were classified by a group of independent judges as either high, average, or low in terms of authoritarian structure and activities. The investigator wishes to compare the proportion of students in each school who joined each of the three types of organizations. What statistical technique should be used to make this comparison?

c. In checking school records, the investigator finds that most seniors in the two high schools had been administered a California F scale (a measure of authoritarianism) during their last year of junior high school. He decides to administer a different but similar authoritarianism measure to seniors who had taken the earlier test, and then see how the senior-level authoritarianism scores differed between students in the two schools when their earlier scores were taken into consideration. What statistical technique should be used?

SUGGESTION SHEET

If your last name starts with letters from Maz to Mor, please complete the Suggestion Sheet at the end of the book while the chapter is still fresh in your mind.

14 EXPLORING RELATIONSHIPS BETWEEN VARIABLES: THE CORRELATIONAL METHOD

OVERVIEW

This chapter describes how the correlational method is used in studies involving prediction or investigation of relationships between variables. Prediction studies involve the practical problem of predicting future behavior from variables measured at an earlier point in time. In relationship research the emphasis is on developing an understanding of cause-and-effect patterns among variables. A variety of correlational statistics are available to estimate the magnitude of relationship or prediction. Selection of a particular correlational technique depends upon the variables to be included in the analysis. Multivariate correlational techniques are widely used because present-day educational research projects tend to investigate relationships between a large number of variables.

OBJECTIVES

After studying this chapter you should be able to:

1. Draw appropriate inferences from research data presented in the form of correlation coefficients.
2. State at least one advantage and one limitation of the correlational method.
3. Describe the procedures involved in conducting a relationship study, including selection of the problem, selection of subjects, data collection, and data analysis.
4. Describe three uses for prediction studies.
5. Describe the procedures involved in conducting a prediction study, including selection of the problem, selection of subjects, data collection, and data analysis.
6. Explain the use of Taylor-Russell tables and cross-validation in prediction studies.
7. Describe research situations in which the different types of bivariate correlational statistics are used.
8. Plot a scattergram and explain its use in correlational research.
9. Describe research situations in which correction for attenuation, correction for restriction in range, and partial correlation are used.
10. Describe research situations in which multiple regression, discriminant analysis, canonical correlation, path analysis, correlation matrices, factor analysis, and structural equation modeling are used.
11. Interpret the results of a multiple regression analysis, discriminant analysis, canonical correlation, path analysis, correlation matrix, factor analysis, and structural equation model.

12. Formulate subgroups and moderator variables for use in correlational research.
13. Interpret the meaning of correlation coefficients in prediction and relationship studies that differ in magnitude and statistical significance.

THE NATURE OF CORRELATION

Correlational studies include all those research projects in which the purpose is to discover relationships between variables through the use of correlational statistics. (Correlational statistics are also used extensively in test construction and analysis; their use for these purposes is discussed in chapter 7.) Because an understanding of correlation coefficients is essential to what follows, we will briefly discuss their meaning in nonmathematical terms.

Individual differences are of prime importance to researchers. If everyone had the same academic achievement, for example, there would be little interest in studying its determinants, in predicting it, or in measuring it. Yet people do vary with respect to this attribute, and the variations have major personal and social consequences. High academic achievers generally play a different role in society and view themselves more positively than do low academic achievers. If researchers could discover the causes of variability in academic achievement, this knowledge might prove useful in helping both low and high achievers become more personally and socially successful.

To understand how the correlation coefficient helps us in this kind of investigation, consider an achievement test on which a group of students earned scores varying from 40 to 100. How would we know if students' scores on some other measure, such as an intelligence test or personality inventory, are related to their scores on the achievement test? Suppose that students who earned a score of 40 on the achievement test had an IQ of 85 on an intelligence test; those with an achievement score of 41 had an IQ of 86; and so on through the range of scores, so that students with an achievement score of 100 had IQs of 145. If this were the case, we could say that there is a perfect relationship, or correlation, between the two variables.

Suppose, by contrast, that for any given achievement score there are students with widely varying IQs. For example, suppose students with scores of 40 on the achievement test had IQs ranging from 85 to 145. Then we would conclude that there is little relationship, or correlation, between the two variables. Another possibility is a negative relationship between achievement test scores and IQ, which would occur if students with progressively higher achievement scores earned progressively lower IQ scores.

The purpose of the **correlation coefficient** is to express in mathematical terms the degree of relationship between any two variables. If the relationship is perfectly positive (for each increment in one variable there is a corresponding increment in the other), the correlation coefficient will be 1.00. If the relationship is perfectly negative, it will be -1.00. If there is no relationship, the coefficient will be zero. If two variables are somewhat related, the coefficients will have a value between zero and 1.00 (if the relationship is positive) or between zero and -1.00 (if negative). Thus, the correlation coefficient is a precise way of stating the extent to which one variable is related to another. To express the idea another way, the correlation coefficient tells us how effectively persons' scores on one test (e.g., an intelligence test) can be used to predict their scores on another test (e.g., an achievement test). If predictions can be made, this would suggest that the variable measured by the predictor test has a causal influence on the variable measured by the other test.

The square of a correlation coefficient yields a statistic that is generally called the **explained variance.** For example, the square of a correlation coefficient of .30 is .09. If variable A correlates .30 with variable B, we can say that variable A "explains" 9 percent of the variance in variable B.

The mathematical basis of explained variance is fairly complicated. A simple way to understand it is to imagine that scores on variable B range from 30 to 70. If A explained none of the variance in B, we could not predict anyone's score on B other than to say that it could be as low as 30 or as high as 70 (a range of 40 points). If A explained all of the variance B, we could predict anyone's score on B perfectly, and so our range of prediction would be 0 points. If A explained 30 percent of the variance in B, we could use A to predict anyone's score fairly accurately within a certain range; for example, our prediction of B might be a range of scores between 40 to 60 (a range of 20 points). In other words, as the explained variance (i.e., r^2) increases, we can use a person's score on variable A to predict his or her score on variable B within an increasingly narrow range.

Several types of correlation coefficients are presented in this chapter. Different coefficients are necessary because certain variables (e.g., most measures of intelligence) are in the form of interval scales or ratio scales, whereas other variables are in the form of rank orderings (e.g., ranking of teachers in terms of their effectiveness) or dichotomies (e.g., true-false data). Also, the relationship between two variables is not always linear, as we shall find in our discussion of the correlation ratio.

The basic design in correlational research is very simple, involving nothing more than collecting data on two or more variables on the same group of subjects and computing a correlation coefficient. For example, we might select a group of college freshmen and attempt to predict their first-year grades (variable 1) on the basis of their overall Scholastic Aptitude Test scores (variable 2). Many valuable studies in education have done little more than follow this simple design. Recent studies have employed more sophisticated correlational techniques in order to obtain a clearer picture of the relationships being studied.

As is the case with most research, the quality of correlational studies is determined not by the complexity of the design or the sophistication of the correlational techniques used, but by the depth of the rationale and theoretical constructs that guide the research design. In the past, many correlational studies in education have involved little more than locating available scores on several measures for a sample and then correlating these scores with each other in the hope that a meaningful relationship would emerge.

This approach might produce usable bits of information, but the chances of gaining significant knowledge are far less than if the researcher uses theory and the results of previous research to select variables to be correlated with one another.

Correlation and Causality

The correlational approach to analyzing relationships between variables has the same limitations with respect to causal inference as the causal-comparative approach discussed in the preceding chapter. For example, if we found a positive correlation between years of education and level of interest in cultural activities, we might infer that each year of formal schooling is likely to *cause*, *determine*, or *result in* greater interest in cultural activities. Two other causal inferences are equally plausible. Level of interest in cultural activities may determine how much education a student will seek. Also, some third variable may determine both amount of education and level of interest in cultural activities, thus creating a relationship between these two variables. Parents' education is a possible third variable. Parents who are college graduates may encourage their children to stay in school longer and to develop more cultural interests than parents with less formal education. If this is true, then the observed relationship between education and cultural interests is not a cause-and-effect relationship in either direction but rather the result of their common determination by a third variable.

A correlational relationship between two variables is occasionally due to an "artifact." For example, if we correlate two scales from the same personality inventory, a significant relationship between the scales may be found because both scales contain some of the same items, not because the personality dimensions that they measure are causally related. In this situation a statistical technique can be used to correct the correlation coefficient for covariation due to overlapping test items.[1] Also, when raters are used to collect data, relationships between variables may be found because the same rater scores both variables. This is particularly likely when there is rater bias due to halo effect (see chapter 12). We may find, for example, interrelations between several "good" traits if raters form an initial positive or negative impression of a person. If the

1. This statistical technique is described in W. Grant Dahlstrom and G. S. Welsh, *An MMPI Handbook: A Guide to Use in Clinical Practice and Research* (Minneapolis: University of Minnesota Press, 1960), p. 83.

impression is positive, they will probably score the person high on all the traits; if the impression is negative, they probably will assign the person low scores. Any relationship found between the traits would be due to this artifact rather than to a cause-and-effect pattern.

In summary, correlational statistics can be used to explore cause-and-effect relationships between variables, but the obtained results generally do not lead to strong conclusions. A correlation between A and B can mean that A is a determinant of B, that B is a determinant of A, that a third variable X determines both A and B, or that the relationship between A and B is due to an artifact. Only an experiment can provide a definitive conclusion about cause-and-effect. Correlation coefficients are best used to measure the *degree* of relationship between two variables and to explore *possible* causal factors that can later be tested in an experimental design.

Advantages and Uses of the Correlational Method

The correlational method of analyzing research data is very useful in studying problems in education and in other behavioral sciences. Its principal advantage is that it permits one to analyze the relationships among a large number of variables in a single study. In the behavioral sciences we are frequently confronted with situations in which several variables are contributing causes of a particular pattern of behavior. The correlational method allows us to analyze how several variables, either singly or in combination, might affect a particular pattern of behavior. (Path analysis and structural equation modeling, which we discuss later in the chapter, are particularly useful for this purpose.) The experimental method, in contrast, is not well suited to studying the effects of more than a few variables at a time.

Another advantage of the correlational method is that it provides information concerning the degree of relationship between the variables being studied. As discussed in the previous chapter, this is an advantage over the causal-comparative method. For example, causal-comparative studies of teaching ability generally start with the identification of a group of good and a group of poor teachers. Comparisons are then made between the two groups on a number of dependent variables in order to identify possible causes for differences in teaching ability. Such a dichotomy is obviously artificial because, within both of these groups of teachers, some will certainly be better than others. These differences in degree are ignored when using the causal-comparative method. In reality, what we have in this population is not two groups of teachers of distinctly different ability, but a single group ranging in degree of teaching ability from very poor to very good. The correlation coefficient provides a measure of degree of relationship over the entire range of teaching ability or within certain ranges.

The correlational method is used for two major purposes: (1) to explore relationships between variables and (2) to predict scores on a variable from subjects' scores on other variables. In relationship research the variables may be measured at the same point in time or at different points in time. In prediction research the variables used for prediction must be measured prior to the variable to be predicted.

The design of relationship research and prediction research is presented in the next two sections of this chapter. The remainder of the chapter describes the types of correlational statistics that can be used to analyze relational or predictive data. Most of the statistics can be used in either type of research. A few statistical techniques have been developed specifically for prediction research, and these are so noted. In subsequent chapters on the experimental method (chapters 15 and 16) you will find that the same correlational statistics can also be used to analyze data from experiments.

PLANNING A RELATIONSHIP STUDY

The Basic Research Design

The primary purpose of relationship studies is to identify the causes and effects of important educational phenomena such as academic achievement, attitude toward school, teacher morale, and use of particular teaching techniques. This type of research design is especially useful for exploratory studies in areas where little is known. To describe the steps involved in conducting a relationship study, we will use a study by Penelope Peterson and Elizabeth Fennema on classroom instructional phenomena that affect the mathematics achievement of fourth-grade students.[2]

The Problem

The first step in planning a relationship study is to identify specific variables that show promise of being important determinants of the characteristic or behavior pattern being studied. A review of existing research and theory is often helpful in identifying such variables. In the study by Peterson and Fennema, the behavior pattern being investigated was children's gains in mathematics achievement over part of a school year. Their interest was in identifying instructional practices that affect the amount of gain made by students, and in

2. Penelope L. Peterson and Elizabeth Fennema, "Effective Teaching, Student Engagement in Classroom Activities, and Sex-Related Differences in Learning Mathematics," *American Educational Research Journal* 22 (1985): 309–335.

determining whether different types of instruction are effective for girls and boys. Also, they differentiated between low-level mathematics achievement (knowledge and skills) and high-level mathematics achievement (understanding and application) to determine whether different types of instruction are effective for each of these types of mathematics learning. Their research problem was expressed in the form of the following question:

> Do significant relationships exist between the type of mathematics classroom activity in which boys and girls are engaged and their low level and high level achievement, and do these relationships differ significantly for boys and girls?[3]

Fortunately, the researchers were not completely blind as to instructional variables that might affect the types of academic achievement of interest to them. They were able to draw on previous research findings about teacher and student behaviors that correlate with student academic achievement gains. Although relationship studies are usually exploratory, as this one was, they should be guided by previous research findings and theory whenever possible in order to increase the likelihood of finding variables that cause the behavior pattern of interest. Thus, a review of the research and theoretical literature is a critical step in a study designed to explore cause-and-effect relationships between variables.

Selection of Subjects

The next step in a relationship study is to select subjects who can be measured on the variables with which the research is concerned. As we pointed out in our discussion of causal-comparative studies, it is very important to select a group of subjects who are reasonably homogeneous. Otherwise, relationships between variables may be obscured by the presence of subjects who differ widely from each other. This procedure of selecting a homogeneous sample was followed in Peterson and Fennema's study:

> The participants were 36 fourth grade teachers (3 male and 33 female) and their mathematics classes in 15 schools located either in rural areas or in small towns adjoining larger cities in Wisconsin. . . . Most of the students in the classes were white and came from middle-class families.[4]

Also, the researchers formed subgroups from this sample (a procedure we discussed in chapter 13) to make the samples used in the data analysis even more homogeneous. The subgroups were formed on the basis of gender. Six

3. Ibid., p. 311.
4. Ibid., pp. 311–312.

boys and six girls, randomly selected from each class, were chosen for intensive observation during the course of the study.

Data Collection

Data for relationship studies can be collected by various methods, including standardized tests, questionnaires, interviews, or observational techniques. The only requirement is that the data must be in quantified form.

Several measurement techniques were used in the mathematics study we have been describing. Observers were trained to use an observation schedule to record the math activities and behavior of the 12 selected students in each of the 36 classes. Each class was observed for three weeks. The recorded activities and behaviors are listed in table 14.1. Each activity and behavior was scored as the percentage of total class time that it occurred. In addition, each student was administered a standardized test of mathematics achievement in December or January and again in May. Students were given two scores for their performance on the test: a "low level" score for performance on items requiring recall of a specific fact or manipulation of an algorithm; and a "high level" score for performance on items requiring understanding, interpretation, or application of mathematical knowledge.

Data Analysis

In a simple relationship study, the data are analyzed by correlating (1) a measure thought to be related to a complex behavior pattern with (2) a measure of the behavior pattern itself. In the study by Peterson and Fennema, each measure of classroom activities and behaviors was correlated with the students' end-of-year achievement on the low-level and high-level mathematics test. Table 14.1 shows the results for girls. (The results for boys are shown later in the chapter in table 14.11.)

The unit of analysis for each correlation coefficient in table 14.1 is the class mean.[5] In other words, the researchers used the mean score of the six girls who were observed in each teacher's classroom. Because 36 teachers were involved in the study, the sample size for the correlation coefficients shown in table 14.1 is 36. Also, you should note that a particular type of correlation coefficient—a partial coefficient—is shown in table 14.1. Partial coefficients are discussed in more detail later in the chapter. For now, it is sufficient to understand that each coefficient in the table represents the degree of relationship between each classroom activity or behavior and girls' math achievement in May after the influence of their math achievement in December or January was removed

---

5. The selection of a unit of statistical analysis is discussed in chapter 9.

TABLE 14.1

Partial Correlations between Girls' Engaged Time Scores and End-of-Year Mathematics Achievement

Engaged Time Variables	Low-Level Achievement *r*	High-Level Achievement *r*
Type of activity expected by teacher		
Daily math	.17	.14
Other math	.07	.13
Nonmath	−.22*	−.08
Interim activity	−.10	−.20
Social activity	−.30**	−.43**
Setting of activity		
Total class	.06	−.19
Medium group	−.12	.24*
Small group–same sex	.18	.01
Small group–different sex	−.01	.41**
Two students–same sex	−.05	.05
Two students–different sex	−.03	−.13
Teacher–student	.03	−.15
Alone	−.03	.08
Engaged in math activity	.19	.31**
Math–high level	.18	.17
Math–low level	.01	.11
Math–symbolic	−.01	.07
Math–representational	.19	.20
Helping	−.04	−.11
Being helped by student	.03	−.09
Being helped by teacher	.01	−.15
No helping	.18	.32**
Competitive	−.40**	−.05
Cooperative	.25*	.13
Both competitive and cooperative	.25*	.03
Neither competive nor cooperative	.27*	.30**
Nonengaged in math activity	−.19	−.30**
Social	−.37**	−.34**
Waiting for help	.09	−.30**
Academic (nonmath)	−.17	−.09
Interim activities	−.04	−.03
Off-task	−.09	−.24*

SOURCE: Adapted from Penelope L. Peterson and Elizabeth Fennema, "Effective Teaching, Student Engagement in Classroom Activities, and Sex-Related Differences in Learning Mathematics," *American Educational Research Journal* 22 (1985): 319.
One-tailed test * $p < .10$. ** $p < .05$.

statistically. In other words, the partial correlation coefficient takes into account the fact that some classes of girls were higher-achieving and others were lower-achieving at the start of the year. The scores used to measure the girls' achievement, then, are not their actual end-of-year achievement scores. They are more like scores measuring how much gain the girls made in achievement in the interval from the first testing to the second testing.

Inspection of table 14.1 reveals that most of the statistically significant correlation coefficients are negative rather than positive. The study learned more about classroom activities and behaviors that seem to depress girls' learning of math than facilitate it. For example, we find that girls do less well in classes in which teachers allow more opportunity for socializing or discussion of personal and social topics (expected activity is social: $r = -.30$ and $-.43$ with low-level and high-level math, respectively; nonengaged in math because of socializing, $r = -.37$ and $-.34$ with low-level and high-level math, respectively).

The Shotgun Approach

As we have already noted, one advantage of the correlational method is that it permits the researcher to study the relationship between several variables simultaneously. However, this potential advantage can become a weakness if the researcher administers a very large number of measures to a sample of subjects in the hope that some of these measures will turn out to be related to the complex behavior pattern being studied. In the **shotgun approach,** measures are included even though the researcher can think of no theoretical basis or common-sense rationale to justify their inclusion.

In correlational studies, the researcher not uncommonly correlates 20 or more variables with a criterion variable. Sometimes there are several criterion variables, and if each of them is correlated with all of the other variables, the number of correlation coefficients becomes very large.

Although the shotgun approach of correlating many variables with each other sometimes yields significant findings, it should be avoided. A large number of measures must be administered, often at considerable expense. Even if some of the measures correlate with the criterion, they may do so by chance. Upon repeating the study, the researcher will find that many of the correlations do not replicate. The only situation in which the shotgun approach may be justified is when research knowledge is required without regard to cost in an area where previous research is insufficient to form the basis for a more theory-based approach.

A total of 64 correlation coefficients are shown in table 14.1. Although this is a large number of coefficients, the results generally form meaningful patterns because the researchers were careful to base their selection of variables on previous research findings about effective classroom teaching. Had they not done so, the pattern of significant and nonsignificant relationships would be difficult to interpret.

Note that as the number of computed correlation coefficients increases, the task of interpretation becomes more complex. In the published report of their study, Peterson and Fennema simplified the task of interpretation by emphasizing discussion of the statistically significant results. A complete interpretation also would include an attempt to explain the nonsignificant results. For example, the correlation between class time engaged in high-level math activities and high-level math achievement was rather low ($r = .17$). The same situation applies to low-level math activities and low-level achievement ($r = .01$). It seems reasonable, however, that the more time students spend engaged in class doing relevant work, the greater should be their math achievement. These anomalous findings are potentially important, and they should be given the same attention as the statistically significant results.

Limitations of the Relationship Study

We have already discussed the fact that correlations obtained in a relationship study cannot establish cause-and-effect relationships between the variables correlated. For example, the significant r of $-.40$ for the variable labelled "competitive" in table 14.1 suggests that teacher emphasis on competitive learning activities *causes* students to learn math facts and skills less well. Another possibility, however, is that some other teacher characteristic such as a negative orientation to students causes them to emphasize competitive activities and other activities that depress girls' math achievement. In this case, teachers' orientation to students, rather than competitive activities, is the cause of students' level of math achievement.

Many researchers have criticized relationship studies because they attempt to break down complex behavior into simpler components. Although this atomistic approach is appropriate for many research areas in education and psychology, there is some question as to whether a complex characteristic, such as artistic ability, can be meaningful if broken into its elements. Not infrequently, people seem to possess all or most of the specific skills that appear related to artistic ability and yet are unable to produce creative art work. On the other hand, many of the recognized masters in the creative arts have been notably deficient in some specific skill related to their media and yet have produced masterpieces.

Another problem involving the use of the correlational technique to identify variables related to complex skills or abilities is that success in many of the complex activities that interest us can probably be attained in a number of different ways. For example, a study attempting to relate success of high school principals to specific independent variables might fail because of the lack of any set of characteristics common to all successful principals. In one group of administrators, for example, forcefulness might be significantly correlated with success, while in another group of administrators, who employ different administrative techniques, this characteristic might be negatively correlated with success. We know so little about certain behavior patterns, and many of these patterns are so highly complex, that only the most careful interpretation of correlational data can provide us with an understanding of the phenomenon being studied.

PLANNING A PREDICTION STUDY

Types of Prediction Studies

Educational researchers carry out many prediction studies, usually with the aim of identifying variables that forecast academic and vocational success. The scope of prediction studies can be illustrated by the titles of these journal reports:

Carole S. Harrison, "The Validity of the Musical Aptitude Profile for Predicting Grades in Freshman Music Theory," *Educational and Psychological Measurement* 47 (1987): 477–482.

Fred M. Grossman and Gloria A. Galvin, "Clinically and Theoretically Derived WISC-R Subtest Groupings: Predicting Academic Achievement in a Referral Population," *Psychology in the Schools* 24 (1987): 105–110.

William F. Brazziel, "Forecasting Older Student Enrollment: A Cohort and Participation Rate Model," *Journal of Higher Education* 58 (1987): 223–231.

A. E. Johnson, Jr., "Predicting First Year Grade Point Average for Minority Students in Law School," *College and University* 62 (1987): 318–324.

Prediction studies provide us with three types of information: the extent to which a criterion behavior pattern can be predicted; data for theory building about possible determinants of the criterion behavior pattern; and evidence regarding the predictive validity of the test or tests that are correlated with the criterion behavior pattern.

Prediction studies can be differentiated in terms of which of these types of information we are most interested in obtaining. In some studies the emphasis is on a particular criterion behavior (e.g., first-year college grades), and one or more personality and aptitude tests are used to predict this criterion. Those tests that are good predictors are then applied to practical problems, such as selection of students for college admission. In other studies a similar research design is followed, but we are primarily concerned with the theoretical significance of our findings. Finally, we may carry out prediction studies for the purpose of test development. The emphasis is on writing test items and determining the test's predictive validity for one or more criteria. The particular criterion predicted is of secondary importance.

Prediction research has made a major contribution to educational practice. Many prediction studies have been aimed at short-term prediction of the student's performance in a specific course of study, and others have been aimed at long-term prediction of general academic success. The findings of these studies have greatly aided school personnel in choosing students most likely to succeed in a particular academic environment or course of study. Also, prediction studies provide the scientific basis for counselors' efforts to help students plan their academic future. Counselors can administer vocational-interest tests that have proved effective in predicting a person's future occupation and interpret the results to their clients.

Prediction research can also be done to reduce the cost of training new personnel for today's complex vocational skills. For example, a selection system such as that employed by the U.S. Air Force for pilot training can save vast sums of money because it eliminates a certain number of persons who would fail during the training program. Such training is extremely costly, and the cost of training the unsuccessful candidate up to the point of failure must be added to the per-person cost of training successful candidates. A selection process that reduces the number of failures is of great value. Prediction research is done to determine which criteria to incorporate in the selection process.

The Basic Research Design

Prediction studies are similar to relationship studies in that both involve computing correlations between a complex behavior pattern (the criterion) and variables thought to be related to the criterion. However, in prediction studies the other variables (sometimes called *predictor variables*) are measured some time before the criterion behavior occurs. In contrast, in relationship studies the criterion behavior and other variables need not be measured in a particular order; in practice they are often measured at the same point in time. Also, prediction studies tend to be more concerned with maximizing the correlation between the predictor variables and the criterion. As we shall see later in the chapter, correlations sometimes can be increased by use of multiple correlation and moderator variables.

The Problem

As we have already observed, researchers can carry out prediction studies for different purposes. They may be interested in testing the predictive validity of a particular test, in predicting a behavior criterion for use in an applied situation, or in predicting a behavior criterion to test theoretical hypotheses. An example of the first type of research is a prediction study by Richard Butler and Clark

McCauley.[6] The purpose of their study was to determine the validity of the Scholastic Aptitude Test (SAT) and high school class rank in predicting the grade point average (GPA) of students at the United States Military Academy. They were especially interested in determining whether the SAT and high school class rank predicted the students' GPA in years 1, 2, 3, and 4 equally well.

An important aspect of prediction studies is the proper definition of one's criterion behavior pattern. Many studies have failed to find predictive relationships because a poor criterion was specified. For example, GPA is sometimes used as a criterion, as in Butler and McCauley's study. The GPA includes a person's grades in several subjects, such as mathematics, Spanish, and history. Also, the kinds of courses that students take usually change as they progress from their freshman year to senior year of college. Furthermore, some students select easier courses to take than do other students. These observations suggest that GPA is probably a shifting, amorphous criterion and therefore difficult to predict well.

To the researchers' credit, they analyzed the educational program at the U.S. Military Academy to determine the possible influence of these factors on the criterion GPA scores. They found that differential course difficulty was not a factor because,

> about half the core courses each year are science or mathematics courses . . . [and] different instructors teaching the same course use the same syllabus and the same examinations. It seems likely that the size and standardization of the core requirement may prevent less able cadets from seeking out easier courses or instructors.[7]

Moreover, the researchers used the two test scores yielded by the SAT (Verbal and Quantitative) rather than total SAT score to predict students' GPA. This is a desirable feature because each test measure might predict different components of the GPA.

Selection of Subjects

As we discussed with respect to other research designs, it is important to draw subjects from the specific population most pertinent to your study. In the prediction study we have been considering, the researchers were specifically interested in predicting the GPA of students over the course of their four-year program at the U.S. Military Academy. Therefore, their sample consisted of two

6. Richard P. Butler and Clark McCauley, "Extraordinary Stability and Ordinary Predictability of Academic Success at the United States Military Academy," *Journal of Educational Psychology* 79 (1987): 83–86.
7. Ibid., p. 85.

complete classes of graduates of the academy (1982 and 1983). They also included a sample of graduates of the U.S. Air Force Academy, an institution having a similar population of students and a similar academic program.

Data Collection

Standardized tests, questionnaires, interviews, or observational techniques can be used to measure predictor variables and the criterion behavior pattern in a prediction study. Of course, the predictor variables must be measured before the criterion behavior pattern occurs. Otherwise, one cannot claim that a particular test or other measure actually predicted the criterion. In Butler and McCauley's study, scores on the two predictor measures—SAT and high school class rank—were obtained in the students' senior year of high school. The GPAs were calculated during the subsequent four years that the students were in college.

Prediction of events or behaviors that will occur in the near future is generally easier and more accurate than prediction of events or behaviors that will occur in the more distant future. This is because in short-term prediction, more of the determinants of the behavior being predicted are likely to be present. Furthermore, short-term prediction allows less time for important criterion variables to change or for important new determinants to emerge. For example, if we wish to predict the probable success of individuals in management positions, we would probably start with variables that have been found in previous research to be related to later success in management positions. This type of test battery might include such factors as verbal intelligence, social attitudes, emotional maturity, and so on. However, certain variables important to success could not possibly be measured because they are not present at the time the prediction must be made. For example, the individual's ability to work well with superiors in the management hierarchy—a likely determinant of management success—cannot be measured because the superiors are unknown at the time of prediction.

Data Analysis

The basic form of data analysis in a prediction study consists of correlating each predictor variable with the criterion. In the study we have been describing, SAT Verbal scores, SAT Quantitative scores, and high school class rank (the predictor variables) were each correlated with students' GPA in each year of college (the criterion variables). The correlation coefficients are shown in table 14.2. Each of the predictor variables is effective in predicting students' GPAs, but only moderately so. Students' rank in their high school class is overall a slightly better predictor. A similar pattern of prediction was found for the sample of U.S. Air Force Academy graduates.

The statistics shown in table 14.2 are sometimes called *bivariate correlational*

TABLE 14.2

Correlations between Predictor Variables and Grade Point Averages of U.S. Military Academy Students

Year of Grade Point Average	SAT Verbal	SAT Quantitative	High School Rank
1982 Class			
Year 1	.30	.41	.47
Year 2	.30	.43	.51
Year 3	.30	.43	.51
Year 4	.30	.42	.51
1983 Class			
Year 1	.36	.35	.38
Year 2	.32	.40	.41
Year 3	.32	.39	.41
Year 4	.32	.39	.41

SOURCE: Adapted from Richard P. Butler and Clark McCauley, "Extraordinary Stability and Ordinary Predictability of Academic Success at the United States Military Academy," *Journal of Educational Psychology* 79 (1987): 84.
NOTE: All coefficients are statistically significant ($p < .05$, one-tailed). The grade point averages are noncumulative; that is, they are for just one year at a time. Rank in high school was adjusted for class size. SAT = Scholastic Aptitude Test.

statistics, because each coefficient expresses the magnitude of relationship between two (hence "bivariate") variables. This type of statistic is discussed in the next section of the chapter.

Other statistical tools can be applied to improve predictions from subjects' scores on the predictor measures. The primary tool is multiple regression, which uses the subjects' scores on two or more measures to predict their performance on the criterion measures. (Multiple regression is discussed later in the chapter.) By using multiple regression, Butler and McCauley were able to obtain correlation coefficients ranging from .59 to .63 for the class of 1982, and .54 to .57 for the class of 1983.[8] These coefficients are greater than any of those shown in table 14.2.

Moderator analysis, also discussed later in the chapter, is another procedure for improving the predictability of a criterion variable. This procedure involves identifying a subgroup for whom the correlation between a criterion and a predictor variable is significantly greater than the correlation for the total sample from which the subgroup was formed.

8. Multiple regression is not mentioned by name in Butler and McCauley's report, but that undoubtedly is the technique used to determine what they refer to as the "composite variable" of the predictor variables.

Statistical Factors in Prediction Research

Group Prediction

The goal of many prediction studies is to develop measures with sufficient predictive validity to be used in practical selection programs in education or industry. The effectiveness of a measure for selection purposes, however, is not determined solely by its predictive validity. Two other factors influence effectiveness in practical selection problems. The first is the selection ratio. This is the proportion of the available candidates that must be selected. A predictive measure gives better results when only the few candidates scoring highest need be chosen than when all but the few who score lowest must be chosen. In other words, the smaller the proportion of candidates that must be chosen, the more of those chosen will be successful.

The other factor influencing the effectiveness of a predictive measure is the proportion of candidates who would be successful if no selection were applied. In most vocational applications, this is the proportion of employees hired for the given activity, prior to the selection system, whose work was satisfactory. In educational selection it would be the number of students who succeeded in the given course of study prior to the use of selective admission. This number provides a baseline. If the baseline figure is high, the predictive measure will need to have very high validity in order to improve on the success of "natural" selection. If the baseline figure is low, the predictive measure can have low predictive validity yet manage to improve on "natural" selection.

The **Taylor-Russell Tables** were developed to combine the three factors of predictive validity, selection ratio, and proportion successful without selection.[9] If these three factors are known, the researcher can predict the proportion of the candidates selected who will be successful if the predictive measure is used.

Shrinkage

In using correlations for prediction, the usual procedure is to select a test or battery of tests that we believe will predict the behavior with which we are concerned. These tests are then tried out on a sample in order to determine their predictive validity, that is, the degree to which they will predict the behavior that we wish them to predict. The correlation between the prediction made by the test and the later behavior of the individual provides an estimate of the predictive validity of the test. This correlation, however, will almost certainly become smaller if we repeat the study with a new sample.

9. H. C. Taylor and J. T. Russell, "The Relationships of Validity Coefficients to the Practical Effectiveness of Tests in Selection: Discussion and Tables," *Journal of Applied Psychology* 23 (1939): 565–578.

The tendency for predictive validities to decrease when the research is repeated is referred to as **shrinkage.** More shrinkage is likely to occur when the original sample includes a small number of subjects and when the number of predictor variables is large.

Shrinkage is due primarily to the fact that when we initially validate our measures, some of them will yield significant correlations by chance. In other words, characteristics unique to the group of subjects we have tested tend to yield a maximum predictive validity for some of our predictive measures. In fact, we can demonstrate mathematically that if researchers keep adding predictor variables to a multiple regression equation, they eventually will be able to predict each person's score on the criterion variable perfectly. Upon repetition of the study, however, these same chance predictive relationships are not likely to be present, and thus the correlations initially obtained become smaller or disappear.

Because making predictions on the basis of correlations derived from one sample of subjects is of uncertain value, we advise you to conduct a cross-validation of predictor variables before using them in practical prediction situations. Thus, after preliminary validation of the battery, the predictive validity of each variable should be cross-checked using another sample. Those correlations that have dropped to a nonsignificant level should be eliminated.

BIVARIATE CORRELATIONAL STATISTICS

In this section we discuss 10 correlational techniques that can be used to analyze the degree of relationship between two variables. Because two variables are involved, these techniques are sometimes called *bivariate* correlational statistics. The form of the variables to be correlated and the nature of the relationship determine which technique is used. Variables in relationship studies are usually expressed in one of five forms: continuous score, rank, artificial dichotomy, true dichotomy, and category.[10] Table 14.3 lists 10 bivariate correlational techniques and the conditions under which they are used.

Product-Moment Correlation

The **product-moment correlation coefficient *r*** is computed when both variables that we wish to correlate are expressed as continuous scores. For example, if we administer an intelligence test such as the Wechsler Intelligence Scale for Children and an achievement test such as the Stanford Achievement Test to the

---

10. These five types of scores are described in chapter 9.

TABLE 14.3

Bivariate Correlational Techniques for Different Forms of Variables

Technique	Symbol	Variable 1	Variable 2	Remarks
Product-moment correlation	r	Continuous	Continuous	The most stable technique, i.e., smallest standard error
Rank-difference correlation (*rho*)	ρ	Ranks	Ranks	Is a special form of product-moment correlation
Kendall's *tau*	τ	Ranks	Ranks	Preferable to *rho* for numbers under 10
Biserial correlation	r_{bis}	Artificial dichotomy	Continuous	Values can exceed 1—has a larger standard error than r—commonly used in item analysis
Widespread biserial correlation	r_{wbis}	Widespread artificial dichotomy	Continuous	Used when the researcher is interested in persons at the extremes on the dichotomized variable
Point-biserial correlation	r_{pbis}	True dichotomy	Continuous	Yields a lower correlation than r_{bis}
Tetrachoric correlation	r_t	Artificial dichotomy	Artificial dichotomy	Used when both variables can be split at critical points
Phi coefficient	ϕ	True dichotomy	True dichotomy	Used in calculating inter-item correlations
Contingency coefficient	C	2 or more categories	2 or more categories	Comparable to r_t under certain conditions—closely related to chi-square
Correlation ratio, *eta*	η	Continuous	Continuous	Used to detect nonlinear relationships

same group of students, we will have two sets of continuous scores. The product-moment correlation coefficient r would be the appropriate correlational statistic for determining the magnitude of relationship between students' scores on the two measures.

Product-moment correlation is the most used bivariate correlational technique because r has a small standard error and because most educational measures yield continuous scores. In fact, r can be calculated for any two sets of scores, even if one or both measures do not yield scores in continuous form. Researchers frequently compute a correlation matrix in which subjects' scores on

TABLE 14.4

Rank-Order (*rho*) Correlation Matrix for Students' Mean Rankings of Preferences for Different Books

Student Group	Intercorrelations (*rho*)					
	2	3	4	5	6	7
University students						
1. English females	.81***	.50**	.23	.56**	.18	.27
2. Afrikaans females		.45*	.18	.49**	.08	.19
3. English males			.76***	.60***	.74***	.75***
4. Afrikaans males				.54**	.87***	.84***
Technical college students						
5. English females					.61***	.78***
6. English males						.92***
7. Afrikaans males						

Source: Adapted from Victor Nell, "The Psychology of Reading for Pleasure: Needs and Gratifications," *Reading Research Quarterly* 23 (1988): 25.
* $p < .05$. ** $p < .01$. *** $p < .001$.

all of the variables are correlated with each other. (The correlation matrix is discussed later in the chapter.) All of the correlation coefficients in the matrix are product-moment *r*s, even if the measures yield different types of scores.

Correlation of Rank Scores

The Rank-Difference Correlation Coefficient, *rho*

The **rank-difference correlation coefficient** *rho* is a special form of the product-moment correlation coefficient. Rank-difference correlation is used to correlate two variables when one or both of these variables are available only in rank form. If one variable is in continuous form, it must be converted to rank form. Conversion involves the simple procedure of listing the continuous scores in order of magnitude and then assigning ranks to them.

Rank-difference correlation was used in a study of reading preference by Victor Nell.[11] He asked various groups of South African students to rank a list of extracts from 30 books in their order of preference for them. Table 14.4 presents the *rho* coefficients for the rank scores of all possible pairs of scores. We find, for

11. Victor Nell, "The Psychology of Reading for Pleasure: Needs and Gratifications," *Reading Research Quarterly* 23 (1988): 6–50.

example, that the mean rankings of English males and Afrikaan males in technical colleges are very similar (*rho* = .92). The mean rankings of Afrikaan females and Afrikaan males in universities, however, have very little relationship to each other (*rho* = .18).

Table 14.4 is arranged in the form of a correlation matrix, which is a method for reporting a set of correlation coefficients. This method is discussed later in the chapter.

Kendall's *tau,* τ

Tau is another form of rank correlation coefficient that has some theoretical advantage over the better known Spearman's *rho*. Like *rho, tau* can be computed to correlate two sets of ranks. Data not in rank form can be converted to ranks if it is desired to compute *tau*. Its principal advantage is that it has a more normal sampling distribution than *rho* for samples under 10. It is more difficult to calculate than *rho* and yields lower correlation coefficients when computed from the same data. As *rho* very closely approximates the Pearson *r* calculated from the same data, it is less likely than *tau* to be misinterpreted by the educator.

Correlation of Dichotomous Scores

The Biserial Correlation Coefficient, r_{bis}

The **biserial correlation coefficient** r_{bis} is used when one of the variables is in the form of continuous scores and the other variable is in the form of an artificial dichotomy. For example, if we wish to determine the relationship between success and failure in algebra and scores on an algebra aptitude test, we would compute a biserial correlation coefficient. In this case the aptitude test yields continuous scores, while the record of each subject as having passed or failed algebra takes the form of an artificial dichotomy. As a rule, the correlation coefficients obtained using the biserial technique are somewhat higher than those obtained on the same data using the product-moment technique.

Although the theoretical limits of any correlation are +1 to −1, it is mathematically possible to obtain biserial correlation coefficients greater than one if the variables are not normally distributed. This fact should be kept in mind when employing biserial correlation. Otherwise, if you obtain a biserial correlation coefficient greater than 1.00, you will spend a great deal of time looking for an error that does not exist.

In addition to yielding higher coefficients, biserial correlation is somewhat less precise than product-moment correlation, and therefore it has a larger standard error. Therefore, if possible, you should measure continuous variables (e.g., grade point average) rather than dichotomous variables (e.g., pass-fail). In some situations, however, data cannot be obtained in continuous form. You should not hesitate to use the biserial correlation technique under those circumstances.

The Widespread Biserial Correlation Coefficient r_{wbis}

There are many instances in educational research where we want to correlate scores on a continuous variable, such as intelligence, with extreme scores on some other characteristic. Let us say, for example, that we wished to determine whether teaching success is correlated with certain personality traits. The measurement of teaching success is a difficult task for which satisfactory measures are not easily obtained. Evaluations of teaching ability are usually based on a composite evaluation made by two or more raters. In making ratings, raters usually find it easier to pick out the extremes (i.e., the better and poorer teachers in the group) than to discriminate among teachers who are within the average range of teaching ability. For example, if five raters were used to evaluate a hundred teachers, we would find that the raters would agree much more closely in their identification of the 10 best teachers and the 10 poorest teachers than they would agree on the relative ability of teachers close to the average. This situation occurs in many studies where ratings are used as a basis for evaluation.

When only those individuals whose scores are at the two extreme ends on a dichotomized variable are used, the extreme groups constitute a widespread dichotomy. The technique of **widespread biserial correlation** is used to correlate a continuous score with a widespread dichotomy. The cutoff points for identifying extreme cases are defined in such a way that the two extreme groups have an equal number of cases.

The Point Biserial Correlation Coefficient r_{pbis}

The **point biserial correlation coefficient** r_{pbis} is used when one of the variables we wish to correlate is in the form of a continuous score and the other variable is in the form of a true dichotomy. This correlational technique is used in studies relating gender to different continuous variables, such as intelligence, verbal fluency, reading ability, and achievement. In such studies gender provides the true dichotomy, and the other measure provides the continuous variable.

As a rule the point biserial coefficient will be somewhat lower than if the same data were analyzed using the biserial correlation. However, it has several advantages over biserial correlation. It does not yield correlations greater than 1.0. Its standard error is easier to calculate, and its statistical significance can be determined using the product-moment r significance tables, which are found in most elementary statistics texts.

The Tetrachoric Correlation Coefficient, r_t

Occasionally we encounter a situation in educational research where both variables that we wish to correlate are in the form of artificial dichotomies. Under these conditions the technique of **tetrachoric correlation** is used. Use of this coefficient requires the assumption that the variables underlying the dichotomies in the tetrachoric correlation analysis are continuous and normally distributed. Also, the tetrachoric coefficient is considerably less stable than the product-moment coefficient. Thus, this type of correlation should not be used unless the research problem clearly warrants it. The standard error of the tetrachoric correlation coefficient is also quite difficult to compute, which means that considerable effort is required to determine whether the observed correlation coefficient is significant. The tetrachoric correlation statistic is most stable when a large number of cases is used and when the dichotomies divide the sample into approximately equal groups.

The *Phi* Coefficient, ϕ

The *phi* **coefficient** is used to correlate two variables that are both true dichotomies. Because we deal with relatively few true dichotomies in education, *phi* coefficients are seldom calculated in educational research. The main use of this technique is to determine the correlation between two items on a test during item analysis. Each subject's response to each item can be classified as either correct or incorrect, thus giving us two true dichotomies.

The Contingency Coefficient

The **contingency coefficient** C is used when the variables to be correlated are in the form of categories. Although C can be used when the variables are divided into dichotomies, the *phi* coefficient or tetrachoric correlation is preferable under these conditions. When either or both variables are classified into more than two categories, however, ϕ or r_t cannot be applied; instead, the contingency coefficient is used to measure the degree of relationship.

C is closely related to the chi-square statistic (see chapter 13) and is computed using a contingency table. If chi-square has been computed, C can easily be derived from chi-square. Conversely, chi-square can be computed from C; this is usually done because chi-square provides the easiest method of determining the statistical significance of C. The contingency coefficient yields correlations closely comparable to the product-moment r if each variable is split into at least five categories and if the sample is large. C should not be used unless the data are available only in categories or unless converting the scores to categories presents the data in a more logical or understandable form.

Scattergrams and the Correlation Ratio

We have observed that the magnitude of the relationship between two variables can be represented by a correlation coefficient. The magnitude of the relationship can also be pictorially represented by making a **scattergram.** All that is required is to draw an X axis and a Y axis representing the score ranges of the two variables involved. The two scores of each individual in one's sample can then be represented by a single point (i.e., coordinate) on the graph.

Figure 14.1 presents several scattergrams. The first scattergram shows a perfect correlation, indicated by the straight line, since each unit of increment in the X-axis variable is accompanied by a unit of increment in the Y-axis variable. The correlation is 1.00, because if we know a person's score on one variable, we can predict perfectly this person's score on the other. The second scattergram indicates a fairly high degree of positive correlation between the two variables. If we know a person's score on the X-axis variable, we cannot predict the person's score on the Y-axis variable perfectly, but the score given by the straight line ("the line of best fit") will yield a fairly accurate prediction. If the line that described the relationship between two variables slanted down from left to right (instead of down from right to left, as in the second scattergram), the correlation coefficient would be negative. The third scattergram is a graphic representation of a complete lack of relationship between two variables. Knowing a person's score on the X-axis variable is of no value at all in predicting his or her score on the Y-axis variable.

The line of best fit (the straight line in scattergrams 1, 2, and 3 of figure 14.1) can be calculated using the equation

$$Y = bX + a$$

where Y is the variable being predicted, b is the slope of the line (sometimes called "regression weight"), X is the predictor variable, and a is the point where the line intersects with the Y axis. You will see an elaboration of this basic equation when we discuss multiple regression later in the chapter.

Using a scattergram to represent graphically the relationship between the variables involved in a correlational study is particularly helpful in detecting nonlinear relationships. The correlation techniques described previously assume that the relationship is linear, in other words, that a straight line best describes the relationship between the two variables. However, sometimes the relationship is nonlinear, as in the fourth scattergram of figure 14.1. In this example a curved line rather than a straight line best describes the relationship between the two variables and therefore leads to better predictions from scores on the X axis to scores on the Y axis.

Sometimes nonlinear relationships are discovered in correlational studies only after scattergrams have been plotted, but occasionally they are hypothe-

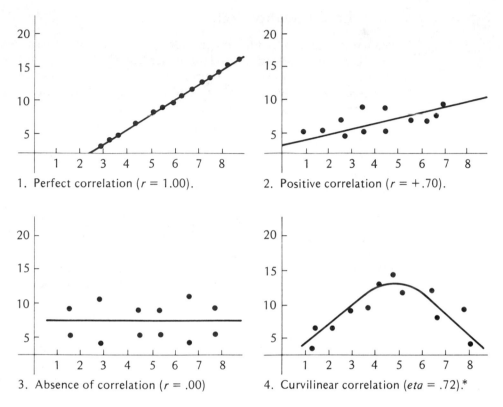

1. Perfect correlation ($r = 1.00$).

2. Positive correlation ($r = +.70$).

3. Absence of correlation ($r = .00$)

4. Curvilinear correlation ($eta = .72$).*

* The product-moment correlation for the same data would be about $+.29$.

Figure 14.1   Examples of Scattergrams

sized to describe the relationship between two variables. For example, some researchers have hypothesized a curvilinear relationship between anxiety and intellectual performance. The rationale for this hypothesis is that persons low in anxiety will not be motivated to do well on a performance task and thus will earn low scores. Persons with a moderate amount of anxiety will be motivated by their anxiety to perform well, and since their anxiety is moderate, it will not disrupt their performance. Therefore, they should earn higher scores than the nonanxious group. By the same reasoning, highly anxious persons should be even more motivated to perform well. If high motivation were the only factor operating, highly anxious persons should earn the highest scores, and the relationship between anxiety and performance would be linear. However, it has been hypothesized that highly anxious persons, though well-motivated, are disrupted by their anxiety and thus will earn low performance scores. Consequently, the hypothesized relationship between anxiety and performance is curvilinear with high- and low-anxiety groups hypothesized to have low performance scores, and the middle-anxiety group hypothesized to have high performance scores.

If the scattergrams for research data indicate that the relationship between two variables is markedly nonlinear, then one should compute the **correlation ratio** (*eta*). The advantage of the correlation ratio is that it provides a more accurate index of the relationship between two variables than other correlational statistics when the relationship is markedly nonlinear. Other types of correlation coefficients will generally underestimate the degree of relationship when nonlinearity exists. Researchers sometimes perform a special statistical test to determine whether the *eta* statistic yields a coefficient that is of significantly greater magnitude than the coefficient yielded by a linear correlation statistic.

The disadvantage of the *eta* coefficient is that it is relatively difficult to compute. This disadvantage has been virtually eliminated by the advent of computer programs designed to compute *etas* and scattergrams with little researcher effort needed.

An alternative to *eta*, especially when several predictor variables are involved, is the technique of multiple regression, which is discussed later in the chapter. This technique can be used to test for nonlinear (sometimes called "curvilinear") relationships between variables.[12]

In addition to revealing nonlinear relationships, scattergrams are useful for detecting outliers in research data. (The phenomenon of outliers was discussed in chapter 9.) The points in each of the scattergrams in figure 14.1 are generally clustered near each other. If one of the points was quite far away from the other points in the scattergram, we would have reason to suspect that the subject represented by that point was an outlier.

ADJUSTMENTS TO THE CORRELATION COEFFICIENT

Correction for Attenuation

When we correlate scores on two measures, the obtained correlation coefficient is lower than the true correlation to the extent that the measures are not perfectly reliable. This lowering of the correlation coefficient due to unreliability of the measures is called attenuation. **Correction for attenuation** provides an estimate of what the correlation between the variables would be if the measures had perfect reliability. In prediction studies correction for attenuation is not usually

12. The use of multiple regression to test for nonlinear relationships is illustrated in Gerald J. Melican and Leonard S. Feldt, "An Empirical Study of the Zajonc-Markus Hypothesis for Achievement Test Score Declines," *American Educatonal Research Journal* 17 (1980): 5–19.

applied because we must make predictions on the basis of the measures we have, and the reliability of these measures, even if low, must be accepted as a limitation.

This correction is sometimes used, however, in exploratory studies. In these studies crude measures of low reliability are often used, thus lowering the obtained correlation coefficient. The correction for attenuation helps the researcher determine what the relationship between two variables might be if perfect measures of the variables were available. Because correction for attenuation is only an estimate, it sometimes yields corrected correlations above 1. These are spurious and are usually dropped to .99 in research reports. Finally, remember that a correlation corrected for attenuation tells us "what might be" rather than "what is."

Correction for Restriction in Range

The **correction for restriction in range** is applied to correlation coefficients when the researcher knows that the range of scores for a sample is restricted on one or both of the variables being correlated. Restriction in range leads to a lowering of the correlation coefficient.

The use of this technique is illustrated in a study by Emily Krohn, Robert Lamp, and Cynthia Phelps.[13] They validated a test of cognitive abilities, the Kaufman Assessment Battery for Children (K-ABC), by correlating children's scores on its various subtests with their scores on a well-established intelligence test, the Stanford-Binet Intelligence Scale (SB). The sample of children was a group of black preschoolers enrolled in a Head Start program.

The standard deviations of the K-ABC and SB for norming groups are 15 and 16, respectively. The standard deviations for the researchers' sample, however, were substantially lower. For example, the sample's standard deviation on the SB was 9.4, which indicates a restricted range of scores relative to the norming group. Therefore, the researchers calculated both the regular correlations (r) between students' K-ABC subtest scores and SB total score, and the same correlations corrected for restriction in range.

The regular and corrected correlation coefficients are shown in table 14.5. Inspection of this table reveals that each corrected coefficient is greater than the corresponding r. The corrected coefficient is an estimate of the magnitude of the relationship between two sets of test scores had the sample earned the same range of scores as the norming group.

Use of the correction for restriction in range requires the assumption that the two variables are related to each other linearly throughout their entire range.

---

13. Emily J. Krohn, Robert E. Lamp, and Cynthia G. Phelps, "Validity of the K-ABC for a Black Preschool Population," *Psychology in the Schools* 25 (1988): 15–21.

TABLE 14.5

Uncorrected Correlations and Correlations Corrected for Restriction in Range between K-ABC Subtests and Stanford-Binet IQ Scale

	Simultaneous	Sequential	K-ABC Mental Processing Scale	Achievement	Nonverbal
K-ABC					
Simultaneous					
Sequential	$r = .24$				
	$r_c = .56^*$				
Mental Processing Scale (MPC)	$r = .83^*$	$r = .74^*$			
	$r_c = .92^*$	$r_c = .84^*$			
Achievement	$r = .52^*$	$r = .43^*$	$r = .61^*$		
	$r_c = .79^*$	$r_c = .68^*$	$r_c = .83^*$		
Nonverbal[a]	$r = .59^*$	$r = .62^*$	$r = .74^*$	$r = .24$	
	$r_c = .77^*$	$r_c = .76^*$	$r_c = .85^*$	$r_c = .60^*$	
Stanford-Binet (L-M)	$r = .58^*$	$r = .29^*$	$r = .58^*$	$r = .65^*$	$r = .41^*$
	$r_c = .82^*$	$r_c = .62^*$	$r_c = .82^*$	$r_c = .87^*$	$r_c = .69^*$

Source: Table 3, Emily J. Krohn, Robert L. Lamp, and Cynthia G. Phelps, "Validity of the K-ABC for a Black Preschool Population," *Psychology in the Schools* 25 (1988): 20.
Note: r_c = correlation coefficients corrected for restriction of range.
[a] Since the Nonverbal Scale requires the child to be at least four years of age or older, the sample size for this measure was reduced to 23.
* $p < .01$.

If the relationship for the total range of scores is curvilinear, the correction for restriction in range is not applicable.

Partial Correlation

Partial correlation is sometimes employed in relationship and prediction studies. This method is useful when we wish to rule out the influence of one or more variables upon the criterion behavior pattern in order to clarify the role of other variables. Its use is illustrated in the study of mathematics instruction by Peterson and Fennema that we described earlier in the chapter. Table 14.1 presents correlational analyses from that study. The coefficients shown in the table are actually partial correlation coefficients.

We can understand the researchers' use of partial correlation by considering the factors that influence girls' end-of-school-year math achievement.

One influencing factor is undoubtedly the girls' math achievement earlier in the school year. Girls who are doing well in mathematics in December are likely to be doing better in May than girls who are not doing well in mathematics in December. The influence of this factor is shown by arrow A in Figure 14.2. The teacher's instruction is also likely to influence girls' end-of-year achievement. This influence is represented in figure 14.2 by arrow B.

The question arises, How much influence does each of these factors have on girls' end-of-year achievement? The technique of partial correlation allows us to answer this question. It was used in the analysis reported earlier in table 14.1 to show us the extent of influence of instructional factors *on their own* (arrow B in figure 14.2). Had the researchers wished, they also could have used partial correlation to determine how much beginning-of-the-year achievement level influenced end-of-the-year achievement level (arrow A in figure 14.2).

Analyzing the situation still further, we realize that girls' beginning-of-the-year achievement can influence teachers' instruction (arrow C in Figure 14.2) in addition to their end-of-the-year achievement. Teachers who have higher-achieving girls in their classes may instruct them differently from teachers who have lower-achieving girls. The technique of partial correlation also eliminates this possible influence so that we can determine the influence of instructional factors on end-of-the-year achievement independently of the influence of (a) beginning-of-the-year achievement on end-of-the-year achievement *and* (b) beginning-of-the-year achievement on instructional factors. If the researchers had been interested in removing the influence of beginning-of-the-year achievement from just one of the variables (e.g., its influence on instructional factors), the statistical method of **part correlation** would be used instead of partial correlation.

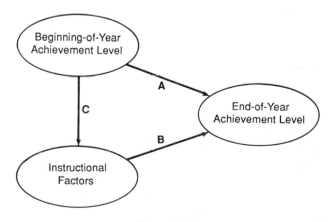

Figure 14.2

A complex causal pattern may well underly the variables studied by Peterson and Fennema. Partial correlation simplifies the situation so that just one part of the pattern (arrow B in figure 14.2) is analyzed. Other statistical techniques—path analysis and LISREL—provide a way to examine the full causal pattern with all its possible influences among variables. These techniques are described later in the chapter.

MULTIVARIATE CORRELATIONAL STATISTICS

The correlation techniques presented above are intended to help you measure the degree of relationship between two variables. Most of the research problems we study in the field of education, though, involve three or more variables. The multivariate techniques presented in the following sections allow you to measure and study the degree of relationship among various combinations of three or more variables. You should study these techniques in depth. They are used to analyze correlational data, but they are also used increasingly to analyze data from experiments. We shall discuss this latter use of multivariate techniques in chapters 15 and 16. Furthermore, they can be used in place of or as a supplement to the statistical techniques that have been used traditionally in causal-comparative research (see chapter 13).

Multiple Regression

Multiple regression is a multivariate technique for determining the correlation between a criterion variable and a combination of two or more predictor variables. It has become one of the most widely used statistical techniques in educational research.

The popularity of multiple regression stems from its considerable versatility and information yield about relationships among variables. It can be used to analyze data from any of the major research designs: causal-comparative, correlational, and experimental. It can handle interval, ordinal, or categorical data. And it provides estimates both of the magnitude and statistical significance of relationships among variables.

The use of multiple regression is illustrated in a relationship study conducted by Paula Jorde-Bloom and Martin Ford.[14] The purpose of their study was to identify factors that distinguish administrators of early childhood education programs who have adopted the use of microcomputers from

---

14. Paula Jorde-Bloom and Martin Ford, "Factors Influencing Early Childhood Administrators' Decisions Regarding the Adoption of Computer Technology," *Journal of Educational Computing Research* 4 (1988): 31–47.

administrators who have not. Jorde-Bloom and Ford observed that educational innovations keep appearing, and so administrators are responsible for deciding which innovations to consider for adoption and for managing the change process. They justified the need for their study in this way: "Thus, an awareness of some of the factors that help explain or predict innovation acceptance may broaden our understanding of how education professionals cope with a changing society."[15]

The researchers hypothesized that an administrator's decision to adopt computers would be influenced by four sets of factors: (1) relevant past experiences, (2) expectancies about what would happen if one decided to adopt computers, (3) openness to change, and (4) presence of support and encouragement from outside the organization. Eight measures of these factors were administered to the sample, as described below:

Relevant Past Experiences

1. *Computer experience.* Thirty-one questions about the administrator's experience with computer-related technology and microcomputers.
2. *Innovation experience.* Eight questions about experiences with other educational innovations.
3. *Math/science background.* Number of completed high school courses in math and science.

Expectancies

4. *Self-efficacy.* Fifteen questions about self-perceived ability and confidence to implement computer use.
5. *Consequences of use.* Twenty-one questions about appreciation of computers, computer anxiety, and beliefs about the societal impact of computers.

Openness to Change and Presence of Support

6. *Innovativeness.* Thirty-two questions about one's perceived tendency to innovate.
7. *Professional orientation.* Twenty-four questions about various aspects of the administrator's role: complexity of the organization, on-the-job activities, outside activities, highest degree obtained.
8. *Outside support.* Ten questions about the support for computer implementation that an administrator has received from spouse, friends, colleagues, or others.

15. Ibid., p. 32.

The administrator's age and gender also were viewed as possible influences on the decision to adopt computers, and so they were measured, too.

A sample of 80 administrators of early childhood programs in the state of Illinois completed the measures described above. They also completed measures of two criterion variables: (1) their level of computer implementation for administrative purposes, and (2) their level of computer implementation for instructional uses. The measure of each criterion variable assessed how far they had proceeded along a continuum of implementation: awareness, active information seeking, assessment, tentative adoption, and institutionalization. These two variables are listed at the top of the second and third columns of table 14.6. The intersects of these columns and rows show the correlation between each influence variable and each implementation variable. For example, the correlation between amount of outside support and level of computer implementation for administrative use is .40. This correlation is statistically significant at the .001 level.

The correlational analyses shown in table 14.6 form the basis for multiple regression. The purpose of this statistical technique is to determine which of the influence variables can be combined to form the best prediction of each criterion variable. In other words, the objective of multiple regression is to use the

TABLE 14.6

Correlations between Influence Variables and Computer Implementation Variables

Influence Variables	Administrative Use r	Instructional Use r
Computer experience	.74***	.57***
Innovation experience	.19*	.14
Math/science background	.34***	.19*
Self-efficacy	.69***	.61***
Consequences of use	.66***	.50***
Innovativeness	.45***	.46***
Professional orientation	.60***	.55***
Outside support	.40***	.31**
Age	.02	.07
Gender	−.20*	−.42***

SOURCE: Adapted from Paula Jorde-Bloom and Martin Ford, "Factors Influencing Early Childhood Administrators' Decisions Regarding the Adoption of Computer Technology," *Journal of Educational Computing Research* 4 (1988): 42.
* $p < .05$.
** $p < .01$.
*** $p < .001$.

subjects' scores on *some or all* of the influence measures to predict their scores on each criterion measure. In contrast, each bivariate correlation coefficient shown in table 14.6 represents the use of subjects' scores on *one* influence measure to predict each criterion measure.

A typical multiple regression analysis generated by a computer program will produce many statistics and equations. Only a few of them may appear in the published report. Others can be calculated if appropriate statistics are provided by the authors of the report. We can explain this point further by examining the multiple regression results presented in table 14.7.

The first column of table 14.7 lists the variables in the multiple regression analysis. Note that two multiple regression analyses were done, one for each criterion variable. In the first analysis, the criterion variable of level of computer implementation for administrative purposes was predicted from four influence variables: computer experience, professional orientation, self-efficacy, and math/science background. In the second analysis, the criterion variable of level of computer implementation for instructional use was predicted from a similar set of influence variables, but they entered the multiple regression at different steps.

We begin our explanation of table 14.7 by considering the third column. It presents the product-moment correlation coefficient between each influence variable and the pertinent criterion variable. These coefficients are the same as

TABLE 14.7

Stepwise Multiple Regression of Influence Variables on Administrators' Level of Computer Implementation

Influence Variables	Beta	Correlation Coefficient (r)	Multiple Correlation (R)	R^2	R^2 Increment
Implementation for Administrative Use					
1. Computer experience	.40	.74	.74	.54	
2. Professional orientation	.30	.60	.81	.66	.12
3. Self-efficacy	.28	.69	.83	.70	.04
4. Math/science background	.20	.34	.86	.73	.03
Implementation for Instructional Use					
1. Self-efficacy	.26	.61	.61	.37	
2. Professional orientation	.28	.55	.69	.47	.10
3. Gender	−.20	−.42	.71	.50	.03
4. Computer experience	.25	.57	.73	.54	.04

SOURCE: Adapted from Paula Jorde-Bloom and Martin Ford, "Factors Influencing Early Childhood Administrators' Decisions Regarding the Adoption of Computer Technology," *Journal of Educational Computing Research* 4 (1988): 43–44.

those that appear in table 14.6. For example, the correlation between computer experience and implementation for administrative use is .74 in table 14.6. This is the same value as the coefficient shown in table 14.7 (see the intersect of the first row of coefficients and the third column).

In explaining the other parts of table 14.7, we will concentrate on the analysis of level of computer implementation for administrative use (the top set of rows). You can extend the analysis on your own to the multiple regression results for level of computer implementation for instructional use.

The first step in multiple regression is usually to compute the correlation between the best predictor and the criterion variable. This procedure yields a multiple correlation coefficient (R), which is shown in the fourth column of table 14.7. Because computer experience is the best predictor ($r = .74$), it is the first predictor entered into the multiple regression. Note that the correlation coefficient ($r = .74$) is the same as the multiple correlation coefficient ($R = .74$).

Unless you specify otherwise, the computer program will start the multiple regression analysis with the most powerful predictor of the criterion variable. There are situations, however, in which you will want to enter a less powerful predictor first. For example, if the predictor variables can be ordered chronologically, you may wish to start the multiple regression analysis by entering the "earliest" predictor first. Another situation occurs when one of the predictors is well established in the field of education and another predictor is novel. For example, IQ as a predictor of school achievement is well established. Suppose you have developed a new measure of scholastic aptitude and are testing its predictive validity relative to an IQ measure. It makes sense to enter IQ scores first in the multiple regression—irrespective of their correlation with the criterion—and then to see how well the new measure improves upon the prediction.

Suppose you have not specified the order in which the predictor variables are to be entered into the multiple regression analysis. In this case, after selecting the best predictor, the computer program will search for the next best predictor of the criterion variable. This second predictor is not chosen on the basis of its product-moment correlation (r) with the criterion. Rather, the second predictor is chosen on the basis of how well it improves upon the prediction achieved by the first variable.

What qualities should a variable have to be a good second predictor? First, it should correlate as little as possible with the first predictor variable. If it correlates with the first variable entered in the multiple regression analysis, there is the possibility that it will predict the same variance in the criterion variable as the first variable. For example, suppose an IQ test and a scholastic aptitude test are used to predict fifth-grade reading achievement. The two predictor variables are likely to correlate highly with each other because they measure the same underlying factor. If IQ scores are entered in the multiple regression first, the scholastic aptitude test is unlikely to improve upon the prediction since it mostly represents the same factor as the IQ test. The situation is comparable to using the same IQ scores a second time to improve upon the prediction achieved by using them the first time.

The second quality of a good second predictor is obvious: It should correlate as highly as possible with the criterion variable. In short, a good second predictor is one that correlates as little as possible with the first predictor and as highly as possible with the criterion.

Table 14.7 indicates that professional orientation was the second variable entered in the multiple regression analysis. The two predictor variables together yield a multiple correlation coefficient of .81. This is a moderate improvement upon the prediction achieved by just using computer experience as a predictor ($R = .74$).

At this point you may ask why professional orientation improves the prediction relatively little, given that professional orientation on its own correlates .60 with the criterion. The reason for this phenomenon was discussed above. Administrators' scores on the measures of computer experience and professional orientation are undoubtedly correlated (in fact, $r = .38$). Because of this overlap, professional orientation does not have a chance to improve dramatically upon the prediction made by computer experience, which entered the multiple regression analysis first.

The overlap between two predictor variables, that is, the extent to which they intercorrelate with each other, is called **collinearity.** If there is a lot of collinearity between the predictor variables, only some of them will enter the multiple regression analysis as predictors, even though all of them may predict the criterion variable to an extent. This was evidently the case in this analysis. All of the influence variables, except age, correlated significantly with the criterion variable (see table 14.6, column 2), but only a few of them contributed to the multiple regression analysis.

The third predictor entered in the multiple regression analysis is determined by whether it improves upon the prediction made by the first two predictors. We see in table 14.7 that self-efficacy improves the multiple correlation coefficient slightly to .83.

The computer program will keep adding predictor variables until there are none left. Each new predictor variable will contribute less to R than the preceding predictor, however, in which case there are rapidly diminishing returns for adding new predictors. A test of statistical significance can be used to limit the number of predictor variables that are used. The researcher can specify in the computer program that new predictor variables are not to be added to the multiple regression analysis unless their contribution to R is statistically significant.

At this point we can consider further the meaning of R. The **multiple correlation coefficient (R)** is a measure of the magnitude of relationship between a criterion variable and a predictor variable or some combination of predictor variables. The value of R will increase with each variable that enters the multiple regression analysis. Thus, we see that in table 14.7 that the value of R gradually increases from .74 to .86 as each predictor variable is added. The value of .86 represents the best prediction one can make of level of computer implementation for administrative use from the influence variables listed in table 14.6. The value of R can range from 0.00 to 1.00; negative values are not possible. The larger the R, the better the prediction.

If R is squared, it will yield a statistic known as the **coefficient of determination (R^2)**. The fifth column of table 14.7 shows the R^2 coefficients corresponding to the Rs in the fourth column. For example, the topmost R^2 coefficient is .54, which is the square of the corresponding R coefficient (.74). R^2 expresses the amount of variance in the criterion variable that is predictable from a predictor variable or combination of predictor variables.

The final column of table 14.7 presents the R^2 increments for the multiple regression analysis. The **R^2 increment** is a statistic that expresses the additional variance in the criterion variable that can be explained by adding a new predictor variable to the multiple regression analysis. For example, the addition of professional orientation to the analysis explains 12 percent more of the variance in the criterion variable (.66 − .54 = .12) than can be explained by computer experience alone. Adding self-efficacy to the analysis results in an R^2 increment of just 4 percent, meaning that it predicts 4 percent more of the variance in level of computer implementation for administrative use than can be predicted by computer experience and professional orientation together.

Two tests of statistical significance are commonly done in multiple regression analysis. One test is done to determine whether the obtained value of R is significantly different from 0. The other test, as we explained above, is done to determine whether the R^2 increment is statistically significant. For example, one could test whether the R^2 of .66 that is obtained by adding professional orientation to the multiple regression analysis is significantly different from the R^2 of .54 obtained without using this variable as a predictor.

The mathematical basis for multiple regression is an equation that links the predictor variable(s) to the criterion variable. Suppose that level of computer implementation for administrative use = Y, computer experience = X_1, professional orientation = X_2, self-efficacy = X_3, and math/science background = X_4. Using C to stand for a constant term, we may state the multiple regression equation as:

$$\hat{Y} = b_1X_1 + b_2X_2 + b_3X_3 + b_4X_4 + C$$

Note that $\hat{Y}$ has a circumflex above it to indicate that the Y scores are being predicted from the X variables. The predicted values of $\hat{Y}$ will deviate from students' actual Y scores because X_1, X_2, X_3, and X_4 are not perfect predictors. Note, too, that this equation is similar to the straight-line equation for bivariate correlation ($\hat{Y} = bX + a$).

Each b value in the multiple regression equation is a **regression weight,** which can vary from −1.00 to +1.00. A separate regression weight (sometimes called a b weight) is calculated for each predictor variable. When each student's scores on the predictor variables are multiplied by their respective regression weights and then summed, the result is the best possible prediction of the student's score on the criterion variable.

Sometimes b weights are converted to beta (β) weights. **Beta weights** are the regression weights in a multiple regression equation in which all of the variables in the equation are in standard score form. Some researchers prefer beta weights because they form an absolute scale. For example, a beta weight of $+.40$ is of greater magnitude than a beta weight of $+.30$ irrespective of the predictor variable with which it is associated. In contrast, the magnitude of a b weight is dependent upon the scale form of the predictor measure with which it is associated. Beta weights can be converted to b weights, and vice versa, using the formula $b = \beta (S_y/S_x)$ where S_y and S_x are the standard deviations of the Y and X variables, respectively.

If you look at table 14.7, you will see that beta weights for each of the predictor variables are presented. With this information, we can construct the multiple regression equation as follows:

$$\hat{Y} = .40X_1 + .30X_2 + .28X_3 + .20X_4 + C$$

where each of the variables is in standard score form. In other words, we can predict an administrator's level of computer implementation for administrative use quite well if we multiply his or her computer experience score by .40, professional orientation score by .30, self-efficacy score by .28, and math/science background score by .20.

The magnitude of a predictor variable's beta weight should not be confused with its importance. A predictor variable can be theoretically significant and highly correlated with the criterion, yet have a low beta weight. The beta weight is arbitrary to an extent, because it depends on the predictor variable's correlation with the other predictors. If the researcher has chosen to enter the predictors in a prespecified order, the beta weights will be dependent on that factor, too.

There are several variations of multiple regression analysis: stepup (also called "forward"), stepdown (also called "backward"), and stepwise. Each variation uses a different procedure for selecting a subset of predictor variables that yields the best prediction of a criterion variable. The title of table 14.7 indicates that Jorde-Bloom and Ford used a stepwise multiple regression procedure.

Multiple regression analysis is sometimes misused by researchers. One common problem is to confuse prediction with explanation. The procedures are relatively straightforward if the purpose is to optimize prediction of a criterion variable. You should be careful, however, if you have a theory that attributes causal significance to the predictor variables. In this situation, you should not confuse the causal significance of a predictor variable with its regression weight or R^2 increment value in a multiple regression equation. If you wish to test a causal theory by using multivariate correlational data, you are advised to consider path analysis or LISREL (both techniques are discussed later in the chapter) rather than multiple regression.

We also caution you to retain a reasonable balance between sample size and number of predictor variables. In the extreme case where sample size equals number of predictors, R will equal 1.00 (perfect prediction), even if none of the predictors is correlated with the criterion. The multiple regression equation resulting from this analysis will almost certainly yield very poor predictions for a new sample of subjects. A rough rule of thumb is to increase sample size by at least 15 subjects for each variable that will be included in the multiple regression. Using this rule, you would select a sample of at least 45 subjects for a multiple regression analysis involving three predictor variables.

Discriminant Analysis

Discriminant analysis is similar to multiple regression in that both statistical techniques involve two or more predictor variables and a single criterion variable. Discriminant analysis, however, is limited to the special case in which the criterion is a person's group membership. Examples of group membership are male versus female; high-achieving student versus low-achieving student; engineer versus physicist versus doctor. The discriminant analysis equation uses a person's scores on the predictor variables in an attempt to predict the group of which the person is a member.

Discriminant analysis was used in a study of high-achieving and low-achieving students in the tenth grade by Barry Zimmerman and Manuel Pons.[16] The purpose of their study was to determine whether these two groups of students differ in use of "self-regulated learning strategies," which are similar in meaning to what is meant by "study skills." Forty high-achieving and 40 low-achieving students were interviewed to collect data on their use of the 15 self-regulated learning strategies listed in the first column of table 14.8. The next two columns of that table report each group's mean score on a measure of their frequency of use of each strategy.

One way to analyze the results shown in table 14.8 would be to do fifteen *t*-tests, each one comparing the mean scores of the high-achieving and low-achieving group on a different strategy. Another approach is to do a discriminant analysis to determine how well the students' scores on the measures of the

16. Barry J. Zimmerman and Manuel Martinez Pons, "Development of a Structured Interview for Assessing Student Use of Self-Regulated Learning Strategies," *American Educational Research Journal* 23 (1986): 614–628.

TABLE 14.8

Differences between High-Achieving and Low-Achieving Students on Self-Regulated Learning Strategies

Strategy	High-Achieving M	Low-Achieving M	Discriminant Function Coefficients[a]
Self-evaluating one's work	.97	.78	.17
Organizing study material	3.86	1.18	.42
Goal-setting and planning	3.03	1.55	.41
Seeking information	4.40	1.41	.58
Keeping notes and monitoring	3.98	1.65	.43
Structuring study settings	1.90	.97	.29
Arranging consequences for success or failure	1.70	.30	.13
Rehearsing and memorizing	2.27	.98	.41
Seeking peer assistance	1.75	.57	.00
Seeking teacher assistance	2.25	.67	.36
Seeking adult assistance	1.10	.17	.31
Reviewing tests	1.05	.40	−.11
Reviewing notes	4.65	2.48	.15
Reviewing text	2.85	1.05	.31
Total	35.77	14.16	
Other	1.17	2.21	−.09

SOURCE: Adapted from Barry J. Zimmerman and Manuel Martinez Pons, "Development of a Structured Interview for Assessing Student Use of Self-Regulated Learning Strategies," *American Educational Research Journal* 23 (1986): 621.
[a] Coefficients in this column are standardized.

15 strategies (the predictor variables) discriminate between students who are high or low in academic achievement (the criterion variable). Using this approach, the researchers found that high-achieving and low-achieving students differed significantly in their use of the 15 learning strategies. The discriminant analysis equation correctly classified the group membership (high or low achievement) of 93 percent of the students in the sample.

The discriminant analysis equation applies a weight, called a *discrimination function coefficient*, to each student's score on each variable. The weights, which are similar to beta weights in a multiple regression equation, are shown in the fourth column of table 14.8. A student's standardized score on each variable is multiplied by this weight to predict his or her group membership. Greater weights, whether positive or negative, contribute more to predicting the student's group membership. We find in table 14.8 that the self-regulated learning strategies of seeking information, keeping notes and monitoring, organizing study material, and goal-setting and planning are especially important in predicting students' achievement level.

We need to realize that the discrimination function coefficients do not indicate the magnitude of correlation between each of the predictor variables and the criterion variable.[17] Two predictor variables may predict the criterion variable almost equally, but if they correlate with each other highly, the predictor variable that is entered into the discriminant analysis equation first will have a high discrimination function coefficient, and the other will have a low discrimination function coefficient. A bivariate correlational statistic, such as the product-moment *r*, can be used to determine the degree of relationship between each predictor variable and the criterion variable.

Discriminant analysis is elegant in its conciseness because it yields a single equation linking the predictor variables and criterion variable. It requires, however, complex computations and a sophisticated knowledge of the mathematical basis of statistics to interpret the results. For this reason, if you are planning to use this technique, we advise you to work alongside an expert statistician. You may wish to supplement the discriminant analysis by using simpler statistical methods such as product-moment correlation.

Canonical Correlation

Canonical correlation is a multivariate correlational technique in which a combination of several predictor variables is used to predict a combination of several criterion variables. This technique is similar to multivariate analysis of variance (described in the previous chapter), which has a dependent variable that is a composite of two or more variables. Canonical correlation is also similar to multiple regression, which involves the combination of several predictor variables to predict a criterion. In multiple regression, however, there is a single criterion variable to be predicted. In canonical correlation, two or more variables form the criterion.

Suppose that you have access to students' scores on a set of predictor variables such as scholastic aptitude, family socioeconomic status, high school gradepoint average, vocational interests, and extraversion-introversion. Also available are students' scores on criterion variables measured later in life, such as years of postsecondary education, annual salary, levels of physical and mental health, and contributions to the community. One method for understanding the relationships between the predictor variables and criterion variables is to correlate each predictor variable with each criterion variable using the bivariate

---

17. Similarly, regression weights or beta weights in a multiple regression equation do not indicate the magnitude of correlation between each predictor variable and the criterion variable.

correlational techniques (e.g., the product-moment correlation coefficient) described earlier in this chapter. Another approach is to ask the question, What *set* of predictor variables best predicts what *set* of criterion variables? The method used to answer this question is canonical correlation.

A research study by Michael Kerr, Sidney McPhee, and Paul Kleine illustrates the use of canonical correlation.[18] The purpose of the study was to test the validity of the Oklahoma Curriculum Proficiency Examination, which is a state-mandated teacher competency test. The researchers reasoned that the scores of secondary teaching candidates on it would have a positive correlation with their academic grades, because the content of the test was intended to reflect somewhat the content of the students' academic program.

The sample of teaching candidates took a version of the teacher competency test corresponding to their subject area specialization. The four versions of the test are listed in the first column of table 14.9. The four or five subtests that make up each version are also listed in this column.

The teaching candidates' achievement was measured by three variables: (1) GPA for courses taken in a candidate's fields of specialization; (2) GPA for professional education courses taken; and (3) cumulative GPA across all subjects. The total number of variables, then, was seven or eight: three GPA variables and four or five teacher competency subtest variables.

The researchers determined the relationship between the GPA variables and the subtest variables by using the technique of canonical correlation. This technique yields a canonical correlation coefficient R, which indicates the magnitude of the relationship between the two sets of variables. The R value for teaching candidates who took each version of the teacher competency test is shown in the last column of table 14.9. Only the R value for the Language Arts test is statistically significant, meaning that the composite variable representing the GPA variables is a statistically significant predictor of the composite variable representing the subtests of the Language Arts test. Each of these composite variables is called a **variate.** They are similar to the "factors" in factor analysis, a technique that is described later in the chapter.

The finding of nonsignificant R values for three of the four versions of the Oklahoma Curriculum Proficiency Examination led the researchers to conclude that its validity is questionable.

The mathematical basis for canonical correlation is quite complex, as are the computational procedures and interpretation of the results. Yet canonical correlation appears with increasing frequency in the research literature, as researchers become interested in including more variables in their projects. Canonical correlation can be used in practical prediction, although this application seems limited because the purpose of practical prediction usually is to select

18. Michael E. Kerr, Sidney A. McPhee, and Paul Kleine, "Scholastic Aptitude and Achievement as Predictors of Performance on Teacher Competency Tests: A Further Investigation," *Journal of Educational Research* 80 (1987): 266–271.

TABLE 14.9

Canonical Correlations between Teacher Competency Test Variables and GPA Variables

Teacher Competency Test Variables	Canonical R	Canonical R^2
Language arts test	.68	.47*
Grammar and composition		
Reading skills		
Literature		
Research skills		
Additional areas		
Mathematics test	.45	.21
General math		
Geometry		
Algebra		
Advanced math		
Science test	.47	.22
Science education		
Life sciences		
Earth science		
Physical science		
Social studies test	.44	.19
Political science		
Geography		
History		
Oklahoma history		
Additional areas		

SOURCE: Adapted from Michael E. Kerr, Sidney A. McPhee, and Paul Kleine, "Scholastic Aptitude and Achievement as Predictors of Performance on Teacher Competency Tests: A Further Investigation," *Journal of Educational Research* 80 (1987): 267–269.
* $p < .05$

persons who are likely to do well on a single important criterion. Canonical correlation is most often used when the researcher plans to undertake an exploratory relationship study to determine how a large number of variables measured at the same or different points in time relate to one another.

Path Analysis

Path analysis is a method for testing the validity of a theory about causal relationships between three or more variables that have been studied using a correlational research design. Path analysis is similar to the other multivariate methods described above—multiple regression, discriminant analysis, canonical correlation, and factor analysis—in that its concern is with the relationships among *three* or more variables. The primary difference between path analysis and the other multivariate methods is in its purpose. Path analysis is used solely to test theories about hypothesized causal links between variables. In contrast, the other multivariate methods are used primarily to maximize the correlation between various combinations of variables. Occasionally they are used to examine hypotheses about causal relationships between variables, but they are much less powerful than path analysis for this purpose.

Path analysis has a complicated rationale and set of statistical procedures associated with it. Despite its difficulty, you are advised to become familiar with path analysis for several reasons. First, knowledge about the method of path analysis should deepen your understanding of the limitations and uses of correlational research design. Second, path analysis provides a better basis for examining causal relationships in correlational data than other methods, even though some of the other methods are simpler to apply.

To illustrate path analysis, we will consider a study by Edwin Bridges and Maureen Hallinan on teacher absenteeism in school districts.[19] These research- ers were interested in identifying factors that explain why some teachers more often do not show up for work than other teachers. The basic theory guiding their search for explanatory variables is that teacher absenteeism is sometimes used to achieve temporary relief from an unrewarding work context.

Teacher absenteeism was measured in this study by counting the number of one-day absence episodes occurring on Mondays and Fridays over an entire school year. For the primary analysis, the following variables were also measured:

1. *Work system interdependence.* Measured by having teachers rate the extent to which they interact with others in various school activities.
2. *Group cohesion.* Measured by having teachers complete a scale of how well they like their co-workers.
3. *Communication.* Measured by having teachers estimate the frequency with which they talk to other teachers about certain topics.
4. *Subunit size.* Measured by the number of full-time teachers spending their entire workday in the school.

With the exception of subunit size, all the variables were measured for each teacher in a participating school and then averaged to yield a single score for that school. Thus, the unit of analysis was the school. A total of 57 K-6 elementary schools participated in the study.

Table 14.10 presents the correlation matrix of all the variables mentioned above. How are we to interpret these results? As the purpose of the study was to

---

19. Edwin M. Bridges and Maureen T. Hallinan, "Subunit Size, Work System Interdependence, and Employee Absenteeism," *Educational Administration Quarterly* 14 (1978): 24–42.

TABLE 14.10

Correlation Matrix for Variables in Teacher Absenteeism Study

	Work System Interdependence	Communication	Group Cohesion	Absenteeism
Subunit size	.00	.24*	−.14	.35*
Work system interdependence		.51*	.34*	−.24*
Communication			.28*	.10
Group cohesion				−.32*
Absenteeism				

Source: Adapted from Edwin M. Bridges and Maureen T. Hallinan, "Subunit Size, Work System Interdependence, and Employee Absenteeism," *Educational Administration Quarterly* 14 (1978): 32.
$* p < .05.$

identify possible causes of teacher absenteeism, we can examine how well each of the other variables predict it. Three of the four variables are statistically significant predictors of teacher absenteeism: subunit size ($r = .35$), work system interdependence ($r = −.24$), and group cohesion ($r = −.32$). However, just because these variables predict teacher absenteeism does not mean they "cause" the absenteeism. Also, a very real problem is created by the fact that the predictor variables correlate with each other. For example, work system interdependence and group cohesion both predict teacher absenteeism, and they also correlate with each other ($r = .34$). Does group cohesion affect absenteeism independently of work system interdependence? Does work system interdependence affect absenteeism independently of group cohesion? And what about the fact that the variable of communication correlates significantly with both work system interdependence ($r = .51$) and group cohesion ($r = .28$)? Partial correlation, which was described earlier in the chapter, might be used to illuminate some of the relationships stated in these questions. Path analysis, however, is a more powerful method for disentangling the varied connections between variables suggested by the correlation matrix.

Path analysis consists basically of three steps. The first step is to formulate a theory linking the variables of interest. Bridges and Hallinan formulated two theories. The first theory linked size of the work unit to teacher absenteeism by positing the following causal connections: "Large size increases the difficulties of maintaining communications among employees; lower levels of communications reduce group cohesiveness; low group cohesiveness leads to higher rates of employee absenteeism."[20] The second theory linked work system

20. Ibid., p. 25.

interdependence (the extent to which an organization's primary mission is planned and carried out collaboratively by employees) to teacher absenteeism. The theory posited that higher degrees of interdependence in school work systems will increase the rate of interaction (communication) among teachers; increased interaction will be reinforcing to teachers and thus group cohesion will increase over time; and increased group cohesion will lead to reduced teacher absenteeism.

After a theory has been formulated, the next step in path analysis is to select or develop measures of the variables (sometimes called "theoretical constructs" in this context) that are specified by the theory. This step is important because the path analysis will yield invalid results if the measures are not valid representations of the variables. You may want to identify more than one measure for each variable. Alternate measures of important educational variables are often available.[21]

The third step in path analysis is to compute the statistics that show the strength of relationship between each of the pairs of variables that are causally linked in the theory. Finally, you must interpret the statistics to determine whether they support or disconfirm the theory.

We can illustrate the procedures of path analysis by considering again Bridges and Hallinan's study of teacher absenteeism. You will recall that their basic theory was that teachers resort to absenteeism because they are trying to achieve temporary relief from an unrewarding work context. In the more articulated form of the theory, subunit size and work system interdependence were linked to teacher absenteeism through their effects on communication and group cohesion. These connections are shown in figure 14.3. This type of figure is the standard way of representing path analysis variables. Note that each variable in the theory is represented in the figure. Also note the use of arrows in the figure. Each straight arrow indicates a hypothesized causal relationship in the direction of the arrow; for example, size of subunit influences communication, communication influences group cohesion, and so on.

Several other features of the path analysis in figure 14.3 should be observed at this time. Note that all the straight arrows point in one direction. For example, communication is hypothesized to influence group cohesion, but group cohesion is not hypothesized to influence communication. When a path analysis is ordered in this way, it is said to be based on a recursive model. A **recursive model** is one which only considers unidirectional causal relationships. If variable A is hypothesized to influence variable B, you cannot also hypothesize that variable B influences variable A. A **nonrecursive model** should be used if you wish to test hypotheses involving reciprocal causation between pairs of variables.

21. If alternate measures of variables are administered, the researcher should consider using LISREL (discussed later in the chapter) rather than path analysis to analyze the data.

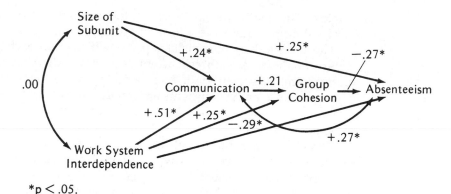

*p < .05.

Figure 14.3   Path Analysis of the Effects of Subunit Size and Work System Interdependence on Teacher Absenteeism.

Source: Adapted from Edwin M. Bridges and Maureen T. Hallinan, "Subunit Size, Work System Interdependence, and Employee Absenteeism," *Educational Administration Quarterly* 14 (1978): 33.

Two of the arrows in figure 14.3 are curved and double-headed. This type of arrow linking two variables indicates that the researcher has not hypothesized how the variables might be causally related to each other. Figure 14.3 indicates that in designing their path analysis, Bridges and Hallinan did not hypothesize how subunit size and work system interdependence might be causally related, nor how communication and absenteeism might be causally related. To clarify, a curved arrow in a path analysis indicates the lack of a hypothesis about causality. A straight arrow indicates the presence of a hypothesis about causality. The hypothesis can predict no correlation, a positive correlation, or a negative correlation between the two variables.

Two types of variable are commonly distinguished in path analysis. **Exogenous variables** are variables that lack hypothesized causes in the path analysis model. Subunit size and work system interdependence are exogenous variables because no variables are hypothesized to influence them. **Endogenous variables** are variables that have at least one hypothesized cause in the path analysis model. For example, group cohesion is an endogenous variable because it is hypothesized to be influenced by communication.

The next step in path analysis is to measure each of the variables specified in the model. You will recall that we described above how each of the variables in figure 14.3 was measured by the researchers.

At this point in the path analysis, the exogenous and endogenous variables have been identified and measured; and the causal links specified by the researchers' theory have been identified by arrows. The next step is to perform a statistical analysis to determine the strength of association between each set of variables. The mathematical basis of the statistical procedures is complex. Basically the procedures are a form of multiple regression.

The statistical analysis yields a path coefficient for each pair of variables in the path analysis. A **path coefficient** is a standardized regression coefficient indicating the direct effect of one variable on another variable in the path analysis. Because path coefficients are standardized regression coefficients, they have the same meaning as the beta (B) coefficients calculated in multiple regression.

What does the numerical value of a path coefficient mean? The path coefficient can be viewed as a type of correlation coefficient. Like correlation coefficients, path coefficients can range in value from -1.00 to $+1.00$. The larger the value, the stronger the association between the two variables. The meaning of the path coefficient differs, though, depending on the two variables being correlated. Consider first the case of two variables that are dependent on no other variables (viewed as causes) within the path analysis model. Size of subunit and work unit interdependence in figure 14.3 are two such variables. Neither variable is caused by any other variable within the model. In this case the path coefficient is equal to the product-moment correlation (r) for the two variables. If you refer to table 14.10 and figure 14.3, you will see that the path coefficient and correlation coefficient for subunit size and work unit interdependence are exactly the same ($p = r = .00$).

The path coefficient also equals the product-moment coefficient when one variable (A) is viewed as dependent on a single cause (variable B) within the path analysis model. For example, in the following figure variable A is viewed as the single cause of variable B, and therefore the path coefficient (P_{ab}) is equal to the product-moment correlation coefficient for these variables.

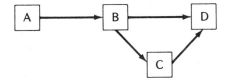

Still another situation where p equals r is the case of a variable that is dependent on more than one cause within the path analysis, but the causes are viewed as independent of each other.

Now we can consider the case of path coefficients that do not satisfy the requirements described above. In fact, none of the path coefficients in figure 14.3—except the path coefficient for subunit size and work system interdependence—satisfies the requirements. These path coefficients are similar, but not identical, to partial correlation coefficients in that they represent the strength of association between two variables with the effect of other pertinent variables partialed out. For example, the path coefficient between subunit size and absenteeism in figure 14.3 is .25, which represents their strength of association with communication and group cohesion partialed out.

You will note that the path coefficient (.25) is somewhat less than the product-moment r for the same variables ($r = .35$, as shown in table 14.10). This result means that subunit size has some direct effect on teacher absenteeism, but that part of its effect is indirect. The "indirect" effect means that part of the effect of subunit size on teacher absenteeism is due to its effect on communication. The total indirect effect of a variable is equal to the r between it and the dependent variable minus the corresponding path coefficient. For the effect of subunit size on teacher absenteeism, the direct effect is .25 and the indirect effect is .10 (.35 − .25). This analysis indicates that the direct effect of subunit size upon teacher absenteeism (.25) is substantially more potent than its indirect effects (.10).

The final step in path analysis is to determine whether the results support the theory. In the research study we have been considering, Bridges and Hallinan concluded that their theory was not supported since the effects of subunit size and work system interdependence on teacher absenteeism are not entirely mediated by communication and group cohesion.[22]

In summary, the major advantage of path analysis is that it enables the researcher to test causal theories using correlational data. Other multivariate techniques, such as multiple regression and canonical correlation, are not well suited for this purpose. Rather, these techniques are best used to maximize the prediction of one or more criterion variables from a set of predictor variables.

If you plan to do a path analysis, you should study this method carefully and consult an expert statistician if necessary. The calculation of path coefficients and testing them for statistical significance are difficult procedures. The data need to satisfy certain assumptions, and the results of the path analysis can be misleading if the variables are not well measured, if important causal variables are left out of the theoretical model, or if the sample size is insufficient for the number of variables being considered.

Of these problems, underspecification of the causal model is probably the most serious. Thomas Cook and Donald Campbell provide an example of how underspecification can distort the interpretation of path results.[23] They note that students who have attended a Head Start program (HS) are likely to have lower first-grade achievement scores (Ach) than students who have not attended such a program. Thus, if HS → Ach specifies a complete causal model, the path coefficient will be negative ($B = -.19$), as shown in figure 14.4a. We would conclude that Head Start has a harmful effect on student learning.

22. Bridges and Hallinan's results have been simplified for our purposes. Additional data analyses related to their theory can be found in their journal report.
23. Thomas D. Cook and Donald T. Campbell, *Quasi-Experimentation: Design and Analysis Issues for Field Settings* (Chicago: Rand McNally, 1979).

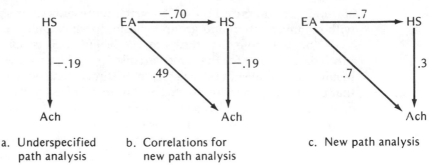

a. Underspecified   b. Correlations for   c. New path analysis
   path analysis   new path analysis

Figure 14.4   Underspecified and Better-specified Path Analyses
SOURCE: Adapted from Thomas D. Cook and Donald T. Campbell, *Quasi-Experimentation: Design and Analysis Issues for Field Settings* (Chicago: Rand McNally, 1979), p. 306.

The problem with this causal model is that it omits an important cause of first-grade achievement. We can call this causal variable Educational Advantage (EA), which is usually measured by some index of socioeconomic status. Students from high socioeconomic status homes usually perform better in school, and so the correlation between EA and Ach is positive (.49) in figure 14.4b. Students with high EA are also less likely to attend a Head Start program; hence, the negative correlation between EA and HS (−.70).

Now examine the path analysis in 14.4c based on the correlation coefficients of figure 14.4b. You will note that the path coefficient for the HS → Ach link is positive ($B = .3$), whereas in figure 14.4a the path coefficient is negative. This example thus provides a demonstration of how a path coefficient can change signs depending on how completely the model is specified. Underspecified models should be avoided because they can lead to serious errors of causal inferences.

The Correlation Matrix and Factor Analysis

Factor analysis is one of the most frequently used techniques in multivariate research, because researchers often measure a large number of variables in a single research project. Data analysis and interpretation are unwieldly in situations involving many variables. **Factor analysis** is helpful to the researcher because it provides an empirical basis for reducing the many variables to a few factors by combining variables that are moderately or highly correlated with each other. Each set of variables that is combined forms a **factor,** which is a mathematical expression of the common element that cuts across the combined variables.

The use of factor analysis is illustrated in a study by Robert Kottkamp, John Mulhern, and Wayne Hoy.[24] The purpose of their study was to develop an instrument to measure school climate at the secondary school level. Factor analysis was used twice in the development of the instrument, called the Rutgers Organizational Climate Description Questionnaire for Secondary Schools (OCDQ-RS). The first use was to identify commonalities in a large pool of items written to measure various aspects of school climate.

Through this use of factor analysis and other techniques, the researchers eventually developed an instrument, the OCDQ-RS, consisting of five subscales that measure five dimensions of school climate. The labels for the subscales and a sample item from each one are as follows:

1. *Supportive principal behavior.* "The principal uses supportive criticism."
2. *Directive principal behavior.* "The principal rules with an iron fist."
3. *Engaged teacher behavior.* "Teachers spend time after school with students who have individual problems."
4. *Frustrated teacher behavior.* "Assigned nonteaching duties are excessive."
5. *Intimate teacher behavior.* "Teachers invite other faculty members to visit them at home."

The instrument is completed by the school's teachers, who rate each item for its frequency of occurrence.

The second factor analysis was done to determine whether the five subscales of the OCDQ-RS could be grouped into a smaller number of factors. The first step in the factor analysis procedure is to compute a **correlation matrix,** which shows the correlation between every possible pair of variables to be analyzed. The correlation matrix for the five OCDQ-RS subscales is shown in table 14.11. Each subscale is listed on a separate row and column. Because there are five subscales, the matrix has five rows and four columns. The correlation between any two variables is given at the point where the row and column corresponding to the variables cross. For example, the correlation between directive principal behavior and frustrated teacher behavior is .41, which is located at the intersect of row 2 and column 4.

Only half of a row-by-column matrix is necessary to show the correlation between all possible pairs of variables. That is why the space below the diagonal is blank. Also, there is no column 1 corresponding to variable 1. That is because the correlation between variable 1 and itself is 1.00. The same is true of the other variables: The correlation between variable 2 and itself is 1.00, and so on. The

24. Robert B. Kottkamp, John A. Mulhern, and Wayne K. Hoy, "Secondary School Climate: A Revision of the OCDQ," *Educational Administration Quarterly* 23 (1987): 31–48.

TABLE 14.11

Correlation Matrix and Factor Analysis of the Five Subtests of the OCDQ-RS

Subtest	Intercorrelations				Factors	
	2	3	4	5	1	2
1. Supportive principal behavior	−.09	.36**	−.30*	.05	.56	.28
2. Directive principal behavior		−.20	.41**	−.04	−.62	.27
3. Engaged teacher behavior			−.51**	.16	.73	.33
4. Frustrated teacher behavior				.00	−.85	.09
5. Intimate teacher behavior					.01	.89

SOURCE: Adapted from Robert B. Kottkamp, John A. Mulhern, and Wayne K. Hoy, "Secondary School Climate: A Revision of the OCDQ," *Educational Administration Quarterly* 23 (1987): 45.
* $p < .01$. ** $p < .001$.

correlation between a variable and itself is not usually shown in a correlation matrix.

After preparing the correlation matrix, the researchers did a factor analysis to determine whether the five variables represented by the subscales could be described by a smaller number of factors. The factors identified as a result of the analysis are presented in the last two columns of table 14.11.

The mathematical basis for factor analysis is complex. Basically, it involves a search for clusters of variables that are all intercorrelated with each other. The first cluster of variables that is identified is called the first factor; it represents the variables that are most intercorrelated with each other. The factor is represented as a score, which is generated for each subject in the sample. Thus, it is possible to compute a correlation coefficient between students' factor score and their score on a particular variable that was entered into the factor analysis. These coefficients are presented under the heading, Factor I, in table 14.11. The individual coefficients are sometimes called the **loading** of each variable on the factor.

Inspection of the Factor I loadings indicates that the first four variables correlate moderately or highly with the factor. The researcher needs to interpret the pattern of correlation to determine the conceptual meaning of the underlying factor. In the case of this study, the researchers decided that the construct underlying Factor I was openness, which they defined as follows:

openness refers to a school climate where both the teachers' and principal's behaviors are authentic, energetic, goal-directed, and supportive, and in which satisfaction is derived from both task-accomplishment and social need gratification.[25]

This interpretation of Factor I fits the observed correlations well. The variables of supportive principal behavior and engaged teacher behavior both correlate positively with the factor (.56 and .73, respectively); and the variables of directive principal behavior and frustrated teacher behavior both correlate negatively with it (−.62 and −.85, respectively).

Table 14.11 indicates that the variable of intimate teacher behavior does not correlate with the first factor ($r = .01$). Instead, it is heavily loaded on the second factor ($r = .89$). The other variables have low correlations with this second factor. Therefore, the researchers identified the construct underlying this factor as intimacy, which they defined as follows:

> Intimacy . . . reflects a strong and cohesive network of social relationships among the faculty. Teachers know each other well, have close personal friends among the faculty, and regularly socialize together. The friendly social interactions that are the essence of this construct are limited, however, to social needs; in fact, task accomplishment does not seem germane to this dimension.[26]

The two factors of openness and intimacy represent much of the information contained in the larger correlation matrix. Each factor can be treated as a variable, and each student can be given a score on it, called a **factor score.** The factor scores can be used in subsequent statistical analyses. For example, a t-test can be done to determine whether public and private secondary schools differ significantly on the first factor.

Factor analysis is a valuable tool in educational research, but it needs to be used carefully. A frequent caution given to the novice researcher is "Garbage in, garbage out," meaning that the factors generated by a factor analysis are only as interpretable as the variables entered into the correlation matrix. Therefore, the researcher should carefully consider the number and types of variables that are to be entered into the factor analysis. If the variables have little or nothing conceptually in common, a factor analysis would be inappropriate.

Several variations of factor analysis are available. For example, a factor analysis can be done to yield an **orthogonal solution,** meaning that the resulting factors are uncorrelated with each other. An orthogonal solution is desirable if we seek a "pure" set of factors, with each measuring a construct that does not overlap with constructs measured by other factors. In certain situations,

25. Ibid., p. 46.
26. Ibid., p. 46.

however, it is desirable to do a factor analysis with an **oblique solution,** meaning that factors can be derived that do correlate with each other. For example, a factor analysis of tests of intellectual ability may yield such factors as verbal ability, mathematical ability, logical reasoning ability, listening ability, and so on. These factors may correlate with each other because part of each factor measures an underlying construct of general intelligence.

The decision as to which type of factor analysis to use involves many considerations. Therefore, we advise you to consult an expert statistician for assistance in planning a factor analysis for a particular set of data.

Structural Equation Modeling

A sophisticated new method for multivariate correlational analysis has become available in recent years. The method is similar to path analysis in that it can be used to test theories or models of causal relationships between variables. It is more powerful than path analysis, however, because it yields more valid and reliable measures of the variables to be analyzed. Because the measures are more valid and reliable, a more powerful test of a causal theory or model can be made.

This statistical method is called **structural equation modeling.** It is also sometimes called **LISREL,** which is the name of the computer program that was developed to run it.[27] LISREL is an acronym for "Analysis of Linear Structural Relationships." The method sometimes is called **latent variable causal modeling** because it is used to test causal models and theories, and because, as we shall see below, it involves the measurement of latent variables.

The essential elements of LISREL are illustrated in a study by Suzanne King and Lee Wolfle.[28] The purpose of their study was to identify factors that contribute to the reputation of graduate departments, as determined by ratings of quality in a national survey. The sample consisted of a large number of departments of English, French, philosophy, geography, political science, and sociology.

The researchers hypothesized that the rating of a department's quality would be influenced by three factors: size, quality of the graduate students, and research productivity of the faculty. This causal model is depicted in figure 14.5. The model is similar to models used in path analysis (for example, see figure 14.3). Each straight arrow leading to the right indicates a hypothesized causal relationship in the direction of the arrow; for example, department size is

---

27. K. Joreskog and D. Sorbom, *LISREL VI Users Manual* (Chicago: International Educational Services, 1986). Another program for doing a structural analysis is EQS, which is described in Peter M. Bentler, *Theory and Implementation of EQS: A Structural Equations Program* (Los Angeles, BMDP Statistical Software, 1985).
28. Suzanne King and Lee M. Wolfle, "A Latent-Variable Causal Model of Faculty Reputational Ratings," *Research in Higher Education* 27 (1987): 99–105.

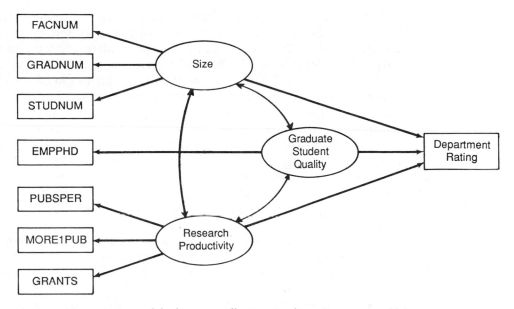

Figure 14.5   LISREL Model of Factors Affecting Graduate Department Ratings
Source: Adapted from figure 1 in Suzanne King and Lee M. Wolfle, "A Latent-Variable Causal Model of Faculty Reputational Ratings," *Research in Higher Education* 27 (1987): 101.

hypothesized to influence a department's reputation. Also, as in path analysis, the curved, double-headed arrows indicate the absence of a hypothesis about how two variables are related to each other. For example, the researchers' causal model contained no hypothesis about how department size and graduate student quality would affect each other.

The LISREL model shown in figure 14.5 differs from a path analysis in its use of the boxes at the left of the figure. The variables shown in ellipses (size, graduate student quality, and research productivity) are viewed as **latent variables,** which are the theoretical constructs to be measured. The rectangles to the left are the **manifest variables,** which are the variables that were actually measured by the researchers. Because educational measurement is imprecise, each latent variable should be measured whenever possible by several instruments, each of which measures a manifest variable conceptually related to it.

A similar principle is used in the development of test items. Because a single item is seldom a perfect measure of a construct, researchers combine a variety of items, each of which measures a related aspect of the construct, to form a test. In test construction, however, the items are usually summed to yield a total score. In LISREL, the measures of the manifest variables are factor-analyzed to identify their common variance, that is, the factor that they share in common.

In the study we are considering, the latent variable of department size was represented by three manifest variables: number of faculty members in the department in 1980 (FACNUM); number of graduates of the program between 1976 and 1980 (GRADNUM); and number of full- and part-time doctoral students in 1980 (STUDNUM). The latent variable of graduate-student quality was represented by just one manifest variable: percentage of graduates who, at the time of graduation, had definite employment commitments with Ph.D.-granting institutions (EMPPHD). Finally, the latent variable of research productivity was represented by three manifest variables: number of published articles attributed to faculty members divided by number of faculty in the department (PUBSPER); proportion of faculty with one or more published articles between 1978 and 1980 (MORE1PUB); and percentage of faculty members holding research grants from specified agencies between fiscal years 1978–1980 (GRANTS).

An initial step in LISREL is to factor-analyze each set of manifest variables to confirm that each manifest variable has an adequate correlation with the factor that will be used to represent the latent variable. A subsequent step is to compute path coefficients for each arrow leading out from each manifest variable. For example, in the case of ratings of geography departments, the researchers obtained path coefficients of .59 for size, .07 for graduate-student quality, and .60 for research productivity. Because a larger path coefficient indicates a large influence, we can conclude that a geography department's size and faculty research productivity have more influence on its reputation than does the quality of its graduate students.

In summary, LISREL is a multivariate correlational method that is used to measure latent variables reliably and validly, and to test the validity of causal theories or models. It is a powerful method, but difficult to use. Also, it makes several assumptions about the data that are entered into the analysis. Unless you are an expert in the use of LISREL, you should work with a consultant to determine whether this method, or similar method, is appropriate for your data analysis. If LISREL is appropriate, a consultant probably will be needed to help you correctly execute the LISREL computer program.

Differential Analysis

Subgroup Analysis in Relationship Studies

In discussing causal-comparative research, we stressed the importance of forming well-defined groups as a basis for studying possible causal factors. The same principle also applies to relationship studies. The formation of homogeneous subgroups may uncover relationships that are obscured when correlations are computed for the total sample.

The importance of this point is illustrated in the study by Peterson and Fennema described in the first part of the chapter. You will recall that the purpose of their study was to identify instructional practices that possibly facilitate or depress the math achievement (both low level and high level) of fourth-grade students. Table 14.1 presents the correlations between these two sets of variables for the sample of girls. The researchers also calculated correlation coefficients for the sample of boys. Table 14.12 presents these coefficients and also the corresponding coefficients for girls (taken from table 14.1). To simplify the presentation, only the correlations for low-level math achievement are shown.

Inspection of table 14.12 reveals the usefulness of analyzing data separately for different subgroups. Some of the correlation coefficients are statistically significant for girls but not for boys (e.g., nonmath activity expected); some are significant for boys but not for girls (e.g., interim activity expected); and some are significant for both boys and girls (social activity expected).

Had the data not been analyzed separately by student gender, the researchers could have reached false conclusions about the possible effects of instructional practices. For example, they could have overgeneralized the effects of particular practices by concluding that they affect all students equally. Also, a correlation coefficient that is significant for students of one gender is not always significant for the total sample. In this case, the researchers would conclude that an instructional practice has no effect when actually it does have an effect for a particular subgroup.

We see in table 14.12 that no pair of correlation coefficients is identical. For example, the correlation between daily math expected and math achievement is .17 for girls and .12 for boys. The question arises as to whether this difference in magnitude of correlation is a chance fluctuation or whether it represents a true difference in the population of girls and boys that this sample of girls and boys represents.

The question can be answered by doing a t-test of the statistical significance of the difference between two correlation coefficients. The last column of table 14.12 indicates which of the correlation comparisons yielded a statistically significant t value. We find, for example, that the difference between the rs for the variable—time spent on competitive activities—is statistically significant. Competitive activities appear to have a moderately negative effect on girls' math achievement ($r = -.40$), but a slightly positive effect on boys' ($r = .13$).

A useful strategy for identifying variables for differential analysis is to ask yourself what characteristics or relationships, other than the one you have hypothesized, could have contributed to the correlation you have obtained. Then select subjects from your sample that have the characteristic and recompute the correlation for the two subgroups, that is, those having and those not having the characteristic in question. If the resulting correlations are about the same, you may conclude that the characteristic in question has not contributed

TABLE 14.12

Partial Correlations between Boys' and Girls' Engaged Time Scores and End-of-Year Low-level Mathematics Achievement

Engaged Time Variables	r for Girls	r for Boys	t[a]
Type of activity expected by teacher			
Daily math	.17	.12	
Other math	.07	.08	
Nonmath	−.22	−.03	
Interim activity	−.10	−.23	
Social activity	−.30	−.38	
Setting of activity			
Total class	.06	.09	
Medium group	−.12	.13	
Small group—same sex	.18	−.10	
Small group—different sex	−.01	.02	
Two students—same sex	−.05	−.10	
Two students—different sex	−.03	.11	
Teacher—student	.03	−.53	.05
Alone	−.03	−.14	
Engaged in math activity	.19	.34	
Math—high level	.18	.06	
Math—low level	.01	.27	
Math—symbolic	−.01	.29	
Math—representational	.19	.03	
Helping	−.04	.17	
Being helped by student	.03	−.10	
Being helped by teacher	.01	−.35	.10
No helping	.18	.37	
Competitive	−.40	.13	.05
Cooperative	.25	.03	
Both competitive and cooperative	.25	.08	
Neither competitive nor cooperative	.27	.30	
Nonengaged in math activity	−.19	−.35	
Social	−.37	−.41	
Waiting for help	.09	−.15	
Academic (nonmath)	−.17	−.01	
Interim activities	−.04	−.05	
Off-task	−.09	−.34	

SOURCE: Adapted from Penelope L. Peterson and Elizabeth Fennema, "Effective Teaching, Student Engagement in Classroom Activities, and Sex-Related Differences in Learning Mathematics," *American Educational Research Journal* 22 (1985): 319.
[a] one-tailed test.

to your initial correlation, but if these two correlations are significantly different, you have gained a new insight into the relationship you are studying.

Moderator Variables in Prediction Studies

Sometimes a test is more effective in predicting the behavior of certain subgroups than in predicting the behavior of other subgroups. In this situation we can use differential prediction, which is a form of differential analysis. For example, it has been found that aptitude test scores generally predict school grades better for females than for males. In this instance, sex is designated a **moderator variable** because it moderates the predictive validity of a test. Age, gender, education, and socioeconomic status are frequently used as moderator variables. Also, one test is sometimes used as a moderator variable to improve the predictive validity of another test. In a study by Lawrence Malnig, the Taylor Manifest Anxiety Scale (TMAS) was used as a moderator variable to improve the correlation between scores on the School and College Aptitude Test (SCAT) and college grades.[29]

The use of a moderator variable to improve a test's predictive validity is illustrated in a study by Moshe Zeidner.[30] The purpose of the study was to determine the validity of a scholastic aptitude test for predicting the first year grade point average (GPA) of students enrolled in an Israeli university. Zeidner hypothesized that the aptitude test might be less valid for older students than for younger students. In other words, he hypothesized that age would act as a moderator variable for the relationship between aptitude test performance and GPA. He offered the following rationale for this hypothesis:

> Older student candidates may differ from their younger (i.e., late adolescent or early young-adult) counterparts not only in age per se but also in a number of potentially important variables, associated with age or cohort, that might affect test performance. These include: quality of primary and secondary school experience, cultural, and social experiences accumulated through the course of day-to-day living, occupational training, and so on. In addition, older examinees, who have long since graduated from high school, may differ from younger examinees on a host of other variables that may also bear on the level of test performance, such as the recency of their test taking experience, test wiseness, test attitudes, motivations and anxieties.[31]

The results of the correlational analysis are shown in table 14.13. The correlation between aptitude test performance and GPA is positive and statisti-

29. Lawrence R. Malnig, "Anxiety and Academic Prediction," *Journal of Counseling Psychology* 11 (1964): 72–75.
30. Moshe Zeidner, "Age Bias in the Predictive Validity of Scholastic Aptitude Tests: Some Israeli Data," *Educational and Psychological Measurement* 47 (1987): 1037–1047.
31. Ibid., p. 1038.

TABLE 14.13

Correlation between Scholastic Aptitude Test Scores and Grade Point Average for Different Age Groups

Age Group	N	r
18–21	238	.30**
22–25	314	.21*
26–29	72	.41***
30+	121	−.08

SOURCE: Adapted from Moshe Zeidner, "Age Bias in the Predictive Validity of Scholastic Aptitude Tests: Some Israeli Data," *Educational and Psychological Measurement* 47 (1987): 1043.
* $p < .05$. ** $p < .01$. *** $p < .001$.

cally significant for the three age groups between 18 and 29. The correlation coefficient for the 30+ age group, however, is negative and not statistically significant. Thus, the results support the researcher's hypothesis that aptitude tests have lower predictive validity for older applicants to college. Also, the coefficients for the four groups range from −.08 to .41. Had Zeidner calculated the coefficient for the total sample (i.e., all four groups combined), the resulting *r* probably would have been in the middle of this range. By using age as a moderator variable, he was able to find subgroups for whom the *r* was higher, notably, students between ages 18 and 21, and between ages 26 and 29.

To identify possible moderator variables, undertake a careful analysis of how various factors interact in determining academic or occupational success. An example of this kind of analysis occurred in a study by air force psychologists to determine whether success in pilot training could be predicted from the cadet's interest in aviation. The psychologists developed a test containing many items of general information about aviation. They hypothesized that an individual interested in aviation would have gained the information needed to answer the questions, while persons not interested would not have this information. The test was tried on a sample of aviation cadets and found to correlate moderately with the later success in pilot training. The researchers then hypothesized that the test would be a more satisfactory predictor for individuals with low interest in reading than individuals with high interest in reading. This hypothesis was based upon the premise that the individual who did a great deal of reading might have gained much of the information on the test without having a strong interest in aviation. On the other hand, individuals who had little interest in reading would almost surely not have the information on the test unless they had a strong interest in aviation. The findings of subsequent research supported this hypothesis.

INTERPRETATION OF CORRELATION COEFFICIENTS

Statistical and Practical Significance of Correlation Coefficients

Beginning researchers often have a difficult time interpreting the correlation coefficient after computing it. In fact, a correlation coefficient is a mathematical way of expressing the degree of relationship between two or more variables. To state it another way, the coefficient expresses the degree to which the variables covary. A coefficient of .50 does not mean that the two measures have 50 percent of their variance in common. Rather, the square of the correlation gives this "common variance." Two tests that are correlated .50 have $(.50)^2$ or 25 percent of their variance in common. As a statement of prediction, a correlation of .50 means that the variance in one variable predicts 25 percent of the variance in the other variable.

Statistical significance of a correlation coefficient usually expresses whether the obtained coefficient is different from zero at a given level of confidence. If the coefficient is not significantly different from zero, the null hypothesis of no difference cannot be rejected. If the coefficient is statistically significant, we can conclude that the relationship between the variables is nonzero. You should keep in mind, though, that the population coefficient may be greater or less than the obtained correlation coefficient. If you wish, you can calculate confidence limits to estimate the range of coefficients within which the population coefficient is likely to fall. (Confidence limits are discussed in chapter 9.).

Most statistics texts include a table from which the statistical significance of a product-moment correlation can be determined directly. The level of statistical significance of a correlation coefficient is determined in large part by the number of cases upon which the correlation is based. For example, with 22 cases, a product-moment coefficient of .54 is needed to be significant at the .01 level. If 100 cases are available, however, a correlation of .25 is significant at the .01 level, and with 1,000 cases a correlation of only .08 is significant at the .01 level.

Statistical significance is also dependent on whether a one-tailed or two-tailed test is performed. In a two-tailed test the researcher determines whether the obtained coefficient (ignoring its sign) is at either tail of the normal curve of positive and negative coefficients that could occur by chance in samples drawn by chance from a population in which $r = .00$. In a one-tailed test, only coefficients on one side of the normal curve distribution are considered.

Relationship studies are aimed primarily at gaining a better understanding of the complex skills or behavior patterns being studied, and therefore low correlation coefficients are as meaningful as high coefficients. Prediction studies are concerned with forecasting certain kinds of future behavior and therefore require higher correlation coefficients than those usually found in relationship studies. In prediction studies statistical significance is of little consequence because correlations usually must exceed this point to be of practical value. In other words, practical significance is more important than statistical significance.

Interpreting Magnitude of Correlation Coefficients in Prediction Research

The following rules provide a basis for interpreting correlating coefficients obtained in prediction research. These rules are, of course, only a general guide, but they will be appropriate for most types of educational research.

Correlation coefficients ranging from .20 to .35 show a slight relationship between the variables, although this relationship may be statistically significant. Correlations at this level are of little value in practical prediction situations.

With correlations around .50, crude group prediction may be achieved. As a correlation of .50 between a test and the performance predicted only indicates 25 percent common variance, we can obviously expect predictions based on a correlation this low to be frequently in error. Correlations within this range, however, are useful when combined with other correlations in a multiple regression equation. Combining several correlations in this range can in some cases yield individual predictions that are correct within an acceptable margin of error. Correlations at this level used singly are of little or no use for individual prediction because they yield only a few more correct predictions than could be accomplished by guessing or by using some chance selection procedure. The exception is when a very favorable selection ratio is present.

Correlation coefficients ranging from .65 to .85 make possible group predictions that are accurate enough for most purposes. As we move toward the top of this range, group predictions can be made very accurately, usually predicting the proportion of successful candidates in selection problems within a very small margin of error. Near the top of this correlation range individual predictions can be made that are considerably more accurate than would occur if no such selection procedure were used.

Correlation coefficients over .85 indicate a very close relationship between the two variables correlated. A correlation of .85 indicates that the measure, or combination of measures, used for prediction has about 72 percent variance in common with the performance being predicted. Prediction studies in education very rarely yield correlations this high. When obtained at this level, however, correlations are very useful for either individual or group prediction.

Interpreting Magnitude of Correlation Coefficients in Relationship Research

Many of the relationship studies done by educational researchers concern factors that possibly influence student learning, teacher morale, adoption of innovations, or other valued outcome. For example, the studies of mathematics

TABLE 14.14

Results of a Hypothetical Study of the Relationship between Use of a Teaching Technique and Student Performance

Student Course Performance	Percentage of Students	
	Technique Present	Technique Absent
Pass	60	40
Fail	40	60
Total	100	100

SOURCE: Adapted from N. L. Gage, *Hard Gains in the Soft Sciences: The Case of Pedagogy* (Bloomington, IN: Phi Delta Kappa's Center on Evaluation, Development and Research, 1985), p. 12.

achievement (by Peterson and Fennema) and college grade point average (by Zeidner and by Butler and McCauley) are of this type. The correlations between these outcomes and factors that may influence them typically range from .20 to .40. Although the magnitude of these correlation coefficients is lower than those needed for effective prediction, they nonetheless can signify important relationships between variables.

Consider a situation in which the observed relationship between two variables is only .20.[32] Suppose that one variable being investigated is a particular teaching technique. Each teacher in the sample is observed to determine whether he or she uses the technique. The outcome variable is student performance in the teacher's course. Each student is classified as having passed or failed the course. Suppose we obtain the results shown in table 14.14. The correlation between the two variables of teaching technique and student performance is only .20. (Note that a phi coefficient was used because both variables are dichotomous.) This is a low correlation coefficient even though the findings have practical significance: Use of the technique leads to a 50 percent increase in the number of students who pass the course.[33]

You should realize that in this example we examined relationships between variables, not prediction of one variable from another. We did not try to predict the particular students who passed the course and the particular

32. The statistics for this example are taken from a hypothetical experiment described in N. L. Gage, *Hard Gains in the Soft Sciences: The Case of Pedagogy* (Bloomington, IN: Phi Delta Kappa's Center on Evaluation, Development and Research, 1985).
33. Sixty percent of students whose teachers use the technique pass the course. Only 40 percent of students whose teachers do not use the technique pass the course. This is a 20 percentage point difference. Twenty percent divided by the 40 percent of students who pass the course from teachers who do not use the technique represents a 50 percent increase.

students who failed it. Instead, we examined the possible effect of the teaching technique on the entire group. The obtained r of .20 tells us that if a teacher uses the technique, a higher percentage of students will pass the course, but not which students.

Medical researchers have found that correlations even lower than .20 can have practical significance. For example, a medical research study found a positive relationship between lowering of men's cholesterol level and incidence of heart attacks.[34] The correlation coefficient for these two variables was only .03, yet the finding was considered an important breakthrough in the treatment of heart disease.

Another point to consider in interpreting correlation coefficients obtained in relationship research is that many factors influence most of the behavior patterns and personal characteristics of interest to educators. Therefore, the influence of any one factor is not likely to be large. Correlations in the range of .20 to .40 may be all that we should expect to find for many of the relationships between variables studied by educational researchers.

MISTAKES SOMETIMES MADE IN DOING CORRELATIONAL RESEARCH

1. The researcher assumes correlational findings to be proof of cause-and-effect relationships.
2. Relies on the "shotgun" approach rather than theory and previous research findings in selecting variables for correlational studies.
3. Fails to develop satisfactory criterion measures for use in prediction or relationship studies.
4. Does not do a cross-validation study to determine the extent of shrinkage of multiple correlation coefficients obtained in the original prediction study.
5. Selects a bivariate correlational statistic that is inappropriate for the types of scores to be analyzed.
6. In studies incorporating many variables, limits analyses to bivariate correlational statistics rather than also using multivariate correlational statistics to clarify how all of the variables relate to each other.
7. Fails to specify an important causal variable in planning a path analysis.
8. Does not check whether the data satisfy the assumptions underlying path analysis and structural equation modeling.
9. Misinterprets the practical and statistical significance of correlation coefficients obtained in a prediction or relationship study.

---

34. This study and the topic of magnitude of correlation coefficients are discussed in Gage, *Hard Gains in the Soft Sciences*, pp. 12–14.

ANNOTATED REFERENCES

Bruning, James L., and Kintz, B. L. *Computational Handbook of Statistics*, 3rd ed. Glenview, IL: Scott, Foresman, 1987.

Provides easy-to-follow computational procedures for these correlational techniques: product-moment correlation, Spearman rank-order correlation, Kendall rank-order correlation, point biserial correlation, the correlation ratio, *phi* coefficient, contingency coefficient, partial correlation, multiple regression, and the test for difference between independent/dependent correlations.

Cohen, Jacob, and Cohen, Patricia. *Applied Multiple Correlation/Correlation Analysis for the Behavioral Sciences*, 2nd ed. Hillsdale, NJ: Lawrence Erlbaum, 1983.

Presents research applications and computational procedures for the statistical techniques presented in this chapter: bivariate correlation, multiple regression, factor analysis, and path analysis. The authors also discuss procedures for handling missing data, computer analysis, and the relationship between analysis of variance and multiple regression.

Cook, Thomas D., and Campbell, Donald T. *Quasi-Experimentation: Design and Analysis Issues for Field Settings.* Chicago: Rand McNally, 1979.

Chapter 7 of this book contains a discussion of sophisticated statistical techniques for making causal inferences from correlational data. A critical review of path analysis procedures is included.

Pedhazur, Elazar J. *Multiple Regression in Behavioral Research: Explanation and Prediction*, 2nd ed. New York: Holt, Rinehart and Winston, 1982.

Provides an in-depth discussion, with many examples, of the multivariate correlation techniques presented in this chapter: partial correlation, multiple regression, path analysis, LISREL, discriminant analysis, and canonical correlation; discusses their applications in prediction and relationship studies.

SELF-CHECK TEST

Circle the correct answer to each of the following questions. An answer key is provided on page 884.

1. A perfect negative correlation is described by a correlation coefficient of
   a. 0.00.
   b. +1.00.
   c. −1.00.
   d. −.50.
2. A principal advantage of the correlation method is that it allows
   a. establishment of cause-and-effect relationships.
   b. simultaneous study of relationships between a great number of variables.
   c. many types of experimental designs to be used.
   d. for adjustment in pretreatment measures.

3. In contrast to relationship studies, prediction studies are more concerned with
   a. reducing restriction in range.
   b. maximizing the correction for attenuation.
   c. maximizing the correlation of each variable with a criterion.
   d. criterion measures.

4. A correlational technique appropriate when both variables are expressed as continuous scores is the
   a. product-moment correlation.
   b. rank-difference correlation.
   c. biserial correlation.
   d. *phi* coefficient.

5. Spearman's *rho* and Kendall's *tau* are both used to correlate two sets of
   a. continuous scores.
   b. true dichotomies.
   c. artificial dichotomies.
   d. ranked scores.

6. The scattergram is useful for
   a. deciding whether to compute a partial coefficient.
   b. deciding whether to do a factor analysis.
   c. correcting for restriction in range.
   d. studying nonlinear relationships between variables.

7. The lowering of a correlation coefficient between two sets of scores due to lack of reliability of the measures is called
   a. attenuation.
   b. restriction in range.
   c. regression.
   d. correlation ratio.

8. The process used to rule out the influence of one or more variables upon the criterion behavior pattern is called
   a. regression.
   b. partial correlation.
   c. correction for attenuation.
   d. analysis of variance.

9. The process of determining the correlation between the criterion behavior and a combination of predictor measures is called
   a. simple correlation.
   b. multiple regression.
   c. differential analysis.
   d. moderator analysis.

10. The purpose of canonical correlation is to determine the magnitude of the relationship between
    a. a set of predictor variables and a set of criterion variables.
    b. a set of predictor variables and a person's group membership.
    c. two or more factor scores.
    d. two or more discriminant functions.

11. A systematic representation of the correlations between all variables measured in a study is called a
    a. scattergram.
    b. correlation ratio.
    c. plot.
    d. correlation matrix.

12. A useful correlational technique for testing causal hypotheses is
    a. factor analysis.
    b. path analysis.
    c. discriminant analysis.
    d. moderator analysis.
13. In factor analysis the term *factor* refers to
    a. product-moment correlations.
    b. test scores.
    c. mathematical constructs.
    d. regression equations.
14. LISREL combines the use of
    a. path analysis and factor analysis.
    b. path analysis and discriminant analysis.
    c. canonical correlation and factor analysis.
    d. differential analysis and factor analysis.
15. If a set of tests predicts a criterion variable better for males than for females, gender is said to be a
    a. predictor variable.
    b. regression element.
    c. moderator variable.
    d. group predictor.

APPLICATION PROBLEMS

The following problems are designed to give you practice in applying significant concepts and research procedures explained in the chapter. Most do not have a single correct answer. For feedback, compare your answers with the sample answers on pages 899–900.

1. A researcher intercorrelates a number of measures she has collected on a sample of college seniors. She finds a correlation of +.65 between (1) the amount of time a student has been employed during his or her college years and (2) a paper-and-pencil measure of the student's personal maturity. On the basis of this finding, would you be justified in concluding that:
   a. The college should institute a work-study program in order to increase the maturity level of its students? Explain your answer.
   b. It is probable that the *longer* a student has worked during college, the *higher* will be his score on the personal maturity measure? Explain your answer.
   c. More mature students are better able to obtain jobs while in college than their less mature peers? Explain your answer.
2. A researcher decides to investigate possible determinants of interest in science among elementary school children. First he develops and validates a measure of this variable. Then he locates tests that measure as many variables as possible in as short a time as possible to correlate with his interest test. He figures that he will increase the likelihood of discovering significant relationships if he maximizes the number of variables included in his correlational design. What is wrong with the researcher's reasoning?
3. A researcher has collected a large amount of data on a sample of college students: scores on the Stanford-Binet Intelligence Scale, scores on the Wechsler Adult Intelligence Scale, scores on the Scholastic Aptitude Test, high school class rank, scores on a test anxiety scale,

and whether or not they successfully completed the first year of college (pass-fail and gradepoint average). The following are statistical analyses to be made of these data:

a. Correlation of scores on the Stanford-Binet Intelligence Scale with scores on the Wechsler scale. What statistical technique should be used, and why?

b. The researcher finds that test anxiety correlates significantly with the criterion variable of gradepoint average in the first year of college. The Scholastic Aptitude Test (SAT) also correlates significantly with test anxiety and the criterion. What statistical technique should be used to determine the correlation between test anxiety and college gradepoint average after the influence of SAT on both variables has been removed?

c. Correlation of Scholastic Aptitude Test scores with the dichotomous variable of pass-fail in the first year of college. What statistical technique should be used, and why?

d. Determine whether all of the measures used in this study, when intercorrelated with each other, measure a common factor. What statistical technique should be used, and why?

e. Determine whether the relationship between scores on the test anxiety scale and high school class rank is nonlinear. What statistical technique should be used, and why?

4. A researcher administered a battery of 20 different tests to a group of entering medical students. She also collected their gradepoint average at the end of their first year of medical school. What statistical technique should be used to maximize the usefulness of the 20 tests as predictors of the gradepoint average, and why?

5. In the table that follows, the criterion variable is gradepoint average. What are the moderator variables? What are the predictor variables?

Group	N	Verbal Aptitude and GPA*	Quantitative Aptitude and GPA*	Creative Aptitude and GPA*
High self-esteem	35	.65	.60	.35
Middle self-esteem	35	.34	.45	.10
Low self-esteem	35	.27	.10	−.27

* GPA = gradepoint average.

SUGGESTION SHEET

If your last name starts with the letters from Mos to Osb, please complete the Suggestion Sheet at the end of the book while the chapter is still fresh in your mind.

15 EXPERIMENTAL DESIGNS: PART 1

OVERVIEW

The experiment is a powerful research method. Unlike the correlational and causal-comparative methods, it can be used to establish cause-and-effect relationships between two or more variables. Experiments are not easy to conduct, however. This chapter describes the major problems that arise in conducting experimental research, and methods for solving them. Commonly used experimental designs are introduced here, with additional designs presented in the next chapter.

OBJECTIVES

After studying this chapter you should be able to:

1. Critically evaluate possible threats to the internal validity of an experiment.
2. Critically evaluate possible threats to the external validity of an experiment.
3. Describe procedures for increasing the representativeness of experimental designs.
4. Explain how experimenter bias can affect the outcome of an experiment, and state procedures for reducing experimenter bias.
5. Explain why it is not usually possible to assign students randomly within a classroom to different experimental treatments.
6. Create commonly used experimental designs, including specifications for random assignment, formation of experimental and control groups, and use of pretests and posttests.
7. State threats to the internal and external validity of commonly used experimental designs.
8. Specify statistical techniques for analyzing data yielded by experiments.

INTRODUCTION

The experiment provides the most rigorous test of causal hypotheses available to the researcher. Although correlational and causal-comparative research designs can suggest causal relationships between variables, experimentation is needed to determine whether the relationship is one of cause and effect.

An example of the correlational-experimental loop in research was described by Barak Rosenshine and Norma Furst.[1] They reviewed a set of studies

1. Barak Rosenshine and Norma Furst, "The Use of Direct Observation to Study Teaching," in *Second Handbook of Research on Teaching*, ed. R. M. W. Travers (Chicago: Rand McNally, 1973), pp. 122–183.

concerning teaching, which were done over a period of several years at Canterbury University, New Zealand. In a correlational study the researchers found a significant correlation ($r = .54$) between level of student learning and the extent to which a teacher followed a student's answer by redirecting the question to another student for comment. In other words, teachers who made extensive use of redirection generally had better-achieving classes than teachers who made little use of this technique.

This research finding appears to justify training teachers in the redirection technique in the expectation that this will improve their classroom performance. Rosenshine and Furst report, however, that the Canterbury researchers conducted experiments in which they manipulated teachers' use of redirection. No differences in student learning were found between redirection-present and redirection-absent conditions. Thus correlational studies demonstrated a relationship between two variables, but experiments indicated that the relationship was not one of cause-and-effect. A third variable may have created the relationship, or perhaps student performance affected teachers' use of redirection, which is the reverse of the causal pattern that the researchers hypothesized.[2]

Many experiments carried out by educational researchers are concerned with testing the effect of new educational materials and practices on students' learning. Thus, the results of educational experiments may have a direct impact on the adoption of new curriculum materials and teaching methods in the schools. The scope of present-day experimentation in education is illustrated by the titles of these journal articles:

Jan H. Spyridakis and Timothy C. Standal, "Signals in Expository Prose: Effects on Reading Comprehension," *Reading Research Quarterly* 22 (1987): 285–298.

Rhonda M. Wilkerson and Kinnard P. White, "Effects of the 4MAT System of Instruction on Students' Achievement, Retention, and Attitudes," *The Elementary School Journal* 88 (1988): 357–368.

Ann Weaver Hart, "A Career Ladder's Effect on Teacher Career and Work Attitudes," *American Educational Research Journal* 24 (1987): 479–503.

Joyce Sprafkin, Kenneth D. Gadow, and Gail Kent, "Teaching Emotionally Disturbed Children to Discriminate Reality from Fantasy on Television," *Journal of Special Education* 21 (1987/1988): 99–107.

Allan Wigfield, "Children's Attributions for Success and Failure: Effects of Age and Attentional Focus," *Journal of Educational Psychology* 80 (1988): 76–81.

Most experiments in education employ some form of the classic single-variable design. **Single-variable experiments** involve the manipulation of a

2. See chapter 14 for a discussion of causal inference in correlational research.

single treatment variable followed by observing the effects of this manipulation on one or more dependent variables.[3] The variable to be manipulated is referred to in this chapter as the **experimental treatment.** (It is sometimes called instead the *independent variable, experimental variable,* or *treatment variable.*) Most experiments in education also employ a comparison group that does not receive the experimental treatment. We use the term **control group** to refer to this group.

The variable that is measured to determine the effects of the experimental treatment is usually referred to as the *posttest, dependent variable,* or *criterion variable.* In this chapter we use the term **posttest** to describe a measure of this variable. If a variable is measured before administering the experimental treatment, it is called the **pretest.**

To understand how these terms are used, consider an experiment to determine the effect of a new reading program on students' reading achievement. The *experimental treatment* would be the introduction of the new reading program into the daily schedule of learning activities of a group of students. The *control group* would receive its regular reading program. The *pretest* would be the measurement of students' reading achievement before the new reading program had been introduced into the curriculum. The *posttest* would be the measurement of students' reading achievement after the introduction of the new program.

The key problem in experimentation is establishing suitable control so that any change in the posttest can be attributed only to the experimental treatment that was manipulated by the researcher. As we shall find in the next sections of this chapter, many extraneous variables need to be controlled in order to allow an unequivocal interpretation of experimental data. Also, there is no single correct approach to designing and carrying out experiments. Rather, different experimental designs can be used depending upon the variables that you wish to "control," that is, rule out as possible causes of changes on the posttest.

We stated above that the experiment is the most powerful research design currently available for testing hypotheses about causal relationships between variables. Yet it is also important to note that the experiment is not a perfect method. Even the findings of a well-designed experiment are potentially refutable. This point is made well by the philosopher Karl Popper:

> But what, then, are the sources of our knowledge? The answer, I think, is this: there are all kinds of sources of our knowledge but *none has authority.* . . . I do not, of course, deny that an experiment may also add to our knowledge, and in a most important manner. But it is not a source in any ultimate sense.[4]

3. Experiments in which more than one treatment variable is manipulated are called *factorial experiments.* They are discussed in chapter 16.
4. Karl Popper, *Conjectures and Refutations* (New York: Harper Torchbooks, 1968), p. 24.

As you read this and the next chapter, you will find that many factors can threaten the validity of an experiment. By controlling these factors, the power of an experiment to demonstrate a cause-and-effect relationship is strengthened. As Popper observed, however, it is not possible to do an experiment that provides an irrefutable demonstration of cause-and-effect. Therefore, replications of experiments—especially ones that test alternative causal hypotheses—are desirable.

INTERNAL AND EXTERNAL VALIDITY OF EXPERIMENTS

Holding Variables Constant

As we just stated, the most difficult task in applying experimental methods to educational problems is holding all variables in the educational situation constant except the administration of the experimental treatment. The classic single-variable experiment was first developed in the physical sciences, where it has been most fruitful in the production of knowledge. This is because physical matter is very adaptable to the rigorous requirements of the experimental laboratory. It is doubtful whether the rigorous control of the physical science laboratory can ever be achieved in the behavioral sciences, where human subjects are the object of experimentation.

Donald Campbell and Julian Stanley wrote a classic paper distinguishing between experimental designs in terms of their internal validity.[5] The **internal validity** of an experiment is the extent to which extraneous variables have been controlled by the researcher. If extraneous variables are not controlled in the experiment, we cannot know whether observed changes in the experimental group are due to the experimental treatment or to an extraneous variable.

To demonstrate the importance of controlling for extraneous variables, we will consider an experiment conducted by William Kyle, Ronald Bonnstetter, and Thomas Gadsden, Jr.[6] These researchers examined the effects of introducing a new science curriculum into a school district. The curriculum, the well-known Science Curriculum Improvement Study (SCIIS), emphasizes an inquiry-oriented, process approach to science. The district's existing curriculum emphasized reading a text, answering questions from it, and completing worksheets. The focus of the curriculum was on low-level cognitive skills.

---

5. Donald T. Campbell and Julian C. Stanley, "Experimental and Quasi-Experimental Designs for Research on Teaching," in *Handbook of Research on Teaching*, ed. N. L. Gage (Chicago: Rand McNally, 1963), pp. 171–246.
6. William C. Kyle, Jr., Ronald J. Bonnstetter, and Thomas Gadsden, Jr., "An Implementation Study: An Analysis of Elementary Students' and Teachers' Attitudes toward Science in Process-Approach vs. Traditional Science Classes," *Journal of Research in Science Teaching* 25 (1988): 103–120.

During the first year of implementation, SCIIS was introduced into six of the 35 elementary schools in the district. At the end of the school year, the researchers administered measures of attitudes toward science to teachers and students in these six schools. They also administered the same measures to a sample of teachers who had used the regular science curriculum that year but who would be teaching SCIIS the following year.

Table 15.1 presents some of the results of the experiment. There are no significant differences in the percentage of SCIIS and non-SCIIS teachers who expressed a positive attitude on the various measures. By contrast, a significantly higher percentage of SCIIS students expressed a positive attitude toward science on each of the measures.

Can the researchers conclude that the more positive attitude of SCIIS students was *caused* by students' exposure to SCIIS? Can they also conclude that SCIIS did not *cause* any change in teachers' attitudes toward science? The answer to these questions depends on how well extraneous variables were controlled in the experiment. **Extraneous variables** refer to aspects of the situation that occur while the experimental treatment is in progress; these aspects are irrelevant to

TABLE 15.1

Percentage of SCIIS and non-SCIIS Participants Having Positive Perceptions of Their Science Class

Item	Students			Teachers		
	SCIIS	Non-SCIIS	X^2	SCIIS	Non-SCIIS	X^2
Science is (was):						
fun	85	53	60.13**	30	35	.41
interesting	88	64	36.24**	45	51	.43
exciting	70	44	33.06**	25	22	1.44
boring	13	35	32.65**	41	38	1.05
Science makes me feel:						
successful	59	45	12.23*	36	32	38
uncomfortable	11	24	14.30**	31	26	1.08
curious	76	56	21.65**	49	49	.18

SOURCE: Adapted from William C. Kyle, Jr., Ronald J. Bonnstetter, and Thomas Gadsden, Jr., "An Implementation Study: An Analysis of Elementary Students' and Teachers' Attitudes toward Science in Process-Approach vs. Traditional Science Classes," *Journal of Research in Science Teaching* 25 (1988): 110. * $p < .01$. ** $p < .001$.

the treatment, but because they occur concomitantly with the treatment, they can become confounded with it. Campbell and Stanley identified eight types of extraneous variables, some of which are pertinent to the experiments that we have been been considering. They are as follows:

1. *History.* Experimental treatments extend over a period of time, providing opportunity for other events to occur besides the experimental treatment. The students in the experiment we are considering participated in SCIIS or the regular science curriculum for an entire school year. Also, the two groups of students were in different schools. Perhaps the SCIIS schools had an overall better learning environment than did the non-SCIIS schools. As a result of exposure to this environment over the course of a school year, students in SCIIS could have developed a more positive attitude toward all of their school subjects, not just science. If this were true, the school's learning environment would have produced the attitude effect, not the SCIIS curriculum. To avoid this problem in interpreting effects, the researchers need to ensure that the SCIIS and non-SCIIS schools are similar in all respects except their science curriculum.

2. *Maturation.* While the experimental treatment is in progress, biological or psychological changes in students are likely to occur. For example, they may become stronger, more cognitively able, more self-confident, and more independent. In our example, students in the SCIIS and non-SCIIS schools were at the same grade level (a nice experimental control), but the SCIIS students may have had higher ability and socioeconomic levels than the non-SCIIS students. This is especially possible because the SCIIS and non-SCIIS students came from different schools, and different schools in a district often serve communities varying in socioeconomic level. If SCIIS students were in fact more able and came from more advantaged families, they might have more positive attitudes toward science than non-SCIIS students irrespective of the science curriculum being used. Because the researchers did not assess background characteristics of students in the two treatment conditions, we cannot rule out these characteristics as causes of the observed group differences in attitudes toward science.

3. *Testing.* In most educational experiments a pretest is administered, followed by the experimental treatment and then a posttest. If the two tests are similar, students may show an improvement simply as an effect of their experience with the pretest, that is, they have become "test-wise." In the case of our research example, this extraneous variable is not a problem.

4. *Instrumentation.* A learning gain may be observed from pretest to posttest because the nature of the measuring instrument has changed. In experiments involving observational measurements, instrumentation effects can be a special problem. Observers who assess teachers or students before and after an experimental treatment may be disposed to give more favorable ratings the second time simply because they expect (consciously or subconsciously) a change to have occurred.

Because no premeasures were administered in the science curriculum experiment, the extraneous variable of instrumentation is not a threat to its internal validity.

5. *Statistical regression.* Whenever a test-retest procedure is used to assess change as an effect of the experimental treatment, the possibility exists that **statistical regression** can account for observed gains in learning. We will not present the mathematical basis for statistical regression here, but simply describe its effects on test scores.[7] For example, suppose a group of students was selected who fell below the 15th percentile on a test of reading achievement. If the same students are tested again on a similar test (i.e., one that is correlated with the first test), they will earn a higher mean score because of statistical regression, with or without an intervening experimental treatment. Furthermore, if another group of students was selected who earned very high scores on the first test, for example, above the 85th percentile, these students would earn a lower mean score when retested on a similar measure, again as a result of statistical regression. You should be alert to the confounding effects of statistical regression whenever students have been selected for their extreme scores on a test and are retested later on a measure that is correlated with the first test. Upon retesting, regression always tends to move the subject's score toward the mean. The probable regression can be estimated and considered in the results.

No premeasures of attitudes were administered in the science curriculum study, so it is not possible to determine whether teachers and students in the SCIIS and non-SCIIS schools had unusually positive or negative attitudes at the start of the experiment. Thus, we have no way of knowing whether differences in their expressed attitudes at the end of the school year reflect a differential statistical regression effect rather than, or in addition to, the effect of the SCIIS curriculum.

6. *Differential selection.* In experimental designs in which a control group is used, the effect of the treatment sometimes can be confounded because of differential selection of subjects for the experimental and control groups. This can be a major problem in the science curriculum experiment. The researchers do not explicitly state that schools were randomly assigned to the SCIIS and non-SCIIS treatments. (Random assignment, as we discuss a bit later in the chapter, is the best safeguard against differential selection.) The likelihood is that the schools that implemented SCIIS in the first year were chosen to do so because in fact they were different from other schools in the district.

Suppose the SCIIS schools were selected to implement this curriculum because their students were more academically able than were students at other schools. If this were true, the observed differences in science attitudes of the

7. A discussion of statistical regression can be found in Campbell and Stanley, "Experimental and Quasi-Experimental Designs," pp. 180–182. Also, see the discussion of gain scores in chapter 16.

SCIIS and non-SCIIS groups at the end of the school year could be attributed to the fact that different types of students were selected into the two groups.

The lack of a difference in science attitudes between SCIIS and non-SCIIS teachers at the end of the school year might indicate that similar teachers taught at the two groups of schools. In this case, differential selection of teachers would not be a problem in interpreting the results of the experiment. However, because no information about teacher and student characteristics prior to the experiment is available, we do not know whether differential selection, rather than SCIIS, caused the observed differences between groups on the postmeasures.

7. *Experimental mortality* (sometimes referred to as *attrition*). Subjects are lost from an experiment if they drop out of it or are absent during pre-post testing. This attrition results from extraneous factors such as illness or because subjects resent being in what they perceive as the less desirable treatment. Whatever the reason, attrition threatens an experiment's internal validity if it causes differential loss of subjects across treatments. For example, suppose low-performing students feel less positively about SCIIS, and also drop out of school in greater numbers during the year. In this case, fewer such students would complete the postmeasures of science attitudes, thereby artificially inflating the percentage of students with positive attitudes shown in table 15.1.

You can minimize the problem of experimental mortality by randomly assigning students to treatment groups *and* by making the treatments equally desirable. (A procedure for equating desirability of treatments is described on pages 666–667.) Also, you should keep records for each treatment of subjects' absenteeism or withdrawal from the experiment.[8] This information is not reported for the science curriculum experiment. The researchers stated, for example, that 92.3 percent of the total sample of teachers completed the questionnaires that provided the data for table 15.1. They did not indicate, however, whether the respondents were distributed equally across the experimental and control treatments.

8. *Selection-maturation interaction.* This extraneous variable is similar to differential selection (see number 6 above), except that maturation is the specific confounding variable. Suppose, for example, that the science curriculum study had been done in two different school districts. Further suppose that because of a differential admissions policy, the average age of the experimental group is six months older than that of the control group. In this case, any group differences in science attitudes can be attributed to the effects of students' age rather than to the effects of the science curriculum that each group studied.

8. Procedures for analyzing research data to determine the presence of systematic bias in loss of subjects from experimental and control groups are described in Stephen G. Jurs and Gene V Glass, "The Effect of Experimental Mortality on the Internal and External Validity of the Randomized Comparative Experiment," *Journal of Experimental Education* 40 (1971): 62–66.

Campbell and Stanley's list of eight extraneous variables was subsequently extended by Campbell and co-author Thomas Cook.[9] They added four more extraneous variables, which are described below.

9. *Experimental treatment diffusion.* If the treatment condition is preceived as very desirable relative to the control condition, members of the control group may seek access to the treatment condition. Experimental treatment diffusion is especially likely if the experimental and control subjects are in close proximity to each other. For example, some teachers in a school building (the treatment group) may be assigned to use an innovative, attractive curriculum, whereas other teachers in the same school (the control group) may be assigned to continue using the regular curriculum. As the experiment progresses, some of the control group teachers may discuss the new curriculum with treatment group teachers, even if instructed not to do so. They may even borrow some of the materials and activities to use in their classrooms. Thus, over time the treatment "diffuses" to the control group.

If experimental treatment diffusion occurs, the effect of a treatment on the posttest will be clouded. To avoid this problem, you should try to arrange conditions so that contact between the experimental and control groups is minimized. Also, you can directly tell members of each group not to speak to each other about the experiment while it is in progress. After the experiment is completed, interview some or all of the sample to determine whether experimental treatment diffusion in any form occurred.

As we examine table 15.1, we find that many teachers in both groups had negative attitudes and perceptions about their science classes. For example, approximately 40 percent of teachers in both groups found that science was boring. What we do not know is the percentage of teachers who found science boring at the start of the school year. The percentage may have been even higher. If so, the introduction of SCIIS reduced the percentage of teachers who found science instruction boring. If the percentage was reduced in the control group as well, this could indicate a treatment diffusion effect.

10. *Compensatory rivalry by the control group.* This extraneous variable refers basically to the same phenomenon as the John Henry effect described in chapter 5. The John Henry effect involves a situation in which control group subjects perform beyond their usual level because they perceive that they are in competition with the experimental group. If this phenomenon occurs, the observed difference, or lack of difference, between the experimental treatment and control groups on the posttest can be attributed to the control group's unusual motivation rather than to treatment effects.

11. *Compensatory equalization of treatments.* This extraneous variable can occur if the experimental group receives a treatment that provides goods or

9. Thomas D. Cook and Donald T. Campbell, *Quasi-Experimentation: Design and Analysis Issues for Field Settings* (Chicago: Rand McNally, 1979).

services perceived as desirable. Under these conditions, administrators may attempt to compensate the control group by giving it goods and services. If these goods or services affect the control group's posttest scores, they would obscure the effects of the experimental treatment. The reason is that the researchers, instead of comparing the treatment with a no-treatment control condition, would be comparing one treatment with another treatment.

Cook and Campbell observed that this problem almost certainly operated some years ago in experiments testing the effects of Follow Through and similar compensatory education programs. The control schools tended to be given Title I funds for their disadvantaged students in similar amounts to those given to Follow Through schools. Therefore, although the control schools did not have a Follow Through program, they had resources that could be used to purchase similar services for their disadvantaged students.

12. *Resentful demoralization of the control group.* A control group can become artificially demoralized if it perceives that the experimental group is receiving a desirable treatment that is being withheld from it. As a result, its performance on the posttest would be lower than normal. In turn, the experimental treatment would appear to be better than it actually is, because the difference between the posttest scores of the experimental and control groups was artificially increased by the demoralization of the control group.

You will recall that in the science curriculum experiment we have been considering, the control group consisted of teachers who would be implementing SCIIS the year following completion of the experiment. Therefore, it seems unlikely that any of the three extraneous variables just described—compensatory rivalry, compensatory equalization, and resentful demoralization—would have affected their teaching performance or attitudes during the course of the experiment.

We have seen now how twelve different extraneous variables can threaten the internal validity of an experiment. The science curriculum experiment did not control these variables well, primarily because teachers and students were not randomly assigned to the experimental and control groups, and because premeasures were not administered. Therefore, the researchers probably drew too strong a conclusion when they stated that, "the nature of the science taught does affect student attitudes toward science."[10] The results are consistent with this conclusion, but they are also consistent with other interpretations involving the operation of extraneous variables.

In summary, the goal in designing an experiment is to create a set of conditions such that any observed changes can be attributed with a high degree of confidence to the experimental treatment rather than to extraneous variables. Random assignment and pre-post testing are central to creating such conditions.

10. Kyle, Bonnstetter, and Gadsden, "An Implementation Study," p. 117.

Therefore, these features of experimental design are emphasized in this chapter and the next.

Generalizability of Findings

As we just stated, a variety of controls are needed so that the effect of the experimental treatment is not confounded by extraneous variables. However, the educational researcher is faced with a dilemma: As more rigorous controls are applied to the experiment, less carryover can be expected between the experiment and related field situations. In other words, the behavioral sciences are constantly faced with the choice of obtaining rigorous laboratory control at the cost of realism or of maintaining realistic experimental situations at the cost of losing scientific rigor in the process.

Most educational studies aim at a compromise between these goals. They attempt to attain sufficient rigor to make the results scientifically acceptable while maintaining sufficient realism to make the results reasonably transferable to educational situations in the field.

Campbell and Stanley identified four general factors that affect the generalizability of findings from experiments—what they call the experiment's external validity.[11] **External validity** is the extent to which the findings of an experiment can be applied to particular settings. The findings of an educational experiment may be externally valid for one setting, less externally valid for a different setting, and not externally valid at all for some other setting.

Glenn Bracht and Gene Glass subsequently differentiated Campbell and Stanley's four general factors into more specific sources of external validity.[12] The following section is a description of Bracht and Glass's list of factors that affect the generalizability of findings from experiments.

Population Validity

Population validity concerns the extent to which the results of an experiment can be generalized from the specific sample that was studied to a larger group of subjects. Bracht and Glass distinguish two types of population validity.

The first type is *the extent to which one can generalize from the experimental sample to a defined population.* To illustrate, suppose you are concerned with

---

11. The four general factors are: the reactive effect of testing; the interaction of the experimental treatment with particular student characteristics, measuring instruments, and the time of the study; the possible artificiality of the experimental treatment and the students' knowledge that they are involved in an experiment; and multiple-treatment interference. The meaning of these factors is explained in the following discussion of Bracht and Glass's list of external invalidity sources.

12. Glenn H. Bracht and Gene V Glass, "The External Validity of Experiments," *American Educational Research Journal* 5 (1968): 437–474.

determining whether a programmed instruction format leads to greater achievement gains than conventional textbook presentation. You perform the experiment on a sample of 125 high school students randomly selected from a particular school district. The experiment demonstrates that programmed instruction leads to greater achievement gains. Although you might wish to generalize the findings to the population of "all" students, strictly speaking you can generalize only to the population from which the sample was drawn—namely, high school students in the particular school district. Bracht and Glass call this limited group the **experimentally accessible population,** defined as the population from which the sample is drawn. The accessible population is usually "local," normally within driving distance of the experimenter's office or laboratory. Assuming that the sample described above has been randomly selected, you can validly generalize the research findings from the 125 participating students to the experimentally accessible population (i.e., all high school students in the school district).

Often the researcher or the reader of a research report wishes to generalize from the experimentally accessible population to a still larger group (e.g., all high school students in the United States). This larger group of subjects is called the **target population.** Generalizing research findings from the experimentally accessible population to a target population is risky. We must compare the two populations to determine whether they are similar in critical respects. For example, if the experiment was done in a school district composed almost entirely of middle-class suburban families, generalization of the research findings to all U.S. high school students may be invalid.

The second type of population validity is *the extent to which personological variables interact with treatment effects.* In the experiment described above, you do not know whether instructional format interacts with student characteristics. That is, although programmed instruction was found to be superior to conventional textbook presentation for high school students, different results might be obtained with students at other grade levels. If so, the differential effects would limit the generalizability of the experiment's findings.

Student's ability, gender, extroversion-introversion, anxiety level, and level of independence are examples of other personological variables that may affect the generalizability of findings from experiments. The systematic study of these interactions is called *aptitude-treatment interaction research.* This topic is discussed in the next chapter.

Ecological Validity

Ecological validity concerns the extent to which the results of an experiment can be generalized from the set of environmental conditions created by the researcher to other environmental conditions. If the treatment effects can be obtained only under a limited set of conditions or only by the original researcher, the experimental findings are said to have low ecological validity. Bracht and Glass identified ten factors that affect the ecological validity of an experiment. They are as follows:

1. *Explicit description of the experimental treatment.* The researcher needs to describe the experimental treatment in sufficient detail so that other researchers can reproduce it. Suppose you find that the discussion method is more effective than the lecture method in promoting higher cognitive learning, but your description of the discussion method is so vague and incomplete that other researchers cannot know whether they are using the method in the same way. In this case the experimental findings have virtually no generalizability to other settings.

2. *Multiple-treatment interference.* Occasionally a researcher will use an experimental design in which each subject is exposed to more than one experimental treatment. Suppose that each subject in the experiment receives three different treatments: A, B, and C. Treatment A is found to produce significantly greater learning gains than treatments B and C. Because of the experimental design that was used, you cannot safely generalize the finding to a situation in which treatment A is administered *alone*. The effectiveness of treatment A may depend on the coadministration of the other two treatments. Whenever it appears that multiple-treatment interference will affect the generalizability of your findings, you should choose an experimental design in which only one treatment is assigned to each subject.

3. *Hawthorne Effect.* In chapter 5 we discussed how the Hawthorne Effect and the placebo effect often occur when researchers perform experiments to determine the effectiveness of innovative educational practices. Researchers often give participating teachers and students special attention; this factor, not the experimental treatment itself, may cause a change in their behavior. Should the Hawthorne Effect or the placebo effect occur, the external validity of the experiment is jeopardized because the findings may not generalize to a situation in which researchers or similar personnel are not present.

4. *Novelty and disruption effects.* A novel experimental treatment may be effective simply because it is different from the instruction that subjects normally receive. If this is true, the results of the experiment have low generalizability because the treatment's effectiveness is likely to erode as the novelty wears off. The reverse problem occurs with experimental treatments that disrupt the normal routine. This type of experimental treatment may be ineffective when tried out initially. With continued use, subjects may assimilate the treatment into their routine and find that it is effective. Thus, the findings of the initial tryout are not generalizable to a condition of continued use.

5. *Experimenter effect.* An experimental treatment may be effective or ineffective because of the particular experimenter (teacher) who administers it. The treatment effects, then, cannot be generalized to conditions in which a different person is the experimenter (often a classroom teacher). The various

ways in which experimenters can influence and bias the administration of a treatment are discussed below in the section on experimenter bias.

6. *Pretest sensitization.* In some instances the pretest may act as part of the experimental treatment and thus affect research results. If the experiment is repeated without the pretest, different research results will probably be obtained. Let us consider a hypothetical experiment in which this reactive effect could occur. Suppose you are interested in the effect of point of view in a film on students' attitudes. You might develop a film in which the narrator takes a strongly slanted, positive view of controversial decisions made by a contemporary politician. To assess the effect of the film, you might administer a pretest and posttest of students' attitudes toward the politician.

Suppose there is a significant positive shift in students' attitudes, which you attribute to the experimental treatment, that is, the film. Can you generalize this finding and assert that the film will have the same effect when used in other situations? The generalization is not warranted unless you can demonstrate that the pretest has no effect on the experimental treatment. The possibility exists that the pretest activates students' awareness of their attitudes toward this politician and sensitizes them to the narrator's attitude. This sensitization, induced by the pretest, may be the factor that interacts with the film to produce the attitude shift. By contrast, if they are shown the film alone, students might be most sensitized to learning the facts presented in the film. Thus, they might show little or no attitude shift because they did not have a set to attend to the narrator's point of view.

Bracht and Glass's review of the literature on pretest sensitization indicated that it is most likely to occur when the pretest is a self-report measure of personality or attitude. A more recent review of the research on pretest sensitization effects was conducted by Victor Willson and Richard Putnam.[13] They located 32 studies of this phenomenon and did a meta-analysis (see chapter 4) to determine the average effect size across studies. Willson and Putnam found a substantial effect of pretests on posttest performance. In other words, an experimental group that receives a pretest is likely to perform at a higher level on the posttest than a corresponding experimental group that does not receive a pretest. This effect occurs even when the posttest is different than the pretest. In fact, the meta-analysis revealed that the pretest effect was stronger when pretest and posttest were different. Furthermore, administration of a pretest was usually found to have a positive effect irrespective of the outcome being measured—cognitive, attitudinal, or personality.

7. *Posttest sensitization.* This source of ecological invalidity is similar to pretest sensitization. The results of an experiment may be dependent upon the administration of a posttest. This can happen if the posttest is a learning

---

13. Victor L. Willson and Richard R. Putnam, "A Metaanalysis of Pretest Sensitization Effects in Experimental Design," *American Educational Research Journal* 19 (1982): 249–258.

experience in its own right. For example, the posttest may cause certain ideas presented during the treatment phase to "fall into place" for some of the participating students. When the experiment is repeated without a posttest, the treatment may be of diminished effectiveness. Although posttest sensitization is plausible, it has not been studied as an experimental phenomenon to the extent of its counterpart, pretest sensitization.

8. *Interaction of history and treatment effects.* In a strict sense one cannot generalize beyond the time period in which the experiment was done. An experiment evaluating an innovative educational method might be done at a time when teachers are particularly disenchanted with a corresponding conventional method. They might be exceptionally motivated to demonstrate the superiority of the new method. At a later time, we might repeat the experiment and find no difference because teachers no longer see the method as "innovative."

9. *Measurement of the dependent variable.* The generalizability of the experiment may be limited by the particular pretest and posttest designed to measure achievement gains or other outcome variable. Suppose the superiority of the programmed instruction format over a regular textbook-oriented format was demonstrated using multiple-choice tests. As programmed instruction is well adapted to the multiple-choice format, the results could be due to this similarity between programmed content and multiple-choice questions. Thus, the experiment does not permit us to generalize the findings to other measuring instruments. For example, no difference between instructional formats might be found if essay-type pretests and posttests were administered.

10. *Interaction of time of measurement and treatment effects.* Administration of a posttest at two or more different points in time may result in different findings about treatment effects. The usual practice is to administer the posttest immediately after subjects have completed the experimental treatment. Conclusions about treatment effectiveness are based on the results of this posttest administration. Nevertheless, we advise you to administer the same or a parallel posttest several weeks or months later to measure retention of learning. Bracht and Glass cite several examples in the research literature in which treatment effects change from posttest to delayed posttest; the effects may be enhanced, remain the same, or diminish over time.[14]

In designing an experiment, carefully consider the "real-life" educational setting to which you wish to generalize the results of the experiment. Then review the design of the experiment using the 10 factors described above to determine the extent of discrepancy, if any, between the experimental conditions and the "real-life" educational setting. If a discrepancy cannot be minimized, it should at least be noted in the research report as a limit on the generalizability of the research findings.

14. Bracht and Glass, "Validity of Experiments," p. 466.

Representative Design

In recent years some educational researchers, most notably Richard Snow,[15] have criticized conventional experimental design for its artificiality and lack of generalizability. Building upon the earlier work of Egon Brunswick, Snow used the label "systematic design" to characterize the usual form of experimentation. In systematic design a few treatment variables and pretest-posttest measures are administered. All other variables are either controlled or ignored. Most of the experiments reported in journals of educational research are based on systematic design principles.

The problem with systematic design is that it often produces artificial learning situations and unnatural behavior in the learner. Snow advocates the use of representative design to combat these problems and also to increase the generalizability of findings from experiments. **Representative design** is a process for planning experiments so that they reflect accurately: (1) real-life environments in which learning occurs, and (2) the natural characteristics of learners.

The need for representative design is based on a number of assumptions about the environment and the human learner. One assumption is that the characteristics of the natural environment are complex and interrelated. We cannot simply choose to vary one environmental characteristic and hold others constant; as one characteristic changes, so do others. We need to study the learning environment as an ecology in the same way that biologists study the ecology of the natural environment.

Another assumption of representative design is that humans are active processors of information; they do not react passively to experimental treatments. Therefore, the active nature of human learners needs to be considered in designing experiments. A related assumption is that human learners, if allowed, will adjust and adapt to their environment. Systematic experiments are artificial in that they constrain the range of behavior that might be exhibited if the learner is allowed to act naturally. Finally, representative design assumes that, because the behaving organism is complex, any experimental intervention is likely to affect the learner in complex ways. An instructional method may be designed only to increase students' knowledge of a specific subject, but the effect may generalize to affect students' attitudes and also may affect their knowledge of other subjects. Furthermore, the instructional intervention might be designed primarily to affect short-term performance, but the effects may "radiate" out to affect long-term performance as well.

Snow believes that educational researchers should design experiments to reflect this view of the environment and the learner. That is, experiments should

---

15. Richard E. Snow, "Representative and Quasi-Representative Designs for Research on Teaching," *Review of Educational Research* 44 (1974): 265–291.

become more *representative* of the natural environment and of human subjects as active learners. Snow notes that true representative designs are very difficult to achieve in education, but he suggests compromises that will make experiments more representative. The following are some of his recommendations:

1. When appropriate, conduct the research in an actual school setting or other environment to which you wish to generalize your findings.

2. Incorporate several environmental variations into the design of the experiment. For example, if the purpose is to evaluate a new instructional method, have not just one teacher but rather a sample of teachers use it. Also, vary the educational setting. For example, an instructional method could be tested in a sample of inner-city schools, suburban schools, and rural schools.

These planned variations are most meaningful if you can conceptualize relevant dimensions of the educational ecology. Suppose you are interested in the possible effects of inserting questions into instructional materials. What are "instructional materials" in this context? Are they the first textbook that you happen to pick off a shelf, or the textbook that the sample of subjects happens to be studying? A more systematic approach is to conceptualize relevant dimensions of instructional materials: readability of prose (difficult, average, easy), modality (film, audiotape, print), subject area (math, social studies, language arts), and so forth. Then you can select instructional materials that sample one or more of these dimensions.

3. Observe what students are actually doing during the experiment. These observations may prove helpful in interpreting the results of the experiment. For example, you may observe that the subjects were not attentive to a particular treatment or were distracted by other events. If the research data later indicate that the treatment was not effective, the observations would be helpful in interpreting this result and in planning future research.

4. A related technique to the one preceding is to observe the social context in which the experiment is being conducted. Certain events that occur in schools or in other educational settings may affect the experimental treatments. If these events are observed and recorded, the research findings should be more interpretable.

5. Prepare students for the experiment. Snow claims that the typical practice is for researchers to give students simple instructions and perhaps a few minutes' training prior to the start of an experiment. More extensive preparation may be necessary to ensure a smooth transition from students' current mental set to the one required by the experimental task.

6. Incorporate a control treatment that allows students to use their customary approaches to learning. Suppose an experiment is designed in which students are formed into dyads and trained to ask questions of each other about curriculum materials. An appropriate control treatment might be to form some students into dyads and allow them to use any procedures they wish to review the same materials. The control groups form a naturalistic baseline against

which the behavior and learning of the experimental group can be evaluated. This use of control groups is analogous to animal research in which the behavior of animals in captivity is studied by comparing it with their behavior "in the wild." Educational researchers make decisions about how to represent the natural environment and the natural behavior of learners each time they design an experiment. Effective use of the procedures described here should increase the generalizability of findings from experiments to the real world of educational practice.

Experimenter Bias

Robert Rosenthal's studies of experimenter bias effects have made a significant contribution to experimental methodology.[16] Researchers will frequently have expectancies about the outcomes of their experiments, and Rosenthal has demonstrated that these expectancies are sometimes transmitted to subjects in such a way that their behavior is affected. This phenomenon is known as the **experimenter bias effect.** The phenomenon typically occurs outside the awareness of the experimenter. The experimenter bias effect does not refer to situations in which an experimenter, with full awareness of his or her actions and intentions, manipulates subjects' behavior or falsifies data in order to yield an "expected" finding.

Rosenthal and his associates carried out many experiments on the experimenter bias effect, and we shall describe one of them here.[17] A group of undergraduates was instructed in procedures for running albino rats through a simple T maze and for training the rats to solve a discrimination learning problem. The student experimenters were told that, as a result of generations of inbreeding, some rats they would train were "maze-bright" while others were "maze-dull." They were then given instructions regarding expected findings:

> Those of you who are assigned the Maze-Bright rats should find your animals on the average showing some evidence of learning during the first day of running. Thereafter performance should rapidly increase.
>
> Those of you who are assigned the Maze-Dull rats should find on the average very little evidence of learning in your rats.[18]

In fact, though, a homogeneous group of albino rats (not varying on the dimension of maze brightness-dullness) was randomly assigned to the experi-

16. Robert Rosenthal, *Experimenter Effects in Behavioral Research, Enlarged Edition* (New York: Irvington, 1976).
17. Robert Rosenthal and K. L. Fode, "The Effect of Experimenter Bias on the Performance of the Albino Rat," *Behavioral Science* 8 (1963): 183–189.
18. Ibid., p. 184.

menters for training. Nevertheless, Rosenthal and Fode found that rats trained by experimenters who thought their rats were maze-bright earned significantly higher learning scores than rats trained by experimenters with the opposite expectancy. The differential learning gains were the result of an experimenter bias effect rather than genetic differences between groups of rats.

The implication of this finding for educational experiments is obvious. An educational researcher might do an experiment to determine whether a technique or product he or she has developed is superior to conventional practice. If the researcher has a strong expectancy that the innovation is superior to conventional practice, the experiment might yield this finding. In this case the finding is attributable to an experimenter bias effect rather than to the innovation per se. Should impartial researchers carry out further experiments to evaluate the innovation, they are not likely to replicate the original finding since the experimenter bias effect is no longer operating.

The method of transmission of the experimenter's expectancy to the subject is not clearly understood, although Rosenthal and others have conducted studies directed at this problem.[19] Yet the experimenter bias effect does appear to be a real threat to the internal validity of experiments. You should take steps to avoid the operation of this effect in designing and carrying out an experiment. One effective technique is to train naive experimenters to work with students or teachers participating in the study. Whenever possible do not work directly with the subjects. Also, you should avoid suggesting to the experimenters, directly or indirectly, that one experimental treatment is better than another.

To some degree the tools used to measure the dependent variables can be selected so as to reduce the chance of experimenter bias. For example, if the rats in the Rosenthal and Fode experiment had been trained in mazes having sensitized pathways so their progress was measured and recorded automatically, there would have been much less chance of observer bias influencing the results. Observer expectations are most likely to influence research results when scores on the dependent variable rely upon subjective judgment by the observer, or when the investigator can make inputs (often subconsciously) into the experimental treatment itself.

A researcher conceivably can go too far in trying to eliminate experimenter bias. For example, you can be so neutral or even skeptical about the procedure being tested that the participants get turned off to it. Also, you might put the procedure to too difficult a test in the interest of appearing neutral. For example, the procedure might be tried in schools that are experiencing administrative

19. Robert Rosenthal and Lenore Jackson also reported a classic experimental study of how teachers' expectancies affect their students' behavior in *Pygmalion in the Classroom* (New York: Holt, Rinehart and Winston, 1968). Although their experimental procedures provoked considerable controversy, their book stimulated much interest and further research on teachers' expectancies.

problems. If the initial test is under difficult conditions such as these, it might be labeled ineffective and abandoned. Generally speaking, it is better initially to identify a set of conditions under which the procedure has a good chance of working. Subsequent experiments can determine the limiting conditions of its effectiveness.

Joshua Klayman and Young-Won Ha labeled this approach of testing cases that offer the best chance of supporting one's hypotheses a **positive test strategy.**[20] They demonstrated that under certain conditions, which would include the testing of hypotheses about new educational procedures, we should in fact seek instances that support our hypotheses rather than instances that refute them.

Treatment Fidelity

Theodore Barber extended the work of Rosenthal by identifying additional sources of investigator and experimenter bias.[21] The investigator is the person who designs the experiment and interprets the data. The experimenter is the person who administers the experimental treatments and collects the data. The investigator and experimenter often are one and the same person, but this is not always so.

One type of bias identified by Barber occurs when the experimenter fails to follow the exact procedures specified by the investigator for administering the treatments. Barber labeled this type of bias "experimenter failure to follow the protocol effect" and cited several studies in which it was demonstrated empirically to occur. Other researchers refer to this type of bias as lack of treatment fidelity. **Treatment fidelity** is the extent to which the treatment conditions, as implemented, conform to the researcher's specifications for the treatment.

Researchers should try to maximize treatment fidelity, and also to assess it. This is done too seldom in educational experiments. James Shaver reviewed studies published in the *American Educational Research Journal (AERJ)* for the years 1969 to 1981.[22] He identified 22 reports of teaching methods research in which checking treatment fidelity would have been appropriate. Less than half of the reports ($N = 9$) actually made such a check.

20. Joshua Klayman and Young-Won Ha, "Confirmation, disconfirmation, and information in hypothesis testing," *Psychological Review* 94 (1987): 211–228.
21. Theodore Barber, "Pitfalls in Research: Nine Investigator and Experimenter Effects," in *Second Handbook of Research on Teaching,* ed. R. M. W. Travers (Chicago: Rand McNally, 1973), pp. 382–404.
22. James P. Shaver, "The Verification of Independent Variables in Teaching Methods Research," *Educational Researcher* 12, no. 8 (1983): 3–9. See also Annotated References at the end of this chapter.

Treatment fidelity can be maximized by careful training of the persons—often teachers—who are to implement the training. For example, in the science curriculum experiment that we reviewed above, the training of teachers who were to implement SCIIS occurred in the form of inservice workshops. From the descriptions provided by the researchers, these workshops appear to have lasted only a few days. This amount of training may not be sufficient to change teacher behavior in the direction of using the process-oriented inquiry approach required by SCIIS.

Treatment fidelity can be assessed by first writing precise specifications for each experimental treatment. Then the investigator must carefully train the experimenters to follow these specifications. Finally, during the actual experiment the investigator should collect data on the experimenter's behavior to determine the congruence between behavior and treatment specifications. Data on experimenter behavior can be collected by a variety of observational techniques (see chapter 12).

An example of careful attention to procedures for maximizing and assessing treatment fidelity can be found in an experiment by Jerry Pratton and Loyde Hales.[23] The purpose of their experiment was to determine the effect of having teachers use active participation, a technique popularized by the educator Madeline Hunter and her associates. They defined active participation as

> a deliberate and conscious attempt on the part of the teacher to cause students to participate overtly in a lesson. For example, a teacher presenting a lesson in division may ask students to indicate the number of digits that are in a dividend by holding up the correct number of fingers or writing the number on their pages.[24]

Each of five teachers was trained to deliver a lesson that included active participation (the experimental treatment) and the same lesson but without active participation (the control treatment). Following the training period, each teacher taught each form of the lesson to two fifth-grade classes. Each lesson was videotaped, and, in addition, the teachers completed a questionnaire about the number of students present, time of day, unusual occurrences, and so on.

The researchers analyzed the videotape and questionnaire data to determine the extent to which the teachers taught the lessons in the same way and under the same conditions except for use of active participation. Table 15.2 reports the results of the analysis. The results indicate good treatment fidelity, meaning that any difference between the treatment and control groups on the dependent variable (student achievement on a posttest covering the lesson

23. Jerry Pratton and Loyde W. Hales, "The Effects of Active Participation on Student Learning," *Journal of Educational Research* 79 (1986): 210–215.
24. Ibid., p. 211.

TABLE 15.2

Fidelity of Treatment in Active Participation Experiment

Observed Factors	Active Participation *M*	Non-Active Participation *M*
External factors (atypical)		
Unusual classroom interruptions	.10	.00
Unusual weather	.00	.00
Unusual school event	.00	.00
Day of the week dirsuptive	.00	.00
Afternoon lesson	.00	.00
Different physical environment	.00	.00
Homeroom teacher influence	.00	.00
Unusual class size	.00	.00
Lesson taught in different room	.00	.00
Student factors (unusual)		
Students' experiences affect lesson	.00	.00
Hostile atmosphere	.00	.00
Unusual student disruptions	.10	.10
Abnormal group behavior	.00	.00
Teacher factors (atypical)		
Teacher experience influence lesson	.00	.00
Excessive praise	.00	.00
Unusual teacher enthusiasm	.00	.00
Unusual teacher behavior	.00	.00
Different teaching style	.00	.00
Different management approach	.00	.00
Different lesson approach	.00	.00
Inappropriate active participation	.00	.00
Teacher gave test answers	.00	.00
Other factors		
Typical external interruptions	.80	.40
Typical student disruptions	.80	.30
Teacher use of praise	14.70	14.90
Teacher varies from lesson	.20	.10
Use of active participation	6.00	.00
Inappropriate use of active participation	.00	.90
Level of teacher enthusiasm (scale: 1–5)	2.90	2.90
Enrollment	24.90	25.20
Attendance	21.50	23.50
Length of lesson	29.60	29.10

SOURCE: Adapted from tables 1 and 2 in Jerry Pratton and Loyde W. Hales, "The Effects of Active Participation on Student Learning," *Journal of Educational Research* 79 (1986): 213.

TABLE 15.3

Characteristics of Three Experimental Chemistry Texts

Text	Topic	Length (words)	Conceptual units length	Percentage of density	Percentage of lexical difficulty	Syntactic difficulty
1	Permanent polarity	62	6	3	9.60	33.00
2	Nuclear bonding	82	8	4	12.00	45.00
3	Induced polarity	161	13	3	10.55	47.00

Source: Table 1, Sandra Castañeda, Miguel Lopez, and Martha Romero, "The Role of Five Induced Learning Strategies in Scientific Text Comprehension," *Journal of Experimental Education* 55 (1987): 136.

content) can be attributed to the treatment (active participation) rather than to extraneous variables.

The treatment variable in some experiments consists of instructional materials rather than a teaching method. Treatment fidelity should be checked in this situation, too. For example, an experiment by Sandra Castañeda, Miguel Lopez, and Martha Romero tested the effect of three types of chemistry text on student reading processes.[25] The researchers analyzed the three text samples to check that they varied in the ways intended. The results of their analysis are shown in table 15.3. The texts were found to vary in the way intended.

Researchers wishing to test the effects of other instructional materials similarly need to (1) conceptualize the relevant dimensions on which they vary, (2) develop measures for quantifying each dimension, and (3) analyze the materials using the measures.

Strong versus Weak Experimental Treatments

One of the major problems of experimental research is producing a treatment that is strong enough to have an effect on the dependent variable. For example, you may do an experiment to determine whether a particular teaching method affects student achievement. The experimental design might require a group of

25. Sandra Castañeda, Miguel Lopez, and Martha Romero, "The Role of Five Induced Learning Strategies in Scientific Text Comprehension," *Journal of Experimental Education* 55 (1987): 125–130.

teachers to use the method for a period of one week, with student achievement measured at the beginning and end of this time period. Also, there might be a control group of teachers that uses a conventional teaching method for the same period; the achievement of their students would be measured in the same way as that of the experimental students.

Suppose no differences are found between the experimental and control groups. Should you conclude that the experimental teaching method does not produce greater achievement gains? Perhaps, but we can raise the criticism that you used a "weak" treatment. That is, we might argue that the experimental teaching method would have produced greater achievement gains than the control method had it been used over a longer time period, perhaps an entire school year.

Of course, as you increase the strength of the treatment, the experiment is likely to increase in complexity, time, and cost. Thus, many educational problems amenable to an experimental approach cannot be tackled by student researchers. They require a well-funded and well-staffed organization in order to be investigated properly. Before doing an experiment, you should determine whether you have the resources necessary to design a treatment that can reasonably be expected to have an effect on student achievement or other dependent variables.

EXPERIMENTAL DESIGNS AND STATISTICAL ANALYSIS TECHNIQUES

This section discusses types of experimental designs in educational research that incorporate random assignment of subjects to treatments. Experimental designs that do not involve random assignment are presented in the next chapter.

Earlier in this chapter we discussed Campbell and Stanley's ideas about the internal and external validity of experiments. These researchers also classified types of experimental designs. Table 15.4 provides a schematic presentation of their classification of single-group designs and control-group designs with random assignment. Some of the designs are more complex than others. They vary in use of control groups and administration of a pretest. The table shows that some experimental designs are much more likely than others to possess high internal and external validity. As we shall find, however, all have application in educational research. The selection of a particular design will depend upon the type of problem you are attempting to solve and the conditions under which you must work.

In presenting each experimental design, we shall briefly discuss the statistical procedures used to analyze the data yielded by the design. The *t*-test, analysis of variance, and analysis of covariance are widely used in experimental research. Multiple regression techniques are becoming increasingly popular, too, particularly as educational experiments become more complex. All these

TABLE 15.4

Experimental Designs and Their Sources of Invalidity

	Sources of Invalidity	
Design	Internal	External
Single-group designs		
1. One-shot case study X O	History, maturation, selection, mortality	Interaction of selection and X
2. One-group pretest-posttest design O X O	History, maturation, testing, instrumentation, interaction of selection and other factors	Interaction of testing and X; interaction of selection and X
3. Time-series design O O O O X O O O O	History	Interaction of testing and X
Control group designs with random assignment		
4. Pretest-posttest control-group design R O X O R O O	None	Interaction of testing and X
5. Posttest-only control-group design R X O R O	Mortality	None
6. Solomon four-group design R O X O R O O R X O R O	None	None

SOURCE: Adapted from tables 1, 2, and 3 in Donald T. Campbell and Julian C. Stanley, "Experimental and Quasi-Experimental Designs for Research on Teaching," in *Handbook of Research on Teaching*, ed. N. L. Gage (Chicago: Rand McNally, 1963), pp. 171–246.

NOTE: In Campbell and Stanley's tables, some invalidating factors are shown as possible sources of concern in certain designs. Only definite weaknesses in experimental designs are indicated here.

KEY: R = Random assignment.
       X = Experimental treatment.
       O = Observation, either a pretest or posttest of the dependent variable.

techniques were introduced in chapters 13 and 14, in the context of analyzing data from nonexperimental research.

The experimental designs presented here often involve the measurement of change, which poses difficult methodological problems. We shall discuss this topic at some length in chapter 16. We suggest that you also review chapter 9, which provides an overview of statistical analysis and its relationship to research design.

Random Selection and Random Assignment

We previously discussed randomization in terms of selecting a sample of persons to participate in one's study (see chapter 6). Briefly stated, **randomization** means that each person in a defined population has an equal chance of being selected to take part in the study. When doing an experiment, you need to consider another type of randomization, namely, random assignment of persons to experimental treatments. **Random assignment** means that each sampling unit (e.g., student, class, school district) has an equal chance of being in each treatment in the experiment. Random assignment is not relevant to single-group designs (designs 1 and 2 in table 15.4) because they incorporate only a single treatment.

In designing an experiment, you should make every effort to incorporate random assignment in your experimental design. Random assignment is the best technique available for assuring initial equivalence between different treatment groups. To illustrate this point, suppose you wish to compare the effectiveness of two worksheet formats. You have available a sample of 50 students for the experiment, and wish to form them into two treatment groups. Treatment group 1 will use one of the worksheet formats. Treatment group 2 will use the other format.

How is random assignment of students to treatment groups accomplished? The procedures are basically the same as for drawing a random sample from a defined population (see chapter 6). One good procedure is to use a table of random numbers. The students on the list can be numbered from 1 to 50; it does not matter that the names are in alphabetical order. Next consult a table of random numbers, such as the one in Appendix C. Identify an arbitrary starting point, let's say, the top of the fourth column on the first page of Appendix C (number = 81292). Because 50 students must be assigned, we will need to use two of the columns of each number. Let's use the first two columns beginning with column 4. The first 10 numbers selected by this procedure are: 81, 25, 38, 78, 99, 37, 34, 68, 50, 17. The numbers 81-78-99-68 are of no use to us. The first usable number, 25, identifies the 25th student on the list, who is assigned, let's say, to treatment group 1. The 38th student on the list is assigned to treatment group 2, the 37th student is assigned to treatment group 1; the 34th student is assigned to treatment group 2; and so on. You would keep using the table of random numbers until all 50 students had been assigned—by chance—to one treatment group or the other.

Random assignment does not *ensure* initially equivalent treatment groups, especially when a small sample is involved. A disproportionate number of subjects in one experimental group may have a certain characteristic. For example, the treatment group may have more low-achieving students, or more boys, or more white students. If so, it will be difficult to determine whether it was the characteristic or the treatment that caused group differences on the posttest. Methods for avoiding this problem are described below in the section on faulty randomization procedures.

Although random assignment is not a perfect method for assuring treatment group equivalence, it is the best method available. In turn, treatment group equivalence is essential to the internal validity of an experiment. To the extent that threats to the internal validity of the experiment are present, they should affect each treatment group to an equal extent if the groups are initially equivalent. Therefore, differences between the groups on the posttest can be attributed, with a high degree of confidence, to the treatment rather than to extraneous factors.

Random assignment can be easily achieved in brief experiments that occur under laboratory conditions. The situation is much different in field experiments conducted in schools, students' homes, or elsewhere. It may be difficult to obtain subjects' cooperation or establish conditions necessary for random assignment. Furthermore, even if initially equivalent groups are formed through random assignment, the equivalence may break down as the experiment proceeds. Thomas Cook and Donald Campbell identified a number of specific obstacles to forming and maintaining equivalent treatment groups in field experiments.[26] We turn now to a discussion of some of these obstacles, and how they might be avoided or overcome.

1. *Withholding the treatment from the control group.* If one treatment is perceived as more desirable than the other, you may encounter strong resistance to the use of random assignment. For example, suppose an experiment is planned to test the effects on student achievement of introducing a computer-enhanced videodisc system in elementary school classrooms. You wish to randomly assign 10 classrooms to receive the system (the treatment group), and another 10 classrooms (the control group) to continue functioning without the system for the duration of the experiment.

Upon hearing about the proposed experiment, teachers in the district may desire to have the system in their classrooms. They may view a computer-enhanced videodisc system as innovative and exciting—a real "plus" for their school and classroom. They may solicit parent support and lobby central office administrators to be in the favored group that receives the system. They are likely to express resistance to being in the low-prestige control group. In short, they will fight against the use of random assignment to allocate what is

---

26. Cook and Campbell, *Quasi-Experimentation.* Some of their obstacles to treatment group equivalence are not listed here because they are discussed elsewhere in this chapter.

perceived as a scarce and valuable resource—a computer-enhanced videodisc system.

If you ignore the protests and carry out the experiment as planned, you are likely to experience one or more of the internal validity threats described above: compensatory rivalry by the control group, compensatory equalization of treatments, or resentful demoralization of the control group. Therefore, you should explore the situation to find a solution that addresses the protests while at the same time maintaining the integrity of the experiment.

One solution is to tell the control-group participants that they will receive the treatment after the experiment is concluded. In the example above, the 20 teachers and their principals could be told that 10 of the teachers will receive the system the first year, and the other 10 teachers will receive it the second year.

Educators are usually amenable to this solution. The major difficulty with it obviously is that it creates additional work for the researcher. The length of the experiment is effectively doubled. You can save a great deal of effort simply by not collecting data during the administration of the treatment to the control group. On the other hand, by collecting the additional data, you will have a replication of the experiment. The first treatment group can be compared with the control group, and the control group can be compared with itself (before and after receiving the treatment).

A different solution is feasible in certain situations. Suppose you anticipate that some subjects will refuse to participate in the experiment because they do not want to be in a no-treatment control group or for some other reason. In this case, you can contact potential subjects and ask them if they would be willing to participate in the experiment irrespective of whether they are assigned to the treatment group or control group. Persons willing to abide by this condition would form the sample, which then would be randomly assigned to the treatment conditions.

The advantage of this procedure is that you do not have to administer the treatment to the control group subsequent to the main experiment; and subjects will rarely refuse to participate after randomization has occurred because they found that they were assigned to the control group. The major disadvantage of this procedure is that the experiment is conducted on a volunteer sample, hence limiting severely the external validity of the research results.

The senior author developed still another solution that will work in certain situations.[27] The solution is to give the control-group subjects an alternative treatment that they perceive as equally desirable as the experimental treatment. This treatment should be similar in both duration and procedure to the experimental treatment, but it should be concerned with a different set of dependent variables. For example, the senior author of this text along with

27. Walter Borg, "Dealing with Threats to Internal Validity That Randomization Does Not Rule Out," *Educational Researcher* 13, no. 10 (1984): 11–14.

Frank Ascione did an experiment to test the effectiveness of an inservice education program that they had developed to improve teachers' classroom management skills.[28] The experimental group participated in this program, while the control group participated in an equally desirable program of similar format but addressed to a different set of skills, namely, teaching skills to improve students' self-concept.

Applying this solution to the problem of testing a computer-enhanced videodisc system, we might recommend that the researchers introduce a similarly desirable, but different kind of technology in the control-group classes. Another possibility would be to introduce the system in both the experimental and control-group classes, but to have the teachers in the two groups use it for different but equally desirable purposes. For example, the experimental-group teachers could use it in teaching mathematics and science, while the control-group teachers could use it in teaching language arts and reading. If the computer-enhanced videodisc system is effective, the experimental-group students should outperform control-group students on measures of achievement in mathematics and science, whereas the reverse should occur for measures of language arts and reading.

2. *Faulty randomization procedures.* A defect in the researcher's random assignment procedure may result in nonequivalent treatment groups. Cook and Campbell cite the famous case of the 1969 military draft lottery. Each day of the year was put on a slip of a paper, and the slips were put in an urn. The order in which the slips were drawn out of the urn determined the order in which draft-age males would be drafted into military service. For example, if February 12 was drawn first, men with that birth date would be drafted first. Evidently the urn was not shaken well because the slips of days put into it last (those of December, November, October) remained near the top and were drawn out first. The solution to the problem is obvious.

Another problem that can occur with randomization procedures is that participants in the experiment may not believe the researcher's statement that random assignment to treatment groups occurred. This problem may be more likely to occur if the researcher is well known to the participants, and if they have reason to believe that the researcher is positively or negatively biased toward some of the participants. To avoid this problem, we suggest you have a credible witness observe the random assignment process. For example, if teachers in a school district are to be assigned to treatment groups, you might ask a teachers union or association representative to observe the randomization process.

As we indicated earlier, random assignment does not ensure equivalent treatment groups. Suppose you notice that randomly constituted groups are

28. Walter R. Borg and Frank R. Ascione, "Classroom Management in Elementary Mainstreaming Classrooms," *Journal of Educational Psychology* 74 (1982): 85–95.

obviously not equivalent based on available data about the sample—one group may have a disproportionate number of males, students from a particular grade level, students with high scholastic aptitude scores, and so on. If nonequivalence occurs at the time of random assignment, you have two alternatives. First, you can start again with the total sample and redo the random assignment procedures; for example, you can pick a new starting point in a table of random numbers and reassign each subject to a treatment group. Hopefully, a second—or even third—attempt at randomization will result in treatment group equivalence on known dimensions.

The second alternative is to stratify the total sample on the factor or factors for which equivalence is desired. (Stratification procedures are discussed in chapter 6.) After the total sample has been stratified, subjects can be randomly assigned within strata to treatment groups. This procedure ensures treatment group equivalence on the stratified factors.

3. *Small sample size.* The probability that random assignment will produce initially equivalent treatment groups increases as sample size in each group increases. For example, equivalent groups will more likely result if 100 subjects are randomly assigned to two treatment groups ($N = 50$ per group) than if they are assigned to four treatment groups ($N = 25$ per group).

There are several solutions to the problem of a small sample that is to be randomly assigned to two or more treatment groups. One obvious solution is to attempt to increase sample size. The additional expenditure of resources is well worth it if the result is equivalent treatment groups, and consequently, more interpretable research results. Another solution is to use matching procedures, which are discussed later in the chapter.

The third solution is to consider whether one or more treatment groups can be eliminated. Suppose, for example, that you are interested in testing the relative effectiveness of four training variations for an unusual learning disorder. You can only locate a sample of 16 students having the disorder. If the students are randomly assigned to the four treatments, there will only be four students per treatment group. Even if there are real differences between treatments, statistical power (see chapter 9) probably will be so low that the null hypothesis of no difference between treatments will not be rejected. In this situation you should consider comparing just the two most theoretically interesting or most promising treatments, in which case there will be eight students per treatment group.

4. *Intact groups.* Although not mentioned specifically by Cook and Campbell, intact groups in education pose a difficult obstacle to using random assignment procedures. An **intact group** is a set of individuals who must be treated as members of an administratively defined group rather than as individual persons. For example, most school classes are intact groups. The intact group is usually defined in terms of a particular grade level, teacher, and classroom (e.g., the fourth-grade class taught by Ms. Jones in Room 16).

Suppose that you wish to do an experiment in which the individual student is the appropriate sampling unit. You have available a sample of 50 fourth-grade students—25 from a classroom in school A and another 25 from a classroom in school B. Random assignment requires that each student be assigned, by chance, to the experimental or control group. School administrators and teachers, however, may require you to deal with students, not as individuals, but as members of an intact group. Thus, all students in a classroom must be given the same treatment in order to preserve the "intact" nature of the classroom group.

Given this situation, you can opt to increase the number of classrooms in the sample and institute one treatment condition per classroom. This procedure should result in an experiment with good internal validity if: (1) classrooms are randomly assigned to the experimental and control groups; (2) the issue of unit of statistical analysis is carefully addressed;[29] and (3) the problems that can occur with random assignment, described above, are avoided.

In practice the random assignment of classrooms to experimental and control groups may be difficult. If classrooms in several schools are involved, one classroom in a school may be assigned by chance to the experimental group, whereas another classroom in the same school is assigned by chance to the control group. Administrators tend to view each school as an intact group of teachers and students, however, and want everyone in the school to be treated the same way. Therefore, they are likely to press you to assign one treatment per school. For example, students in the fourth-grade class of school A could be assigned to the treatment condition (a new instructional method designed to improve learning) and students in the fourth-grade class of school B could be assigned to the no-treatment control condition. The integrity of the public school structure is thus preserved.

Several problems arise with this procedure, though, because students have not been randomly assigned to the treatment conditions. Consider, for instance, what would happen if students in school A came from predominantly upper-middle-class families and students in school B came from lower-class families. Because scholastic achievement is correlated with social class, students in school A are likelier to have higher posttest achievement scores than students in school B, with or without the instructional treatment. Thus, we cannot conclude on the basis of the findings that the instructional treatment is superior to conventional instruction. An equally plausible interpretation is that the differential achievement gain results from initial differences in the treatment groups.

The preceding illustrations typify the thorny problems we encounter doing a field or laboratory experiment in which random assignment to experimental treatments is not possible because the subjects are members of intact groups.

---

29. The topic of units of statistical analysis is discussed in chapter 9.

Nonetheless, it is possible to design an experiment in which the limitations of nonrandom assignment are partially or wholly overcome. Experimental designs of this type have been designated "quasi experiments" by Campbell and Stanley to distinguish them from "true" experiments, that is, experiments having random assignment. In the next chapter we discuss procedures for developing equivalence between intact groups receiving different experimental treatments.

SINGLE-GROUP DESIGNS

The One-Shot Case Study

The **one-shot case study design** hardly qualifies as an experimental design. In this design an experimental treatment is administered, and then a posttest is administered to measure the effects of the treatment. As table 15.4 shows, this design has poor internal validity. Suppose we select a group of students, give them remedial instruction (the experimental treatment), and then administer a measure of achievement (the posttest). How can we determine the influence of the treatment on the posttest? Unfortunately, we cannot. The students' scores on the posttest could be accounted for by their regular school instruction or by maturation, as well as by the treatment. Also, the fact that students were tested only once makes it impossible to measure change in their performance. Without a measure of change, we cannot even determine whether the students' achievement improved over time, regardless of whether this change was due to the treatment or to some other variable.

In short, the one-shot case study, although relatively simple to carry out, yields meaningless findings. Researchers who are limited to studying a single group of subjects should administer at the very least both a pretest and a posttest.

One-Group Pretest-Posttest Design

The **one-group pretest-posttest design** involves three steps: first, the administration of a pretest measuring the dependent variable; second, the application of the experimental treatment (independent variable) to the subjects; and finally, the administration of a posttest measuring the dependent variable again. Differences due to application of the experimental treatment are then determined by comparing the pretest and posttest scores.

The one-group pretest-posttest design was used in an experiment conducted by Eleanor Semel and Elisabeth Wiig.[30] Their purpose was to determine

---

30. Eleanor M. Semel and Elisabeth H. Wiig, "Semel Auditory Processing Program: Training Effects Among Children with Language-Learning Disabilities," *Journal of Learning Disabilities* 4 (1981): 192–196.

whether a new training program—based on an auditory processing model—would improve the language skills of learning-disabled children. The sample consisted of 45 elementary school students who were diagnosed as learning disabled in language because they scored two or more grades below age-grade expectation in two or more academic areas, one of them being reading.

All children in the sample received the training program, which was provided 30 minutes daily for 15 weeks. We might reasonably expect that the children, though language disabled, would make some language gains over this long a time period even without special instruction. Realizing this, the researchers made a generous estimate of gains that might be expected due to regular instruction (i.e., history), maturation, and so on; then they judged the effectiveness of the training program by whether it exceeded this estimate. Semel and Wiig explained their reasoning and procedures as follows:

> . . . standardized and age referenced tests were used as pre- and posttraining measures. In fact, then, the standardization samples were considered to be acceptable as a substitute for a control group. A rigid criterion of performance gains (+ 6 months) was set for the magnitude of gains which could be considered educationally significant. In reality, children with language-learning disabilities would not be expected to gain language skills at the rate expected for children with normal language development.[31]

The same battery of language proficiency tests was administered before and after the training program. The performance of the students on the pretest and posttest measures is shown in table 15.5. Mean raw score gains were observed on each of the measures (see columns 1 and 2). To determine whether the gains were educationally and statistically significant, the researchers first converted students' raw scores on each measure to an age-level equivalent (see chapter 9). The pretest age-level equivalent then was subtracted from the posttest age-level equivalent to yield an age-level gain score. The mean age-level gain on each measure for the total sample is shown in column 3 of table 15.5.

Next the researchers determined the percentage of students whose age-level gain on a particular measure was more than six months. These percentages are shown in the last column of the table. For example, 75 percent of the students made age-level gains of more than six months on the ITPA Grammatic Closure Test. The researchers tested whether these percentages were significantly different from a "chance" figure of 50 percent. The chi-square test revealed that more students made gains of 6+ months than could be expected if this was a chance event.

The researchers used the one-group pretest-posttest design in this experiment because the school system in which it was conducted did not permit differential services for its students. The absence of a control group was not a

31. Ibid., pp. 195–196.

TABLE 15.5

Pretest and Posttest Results for Students Receiving a Language Training Program

Test	Pretest M	Posttest M	Age-Level Gain (in months)	Percentage of Students with Gains > 6 mos.
1. ITPA Grammatic Closure	17.51	23.09	15.48	75.57% $\chi^2 = 11.76$**
2. DTLA: Auditory Attention Span for Unrelated Words	32.67	37.68	15.73	68.92% $\chi^2 = 6.42$*
3. DTLA: Auditory Attention Span for Related Syllables	30.89	39.29	10.13	51.13% $\chi^2 = .02$
4. DTLA: Verbal Opposites	19.44	23.64	7.27	37.79% $\chi^2 = 2.68$
5. DTLA: Verbal Absurdities	.96	5.36	22.00	71.13% $\chi^2 = 8.02$**
6. Carrow Elicited Language Inventory	36.12	40.00	30.37[a]	76% $\chi^2 = 8.76$**

SOURCE: Adapted from Eleanor M. Semel and Elisabeth H. Wiig, "Semel Auditory Processing Program: Training Effects Among Children with Language-Learning Disabilities," *Journal of Learning Disabilities* 4 (1981): 194–195.
[a] This score is the mean percentile gain using the percentile norms for this measure.
* $p < .05$.
** $p < .01$.

serious threat to the internal validity of the experiment, though, because the researchers had a good idea of pretest-posttest gains due to extraneous factors. The gains of the experimental group could be evaluated against estimated gains under normal, nonexperimental conditions.

The researchers' results, shown in table 15.5, indicate that the new training program was quite effective. However, even though the rationale for their experimental design appears sound, replications of the experiment would be desirable to increase educators' confidence in the effectiveness of the training program. For example, the program should be tested in a school district that would permit use of a pretest-posttest control group design.

The one-group pretest-posttest design is especially appropriate when you are attempting to change a behavior pattern or internal process that is very stable. For example, attitudes are quite stable in most individuals by adulthood and are unlikely to change unless some significant effort is made. The one-group design is also justified when the behavior pattern or characteristic is out of the ordinary or recalcitrant to change. For example, if I participate in an experimental program to learn how to speak Ukrainian (an out-of-the-ordinary behavior), the likelihood that extraneous factors could be involved to account for the change is small. Similarly, if an experimenter trains a cat to say a few human words, we would hardly dismiss the results as due to extraneous factors.

In summary, the one-group pretest-posttest control group design is most justified when extraneous factors can be estimated with a high degree of certainty or can be safely assumed to be nonexistent.

Statistical Analysis

The data in the Semel and Wiig study were analyzed by comparing whether an observed measure of pre-post gains (6+ months of age-level gain) differed significantly from a chance distribution of gain—a 50-50 split. The more usual procedure for analyzing data from a one-group pretest-posttest design is to do a *t*-test for correlated means. This test determines whether the difference between the pretest and posttest mean is statistically significant. The *t*-test for correlated means—rather than the *t*-test for independent means—is used because the same subjects take both the pretest and posttest.

If the scores on either the pretest or posttest show marked deviation from the normal distribution, a nonparametric statistic should be used. Most likely you would select the Wilcoxon signed-rank test. Each of the statistical tests mentioned above is also discussed in chapter 13.

Time-Series Design

In the **time-series design** a single group of subjects is measured at periodic intervals. The experimental treatment is administered between two of these time intervals. The effect of the experimental treatment, if any, is indicated by a discrepancy in the measurements before and after its appearance.

Campbell and Stanley classify the time-series experiment as a type of single-group design (see table 15.4) because it involves a single group of subjects all of whom receive the experimental treatment. The procedures used to maximize the internal validity of this type of experimental design and to analyze the data are similar to those used in single-subject designs. In fact, the labels for the two types of experimental design (single-group design and single-subject design) are very similar. Therefore, we discuss the time-series design in conjunction with single-subject designs in chapter 16.

CONTROL-GROUP DESIGNS
WITH RANDOM ASSIGNMENT

We discuss in this section two of the experimental designs shown in table 15.4: the pretest-posttest control-group design (no. 4); and the posttest-only control-group design (no. 5). We also present two variations on these designs: the pretest-posttest control-group design with matching; and the multiple-treatment group design.

The Solomon four-group design is shown in table 15.4, but we will defer our discussion of it until the next chapter. This is because the Solomon four-group design is an example of a factorial design. Therefore, to understand how this design works, you need to understand the logic of factorial design—a topic covered in chapter 16.

Pretest-Posttest Control-Group Design

Nearly any study that can be conducted using a single-group design can be carried out more satisfactorily using a control-group design. The essential difference between the single-group design and the control-group design is that the latter employs at least two groups of subjects, one of which is called the **control group** and is included primarily to make it possible to measure the effect of extraneous factors upon the posttest. The experiences of the experimental and control groups are generally kept as identical as possible with the exception that the experimental group is exposed to the experimental treatment. If extraneous variables have brought about changes between the pretest and posttest, these will be reflected in the scores of the control group. Thus, only the posttest change of the experimental group that is over and above the change that occurred in the control group can be attributed to the experimental treatment.

The pretest-posttest control-group design is among the most commonly used experimental designs in educational research. If properly carried out, it effectively controls for the eight threats to internal validity identified by Campbell and Stanley: history, maturation, testing, instrumentation, regression, selection, mortality, and interaction effects. However, table 15.4 indicates that the external validity of this design may be affected by an interaction of the pretest with the experimental treatment, that is, the experimental treatment may produce significant effects only because a pretest was administered. When it is tried on a group that has not been pretested, the treatment may not work as well. If you think that your experimental treatment is affected by pretesting, you should use the posttest-only control group design or the Solomon four-group design.

The following steps are involved in using a pretest-posttest control-group design: (1) random assignment of subjects to experimental and control groups, (2) administration of a pretest to both groups, (3) administration of the treatment to the experimental group but not to the control group, and (4) administration of a posttest to both groups. The experimental and control groups must be treated as nearly alike as possible except for the treatment variable. For example, both groups must be given the same pretests and posttests and be tested at the same time.

In some experiments, the control group receives no treatment except a pretest and posttest. In other experiments, however, you may want to administer an alternative experimental treatment to the control group. For example, as we discussed above, you may administer an equally desirable but different treatment to the control group in order to avoid the internal validity threats of compensatory rivalry, compensatory equalization, and resentful demoralization. Frequently, researchers compare an educational innovation with conventional practice. In this situation, the experimental group receives the innovation and the control group receives the alternative treatment, namely, conventional practice.

If the control group receives a treatment rather than a no-treatment condition, researchers sometimes refer to it as a *comparison group* rather than as a *control group*. Another option is to refer to the two groups by labels that describe the two treatment conditions, for example, the *computer lab group* and the *computer-in-classroom group*.

The pretest-posttest control-group design was used in a study of test-taking instruction by Moshe Zeidner, Avigdor Klingham, and Orah Papko.[32] The purpose of their experiment was to test the effectiveness of a training program to improve students' test-taking ability and to reduce their test anxiety. The program provides training in the nature of test anxiety, relaxation techniques, rational thinking, coping imagery, attention focusing, and time management.

The sample consisted of 24 fifth- and sixth-grade classes, because previous research had discovered that test anxiety increases among students when they reach upper elementary school. The 24 classes were randomly assigned to treatment (12 classes) and control (12 classes) conditions. The treatment classes received the test-taking program during homeroom periods in five one-hour sessions held two weeks apart. In a check of treatment fidelity, all teachers but one were found to be implementing the program as intended. The control classes did not receive any instruction in test-taking skills.

The dependent variables included three cognitive tests and two affective inventories. The cognitive tests were: the Digit Symbol Coding Scale of the Wechsler Intelligence Scale for Children; a vocabulary test; and a mathematics test. One of the affective inventories was the Test Anxiety Inventory, which includes two subscales: a Worry Scale, which measures students' cognitive

32. Moshe Zeidner, Avigdor Klingham, and Orah Papko, "Enhancing Students' Test Coping Skills: Report of a Psychological Health Education Program," *Journal of Educational Psychology* 80 (1988): 95–101.

concerns about the consequences of failure; and an Emotionality Scale, which measures autonomic stress reactions such as sweating, stomachache, and trembling. Higher scores on the inventory indicate greater worry and stress. The other inventory was the Teacher Awareness Inventory, on which higher scores indicate greater sensitivity to test anxiety as a student concern. All of the measures were administered to the experimental and control classes both before (pretest) and after (posttest) the training program.

Statistical Analysis

The pretest-posttest control-group experiment typically yields four mean scores for each measure. As shown in table 15.6, there are two pretest means and two posttest mean scores for each of the measures in the test-taking study. You will note that the experimental and control groups had almost identical mean scores on the pretest cognitive measures, but there were small differences in mean scores on the pretest affective measures. This result illustrates the principle that random assignment does not ensure initial equivalence between groups. Random assignment only ensures absence of systematic bias in group composition.

Campbell and Stanley observed that researchers often use the wrong statistical procedure to analyze such data. The incorrect procedure is to do a *t*-test on the pretest and posttest means of the experimental group (e.g., 23.5 vs. 28.9 on the Digit Symbol Test) and another *t*-test on the corresponding means of the control group (24.2 vs. 24.1). If the *t*-value for the experimental group is statistically significant, but the *t* value for the control group is not, the researcher would conclude—wrongly—that the experimental treatment was superior to the control treatment. This method of statistical analysis is wrong because it occasionally yields statistically significant differences that do not really exist between the experimental and control groups; in other words, it has a tendency to produce Type I errors.

The preferred statistical method is analysis of covariance in which the posttest means are compared using the pretest scores as a covariate. If the assumptions underlying analysis of covariance cannot be satisfied, you might consider an analysis of variance of the posttest means. (Because there are two posttest means, one for the experimental group and one for the control group, this is equivalent to doing a *t*-test). Another approach is to do a two-way analysis of variance for repeated measures; this statistical technique is discussed in the next chapter, in the section on factorial designs.

Zeidner and his associates tested the statistical significance of their results using analysis of covariance (ANCOVA).[33] You will recall from chapter 13 that

33. The ANCOVAs for the cognitive test measures in table 15.6 were preceded by a multivariate analysis of covariance (MANCOVA). The MANCOVA revealed a statistically significant difference between the experimental and control groups on the three test measures considered together.

TABLE 15.6

Effects of Test-taking Instruction on Students' Test Performance, Student's Test Anxiety, and Teacher Awareness

Measures	Experimental Group	Control Group	F
Digit Symbol Test			
Pre M	23.5	24.2	
Post M	28.9	24.1	
Adj M	29.2	23.8	56.93**
Vocabulary Test			
Pre M	15.5	15.2	
Post M	16.4	14.5	
Adj M	16.3	14.6	53.66**
Mathematics Test			
Pre M	9.3	9.3	
Post M	10.4	8.7	
Adj M	10.4	8.7	51.50**
Worry Scale			
Pre M	13.8	15.2	
Post M	14.1	15.9	
Adj M	14.7	15.5	4.50*
Emotionality Scale			
Pre M	17.1	17.5	
Post M	17.3	17.4	
Adj M	17.5	17.2	.74
Teacher Awareness			
Pre M	16.6	17.8	
Post M	21.5	17.4	
Adj M	21.9	16.9	44.66**

SOURCE: Adapted from Moshe Zeidner, Avigdor Klingham, and Orah Papko, "Enhancing Students' Test Coping Skills: Report of a Psychological Health Education Program," *Journal of Educational Psychology* 80 (1988): 98–99.
* $p < .05$. ** $p < .001$.

ANCOVA adjusts the posttest scores for differences between the experimental and control group on the corresponding pretest. The adjusted posttest means are shown in the rows labeled "Adj *M*" in table 15.6. Note, for example, that the adjusted posttest mean score of the experimental group on the Digit Symbol Test (29.2) is slightly higher than its actual posttest mean score (28.9). This is because the experimental group had a slightly lower mean score (23.5) than the control group (24.2) on the pretest. The effect of the ANCOVA adjustment is to compensate the experimental group for this initial disadvantage by increasing its posttest score to the level that would be predicted on the basis of the correlation between pretest and posttest Digit Symbol Test scores.

The results of the ANCOVAs are shown in the last column of table 15.6. The ANCOVAs yielded a significant F value for all measures except the Worry Scale. Thus, the researchers were able to conclude that a training program in test-taking skills improves students' test-taking ability and reduces their autonomic stress reactions to test-taking. The training program also increases teachers' sensitivity to their students' test anxiety. We can be fairly confident that these effects are attributable to the training program for three reasons: (1) classes were randomly assigned to the experimental and control classes; (2) the observed differences between groups on the posttest were statistically significant; and (3) extraneous variables were effectively controlled.

Pretest-Posttest Control-Group Design with Matching

A variation on the pretest-posttest control-group design is the use of the matching technique to obtain additional precision in the statistical analysis of the data. **Matching** in such designs refers to the selection of subjects for experimental and control groups in such a manner that they are closely comparable on a pretest that measures the dependent variable or variables correlated with the dependent variable. The main purpose of matching is to reduce initial differences between the experimental and control groups on the dependent variable or a related variable.

Matching is most useful in studies where small samples are to be used and when large differences between an experimental and control group on the dependent variable are not likely to occur. Under these conditions the small differences that do occur are more likely to be detected if sampling errors are reduced by the use of matching. The more closely the matching variable correlates with the dependent variable, the more effective the matching will be in reducing these errors. Thus, if matching is to be employed, we need to have available a matching variable that correlates highly with the dependent variable. For example, in studies concerned with achievement gains that occur under different conditions of learning, alternate forms of the same achievement test usually are available for the initial matching and for posttesting.

The measure of standard error used in tests of statistical significance is reduced considerably by the matching technique. This increase in precision is reflected in the difference between (a) the standard error of the difference between correlated means; and (b) the standard error of the difference between uncorrelated means. The formula for the standard error of the difference between uncorrelated means is

$$\sigma_D = \sqrt{\sigma^2_{m1} + \sigma^2_{m2}}$$

whereas the formula for the standard error of the difference between correlated means for matched groups is

$$\sigma_D = \sqrt{\sigma^2_{m1} + \sigma^2_{m2} - 2r_{12}\sigma_{m1}\sigma_{m2}}$$

The two formulas are identical except for the last factor in the matched-group formula. Because this factor is subtracted, it reduces the standard error, with the size of the reduction increasing as the size of the correlation increases.

Steps

The usual steps in carrying out a study using the pretest-posttest control-group design with matching are as follows:

1. Administer measures of the dependent variable or of a variable closely correlated with the dependent variable to the research subjects.
2. Assign subjects to matched pairs on the basis of their scores on the measures described in step 1.
3. Randomly assign one member of each pair to the experimental group and the other member to the control group.
4. Expose the experimental group to the experimental treatment and administer no treatment or an alternative treatment to the control group.
5. Administer measures of the dependent variables to the experimental and control groups.
6. Compare the performance of the experimental and control group on the posttest(s) using tests of statistical significance.

A method of matching that many statisticians favor is to place all subjects in rank order on the basis of their scores on the matching variable. After subjects have been placed in rank order, select the first two subjects (regardless of the difference in their scores on the matching variable) and by random means, such as flipping a coin, assign one subject to the experimental group and the other to the control group. Then select the next two subjects on the rank list and again randomly assign one to the experimental group and the other to the control group. Continue this procedure until all subjects have been assigned.

Edelwina Rivera and Michael Omizo used this matching procedure in an experiment that evaluated a method for increasing attention and reducing impulsivity among hyperactive children.[34] Their procedure for matching and randomly assigning students to treatments was as follows:

The sample consisted of 36 male hyperactive children between the ages of seven and eleven years ($M = 9.5$). . . .

---

34. Edelwina Rivera and Michael M. Omizo, "The Effects of Relaxation and Biofeedback on Attention to Task and Impulsivity Among Male Hyperactive Children," *Exceptional Child* 27 (1980): 41–51.

Subjects were identified through teachers' ratings on Conners' Behavior Rating Scale, Abbreviated Form . . . which has been reported to be the most extensively used teacher rating scale in existing research identifying and diagnosing hyperactive children. . . . Subjects were matched by ranking them on their behavior rating scores. Starting from the highest score, two subjects were taken at a time and randomly assigned to one of two groups by flipping a coin. After the groupings had been established, the two groups were randomly assigned to either experimental ($N = 18$) or control ($N = 18$) condition again by flipping a coin.[35]

The teacher ratings were not used as a posttest measure. However, the ratings correlated significantly ($r = .43$, $p < .01$) with pretest electromyogram (EMG) scores, which are a measure of muscular relaxation-tension, and which were readministered as a posttest. Because of this matching procedure, the pretest EMG means of the experimental and control groups were almost identical.

An alternative approach to matching is to stratify the sample on a pertinent variable and then to randomly assign subjects to treatment groups by stratum. The advantage of stratified random assignment is that the researcher can test whether treatment effects on a posttest measure vary from one stratum (i.e., subgroup) to another. Because of this advantage, stratified random assignment has been used with increasing frequency in recent years. We shall discuss this procedure in more detail in the section on factorial designs in chapter 16.

Posttest-Only Control-Group Design

This design is similar to the pretest-posttest control-group design except that pretests of the dependent variable are not administered to the experimental and control groups. The steps involved in the **posttest-only control-group design** are as follows: (1) randomly assign subjects to the experimental and control groups, (2) administer the treatment to the experimental group and no treatment or an alternative treatment to the control group, and (3) administer the posttest to both groups.

This design is recommended when you are unable to locate a suitable pretest or when there is a possibility that the pretest has an effect on the experimental treatment. In choosing this experimental design, consider three possible disadvantages of not administering a pretest of the dependent variable. First, random assignment may not be fully successful in eliminating initial differences between the experimental and the control groups. If initial differences still exist, then any differences found on the posttest can be attributed to them rather than to the effect of the experimental treatment. Because random assignment is most effective in equating groups when large numbers of subjects are involved, the posttest-only control-group design is best employed when you have a large pool of subjects available for study.

35. Ibid., p. 43.

The second disadvantage of not administering a pretest is that you cannot form subgroups to determine whether the experimental treatment has a different effect on subjects at different levels of the variables measured by the pretest.

The third disadvantage of not administering a pretest occurs when there is differential attrition during the course of the experiment. For example, if subjects in the control and the experimental group drop out of the experiment before it is over, then any differences on the posttest may be due to differential dropout characteristics of the two groups, rather than to the effect of the experimental treatment. Thus, the posttest-only control-group design should not be used when considerable attrition of subjects during the course of the study is a likely possibility.

An example of a posttest-only control-group experiment is provided below in the next section of the chapter.

Statistical Analysis

The data yielded by this experimental design can be analyzed simply by doing a *t*-test comparison of the mean posttest scores of the experimental and the control group. If more than two groups have been studied, then the mean posttest scores can be analyzed using analysis of variance. If the scores depart radically from the normal distribution, then a nonparametric test should be done.

Single-Factor Multiple-Treatment Design

The single-factor multiple-treatment design is a simple extension of the control-group designs that we presented in this chapter. The pretest-posttest control-group design, the pretest-posttest control-group design with matching, and the posttest-only control-group design involve random assignment of a sample to *two* groups. Each of these designs can be extended to include cases where a sample is randomly assigned to *three* or more groups.

We call such extensions **single-factor multiple-treatment designs.** The *single-factor* designation indicates that the groups differ on only one factor, which is the type of treatment they receive. The *multiple-treatment* designation indicates that more than two treatment conditions are involved.

An example of such a design is an experiment on instructional media conducted by Michael Simonson, Roger Aegerter, Timothy Berry, Terryl Kloock, and Robert Stone.[36] The purpose of their experiment was to determine the

36. Michael R. Simonson, Roger Aegerter, Timothy Berry, Terryl Kloock, and Robert Stone, "Four Studies Dealing with Mediated Persuasive Messages, Attitudes, and Learning Styles," *Educational Communications and Technology Journal* 35 (1987): 31–41. The experiment described above included an additional factor, which is not discussed in order to simplify the presentation.

effects of different instructional media on children's attitudes toward disabled persons. The specific hypothesis was that instructional media that present a message more realistically will cause greater attitude change than instructional media that present the message less realistically.

A total of 140 fifth- and sixth-grade students were randomly assigned to three treatments. One treatment was a film on employment of the handicapped. It had been selected by a jury of media specialists as an excellent persuasive film. Another treatment was a less realistic presentation of the message delivered in the film. It consisted of a slide presentation of still scenes in the film plus an accompanying audiotape of the film's narration. The third treatment involved no instruction.

The dependent variable in the experiment was a measure of attitudes toward disabled persons. A measure of this variable was administered as a posttest only. Therefore, the experiment involved a posttest-only control-group design. If the measure also had been administered as a pretest, it might have sensitized the students to the researchers' expectations. Had this occurred, the effects of the two treatments (film and slide-tape presentation) would have been confounded with the effects of the pretest.

Note, too, that the experiment could have been done with two treatment conditions, but it would have been less informative. For example, the researchers could have just compared the effectiveness of a film versus a slide-tape presentation. Suppose the film was found to cause more positive attitudes than the slide-tape presentation. This is useful knowledge, but we would be left wondering whether the film was more effective than just leaving the students alone.

Each of the three treatment conditions, then, serves a useful purpose in the experiment. In fact, a case can be made for adding even more treatment conditions. You will recall that the researcher's hypothesis was that the realism of an instructional message contributes to its effectiveness in creating attitude change. Films and slide-tape presentations are just two variations along the continuum of realism. In the context of this experiment, a disabled person speaking to the students can be considered more realistic than a film; and a textbook chapter on disabled persons could be considered less realistic than a slide-tape presentation. If these conditions were added to the experiment, the result would be a single-factor multiple-treatment design with five treatments: (1) live speaker, (2) film, (3) slide-tape, (4) text, and (5) no-treatment control.

Statistical Analysis

The results of the attitude change experiment are shown in table 15.7. The mean and standard deviation of each treatment group's scores on the attitude measure are shown in the second and third data columns.

TABLE 15.7

Effects of Film, Slide-Tape, and a No-Treatment Control on Students' Attitudes toward Disabled Persons

Treatment Group	N	Mean	SD	F
Film	49	85.63	15.67	6.41*
Slide-Tape	45	80.84	17.91	
Control	46	73.09	19.52	

SOURCE: Adapted from Michael R. Simonson, Roger Aegerter, Timothy Berry, Terryl Kloock, and Robert Stone, "Four Studies Dealing with Mediated Persuasive Messages, Attitudes, and Learning Styles," *Educational Communications and Technology Journal* 35 (1987): 36.
NOTE: Higher scores indicate a more positive attitude toward disabled persons.
* $p < .05$.

An analysis of variance was done to determine whether the mean scores of the three groups differed significantly from each other. The analysis of variance yielded a statistically significant F ratio (6.41) shown in the last column of table 15.7. Follow-up *t*-tests revealed that both the film and slide-tape groups had significantly more positive attitudes than the control group. Also, as predicted, the mean attitude score of the film group was higher than that of the slide-tape group, although the difference was not statistically significant.

Multiple-treatment experiments generally yield three or more mean scores or similar descriptive statistic. Therefore, the usual test of statistical significance in such experiments is univariate or multivariate analysis of variance, univariate or multivariate analysis of covariance, or a nonparametric equivalent.

MISTAKES SOMETIMES MADE IN CONDUCTING EXPERIMENTS

1. The researcher selects an experimental design that is inappropriate for the research problem.
2. Does not consider confounding variables such as history, maturation, statistical regression, and differential loss of subjects, which might have brought about changes attributed to the experimental treatment.
3. Generalizes the research findings to other situations and populations not warranted by the experimental design and sampling procedures.
4. Does not take steps to reduce the possibility of experimenter bias.
5. Designs an experimental treatment that is too weak to have an effect on the dependent variable.

6. Confuses the concept of random selection of subjects with the concept of random assignment of subjects to different experimental conditions.
7. When using a control-group design, matches the subjects on variables that do not correlate sufficiently with the dependent variable.
8. Uses the posttest-only control-group design with a small sample of subjects.

ANNOTATED REFERENCES

Keppel, Geoffrey. *Design and Analysis: A Researcher's Handbook*, 2nd ed. Englewood Cliffs, NJ: Prentice-Hall, 1982.

Provides a good perspective on the nature of experimentation in the behavioral sciences for the student who can follow it. A background in statistical analysis is necessary to follow the discussion of the various experimental designs.

Phillips, D. C. "Toward an Evaluation of the Experiment in Educational Contexts." *Educational Researcher* 10, no. 6 (1981): 13–20.

This philosopher of education carries on an entertaining dialogue with himself about the experimental method. While acknowledging its usefulness in educational research, he also makes convincing arguments about its inherent limitations. His central point is that no research method, including experimentation, yields irrefutable knowledge.

Richey, Harold W. "Avoidable Failures of Experimental Procedure." *Journal of Experimental Education* 45 (1976): 10–13.

Provides much down-to-earth advice about conducting experiments based on a personal experience in which an experiment failed. Most of the reasons for the failure are described in other sources, but the author's presentation is especially convincing. Provides recommendations to other investigators, including the suggestion that you imagine yourself a subject in the experiment and then intuit how you would react to each experimental procedure.

Shaver, James P. "The Verification of Independent Variables in Experimental Procedure." *Educational Researcher* 12, no. 8 (1983): 3–9.

Identifies weaknesses in the way that treatment fidelity is typically assessed, and suggests procedures for a stronger assessment. In particular, argues that fidelity of a treatment should be assessed by whether its implementation conforms to prespecified standards, rather than by whether its implementation differs from the implementation of the control treatment.

SELF-CHECK TEST

Circle the correct answer to each of the following questions. An answer key is provided on page 884.

1. A posttest in an experiment is sometimes called the
   a. dependent variable.
   b. experimental treatment.
   c. experimental variable.
   d. treatment variable.
2. An experiment in which the extraneous variables are controlled is said to be
   a. internally reliable.
   b. internally valid.
   c. externally valid.
   d. externally reliable.
3. If students' scores tend to move toward the mean upon retesting, _____ is said to have occurred.
   a. experimental mortality
   b. statistical regression
   c. maturation
   d. reactive effect of pretesting
4. If a pretest functions as part of the experimental treatment, the _____ of the experiment would be weakened.
   a. internal validity
   b. internal reliability
   c. external validity
   d. external reliability
5. Representative design of experiments assumes that
   a. the learning environment is a complex, interrelated ecology.
   b. the human learner is an active processor of information.
   c. the intended effects of an experimental intervention may radiate out to affect other aspects of performance.
   d. All of the above are correct.
6. Researchers often give participating teachers and students special attention that, though not part of the experimental treatment, may cause change. This phenomenon has been called the
   a. Hawthorne Effect.
   b. placebo effect.
   c. effect of multiple-treatment interference.
   d. reactive effect of experimentation.
7. A useful technique to minimize the effects of experimenter bias upon the outcome of an experiment is to
   a. train naive experimenters to collect the data from subjects.
   b. use objective measuring instruments.
   c. avoid suggesting to the experimenters that one experimental treatment is better than another.
   d. All of the above are correct.

For questions 8–10, use the following key:
   R = random assignment
   X = experimental treatment
   O = observation (pretest or posttest)

8. O X O describes the
   a. one group pretest-posttest design.
   b. one-shot case study.
   c. pretest-posttest control-group design.
   d. posttest-only control-group design.

9. R O X O describes the
      O O
   a. posttest-only control-group design.
   b. Solomon two-group design.
   c. counterbalanced design.
   d. pretest-posttest control-group design.
10. R   X O is a useful design if
         O
    a. it is thought the pretest will have an effect on the experimental treatment.
    b. no matching group is available.
    c. no control group is available.
    d. a large sample is available.

APPLICATION PROBLEMS

The following problems do not have a single correct answer. For feedback, you can compare your answers with the sample answers on pages 900–901.

1. A researcher is planning an experiment to test the effectiveness of the discussion method at the high school level. One teacher has agreed to use the discussion method in her class several times a week for a semester. Another teacher has agreed to teach the same content, but without using the discussion method. The researcher will collect the following data: student scores on an achievement test and on a scale measuring attitudes toward the instruction. What are three recommendations that you can offer to improve the representativeness of this experimental design?

2. A researcher has developed a new training program for teachers, which he firmly believes will bring about observable changes in their classroom behavior. To test its effectiveness, he plans to conduct an experiment in which he observes and compares teacher behavior before and after training.

   a. What type of methodological flaw has been introduced into the study at this point?
   b. What is an alternative procedure that might eliminate this flaw?

3. A researcher wants to test the effectiveness of providing high school students with a note-taking outline of each chapter they are assigned to read in a history class. She has permission to conduct the experiment with two history classes, each containing 30 students. She randomly forms two groups within each class. The experimental group receives a note-taking outline each time they are assigned a chapter; the control group receives the same assignment, but not a note-taking outline. On the basis of this information, what flaw has the researcher introduced into the experimental design?

4. A researcher is planning to test the effectiveness of a new reading program. A sample of 40 teachers distributed evenly among five schools in one school district has volunteered to use the program for a semester. Using only this sample, the researcher wishes to form two equivalent groups, one of which will participate in the special program while the other receives its regular program. State two methods by which equivalence can be achieved through random assignment.

5. A researcher carried out an experiment in mathematics instruction involving a pretest-posttest control-group design. The mean achievement scores for the experimental group were 35 on the pretest and 65 on the posttest. The mean scores for the control group were

45 on the pretest and 55 on the posttest. What statistical technique would most likely be used to analyze these data, and why?

SUGGESTION SHEET

If your last name starts with the letters from Osc to Pri, please complete the Suggestion Sheet at the end of the book while the chapter is still fresh in your mind.

16 EXPERIMENTAL DESIGNS: PART 2

OVERVIEW

This chapter applies principles of experimentation discussed in chapter 15 (especially internal and external validity) to three other types of experimental designs. Quasi-experimental designs are used when random assignment of subjects to experimental and control groups is not possible. Factorial designs, in contrast to the single-factor designs described in chapter 15, involve simultaneous manipulation of two or more variables. The third type of design is the single-subject experiment, which involves studying the effects of a treatment on a single individual or group. The chapter concludes with a consideration of problems involved in measuring change, an important topic because experiments in educational research are often done to determine the effect of a training procedure on student gain in achievement or other change in performance.

OBJECTIVES

After studying this chapter you should be able to:

1. Describe three procedures to lessen initial group differences that occur because of nonrandom assignment of students to experimental and control treatments.
2. Describe the methods and statistical procedures used in the following quasi-experimental designs: static-group comparison, nonequivalent control-group, and counterbalanced.
3. State threats to the internal and external validity of quasi-experimental designs.
4. Classify the independent variables that appear in factorial research designs into five types.
5. Explain the purpose, design, and statistical analysis of aptitude-treatment interaction experiments.
6. Compare the nature and uses of single-subject and group experimental designs.
7. Create several variations of A-B-A and multiple-baseline designs in single-subject research, and describe statistical techniques for analyzing the data yielded by these designs.
8. State several threats to the internal and external validity of single-subject experiments.
9. Describe problems in using gain scores to measure change, and state two statistical techniques for solving them.

QUASI-EXPERIMENTAL DESIGNS

We explained in chapter 15 that random assignment of subjects to the experimental and control groups is a very important feature of experimental design. Nonetheless, random assignment of subjects is sometimes not possible, particularly in field studies. Such experiments have been termed **quasi-experiments** by Campbell and Stanley[1] to indicate that random assignment of subjects to treatment groups was not accomplished. Quasi-experiments, if carefully designed, can yield useful knowledge. However, you should be aware of the special problems that may arise when subjects are not assigned randomly to groups, and should take steps to solve them.

Static-Group Comparison Design

The **static-group comparison design** is a type of experiment in which two treatment groups are administered a posttest but not a pretest; and subjects are not randomly assigned to the treatment groups. This design is identical to the posttest-only control-group design discussed in chapter 15, except for the absence of random assignment.

The steps involved in the static-group comparison design are as follows: (1) one group of subjects is administered the experimental treatment and is then posttested, and (2) another group of subjects is given the posttest only. These steps are represented in the following diagram:

$$- \frac{X \ O}{O} -$$

where X represents the experimental treatment, O represents measurement of the dependent variable after the treatment phase has ended, and the broken line indicates that the experimental and control groups are not formed randomly.

The main threat to internal validity affecting this design is that posttest differences between groups can be attributed to characteristics of the groups as well as to the experimental treatment. For example, suppose teachers in one school are given the experimental treatment and posttest, and teachers in another school are given only the posttest. If differences on the posttest are found, it can be argued that they are due to differences between teachers in the two schools rather than to the effect of the experimental treatment.

The static-group comparison design is weak. If you are planning to use it, consider carefully the feasibility of administering a pretest to the subjects. If this simple addition can be made, the resulting experiment will be a nonequivalent control-group design, which allows much stronger inferences concerning the effect of the experimental treatment on the posttest. This design is discussed in the next section.

1. Donald T. Campbell and Julian C. Stanley, "Experimental and Quasi-Experimental Designs for Research on Teaching," in *Handbook of Research on Teaching*, ed. N. L. Gage (Chicago: Rand McNally, 1963), pp. 171–246.

Statistical Analysis

The data yielded by a static-group comparison design can be analyzed by doing a *t*-test on the posttest mean scores of the two groups. If the scores deviate considerably from the normal distribution, a nonparametric test (most probably the Mann-Whitney *U* Test) would be used instead.

Nonequivalent Control-Group Design

The most widely used quasi-experimental design in educational research is probably the nonequivalent control-group design. This design is represented by the following diagram:

$$\frac{-\ -\ O\ X\ O\ -\ -}{O\quad\ \ O}$$

where X represents the experimental treatment, O represents pretest or posttest measurement of the dependent variable, and the broken line indicates that the experimental and control groups are not formed randomly. Thus, the distinguishing features of the **nonequivalent control-group design** are: administration of a pretest and posttest to both treatment groups, and nonrandom assignment of subjects to the groups.

The above diagram shows two groups. It is also possible to have a nonequivalent control-group design with more than two groups. Furthermore, it is possible to have all groups receive a treatment, with no group being a no-treatment control condition. The only essential features of this particular design, then, are nonrandom assignment of subjects to groups and administration of a pretest and posttest to all groups.

The nonequivalent control-group design was used in an experiment testing the effectiveness of an alternative to the use of resource rooms for mildly handicapped elementary students.[2] The study was conducted by James Affleck, Sally Madge, Abby Adams, and Sheila Lowenbraun.

The traditional approach to educating mildly handicapped children has been to place them in special resource rooms for all or part of their instruction. This approach is expensive, however, and it tends to isolate these children from their nonhandicapped peers. Therefore, the researchers and other educators developed the Integrated Classroom Model (ICM) in which mildly handicapped children are taught in regular classrooms administered jointly by regular and special education teachers. An ICM classroom typically includes one-third

2. James Q. Affleck, Sally Madge, Abby Adams, and Sheila Lowenbraun, "Integrated Classroom Versus Resource Model: Academic Viability and Effectiveness," *Exceptional Children* 54 (1988): 339–348.

mildly handicapped students and two-thirds average and above-average regular students.

The researchers were unable randomly to select and assign teachers and students to the experimental groups. In school districts, schools or classrooms are selected to try out a new program like ICM for a variety of reasons. For example, some schools may be selected because they have a staff that is particularly supportive of experimentation. In the experiment we are describing, the Integrated Classroom Model was tried out in two schools the first year of the project.[3] The reasons for selecting these two schools were not specified.

The control group consisted of mildly handicapped students in two other schools that had a resource room program. The researchers did not explain why these two schools were selected. Suppose, however, that five schools in the district had a resource room program. In this situation the researchers should examine each school carefully and then select the school or schools that are most similar to the experimental schools. This essentially is a matching procedure, which is better than selecting a school or schools at random from those having a resource room program. The random selection process, while desirable in other research situations, could result here in a sample of control schools that have very different characteristics from the experimental schools.

Because subjects in a nonequivalent control-group experiment are not randomly assigned to groups, it is particularly important to describe the characteristics of each group at the outset of the experiment. The description will help the researchers and others decide whether observed group differences on the posttest were caused by the treatment or by preexisting group differences on some variable. In the case of the ICM experiment, the researchers compared the experimental and control groups on several variables, which are shown in table 16.1, and found them to be similar. In addition, they reported that:

> All of the students in both groups were Caucasian, and both groups had equal socioeconomic status as determined by the district's reduced school lunch data. . . . The teachers of both the ICM and resource room model had similar experience and background. Similar specialized materials and methods were used in both models.[4]

Only students identified as learning disabled were included in the data analysis. Thus, both groups were similar with respect to handicapping condition.

Each student in the experiment was administered the reading, math, and language tests of a standardized test battery in October (pretest) and again the following May (posttest).

---

3. The researchers continued the experiment for years 2 and 3 of the project, but we only discuss year 1 results here in order to simplify the presentation.
4. Affleck, Madge, Adams, and Lowenbraun, "Integrated Classroom versus Resource Model," p. 342.

TABLE 16.1

Comparison of Group Characteristics in Integrated Classroom Experiment

Variable	Integrated Classroom Group	Resource Room Group
N	29	17
Gender		
male	19	12
female	10	5
Mean IQ score	95.9	99.4
Age range	8–0 to 12–2	7–3 to 11–9
Number of classrooms	5	5
Mean number of students per classroom	24	26
Mean number of learning-disabled students per classroom	7	3

SOURCE: Adapted from James Q. Affleck, Sally Madge, Abby Adams, and Sheila Lowenbraun, "Integrated Classroom Versus Resource Model: Academic Viability and Effectiveness," *Exceptional Children* 54 (1988): 343.

Statistical Analysis

The main threat to the internal validity of nonequivalent control-group experiments is the possibility that group differences on the posttest are due to preexisting group differences rather than to a treatment effect. Analysis of covariance (first discussed in chapter 13) is frequently used to handle this problem. Analysis of covariance reduces the effects of initial group differences statistically by making compensating adjustments to the posttest means of the two groups.

In the ICM experiment, the researchers used the students' October scores (the pretest) on each achievement test as the covariate for their May scores on the same test. First, however, the raw scores were converted to normal curve equivalent (NCE) scores, which are a type of standardized test score (see chapter 9). NCE scores have a mean of 50 and a standard deviation of 21.06.

Table 16.2 shows the posttest mean scores and adjusted posttest mean scores of both ICM and resource room students. We see that these scores range from 26.0 to 38.6. An NCE score of 29 is one standard deviation below the mean score of the norming group. Therefore, the students would be considered low-achieving (approximately the 15th percentile), which corresponds to their diagnosis of being learning-handicapped.

NCE scores allow comparisons between results of different tests. For example, table 16.2 shows that ICM students' adjusted mean NCE score on the

TABLE 16.2

Comparison of Integrated Classroom Students and Resource Room Students on End-of-Year Tests

Measure	Integrated Classroom Group	Resource Room Group	F
Language posttest			2.2
M	36.3	26.0	
Adjusted M	33.1	29.2	
Reading posttest			.1
M	38.1	29.8	
Adjusted M	34.3	33.6	
Math posttest			4.2*
M	38.0	31.5	
Adjusted M	38.6	30.9	

Source: Adapted from James Q. Affleck, Sally Madge, Abby Adams, and Sheila Lowenbraun, "Integrated Classroom Versus Resource Model: Academic Viability and Effectiveness," *Exceptional Children* 54 (1988): 343.
* $p < .05$

reading test was 34.3, whereas it was 38.6 on the math test. The fact that the math test score is higher means that the students were achieving at a higher level in math than in reading at the end of the school year.

The last column of table 16.2 shows the F ratio for the analysis of covariance of the two groups' adjusted posttest scores on each achievement test. The ICM and resource room students did not differ significantly in language and reading achievement. The treatment effect for math achievement, however, was statistically significant and favored the ICM students. The researchers concluded from these and other data analyses that "The results . . . support the integrated classroom model as a viable alternative service delivery model for students with learning disabilities."[5]

FACTORIAL DESIGNS

The classic single-factor experiment aims at holding all elements of the experimental situation constant except the treatment variable. This is true of the experiments described in chapter 15 and also the Integrated Classroom Model

5. Ibid., p. 345.

(ICM) experiment that we just described. In most educational situations, however, the experimental treatment cannot realistically be considered in isolation from other factors. For example, all of the children in the ICM experiment were white, but many school districts serve students from a variety of ethnic backgrounds. Therefore, further research on ICM instruction should consider the effects of *two* factors: treatment (ICM vs. resource room) and student ethnicity (white, black, chicano, etc.). It is also necessary to determine whether the two factors *interact* to affect student achievement. For example, ICM instruction may be ineffective for white children but not for children of other ethnic backgrounds. Factorial experiments make such investigation possible.

A **factorial experiment** is an experiment in which the researcher determines the effect of two or more independent variables (i.e., factors)—each by itself and also in interaction with each other—on a dependent variable. The effect of each independent variable on the dependent variable is called a **main effect.** The effect of the interaction of two or more independent variables on the dependent variable is called an **interaction effect.**

Two-Factor Experiments

The simplest type of factorial experiment involves a 2×2 design. The expression "2×2" means that two variations of one factor (A_1 and A_2) and two variations of another factor (B_1 and B_2) are manipulated at the same time. This factorial design requires the formation of four treatment groups, with each group receiving a different combination of the two factors: A_1B_1, A_1B_2, A_2B_1, and A_2B_2. Subjects should be randomly assigned to the four treatment groups. If random assignment procedures are not used, the design is a quasi-experiment. The data resulting from a factorial quasi-experiment are very difficult to interpret because main effects and interaction effects must be disentangled from possible selection effects due to initial differences between subjects in the various treatment groups.

Walter Saunders and Joseph Jesunathadas conducted a factorial experiment to identify factors that affect students' ability to engage in proportional reasoning.[6] They defined proportional reasoning as the ability to solve problems requiring the use of proportions (e.g., 2:3). This type of reasoning is important to student success in mathematics courses and also in science courses, especially physics and chemistry.

The experiment actually involved three factors, but we will simplify our description of it by considering it as a two-factor experiment. We will introduce the third factor a bit later.

The first factor in the experiment was familiarity of curriculum content.

6. Walter L. Saunders and Joseph Jesunathadas, "The Effect of Task Content Upon Proportional Reasoning," *Journal of Research in Science Teaching* 25 (1988): 59–67.

The researchers were interested in knowing whether students could engage in proportional reasoning better if the content was familiar than if the content was unfamiliar, as is often the case in science classes. They gave the following reason for their interest in this factor: "The obvious implication is that if students perform proportional reasoning better with familiar than with unfamiliar content, then instructional activities designed to promote familiarity of science content would be in order.[7]

The second factor in the experiment was level of difficulty of the proportions involved in solving problems. Three levels of difficulty were manipulated in the experiment: easy proportions (e.g., 2:3), moderately difficult proportions (e.g., 4:15), and difficult proportions (4:8.9).

A total of 76 typical ninth-grade students took a test in which the two factors were manipulated. The test contained 12 proportional reasoning problems, four at each level of difficulty. Two of the four problems at each level of difficulty involved content that would be familiar to ninth-grade students. The other two problems involved unfamiliar science textbook content.

In summary, the experiment involved a 3 × 2 factorial design: three levels of proportion difficulty and two levels of familiarity. The different combinations of the two factors are depicted below:

Because the experimental design has six combinations of factors, it normally would require six groups of students. However, the researchers had all of the students take the complete test, because it was not very long—a total of 12 items, two in each of the cells shown in the above diagram. Thus, the effect of each combination of the factors was examined with a total of 76 students (the complete sample). If each combination of factors had involved many test items, the researchers could have randomly assigned the 76 students to each combination (approximately 12 students per combination).

Statistical Analysis

The first step in analyzing the results of a factorial experiment is usually to compute descriptive statistics for the groups representing each combination of factors. The mean score of the students on the problems representing each of the

7. Ibid., p. 60.

TABLE 16.3

Mean Scores of Students on Problems Varying in Difficulty and Content Familiarity in Proportional Reasoning Experiment

Difficulty Level	Familiar Content	Unfamiliar Content	Total
Easy	1.44	.93	2.37
Moderate	.61	.70	1.31
Difficult	.64	.57	1.21
Total	2.69	2.20	4.89

SOURCE: Adapted from Walter L. Saunders and Joseph Jesunathadas, "The Effect of Task Content Upon Proportional Reasoning," *Journal of Research in Science Teaching* 25 (1988): 63.

six combinations of factors is shown in table 16.3. Also shown is the mean score of the students on each factor. For example, we see that students' mean score for test items having familiar content, ignoring the effect of item difficulty, is 2.69.

The next step in analyzing the results of a factorial experiment is to do an analysis of variance (ANOVA), analysis of covariance (ANCOVA), or multiple regression analysis to determine whether the differences between mean scores are statistically significant. Saunders and Jesunathadas did an ANOVA, the results of which are shown in table 16.4.

Table 16.4 shows that the main effect of content familiarity yielded a statistically significant F ratio of 10.03, meaning that students did significantly better on test items with familiar content ($M = 2.69$) than on test items with

TABLE 16.4

Analysis of Variance of Student Performance on Problems in Proportional Reasoning Experiment

Source	F	p
Content familiarity (C)	10.03	.002
Difficulty of proportions (D)	37.38	.001
$C \times D$ interaction	18.58	.001

SOURCE: Adapted from Walter L. Saunders and Joseph Jesunathadas, "The Effect of Task Content Upon Proportional Reasoning," *Journal of Research in Science Teaching* 25 (1988): 64.

unfamiliar content ($M = 2.20$). The main effect of proportion difficulty also yielded a statistically significant F ratio of 37.38. Because this factor has three levels (easy, moderate, and difficult), the researchers needed to do post hoc t-tests to determine which of the mean scores (2.37, 1.31, and 1.21 in table 16.3) differed significantly from each other. This analysis revealed that the students did significantly better on the easy items than on the moderate or difficult items. Their performance on the moderate and difficult items did not differ significantly.

We also see in table 16.4 that the interaction between the two factors yielded a statistically significant F ratio of 18.58. The nature of the interaction is depicted in figure 16.1. The students' mean score for each combination of factors, shown in figure 16.1, indicates that the students only do better on test items with familiar content when they involve easy proportions. They do not do better on test items with familiar content if the proportions are moderately difficult or difficult.

The study of interaction effects in a factorial experiment leads to important insights, as we see above. If we only compared students' performance on test items with familiar content and test items with unfamiliar content (see bottom row of table 16.3), we would conclude that students do better on the former type of item. This conclusion oversimplifies the actual situation, however. The conclusion only applies to a certain type of test item, namely test items whose solution involves simple proportions.

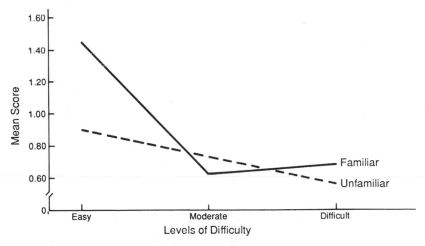

Figure 16.1   Plot of Two-Way Interaction Involving Difficulty Level and Content Familiarity in Proportional Reasoning Experiment.

Source: Adapted from Walter L. Saunders and Joseph Jesunathadas, "The Effect of Task Content Upon Proportional Reasoning," *Journal of Research in Science Teaching* 25 (1988): 65.

Three-Factor Experiments

A factorial experiment is not limited to the manipulation of two factors. We can find published reports of experiments involving three, four, and even five factors. Experiments involving more than three factors are not common, however, because developing all of the treatment variations is difficult and because a large sample is usually required.

As we stated above, the experiment on proportional reasoning by Saunders and Jesunathadas involved three factors. The third factor was student gender. Student performance on the test items was analyzed separately for male students ($N = 34$) and female students ($N = 42$). Mean scores for students of each gender are shown in table 16.5. We see in this table that there are 12 combinations of factors. This is because the actual experiment involved a $3 \times 2 \times 2$ factorial design: 3 levels of item difficulty (easy, moderate, and difficult); 2 levels of test content familiarity (familiar and unfamiliar); and 2 levels of gender (male and female).

The analysis of variance shown in table 16.4 should include four more F ratios. One F is for the main effect of gender (10.33), which is statistically significant. This means that the mean score summed across all items for males (6.14) is significantly different from the mean score for females (3.60).

TABLE 16.5

Mean Scores of Male and Female Students on Problems in Proportional Reasoning Experiment

Difficulty Level		Familiar Content		Unfamiliar Content	
		Male	Female	Male	Female
Easy	M	1.56	1.31	1.09	0.76
	SD	0.66	0.75	0.90	0.85
	N	34	42	34	42
Moderate	M	0.82	0.40	1.00	0.40
	SD	0.90	0.73	0.85	0.77
	N	34	42	34	42
Difficult	M	0.94	0.33	0.73	0.40
	SD	0.85	0.61	0.90	0.73
	N	34	42	34	42

SOURCE: Adapted from Walter L. Saunders and Joseph Jesunathadas, "The Effect of Task Content Upon Proportional Reasoning," *Journal of Research in Science Teaching* 25 (1988): 63.

The other three F ratios involve interaction effects, which are shown below:

1. Gender by Content Familiarity $F = 1.31$ $(p = .27)$
2. Gender by Difficulty of Proportions $F = .01$ $(p = .93)$
3. Gender by Familiarity by Difficulty $F = 2.81$ $(p = .06)$

The first two F ratios, which are not statistically significant, mean that the significant main effects for item difficulty and content familiarity (see table 16.4) are not affected by students' gender. The three-way interaction, however, is very nearly statistically significant $(p = .06)$.

The three-way interaction can be detected by comparing the results shown in tables 16.3 and 16.5. We find in table 16.3 that on easy items, students did better on those with familiar content than on those with unfamiliar content. Looking now at table 16.5, we find that this difference pattern holds true for both male and female students.

Next, we find in table 16.3 that for items of moderate difficulty, students do slightly better on those with unfamiliar content. Looking now at table 16.5, we find that this difference pattern is found for male students but not for female students. In other words, the difference in performance on items varying in content familiarity (factor 1) at a moderate level of difficulty (factor 2) is affected by student gender (factor 3).

A similar three-way interaction is found for difficult test items. Looking at table 16.3, we find that students do slightly better on difficult test items if the content is familiar. Looking now at table 16.5, we find that the difference pattern again applies to male students but not to female students.

Three-way interactions are difficult to interpret and are often of small magnitude. Thus, even if they are statistically significant, they are usually ignored by researchers. Most computer programs for ANOVA and ANCOVA routinely report F ratios for three-way interactions, however, so you should at least understand what they represent. The focus of interpretation is usually on the reported F ratios for main effects and two-way interactions.

Types of Treatment Variables

In discussing Saunders and Jesunathadas' experiment on proportional reasoning, we stated that three variables were manipulated. Strictly speaking, only the difficulty and familiarity of test items were "manipulated." One cannot manipulate their third factor, which was the subjects' gender; it is a given of the situation (i.e., the experimenter cannot manipulate subjects to make them male or female). Campbell and Stanley[8] have provided a useful classification of the

8. Campbell and Stanley, "Designs for Research on Teaching," p. 200.

types of independent variables that might appear in an educational experiment along this dimension of manipulability:

1. Manipulated variables, such as teaching method, assignable at will by the experimenter
2. Potentially manipulable aspects, such as school subject studied, that the experimenter might assign in some random way to the pupils he or she is using, but rarely does
3. Relatively fixed aspects of the environment, such as community or school or socioeconomic level, not under the direct control of the experimenter but serving as explicit bases for stratification in the experiment
4. "Organismic" characteristics of pupils, such as age, height, weight, and sex
5. Response characteristics of pupils, such as scores on various tests.

As Campbell and Stanley point out, the experimenter's primary interest is usually in the class 1 variable. Variables in classes 3, 4, and 5 are used to group subjects in order to determine how generalizable the effects of manipulated variables are. For example, your primary independent variable may be a new teaching method. In addition, you might be interested in grouping students by intelligence level (a class 5 variable, as intelligence is usually determined by a test score) in order to determine whether the teaching method is effective for students of all intelligence levels or just for students of a particular intelligence level. This type of research is discussed in the section immediately following.

Aptitude-Treatment Interaction Research

Different students have different learning styles and aptitudes. Therefore, a single instructional method or program may not be suitable for all students. Improvement in education may result from efforts to match instructional methods and programs with students who are best able to learn from them. A line of educational experimentation, called aptitude-treatment interaction (ATI) research, has explored this possibility.[9] The purpose of **ATI research** is to determine whether the effects of different instructional methods are influenced by the cognitive or personality characteristics of the learner.

ATI research does not assume that one instructional method is better than another; nor is it assumed that students with certain characteristics are better learners than others. Instead, ATI research proceeds under the assumption that the two factors (method and learner characteristics) may interact in ways that have educational significance. Interactions are revealed by designing factorial

9. A comprehensive survey of ATI research was done by Cronbach and Snow (see the Annotated References at the end of this chapter).

experiments similar to the experiment on proportional reasoning that we described above.

An ATI experiment usually has two independent variables. The first independent variable may be teaching method, curriculum materials, learning environment, or similar instructional variable. The other independent variable is a student characteristic such as an aptitude, personality dimension, level of academic achievement, or learning style.

The initial focus of ATI research was on aptitudes, hence the label *aptitude-treatment interaction*. Subsequently, the label *attribute-treatment interaction* was introduced to indicate that a wide range of learner characteristics—not just aptitude—may interact with instructional methods.[10] Attribute variables correspond to the last two types of independent variables (4 and 5) in Campbell and Stanley's classification described above: organismic characteristics and response characteristics.

An example of ATI research is the experiment on mastery learning by Kim Chan and Peter Cole.[11] Mastery learning is an instructional method developed by Benjamin Bloom to improve the learning process. Its features include the following:

> Course content is typically organized into a set of sequential learning tasks and a mastery criterion is specified for each task. Formative tests are constructed and feedback and corrective procedures are developed at every stage of the learning sequence. Adequate learning time is provided to ensure that the prescribed criterion level is attained by all students on each task before advancing to the next task in the series.[12]

The specific hypothesis tested by Chan and Cole was that mastery learning would be of more benefit to low-aptitude students than to high-aptitude students. This is a typical ATI hypothesis, because an instructional method is predicted to have differential effects for learners varying in entry characteristics.

The experiment involved 180 third-grade students in Australia who were randomly assigned to four treatment groups:

1. *90% mastery group.* The students received mastery learning instruction, and needed to answer correctly 90 percent of the items on a criterion test before proceeding to a new learning task.
2. *70% mastery group.* Similar to the 90 percent condition, except that students only needed to answer 70 percent of the criterion test items correctly before proceeding to a new learning task.

10. The significance of this broader label is explained in Sigmund Tobias, "Achievement Treatment Interactions," *Review of Educational Research* 46 (1976): 61–74.
11. Kim Sang Chan and Peter G. Cole, "An Aptitude-Treatment Interaction in a Mastery Learning Model of Instruction," *Journal of Experimental Education* 55 (1987): 189–200.
12. Ibid., p. 189.

3. *Nonmastery group.* The students proceeded from one learning task to the next irrespective of how well they did on each criterion test.
4. *Control group.* The students received no instruction.

The set of three learning tasks were designed to improve students' reading comprehension.

All students took several cognitive tests prior to the instructional phase of the experiment. One of them was a word recognition skill test designed to measure students' ability to read words aloud. This was the attribute variable. Following the instructional phase, students took several posttests, including a test of reading comprehension.

Statistical Analysis

The data from an ATI experiment can be analyzed in the same way as any other factorial experiment. The first step is to compute descriptive statistics, usually the mean and standard deviation, for each of the treatment groups. In the case of the mastery learning experiment, means and standard deviations were computed for each pretest and posttest for each of the four treatment groups. Descriptive statistics for the reading comprehension posttest are presented in table 16.6. It is apparent that the 90 percent mastery group did somewhat better on this measure than the other three treatment groups.

Analysis of variance or analysis of covariance is often used to determine the statistical significance of mean score differences between the various treatment groups in an ATI experiment. You will recall, for example, that

TABLE 16.6

Descriptive Statistics for Reading Comprehension Posttest in Mastery Learning Experiment

Treatment Group	Reading Comprehension Posttest	
	M	*SD*
90% Mastery	54.91	3.55
70% Mastery	51.51	4.94
Nonmastery	51.96	4.85
Control	50.93	4.35

SOURCE: Adapted from Kim Sang Chan and Peter G. Cole, "An Aptitude-Treatment Interaction in a Mastery Learning Model of Instruction," *Journal of Experimental Education* 55 (1987): 193.

TABLE 16.7

Summary of Multiple Regression Analysis for Reading
Comprehension Posttest in Mastery Learning
Experiment

Source	F	p	R^2 Increment
Cognitive pretests (CP)	42.50	.01	.49
Treatment (T)	11.31	.01	.08
$CP \times T$ interaction	1.86	.05	.05

SOURCE: Adapted from Kim Sang Chan and Peter G. Cole, "An
Aptitude-Treatment Interaction in a Mastery Learning Model of
Instruction," *Journal of Experimental Education* 55 (1987): 194.

analysis of covariance was used in the experiment on proportional reasoning
described above. Another approach is to use multiple regression (see chapter
14), as was done in the mastery learning experiment.

A summary of the multiple regression analysis for the reading comprehension posttest is shown in table 16.7. The first row of this table shows the
combined effect of the various cognitive pretests (including the word recognition
test) on the reading comprehension posttest. The F ratio for this effect, which is
statistically significant ($p = .01$), is similar in meaning to an F ratio in an analysis
of variance or analysis of covariance. The R^2 increment of .49 means that the
cognitive tests account for 49 percent of the variance in the posttest; or, to state it
another way, the combined pretests correlate .70 with the posttest. This high a
correlation is not surprising. Students of higher aptitude are likely to do better
on an achievement posttest, irrespective of the instructional method that is
used.

The next row of table 16.7 shows the effect of the treatment variable on the
reading comprehension posttest. This effect, which is also statistically significant, accounts for an additional 8 percent of the variance in the posttest beyond
that accounted for by the cognitive pretest. The significant treatment effect is
due to the fact that the 90 percent mastery treatment was superior to the other
three treatment variations (see table 16.6).

Finally, we see in table 16.7 that the interaction effect between the
cognitive pretests and the treatment variable is statistically significant. This
means that the effectiveness of the various treatments is affected by students'
prior academic achievement, as measured by the cognitive pretests.

The nature of this interaction effect can be examined in a particular way
using multiple regression. The researcher considers each treatment group
separately and uses the students' scores on each aptitude test to predict their

scores on the posttest. The result is an equation. (You may wish to review chapter 14 for a description of how these equations are developed.) Because the mastery learning experiment involved four treatment groups, there were four such equations for each cognitive pretest. The equations for the word recognition test are shown below:

90% Mastery	$Y = .12X + 49.82$
70% Mastery	$Y = .29X + 39.36$
Nonmastery	$Y = .28X + 40.40$
Control	$Y = .25X + 40.96$

In each equation, Y equals the student's predicted score on the reading comprehension posttest, and X equals the student's score on the word recognition test.

The X and Y values for each equation can be plotted on a graph, as is shown in figure 16.2. The equations for three of the groups (70 percent mastery, nonmastery, and control) were plotted together on the graph because they are so similar and because doing so simplifies the presentation.

The nature of the interaction effect is now apparent. For students with low cognitive ability (scores of approximately 0–20 on the word recognition test, 90 percent mastery learning instruction is substantially better than the other treatment conditions. For students with higher cognitive ability, the superiority of mastery learning instruction is negligible. In other words, we cannot conclude

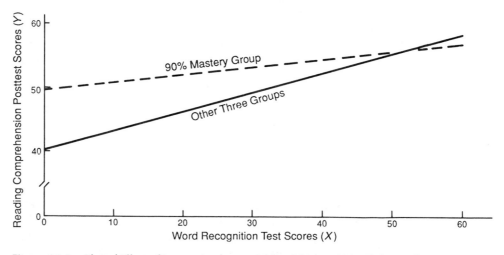

Figure 16.2   Plot of Effect of Interaction between Word Recognition Ability and Treatments in Mastery Learning Experiment.

SOURCE: Adapted from Kim Sang Chan and Peter G. Cole, "An Aptitude-Treatment Interaction in a Mastery Learning Model of Instruction," *Journal of Experimental Education* 55 (1987): 195.

from the results of this experiment that mastery learning is generally superior to other methods. It is only superior for those students with low initial cognitive ability. This more limited conclusion supports the researchers' hypothesis, which we stated in our initial description of the experiment.

In summary, an ATI experiment allows for a more sophisticated analysis of the effects of instructional methods than would be possible by just comparing one treatment group with another. ATI designs include at least two factors (treatment and learner characteristics), whereas the experimental designs described in chapter 15 involve only a single factor (the treatment variable).

Solomon Four-Group Design

The Solomon four-group design is a special case of a factorial design. The **Solomon four-group design** is used to achieve three purposes: (1) to assess the effect of the experimental treatment relative to the control treatment; (2) to assess the effect of a pretest relative to no pretest; and (3) to assess the interaction between pretest and treatment conditions.

You will recall from the preceding chapter that pretest sensitization is a possible threat to the ecological validity of an experiment. Different results might occur if a pretest is administered to the experimental and control groups than if a pretest is not administered. The pretest might have an effect on student achievement or attitudes because it provides an opportunity to *practice* or think about the content incorporated in the pretest. Also, the pretest might have a special effect on the experimental-group students because it *sensitizes* them to study specific content incorporated in the experimental treatment. The pretest would not have this effect on the control group because, by definition, they are not exposed to the experimental treatment content.

A systematic investigation of pretest effects can be made by using the Solomon four-group design. Two factors—pretest and treatment—are varied in this design, as shown in this diagram:

$$
\begin{array}{lllll}
\text{Group 1.} & \text{R} & \text{O} & \text{X} & \text{O} \\
\text{Group 2.} & \text{R} & \text{O} & & \text{O} \\
\text{Group 3.} & \text{R} & & \text{X} & \text{O} \\
\text{Group 4.} & \text{R} & & & \text{O}
\end{array}
$$

     Key: R = random assignment.
                X = experimental treatment.
                O = observation, either a pretest or posttest.

If the pretest provides a practice effect, this should result in higher posttest performance by groups receiving the pretest (1 and 2), than by groups not receiving the pretest (3 and 4). If the pretest sensitizes the experimental group to study specific content, this should result in a pretest-treatment interaction.

Specifically, there should be a greater difference on the posttest between groups 1 and 3 than between groups 2 and 4. This is because a sensitization effect means that the pretest facilitates the learning of the experimental group but not of the control group.

The Solomon four-group design was used in an experiment by Rosaland Edwards.[13] The main purpose of the experiment was to determine the effect of performance standards on motor skill development in elementary school children. Edwards hypothesized that "an individual with a difficult, specific standard or goal, but one that is attainable, will have a higher level of performance than an individual with no standards or with an easy, nonspecific goal."[14]

The experiment involved eight intact fourth-grade and fifth-grade classes, which were assigned to the four groups (two classes per group) of the Solomon design. All of the groups were taught the motor skill of making a hockey flip shot. This skill involves using a hockey stick to shoot a floor hockey ball through a target 0.31 meters square, 25 centimeters from the floor, and located 1.86 meters from the shooting line. Also, all students were given a total of six 2-minute sessions distributed evenly over two days.

All students in the two experimental treatment groups (O X O and −X O) were given a performance standard to attain by their teacher. This standard was to make two more successful shots per session than they had averaged the previous day. Based on pilot study results, this standard was considered difficult but attainable. The two control groups (O − O and − − O) participated in similar practice sessions but without explicit performance standards.

The pretest consisted of having students take 45 shots at the target. The student received two points for hitting the hockey ball through the target hole, one point if the hockey ball traveled in the air and hit the target, and zero points otherwise. The pretest score was the total points accumulated in the 45 attempts.

Edwards was concerned that the pretest might function as a treatment in its own right. Therefore, two of the groups (O X O and O − O) received a pretest, and two groups (− X O and − − O) did not receive a pretest. The inclusion of a pretest factor in the experimental design allowed Edwards to test the effects of the pretest on measures of the dependent variables.

Two dependent variables were measured. First, the behavior of the students during the practice sessions in the instructional phase of the experiment was assessed. The primary measure of student behavior was the total number of shots (called "trials") the students took at the target during the six 2-minute practice sessions. The other dependent variable, flip-shot skill, was measured by a posttest that was identical in form and scoring to the pretest.

13. Rosaland Edwards, "The Effects of Performance Standards on Behavior Patterns and Motor Skill Achievement in Children," *Journal of Teaching in Physical Education* 7 (1988): 90–102.
14. Ibid., p. 90.

Statistical Analysis

The Solomon four-group experiment can be viewed as a 2 × 2 factorial design. The two factors are pretest (present or absent) and treatment (performance standards present or absent). As we saw above in the experiment on proportional reasoning, group differences in a factorial experiment can be tested for statistical significance using an analysis of variance procedure. This was the case in the experiment on motor skill development. The researcher first did a multivariate analysis of variance (MANOVA) on the two dependent measures—practice trials and posttest score—considered together. Then she did a univariate analysis of variance (ANOVA) separately for each dependent measure.

The results of the two ANOVAs are shown in table 16.8. The only statistically significant effect on students' posttest scores was the treatment variable. Students receiving performance standards earned a significantly higher mean score ($M = 15.58$) than students not receiving performance standards ($M = 12.58$).

There were two statistically significant effects on the number of trials that students made during the practice sessions. Students receiving performance standards had significantly more trials ($M = 70$) than students not receiving performance standards ($M = 54$). A significant interaction also existed between the pretest and the treatment variable.

The nature of this interaction is illustrated in figure 16.3. We see that the pretest had a modest effect on the control group: Pretested students only had about 10 more trials on average than did nonpretested students. The pretest, however, had a dramatic effect on the treatment group: Pretested students had about 30 fewer trials on average than did nonpretested students. Edwards

TABLE 16.8

Analysis of Variance Results for Solomon Four-Group Experiment on Motor Skill Development

Source	Posttest Scores F	Trials F
Treatment (*T*)	25.19*	13.51*
Pretest (*P*)	____.ᵃ	____ᵃ
T × *P* interaction	____.ᵈ	18.14*

SOURCE: Adapted from Rosalind Edwards, "The Effects of Performance Standards on Behavior Patterns and Motor Skill Achievement in Children," *Journal of Teaching in Physical Education* 7 (1988): 95–96.
ᵃ The *F* values were not included in the report; only the fact that they were not statistically significant. * $p < .05$.

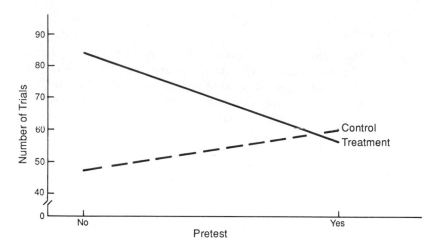

Figure 16.3   Plot of Effect of Interaction between Pretest and Treatment on Number of Trials in Motor Skills Experiment.

Source: Adapted from figure 1 in Rosaland Edwards, "The Effects of Performance Standards on Behavior Patterns and Motor Skill Achievement in Children," *Journal of Teaching in Physical Education 7* (1988): 96.

interpreted the interaction effect to mean that: "Having an adult give the test appears to set the pace or perhaps tends to standardize the number of practice trials taken during the allotted practice sessions."[15] As we see in figure 16.3, the treatment group with a posttest had both a performance standard and a pretest experience to guide their behavior. Evidently, the pretest experience had more of an effect, because their trial frequency was more similar to the control group that had a pretest than it was to the other treatment group, which also had a performance standard but no pretest experience. Edwards cautioned other researchers to be careful about using pretests in studies of motor skill development because they can mask the effects of instruction.

If a pretest effect seems likely, you can use either a posttest-only control-group design (see chapter 15) or a Solomon four-group design. The latter is the more powerful experimental design, but it requires a rather large sample and much researcher effort. The effort is justified if there is a high probability that pretesting will have an effect on the experimental treatment and if you wish to measure this effect.

Counterbalanced Experiments

Each subject is assigned to just one treatment in most experiments. In a typical 2 × 2 factorial experiment, for example, there are four treatment conditions. Each subject is assigned to just one of these conditions. Some research

15. Ibid., p. 98.

problems, however, can be investigated by assigning each subject to more than one treatment condition. You will recall that this is what was done in Saunders and Jesunathadas' experiment on proportional reasoning. The advantage of assigning subjects to several treatments is that the experiment can be done with fewer subjects. Thus, subject recruitment is easier, and financial expenses of conducting the experiment may be reduced. Another advantage is that the statistical analysis of the data is more sensitive because each subject is "matched" with himself across treatments.

If subjects participate in more than one treatment, the effect of a treatment can become confounded with its order of administration relative to the other treatments. The influence of order of treatment administration on a dependent variable is called an **order effect.** For example, an order effect can occur if subjects become fatigued by participating in several treatments. They may do less well on the posttest associated with the last-administered treatment, not because this treatment is less effective, but because they are fatigued from responding to the demands of the previously administered treatments.

Order effects can also occur due to the subject's opportunity to practice during each treatment. In many educational experiments the treatments represent different instructional methods. A subject who is assigned to several such treatments may do better on the posttest associated with the last-administered treatment than on the other posttests. The reason for the improved performance may be because the subject had the opportunity to practice the skills measured by the posttest during earlier-administered treatments, rather than because the last-administered treatment is superior.

Counterbalanced designs are used to avoid the problems of interpretation due to order effects. In a **counterbalanced experiment,** each subject is administered several treatments, but the order of administering the treatments is varied across subjects to eliminate the possible confounding of order effects with treatment effects. An example of counterbalancing is an experiment on reading conducted by Philip DiStefano, Michael Noe, and Sheila Valencia.[16] These researchers were interested in the effects of purpose for reading and text difficulty on reading rate. The basic design involved the manipulation of two factors (a 2 × 2 factorial experiment).[17] One factor was text difficulty. Two text passages of approximately 1,400 words each were used to represent this factor. One passage had a readability level of eighth grade, and the other had a readability level of eleventh grade. The other factor was purpose for reading. Half the subjects were asked to read each passage for the purpose of gaining an *overview* of it. The other half of the subjects read each passage for the purpose of gaining *detailed* knowledge of its content.

16. Philip DiStefano, Michael Noe, and Sheila Valencia, "Measurement of the Effects of Purpose and Passage Difficulty on Reading Flexibility," *Journal of Educational Psychology* 73 (1981): 602–606.
17. The experiment included additional elements (a grade-level factor and a practice test) not discussed here.

This type of 2×2 design would normally require the formation of four treatment groups, shown in the following diagram:

	Overview	Detail
8th-Grade Level	Group A	Group B
11th-Grade Level	Group C	Group D

The researchers only needed to form two treatment groups, though, because each subject participated in two of the treatment variations. Half of the subjects were randomly assigned to read the eighth-grade passage for detail and then to read the 11-grade passage for overview. The other half of the subjects first read the eleventh-grade passage for overview and then the eighth-grade passage for detail. This design can be represented as follows:

Group A: 8—Detail   11—Overview
Group B: 11—Detail   8—Overview

You will note that the order of administering the easy (8th-grade level) and difficult (11th-grade level) passages was counterbalanced: Group A read the easy passage first, whereas group B read it second. You will also note that the purpose-for-reading factor was not counterbalanced; both groups read for detail in the first-administered treatment. DiStefano and his colleagues explained that this factor was not counterbalanced because previous researchers had found that the purpose-for-reading treatments are not susceptible to order effects.

Analysis of variance is generally used to examine the data resulting from a counterbalanced experiment. In the experiment described above, statistically significant differences were found for the main effects of purpose-for-reading ($F = 262.43$, $p < .001$) and for passage difficulty ($F = 13.24$, $p < .001$). The interactive effect of these two factors was also significant ($F = 13.24$, $p < .001$). When specific comparisons were done, it was found that students read the easy and difficult passages at the same rate when they were concentrating on detail. Students read the easy passage much faster than the difficult passage, however, when their purpose was to get an overview.

We conclude this discussion of counterbalancing by noting that it can be used in situations other than the assignment of subjects to more than one treatment. In an experiment conducted by the second author of this text and his colleagues, each teacher-experimenter was assigned to teach four different treatments.[18] (Each student participated in a single treatment, so there was no

18. Meredith D. Gall, Beatrice A. Ward, David C. Berliner, Leonard S. Cahen, Philip H. Winne, Janet D. Elashoff, and George C. Stanton, "Effects of Questioning Techniques and Recitation on Student Learning," *American Educational Research Journal* 15 (1978): 175–199.

need to counterbalance treatments with respect to students.) To avoid the possibility of an order effect, each experimenter taught the four treatments in a different order. Thus, the treatments were counterbalanced with respect to the order in which the experimenter taught them.

Another situation that may require counterbalancing is order of testing. Suppose two posttests are to be administered to each subject in an experiment. If there is a possibility that the order in which the posttests are given will affect subjects' scores, this factor can be counterbalanced. A random half of the subjects in each treatment group can take posttest A followed by posttest B. The other half of the subjects can take posttest B followed by posttest A.

Variations in Factorial Experiments

The design and analysis of factorial experiments is a complicated matter. There are many factorial designs to select from, depending upon: the number of independent variables, the nature of the independent variables, whether subjects receive repeated measures of the same variable, whether there are unequal numbers of subjects in each treatment group, the scale and distribution properties of scores on the dependent variables, and the need for a covariate to compensate for initial differences between treatment groups. It is useless to develop a sound research hypothesis and to carefully execute the experiment unless the proper factorial design has been chosen. If you are planning a factorial experiment, we advise you to consult a reference textbook on experimental design (see Annotated References) and to consult an expert in the area of factorial design and statistical analysis.

SINGLE-SUBJECT DESIGNS

As its label implies, the distinguishing feature of a **single-subject experiment** is the fact that the sample of subjects is one. If two or more subjects are treated as one group, this also is considered a single-subject experiment.

The single-subject experiment is particularly well suited to research on behavior modification. The field of behavior modification seeks to change the behavior of individuals by applying experimentally validated techniques such as social and token reinforcement, fading, desensitization, and discrimination training.[19] As an educational strategy, behavior modification is used extensively

19. There are many publications on the educational uses of behavior-modification techniques, including Richard M. Wielkiewicz, *Behavior Management in the Schools: Principles and Procedures* (Elmsford, NY: Pergamon, 1986).

in classroom management, skill development, and training of the handicapped. It also is employed widely in counseling, psychotherapy, institutional caretaking, and in drug research. Many single-subject experiments of interest to educators appear in the *Journal of Applied Behavior Analysis*, but this type of experiment appears in other journals as well.

Single-subject experiments should not be equated with the case-study method of investigation (see chapter 10). Both focus on the single individual, yet they differ in degree of experimental control. As we discuss below, single-subject designs use several procedures to achieve experimental control: reliability checks on the experimenter's observations of the subject's behavior, frequent observations of the behaviors targeted for change, description of the treatment in sufficient detail to permit replication, and replication of treatment effects within the experiment. In contrast, case studies usually have a broader focus and rely heavily on qualitative data and the researcher's subjective impressions. Quantitative data and replications are not usually reported.

Some researchers think that the single-subject experiment is a watered-down, easier version of one of the group designs presented earlier in this chapter and in chapter 15. This is not true. Researchers who work with single-subject designs are equally as concerned with problems of internal validity and external validity as researchers who do group experiments. Most single-subject designs are rigorous, time-consuming, and may involve as much data collection as a design involving experimental and control groups.

A study by Hans van der Mars illustrates the use of the single-subject experiment.[20] The purpose of his experiment was to test a particular method for increasing teacher's use of verbal praise to reward good conduct. The need for the study was established by referring to previous research findings that verbal praise promotes good student conduct, but that teachers seldom use verbal praise unless specifically trained to do so.

The subject of the experiment was a student teacher of physical education. The experimental intervention was an audiocueing device, which consisted of a microcassette recorder on a waist belt and a mini-earphone. While wearing the device unobtrusively, the teacher received audiocueing:

> The subject was cued in to specific managerial events and student behaviors by the type of cues, such as (a) "Praise two students for getting to their squads quickly"; (b) "When the activity starts, look for those students who get started quickest. Praise them!" (c) "Praise the group for paying attention and being quiet during instructions"; and (d) "Look for hard workers. Praise them!"[21]

20. Hans van der Mars, "Effects of Audiocueing on Teacher Verbal Praise of Students' Managerial and Transitional Task Performance," *Journal of Teaching in Physical Education* 6 (1987): 157–165. The experiment involved a second teacher, but the data for this teacher are not presented here in order to simplify the presentation.
21. Ibid., p. 159.

An audio-recording of each lesson that the teacher taught was made. Each recording was analyzed to determine the teacher's rate of verbal praise of good student conduct. Rate was computed by dividing the frequency of verbal-praise statements in the lesson by the number of minutes in the lesson.

In the first phase of the experiment, the teacher taught five lessons without training in verbal praise or use of the audiocueing device. The teacher's rate of verbal praise during these lessons is shown in figure 16.4. These lessons are called a **baseline** because they show the teacher's natural behavior without experimental intervention. The baseline is similar in purpose to a pretest in the experimental designs presented in chapter 15 and the first part of this chapter.

Following the baseline period, the teacher was trained in how to recognize and praise good student conduct, and was asked to use the audiocueing device for eight lessons. The prerecorded audio cues were presented at an average rate of two per minute. Figure 16.4 shows that the teacher's rate of verbal praise increased substantially during this treatment phase.

In the next baseline period, the teacher was given no audiocues for four lessons. The act of withdrawing a treatment in this manner is sometimes called **extinction** by behavioral researchers. Figure 16.4 shows that the teacher's rate of verbal praise declined. This second baseline period is similar in meaning to a posttest in a group experimental design.

The final phase of the experiment involved reintroduction of audiocues for six lessons. As in the first treatment phase, the teacher's rate of verbal praise increased.

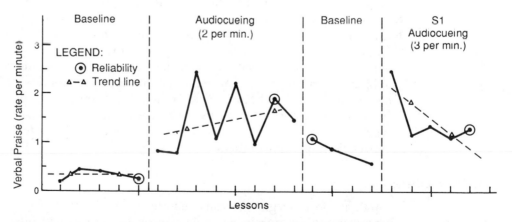

Figure 16.4   Rate of Verbal Praise across Baseline and Treatment Conditions in Audiocueing Experiment.

Source: Adapted from Hans van der Mars, "Effects of Audiocueing on Teacher Verbal Praise of Students' Managerial and Transitional Task Performance," *Journal of Teaching in Physical Education* 6 (1987): 161.

Note: The reliability points are sessions in which observer reliability was checked.

A single-subject experiment typically yields the type of data graphed in figure 16.4. The researcher must examine the data and decide whether the data indicate that the treatment had an effect on the dependent variable. This decision is usually made in two ways. One approach is to examine the form of the graphed data. The following statement about figure 16.4 by van der Mars illustrates this approach:

> The changes established were found to be experimentally significant in light of (a) baselines that were minimally variable and either stable or directed in a downward trend, (b) the absence of overlap between baseline and treatment data, and (c) the change of level from final baseline sessions to initial treatment sessions.[22]

The other approach is to organize the data so that they can be analyzed using a conventional test of statistical significance. For example, van der Mars used a t-test to compare the pooled mean of the two baseline phases and the pooled mean of the two treatment phases. The t value of 3.72 was statistically significant ($p < .01$), leading him to conclude that the audiocueing treatment produced a real effect.

Baseline-treatment-extinction-treatment is one of many single-subject designs. In the following sections we describe general features of single-subject design, steps to follow in using some of the more common designs, and statistical techniques for analyzing single-subject data. We conclude by discussing factors to consider in choosing between group and single-subject designs.

General Design Considerations

Single-subject experiments should be designed to have high internal validity. As is true of group designs, the internal validity of a single-subject design is a function of the researcher's ability to rule out factors other than the treatment variable as possible causes of changes in the dependent variable. In group experiments, internal validity is achieved primarily by random assignment of subjects to the experimental treatment and a control condition. Since $N = 1$ in single-subject research, random assignment and control groups are not possible. Internal validity is achieved by other design techniques, which are described below. These techniques are not exclusive to single-subject designs, but they are especially important to them.

Reliable Observation

Single-subject designs typically require many observations of behavior. If the observations are unreliable, they will obscure treatment effects. Certain precautions and procedures should be followed in making observations, including

22. Ibid., p. 162.

careful training of observers, operational definition of the behaviors to be observed, periodic checks of observer reliability, and control of observer bias. When appropriate, you can consider measurement of behavioral products (e.g., number of problems solved in a school assignment) as a substitute for observation of behavior. These procedures are discussed in chapter 12 and in works on single-subject design (see Annotated References, especially Barlow and Hersen).

The simplest procedure is to target one behavior for observation throughout the experiment. For example, the teacher's rate of verbal praise for conduct was the only behavior that was observed in the experiment on audiocueing. It is possible to monitor additional behaviors, but as each new behavior is added to the research design, observational procedures become increasingly complicated.

Repeated Measurement

In the typical group-experiment design, data are collected at two points in time: before (pretest) and after (posttest) the experimental treatment. Single-subject designs require many more measurements, because the behavior of individuals varies even within short time intervals. Consider the fact that the experiment on audiocueing had four phases: baseline, treatment, baseline, treatment. If the student-teacher's verbal praise behavior were measured only once in each phase, it would be impossible to interpret whether variations in rate of praise were a function of the treatment variable or of other naturally occurring events. The use of frequent measurements provides a clearer, more reliable description of how the student-teacher's behavior naturally varied and how it varied in response to the treatment condition. Furthermore, statistical significance tests of single-subject data are more powerful if many measurements of the dependent variable are available.

Because of the need for repeated measurements in single-subject design, it is important to standardize the measurement procedure. Preferably each measurement occasion would involve the same observers, the same instructions to the subject, and the same environmental conditions. Otherwise, treatment effects are likely to be contaminated with measurement effects.

Description of Experimental Conditions

The researcher should provide a precise description of each experimental condition that is important for replication. Some single-subject designs require reintroduction of the baseline and the treatment variable. For example, the baseline and treatment conditions appeared twice in the experiment on audiocueing. If the conditions involving the baseline or the treatment variable are not specified precisely, they will be difficult to replicate within the experiment. As a consequence, the internal validity of the experiment is threatened. Furthermore, imprecise specification makes it difficult for other researchers to replicate the treatment and baseline conditions, thus threatening the external validity of the experiment.

Baseline and Treatment Stability

The baseline in single-subject designs is the natural frequency of the target behavior before introduction of the experimental variable. If the baseline frequency of occurrence did not vary at all during the period of observation, it would be easy to assess the effect of the treatment variable. Yet most behaviors vary. If the variation is too great, you will have difficulty in separating treatment effects from naturally occurring changes in the subject's behavior.

You may use a standard for determining when a baseline has stabilized, for example, no more than 5 percent range of variation from the mean over a period of 10 observations. There are occasions, though, when this type of standard is inappropriate. For example, suppose you plan to use an experimental intervention with a subject whose behavior is systematically worsening or improving. If the subject's behavior is systematically improving during the baseline period, you are faced with a difficult problem. If the subject continues to improve during the treatment phase, we could easily argue that the continued improvement was due to some condition that existed during the baseline period rather than to a treatment effect. In this situation you should consider withholding the treatment variable until baseline improvement has peaked and then stabilized.

The same need for stability applies to the treatment phase of a single-subject design. Suppose you have planned four treatment sessions. No effects appear after the first three sessions, but improvement is apparent after the fourth session. Should you discontinue treatment, as planned? It is probably advisable in this situation to continue treatment until a stable, interpretable pattern of treatment effects has emerged.

Length of Baseline and Treatment Phases

As a general rule, there should be approximately the same length of time and number of measurements in each phase of a single-subject design. Otherwise, the imbalance complicates the statistical analysis and interpretation of treatment effects. There are occasions, though, when the rule of equal phases conflicts with the need to maintain baseline or treatment conditions until a stable pattern of measurements has emerged. You may also need to maintain baseline or treatment conditions longer than intended because of institutional or ethical factors. One way to overcome this problem is to do several pilot studies to investigate baseline and treatment parameters. These parameters can be used to design a more rigorous experiment in which baseline and treatment conditions are equalized in duration and number of measurements.

A-B-A Designs

A-B-A designs are used in single-subject or single-group experiments having one treatment. The *A* stands for the baseline condition, and the *B* stands for the treatment.

A-B Design

The **A-B design** is the simplest of the single-subject designs. Begin by selecting a subject for the experiment, one or more target behaviors, measures of the target behaviors, and experimental treatment. Then measure the target behavior repeatedly during the baseline period (A). Finally, administer the experimental treatment (B) while continuing to measure the target behavior.

The A-B design is low in internal validity.[23] If the difference between the means of the A measurements and the B measurements is statistically significant, we can conclude that a reliable change occurred from the baseline phase to the treatment phase. Attributing the change to a treatment effect is difficult, however, because the influence of other factors cannot be ruled out. These factors might be other events occurring during the treatment phase or the effects of testing during the baseline period. The A-B design should be used only when no suitable alternative is available or when the researcher intends it as a pilot study to be followed by an experiment using a more rigorous design.

A-B-A Design

The **A-B-A design** follows the same steps as the A-B design, except that a second baseline condition is added. The second baseline typically involves **withdrawal** of the treatment, as in the experiment on audiocueing. You can also bring about **reversal** of the treatment in the second baseline condition. For example, in the experiment on audiocueing, the researcher might have given the teacher audiocues to ask students to engage in good conduct, but not to give them verbal praise for doing so.

The A-B-A design has good internal validity. If the target behavior changes as expected in each phase of the experiment, we can conclude that the changes were due to the effect of the treatment variable. One difficulty with this design is that the experiment ends on a negative note, since the treatment (presumably positive in nature) is withdrawn or reversed. This condition may be ethically unacceptable to the researcher and to others involved in the experiment.

Another limitation of this design, and of all baseline designs, is that the

---

23. The uses and internal validity problems of the A–B design are discussed in D. T. Campbell, "Reforms as Experiments," *American Psychologist* 24 (1969): 409–429.

observed treatment effect is dependent upon the particular baseline conditions included in the experiment. Assuming a reliable A-B change is found, we can conclude only that the effect will occur reliably for that particular baseline. Therefore, the baseline conditions must be described precisely. This restriction is similar to the pretest limitation in group designs that include a pretest (see discussion of internal validity in previous chapter). Reliable treatment effects found in such designs cannot be presumed to be independent of the particular pretest that was used to discover the effects.

A-B-A-B Design

This design overcomes the ethical issue that may arise with the A-B-A experiment. In the **A-B-A-B design,** the experiment ends with reintroduction of the treatment variable. The experiment on audiocueing described above exemplifies this type of design. Each of the four phases of the A-B-A-B design were present: initial period of baseline observation, initial introduction of the treatment variable, withdrawal or reversal of the treatment variable (second baseline), and reintroduction of the treatment variable.

An experiment by D. S. Guza and T. F. McLaughlin illustrates two interesting variations of the A-B-A-B design.[24] First, the sample consisted of a single group (a group of 13 fourth-grade students enrolled in a combination fourth/fifth-grade class), rather than a single individual. Second, the baseline condition was an alternative treatment rather than a withdrawal or reversal of the treatment.

The purpose of the experiment was to evaluate the effectiveness of two alternative approaches to spelling instruction. The baseline treatment involved giving students a weekly list of 20 spelling words at the beginning of the week. Students took a pretest on the list, engaged in practice activities during the week, and then took the 20-word review test on the last day of the school week. The alternative treatment involved dividing the 20 words into four lists of 5 words each. Students practiced spelling each list one day and taking a test the following day. This test was similar in format to the pretest of the baseline condition. In this way, the students had the opportunity to study all four lists during the school week. The students took a 20-word review test (similar to the review test in the baseline treatment) on the last day of the school week. Guza and McLaughlin hypothesized that this instructional method (labeled the *daily partial list treatment*) would be more effective than the baseline treatment.

The A-B-A-B design was carried out over a period of 20 school weeks. The baseline treatment (A) was in effect for five weeks, followed by five weeks of the daily partial list treatment (B). The baseline treatment was reinstituted for

---

24. D. S. Guza and T. F. McLaughlin, "A Comparison of Daily and Weekly Testing on Student Spelling Performance," *Journal of Educational Research* 80 (1987): 373–376.

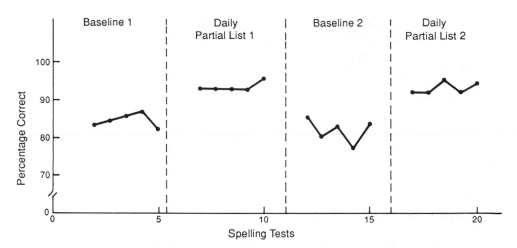

Figure 16.5   Average Percentage of Words Spelled Correctly across Baseline and Treatment Conditions in Spelling Experiment.

SOURCE: Adapted from Figure 1 in D. S. Guza and T. F. McLaughlin, "A Comparison of Daily and Weekly Testing on Student Spelling Performance," *Journal of Educational Research* 80 (1987): 375.

another five weeks, followed by reinstitution of the daily partial list treatment for the final five weeks. The dependent variable was the percentage of words spelled correctly on the end-of-the-week test on the 20-word list.

A graph of the resulting data is presented in figure 16.5. Inspection of the graph reveals the superiority of the daily partial list treatment. The mean percentage of words spelled correctly for baselines 1 and 2 were 83.8 percent and 83.3 percent, respectively. The corresponding means for the daily partial list treatment were 94.8 percent and 95.6 percent.

Inspection of the graph was supplemented by Wilcoxon signed-rank tests (see chapter 13) comparing baseline 1 and daily partial list 1 results, and comparing baseline 2 and daily partial list 2 results. In both cases, a statistically significant difference between the baseline and daily partial list treatments was found.

This A-B-A-B experiment involved a single group of subjects, but it has much better internal validity than the single-group experiments described in the previous chapter: the one-shot case study; the one-group pretest-posttest design; and the time-series design. One reason for its superiority is that the treatment was instituted twice during the experiment. The other reason is that the dependent variable was measured many times during the experiment. In contrast, the dependent variable is measured just once in the one-shot case study and only twice in the one-group pretest-posttest design. The dependent variable is measured many times in a time-series design, but the treatment variable is just instituted once. By simply introducing the treatment twice during an experiment, the researcher can convert a time-series design into an A-B-A-B design, and thereby make a more internally valid test of a treatment's effectiveness.

Other A-B-A Designs

The preceding discussion presented the basic A-B-A designs. There are several other A-B-A designs, including several for investigating interaction effects involving treatments. These designs are discussed in surveys of single-subject research (see Annotated References).

Multiple-Baseline Designs

As described above, time-series designs (A-B-A) generally use the natural occurrence of the target behavior as a control condition for assessing treatment effects. In contrast, **multiple-baseline designs** are experiments in which conditions other than the naturally occurring target behavior are used as controls for assessing treatment effects.

Multiple-baseline designs are used when reinstatement of baseline conditions in an A-B-A type design is not possible. This problem may occur if the researcher is unable to withdraw or reverse the treatment for ethical reasons. Also, it may not be possible to demonstrate a treatment effect using an A-B-A design. That is, the target behavior may not return to the pretreatment baseline rate after the treatment is withdrawn or reversed. If this occurs, we cannot conclude that the treatment had an effect, even though the target behavior changed reliably from the initial baseline phase to the treatment phase. As an alternative, we can use a multiple-baseline design to investigate the treatment.

In one of the more commonly used multiple-baseline designs, two or more subjects are used to control for extraneous variables in assessing treatment effects. This was the case in an experiment conducted by George Stern, Susan Fowler, and Frank Kohler.[25] The purpose of their experiment was to determine the effects of using a peer-mediated intervention to help students who engage in inappropriate behavior. In a peer-mediated intervention, one student monitors and gives points to another student. A question of special interest to researchers was whether the role of monitor/point-giver or the role of point-receiver results in greater behavior change.

Two students in a combination fifth/sixth-grade class, Robert and Karen, were selected as subjects because they were disruptive during math seatwork and were members of the lowest-performing math group. Three other low-

---

25. George W. Stern, Susan A. Fowler, and Frank W. Kohler, "A Comparison of Two Intervention Roles: Peer Monitor and Point Earner," *Journal of Applied Behavior Analysis* 21 (1988): 103–109. The experiment involved several additional subjects not discussed here.

performing peers worked as their partners. Partners A and B worked with Karen, and Partner C worked with Robert.

Figure 16.6 illustrates the design and results of the experiment. The dependent variable shown on the vertical axis is total inappropriate behavior,

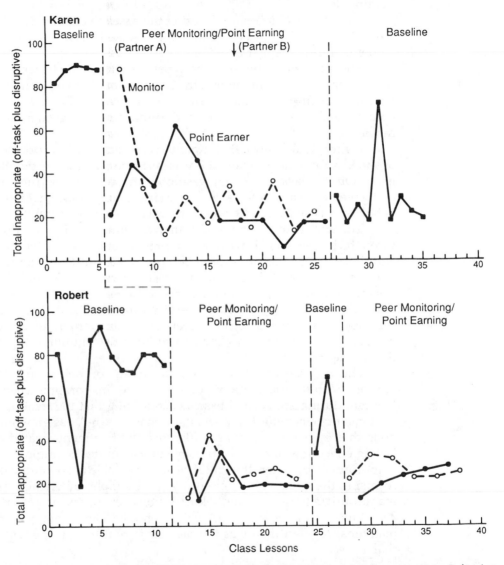

Figure 16.6   Percentage of Intervals in Which Students Engaged in Inappropriate Behavior across Baseline and Treatment Conditions in Peer-Mediation Experiment.

SOURCE: Adapted from figure 1 in George W. Stern, Susan A. Fowler, and Frank W. Kohler, "A Comparison of Two Intervention Roles: Peer Monitor and Point Earner," *Journal of Applied Behavioral Analysis* 21 (1988): 107.

which includes both off-task behavior and disruptive behavior (any behavior that interfered with the work of another child). These observations were made at intervals of every 10 seconds during math seatwork each day. The measure was the percentage of intervals in which Karen and Robert were off-task or disruptive.

No intervention occurred during the baseline conditions. You will note in figure 16.6 that the percentage of inappropriate behavior is quite high for both students during the first baseline.

The intervention phase of the experiment for Karen began on the sixth day. On alternate days she monitored the seatwork of her two partners, A and B, and gave them points for meeting a criterion of good behavior. If enough points were accumulated over a period of days, the entire class received a reward, usually a movie.

Figure 16.6 shows that Karen's percentage of inappropriate behavior dropped substantially when she was put into this role of monitor and point-giver. On the days that Karen was not in this role, her partners monitored her and gave her points in the same way. Figure 16.6 shows that her inappropriate behavior was similarly low when she was in the role of point-earner.

You will note in figure 16.6 that the first baseline for Robert extended through class session 11, whereas it terminated for Karen after session 5. The six additional baseline sessions for Robert provide a control for extraneous variables that could confound the treatment effects observed in Karen. Both Karen and Robert were in the same class with the same teacher during these six sessions. The only difference is that Karen received the treatment. Therefore, we can be confident that Karen's lower percentage of inappropriate behavior, both in comparison to her first baseline and to Robert's continuing first baseline, was due to the treatment.

The baseline condition was reinstituted for Karen after the 26th class session. With the exception of one session, her inappropriate behavior was at a low rate during this second baseline, indicating that the treatment produced a good maintenance effect. We see, then, that an A-B-A design would have been a poor choice for this experiment. Because the treatment created an apparently lasting effect, it would not be possible to reinstitute the original baseline rate of inappropriate behavior. It might have been possible to reinstitute the baseline by reversing the treatment in some way, for example, by giving Karen points for inappropriate behavior. This solution, however, poses ethical problems.

You will note that Robert's second baseline demonstrated less of a maintenance effect than was the case for Karen. In fact, the researchers stated that

Robert responded to the withdrawal of treatment by increasing his rate of inappropriate behavior somewhat and by repeatedly asking for a resumption of the peer-monitoring procedure. Because of his requests and the teacher's request, we reimplemented the intervention after only three days of baseline.[26]

Following reinstitution of the treatment, Robert's percentage of inappropriate behavior again dropped. The effectiveness of the treatment did not seem to depend on whether Robert was in the role of monitor/point-giver or point-earner.

The researchers did not perform tests of statistical significance on their data. Instead, they relied on analysis of the descriptive graphs shown in figure 16.6. The treatment effect is convincing because it was tested three times (once in the case of Karen and twice in the case of Robert), and each time the student's rate of inappropriate behavior dropped well below the preceding baseline condition.

Other Multiple-Baseline Designs

A variety of multiple-baseline designs have been developed to solve different research problems. Some of these designs involve use of multiple target behaviors or multiple stimulus settings to provide baseline control. The design discussed above used multiple subjects to provide baseline control. These designs are discussed in more detail elsewhere (see the Annotated References to this chapter).

Statistical Analysis of Single-Subject Data

Many researchers rely exclusively on raw data and a few descriptive statistics for interpreting the results of single-subject experiments. Figures 16.4, 16.5, and 16.6 are typical graphic representations of single-subject data. The abscissa (horizontal line) represents units of time, and the ordinate (vertical line) represents units of the target behavior. Each data point is plotted separately on the graph, and the data points may be connected by lines. Vertical broken lines are used to indicate the transition from one phase to another (e.g., from baseline to treatment).

You should note several features of the graphical data plot, and within each phase analyze the data points for measures of the target behavior for mean level and presence and direction of slope. Compare adjacent phases with respect to change in mean level, change in slope, and change in level between the last data point for one phase and the first data point for the next phase.

Some researchers also recommend determining the magnitude of a treat-

26. Ibid., p. 109.

ment effect by computing the percentage of nonoverlapping data.[27] This percentage is the number of treatment data points that exceed the highest (or lowest, if appropriate) baseline data point, divided by the total number of treatment data points. For example, in figure 16.6, all but one of the 11 data points for Robert's second treatment phase are lower (the desirable direction) than the lowest data point in the preceding baseline. Therefore, the percentage of nonoverlapping data is 91 percent.

The use of visual analysis of graphs to interpret treatment effects in single-subject experiments has been criticized.[28] One criticism is that the ordinal scale of a graph can be modified to accentuate or mask treatment effects. For example, the same data are plotted in figure 16.7a and figure 16.7b, yet the two graphs create quite different impressions of the magnitude of the treatment effect. Another criticism of visual analysis is that empirical studies have shown low interrater reliability in using visual analysis to determine whether or how much of a treatment effect occurred.[29]

The alternative to visual analysis is the use of inferential statistics. For example, you will recall that in the experiment on audiocueing, the researcher used a t-test to compare the pooled mean of the two baseline phases and the pooled mean of the two treatment phases. Like visual analysis, however, the use of inferential statistics in single-subject experiments has been criticized.[30] One criticism is that inferential statistics are not appropriate to the logic of the single-subject experiment, which involves intensive study of the individual rather than of samples from populations.

Another criticism is that inferential statistics involve an assumption that observations are independent of each other. This assumption is seldom satisfied in single-subject experiments. The behavior that is observed in any given session is probably dependent on the behavior that occurred in previous sessions. The technical term for this phenomenon is **serial dependency.** The extent of serial dependency in data from a single-subject experiment, plus the presence of a treatment effect, can be detected through the use of **time-series statistics.**[31] The

27. Thomas E. Scruggs, Margo A. Mastropieri, and Glendon Casto, "The Quantitative Synthesis of Single-Subject Research: Methodology and Validation," *Remedial and Special Education* 8 (1987): 24–33. These researchers also recommend the percentage of nonoverlapping data as a measure of effect size for meta-analyses of single-subject experiments. Several articles criticizing this recommendation appear in the same issue of the journal.

28. Christopher F. Sharpley, "Some Arguments Against Analyzing Client Change Graphically," *Journal of Counseling and Development* 65 (1986): 156–159.

29. A. DeProspero and S. Cohen, "Inconsistent Visual Analyses of Intrasubject Data," *Journal of Applied Behavior Analysis* 12 (1979): 573–579; R. R. Jones, R. S. Vaught, and M. Weinrott, "Time-series Analysis in Operant Research," *Journal of Applied Behavior Analysis* 11 (1978): 277–283.

30. Roger F. Bass, "The Generality, Analysis, and Assessment of Single-Subject Data," *Psychology in the Schools* 24 (1987): 97–104.

31. The use of time-series statistics in single-subject experiments is explained in Sharpley, "Some Arguments." Also see G. V Glass, V. L. Wilson, and J. M. Gottman, *Design and Analysis of Time-Series Experiments* (Boulder: Colorado University Press, 1975).

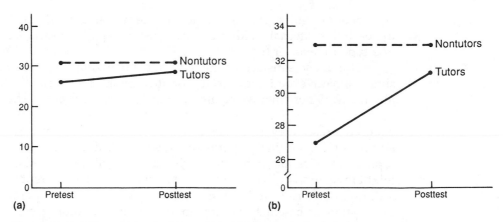

Figure 16.7   Plots of Identical Data Using Different Ordinal Scales
Source: Adapted from figure 1 in Christopher F. Sharpley, "Some Arguments Against Analyzing Client Change Graphically," *Journal of Counseling and Development* 65 (1986): 157.

computations for this statistical technique are complex, however, and many data points are necessary to yield interpretable results.

In summary, researchers can be misled both by visual analysis and inferential statistics in interpreting data from single-subject experiments. Therefore, we need to exercise good judgment in using either or both techniques. Good judgment requires both a technical understanding of these techniques and a thorough understanding of relevant theory, previous research findings, and circumstances surrounding the conduct of the experiment. Incorporating replications into the design of the experiment, as in the peer-monitoring experiment described above, also promotes sound interpretations of treatment effects.

External Validity

One of the major criticisms directed at single-subject designs is that they have low external validity: The findings cannot be generalized beyond the single subject used in the experiment. The same critics are likely to look with favor on the traditional group experiment, in which the findings can be generalized from the sample to the population from which it was drawn. However, many group experiments do not involve random selection of the sample from a defined population. Rather, the particular sample is chosen because it is readily accessible and the results are generalized through logical inference to a larger population having similar characteristics. Also, researchers such as Richard Snow (see chapter 15) have questioned the generalizability of some group experiments because they do not accurately reflect the natural environment. In balance, it appears that both single-subject and group experiments can be criticized on similar grounds for lack of external validity. The real issue is how to increase the external validity of each type of experiment, rather than rejecting one type in favor of the other.

The most satisfactory method for increasing the external validity of single-subject experiments is to conduct replication studies. Replication can involve variation in investigators, settings, and subjects. The investigators, settings, and subjects can be the same or similar to those of the original experiment, or they can vary along specified dimensions. For example, the subject of the original experiment might be a fifth-grade male student. The replication experiment might involve another fifth-grade male student, or it might involve an individual who is representative of a different population (e.g., a 12th-grade female student). Essential to any replication experiment is a careful description of baseline and treatment conditions, subject characteristics, and measurement procedures. This description provides a basis for determining the degree of generalizability from one experiment to another.

Choosing between Group and Single-Subject Designs

Single-subject designs place the focus of investigation on the individual. The group designs presented earlier in this chapter and in chapter 15 tend to subordinate the individual to the population of which he or she is a member. In planning your own experiments, you will need to choose between one or the other type of design.

One important basis for choosing between these types of design is whether you are more concerned with how populations and samples function, or how the individual learner functions. Both levels of inquiry are legitimate and complementary. Generalizations about education derived from research on samples or populations eventually need to be applied to the individual learner. Sometimes this is difficult to do. For example, learning curves based on averaging the performance of many students may not represent the performance of any individual student in the group. On the other hand, conclusions from single-subject research need to be replicated continually in order to determine their generalizability to populations of individuals.

Another important basis for choosing between group and single-subject designs is the methodological requirements of the research problem. Single-subject designs ideally require many measurements of the dependent variable over time, but many dependent variables are not easily measured on this basis. Behavior change appears to lend itself well to repeated observational measurements. Cognitive and affective learning outcomes require more complex measurement procedures, and it is difficult to administer the same procedure repeatedly.

Many, if not most, teaching methods and curriculum materials are designed for groups of students rather than for the individual student. In research on group-administered methods and materials, then, group designs may yield more useful data than single-subject designs. On the other hand, research on methods of individualized instruction probably should make more use of single-subject designs than is currently found in the literature.

You will recall that we described above an experiment on spelling instruction that employed an A-B-A-B design. The sample was a group of 13 fourth-grade students from one classroom. Does the fact that there were 13 students make this a group experiment rather than a single-subject experiment? We consider it to be a single-subject experiment because the students were treated as a single group: They were taught together by one teacher and the unit of statistical analysis was the group. If a *sample* of fourth-grade classes had been studied instead, the experiment would be considered to involve a group design.

Some educators suggest that exploration of new educational techniques should begin with single-subject designs. This strategy enables the researcher to make intensive observations over a reasonably long period of time, to "play with" treatment variations, and to formulate hypotheses. Insights derived from single-subject data then can be tested for generalizability in a multisubject design.

OTHER EXPERIMENTAL DESIGNS

In chapter 15 and in this chapter we have presented the main designs used in experimental research. Our presentation is by no means exhaustive. There are many factorial designs that we have not considered here. Also, Campbell and Stanley discuss additional experimental designs that have application to some educational research problems.[32] These designs are essentially variations on designs presented in this chapter. For example, the equivalent-time-samples design uses a single group of subjects who are measured repeatedly; sometimes the experimental treatment is presented before the measurement, and other times it is not. In an experiment using this design, a researcher compared the effect of 56 days of music on industrial production interspersed with 51 days of no music.[33] Essentially, this design is the same as the time-series design except for the repeated introduction of the experimental treatment.

At this point it should be apparent to you that a wide range of experimental designs can be used in educational research. In selecting a design, you should

---

32. Campbell and Stanley, "Designs for Research on Teaching."
33. W. A. Kerr, "Experiments on the Effect of Music on Factory Production," *Applied Psychology Monographs*, no. 5 (1945).

consider its internal and external validity carefully. The main objective is to select a design that will give the clearest picture of the effect of the experimental treatment, unconfounded by the effect of such variables as history, maturation, and so forth. Another important objective is to select a design that will yield results that can be generalized to other situations in which one is interested. This is not an easy task. Therefore, you should consider a range of experimental designs before selecting one to use in your research project.

MEASUREMENT OF CHANGE

All experiments are attempts to determine the effect of an independent variable on a dependent variable. In educational research the independent variable is often a new educational practice or product, and the dependent variable is a measure of student achievement, attitude, or personality. If it has an effect, the independent variable should be reflected as a *change* in students' scores on the measure that was administered before (the pretest) and after (the posttest) the experimental treatment. Thus, an important aspect of experimental design is the measure of change from pretest to posttest scores.

To measure change one might think it sufficient to subtract students' pretest scores from their posttest scores. For example, if a student's initial score on a measure of achievement was 50, and the score rose to 65 after administration of the experimental treatment, the gain score—also called a *change* or *difference* score— would be 15. However, there are serious difficulties in using gain scores to determine the effects of an experimental treatment.

These difficulties can be illustrated by considering a study of achievement gains from the beginning to the end of the freshman year of college conducted by Paul Dressel and Lewis Mayhew.[34] Table 16.9 lists gains made by students in nine colleges on various tests of achievement.[35] The gain scores are presented separately for subgroups formed on the basis of their pretest scores on each test. There is evidently a strong inverse relationship between pretest score and achievement gain. For example, on the test Critical Thinking in Social Science, the students whose scores were lowest at the beginning of the year made considerably larger gains (6.89 points) than the students whose scores were initially highest (an average gain of 2.26 points).

How are we to interpret such data? Do they mean that students with low initial achievement are likely to learn more (as measured by their change scores)

34. Paul L. Dressel and Lewis B. Mayhew, *General Education: Explorations in Evaluation* (Washington, DC: American Council on Education, 1954).
35. Table 16.9, reporting Dressel and Mayhew's results, is from Paul B. Diederich, ''Pitfalls in the Measurement of Gains in Achievement,'' *School Review* 64 (1956): table 1, p. 60.

TABLE 16.9

Average Gains of Students on Posttests, Classified according to Pretest Standing

Test	Low Group	Low Middle Group	Middle Group	High Middle Group	High Group
Critical thinking in social science	6.89	5.48	3.68	4.20	2.26
Science reasoning and understanding	6.26	5.16	2.93	2.04	0.31
Humanities participation inventory	18.00	5.05	4.94	1.39	−2.07
Analysis of reading and writing	5.33	2.89	1.81	1.22	0.25
Critical thinking	6.68	4.65	3.47	2.60	1.59
Inventory of beliefs	9.09	5.31	4.65	3.32	1.01
Problems in human relations	3.19	1.67	1.31	1.51	−0.36

SOURCE: Reprinted from "Pitfalls in the Measurement of Gains in Achievement," by Paul B. Diederich, by permission of the University of Chicago Press. Copyright © 1956 by The University of Chicago. Reprinted from *School Review* 64 (1956), table 1, p. 60.

than students with initially high achievement? Although this interpretation is conceivably correct, the inverse relationship between pretest scores and achievement gain scores is more likely an artifact produced by measurement error in the pretest and posttest.

The following is a description of five problems of interpretation if the raw gain score (post score minus pre score) is used to measure the amount of change that has occurred in individuals as the result of an intervention or natural growth process.

1. Gain scores are subject to a ceiling effect. The concept of **ceiling effect** means that the range of difficulty of the test items is limited. Therefore, the test does not measure the entire range of achievement possible on the dimension being measured. For example, if a student answers 90 items correctly on a 100-item pretest, the student may only improve his or her score by 10 points on the posttest. In contrast, a student with a score of 40 on the pretest can make a potential gain of 60 points. Thus, the ceiling effect places an artificial restriction on the distribution of gain scores across levels of initial ability.

The tests used in Dressel and Mayhew's study may have been subject to a ceiling effect. Students in the high-middle and high groups may have scored near the ceiling of the pretest. Thus, they could earn only a minimal gain score when they took the posttest.

2. The interpretation of gain scores is also confounded by the phenomenon of **regression toward the mean.** The regression effect means that students who earn a high score on the pretest will earn a somewhat lower score on the

posttest, whereas students with a low pretest score will earn a somewhat higher score on the posttest.[36] The regression effect occurs because of errors of measurement in the pretest and posttest and because the tests are correlated with each other.

To explain the regression effect in nonstatistical terms, suppose that a student earns a very high score on a multiple-choice achievement test. This is probably not the student's "true" score. At least one determinant of the high score was probably the operation of chance factors. For example, the student may have made lucky guesses on some of the multiple-choice items of which he or she was unsure; or the test by chance may have included a high proportion of items that the student knew. Now the student probably will not have the same good luck when he or she next takes a parallel form of the test (equivalent to a posttest in an experiment). Thus, the student will probably earn a somewhat lower score. The reverse situation applies to the initially low scorer. This student has probably earned the low score in part because of exceptionally bad luck. Because of the laws of probability, the student's luck will probably improve when the posttest is administered. Thus, he or she will earn a somewhat higher score. We can see now that gain scores are distorted in part because of the regression effect. In table 16.9 the students with initially low achievement have regression working for them to produce a larger gain score, whereas the students with initially high achievement have regression working against them.

3. Gain scores assume equal intervals at all points of the test, yet this assumption is almost never valid for educational measures. For example, on a 100-item test, a gain in score from 90 to 95 is assumed to be equivalent to a gain in score from 40 to 45. In fact, it is probably much harder to make a gain of 5 points when one's initial score is 90 (because of ceiling and regression effects) than when one's initial score is 40. If the test measures knowledge of word definitions, for example, a student whose initial score is 45 can perhaps earn 5 points by learning the meaning of easy, frequently used words, whereas the student with the initially high score may have to learn the meanings of difficult, rarely used words to improve his or her score.

4. With the exception of factorially pure tests, a given score on a test may reflect different levels of ability for different students. For example, a mathematics achievement test may include a variety of subtests in addition, subtraction, mathematical reasoning problems, algebra, and so on. Two students may earn the same score on the test, yet this score may reflect a different pattern of

36. You will recall that the regression effect was discussed in the previous chapter as a threat to the internal validity of an experiment. It is possible to get significant achievement gains in an initially low-achievement group of students because of the regression effect, even if the experimental treatment has no effect.

strengths and weaknesses. For example, one student may be weak in subtraction but strong in reasoning problems, whereas another student may be strong in subtraction but weak in reasoning problems. After a period of time, the two students may earn the same gain score because they overcame their respective deficiencies. Thus, the gain score for the first student reflects improvement in subtraction, whereas the gain score for the second student reflects improvement in mathematical reasoning. Because the gain scores are not equivalent in meaning, it is questionable whether they can be compared statistically.

5. Still another difficulty with gain scores is that they usually are not reliable.[37] The higher the correlation between pretest and posttest scores, the lower the reliability of the change scores. Also, the reliability of change scores is affected by the degree of unreliability of the pretest and posttest themselves.

Statistical Analysis of Change

Many factors adversely affect the meaning and reliability of change scores, yet some measure of change is necessary if the researcher is to compare the effects of different experimental treatments. Although the limitations of change scores cannot be overcome entirely, statistical procedures are available for overcoming some of the limitations.

First, we will consider the situation in which the researcher is interested in the change scores of individual students. For example, you may want to know why, as shown in table 16.9, some freshman college students showed more gain on the measure *Critical Thinking in Social Science* (abbreviated here CTSS), than other students. Suppose you hypothesized that the gain scores are correlated with the students' high school gradepoint average (GPA). To test this hypothesis, you should not simply correlate GPA with the CTSS gain scores, because the CTSS scores are contaminated by regression and ceiling effects. A sounder procedure is to use part correlation (see chapter 13), in which students' high school GPA scores are correlated with their CTSS gain scores adjusted statistically so that initial score is held constant.

An equivalent procedure is multiple regression (see chapter 14), in which students' posttest CTSS scores are the dependent variable and pretest CTSS scores and high school GPA scores are the predictor variables. Pretest CTSS scores are entered first into the prediction equation. A slight variation is to do the multiple regression using only the pretest CTSS scores as a predictor variable. The resulting multiple regression equation can be used to determine a

37. Gain scores are reliable under a limited set of circumstances. See J. K. Gupta, A. B. L. Srivastava, and K. K. Sharma, "On the Optimum Predictive Potential of Change Measures," *Journal of Experimental Education* 56 (1988): 124–128.

predicted posttest CTSS score for each student. These scores are called **residual gain scores** or **adjusted gain scores.** Students' high school GPA scores can be correlated with the residual gain scores.

The other situation in which change scores are used is the analysis of mean change. Suppose you administer an achievement pretest to two groups—one group is to receive an experimental treatment and the other is to serve as a control group. If they have been randomly assigned to the two groups, subjects should have equivalent means on their pretest scores. If this is the case, then you can use t-tests to determine the statistical significance of the mean change scores.

Occasionally the mean pretest scores will differ significantly by chance even when the subjects have been assigned randomly to treatment groups. Also, pretest means may differ when quasi-experimental designs are used. To adjust for initial differences in pretest means, analysis of covariance should be used. This statistical technique permits you to attribute mean change scores to the effect of the experimental treatment rather than to differences in initial scores. For example, analysis of covariance could be applied to the data of table 16.9. By using this statistical technique, we could compare the mean achievement gain scores of each of the five subgroups *as if* they had all earned the same mean achievement score at the beginning of the freshman year. As we discussed in chapter 13, the data need to be examined to determine whether they satisfy certain assumptions underlying analysis of covariance.

Still another approach for determining the statistical significance of pretest-posttest change in experiments is **analysis of variance for repeated measures.** In this form of analysis of variance the occasions on which the measure of the dependent variable is administered (pretest and posttest) are considered one factor; the experimental and control treatments are the other factor.

The F ratios for the two factors (sometimes called main effects) are not of interest in this analysis of variance. For example, it is not meaningful to compare the mean of all the pretest scores with the mean of all the posttest scores, ignoring whether the scores are from experimental or control students. Of interest instead is the *interaction* between time of measurement and treatment; that is, we are interested in whether the difference between the pretest and posttest means of the experimental group is significantly greater or less than the difference for the control group.

This type of statistical analysis is illustrated in a study conducted by Norbert Johnson, Jerome Johnson, and Coy Yates.[38] The purpose of their experiment was to evaluate the effectiveness of a particular counseling program (the Vocational Exploration Group) in improving the career maturity of

38. Norbert Johnson, Jerome Johnson, and Coy Yates, "A Six-Month Follow-up on the Effects of the Vocational Exploration Group on Career Maturity," *Journal of Counseling Psychology* 28 (1981): 70–71.

TABLE 16.10

Pretest, Posttest, and Follow-Up Mean Differences on the Career Maturity Inventory (CMI)

CMI Scale	Pretest		Posttest		Follow-Up		Pre-Post Difference	Pre-Follow-Up Difference
	Exp. M	Control M	Exp. M	Control M	Exp. M	Control M	F	F
Attitude	34.3	34.3	38.1	35.1	38.0	34.7	4.15*	4.57*
Competence scale								
Knowing yourself	9.3	9.6	12.1	10.3	10.4	10.4	N.S.	N.S.
Knowing about jobs	10.1	10.6	15.8	11.3	13.4	11.2	16.13**	12.92**
Choosing a job	11.3	11.6	13.9	12.2	11.9	12.2	N.S.	N.S.
Looking ahead	10.6	11.6	13.1	12.2	12.7	11.8	N.S.	N.S.
What should they do?	9.9	10.1	11.4	10.8	11.4	10.8	N.S.	N.S.

SOURCE: Adapted from Norbert Johnson, Jerome Johnson, and Coy Yates, "A Six-Month Follow-up on the Effects of the Vocational Exploration Group on Career Maturity," *Journal of Counseling Psychology* 28 (1981): 71.

NOTE: N.S. = not significant.

$* p < .05. ** p < .001.$

students. Sixty eighth- and ninth-grade students were randomly assigned to the counseling program or a no-treatment control group. The Career Maturity Inventory (CMI) was administered to all students as a pretest, posttest (immediately following conclusion of the experimental program) and as a follow-up posttest (six months following the program). The CMI, which consists of six scales, measures maturity of attitudes and competencies necessary for making realistic career decisions.

Table 16.10 presents the pretest, posttest, and follow-up means on the CMI for the experimental and control groups. It is apparent that the pretest-posttest difference on each scale is greater for the experimental group than for the control group. For example, the pretest-posttest difference on the Attitude Scale is greater for the experimental group (3.8) than for the control group (0.8).

The statistical significance of these differences is determined by doing a two-way (Treatment Group × Time of Testing) analysis of variance. A statistically significant F ratio for the interaction effect indicates that the pretest-posttest difference for one group is reliably greater or less than the pretest-posttest difference for the other group. The last two columns of table 16.10 present these F ratios for the pre-post difference and pre-follow-up difference on each CMI scale. Significant F ratios were obtained for the Attitude scale and the Knowing Yourself Competence scale. A series of t-tests for multiple comparisons (see chapter 13) revealed significant gains on these scales for the experimental group, but no change for the control group.

MISTAKES SOMETIMES MADE
IN CONDUCTING EXPERIMENTS

1. The researcher does not consider confounding variables such as selection of subjects, history, regression, and loss of subjects, which might have brought about changes attributed to the treatment in quasi-experimental and single-subject designs.
2. Does not use a factorial design when possible in order to study the effects of several independent variables at once on the dependent variable.
3. In conducting single-subject research, does not check on reliability of measurement procedures.
4. In conducting single-subject research, does not collect enough data to yield a stable baseline or treatment effect.
5. Attempts to use a counterbalanced design even though each treatment tends to alter performance on subsequent treatments.
6. In analyzing experimental data, attempts to work with simple change scores when it might be more appropriate to use partial correlation or analysis of covariance.

ANNOTATED REFERENCES

In addition to the following sources, you may wish to review the Annotated References in chapter 15; some of them are pertinent to topics discussed in this chapter.

Achen, Christopher H. *The Statistical Analysis of Quasi-Experiments*. Berkeley: University of California Press, 1986.

Investigates two common problems in experimental and correlational research—nonrandom assignment to experimental and control groups, and nonrandom samples from the population of interest. The author gives interesting examples of how conventional statistical techniques distort the estimation of treatment effects in these situations, and he demonstrates how other techniques provide better estimates. A sophisticated understanding of statistics is needed to follow the author's arguments.

Barlow, David E., and Hersen, Michael. *Single Case Experimental Design Strategies for Studying Behavior Change*, 2nd ed. New York: Pergamon, 1984.

A comprehensive discussion of the methodology of single-subject experiments. Examples of single-subject studies in education, counseling, psychiatry, and medicine illustrate design techniques. There are several chapters on A-B-A and multiple baseline designs, and a chapter on statistical techniques for analyzing single-subject data.

Cook, Thomas D., and Campbell, Donald T. *Quasi-Experimentation: Design and Analysis Issues for Field Settings*. Chicago: Rand McNally, 1979.

Worth careful study. Chapter 3 discusses the quasi-experimental designs presented here and also includes several more sophisticated designs that may yield interpretable data even though random assignment was not used. Chapter 4 discusses possible problems in using analysis of variance or analysis of covariance to detect treatment effects in quasi-experiments.

Cronbach, Lee J., and Snow, Richard E. *Aptitudes and Instructional Methods.* New York: Irvington, 1977.

Book-length survey of the field of aptitude-treatment research. The authors review findings and methodological problems of previous research, and they make recommendations for future work in this field.

Linn, Robert L. "Quantitative Methods in Research on Teaching." In *Handbook of Research on Teaching*, 3rd ed., edited by Merlin C. Wittrock. New York: Macmillan, 1986, pp. 92–118.

Describes a variety of topics concerning randomized experiments, quasi-experiments, and correlational studies. Of particular relevance is the discussion of procedures for measuring change in subjects attributable to an experimental treatment. The author notes strengths and weaknesses of each of the major procedures for analyzing change: gain scores, standardized gain scores, residual gain scores, and analysis of covariance.

SELF-CHECK TEST

Circle the correct answer to each of the following questions. An answer key is provided on page 884.

1. The distinguishing characteristic of the nonequivalent control-group design is that
   a. the control group does not receive a posttest.
   b. subjects are not randomly assigned to the experimental and control groups.
   c. repeated measurements are made on the experimental group but not on the control group.
   d. the experimental treatment has external validity, but the control treatment does not.
2. The difference between treatment group means in a nonequivalent control-group design is usually tested for statistical significance by
   a. a *t*-test on the posttest means.
   b. the *t*-distribution for the correlation between pretest and posttest scores.
   c. analysis of covariance on the posttest means.
   d. separate *t*-tests of the pre-post difference for the experimental group and for the control group.
3. Factorial designs are used in order to
   a. control for the effects of nonrandom assignment to treatments.
   b. collect data that can be entered into a factor analysis.
   c. control for statistical regression.
   d. test for the interaction of several variables in the same experiment.
4. A $2 \times 2 \times 2 \times 2$ factorial design means that the experiment includes
   a. 2 dependent variables.
   b. 4 dependent variables.

   c. 2 independent variables.
   d. 4 independent variables.
5. Which of the following variables is most experimentally manipulable?
   a. student ability
   b. student age
   c. socioeconomic level of community in which a school is located
   d. teaching method
6. The effect of a pretest on the dependent variable in an experiment is best investigated using a
   a. Solomon four-group design.
   b. counterbalanced design.
   c. aptitude-treatment interaction design.
   d. A-B-A design.
7. Research on aptitude-treatment interaction seeks to discover whether
   a. students with certain characteristics are better learners than others.
   b. certain instructional methods are better than others.
   c. certain students learn better under one instructional method than under another instructional method.
   d. the interactions between students of differing ability are ordinal or disordinal.
8. Counterbalanced experiments are particularly susceptible to
   a. regression effects.
   b. order effects.
   c. maturation effects.
   d. ATI effects.
9. Within-subject replication of the treatment variable is provided by
   a. the A-B design.
   b. the A-B-A design.
   c. the A-B-A-B design.
   d. All of the above are correct.
10. Multiple-baseline designs are used instead of A-B-A type designs when
    a. only one subject is available for the experiment.
    b. reinstatement of baseline conditions is not possible
    c. reinstatement of treatment conditions is not possible.
    d. All of the above are correct.
11. Data of single-subject experiments are often analyzed to determine
    a. change in mean performance level from one phase of the experiment to another.
    b. change in performance level between the last data point for one phase and the first data point for the next phase.
    c. change in slope from one phase of the experiment to another.
    d. All of the above are correct.
12. The higher the correlation between pretest and posttest scores, the
    a. lower the reliability of the change score.
    b. higher the reliability of the change score.
    c. more difficult will be prediction of posttest scores based on pretest scores.
    d. lower the validity of the posttest.
13. When doing an analysis of variance for repeated measures, the researcher is most interested in
    a. the main effect for treatment.
    b. the main effect for testing occasion.
    c. the interaction between treatment and time of testing.
    d. the interaction between treatment and multiple baselines.

APPLICATION PROBLEMS

The following problems are designed to give you practice in applying significant concepts and research procedures explained in the chapter. Most of them do not have a single correct answer. For feedback, you can compare your answers with the sample answers on pages 901–902.

1. A school district has made available 12 elementary school classes for an experiment to determine which of two comprehensive reading programs is superior. Of the 12 classes, 4 are first grade, 6 are second grade, and 2 are third grade. The district administrators have imposed the requirement that students within classrooms cannot be randomly assigned to treatments. Under these conditions, what are two procedures that the researcher can use to help ensure equivalence of the two treatments (reading program A and reading program B)? If the two treatments are found to differ on the pretest, how can these differences be controlled statistically?

2. A researcher plans to test the effectiveness of self-paced instruction vs. conventional instruction for male and female students of varying levels of ability. There are a total of 150 students: 60 boys and 90 girls. Within each of these groups (boys and girls), there are an equal number of high-, middle-, and low-ability students. Make a chart that illustrates the experimental design for this research project, and show the number of students in each experimental group. Also, list each interaction effect that can be analyzed.

3. The purpose of an experiment was to decrease the frequency with which a college professor said "uh" and "you know" during lectures. The treatment consisted of a small signal at the rear of the room which the experimenter flashed each time that the professor uttered one of the verbal behaviors targeted for extinction. An A-B-A design was used to assess the treatment effect. The results indicated a high baseline frequency of behaviors, followed by a dramatic decrease in frequency when the treatment was instituted. The behaviors did not increase again when the treatment was withdrawn. Since reinstatement of baseline conditions is required in an A-B-A design, describe an alternative single-subject design that can be used to demonstrate a treatment effect.

4. A new program has been developed to increase students' speed and accuracy in doing simple arithmetic computations. You have been asked by the school district's curriculum specialist to evaluate its effectiveness. One of the first decisions you must make is whether to use a multisubject or single-subject experimental design. What are several questions you might ask the curriculum specialist about the program and about the purpose of the experiment that will help to determine the more appropriate type of experimental design to be used?

5. A researcher conducted an experiment in which he administered an arithmetic test before and after students had participated in a new individualized curriculum. Parallel forms of the tests were used as pretest and posttest, and the range of possible scores was 0–100 on each. In analyzing data from the experiment, the researcher found that students in the lowest quartile of the pretest ($M = 15.5$) made a good gain (posttest $M = 37.6$), whereas students in the highest quartile ($M = 83.7$) declined slightly ($M = 80.1$). From these differences in gain scores, he concluded that the new curriculum is more effective for students of low ability than for students of high ability. What are two other interpretations that could be made of the differences in gain scores?

SUGGESTION SHEET

If your last name starts with letters from Pro to Rur, please complete the Suggestion Sheet at the end of the book while this chapter is still fresh in your mind.

Part VI

OTHER TYPES OF EDUCATIONAL RESEARCH

This part of the book deals with three different types of educational investigation: evaluation research, research and development, and historical research. They draw to varying degrees on the quantitative and qualitative traditions of research described in Part IV, and on the descriptive, correlational, and experimental research designs described in Part V.

Your decision to do one of these types of research will depend primarily on your interests. If you are interested in testing the merits of different educational programs and materials, evaluation research is likely to appeal to you. On the other hand, if you are more interested in developing new programs and materials, educational research and development would be an appropriate methodology. And if you are intrigued by the past and its significance for the present, you should consider doing historical research.

We do not take the view that one type of research is more valuable than another. Each type addresses different types of questions, and each is necessary for advancing the field of education.

17 EVALUATION RESEARCH

OVERVIEW

Evaluation studies in education are an important tool of policy analysis, program management, and political action. The chapter discusses the steps involved in doing an evaluation study, with emphasis on procedures for involving the client in the evaluation process. Thirty criteria for judging the quality of an evaluation study are presented. The chapter concludes with a survey of the major evaluation models. Some of them are more quantitatively oriented, whereas others are more qualitatively oriented. Similarities and differences between evaluation studies and educational research are noted throughout the chapter.

OBJECTIVES

After studying this chapter you should be able to:

1. Describe the major uses of educational evaluation.
2. State the major differences between educational research and educational evaluation.
3. Describe procedures for clarifying the reasons for doing a particular evaluation study, and for identifying stakeholders.
4. Describe procedures for analyzing what is to be evaluated, and for converging on a set of questions to be answered by the study.
5. Identify several considerations involved in creating an evaluation design that are not usually involved in creating a research design.
6. Describe procedures for collecting and analyzing evaluation data.
7. Explain how the reporting of an evaluation study typically differs from the reporting of a research study.
8. State the major quantitatively oriented models of evaluation, and describe the primary characteristics of each model.
9. State the major qualitatively oriented models of evaluation, and describe the primary characteristics of each model.

THE NATURE AND PURPOSE OF EDUCATIONAL EVALUATION

The wide range of educational phenomena that have been the object of evaluation studies is shown in the following list:

1. Instructional methods (e.g., lectures, inquiry teaching, linguistic approach to reading instruction, manipulatives in mathematics instruction)
2. Curriculum materials (e.g., textbooks, slide-tapes, multimedia packages)
3. Programs (e.g., Head Start, language arts programs, teacher education programs, after-school programs)
4. Organizations (e.g., kindergartens, alternative schools, resource centers)
5. Educators (e.g., inservice teachers, teacher aides, school principals, volunteer tutors)
6. Students (e.g., elementary students, college students, gifted students, students with behavior problems)

We use the term "program" occasionally in this chapter as a generic label for all of these objects of educational evaluation.

Educational evaluation is the process of making judgments about the merit, value, or worth of educational programs. This type of inquiry has grown remarkably in the past 25 years. For example, the budget for the Office of Planning, Budgeting, and Evaluation in the U.S. Office of Education grew more than 1,600 percent in the period from 1968 to 1977.[1] Evaluation of all federal programs for education has become mandated. A large number of school districts have established departments of evaluation as part of their central administration. Many educational researchers have moved into the field of evaluation because of the widespread demand for their services.

Why has educational evaluation attracted so much interest from government? The main reason is that public administrators have come to view evaluation as an important tool in policy analysis, in the political decision-making process, and in program management. With respect to policy analysis, evaluation research yields important data about the costs, benefits, and problems of various program alternatives. Policy analysts can use these data to prepare position papers, which are then reviewed by persons with decision-making authority. The growth in this type of evaluation research is demonstrated by the fact that in 1979 the American Educational Research Association initiated a journal called *Educational Evaluation and Policy Analysis.*

With respect to the political process, evaluation findings are used by politicians to create advocacy for particular legislation and for budget appropriations. Opponents of the legislation are then pressed to sponsor their own evaluations to generate data favoring their cause. We need only think of the data cited by proponents and opponents of nuclear power and of military build-ups to realize that evaluation has become closely intertwined with the political process. Adversary evaluation, discussed later in the chapter, formalizes this use of evaluation.

---

1. Milbrey W. McLaughlin, "Evaluation and Alchemy," in *Educational Evaluation in Public Policy Settings,* ed. J. Pincus (Santa Monica, CA: Rand Corporation, 1980).

Finally, evaluation research is becoming an increasingly important tool of program management. For example, cost-benefit evaluations (also called "efficiency evaluations") are done to determine whether programs are producing benefits that justify their costs. Another use of evaluations is to hold managers accountable for producing results. Evaluations are done, too, to generate data that will help managers make sound decisions relating to program design, personnel, and budget.

Educational Evaluation and Educational Research

Is evaluation research the same as educational research? This question is frequently raised. For example, you may wonder whether an educational researcher is qualified to fill a position involving program evaluation duties; or whether the graduate preparation required to train an educational researcher is different from that required to train an educational evaluator.

The generally accepted view is that educational research and educational evaluation overlap to a great extent. In practice, evaluators make considerable use of qualitative and quantitative research designs, measurement tools, and statistical analyses that constitute the methodology of educational research. Yet there are important differences between the two fields in purpose. We describe three of them here.

First, evaluation research is usually initiated by someone's need for a *decision* to be made concerning policy, management, or political strategy. The purpose of the research is to collect data that will facilitate decision making. In contrast, educational research is usually initiated by a *hypothesis* about the relationship between two or more variables. The research is conducted in order to reach a conclusion about the hypothesis—to accept or reject it. Of course, the findings of educational research also can be used to guide decision making; and evaluation data may be relevant to the testing of a research hypothesis. The critical difference between the two fields is in the emphasis that is placed on making practical decisions versus accepting, rejecting, or formulating a hypothesis.

The second difference between educational research and educational evaluation is in the extent to which findings are generalized. Evaluation is often done for a limited purpose. Decision makers may be interested in how well their program works, and thus they commission a site-specific evaluation study to collect data relevant to their special concerns. In contrast, researchers are more likely to be interested in discovering widely applicable principles explaining relationships between variables. Researchers may use a particular set of curriculum materials or group of teachers to test a hypothesis, but they typically view these as samples of larger populations of materials or groups to which the research findings will be generalized. Again, the difference is not pure: Some evaluation research is designed to yield widely generalizable results, and some basic research has limited generalizability.

The third difference concerns judgments of value. Evaluators design their studies to yield data concerning the worth, merit, or value of educational phenomena. Their findings tend to be stated in such phrases as "This reading program is better than the other program because . . ." or "The respondent group of teachers preferred this mode of inservice training because. . . ." Researchers, though, design their studies to discover the truth about educational phenomena. Their findings tend to be couched in such terms as "It appears that variable X is a determinant of variable Y" or "A moderate relationship between variables X, Y, and Z was observed." Educators may make value judgments and decisions based on research findings, but this is a secondary use of the findings. The primary use of research is to contribute to basic understanding of educational phenomena.

As we stated above, educational evaluators draw extensively on methodology used by researchers despite their different goals. For this reason, this book can serve as a primer on evaluation even though it is intended primarily as a survey of research methods. The next section of the chapter describes procedures for conducting an evaluation study. You will find that most of the procedures and terminology are the same as those described elsewhere in the text.

STEPS IN CONDUCTING AN EVALUATION STUDY

An evaluation study follows essentially the same steps as those involved in doing a research study. A few additional factors must be considered, however, depending upon the evaluation model that is used. These factors are highlighted below, using as an example a study conducted by Charles Maher,[2] the purpose of which was to evaluate a school especially designed for troubled adolescents. The 45 students in the school had been classified as emotionally disturbed and socially maladjusted because of such behavior as truancy, absenteeism, fighting, and failure to complete school assignments.

Clarifying Reasons for Doing the Evaluation

An evaluation study can be initiated because of the evalutor's personal interest in doing it or because some person or agency requested it. Both reasons can be

---

2. Charles A. Maher, "Program Evaluation of a Special Education Day School for Conduct Problem Adolescents," in *Evaluation Studies Review Annual*, Vol. 7, eds. Ernest R. House, Sandra Mathison, James A. Pearsol, and Hallie Preskill (Beverly Hills, CA: Sage, 1982), pp. 406–412.

involved in initiating the study, as when the evaluator's personal interests and an agency's need for evaluation happen to coincide.

If the evaluation study is done to answer questions primarily of interest to you, then you will only need to clarify for yourself why the study is being done. Such was the case in a study described later in the chapter in the section on expertise-oriented evaluation. The study was motivated by the researcher's interest in using the method of educational criticism to illuminate certain aspects of fourth-grade classroom instruction.

The situation was different in Maher's study, which was initiated because of a request from the school:

> The program evaluation was undertaken by the author (evaluator) at the request of the principal and professional staff of the school. These program decision makers indicated a general need to know how effective their school was in terms of individual pupils and in terms of the 12 Educational Programs [described below].[3]

When an evaluation is requested in this way, the evaluator should consider probing the matter to determine *all* of the reasons for the evaluation request. Evaluations can be requested because they are required by an accreditation board or by a funding agency. Such evaluations are usually legitimate. Evaluations also can be requested for more dubious reasons. Someone may want to use the evaluation to shape up the behavior of the program staff; in this case, the evaluation serves a watchdog function. Someone may want the evaluator to gather evidence that can be used to justify an already-made decision to terminate the program or reduce its funding; in this case, the evaluator is a "hired gun." Or someone may want the evaluator to gather information that can be used to harm the reputation of a member or members of the program staff. If program staff members perceive that any of these purposes underlie the evaluation, they may work to sabotage the evaluator's efforts.

An evaluation request, then, can be made for various reasons, some of them covert. Therefore, the evaluator needs to spend time interviewing key individuals to determine whether the request is aboveboard and ethical. Evaluation experts recommend that you refuse to conduct an evaluation if any breach of ethics has occurred or is likely to occur. The ethics of evaluation are discussed further below in the section on criteria of a good evaluation study.

Clarifying the reasons for an evaluation request is also useful in selecting an appropriate evaluation model. Later in the chapter, we present six evaluation models, each appropriate for a different purpose. In the study we are considering here, Maher stated that the purpose of his evaluation was to guide decision making:

3. Ibid., p. 407.

The evaluation procedure . . . is based upon a concept of program evaluation as a process whereby information is obtained so that judgments (decisions) can be made about the worth of various aspects of a program.[4]

The CIPP model and the responsive evaluation model, both described later in the chapter, emphasize this purpose for evaluation. Maher's study exemplifies elements of both models.

Identifying the Stakeholders

A **stakeholder** is anyone who is involved in the program being evaluated or who might be affected by or interested in the findings of the evaluation. It is important to identify the stakeholders at the outset of an evaluation study. They can help you clarify the reasons why the study was requested, the questions that should guide the evaluation, the choice of research design, the interpretation of results, and how the findings should be reported and to whom.

Ignoring some of the stakeholders can have serious political consequences. Stakeholders can sabotage the evaluation process or discredit the results if they find that the evaluator is not sensitive to their need for involvement. This potential for catastrophe does not mean, however, that you must involve all stakeholders to an equal degree. Some stakeholders may wish simply to be kept informed, whereas others may want to influence the questions that guide the study and the evaluation design.

Maher chose in his study to obtain stakeholder involvement by forming a program evaluation committee at the start of the school year. The committee included the evaluator, three teachers representing different programs, and the school psychologist. Involvement of other significant stakeholders—the principal and executive board—was obtained by submitting the committee's evaluation plan to them for their approval. Maher did not refer to involvement of students and their parents, or staff of local schools, in his report, although they would appear to be significant stakeholders. Perhaps they were represented on the school's executive board.

Deciding What Is to Be Evaluated

One of the first tasks that confronts the evaluator is to delineate carefully the salient characteristics of the program. For example, if a set of curriculum materials is to be evaluated, you should include, at a minimum, the following kinds of information about it: author, publisher, publication date, list of materials, purchase cost, maintenance and replacement costs, and reports of

4. Ibid., p. 406.

previous evaluation studies. Careful program delineation is important even in local evaluation research. **Program delineation** is the process of analyzing and describing the significant characteristics of an educational program. It is not uncommon for persons working in a program to know only those aspects that affect them directly. Unless all program components are delineated, an important component may be overlooked in the evaluation process.

Following program delineation, you need to analyze the program to determine which of its aspects or components are to be included in the evaluation study. Aspects and components can be grouped into the following categories: goals, resources, procedures, and management. These categories are useful for designing an evaluation irrespective of the evaluation model that is used.

Program Goals

Judgments about the merit of program goals are central to most evaluation studies. If a program does not have goals, or does not have worthwhile goals, it is hard to imagine how it can be worthwhile in any other respect. A **goal** is the purpose, effect, or end-point that the program developer is attempting to achieve.

Some programs have carefully specified goals. In other programs the evaluator must infer the goals that the developer has in mind. Once the program goals have been identified, your major task may be to determine the extent to which the program achieves the goals in practice. In formative evaluation, your task may be to help the developers determine what the goals of the program should be.

Achievement of program goals was a major focus of Maher's evaluation of the school for troubled adolescents. The school curriculum consisted of 12 "educational programs": the academic subject programs of mathematics, language arts, science, reading, and social studies; special subject programs of art, music, and physical education; and life skills programs of employment training, social education, work study, and group counseling. The school's identification of 12 distinct programs greatly simplified Maher's task of analyzing the school's curriculum. The decision was made to assess students' achievement of the goals specified for each program.

Resources and Procedures

Resources and procedures are the means used by developers to achieve program goals. Many evaluation studies are focused exclusively on goal identification and goal attainment, but program resources and procedures are also a legitimate focus for evaluation.

Resources are the personnel, equipment, space, and other cost items needed to implement program procedures. Decision makers may want to know the answers to such questions as, Are our present resources sufficient to operate the program as intended by its developers? Is the program too expensive? Are there "hidden" costs in the program? Will the program take away resources needed by other programs? Each of these questions requires the evaluator to focus on program resources.

Procedures are the techniques, strategies, and other processes used in conjunction with resources to achieve program goals. Some evaluation research is concerned primarily or exclusively with procedures. Examples of evaluation questions that concern program procedures are: How long did teachers need to use the materials before students mastered the content? Did teachers have difficulty in using the inquiry approach to science teaching? To what extent did teachers actually use the inquiry approach? Answers to these questions usually require close and repeated observation of the program while it is in operation.

Evaluation of program resources and procedures is especially helpful for understanding the observed effects of the program. Suppose a program is observed to have negligible effects on student achievement. Decision makers may choose to discontinue the program because the evaluation was negative. Yet the program may have been ineffective because needed materials did not arrive on time, or because teachers experienced many interruptions that reduced the total time allotted to program implementation. If the evaluator had collected data on these resource and procedural problems, the decision makers might have chosen an alternative course of action (e.g., to remove the "bugs" from the program and try it again). Indeed, collection of data on both resources/procedures and program-goal attainment is very important in any type of formative evaluation. Decisions about the program revision can be made more effectively if developers know both how well the current version of the program is working *and* why.

Program Management

Most programs have a **management system** to monitor resources and procedures so that they are used effectively to achieve program goals. We usually think of management only in relation to large-scale programs such as a system of secondary education or curriculum coordination in a school district. Yet many curriculum materials contain built-in management procedures to monitor the student's instructional progress. One may also think of self-management (e.g., teachers monitoring their classroom teaching in order to improve on-the-job performance).

Evaluation research may be focused on management systems as they relate to resource utilization and program procedures. Or the evaluation may be concerned with the impact of the management system on program-goal attainment. Decision makers may need answers to such questions as: Is the management system ensuring the effective use of program resources? Is the management system as efficient as it can be? Are the management procedures being used as intended by the program developers? Each of these questions requires the evaluator to design research that delineates the management system and examines its workings.

Identifying Evaluation Questions

We stated in chapter 2 that a research problem can be stated in the form of questions, hypotheses, or objectives. The same range of formats can be used in evaluation studies, although it is most common to state questions.

Lee Cronbach distinguished two phases in selecting questions for an evaluation study.[5] The **divergent phase** involves generating a comprehensive list of questions, issues, concerns, and information needs that might be addressed in the evaluation study. (Note that issues, concerns, and information needs can be rephrased subsequently as questions to maintain a constant format.) The evaluator should invite all stakeholders to contribute to this list. In addition, you can suggest possible questions for study. If you have selected an evaluation model to guide the study, it too can prompt ideas for questions. For example, in the section on the summative model later in the chapter, we included a checklist of 39 criteria for evaluating curriculum materials. Stakeholders could be asked to nominate some or all of the criteria for inclusion in the study. These criteria, which are conveniently stated in the form of questions, could be added to the list of questions generated by other means.

The second of Cronbach's two phases is the **convergent phase.** It involves reducing the initial list of evaluation questions to a manageable number. This phase is necessary because of the expense involved in answering each evaluation question. The evaluator, in collaboration with significant stakeholders, must winnow the list to the most important questions that can be answered with available resources.

The report of Maher's study suggests that a convergent phase of question identification occurred:

> By means of a series of structured interviews and small group meetings with principal, teachers, and specialists, the evaluator identified three specific evaluation information needs that were agreed upon by these groups as priority needs. First, the principal and executive board desired substantive data regarding the overall effectiveness of the programs provided in the school. Second, the staff desired information that would help pinpoint strengths and weaknesses of these programs, including information about the social validity of the programs as

5. Lee J. Cronbach, *Designing Evaluations of Educational and Social Programs* (San Francisco: Jossey-Bass, 1982).

perceived by the pupils. Third, since the school initially had been designed to facilitate the educational planning process by means of individual goal setting and concretizing educational outcome expectations for each pupil, the principal and staff wanted information about the extent to which that purpose was being fulfilled. These three evaluation information needs served to focus the manner in which the evaluation was designed and implemented.[6]

Note that the evaluation objectives were stated as information needs rather than as questions. With simple rephrasing, they could be stated as questions.

As an evaluation study proceeds, new questions are likely to arise in the minds of the evaluator and stakeholders. Some of the evaluation models described later in the chapter—especially the qualitatively oriented models—explicitly acknowledge this possibility. In our discussion of adversarial evaluation, we list additional questions that arose in the course of doing an evaluation study of this type. If possible, you should set aside time and other resources that can be used to answer important questions that arise after data collection begins.

Developing an Evaluation Design and Timeline

Any of the research procedures described in the preceding chapters can be incorporated into the design of an evaluation study. This is why many evaluation studies are similar to research studies in design, execution, and reporting.

Some issues are more likely to affect the design of an evaluation study than the design of a research study. One issue is whether the evaluation should be done by an internal evaluator or an external evaluator. An **internal evaluator** is someone who is a member of the program staff. For example, some students do thesis or dissertation projects in which they evaluate some aspect of a program for which they work. They may do the evaluation while they are on leave to work on their degrees, but even in this situation they function as internal evaluators.

An **external evaluator** is someone not in the regular employ of the program who is employed specifically to do the evaluation. This person sometimes is called a *third-party evaluator* or *evaluation contractor*.

Most types of evaluation can be done by an internal evaluator, especially when the evaluation findings will be used to guide program management and decision making. Summative evaluation, which is described more fully later in the chapter, is best done by an external evaluator. The purpose of summative evaluation is to determine the merits of a fully operational program and possibly to compare it with a competing program. The evaluator is obliged to represent

6. Maher, "Program Evaluation," p. 407.

the interests of the consumer or the external agency that is sponsoring the evaluation. An external evaluator is in a much better position than an internal evaluator to represent these interests. Even so, an external evaluator can come under pressure to bias the evaluation design to produce positive or negative results. This can also happen to an internal evaluator. If the pressure becomes too intense, the evaluator's only recourse may be to terminate the evaluation on ethical grounds.

The evaluation design is created to answer the questions formulated in the convergent phase described above. The process of creating the design is heavily influenced by the evaluator's choice of a quantitatively oriented or qualitatively oriented evaluation model. Quantitatively oriented models tend to involve research designs that are executed without change once data collection begins. In contrast, qualitatively oriented models encourage the evaluator to pose new questions and to generate new research designs as the study progresses.

Many evaluation studies involve an experimental or quasi-experimental design, because the primary question often is how well the program works. (The program can be viewed as an experimental treatment.) A common issue in this situation is how much internal and external validity to build into the evaluation design. More resources are required to include a control group and other experimental design features that increase one's confidence that observed effects are attributable to the program and that the effects are generalizable. The program staff, however, may not wish to pay the costs needed to improve the experiment's validity.

The resolution of this issue seems to depend on who is in control of the evaluation process. Some evaluators do evaluation studies out of personal interest, as was the case in a study that used the method of educational criticism, described later in the chapter. These evaluators can design more or less rigorous studies as they wish. When you are doing a study that involves collaboration with stakeholders, the situation is different. You must be sensitive to the quality of information that will satisfy the stakeholders' needs and budgetary constraints. This may mean designing a less rigorous study than you might wish. Again, if the resulting design compromises your standards too much, you can choose either to terminate the study or withdraw from it.

In designing an evaluation study, you should be aware that evaluation activities can be both beneficial and harmful. Gene Glass described this problem as a paradox.[7] On the one hand, persons involved in a program appear to do best when they feel that they are valued unconditionally and do not have an evaluator watching over their shoulder. On the other hand, Glass observed, "it appears that people move truer and more certainly toward excellence to the extent that they clarify their purposes, measure the impact of their action, judge

7. Gene V Glass, "A Paradox About Excellence of Schools and the People in Them," *Educational Researcher* 4 (1975): 9–13.

it, and move on—in a few words, evaluate their progress."[8] The perils of evaluation involve not only people, but the program itself. A program may be good, but a poor evaluation can misjudge it and contribute to its downfall. A program may have the potential to be good, but a negative evaluation while it is under development can lead administrators to withdraw funding. Furthermore, evaluation activities use up resources that could be allocated to support good program development.

The beneficial and harmful effects of evaluation are difficult to reconcile. Some evaluators recommend that you weigh all possible consequences of a planned evaluation activity. The potential benefits should outweigh the potential harm before you make a decision to proceed with the evaluation.[9] Also, you should design the study to minimize potentially harmful effects. One way to accomplish this goal is to involve significant stakeholders in the design of the study. For example, they can assist in selecting or developing measures that reflect the outcomes most likely to be achieved by the program. Including the stakeholders' measures will make the evaluation less threatening to them. Also, the measures may reveal effects that cast a positive light on the program.

The final issue we will consider here involves timelines. Many research studies can be done at your own pace. Not so with evaluation studies. If stakeholders are involved, they usually want the final report by a certain date. The evaluator in these situations will need to create a timeline as part of the evaluation design to ensure that the study is completed by the requested date. The timeline can be generated using a PERT chart or similar technique.[10] One advantage of creating a PERT chart is that it can be used to identify and document the resources needed to complete a study by the requested date. You can use this chart to convince stakeholders to increase resources if the requested date can not be met using the resources originally budgeted for the study.

Collecting and Analyzing Evaluation Data

Data collection and analysis in both evaluation studies and research studies are similar. For example, Maher's evaluation study involved a single-group pretest-posttest experimental design, which is described in chapter 15. A quantitative measurement technique, called Goal Attainment Scaling, was used to assess how much progress each student made toward achieving each of the goals of the school's 12 programs. Use of the technique by trained raters yielded a stan-

8. Ibid., p. 12.
9. See p. 301 of Egon G. Guba and Yvonna S. Lincoln, *Effective Evaluation* (San Francisco: Jossey-Bass, 1981).
10. PERT charts are discussed in chapter 2. The use of PERT charts and similar techniques in evaluation studies are described in chapter 16 of Blaine R. Worthen and James R. Sanders, *Educational Evaluation* (New York: Longman, 1987).

dardized goal attainment score for each goal for each student at the beginning and end of the school year. Also, students completed a posttest set of scales on which they rated how helpful each program had been to them. Students' perceptions of the strengths and weaknesses of each program were elicited by open-ended questionnaire items.

One of the primary data analyses involved computing students' mean standardized goal attainment scores at the beginning of the school year ($M = 35.20$) and at the end of the school year ($M = 45.21$). The difference between the means was statistically significant ($p < .05$). Also, students' change scores for each program and other data were used to rank the programs for instructional effectiveness. The employment training, mathematics, and reading programs were found to have had the most impact on the students.

Reporting the Evaluation Results

A typical research study will yield a single report—a master's thesis, doctoral dissertation, or technical report. A condensed version of the report subsequently may be presented as a paper at a professional conference or published as a journal article.

The reporting of an evaluation study is often more complicated because various stakeholder audiences are involved, and each has different information needs. The reporting of the evaluation study that we have been considering exemplifies this principle. Maher described his reporting procedure as follows:

> Following data analysis . . . the evaluation information was disseminated in three ways by the Committee. First, an executive summary report was provided to the principal and executive board, that consisted of a digest version of the evaluation information obtained. Second, a more detailed report was provided to school staff, that consisted of a narrative description of the results, graphical and tabular presentation of data, and evaluation conclusions. Third, an "Evaluation Forum" was held at which evaluator, principal, and staff discussed the evaluation, considered questions and issues raised from reading the evaluation reports, and delineated tentative recommendations for program development and improvement.[11]

If you do an evaluation study for a master's or doctoral degree, you may need to write several reports similar to those prepared by Maher. In addition, you will need to report the results in a thesis or dissertation. Your thesis or dissertation committee probably will require you to use the same format as for reporting a research study (see chapter 21). For example, you may need to write

11. Maher, "Program Evaluation," p. 410.

an extensive review of the literature, which is not generally found in program evaluation reports.

Your thesis or dissertation should include a discussion of how the evaluation findings were used. This is a matter of considerable interest to evaluation experts. In fact, research has been done on how evaluation findings actually are utilized by decision makers.[12] In the case of Maher's study, he noted the following uses of the evaluation findings:

> Following the dissemination of evaluation information, two meetings were held between the evaluator and the principal and staff of the school to assess the utility of the evaluation. Feedback suggested that the evaluation information gathered and reported satisfied the information needs of these program decision makers. . . . Moreover, the information derived from the evaluation was publicly acknowledged by the school's executive board as being used in their decision to expand the size and scope of the school during the ensuing school year. Also, the evaluation procedure has been made a routine part of the school's operational procedure.[13]

Another common feature of evaluation studies reported as theses or dissertations is a discussion of the larger significance of the study. For example, your study's findings may have theoretical significance or may serve as a replication of previous findings on the same problem. If so, you should discuss the study from these perspectives.

Many evaluation projects can be viewed as case studies of the application of a particular evaluation model. If appropriate, the discussion section of your thesis or dissertation should consider the study from this perspective. You can discuss your ideas about the model's applicability to the situation you studied, the shortcomings of the model, and how they might be overcome in future studies. In this way, you can contribute to the improvement of evaluation methodology in education.[14]

Finally, the discussion section of your thesis or dissertation should include a **meta-evaluation.** A meta-evaluation is an evaluation of an evaluation. Researchers are obligated to include in their reports a discussion of weaknesses in their research design or in the execution of the study that might affect the validity of the findings. Evaluators have a similar obligation. Professional organizations have published criteria of a good evaluation study that can be used to judge the adequacy of your own study. These criteria are discussed below.

12. An example of such a study is Karolynn Siegel and Peter Tucker, "The Utilization of Evaluation Research: A Case Analysis," *Evaluation Review* 9 (1985): 307–328.
13. Maher, "Program Evaluation," p. 411.
14. Good examples of contributions to evaluation methodology, derived from analyses of evaluation case studies, can be found in the journal *Educational Evaluation and Policy Analysis*.

CRITERIA OF A GOOD EVALUATION STUDY

The publication of *Standards for Evaluations of Educational Programs, Projects, and Materials* in 1981 marked an important advance in evaluation research.[15] The 30 standards described in the report can be helpful if you intend to do evaluation research for your thesis or dissertation project. You can use the standards as criteria for judging the soundness of your evaluation design and for judging previous evaluation studies in your area of interest.

The standards were developed by the Joint Committee on Standards for Educational Evaluation. The Joint Committee, under the direction of Daniel Stufflebeam, represented many important organizations in education: American Association of School Administrators, American Educational Research Association, American Federation of Teachers, American Personnel and Guidance Association, American Psychological Association, Association for Supervision and Curriculum Development, Council for American Private Education, Education Commission of the States, National Association of Elementary School Principals, National Council on Measurement in Education, National Education Association, and National School Boards Association. Several hundred educators nationwide were involved in developing and field-testing the standards.

The standards were created by the Joint Committee for use in judging the quality of educational evaluations, just as the *Standards for Educational and Psychological Tests* (see chapter 7) were developed for judging the quality of tests. A total of 30 standards are described in the Joint Committee's book-length report.

The standards were developed for several reasons. First, there was a growing awareness that the technical quality of some evaluation studies was poor and that some studies were insensitive to the entity being evaluated. Another realization was that the process of evaluation could be corrupted by persons with ulterior motives. As we noted in the introduction, educational evaluation usually involves political considerations. Evaluators and clients can bend the evaluation process to produce results that reflect their biases or self-interests. Third, the Joint Committee felt that a published set of standards could help to improve the professionalism of educational evaluation. Also, the Joint Committee found that no adequate standards were available at the time they began their work.

The Joint Committee concluded that a good evaluation study satisfies four important criteria: utility, feasibility, propriety, and accuracy. An evaluation has **utility** if it is informative, timely, and useful to the affected persons. **Feasibility** means, first, that the evaluation design is appropriate to the setting in which the study is to be conducted, and second, that the design is cost-effective. An

---

15. Joint Committee on Standards for Educational Evaluation, *Standards for Evaluations of Educational Programs, Projects, and Materials* (New York: McGraw-Hill, 1981).

evaluation has **propriety** if the rights of persons affected by the evaluation are protected. The ethics of educational research described in chapter 3 are pertinent to this standard. Finally, **accuracy** refers to the extent to which an evaluation study has produced valid, reliable, and comprehensive information about the entity being evaluated.

Each criterion for judging an educational evaluation was operationalized in terms of specific standards. The following is a brief description of the 30 standards. Each standard is listed below the criterion to which it most closely relates.

Utility

1. *Audience identification.* All of the audiences affected by the evaluation should be identified.
2. *Evaluator credibility.* The evaluator should be competent and trustworthy.
3. *Information scope and selection.* The questions to be answered by the evaluation should be pertinent and responsive to the affected audiences.
4. *Valuational interpretation.* The bases for interpreting the results and for making value judgments should be clearly described.
5. *Report clarity.* The affected audiences should find it easy to understand the evaluators' reports.
6. *Report dissemination.* Evaluation reports should be disseminated to all clients and right-to-know audiences.
7. *Report timeliness.* The evaluation findings should be reported in a timely manner.
8. *Evaluation impact.* The evaluation should be conducted so as to encourage appropriate action by the affected audiences.

Feasibility

9. *Practical procedures.* The evaluation procedures should be practical and minimally disruptive to participants.
10. *Political viability.* The evaluators should obtain the cooperation of affected interest groups and should keep any group from subverting the evaluation process.
11. *Cost-effectiveness.* The benefits produced by the evaluation should justify the resources expended on it.

Propriety

12. *Formal obligation.* Obligations of all involved parties should be agreed to in writing.
13. *Conflict of interest.* Conflicts that arise in the evaluation process should be treated openly and honestly.

14. *Full and frank disclosure.* Evaluation reports should be direct and honest.
15. *Public's right to know.* The public's right to know about the evaluation should be assured whenever legally or ethically permissible.
16. *Rights of human subjects.* The rights and welfare of persons involved in the evaluation should be protected.
17. *Human interactions.* Evaluators should respect the worth and dignity of persons involved in the study.
18. *Balanced reporting.* The strengths and weaknesses of the entity being evaluated should be reported completely and fairly.
19. *Fiscal responsibility.* Expenditure of resources for the evaluation should be prudent and ethically responsible.

Accuracy

20. *Object identification.* All pertinent aspects of the entity being evaluated should be described.
21. *Context analysis.* All pertinent aspects of the conditions that surround the entity being evaluated should be described.
22. *Described purposes and procedures.* A careful record of the evaluation purposes and procedures should be kept.
23. *Defensible information sources.* Sources of data should be described in sufficient detail that their adequacy can be judged.
24. *Valid measurement.* A range of validated measures should be used in the data collection process.
25. *Reliable measurement.* The measures should have adequate reliability for their intended uses.
26. *Systematic data control.* Human error in data collection should be minimized.
27. *Analysis of quantitative information.* Analysis of quantitative data in an evaluation study should be accurate and thorough, and should yield clear interpretations.
28. *Analysis of qualitative information.* Analysis of qualitative data in an evaluation study should be accurate and thorough, and should yield clear interpretations.
29. *Justified conclusions.* The conclusions of an evaluation must be based on sound logic and appropriate data analyses.
30. *Objective reporting.* Evaluation reports should be thorough and free of biases of pressure groups.

Helpful case studies that illustrate each standard are presented in the Joint Committee's report.[16] The evaluation models and procedures described in this chapter reflect many of the standards.

---

16. Ibid.

Application of the 30 standards is not always straightforward. For example, the evaluators' efforts to produce an accurate evaluation (standards 20–30) may conflict with their desire to issue timely reports (standard 7). Also, some of the persons involved in the evaluation may be more committed to achieving the standards than are other persons. If it appears that important standards have been compromised, the Joint Committee recommends that the evaluators should consider dropping the project.

The importance of individual standards will vary depending upon the situation. For example, the public's right to know (standard 15) may not be an important consideration in a privately funded, inhouse evaluation of a product under development. However, the use of valid, reliable measures (standards 24 and 25) may be quite important to the developers whose product is being evaluated. You should keep in mind, too, that the standards were specifically intended for evaluations of programs (educational activities that provide services on a continuing basis), projects (activities that are funded for a defined period of time), and materials (physical items such as books, films, tapes, and other instructional products). The standards were not intended for judging evaluations of institutions, professional personnel, or students.

QUANTITATIVELY ORIENTED EVALUATION MODELS

We have made the point throughout this book that there is not one way to do educational research, but rather many ways. You can do basic or applied research, quantitative or qualitative research, and descriptive, correlational, or experimental research. Also, these broad categories of research have many variations reflecting different objectives, philosophies of scientific inquiry, and methodologies.

Like educational research, educational evaluation takes diverse forms. This is because evaluators over time have developed different purposes for doing evaluation, different philosophies, and different methodologies. These differences gradually led to the development of different formal models of doing evaluation. The remaining sections of this chapter describe the major models.[17] If you are planning to do evaluation studies, you should review these models to determine which one best suits your purpose and philosophical approach to inquiry.

The quantitatively oriented models described below rely primarily on positivistic methods of inquiry. They emphasize objective measurement, representative sampling, experimental control, and use of statistical techniques to

---

17. Our characterization of evaluation models is based primarily on Worthen and Sanders, *Educational Evaluation.*

analyze data. The models emphasize a concern for determining what is generally true and worthwhile about the program being evaluated rather than a concern for the individual case and idiosyncratic phenomena.

Evaluation of the Individual

Evaluation research can be traced back to at least the early 1900s when the testing movement began. Binet's intelligence test was published in 1904, and group ability testing began during World War I. Evaluation primarily involved the assessment of individual differences in intelligence and school achievement. This model of evaluation is still widely followed in American education. Also, evaluation of teachers, administrators, and other school personnel has become a matter of increasing interest to researchers and administrators.[18] Like assessment of students, personnel evaluation focuses on measurement of individual differences, and judgments are made by comparing the individual with a set of norms or a criterion.

Objectives-Based Evaluation

Ralph Tyler's work on curriculum evaluation in the 1940s brought about a major change in educational evaluation.[19] Tyler's view was that curriculum should be organized around explicit objectives and that the success of the curriculum should be judged on the basis of how well students achieve the objectives. The Tyler model marked a shift from evaluating individual students to evaluating the curriculum. Also, the Tyler model implied that students might perform poorly not because of lack of innate ability, but because of weaknesses in the curriculum.

The Tyler model has had an important influence on subsequent developments in educational evaluation. The National Assessment of Educational Progress (see chapter 1) was originated in the 1960s under Tyler's leadership. This federal program continues to the present day to collect data on the academic achievement of the nation's youth. Many state testing programs collect similar data using this program's methods. The increasing practice of competency testing of students and teachers is another outgrowth of the Tyler model.

Educational evaluators have developed other evaluation models that reflect Tyler's emphasis on measurement of explicit objectives as the basis for determining the merits of an educational program. For example, Malcolm

18. For example, see Jason Millman, ed., *Handbook of Teacher Evaluation* (Beverly Hills, CA: Sage, 1981).
19. Ralph W. Tyler, *Basic Principles of Curriculum and Instruction: Syllabus for Education 360* (Chicago: University of Chicago Press, 1949).

Provus developed **discrepancy evaluation,** which emphasizes the search for discrepancies between the objectives of a program and students' actual achievement of the objectives.[20] The resulting information about discrepancies can be used to guide program management decisions.

Another objectives-based model is **cost-benefit evaluation.**[21] Evaluators using this model seek to determine the relationship between the costs of a program and the objectives that it has achieved. Different programs can be compared to determine which is most cost-effective, that is, which promotes the greatest benefits for each unit of resource expenditure.

If you are planning a study of students' achievement of instructional objectives, one of your major concerns will be measurement of the objectives. To facilitate measurement, you probably will find it helpful to state objectives in behavioral terms, meaning that the program outcomes are stated as behaviors that anyone, including evaluators, can observe in a program participant.[22] This type of objective, commonly called a **behavioral objective,** usually has three components: statement of the program objective as an observable, behavioral outcome; criteria for successful performance of the behavior; and the situational context in which the behavior is to be performed. "Given a set of 20 single-digit multiplication problems, the learner will be able to solve them by writing the correct answer beneath each problem in less than three minutes with no more than two errors" is an example of a behavioral objective.

Behavioral objectives have been critized on the grounds that they reduce education to a matter of only teaching that which can be stated and measured in the language of behavioral objectives. Of course, behavioral objectives, like any other technique, can be misused. Used appropriately, however, they simplify the task of developing suitable instruments (especially domain-referenced instruments[23]) to measure the learner's achievement of an objective.

Another issue in evaluating program objectives concerns which objectives to measure. Evaluators often rely on the program's developers or experts to make this decision. Michael Scriven, however, argued that evaluators should not know the program goals in advance.[24] Instead, the evaluators should conduct research to discover the actual effects of the program in operation. The actual effects may differ markedly from the program developers' stated goals. An evaluator who knows the goals in advance may become co-opted by them and overlook other effects of the program, especially adverse side effects. Scriven's strategy for evaluation has come to be known as **goal-free evaluation.**

20. Malcolm Provus, *Discrepancy Evaluation* (Berkeley, CA: McCutchan, 1971).
21. This type of evaluation research is discussed in Henry M. Levin, *Cost-Effectiveness: A Primer* (Beverly Hills, CA: Sage, 1983).
22. Procedures for writing behavioral objectives are explained in many sources. The classic work is Robert F. Mager, *Preparing Instructional Objectives*, rev. ed. (Belmont, CA: David S. Lake, 1984).
23. Domain-referenced measurement is discussed in chapter 7.
24. Michael Scriven, "Goal-Free Evaluation," in *School Evaluation: The Politics and Process*, ed. Ernest R. House (Berkeley, CA: McCutchan, 1973), pp. 319–328.

Although this method has merit, there are many situations in which an evaluator is employed to collect evaluative data about specific program goals. In these situations the evaluator is required to attend to certain goals; yet it is advisable to remain alert to the possibility that the program may have actual effects, both beneficial and adverse, that are quite different from those intended by the program developers.

An example in education of this phenomenon is the evaluations of DISTAR, an academic program intended to develop the cognitive skills of low-income disadvantaged children. Although the evaluation research has focused on measurement of these cognitive skills, self-concept instruments have been routinely administered as well. The evaluation findings indicate that DISTAR affects students' cognitive growth and also has a positive effect on their self-esteem.[25]

Needs Assessment

A **need** can be defined as a discrepancy between an existing set of conditions and a desired set of conditions. For example, suppose an educator makes the assertion, "We need to place more emphasis on science education in our elementary school curriculum." The educator is saying in effect that there is a discrepancy between the existing curriculum and a desired curriculum. This statement of need reflects a judgment about the present merit of the curriculum. For this reason professional evaluators are interested in the determination of need states in education. Also, note that the assessment of need states provides a basis for setting objectives for curriculum or program development. That is why we consider needs assessment to be closely related to objectives-based models of evaluation.

Educational needs can be assessed systematically using quantitative research methods. An example of this type of needs assessment is a study conducted by Morris Lai, Sandra Shimabukuro, Nao Wenkam, and S. Pattabi Raman.[26] The purpose of their study was to identify nutritional weaknesses in food habits of Hawaiian students in grades 1–12. The nutritional weaknesses were viewed as needs to be addressed in the development of a statewide nutrition education program.

The sample consisted of approximately 900 students in elementary, junior high, and high school classes representing seven regional districts of Hawaii. With the aid of interviewers, students completed forms on which they recorded

25. Linda B. Stebbins, Robert G. St. Pierre, Elizabeth C. Proper, Richard B. Andersie, and Thomas R. Cerva, "An Evaluation of Follow Through," in *Evaluation Studies Review Annual*, Vol. 3, eds. Thomas D. Cook, Marlyn L. Del Rosario, Karen M. Hennigan, Melvin M. Mark, and William M. K. Trochim (Beverly Hills, CA: Sage, 1978), pp. 571–610.
26. Morris K. Lai, Sandra K. Shimabukuro, Nao S. Wenkam, and S. Pattabi Raman, "A Nutrient Analysis of Students' Diets in the State of Hawaii," *Journal of Nutrition Education* 14 (1982): 67–70.

TABLE 17.1

**Percentage of Students with Daily Intake below Two-Thirds
of the Recommended Dietary Allowance of Each of Nine Nutrients**

Nutrient	Elementary		Junior High		Senior High	
	Male ($n = 170$)	Female ($n = 159$)	Male ($n = 145$)	Female ($n = 137$)	Male ($n = 164$)	Female ($n = 115$)
Protein	0%	1%	1%	3%	3%	6%
Vitamin A	35	42	56	57	40	59
Thiamin	32	40	39	36	33	37
Riboflavin	8	14	9	16	15	21
Niacin	20	31	23	28	18	28
Vitamin C	25	27	37	35	32	33
Calcium	22	29	40	66	38	70
Phosphorus	4	6	9	26	16	32
Iron	9	13	49	73	38	77

Source: Adapted from table 1 in Morris K. Lai, Sandra K. Shimabukuro, Nao S. Wenkam, and S. Pattabi Raman, "A Nutrient Analysis of Students' Diets in the State of Hawaii," *Journal of Nutrition Education* 14 (1982): 68.

everything they ate over the 24-hour period immediately prior to data collection. The researchers analyzed the data by a computer program that identified the nutrient composition of all food items consumed by the students.

One of the primary data analyses concerned the sample's daily intake of nine important nutrients. They are listed in the first column of table 17.1. The evaluators calculated the percentage of students whose intake of each nutrient fell below two-thirds of the Recommended Dietary Allowance (RDA), a standard established by the National Academy of Sciences. The percentages are shown separately for each gender and school level in table 17.1.

The results indicate that protein intake was satisfactory but that intake of the other nutrients—especially vitamin A, thiamin, and calcium—was a problem. Risk of iron deficiency was particularly high among junior high and high school students. Supplemental analyses indicated nutritional deficiencies linked to ethnicity: Asian and Polynesian students had low calcium intake, and Japanese students had low vitamin A intake.

These and other findings of the study revealed specific needs (discrepancies between actual and recommended food habits) of students in the sample. Consequently, the researchers made the following recommendations:

> To a curriculum developer, the results of our study show that differences in dietary intake among age groups necessitate a curriculum geared to each grade level and

designed sequentially to meet the needs of children as they grow older. . . . Furthermore, the evidence of ethnic influences on dietary intake supports the need for a curriculum unique to the population mix in Hawaii.[27]

Curriculum specialists could develop a nutrition education program without benefit of these recommendations derived from a formal needs assessment. However, the program might overlook certain objectives, give them inappropriate emphasis, or fail to address the needs of particular students.

The typical needs assessment is a feasible evaluation project to do as a master's or dissertation study. The primary requirement is a measure of the target group's current behavior or achievement and a standard against which to compare it. If you are interested in doing curriculum development as part of your professional career, you may wish to do a needs assessment in the curriculum content area that particularly interests you.

Several problems can arise in doing a needs assessment. One of them concerns the definition of *need*. Exactly what is a *desired* set of conditions? J. Roth identified five types of desired states: ideals, norms, minimums, desires (wants), and expectations.[28] A need can be a discrepancy between an actual state and any one of these five desired states. The goal of a college degree for all citizens (ideal desired state) is certainly a different kind of desired state from the goal of basic skill in reading for all children (a minimum desired state).

Many needs assessments do not make clear how urgent or optional are the desired states that are being determined. For example, the evaluators who did the nutrition study used the quantity, two-thirds of the Recommended Dietary Allowance, as a standard of nutritional adequacy. It is not clear from their report whether this standard is a minimum desired state or an accepted norm.

Another problem with the needs assessment process is that the values underlying needs are often left unarticulated. It is helpful to determine quantitatively whether certain groups view elements of education (e.g., small class size, compulsory school prayer, computer-assisted instruction) as needs. These quantitative expressions of need just scratch the surface, though. Personal values and standards are important determinants of needs, and they should be assessed to round out one's understanding of needs among the groups being studied.

You should also be aware that needs assessment data are usually reported as group trends. There may be important individual differences in stated needs that should be explored. A nice feature of the nutrition study is that gender, age, and ethnic differences in nutritional intake were analyzed. These analyses revealed important individual differences that would have been obscured if the sample had been viewed as a homogeneous group.

27. Ibid., p. 69.
28. J. Roth, "Needs and the Needs Assessment Process," *Evaluation News* 5 (1977): 15–17.

Formative and Summative Evaluation

Educational products—textbooks, films, computer software, workbooks, etc.—play a major role in classroom instruction. Therefore, the effectiveness of these products is a matter of some concern to educators. Because several competing products may be available for the same purpose, information about their relative effectiveness is needed to help educators make a good purchase decision.

Michael Scriven developed a useful evaluation model for evaluating educational products.[29] He observed that product evaluation serves two different functions. The function of **formative evaluation** is to collect data about educational products while they are still being developed. The evaluative data can be used by developers to design and modify the product. In some instances the evaluation findings may lead to a decision to abort further development so that resources are not wasted on a product that has little chance of ultimately being effective.

The summative function of evaluation occurs after the product has been fully developed. **Summative evaluation** is conducted to determine how worthwhile the final product is, especially in comparison with other competing products. Summative data are useful to educators who must make purchase or adoption decisions.

The distinction between formative and summative evaluation applies not only to education but to many other fields as well. Industry frequently uses techniques of formative evaluation to guide the development of new products. The results of each evaluation provide data to help engineers and others improve the design or functioning of the product. The same formative data may also help managers decide how much and what kinds of resources to commit to further development of the product. When the completed product reaches the marketplace, other groups are likely to conduct summative evaluations. Each potential purchaser will evaluate the product against personal criteria and perhaps against other products that are commercially available. Summative evaluations of high rigor are conducted by such groups as Consumers Union, the publisher of *Consumer Reports*. Ralph Nader and his associates have become widely known because of their summative evaluations of certain products and programs.

The distinction between the formative and summative function of evaluation is important because it affects the process by which evaluation is carried out. Formative evaluation is often done by an "in-house" evaluator, whose job it is to help the team of developers. In fact, during the program development process, some members of the team may perform a dual function, being both developers and evaluators. Summative evaluation, however, is usually done by an external evaluator. This person should not be associated with the develop-

29. Michael Scriven, "The Methodology of Evaluation," in *Curriculum Evaluation*, ed. Robert E. Stake (Chicago: Rand McNally, 1967).

ment team, in order to avoid being biased or co-opted by team members. Rather, the summative evaluator should be responsive to the needs and requirements of educational decision makers, potential users of the product, and the agency that funded the development of the product.

Objectives play an important role in formative and summative evaluations. They provide the criteria for judging the merits of the product. The objectives usually include behavioral objectives and state the learning outcomes to be achieved by the student using the product. Other objectives refer to product qualities desired by the purchaser or user—for example, low cost, absence of gender or ethnic bias, durability, and motivational appeal.

Various checklists and product analysis systems have been developed for judging the different characteristics of educational products.[30] One such system, developed by the second author of this text, is shown in the list below, which is an inventory of evaluation criteria stated as questions.

Publication and Cost

1. Authors: *Are the authors known and respected professionally?*
2. Cost: *Is the cost of the materials reasonable relative to other, comparable materials?*
3. Development History: *Were the materials adequately field-tested and revised prior to publication?*
4. Edition: *Is this edition to be in publication for several years, or is a new edition to be released shortly?*
5. Publication Date: *Were these materials published within the last two years?*
6. Publisher: *Does the publisher of these materials have a good reputation among educators?*
7. Purchase Procedures: *Are the purchase procedures clear and easy to use?*
8. Quantity: *Are there likely to be difficulties in obtaining sufficient quantities of the materials for each student who will be using them?*
9. Special Requirements: *Do our schools have the special resources required for use of the materials?*
10. Teacher Training: *Does use of the materials require skills that our district teachers are not likely to possess?*

Physical Properties

11. Aesthetic Appeal: *Are the materials likely to appeal to the user's aesthetic sense?*
12. Components: *Do the materials contain so many components that teachers will have difficulty in keeping track of them and using them?*

30. Michael Scriven, "Standards for the Evaluation of Educational Programs and Products," in *Evaluating Educational Programs and Products*, ed. Gary D. Borich (Englewood Cliffs, NJ: Educational Technology Publications, 1974); G. K. Tallmadge, *Ideabook: Joint Dissemination Review Panel* (Washington, DC: U.S. Government Printing Office, 1977) (ERIC DL 48329).

13. Consumables: *Does the product make unnecessary use of consumable materials?*
14. Durability: *Do the materials have components that are especially vulnerable to wear?*
15. Media: *Does the developer make appropriate use of the media included among the materials?*
16. Quality: *Did the publisher use high-quality materials in the production process?*
17. Safety: *Are there possible hazards to students or teachers in using the materials?*

Content

18. Approach: *Does the developer use an approach consistent with the district's curriculum?*
19. Instructional Objectives: *Are the materials' objectives compatible with the district's curriculum and acceptable to teachers?*
20. Instructional Objectives—Types: *Do the materials contain affective objectives in addition to cognitive objectives?*
21. Issues Orientation: *Are the materials free of biases that are misleading or that are likely to be unacceptable to teachers, students, and the community?*
22. Multiculturalism: *Do the materials reflect the contributions and perspectives of various ethnic and cultural groups?*
23. Scope and Sequence: *Are the scope and sequence of the materials compatible with the district's curriculum?*
24. Sex Roles: *Is the content of the materials free of sex stereotypes?*
25. Time-Boundedness: *Does the content of the materials reflect current knowledge and culture?*

Instructional Properties

26. Assessment Devices: *Do the materials contain tests and other assessment devices that will be helpful to the teacher and his or her students?*
27. Comprehensibility: *Will the materials be clearly understood by the students who will be using them?*
28. Coordination with the Curriculum: *Are the materials compatible with other materials currently being used in the school?*
29. Individualization: *Does the design of the materials allow teachers to use them differently according to student needs?*
30. Instructional Effectiveness: *Does the publisher provide any data on the effectiveness of the materials in actual use?*
31. Instructional Patterns: *Is the primary instructional pattern likely to help the learner achieve the materials' objectives?*
32. Learner Characteristics: *Are the materials appropriate for the students who will be using them?*
33. Length: *Are the materials an appropriate length so that they can fit conveniently into the teacher's instructional schedule?*

34. Management System: *Is the use of the materials easily managed by the teacher?*
35. Motivational Properties: *Are the materials likely to excite the interest of students and teachers?*
36. Prerequisites: *Are the students likely to have the prerequisite knowledge or skills necessary for learning the content of the materials?*
37. Readability: *Are the materials written at an appropriate reading level for students who will be using them?*
38. Role of the Student: *Do the materials include activities that students are capable of doing and that they will enjoy doing?*
39. Role of the Teacher: *Do the materials include activities that teachers will find interesting and rewarding?*[31]

Note that only one of the evaluative criteria (no. 30) concerns learning outcomes. The other criteria may be just as important, however, to particular purchasers or users of a product. Also note that this and similar lists of educational product criteria can be useful in both formative and summative evaluation.

This evaluation model plays a major role in educational research and development (R & D). Therefore, if you are interested in doing a formative or summative evaluation, we recommend that you first develop an understanding of educational R & D methods, which is the subject of chapter 18.

Evaluation to Guide Program Management

The models described above tend to focus on arm's-length evaluations of completed programs. As evaluators began to work more closely with staff of ongoing programs or programs under development, they became interested in how they might contribute to this process. Evaluators saw that critical *decisions* needed to be made by program managers and that they could collect evaluative data that could help the managers make these decisions.

The CIPP model was formulated by Daniel Stufflebeam and his colleagues to show how evaluation could contribute to the decision-making process in program management.[32] CIPP is an acronym for the four types of educational evaluation included in the model: context evaluation, input evaluation, process evaluation, and product evaluation. Each type of evaluation is tied to a different set of decisions that must be made in planning and operating a program.

Context evaluation involves identification of problems and needs in a specific educational setting. You will recall from our discussion of needs

31. Meredith D. Gall, *Handbook for Evaluating and Selecting Curriculum Materials* (Boston: Allyn and Bacon, 1981), 118–120.
32. The CIPP model is described in Daniel L. Stufflebeam and others, *Educational Evaluation and Decision Making* (Itaska, IL: F.E. Peacock, 1971).

assessment above that a need is a discrepancy between an existing condition and a desired condition.

Input evaluation concerns judgments about the resources and strategies needed to accomplish program goals and objectives. Information collected during this stage of evaluation should help decision makers choose the best possible resources and strategies within certain constraints. Input evaluation deals with such issues as whether certain resources are too expensive or unavailable, whether a particular strategy is likely to be effective in achieving program goals, whether certain strategies are legally or morally acceptable, and how best to utilize personnel as resources. Input evaluation requires the evaluator to have a wide range of knowledge about possible resources and strategies, as well as knowledge about research on their effectiveness in achieving different types of program outcomes.

Process evaluation involves the collection of evaluative data once the program has been designed and put into operation. The evaluator might be called upon to design a data collection system for monitoring the day-to-day operation of a program. For example, you might keep attendance records on an inservice teacher-training program based on voluntary participation. If attendance data reveal deviations from what was anticipated, the program's decision makers can take action based on their appraisal of the data. Without such a record-keeping system, the program might deteriorate, perhaps irreversibly, before the decision makers become aware of what is happening. Another function of process evaluation is to keep records of program events over a period of time. These records may prove useful at a later time in detecting strengths and weaknesses of the program that account for its observed outcomes.

The fourth element of the CIPP model is **product evaluation.** The task of product evaluation is to determine the extent to which the goals of the program have been achieved. Measures of the goals are developed and administered. The resulting data can be used by program administrators to make decisions about continuing the program and modifying it.

Each of the types of evaluation described above requires that three broad tasks be performed: delineating the kinds of information needed for decision making, obtaining the information, and synthesizing the information so that it is maximally useful in making decisions. The first and third steps (delineation and synthesis) should be done as a collaborative effort between evaluator and decision maker. Obtaining information is a technical activity and should be delegated primarily to the evaluator.

You may have noted that the CIPP model incorporates elements of the other evaluations described above—objectives-based evaluation, needs assessment, and formative and summative evaluation. The CIPP model is distinguished by its comprehensiveness, by the fact that it is an ongoing process, and by its purpose, which is to guide the decision-making function in program management.

This model has proved useful in guiding the work of evaluation staffs in school districts and governmental agencies. Because the CIPP model is complex, it would be difficult to use, at least in its entirety, in a thesis or dissertation project. The other models described above are more manageable. However, you may happen to do an evaluation study involving collaboration with an agency that uses the CIPP model. In this case you should be familiar with the model so that you can determine how your study fits into the agency's total evaluation process and also the kinds of data and other resources that may be available to you.

QUALITATIVELY ORIENTED EVALUATION MODELS

The evaluation models described above are useful, but they do not satisfactorily address a number of important problems of evaluation. The objectives-based models, for example, tend to take a program's objectives or observed effects as givens. They do not offer much guidance if you wish to understand why particular objectives are considered worthwhile or why the stakeholders agree or do not agree on the worth of objectives.

The politics of evaluation also are not given serious attention in quantitatively oriented models. Various groups have a stake in the outcome of an evaluation study, and they may try to influence the evaluation process accordingly. Should you resist these political influences or incorporate them into the design of the evaluation study? Another problem is that under certain conditions evaluations may do more harm than good. As we stated above, people generally do not like being evaluated, and the evaluation process may hamper the very performance that is being assessed. How can you work with the client so that the evaluation produces the most benefit and least harm?

In the opinion of some evaluators, the most serious limitation of the evaluation models described above is their reliance on positivistic research methodology. We discussed in chapter 1 the assumptions underlying positivism and the criticisms directed at them. Similar criticisms have been directed at evaluation models that we characterized as quantitatively oriented.

We also discussed in chapter 1 that some educational researchers, having rejected quantitative methodology, turned their attention to qualitative methods. Some evaluators did likewise. The following sections of the chapter describe the evaluation models that they developed over the past decade or so. These models rely heavily on the qualitative methods described in chapter 10, and they address aspects of evaluation ignored or given little emphasis in quantitatively oriented models.

These models differ most strongly from quantitatively oriented models in not assuming that there are objective criteria for judging the worth of an educational program or product. Rather, qualitatively oriented models assume that the worth of an educational program or product depends heavily on the values and perspectives of those doing the judging. Therefore, the selection of persons or groups to be involved in the evaluation is critical. In contrast, quantitatively oriented models have tended not to explore differences in perceptions of worth. For example, in the nutrition education study described above, the Recommended Dietary Allowance was used as the basis for judging good nutritional intake. Some individuals or groups, however, may have other ideas about what constitutes good nutritional intake. This issue was not explored in the study.

Responsive Evaluation

Robert Stake pioneered the qualitative approach to educational evaluation.[33] His evaluation model, called **responsive evaluation,** focuses on the concerns and issues affecting the stakeholders. The **stakeholders** are the persons who are involved in or affected by the program being evaluated. A **concern** is any matter about which a stakeholder feels threatened or any claim that they want to substantiate. An **issue** is any point of contention among the stakeholders. Concerns and issues provide a much wider focus for evaluation than do the behavioral objectives that are the primary focus for traditional evaluation.

Egon Guba and Yvonna Lincoln identified four major phases that occur in an evaluation of this type.[34]

The first major phase involves initiating and organizing the evaluation. Guba and Lincoln recommend that the evaluator and client negotiate an evaluation contract that specifies such matters as identification of the entity to be evaluated, the purpose of the evaluation, rights of access to records, and guarantees of confidentiality and anonymity. They also emphasize the importance of identifying the stakeholders in the evaluation. Each stakeholder has the right to have his or her concerns reflected in the evaluation process.

It is also important to identify political factors that can affect the evaluation process. Guba and Lincoln cited the example of an evaluator who was asked to evaluate the effectiveness of paraprofessional teacher aides in improving student learning. It became apparent to the evaluator, though, that the position of teacher aide also served important political purposes: It provided linkages between school and community, and it provided jobs for community members. Thus, there was much pressure on the evaluator by school officials to show teacher aides in a positive light.

The second phase of a responsive evaluation is to identify the concerns,

33. Robert E. Stake, "The Countenance of Educational Evaluation," *Teachers College Record* 68 (1967): 523–540; Robert E. Stake, "The Case Study Method in Social Inquiry," *Educational Researcher* 7 (1978): 5–8.
34. Guba and Lincoln, *Effective Evaluation.*

issues, and values of the stakeholders. These factors are usually identified by a series of interviews and questionnaires administered to all or a sample of stakeholders. Guba and Lincoln cited the example of a responsive evaluation of the governance structure in a particular school system. The special focus of the evaluation was whether the governance structure was open to inputs from various stakeholding audiences in establishing school policy. Stakeholders included the school board, school administrators, teachers, students, parents, the city's mayoral staff, and influential members of the community.

Interviews with the stakeholders revealed several serious concerns, such as citizen lockout in decision making (for example, the school board cut out elementary art despite parental opposition) and arrogation of power by a small elite (for example, school staff felt that they had little say in school affairs). Several issues were also identified: whether school policy formulation should be centralized or decentralized; whether policy should be formulated by professionals or by lay groups; and whether the school board should be elected or appointed. These issues and concerns express the underlying values of the stakeholders. For example, some of the stakeholders were found to value a high-quality curriculum, a rational decision-making process, equality of representation in decision making, and accountability.

The third phase of a responsive evaluation is to gather information that pertains to the concerns, issues, and values identified by the stakeholders. The evaluator also should collect descriptive information about the entity being evaluated and about standards that will be used in making judgments concerning the entity. Information in responsive evaluations can be gathered by a variety of methods: naturalistic observation, interview, questionnaire, standardized tests. Consider the example of evaluating a school system's governance structure. A concern of some stakeholders was that the school board cut out elementary art despite parental opposition. The evaluator could reconstruct this occurrence to determine what kind of evidence there is to substantiate this concern. The evaluator also needs to work extensively with the various stakeholders to gain a deeper understanding of the issues, values, and standards involving the entity that is being evaluated.

The final phase of a responsive evaluation is to prepare reports of results and recommendations. The case study format is used frequently in such reports, but when appropriate, a traditional research reporting format (see chapter 21) can be used. A responsive evaluation report will contain extensive descriptions of the concerns and issues identified by the stakeholders. Guba and Lincoln also recommend that the evaluator—in negotiation with the stakeholders—make judgments and recommendations based on the gathered information.

Unlike the other types of evaluation research described above, responsive evaluators do not specify a research design at the outset of their work. Instead, responsive evaluators use **emergent designs,** meaning that the design of the research changes as the evaluator gains new insights into the concerns and

TABLE 17.2

Comparison of Quantitatively Oriented Evaluation Models and Responsive Evaluation

Comparison Item	Type of Evaluation	
	Quantitatively Oriented	Responsive
Orientation	Formal.	Informal.
Value perspective	Singular; consensual.	Pluralistic; possibility of conflict.
Basis for evaluation design (organizer)	Program intents, objectives, goals, hypotheses; evaluator preconceptions: performance, mastery, ability, aptitude, measurable outcomes; instrumental values of education.	Audience concerns and issues; program activities; reactions, motivations, or problems of persons in and around the evaluand.
Design completed when?	At beginning of evaluation.	Never—continuously evolving.
Evaluator role	Stimulator of subjects with a view to testing critical performance.	Stimulated by subjects and activities.
Methods	Objective; "taking readings," for example, testing.	Subjective—observations and interviews; negotiations and interactions.
Communication	Formal; reports; typically one stage.	Informal; portrayals; often two stage.
Feedback	At discrete intervals; often only once, at end.	Informal; continuously evolving as needed by audiences.
Form of feedback	Written report, identifying variables and depicting the relationships among them; symbolic interpretation.	Narrative-type depiction, often oral (if that is what the audience prefers); modeling what the program is like; providing vicarious experience; "holistic" communication.
Paradigm	Experimental psychology.	Anthropology, journalism, poetry.

SOURCE: Reprinted from Egon G. Guba and Yvonna S. Lincoln, *Effective Evaluation* (San Francisco: Jossey-Bass, 1981), p. 28. By permission of the publisher.

issues of the stakeholders. For example, Guba and Lincoln compared sampling techniques in emergent and traditional research design: "Sampling is almost never representative or random but purposive, intended to exploit competing views and fresh perspectives as fully as possible. Sampling stops when information becomes redundant rather than when subjects are representatively sampled."[35]

The preceding description of the four phases of responsive evaluation demonstrates that it differs from quantitatively oriented evaluation models in important ways. The differences are summarized in table 17.2.

Responsive evaluation is an important development in educational evaluation. However, we caution the student who is thinking about doing a responsive evaluation as a thesis or dissertation. Responsive evaluations are usually complex and are best done by a team of evaluators rather than by an individual working alone. Members of a team can act as a check on each other and ensure that a comprehensive picture of the entity being evaluated is formed. Also, the responsive evaluator should be conversant with a variety of research designs ranging from formal experiments to ethnographic inquiry. The reason for this requirement is that emergent design requires the selection of different research methodologies depending upon the phenomena being investigated at a particular point in the evaluation.

If you plan to use responsive evaluation as a model to guide your thesis or dissertation study, you should consider finding an experienced team of evaluators with whom you can work. Perhaps the team is engaged in planning or conducting a responsive evaluation study. You can select one set of concerns or issues as a focus for your project.

Adversary Evaluation

Adversary evaluation is a model of evaluation that is related in certain respects to responsive evaluation, described above. This model was derived from procedures used in jury trials and administrative hearings in the field of law.[36] The distinguishing features of adversary evaluation are its use of a wide array of data; its reliance on human testimony; and, most importantly, the fact that it is "adversarial," meaning that both positive and negative judgments about the program are encouraged. Adversary evaluation is more structured and limited than the responsive evaluation model.

Adversary evaluation has four major stages. The first stage is to generate a broad range of issues. To do this, the evaluation team surveys various groups involved in the program (users, managers, funding agencies, etc.) to determine what they believe are relevant issues. Examples of such issues are: "Should this program be terminated, so that the alternative program can be instituted?" "Should funding for this program be increased by at least 50 percent?" "Are students making the learning gains that we expect them to make?"

The second stage involves reducing the list of issues to a manageable

35. Ibid., p. 276.
36. Robert L. Wolf, "Trial by Jury: A New Evaluation Method," *Phi Delta Kappan* 57 (1975): 185–87.

number. One method of doing this is to have a group of respondents list the issues in order of importance. The third stage is to form two opposing evaluation teams (the adversaries) and provide them an opportunity to prepare arguments in favor of or in opposition to the program on each issue. As part of this process, the teams can interview potential witnesses, study existing evaluation reports, and collect new data. The final stage is to conduct prehearing sessions and a formal hearing. In the formal hearing the adversarial teams present their arguments and evidence before the program's decision makers.

A large-scale adversary evaluation of minimum competency testing was conducted by the former National Institute of Education (NIE).[37] A "pro" team and a "con" team were formed to argue the merits of this practice. A hearing officer arbitrated disagreements over the qualifications of witnesses and admissibility of testimony. Although adversary evaluation can include a jury, this feature was not included.

The pro and con teams were asked to focus their arguments on these issues:

1. Will minimum competency programs that use test results for student certification and/or classification have beneficial or harmful effects on students?
2. Will minimum competency programs that use test results for student certification and/or classification have beneficial or harmful influences on curriculum and teaching?
3. Will minimum competency programs that use test results for student certification and/or classification have positive or negative effects on public perceptions of educational quality?

Earlier in the chapter, in the section on identifying evaluation questions, we stated that new questions sometimes arise in the course of doing an evaluation study. Such was the case in this study. As the adversarial hearings proceeded, a more specific set of questions concerning minimum competency testing emerged.

1. Is minimum competency testing (MCT) a valuable technique for improving the quality of instruction?
2. Does MCT unfairly discriminate against racial minorities and bilingual students, or does it provide neutral measures of basic skills for which all students ought to be held accountable, both for their own good and for that of society?
3. Is MCT technology sufficiently sophisticated to carry the burden that is placed on it?

37. Paul Thurston and Ernest R. House, "The NIE Adversary Hearing on Minimum Competency Testing," *Phi Delta Kappan* 63 (1981): 87–89.

4. Why do states differ widely in their enthusiasm about MCT and in the type of MCT programs they mandate?
5. Do the positions of the pro and con groups reflect basic differences in educational philosophy?

The formulation of these new questions out of the adversarial hearings is useful. The questions provide a compelling agenda for further inquiries into the technology and merits of minimum competency testing.

In addition to its benefits, evaluators have discovered that adversary evaluation has shortcomings.[38] It is expensive and time-consuming. Also, its results can be biased if one of the evaluation teams is more skilled in argumentation than the other. Some evaluators have modified elements of the model to deal with these problems.[39]

Expertise-Based Evaluation

The use of experts to make judgments about the worth of an educational program is a time-honored and widely used method of evaluation. For example, most institutional programs are reviewed periodically by accreditation boards composed of experts. Commissions that include experts and laypersons are often used to appraise the status of some aspect of the educational enterprise. An example is the National Commission on Excellence in Education, which produced the influential report *A Nation at Risk.* If you do a thesis or dissertation project, its quality will be judged by a panel of professors who are in this role because of their presumed expertise.

Expertise-based evaluation has taken a new form with the emergence of a qualitative research tradition in education. Educational anthropologists, for example, can use the qualitative research method of ethnography to evaluate, as well as describe, the phenomena that interest them. Other qualitative methods described in chapter 10—participant observation, case studies, interviewing—can be adapted by the researcher to do an "expert" evaluation.

Educational connoisseurship and criticism is a qualitative research method that was specifically developed for the purpose of educational evaluation.[40] Elliott Eisner, an art educator, derived the method from literary and art criticism. One aspect of it is connoisseurship, which is the process of appreci-

38. W. James Popham and Dale Carlson, "Deep Dark Deficits of the Adversary Evaluation Model," *Educational Researcher* 6 (1977): 3–6. See also Paul Thurston, "Revitalizing Adversary Evaluation: Deep Dark Deficits or Muddled Mistaken Musings," *Educational Researcher* 7, no. 7 (1978): 3–8.
39. See, for example, Kit C. Wood, Sarah E. Peterson, James S. De Gracie, and James K. Zaharis, "The Jury Is In: Use of a Modified Legal Model for School Program Evaluation," *Educational Evaluation and Policy Analysis* 8 (1986): 309–315.
40. Elliott W. Eisner, *The Educational Imagination: On the Design and Evaluation of School Programs* (New York: Macmillan, 1979).

ating (in the sense of becoming aware of) the qualities of an educational program and their meaning. To perform this role well, the connoisseur must have expert knowledge of the program being evaluated as well as of other relevant programs. This expertise is similar to that of an art critic who has a special appreciation of an art work because of intensive study of related art works and of art theory. An educational connoisseur, then, will be more aware of more nuances of an educational program than will a novice educator or layperson.

The other aspect of the method is criticism, which is the process of describing and evaluating that which has been appreciated.

The validity of educational criticism (as we shall label the method here) depends heavily on the expertise of the evaluator. This is also a prominent feature of the other qualitatively oriented evaluation models described above. Educational criticism differs from adversary evaluation and responsive evaluation, however, in that it tends to be a solitary endeavor, and the questions that motivate the inquiry are usually set by the evaluator alone rather than in conjunction with stakeholders.

Gail McCutcheon used the method of educational criticism in a study of a fourth-grade classroom.[41] The purpose of the study was to answer several questions about this classroom: What is going on here? Is it worth doing? Was it done well? What are children likely to learn as a result? Notice that several of the questions call for description, and several clearly call for evaluation.

McCutcheon did six weeks of field work in the teacher's classroom, and she collected data by means of observation, videotaping, interviews, and inspection of student work. The descriptive part of her report used a literary style to capture certain qualities of the teacher's classroom. The opening paragraph of the report exemplifies her writing style:

> Myriad sounds, smells, and sights greet the newcomer to Mr. Clement's room. The squeal of a guinea pig and the scrabbling of rats in their wire cages mingle with the voices of children as they discuss their private lives and schoolwork. Penny wants to know whether Maria and Freddie like each other because they sit together. Laura asks Mr. Clement if she may go to the library as another girl returns triumphantly, holding up *Mrs. Piggle Wiggle,* apparently a treasure. The smells of guinea pigs, rats, clean wood shavings, school disinfectant, and a freshly peeled orange intermix. Randy is eating raisins.[42]

Later parts of the report are evaluative, as illustrated by the following comments:

> In this lesson, then, children had the opportunity to learn many things—things about the solar system, construction, visual problem-solving, self-control, and

---

41. Gail McCutcheon, "Of Solar Systems, Responsibilities, and Basics: An Educational Criticism of Mr. Clement's Fourth Grade," in *Qualitative Evaluation: Concepts and Cases in Curriculum Criticism,* ed. George Willis (Berkeley, CA: McCutchan, 1978), pp. 188–205.
42. Ibid., p. 192.

social interaction. We might wonder, though, whether responsibility for decision-making, planning socially, and self-control are worthwhile lessons . . . don't children learn these responsibilities anyway—in the home, the community, and school without so much emphasis being placed upon them?[43]

When school is seen as an integral part of children's lives, children may be more likely to apply school learning and to consider doing schoollike things at home. A more unified life may make schooling seem more relevant. The less formal setting of this classroom and Mr. Clement's acknowledging the existence of children's personal interests may work toward this end.[44]

Note that the first evaluative comment is critical, whereas the second is complimentary. An evaluator needs to be sensitive to both the strengths and the weaknesses of the program being evaluated.

This study illustrates how educational criticism can illuminate the nature and value of a program—in this case, fourth-grade instruction—in a way that would be difficult to accomplish using quantitative research methodology. At the same time, the validity of the findings is entirely dependent on the expertise of the researcher-critic. Therefore, it seems necessary to replicate the findings by additional case studies, preferably carried out by other researcher-critics. Alternatively, the findings can be considered tentative knowledge claims and further tested for validity using the methods of quantitative research.

If you are planning to do an evaluation study using educational criticism, you first should make a careful study of this method and related qualitative methods described in chapter 10. Also, you should develop expertise about the program or other educational phenomena you intend to describe and evaluate. This means becoming knowledgeable about other programs, past and present, that are similar to the one you selected for study. You should keep in mind that expertise is one of the most important qualifications of an educational critic, just as it is one of the most important qualifications of a literary or art critic.

MISTAKES SOMETIMES MADE IN DOING EVALUATION STUDIES

1. The evaluator does not explore the various reasons (especially political reasons) underlying a request for an evaluation study.
2. Fails to identify or involve significant stakeholders affected by the evaluation study.
3. Fails to delineate all aspects of the program being evaluated.
4. Is not open to new evaluation questions that arise as the evaluation proceeds.

43. Ibid., p. 199.
44. Ibid., p. 202.

5. Does not write reports geared to the specific needs of different stakeholder groups.
6. Does not consider alternative models of evaluation in designing a study.
7. Does not use measures that are directly linked to program goals.
8. Ignores possible side effects not included in the formal statement of program goals.
9. Attempts to do a qualitatively oriented evaluation without sufficient training in qualitative research methodology.

ANNOTATED REFERENCES

Bryk, Anthony S., ed. *Stakeholder-Based Evaluation.* San Francisco: Jossey-Bass, 1983.

Examines how a particular evaluation model (similar to what we labeled *responsive evaluation* in this chapter) was used in actual evaluations of programs. Contributors found benefits, but also problems. For example, the evaluators had difficulty incorporating the various viewpoints of stakeholders into the evaluation design. Worth studying if you are planning to do a responsive evaluation.

Herman, Joan L., ed. *Program Evaluation Kit,* 2nd ed. Newbury Park, CA: Sage, 1988.

Practical, step-by-step guide to planning and conducting any type of program evaluation. The "kit" includes nine volumes that can be used separately or together: (1) overview of program evaluation, (2) how to focus an evaluation, (3) how to design an evaluation, (4) how to use qualitative methods, (5) how to assess program implementation, (6) how to measure attitudes, (7) how to measure performance and use tests, (8) how to analyze data, and (9) how to communicate evaluation findings.

Shadish, Jr., William R., and Reichardt, Charles S., eds. *Evaluation Studies Review Annuals*, vol. 12. Newbury Park, CA: Sage, 1988.

Deals with such topics as the utility of program evaluation, the role of values in evaluation, and recent developments in evaluation methodology. (Annual publication, approximately 30 chapters per volume.)

Stufflebeam, Daniel L., and Welch, Wayne L. "Review of Research on Program Evaluation in United States School Districts." *Educational Administration Quarterly* 22 (1986): 150–170.

Reviews the research literature on school district evaluation to answer six questions: (1) what gets evaluated? (2) what are the purposes of evaluation? (3) what methodological approaches are used? (4) who are the participants? (5) how is evaluation organized and funded? and (6) how are evaluation findings utilized, and what factors affect their utilization? Provides useful background information if you are planning to evaluate a school district program.

Worthen, Blaine R., and Sanders, James R. *Educational Evaluation: Alternative Approaches and Practical Guidelines.* New York: Longman, 1987.

Comprehensive survey of evaluation methodology. First half provides overview of the field and of the major evaluation models; second half analyzes the steps involved in conducting an evaluation study and provides specific guidelines for carrying out each step. The authors' guidelines should prove useful no matter what kind of evaluation study you plan to do.

SELF-CHECK TEST

Circle the correct answer to each of the following questions. An answer key is provided on page 884.

1. Educational evaluation can be used to assist
   a. program management.
   b. policy analysis.
   c. political decision making.
   d. all of the above.
2. Educational evaluation and educational research
   a. have the same purpose, but use different methodologies.
   b. have the same purpose, but are conducted in different settings.
   c. have different purposes, but use the same methodologies.
   d. use the same methodologies, but differ in degree of experimental control.
3. The propriety standard in educational evaluation means that
   a. the evaluation design is appropriate to the settings in which the study will be conducted.
   b. the rights of persons affected by the evaluation are protected.
   c. reports are submitted to stakeholders in a timely manner.
   d. the criterion tests used in the evaluation are content-valid.
4. An external evaluator
   a. does not need to identify stakeholders affected by the program being evaluated.
   b. is a specialist in using the CIPP model.
   c. is desirable when doing a summative evaluation of a program.
   d. is more likely to do a qualitatively oriented evaluation than a quantitatively oriented evaluation.
5. A basic principle of goal-free evaluation is that
   a. the evaluator should not know in advance the program goals.
   b. the evaluator should not know in advance the decisions that need to be made about the program.
   c. the evaluation design should not have goals.
   d. the evaluation should be organized around behavioral objectives rather than goals.
6. Objectives-based evaluation is used primarily to
   a. determine how well a program is achieving its objectives.
   b. compare the performance of an individual student with group norms.
   c. identify concerns of stakeholding audiences.
   d. help evaluators identify their objectives for doing an evaluation study.
7. In the CIPP model, close collaboration between evaluators and program decision makers
   a. is strongly encouraged throughout the evaluation process.
   b. is strongly discouraged throughout the evaluation process.

   c. is strongly discouraged once the goals of the evaluation research have been settled.
   d. is encouraged only for the purpose of summative evaluation.
8. Adversary evaluation is characterized by
   a. use of various data sources.
   b. reliance on human testimony.
   c. encouragement of positive and negative judgments about a program.
   d. all of the above.
9. In evaluation research, a discrepancy between an existing condition and a desired condition is called a
   a. standard.
   b. need.
   c. cost-benefit.
   d. input-output.
10. An emergent design in research is one that is specified
   a. by the stakeholding audiences.
   b. by the contractor.
   c. during the course of the evaluation process.
   d. after concerns have been identified, but before issues are identified.
11. The method of educational criticism depends heavily on
   a. stakeholders' criticisms of the program being evaluated.
   b. program managers' criticisms of the program being evaluated.
   c. a special appreciation of the program by the person doing the evaluation.
   d. criticism of program documents and artifacts.

APPLICATION PROBLEMS

The following problems do not have a single correct answer. For feedback, you can compare your answers with the sample answers on pages 902–903.

1. The manager of a new program is preparing an annual budget. She needs to decide how much money, if any, should be spent on program evaluation. She realizes that the less spent on evaluation, the more is available for program operations. What arguments can you present in favor of allocating at least 10 percent of the budget for program evaluation?
2. A curriculum developer plans to pilot-test a set of self-instructional materials designed to improve the writing skills of college freshman. List five questions that a developer might want to have answered about the materials' effectiveness.
3. You are asked by an elementary school principal to conduct an evaluation of the school. When you, as evaluator, ask the principal what it is about the school that he wishes to have evaluated, he responds, "I don't know. What do you usually evaluate?" How might you respond to this question?
4. A program has one stated goal—to train high school nonswimmers to swim freestyle two lengths of an Olympic-size pool. You are a "goal-free" evaluator who is called in to evaluate the program's success. How would you approach the task of evaluation?
5. Suppose a nutrition education program was being developed based on the study described in the needs assessment section of the chapter. What audiences are likely to have a stake in the evaluation? What concerns might be expressed by each of these audiences?

SUGGESTION SHEET

If your last name starts with letters from Rus to Sme, please complete the Suggestion Sheet at the end of the book while the chapter is still fresh in your mind.

18 EDUCATIONAL RESEARCH AND DEVELOPMENT

OVERVIEW

This chapter describes a strategy for developing educational products of proven effectiveness. This strategy is called *research and development (R & D)*. It consists of a cycle in which a version of the product is developed, field-tested, and revised on the basis of field-test data. Although product development sometimes occurs in basic and applied research studies, their primary goal is to discover new knowledge. In contrast, the goal of R & D is to take this research knowledge and incorporate it into a product that can be used in the schools. In a sense, the purpose of R & D is to bridge the gap that frequently exists between educational research and educational practice. The various steps of the R & D cycle are described in this chapter as well as some of the problems and issues that confront developers as they design a new product.

OBJECTIVES

After studying this chapter you should be able to:

1. State two deficiencies of basic and applied research as strategies for developing educational products.
2. Describe the 10 steps of the R & D cycle.
3. State the criteria that can be used to select an educational product to be developed.
4. Defend the importance of stating behavioral objectives in educational R & D.
5. Describe why it is important to field-test a product in a setting similar to that in which it will be used when fully developed.
6. Explain the function of the main field test in the R & D cycle.
7. Give arguments for and against refinement of educational materials during the initial stages of development.
8. Describe two opportunities for a graduate student to do an R & D project.

WHAT IS EDUCATIONAL RESEARCH AND DEVELOPMENT?

Research and development (R & D) is a powerful strategy for improving practice. Expenditures for R & D in industry have averaged approximately 4 percent of sales during the past quarter century.[1] R & D expenditures in some

---

1. Zvi Griliches, "R & D and Productivity: Measurement Issues and Econometric Results," *Science* 237, no. 4810 (1987): 31–35.

industries, such as pharmaceuticals and computer manufacture, are much higher than this. As a result, technological advances in these fields have been rapid and have brought striking benefits for the consumer. Unfortunately, R & D still plays a minor role in education. Less than one percent of education expenditures are for this purpose.[2] This is probably one of the main reasons why progress in education has lagged far behind progress in other fields.

What is **research and development (R & D)**? It is a process used to develop and validate educational products. By "product," we mean not only such things as textbooks, instructional films, and computer software, but also methods, such as a method of teaching, and programs, such as a drug education program or a staff development program. The focus of present-day R & D projects appears to be primarily on program development. Programs are complex learning systems that often include specially developed materials and personnel trained to work in a particular context.

The steps of the R & D process are usually referred to as the **R & D cycle,** which consists of studying research findings pertinent to the product to be developed, developing the product based on these findings, field testing it in the setting where it will be used eventually, and revising it to correct the deficiencies found in the field-testing stage. In more rigorous programs of R & D, this cycle is repeated until the field-test data indicate that the product meets its behaviorally defined objectives.

In contrast, the goal of educational research is not to develop products, but rather to discover new knowledge about fundamental phenomena (through basic research) or about educational practice (through applied research). Of course, many applied research projects involve development of educational products. For example, in a project concerned with comparing the effectiveness of two methods for teaching reading, the researcher may develop materials that incorporate each method because suitable materials are not available. Typically, however, these materials are developed and refined only to the point where they can be used to test the researcher's hypotheses. Furthermore, the tests are made in settings that do not reflect actual school conditions. For these reasons applied research rarely yields products that are ready for operational use in the schools.

One way to bridge the gap between research and practice in education is to do R & D. It takes the findings generated by basic and applied research and uses them to build tested products that are ready for operational use in the schools. We should emphasize here, though, that educational R & D is not a substitute for basic or applied research. All three research strategies—basic, applied, and R & D—are required to bring about educational change. In fact, R & D increases the potential impact of basic and applied research findings upon school practice by translating them into usable educational products.

2. W. Vance Grant and Leo J. Eiden, *Digest of Education Statistics* (Washington, DC: U.S. Government Printing Office, 1981).

Evaluation methods—especially formative and summative evaluation—play a major role in R & D. Therefore, if you plan to do an R & D study, you should study carefully the evaluation methods described in chapter 17.

Educational R & D should not be equated with curriculum development. Curriculum development is often guided by a curriculum philosophy or academic discipline rather than by the findings of empirical research. Also, the development of curriculum guides and materials often does not involve field test and revision cycles. Some curriculum developers, however, do use elements of R & D methodology in their work. As more of these elements are used, curriculum development approximates the R & D process.

Educational R & D bears a close relationship to the field of instructional technology. Instructional technologists used to be concerned primarily with audiovisual equipment and materials, but in recent years their primary interest has been the design and validation of learning systems. Reflecting this trend, we define **instructional technology** as the systematic use of research knowledge and methods to design and validate learning systems. Many instructional technologists work in medical, military, and business settings where they primarily develop training programs for employees.

If you plan to do an R & D project for your thesis or dissertation, we advise you to study instructional technology to determine whether some of its methods and conceptual models are appropriate to your project. These methods and models include: front-end analysis (needs assessment, systems analysis, task analysis, analysis of skill hierarchies); typologies of learning outcomes; match of instructional techniques to learning outcomes; match of learner characteristics to instructional methods; cognitive processes in learning; individualized instruction (Keller Plan, auto-tutorial instruction, mastery learning, etc.); and domain-referenced assessment. These methods and models are described in several textbooks mentioned in the Annotated References at the end of this chapter. Also, it is useful to become acquainted with professional organizations of instructional technologists and their publications: National Society for Performance and Instruction (*Performance and Instruction Journal*); Association for Educational Communications and Technology (*Tech Trends; Educational Communications and Technology Journal*), and American Society for Training and Development (*Training and Development Journal*).

THE R & D CYCLE

In the remainder of this chapter we shall discuss each of the major steps in the R & D cycle. The specific R & D cycle that will be presented was developed by the staff of the Teacher Education Program at the Far West Laboratory for Educational Research and Development, with which the authors were formerly affiliated. The Far West Laboratory is one of 10 regional laboratories funded by the U.S. Office of Education to bring about educational improvement through R

& D. The Teacher Education Program developed products called minicourses, which were designed to improve teachers' use of specific classroom skills.[3]

Since we will be using the development of our first minicourse to illustrate the R & D cycle, we will briefly describe here the characteristics of this product. Each minicourse involves about 15 hours of teacher training in either the preservice or inservice setting. During this time, the teacher being trained is introduced to a number of specific classroom skills. These skills are first described and illustrated in an instructional film. The teacher then sees the skills demonstrated in a "model film," that is, a film of a brief classroom situation conducted by a model teacher. Then the teacher plans a short lesson in which the skills can be applied, teaches the lesson to a small group of students, and records the lesson on videotape. Immediately after the lesson, the teacher views the videotape, focusing attention on the specific skills to be learned.

This lesson is called a *microteach lesson* because the regular classroom situation is scaled down in time and number of pupils. Having seen and evaluated the videotape recording of the lesson, the teacher then replans the same lesson and reteaches it the following day to another small group of pupils. This lesson is also recorded on videotape, so that the teacher can again view and evaluate his or her performance immediately after the lesson is completed. The teacher then proceeds to the next sequence of instructional lesson, model lesson, microteach, and reteach.

The major steps in the R & D cycle used to develop minicourses are as follows:

1. *Research and information collecting*—Includes needs assessment, review of literature, small-scale research studies, and preparation of report on state of the art.
2. *Planning*—Includes defining skills to be learned, stating and sequencing objectives, identifying learning activities, and small-scale feasibility testing.
3. *Develop preliminary form of product*—Includes preparation of instructional materials, procedures, and evaluation instruments.
4. *Preliminary field testing*—Conducted in from 1 to 3 schools, using 6 to 12 subjects. Interview, observational, and questionnaire data collected and analyzed.
5. *Main product revision*—Revision of product as suggested by the preliminary field-test results.
6. *Main field testing*—Conducted in 5 to 15 schools with 30 to 100 subjects. Quantitative data on subjects' precourse and postcourse performance are collected. Results are evaluated with respect to course objectives and are compared with control group data, when appropriate.

3. Walter R. Borg, Marjorie L. Kelley, Philip Langer, and Meredith D. Gall, *The Minicourse: A Microteaching Approach to Teacher Education* (New York: Macmillan, 1970).

7. *Operational product revision*—Revision of product as suggested by main field-test results.
8. *Operational field testing*—Conducted in 10 to 30 schools involving 40 to 200 subjects. Interview, observational, and questionnaire data collected and analyzed.
9. *Final product revision*—Revision of product as suggested by operational field-test results.
10. *Dissemination and implementation*—Report on product at professional meetings and in journals. Work with publisher who assumes commercial distribution. Monitor distribution to provide quality control.

If this sequence of 10 steps is followed properly, it yields a validated educational product that is fully ready for operational use in the schools. Each of the steps is described below. Some of the steps described above, especially step 6 (main field testing), involve research methods described in previous chapters.

Research and Information Collection

Needs Assessment

Several criteria should be considered in selecting a product for development. The criteria used at the Far West Laboratory included the following:

1. Does the proposed product meet an important educational need?
2. Is the state of the art sufficiently advanced that there is a reasonable probability that a successful product can be built?
3. Are personnel available who have the skills, knowledge, and experience necessary to build this product?
4. Can the product be developed within a reasonable period of time?

The first criterion—need—can be addressed by doing a needs assessment. Procedures that an independent developer might use to assess needs are described in chapter 17. Procedures that are used by educational R & D organizations to assess needs may take a different form.[4] For example, they often must address needs that are stated in funding proposals, irrespective of whether the target audience perceives these needs.

It was apparent to the staff of the Teacher Education Program that there was a pressing need to develop effective products for inservice teacher education. School districts at that time generally provided very little inservice

4. Kay A. Adams, "Needs Sensing: The Yeast for R & D Organizations," *Educational Evaluation and Policy Analysis* 5 (1983): 55–60.

education, and what was available suffered from four serious weaknesses: (1) Teachers were told what to do rather than being given the opportunity to practice good teaching techniques; (2) they were taught vague generalities, such as "individualize your instruction," rather than being given training in specific classroom skills; (3) they were not shown effective models to emulate; and (4) they were given little or no feedback on their classroom performance. The minicourses were designed to overcome these weaknesses.

Literature Review

Once the nature of the educational product has been tentatively identified, a literature review is undertaken to collect research findings and other information pertinent to the planned development. As in basic or applied research, one purpose of the literature review is to determine the state of knowledge in the area of concern. In R & D projects, the developer also must be concerned with how this knowledge can be applied to the planned product.

A preliminary review of the literature on teaching methods suggested that questioning techniques in classroom discussions would be a good choice for our first minicourse. The title eventually given to Minicourse 1 was "Effective Questioning—Elementary Level."

Since Minicourse 1 was the first product developed by the Teacher Education Program, it was necessary to conduct two literature reviews. The purpose of the first review was to locate research that could be used to develop a basic instructional model for training teachers. Research in four areas was studied: microteaching, learning from films, feedback in learning, and modeling in learning. Through this review we were able to identify several instructional techniques that improve learning. For example, research has found that providing teachers with videotape feedback on their teaching performance is an effective technique for developing new classroom skills. Another effective technique is to provide a model of the skills to be learned.

Our second literature review was concerned with questioning and discussion skills. We found that research in this area extended back to Stevens's 1912 study of high school classrooms.[5] Stevens found that two-thirds of teachers' questions required students to recall facts rather than to think about facts. Furthermore, teachers talked two-thirds of the discussion time, thus allowing students to participate only one-third of the time. Similar findings have been obtained in more recent studies.[6] It appears that even though they have known about the prevalence of such undesirable teaching practices for a long time, educators have not succeeded in bringing about needed improvements in

5. R. Stevens, "The Question as a Measure of Efficiency in Instruction," *Teachers College Contributions to Education* 48 (1912).

6. Meredith D. Gall, "Synthesis of Research on Teachers' Questioning," *Educational Leadership* 42, no. 3 (1984): 40–47.

teachers' classrom skills. We decided that major goals of Minicourse 1 would be to reduce teacher talk and correspondingly to increase student talk, and to increase the percentage of teachers' thought questions.

In the next phase of the literature review, it was necessary to identify specific techniques that teachers could use to accomplish these goals. Although some pertinent research studies were available, it was also necessary for us to give considerable attention to the opinions and experience of practitioners. For example, Grossier advocates several teaching strategies which were included in Minicourse 1, but he presents no evidence on their effectiveness.[7] Since our later field experience with Minicourse 1 indicated that most of the strategies bring about improved class discussion, they were included in the final form of the course.

Small-Scale Research

Developers often will have questions that cannot be answered by referring to research studies or professional texts. These questions can be answered at least tentatively by doing small-scale studies prior to developing the product. For example, in Minicourse 5, which is concerned with mathematics tutoring skills, we could find no research findings about what occurs between pupil and teacher in the typical tutoring sequence. In order to partially fill this gap, we sent observers into a number of classrooms to study tutoring interactions between teachers and pupils. We learned from these observations that the usual tutoring contact between the teacher and the individual pupil was brief, averaging only 15 seconds. The content of these tutoring contacts suggested that the teacher typically gave the pupil an answer or pointed out the pupil's error and then moved on. Efforts to guide the pupil toward the identification of his or her errors or to develop understanding of mathematical concepts and problem solving procedures were rare. Although they were not collected in a tightly controlled research setting, these data gave us at least a tentative empirical basis for determining a direction in which to improve teachers' tutoring skills.

Planning

Once the developer has completed a literature review and collection of other pertinent information, the next step is to make a plan of the product. This plan should include: (1) the product's objectives, (2) the product's target audience, and (3) a description of the product's components and how they will be used.

The product often changes substantially during the development process. This does not mean that the initial planning should be taken lightly. It provides

7. P. Grossier, *How to Use the Fine Art of Questioning* (New York: Teachers Practical Press, 1964).

the information upon which later revisions are built. Without careful planning at the start, the likelihood of building a good product is much reduced.

The most important aspect of the plan is the statement of the objectives to be achieved by the product. For example, an objective of an R & D product in social studies might be, "At least 75 percent of the students who complete the program will earn a score of 90 or better on a test measuring various map skills." Such student-based objectives enable educators to determine in quantitative terms whether the program "works." Objectives also provide the best basis for developing an instructional program, because the program can be field-tested and revised until it meets its objectives. Precise specification of educational outcomes—or **behavioral objectives,** as they are also called—requires considerable skill on the part of the developer.[8] In some ways developing a behavioral objective for an educational product is similar to developing a good criterion in a research study.

During the planning phase, behavioral objectives are usually stated somewhat loosely. For example, in the initial planning of Minicourse 1, one of our objectives stated that after the course most teachers would increase their use of thought questions in a discussion situation. We did not have sufficient knowledge in the planning phase, though, to specify the percentage of thought questions that we would expect teachers to ask in order for the course to be considered effective. As we proceeded through the R & D cycle and accumulated research data, we were able to refine the statement of the behavioral objective so that it took the following form: "Given a 20-minute discussion lesson, at least half of all questions asked by teachers will be classified as thought questions. This criterion will be met by at least 75 percent of teachers who complete Minicourse 1."

Another important element of the planning phase is estimation of the money, personnel, and time required to develop the product. Generally, ample resources are needed to carry out a single R & D project. The cost of developing a single minicourse, which provides about 15 hours of instruction, was in excess of $100,000 in the early 1970s. A major curriculum project today will cost several million dollars. Personnel needs are considerable, too. The development of a minicourse requires an average of 104 person-weeks of professional work, 50 person-weeks of clerical work, and 50 person-weeks of production work. In contrast, most research projects involve small sums of money, often just a thousand dollars or so, and the efforts of a single investigator with perhaps a few part-time graduate assistants.

Unless careful planning is done, developers may find that their resources have run out before the product has been fully developed. Planning is necessary in order to anticipate needed materials, professional help, and field-test sites. Consideration of field-test sites is especially important when testing is done in

---

8. See text by Robert Mager in the Annotated References at the end of this chapter.

the schools, which generally are receptive to testing only at certain times of the year. For example, if the product is ready for testing in June, one may have to wait until September or October unless the product can be tested during a summer school session. Also, school administrators generally require a few months' notice before agreeing to have their schools serve as a test site.

Although developers must devote a considerable amount of time to initial planning, the planning function is never really ended. As work progresses, they are likely to discover several areas in which initial planning was insufficient or in error. Replanning must then be done. Nonetheless, it is wise to devote major effort to building a sound initial plan. A good plan can help developers avoid much wasted work during later phases of the R & D cycle.

Development of the Preliminary Form of the Product

After the initial planning has been completed, the next major step in the R & D cycle is to build a preliminary form of the educational product that can be field tested. In the case of Minicourse 1, this involved a wide range of tasks. Scripts describing the specific skills that teachers are to learn were written for each instructional sequence. The scripts were then produced on videotape and edited to include clips showing the skills being used in classroom situations. Prospective model teachers were located, observed, and trained to conduct model lessons designed to further illustrate the minicourse skills. The model lessons were then recorded on videotape and edited. A teacher handbook designed to supplement the videotaped instructional lessons was drafted, revised, and printed. A set of forms for teachers to use in self-evaluation of the microteach and reteach lessons was developed and printed.

An important principle to follow at this stage of product development is to include procedures for obtaining lots of feedback from the product's users. Therefore, we developed several questionnaires and interview guides to use in the preliminary field test, and we trained laboratory staff members to administer them.

Another important principle that applies to most educational R & D projects is to strive from the outset to develop products that are fully ready for use in the schools. Partially developed products force local practitioners to make adjustments to fill in the gaps. Because few schools are equipped to make such adjustments, a partially developed product cannot be used effectively and is often badly misused. In the small-scale R & D project described later in the chapter, the focus of development was a textbook chapter. This product was not sufficient for field testing, however. The developer also needed to write a teachers manual so that the field-test teachers would know how to use the chapter in their classrooms.

Preliminary Field Test and Product Revision

The purpose of the **preliminary field test** is to obtain an initial qualitative evaluation of the new educational product. For the minicourse this evaluation was based primarily upon the feedback of a small group of teachers who take the course and the observations of laboratory personnel who coordinate the field test. As a rule, from four to eight teachers have been sufficient for the preliminary field test, since the emphasis of this evaluation is upon qualitative appraisal of course content rather than quantitative appraisal of course outcomes.

In all phases of the R & D cycle involving product evaluation, it is important to establish field sites similar to those in which the product will be used when it is fully developed. If a different type of field site is used, the developer faces the problem of generalizing findings obtained in one setting to another. For example, Minicourse 1 was designed to be used by elementary school teachers during their regular school day. Therefore, the preliminary field test was carried out with six teachers from two elementary schools. Instead of this procedure, we might have invited the teachers and some of their students to our laboratory to take the course, perhaps on a speeded-up basis. The major problem with this procedure is that we might have obtained a very unrealistic impression of the course. Elements of the course that raise no problem in a laboratory setting might create havoc when used in the schools, causing an adverse effect on the course outcomes.

Throughout the preliminary field test of Minicourse 1, two field representatives from the laboratory worked closely with the six teachers in order to obtain as much teacher feedback and observational data as possible. Each teacher was interviewed individually three times during the field test. These interviews focused upon specific problems and course deficiencies as well as suggestions for improvement. At the end of the course, each teacher completed a questionnaire regarding the course and participated in a group discussion with laboratory personnel. In addition to these formal contacts, each teacher had informal contacts with one of the laboratory representatives each day.

Teachers or other user groups receive a great deal of attention from developers because of the need to receive extensive feedback from them. This attention can produce the Hawthorne Effect, which will lead developers to overestimate the effectiveness of their product.[9] Thus, developers must strive for a delicate balance in which feedback is obtained without giving the field-test participants an undue amount of attention.

Observing the participating teachers near the end of the preliminary field test of Minicourse 1 revealed that the teachers were generally unable to use the course skills effectively either in their regular classrooms or in their microteach

9. The Hawthorne Effect is discussed in chapter 5.

lessons. Thus, from the standpoint of bringing about specific changes in the classroom behavior of these teachers, the preliminary form of the course was a failure. End-of-course interviews and questionnaires obtained from these teachers, however, indicated that they perceived the course as being very effective and as providing them with a great deal of help in improving their teaching.

This experience suggests that global ratings are of little value in evaluating specific educational objectives. Furthermore, they can be detrimental if they mislead developers into believing that a product achieves its objectives and is ready for use when actually it is not. In the case of Minicourse 1, the favorable testimonials were perhaps in part a result of the extremely poor quality of most previous inservice teacher education programs, which teachers used as a standard of comparison.

After the preliminary field test of Minicourse 1, all data were compiled and analyzed. The development team used these results to replan the course and then went on to make the necessary revisions.

Main Field Test and Product Revision

The purpose of the **main field test** in the minicourse R & D cycle is to determine whether the educational product under development meets its performance objectives. Generally an experimental design is used to answer this question. In the case of Minicourse 1, a single-group pre-post design (see chapter 15) was used to determine whether teachers would significantly increase their use of questioning skills. About 50 teachers participated in the experiment. Shortly before the course began, each teacher was asked to conduct a 20-minute discussion in his or her regular classroom, and this discussion was videotaped. After the course was completed, each teacher again conducted a 20-minute videotaped discussion.

Each videotape was viewed by trained raters who made quantitative observations of teachers' use of the skills and behavior patterns presented in the minicourse. As each videotape was coded and given to raters in random order, the raters did not know which were pretapes and which were posttapes. Table 18.1 presents the major findings of the experiment.

Most of the changes in teacher and student behavior brought about by Minicourse 1 are not only statistically significant, but are also significant in their implications for educational practice. Although a control group was not used in the main field test, subsequent studies have indicated that teachers who take the course make substantially larger gains than teachers who either do not have the course or who receive some form of minimal treatment.

In addition to the primary purpose of the main field test, which is to determine the success of the new product in meeting its objectives, the secondary purpose is to collect information that can be used to improve the

TABLE 18.1

Main Field-Test Results from Minicourse 1

Behavior Compared	Pretape Mean ($N = 48$)	Posttape Mean ($N = 48$)	t	Significance Level
Increase considered desirable				
1. Number of times teacher used redirection.	26.69	40.92	4.98	.001
2. Number of times teacher used prompting.	4.10	7.17	3.28	.001
3. Number of times teacher used further clarification.	4.17	6.73	3.01	.005
4. Number of times teacher used refocusing.	0.10	0.02	0.00	NS[a]
5. Length of pupil responses in words (based on 5-min. samples of pre- and post-tapes).	5.63	11.78	5.91	.001
6. Length of teacher's pause after question (based on 5-min. sample of pre- and posttapes).	1.93	2.32	1.90	.05
7. Proportion of total questions that call for higher cognitive pupil responses.	37.30	52.00	2.94	.005
Decrease considered desirable				
8. Number of times teacher repeated own questions.	13.68	4.68	7.26	.001
9. Number of times teacher repeated pupil answers.	30.68	4.36	11.47	.001
10. Number of times teacher answered own questions.	4.62	0.72	6.88	.001
11. Number of one-word pupil responses (based on 5-min. samples of pre- and post-tapes).	5.82	2.57	3.61[b]	.001
12. Frequency of punitive teacher reactions to incorrect pupil answers.	0.12	0.10	0.00	NS
13. Proportion of discussion time taken by teacher talk.	51.64	27.75	8.95	.001

SOURCE: Adapted from Walter R. Borg, Marjorie L. Kelley, Philip Langer, and Meredith Gall, *The Minicourse: A Microteaching Approach to Teacher Education* (New York: Macmillan, 1970), p. 76.
[a] Not significant.
[b] Means would have been about four times larger if entire tape had been analyzed; *t*-value would have been higher.

course in its next revision. Therefore, questionnaire and interview data should be obtained from all participants in the main field test.

If the main field-test findings indicate that the new product falls substantially short of meeting its objectives, it is necessary to revise the product and conduct another main field test. This cycle of field testing and revision would continue until the product meets the minimum performance objectives set for it. In practice the product would probably be abandoned if substantial progress was not made in the second main field test.

Operational Field Test and Final Product Revision

The purpose of the **operational field test** is to determine whether an educational product is fully ready for use in the schools without the presence of the developer or his staff. In order to be fully ready for operational use, the package must be complete and thoroughly tested in every respect. In the case of the minicourse, all materials needed to coordinate the course are normally tried out during the preliminary and main field tests. Because these field tests are conducted by laboratory personnel, however, a satisfactory test of how well the total course package works "on its own" cannot be made.

The operational field test is set up and coordinated by regular school personnel and should closely approximate regular operational use. Feedback from both the coordinators and the teachers taking the course are collected by means of questionnaires which are mailed to the laboratory. The main use of these data is to determine whether the course package is complete. Interviewers focus on parts of the course that fail to do their job or on materials that are needed in order to make the operation of the course easier or more effective. Precourse and postcourse videotapes are not obtained during the operational field test.

After the operational field test is complete and the data have been analyzed, a final revision of the total course package is carried out. In the case of the minicourses, the Far West Laboratory made a final revision of all scripts and printed materials and turned them over to a commercial publisher for final production. The courses were then sold or rented to schools for operational use in their inservice training programs.

Dissemination, Implementation, and Institutionalization

The R & D cycle is a time-consuming and expensive process. The way to justify the costs is by demonstrating effective dissemination of the resulting product to its intended audience. **Dissemination** refers to the process of helping potential users become aware of R & D products. Also, it is necessary to demonstrate that the R & D product is implemented according to the developers' specifications so that it produces the intended effects. **Implementation** refers to the process of helping adopters of an R & D product to use it in the manner intended by the developers.

Successful implementation does not mean necessarily that the product will be used on a regular, continuing basis by the adopters. Therefore, developers also need to be concerned with **institutionalization,** which is the process of making the R & D product an integral part of the adopting institution's structure and functions. The term "implementation" is sometimes used to include the institutionalization process. We follow this convention here.

Despite the importance of R & D dissemination and implementation, these processes were seldom studied until the mid-1970s. The concern of educational R & D personnel prior to this time was on the conceptualization and development of large-scale curriculum products using the R & D cycle of develop-test-revise. Little funding was available for monitoring these products after they had been developed. Priorities shifted dramatically in the mid-1970s, though. Many educators stopped using the term "research and development," preferring instead to talk about "research, development, and dissemination" (R, D, & D). **Research, development, and dissemination** refers to the research-based development of products that meet behaviorally defined objectives and dissemination and implementation criteria.

The ratio of 1:10:10 is sometimes used in industry to estimate funding requirements for R, D, & D. For example, suppose it requires $1 million to do the basic research for a new product. It will then require $10 million to develop the product through the operational field test revision. Ten times that amount ($100 million) will be required to manufacture and disseminate the product.

Educators are not accustomed to think about the large sums of money implied by the 1:10:10 ratio for the dissemination of R & D products. Commercial educational publishers do expend large sums of money for production facilities, inventory storage and shipping departments, branch offices, advertising, sales forces, and inservice trainers. Even today, though, these facilities and personnel are largely nonexistent in the federal and state educational systems. For example, when the first minicourses completed their development cycle in the early 1970s, there were no official plans either at the Far West Laboratory or at the U.S. Office of Education for their dissemination. A dissemination plan was developed piecemeal with a commercial publisher. This plan was based largely on the publisher's established distribution procedures rather than on a rational analysis of the dissemination and implementation requirements for the particular product.

A dissemination and implementation capability for R & D products is slowly developing in this country. For example, the **National Diffusion Network (NDN)** was established by the U.S. Office of Education to disseminate successful R & D products.[10] This dissemination agency links successful products with school systems that might benefit from them.

Dissemination and implementation logically occur at the end of the R & D cycle. This does not mean, however, that developers can avoid thinking about these matters until then. Rather, they need to consider dissemination and implementation issues in the initial stages of planning. There is no point in developing a product whose target audience is difficult to reach or whose implementation requires inordinately expensive staff development. By planning for dissemination and implementation at the outset of product planning, developers may avoid creating a white elephant.

If you are interested in educational R & D, one of your options is to do a study on some aspect of the R & D process. For example, research on implementation processes has attracted much interest in recent years. This research concerns such problems as the identification of stages in the implementation process,[11] factors that facilitate or inhibit implementation,[12] and the use of staff development as a strategy for promoting implementation.[13]

PROBLEMS AND ISSUES IN EDUCATIONAL R & D

Virtually no R & D technology was available when the Far West Laboratory started its development work in 1966. Therefore, we needed to develop our own procedures for handling problems and issues as we encountered them. Because you are likely to face similar problems and issues if you do an R & D project, we discuss some of them below.

Learning versus Polish

The first problem concerns how far the educational developer should go in building the preliminary form of a product involving an expensive component, such as instructional films or tapes. The development of the preliminary form of Minicourse 1 presented us with an interesting dilemma. On the one hand, it was desirable to spend as little money as possible on initial development, since the feedback obtained from the preliminary field test would almost surely call for

10. Tom Lo Guidice, "The National Diffusion Network: A Report on a Resource for America's Elementary and Secondary Schools," *Clearing House* 59 (1985): 33–34.
11. Gene E. Hall and Shirley M. Hord, *Change in Schools: Facilitating the Process* (Albany: State University of New York Press, 1987).
12. Michael Fullan, *The Meaning of Educational Change* (New York: Teachers College Press, 1982).
13. Georgea G. Mohlman, Theodore Coladarci, and N. L. Gage, "Comprehension and Attitude as Predictors of Implementation of Teacher Training," *Journal of Teacher Education* 33 (1982): 31–36.

extensive revision. On the other hand, a poorly developed set of materials might produce poor results even though the ideas underlying the development were sound.

The most defensible resolution of this dilemma is to put most of the initial development effort into a simple product that makes maximum use of learning principles, that is, a theoretically sound product. Little or no effort should be devoted to such activities as correcting minor errors in narration, building attractive charts where crude ones would serve the purpose, or reshooting motion picture footage because of poor camera work.

In summary, our strategy called for giving the essentials our best effort and doing everything else as cheaply and quickly as possible. This strategy was supported by the many research studies that have found little effect on learning outcomes as the result of variations in technical quality of audiovisual media.[14]

Our experience indicates that developers will not find this an easy road to follow. Media specialists on the development team, such as artists, actors, and television production personnel, may apply great pressure to improve the nonessential aspects of the product. If these pressures are not controlled by the developers, they will see most of their resources going into unnecessary polish.

It is even more important to resist efforts to apply polish during the development cycle if the product fails to achieve its objectives in field tests. One reason is that the developers have spent a great deal of money, which they do not want to admit has been wasted. Second, the product looks good, and some educators may use it for this reason even if it is not effective. Finally, even though the product fails to achieve its objectives, it is easy to rationalize that it is probably better, or surely no worse, than competing products currently in use.

Realism versus Pertinence

Another question of development strategy concerns the extent to which developers should strive to use typical real-life examples in their products. Our work with model lessons for Minicourse 1 brought us face to face with this question. Initially, we believed that our model lessons should be as realistic as possible. Therefore, we started by selecting teachers who were reported to have outstanding teaching skills by principals and supervisory personnel. We then worked individually with each teacher, describing the skills that were to be displayed in the model lesson and discussing in general terms methods for fitting these skills into a lesson and modeling them effectively. We then brought videotape recording equipment into the classroom, and teachers conducted the lessons that they had planned.

14. M. A. May and A. A. Lumsdaine, eds., *Learning From Films* (New Haven, CT: Yale University Press, 1958).

The typical outcome of these early efforts was a very long model lesson that contained very few examples of the skills that we wished the teacher to model. For example, one of our first model lessons ran for a full hour. During this time the specific skills that the teacher was to model were demonstrated less than five minutes. Though providing a realistic picture of typical classroom teaching, this model was extremely inefficient in terms of the objectives we had set up for the model lesson. Furthermore, if this realistic lesson had been edited to reduce the amount of time that the viewer was required to watch irrelevant behavior, the lesson would have become highly unrealistic, since large segments would have been removed.

It became increasingly apparent that if the model lesson were to provide numerous examples of the skills to be learned and contain a minimum of nonpertinent teaching behavior, it would be necessary to plan the model lesson very thoroughly with the model teacher. Thus, although the model lessons for Minicourse 1 were not scripted (the teacher and pupils went through the lesson using their own words), they presented a less natural situation than one finds in the typical classroom. In developing other minicourses, we found it necessary on occasion to prepare complete scripts so that the model lessons would provide enough clear-cut examples of the skills to be learned within a reasonable period of time.

If you do an R & D project, you probably will find that examples are generally effective in helping students learn the concepts, principles, and skills intended by the product. You should not assume, however, that an example is effective just because it presents a typical situation or is drawn directly from real life. Instead, you should test different types of examples to determine which ones best help the learner achieve the product's objectives.

Other Lessons

Our experience in developing Minicourse 1 also taught us other lessons about educational R & D. First, we learned that the rule so often stated by researchers—if anything can go wrong in a research project, it will—seems to be equally true of R & D. For example, during the preliminary development of Minicourse 1 in 1966, portable videotape equipment was still at a rather primitive stage of development. Yet we were building a product that relied heavily upon the use of this equipment for presenting instructional and model lessons and for providing feedback during the microteach and reteach sessions. Therefore, we needed to develop procedures that would reduce the problems caused by the bulkiness of the equipment and its occasional malfunctions.

Finally, we began to see that developing an educational product was a far more difficult and time-consuming task than we had anticipated. Major development work in education requires a large and competent professional staff and significant long-term financial support. Surprisingly, we frequently encounter local school administrators who wish to develop their own minicourses and other products. Very few school districts have the resources to develop a validated product using R & D methodology.

Other fields sometimes solve the problem of obtaining the substantial resources needed for R & D by forming collaborative arrangements. Projects that involve the sharing of personnel and facilities in universities and industrial firms are increasingly common.[15] These projects require resources that are unavailable to either organization working alone.

Similar to university-industry collaboration, some schools and universities have become involved in collaborative arrangements for the purpose of doing R & D.[16] Also, some of the regional laboratories funded by the U.S. Office of Education are involved in collaborative R & D projects. If you wish to do an R & D study for a thesis or dissertation, you should consider linking up with an ongoing project of this type. These projects may be able to make resources available to you that would greatly facilitate your study. In return, your study might contribute to the progress of the overall project.

AN EXAMPLE OF SMALL-SCALE R & D

We have already discussed the considerable resources required to carry out even a single educational R & D project. It is highly unlikely that a graduate student will be able to find the financial and personnel support to complete a major R & D project. In fact, educational R & D is beyond the abilities of most school districts.

If you plan to do an R & D project for a thesis or dissertation, you should keep these cautions in mind. It is best to undertake a small-scale project that involves a limited amount of original instructional design. Also, unless you have substantial financial resources, you will need to avoid expensive instructional media such as film and synchronized slidetape. Another way to scale down the project is to limit development to just a few steps of the R & D cycle.

An example of an R & D dissertation is the project undertaken by Lawrence Cunningham to develop a history textbook about the ancient Chamorros of Guam and an accompanying teachers guidebook.[17] (The Chamorros are the indigenous people of Guam.) The study of Guam history is a required subject in the Guam public schools. Cunningham's long-term goal was to develop a complete textbook and guide, but he limited the scope of his dissertation study

15. K. W. McHenry, "University-Industry Research Cooperation: An Industrial View," *Journal of the Society of Research Administrators* 17 (1985): 31–43.
16. Lynne O'Brien and William E. Pulliam, "Collaborative Research and Development: A Source of Optimism for the Future," *Clearing House* 58 (1984): 101–103.
17. Lawrence J. Cunningham, "The Development and Validation of a High School Textbook on the Ancient Chamorros of Guam" (Ed.D. dissertation, University of Oregon, 1987).

to one chapter of the textbook and the section of the teacher's guide pertaining to it. (Hereafter, the term "chapter" refers to both the chapter and the teacher's guide.)

The objectives of the study were as follows:

1. to review the relevant literature on textbook instructional design and Chamorro history
2. to plan chapter objectives
3. to develop a preliminary form of the chapter
4. to field-test the preliminary form of the chapter
5. to revise the preliminary form of the chapter based on the field-test results
6. to conduct a main field test of the revised chapter.[18]

Each step of the R & D process used to develop the product is described in a separate chapter of the dissertation. Chapter 2 presents the results of Cunningham's research and information-collecting activities. These activities included a search for existing relevant curriculum materials, a study of learner characteristics on Guam, a review of the literature on characteristics of effective text, and a review of the literature on the ethnohistory of Guam.

Chapter 3 describes his initial planning activities, which focused on identifying objectives for the proposed chapter. The following are examples of the objectives Cunningham identified:

1. Given pictures of 15 ancient Chamorro artifacts, you will be able to match at least 12 with their descriptive labels.
2. Given paper, pencil, and a simulated situation in which you find an ancient Chamorro artifact, you will state the proper things to do and not to do, as stated in this chapter.
3. Given a drawing of a latte stone, you will label the two parts of the latte stone and identify the latte stone's purpose with 100 percent accuracy.
4. Given a map showing different environmental zones, you will identify good locations for building a village. Your reply will be judged on the basis of what archaeologists have discovered about ancient Chamorro settlement patterns.[19]

These objectives are written in the form of behavioral objectives, which were discussed earlier in the chapter.

Chapters 4 and 5 of the dissertation describe the development of the preliminary form of the product and the preliminary field test. Two versions of the chapter were developed: an expository version (conventional text format)

18. Ibid., p. 6.
19. Ibid., pp. 34–35.

and a narrative version, which covered the same content but in a story format. Cunningham developed the two versions because he was uncertain about which format would be more effective. It was feasible to develop and test both versions because he limited the scope of R & D to just one chapter of the proposed textbook. In addition, Cunningham developed a variety of evaluation instruments: a domain-referenced achievement test, a teacher questionnaire, student attitude scales, and a student interview schedule.

A total of 16 students drawn from two representative Guam history classes participated in the preliminary field test. They were formed into two groups, with one group studying the expository version and the other group studying the narrative version. Both groups completed each of the student instruments. In addition, the materials were reviewed for accuracy by two archaeologists; for community acceptability by several Chamorro leaders; for quality of instructional design by an instructional technologist; for curriculum appropriateness by one of Guam's associate school superintendents; and for lack of sex bias by experts on this subject. The results of the field test were reported in the dissertation, and also the revisions made in the materials on the basis of the results.

Chapter 6 of the dissertation presents the results of the main field test of the two revised versions of the product. This field test involved a pretest-posttest control-group experiment. The sample included five teachers and four Guam history classes taught by each teacher (total $N = 20$ classes). Each teacher's four classes were randomly assigned to the two treatment conditions—studying the expository version, or studying the narrative version. Each teacher taught both treatment conditions, thus controlling for the variable of teaching effectiveness. Checks for fidelity of treatment implementation were made.

Analysis of the experimental data revealed that both treatment groups made significant gains in achievement and attitudes. No significant differences between groups on measures of these variables were found. Table 18.2 presents a typical statistical analysis, in this case for the pre and post administrations of the domain-referenced achievement test. In a subsequent face-to-face comparison of the two versions, the majority of the students preferred the narrative version. Conversely, the majority of the teachers preferred the expository version. Advocates of the narrative version felt that the story made ancient Guam history more interesting and easier to learn. Advocates of the expository version felt that the story was a distraction from what they felt was their primary task, which was to learn the information and pass a test on it.

Cunningham reached the following conclusions from these results:

> It appears, then, that expository and narrative text work equally well in ecologically-valid situations. They both contribute to student achievement. Therefore, decisions to choose expository or narrative text may be based on other considerations, such as student preferences or the nature of the subject matter.[20]

TABLE 18.2

Performance of Expository and Narrative Text Groups on Achievement Test in Main Field Test

Treatment Group	N	Pretest M (SD)	Posttest M (SD)	Adjusted Posttest M	F
Expository text	157	5.25 (3.91)	24.97 (7.88)	25.04	.00
Narrative text	156	5.55 (4.14)	25.12 (6.86)	25.05	

Source: Adapted from Lawrence J. Cunningham, "The Development and Validation of a High School Textbook on the Ancient Chamorros of Guam," (Ed.D. dissertation, University of Oregon, 1987), p. 95.

If you are planning to do an R & D project, you should give careful consideration to the time required. The dissertation described above took well over a year for completion of product development through the field-test phase. A research project for the master's thesis or doctoral dissertation typically can be completed in much less time. The additional time required for an R & D project is worthwhile, however, if you are interested in making a contribution that will lead to an immediate tangible improvement in educational practice.

In the case of the dissertation described above, the developer was able to make a contribution not only to practice but also to research knowledge. You will recall that his main field test involved an experimental comparison of expository and narrative presentation of information. The results of the field test contributed new knowledge, and raised new questions, about the effects of variations in text characteristics on learners. In planning an R & D project, you too may find yourself considering alternatives about such matters as product design, product content, and target audience. It may be possible to compare several alternatives through informal or systematic experiments incorporated in the field-test phases of the R & D cycle.

The dissertation described above took the development of a product through the main field-test step of the R & D cycle. It may be feasible to take other products through all steps of the cycle. For other products, the development task may be sufficiently complex to justify a dissertation study that ends at the preliminary field-test phase. You and your dissertation committee will need to consider the nature of the proposed product and decide how much of the R & D cycle would constitute an acceptable study.

20. Ibid., p. 142.

MISTAKES SOMETIMES MADE IN DOING RESEARCH AND DEVELOPMENT

1. The developer does not draw upon research-based principles of instructional design in planning a product.
2. Does not determine at the outset whether there is a need for the product.
3. Overlooks certain aspects of the product in listing topics to be included in the literature review.
4. Does not state the product's objectives in a form that enables them to be measured clearly.
5. Obtains insufficient feedback from users during each field test of the product.
6. Does not plan for the dissemination and implementation of the product while it is still under development.
7. Pays too much attention to the cosmetic aspects of the product and too little attention to its instructional effectiveness.

ANNOTATED REFERENCES

Borg, Walter R. "The Educational R & D Process: Some Insights." *Journal of Experimental Education* 55 (1987): 181–188.

Describes pitfalls to avoid in doing R & D, as well as techniques that are likely to yield an effective product. The author's advice is based on his 20 years' experience doing educational R & D.

Gagné, Robert M., and others. *Principles of Instructional Design,* 3rd ed. New York: Holt, Rinehart and Winston, 1987.

Describes effective instructional techniques that can be incorporated in the design of educational products. The authors stress the importance of analyzing learning outcomes (e.g., verbal information, intellectual skills, attitudes, motor skills), since each type of learning outcome requires the use of different instructional techniques.

Gall, Meredith D. *Handbook for Evaluating and Selecting Curriculum Materials.* Boston: Allyn & Bacon, 1981.

One way to understand the development of effective educational products is to consider the process from the perspective of consumers. This book describes research on curriculum materials selection, textbook adoption policies, and 39 criteria for analyzing and evaluating materials.

Mager, Robert F. *Preparing Instructional Objectives,* rev. ed. Belmont, CA: David S. Lake Publishers, 1984.

Classic text on how to write behavioral objectives. Mager also has written other texts, available from the same publisher, that would be useful in designing an educational product. Their titles are: *Making Instruction Work; Measuring Instructional Results,* 2nd ed.; *Analyzing Performance Problems,* 2nd ed.; *Goal Analysis,* 2nd ed.; *Developing Attitudes Toward Learning,* 2nd ed.

SELF-CHECK TEST

Circle the correct answer to each of the following questions. An answer key is provided on page 884.

1. The basic goal of educational R & D is to
   a. discover new knowledge through action research.
   b. develop research-based products.
   c. test educational materials.
   d. improve existing educational products.
2. The first major step of the R & D cycle involves
   a. doing a review of the literature.
   b. making classroom observations.
   c. preparing a report on the state of the art.
   d. All of the above are correct.
3. In the R & D cycle the general aim of the literature review is
   a. focused on product evaluation.
   b. focused on R & D strategies.
   c. the same as in basic and applied research.
   d. narrower than in basic or applied research.
4. The most important aspect of planning in the R & D cycle is
   a. defining skills.
   b. determining course sequence.
   c. feasibility testing.
   d. stating product objectives.
5. Developing behavioral objectives for an educational product is similar in some ways to developing a
   a. proposal for a research study.
   b. good criterion for a research study.
   c. product for assessment of learning.
   d. All of the above are correct.
6. When initial planning has been completed, the next logical step in the R & D cycle is to
   a. do a literature review.
   b. conduct preliminary field testing.
   c. construct a preliminary form of the product.
   d. prepare a report on the state of the art.
7. In conducting product evaluation, the developer should use field-test sites that
   a. have been randomly selected.
   b. are similar to the sites in which the completed product will be used.
   c. approximate an experimental laboratory setting in terms of control over extraneous variables.
   d. provide the most difficult test of the product's effectiveness.
8. The need during preliminary testing for extensive feedback from the learner may create the problem of
   a. observer bias.
   b. observer contamination.
   c. the Hawthorne Effect.
   d. the placebo effect.
9. The primary purpose of the main field test in the R & D cycle is to determine whether
   a. sampling is accurate.
   b. observer bias is minimal.
   c. the criterion measures are valid.
   d. the product meets its objectives.

10. According to Borg and Gall, the answer to the "learning versus polish" question is to
    a. give essentials best effort, and do everything else as cheaply and quickly as possible.
    b. follow carefully the suggestions of team media specialists.
    c. produce a polished product for initial testing.
    d. produce a polished product only for the main test.

APPLICATION PROBLEMS

The following problems are intended to give you practice in applying significant concepts and research procedures explained in the chapter. Most do not have a single correct answer. For feedback, compare your answers with the sample answers on pages 903–904.

1. Suppose you are asked to develop a brief training program to help students overcome 15 common spelling errors involving homonyms (e.g., "principal" and "principle"). As part of the development of the program, you are asked to collect evidence that it is effective. Make up a brief plan with specific steps that you would take to accomplish this objective.
2. An educational R & D specialist has a choice of four products he can develop. Product A probably would be very popular and well received by school personnel. Product B probably would qualify for additional funds so that audiovisual aids could be developed. Product C has well-defined behavioral objectives. Product D is supported by a base of research knowledge concerning learners' achievement of the product's objectives. Given this information, which product has the best chance of successfully completing an R & D cycle? Why?
3. An R & D specialist is developing a new set of curriculum materials. As it is very complicated to test a preliminary version of the materials in a regular classroom, she arranges to take students from class and have them use the materials in a special classroom at a school site set aside for this purpose. What is one risk that she takes by following this strategy?
4. A group of developers conducted a main field test of some new audiovisual aids. They found that the materials achieved three behavioral objectives quite satisfactorily, but not the other two objectives. However, the developers feel they acquired insight from the field test concerning why the materials failed to achieve these objectives. Given this information, what is a reasonable course of action for the developers to follow next?
5. An R & D specialist has a certain amount of development money to work on a new approach to teaching introductory statistics. He wants to use attractive printed media; a series of pamphlets instead of a single book; ample use of illustrations; typeface in several colors. For his preliminary field test, however, he is intending to try out cheap photocopies of the text. A colleague points out that this cheap version may produce poor results, even though his approach is basically sound. What is one argument that he can use in defense of a cheap printed version?

SUGGESTION SHEET

If your last name starts with letters from Smf to Stu, please complete the Suggestion Sheet at the end of the book while this chapter is still fresh in your mind.

19 TECHNIQUES OF HISTORICAL RESEARCH

OVERVIEW

Historical research in education is important for several reasons. The findings of historical research enable educators to learn from past discoveries and mistakes; to identify needs for educational reform; and, to a certain extent, to predict future trends. This chapter presents the major steps and techniques in historical research: (1) identifying a problem or topic, (2) searching for and recording relevant sources of historical evidence, (3) evaluating the evidence for authenticity and validity, and (4) synthesizing historical facts into meaningful chronological and thematic patterns. The chapter emphasizes the various interpretive processes that the historian uses in a research project.

OBJECTIVES

After studying this chapter you should be able to:

1. Describe the major differences between contemporary and nineteenth-century historical research.
2. State several uses of historical research.
3. List the major steps involved in doing a historical research project.
4. Describe five types of historical research in education.
5. Distinguish between documents, quantitative records, spoken sources of information, and relics.
6. Distinguish between primary and secondary sources of historical information.
7. State several procedures and considerations involved in recording information from historical sources.
8. Explain the various features of a document that are examined in the process of external criticism.
9. Distinguish between subjectivity and bias in reporting an event.
10. Explain the statement "History means interpretation."
11. Describe how the use of concepts affects historical interpretation.
12. Explain the interpretive problems and processes involved in making causal inferences or generalizations from historical evidence.
13. Discuss factors involved in organizing the historical research dissertation.

INTRODUCTION

The British historian Edward Carr, in response to the question, What is history?, stated that "it is a continuing process of interaction between the historian and his facts, an unending dialogue between the present and the past."[1] Consistent with Carr's view, we define **historical research** as the systematic search for facts relating to questions about the past, and the interpretation of these facts. By studying the past, the historian hopes to achieve a better understanding of present institutions, practices, and issues in education.

Historical investigation generally is considered part of the qualitative research tradition in education. In support of this view, C. H. Edson identified four characteristics of historical investigation that it shares with other qualitative research methodologies: (1) emphasis on the study of context, (2) the study of behavior in natural rather than laboratory settings, (3) appreciation of the wholeness of experience, and (4) the centrality of interpretation in the research process.[2] As you will learn later in the chapter, historical investigation is not completely qualitative. Some historians also make use of quantitative research methods.

The importance of interpretation in historical research is apparent from even a superficial analysis of what is involved in doing this kind of investigation. Historical research necessarily deals with events that occurred prior to the historian's decision to study them. Therefore, historians must rely on a recording of the events—for example, by a journalist, court reporter, diarist, or photographer. The recording of the event (a "historical source") involves an interpretative act by journalists or other recorders because their biases, values, and interests will cause them to attend to some details and omit others. Thus, historical sources are cloaked in interpretation before historians touch them. Historians add another layer of interpretation in the way they choose to emphasize or ignore facts about the past and in the way they fit facts into categories and patterns. Little wonder, then, that the historian Joan Burstyn described history as "constructed reality."[3]

The contemporary emphasis on interpretation in historical research contrasts with the popular nineteenth-century view that "history consists of the compilation of a maximum number of irrefutable and objective facts."[4] Consequently, nineteenth-century histories often consisted of multivolume compilations of details about rather limited topics. Contemporary historians tend to dismiss these writings as being merely historical narratives. Their own writings

---

1. Edward H. Carr. *What Is History?* (New York: Random House, 1967), p. 35.
2. C. H. Edson, "Our Past and Present: Historical Inquiry in Education," *The Journal of Thought* 21, no. 3 (1986): 13–27.
3. Joan N. Burstyn, "History as Image: Changing the Lens," *History of Education Quarterly* 27 (1987): 167–180.
4. Carr, *What Is History?* p. 14.

tend to be shorter, and they subordinate historical facts to an interpretive framework within which they are given meaning and significance.

Historical research in education differs from other types of educational research in that the historian *discovers* data through a search of historical sources such as diaries, official documents, and relics. In other types of educational research, the researcher *creates* data by making observations and administering tests in order to describe present events and present performance.

The Subject Matter of Historical Research

The subject matter of historical research in education is as broad as the field of education. Arthur Moehlman and his colleagues at the University of Texas have developed a set of categories for classifying the various types of historical research that appear in the literature.[5] Their classification scheme, in adapted form, is presented here:

1. General educational history.
2. History of educational legislation, which includes such topics as taxation, bonds, school land boards and districts, equalization programs, curriculum, state-supported schools and universities, and court cases
3. Historical biographies of major contributors to education
4. History of major branches of education, which includes such topics as school goals, school accreditation and attendance laws, community education, school organization and administration, school finance, school enrollment, school personnel, school plant, instructional methods and materials, and school curriculum
5. Institutional history of education, which includes such topics as kindergarten, elementary school, secondary school, colleges and universities, correspondence education, vocational schools, armed forces schools, mass media, research organizations, and foundations
6. Cultural history of education, which includes such topics as ethnology, anthropology, sociology, and technology
7. History of educational planning and policy
8. Historical critiques of education
9. Comparative history of international education.
10. History of contemporary problems in education.

A study of this classification scheme may help you to define the type of problem you wish to investigate in a historical study.

---

5. Adapted from A. H. Moehlman et al., *A Guide to Computer-Assisted Research in American Education* (Austin: University of Texas, 1969), pp. 76, 83–94.

The Uses of History

Histories of education are written for various reasons. Some historians are simply entranced with the past for its own sake. They become intrigued with a particular historical period, and they spend their time documenting the events and objects that make it distinctive. Historians of this type are sometimes called *antiquarians*.

A more serious purpose for studying the past was offered by Sol Cohen, an educational historian:

> To Freud, neurosis is the failure to escape the past, the burden of one's history. What is repressed returns distorted and is eternally reenacted. The psychotherapist's task is to help the patient reconstruct the past. In this respect the historian's goal resembles that of the therapist—to liberate us from the burden of the past by helping us to understand it.[6]

As an example of this liberating function, consider what might happen if educational researchers did not do reviews of the literature in their areas of interest. Researchers might "discover" what was already known to past researchers; they might test hypotheses that previously had been shown to be unproductive; and they would reinvent research methodology or continue to make the same methodological errors as their predecessors. Indeed, without continually updated historical reviews of the research literature, progress would be impossible.

The same liberating function of history applies to educational practice. For example, educators who are ignorant of past bond issues in their school district might campaign for a new bond issue, making unjustified historical assumptions and overlooking effective techniques used by their predecessors.

Another purpose of historical research is to provide a moral framework for understanding the present. Robert Bellah and his colleagues argued that present-day individualism and scientific rationalism provide little guidance for making sense of life and for making moral judgments.[7] Study of the past reminds us of other traditions—traditions that involved a defined moral order and that connected the individual to a community. It is probably for this reason that religious and ethnic groups attempt to keep their collective pasts alive. One can argue that the same need exists in education. The founding of our educational institutions was predicated on values and a view of society, the study of which can inform the way in which we view and judge these institutions as they exist today.

Historical research in education sometimes serves the function of social

---

6. Sol Cohen, "The History of the History of American Education, 1900–1976: The Uses of the Past," *Harvard Educational Review* 46 (1976): 298–330.
7. Robert Bellah et al., *Habits of the Heart: Individualism and Commitment in American Life* (Berkeley: University of California Press, 1985).

reform. This use of history characterizes the work of recent revisionist historians of education. These historians have attempted to sensitize educators to unjust or misguided practices in the past that, perhaps unwittingly, have persisted into the present and require reform. Because the past provides a detached perspective, it may be easier for educators to detect and achieve an understanding of misguided practices than if their perspective were limited to the immediate present.

To a certain extent, historical research can assist the educator in predicting future trends. If we know how an educator or group of educators has acted in the past, we can predict how they will act in the future. The educator whose past actions have been motivated by a desire for liberal reform is likely to be similarly motivated in the future. As in other types of educational research (see chapter 14), however, prediction is rarely perfect. For example, new social, political, or economic conditions may arise that create fundamental changes in the conditions under which educators work. These new conditions may well invalidate predictions based on past performance. Indeed, historical research can help prevent poor decisions by demonstrating that two situations (one in the past and one in the present), which appear similar on the surface, are in fact different in important ways.

Historians of education traditionally have influenced practice through the training of educators. For example, preservice teachers are usually required to take a course in the history of education. In recent years historians have become more involved in educational policy making. A notable example is Patricia Graham, a historian who was director of the National Institute of Education from 1977 to 1979.[8]

Some educational researchers think that historical methodology is irrelevant to their work. In their view, research belongs to the sciences, whereas history belongs to the humanities. In fact, any competent researcher is a historian. This is because research involves reviewing the literature to determine what investigations and theoretical work have already been done on a particular problem. The search for relevant documents (journal articles, technical reports, unpublished manuscripts, etc.) and the interpretation of their significance are tasks that characterize the work of empirical researchers and historians alike. The study of historical methodology should help you become a better researcher, whether or not you choose to do a study that is primarily historical.

Steps in Doing Historical Research

C. H. Edson claimed, "There is no single, definable method of historical inquiry."[9] This is certainly true, because historical inquiry is so dependent on

---

8. Patricia Graham described her experiences as director of the NIE in "Historians as Policy Makers," *Educational Researcher* 9, no. 11 (1980): 21–24.
9. Edson, "Our Past and Present," p. 20.

the idiosyncratic ways in which different historians interpret and judge the past. Nonetheless, we think it is possible to identify some steps that are common across most historical studies. These steps are as follows: Define the problems or questions to be investigated; search for sources of historical facts; summarize and evaluate the historical sources; and present the pertinent facts within an interpretive framework. Each of these steps is discussed in the next sections of the chapter.

The search for historical facts and the interpretation of these facts are not necessarily discrete, sequential phases of a historical research project. Edward Carr provided the following description of how a historian engages in research:

> Laymen . . . sometimes ask me how the historian goes to work when he writes history. The commonest assumption appears to be that the historian divides his work into two sharply distinguishable phases or periods. First, he spends a long preliminary period reading his sources and filling his notebooks with facts; then, when this is over, he puts away his sources, takes out his notebooks, and writes his book from beginning to end. This is to me an unconvincing and unplausible picture. For myself, as soon as I have got going on a few of what I take to be the capital sources, the itch becomes too strong and I begin to write—not necessarily at the beginning, but somewhere, anywhere. Thereafter, reading and writing go on simultaneously. The writing is added to, subtracted from, re-shaped, cancelled, as I go on reading. The reading is guided and directed and made fruitful by the writing: the more I write, the more I know what I am looking for, the better I understand the significance and relevance of what I find.[10]

Researchers who use other methodologies (e.g., controlled experimentation) often interpose similar processes. As a first step, researchers may formulate a few tentative hypotheses and plan a research design for testing them. After reviewing the literature and conducting pilot studies, they may decide to make further changes in the hypotheses and research design. Even after the formal experiment has been conducted and all the data collected, researchers may formulate new hypotheses that they never intended at the outset, but which can be tested by the available data.

This analysis of the historical research process does not imply that researchers can follow any sequence they desire. A structured sequence of steps is needed to guide the project. Variations within this sequence will occur, depending upon the particular circumstances of the search for historical facts and upon the interpretive framework used to understand the facts.

10. Carr, *What Is History?* pp. 32–33.

DEFINING A PROBLEM OR TOPIC
FOR HISTORICAL RESEARCH

As with other types of educational research, the first step in planning an historical research project is to define the problems or topics to be investigated. A review of problems and topics studied by other educational historians is often useful for initiating this process.

Mark Beach analyzed the problems and topics that prompt historical inquiry into five types.[11] Current social issues are the most popular source of historical problems in education. For example, loyalty oaths in educational institutions, urban education, proposals for radical reform in education, and intelligence testing are social issues that have provided a focus for recent historical research projects.

Histories of specific individuals (i.e., biographies), histories of specific educational institutions, and histories of educational movements form a second type of historical inquiry. These studies are often motivated by "the simple desire to acquire knowledge about previously unexamined phenomena."[12] Even when a history of an educator, institution, or movement exists, researchers needs to determine whether it adequately explores the events in which they are interested. In fact, gaps in knowledge of the past often provide the basis for a historical study. Bernard Bailyn, an educational historian, offered the following rationale for this type of research:

> The motivation here is to learn something new and to present this new information; but the precise issues are not defined. There are no specific questions and no hypothetical answers. Thus the motivation for writing a narrative of a battle may be simply to discover what happened in it; to find out how it was that the victors won it. Or, again, one decides to do research and write about Wilson's Administration because we are ignorant of it, and any thorough, clear narrative of it will be valuable because it fills an important gap, an evident vacuum.[13]

The third type of historical inquiry in education involves an attempt to interpret ideas or events that previously had seemed unrelated. For example, a researcher may find that histories of textbook publishing have been written and that separate, unrelated histories of school curriculum also have been written. In the process of reviewing these separate histories, the researcher may detect relationships and raise questions that did not concern the other historians. These perceived relationships and questions may provide the basis for an

---

11. Mark Beach, "History of Education," *Review of Educational Research* 39 (1969): 561–576.
12. Ibid., p. 562.
13. Bernard Bailyn, "The Problems of the Working Historian," in *The Craft of American History*, ed. A. S. Eisenstadt (New York: AHM Publishing, 1969), pp. 202–203.

original historical inquiry. A fourth, related type of historical inquiry occurs when the researcher attempts to synthesize old data or to merge it with new historical facts that have been discovered.

The fifth type of historical inquiry involves reinterpretation of past events that have been studied by other historians. These reinterpretations are sometimes called **revisionist history,** in that they are attempts to revise existing histories within the framework of new (and sometimes politically radical) interpretive frameworks.

As in any type of research, the beginning researcher planning a dissertation or thesis should review the literature and talk with experienced researchers before attempting to define a set of problems or topics for historical inquiry. Sometimes you will find through a review of the literature that other historians have formulated important problems and questions for investigation. For example, Guadalupe San Miguel, Jr. recently reviewed the status of historical research on Chicano education.[14] He concluded his review by identifying questions not yet answered by historians. Some of these questions are as follows:

> First, little is known about the roots and evolution of the Mexican American commitment to education referred to in several of the studies. Who in the community, for instance, supported education, what type of education, and for what purposes? . . .
>
> Second, we do not know who attended school nor for how long they attended. . . .
>
> Finally, new studies comparing and contrasting the educational experiences of Mexican Americans with other minority and immigrant groups are needed. It is unclear yet the extent to which the educational experiences of Mexican Americans were similar or dissimilar to historically dispossessed groups such as blacks and native Americans, or to other language minority groups of European descent.[15]

Questions such as these, formulated by an experienced historian, can be very helpful in identifying a problem for your own study.

An important guideline in identifying a problem or topic for historical research is to check that the sources needed for the investigation are available. It would be unwise to select a problem that required use of documents in a language that the researcher does not know, or documents that might be difficult to access (e.g., classified records in government archives).

14. Guadalupe San Miguel, Jr., "Status of the Historiography of Chicano Education: A Preliminary Analysis," *History of Education Quarterly* 26 (1986): 523–536.
15. Ibid., pp. 535–536.

SEARCHING FOR HISTORICAL SOURCES

Types of Historical Sources

Virtually any object or written record that one can imagine is a potential source of information about the past. We will distinguish four types of historical sources here: documents, quantitative records, oral records, and relics.

The most commonly used type of historical source is written or printed materials (sometimes called **documents**). These materials can take varied forms: diaries, memoirs, legal records, court testimony, newspapers, periodicals, business records, notebooks, yearbooks, diplomas, committee reports, memos, institutional files, tests. They can be classified in several ways: handwritten (i.e., in manuscript form) or printed, published or unpublished, prepared for public use or for private use.

Another distinction is whether the document was prepared intentionally as a historical record or whether it was unpremeditated. Some documents, such as memoirs and yearbooks, are written primarily to serve as a record of the past. Other documents, such as memos and teacher-prepared tests, are intended to serve an immediate purpose, with no thought that at a later time they might be used as a historical record. The distinction between **intentional documents** and **unpremeditated documents** may be important to consider when evaluating the source for authenticity and genuineness (see later section on historical evaluation).

Quantitative records can be considered as a separate type of historical source or as a subtype of document. Census records, school budgets, school attendance records, test scores, and similar compilations of numerical data provide a valuable source of facts for the historical researcher. Historians are making increasing use of computers to analyze the large amounts of numerical data that these documents often contain.

Another important type of historical source is the spoken word. Ballads, tales, sagas, and other forms of the oral tradition have been used to convey a record of events for posterity. Also, historians can conduct oral interviews of persons who have witnessed and participated in events of potential historical significance. The interviews are recorded on audiotape and may be transcribed to form a written record. This branch of historical research, known as **oral history,** currently is quite active. For example, the oral history program at Columbia University, initiated in the 1940s, includes records of interviews with more than 2,700 people who supplied more than 14,000 hours of recollections.[16]

16. Charles W. Crawford, "Oral History—the State of the Profession," *Oral History Review*, 1974, pp. 1–9.

The Oral History Association is an organization of historians interested in this type of research.[17]

Relics are the fourth type of historical source. **Relics** include any object whose physical or visual properties provide information about the past. School buildings, school furniture, architectural plans for school physical plants, textbook drawings, and instructional devices are examples of objects that can be used as relics in the study of past practices in education.

Some objects can be classified as both documents and relics, depending on how they are used in a historical research project. For example, in a study of printing methods used in the production of textbooks, the textbooks would be classified as a relic. This is because one of their physical properties is being examined. On the other hand, the textbook would be used as a document in a study of how textbooks of different periods treated an important historical event. The reason for classifying the textbooks as documents is that the verbal communications contained in them are the focus of the historical research.

Another basis for classifying historical sources is whether they are "primary" or "secondary." The distinction between primary and secondary sources is the same as in other types of educational research (see chapter 4). In historical research, **primary sources** are defined as those documents in which the individual describing the event was present when it occurred. **Secondary sources** are documents in which the individual describing the event was not present but obtained a description from someone else, who may or may not have directly observed the event. Thus, reports of historical research generally are classified as secondary sources because the historian rarely is a direct witness to the past events described in the reports. Instead, the report usually is based on the historian's interpretation of other primary and secondary sources.

A Tentative Search Plan

The search for historical facts relating to the problem or topic should be systematic. To a certain extent, historians need to know what they are looking for even before the search begins. Otherwise, they are likely to search aimlessly and to overlook important sources of relevant facts. Philip C. Brooks suggests the following approach for initiating a search for historical sources:

> Resourcefulness and imagination are essential in the preliminary exploration as well as in the later actual study. One can suppose that certain kinds of sources would exist if he thinks carefully about his subject, the persons involved, the government or institutions concerned, and the kinds of records that would

17. Oral History Association, University of Vermont, Burlington. The association has several publications, including the *Oral History Review*, published annually.

naturally grow out of the events that he will be studying. He should ask himself who would have produced the useful documents in the transaction he is concerned with. What would be the expected flow of events? What kinds of records would have been created? What would be the life history of the documents, from their creation through current use, filing, temporary storage, and eventual retention in a repository where he can consult them? What kinds of materials would one expect to be kept rather than discarded?[18]

The search for historical facts in primary and secondary sources cannot be entirely determined in advance, however. A tentative search plan should be created and revised as one's interpretive framework develops. Changes in one's plan will occur as a particular primary or secondary source reveals other pertinent sources whose existence the historian had not anticipated.

Preliminary Sources

The first step in a search plan is to identify and consult relevant preliminary sources of historical information. A number of published aids for identifying the secondary source literature in history are available. These are called *preliminary sources*. An important requirement for using these aids effectively is to list key descriptors for one's problem or topic. Procedures for identifying descriptors are presented in chapter 4.

Published Bibliographies

Published bibliographies are a useful starting point for historians in constructing their own bibliography. One way to find published bibliographies is to consult *bibliographies of bibliographies,* which include the following references.

Sheehy, Eugene P. *Guide to Reference Books*, 10th ed. Chicago: American Library Association, 1986.

Walford, A. J. *Walford's Guide to Reference Material, Vol. 1. Science and Technology*, 4th ed. Phoenix: Oryx, 1980.

Walford, A. J. *Walford's Guide to Reference Material, Vol. 2. Social and Historical Sciences, Philosophy, and Religion*, 4th ed. Phoenix: Oryx, 1982.

Bibliographic Index. A Cumulative Bibliography of Bibliographies. New York: H. W. Wilson, 1938—.

A number of other bibliographic aids are described in chapter 4.

Several compilations of bibliographies of historical works are available.

18. Philip C. Brooks, *Research in Archives: The Use of Unpublished Primary Sources* (Chicago: University of Chicago Press, 1969), pp. 19–20.

One of them is *Historian's Handbook: A Descriptive Guide to Reference Works* by Helen J. Poulton and Marguerite S. Howland (Norman: University of Oklahoma Press, 1986). An especially helpful reference for the educational historian is *A Bibliography of American Educational History: An Annotated and Classified Guide* edited by Francesco Cordasco and William W. Brickman (New York: AMS Press, 1975). This is a comprehensive annotated bibliography of references. Part 1 lists general reference works on American education. Part 2 is organized under the following headings: elementary education and curriculum; secondary education and curriculum; vocational education; education in the individual states; higher education; school books; the teaching profession; church, state, and education; the federal government and education; the education of women; biographies, foreign influences on American education; and contemporary issues in American education. Part 3 lists references dealing with specific historical periods in American education.

The journal *History of Education Quarterly* occasionally includes specialized bibliographies intended for the educational historian.

Reference Works

Biographical directories are a useful aid for historical studies of persons who played a critical role in past events. *The Biography Index*, published by H. W. Wilson (New York), lists biographical material that has appeared in journals and in books; it is updated quarterly. There are many collections of brief biographies, including these.

American Council of Learned Societies, ed. *Dictionary of American Biography*. 17 vols., 7 suppl., & Index Guide. New York: Scribner's, 1927–1981.

Dictionary of National Biography. 22 vols., 8 suppl. New York: Oxford University Press, 1882–1981.

Who's Who in America. Editions 1–present. Chicago: Marquis Who's Who, 1899–present.

Encyclopedias are another useful source of biographical information.

Historical researchers also need to know about places, events, and things. An atlas can be consulted to determine the location of an unfamiliar place. Many atlases are available, including: William R. Shepherd, *Shepherd's Historical Atlas*, 10th rev. ed. (New York: Barnes & Noble, 1980). *Webster's New Geographical Dictionary*, rev. ed. (Springfield, MA: Merriam-Webster, 1984) is another useful reference for identifying locations. Specialized chronologies, dictionaries of terms, and dictionaries of quotations have been prepared to help the historical researcher determine dates of past events, the meaning of words no longer in common use, and the origin of sayings.

Secondary Sources

The search of preliminary sources will result in a tentative bibliography of secondary sources, usually published histories relating to your problem or topic. These histories will include the historian's interpretations and conclusions, historical information, references to other secondary sources, and references to primary sources, which provide the ultimate basis for the historian's "facts."

An important issue is whether to use another historian's facts without personally checking the primary sources from which they were derived. You will need to exercise judgment in this matter, considering such factors as the other historian's reputation, likelihood of bias, and accessibility of the primary source documents. If you choose to use the other historian's facts without further check, you should footnote the other historian's work as the source for the historical facts used in your own work.

Primary Sources

Primary sources of historical information (e.g., diaries, manuscripts, school records) are often contained in institutional repositories or archives. This is especially true of primary sources relating to historical events in which the principal witnesses are deceased or otherwise inaccessible. For histories of events that have occurred in the recent past, the historical researcher may contact witnesses on an individual basis in order to study documents in their possession or to interview them.

There are many repositories of primary sources relating to American history. They are maintained by many institutions and groups: federal, state, and local governments; religious institutions; professional societies; business firms; and newspapers.

A Guide to Manuscripts and Archives in the United States, edited by Philip M. Hamer (National Historical Publications Commission, 1961), describes the holdings of 1,300 repositories. Another guide to historical repositories is the *National Union Catalog of Manuscript Collections,* 2 vols. (Hamden, CT: Shoestring Press, 1964). Most of these repositories contain handwritten or printed documents. In recent years some oral history repositories have been instituted.

Repositories vary in the ease of access of their primary sources. The holdings of official archives are often well-indexed, and archivists may be available to assist you in your work. In other situations you will be on your own, and therefore you will need to learn the filing system that was used. Records also may be stored on microfilm or microfiche, in which case you will need to learn specialized information-retrieval skills.

Researchers who are interested in quantitative data will almost certainly need to enlist the aid of a staff member to interpret them. For example, quantitative data often are on printouts generated from computer programs prepared specifically for the institution's needs. The data cannot be interpreted unless a staff member explains the computer program to the researcher.

The search for primary historical sources is time-consuming and difficult. The task is manageable, however, if the research problem has been carefully delimited and if a search plan has been constructed. Also, you will be motivated by knowing that you are dealing with the ultimate "stuff" from which history is made.

RECORDING INFORMATION FROM HISTORICAL SOURCES

In examining a primary or secondary source, the historical researcher may not know what information will prove useful at a later phase of the study. Quite possibly the interpretive phase of the study will involve searching for new facts that were not viewed as relevant earlier in the study. The problem of deciding what information to abstract from a historical source becomes critical when the source is not easily accessible. For example, you may need to travel to repositories where historical sources are stored. Unlike libraries, repositories usually do not allow their materials to leave the premises. Thus, you will need to decide, then and there, what information to record for later use.

Before deciding what information to record, you will need to deal with two preliminary issues. The first issue is whether the materials—especially primary sources—will be made accessible to you. Institutional records are often available for study, but this does not mean that someone can automatically examine them. You may need to make a formal request for permission to study the records. Some documents may be inaccessible or accessible for study only under certain conditions.

The other issue concerns the types of material that can be copied and reproduced in the dissertation. An institution may allow you to examine documents but not to quote directly from them; or the institution may allow only certain portions to be copied. You may wish to reproduce documents that are considered "literary property"; for example, a series of essays or speeches that could be published for profit. In this situation you need to take care not to infringe on someone's actual or potential copyright. Under the doctrine of fair use established by the U.S. Congress, you can quote short passages of a primary or secondary source without infringing copyright.

Note Taking and Photocopying

One procedure for recording information from historical sources is to make written or typed notes. Reports of empirical research usually can be outlined on a single note card (see chapter 4), but historical sources are best reviewed by placing only one item of information on each card. The difference in procedure is necessary because many small bits of information relating to your research questions may be obtained from one important document, such as an autobiography or a diary. Each card may be coded to indicate the question or topic to which the note relates. If all notes from the document were copied on a single card, the process of rearranging the information would be quite difficult.

Many historical researchers now simply photocopy documents that are of interest to them. Modern technology has made photocopying quick and relatively inexpensive. Some repositories have facilities that enable researchers to photocopy microfilmed documents. Although photocopies do not necessarily eliminate the need for note taking, they often reduce the amount required. The purpose of the notes should be to provide brief reminders to the researcher of information presented in detail in the photocopied document.

Photocopying has its limitations. It may not be possible to photocopy old historical documents because the exposure to the photocopy process may damage them. Some documents, especially newspaper clippings, may not photocopy well. Special photographic techniques may be necessary to reproduce oversize documents, maps, and charts.

Summarizing Quantitative Data

If you intend to collect large amounts of quantitative data about past events, you will need to plan how to record and summarize them. It may be advantageous to use the computer for these purposes.

The first step is to think carefully about the kinds of data that are necessary to the investigation. Keep in mind that the more data you collect, the more time-consuming will be the data analysis. You should define variables carefully (e.g., income, socioeconomic status, voting records) and appropriate measures of them. Also, you should define in advance the sample or population for which data are to be recorded. In other words, you should not just record whatever data you happen to come across.

Once the relevant data have been "discovered" through a search of quantitative historical records, you probably will analyze them using descriptive statistics. If the data were collected from samples representing defined populations, you also can use tests of statistical significance.

Quantitative analysis of historical data has emerged as a topic of considerable interest to historians in the past two decades. The reason for this trend is that historical conclusions based on large amounts of carefully selected quantitative data are likely to be more representative of the past than conclusions based on a few case studies. Also, quantitative analysis makes it possible to study the "average" citizen rather than the few "great" men and women who have dominated traditional historical research. H. Warren Button commented on this approach to historical research:

A part of the advantage of quantification in social and educational history is that it allows historians to follow a recent interest, an interest in the history of the common man—no depreciation intended—"history from the bottom up"— grassroots history. Records for history in this vein are likely to be thin and fragmentary; for coherence it is necessary to mine every source. For instance, for a quantitative study of Buxton, a black antebellum haven in Ontario, it is necessary to assemble data from perhaps fifteen thousand entries in the census manuscripts of 1861, 1871, and 1881; from town auditors' accounts, and church records.[19] The research necessity for compilation and statistical treatment, by unfortunate paradox, produces history almost without personalities, even without names. Still, this new history has and will produce new understandings and will counterweight our longstanding concern for "the better sort."[20]

A quantitative history project requires the ability to use sampling techniques, to define and measure variables, to create a research design, and to conduct statistical analyses. Therefore, if you plan to do this type of study, you should refer to other sections of this book and to specialized works on quantitative history.

EVALUATION OF HISTORICAL SOURCES

Researchers need to adopt a critical attitude toward documents, quantitative data, and relics found in the search for historical facts. A historical source may be genuine, or it may be forged. A document may have been written by someone other than the person whose name appears as author. It may refer to events that did not occur or that occurred differently from the description given by the witness. If your evaluation of a historical source leads you to doubt its genuineness or credibility, you should note this in the research project.

You can never be completely certain about the genuineness and accuracy of historical sources. All you can do is to generate and test hypotheses about each source. For example, you can ask, "Was this document really written by the person designated as the author?" As these hypotheses are shown to be untenable, you increase the probability—although never to the point of absolute certainty—that the sources are genuine and credible. Some historical sources may prove to be of mixed value, accurate in some respects and highly biased in other respects.

The evaluation of historical sources is usually referred to as **historical criticism.** This process is generally divided into two major categories: external criticism, which is the evaluation of the nature of the source; and internal

---

19. Beverly H. Nenno, dissertation in progress, State University of New York at Buffalo.
20. H. Warren Button, "Creating More Usable Pasts: History in the Study of Education," *Educational Researcher* 8, no. 5 (1979): 4.

criticism, which is the evaluation of the information contained in the source. The following discussion of external and internal criticism is directed toward evaluation of documents, although the principles also apply to the evaluation of oral records, quantitative data, and relics.

As one primer of historical research methods indicates, historical criticism is a complex, sophisticated process:

> It relies on attention to detail, on common-sense reasoning, on a developed "feel" for history and chronology, on familiarity with human behavior, and on ever enlarging stores of information. Many a "catch question" current among school-boys calls forth these powers in rudimentary form—for instance the tale about the beautiful Greek coin just discovered and bearing the date "500 B.C." Here a second's historical reflection and reasoning is enough for verification: the "fact" is readily rejected.[21]

The ultimate value of a historical study is determined in large part by the researcher's ability to evaluate the worth and meaning of historical sources that come to light in the process of doing the study.

External Criticism

In **external criticism** the researcher raises questions about the nature of the historical source: Is it genuine? Is it the original copy? Who wrote it? Where? When? Under what conditions? Many factors must be considered in answering these questions. We can suggest only a few of them here.

Some historical sources have been shown to be **forgeries,** that is, fabrications claimed to be genuine. Educational historians are less likely to encounter forged and spurious documents than are historians studying some political or religious movement, where stronger motivations exist for creating forgeries.

The existence of **variant sources** may prove to be a problem in determining whether one has the original copy of a primary source. For example, in going through the files of an educational institution, you may discover copies of internal memoranda that relate to the topic. But perhaps the file copy was not distributed in exactly that form to its intended receiver or receivers. Sometimes the writer of a memo adds a personal note or qualification to one of the receivers. Thus, you may find a slightly different version of the memo in the receiver's files than was placed in the sender's file. In this situation, both versions of the memo may be considered original primary sources and both may reveal relevant, but different, information about a past event.

21. Jacques Barzun and Henry F. Graff, *The Modern Researcher*, 3rd ed. (New York: Harcourt Brace Jovanovich, 1977), p. 91.

Variant sources present a special challenge in working with documents predating the introduction of the typewriter (circa 1880). Copies of these documents, called manuscripts, were written in longhand, often resulting in small errors. In working with old manuscripts, you should make an effort to determine whether they are the only version or whether copies were made. If copies are known to exist, you can be on the alert for them.

Authorship of a document is usually listed on the document itself. This is not always a reliable indicator. Some publications, especially recorded speeches, may be ghostwritten; and occasionally an author will use a pseudonym to conceal his or her real identity. Barzun and Graff cite the example of a historian who spent 35 years in an attempt to identify the author of a series of unsigned installments that appeared in a periodical at the time of the Civil War.[22] If a document has multiple authors, it may be impossible to determine who wrote the parts of it that are of particular relevance to your study.

The place of origin of a document is often apparent from where it is stored, or from indications in the document itself. The date when it was written may be indicated on the document. Sometimes it can be ascertained from statements in the document or from its location in a set of records or files. Dates indicated on the document should be viewed critically, for people often make innocent, but misleading, errors. For example, at the start of a new year it is not uncommon for someone to make the mistake of entering the previous year.

Knowledge of the conditions under which a document was prepared is most helpful in determining its nature and usefulness to the problem under investigation. For example, if you are studying documents from a particular institution, it is very helpful to learn everything that you can about the institution's table of organization and operating procedures. This knowledge will help you understand the purpose of certain documents and for whom they were intended. Furthermore, having this knowledge in the early stages of the study will help you limit your search to certain kinds of documents in the institution.

Internal Criticism

Internal criticism involves evaluating the accuracy and worth of the statements contained in a historical document. In examining the statements, you need to ask yourself such critical questions as, Is it probable that people would act in the way described by the writer? Is it physically possible for events to have occurred this quickly? Do the budget figures mentioned by the writer seem reasonable? In making these judgments, you need to be careful not to reject a statement just

22. Ibid., p. 107.

because the event it describes appears improbable. Most of us can recall several highly improbable events that have occurred in our own lives.

Although internal criticism can be directed at the statements themselves, it also is necessary to evaluate the person who wrote them. For example, it is important to know whether the writer was a competent observer of the events to which he or she refers. Was the writer present at the events? Was he or she an expert on the matters discussed? Was the source considered an accurate, truthful observer? Many studies in psychology have demonstrated that eyewitnesses can be extremely unreliable, especially if they are emotionally aroused or under stress at the time of the event. Even under conditions where no emotional involvement occurs, some individuals are a great deal more competent as observers than others.

Even if witnesses are competent and truthful, they may still record different accounts of the events that took place. One has only to read accounts of an event (e.g., a school board meeting) in different newspapers to determine how widely witnesses can vary in their perceptions. This does not mean necessarily that one witness is correct and the others are wrong. Nor is the converse necessarily true: that because the majority of witnesses agree in their accounts, they are right and the witness with a different perception is wrong.

Should you come across widely differing accounts of an event, your reaction might be to think there is no objective historical truth. Rather, all acounts are equally valid or equally false. (You will recall from chapter 1 that this is essentially the same view taken by some postpositivistic philosophers of science.) We question this view. Although each person's account is subjective to an extent, there is still an objective reality to be discovered. As Edward Carr noted, "It does not follow that, because a mountain appears to take on different shapes from different angles of vision, it has objectively either no shape at all or an infinity of shapes."[23] The task of the historian is to combine one or more witnesses' accounts, admittedly subjective, and to interpret them (admittedly, also a subjective process) in an attempt to discover what actually happened.

Although all accounts of historical events are subjective, they are not all necessarily biased or prejudiced. A **bias** or prejudice is a set to perceive events in such a way that certain types of facts are habitually overlooked, distorted, or falsified. The person who has an ax to grind or who has strong motives for wanting a particular version of a described event to be accepted can usually be expected to produce biased information. For example, a school superintendent, when writing an account of a school board meeting in which a dispute occurred between himself and members of the school board, will tend to present his side of the argument in the most favorable light, may subconsciously alter his position to agree with facts that have become apparent since the meeting, and may forget or deliberately omit statements of his opponents that have been

23. Carr, *What Is History?* pp. 30–31.

found to have merit since the meeting occurred. Historians must often delve to a considerable degree into the race, political party, religious group, and social status of the observer in an effort to appraise the likelihood of prejudice or bias. The use of emotionally charged or intemperate language, whether of a favorable or unfavorable nature, suggests bias and should be watched for.

People often exaggerate their own roles in important affairs. The exaggeration may not be deliberate but merely reflects the occurrences from their point of view. Many false reports can be traced to the tendency of some individuals to distort their description of events in order to make a more interesting story or call more attention to their role in them. False reports also can occur when the social or political position of individuals is such as to require them to make conventional statements rather than honest ones. For example, a school superintendent, upon being questioned about internal difficulties with principals or other members of the organization, might make claims about the high staff morale and cohesiveness. Such claims may be made to avoid compounding the problem and to avoid putting himself or herself in a negative light. For similar reasons people in public life frequently make conventional statements about political opponents. These statements may have little or no relation to their true feelings.

If you find a discrepancy between someone's public and private statements, this does not necessarily mean that they have no value as historical evidence. Rather, the discrepancy itself is evidence concerning the person involved in making the statement and about the social environment in which he or she functioned.

INTERPRETATION IN HISTORICAL RESEARCH

The Historian as Interpreter

In discussing internal criticism, we noted that witnesses to an event will report different impressions based on their competence, biases, and relationship to the event. The historian is in a similar situation:

> The facts are really not at all like fish on the fishmonger's slab. They are like fish swimming about in a vast and sometimes inaccessible ocean; and what the historian catches will depend partly on chance, but mainly on what part of the ocean he chooses to fish in and what tackle he chooses to use—these two factors being, of course, determined by the kind of fish he wants to catch. By and large, the historian will get the kind of facts he wants. History means interpretation.[24]

24. Ibid., p. 26.

If you choose to do historical research, you will need to become aware of your biases, values, and interests as they relate to the topic that you selected. Biases, values, and personal interests allow you to "see" certain aspects of past events, but not others. As you become aware of your own interpretive framework, you also will have increased sensitivity to interpretive biases of other historians who conducted research on the same or similar topics.

Because "history means interpretation," historians are constantly re-writing the past, as their interests and concerns change. The last few decades of historical research in education have seen the emergence of a **revisionist** (also called "reconstructionist") group of researchers who are viewing American educational history from a new interpretative framework:

> [Reconstructionist] Historians of education are questioning stereotyped notions of the words *reform* and *progressive* and are thinking in terms of the *irony* of school reform. Historians of education are now ready to examine the public schools as instruments of social control. Historians of education are now disclosing phenomena long hidden by official pieties: the maltreatment of immigrants and ethnic groups, the discriminatory treatment of women and minority groups, the connections between schools and politics and between education and social stratification.[25]

In contrast, earlier historians tended to look for evidence in the past of how American education contributed to the improvement of our society and of students' lives. Recent historians, it appears, have a "radical" bias in their interpretation of the past, whereas older historians had a "liberal reform" bias.

Another bias of educational historians was exposed by Bernard Bailyn in a landmark historical study published in 1960.[26] Bailyn observed that historians of American education had interpreted education predominantly as a process of formal schooling. He urged historians to overcome this bias so that they could view education "not only as formal pedagogy but as the entire process by which a culture transmits itself across the generations" (p. 14). Partly as a result of Bailyn's influence, educational historians have enlarged their perspective to conduct research on many nonschool influences that affect the learning and socialization of citizens.

Presentism is another form of bias that the educational historian needs to avoid. Presentism is the tendency to interpret past events using concepts and perspectives that originated in more recent times. For example, there has been much interest recently in educational "accountability." The historical researcher who is interested in this problem may look for evidence of how earlier educators viewed their responsibility to be accountable to the public and to the students

25. Cohen, "History of American Education," p. 329.
26. Bernard Bailyn, *Education in the Forming of American Society: Need and Opportunities for Study.* Chapel Hill: University of North Carolina Press, 1970 (reprint of 1960 ed.).

whom they served. Historians may find information in primary sources that, to them, reflects concern for accountability. Yet this may not have been at all how earlier educators viewed their sense of responsibility to the community. They may have used concepts similar in name to "accountability" but having quite different meanings. Therefore, the historian needs to discover how the various concepts were used in their own time and settings, rather than attach present meaning to them.

David Tyack's study of compulsory education illustrates well the role of interpretation in historical research.[27] As Tyack observes, the rise of compulsory education is a remarkable part of American educational history:

> I see two major phases in the history of compulsory school attendance in the United States. During the first, which lasted from [the] mid-nineteenth century to about 1890, Americans built a broad base of elementary schooling which attracted ever-growing numbers of children. Most states passed compulsory attendance legislation during these years, but generally these laws were unenforced and probably unenforceable. The notion of compulsion appears to have aroused ideological dispute at this time, but few persons paid serious attention to the organizational apparatus necessary to compel students into classrooms. Therefore, this phase might be called the *symbolic* stage. The second phase, beginning shortly before the turn of the twentieth century, might be called the *bureaucratic* stage. During this era of American education, school systems grew in size and complexity, new techniques of bureaucratic control emerged, ideological conflict over compulsion diminished, strong laws were passed, and school officials developed sophisticated techniques to bring truants into schools. By the 1920s and 1930s increasing numbers of states were requiring youth to attend high school, and by the 1950s secondary school attendance had become so customary that school-leavers were routinely seen as dropouts.[28]

The question arises, Why did schooling in the United States gradually become compulsory under force of law? Tyack examined five interpretations to see how well each answered this question. For example, the ethnocultural interpretation argues that compulsory education came about because of the belief that it would inculcate a single "correct" standard of behavior, especially among the nineteenth-century immigrants from Southern and Eastern Europe who were provoking much concern among certain religious and ethnic groups already established in this country. Another interpretation, drawn from the economic theory of human capital, states that compulsory schooling grew out of a belief that education would improve the productivity and predictability of the work force. In the words of the noted educator Horace Mann, education is "the most prolific parent of material riches."[29]

27. David B. Tyack, "Ways of Seeing: An Essay on the History of Compulsory Schooling," *Harvard Educational Review* 46 (1976): 55–89.
28. Ibid., p. 60.
29. Ibid., p. 79.

Each of the five interpretations explains some of the historical evidence, leaves other evidence unexplained, and suggests new lines of research. In Tyack's view, alternative interpretations help the historian "to gain a more complex and accurate perception of the past and a greater awareness of the ambiguous relationship between outcome and intent—both of the actors in history and of the historians who attempt to recreate their lives."[30] In planning your own historical study, you are advised to consider at least two interpretive frameworks for explaining the phenomena. Even if you choose to operate primarily within one interpretive framework, the other framework will provide a basis for assessing the worth of your research procedures and thinking.

Use of Concepts to Interpret Historical Information

Concepts are indispensable for organizing the phenomena that occurred in the past. **Concepts** group together those persons, events, or objects that share a common set of attributes. For example, without a concept such as "progressive education," a great many historical phenomena would remain separate from each other; they could not be formed into a meaningful pattern. Concepts, however, also place limits on the historical researcher's interpretation of the past. For example, a researcher who is doing a historical study of teachers may assume that the defining attribute of this concept is "holds a state certificate acknowledging completion of a college-level teacher education program." This definition of "teacher" will cause the researcher to study certain persons in a certain historical period but not others—for example, teacher aides, school volunteers, resource personnel—who would be considered teachers using a different definition.

We see then that concepts are necessary in historical research, but you need to use them cautiously. At the least, you should check the definition of each concept to determine whether it applies to the historical phenomena being studied. If necessary, provide a definition of the concept in the report.

Recent historical research has made much use of concepts from other disciplines. T. C. R. Horn and Harry Ritter made the following observation about this development:

> In general, the trend has been to look primarily to the "social sciences"—sociology, economics, political science, psychology, and anthropology—for new ideas, and lately to statistics and mathematics; to a lesser degree, historians have turned to "humanistic" disciplines such as language studies, poetics, literary criticism, and philosophy.[31]

30. Ibid., p. 89.
31. T. C. R. Horn and Harry Ritter, "Interdisciplinary History: A Historiographical Review," *The History Teacher* 19 (1986): 427.

Horn and Ritter found that all of the historical studies that won major prizes in a recent year drew upon conceptual frameworks from other disciplines.

Interdisciplinary concepts are useful tools. You should be aware, however, of how these concepts are defined in the discipline from which they originate to ensure that they are used appropriately in your study.

Causal Inference in Historical Research

An essential task of historical research consists of investigating the causes of past events. As Edward Carr stated, "The study of history is a study of causes."[32] What were the forces and events that gave rise to the intelligence-testing movement? Why did American educators adopt so readily the British open-classroom approach? How did the role of the principal originate in this country? These are the types of "causal" questions that guide many historical studies.

Causal inference in historical research is the process of reaching the conclusion that one set of events brought about, directly or indirectly, a subsequent set of events. Historians cannot "prove" that one event in the past caused another, but they can be aware of, and make explicit, the assumptions that underlie the act of ascribing causality to sequences of historical events.

An assumption that some historians make is that humans act similarly across cultures and across time. Thus, they may use a currently accepted causal pattern to explain an apparently similar pattern in the past. For example, a historian might find an instance in nineteenth-century American education when college students stopped attending classes and started attacking the school's administration; this event was preceded in time by administrative rulings abridging students' rights and privileges. The historian might infer— perhaps correctly—that the rulings led to the student revolt, reasoning that this was the apparent chain of events in the student revolts of the 1960s. Other historians, however, believe that historical events are unique; that is, history does not repeat itself. Occurrences at one point in history cannot be used to help explain occurrences at another point in historical time.

In making causal inferences, historians should be aware of their assumptions about the causative factors sometimes invoked to explain the course of history. Historians have emphasized various types of causes in their attempts to explain past events. They have attributed significant historical occurrences to the actions of certain key persons (the "great man" view of history), the operation of powerful ideologies, advances in science and technology, economic factors, geographical factors, sociological factors, and psychological factors. Some historians take an eclectic view and explain historical events in terms of a combination of all these views.

32. Carr, *What Is History?* p. 113.

It appears that the more we know about the antecedents of a historical event, the more likely we are to discover possible causes of the event. In the example stated above, the historian could make a plausible inference that the school's administrative rulings were a factor in causing the student revolt. But was it *the* cause? Suppose the historian also discovered that other events were occurring simultaneously that might upset students, e.g., the imminence of war, revolts of the citizenry against government tax increases, or a rapidly increasing enrollment that strained the college's facilities. All these circumstances are potential causes, and there may be others that the historian has not yet discovered. Therefore, the historian would have difficulty in justifying the attribution of a historical event to a single cause.

It is more defensible to identify an antecedent event as *a* cause than as *the* cause. Also, historians, by their choice of language, can convey their interpretation of the certainty of the causal link ("it is highly likely that" or "it is possible that") and strength of the causal link ("it was a major influence" or "it was but one of many events that influenced").

Generalizing from Historical Evidence

As in other types of educational research, historians cannot study the entire population of persons, settings, events, and objects that interest them. Instead, they usually study only a small sample. This sample is determined by the available records, which may not be at all representative. For example, suppose a historian studied the diaries, correspondence, and other written records of teachers in the 1800s in order to understand teaching conditions then. The study necessarily will be limited to documents that remain from this period. Therefore, the historian needs to bear in mind that teachers who were interested in making a written description of their work may not have been typical of teachers in general. One way to determine generalizability is to look for consistency across teachers in different circumstances. For example, did teachers who wrote about their work for publication describe similar conditions as did teachers who wrote about their work in private diaries and correspondence?

Another problem of **generalizability in historical research** occurs in interpretation of historical evidence relating to a single individual. For example, the historian may come across a document in which the individual being studied takes a stand on a particular educational issue of the time. It is difficult to generalize from this one document that the individual consistently held the same opinion across time.

As in any research project the findings are strengthened by increasing the sample of data on which they are based. Therefore, it is advisable to search for as many primary and secondary sources relating to the topic as possible. Where the evidence is limited, researchers should limit the generalizability of their interpretations accordingly.

The branch of historical research known as *quantitative history* is improving the historian's ability to study representative samples of the phenomena in which they are interested. The computer has made possible the analysis of data about large groups of people represented in census reports, school records, and similar documents.

WRITING THE HISTORICAL RESEARCH DISSERTATION

The organization of the historical research dissertation does not usually follow the chapter outline for educational research dissertations presented in chapter 21. Reports of historical research have no standard format. The particular problem or topic investigated determines how the presentation of findings will be organized.

One obvious method of organization is to present the historical facts in chronological order. Thus, each chapter of the dissertation might cover a discrete period of time in the life of an individual, institution, or educational movement. The other obvious method of organization is to present the historical facts according to topic or theme. For example, if the purpose of the study was to examine how different school districts came to establish a kindergarten program, the dissertation might have a separate chapter for each school district included in the study.

Neither method of organization is satisfactory for some studies. Suppose the researcher's purpose is to describe the development of a particular university. The researcher may organize the dissertation chronologically, with each chapter devoted to different periods of time. This approach, though, may obscure certain themes that have continuity across time periods (e.g., the development of the university's relationship to the government as a prime research contractor, the development of its graduate school, and the development of its undergraduate curriculum). Thematic continuity could be achieved by having a separate chapter for each aspect of the university's development, but then one would lose a sense of the institution's unity and overall state of development at particular points in time. Also, it would be difficult for the researcher to show how the various areas of the university's development influenced and related to each other.

A possible solution to this problem is to combine the chronological and thematic approach. Each chapter might cover a discrete time period, but the internal organization of the chapters might be thematic. Ultimately, the decision to use a particular organizational pattern depends upon the questions that the historical researcher has chosen to ask.

The major part of the dissertation probably will consist of the chapters in which the researcher's findings are presented. In addition, the researcher may wish to have a separate chapter that reviews other historians' interpretation of the same or a similar topic. The methodology used in the study may be presented in a separate chapter, especially if the historical sources posed unusual problems of external or internal criticism. The researcher's interpretations and reflections on the interpretive process are sometimes presented in a separate chapter.

Choice of words must be considered carefully in writing the dissertation, because they reflect the researcher's interpretive framework. We have noted above, for example, how the use of certain words can convey differences in probability and degree of causal relationships between past events. Adjectives have particular interpretive significance. Suppose that the researcher decides to describe a particular institution as a "major" university. The use of this adjective is interpretive, but does it reflect the researcher's own awe of the institution or does it reflect the expert judgment of other educators? The researcher needs to think carefully about the reasons for choosing this particular word in describing the topic of the research study. This is not to suggest that the use of words having affective or value connotations should be avoided. Without the presence of such words, the historical research dissertation would be exceedingly boring; and it would fail in its responsibility to reconstruct the past so that it becomes alive for the reader.

EXAMPLES OF HISTORICAL RESEARCH IN EDUCATION

The Development of Japanese Educational Policy

As we stated earlier in the chapter, current social issues often provide the stimulus for historical studies in education. Such was the case in a recent study of changes in Japanese educational policy during the past century.[33] The study was conducted by Edward Beauchamp, who began his report by observing.

> The appointment of an Ad Hoc Reform Council, or *Rinkyoshin*, on 21 August 1984 was a logical culmination to a lengthy period of concern in Japan over a set of widely perceived educational problems and the future prospects for Japanese education. The charge given to the council by Prime Minister Yasuhiro Nakasone was clear: "to consider basic strategies for necessary reforms . . . so as to secure such education as will be compatible with the social changes and cultural developments of our country."[34]

33. Edward R. Beauchamp, "The Development of Japanese Educational Policy, 1945–1985," *History of Education Quarterly* 27 (1987): 299–324.
34. Ibid., p. 299.

By studying past educational reforms in Japan, Beauchamp provided us with a basis for understanding that country's present problems in education and the directions that reform might take.

The primary data for the study were key policy and legal documents issued by governmental agencies over the past century: the 1890 Imperial Rescript on Education issued by the Emperor Meiji; the Fundamental Law of Education and the School Education Law of 1947; the Report on the Long-Range Educational Plan Oriented Toward the Doubling of Income issued by the Economic Council of Japan's Economic Planning Agency in 1960; the Ministry of Education's *Educational Standards in Japan,* published in 1970; and a report issued by the Organization for Economic Cooperation and Development in 1971. Beauchamp also referred to secondary sources containing information and interpretations about Japanese education.

The primary method for organizing the data and interpretations was chronological. This method of organization is reflected in the report's headings: Japanese Education, 1868–1945; The Occupation of Japan, 1945–52; The Post-Occupation Period, 1952–60; Expansion in the 1960s and 1970s; The Third Major Reform Period, 1978–Present. Beauchamp organized policy developments in each of these chronological periods more or less thematically. The primary theme was policy developments at different levels of schooling—elementary, secondary, and postsecondary. One of the interesting features of Beauchamp's report is his analysis of how changes in policy rippled through each of these levels of schooling.

The key concepts used by Beauchamp to make sense of changes in Japanese education are "reform" and "policy." Each of these concepts is widely used in current discussions of American education. We need to ask, however, whether the meaning that Americans ascribe to these terms applies to Japanese education. For example, the term "reform" implies perceived weaknesses in the educational system and also that these weaknesses are so serious as to require a radical change in the system. It is not clear from Beauchamp's report whether the changes in Japanese education that he highlights as significant had these qualities.

The concept of "policy" is even more problematic. Just what is a policy? Beauchamp's primary data were documents, which can be considered official statements of policy. In the United States at least, there are often significant differences between stated policy and implemented policy. Stated policy (e.g., school board directives, adopted curriculum guides) is often ignored or modified in practice by those to whom the policy is directed. Beauchamp did not address the issue of whether the same discrepancies might exist in Japanese education.

Another point to consider is that members of commissions or governing bodies that prepare the type of documents analyzed by Beauchamp often disagree strongly among themselves. The final policy document is often a compromise statement that does not reflect conflicts between members representing different interest groups. An analysis of these conflicts might reveal more about the status of policy in an educational system than would a public document.

These criticisms do not necessarily invalidate Beauchamp's conclusions. Their intent is to demonstrate the importance of carefully analyzing the key concepts used to interpret historical data, especially when the data pertain to another culture.

We stated earlier in the chapter that a major purpose of historical research is to identify the cause-and-effect patterns in past events. This purpose is reflected throughout Beauchamp's report, as in this statement:

> Educational policy during the 1960s and much of the 1970s was consciously designed to foster economic development. Indeed, there is little doubt that since the middle of the 1950s the interests of industry have been extremely influential in shaping educational policy.[35]

Beauchamp's argument in this statement is that lobbying by industry (cause) was a major influence on the development of educational policy (effect) during the time period being studied. Various types of evidence are presented in the report to support this causal argument.

Beauchamp also attempted to explain the persistence of Japan's extremely demanding entrance examinations for college, despite the fact that they are criticized by most Japanese. He found evidence to support three different explanations for their persistence: "(1) a deeply ingrained Confucian legacy; (2) powerful vested interests; and (3) too few places for too many applicants."[36] This is a good example of the principle that significant societal phenomena often have multiple causes, as well as multiple effects. Therefore, historians need to study as much of the historical context as possible in order to avoid oversimplifying the progression of cause and effect in past events.

One of Beauchamp's major generalizations is that each major reform in Japanese education over the past century was followed by a period of reflection and subsequent modification to bring it in line with traditional Japanese values. Therefore, in attempting to understand Japan's current reform efforts, we would be well advised to learn as much as possible about that country's traditional values.

Another generalization is that each reform was influenced by foreign educational models. Beauchamp was careful to note, however, that this generalization is not likely to apply to the current wave of reform in Japan. This is because all of the countries to which Japan has looked for models in the past are themselves engaged in reform. This discontinuity in a historical pattern raised for Beauchamp a significant question:

35. Ibid., p. 310.
36. Ibid., p. 315.

Can the Japanese *create* a new model which will not only meet their needs in the twenty-first century, but will also serve as a model from which the rest of the world might learn?[37]

It is customary to think of historical research as the study of the past. Beauchamp's study illustrates that historical research is much more than this. The study of Japan's past educational policies provides a valuable basis for understanding its current policy-making activities; for making predictions about the outcomes of these activities; and for suggesting the significance of these activities for policymakers in other countries.

Antecedents of Village High Schools in Alaska

A doctoral dissertation by Margo Zuelow provides an example of how historical research can form one part of a larger study.[38] The major purpose of her study was to examine the recent development of self-contained village high schools in isolated areas of Alaska. The study was in three parts: a formative evaluation (see chapter 17) of a school district that had instituted these schools, a review of the literature to determine techniques that other societies have developed for delivering instruction to geographically isolated areas, and research on historical antecedents of the new village high schools.

The search for primary sources relating to Alaskan secondary education required two trips to Alaska, according to Zuelow. One trip was to the Alaska State Department of Education and the Historical Library in Juneau; the other was to the Center for Northern Education Research in Fairbanks. Among the documents examined were: the minutes of the State Department of Education; the reports of the Alaska commissioner of education; the annual reports of the U.S. secretary of the interior; the *Alaska Teacher*, which is the journal of the National Education Association affiliate in Alaska; and clippings from major Alaskan newspapers on education issues.

Zuelow noted that early Alaskan documents usually were based on personal observation. For example, the early reports of the Alaska commissioner of education were typed by the commissioner and were in the form of a travel narrative describing his inspection trips to all the schools in the territory. As the Alaskan agencies concerned with education grew, the reports generally were written by department heads, who described the work and observations of their subordinates. Zuelow found that different reports often conflicted on the specific date that an event occurred, although they usually agreed on the month.

37. Ibid., p. 324.
38. Margo C. Zuelow, "An Historical Perspective for, and Evaluation of, Changes in Secondary Education Programs for Rural Alaskans in One Regional Education Attendance Area" (Ph.D. dissertation, University of Oregon, 1977).

Zuelow chose a chronological format to present the historical antecedents of current Alaskan secondary education policy. Her two major chronological divisions and stages within each are:

1. Pre-Statehood (–1959)
   a. Alaska's First Settlers (–1741)
   b. Russian Discovery (1741–85)
   c. Russian Control of Education (1785–1867)
   d. United States Governmental Neglect (1867–99)
   e. United States Governmental Schools (1884–99)
   f. Introduction of Reindeer (1890–1959)
   g. Territorial Schools for Non-Native Children (1890–1959)
   h. Schools outside Incorporated Towns (1901–59)
2. Statehood and the Alaska Constitution (1959–76)
   a. State Responsibility Recognized (1959–64)
   b. Johnson-O'Malley Act Reorganized (1965–76)

These stages and divisions reflect Zuelow's interpretation of patterns of events and influences on Alaskan education policy. Note that the stages are not necessarily discrete phases, but sometimes overlap each other (e.g., 1d and 1e).

Zuelow identified several themes that characterize the development of Alaskan secondary education. Probably the most significant is the issue of local control of education by Native Alaskans. She found that "up until the 1960's, Alaska Natives were not consulted on legislative action which would affect the education of their children."[39] A critical event occurred in April 1969, when Native Alaskan spokesmen had an opportunity to present their views before a hearing of the Special Indian Subcommittee of the U.S. Senate. The spokesmen strongly criticized the boarding schools, which at that time provided much of the secondary education for rural Native Alaskan students. The boarding schools required the students to live away from their home communities, with adverse consequences. The spokesmen advocated the development of local village high schools and greater involvement of the Native Alaskan community in school matters.

Zuelow's historical analysis provides a valuable perspective for examining recent developments in Alaskan education. The formation of small village high schools, which may serve as few as five students, can be questioned from the standpoint of economic efficiency and educational quality. Yet history suggests other factors, such as local control and appropriateness of curriculum, that need to be considered in judging these schools. It may be that the village high school provides benefits that offset the high costs and other apparent disadvantages.

---

39. Ibid., p. 74.

Also, Zuelow's historical analysis identified solutions that did not work in the past, especially the notion of the regional boarding school. Although the past is by no means a certain guide to the future, it is useful in suggesting caution. Any future proposal for a regional boarding school (or other change) should cause one to ask whether conditions have changed sufficiently to augur success despite failures in the past.

MISTAKES SOMETIMES MADE IN DOING HISTORICAL RESEARCH

1. The researcher selects a problem or topic for which historical sources are inaccessible or nonexistent.
2. Makes excessive use of secondary historical sources.
3. Fails to subject historical sources to external and internal criticism.
4. Is unaware of personal values, biases, and interests that influence selection and interpretation of historical sources.
5. Uses concepts from other disciplines inappropriately to explain past events.
6. Makes unwarranted causal inferences or refers to a particular factor as *the* cause rather than *a* cause.
7. Generalizes to a larger set of people, places, or institutions than is justified by the available historical information.
8. Lists facts without synthesizing them into meaningful chronological and thematic patterns.

ANNOTATED REFERENCES

Barzun, Jacques, and Graff, Henry F. *The Modern Researcher*, 4th ed. San Diego: Harcourt, Brace Jovanovich, 1985.

Provides a comprehensive survey of the historian's work. Techniques of fact finding, historical criticism, and interpretation are presented. In addition, there is an extensive section on procedures for writing the historical report.

Brickman, William W. *Educational Historiography: Tradition, Theory, and Technique.* Cherry Hill, NJ: Emeritus, Inc., 1982.

A revised edition of a classic textbook on methods of historical research. It includes an extended discussion of most of the topics discussed in the chapter.

Button, H. Warren. "Why and When History Doesn't Work: The Case of Miss Purington." *American Behavioral Scientist* 30 (1986): 28–41.

An entertaining, brief discussion of various flaws of historical reasoning and writing. It would be a good article to read before undertaking a historical study as a reminder of what *not* to do.

Carr, Edward Hallett. *What Is History?* New York: Random House, 1967.

Published lectures. A classic reference on the nature of historical investigation. The problem of causal inference in historical research, the nature of historical facts, the historian's role as interpreter, and the uses of history are among the topics covered by this eminent historian. "Must" reading for the student who wishes an in-depth understanding of what history is.

Graff, Harvey J. " 'The New Math': Quantification in the 'New' History, and the History of Education." *Urban Education* 11(1977): 403–440.

Discusses how recent historical research has been influenced by the use of quantification, which the author defines as "a reliance and a recognition of the peculiar value of standard and comparable numerical data for the examination of a wide range of important questions." Also contains a brief review of quantitative historical studies of literacy, school attendance, higher education, the family, the economics of education, and the role of elite groups in municipal educational reform.

Sherman, Robert R., ed. *Understanding History of Education*, 2nd ed. Cambridge, MA: Shenkman, 1984.

Collection of readings. Covers several important topics relating to historical research—the uses of educational history, the nature of historical facts, causation, oral history, and quantitative history.

Tuchman, Barbara W. *Practicing History.*New York: Knopf, 1981.

Collection of essays by one of the most popular historians of our time. The three parts of the book cover the craft of doing historical research, the uses of history, and examples of the author's historical studies. The essays are worth reading not only for their content, but also as models of good historical writing.

SELF-CHECK TEST

Circle the correct answer to each of the following questions. An answer key is provided on page 884.

1. In historical research the wide range of written and printed materials recorded for the purpose of transmitting information is called
   a. relics.
   b. documents.
   c. primary sources.
   d. preliminary sources.
2. In historical research the physical objects related to the period being studied are called
   a. documents.
   b. primary documents.
   c. secondary sources.
   d. relics.
3. In other forms of research the review of the literature is considered a preliminary step to gathering data. In historical research the review of the literature is usually

    a. omitted.
    b. the step providing the research data.
    c. the step conducted after the data-gathering phase.
    d. not of great importance.
4. The type of evaluation aimed at determining whether the evidence being evaluated is authentic is termed
    a. internal criticism.
    b. external criticism.
    c. external validation.
    d. historical criticism.
5. Internal criticism of a document
    a. is usually more difficult than external criticism.
    b. is directed at evaluating the writer.
    c. is assisted by other accounts of the same events.
    d. All of the above are correct.
6. Presentism is defined as
    a. the belief that the present is more important than the historical past.
    b. the use of contemporary concepts to interpret past events.
    c. the belief that the present cannot be understood by study of past events.
    d. the set of assumptions underlying contemporary revisionist history.
7. Causal inference in historical research is a process in which the historian
    a. proves that one historical event determined another event.
    b. uses internal criticism to establish causal links between documents written at different points in time.
    c. uses interpretation to ascribe causality to a sequence of historical events.
    d. demonstrates the unique nature of each historical event.
8. Reports of historical research
    a. are organized chronologically.
    b. are organized thematically.
    c. can be organized chronologically or thematically.
    d. are organized no differently from reports of experimental research.
9. One of Bernard Bailyn's contributions to historical research in education was
    a. to originate the "liberal reform" framework for reinterpreting historical events in education.
    b. to originate a new theory of causal inference in historical research.
    c. to bring "accountability" to historical research in education.
    d. to include nonschool influences on learning as a legitimate topic for historical research in education.
10. Quantitative analysis of historical data is intended primarily to facilitate
    a. external criticism.
    b. internal criticism.
    c. study of large samples of populations.
    d. study of secondary sources.

APPLICATION PROBLEMS

The following problems are designed to give you practice in applying significant concepts and research procedures explained in the chapter. Most do not have a single correct answer. For feedback, compare your answers with the sample answers on pages 904–905.

1. A historian is planning to do research on the origins of intelligence testing in this country. List three preliminary sources he or she might consult, and three possible repositories of historical data relating to intelligence testing.

2. Suppose you were doing a historical study concerned with allocation of funds to teacher salaries, books, other instructional materials, plant maintenance and operation, and administrative costs in three rural elementary schools during the period from 1900 to 1930. Your main sources for this study are the account books for each school, in which the principals listed by date each expenditure as it occurred and entered a brief description. In studying these sources, how would you prepare note cards for use in your research?

3. Suppose you are doing a historical study on the teaching of pseudo sciences in U.S. public schools during the period 1870–99. You find the following article in the April 15, 1891, issue of the *Sonoma Farmer,* a rural weekly published in California:

Wonders of the Science of Phrenology

Local citizens attending the County Fair this week are being amazed by Professor Horatio Horton, a leading practitioner of the science of Phrenology. Professor Horton can make infallible analyses of the character and personality of any man or woman by feeling the bumps on the individual's head. Most persons overheard by your reporter agreed that the Professor's analyses of people out of the audience were uncanny.

After the performance your reporter interviewed the Professor in his dressing room and learned that he is a leader in the movement to teach Phrenology in the public schools. The Professor himself has taught the science to thousands of students in colleges and high schools throughout most of the civilized nations of the world. Phrenology is now a required subject in the secondary schools of France, Italy and several other European countries. Students in these countries usually devote a year to the study of this valuable science.

The Professor strongly recommends that local citizens apply pressure to county officials to bring about inclusion of Phrenology in the local curriculum. He is available to give teachers a short course in the science and has also written several books and pamphlets that would be useful to students.

Your reporter feels that adequate training in Phrenology should be provided in our schools as soon as possible. After all, your children are entitled to a modern education.

List four reasons why the accuracy of the information might be questioned.

4. A historian is planning to do research on how early-nineteenth-century school officials and psychologists influenced each other with respect to advocacy of intelligence testing. (a) What concepts does the historian need to define in doing this research? Why? (b) What are several factors that will affect the generalizability of the historian's findings?

SUGGESTION SHEET

If your last name starts with letters from Stv to Tuc, please complete the Suggestion Sheet at the end of the book while this chapter is still fresh in your mind.

Part VII

DATA PROCESSING AND REPORTING

Procedures for processing research data should be planned before the data actually are collected. This planning can suggest ways of recording data at the time of collection that will speed up subsequent processing and reduce costs. The computer has emerged as the dominant tool for data processing and analysis, and so you should become conversant with this technology. These topics are discussed in chapter 20.

Most scientific advances are the culmination of small contributions made by many researchers. For this reason it is important to report the findings of your study, even if it is small in scale. The two most common ways of reporting research findings are to give a paper at a professional meeting and to publish an article in a professional journal. These topics are discussed in chapter 21.

OVERVIEW

Even small studies can generate a substantial amount of data. This chapter describes ways to process the data efficiently and accurately. It begins by explaining how to score standard tests and other measures, and how to organize the scores for statistical analysis. The main part of the chapter concerns procedures for using a mainframe computer, personal computer, or handheld calculator to do statistical analyses. The chapter concludes with procedures for storing data and calculations for later reference.

OBJECTIVES

After studying this chapter you should be able to:

1. Describe procedures for handscoring or machine-scoring tests and other objective instruments.
2. Describe procedures for scoring unstructured or self-developed measures.
3. Prepare hand data cards to organize small amounts of data.
4. Prepare an I.D. code that includes a unique identifier and subgroup codes.
5. Describe the types of computers and statistical software available for processing research data.
6. Organize research data using a computer recording form.
7. Describe procedures for using a computer to enter, analyze, display, and manage research data.
8. Explain how to check data analyses done by calculator or computer for accuracy.
9. Describe at least two desirable procedures to follow in storing research data.

INTRODUCTION

After collecting research data, you will need to convert them to a form that permits efficient, accurate statistical analysis. Tests and other objective instruments must be scored using an answer key. Qualitative data collected by interview or observation must be coded if they are to be subjected to statistical analysis. The resulting scores must be recorded in such a way that they can be analyzed by means of a calculator or computer. These tasks require careful planning so that you can learn as much as possible from the data and be confident that your statistical findings are accurate.

SCORING OF TESTS AND OTHER MEASURES

Steps in Scoring Standard Tests

The first step in scoring standard tests is to review the test manual and the test itself in order to become completely familiar with the scoring procedures. Scoring keys are provided with standard tests. The key that you plan to use should be checked against the test items to ensure that it is correct.

Standard tests generally are designed so that students record their responses on a separate answer sheet rather than in the test booklet. If you wish, you can use a window key to score the answer sheets. A **window key** (also called a "template") is a sheet of stiff paper approximately the same size as the test sheet on which students record their answers. Small holes ("windows") that overlay the correct choice for each test item are cut in the sheet of stiff paper. The scorer then can place the window key over each student's test sheet and quickly count the number of correct test items by checking each "window" to determine whether a pencil mark has been placed there. The scorer should check whether the student marked more than one choice for a particular test item. The test manual may specify scoring rules for dealing with multiple responses to an item. Otherwise you will need to develop your own rules.

When faced with a lengthy test-scoring job, you should work for periods of one or two hours rather than attempt to complete the entire job at one sitting. After an hour or two, most people become tired and bored, which leads to mistakes. If periods of study or recreation are alternated with periods of test scoring and other clerical work, you will find the work less fatiguing and will make fewer errors.

After scoring all the answer sheets, you should select every tenth copy or so for rescoring. Each error that you detect should be tallied, with an indication of its size and direction, and the test item on which it occurred. After rescoring the sample of answer sheets, you should examine the error pattern and decide whether it warrants rescoring all the answer sheets. If only a few small errors are found, they are not likely to affect the research results.

Following the scoring process, the tests should be packaged and labeled with the date of testing, the subjects tested, and other pertinent information. This step is critical. You may forget these details between the time of scoring and the time when you analyze the data and write your report. Hours can be wasted in tracking down details at a later time, whereas only a few minutes are needed to record them at the time of scoring the tests.

Machine Scoring of Answer Sheets

Many universities and school districts have scoring machines that you can use at low cost. These machines will save you a great deal of time if you have many answer sheets to score.

If you plan to use a scoring machine, you should determine how it operates prior to data collection. Many of these machines will only score a certain kind of answer sheet called an NEC form. There are a variety of NEC forms, each having a different configuration of bubbles. Subjects fill in a bubble—usually with a number 2 pencil—to indicate their response to an item. You should select an appropriate NEC form on which subjects can record their responses to your research test, attitude scale, questionnaire, or other instrument.

One part of the scoring machine consists of a **scanner.** It scans the bubbles on each answer sheet and records the ones that have been filled in by the subject. The scanner is easily confused by stray pencil marks. Therefore, you should check the answer sheets beforehand and erase stray marks that could interfere with the scanner's operation. Also, prior to feeding in the answer sheets, you will need to use the scanner's programing feature to indicate how each item on the answer sheet is to be scored. This step is equivalent to creating a window key, or template, which was described above. The scanner can be programmed to mark an item wrong, or as a nonresponse, if the subject filled in more than one bubble for an item.

The other part of a scoring machine is a computer and printer. Most scoring-machine computers can compute a total score for each sheet and prepare a printout listing the names of all the subjects and their total score on the measure. Some of these computers also can do descriptive statistics on the total scores and item scores. Another good feature of these computers is that they can prepare a computer tape of the subjects' total scores and item scores. This tape can be used to transmit the score data directly into the computer that you will use for more complex statistical analyses. This capability saves you the job of having to type each and every bit of data into the other computer.

Scoring Unstructured or Self-Developed Measures

The measurement of some variables requires the development of new measures or new ways of scoring existing measures. In either case the procedures for scoring the variables should be fully developed in a pilot study.

The pilot study should include subjects similar to those who will be tested in the main study. You can make any changes in scoring rules that seem appropriate, and you can make changes in the measure itself. After developing the scoring rules, you will need to administer the measure to another pilot group in order to determine whether these rules yield valid, reliable scores. The scoring rules should not be used on data from the main sample until they are completely satisfactory.

Once the scoring of the measure for the main sample has started, the scoring procedure must not be changed even if you see problems with it. Otherwise some subjects will be scored on one basis and others on a different basis. The alternative of rescoring the responses of all subjects is also questionable unless the measure is highly objective. This is because the previous scoring may affect your perception of the subjects' responses. One solution to the problem is to revise the scoring system and have new raters use it. The best solution, however, is to avoid the problem altogether by developing and testing the scoring procedures with a pilot sample.

It is important to prepare a document recording the scoring procedures developed specifically for the study. It should be written as a set of specific steps to be followed. Also, definitions and procedures for handling ambiguous responses should be provided. During the scoring of the measures, you should refer back to this document, or there may be a tendency to drift away from the procedures. The document should be included in the research report to help others understand the scoring procedures and to enable others to use them in their own studies.

ORGANIZING DATA FOR STATISTICAL ANALYSIS

Hand Data Cards

After all the measures have been scored, you should enter the data on a form that lends itself to the planned statistical analysis. A suitable form for data that will be analyzed by computer is described later in the chapter. In this section we describe the use of **hand data cards,** which are suitable for small amounts of data that can be analyzed by hand.

All the data for a subject are placed on a separate hand data card. An example of a hand data card with a key describing each entry label is shown in figure 20.1. Note that the card includes a few extra blanks in case additional variables are generated in the course of the data analysis. Once you have prepared one card with the entry labels printed on it, you can have others photocopied at little expense.

Test scores and other quantitative information can be recorded directly on the hand data card. Some information must be quantified, however, so that it can be analyzed by statistical techniques. For example, a number code can be assigned to such information as gender, social class, homeroom teacher, and school district. In figure 20.1, the three schools in the study are designated by this type of number code.

I.D. Codes

Subjects in a research sample usually are assigned an **I.D. code** (identification code) for two purposes. The first purpose, as explained in chapter 3, is to protect the subject's privacy. Make a list of each person's name accompanied by an I.D.

I.D.	_____	Ach 9/81	_____
Sex	_____	Ach 5/82	_____
D.B.	_____	CEFT	_____
School	_____		_____
Group	_____		_____
F.O.	_____		_____
IQ	_____		_____

I.D.   Pupil's identification number
Sex   1 = boy; 2 = girl
D.B.   Date of birth: first two digits give month, second two give year (Example: 0273 = February 1973)
School   1 = Harrison; 2 = Washington; 3 = Horace Mann
Group   1 = Experimental; 2 = Control
F.O.   Level of father's occupation using Warner scale
IQ   Wechsler Intelligence Scale for Children, total IQ score
Ach 9/81   Comprehensive Test of Basic Skills, level 1, form S, total score
Ach 5/82   Comprehensive Test of Basic Skills, level 1, form T, total score
CEFT   Children's Embedded Figures Test, total score
—   Other blanks may be used to record additional data

Figure 20.1   Sample Hand Data Card and Key

code. Access to the list is restricted and is used only when necessary for research purposes. The subjects are identified by their I.D. code in all data analyses. The second reason for using an I.D. code is that it is easier to identify a subject by numerical characters than by the subject's actual name, which involves alphabetic characters.

Each subject in the research sample must be given a unique number as part of the I.D. code. This is easily accomplished by giving the first person in the list of subjects an I.D. code of 01, the second person an I.D. code of 02, and so on. This unique identifier should have as many digits as there are in the number that represents the size of the total sample. If there are 250 students in the sample, then the first student on the list would be assigned an I.D. code of 001, the second student an I.D. code of 002, and so on.

Sometimes you will want to extend the I.D. code in order to identify the subjects further as members of particular subgroups. For example, the first three digits of an I.D. code could be used as the unique identifier; the fourth digit could be used to identify the subject as male (0) or female (1); and the fifth digit could be used to identify whether the subject attended a public school (1), a private school (2), or a denominational school (3). A subject with an I.D. code of 09512 would be a female attending a private school who is identified on the master list as subject number 95. Extended codes of this type are useful if you plan to do subgroup analyses.

Research variables also can be identified by an I.D. code. Computer programs generally require that each variable be labeled by a discrete number or by a brief descriptor. For example, the variable "reading achievement" might be identified by the numerical code 01 or by the descriptor READACH. In the computer printout that presents the results of the statistical analyses, the I.D. code is used as a label to identify the results pertaining to a particular variable.

USE OF THE COMPUTER TO PROCESS DATA

Computer Hardware and Software

Computers have two main parts: hardware and software. The **hardware** is the machine itself. If you have a large amount of data to analyze, you will need to use a mainframe computer, which has the capacity to perform many millions of calculations per minute. These computers are very expensive, and therefore they usually are only available at university and college computer centers. One mainframe computer, such as the IBM 360 or DEC-VAX, can use its time-sharing features to serve the computing needs of an entire campus.

Many personal computers, especially the IBM PC and PC-compatibles, now have the capability to perform sophisticated statistical analyses on fairly large amounts of data. The main advantage of these computers over a mainframe computer is their convenience. A personal computer can be used when and where you wish. Use of the mainframe computer requires a trip to the computer center or computer terminal. Also, there may be restrictions on its availability and charges for its use.

Some handheld calculators have the capability of performing statistical analyses by simply having you press an appropriate function key. Less sophisticated calculators are also useful if you have just a small amount of research data to be analyzed, and if the analyses are limited to simple descriptive and inferential statistics.

The other part of a computer is the software. **Software** consists of the programs that actually manage and analyze the data that you enter into the computer.

The most commonly used set of computer programs in educational research is SPSS-X, which is an acronym for "Statistical Package for the Social Sciences—Version 10." **SPSS-X** is a comprehensive, integrated collection of computer programs for managing, analyzing, and displaying data. SPSS-X programs can perform virtually every statistical procedure described in the preceding chapters of this book. Most universities and colleges have SPSS-X available for their mainframe computers. A version of SPSS-X is also available for some personal computers.

Another widely available set of integrated statistical programs for mainframe computers is **SAS** (pronounced "sass"). It is more difficult to use than SPSS-X, but it has more capabilities.

An increasing amount of statistical analysis software is available for personal computers. You should check the soundness of this software before using it. Some programs have not been fully tested for "bugs" (errors) or do not follow standard algorithms to arrive at a solution; they may therefore give spurious results.

Organizing Data for Entry into a Computer

Most quantitative research studies generate sufficient data to warrant use of a computer for data analysis. The initial step in planning a computer analysis is to organize the data for entry into the computer. This step is necessary because data cannot be keyboarded into the computer any way you wish. (By "keyboarding," we mean the act of typing the data using the computer's keyboard.)

Planning for data entry is facilitated by use of a **computer recording form.** These forms can be purchased at office supply stores and computer centers, or you can make your own. A sample computer recording form is shown in figure 20.2. Note that the form is a grid—also called a matrix—containing 80 columns and a set of rows. The reason for the 80 columns is that the typical computer screen can display 80 columns of information.

The data for each subject in the sample are put on one row of the form. With rare exceptions, data for two or more subjects are never put on the same row. Thus, the five rows on which data are recorded in figure 20.2 represent data for five different subjects.

Each column, or set of columns, on the form is used to represent a different variable. Scores for two or more different variables are never recorded in the same columns. The number of columns required to record data for a variable is called the **variable field length.** In figure 20.2, columns 20–28 are students' scores on three subtests. Scores on each test can range from 0 to 80.0 in 0.5 increments. Therefore, the variable field length for each subtest is 3 columns. Although the scores have a decimal value, the decimal points usually are not recorded on the form. A procedure that is described below is used to tell the computer program the location of the decimal point in the variable field.

Some columns can be left blank so as to organize the data visually. For example, columns 6, 19, and 29 are left blank to set off the I.D. code and another piece of information (columns 1–5), the data for test A (columns 7–18), the data for test B (columns 20–28), and the data for a questionnaire (columns 30–39).

Suppose the research data for each subject will not fit in 80 columns. It is necessary then to split the data into several records. A **record** is the amount of data that is included in the 80 columns. (Under certain conditions explained

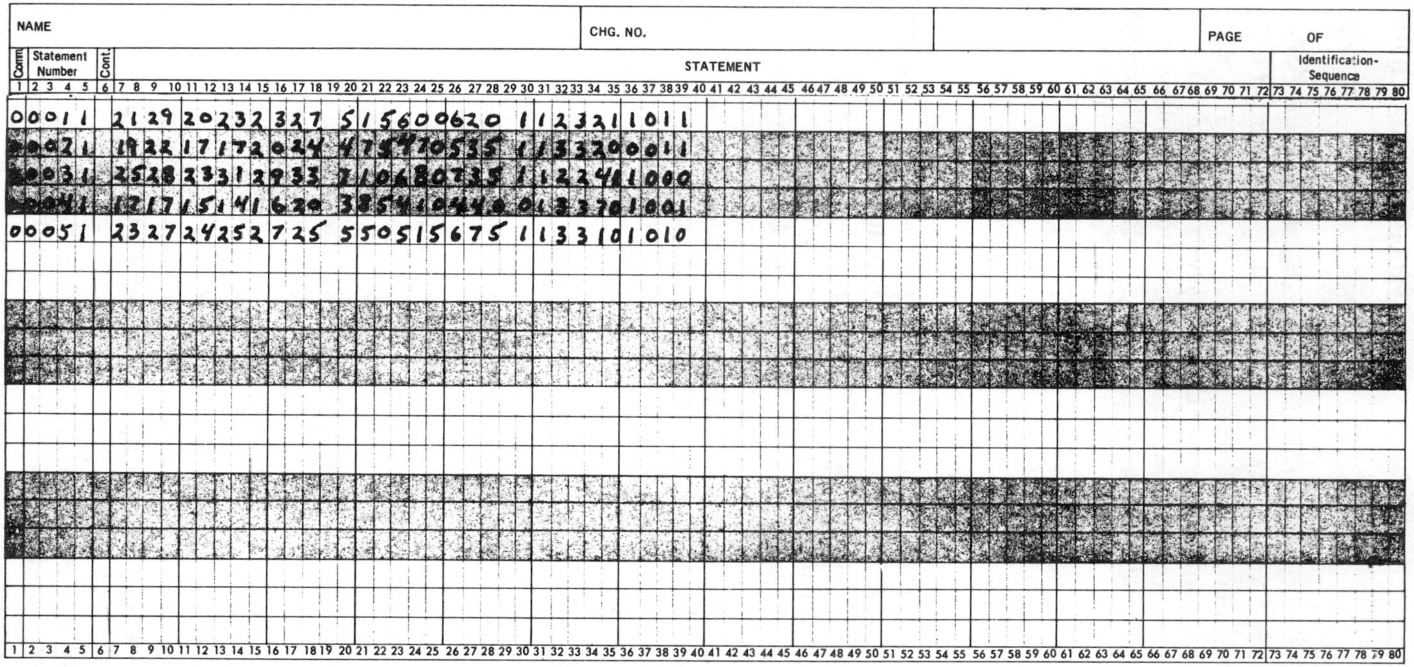

Figure 20.2 Computer Recording Form and Key

LEGEND:
1–4 Student number
5 Record number
7–18 Test A scores (2 column fields)
20–28 Test B scores (3 column fields)
30–39 Questionnaire scores

below, a record can include more than 80 columns.) When the 80 columns are filled, you can create a new record and continue recording the subject's data. Each record is given a sequence number so that it can be easily identified. The record number for the 80 columns shown in figure 20.2 is in column 5 ("1"). Each record repeats the subject's I.D. code (usually in the first columns) so that the different records for each subject can be compiled for the statistical analysis.

Some computer programs do not require you to organize your data into 80-column records. Instead, you can enter the data for each subject in a continuous "stream." The advantage of a continuous data stream is that you do not need to create and keep track of multiple records. The disadvantage is that because of the 80-column limit of most computer screens and printers, a record that exceeds this limit must be "wrapped around" several lines. It is not easy to view and interpret data displayed in wrapped-around fashion.

The data shown in figure 20.2 are numerical. Data in the form of alphabetical characters can be recorded as well. For example, suppose you wish to use a computer program to do a content analysis of textbook passages. (Content analysis is described in chapter 12.) The passages can be entered on the computer recording form as a series of words, punctuation, and spaces between words. Each passage can be given an I.D. code. Because text is continuous, there is no advantage or need to organize the text data for each passage into variable fields and records. Instead, the text can be entered as a continuous data stream for each passage.

It is time-consuming to record all your research data on a computer recording form. Also, once the data have been recorded this way, they will need to be recorded once again by keyboarding them into the computer. Therefore, many researchers only use the form to plan their data-entry procedure. They do so by selecting a few subjects from their sample. They use these subjects' data to plan the order of entering the variables, the grouping of variables, the number of records to create, and so on. Once this planning is completed, the data for all the subjects are keyboarded directly into the computer.

There is at least one situation in which it is worthwhile to record all of your data on a computer recording form. This is the situation in which someone other than yourself will keyboard the data into the computer. If this person works directly from questionnaire forms, answer sheets, and other materials on which data have been recorded, the potential for keyboarding errors is great. You can minimize errors by personally entering all the data in these materials on a computer recording form. The other person then only needs to keyboard the data exactly as they were recorded on this form. If you plan to keyboard the data, however, there is no need to communicate with another person, and so you can skip the intermediate step of recording all the data on the form.

Steps in Computer Processing of Research Data

Once you have organized your research data for the computer, you are ready to start interacting with the computer and the statistical analysis program you have chosen. In this section we describe the three main steps in using the computer: (1) data entry, (2) statistical analysis, and (3) display of statistical results. We refer to SPSS-X in our discussion, but the terms and procedures apply to other computer programs as well.

Data Entry

Research data are keyboarded into the computer using a **data entry program.**[1] This program enables you to communicate such information as the number of variable fields you will be entering, the characteristics of each field (e.g., whether the numerical values have a decimal point), and the maximum and minimum values of each variable. In turn, the data entry program creates a "template" that assists you in keyboarding the data. For example, after you create the first data record for each subject, the data entry program automatically can enter the subject's I.D. code and record number for each succeeding record. Also, if you make a keyboarding error, the data entry program can catch it if the invalid value happens to exceed the maximum or minimum value that you specified for the variable.

After all the data have been entered, you can have SPSS-X generate a printout of the resulting data file on computer paper. Another option is to have SPSS-X display the data file on the computer screen. A **data file** is the data in the form that they were keyboarded into the computer. You can also display the frequency distribution of scores for each variable.

You should check the display of the data file and frequency distributions for data entry errors. This process sometimes is called "cleaning" the data, and is a critical step. If just one variable is entered in the wrong columns or one subject is given an incorrect I.D. code, all the subsequent statistical analyses are likely to be useless.

After the data have been entered, SPSS-X can create a **system file.** This is a representation of the data file that has been organized so that it can be analyzed by other SPSS-X programs. In other words, SPSS-X analyzes the system file, rather than the data file.

Statistical Analysis

The next step is to request SPSS-X to perform statistical analyses on the data file. These requests are communicated to SPSS-X using a set of standard **commands,** such as ANOVA (for analysis of variances) and DESCRIPTIVE (for

---

1. At the time of this writing, SAS, but not SPSS-X, has a data entry program. Other data-entry programs that can be used in conjunction with SPSS-X are available.

frequencies, means, standard deviations, etc.). The commands will initiate a statistical analysis on the entire data file, or on a subset of the variables you select from the data file.

Commands can be entered into a mainframe computer in two ways: batch mode and interactive mode. In the **batch mode,** you keyboard all the commands into a command file at one time. The list of commands can include requests to do multiple statistical analyses on the data file. In fact, it is possible to do all the data analyses for your study in one "run" through the computer, using SPSS-X's batch mode. The analyses can be done immediately or at a later time. The advantage of deferring the analyses (called a "computer run") until a later time is that computer centers often charge a lower rate if the runs are done at an off-peak time, such as late at night.

In SPSS-X's **interactive mode,** each command is executed as soon as it is entered into the computer. Thus, it is possible to do one statistical analysis, display the results on the screen, and make a decision about the next analysis based on your interpretation of the results. Having made your decision, you can enter the next command and almost immediately see the results of that analysis.

The obvious advantage of the interactive mode is that it facilitates decision making. Also, the interactive mode of SPSS-X includes an extensive help menu to guide you in using its various capabilities. A possible drawback is that the interactive mode uses more computer time than the batch mode. If you are paying a cost-per-minute fee for use of the mainframe computer, it is likely to cost you more to process your data in the interactive mode than in the batch mode.

Display of Results

As we indicated above, you can request SPSS-X to display the results of a statistical analysis on the computer screen. Even if you use this option, it is still desirable to request a printout of the results as a permanent record of the statistical analysis. SPSS-X includes commands that allow you to print the results in different formats and to display more or less of the information from the analysis.

Some or all of the printed results can be photo-reduced and included directly in the dissertation or research report. If you wish to do this, you can generate a preliminary printout to use in deciding what the final printout should look like. Then you can generate the final printout. This procedure saves you the tedious and sometimes error-ridden task of typing large amounts of statistical information. Also, you can check with the computer center about the kind of paper on which the results will be printed. It may be possible to choose a paper that is particularly good for photocopying.

You may want to print and save other parts of the statistical analysis besides the actual statistical results (e.g., means, standard deviations, t and F values). It usually is desirable to print and save the data file; the command file, which is the list of commands that generated the analysis; and the listing file (also called the output file), which generates the printout and which can be used to make extra copies of the printout at a later time without doing the analysis over again. These files are best saved on a computer tape. This procedure is described later in the chapter.

Data Base Management

In computer processing of research data, the major task is to perform statistical analyses on a data file. Another task is to create and manipulate the data file. This aspect of computer processing is called **data base management.**

To illustrate a common situation requiring data file management, suppose a data file consists of the scores of 30 students on five attitude scales, each having 10 items scored 1 to 5. Because students' scores on each item have been entered, the data file will consist of 30 records (one record for each of the 30 students), with each record containing 50 variables (each item of each scale being a variable). If we think of the data file as a grid, we see that it has 30 rows and 50 columns—not counting the columns required for the I.D. code and record number.

This data file is useful for investigating the item properties of the five attitude scales. Once the analyses are completed, it is likely that the remaining statistical analyses will involve students' total scores on the five scales. In this case, it is desirable to create a new data file. SPSS-X can be used to compute total scores from the item scores and then to transfer these scores to a new data file. This file would be a grid containing 30 rows and 10 columns (each total score being a two-digit variable).

Transformation of data files from one form to another is fairly common in computer processing of research data. For example, the master data file may consist of subjects' raw scores on several tests. It is often desirable to create new files in which these scores are expressed as standard scores, percentile equivalents, or grade-level equivalents.

Sometimes a data file becomes so large that it is unwieldy. In this case, it is desirable to break it into smaller data files, especially if the different files will be used for different statistical analyses. Conversely, you may have several small data files, each containing only a few variables. This situation sometimes occurs when data processing has proceeded in several stages. In this case, it may be desirable to merge the separate data files into a single data file. SPSS-X and related programs have the capacity to perform this function, called **data file merging.**

Another aspect of data file management is **data file transfer.** For example, suppose you have created a data file on a personal computer, but it does not have the capacity to perform the desired statistical analysis. In this situation, it is necessary to transfer the data file to a larger computer. Programs are available to effect this transfer.

We mentioned another situation involving data file transfer in a preceding section of the chapter. Some scoring machines can create a computer tape while scoring data recorded on answer sheets. The data on the tape constitute a data file that can be transferred to the computer that will be used for the major statistical analyses.

Some research studies make use of an existing **computer data base,** which is a set of data files and a directory to the information contained in them. The data base may have been generated in another research study or by an institution, for example, a school district having computerized record-keeping systems.

It is relatively easy to transfer data files from an existing data base into the computer that will do your statistical analyses. There is not even the need to transfer the files physically. They can be transmitted over telephone lines using *modems* or special networks. This is much easier than the alternative of making a printout of the data files and then keyboarding the information into a local computer to create new data files.

Learning to Use the Computer

Universities and colleges that have a mainframe computer usually offer courses in its use. They also may offer courses on how to use microcomputers to perform statistical analyses. If you plan a career in educational research, we recommend that you get this training. Quantitative research in education has reached a level of sophistication that most studies of this type generate data requiring analysis by computer.

Use of SPSS-X and similar computer software is fairly complicated. Many graduate students find it necessary to hire a computer consultant to assist them in analyzing the data for their thesis or dissertation. You should try to find a consultant who has not only a good understanding of computers, but also of educational research methods and statistics. It is not advisable, however, to turn over your data completely to a consultant. The consultant is not likely to have the same "feel" for the data or methodology as you do, and therefore he or she may wind up doing inappropriate and inaccurate analyses.

These problems can be avoided by asking the consultant to explain each step of data file management and statistical analysis when it is executed. Also, you should specify the statistical techniques to use in answering your research questions or testing your hypotheses, rather than to allow the consultant to choose them.

When possible, you should work alongside the consultant. For example, you can observe the consultant create the data entry program and enter the first few records. When you understand how the process works, you can enter the remaining data on your own. Also, you can ask the consultant to use SPSS-X or related software in an interactive mode. As the consultant keyboards each set of commands, you can ask what they mean; and you can see on the computer screen the statistical results produced by the commands. This procedure is far preferable to the alternative of trying to make sense of a stack of computer printouts generated by the consultant without your participation.

Checking Data Analyses for Accuracy

Whether you use a calculator, personal computer, or mainframe computer, you should check continuously for accuracy. The first thing to check is the data file. Some calculators facilitate this check by making a paper tape of each data entry. This tape constitutes the data file. Computers show the data file on a screen or printout. Visual inspection of these displays can pick up obvious errors like unusually large or small values of a variable, or misaligned columns. A data entry program also can pick up these errors.

The next task is to make spot checks of parts of the data file. If these checks reveal unacceptable errors, you will need to enter the data again. Data entry programs allow you to keep the original data file and re-keyboard the new entries over it. The computer will signal you whenever there is a discrepancy between the original entry and the new entry. You can check the discrepancy to determine which entry is in error.

The results of a statistical analysis can be checked in several ways. You can redo the analysis, or you can check the command file to ensure that the proper commands were used. If you did the analysis by computer, you can check part of it by using a calculator. For example, if the computer program calculated a large number of correlation coefficients, you can compute one of them on a calculator. Generally, if the calculator result matches the computer result (within rounding errors), you can be confident that the computer computed all the other correlations without error.

If the results of a statistical analysis are implausible, you should be extra sensitive to the possibility that an error occurred. Even if the results are plausible, however, they still should be checked.

STORING RESEARCH DATA

After you have completed the data analyses for your study, you should file the raw data, hand computations, and computer printouts. The printouts should include the results of the statistical analyses, the data files, and the command files for major analyses. If you used a mainframe computer, an alternative is to store this information on a computer tape. A computer tape is more compact than a stack of printouts and is relatively inexpensive. A single tape is sufficient to store all the files for even a very large research study. If you used a personal computer, the various files can be saved on floppy disks.

It is particularly important to retain the raw data, which are the test answer sheets, observation forms, recordings of interviews, and other research material as initially received from subjects. For example, you may wish to refer back to the raw data to check a particular score that seems doubtful. Also, retaining the raw data makes it possible to use the data in future research. It is not uncommon to hit upon an idea for reanalyzing data after the original study has been completed. The reanalysis may yield new and interesting information that would be lost if the raw data had been destroyed at the end of the original analysis. If any research findings are challenged, the raw data provide the only fully satisfactory source for rechecking them.

The process of checking will be greatly simplified if you record the steps neatly and systematically, and label each step for future reference. The time consumed in keeping systematic records is a good investment. It is much less than the time that would be required to decipher unlabeled raw data or to redo lost calculations.

MISTAKES SOMETIMES MADE IN PROCESSING RESEARCH DATA

1. The researcher does not check the window key or scoring machine template for accuracy when scoring answer sheets.
2. Does not document scoring procedures specifically developed for the study.
3. Does not create an I.D. code that uniquely identifies each subject in the sample.
4. Does not organize the data on a computer recording form or similar aid before entering them into the computer.
5. Completely turns over the data to a consultant for computer processing.
6. Does not check each data file and statistical analysis for accuracy.
7. Does not label and store the raw data, data files, and results of statistical analyses so that they can be retrieved easily for subsequent use.

ANNOTATED REFERENCES

Bruning, James L., and Kintz, B. L. *Computational Handbook of Statistics,* 3rd ed. Glenview, IL: Scott, Foresman, 1987.

Appendix contains computer programs written in BASIC for commonly used statistical techniques. The programs are coordinated with computational examples presented in the book.

Greenberg, Barry. *Using Microcomputers and Mainframes for Data Analysis in the Social Sciences.* Columbus, OH: Merrill, 1987.

An introduction to the use of computers for analysis of research data. The emphasis is on SPSS and SPSS-X, but the author also provides step-by-step descriptions of other programs designed for the IBM PC, Apple II, and Apple Macintosh.

SAS User's Guide: Basics, Version 5 ed. Cary, NC: SAS Institute, 1985.

A comprehensive guide to SAS terminology and procedures for data processing, summarizing, and reporting.

SPSS-X User's Guide, 3rd ed. Chicago: SPSS Inc., 1988.

Explains the SPSS-X Data Analysis System, Release 3.0. The previous edition explained SPSS-X releases through 2.2. The three parts of the manual introduce the system, set forth procedures for data management, and outline procedures for statistical analysis. Also available are manuals that provide simpler introductions to the system: *The SPSS-X Guide to Data Analysis* and *SPSS-X Introductory Statistics Guide.* Both are published by SPSS Inc.

Stoloff, Michael L., and Couch, James V. *Computer Use in Psychology: A Directory of Software.* Washington, DC: American Psychological Association, 1987.

Statistics and research section describes 43 computer programs for data analysis and presentation.

SELF-CHECK TEST

Circle the correct answer to each of the following questions. An answer key is provided on page 884.

1. The first step in scoring standardized tests used in research is to
   a. restudy the test manual and the test.
   b. check the *Mental Measurements Yearbooks* concerning the test.
   c. check for interrater reliability.
   d. prepare an answer key.
2. The first step in using a test scoring machine is to
   a. run all answer sheets through the machine and check for scoring errors.
   b. check all answer sheets, darkening pencil marks if needed, and erasing random pencil marks.
   c. prepare the command statements.
   d. select an appropriate computer-scoring program.
3. The procedures and rules for scoring unstructured measures should be recorded in detail in order to
   a. make them available to other researchers.
   b. be able to state them precisely in the research report.
   c. control the actual scoring of the measures with greater accuracy.
   d. All of the above are correct.

4. A variable field is
   a. a data grid that has a varying number of rows.
   b. a data grid that has a varying number of columns.
   c. the number of columns occupied by a variable in a computer record.
   d. the number of rows occupied by a variable in a computer record.
5. SPSS-X was designed to
   a. create and manage data files.
   b. perform statistical analyses.
   c. display statistical results on a computer screen or printout.
   d. All of the above are correct.
6. Each row in a data grid represents a discrete
   a. command statement.
   b. system file.
   c. variable.
   d. subject in the sample.
7. The batch mode of computer processing
   a. executes a series of command statements together.
   b. executes a series of command statements one at a time.
   c. is used primarily for data file merging.
   d. is used primarily for data base transfer.

APPLICATION PROBLEMS

The following problems are designed to give you practice in applying significant concepts and research procedures explained in the chapter. Most of them do not have a single correct answer. For feedback, you can compare your answers with the sample answers on page 905.

1. Suppose you are handed 100 answer sheets for the *California Psychological Inventory*, a test not familiar to you. Your task is to score the answer sheets for the standard scales of this inventory. What would be the recommended first step in performing this task?
2. The following is a partially completed hand data card for a subject who participated in a research study:

I.D.	06	Social Class	upper middle class
Sex	male	Pretest Score	37
School	Westhaven Junior High	Posttest Score	55

What procedure would you recommend for simplifying the information on this card to facilitate later data analysis?
3. The third computer record for a research subject whose I.D. is 143 is to contain his scores on six attitude scales (52, 57, 63, 49, 62, 47), his scores on three behavior rating scales (1.2, 2.2, 1.8), and his occupation (stockbroker), age (47), and annual income ($48,561). How might this information be represented on a computer recording form?

SUGGESTION SHEET

If your last name starts with letters from Tud to Wex, please complete the Suggestion Sheet at the end of the book while this chapter is still fresh in your mind.

OVERVIEW

This chapter presents guidelines for preparing a thesis, dissertation, journal article, or professional paper. The section on writing a thesis or dissertation presents its main headings and the type of content usually included under each heading. The section on writing a journal article emphasizes the need for brevity and careful selection of a journal to which to submit it. The chapter concludes with suggestions for preparing a paper to be read at a professional meeting.

OBJECTIVES

After studying this chapter you should be able to:

1. Describe the content and purpose of each section of a dissertation.
2. Write dissertation titles that are descriptive yet brief.
3. State the criteria considered most important by editors in evaluating manuscripts for journal publication.
4. Describe the procedures for submitting a research article to a professional journal.
5. Describe the procedures for submitting a research paper to be read at a professional meeting.

INTRODUCTION

The purpose of this chapter is to provide general guidelines for preparing a thesis, dissertation, journal article, or professional paper. We do not attempt to present detailed information on format, however. Most colleges and universities have their own format requirements.

A distinction between the terms "thesis" and "dissertation" usually is made. A thesis is a report of a research project done as a requirement for the master's degree. A dissertation is the corresponding report for the doctoral degree. Both the thesis and dissertation follow similar formats, although the dissertation is typically longer. This is because research projects undertaken for the doctoral degree tend to be more complex and involve more data collection than master's degree projects. We use the term *dissertation* in this chapter to refer to both types of report.

THE DISSERTATION

In doing a literature review, you will observe that most research articles are organized similarly. Dissertations follow this same organization, but they tend to be much longer. A typical research article is 15 to 20 manuscript pages (typed double-space), whereas dissertations typically range from 50 to 200 pages.

The following list presents an outline of the typical dissertation. Some variations in this outline will be found in the requirements of different universities and colleges.

The outline applies generally to dissertations reporting either quantitative or qualitative research studies. As we discuss below, the only substantial differences are likely to be in chapters 3 and 4. Qualitative studies generally require a more extensive description of each subject in the sample than is required in quantitative studies. Also, the reporting of case studies is generally different from the reporting of quantitative results. Chapter 10 describes procedures for organizing and reporting case study data. Chapter 19 describes procedures for reporting historical studies that are of a qualitative nature.

Front Matter

1. Title page
2. Preface and Acknowledgments
3. Table of contents
4. List of tables
5. List of figures

Body of the Dissertation

Chapter 1. Introduction
   a. General statement of the problem
   b. Significance of the study
   c. Research hypotheses, questions, and objectives
   d. Definition of terms
Chapter 2. Review of the literature
   a. Review of previous research and opinion
   b. Interpretative summary of the current state of knowledge
Chapter 3. Research method

    a. Research design
    b. Sampling procedures
    c. Experimental treatments and procedures
    d. Measures
Chapter 4. Research findings
    a. Overview of statistical procedures
    b. Description of results for each hypothesis, question, or measure
    c. Supplemental analyses
Chapter 5. Summary and Discussion
    a. Summary of research problem and method
    b. Interpretation of each result
    c. Limitations of the study
    d. Implications

Back Matter

1. Bibliography
2. Appendix

Some students wait until all data have been collected and analyzed before starting to write the dissertation. A more efficient procedure is to write some sections of the dissertation earlier. You are likely to encounter some periods of time when you are extremely busy collecting or analyzing data, and other periods of time when you must sit and wait. These lulls can be used to draft the first chapters of the dissertation.

The easiest way to write a good dissertation is to start by outlining each part in detail. The outline at first can be merely a list of all major topics that are to be discussed in each part. Next, the topics can be stated as headings and placed in a meaningful order. Finally, you can add subheadings and the points to be discussed under them. Headings and subheadings help the reader to understand the nature of the research project and the organization of the dissertation.

In chapter 2 we recommended that you write a detailed dissertation proposal as part of the research planning process. If you did so, it can be used in whole or in part for the first three chapters of the dissertation.

Format Considerations

When you are ready to start writing the dissertation, you should obtain information about your university's format requirements. Some universities prepare a style manual for graduate students, whereas others refer them to a published style manual.

It is helpful to ask your dissertation chairperson to refer you to several outstanding dissertations recently completed at your institution. An examination of these dissertations, together with the prescribed style manual, will give you most of the information needed to satisfy dissertation requirements. Also, study of the dissertations will give you an idea of your chairperson's standards and expectations.

Questions of style not addressed by your university's style manual usually can be answered by referring to the *Publication Manual of the American Psychological Association* (see Annotated References). You should be particularly careful to use nonsexist language in your thesis or dissertation. For example, it is considered sexist to write: "Subjects were 16 boys and 16 girls. Each child was to place a car on his board so that two cars and boards looked alike." A nonsexist alternative would be: "Each child was to place a car on his or her board so that two cars and boards looked alike." Similarly, it is considered sexist to state: "The use of experiments in education presupposes the mechanistic nature of man." A nonsexist alternative would be: "The use of experiments in education presupposes the mechanistic nature of the human being." Accepted guidelines for nonsexist technical writing have been prepared by the American Psychological Association.[1]

A common problem in writing a dissertation or other research report is figuring the proper tense to use. The general rule is to use the past tense to describe events that occurred at a point in time prior to the writing of the report. For example, one might write: "Sixty students were selected from a local school district . . ."; "Harber (1968) found in her study that . . ."; "The Stanford Achievement Test was developed to measure . . ."; "A *t*-test was done. . . ." Each of these statements refers to an event or activity that occurred prior to the writing of the report.

The present tense is used to refer to assertions that continue to be true at the time the report is written. For example, one might write: "Research has shown consistently that inserted questions in text facilitate retention of the text content." The research has already occurred; hence the past tense ("has shown") is used. We can presume that the relationship between inserted questions and retention continues to be true beyond the observations made by the researchers; hence the present tense ("facilitate" is used). Similarly, one might write, "the Stanford Achievement Test measures various aspects of academic performance" because this feature of the test continues to be true at the time the report is written. Also, one would state that, "table 2 shows that" because the table continues to perform a function. The table did not show a phenomenon just at one point in time. By the same logic, one would state that "this *t* value is statistically significant" because the results of a statistical significance test continue to be true beyond the point that the test was performed.

1. American Psychological Association, "Guidelines for Nonsexist Language in APA Journals," *Educational Researcher* 7, no. 3 (1978): 15–17.

Use of a Word Processing Program

Many students now prepare their dissertation on a computer using a word processing program such as *Macwrite* or *Microsoft Word*. The obvious advantage of a word processing program is that it facilitates the many revisions involved in writing a dissertation. One reason why many revisions are needed is that dissertation committees typically include four or five faculty members, each of whom is likely to see different flaws and different improvements that can be made. The other reason is that format requirements of dissertations tend to be complicated. For example, margins, footnotes, and page numbers usually must be precisely positioned on the page. Use of a word processing program makes it easy to adjust the manuscript to satisfy these requirements.

You may find it helpful to prepare your dissertation in two stages. First, you can use a word processing program to get the dissertation in the best form you can. Then you can employ a typist who is familiar with university dissertation requirements to prepare the final version. If the typist has the same type of computer as you do, he or she can work directly from a disk copy of the dissertation. Thus, there is no need to have the dissertation retyped from scratch. If the typist uses a different computer, there are ways to make a disk copy that will work on it. Most computer consultants are familiar with disk copy technology.

Manuscript Manager:APA Style is a useful piece of computer software for writing dissertations and journal articles. It is a word processing program, and it also automatically formats a document (dissertation, journal article, professional paper) so that it follows the editorial rules of the *Publication Manual of the American Psychological Association*, 3rd edition. For example, it formats each citation according to APA rules, and it automatically checks that each citation in the text has a reference and vice versa. *Manuscript Manager* is available for the IBM PC, PC compatibles, and Apple IIe and IIc.

Front Matter

As shown in the dissertation outline presented earlier, the *front matter* includes the title page, preface and acknowledgments, table of contents, list of tables, and list of figures. Your university is likely to have its own format requirements for this material.

A dissertation title should be brief, yet descriptive. Suppose, for example, that a student has done an experiment comparing the achievement gains of sixth-grade students who used computers while learning American history with the achievement gains of a matched group of students who did not use computers. An appropriate title would be "An Experiment Comparing Conventional and Computer-Augmented Instruction in Sixth-Grade American History." This title is brief, yet it gives the reader a good sense of the study's purpose.

Another title might be "A Study Comparing the Achievement of Sixth-Grade Students Instructed in American History through the Use of Computer-Augmented Instruction with Those Experiencing Conventional Classroom Instruction." This title tells what the study is about, but it is unnecessarily long.

Still another title might be "Teaching with Computers." This title fails in that it does not reveal the purpose of the study, but merely identifies the topic in very general terms. In doing your literature review, you will find such brief titles exasperating. They tell so little that it is necessary to check each reference further, even though the majority of them may have nothing to do with the purpose of your study. Many secondary sources such as *Education Index* list only the title of research reports, and so a general title may mislead the user and often is indexed improperly.

In preparing the table of contents and titles of tables and figures, you should keep in mind that these materials should follow parallel grammatical construction. In other words, chapter titles, headings, and titles of tables and figures should be prepared so they are consistent in wording and grammatical construction.

The Introductory Chapter

The introductory chapter usually starts with a general statement of the problem. This statement should help the reader develop an appreciation for the problem's practical and theoretical significance. Next is a specific statement of the study's research questions, hypotheses, or objectives.

Another section of the introductory chapter is sometimes devoted to definitions of terms. This section is very important because educational terms such as "multicultural education," "gifted child," "learning styles," and many others are defined differently by different educators. Therefore, specific definitions of the terms used in the study are necessary. Some researchers do not define the terms in a separate section. They prefer to define each term the first time that it appears in the text of the dissertation. Thus, each term can be defined in a relevant context. Also, the reader need not flip back and forth to a separate section to determine whether a term has been defined, and if so, what the definition is.

You often can prepare a good rough draft of the introductory chapter while the study is in process. Most writers find that if they prepare a rough draft and then set it aside for a week or two, they will see weaknesses that would not have been apparent if an immediate revision had been attempted. Also, new points and different approaches to organizing the chapter often come to mind during the intervening weeks. If you wait until all the data have been collected and analyzed before writing the dissertation, you may not have sufficient time to lay aside each section for this period of incubation.

Another advantage of drafting the early chapters of the dissertation while the study is in progress is that a less demanding schedule of writing can be followed. Most people find it difficult to write steadily for any period of time. It is much easier to write a few pages and then put the work aside and do something else. This option is not available if you wait too long to start preparing the dissertation.

Review of the Literature

The chapter reviewing the literature is meant to give the reader an understanding of previous relevant contributions to the problem so that they can better understand the purpose and methodology of your study. Before writing this chapter, you may find it helpful to examine the journal *Review of Educational Research*. The research reviews published in it are generally exemplary.

The first step in preparing the chapter is to make a rough outline of the major topics. The coding system applied to the note cards during the review of the literature (see chapter 4) is often useful for this purpose. After preparing this outline, you should read all the note cards and sort them into the topics contained in the outline. You then must decide on the order in which to present the topics. Next, you should review the cards dealing with the first topic until you are thoroughly familiar with their contents. This review will help you decide how the topic should be presented, the order in which studies should be discussed, and which studies should be emphasized.

For each topic you usually will find two or three studies that are most relevant and methodologically sound. These studies should be discussed in detail. If other studies produced similar findings, they can be summarized by a statement such as, "findings of the above studies generally have been supported by other studies that employed essentially the same approach." The supporting studies can be cited using whatever format you have adopted for the dissertation. The advantage of this method is that it provides a review of pertinent findings without a laborious recounting of each and every study.

Another method commonly used by researchers is to organize related studies into a table. The first step is to decide which features of the studies to abstract. Possible features include: nature of the sample, procedures or treatments, dependent variables, and statistical results for each variable. The next step is to review each study and write a capsule description of each feature. Finally, these descriptions are organized into a table. The advantages of this method are its concise presentation style and ease with which studies can be compared. Table 21.1 presents a section from a large table of this type that was prepared by Ron Thorkildsen for a literature review in a dissertation on social

TABLE 21.1

Summary of Research on Social Skills Training Programs for Mildly Handicapped Children

Study Number/ Authors	Social Skills Taught	Subjects/ Design	Type of Assessment	Training Techniques	Maintenance Training/ Assessment	Generalization Training/ Assessment	Results
(1) Ballard, Corman, Gottlieb, & Kaufman (1977)	Cooperative interaction	N = 37 EMR 3,4,5 gr. Group design	Sociometric nomination	Cooperative groups formed	No training specified	In natural environment with non-handicapped peers	1. Peer acceptance of experimental group increased and peer rejection decreased more than controls 2. Acceptance of controls decreased and rejection increased 3. Acceptance of experimental subjects was higher and rejection was lower by peers in 2nd activity group than controls 4. Acceptance of experimental subjects by classmates who did not participate with them in group activity was higher after intervention than acceptance of controls by classmates.
(2) Berler, Gross, & Drabman (1982)	1. Eye contact 2. Initiating social interactions 3. Praising 4. Responding to criticism 5. Making requests	N = 3 LD 8–10 years SS Design	1. Sociometric rating 2. Behavior observation 3. Role play tests	1. Coaching 2. Modeling (videotape) 3. Behavioral rehearsal 4. Feedback	No training 1-month follow-up	Natural role-playing situations	1. Increased use of appropriate skills during role playing 2. Performance maintained above baseline levels during follow-up 3. Performance did not generalize to natural school setting 4. Peer acceptance did not change

Source: Adapted from Ron J. Thorkildsen, "An Experimental Test of a Microcomputer/Videodisc Program to Develop the Social Skills of Mildly Handicapped Elementary Students" (Ph.D. dissertation, University of Oregon, 1984), p. 14.

skills training for mildly handicapped children. Note that it concisely presents a great deal of information about each study, and it facilitates comparisons between studies. Thorkildsen's complete table reviews 18 studies in this manner, two of which are shown in our table 21.1. Supplemental tables in Thorkildsen's literature review chapter synthesize elements of this master table in order to detect patterns of interest. For example, one of the supplemental tables lists types of social skills and shows the number of studies that included training of each type. This table reveals that the primary emphasis of the studies was on training of verbal skills rather than the training of nonverbal skills.

In the process of synthesizing the findings, you will need to interpret their meaning and significance. Your interpretations can repeat those offered by the researchers, but you are also free to disagree with them and offer your own interpretation. Your interpretations of previous research findings can form a separate section of the chapter, or they can be included in the discussion of each topic. The interpretative sections are by far the most difficult to write, because they require that you have a thorough understanding of the research you have reviewed.

You should repeat the procedures described above for each of the topics covered in the literature review. The reviews of the topics then can be combined into a rough draft of the chapter. Unfortunately, some students do not use these procedures, but instead do little more than prepare an abstract of each article they wish to discuss; then they string these abstracts together without any attempt at continuity or logical organization. This type of review tends to be excessively long and fails in its purpose of giving the reader an understanding of the research problem.

Another pitfall to avoid in preparing a literature review is that of presenting each study in essentially the same way. For example, some students treat each article in a separate paragraph and start each article with the name of the researchers who wrote it. Also, they devote the same amount of space to each study without regard to its importance or relevance. This type of review is tiresome to read and usually does not provide a good understanding of what is known about the research problem.

Another weakness of some literature reviews is excessive use of quotations. They should only be used when the author's statement is especially relevant and well written, and when it can be inserted without spoiling the continuity of the presentation. Nothing is more tiresome than a literature review that is merely an accumulation of quotations, each linked to the next by a few sentences written by the reviewer.

Research Method

The chapter on research method should have separate sections describing the research design, sampling procedures, experimental treatments and other procedures, and measures.

The first section provides a description of the type of research design that was used—descriptive, causal-comparative, correlational, or experimental. The extent to which the study relied on qualitative or quantitative methodology should also be discussed.

The chapter continues with a detailed description of the sample. This description is needed by the reader to determine the population to which the research results can be generalized. The description varies with the nature of the study, but it often includes such information as the distribution of gender, socioeconomic status, and ability in the sample. If the sample was organized into groups (e.g., experimental and treatment groups), it is important to describe the characteristics of each group separately so that their comparability can be judged.

The method of selecting the sample should be described in detail. If random sampling was employed, a detailed description of the procedure should be given. If a matching procedure was used, the matching criteria, rationale for the criteria, and number of cases lost because of inability to obtain a satisfactory match should be stated. If stratified sampling was used, the procedure for identifying subjects for each stratum should be described. If a nonrandom selection procedure was used, it is particularly important to describe the procedure in detail so that the reader has a basis for judging the study's generalizability.

Part of the section on sampling should include a description of the schools or other settings from which the sample was drawn. This might include descriptions of the curriculum, the community served by the schools, the characteristics of participating teachers and administrators, the schools' performance on standard achievement measures, and any idiosyncratic characteristics of the schools and community.

If you have done a qualitative study, your study may consist of only one or two subjects or sites. Each subject and each site should be described in much more detail than would be the case in a typical quantitative study. One focus of the description should be your reasons for selecting the particular subjects and sites. These reasons will help the reader understand the sample and the extent to which it is representative of other groups and settings.

Another focus of the description should be on characteristics of the subjects or sites that are relevant to the phenomena being studied. For example, if the study concerns a school's reactions to a new curriculum, it would be relevant to describe previous curriculums introduced to the school, and the school's reaction to them. Even though the study is not about these previously introduced curriculums, a description of them provides a basis for understanding the phenomena being investigated.

The next section of the chapter should provide a description of how the research design was implemented. Any discrepancies between planned procedures and procedures actually used should be noted. If an experimental design was used, the treatments should be described in considerable detail, in case other researchers wish to replicate them or compare them with treatments used in other studies.

Other research designs also involve procedures that are important to understanding the study, and they, too, should be described in detail. Examples of such procedures include those used to obtain cooperation of subjects, to deal with unforeseen problems, and to control for extraneous variables. Presentation of a detailed timeline of the major events in executing the study is often helpful to the reader.

The final section of the chapter should include a description of all measures used in the study. If the measure is well known, the description can be brief. It usually is sufficient to describe the types of scores yielded by the measure, evidence of validity and reliability, and the relationship of the measure to the research questions or hypotheses.

If new or little-known measures were used, a much more detailed description is needed. You should explain the rationale for using the measure, the nature of its items, and its validity and reliability. If the measure involves unusual or new scoring procedures, these should be described in detail. (The preceding chapter of this text discusses this topic.) Sometimes a separate chapter of the dissertation is devoted to describing the development of a new measure that was critical to the study.

The description of measures also should include how they were administered. You should note any unusual occurrences that may have influenced the results; for example, changes in the schedule for administering the tests, disturbances during the testing sessions, and unexpected reactions by subjects. If some of the subjects were absent from a scheduled testing session, follow-up procedures should be described. Also, you should describe procedures used to control the administration of measures—for example, procedures for controlling observer bias or for ensuring that all treatment groups were administered a measure in the same way.

Research Findings

The next chapter of the dissertation presents the research findings. There should be no discussion of the findings, however. This task is left to the next chapter of the dissertation.

General procedures for processing and analyzing the research data can be described at the beginning of the chapter. For example, you may have decided to remove some subjects from the data base because of too much missing data. This decision affects some or all of the data analyses, and so it is appropriate to discuss it at the outset of the chapter. Other matters of general relevance are the computer programs used to analyze the data, transformations of scores to make them amenable to statistical analysis, and the organization of the chapter.

The best way to present the results of statistical or qualitative analyses is to organize them around the study's hypotheses, questions, or objectives. Each hypothesis, for example, would be stated in the same form as it was presented in chapter 1 of the dissertation. Then all findings pertinent to this hypothesis would be presented. If the study tested five hypotheses, there would be five sections of the chapter, each dealing with a separate hypothesis.

The important statistical results in a study usually concern the possible effect of one variable on another. It is important to report both the practical significance and statistical significance of these observed effects. Reporting a statistically significant p value simply tells the reader that the null hypothesis can be rejected. The p value says nothing about the magnitude of the effect, which is critical to judging its practical significance. (Statistical measures of magnitude of effect are discussed in chapter 9 of this text.)

You should be careful to use appropriate language in describing the results of hypothesis testing. The result of a statistical significance test does not *prove* or *disprove* a hypothesis (see chapter 9). You can only say that the result *supports* or *does not support* the hypothesis. Although the term "support" rather than "prove" seems like a small distinction, it alerts readers to the limitations of the null-hypothesis method.

A useful approach in preparing the results chapter is to start by putting the results for each hypothesis, question, or objective in tables and figures. They describe statistical results more clearly and economically than is possible in text presentation. After studying each table or figure, you can write a paragraph or two explaining what it contains and drawing the reader's attention to noteworthy findings. You should avoid discussing every entry in the table or figure whether significant or not. This style of presentation is boring, and it defeats the purpose of using tables and figures.

Each table or figure should contain all the information necessary for the reader to interpret it. This information usually includes the type of statistic reported, a descriptive label for each variable, sample size for each analysis, probability levels if any, and footnotes if necessary. You are advised to study tables and figures in research journals and to follow their format. The preceding chapters of this book contain many tables and figures from such journals, and you can use them as models.

What is the difference between a table and a figure? Any presentation of numerical information or prose in column form is called a **table.** The usual table in a research report consists of a column of variables followed by other columns of descriptive or inferential statistics relating to the variables. A listing of subjects in the sample or research sites also would be labeled as a table.

The typical **figure** in a research report consists of information in pictorial form. Histograms, charts, pie graphs, scatterplots, and time-series plots are common types of figures in research reports. Reproductions of prose from another source in a special format are also labeled as figures. Two examples of this type of figure are the letter to a research participant (figure 3.1) and the sample page from *Psychological Abstracts* (figure 4.1).

Often the results of the planned analyses will suggest questions or hypotheses that were not part of the original dissertation proposal. If the available data can be used to address these questions or hypotheses, then it is entirely appropriate to do supplemental analyses and report them in a separate section of the results chapter. Researchers sometimes are surprised to find that their most important results do not stem from their initial hypotheses, questions, or objectives.

The preceding discussion pertains to the presentation of quantitative analyses. Similar principles of presentation apply to qualitative analyses. The results of the analyses can be organized according to the study's hypotheses, questions, or objectives. If the study consisted of a set of case studies, the analyses for each case study can be presented separately. If possible, each case study should be organized similarly in order to facilitate comparisons between them.

The results of a statistical analysis can be presented consisely in a table and few paragraphs of text. This is not possible with case studies. The presentation of a case study may require 10 to 20 pages of text, or even more. If so, you should consider making each case study the subject of a separate chapter.

The results of a qualitative study generally are presented using words rather than numbers. Therefore, use of language is critical. The writing of a case study requires a literary flair in order to bring the subject of the case study alive for the reader. It usually is necessary to write several drafts of each case study and to elicit critical feedback from colleagues on each draft. The feedback should focus on such matters as whether the writing includes sufficient descriptive detail; the important phenomena are distinguished from the trivial; the researcher's perspectives and values are explicit; and multiple sources, if available, are used to document findings. It generally is much more difficult to write the results chapter or chapters for a qualitative study than for a quantitative study.

We stated above that the results chapter for a quantitative study should not include discussion and interpretation of the results. This is not so with qualitative studies, which by their very nature emphasize interpretation. Therefore, it is important to present an explicit interpretative framework, usually in the first chapter. This framework can be repeated in summary form at the start of the results chapter or chapters to provide a mental set for the reader.

Summary and Discussion

The last chapter of a dissertation usually includes a brief summary of the research problem and method; an interpretation of each result; limitations of the study; and implications of the findings.

The most important task in writing this chapter is to identify and interpret the important statistical results. As you examine each result, you should ask yourself such questions as: Is this a noteworthy result, and if so, why? Is it consistent with the results of previous research? If not, why not? Is there an existing theory that can explain the result? Does the result suggest a new theory? Are there alternative explanations of the result? Is one of these alternative explanations more plausible than the others? Does the result merit further investigation to clarify it? If so, what form might such investigation take?

Your answers to these questions will be of great interest to other researchers for several reasons, including the fact that you were an eyewitness to the data-collection process. As an eyewitness, you have a better feeling for what the data mean than do other researchers, who must rely on your report for an understanding of what happened.

The chapter should include a discussion of the study's methodological limitations. You should note problems that occurred in sampling procedures, instrumentation, data collection, and data analysis. Some of the problems may be inherent in the research design, whereas others may have occurred in the execution of the study. If an observed result was contrary to prediction, you should consider whether this was due to methodological flaws.

It is desirable to add a section on implications of the findings for practice, if there are such implications. You can present speculations that would be out of place in the results chapter.

If you did not do so earlier in the chapter, you should conclude the chapter by suggesting questions for further research. This is a worthwhile exercise, because your experience in doing a study has put you in a good position for judging the important questions that should be answered next. Other researchers can combine your judgments with their own to design studies with the best likelihood of yielding important new knowledge.

Back Matter

The *back matter* of a dissertation usually consists of the bibliography and one or more appendixes.

The bibliography must list all references that were cited in the body of the dissertation. Depending upon the university, it may be permissible also to include pertinent references that were not cited. Compiling the bibliography is not difficult if you used the correct bibliographic format at the time you made bibliography cards for your literature review. All you need do is select the bibliography cards to be referenced, place them in alphabetical order, and type them.

The most common flaw in dissertation bibliographies is inconsistent format. The method of referencing a particular type of source should be consistent down to the last comma. Common errors include inconsistent punctuation, the use of the author's first name in some references and initial only in other references, and the abbreviation of some journal titles but not others.

Appendixes are used to present information that is not critical to the study or that will be of interest only to some readers. Appendixes commonly include: (1) tables that are very long or that contain statistical results not essential to the study; (2) locally developed research materials, such as measures, forms, and descriptions of procedures; (3) psychometric data such as item analyses; and (4) lengthy quotations from primary and secondary sources that are not easily accessible.

PREPARING A JOURNAL ARTICLE

You have much to gain by preparing one or more journal articles based on your dissertation as soon as you have completed it. At this time all phases of the study are fresh in your mind, and so you can prepare the article much more easily than if you put the task aside for a while. Also, most employers of educators with doctorates are interested in their publications. If you are able to list one or more publications (especially research publications) on your *vita*, you will have a decided advantage in obtaining a position.

You will need to decide whether to write the article by yourself or with a co-author. It is common practice for the student to co-author an article with his or her dissertation chairperson, especially if the study was part of a larger project coordinated by the chairperson. In most cases the student would be the senior author of an article directly reporting the dissertation results, and the chairperson or other collaborators would be junior authors.

The first step in preparing a research article is to decide what journal is most likely to publish studies in your field. The best candidates can be identified by checking the bibliography of your dissertation. You are likely to find that a few journals published the majority of studies that you cited as pertinent to your research problem. These journals are the ones most likely to accept your article for publication.

Another factor to consider in selecting a journal is its reputation. Some education journals are more widely read and more influential than others. Also, refereed journals generally are regarded more highly than nonrefereed journals. A **refereed journal** is one in which articles are judged as acceptable for publication by a panel of acknowledged experts. Most refereed journals prominently display their panel of reviewers at the front of each issue.

Terrence Luce and Dale Johnson conducted a survey to determine how members of the American Educational Research Association would rank a sample of 74 education and education-related journals.[2] Approximately 700 members were asked to rank-order the 10 journals in which "you would most

2. Terrence S. Luce and Dale M. Johnson, "Ratings of Educational and Psychological Journals," *Educational Researcher* 7, no. 10 (1978): 8–10.

like to be published and/or those in which you expect to find material important to you as an educator." The 10 highest-ranked journals and their ranks are as follows:

1. *American Educational Research Journal*
2. *Review of Educational Research*
3. *Harvard Educational Review*
4. *Phi Delta Kappan*
5. *Journal of Educational Research*
6. *Educational Researcher*
7. *Journal of Educational Psychology*
8. *Educational and Psychological Measurement*
9. *Journal of Educational Measurement*
10. *American Psychologist*

Most of these journals will publish reports based on dissertation studies if they are well done and important.

Once you decide upon the journal in which you wish to publish, you should examine the typical length and format of recently published articles in it. You probably will find that they are similar in format to the dissertation, but much briefer.

The importance of writing brief journal articles was emphasized in recent advice to prospective authors by Myron Boor.[3]

> In reviewing a few dozen manuscripts for major psychiatric and psychological journals during the past several years, I have noted that almost all submitted manuscripts are too long and usually they are much too long. The veritable contributions of manuscripts often are obscured in a mass of tangential and even totally irrelevant verbiage. Briefer manuscripts would better highlight the contributions of the study to the literature, conserve expensive journal space, save readers' valuable time, require less revision, and have an increased probability of acceptance.[4]

Earlier in this chapter we estimated the length of a typical research article to be 15 to 20 manuscript pages, typed double-space. This estimate includes text, tables and figures, and references. Hence, the typical dissertation must be shortened dramatically to satisfy this page limit.

The general statement of the problem in the dissertation usually is condensed to a paragraph or two. The review of the literature is shortened substantially, with brief reference made only to those studies that are most relevant to your study. The specific research hypotheses and questions are stated, but succinctly. The section on method should provide a capsule

---

3. Myron Boor, "Suggestions to Improve Manuscripts Submitted to Professional Journals," *American Psychologist* 41 (1986): 721–722.
4. Ibid., p. 721.

description of the research design, sample, procedures, and measures. If some aspects of the method are new or unusual, however, they should be described in detail.

The section on findings makes up a greater proportion of a research article than of a dissertation. Tables are used extensively in this section because they can convey a lot of statistical information concisely. Only the most important findings are highlighted in the text. The discussion of the results should be brief and should focus on the most important findings, limitations of the study, and needs for further research. The bibliography must only include the references actually cited in the text.

In summary, the dissertation format allows you to describe virtually everything you did and found. The length restrictions of a journal article require you to decide the most important things you did and found and to focus on them.

Some dissertations deal with a subject that logically can be divided into more than one article. This approach makes it possible to prepare shorter articles that have a better chance of being accepted for publication. For example, suppose you did a major review of the literature as part of the dissertation. In this case you could consider writing two articles: One would be a literature review; the other would be a report of your study.

The final version of the article should be typed double-space. Also, it should be formated according to the journal's specifications. Journals published by the American Psychological Association, and many other journals as well, follow the specifications of the APA publication manual (see Annotated References). You usually can meet a journal's format specifications by following the format of articles published in its recent issues.

You can check a recent issue of the journal to learn where the manuscript should be sent and other requirements, such as number of copies to include. Most refereed journals require submission of multiple copies so that they can be sent to different persons on the editorial board. Because many journals have a policy of "blind" reviews of manuscripts, you should not have your name and institution appear anywhere except on the cover page of the manuscript. It is appropriate to include a cover letter explaining your enclosures and your desire to have the manuscript published in the journal.

After the editor receives the manuscript, a postcard usually is sent to you acknowledging receipt. Copies of the manuscript are sent to members of the editorial board if the journal is refereed. Whether the manuscript is accepted or not, you should receive copies of their critiques. Often the acceptance is contingent upon making minor revisions that respond to the reviewers' criticisms. In some cases, the editor will ask for major revisions. A manuscript that has gone through a major revision may have to go through a whole new round of review before a final publication decision is made. Even if revisions are not necessary, the review process can take several months or more, and there also may be a considerable lag before you receive galley proofs. The galley proofs are the preliminary typeset version of the article. You should check them carefully for any typesetting errors.

If the manuscript is rejected by a journal, you can expect to receive a statement of the reasons for its rejection. These reasons may not necessarily reflect negatively on it. Many factors operate in the review process, such as editorial policy, a particularly heavy backlog of accepted articles, or personal biases of editorial board members. It is entirely possible that a journal will publish a manuscript that was rejected by another journal. We personally have had this experience a number of times.

A study by Bruce Hall, Ann Ward, and Connie Comer provides some insight about criteria that affect a study's publishability in a research journal.[5] They selected a random sample of 128 educational research articles published in 1983 and had them rated by a panel of experienced researchers. The panel judged that 54 of the articles should have been rejected or accepted only after major revisions.

Hall and his colleagues asked the panel to indicate the specific shortcomings that led them to make these judgments. Table 21.2 shows the most

TABLE 21.2

Specific Shortcomings Cited by Judges to Substantiate Decision to Reject or Require Major Revisions in Articles

Specific Shortcoming	Percentage of the 54 Articles Cited
1. Validity and reliability of data-gathering procedures not established	43
2. Research design not free of specific weaknesses	39
3. Limitations of study not stated	31
4. Research design not appropriate to solution of the problem	28
5. Method of sampling is inappropriate	28
6. Results of the analysis not presented clearly	28
7. Inappropriate methods selected to analyze data	26
8. Report is not clearly written	26
9. Assumptions are not clearly stated	22
10. Data-gathering methods or procedures not described	22

SOURCE: Table 8, Bruce W. Hall, Annie W. Ward, and Connie B. Comer, "Published Educational Research: An Empirical Study of Its Quality," *Journal of Educational Research* 81 (1988): 188.

5. Bruce W. Hall, Annie W. Ward, and Connie B. Comer, "Published Educational Research: An Empirical Study of Its Quality," *Journal of Educational Research* 81 (1988): 182–189.

frequently cited shortcomings of the 54 articles. Most of the shortcomings involved flaws in research methodology or inadequacies in the way it was reported. You may find it helpful to review your drafts of a research article using this list of shortcomings as a guide.

PREPARING A PAPER FOR A PROFESSIONAL MEETING

It is desirable to present a paper based on your dissertation at a professional meeting. You can list it on your *vita* as a professional accomplishment. Also, it helps you become better known to your colleagues.

Educational associations such as AERA (American Educational Research Association) and ASCD (Association for Supervision and Curriculum Development) announce a "call for papers" many months in advance of their annual meeting. The call for papers will appear in one of the association's publications, which are sent to all members. Its purpose is to invite members to submit proposals for papers to be delivered at the meeting. The call for papers states who can submit a proposal (nonmembers usually must be sponsored by a member), format for writing the proposal, and directions for submitting the proposal to the association's proposal review committee. The length of the proposal varies with the association. A short abstract of the proposed paper may be all that is required; occasionally the complete paper must be submitted for review.

After the proposal has been reviewed for its merit and appropriateness, you will receive notification of the committee's decision. If the proposal is accepted, you usually are obligated to attend the meeting in order to deliver the paper in person. Therefore, it is inadvisable to submit a paper proposal unless you are reasonably certain that you will be able to attend the meeting.

It is likely that your paper, if accepted, will be grouped with papers on similar topics to form a symposium or paper-reading session. The time allotted to each participant is often too short to permit the actual reading of the paper; besides, doing so is likely to bore the audience. Instead, you probably will be asked to distribute copies of the paper to the audience. In your talk you should stress the highlights of your research. Many associations will make overhead projectors and other devices available for use in your presentation.

Some associations automatically submit copies of papers presented at their meetings to ERIC (see chapter 4) in order to promote wider distribution of the paper. If the association does not do this, you can, on your own initiative, submit a copy of the paper to the appropriate ERIC clearinghouse.

Papers presented at professional meetings generally are similar in form to articles published in research journals. Occasions may arise, however, when you will be asked to present your research study at a meeting of policymakers or practitioners who have rather limited understanding of research methodology.

Research Question Eleven

	High Involvement %	Moderate Involvement %	Some Involvement %	No Involvement %
Does participation in student government contribute significantly to academic success in high school?				
Very High Grades 'A'	100.0	64.7	38.6	18.0
High Grades 'B'	—	35.3	26.5	39.2
Moderate Grades 'C'	—	—	33.7	39.9
Low Grades 'D'	—	—	1.2	2.9

Trends

* All high school students highly involved in student government (100%) earned very high grades.
* All high school students with moderate involvement in student government (64.7 plus 35.3 or 100%) earned very high or high grades.
* Most high school students with some involvement in student government (38.6 plus 26.5 or 65.1%) earned very high or high grades.
* High school students not involved in student government were least likely to earn high or very high grades.

Figure 21.1   Sample Chart from Chart Essay on Extracurricular Activity Study

SOURCE: Figure 4, Patricia A. Haensly, Ann E. Lupkowski, and James F. McNamara, "The Chart Essay: A Strategy for Communicating Research Findings to Policymakers and Practitioners," *Educational Evaluation and Policy Analysis* 9 (1987): 71.

Patricia Haensly, Ann Lupkowski, and James McNamara developed a method called a **chart essay** that meets this need for a less technical presentation style.[6] The chart essay simplifies the elements of a research study by using charts to focus the audience's attention on aspects of the study that are most relevant to policy making.

Haensly and her colleagues illustrated the method using a study that determined the impact of high school curricular activities on learning. A chart essay format was used to present the findings to a conference of educators of gifted children. One of the charts is reproduced in figure 21.1. The chart's

6. Patricia A. Haensly, Ann E. Lupkowski, and James F. McNamara, "The Chart Essay: A Strategy for Communicating Research Findings to Policymakers and Practitioners," *Educational Evaluation and Policy Analysis* 9 (1987): 63–75.

banner states one of the study's research questions. The findings relevant to the question are stated in a form that does not require special expertise in statistics.

The "trends" statements at the bottom part of the chart are concise, nontechnical, and descriptive of the statistical findings. They are one of the most important elements of the chart essay:

> Taken collectively these trend statements provide the executive summary. At any point in the conference briefing session, they can be easily referenced. . . . [We] have found that trends statements are often quoted directly in press releases, administrative reports, and public meetings.[7]

A helpful feature of the chart essay format for reader comprehension is that each aspect of a study—for example, each research question—is shown on a one-page chart.

MISTAKES SOMETIMES MADE IN PREPARING RESEARCH REPORTS

1. The researcher fails to prepare a draft version of each part of a research report while it is still fresh in his or her memory.
2. Organizes the report of a literature review chronologically instead of topically.
3. Treats each study in the literature review in mechanical fashion, devoting about the same amount of space to each study regardless of relevance or importance.
4. Uses too many quotations or selects quotations that do not make their point as well as the researcher could do through skillful paraphrasing.
5. Confounds presentation of statistical results with their interpretation and implications.
6. Equates statistical significance of results with their practical significance, or does not consider the issue of practical significance.
7. Fails to note methodological limitations of the study.

ANNOTATED REFERENCES

Becker, Howard S. *Writing for Social Scientists: How to Start and Finish Your Thesis, Book, or Article.* Chicago: University of Chicago Press, 1986.

Focus is on the writing process rather than on rules of grammar and punctuation. The author deals with such topics as overcoming writer's block,

---

7. Ibid., p. 70.

revising a manuscript, and developing a sense of writing style. Written specifically for social scientists, including educational researchers.

Mullins, Carolyn. *A Guide to Writing and Publishing in the Social and Behavioral Sciences*. Melbourne, FL: Krieger, 1983.

Describes procedures for preparing journal articles and professional books. Discusses such practical matters as working with journal editors, writing a book prospectus, choosing an appropriate publisher, and negotiating a book contract.

Publication Manual of the American Psychological Association, 3rd ed. Washington, DC: American Psychological Association, 1983.

Contains detailed specifications for preparing articles for journals published by the American Psychological Association. Many other social science journals follow the same specifications. Copies can be ordered by writing to Publication Sales, American Psychological Association, 1200 Seventeenth St., N.W., Washington, DC 20036.

Ulrich's International Periodicals Directory, 26th ed. New York: R. R. Bowker, 1987/88.

A guide to more than 70,000 periodicals grouped by subject and also listed alphabetically by title. Hundreds of these periodicals are education journals classified into such categories as teaching methods and curriculum, special education, school administration, adult education, and computer applications. Information about each journal includes frequency of publication, publisher's address, sponsoring professional organization if any, name of editor, and circulation.

Van Til, William. *Writing for Professional Publication*, 2nd ed. Boston: Allyn & Bacon, 1986.

This widely published author in the field of education offers many tips for getting a journal article or book published. Among the topics covered are how to get published for the first time, how to ensure that your manuscript is in publishable shape, and how to deal with editors.

SELF-CHECK TEST

Circle the correct answer to each of the following questions. An answer key is provided on page 884.

1. In a dissertation, the review of literature should conclude with a
   a. definition of terms.
   b. summary of the state of the art.
   c. description of measures to be employed.
   d. bibliography.
2. In a dissertation, the description of a well-known standardized test should probably
   a. be highly detailed.
   b. be rather brief.
   c. include findings of other studies using the same measure.
   d. include detailed data concerning construct validity.
3. In a dissertation, the description of new or little-known measures should include

      a. reliability data.
      b. validity (especially construct) data.
      c. findings of other studies including the measure.
      d. All of the above are correct.
4. The best method of obtaining clarity in reporting research findings is to organize the discussion
      a. according to the order in which the data were analyzed.
      b. according to the order in which the data were collected.
      c. by presenting the most statistically significant findings first.
      d. according to the hypotheses which guided the research.
5. If the researcher obtains positive results with respect to a hypothesis, he or she can state that the results _____ the hypothesis.
      a. verify
      b. prove
      c. confirm
      d. support
6. The appendix is the appropriate place in the dissertation to include
      a. copies of data-gathering instruments used in the study.
      b. sampling techniques used to select subjects.
      c. the results of tests of null hypotheses.
      d. the review of literature.
7. The first step in preparing a research article is to
      a. determine the journal most likely to publish it.
      b. give it a title.
      c. develop an outline of its content.
      d. write the introduction.
8. After identifying a journal to which to submit an article, the researcher should
      a. examine recent issues of the journal.
      b. contact the journal editor.
      c. select two alternative publication sources.
      d. set the date for publication.

APPLICATION PROBLEMS

The following problems are designed to give you practice in applying significant concepts and research procedures explained in the chapter. Most of them do not have a single correct answer. For feedback, you can compare your answers with the sample answers on page 905.

1. Prepare an outline of the major headings and subheadings of a dissertation.
2. Rewrite the following dissertation titles so that they are brief yet descriptive:
      a. "A Study Investigating the Relationship between Selected Personality Factors in First-, Second-, and Third-Grade Children and Their Attitudes Toward School at Various Intervals in the School Year."
      b. "A Preliminary Investigation into the Effects of Participation in a High School Counseling Program on Student Perceptions of Various Aspects of College."

SUGGESTION SHEET

If your last name starts with letters from Wey to Zzz, please complete the Suggestion Sheet at the end of the book while this chapter is still fresh in your mind.

SELF-CHECK TEST ANSWERS

Chapter 1

1*c*, 2*d*, 3*c*, 4*a*, 5*c*, 6*b*, 7*b*, 8*d*, 9*d*, 10*a*, 11*c*.

Chapter 2

1*b*, 2*c*, 3*b*, 4*c*, 5*d*, 6*b*, 7*a*, 8*c*, 9*b*, 10*d*.

Chapter 3

1*c*, 2*c*, 3*d*, 4*c*, 5*b*, 6*b*, 7*c*, 8*c*, 9*d*, 10*a*.

Chapter 4

1*a*, 2*b*, 3*b*, 4*a*, 5*a*, 6*d*, 7*b*, 8*a*, 9*c*, 10*c*.

Chapter 5

1*b*, 2*b*, 3*a*, 4*a*, 5*d*, 6*c*, 7*a*, 8*b*, 9*c*, 10*c*.

Chapter 6

1*a*, 2*a*, 3*a*, 4*b*, 5*a*, 6*c*, 7*a*, 8*c*, 9*d*, 10*b*.

Chapter 7

1*b*, 2*d*, 3*b*, 4*c*, 5*c*, 6*c*, 7*d*, 8*b*, 9*a* or *c*, 10*a*.

Chapter 8

1*c*, 2*b*, 3*a*, 4*c*, 5*b*, 6*a*, 7*d*, 8*c*, 9*a*, 10*c*.

Chapter 9

1*c*, 2*a*, 3*b*, 4*c*, 5*c*, 6*a*, 7*d*, 8*c*, 9*b*, 10*d*, 11*a*, 12*d*, 13*b*.

Chapter 10

1*a*, 2*a*=P, *b*=N, *c*=P, *d*=N, 3*c*, 4*a*, 5*b*, 6*d*, 7*b*, 8*a*, 9*b*, 10*d*.

Chapter 11

1*a*, 2*b*, 3*c*, 4*c*, 5*b*, 6*b*, 7*b*, 8*d*, 9*c*, 10*d*.

Chapter 12

1*b*, 2*c*, 3*a*, 4*d*, 5*c*, 6*a*, 7*b*, 8*a*, 9*b*, 10*d*.

Chapter 13

1*b*, 2*c*, 3*b*, 4*d*, 5*a*, 6*c*, 7*c*, 8*a*, 9*b*, 10*a*, 11*b*.

Chapter 14

1*c*, 2*b*, 3*c*, 4*a*, 5*d*, 6*d*, 7*a*, 8*b*, 9*b*, 10*a*, 11*d*, 12*b*, 13*c*, 14*a*, 15*c*.

Chapter 15

1*a*, 2*b*, 3*b*, 4*c*, 5*d*, 6*a*, 7*d*, 8*a*, 9*d*, 10*a*.

Chapter 16

1*b*, 2*c*, 3*d*, 4*d*, 5*d*, 6*a*, 7*c*, 8*b*, 9*c*, 10*b*, 11*d*, 12*a*, 13*c*.

Chapter 17

1*d*, 2*c*, 3*b*, 4*c*, 5*a*, 6*a*, 7*a*, 8*d*, 9*b*, 10*d*, 11*c*.

Chapter 18

1*b*, 2*d*, 3*b*, 4*d*, 5*b*, 6*c*, 7*b*, 8*c*, 9*d*, 10*a*.

Chapter 19

1*b*, 2*d*, 3*b*, 4*b*, 5*d*, 6*b*, 7*c*, 8*c*, 9*d*, 10*c*.

Chapter 20

1*a*, 2*b*, 3*d*, 4*c*, 5*d*, 6*d*, 7*a*.

Chapter 21

1*b*, 2*b*, 3*d*, 4*d*, 5*d*, 6*a*, 7*a*, 8*a*.

Chapter 1

1. The proposal could be defended by identifying types of research that could be done with the funds. For example:
   a. Basic research to discover the process that students use in studying. Determine whether high-achieving and low-achieving students use different processes.
   b. Applied research to determine study methods that are effective in improving student achievement.
   c. Systematic R & D to develop validated study-skill programs.
   d. Evaluation studies to determine whether study-skill programs are being implemented properly and whether they are producing the desired results.

   A more general defense is that money alone does not produce results. There are many examples of government-funded programs that were well-intended but proved ineffective. Research may mean less money for highly visible programs in the short run, but it may produce more effective impact on practice in the long run.

2. Quantitative researchers try to be neutral, objective researchers; they try to stay detached from the persons they study; try to obtain results that will generalize across many groups and situations; and to rely on statistical analysis and reporting techniques. Qualitative researchers tend to view themselves as a data-collection tool; tend to interact with the persons they study; are more concerned with understanding the individual case than with generalizing across cases; and tend to report results in the form of verbal descriptions.
   One defense of quantitative research is that its findings can be easily replicated by other researchers because it relies on objective research procedures. Another defense is that this type of research seeks to discover generalizations, which are of great value in understanding diverse educational phenomena. One defense of qualitative research is that it is well-suited

for the study of important nonobservable phenomena. Another defense is that it can result in insights about a single case, which may be important in its own right. Also, insights about a single case can be used to generate new hypotheses that can then be tested by using quantitative research techniques.

Chapter 2

1. Sample areas of interest and problems:
   a. Evaluation of teaching effectiveness
      (1) Development of classroom observation systems
      (2) Studies of the relationship between particular teaching techniques and student outcomes
   b. Teacher supervision
      (1) Characteristics of effective supervisors
      (2) Studies of typical interaction patterns between supervisors and teachers
   c. Creativity
      (1) Development of techniques for increasing creativity
      (2) School achievement of creative children

   Sample null hypothesis, problem a(2):
   Mathematics teachers who use specific feedback during math lessons and comparable teachers who use general feedback do not obtain different levels of pupil gain in mathematics achievement.

   Sample directional hypothesis:
   Mathematics teachers who use specific feedback during math lessons obtain higher pupil achievement gains than comparable teacher who use general feedback.

   Sample objective:
   The objective of this study is to determine whether there is a difference in pupil mathematics achievement for mathematics teachers who use specific feedback as compared with those who use general feedback.

2. Topics usually covered in a research plan:
   a. Introduction, including purpose of study and literature review
   b. Hypotheses or objectives
   c. Measures
   d. Subjects
   e. Research design
   f. Data analysis
   g. Chronological list of procedures

3. Advantages of a detailed research plan:
   a. A written plan is easily given to experts for their advice.
   b. A researcher may forget to carry out important steps of a project if she does not put them in writing beforehand.
4. Research hypothesis evaluation:
   The researcher appears to have a definite reason for testing the hypothesis. This is good. Second, the hypothesis appears testable; however, the researcher should identify the specific self-concept measures on which no change is expected. Third, the hypothesis could be shortened by omitting the rationale, "since we believe . . . in the ability-grouped class." A better statement of the hypothesis might be, "Low-ability children placed in an ability-grouped class will show no significant change on self-concept measures (specify) over a certain time period." The hypothesis, and the study itself, could also be improved if the researcher made a prediction about self-concept changes of low-ability students who are not placed in ability-grouped classes.
5. Arguments favoring a pilot study:
   a. The pilot study may help her develop new hypotheses to be tested.
   b. It may help her discover problems that were not mentioned in the report of the previous study.
   c. It may help her discover new procedures that are more effective than those tested in the previous study.
   d. It provides a test of the modifications that she has added to the previous study.

Chapter 3

1. Each individual's consent will be obtained prior to the start of the project. The test data will be kept confidential; names of subjects will be removed from the tests as soon as possible. When the research design permits, tests will be anonymous.
2. No. School people usually will want specific information about details of the research project that will affect them. For example, they will want to know who is to be involved, whether the tests are controversial, how the individual's right to privacy is to be protected, and whether the results will reflect unfavorably on the school district.
3. In this study the investigator should take steps that would assure desensitization of subjects. These steps could include:
   a. Plan a procedure and conduct a small-scale pilot study to be sure you have developed an adequate procedure for desensitizing your subjects. If not, do not conduct study until such a procedure is developed. The procedure should probably include steps such as the following:
   b. Point out that most people tell a great many small lies in situations in which they believe there is no chance to be caught.

    c. Provide evidence to support the above statement, if available. This could include data from previous research as well as the research in question.

    d. Check on whether all subjects have accepted your arguments. If not, carry out individual conferences and if necessary counseling with subjects who are still troubled.

4. Incorrect scores on this test could lead students to develop incorrect self-perceptions and aspirations. Therefore, the investigator should carry out a program to dehoax students at the end of the study. Steps in this program could include the following:

    a. Describe the purpose of the study and explain why the deception was necessary.

    b. Hold individual conferences with subjects, show them their test papers pointing out their correct score and discussing how this score was changed.

    c. Give students a questionnaire to determine if they are dehoaxed; i.e., do they believe your explanation and accept their actual score on the test?

    d. Offer to give students another algebra aptitude test so they can be sure of their actual performance.

5. Ethical and legal steps that should be taken by the researcher.

    a. Inform parents of the purposes of the study and obtain parental permission for subjects to participate.

    b. Describe the specific school records you will need and obtain parental permission to use the records.

    c. Inform participants of the essential features of the research and answer questions they raise.

    d. Be sure that the study is structured so as to remove any serious negative effects such as resentment and more negative attitudes among control-group subjects. For example, such resentment could probably be removed by giving control-group subjects a "large" gift at the end of the study.

    e. Explain the study to all subjects at the end of the research.

    f. Set up procedures to ensure confidentiality of all data related to the study.

Chapter 4

1. A primary source is one in which the writer was a witness to what is being reported. In educational research literature this usually means the writer is reporting on personal investigations. Most articles appearing in journals such as the *Journal of Educational Psychology, Journal of Experimental Education,* and the *Journal of Educational Research* are primary source references.

    On the other hand, a secondary-source author is reporting on events that he did not himself witness. In educational research literature, secondary sources discuss investigations done by other researchers. Textbooks contain secondary source information for the most part. The review of literature you prepare for your graduate research project will also be a secondary source since you will be reviewing the work of other investigators.

2. a. Praise, Positive Reinforcement, Reinforcement, Verbal Reinforcement, Social Reinforcement, Sharing (Social Behavior), Prosocial Behavior.
    b. Positive Reinforcement, Reinforcement, Social Reinforcement, Rewards.
    c. Barton, Edward J. "Developing Sharing: An Analysis of Modeling and Other Behavioral Techniques." *Behavior Modification*, 1981 (July) Vol. 5 (3), 386–398. (Several other articles peripheral to this topic may also be found in 1982 to 1988 Psychological Abstracts; see for example abstracts 1090 and 7530.)

3. To complete this problem you should have carried out the following steps:
    a. Selected two preliminary sources in the faculty member's area, searched the author indexes, and made up bibliography cards.
    b. Searched *Social Science Citation Index* for the name of the faculty member. Put a tally mark on each bibliography card for each time the article was cited. If the selected faculty member was in psychology, you should also have checked *Science Citation Index*.
    c. Selected bibliography card with most tally marks, located article, read and made up note card following procedures described in chapter 4.

4. a. The following data should be included on your bibliography card. The sample is in *Psychological Abstracts* format:
       Richey, Harold W. (Univ. of Missouri) Avoidable failures of experimental procedure. *Journal of Experimental Education*, 1976 (Win), Vol. 45 (2), 10–13.
    b. This article was selected because it contains some very useful information for the student in educational research. If you plan to conduct an experimental study, keep your note card and review these causes of failure when designing your study. This is not a research article so it is recommended that a sentence outline format be used. Your 5-by-8 note card should have the bibliographic data at the top and should include the following information.
       (1) Common reasons for failures of experimental procedures:
           (a) Experimental task is too demanding for ordinary levels of subject motivation.
           (b) Procedures are intellectually too demanding or too unfamiliar for subjects.
           (c) Study imposes requirements that are repugnant or annoying to subjects.
           (d) Study involves inherently funny situations that subjects may not take seriously.
           (e) Study asks subjects to respond in ways that make them look inadequate.
           (f) Experimental manipulation is overly contrived or unbelievable.

(g) Impact of manipulation too weak to offset established behavior patterns.

(h) Experimental confederates not convincing actors.

(i) Study takes insufficient notice of special needs or circumstances of subjects which may affect responses.

(2) Suggestions for avoiding these errors:

(a) Investigator should serve as own prepilot subject.

(b) Run pilot study with subjects and conditions as similar as possible to main study.

(c) During pilot study, check in as many ways as possible the adequacy of the experimental manipulation.

(d) Discuss your plans with other researchers and seek critical feedback.

(e) Consider what possible flaws could result in negative findings and correct them before doing the research.

(f) Do a thorough job of planning; it pays off in better research.

5. Locate descriptors in the *Thesaurus of ERIC Descriptors:*

a. Teacher behavior
b. Teacher influence
c. Teacher characteristics
d. Teacher influence
e. Teacher evaluation
f. Teaching
g. Effective teaching
h. Teaching methods
i. Classroom techniques
j. Teaching procedures
k. Teaching programs
l. Teaching skills
m. Teaching styles
n. Teaching techniques
o. Achievement
p. Academic achievement
q. Knowledge level
r. Achievement gains
s. Achievement ratings
t. Performance

Search Plan:
(1 or 2 or 3 or 4 or 5 or 6 or 7 or 8 or 9 or 10 or 11 or 12 or 13 or 14) and (15 or 16 or 17 or 18 or 19 or 20)

Note the use of a high number of *or* connections used to obtain high coverage. It is doubtful whether any two researchers would plan a search such as this in exactly the same way. If you have employed a high number of relevant descriptors in a similar *and, or* configuration, your search plan may be regarded as correct. You should have included many of the same descriptors given above, but you could have omitted some and added others and still have a satisfactory search plan. If you included only the two descriptors "teaching techniques" and "achievement," you would obtain an inadequate search.

Chapter 5

1. a. Subjects were lost from both treatment and control groups. However, treatment-group losses were greater and probably consisted of students with low motivation.
   b. If the researcher is interested in generalizing the findings to all U.S. college students, the sample is probably nonrepresentative, since it was drawn from one commuter college.
   c. Students were not randomly assigned to the sections (at least, the description makes no mention of this procedure), although sections were randomly assigned to treatments.

2. a. Underlined phrase should be "prove the invalidity of this racist belief once and for all." This statement suggests that the investigator is emotionally involved with the topic, that is, has an ax to grind. This indicates a biased viewpoint and suggests that deliberate bias might have occured.
   b. The investigator uses a high-inference global rating of "warmth" and "understanding." Such ratings are highly susceptible to observer bias. More objective ratings would occur if these general traits were defined in terms of specific teacher behaviors. For example, "warmth" could be defined in terms of the number of times the teacher smiled, the number of times she touched children, etc. The design also permits observer contamination, since the investigator both selects and observes the teachers. Thus, he knows which teachers have small children, and this knowledge could influence his rating of the teacher.

3. a. Because orange juice is given daily as part of the normal school routine, no Hawthorne Effect is likely to take place.
   b. If children are unaware that a supplement is being added to their orange juice, no placebo is necessary. If children in the treatment group are aware that a supplement is added, then a placebo (perceived by the children as the same supplement) should be added for the control group. Nevertheless, in a study of this nature it is usually not necessary for children to know that they are receiving a supplement, although parental approval is required.

4. The correlation of .17 is not of practical significance for prediction. A correlation of .17 indicates that the two variables only have 2.89 percent ($.17^2$) common variance. This amount of common variance is too low to have any practical significance in prediction.

5. a. Both groups are volunteers. However, the most serious problem is sampling bias that occurs because of the loss of teachers from group A. These teachers probably differ in motivation (and perhaps other characteristics) from the 14 who completed the training. For example, the dropouts could be more effective teachers who decided they don't need the training or weaker teachers who are afraid of the achievement comparisons. Thus, group A is likely to differ from group B in ways that could bias the results.

b. Yes, it is a new and nonconventional program. The Hawthorne Effect is likely to occur. There is no control-group program.

c. Yes. The control teachers are likely to feel threatened because they will be compared with the experimental group on pupil achievement.

d. (1) Set up reward and motivational systems to reduce dropouts. Also try to get a firm commitment at outset from all participating teachers.

(2) Introduce a control treatment that deals with some other aspect of teaching that would not affect achievement.

(3) Set up procedures that would reduce the anxieties of the control teachers such as assuring complete confidentiality of the results obtained by individual teachers.

Chapter 6

1. a. Obtain the names of all elementary school principals and the addresses of their schools from the state education directory.

b. Contact each principal by mail and request a roster of fifth-grade pupils enrolled in his schools.

c. Order the rosters randomly, and assign a number to each name.

d. Using a table of random numbers, select 100 subjects.

2. a. Obtain the names, sex, and years of experience of all primary-grade teachers in the district.

b. Divide the population into male and female.

c. Set up several experience classifications. This could be done by making a frequency distribution of years of experience and then selecting cutoff points so as to provide three categories of about equal numbers of teachers. Or a division could be made on some logical basis without regard to numbers of teachers. An example of a logical division could be:

First-year teachers
Teachers who have 1 to 5 years of experience
Teachers who have 6 or more years of experience

d. Divide each sex into subgroups based upon whatever experience categories you have established.

e. Check number of teachers in each subcategory to be sure each contains more than 20. (If not, categories should be changed.)

f. Randomly select 20 teachers from each subcategory (male first-year teachers, female first-year teachers, male teachers with 1–5 years of experience, and so on), using a table of random numbers or by drawing names from a container of name slips.

3. a. Identify the 104 second-grade classrooms and assign each a number.

b. Randomly select 10 classrooms using a table of random numbers or by drawing numbers from a container.

    c. Obtain the names of all students in the selected classrooms. Randomly select 10 subjects from each classroom to give a total of 100 subjects.

4. a. *Small differences anticipated.* Because the treatment lasts only one hour and is concerned only with word problems, the investigator might well expect the treatment to bring about only a small difference in mathematics achievement.

    b. *Groups must be broken into subgroups.* The investigator has broken his sample into subgroups based on IQ. This requires an increase in sample size. Because only about 2–3 percent of his subjects are likely to have IQ scores above 130, he must further increase sample size to get enough subjects in this category.

5. a. Investigator used volunteers for treatment group.

    b. Treatment group suffered large loss of subjects. Subjects who finished the program were probably highly motivated. No control-group subjects were lost since they were not called on to do anything.

    c. Subjects were used because they were available, i.e., not drawn randomly from any defined population.

    d. Subjects not drawn from same subject pool. That is, the experimental group was drawn from the remedial course, whereas the control group was drawn from the regular course. Since subjects were drawn from different populations, they probably differed in ways relevant to the study, such as overall mastery of English.

Chapter 7

1. a. Concurrent validity since test scores and grades were obtained at same time.

    b. Content validity since the training was concerned with a limited content area. Most regular achievement tests would be inappropriate because they deal mainly with content not covered in the new instructional technique. What is needed is a measure that deals only with positive and negative numbers. This can be determined only by comparing the test content with the training content.

2. a. Predictive validity was studied.

    b. Predictive validity is most relevant because the aptitude test will be used to predict students' future performance in algebra.

3. Coefficient of equivalence; this is also known as alternate-form reliability.

4. a. Group measure. It is easier, cheaper, and adequate for investigating these variables with college freshmen.

    b. Individual measure. These children will be too limited in writing skill to express their responses in writing. Thus, each child must be shown the pictures individually and his responses recorded by the examiner.

5. a. Make the testing appear important. Tell the students you will tell them the purpose of the research after the testing is completed.

   b. Before administering the measure, tell students that the individuals' responses will not be revealed to anyone and that results will be reported in group form only. It is also recommended that subjects not be obliged to write their names on the measure; if later identification is needed, code numbers can be used.

Chapter 8

1. a. The Score Index should be used.
      Nine test numbers are listed.

   b. Tests measuring study skills:

Test Number	Test Name
24	Achievement Tests: Grades 1–8
*123	Basic Skills Inventory
168	Bristol Achievement Tests (the Study Skills subtest is the same as 171)
171	Bristol Achievement Tests: Study Skills
660	Mastery: An Evaluation Tool
*670	McCarthy Individualized Diagnostic Reading Inventory, Revised Edition
699	Metropolitan Achievement Test, 5th Edition
*1115	Sequential Tests of Educational Progress, Series III
*1293	The 3-R's Test

   c. The Bristol Achievement Tests were developed and standardized in England and Wales. Therefore, the test content might not be appropriate for American students. Also, this test covers ages 8–14 only; thus it is not appropriate for high school students.

2. a. Low cost and ease of administration.

   b. Susceptibility to faking and response sets such as social desirability and acquiescence.

3. a. Adjective Check List.

   b. Stanford Diagnostic Mathematics Test.

   c. Culture-Fair Intelligence Test; Goodenough-Harris Drawing Test; Safran Culture Reduced Intelligence Test.

   d. Strong/Campbell Interest Inventory.

4. a. The degree of similarity between the content of the achievement test and the content of the district's third-grade reading curriculum.

   b. The extent to which the content of the achievement test is up to date and reflects the students' culture.

    c. Is the test appropriate for testing fourth-, fifth-, and sixth-grade pupils? Is the test ceiling high enough?

5. The *Fairview Development Scale* and the *Fairview Self-Help Scale* provide self-help scores, fit the appropriate age range, and have satisfactory reliability. The *Self-Help Skill Assessment Checklist* could be used if reliability data could be obtained. The author of this measure might have obtained reliability data since *Tests and Measurements in Child Development Handbook II* was published. The researcher would probably contact the author and perhaps even conduct his own reliability study if the measure appeared to meet his needs.

Chapter 9

1. a. A↘   The principal's instructional leadership, teacher morale,
        B→D   and school climate each might independently affect
        C↗   student achievement.

    b. ↗B↘   The principal's instructional leadership affects
       A D   teacher morale and school climate. These two
       ↘C↗   factors in turn affect student achievement.

    c. A→B→C→D   The principal's instructional leadership affects teacher morale, which in turn affects school climate, which in turn affects student achievement.

2. The median would be more accurate than the mean, because it would not be affected as much by the 40 extreme scores.

3. a. True dichotomy.
    b. Continuous variable.
    c. Category score.
    d. Artificial dichotomy.

4. No. Although statistically significant, a mean difference of only 2.5 items on a 200-item test is of virtually no practical significance. In deciding which program to use in a school system, factors other than the small achievement difference would probably be more important.

5. The researcher should use each pair of students in the experimental group as the unit of analysis, because the learning of each student probably was affected by his or her partner. The scores of each pair would be averaged to yield a mean score. Since there are 60 experimental group students, there will be 30 mean scores in the statistical analysis. The unit of analysis for the control group should be the individual, because each student engaged in the learning activity independently of the other students. Thus, there will be 60 control group scores in the statistical analysis.

Chapter 10

1. a. The hypothesis should be grounded in with data, not stated before data are collected.

    b. The hypothesis is much too narrow.

    c. The researcher should not have selected a random sample. It would be better to select a purposive sample (e.g., representatives from each racial group) and better still to observe all students.

    d. The observer should not use a structured observation form but instead should use continuous recording and try to record as much as possible of what went on in the classroom.

    e. The one-week observation period is much too short to collect sufficient qualitative data.

2. Referring to the criteria given in this chapter, the following evaluation may be made:

    a. Quality of direct on-site observation would be high. There would be little chance of masking unless other teachers became suspicious of the observers.

    b. Freedom of access would be good in that the participant observers (PO's) would have access to any meetings that they could legitimately attend in their roles of teachers.

       However, if the study had chosen to use participant observers (PO's) who were known to be conducting research (i.e., no deception) they may have had greater access to some situations from which teachers would be excluded.

    c. Intensity of observation would be high if study extended over an entire school year. If the PO's did not have to carry out their teaching roles, the amount of direct observation would increase. If deception were not being used, the PO's could probably prepare much more extensive field notes.

    d. Both qualitative data and quantitative data could be collected, with the PO's and key informant interviews providing qualitative data, while some quantitative data could be collected during the survey interviews.

    e. Triangulation would be achieved in this study by gathering information on the same topics using both the PO's field notes and the data from the interviews.

    f. Because data would be collected in a variety of school settings, a representative sampling of data would probably be collected. However, the implementation of a sampling plan might be hampered by the half-time teaching demands made on the PO's.

    g. There are many unobtrusive cues in the school situation that can help the observer understand the behavior of students and teachers. PO's should be trained to watch for such cues and record them.

Chapter 11

1. a. What are your current plans for the year following your graduation in June? Check appropriate answers and indicate period of time during which you anticipate doing the activity.

_____ 1. Obtain paid employment.
_____ 2. Attend graduate school.
_____ 3. Travel.
_____ 4. Join the Peace Corps or other volunteer service.
_____ 5. Join the armed forces.
_____ 6. Other (specify)._____

b. What are your current plans for the year following graduation in June? Please state all significant activities that you expect to undertake.

_____

_____

_____

_____

2. Some teachers might express an attitude toward open education on the basis of inadequate information. The short test enables the researcher to determine whether this possibility exists in actuality. If so, the test also provides a method of eliminating these teachers from the sample.

3. a. Describe the purpose of the study.
   b. Describe the importance of the study.
   c. Request that the questionnaire be returned by a specified date.
   d. Appeal to the respondent's professional authority in his field or sense of professionalism.
   e. Offer to provide a summary of the study's findings.

4. a. Send a follow-up letter with another copy of the questionnaire and a self-addressed envelope. The letter could be sent by certified mail.
   b. Telephone the nonrespondents, requesting them to return the questionnaire.
   c. Send a telegram to the nonrespondents, requesting them to return the questionnaire.

5. a. Semistructured interview.
   b. In a semistructured interview, it is advisable to begin with structured questions requiring factual answers.
   c. These are followed by questions that will probably require further probing: 5, 6, 7.

Chapter 12

1. a. (1) Animated vs. unchanging facial expression (e.g., presence of smiles, raised eyebrows).
      (2) Inflected vs. monotone speech.
      (3) Movement about the classroom vs. stationary position.
      (4) Verbal statement reflecting personal interest in and appreciation of the subject being taught (e.g., "This was one of the most exciting discoveries of late nineteenth-century physics").

(5) Presence of arm gestures.
   b. Observe the teacher's face during a 20-minute class discussion. Count the frequency of occurrence of these facial expressions:

Frequency

Smiling _____
Laughter _____
Raised eyebrow _____
Other animated expression _____

2. The research did not include plans to calculate interrater reliability coefficients to determine the degree to which observers are developing a common frame of reference.
3. a. The neatness with which objects are organized in the children's desks.
   b. The amount of litter on the floor at the end of the school day.
   c. The neatness of the children's paperwork.
   d. If there is a cloak room, the neatness with which the children's clothes are arranged in it.
   e. The alignment of desks in an orderly pattern at the end of the school day.
4. a. Sociometry.
   b. Ratings made by the students' teachers.
5. a. Frequency of use of low-frequency words.
   b. Frequency of words denoting abstract concepts, e.g., "nationalism," "logic," "symbolism."
   c. Frequency of connectives such as "if," "but," "therefore," "whereas."
   d. Average length of sentences.
   e. Frequency of cited evidence in support of a position.
   These are all specific, low inference measures that can easily be tabulated.

Chapter 13

1. a. High school teachers of comparable age, sex, and experience who have average or low scores in authoritarianism.
   b. Monolingual first-grade children of Mexican ancestry (i) who speak English only and (ii) who speak Spanish only.
   c. Fourth-grade Pueblo Indian boys who have attended school off the reservation.
2. The t-test for correlated means would be most appropriate, because children were matched for scholastic aptitude, which in turn is probably correlated with the dependent variable, achievement.
3. A one-tailed test would be appropriate, because there is already some evidence that special tutoring increases achievement. Thus, if a difference is found, it will probably favor the group that received the special tutoring.

4. a. A *t*-test for uncorrelated means would be used to compare the authoritarianism scores of the two samples.
   b. A chi-square contingency table would be used. The table would be set up as follows:

Number of Students Belonging to Club Rated:

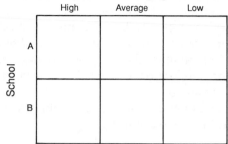

c. Analysis of covariance should be used, because it permits adjusting the senior level scores for differences found in the junior high school scores.

Chapter 14

1. a. No. This conclusion assumes that there is a causal connection between working while in college and degree of personal maturity. Causal inferences cannot be made with a high degree of assurance from correlational data.
   b. Yes. The correlation of +.65 means that the two variables are positively related, that is, an increment in amount of employment is likely to be associated with an increment in personal maturity score.
   c. No. As in (a) above, this conclusion makes a causal assumption that is not warranted on the basis of the correlational data obtained in this study.
2. Increasing the number of variables will not necessarily increase the likelihood of finding significant relationships. Also, some of the variables may correlate significantly with the criterion variables for irrelevant reasons; these relationships will probably disappear when the study is repeated. A better strategy is to include measures which theory and previous research suggest are related to the criterion variable, that is, interest in science.
3. a. Product-moment correlation coefficient, because both scales yield continuous scores.
   b. Partial correlation. This is a statistical technique that is used to determine the degree of relationship between two variables after the effect of a third variable on both has been removed.
   c. Biserial correlation, because the Scholastic Aptitude Test yields continuous scores and the pass-fail criterion is an artificial dichotomy.

    d. Factor analysis, because this technique determines the extent to which all the measures entered into a correlation matrix represent the same basic behavior pattern or characteristic.

    e. Plot a scattergram to represent graphically the relationship between the two variables. If the relationship appears to be nonlinear, compute the correlation ratio *eta*. There are statistical tests that can be used to determine if the regression lines depart significantly from linearity.

4. Multiple regression, because this statistical technique yields a prediction that is more accurate than could be obtained by correlating any single test with the criterion variable, that is, gradepoint average.

5. a. The moderator variable is self-esteem, which has three values: high, middle, and low.

    b. There are three predictor variables: verbal aptitude, quantitative aptitude, and creative aptitude.

Chapter 15

1. a. Recruit a sample of teachers to be in each experimental treatment. The courses represented in each treatment (e.g., English, history) also might be varied.

    b. Plan for observation of in-class activities during the experimental period.

    c. Incorporate an experimental treatment that allows teachers to use their regular instructional methods. These methods may or may not include discussion.

2. a. Because the researcher developed the training program, he probably has a bias that it is effective. This bias can influence his observations of teacher behavior. Even if teachers have not improved after training, the bias may lead him to record observations that show favorable changes.

    b. The reseacher could train persons other than himself to make the observations. Preferably these persons would not know the purpose of the experiment in order to eliminate the influence of their own biases on the observations. Another method of reducing the possibility of experimenter bias is to make videotapes of teacher behavior before and after training. The videotapes could be scored later by observers in random order so that they do not know which are pretapes and which are posttapes.

3. It will be very difficult to ensure that none of the students in the control group will try to obtain the note-taking outline (which is the experimental treatment) from a classmate who is in the experimental group. If some of the control-group students obtain the outline, the experiment is no longer a pure comparison between two types of experimental treatment.

4. One method is to assign teachers randomly to an experimental and control

treatment. Another method is to assign students randomly in each classroom to the experimental and control treatments.

5. Analysis of covariance. The posttest scores of the two groups cannot be compared directly because the groups did not start at the same pretest level (35 vs. 45). The analysis of covariance technique is used to equate their pretest scores statistically.

Chapter 16

1. One procedure is to assign classes randomly to treatments. Preliminary matching by grade level can be done to ensure equivalence of treatment groups. For example, two first-grade classes can be randomly assigned to one treatment, and the other two classes can be assigned to a second treatment. Thus, each treatment will have the same number of classes at each grade level. Analysis of covariance can be used to control for initial differences between groups.

2.

Ability	Conventional Instruction		Traditional Instruction	
	Boys	Girls	Boys	Girls
High	10	15	10	15
Middle	10	15	10	15
Low	10	15	10	15

Interaction effects: A × B
              A × C
              B × C
              A × B × C
Where A = treatment
      B = gender of student
      C = ability level of student

3. A multiple-baseline design can be used. The researcher might elect several target behaviors for experimental manipulation. These would include the verbal mannerisms (i.e., "uh" and "you know") and several other behaviors such as frequency of eye contact with the audience, movement away from the podium, and eliciting student questions. One behavior at a time would be

targeted for experimental manipulation. If each behavior changed as expected, the researcher can conclude that the treatment was responsible for the decrease in frequency of the verbal mannerisms.

4. a. Is the curriculum specialist more interested in the learning of individual students or in the learning of students as a group? (Single-subject designs focus on the individual learner; multisubject designs focus on group trends.)

    b. Is it possible to give students many tests of the computational skills? (Single-subject designs require frequent measurement of the same variable.)

    c. Is it possible to meet the requirements of an A-B-A design (e.g., reinstating baseline conditions after withdrawal of the treatment) or of a multiple-baseline design (e.g., changing one computational skill at a time) in the classes that will participate in the experiment?

5. a. Regression toward the mean could have occurred.

    b. Students in the highest quartile may have made a substantial gain but it was not reflected in the posttest due to a ceiling effect; that is, the posttest may not have measured the entire range of possible achievement for the particular variables of concern.

Chapter 17

1. You can point out that the manager will need to make decisions continuously about the program (e.g., whether to reallocate resources, change timelines, redesign operating procedures). Evaluation can provide data that will improve these decisions. Also, the manager is probably accountable to others (e.g., a funding agency, clients) for program results. Evaluation can provide quantitative data about program results so that the manager does not need to rely exclusively on his or others' subjective impressions.

2. a. To what extent do the materials achieve the objective of improving writing skills?

    b. In what ways are the materials easy or difficult to understand?

    c. Do the materials require more time than is available?

    d. What are college instructors' judgments about the worth of the materials, and what are their recommendations for improving them?

    e. What are college students' judgments about the worth of the materials, and what are their recommendations for improving them?

3. You might point out that the school is composed of several programs (e.g., a college preparation program, a school lunch program, an athletic program). Each program can be evaluated with respect to one or more aspects—goals, resources, procedures, and management. The principal needs to decide which program(s) and which aspect(s) of the program should be evaluated.

4. Either you would not ask what the program's goal is, or you would disregard

it in designing the evaluation. Instead, you will look for the program's actual effects. These effects might include the extent to which the students swim after the program is completed; fear of swimming, even though the students achieve proficiency; other students' expressions of acceptance, avoidance, or ridicule of nonswimmers entered into the program; changes in the pool's regular schedule as a result of the new program.

5. Nutrition experts. They might be concerned about:
   a. the soundness of the needs assessment data being used to develop the program.
   b. the accuracy of the program content.

Students. They might be concerned that:
   a. the program content might be too difficult for them to comprehend.
   b. the program might call for too radical a change in their eating habits.

Parents. They might be concerned that:
   a. the foods recommended by the program will be expensive to purchase.
   b. implementation of the program recommendations will require them to change their cooking and personal eating habits.

Teachers. They might be concerned that:
   a. implementation of the program will take time away from other important subjects they teach.
   b. implementation of the program will require them to change their normal teaching style.

Administrators. They might be concerned about:
   a. costs of implementing the program.
   b. criticism from food manufacturers whose products are cast in an unfavorable light by the program.

Chapter 18

1. Compare your steps with those described on pages 784–785.
2. Product D. A product may be popular (product A), well-funded (product B), with well-defined objectives (product C), but these qualifications do not necessarily mean it will work. However, pertinent research knowledge can guide the developer in designing and evaluating the product so that it will yield significant results.
3. The R & D specialist may overlook problems that would be exposed if she tested the materials in a regular classroom.
4. The developers could revise the materials on the basis of their insights and then submit them to another main field test. An alternative would be to revise

the materials, but first conduct a preliminary field test before another main field test.

5. By not using expensive media, he will have more development money to use in revising the materials. If quality of media is a matter of concern, he can produce a small part of the materials in high-quality format to test its effect.

Chapter 19

1. Possible preliminary sources are:
   a. Eugene P. Sheehy, *Guide to Reference Books*, 9th ed.
   b. *Bibliographic Index.*
   c. *Education Index.*
   d. *A Bibliography of American Educational History.*

   Possible repositories are:
   a. Publishers of tests, especially the publisher of the Stanford-Binet Intelligence Scale.
   b. Libraries that have collections of papers of prominent psychologists and educators involved in the intelligence testing movement.
   c. Professional organizations in education and psychology that were in existence at the time that the intelligence-testing movement began.

2. A separate note card would be made for each entry relevant to the study. The note card would identify the source and give the date, amount, and classification of the entry (teacher, salary, books, etc.), plus anything about the entry that was worthy of special note (such as payment of a teacher in goods rather than money). Once all note cards were completed, they could be sorted in different ways to answer specific questions such as: How similar were the spending patterns of the different principals? What trends occurred in expenditures for educational materials from 1900 to 1930?

   If you used the note-card procedure usually employed for abstracting research articles, you would have only one card for each account book, and these cards would each contain such a large amount of material as to be of little use.

3. a. The reporter had not himself witnessed the teaching of phrenology referred to by the professor.
   b. The professor had an interest in making phrenology appear important.
   c. The professor may be distorting his role in the account.
   d. The professor's entire story could be a fabrication designed to get publicity for his act.

4. a. "School official," "psychologist," "intelligence test," and "early nineteenth century" need to be defined, since these concepts identify the range of phenomena to be included in the historical search.
   b. The number of years in the early nineteenth century for which historical sources are sought; the range of psychologists and school officials whose

views are studied; the geographical locales (e.g., entire United States, individual states, European countries) for which historical sources are sought.

Chapter 20

1. Obtain a copy of the test manual in order to familiarize yourself with the test content and scoring procedure.
2. Use code numbers instead of writing a description. For example, 1 = male, 2 = female. Similarly, the subject's school and social class can be identified by a code number.
3. 1433-525763496247-122218-14748561
   A blank space is used to separate each logical grouping of data: I.D. (143) and record number (3); six attitude scales (52, 57, etc.); three behavior ratings (1.2, 2.2, 1.8); and demographic information (occupation, age, income). Note that the decimal points for behavior rating values are omitted on a computer recording form. Also omitted are the dollar sign and comma in the income figure. The person's occupation (stockbroker) was given a code (1).

Chapter 21

1. Compare your outline with the one presented on pages 861–862.
2. a. "The Relationship Between Personality and Attitudes Toward School in Primary-Grade Children."
   b. "Effect of a High School Counseling Program on Student Perceptions of College."

APPENDIX A

ERIC CLEARINGHOUSES

There are currently 16 ERIC Clearinghouses, each responsible for a major area of the field of education. Clearinghouses acquire, select, catalog, abstract, and index the documents announced in *Resources in Education (RIE)*. They also prepare interpretive summaries and annotated bibliographies dealing with high-interest topics and based on the documents analyzed for *RIE*; these information analysis products are also announced in *Resources in Education*. (Appendix A is reprinted from *CIJE* (regular monthly listing on p. vi), Phoenix: The Oryx Press. By permission of the publisher.)

CE   ADULT, CAREER, AND VOCATIONAL EDUCATION
Ohio State University
National Center for Research in Vocational Education
1960 Kenny Road
Columbus, Ohio 43210-1090
(614) 486-3655; (800) 848-4815

CG   COUNSELING AND PERSONNEL SERVICES
University of Michigan
School of Education, Room 2108
Ann Arbor, Michigan 48109-1259
(313) 764-9492

CS   READING AND COMMUNICATION SKILLS
National Council of Teachers of English
1111 Kenyon Road
Urbana, Illinois 61801-1096
(217) 328-3870

EA   EDUCATIONAL MANAGEMENT
University of Oregon
1787 Agate Street
Eugene, Oregon 97403-5207
(503) 686-5043

EC   HANDICAPPED AND GIFTED CHILDREN
Council for Exceptional Children
1920 Association Drive
Reston, Virginia 22091-1589
(703) 620-3660

FL   LANGUAGES AND LINGUISTICS
Center for Applied Linguistics
1118 22nd St., N.W.
Washington, D.C. 20037-0037
(202) 429-9551

HE   HIGHER EDUCATION
George Washington University
One Dupont Circle, N.W., Suite 630
Washington, D.C. 20036-1183
(202) 296-2597

IR   INFORMATION RESOURCES
Syracuse University
School of Education
Huntington Hall, Room 030
Syracuse, New York
13244-2340
(315) 423-3640

JC   JUNIOR COLLEGES
University of California at
Los Angeles
Mathematical Science Building,
Room 8118
Los Angeles, California
90024-1564
(213) 825-3931

PS   ELEMENTARY AND EARLY
CHILDHOOD EDUCATION
University of Illinois
College of Education
805 West Pennsylvania
Avenue
Urbana, Illinois 61801-4897
(217) 333-1386

RC   RURAL EDUCATION AND
SMALL SCHOOLS
New Mexico State University
Department 3AP, Box 30001
Las Cruces, New Mexico
88003-0001
(505) 646-2623

SE   SCIENCE, MATHEMATICS,
AND ENVIRONMENTAL
EDUCATION
Ohio State University
1200 Chambers Road,
Room 310
Columbus, Ohio 43212-1792
(614) 292-6717

SO   SOCIAL STUDIES/SOCIAL
SCIENCE EDUCATION
Indiana University
Social Studies Development
Center
2805 East 10th St.
Bloomington, Indiana
47405-2373
(812) 335-3838

SP   TEACHER EDUCATION
American Association of
Colleges for
Teacher Education
One Dupont Circle, N.W.,
Suite 610
Washington, D.C. 20036-2412
(202) 293-2450

TM   TESTS, MEASUREMENT,
AND EVALUATION
Educational Testing Service
Rosedale Road
Princeton, New Jersey
08541-0001
(609) 734-5176

UD   URBAN EDUCATION
Teachers College, Columbia
University
Box 40
525 West 120th Street
New York, New York,
10027-9998
(212) 678-3433

APPENDIX B

RESEARCH ARTICLE EVALUATION

A. Introduction

1. Does investigator report on relevant literature?
   a. Review covers three or more sources published within 5 years that appear to be important and relevant.
   b. Review covers only one or two recent and important sources.
   c. No important sources are cited.
2. Is a statement of the problem given? Is it clear?
3. Is a justification given, i.e., why is this research important or worth doing?
4. Is the problem related to theory? Discuss.
5. Is there evidence of bias in the investigator's language? If yes, give examples:

B. Objectives or Hypotheses

1. What form is used to state hypotheses?
2. Evaluate the hypotheses using the criteria given in chapter 2 of Borg and Gall. If objectives are stated, are they clear and specific? Do they describe outcomes rather than procedures?

C. Sample

1. Is the sample appropriate for the study? Discuss.
2. Is the sample large enough?
3. Do the sampling procedures result in possible biases in the sample? If so, describe possible sources of bias.

D. Measures

1. Is evidence of validity and reliability given? If so, describe the data reported, and evaluate.
2. Are there any specific weaknesses in the measures or the measurement procedures?

E. Treatments

1. What type of research design is used?
2. Are the treatments described in sufficient detail? If not, what specific information is omitted?
3. Are there weaknesses in the treatments that could affect the results? If so, describe weaknesses and discuss how results could have been affected.

F. Results and Conclusions

1. Are appropriate statistical tools used? Comment.
2. Are results reported in clear, understandable terms? If not, give example.
3. Does investigator relate his results to his hypotheses or objectives?
4. Does investigator overconclude, i.e., are her conclusions supported by her results? If not, comment.

G. Overview

1. What are the main strengths of this research?
2. What are the most serious deficiencies of this research?
3. In what way and to what extent are these deficiencies likely to have affected the research findings?

APPENDIX C

TABLE OF RANDOM NUMBERS

23795	97005	43923	81292	39907	67758	10202	24311	92262	94571
57096	70158	36006	25106	92601	54650	27591	66340	81852	85246
52750	69765	42110	38252	80201	21099	70577	98650	32570	70616
90591	58216	04931	78274	10943	27273	28333	26528	05363	70678
20809	23068	84638	99566	41598	25664	02400	86856	15690	21895
57292	76721	75277	37751	79009	75957	22333	80932	63678	98611
02266	97120	05055	34236	42475	80604	02227	74799	01606	84330
61795	15534	45465	68798	02943	90934	63729	64185	67378	68604
18021	45643	82756	50833	16365	87969	78079	76533	91675	22641
52404	24573	72667	17693	04332	43579	24459	88992	88875	22902
53104	80180	30612	24735	63414	67892	37053	68277	82713	08798
78245	43321	64458	95647	57757	82849	15238	80647	00195	91936
96198	06398	76790	63703	85749	07026	46901	62065	04240	55270
64823	65665	43284	84972	92214	97669	62556	62765	96414	61991
65083	67708	58513	18046	88476	13211	11675	03250	03976	61793
30047	05312	47866	90067	41508	44709	70493	08790	93571	01781
27052	80915	10914	62544	01245	59280	95348	12568	98058	34935
84438	29174	15154	97010	53558	58741	53713	05690	67826	68041
09083	21005	15203	76311	39195	62019	29929	58151	94437	43455
96548	06390	56577	99863	58951	08673	26284	11180	96169	71823
68927	37828	17069	73928	26582	08496	19678	85603	80533	29303
07519	29067	53047	49285	05174	86393	19820	73942	18184	76756
15246	16092	88491	46453	01504	61322	55766	05181	89467	54054
97306	47296	94565	29597	34592	67680	33930	77474	13161	68380
72590	71948	34123	04318	55899	96852	90471	84147	73053	73654
89228	75728	32272	24197	71581	14731	42090	12581	27281	29504
35188	64410	86923	25630	91336	05930	16148	69690	64229	50576
79344	21677	43388	36013	37128	48252	36783	30953	41674	30600
92450	37916	46903	53061	38117	65493	06579	21503	56726	81829
42567	05694	82727	39689	77779	53564	49126	32864	93794	46365

88541	53575	41679	00275	42844	21185	56205	22097	15512	93679
48490	44531	58369	05146	29999	49853	70192	45752	01891	89879
48498	60958	77913	74738	27821	56080	46295	83244	07909	79598
66570	93573	73521	99191	90791	94440	83853	07269	45272	64172
14134	59770	58818	47782	14536	08728	26317	70618	62286	86600
02628	51111	71749	88386	80882	64862	44220	26333	71612	17538
34303	51306	14555	54950	32979	94909	73544	25237	68846	36997
36555	60193	58493	94436	17809	10573	44606	08827	86732	03596
96123	33332	79671	39903	58640	31862	34378	61853	85252	57568
74657	55345	98139	21947	12934	43220	79446	50791	82101	39841
16357	98838	04651	13592	79790	11164	06929	96812	48725	26200
39257	41070	52928	62728	18733	89729	45718	71281	20705	79362
85385	09094	57205	36910	49021	67081	46062	60302	75730	87285
42990	06851	87583	09817	30589	15822	16152	29534	83027	09408
20095	74511	13101	99675	64987	90859	09421	28141	00471	81498
85634	29225	61789	50214	40938	89135	92887	96677	21520	17625
86485	43039	06163	11600	12947	98321	65895	16677	14185	33029
17387	35584	21532	93242	02735	40710	67210	80906	34297	72084
47896	15137	02461	91770	15902	18042	06513	70892	68573	87932
84184	56437	29770	82718	34059	51473	18661	86916	96651	94597
30544	26847	34801	92192	62034	80502	81955	90455	48695	50967
57943	23208	97061	85407	36072	86131	34986	75316	32620	18339
24378	18075	30285	68126	28612	04809	90668	31212	53287	75156
07562	26987	33492	95717	52625	71019	73339	25848	17942	60477
04290	81873	16024	63178	67665	48912	07004	40560	93696	68208
35047	90224	94622	97187	21471	14521	62568	49439	30594	58235
14302	22399	46015	60528	04465	61708	19844	84106	86489	43088
35326	67950	86153	24999	04348	48990	16602	88466	55509	62742
55637	84138	05740	13206	76209	01011	98869	48213	19290	06185
88114	37944	74658	30615	86141	81485	39630	42042	56132	09058
08393	03099	20248	55960	55318	10078	67927	08282	64522	95902
05617	10105	74931	09584	51870	27165	05194	03762	97149	32865
46085	21887	66245	69041	09346	27206	92883	86026	51453	06910
09019	34355	98391	66641	34424	13823	33256	53010	90047	34647
22398	54887	29195	60132	97777	87900	34890	30510	33341	10944

58588	63524	01478	08462	25803	38837	21958	47809	86052	50529
70258	37280	02450	04668	44812	17163	29204	97396	53437	63681
81321	82945	18083	23736	10014	80676	60415	77122	09602	25499
04686	92158	47128	86932	06775	50713	74466	18569	71250	19115
04391	01898	45790	82710	56848	66167	41540	93622	59639	49386
12894	53767	68758	64614	22875	18221	07808	00270	08686	07785
63217	63546	32102	13928	62441	21844	97625	14146	55840	58707
97703	41682	69641	87876	48778	19165	47177	11837	64577	23292
98539	19670	23783	44554	84825	42986	78079	94383	22338	78442
63597	40735	54417	90536	73859	72462	53993	79332	75583	52779
38517	84270	50087	72740	50600	47352	72497	06823	32505	26791
48604	54578	50541	85598	64948	74747	56505	28597	21571	31350
57455	76026	58884	24939	52421	92135	10189	26563	35104	83107
59673	16955	05138	90140	12025	09015	27187	80682	34332	47894
76965	33580	63541	89825	66164	72315	33482	08281	94365	74500
14360	14144	85161	25472	24570	55298	76043	39105	19844	30345
97013	89823	37948	61157	41459	36370	28550	69530	54504	19993
77340	44427	88820	37504	91115	18138	55880	73067	96291	42137
81614	71577	67147	16496	09674	01166	92134	30464	32758	32617
56664	66094	22935	09396	19055	51817	25412	43499	32673	78425
26898	99502	71809	56125	59522	71932	01420	48187	04168	69516
41654	14153	63170	43854	66892	83658	31487	89733	96068	10647
57764	49562	26137	77068	02133	25312	83798	75131	16163	87866
71945	47769	42025	25824	16825	58159	02778	43604	29476	41023
83584	52050	30789	10836	34717	43809	03376	15216	11433	60356
75441	75429	53040	87861	61959	00313	43971	14943	36697	44871
43182	96919	35016	60367	64910	48288	41834	98977	93610	77952
51798	42888	68819	40101	49411	75175	31774	47688	95759	47900
34747	35088	75466	81577	26417	11784	02602	99474	91981	69855
57556	10196	95300	44530	78200	51578	92014	29247	08203	58119
07418	64410	62954	18034	50763	02451	59299	14454	18751	50819
19150	38401	75128	59161	49054	20858	30631	97256	67871	97608
37927	16126	53019	63467	09774	46307	52037	97127	15291	14392
10780	04029	59044	01725	52129	81525	50568	77550	49856	08063
78016	62918	31163	46180	58803	71302	58383	77846	02395	77173

APPENDIX D

NORMALIZED BISERIAL CORRELATION TABLE

Normalized biserial coefficients* of correlation as determined from proportions of correct responses in upper and lower 27 percent of the group

	Proportion of Correct Responses in the Upper 27 Percent**																									
	02	06	10	14	18	22	26	30	34	38	42	46	50	54	58	62	66	70	74	78	82	86	90	94	98	
02	00	19	30	37	43	48	51	55	58	61	63	66	68	70	72	73	75	77	79	80	82	84	86	88	91	02
06		00	11	19	26	31	36	40	44	47	50	53	56	59	61	64	66	68	71	73	76	78	81	84	88	06
10			00	08	15	21	26	30	34	38	41	45	48	51	54	57	60	63	65	68	71	74	77	81	86	10
14				00	07	12	18	22	27	31	34	38	42	45	48	51	54	57	60	63	67	70	74	78	84	14
18					00	06	11	16	20	25	28	32	36	39	43	47	49	53	56	60	63	67	71	76	82	18
22						00	06	10	15	19	23	27	31	34	38	42	45	49	52	56	60	63	68	73	80	22
26							00	05	09	14	18	22	26	30	33	37	41	44	48	52	56	60	65	71	79	26
30								00	04	09	13	17	21	25	29	33	37	40	44	49	53	57	63	68	77	30
34									00	04	09	13	17	21	25	29	33	37	41	45	49	54	60	66	75	34
38										00	04	08	13	16	20	25	29	33	37	42	47	51	57	64	73	38
42											00	04	08	12	16	20	25	29	33	38	43	48	54	61	72	42
46												00	04	08	12	16	21	25	30	34	39	45	51	59	70	46
50													00	04	08	13	17	21	26	31	36	42	48	56	68	50
54														00	04	08	13	17	22	27	32	38	45	53	66	54
58															00	04	09	13	18	23	28	34	41	50	63	58
62																00	04	09	14	19	25	31	38	47	61	62
66																	00	04	09	15	20	27	34	44	58	66
70																		00	05	10	16	22	30	40	55	70
74																			00	06	11	19	26	36	51	74
78																				00	06	12	21	31	48	78
82																					00	07	15	26	43	82
86																						00	08	19	37	86
90																							00	11	30	90
94																								00	19	94
98																									00	98
	02	06	10	14	18	22	26	30	34	38	42	46	50	54	58	62	66	70	74	78	82	86	90	94	98	

Proportion of Correct Responses in the Lower 27 Percent (row labels, left axis)

SOURCE: Appendix D is abridged from J. C. Flanagan's table of normalized biserial coefficients originally prepared for the Cooperative Test Service. It is included here with the generous permission of Dr. Flanagan.

* Decimal points are omitted.

** If the proportion of correct responses in the lower 27 percent exceeds that in the upper, enter the table with the lower 27 percent proportion at the top and attach a negative sign to the coefficient.

APPENDIX E

EXAMPLES OF UNOBTRUSIVE MEASURES

The following behavioral situations were designed as unobtrusive measures of student attitudes toward various aspects of school experience.[1]

Category 1: Student Willingness to Support Nonacademic School Projects
Behavioral Situation 1: Student body activities
Procedure: A record will be kept of the number of students who purchase student body cards. If this situation is used, a similar sales campaign should be followed each year so that results will be reasonably comparable from year to year.
Scoring: The score to be applied to the total behavior attitude measure will be the number of students purchasing student body cards divided by the total number of students enrolled at the school. A high score indicates favorable attitude.

Category 2: Student Perception of the Importance of Education and Identification with the School's Academic Goals
Behavioral Situation 2: Educational television
Procedure: If the school is within range of an educational television channel, the principal will obtain program notes for the month of March and will select two programs offered between 5 and 7 P.M. and two programs offered between the hours of 7 and 10 P.M. that appear to be of good quality and of general interest to high school students. An announcement of each program will be made the day before the program is to be shown and also the day of the program. On the first school day following the program, students of all classes will be given a very brief test and asked to indicate whether they saw the program and, if so, to answer five multiple-choice questions concerning the program.
Scoring: The score on this measure will be the number of pupils indicating they watched the program who also answered at least three of the five objective

1. The situations were taken from Walter R. Borg, *Behavioral Situations to Be Used in Measuring Overall Student Attitudes* (for the Western States Small Schools Project) (Salt Lake City: Utah State Department of Public Instruction, 1962).

questions correctly divided by the total number of pupils in attendance on the day the program was televised. High score is favorable.

Category 3: Student Respect for School Authority and School Property

Behavioral Situation 3: Promptness in returning library books

Procedure: During the period of February 1 to February 15 inclusive, a special record will be kept of all books checked out by students. As these books are returned, the librarian will indicate whether books have been returned on time or are late.

Scoring: The score will be the number of books returned on time divided by the total number of books checked out.

Category 4: Overall Attitudes toward Teachers and School

Behavioral Situation 4: Truancy data

Procedure: Truancy will be defined as any absence of a pupil from school, for which no excuse is given or for which an inadequate or unsatisfactory excuse is given. The school will maintain truancy data during all school days in the month of April. Students returning from absences will be questioned concerning their reasons for being absent. Unless the student has a written excuse from his parent which the school considers genuine, his excuse should be checked with the parent by telephone. After necessary information has been obtained, the number of days and fractions of days truant should be recorded in the proper classification on the record sheet.

Scoring: The score on this item to be applied to the total attitude measure will be the number of days truant divided by the number of pupils in the school.

APPENDIX F

TEST COLLECTION BIBLIOGRAPHIES

Achievement

Achievement Batteries, Preschool–Gr. 3
Achievement Batteries, Gr. 4–6
Achievement Batteries, Gr. 7 and Above
Achievement Tests, College Level
Algebra Tests
Art
Basic Skills
Biology Achievement
Chemistry–College Level
Chemistry–Gr. 7–12
Composition and Writing Skills
Consumer Competency
Criterion-Referenced Measures, Preschool-Gr. 3
Criterion-Referenced Measures, Gr. 4–6
Criterion-Referenced Measures, Gr. 7 and Above
Economics, Gr. 1 and Above
Environmental Education
French–Foreign Language
Geography
Geometry
German–Foreign Language
Health and Physical Education
History
Home Economics
Industrial Arts–Gr. 7–12

Italian–Foreign Language
Language Development
Language Skills–Preschool-Gr. 3
Language Skills–Gr. 4–6
Language Skills–Gr. 7 and Above
Library Skills
Literature
Mathematics–Preschool-Gr. 3
Mathematics–Gr. 4–6
Mathematics–Gr. 7 and Above
Mathematics–Diagnostic, Preschool-Gr. 3
Mathematics–Diagnostic, Gr. 4–6
Mathematics–Diagnostic, Gr. 7 and Above
Metric System
Minimum Competency Tests
Music
Nutrition
Oral Reading and Listening Skills
Physics and Physical Science
Psychology
Reading–Preschool-Gr. 3
Reading–Gr. 4–6
Reading–Gr. 7 and Above
Reading–Diagnostic, Preschool-Gr. 6
Reading–Diagnostic, Gr. 7 and Above
Reading Readiness
School Readiness

SOURCE: Reprinted from *Test Collection*, Educational Testing Service,® Princeton, NJ. By permission of the publisher. These bibliographies may be purchased from *Test Collection*, Educational Testing Service, Princeton NJ 08541 or call (609) 734-5686. Price in 1988 for individual bibliographies was $11.00 each.

Science–Kindergarten-Gr. 6
Science–Gr. 7 and Above
Sex Education
Social Studies–Kindergarten-Gr. 3
Social Studies–Gr. 4–6
Social Studies–Gr. 7 and Above
Spanish–Foreign Language
Speech Abilities
Speech/Communication
Spelling–Kindergarten-Gr. 6
Spelling–Gr. 7 and Above
Study Skills
United States Government
United States History
Vocabulary, Preschool-Gr. 3
Vocabulary, Gr. 4–6
Vocabulary, Gr. 7 and Above

Aptitude

Cognitive Style and Information Processing
Concept Formation and Acquisition
Creativity and Divergent Thinking
Curiosity
Intelligence-Group Administered, Preschool-Gr. 3
Intelligence-Group Administered, Gr. 4–6
Intelligence-Group Administered, Gr. 7 and Above
Intelligence-Individually Administered, Pre-school-Gr. 3
Intelligence-Individually Administered, Gr. 4–6
Intelligence-Individually Administered, Gr. 7 and Above
Mathematical Aptitude, Gr. 1–3
Mathematical Aptitude, Gr. 4–12
Mathematical Aptitude, College Level
Memory
Non-Verbal Aptitude
Reasoning, Logical Thinking, Problem Solving

Scholastic Aptitude and Mental/Cognitive Ability
Spatial-Perception Relations
Verbal Aptitude

Attitudes and Interests

Academic Interest
Children's Attitude Toward Parents
Curriculum, Attitudes Toward
Educational Techniques, Attitudes Toward
Handicapped Persons, Attitudes Toward
Mathematics, Attitudes Toward
Occupational Attitudes and Job Satisfaction
Racial/Ethnic Attitudes
Reading, Attitudes Toward
Religious Attitudes
School and School Adjustment, Attitudes Toward, Preschool-Gr. 3
School and School Adjustment, Attitudes Toward, Gr. 4–6
School and School Adjustment, Attitudes Toward, Gr. 7 and Above
Sex Roles and Attitudes Toward Women
Social Attitudes
Teacher Attitudes
Values

Personality

Aggression and Hostility
Alienation
Anxiety
Ascendance-Submission
Depression
Independence-Dependence
Introversion/Extraversion
Leadership
Locus of Control
Masculinity-Femininity
Motivation and Need Achievement
Personality–General
Personality Adjustment, Kindergarten-Gr. 3

Personality Adjustment, Gr. 4–6
Personality Adjustment, Gr. 7 and Above
Projective Measures
Psychosexual Development
Responsibility/Perseverance
Self-Concept, Preschool-Gr. 3
Self-Concept, Gr. 4–6
Self-Concept, Gr. 7 and Above
Stress
Task Orientation

Sensory-Motor

Auditory Skills
Motor Skills
Sensory-Motor Abilities
Vision and Visual Perception, Preschool-
  Gr. 3

Special Populations

Adult Basic Education
American Indians
Blind and Visually Handicapped Persons
Brain-Damaged Persons
Deaf and Hearing Impaired Persons
Disadvantaged, Preschool-Gr. 3
Disadvantaged, Gr. 4–6
Disadvantaged, Gr. 7 and Above
Emotionally Disturbed Persons
English as a Second Language
Gifted and Talented Students, Identification
  and Evaluation
Juvenile Delinquents
Learning Disabilities, Identification of, Pre-
  school-Gr. 3
Learning Disabilities, Identification of, Gr.
  4–6
Learning Disabilities, Identification of, Gr. 7
  and Above
Mentally Retarded Persons
Orthopedically Handicapped Persons
Spanish Speakers, Preschool-Gr. 3

Spanish Speakers, Gr. 4–6
Spanish Speakers, Gr. 7 and Above
Vocational Measures for Handicapped
  Persons

Vocational/Occupational

Business Skills
Clerical Aptitude and Achievement
Data Processing
Employment Interviews
Engineering Aptitude and Achievement
Mechanical Aptitude and Knowledge
Nurses
Occupational Knowledge, Skilled Trades
Organizational and Institutional Evaluation
Personality Tests in Industry
Professional Occupations
Salespersons-Selection and Evaluation
Supervisory, Management
Teacher Assessment
Trucking Personnel, Drivers, Diesel
  Mechanics
Vocational Choice-Perception-Development
Vocational/Industrial Aptitude
Vocational Interests
Vocational Rating and Selection Forms

Miscellaneous

Behavior Rating Scales, Preschool-Gr. 3
Behavior Rating Scales, Gr. 4–6
Behavior Rating Scales, Gr. 7 and Above
Biographical Inventories
Child Rearing Practices and Related Attitudes
Classroom Interaction
Counseling Aids
Courtship and Marriage
Culture-Fair Tests
Curriculum and Program Evaluation
Decision-Making Process
Developmental Scales
Drugs-Knowledge and Abuse

Educational Record and Report Forms
Environments
Family Interaction and Related Attitudes
Group Behavior and Influence
Human Sexuality
Infant Development
Item Pools
Learning Style

Manual Dexterity
Moral Development
Piagetian Measures
Social Perception and Judgment
Social Skills, Birth-9
Social Skills, Gr. 4 and Above
Systematic Observation Techniques
Teaching Style

NAME INDEX

Abrahams, N. M., 544
Achen, C. H., 734
Achilles, C. M., 227
Adair, J. G., 84, 94, 190, 202, 203
Adams, A., 690
Adams, K. A., 785
Adams, R., 404
Aegerter, R., 681
Affleck, J. Q., 690
Ahlgren, A., 222
Aiken, L. R., 315
Aitkenhead, M., 91
Ajzen, I., 311
Aletky, P. J., 198
Alf, E. F., Jr., 544
Allen, I. L., 433
Allender, J. S., 25
Altridge, C., 531
Amick, D. J., 568
Andersie, R. B., 761
Anderson, D. S., 23, 40
Anderson, J. F., 431, 467
Aries, E., 529
Asch, W. B., Jr., 444–446
Ascione, F. R., 90, 118, 667
Asher, S. R., 516
Atherton, C. R., 182
Atwell, J. E., 86
Ausbacher, H. L., 510

Dabbie, E. R., 241
Backer, T. E., 314
Bailyn, B., 811, 825
Bakeman, R., 530
Baker, J. G., 498
Barber, T., 658
Barlow, D. E., 734
Barzun, J., 821–822, 836
Basow, S. A., 553, 558–559
Bass, R. F., 724
Bauernfeind, R. H., 190
Baumgartner, R., 426, 432, 438, 440–441, 467
Beach, M., 811
Beane, J. A., 58, 316
Beauchamp, E. R., 831–834
Beauchamp, T. L., 107
Becker, B. J., 203
Becker, H. S., 880
Beecher, H. K., 198
Behling, J. H., 79

Bejar, I. I., 304
Bellack, A. S., 480
Bellah, R., 808
Belson, W. A., 435, 453, 467
Bennett, F., 447
Benson, J., 288
Benson, W., 430
Bentler, P. M., 624
Berdie, D. R., 431, 467
Berelson, R., 519–520
Berger, C. F., 458–460, 498–500
Berk, D. A., 287
Berk, R. A., 266, 287
Berliner, D. C., 58, 364, 372, 388, 710
Berry, M., 459
Berry, T., 681
Besag, F. P., 178
Bettencourt, E. M., 33
Bichler, E., 552–553
Biddle, B. J., 23, 40
Biggers, L., 268
Black, H., 282
Block, J. H., 361
Boatright, B., 493
Boehm, A. E., 530
Bommarito, J. W., 314
Boneau, C. A., 548
Bonnstetter, R. J., 642, 648
Boor, M., 875
Borg, W. R., 90, 118, 479, 487, 511, 666–667, 784, 802
Borich, G. D., 316, 531, 765
Boruch, R. F., 88, 108
Boyer, E. G., 531
Bracht, G. H., 217, 649–653
Bradburn, N. M., 428, 450, 457, 464, 466, 468
Brandhorst, T., 162
Brezezinski, E. J., 440
Brickman, W. W., 816, 836
Bridges, E. M., 614–619
Brinko, K. T., 204
Brite, L. R., 237
Broderick, J. E., 522
Brody, G. H., 59
Bromley, D. B., 408
Brooks, P. C., 815
Brown, B. W., 315
Brown, F. G., 286
Brown, R. M., 522
Bruning, J. L., 375, 568, 635, 857

SUBJECT INDEX